THE PRINCETON REVIEW

GUIDE TO PERFORMING ARTS PROGRAMS

THE PRINCETON REVIEW

GUIDE TO PERFORMING ARTS PROGRAMS

PROFILES OF OVER 600 COLLEGES, HIGH SCHOOLS, AND SUMMER PROGRAMS

BY
MURIEL TOPAZ
&
CAROLE EVERETT

Random House, Inc.
New York

www.randomhouse.com

Princeton Review Publishing, L.L.C.
2315 Broadway
New York, NY 10024
E-mail: info@review.com

Published in the United States by Random House, Inc., New York, and simultaneously in Canada by Random House of Canada Limited, Toronto.

ISBN: 0-375-75095-9

Editor: Gretchen Feder
Production Editor: Kristen Azzara
Production Manager: Greta Englert
Designer: Meher Khambata & Iam Williams

9 8 7 6 5 4 3 2 1

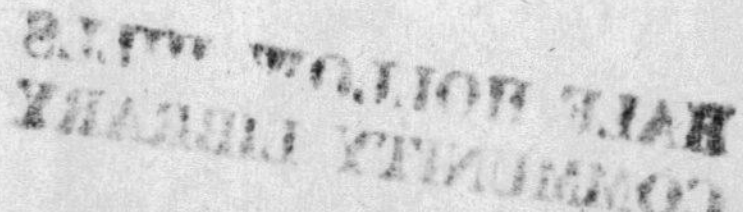

CONTENTS

ACKNOWLEDGMENTS

We are deeply grateful to all the people who helped and supported us while we were writing this book. We are indebted to the following people who contributed in different ways to this project: Christine Eckerle, C.J. and Colin Everett, Jane Gottlieb, Dorothy Hutcheson, Karen Jeanneret, Sayomi Kamimoto, Lisa LaTouche, Daniel Lewis, Daulton Lewis, Phyllis Mahoney, Norton Owen, Heng Ping, Jennifer Rosman, Karin Sunke, Marianna Houston Webber, Kathy Whitbeck, and Lois Wien.

Special thanks to Dr. Eric Martin, for all the hard work he contributed to the directory section. And, our sincere gratitude to all the "Deweys" who worked with him, including Jae Kim, Nathan Leonard, and Jayson Park.

Our appreciation also to the people at the Princeton Review and Random House: John Katzman, Evan Schnittman, Gretchen Feder, Christine Chung, Jackie Jendras, Kristen Azzara, Peter DeGiglio, Amy Touchette, Mary Beth Roche, Iam Williams, Robert McCormack, Stephanie Martin, and Greta Englert.

A NOTE TO PARENTS

Parents of children who are talented in the performing arts have a special responsibility and many challenges. Although *your* child dreams of stardom, or at least of professional fulfillment, *you* may have visions of your youngster resigning herself to a life as a cab driver or waiter. To avoid having your child conflicted and spending years in therapy, it may be useful to consider some helpful parenting behavior.

Parental support of a child's talents can mean the difference between a healthy, gloriously fulfilled young person and a frustrated and tortured adolescent. If your child has musical ability and drive, it may mean renting or borrowing the best instrument available. Countenancing, and even encouraging your budding actor's impromptu backyard performances makes for a productive teenager and lays the groundwork for later commitment and initiative. Providing good training opportunities for the emerging dancer, working out the transportation, and understanding that rehearsals may rank ahead of the family outing to your child will allow your youngster to discover for himself whether this seems to be the right direction.

In all three performing arts—dance, drama, and music—parental help in finding the best teacher; in paying for lessons; in getting a child to and from rehearsals and performances; in attending recitals, shows, and concerts; and in showing your pride and approval of your young artist's accomplishments is critical. It also means scheduling family events around rehearsals or performances. Helping to arrange trial performance opportunities for your child when she is preparing for a high school or college audition will be appreciated. Working with your child on time management and assisting when tensions arise between artistic endeavors and school demands can be useful for both of you. When your teenager is applying to schools or colleges and requesting scholarships, make sure to submit any required forms on time.

The opposite type of parent, however, is the infamous vision of the "stage" mother or father—as best typified by Mama Rose, mother of Gypsy Rose Lee. "Sing out, dear," she screams from the wings. At all costs, avoid being such an aggressive and interfering parent. Unless you are a professional musician, do not accompany your child on the piano. Do not ask endless questions of the teacher, and do not sit in on lessons or classes unless invited. Avoid being your child's constant critic, but do not be a blind and overly enthusiastic cheerleader either. There is a delicate balance. Again, no matter how strongly you doubt the performing arts as a wise career choice, the support you give your "passionate" child at this juncture models a key approach to life. If you want something—go for it! Remember that the decision to devote one's life to art is a difficult, serious, and very personal one that can be made only by the child himself. It must fulfill his dream, not yours.

When your child goes on interviews and/or auditions, do not enter the office or audition room unless you are specifically invited. Never try to influence a teacher or admissions officer; financial inducements are never acceptable.

As we all know, parenting is difficult even without having a performing artist for a child. Every family dynamic is different. We all do our best. If you figure out how to be the perfect parent, please let us know your secret.

1

CHOOSING YOUR EDUCATIONAL FUTURE:

ASKING THE HARD QUESTIONS

The applause is ringing in your ears. You have just finished performing a tricky Bach *Prelude and Fugue* at your piano recital and you feel great. Playing the piano gives you such pleasure that you love to practice, and you feel as though you could do this for your entire life.

Or, running into the wings between scenes as you do a quick costume change in your school play reminds you of how much you love life in the theater. You want to be an actor and there is no doubt in your mind about pursuing this passion.

Or, the holidays are coming and while everyone else is feeling the stress of the season, all you think about night and day is dancing in your next performance of *The Nutcracker*.

Even though it seems clear that you want to spend your life performing, students who are passionate about the arts still have some hard questions to ask themselves. Answer these questions honestly before you even begin to commit seriously to an education and life that focuses on the performing arts:

- How do I like to spend my time? What makes me happy?
- Is there anything other than dance, drama, or music that I would rather do?
- How disciplined am I? How determined am I?
- Am I a self-starter? Can I take responsibility for my own progress?
- How often do I practice?
- What kind of training have I had to date?
- What kind of feedback do I get from my teachers?
- How often have I been cast in major roles? Given solos or important parts?
- Where am I usually seated in the orchestra or band?
- How have I done in auditions for summer programs? All-state? Community or school productions? What ratings have I obtained?
- How well do I handle rejection? Setbacks? Pressure?
- What kind of student am I? How much do I value academics?
- What does my scholastic profile look like? What classes have I taken in school? What are my grades like? Do I enjoy studying?
- What are my SAT or ACT scores?

FOR INTERNATIONAL STUDENTS:

- How well do I speak English?
- What is my TOEFL score?
- How do I feel about being far away from home?
- Can I adjust to living in another culture?
- Can I certify my finances?
- Can I obtain the necessary student visa?

Most everyone who actually has—or has had—a career in the arts will wisely tell you that the life of a performing artist is not all glamour. It is also a great deal of blood, sweat, and tears, not to mention luck. If you are not *totally devoted* to making the arts your focus, then keep your interest in dance, drama, or music as a hobby or an avocation. If you *can* choose something else—do! Becoming a practicing artist is not just a career, it is a lifestyle choice.

Conversely, if you think you have the dedication, drive, passion, and talent—or if you are pre-high school age and want to consider all your options—follow the wisdom this guide offers. Now is the time to learn how to research the places you might want to go for further study and to begin taking the steps toward your dream.

2

PERFORMING ARTS EDUCATIONAL PROGRAMS—HIGH SCHOOL, COLLEGE, SUMMER

IS A HIGH SCHOOL THAT SPECIALIZES IN THE PERFORMING ARTS RIGHT FOR YOU?

For some young people, the decision to attend an arts-oriented high school is obvious. They are already committed to serious study in one of the arts. They have discovered that the hours spent in classes, rehearsals, private lessons, and practicing are among the most satisfying in their lives. Their particular art form is a passion; it is what they want to do most.

For others, the choice is less obvious, though still an option. Attending an arts high school is meaningful even for those who, although finding their art form an enjoyable activity, are not certain that it is how they wish to spend the rest of their lives. A specialty high school offers the opportunity to taste what life as an actor, dancer, or musician will be like while continuing academic preparation for other pursuits. It allows students to choose their future course in an informed fashion rather than by some extraneous standard.

All teenagers are influenced by their peers; however, your friend's lifestyle choice is not necessarily the best choice for you. You need to investigate your possibilities in depth to find the information you need to make an intelligent choice for *your* future. An arts-oriented high school or a high school with a strong arts program is a good place to explore your interest, find out all the information you can, and then make an informed choice about your future.

Specialized high schools usually provide fine academic programs as well as arts training. Most require students to maintain a fairly high standard of academic achievement to remain in the arts program. Additionally, the arts training itself inculcates values that will benefit every young person no matter what future career path she chooses. Such attributes as discipline, self-evaluation, learning how to work single-mindedly toward a given goal, physical and mental stamina, and efficient time management all are important life skills.

Once you have made your decision to attend a performing arts high school, your next step is to determine the one that best suits your needs. Application information differs among the several categories of high school programs, so be sure to read ahead before making your decision.

The best way to find out about audition procedures and admission requirements is to get in touch directly with the institutions that are attractive to you. You should contact the schools no later than the fall of the *year before* you wish to attend, earlier if possible. Some institutions are able to accommodate late applications, but if you wait until the last minute, you will risk the possibility of missing auditions, of there being no more room in the school, or of having financial aid funds already allocated.

Institutions may require any or all of the following, so be prepared:

- Live or videotaped auditions
- School records
- Letters of recommendation
- A personal essay
- A résumé
- A copy of a graded paper
- A photograph
- An interview
- Standardized test scores

Be sure to request written information on the fees and application procedures and to follow all of the instructions carefully and in a timely fashion.

WHAT TYPE OF HIGH SCHOOL SHOULD YOU CHOOSE?

Once you have decided to continue your high school education in a specialized arts school, your next step is to choose from several broad categories and determine the best type of high school for you.

ARTS MAGNET SCHOOLS

These are public schools run by a state's Department of Education. They serve the educational needs of a given community, and only those who live in that particular community can attend. These magnet schools usually draw students from an area that includes several school districts; they attract a wider population than a single school district. Like all public schools, they are tuition free, although some allow out-of-area or out-of-state students to attend if they pay tuition.

Magnet schools have proven to be effective in meeting desegregation goals while providing appropriate education for students with particular career goals or special interests. The programs and class sizes in these schools are typically small, allowing for a generous amount of attention to individual students' needs. The school population is usually racially and ethnically diverse, and includes students from all economic backgrounds. The one thing most students have in common is their talent and commitment to their art. Almost all of the schools have some audition procedure, often based on native talent rather than on previous training. Most require a certain level of academic achievement for admission.

GOVERNOR'S SCHOOLS

In more and more states, you will find either fully or partially state funded governor's schools. Unlike magnet schools, they serve the entire state, although some are open to residents of other states if they pay tuition.

The type of program available differs from one governor's school to the next. Some offer only intensive summer study, some offer short-term study; others are full academic year boarding school programs. Most are designed to aid extraordinarily talented students in their quest for specialized education; therefore, at some schools entrance requirements may be fairly stringent. Check with your state Department of Education for more specific information about programs and admissions requirements.

PRIVATE SCHOOLS

At one end of the wide range of private education is studio and conservatory-type training. These schools offer either on-site academics or classes at neighboring institutions with schedules that accommodate highly specialized, profession-oriented students. At the other end of the spectrum are private institutions that have impeccable academic reputations and also have strong performing arts programs.

Fees differ greatly from one type of private school to the next, ranging from an institution that fully subsidizes all students, to merit or need-based full or partial scholarships, to some of the most costly schools in the nation. Many have residential (boarding) facilities, although there are a number of private day schools, particularly in urban areas.

Admission/audition requirements depend on the type of program to which you apply. Studio and conservatory programs administer highly competitive auditions and pay less attention to academic credentials; more academically oriented schools may not require an audition but place greater weight on scholastic profiles.

RESIDENTIAL (BOARDING) SCHOOLS

Residential schools are either public, such as governor's schools, or private; they may be specifically arts oriented, or they may be academically oriented with strong arts programs. Young people who find that their hometown simply does not offer the quantity or quality of training they seek may choose to attend a residential school. These schools are also helpful for the student who feels that he will function better in a community of peers devoted single-mindedly to an arts-based life, or someone seeking a strong academic program with free time spent, instead, on scholastic pursuits and intensive arts study.

Some students receive both physical and psychological benefits from attending a residential program. Residential students benefit enormously from the integration of their academic and arts programs—all of the teachers are pulling in the same direction rather than making competing demands. All are involved in the development of the student as a whole, and counseling and guidance are usually high priorities. Students conserve time and energy because, in most cases, all their activities are in one place.

Boarding schools in the performing arts are usually best suited to students who are focused, committed to a goal, and mature enough to manage their time without regular parental or other adult supervision. Of course, residential programs are not right for everyone. Only you, along with your parents, can decide whether the benefits of such a program outweigh the disadvantages of leaving home at an impressionable age.

SHOULD YOU CONTINUE YOUR EDUCATION BEYOND HIGH SCHOOL?

DANCE

Whether a young dancer should continue her academic education beyond high school can only be decided in the context of knowing what kind of dancer she wants to be and what opportunities are open to her. If your goal is a major classical company, an academic degree is not something the company is concerned with and the years spent in higher education may present a disadvantage. If your goal is to be a commercial dancer, academic credentials will not be a factor in your career, although the somewhat more mature dancer probably has an edge, depending on the type of show and the type of dancer that is required. Modern dancers who seek employment straight out of high school are definitely at a disadvantage as most modern dance companies are looking for maturity and experience. For other kinds of dancers, the picture is similar—age may or may not be important, and, if it is not, maturity and experience are a plus. The real key is whether or not a company factors in age when choosing future members.

Even for those who aspire to join a classical dance company in which age is critical, there are some good reasons to apply for conservatory or college training. The majority of classical dancers who will "make it" in large companies such as American Ballet Theatre, the New York City, Kirov, San Francisco, Boston, and Houston Ballets, have already been accepted as scholarship students or apprentices by the time they have finished high school. During their senior year of high school and over the summers, serious candidates who want careers with major classical companies are already auditioning or studying at the schools attached to these companies. Another point to consider when deciding whether or not to continue your academic schooling past high school is that most smaller or regionally based companies are not quite as fixated on youth as some of the larger companies. Male dancers should also keep in mind that the age factor is not as crucial for them as it is for females.

No nibbles? No contract or apprenticeship offers? No strong interest exhibited in recruiting you to join a company? Then you should definitely consider continuing your academic education. Apply early in your senior year of high school. If something does come through, it is usually possible to defer enrollment into an institution of higher learning for a year or even longer, if you are really attractive to the institution. If a good dance opportunity arises later, it is usually possible to take a leave of absence from a college or conservatory after a year or more of study.

If you have commercial dance aspirations, or are interested in various national dance forms (African, Flamenco, etc.), the same advice applies. Go after all opportunities, but apply to higher education programs in case the options open to you are not satisfactory.

For modern dancers, higher education is practically a necessity, so plan to continue academic study beyond high school. You probably cannot get a job with a substantial company without it, although smaller pick-up groups are not as stringent in their requirements for experience and maturity.

DRAMA

Years of technical study are not absolutely required in drama. Your appearance and ability to memorize and project, in addition to what many call natural talent, will carry you a long way. Some students will be cast in roles in professional productions while they are still in high school. Some may audition for agents and get representation right away. Age is not so much a factor in the drama world as it is in dance, although the age factor does vary, depending on what kind of actor you would like to be. If you want to pursue a career in television or film, your age may be more important than if you choose to act primarily in the live theater.

But what should you do after high school? Should you get on the audition circuit right away?

> Although some drama students jump directly from high school into performing careers, it is far more common for actors to go on for further training and education. Completing at least two years of liberal arts studies is highly recommended. Extensive reading of English and other world literature, history, art appreciation, and music can help enrich and expand a performer's palate and allow for a deeper, more informed interpretation of dramatic material. The most traditional path for drama students is the completion of four years of high school, four years of liberal arts college—most frequently with a major in English—and then two to four years of conservatory training or serious acting classes.

Whether or not you choose to attend college, it is important to keep developing your dramatic skills. Many acting schools offer evening and weekend classes. Classes and workshops are often very helpful to the developing actor, helping him technically and giving him the opportunity to network with other actors. If you have graduated from a liberal arts college, attended summer programs, or performed in summer stock and taken a few extra classes, beware of falling into the trap of being a "workshop actor," an expert in classes, but not out there auditioning and being cast.

MUSIC

As in so many areas of life now, there seems to be a fascination with youth in music. Although the four-year-old prodigy who can play a Mozart Concerto with pyrotechnics will usually get media attention, there is no substitute for slow and careful development.

Your instrument will also have some bearing on how you shape your educational future. Flute, violin, and piano are highly competitive, thus age *may be* a factor. If you play one of these instruments, you might want to go directly to a conservatory for a Bachelor of Music degree. Other string, brass, percussion, and woodwind players can afford to take more time to develop. Composers and conductors traditionally have studied the liberal arts, and have the luxury of taking time to fully develop their skills.

It is also important for singers to give themselves time to develop. Earning a liberal arts degree is highly encouraged, except in the case of singers who are just not good students. Physiologically, the voice needs time to mature. Studying languages—especially Italian, French, and German—literature, history, and music theory is important for singers.

The dilemma of liberal arts versus conservatory education presents a challenge to many young musicians. It is a highly personal choice, and there are successful musicians who have traveled both paths. Your natural intellectual curiosity, interest in areas outside your instrument, and the level of competition you enjoy may all influence this decision. Some students who start at a liberal arts institution miss the concentrated study of music and transfer to a conservatory. Others enroll at a conservatory and, feeling like they are at trade school, transfer to a liberal arts college. Weigh your options deliberately; you have many choices when pursuing musical study and should thoughtfully consider them all.

WHERE SHOULD YOU STUDY AFTER HIGH SCHOOL?

If you have decided to continue in school, you must decide where to go. Your first step is to determine whether a conservatory or a liberal arts institution will best suit your needs and goals. The next chapter documents the basic difference between these two types of institutions. If you are certain that a performing career is in your future, a conservatory probably will better suit your needs. If this is not a certainty, if you are worrying about an alternate career "just in case," or if you have academic goals and interests, then choosing a liberal arts path is probably wise. These are, however, very general guidelines. Only you, the performer—in consultation with your parents, and paying great attention to the advice of your teacher—can make the final decision. Your teacher can definitely be of enormous help, as he knows a great deal about your potential, your work habits, your ability to improve, and, in the case of dancers, your physical limitations. And, although it may be difficult for a teen to admit it, no one knows you better than your parents.

FACTORS TO CONSIDER

The Faculty

Any school, no matter what its reputation, is only as good as the individual teachers. Get to know who the faculty are, their backgrounds, and their previous experience. Try to ascertain with whom they have studied and performed.

The Curriculum

Read the course requirements and class descriptions carefully. The most important thing is to match your needs with the offerings of the college or conservatory that you choose.

Dance

Most serious dance programs offer at least one daily technical class, often more, particularly in conservatories. Be sure these classes cover the kind of material you want to learn. For example, if you are impassioned about the Graham technique, there is no point in choosing an institution that specializes in Cunningham work. If you want to learn more about choreography, be sure the school offers several levels of courses in dance composition. Examine the other course offerings. Institutions of higher learning should offer a wide range of information about the art of dance, as well as some insight into related arts.

Drama

Acting students should look for a curriculum that offers a wide range of experiences and study. Do you want to study a specific technique such as Meisner or Stanislavsky or Strasberg? Be sure to read the curriculum and do not be afraid to ask what a course such as "Acting Technique" entails. On a basic level, you should also be sure that the school offers good training in voice, speech, and movement. Conservatory training will also usually include classes in stage combat/fight technique, improvisation, mime, masks, Alexander technique, and much more. They may also offer courses in theater history, make-up, and technical aspects of theater (directing, lighting design, stage management, etc.).

Music

The relationship between a student and her individual private teacher is the most critical link in musical study. In evaluating the curriculum, pay attention to how often you will have a private lesson with your chosen teacher; ideally, it should be at least once a week. You must also develop and deepen your proficiency as a musician–studying music theory, history, repertoire for your instrument, ear training, and, for singers, languages and diction. Singers and conductors should become conversant in Italian, French, and German if they are serious about their careers. If you are interested in a particular period or style of music, be sure that there are courses in that area. For example, performance practices in Baroque music, classes in playing contemporary chamber music, and the like should be offered.

If the school does not offer everything you need, find out what classes or private lessons are available off campus. How is outside study regarded? Is it encouraged? Tolerated? Discouraged? Does the program allow the time for off-campus study?

Performing

Dance, drama, and music are performing arts, so it is essential that students have the opportunity to perform during their years in school. Find out what kind of performing opportunities exist and how frequently they occur.

Size and Location

Decide if you want the nurturing atmosphere of a small campus institution, the stimulation of an urban environment, or the competition and the magnitude of choice offered by a large university. Is it important for you to be close to home? Living on your own? The years you spend in higher education and the contacts you make there will be important to you for the rest of your life. They constitute the beginning of your professional network, so try to consider all of the angles.

Costs and Financial Aid Opportunities

This is the time to be practical. Thoroughly investigate the kind and amount of scholarship, financial aid, work/study, and other financial opportunities offered by and through the school. Do not overlook sources such as government scholarships, state scholarships, merit scholarships, arts club scholarships, fraternal club offerings, and any other source you can think of. Be sure to provide all required financial forms on time. Do not count on earning your way through school. Most performing arts programs require extraordinary time and energy commitments that preclude you from being self-supporting.

The Alumni

Find out who has graduated or left the institution and what they are doing now. What percent of alumni go on to professional careers? Who are the renowned alumni that came out of the institution?

The Visit

If at all possible, make arrangements to visit the institutions that interest you. Watch classes, soak up the atmosphere, speak to students, inquire about the daily schedule, check out the living accommodations and the performing facilities, and see what it is really like to study there. If a personal visit is not possible, request a videotape from the college or conservatory; most schools have one. Many also have websites that can help give you a sense of the institution.

A Final Word

Be sure to apply to several institutions. Entrance can be highly competitive. There is no guarantee that you will be chosen by the institution you would most like to attend, so applying to several schools is critical.

WHAT TYPE OF COLLEGE SHOULD YOU CHOOSE?

POST-SECONDARY EDUCATION

The distinctions among post-secondary schools are not rigidly defined. Although most conservatories are freestanding institutions, there are a number of colleges and universities that encompass conservatories within their walls. Distinctions center as much on program philosophy and curricular offerings as they do on definitions of institutions.

Students can choose from two kinds of post-secondary degrees: a professional degree and a liberal arts degree. Institutions that offer a professional degree—called Bachelor of Fine Arts (BFA) or Bachelor of Music (BM)—require that approximately two-thirds of all coursework be done in the studio or in areas related to the art form studied. In some institutions, particularly in conservatory programs, courses in "related areas" (history of dance, music, and theater; theory courses; and the like) are considered part of the academic rather than the art specialty requirements, thus allowing for even more credit hours in the studio or in "practical" or "applied" work such as technique, private study, repertory, and performing.

Students working toward a liberal arts degree—Bachelor of Arts (BA) or Bachelor of Science (BS)—take approximately one-third of their coursework in their art form and more courses that give a general overview of a number of disciplines.

Conservatories

These schools offer the most professionally oriented curricula among all post-secondary institutions. Conservatories do offer some academic courses, but they are clearly secondary to professional study. Performance and preparation for performance are the key ingredients of the program.

For the dancer and the actor, a conservatory will offer at least two or three daily studio courses. Although first-year performance opportunities may be strictly limited in some institutions, by the fourth year it will be an important component of the training. The musician's critical concerns include instrumental study and choosing a private teacher. Musicians will have opportunities for ensemble experiences, but they will be encouraged to perform solo recitals if their instrument has such a tradition. Outside performing will be permitted. Young singers should ask about performing opportunities, as they may be limited for undergraduates.

"Stand-alone" conservatories—those that are not affiliated with another institution—tend to be the least rigid about academic requirements. Conservatories attached to colleges and universities vary greatly in the closeness of that attachment. Several are autonomous for all practical purposes and have the same sort of schedule and requirements as independent conservatories. Others are closely allied to the college with which they are associated. Some even require the student to follow the same academic curriculum as all other university students.

Obviously, a conservatory within a large institution will have a broader range of academics from which to choose. In a small conservatory, course offerings are often restricted to the arts and humanities, with few or none in the sciences and mathematics.

Some stand-alone conservatories have addressed this issue by allowing selected students to cross-register with a nearby, larger academic institution, thus providing a wider range of choices for academic study.

Colleges and Universities

Programs vary, but many offer both professional and liberal arts degrees. Generally speaking, in a college or university, there will be more emphasis on academics and less flexibility in accommodating outside professional activity than in a conservatory. It is important to note, however, that this general statement will not apply in every case to every institution.

In liberal arts institutions, a great deal of arts activity is non-credit; it is seen as extracurricular. There tend to be fewer studio courses and fewer levels of training offered. Although it is certainly possible for a student in a liberal arts program to practice his or her art form as much as a student in a professional program, it takes a bit of ingenuity and a lot of self-starting to juggle the schedule sufficiently to bring this about.

College affords a great opportunity to become knowledgeable about your chosen art form and to broaden your familiarity with many arts. If you choose the college route, expect to learn about everything that makes up the background of an artist—including art history, literature, languages, and writing. Another obvious advantage is that, if you change your mind about becoming a professional performer, you still have the educational training and credentials to follow another career path.

WHERE SHOULD YOU STUDY DURING THE SUMMER?

How do you sort through the bewildering array of options for summer study? Do you choose a place because your friend Suzy Smith loved it last year? Perhaps you have heard through the grapevine that someone from the prior year's course earned a spot in the affiliated company. Or, maybe you have always wanted to study Flamenco dancing and you have found a program that offers it. Maybe you really want to take a million classes a week. Or, you want to experience competitive auditions for orchestral seating. Should you choose a program because it specializes in technical acting classes and productions, and you are dying to participate in them? Although all of these reasons have some merit, it is probably wiser to make your choice of summer study through a more systematic approach.

The way to begin the process is by assessing your goals. What is it that you would like to achieve during the summer? One of the answers should certainly include study that is not possible during the regular school year. Summer is the time to spend more hours studying, practicing, rehearsing, and performing because you don't have to worry about school studies or working around your academic schedule. It should also be the time to broaden your horizons. No matter what community you regularly study in, there are limitations to what is available. Summer study should afford the opportunity to explore different ideas and approaches. Dancers may experience new dance forms or new schools of teaching (i.e., Bournonville if you regularly study Balanchine; RAD if your teacher specializes in Cecchetti; Limón technique if you usually study Graham, etc.). Singers might go to a foreign country to work on the language and repertoire of that nation. Actors could audition for a summer stock company or investigate the world of interning.

What are your other goals? Do you want to spend a great deal of time in dance classes? Then choose a program that offers two or three technical classes daily (certainly no more!). If you take this route, be certain to prepare yourself beforehand for intensive study by regular exercise, slowly increasing the amount of time spent so that you are physically ready for a rigorous experience. Do you want to study with a particular music teacher whose work you admire? Do you want to concentrate on Shakespearean acting? Ask yourself these types of questions to determine your goals.

If you would like to perform more than you do in the winter, make sure the program you choose has a strong performing component. Have you always wanted to try your hand at choreography? Be sure that the program you choose offers this option. If your goal is to see as many dance productions or plays, or hear as many concerts as possible, find a program that includes frequent field trips.

If you regularly study in an urban community, why not choose a campus school for a change of pace? Conversely, perhaps you need to experience the excitement of a big city for the summer.

If you study in large classes during the school year, perhaps a summer that offers more personal tutelage is best for you. Are you the star of your regular school? Then choose a program with more advanced students who will challenge you and offer inspiration.

DANCERS

As you grow older, it is important to assess your long-range goals. If you are a dancer and have targeted a particular dance company in which you would eventually like to work, investigate whether that company has a summer program. This is a good way to "try out" the decision both for you and for the company. Try not to have unrealistic expectations. Being accepted into a company summer school certainly does not guarantee that the company is interested in you in the long term. Obviously, companies accept many more people into the course of study than they consider for company apprenticeship or membership. It is also critical to attend a program linked to a professional company only when you are ready for it, not before. Attending at the right moment can lead to great things; the wrong time can lead to disaster. You don't want to leave a bad impression by trying something before you are ready.

ACTORS

Actors may want to consider auditioning for an apprenticeship with a summer stock company. "Cattle call" auditions (open to all) are usually held in early winter and are advertised in the trade newspapers such as New York's *Backstage*.

MUSICIANS

It is also wise for musicians to think long-range. Do you want to attend the conservatory or university where a particular teacher is a principal faculty member? Studying with that teacher in a summer program is a good way to determine if the chemistry is right between the two of you.

> Be careful when timing your auditions for companies or certain teachers in any of the performing arts. Teachers and directors remember bad auditions. If you need more training and are not ready for company stage work or working with a master teacher, wait. Enroll in a summer program in which you can take more classes and improve your skills.

CHOOSING THE PROGRAM

Once you have narrowed the field to a small group of institutions, be sure to request written information about the program as well as application information. At this point, you can better assess the faculty to see if their backgrounds meet your needs and can establish which faculty members you would actually be studying with, for some might be regular faculty, while others might be guest instructors. Use this guide to find information about costs and scholarship opportunities. Master dance teacher, David Howard, wisely points out that most reputable summer programs offer substantial scholarship aid to only a few deserving students. Offering a small rebate to a large group of students is more of a marketing device than a scholarship program, with the notable exception of a few wholly subsidized summer study programs that are tuition free for all participants.

Consult both your principal teacher and your parents. Teachers are a source of great wisdom, as they know your capabilities and how you work. They can help you with the difficult decision of where you may best flourish. Your parents can help assess your maturity to determine whether or not you will get the most out of a program and whether a program is financially feasible.

To make that final decision easier and to avoid disappointment, be sure to apply to several summer programs—many are highly competitive. Carefully study the entrance requirements and be sure to follow all their instructions. Get ready for that audition! It will be one in a long line that will help to determine your future course.

3

THE APPLICATION PROCESS

GENERAL ADVICE

Some rare students breeze through the application process with little angst and escape the anxiety most feel when asked, "Where do you want to go to school?" Others anguish over every comma they write on an application and treat the process as though it were an extra academic course. With some advance planning, patience, and the ability to ask for help when you need it, the application process does not have to be too painful. Whether you are applying to a high school or college program, the essential steps include the following:

- Establish your criteria
- Obtain catalogs and brochures
- Obtain application forms
- Visit the schools, watch their videos, or visit their websites
- Go on interviews or meet with representatives who visit your school and/or alumni in your area

- Audition, if required
- Take required standardized tests (SSATs or ISEEs, SAT or SAT II, ACT, or TOEFL) and be sure to have copies of your score reports sent directly to the schools that require them
- Write required essays and/or résumés
- Wait, wait, wait until the admissions committee makes its decision
- Decide which school you want to attend and send in your deposit holding your place in class, or endure the waiting list process

In the initial stages of your research, it is not unusual to come up with a fairly long list of high schools or colleges that spark your interest. Consider size, location, climate, housing, friends, the faculty, overall reputation, your own interests (both academic and non-academic), and whether the school is co-educational or single-sex. Your job is much like that of a matchmaker—finding the school, program, or college that is right for you at this point in your development. When you visit a campus, you will often have a visceral response. Close your eyes. Can you picture yourself at this school? Would you make friends and be productive? Could you enjoy living and learning in this environment? Since a great deal of learning at residential schools and colleges takes place outside the classroom, the living part of that question is very important.

You must begin your search for a school at least one year in advance of your intended enrollment. Performing artists who want to apply to a conservatory should review catalogs and audition requirements almost two years in advance, so that they have plenty of time to practice the required repertoire or monologues. For programs that begin in the fall, you should have a narrowed down and balanced list of schools prepared by November of the year before you want to start. The list should include schools that are realistic choices, some that are more competitive ("reach schools"), and others that you have a very good chance of getting into, often called "safeties." This applies to conservatories as well. Because conservatories put much more weight on your audition, and you never know when you might have a bad day, completing more applications or staggering deadlines (doing some early auditions and then doing later auditions if you do not get in) is often a good strategy.

RESEARCHING THE INFORMATION

As you think about your educational future, it is important that you thoroughly research all your options. You should write, call, or e-mail the schools early in the process to obtain catalogs, applications, financial aid information, and audition and admissions requirements. Talk to your teachers, guidance counselor, or college advisor. Talk to students who currently attend the arts high school, boarding school, or college you are considering. Visit campuses. Use this book to research the main performing arts programs at the high school and undergraduate levels. Choose one of our other guides, such as The Princeton Review's *The Best 311 Colleges* or *The Complete Book of Colleges* to get insight into liberal arts programs and to provide the student's point of view concerning life on campus.

Once you have received the catalogs, read them carefully and critically to glean facts about the requirements and the curriculum, faculty, and alumni. Performing arts programs vary. Pay careful attention to what is required for entrance, particularly for the audition. If you do not have the repertoire or monologues ready, start preparing them immediately. Discuss the audition with your current teacher.

Many schools will also send you a videotape. Watching the video will give you some insight into the level of performance and the basic type of person who attends a school. The video, however, has been produced, usually at great expense, and features the most photogenic and articulate students on a campus, on the sunniest days. If you cannot make a personal visit to a school, a video might help you visualize the place, but do not be fooled into thinking that everything will be beautiful and perfect like in the video.

Surf the Internet. Many performing arts high schools have their own websites, and colleges and universities are leaders in using the Internet for marketing purposes. Survey their calendar of events, look at the faculty list, and read the online school newspaper. You can now apply electronically to many colleges and universities. *Just be sure to keep a hard copy of everything you transmit.*

Some schools will give you the names of alumni or currently enrolled students who live in your vicinity. If you speak with either alumni or the students, be sure that you are prepared with very specific questions to ask them about their experience at the school. For a dance program you might ask questions such as: How frequent are the technical classes? What is their level? How much personal correction is given? What kinds of techniques are offered? What are the performance opportunities? In music, your inquiries might include information about how often lessons occur, what juries are like, seating and rotation in the orchestra, casting in operas, and what happens if you want to change your major teacher. Drama students might ask about casting for shows, what happens at conferences, and if students are "cut" from the program. Questions about residential life, what happens on weekends, and the level of competition among students are also appropriate. Remember, however, that the person with whom you are speaking is representing the admissions office and will usually explain most things in a positive light.

THE FACULTY

Finding out about the faculty may take a bit of digging, but it is worth the effort. What kind of qualifications should your teacher(s) have? Obviously, a thorough knowledge of the subject matter is most important. Try to find out from whom the teachers themselves learned their craft, and how intensive their study was.

Not everyone agrees about how important it is for a teacher to have a good professional background. Although it is certainly true that the most accomplished professional is not necessarily the best teacher, it is imperative that serious students of the arts seek teachers who have experienced first hand the rigors of a professional performing career. There is no substitute for having gone through the process of a professional career, and nothing in the classroom can take its place. Going from study directly into teaching is not a substitute for experiencing the real world of the performing arts. Thus, the prospective student should learn about this aspect of faculty qualifications.

A third critical question revolves around whom the faculty or private teacher has trained. Renowned teachers almost always produce at least some renowned students. Beware, however, of the issue of "big name" faculty—although they serve on staff, they may be available to students rarely or not at all. You should inquire about how often they are away performing themselves, leaving their students to fend for themselves or be taught by assistants.

And finally, how will the personalities and expectations of the student and faculty mesh? Some students flourish only in the most competitive atmospheres, with teachers who make the most stringent demands. Some simply need teachers who crack the whip. Others only blossom in a nurturing situation, needing a liberal amount of encouragement and understanding. Not only must the prospective student evaluate the potential teacher, she must also honestly assess her own goals and needs to find the right fit.

The best source of information about the training and accomplishments of the faculty is usually the catalog or bulletin published by the school. It will contain detailed biographical information about its faculty. But the intangible information about personality is harder to come by. Speaking to past and present students can be helpful; however, beware of getting only one opinion for it can be quite slanted. A consensus is much more helpful.

In dance and drama, observing a class or two is sometimes possible and can be illuminating. In music, it is often possible to arrange for a "sample lesson" or "consultation" with a private teacher. Be prepared to pay for the teacher's time in the latter situation. Fees can range from $85 to $200.

ALUMNI

Most reputable institutions will be able to provide information about alumni. Graduates are (or should be) a source of great pride. You can learn two particular pieces of information from alumni: what kind of talent the school attracts and how successful the teaching is.

In addition to the few celebrities that the institution justly prides itself on, it is of interest to find out certain statistics. Investigate what percentage of the student body goes on to professional careers, what kind of companies or musical organizations they join, and what the range of their professional work is. There should be some correlation between alumni achievement and the goals of the student. If, for example, an actor's goal is to perform in commercial theater, it is of little help to learn that the school has produced a great many Shakespearean specialists. Perhaps a string player is most interested in forming a quartet; is there precedent among the alumni? If the majority of dance alumni end up on Broadway, is the school right for the budding ballerina?

Finding out about alumni should not be difficult. Some institutions publish this information in their catalog, or the admissions office will send it to you if you request it. At other schools you may be referred to the alumni office or directly to the dance, drama, or music department.

FILLING OUT THE FORMS

Remember that when filling out application forms, neatness counts. Photocopy the original application and use the copy to prepare a rough draft before you start on the original. Most applications ask for standard information such as your name, address, social security number, and then various lists and short essays about your interests and extracurricular activities. Although typing your application is best, neat, legible handwriting in black or blue ink is also acceptable.

If you are asked about extracurricular activities and only play the oboe or dance or have been doing commercials, do not be afraid to list only that. Long laundry lists of activities do not overly impress admissions officers. Someone who has spent time developing a talent in depth is often far more appealing and interesting, demonstrating discipline and commitment.

At many colleges and universities, and at some performing arts high schools, summer programs, and conservatories, you can apply electronically through the school's website. Before you transmit the form, be sure to proofread it carefully and to print out a copy of what you have sent. Some programs will also require you to mail a hard copy with the application fee.

Other programs make their application forms available on software. Apply!, CollegeNET, and College Link are three sources to investigate. If you do not have access to a personal computer, your college advisor or public library may have ExPan or College Connector, other programs that let you fill out applications on the computer.

It is important that you fill out the forms and mail or transmit them well ahead of the deadline. Since many schools schedule auditions on a first-come, first-served basis, applying in advance can be to your advantage.

RECOMMENDATIONS

High schools, colleges, or conservatories may ask you to submit recommendations from your teachers. Sometimes they will specify that a math and an English teacher, or your principal instructor in dance, drama, or music write the recommendations. Other times, they will allow you to choose who writes on your behalf.

You should ask the person well in advance, giving them the forms and a stamped, self-addressed envelope. Sometimes it is helpful to give them a copy of your résumé, a list of activities, or other documents that will help the person write a balanced portrait of you. As a gesture of courtesy and appreciation, send a thank you note to the people who write your recommendations. It is especially nice to let those who recommended you know once you find out if you are accepted or not.

Avoid the temptation to send more recommendations than are required. If the school or program to which you are applying does not request a letter from someone in your major area of arts concentration, you might send one letter of this nature anyway, documenting your special talent. An entire dossier of every program you have performed in or review you have received is overkill and not regarded favorably by admissions officers, who are engulfed in application material.

RÉSUMÉ

Although some colleges and universities welcome your résumé, they rarely ask you to include it. A conservatory, however, may require that you include your performance résumé. Some arts magnet high schools and summer programs require a résumé as well. We recommend that all performing arts students include a résumé with their applications. The following are a few things to remember when writing a résumé:

- It should be typed.
- The grammar and spelling should be correct and consistent throughout.
- It should be honest. Faculty in dance, drama, and music can detect a hyperbolic résumé immediately. Represent your experience—no matter how limited—with complete truth.
- It should include current work. For students applying to arts high schools, include any summer program you have attended or extracurricular lessons or classes. For college applications, the résumé might include your work history over the four years of high school. Do not go back to your childhood.

You can find sample résumés in the appendix of this book to serve as models.

PHOTOGRAPHS

Institutions sometimes ask dancers, actors, and singers to include a photograph with their applications. This does not mean that you must rush right out to an expensive photographer to have your "head shot" professionally taken. Admissions committees usually use these photographs as a reminder after your audition or interview, and also to help put together a specific class. Dance faculty will look at your body type, your feet, and your placement in the photo. Drama teachers may be thinking of the repertoire planned for the next season and be looking to add certain "types" for the incoming group. When you submit a photograph, be sure to write your name, address, and telephone number on the back of it.

PHOTO GUIDELINES: DANCERS

Read the application guidelines carefully. The photograph requirement is usually quite specific. For example, the admissions panel may request a frontal photograph in *tendu à la seconde* or a profile in *arabesque*. Others may want photographs taken from a dance concert. Be sure the shot fulfills the requirements and send in only what is asked for.

PHOTO GUIDELINES: ACTORS

A head shot is usually fine, but check to see if the application specifies a full-body shot. Do not submit photos that are overly suggestive or in which you appear in an outrageous costume.

PHOTO GUIDELINES: MUSICIANS

It is usually only singers, not other instrumentalists, who may be asked to include a photograph. Submit a simple head shot or a casual picture. Do not send in a photo in which you are wearing a costume.

THE ESSAY

Being able to write well could tip the balance in your favor for high school, college, or university admissions committees. For conservatories, however, it is always your audition that carries the most weight. Some conservatories are now asking for written statements, especially for drama students. Your application essays are an opportunity for you to personalize the process. Spend time working on your essay and be prepared to write several drafts. Edit your essay carefully and avoid spelling and grammatical errors.

Make sure always to meet the deadline when sending applications. Sending in your admissions materials early is an even better idea, because it allows the program to enter you into their applicant records sooner. Always keep copies of everything you send for your own records; things do get lost in the mail.

Choosing the essay topic can be a challenge. Write about something meaningful to you, not something you think a committee wants to read. Most admissions officers agree that, when well written, almost any topic can make a good essay. For performers, avoid the cliché essays, such as your school choir's trip to France, your first *Nutcracker* performance, or your first play. A special experience that happened on that trip—how you tripped walking onto the risers and dropped all your music and how you handled that situation, or how a soloist got sick and you learned and performed that solo—reflects more of your personal characteristics and will be more interesting.

Write well, do many drafts, and mail applications before the deadlines.

THE INTERVIEW

If a high school or college requires an interview, be sure that you are properly prepared. Dress neatly and avoid using slang when speaking. Be positive and conversational. Nothing is worse for an interviewer than students who reply to questions with monosyllabic responses. Drama applicants and singers generally tend to be more loquacious. If you have this trait, beware of the tendency to go on endlessly.

A personal interview is an opportunity for an institution's representative to get to know you better as a real person; not just as a stack of essays, recommendations, and test scores. It is also an opportunity for you to talk about your involvement in the arts. For example, if you are a trombonist, play in a band and orchestra, and take private lessons, talk about how much you practice every day. Mention what attracted you to your instrument in the first place. The interview is also a chance for you to ask questions, so read the catalog and prepare salient questions based on your criteria for a school; however, avoid being confrontational. Questions that seek relevant information are fine; questions that challenge will only antagonize the interviewer.

If a representative from a school or college visits your current school, be sure to meet with this person, as he may end up being your advocate on the admissions committee; personal contact can be a big help. After an interview or personal contact with a representative, always send a thank you note as a courtesy.

ENTRANCE EXAMS

HIGH SCHOOL

Many high schools, whether public or private, require applicants to take standardized tests and have the results sent directly to the admissions office at the school. The two most common tests at the high school level are the SSAT (Secondary School Admission Test, 800-442-7728), required mainly for boarding schools, but also for some day schools, and the ISEE (Independent School Entrance Exam, 800-446-0320), used primarily at day schools. The SSAT and the

ISEE are multiple choice exams with sections that test verbal and mathematical ability and achievement. They also include reading comprehension passages. It is also common at the high school level to require applicants to take school-designed tests that usually include an essay and math problems. As part of the audition, students applying to a specialized music program often must take a test that measures musical aptitude. This test generally asks the applicant to repeat musical melodies, patterns, and rhythms.

POST-SECONDARY

Most colleges and universities in the United States require applicants to take standardized tests, sometimes called College Boards, which sound like an alphabet soup of letters. Educational Testing Service (ETS) administers the SAT, and the American College Testing program administers the ACT—the two standard college boards. It is important that you read each individual college, university, or conservatory's catalog and work out your standardized testing timetable well in advance. Your application will be incomplete and the admissions committee will not make a decision about your acceptance (or rejection) if you fail to present the required test results.

Whether you take the SAT or ACT can also depend on what part of the country you live in. Residents of most Midwestern states are more likely to take the ACT, but students in all areas can take either test. Take sample tests for both the SAT and ACT to help you judge which you score higher on. Most students take the PSAT (Preliminary SAT) in eleventh grade. How well you score on the PSAT may also help you to assess which test to take. Most schools accept scores from either exam, but some prefer the SAT over the ACT.

Other American colleges and universities will also require that you submit scores from SAT IIs, formerly called Achievement Tests. SAT IIs cover twenty different subjects, such as Chemistry, French, and English Literature. Speak with your teacher while you are taking a course to determine if you should take that specific test. For instance, if you are in eleventh grade and finishing your study of Spanish, are you prepared to take—and do well on—the SAT II: Spanish test?

Although some American conservatories require standardized tests—especially those conservatories that are part of universities or have a more academic component—most will require only that applicants who do not speak English as their native language take the Test of English as a Foreign Language (TOEFL). International students applying to colleges, conservatories, or universities in the United States should be certain to ask about any other special exams that test English fluency. If you are an American applying to a program abroad, it is usually expected that you be at least conversationally fluent in that country's native language. Most programs use either a written or oral exam to test your knowledge of the foreign language.

Conservatories may also ask musicians applying to their program to take examinations in music history, music theory, and ear training.

Preparing for all of these examinations is important. Although there is still debate about test preparation for standardized tests, most agree that test-takers who have experience in taking multiple-choice tests and know what types of questions to anticipate earn higher scores. The SAT registration materials include a sample SAT that you should take. Speak with your college advisor and your parents about taking The Princeton Review's test preparation class, or buying its test preparation books and software. Courses and tutors that teach test-taking strategies and build your confidence have been useful in boosting many students' scores.

If you are a musician and know that you must take exams other than standardized tests, be sure to review the material well in advance. Ask what music textbooks the school uses in theory, history, or ear training classes. Study those specific books to gain some insight into what to expect on a basic music entrance test.

WAITING

After you have submitted all of your applications and had your interviews and auditions, do not be surprised if you feel tense during the waiting period. Many students have nightmares, wake up in a cold sweat, and are convinced that every thin envelope the mailman delivers is a rejection letter from their top-choice school. Other students become so anxious that they submit last-minute applications to a few more schools. If the list of high schools, colleges, or conservatories that you applied to has been balanced from the start, and if your auditions have not been disasters, resist the urge to send out additional applications.

If you need a positive outlet to channel your nerves, consider sending the institutions to which you applied additional information about an accomplishment or achievement you have realized since sending in the original application. Do not overdo this, however. Sending a copy of an outstanding paper or a program from a recent performance will do.

If your auditions have not gone well, talk to your teacher and college advisor about trying to arrange a late audition. Many conservatories have rolling deadlines, and some music departments do not always meet their quotas in various instruments. Think about what went wrong in previous auditions. Were you sufficiently prepared with the repertoire? Did you follow instructions? Did you get nervous? Learn from your mistakes so you can approach the next set of auditions with greater confidence.

THE DECISION

Despite the agony of the waiting period, there will come a fateful day when the high schools, colleges, conservatories, or universities you applied to will send you their admissions decisions. You will learn one of three things: you are accepted, you are rejected, or you have been put on the waiting list. If the school has placed you on the waiting list, try not to get overly stressed; your chances of getting in are not over. Do not despair over a rejection. You can usually re-apply in the future, but most times it just was not meant to be.

If you receive multiple acceptances, celebrate your good fortune and success, but don't celebrate for too long. You need to start giving some serious thought to which school will be best for you. Follow these guidelines in your decision-making process:

- Do not immediately accept the biggest name school on your list unless you are absolutely in love with it.
- Do not make your decision based on what your peers are doing.
- Try to revisit campuses—stay overnight, sit in on classes, and eat in the cafeteria. These activities can be very enlightening after you have been admitted.
- Although an important deciding factor is whether or not the school is financially feasible for you and your family, beware of accepting a school based solely on financial considerations. Evaluate financial aid packages and discuss them with your parents and the school's financial aid officer (see Financial Aid page 31).

After giving thoughtful and careful consideration, be sure to meet the deadline for informing the school of your choice, and to tell your other acceptances that you will not be enrolling.

4

FINANCIAL AID

Paying for higher education is a critical concern for most parents and students. After years of absorbing the costs of lessons, summer programs, instruments, and costumes, your family's budget may be lean. Do not despair, and do not limit your search for a school based on tuition. One of the biggest mistakes you can make in the entire admissions process is failing to consider a school because you think it might be too expensive. Do not judge a program by its price tag! Some of the most expensive schools have the most money to spend on financial aid. Private boarding and day schools often offer substantial scholarship help, as do colleges, conservatories, and universities. You must apply for scholarships, however, and you must do so in a timely fashion. The forms are complex, labor-intensive, and it seems that the rules are forever changing. Do not hesitate to ask for help with the financial aid process. Financial aid officers, college advisors, as well as accountants and consultants who specialize in financial aid are all resources available to you. Most importantly, remember this is an occasion when your special talent may help you. Performing arts applicants often get a "free ride" as a result of "bidding wars" that virtually buy talent as schools compete for students.

Even if your parents earn high incomes, you may still qualify for some financial aid in the form of merit-based scholarships. Ask the institution you are applying to about these scholarships. Some private schools, colleges, or universities may award financial aid to families who earn what may be perceived to be high incomes if these families have mitigating circumstances that might include having several children in college simultaneously, supporting elderly relatives, or other demanding financial obligations or unusual expenses. Harvard is reported to have recently given aid to 300 families with incomes of more than $100,000 a year after assessing the families' special situations and need. If money is not an issue, however, don't even bother applying for aid. Some performing artists and their parents seem to have a sense of entitlement, believing that the world owes them subsistence through their education. Do not fall into this trap. It is rare that a financial aid committee will reward this sort of attitude with any tuition assistance. If your family, however, has a real cash flow issue, then definitely inquire about payment plans.

A Word to Parents:
It is your job to complete all the forms. For high school financial aid, you must complete the Family Financial Statement (FFS). For colleges, you may be required to file a Free Application for Federal Student Aid (FAFSA) and possibly the College Board's PROFILE form. You can receive most of these forms by calling the School and College Scholarship Service at 800-778-6888. Many institutions require a copy of your federal income tax form as well, and some also request an asset/liability statement.

Financial aid offers may include a grant, loan, and/or work/study opportunity. It is not uncommon these days for parents to evaluate all the financial aid offers, and then call the institutions involved to try and negotiate. Although some financial aid officers remain firm in the initial offer and find this sort of negotiation offensive, others will respond to this "dialing for dollars" approach. An institution won't necessarily take offense if you explain that you have your heart set on attending that specific program, but feel you cannot turn down an offer from another school that would be of great help to your parents' financial stability.

SCHOLARSHIPS

Many other scholarship sources are out there—you just need to do comprehensive research to learn about them. Avoid costly scholarship search services and do your homework on your own. The Princeton Review publishes a helpful guidebook—*The Scholarship Advisor*—that lists many scholarship opportunities. Ask every school you apply to about merit scholarships. Many corporations such as Metropolitan Life, Bank of America, General Electric, and General Mills also have scholarship programs for employees' children. Educational institutions themselves sometimes help subsidize schooling for faculty offspring through tuition remission programs or grants. Alumni groups, clubs, churches, civic organizations, and some specialized arts organizations such as the American Society of Composers, Authors, and Publishers (ASCAP) provide some funds, although usually not large amounts.

The ARTS program is of particular interest to young performing artists. As part of the National Foundation for Advancement in the Arts (NFAA), the ARTS program is designed to identify, recognize, and encourage young people who demonstrate excellence in dance, music, jazz, theater, and other areas. ARTS holds a scholarship competition each year and award winners receive national recognition and cash prizes. Call 800-970-2987 for more information.

5

SPECIAL ADVICE FOR DANCERS

After you complete the application process, you will have to get through your audition. In this chapter, we give the dancer essential information about how to make it through this step. And of course, if you are accepted, it is then your turn to audition the school. This chapter offers some practical advice, questions to ask, and what to look for in terms of curriculum, faculty, facilities, and the like in a dance program. Take time to consider all of the following—don't make a hasty decision just because it is the first offer you get. Weigh your options, and give this choice serious consideration.

THE AUDITION

Why is it that some people breeze through auditions and others freeze? In most cases, those people who appear confident are just as nervous as those who freeze, sweat, and shake. Chances are that everyone is nervous at an audition. So why do people project themselves so differently?

Part of the answer is certainly a matter of personality and nature—something you cannot do much about. But another large component is preparation. If you are properly prepared, you will feel more confident. For example, be sure that you allow much more time than is necessary to arrive at the audition. Allow yourself time to get lost (just in case), to find the right room, to find the dressing room, to pay fees, and to warm up thoroughly. Nothing can be as unsettling as flying into the studio at the last minute with everything spilling out of your dance bag—everything, that is, but what you need.

WHAT TO WEAR

The first rule is to look your very best. Neatness definitely counts. Be sure your outfit is attractive, clean, and in excellent repair. If a particular type of attire is specified for the audition, be sure to wear it.

A ballet audition often requires women to wear black leotards, and pink tights and shoes, both soft technique and pointes. Schools usually require that men wear white close fitting tee shirts, black tights, white socks, and black or white shoes. For modern dance, it is essential to be barefoot, and it is usually acceptable to wear a leotard or unitard that has some color in it; jazz auditions usually allow more leeway and individuality in attire, but beware of too much showmanship. Choose the leotard with the most flattering neckline and cut, or the tee shirt that fits just right. Wear something that helps identify you without being flamboyant.

Dancewear is designed to show the line of the body, and it is this line that the auditioners are looking for. Leave sweats, plastic pants, leg warmers, floppy sweaters, and the like on the sidelines to keep you warm while another group is working. Such clothing has no place during the audition. If you wear them onto the floor, you will probably be asked, rather testily, to remove them.

It is an absolute necessity to have neatly coifed hair. Women should wear light and attractive street makeup. Leave all the bangles, bracelets, and jewelry at home. If you have pierced ears, it's fine to wear small, discrete earrings. Looking your best both attracts the eye of the auditioners and gives you a nice jolt of self-esteem. No one will notice the mouse in the back of the room whose hair is unkempt, or the person who is trying to fade into the woodwork.

HOW TO BEHAVE

Being polite to the other dancers is not only a matter of courtesy, it also will help your case with the examiners. No school wants to enroll a troublemaker or someone with a difficult personality.

WHAT TO BRING

Unless you have already submitted it, bring a concise résumé (limited to a single page or two) to the audition. It should highlight the most important things you have done thus far. Be sure to include your name, address, telephone number, fax and e-mail address, the roles you have danced, and where you danced them. The résumé might also include your major teachers and any choreographic experience you have had. It is easy for a professional to spot a false résumé, so be honest but not humble. Do not inflate or denigrate your experience. (See the appendix for sample résumés.)

Be sure to carefully read the instructions you have been given, and do not deviate from them. If a photograph is required, have it with you unless, of course, you have already submitted it. The same is true for letters of recommendation, essays, health forms, and any similar material.

WHAT TO PERFORM

If you are required to perform a solo, KEEP IT SHORT. There is nothing more discouraging to auditioners than a piece that drags on and on when many others are waiting to audition. Whatever selection you choose, be sure you have rehearsed it sufficiently, so there will be no unwanted surprises. By all means show it to your teacher, your parents, your friends, or anyone else you can corral beforehand, so you are as confident as possible about your performance. Be prepared to announce the name of your piece, the choreographer, and the name and composer of the music.

Choose something that you can do very, very well. Never choose a piece that is beyond you technically; pyrotechnics are only interesting if performed securely and magnificently. Choose something that shows your performing skills, the breadth of your movement, and your ability to project to an audience. Confidence in your performance is essential, especially since there will undoubtedly be other parts of the audition that deal with your technical skills.

In most cases, the class is the core of the audition. Pay close attention, and do exactly what you are asked. This is the time to follow instructions, not the time to assert your individuality. That is what the solo is for. Practice the combinations discreetly on the sides, out of the line of vision of the auditioners, so that you do not distract them from the dancers they are trying to watch. Try not to get thrown if you make a mistake; everybody makes mistakes. Do not indulge in the desire to go to the corner and sulk. For auditioners, seeing a dancer work through material and succeed in getting it right is just as impressive as seeing him get it right the first time. It shows determination and the ability to learn and to improve, things every examiner is looking for. Try to dance the material as full out as possible. You are demonstrating your discipline, your ability to take direction, and, most of all, your joy in moving.

We informally surveyed seasoned professionals to see what they look for in dancers. The following are the top responses:

- Those who truly love to dance
- Dancers who bring quality to their movement
- Dancers who can take the phrase and make it their own without changing the steps or the intent
- Dancers who are a pleasure to watch, who capture the audience's attention
- Those who demonstrate discipline with poetry

THE MUSIC

Part of being prepared is to check and double check that you have your music in the appropriate format. A CD is useless if the school only has a cassette recorder. Be sure the music is properly cued up; no one wants to wait around while you fish for the start of your dance. Always come with a back-up tape; in fact, if you have access to a back-up tape recorder, come equipped with that as well, just in case. If you are working with live music, be sure you and your musician come to the audition together. That way you can avoid those last-minute jitters while awaiting her arrival. Try not to use the accompanist provided at the auditions; however, if you must, be sure to consult about tempi, repeats, and cuts before you begin.

THE CURRICULUM

A critical factor in choosing an institution to attend is the type of curriculum it offers. Not only should technical classes be of the highest quality, at an appropriate level, and inspirational, but the course offerings should also encompass everything crucial to training the dancer of today, as well as the topics that are particularly of interest to you.

Today, most companies want dancers to have a broad knowledge of the various techniques in the field. Even if your sole passion is classical ballet, you will find it difficult to get a job if you have never taken a modern dance class (although there are a few companies that are notable exceptions). It is also absolutely true that a modern dancer, dancers in the commercial fields, and most national dance specialists should have some experience in ballet. Almost every company commissions work from contemporary choreographers, most of whom have been exposed to various techniques and influences. Since the full range of movement and its control is the goal, it is important that the curriculum you choose offers other technical styles in addition to the one or two that are of greatest interest to you. In addition, your tastes and goals may change after you have been exposed to new ideas and new ways of moving, so be adventurous and open.

Be sure to find out about the school's policy concerning guest artists and/or master classes. Are they a regular part of the program? Are outside choreographers invited to work with the students? How long do guests stay—a single day, a week or two, a semester? Keep in mind that the contacts you make with outside choreographers and teachers can be helpful to you in your future job searches.

The school should also provide information about dance that is unavailable or impractical for studio schools. Make sure that the school offers at least some of the following courses:

- anatomy
- choreography
- dance history
- improvisation
- injury prevention
- interdisciplinary work
- Labanotation
- multiple dance forms (jazz, tap, classical Spanish, ballroom, African dance, etc.)
- music
- nutrition
- *pas de deux* or partner work
- production
- remedial body work
- repertory
- variations
- writing and criticism

As an intelligent, educated dancer, you should also have the opportunity to study such subjects as literature, art history, creative writing, languages, research techniques, dance and technology, and other similar topics. Obviously, only a huge department could provide all of these courses, but make sure the curriculum encompasses the particular course offerings that are of greatest interest to you.

It is also important to find out before you start a program just how much personal choice the curriculum allows. All dance programs have a preponderance of required courses. In some institutions, the path of study is totally or almost totally laid out; others offer considerable choice. If the curriculum is fixed, ask yourself if you will be happy with it. On the other hand, are you disciplined enough to enroll in the courses you need if there is a lot of leeway? Will you receive adequate curricular guidance? Consider these issues carefully before you choose your school, as they will all influence how satisfied you will be with the program.

PERFORMING

If your goal is to be a performer, thoroughly investigate the performing opportunities available. Find out if the school offers a range of performances from fully produced evenings to informal studio or workshop showings. Who choreographs such events? Who gets to perform? How is casting done? Are rehearsals extracurricular or are they a regular part of the credit-granting program? What kinds of facilities exist? Is there a dedicated theater or shared performance space? Do dancers perform with live music? Find out if it is possible for dance students to collaborate with their peers in other disciplines—for example, teaming up with poets, percussionists, singers, or composers on a project might be of great interest to you. Comparing and matching the answers to these questions with your own interests will have a profound bearing on how satisfied you will be with your experience at the school.

OTHER CURRICULAR OPTIONS

If you think you will go on to an alternate, non-performing, dance-related career, such as dance writing, dance criticism, or dance teaching, be sure that the institution you choose offers the course work you will need. If your plans include graduate study, make sure that you will be able to meet the entrance requirements of the graduate program you might wish to attend.

THE FACULTY

To obtain specific information about the dance faculty, start with the catalog. Evaluate where your prospective teachers have studied, what particular area or school of dance they teach, and what professional qualifications they hold. Make sure that they are expert in the specific area they will be teaching, not just in *some* area of dance.

Find out who will actually be instructing you. Some schools assign faculty by year (freshman, sophomore, etc.), others by level (intermediate, advanced, etc.). Will you have the same teacher five days a week, or does each year or level have several teachers? In general, it is more productive to study several times a week with the same teacher, although that is not always possible. Most dance departments offer little free choice concerning who your instructor will be, so it is important to find out in advance if the pool of teachers are professionals you respect. Sometime during your course of study, you should be able to work with the teacher who most interests you.

If your goal is to perform, be wary of an institution that features faculty whose greatest qualifications are their academic degrees. Although professional qualifications do not guarantee good teaching methodology, they do guarantee the teacher's knowledge of a particular technique, a familiarity with the requirements of the profession, and—quite importantly—a network of fellow artists whom they can contact to help your career move forward. This is especially important; the faculty should be able to help with practical information about how to go about getting a job and how to keep it.

HEALTH SERVICES

Dance is a dangerous profession. The statistics on injuries are worrisome. Every season, one-third of the dancers in major companies misses performing because of injury. Knowing this, many institutions offer special health services to their dancers.

INJURY CARE AND PREVENTION

More and more institutions have started to make Pilates' work and equipment, with regular training sessions led by qualified instructors, available to students. Other body-oriented work such as the Alexander Technique, Bartenieff Fundamentals, special anatomy laboratories devoted to Ideokinesis, or similar theories are often a welcome part of the program. Injury prevention training is often part of the formal curriculum or is available informally through faculty conferences. Knowing how to care for the body is essential for all dancers.

Many institutions have a physical therapist either as part of the faculty, as a regular visitor, or on call from a nearby health facility. Schools have discovered that it is economically sound to provide this service to students.

Large institutions often have an entire medical establishment, including clinics and a variety of services for their students, while smaller schools usually have a nurse on the premises with visiting doctors and/or arrangements with neighboring medical facilities. Many institutions also have confidential psychological counseling available to students.

NUTRITION

Nutrition advice and training are often part of the formal curriculum or are available informally through faculty conferences. Institutions know the importance of providing this information. It is essential to learn early in your career how to take care of your body.

A Cautionary Word

Much has been written about the dangers of yo-yo dieting and eating disorders. Although it is essential in the profession to keep a svelte body, it is counterproductive to starve yourself or to resort to extreme measures to keep your weight under control. Question whether the program you are considering overemphasizes thinness. The only acceptable solution to weight control is to practice proper nutrition, which means eating a healthy diet to maintain maximum energy and a good calcium supply. Information on nutrition should be available to every dance student.

INSURANCE

All institutions offer some kind of health insurance plan to students. Because the odds strongly indicate that most dancers will need medical insurance coverage sometime during their school career, it is important for you to enroll in the plan, (even if it is optional) and to subscribe to all supplementary insurance.

Make it a top priority to familiarize yourself with all health services the institution offers as soon as you enroll—and well in advance of needing to use them.

FACILITIES

It is the rare institution whose students are lucky enough to have access to all of the facilities described below. Knowing the ideal, however, helps you understand what facilities are essential and what facilities institutions can sacrifice while still providing an acceptable standard of training.

STUDIOS

In dance, studio size is of more than passing importance. You will never learn to move expansively if you are always cramped for space. This does not mean that you should pick up your dance bag and leave if one of your classes is in a small studio, but at least some classes should be in a space that measures about thirty feet by forty to sixty feet, depending on class size. Ideal class size is between twelve and twenty-five students.

Keep dreaming—no matter what, there will probably never be an adequate number of studios, but a ratio of one studio for every twenty students is a workable number. Clearly, not every school is that well equipped; others surpass that mark.

Studio flooring is a topic endlessly discussed among dance professionals. Thanks to modern materials, most studio flooring is at least adequate. Marley covering laid over a sprung floor construction is common; an untreated wood surface over sprung construction for barefoot dancing is excellent if kept in constant repair to avoid splintering and slick spots. Studios that permit the use of resin should be separate from those used for barefoot activity. Cement underfloors, no matter how they are surfaced, are dangerous.

PERFORMING SPACE

Students and faculty dream of having a dedicated theater and/or black box performing space. Most institutions, however, expect several departments to share performing spaces. Ideally, the dance department should have a dedicated, informal performing space (such as a large convertible studio with lighting facilities and graduated seating), and a small-to mid-sized, well-equipped theater for more formal presentations. Staffed scene shops and costume shops are a delicious luxury, and, believe it or not, some institutions actually have them.

THE RECORDING FACILITY

Dancers should also have access to some sort of recording studio. Such a facility allows students to make tapes or CDs, splice and edit them, record live music, copy and edit videos, and so forth.

THE LIBRARY

There should certainly be access to adequate library facilities—meaning not only books, but also computers, periodicals, and an audio-visual center.

PERFORMING OPPORTUNITIES

The opportunity to perform a variety of works is one of the advantages of higher education. It is an integral element in the training of a young dancer. Without exception, institutions offer the young dancer a broader scope of performance possibilities than he may ever find again.

Both informal and fully produced formal performances are part of dance training, although it is not uncommon for formal performances to be restricted to students in their junior or senior years. Informal workshop performances are the first step to learning the craft of projecting to an audience. Such workshops should occur fairly frequently throughout the year–usually weekly, monthly, or at least several times a semester. Often the dancers are not in costume, and the audience consists only of fellow students and some faculty.

Fully produced formal concerts obviously occur much less frequently; once a semester or even once a year is common. Two concerts a year allows more opportunity for all eligible dancers to perform, but it is always a balancing act to prepare for formal concerts without sacrificing too much of the essential daily technical work.

Throughout the year, you may find the opportunity to dance in other performances. A peer's choreography, a senior project concert, special school celebrations, concerts with colleagues from other departments, and tours to nearby primary and secondary schools are all possibilities.

Many institutions recruit guest choreographers. Working with a guest provides a wonderful opportunity for students; it opens their horizons, challenges their technical and performing skills, and builds a network of contacts that may be helpful in future job searches.

A Note of Caution:
Do not allow your fascination with performing to take over so much of your energy that you miss classes or suffer injuries. Missing classes defeats the purpose of your school experience. Being overly tired leads to lack of concentration, and is the single most common cause of injury.

CAREER SEARCH

Almost all company membership and all jobs in the dance field are decided either by audition or by personal knowledge of the candidate. No one can get you a job or into a company if you are not good enough. That said, personal acquaintances and professional contacts can be of great help.

The most a placement office or career counselor can do for aspiring dancers is to keep them informed of openings, auditions, and opportunities. Faculty members, however, can make those all-important telephone calls to their contacts—if they have any. Such contacts can open many doors and are invaluable. Institutions that boast professionals among their faculty are in an enviable position to give their students' emerging careers a push. Clearly, the faculty will only do this for students whom they believe have the talent to make a contribution to a company or production. After all, if the faculty were to recommend everyone, their opinion would no longer carry any weight.

Your other hidden career aid is the contacts that you make during your school years. If you have the opportunity to work with a guest choreographer or teacher, and you do well, you will have made a contact that may help you in later years. Choreographers are most interested in dancers who are gratifying to work with. They cannot spend their time and energy catering to the needs of difficult, temperamental, or rigid dancers—no matter how talented.

After graduation, be prepared to go to lots of auditions. Also be prepared to face reality—*you will be rejected many times*. For each audition, the choreographer will be searching for a specific type of dancer. If you are not that type, you will not be hired, no matter how good your audition may have been. Try to stay positive despite rejection, and try not to take it too personally. You may be rejected ten times in a row, but don't let that dissuade you from going to the eleventh audition. That may well be the time you are exactly the type of dancer the choreographer is looking for.

6

SPECIAL ADVICE FOR ACTORS

After you complete the application process, you will have to get through your audition. In this chapter, we give the actor essential information about how to make it through this step. And, of course, if you are accepted, it is your turn to audition the school. This chapter offers some practical advice, questions to ask, and what to look for in terms of curriculum, faculty, facilities, and the like in a drama program. Take time to consider all of the following—don't make a hasty decision just because it is the first offer you get. Weigh your options and give your choice serious consideration.

THE AUDITION

Most arts high schools and conservatories (but usually not colleges) require drama students to audition. Some are specific about what they would like you to present: perhaps a Shakespearean monologue or another piece in verse, or perhaps two contrasting monologues—one comic and one serious, or one contemporary and one classical. Some will have you take a movement class, sing *a cappella*, do an improvisation, or even perform a cold reading.

An important thing to remember is that your audition begins the very moment you step into the audition room or onto the stage. Your "off-stage" personality and how you present yourself is of great interest to drama teachers.

The actual audition format varies from school to school; usually a faculty panel of from two to four members will watch or listen to the audition. At some schools, the vibe will be friendly and informal; the panel may even ask you to talk with them a little bit before launching into your monologue. Be conversational but not overly chatty. Telling them your entire life story in an exaggerated theatrical manner is a definite turn-off. At other auditions, the tone will be quite formal, very professional, even intimidating. Remember that you have paid for this chance to audition. This is your moment. Do not be afraid. Perform your monologues with conviction. Determine in advance if there will be a call back, and if so, where and when that list will be posted.

WHAT TO PERFORM

Know what the audition panel expects of you and follow the instructions precisely. If you are given a list of suggested monologues, it is not a bad idea to choose from these suggestions, or perhaps from one of the many books of standard monologues available. Choose your pieces wisely. They should be age appropriate, within the realm of good taste, and within stipulated time guidelines—usually not more than two minutes. Auditioners will *not* favorably view something too unfamiliar, something you or a friend have written, or something off the wall. Nor will they be happy with selections that are too long.

Be sure that you are thoroughly familiar with both the monologue and its context within the play. Young acting students often make the mistake of preparing a monologue without understanding the character, reading the entire play, or even knowing who *wrote* the piece. Practice your monologue for several months. Perform it for your drama teacher, your parents, and your friends. The more you do it in front of people, and not just in front of the mirror, the more prepared you will be for the audition.

Plan to move around somewhat during the audition, as the panel will want to see how you move and speak at the same time. If you plan to use a prop, limit it to one small thing—nothing gimmicky. For example, if you do a letter scene, a piece of paper would be fine. Bringing an entire desk, chair, and stationery set would not be appropriate.

LIVE OR TAPED

It is definitely best to do your auditions live whenever possible. International students, students who cannot travel great distances, or students who have schedule conflicts, may have to videotape their audition and send it in. If you must submit a videotape, make sure to adhere to a few basic principles. Be sure that the quality of the video is good. It does not have to be professionally produced, but must be well lit, in focus, and have decent sound quality. Also, be sure to label both the videotape and the box you send it in with your name, address, and telephone number. Announce your monologues clearly on the tape. You should include the name of the play, author, character, and which act your monologue is from. Make sure you state your name, age, and your address.

WHAT TO WEAR

Actors at auditions are often "PIBs"—People in Black—as that seems to be the most popular color to wear. It need not be, however, as long as you dress in a manner that is comfortable and professional. Be sure that if you are required to take a movement class, you bring the appropriate attire (usually sweats) and that you do not call more attention to your clothes than to the quality of your acting.

An informal survey of drama teachers revealed that, when auditioning young actors, they look for the following qualities:

- a burning desire to act
- potential and natural talent
- a receptive personality
- ability to work with others
- ability to memorize and project
- discipline
- interesting voice quality
- ability to take direction and work with it

THE CURRICULUM

If you want to be an actor, you do not need the years of technical study that dancers and musicians require. Most actors, however, should have specialized training in their craft. Look for programs that offer voice, speech, and movement classes, along with more specialized courses such as stage combat and improvisation.

You also want to know that your personal philosophy matches that of your drama program. You can inquire what the mission and vision of the program is, and make sure that the curriculum is designed to realize that mission. If your goals do not match the goals of a drama program, look elsewhere to avoid inevitable conflict and disappointment.

In evaluating a drama curriculum, look for a variety of offerings that interest you. Find out if the school offers courses in areas such as costume design, lighting design, scenic design, directing, technical direction, stage management, theater management, playwriting, mime, masks, and the Alexander technique. You will want to know which acting technique the school teaches. Read course descriptions carefully to determine what the curriculum encompasses.

HIGH SCHOOL

At the high school level, institutions usually offer students academic courses in all aspects of theater, practical exploration of the discipline, and the opportunity to present their work before an audience.

Typical course offerings for high school students might include the following: Introduction to Acting, Public Speaking, Technical Theater, Theater and History, Introduction to Directing, Advanced Acting, Directing Workshop, Play Production, Shakespearean Workshop, and Movement Workshop.

COLLEGE

At the college level, actors need to determine whether to pursue a Bachelor of Fine Arts program (BFA) or a Bachelor of Arts (BA). It really depends on how you want to focus your time. BFA programs, or "conservatory" programs, may require students to perform in productions and will offer only about one-third of their courses in the liberal arts. The training is specialized and focused. Students who enroll in BA programs usually have a passion for the theater, but also have interests in other areas. A good BA program will give you technical training in acting, along with a broad academic education.

NON-DEGREE COURSES

If you want to improve a certain skill, brush up on a particular technique, or just are not interested in getting a degree, look for some of the many non-degree granting theater programs. These programs usually offer very specialized courses such as audition techniques, acting for film, daytime drama, commercials, and voiceover techniques. Some actors who take a class or two in these programs find them tremendously helpful, both for their craft and for networking with other students and teachers.

THE FACULTY

Read the institution's catalog carefully to obtain information about the drama faculty. Are they active professionals with links to companies and first-hand knowledge of the business? Many actors believe that the best training comes from faculty who are practicing in their field and bring their expertise to the classroom.

Determine the size of the department. How many faculty members are there? How many are full time and how many are part time? How many faculty members have more of an academic background and approach?

Guest artists, including renowned alumni, can add depth to a faculty. Many will come in to teach master classes in their specialty, and also to give students an honest analysis of what is happening in the business.

If you decide to take classes outside of a degree-granting institution, finding a good teacher (let alone a mentor) among scores of reputable teachers is difficult—but well worth your effort. Your body and your psyche are your acting instruments, and you want to work with people who will be positive and supportive. Talk to current or former students, ask to audit some classes, and interview the teacher. Your chemistry with a teacher is very important.

FACILITIES

Not every drama student dreams of having the perfect performing space. Actors can present plays in classrooms, courtyards, and other "alternative" spaces. In a high school, college, conservatory, or university, however, there should be at least one theater or auditorium available. You might ask about what other performing facilities are available to students. Is there a proscenium theater? A black box theater? Are rehearsal facilities adequate? Where are sets and props built and stored? Does the program have its own costume collection? Is there a costume shop on campus? What is the wing space like in the theaters?

When you are on a campus tour, look carefully at the theater spaces. Is the lighting and sound state-of-the-art? Given the number of performances each year, how is booking done for theaters? What do current students say about the facilities?

It is wonderful for drama students to have the opportunity to work in a variety of spaces. The intimacy of the black box and the expanse of the proscenium require different kinds of projection. There never seems to be enough space in the wings, never enough room in the dressing areas. You might as well learn to cope with this while in high school, because even the finest conservatories have to stretch their facilities. Current students can tell you how hard it is to get rehearsal time and space and just how adequate the facilities are.

PERFORMING OPPORTUNITIES

For every actor, the ultimate experience is getting to perform on stage. Having the chance to perform publicly that monologue you've been working on in class for weeks will also be a tremendous learning experience. Acting is a public activity and practicing in front of an audience is essential, so you need to find out everything you can about performance opportunities at each of the institutions you are considering.

It is important to ask institutions what types of performances you will be involved in as a student and how often they will take place. Are there fully produced productions? Informal workshops? In-school performances? Off-campus opportunities? Are there cabaret appearances? Cabarets are often the forum for the most original and outrageous student work. Ask current students what they think of the casting policy. Some schools reserve key roles for junior and senior year students. Ask each school if it places any restrictions on first-year students being cast in productions. Find out whether the school tolerates student-initiated productions. Are such productions encouraged? Frowned upon? Is there a budget to support these types of projects? If you need an avenue outside of the classroom to channel your creativity, finding a school that budgets for such projects might be important.

Review the repertoire of plays performed by students in the last two years. Who directed them? If it is the in-house drama professor, and you get along well with her, having her direct all of the plays may work quite nicely for you. On the other hand, will this person typecast you? What happens if you don't get along? Who will be directing in the next two years? A selection of in-house faculty/directors, combined with guest directors would be ideal.

Does the repertoire list include musicals? Straight plays? Contemporary, period, and experimental plays? If you are particularly interested in one type of dramatic literature, be sure to check that the institution favors that kind of play.

CAREER SEARCH

Career opportunities for actors are extremely competitive. Some conservatories invite casting agents, directors, and other industry people to a showcase highlighting their graduates. Some schools make their facilities available to companies who come in to hold auditions for film, television, and theater.

> For anyone launching a job search in the theater—be wise. Although the rare actor does get "discovered," these instances are few and far between. Beware of anyone offering you overnight success, and if you do get an offer, make sure to always get everything in writing.

At some point in your career search, you will need to decide what kind of acting you want to pursue. If you are interested in performing regionally, investigate every opportunity in your area. Do not, however, limit yourself to the obvious. Although many actors have launched their careers by performing in children's theater, dinner theater, industrial shows, comedy and improvisational groups, or even on cruises and at theme parks, most actors come to realize that they must spend time in either New York or Los Angeles—the two major hubs for theater. Chicago and Miami are other urban areas with opportunities for acting.

NETWORKING

In your job search, use alumni contacts, and realize that faculty members provide one of your best avenues for networking. If a faculty member believes in your talent and has witnessed your growth and hard work, he may open many doors for you. It helps to have contacts. If you know someone connected with show business, ask for their counsel and recommendation of a reputable licensed agent or manager.

CAREER SEARCH RESOURCES

Backstage is a weekly newspaper that lists acting classes and open calls for auditions—usually only those in New York City, but sometimes Los Angeles is covered as well. It also contains information about agents, managers, and photographers. A subscription to this publication is a good investment for anyone interested in a theater career, whether stage, film, television, Broadway, cabaret, or even the technical side of theater. You will often find useful articles in this newspaper about everything from how to get your equity card as a member of one of the actor's unions—Actors' Equity Association (AEA) or the Screen Actors Guild (SAG)—to how to do your make-up for your head shots.

To pursue your career goals, you will eventually need to get an agent or manager. It is most common to audition for agents early on in your career. You can find reputable agents and managers in any trade publication such as the following:

- *Backstage* (330 West 42nd Street, New York, NY 10036, 212-947-0020)
- *Stern's Performing Arts Directory* (*Dance Magazine,* 33 West 60th Street, New York, NY 10023, 212-245-9050)
- *Ross Reports USA* (Television Index, Inc., 40-29 27th Street, Long Island City, NY 11101)

Or visit a specialized bookstore that has aisles of career-related advice books and listings of agents and managers. Many of these bookstores will ship internationally. Two recommended bookstores in New York are:

- Applause Theatre Books (211 West 71st Street, New York, NY 10023, 212-496-7511)
- Drama Bookshop (723 Seventh Avenue at West 48th Street, Second Floor, New York, NY 10019, 212-944-0595)

Make sure to check if the agent or manager is a SAG-franchised agent or a member of the National Conference of Personal Managers, and thus possesses all the necessary union and license designations.

BACK-UP PLAN

A recent study revealed that of all drama majors, only 12 percent actually found full-time work acting. Another 15 percent found part-time acting jobs, and augmented their income with related work. Although an emerging actor must be positive, optimistic, and tough-skinned in the face of rejection, most will also need to have something "to fall back on." Such back-up skills can help avoid many years of driving taxis or waiting tables. During your years of study, you might want to take technical theater classes—stage management, lighting design, costuming, directing, and so on—so that if you want to teach or work in these related fields, you will have had the appropriate experience and education.

An outgoing personality, drama training, and your college degree will allow you to go into any field. How many lawyers were theater majors in college? How many people in sales took acting classes? Most corporations look for someone who can write well and think critically, who has self-discipline, and who possesses a strong work ethic. These are the very traits that are usually well developed in students of the performing arts.

7

SPECIAL ADVICE FOR MUSICIANS

After you complete the application process, you will have to get through your audition. In this chapter, we give the musician essential information about how to make it through this step. After you audition, if you are accepted, it is then your turn to audition the school. This chapter offers some practical advice, questions to ask, and what to look for in terms of curriculum, faculty, facilities, and the like in a music program. Take time to consider all of the following—don't make a hasty decision just because it is the first offer you get. Weigh your options and give your choice serious consideration.

THE AUDITION

Entire books have been written about how to approach a music audition. Great virtuosi have been known to freeze when confronted with the screen behind which some professional auditions are held. To be successful in auditions, you must make a mental adjustment. Try not to think that the panel is judging you. Beverly Sills, the great American soprano, once stated, "There are no such things as auditions. There are only performances." If you think of the audition as another performance instead of a trial, you may capture the interest of the panel.

PREPARATION

Preparation is paramount. Determine your repertoire early—months, if not years in advance, and practice, practice, practice. Some schools are quite explicit about what they require you to perform—certain Bach Preludes and Fugues, specific orchestral excerpts, art songs in specified languages, etc. Read the instructions carefully, and thoroughly prepare the required repertoire. Perform it for your teacher, your school, your friends, and your family. The more you practice, the more it will become part of your musical memory. Those who are well prepared tend to be less nervous on audition day.

Determine your opening piece in advance. It need not be the flashiest, hardest composition in your repertoire, but it should be the one with which you feel the most comfortable. Although audition committees usually have rather lengthy lists of requirements, they will seldom sit and listen to all the required pieces. They usually ask you to start with the selection of your choice. After the first piece, the music audition panel will look at your other offerings and ask you for a piece in a style that contrasts with the one you have just performed. This does not mean that you should have only two compositions in top form; you can never predict which and how many pieces the panel will ask you to perform.

When you leave for your audition, be certain that you have everything with you that you will need. Do you have your instrument, your music, and your equipment—such as a baton for a conductor, copies of compositions for composers, a stick bag for a percussionist, and perhaps even a music stand? It is embarrassing the number of times audition panels witness students walking in and opening empty instrument cases. Many performers who are prone to dryness of the mouth now bring their own bottles of water to the audition. It has become an accepted practice.

LIVE OR TAPED

It is best to audition in person. Audio and videotapes never do justice to the nuances of your performance. If you cannot audition in person because of distance or schedule conflicts, be sure that you prepare a tape with very good audio quality. You do not necessarily need to go to a recording studio to make a professionally produced tape, but a cassette that has lots of street noise or other background distraction is not going to represent you at your best.

WHAT TO WEAR

Try on your audition attire well before the audition. It should be fairly formal, but not overly dressy. Sport jackets and ties for men are fine. Women should wear a nice blouse and a pair of tailored pants or a dress. Singers should *not* wear gowns, and along with wind and brass players, must make sure to leave themselves room to breathe without popping zippers or seams. Make sure the neck size on your shirt is big enough, even with a tie, so that you can breathe easily. Women should practice walking in the shoes they intend to wear for the audition. If you are not accustomed to high heels and intend to wear them, walk back and forth across a hardwood floor many times to rehearse your entrance and exit.

ACCOMPANIMENT

Accompanists can really make or break your audition, so rehearsing ahead of time with the person assigned to you is imperative. Call in advance of your audition and ask to make an appointment with the person assigned to play along with you. Although you will usually have to pay extra for the rehearsal time, it is money well spent. You can use the rehearsal time to establish tempi, talk about what you would like to start with, and be sure that the pianist knows all the selections you have prepared. Bringing your own accompanist, if you can afford it, can be a real advantage, as long as that person is *not* your parent. For the audition, make sure your music is in good shape, with pages in order. Avoid using photocopies of music that may fall off a piano. Use a three-hole punch and assemble the music in a notebook.

> If, for some reason, something does go wrong during your audition—music falling off the piano, the pianist sight-reading and not changing key, the tempo straying back and forth—you must assess whether to stop or move on. In most cases, it is best to keep going. The audition panel can see what is happening and it may not be as disastrous as you think at the moment. Keep your cool, and always be cordial to the pianist.

THE CURRICULUM

Whether you are a singer or an instrumentalist, the study of traditional Western music has a fairly standard curriculum. Make sure the school you choose offers courses in music theory (including species counterpoint and harmony through analysis), orchestration, music history, and ear training, as all of them should be part of your studies. Conservatories usually offer specialized studies in every instrument, including solo and orchestral repertoire.

Curriculum offerings in non-Western traditions or world music are increasingly popular, especially in good music departments at liberal arts colleges. Electronic music is also sometimes available as part of a composition program. Composers should find out about opportunities to have their works performed and taped.

For singers, foreign language diction and conversation classes are an essential part of the curriculum. Conductors, both choral and instrumental, should make sure that they will be able to work regularly with ensembles.

It is always helpful for musicians to gain the practical knowledge that courses in audition preparation and the business of music provide. Find out if the institutions you are considering offer such opportunities.

THE FACULTY

As we stated in the chapter on the application process, be sure to review the faculty before you settle on a school. It is vital that you choose your principal teacher carefully, as she must be someone with whom you get along personally as well as musically. This is the person with whom you will be spending many hours, working one on one to perfect your craft. Read about the teacher's background, look at the list of students she has trained, check the students' musical careers, and speak to current students. A performer with a big name may not necessarily be the best teacher for you. How often does the teacher travel? Will you get regular lessons from her, or does an assistant often cover them? What kind of technique does this person teach? You might arrange for a sample lesson or "consultation." Be prepared to pay for this service; fees range from $85 to $200. Taking up a famous teacher's time, either on the telephone or in the studio, is not good form. Since there is no "shopping" period for a teacher and personal interviews are not normal practice, it is tricky to find the right way to arrange such a consultation. It is best to do your research, try for the paid sample lesson, and then hope for the best.

CHANGING TEACHERS

Private music teachers and their students sometimes just do not get along. Or after a certain amount of time with a teacher, you might wish to seek the point of view of another. Although this is a highly sensitive issue, it is not uncommon. Remember that you and the teacher have entered not only into a personal and musical relationship, but also into a business arrangement. You are paying for those lessons.

If you decide to change teachers for whatever reason, follow the school's guidelines precisely. Since this is often an emotionally charged situation, you must also use your best communication skills to inform the teacher. One good way to handle this is to write a thank you note to the teacher. Talk about how much you have learned, and only after that, get to the "now it is time for me to seek other opinions and guidance" part. You might say, "I hope that you will allow me to come back to check in with you from time to time," or something of that sort. After writing the note, follow up by making an appointment to speak with the teacher in person.

The music world is really quite small, and you do not want to ever alienate a teacher. You never know when that teacher will be judging you in a competition or talking to a music director or agent. If you treat this situation with sensitivity, maturity, and human kindness should it arise, you should not have to worry about having doors shut on future opportunities.

FACILITIES

PRACTICE SPACE

Ideally, a musician should have access to a practice facility that is soundproofed and well-ventilated, with a mirror, a good piano, music stands, and chairs or stools appropriate for each instrument. There should also be rooms large enough for ensemble rehearsals that can range in size from duos to entire orchestras.

TECHNICAL FACILITIES

An institution should provide students access to a recording and video facility. Ideally, it should stay open from early morning until late evening. The long hours allow for flexibility in scheduling, which will place considerably less stress on your school and rehearsal obligations. Another facility that should be part of the ideal music institution is a computer lab—often combined with electronic music studios—with software that allows composers and other musicians to generate both full scores and parts.

LIBRARIES

Investigate whether the school's music library includes all the music trade journals and periodicals, as well as a collection of standard repertoire and contemporary pieces. It is important for students of music to have access to such resources. In addition, archival collections of specialized repertoire are extremely valuable for musicians who want to perform period pieces.

Many conservatories have instrument libraries, which house valuable instruments that can be lent to recommended students. For instance, if a violinist is scheduled to audition for an important orchestra but her instrument is not first class, she would be allowed to borrow a great violin from the school's collection.

PERFORMING OPPORTUNITIES

Musicians spend many long hours alone in practice rooms. It is important to get outside those four walls and to make music in the public arena. The more you perform in front of others, the fewer symptoms of nervousness you will have. A good study program, whether at the high school, college, or conservatory level, should provide you with many opportunities to perform. In addition, you should try to find your own performance venues and share your gift with others.

Although schools and programs may have regularly scheduled, fully produced performances, take the initiative and offer your musical services. Nursing homes, schools, and hospitals often welcome performers. Some may pay and be "gigs;" others will expect you to donate your musical offering. And getting together and jamming with friends is often refreshing, renewing, and just plain fun.

A Cautionary Note

Be careful not to commit to a performance schedule that causes you to miss classes, or one that forces you to expend so much energy that you get overtired. Fatigue is a major cause of over-use syndrome (tendonitis).

INSTRUMENTALISTS

Conservatories usually have specific requirements regarding performance. Beyond what is required, an instrumentalist should have experience performing as a soloist, as part of an orchestra, and as a chamber musician. He should also have the opportunity to compete as a soloist with an orchestra. You may wish to play in a contemporary ensemble, a jazz group, a string quartet, or an opera orchestra. In your formative years, it is important to explore as broad a range of musical opportunities as possible. Because most musicians earn their living playing in the pit, it is important to have this experience while in school.

SINGERS

Singers should be sure to ask if teachers or institutional policies restrict public performance or casting for operas or shows. Some schools will not allow young singers to perform until they complete one or two years of technical study. Singers should also explore as many different kinds of musical styles as possible. Performing with an orchestra, in a chorus, in opera scenes and workshops, or in musical theater; collaborating with composers on new pieces; or singing with chamber musicians and baroque ensembles are all opportunities for artistic growth.

CONDUCTORS

Conductors should put together their own ensembles as often as possible. Get your friends to sight-read through scores with you, in order to work on your rehearsal technique. Make sure that you get as many videotapes as possible of yourself in front of an ensemble.

COMPOSERS

Composers should not overlook the opportunity of collaborating with other musicians and conductors, and also with dancers and drama students.

CAREER SEARCH

Musical careers can take a variety of twists and turns. If you are an instrumentalist, you must think about whether you would like to play in an orchestra, chamber music group, string quartet, band, or any combination of these, or pursue a career as a soloist.

For singers who wish to become soloists in opera, it is essential to keep up with regular auditions, lessons, and language study. Other niches that singers could choose include the following:

- being a professional chorister
- singing on Broadway
- being a church musician
- specializing in early or new/contemporary music

NETWORKING

How do you go about finding a job in music? Start with your best resource—your teacher. His contacts in the profession will open doors and provide you with opportunities that are never advertised. If you know, for instance, that you would like to take orchestral auditions, be sure to speak with your teacher, who may have contacts with orchestras holding auditions. Join the musician's union and read the ads in the trade paper published by them. If you are a graduate of a conservatory, keep in touch with the placement office and read the bulletin board or any newsletters they send. Network and talk to people; word of mouth can often be the best way to find a job.

ADVERTISEMENTS

Every instrument has a trade publication devoted to it, and you should subscribe to one whether you are looking for a job or not. If you are in the job market, such journals are also some of the best places to find job announcements.

MANAGEMENT

If you decide that you would like a solo career, you will need management at some point. Do not sign on with a manager or an agent until you have something to manage, until you are getting bookings for concert engagements. This is sometimes a real Catch-22, as some auditions will only consider you if you have been presented by management. *Musical America,* an expensive annual journal, is the best resource for information about management. If you don't want to invest in your own copy, check the library or its new website. The journal includes a list of musical agents and managers—domestic and international—along with essential information such as concert series, sponsors, and rosters of artists. It is worth auditioning for management when you are ready; however, be wary of agents who ask for monthly retainers.

BACK-UP PLAN

Whether you are a composer seeking a venue for your compositions, a conductor looking for an orchestra to lead, a bassist searching for that winning band, or a singer trying to make it on Broadway, you have to pay the bills while you search for your big break. It's always smart to have a back-up plan in case your big break never comes.

You will find trained musicians working in all kinds of professions. Some may be music-related, such as music copying or arranging, now done primarily on computers, working in music publishing or promotion, instrument repair, or piano tuning. Others may become music critics or work for record companies. The radio, television, and motion picture industries also employ music specialists. Many hospitals and schools for students with special needs employ music therapists. Arts management has attracted thousands of career-seekers to the business side of the cultural field.

Many musicians teach to supplement their income. If you do so privately or in private schools, you do not need any special certification. If you intend to teach in a public school, however, you will need to earn certification. To become a college-level teacher you will definitely need a degree—usually, but not always a master's or doctorate—unless you are thinking of one-on-one instrumental teaching in a conservatory. Musicians who want to teach, particularly at the elementary or secondary level, must have excellent keyboard skills, so keep practicing your piano and pay attention in your keyboard harmony classes.

> Opportunities for careers in music are diverse and can be rewarding. They also bring happiness to the lives of others. Whatever career path you choose—whether in the music world or not—your intense training will serve you well. You have a special talent that many people will envy. Your discipline, dedication, and ability to work well with others are traits sought by employers in all professions.

PROFILES OF HIGH SCHOOLS, COLLEGES, CONSERVATORIES, AND UNIVERSITIES, AND SUMMER PROGRAMS

WHO IS LISTED

The Princeton Review staff mailed questionnaires to summer programs known by reputation, and programs that we found through research on the Internet. We decided that programs that are solely local could not be included in the summer listings.

We mailed high school questionnaires to schools that are members of the Network of Performing Arts Schools and other secondary independent schools known for excellence in the performing arts. Middle schools and community music schools are not included.

Questionnaires for colleges, universities, and conservatories were sent to members of the National Association of Schools of Music and of Dance, as well as to other selected colleges and conservatories known worldwide for their performing arts programs. We then followed up with a second mailing and repeated telephone calls, usually to the admissions office or department chairs at these institutions.

Unfortunately, some schools and programs did not respond, and we have had to exclude them for lack of information. Omission of certain programs, however, would have been truly egregious, presenting a glaring hole. Thus, we read catalogs to glean information about these schools, and used the wealth of information about colleges that the Princeton Review collects for their other publications. We then included these schools herein with a limited profile listing. If your favorite programs are not included in this edition, please ask them to contact:

The Princeton Review Publishing
Guide to Performing Arts Programs
2315 Broadway, Third Floor
New York, NY 10024
info@review.com

ICONS

Dance Programs

Drama Programs

Music Programs

DEFINITIONS OF ENTRANCE SELECTIVITY

Highly selective: approximately 10% admitted.

Selective: approximately 33% admitted.

Competitive: approximately 60% admitted.

Non-competitive: most admitted, but not all.

Open enrollment: admit all who apply.

8

HIGH SCHOOL PROGRAM PROFILES

ALABAMA

ALABAMA SCHOOL OF FINE ARTS

1800 8th Avenue North, Birmingham AL 35203
Tel: 205-252-9241
Fax: 205-251-9541
Email: admissions@asfa.k12.al.us
Web: www.asfa.k12.al.us
Contact: Randy Marsh

General

Type of Institution: public, boarding. *Environment:* urban. *Academic education is offered on-site.*

Total enrollment of institution: 350. *Total student body from other countries:* 1%. *Degrees offered:* high school diploma.

Entrance Requirements

Audition required: live. *Other requirements:* interview, recommendation, essay.

Costs & Financial Aid

Deposit: $65. *Other fees:* $70 per semester matriculation, $35 per semester residential life activity fee.

Percent of students receiving financial aid: 5%. *Types of scholarships and aid awarded:* need-based. *Forms required for scholarships:* FAFSA. *Financial aid offered to international students.*

Services

Housing options: on-site dorms.

Support staff: college advisor, dorm parent, resident assistant.

Comments

There is also a program for theater technicians.

DANCE

Curriculum, Students, and Faculty

Required courses: African dance, character (2 classes per week, 1 year to complete), ballet (5 classes per week, 2 years to complete), dance composition/choreography, dance history, jazz, master classes, men's class (2 classes per week, 2 years to complete), music, pas de deux (2 classes per week, 2 years to complete), pointe (5 classes per week, 2 years to complete), rehearsal and performance, repertory, variations (2 classes per week, 2 years to complete).

Selectivity for males: approximately 60% admitted. *Selectivity for females:* approximately 10% admitted. *Total enrollment:* 29. *Entering class size:* 7. *Graduating class size:* 7.

Renowned alumni: Kathleen Moore, Shawn Black, Wes Chapman, Petra Adlefang, David Moore.

Total full-time faculty: 2. *Total part-time faculty:* 1. *List of current faculty and past affiliations:* Dame Sonia Arova, Alabama Ballet, Ballet South; Thor Sutowski, Cleveland Ballet, Atlanta Contemporary Dance Company, Boston Ballet, Jackson International Ballet Company. *Program contact person:* Therese Laeger.

Audition Information

No audition fee. Audition consists of the following: ballet, orthopedic evaluation, pointe work. *Accompanist provided. Cassette player available; CD player available. Dress requirements for males:* t-shirt, tights, ballet shoes. *Dress requirements for females:* tights, leotards, ballet and pointe shoes.

Audition evaluation criteria: physical evaluation for suitability for classical dance, student's determination, musicality.

Performance Information

Performance opportunities available (frequency): Fully produced concerts (3 per year), on-site performances (10 per year), touring (2 per year).

Performances choreographed by: faculty, guests. *Recent guest choreographers:* Thor Sutowsk, Cornelius Carter.

Facilities

Number of studios available: 3. *Approximate studio dimensions and flooring:* 60' x 40' sprung floor with linoleum, 42' x 40' sprung floor with linoleum, 42' x 40' sprung floor with linoleum. *Performance facilities:* theater in the building.

DRAMA

Curriculum, Students, and Faculty

Required courses: acting, audition preparation, directing, improvisation, make-up, mime, movement, scene study, speech, stage combat, text analysis, verse drama, scene study.

Number of years required to complete program: 2-6. *Summer program not available. No affiliation with a professional theater company.* Students can audition and, if cleared by the department and the school, may participate in productions outside of the school. Birmingham Children's Theatre, Town and Gown, and Summerfest all employ professionals who work with community people.

Selectivity for males: approximately 10% admitted. *Selectivity for females:* approximately 10% admitted. *Total enrollment:* 38. *Entering class size:* 8. *Graduating class size:* 3.

Renowned alumni: Kim Wharton, Erin Underwood, Chuck Yates.

Total full-time faculty: 2. *List of current faculty and past affiliations:* Jesse M. Bates, III.

Audition Information

Audition consists of the following: comedic monologue, improvisation, interview; call back improvisation for those scoring high enough to be seen again. *Dress requirements for males:* casual clothes suitable for movement. *Dress requirements for females:* casual clothes suitable for movement. *Repertoire that students should avoid?* Star-Spangled Girl, Tuna Section from Laughing Wild.

Performance Information

Performance opportunities available (frequency): fully produced performances (2 per year), informal performances (4-8 per year), workshops (1 per year), off-site performances (2 per year). Casting is by audition.

Facilities

Rehearsal facilities and hours: rolling screens used to divide the two theatre spaces into smaller rehearsal areas, can be booked up to 10:00 pm. *Number of theaters on campus:* 2. *Type and capacity:* black box/proscenium 500, proscenium 80.

MUSIC

Curriculum, Students, and Faculty

How are major teacher assignments made? made by the school according to teacher availability. Faculty is not informed of a student's teacher preference at the time of the audition. 34 lessons with major teacher. *May a student change major teachers during the course of study?* possibly. *Study of secondary instrument or discipline is allowed.*

Selectivity for instruments or programs offered (rating): bassoon (non-competitive), choral singing (highly selective), clarinet (highly selective), composition (highly selective), double bass (selective), flute or piccolo (highly selective), French horn (selective), guitar (competitive), harp (selective), jazz (highly selective), oboe/English horn (selective), percussion (selective), piano (highly selective), saxophone (selective), trombone (selective), trumpet (selective), tuba (selective), viola (non-competitive), violin (highly selective), violoncello (selective), voice (highly selective).

Total enrollment: 44. *Entering class size:* 7. *Graduating class size:* 14.

Renowned alumni: Dr. Charles Staples, Thomas Bagwell, Elisa Nelson, Frank E. Adams Jr.

Total full-time faculty: 3. *Total part-time faculty:* 10. *Program contact person:* Les Fillmer.

Audition Information

No audition fee. Audition consists of the following: scales, music theory, rhythmic dictation, arpeggios, sight reading, improvisation, melodic dictation. *Instruments provided for:* harpists, percussionists, pianists.

Performance opportunities available (frequency): chamber music (frequently), jury examinations (frequently), recitals (frequently), touring, chorus.

Facilities

Number of practice rooms and hours: 12; 14 hours per day. *Recital hall?* yes. *Concert hall?* no. *Recording studio?* no.

BOOKER T. WASHINGTON MAGNET HIGH SCHOOL

632 South Union Street, Montgomery AL 36104
Tel: 334-269-3617 or 6186
Fax: 334-269-3974

General

Type of Institution: governor's, magnet-public. *Environment:* urban. *Academic education is offered on-site.*

Total enrollment of institution: 617. *Total student body from other countries:* 1%. *Degrees offered:* high school diploma.

Entrance Requirements

Audition required: live, audio, video. *Other requirements:* interview, recommendation, essay.

Geographic restrictions: primarily in-district; summer is exception.

Costs & Financial Aid

Other fees: course fees.

Types of scholarships and aid awarded: full, partial, merit-based, need-based, named, institutional aid, government aid, reduced tuition, office gig. *Procedure for applying for loans:* school assists students, primarily through their specialty.

Services

Housing options: off-campus housing.

Support staff: college advisor, psychological counselor, resident assistant, resident nurse, student affairs officer.

DANCE

Curriculum, Students, and Faculty

Required courses: ballet, dance composition/choreography, jazz, Horton-based modern dance, pointe, rehearsal and performance, tap, Dunham-based modern (5 classes per week, 2 years to complete).

Total Enrollment: 55. *Entering class size:* 25. *Graduating class size:* 20.

Renowned alumni: Wendy White, Thad Davis, Foye Dubose, Joy Kennamer.

Total full-time faculty: 3. *List of current faculty and past affiliations:* Gary Moore; Cathy Hess Wright; Kate Levitz, Joyce Trisler Modern Dance Company. *Program contact person:* Cathy Hess Wright.

Audition Information

No audition fee. Audition consists of the following: ballet, improvisation, modern dance, orthopedic evaluation, pointe works, evaluation based on classical placement with a given combination in modern or jazz. *Accompanist not provided. Cassette player available; CD player available. Dress requirements for males:* black tights, white shirt, white socks, white technique shoes. *Dress requirements for females:* black leotard, pink tights, pink technique or pointe shoes, hair in bun.

Audition evaluation criteria: evalution is based on classical placement and a given combination in modern dance or jazz.

Performance Information

Performance opportunities available (frequency): Fully produced concerts (2 per year), informal concerts (3 per year), workshops (5 or more per year), on-site performances(5 per year), touring (1 per year).

Performances choreographed by: faculty, guests. *Recent guest choreographers:* Foye Dubose, Annie Day, Marcus Alford.

Facilities

Number of studios available: 3. *Approximate studio dimensions and flooring:* 40' x 40' sprung dance floor, Marley surface. *Performance facilities:* City Theatre.

DRAMA

Curriculum, Students, and Faculty

Required courses: acting, improvisation, movement, scene study, speech, Stanislavski exercises, text analysis, voice, verse drama, make-up, mime.

Elective courses: directing, drama criticism.

Number of years required to complete program: 4. *Summer program not available. Selectivity for males:* approximately 60% admitted. *Selectivity for females:* approximately 33% admitted. *Total enrollment:* 80. *Entering class size:* 35. *Graduating class size:* 15.

Total full-time faculty: 3. *List of current faculty and past affiliations:* Russ Wendt, Arizona State University, Lamar University, Alabama Shakespeare Festival.

Audition Information

Audition consists of the following: improvisation. *Dress requirements for males:* dress slacks and shirt. *Dress requirements for females:* dress slacks and blouse. *Repertoire that students should avoid?* classical.

Audition evaluation criteria: characterization, movement, voice, speech, honesty. Each is given value, listed in order of most to least valued.

Performance Information

Performance opportunities available (frequency): fully produced performances (5 per year), workshops (2 per year), off-site performances (2 per year), casting is by audition.

Facilities

Rehearsal facilities and hours: theater, 4:00 pm-6:00 pm (Mon-Fri), 9:00 am-3:00 pm (Sat). *Number of theaters on campus:* 1. *Type and capacity:* black box 100.

MUSIC

Curriculum, Students, and Faculty

Unique or innovative music curriculum: showband, vocal jazz program, youth orchestra, strings ensemble, music theory lab with computers, computer-driven instruction. *How are major teacher assignments made?* Students may choose, made by the school according to teacher preference and teacher availability. Faculty is not informed of a student's teacher preference at the time of the audition. *May a student change major teachers during the course of study?* never. *Study of secondary instrument or discipline is allowed.*

Selectivity for instruments or programs offered (rating): accompanying (highly selective), bassoon (non-competitive), choral singing (competitive), clarinet (non-competitive), composition (non-competitive), electronic music (non-competitive), flute or piccolo (non-competitive), French horn (non-competitive), guitar (competitive), jazz (non-competitive), oboe/English horn (non-competitive), percussion (non-competitive), piano (selective), saxophone (non-competitive), trombone (non-competitive), trumpet (non-competitive), tuba (non-competitive), viola (non-competitive), violin (non-competitive), violoncello (non-competitive), voice (non-competitive).

Total enrollment: 200. *Entering class size:* 100. *Graduating class size:* 65.

Renowned alumni: Bryan Roughton, Joey Ikner, George Davis.

Total full-time faculty: 8. *Total part-time faculty:* 1. *Program contact person:* Phillip Sprayberry.

Audition Information

No audition fee. Audition consists of the following: scales, music theory, rhythmic dictation, arpeggios, sight reading, melodic dictation, repertoire. *Instruments provided for:* percussionists, guitars, and strings.

Required repertoire: 2 memorized, contrasting, standard repertoire classical pieces for piano. *Repertoire that students should avoid?* Hard gospel. *Performance opportunities available (frequency):* chamber music (frequently), band (frequently), jury examinations (frequently), opera workshops (frequently), orchestral concerts (frequently), recitals (frequently), touring (frequently), produced operas.

Comments

This represents a compilation from show band, concert band, classical guitar, piano, strings, classic viola, jazz choir and choral areas. Music theory is also offered.

ARIZONA

SOUTH MOUNTAIN HIGH SCHOOL

5401 South 7th Street, Phoenix AZ 85040
Tel: 602-271-2845
Fax: 602-271-2880
Email: Sarah.Maresco@qm.phxhs.k12.az.us
Contact: Dance Department

General

Type of Institution: magnet-public. *Environment:* urban. *Academic education is offered on-site.*

Degrees offered: high school diploma.

Entrance Requirements

Audition required: live.

Geographic restrictions: live in attendance zone or complete paper work.

Services

Support staff: college advisor.

DANCE

Curriculum, Students, and Faculty

Required courses: anatomy, ballet, dance composition/choreography, dance history, dance theory, dance writing, research and criticism, jazz, master classes, modern dance, music, nutrition, pointe, rehearsal and performance, repertory, stagecraft, tap, Spanish (2 classes per week, 1 year to complete).

Selectivity for males: admit all who apply. *Selectivity for females:* admit all who apply.

Renowned alumni: Germaul Barnies, Bill T. Jones Company; Heather Adams, Philadanco.

Total full-time faculty: 2. *Total part-time faculty:* 1. *List of current faculty and past affiliations:* Sarah Manesco, Chicago Ballet, Radio City Music Hall Ballet, Austin Ballet Theater; Susan St. John, Aurora Mime Theater; Eyvonne Cratz, RAD certification. *Program contact person:* Sarah Maresco, Susan St. John.

Audition Information

No audition fee. Audition consists of the following: ballet, modern dance. *Accompanist provided. Cassette player available; CD player available. Dress requirements for males:* white and/or black t-shirt and sweatpants. *Dress requirements for females:* all black for modern, pink and black for ballet.

Repertoire that students should avoid? no hip-hop.

Performance Information

Performance opportunities available (frequency): Fully produced concerts (4 per year), informal concerts (2 per year), workshops (5-10 per year), on-site performances (4-5 per year), touring (4-5 per year).

Performances choreographed by: faculty, students, guests.

Facilities

Number of studios available: 2. *Approximate studio dimensions and flooring:* 30' x 50' wood, spring, Marley-covered. *Performance facilities:* school auditorium, informal space—dance studio.

DRAMA

Curriculum, Students, and Faculty

Required courses: acting, audition preparation, directing, drama criticism, improvisation, make-up, martial arts, mime, movement, musical theater, scene study, stage combat, Stanislavski exercises, text analysis, voice.

Number of years required to complete program: 4. *Summer program not available. Affiliation with a professional theater company: Phoenix Theater.*

Selectivity for males: admit all who apply. *Selectivity for females:* admit all who apply.

Total full-time faculty: 1. *List of current faculty and past affiliations:* Barbara Wood.

Audition Information

No audition fee. Audition consists of the following: cold readings, comedic monologue, movement class, Shakespearean monologue, group warm-up.

Audition evaluation criteria: concentration and improvement, focus, diction, etc.

Performance Information

Performance opportunities available (frequency): fully produced performances (3 per year), informal performances (5 per year), workshops (10 per year), off-site performances (5 per year), casting is by audition.

Recent guest artists: David Barker, Charles St. Claire, Edward Marston.

Facilities

Type and capacity: proscenium 1,300.

MUSIC

Curriculum, Students, and Faculty

Unique or innovative music curriculum: Recording program, Midi-program, Mariachi program. *How are major teacher assignments made?* made by the school. *20 lessons with major teacher. Study of secondary instrument or discipline is allowed.*

Selectivity for instruments or programs offered (rating): choral singing (open), clarinet (open), composition (open), double bass (open), electronic music (open), flute or piccolo (open), French horn (open), guitar (open), harp (open), harpsichord (open), jazz (open), oboe/English horn (open), organ (open), percussion (open), piano (open), saxophone (open), trombone (open), trumpet (open), tuba (open), viola (open), violin (open), violoncello (open), voice (open).

Total full-time faculty: 2. *Program contact person:* Stuart Bailey, Bob Diaz.

Audition Information

No audition fee. Instruments provided for: harpists, percussionists.

Performance opportunities available (frequency): jury examinations, recitals.

Facilities

Number of practice rooms and hours: 10; 8-10 hours. *Recital hall?* no. *Concert hall?* no. *Recording studio?* yes.

TUCSON HIGH MAGNET SCHOOL

400 North Second Avenue, Tucson AZ 85705
Tel: 520-617-7500
Fax: 520-617-7546
Email: volpem@mail.thms.k12.az.us
Web: www.thms.k12.az.us
Contact: Marcia Volpe

General

Type of Institution: magnet-public. *Environment:* urban.

Total enrollment of institution: 2,400. *Degrees offered:* high school diploma.

Entrance Requirements

Audition not required.

Geographic restrictions: THMS is a magnet school designed to create an ethnic balance of talented students.

Costs & Financial Aid

Types of scholarships and aid awarded: institutional aid.

Services

Support staff: financial aid advisor, psychological counselor, resident nurse.

DANCE

Curriculum, Students, and Faculty

Elective courses: ballet, dance composition/choreography, dance history, jazz, modern dance, pas de deux, pointe, Spanish, stagecraft, tap.

Selectivity for males: most admitted, but not all. *Selectivity for females:* most admitted, but not all. *Total enrollment:* 500. *Entering class size:* 25. *Graduating class size:* 10.

Renowned alumni: Ellen Bromburg.

Total full-time faculty: 3. *Total part-time faculty:* 2. *List of current faculty and past affiliations:* Eva Tessler, Zenith Dance Collective (Tucson), Professor in Brazil; Sherly Oden, Zenith Dance

Collective (Tucson); Darain Harris; Lis Almgrin; Marcella Cardinas, Ballet Folklorico Del Norte (Tucson). *Program contact person:* Marcia Volpe.

Audition Information

No audition fee. Audition consists of the following: ballet, improvisation, modern dance, pas de deux, pointe works. *Accompanist not provided. Cassette player available; CD player available.*

Performance Information

Performance opportunities available (frequency): Fully produced concerts (1 per semester), informal concerts (1 second semester), workshops (2 per year), on-site performances(2 per year).

Performances choreographed by: faculty, students.

Facilities

Number of studios available: 4. *Approximate studio dimensions and flooring:* 32' x 72' Harlequin floor sprung plywood with heavy varnish. *Performance facilities:* black box theater, auditorium.

DRAMA

Curriculum, Students, and Faculty

Elective courses: acting, movement.

Number of years required to complete program: 4. *Summer program not available. No affiliation with a professional theater company. Selectivity for males:* most admitted, but not all. *Selectivity for females:* most admitted, but not all. *Total enrollment:* 150. *Entering class size:* 25. *Graduating class size:* 10.

Total full-time faculty: 1. *Total part-time faculty:* 2. *List of current faculty and past affiliations:* Art Almgrust, Kathleen Erickson, Brian McGinn.

Audition Information

No audition fee. Audition consists of the following: cold readings, comedic monologue, improvisation.

Performance Information

Performance opportunities available (frequency): fully produced performances (2 per year), informal performances (2 per year), casting is assigned.

Facilities

Rehearsal facilities and hours: THMS Little Theater after school hours. *Number of theaters on campus:* 3. *Type and capacity:* theater 100, black box 100, auditorium 1,000.

MUSIC

Curriculum, Students, and Faculty

How are major teacher assignments made? made by the school, according to teacher preference and teacher availability. Faculty is not informed of a student's teacher preference at the time of the audition. *May a student change major teachers during the course of study?* never. *Study of secondary instrument or discipline is allowed.*

Selectivity for instruments or programs offered (rating): accompanying (competitive), bassoon (non-competitive), choral singing (non-competitive), clarinet (non-competitive), double bass (non-competitive), flute or piccolo (non-competitive), French horn (non-competitive), guitar (non-competitive), jazz (non-competitive), oboe/English horn (non-competitive), percussion (non-competitive), piano (non-competitive), saxophone (non-competitive), trombone (non-competitive), trumpet (non-competitive), tuba (non-competitive), viola (non-competitive), violin (non-competitive), voice (non-competitive).

Total enrollment: 500. *Entering class size:* 25. *Graduating class size:* 20.

Total full-time faculty: 6. *Program contact person:* Marcia Volpe.

Audition Information

Audition consists of the following: scales, orchestral excerpts, ensemble playing, sight reading. *Instruments provided for:* percussionists.

Performance opportunities available (frequency): band, touring.

Facilities

Number of practice rooms and hours: 4; before, during and after school. *Recital hall?* yes. *Concert hall?* yes. *Recording studio?* yes.

CALIFORNIA

COLBURN SCHOOL OF PERFORMING ARTS

3131 South Figueroa Street, Los Angeles CA 90007
Tel: 213-743-2306
Fax: 213-746-7017
Contact: John Bancroft

General

Environment: urban.

Total enrollment of institution: 800.

Entrance Requirements

Audition required: live. *Other requirements:* interview.

Costs & Financial Aid

Percent of students receiving financial aid: 15%. *Types of scholarships and aid awarded:* full, partial, merit-based, named, reduced tuition, tuition payment plan. *Forms required for scholarships:* income tax return. *Procedure for applying for loans:* request information and forms. *Financial aid offered to international students.*

DANCE

Curriculum, Students, and Faculty

Elective courses: Japanese, Indian dance, movement techniques, body conditioning, Feldenkreis, dance composition/choreography, dance writing, research and criticism, rehearsal and performance, African dance.

DRAMA

Curriculum, Students, and Faculty

Required courses: movement, speech.

MUSIC

Conservatory program.

Comments

Music center due to be completed spring 1998. Includes a 416-seat concert hall, 100-seat recital hall. Plans also include adding a four-year, college-level conservatory.

CROSSROADS SCHOOL

1714 21st Street, Santa Monica CA 90404
Tel: 310-829-7391
Fax: 310-828-5636
Web: xrdseorg.com
Contact: Gennifer Yoshimaru

General

Type of Institution: private, day, coed. *Environment:* urban.

Total enrollment of institution: 488. *Total student body from other countries:* 3%. *Degrees offered:* high school diploma.

Entrance Requirements

Audition not required. Other requirements: interview, recommendation, essay, photograph. *Standardized test requirements:* ISEE; TOEFL.

Costs & Financial Aid

Application fee: $100. *Deposit:* $1,500. *Tuition:* $14,344. *Other fees:* $1,000 new student fee, books, $300 supply fee.

Percent of students receiving financial aid: 14% *Types of scholarships and aid awarded:* full, partial, need-based, tuition payment plan. *Financial aid offered to international students. Other aid available to international students:* only need-based aid available for all students.

Services

Support staff: college advisor, foreign student advisor, housing advisor, psychological counselor, resident nurse.

DANCE

Curriculum, Students, and Faculty

Elective courses: African dance, modern dance.

Selectivity for males: most admitted, but not all. *Selectivity for females:* approximately 60% admitted. *Total enrollment:* 31.

Renowned alumni: Echo Gustafson, recent graduate now with Martha Graham. *Total part-time faculty:* 3. *List of current faculty and past affiliations:* Ron Brown, UCLA; Alvin Ailey; Pat Taylor, Jazzantiqua; Shida Pegani, Naneva (Persian) Dance Company. *Program contact person:* Davida Wills.

Audition Information

No audition fee. Audition consists of the following: auditions generally for company only. *Accompanist provided. Cassette player available; CD player available. Dress requirements for males:* black tights, dance belt, black t-shirt. *Dress requirements for females:* black leotard, tights.

Performance Information

Performance opportunities available (frequency): fully produced concerts (2 per year), informal concerts (varies).

Performances choreographed by: faculty, students, guests.

Facilities

Number of studios available: 2. *Performance facilities:* black box theater.

DRAMA

Curriculum, Students, and Faculty

Required courses: acting, audition preparation, directing, improvisation, make-up, movement, musical theater, scene study, speech, stage combat, Stanislavski exercises, voice.

Number of years required to complete program: 4. *Summer program available. Selectivity for males:* most admitted, but not all. *Selectivity for females:* approximately 60% admitted. *Total enrollment:* 83.

Renowned alumni: Jack Black.

Total full-time faculty: 2. *Total part-time faculty:* 3. *List of current faculty and past affiliations:* Davida Wills Hurwin, David Collott, UCLA, ACT, Brian Mulligan, Judith Flaherty, Second City Improv.

Audition Information

Audition consists of the following: a cappella singing, comedic monologue, movement class, group warm-up.

Performance Information

Performance opportunities available (frequency): fully produced performances (4 per year), informal performances (3 per year), workshops (varies), off-site performances and workshops during summer tour program, students assigned to performance modules, parts decided through casting.

Recent guest artists: Lindsay Crouse, John Ritter, Jim Belushi, Paul Michael Glaser.

Facilities

Rehearsal facilities and hours: performance modules run 1:00 pm-5:00 pm (4 days per week) in theater or dance studio. *Type and capacity:* black box 120.

MUSIC

Curriculum, Students, and Faculty

Unique or innovative music curriculum: a comprehensive and rigorous sequential music major programs for both instrumentalists and vocalists. *How are major teacher assignments made?* made by the school. *Faculty is not informed of a student's teacher preference at the time of the audition.*

Selectivity for instruments or programs offered (rating): choral singing (open), clarinet (open), electronic music (open), flute or piccolo (open), guitar (open), jazz (open), percussion (open), piano (non-competitive), saxophone (open), trombone (open), trumpet (open), tuba (open), viola (highly selective), violin (highly selective), violoncello (highly selective), voice (selective).

Total enrollment: 107. *Percent international:* 58%. *Countries most represented:* Korea.

Renowned alumni: Gianna Abondolo, Los Angeles Philharmonic; Sharon Yamata, New York Philharmonic; Sharon Maunther, Cleveland Orchestra; Max Revimson, Columbia Artists; En Sik Choi; Nokuthula Ngwenyama.

Total full-time faculty: 2. *Total part-time faculty:* 5. *Program contact person:* Betty Walsh, Zain Kahn.

Audition Information

Audition consists of the following: sight reading, melodic dictation.

Performance opportunities available (frequency): band, chamber music, orchestral concerts, recitals, chorus.

Facilities

Number of practice rooms and hours: 4; during and after school. *Recital hall?* yes. *Concert hall?* no. *Recording studio?* yes.

IDYLLWILD ARTS ACADEMY

P.O. Box 38
52500 Temekla Drive, Idyllwild CA 92594
Tel: 909-659-2171 ext. 223
Fax: 909-657-2058
Email: Behnke@pe.net
Contact: Anne Behnke

General

Type of Institution: private, boarding. *Academic education is offered on-site.*

Total enrollment of institution: 245. *Degrees offered:* high school diploma, certificate.

Costs & Financial Aid

Application fee: $35. *Deposit:* $2,500. *Other fees:* $1,350 per year private instruction, music, $166 English as a second language.

Percent of students receiving financial aid: 58%. *Types of scholarships and aid awarded:* full, partial, merit-based, need-based, named, institutional aid. *Forms required for scholarships:* income tax return, income asset verification, SSS form. *Procedure for applying for loans:* submit SSS form, submit IRS forms, Financial Aid Committee meets to evaluate, must apply for admission first. *Financial aid offered to international students. Percent of international students receiving scholarships:* 41%. *Other aid available to international students:* all financial aid is available to all students.

Services

Housing options: on-site dorms, family.

Support staff: college advisor, dorm parent, financial aid advisor, foreign student advisor, housing advisor, psychological counselor, resident assistant, resident nurse, student affairs officer.

DANCE

Curriculum, Students, and Faculty

Required courses: anatomy, character, ballet, dance composition/choreography, dance history, jazz, master classes, men's class, modern dance, movement techniques, music, pas de deux, pointe, rehearsal and performance, repertory, variations, modern dance partnering.

Elective courses: tap.

Selectivity for males: approximately 60% admitted. *Selectivity for females:* approximately 60% admitted. *Total enrollment:* 40.

Renowned alumni: Graham Smith, Basel Dance Theatre; Michael Morales, with a ballet company in Florida; Milan Valko, Louisville Ballet; Koji Aoyama, freelance in Japan, danced in Beethoven's 9th for the Winter Olympics opening.

Total full-time faculty: 2. *Total part-time faculty:* 10. *List of current faculty and past affiliations:* Anne Krampen, National Ballet of Canada; Kathleen Haigney, New York City Ballet; Sean Greeive, Lewitzky Dance Company; Stephanie Gilliland, U.C. Riverside; Deborah Brockus, U.C. Irvine; Jean-Marie Martz, Stuttgart Ballet. *Program contact person:* Jean Marie Martz.

Audition Information

No audition fee. Audition consists of the following: ballet, pas de deux, pointe works, prepared solo, ballet, jazz, modern dance, videotape or live on-campus audition *Accompanist provided. Cassette player available; CD player available.*

Performance Information

Performance opportunities available (frequency): Fully produced concerts (2 per year), informal concerts (2 per year), on-site performances(3-4 per year).

Performances choreographed by: faculty, students.

Facilities

Number of studios available: 3. *Approximate studio dimensions and flooring:* 28' x 42' sprung floor, 36' x 44' sprung floor, 36' x 50' sprung floor. *Performance facilities:* Idyllwild Arts Foundation Theatre, Dance Studio Theatre.

DRAMA

Curriculum, Students, and Faculty

Required courses: acting, audition preparation, movement, musical theater, speech, stage combat, verse drama, voice.

Elective courses: directing.

Number of years required to complete program: 1-4. *Summer program available. no affiliation with a professional theater company. Selectivity for males:* approximately 60% admitted. *Selectivity for females:* approximately 60% admitted. *Total enrollment:* 50. *Countries most represented:* Korea.

Renowned alumni: Mare Winningham, Jennifer Jason Leigh.

Total full-time faculty: 4. *Total part-time faculty:* 4. *List of current faculty and past affiliations:* Rob Jansen; Matt Zettee; Jude Levinson, Western Michigan University-Interlochen, School of the Arts; Tim Durwon.

Audition Information

No audition fee. Audition consists of the following: a cappella singing, comedic monologue, Shakespearean monologue, one or more of the monologues is "workshopped" in the audition. *Repertoire that students should avoid?* over-performed monologues that run in fads.

Audition evaluation criteria: assess student's understanding of material; physical, vocal action; goals and seriousness; receptiveness to direction; maturity; willingness to work in intensive program; goals after graduation; interest in college.

Performance Information

Performance opportunities available (frequency): fully produced performances (3 per year), informal performances (2-4 per year), workshops (occasionally), off-site performances (3-5 per year), on campus theater day events assigned, auditioned. Classroom projects assigned, main stage auditioned.

Recent guest artists: Andrew Foster, Ronni Steward.

Facilities

Rehearsal facilities and hours: theater, 4:00 pm-6:30 pm daily and 2 nights per week, Rush Hall, 4:00 pm-6:30 pm daily and evenings as needed. *Number of theaters on campus:* 1. *Type and capacity:* proscenium 350.

MUSIC

Curriculum, Students, and Faculty

Unique or innovative music curriculum: students play solo, chamber orchestra and chamber music literature. *How are major teacher assignments made?* students may choose, made by the school. Faculty is informed of a student's teacher preference at the time of the audition. 24 lessons with major teacher. *May a student change major teachers during the course of study?* possibly. *Study of secondary instrument or discipline is allowed.*

Selectivity for instruments or programs offered (rating): bassoon (selective), clarinet (selective), composition (selective), double bass (selective), flute or piccolo (selective), French horn (selective), guitar (selective), harp (selective), harpsichord (selective), jazz (selective), oboe/English horn (selective), organ (selective), percussion (selective), piano (selective), saxophone (selective), trombone (selective), trumpet (selective), tuba (selective), viola (selective), violin (selective), violoncello (selective), voice (selective).

Total enrollment: 80. *Countries most represented:* China, Taiwan, Korea, Bulgaria.

Renowned alumni: Michael Tilson Thomas; Nikolai Kurganev, Los Angeles Philharmonic; Frank Zappa.

Total full-time faculty: 6. *Total part-time faculty:* 5. *Program contact person:* Terry Graves.

Audition Information

No audition fee. Audition consists of the following: scales, arpeggios, sight reading, repertoire. *Instruments provided for:* harpists, percussionists, pianists.

Required repertoire: student's choice. *Repertoire that students should avoid?* no. *Performance opportunities available (frequency):* chamber music (frequently), jury examinations, orchestral concerts (frequently), recitals (frequently), touring (frequently).

Facilities

Number of practice rooms and hours: 30; 24 hours a day. *Recital hall?* yes. *Concert hall?* yes. *Recording studio?* no.

INDEPENDENCE HIGH SCHOOL

Performing Arts Academy
1776 Educational Park Drive, San Jose CA 95133
Tel: 408-729-3911
Contact: Jan DeShera

General

Type of Institution: public. *Environment:* suburban.

Total enrollment of institution: 4,200. *Degrees offered:* high school diploma.

Entrance Requirements

Audition not required. Other requirements: interview, recommendation, essay.

Geographic restrictions: students entering program must live within the district or prove that they do not have an arts program at their home school.

Services

Housing options: off-campus housing.

Support staff: college advisor, dorm parent, financial aid advisor, foreign student advisor, housing advisor, physical therapist, psychological counselor, resident assistant, resident nurse, student affairs officer.

DANCE

Curriculum, Students, and Faculty

Elective courses: anatomy, ballet (5 classes per week), dance composition/choreography (5 classes per week), dance history, dance writing, research and criticism, jazz (5 classes per week), Labanotation, master classes, Cunningham-based, Graham-based dance, Limon-based modern dance, music, pointe (5 classes per week), rehearsal and performance, repertory, stagecraft (5 classes per week).

Selectivity for males: admit all who apply. *Selectivity for females:* admit all who apply. *Total enrollment:* 165. *Entering class size:* 45.

Renowned alumni: Robert Regalia, dancing with Limon Dance Company, New York City; Khai Tran; Aimee Lam; Jenni Lee; Melissa Wynn; Arnie Apostle; Margret Wingrove; Gerald Casel, Stephan Petronio Co.

Total full-time faculty: 1. *Total part-time faculty:* 1. *List of current faculty and past affiliations:* Kellye Dodd, SJSU, Laban Centre for Movement and Dance, Leda Dance Company; Lesley Ruzon, Icefure Theatre, Vermont. *Program contact person:* Kellye Dodd/Lesley Ruzon.

Audition Information

No audition fee. Audition consists of the following: ballet, modern dance, jazz, ballet class and moderm dance class audition required only for advanced class *Accompanist not provided. Cassette player available; CD player available. Dress requirements for males:* leggings, leotard, appropriate shoes or no shoes. *Dress requirements for females:* leggings, leotard, appropriate shoes or no shoes.

Audition evaluation criteria: must perform a combination in modern, jazz, and ballet.

Performance Information

Performance opportunities available (frequency): Fully produced concerts (3 per year), informal concerts (2 per year), workshops (weekly), on-site performances(2 per year).

Performances choreographed by: faculty, students, guests. *Recent guest choreographers:* Gary Masters—Limon West Dance Company; Ehud Krauss—Zocho Dance Company; James Brenneman, Luigi, Donald McKayle, Fred Masters, State Street Ballet.

Facilities

Number of studios available: 2. *Approximate studio dimensions and flooring:* 30' x 60' sprung wood floor, 25' x 40' sprung wood floor. *Performance facilities:* 500-seat fully equipped stage, new lighting systems and Marley dance floor.

DRAMA

Curriculum, Students, and Faculty

Elective courses: acting, audition preparation, directing, make-up, musical theater, scene study, speech, stage combat, Stanislavski exercises, voice.

Number of years required to complete program: 4. *Summer program not available. Selectivity for males:* admit all who apply. *Selectivity for females:* admit all who apply. *Total enrollment:* 160. *Entering class size:* 40.

Renowned alumni: Bridgette Loriaux, Ashland Oregon Shakespeare Festival; Duc Luu.

Total full-time faculty: 1. *List of current faculty and past affiliations:* Pam Melvin, San Jose State University.

Audition Information

Audition consists of the following: cold readings, comedic monologue; auditions only for drama projects and plays, not for classes. *Dress requirements for males:* clothes that allow movement. *Dress requirements for females:* clothes that allow movement.

Audition evaluation criteria: this depends greatly on which production is being prepared.

Performance Information

Performance opportunities available (frequency): fully produced performances (2 per year), informal performances (4-5 per year), workshops (2 per year), off-site performances (2 per year), casting is by audition.

Recent guest artists: American Musical Theatre of San Jose, Limón Dance Company.

Facilities

Rehearsal facilities and hours: use stage area. *Type and capacity:* proscenium 500.

MUSIC

Curriculum, Students, and Faculty

How are major teacher assignments made? made by the school. Faculty is not informed of a student's teacher preference at the time of the audition. *Study of secondary instrument or discipline is allowed.*

Selectivity for instruments or programs offered (rating): accompanying (highly selective), bassoon (selective), choral singing (open), clarinet (selective), double bass (open), flute or piccolo (selective), French horn (open), guitar (open), jazz (selective), oboe/English horn (selective), percussion (open), piano (open), saxophone (open), trombone (open), trumpet (open), tuba (open), viola (open), violin (open), violoncello (open), voice (open).

Total enrollment: 200. *Entering class size:* 30.

Total full-time faculty: 2. *Total part-time faculty:* 1. *Program contact person:* Mike Kambeitz, Jan DeShera.

Audition Information

Instruments provided for: percussionists; violas, cellos, string basses, alto sax, tenor sax, alto clarinet, bass clarinet, contrabass clarinet, baritone horn, trombones, sousaphones, tubas, baritone sax, bass clarinet.

Facilities

Number of practice rooms and hours: 4; 8:00 am-3:00 pm. *Recital hall?* no. *Concert hall?* yes. *Recording studio?* no.

LOS ANGELES HIGH SCHOOL FOR THE ARTS

5151 State University Drive
Los Angeles CA 90032
Tel: 213-343-2787
Contact: Bo Vitolo

SAN DIEGO SCHOOL OF CREATIVE AND PERFORMING ARTS

2425 Dusk Drive, San Diego CA 92139
Tel: 619-470-0555
Fax: 619-470-9430
Contact: Ole Kittlesen

General

Type of Institution: public, magnet-public. *Environment:* suburban.

Total enrollment of institution: 1,459. *Degrees offered:* high school diploma.

Entrance Requirements

Audition not required.

Geographic restrictions: resident of San Diego City school district.

Services

Housing options: family.

Support staff: college advisor, financial aid advisor.

DANCE

Curriculum, Students, and Faculty

Elective courses: character, ballet, dance composition/choreography, jazz, master classes, men's class, modern dance, movement techniques, music, pas de deux, pointe, rehearsal and performance, repertory, Spanish, stagecraft, tap, variations, modern dance partnering, body conditioning.

Selectivity for males: most admitted, but not all. *Selectivity for females:* most admitted, but not all.

Total full-time faculty: 5. *Total part-time faculty:* 1. *Program contact person:* Donald Robinson.

Audition Information

No audition fee.

Performance Information

Performance opportunities available (frequency): Fully produced concerts (2 per year), informal concerts (2 per year), workshops (occasionally), on-site performances(2 per year), touring (2 per year), musical theater performances.

Performances choreographed by: faculty, students, guests. *Recent guest choreographers:* Jean Isaacs.

Facilities

Number of studios available: 5. *Approximate studio dimensions and flooring:* 30' x 40' oak. *Performance facilities:* full-sized proscenium theater, amphitheater, theater-in-the round.

DRAMA

Curriculum, Students, and Faculty

Required courses: acting, mime.

Elective courses: martial arts, movement, musical theater.

Number of years required to complete program: 3-5. *Summer program not available. Affiliation with a professional theater company: Starlight Opera, Old Globe Theater.*

Selectivity for males: most admitted, but not all. *Selectivity for females:* most admitted, but not all.

Total full-time faculty: 4.

Audition Information

No audition fee.

Performance Information

Performance opportunities available (frequency): fully produced performances (4 per year), informal performances (frequently), casting is by audition.

Facilities

Rehearsal facilities and hours: proscenium theatre, theater-in-the-round, amphitheater. *Number of theaters on campus:* 3. *Type and capacity:* proscenium 500, theater-in-the-round 500, amphitheater 500.

MUSIC

Curriculum, Students, and Faculty

How are major teacher assignments made? made by the school, according to teacher preference. Faculty is not informed of a student's teacher preference at the time of the audition. *May a student change major teachers during the course of study?* Possibly. *Study of secondary instrument or discipline is allowed.*

Selectivity for instruments or programs offered (rating): accordion (non-competitive), bassoon (non-competitive), choral singing (non-competitive), clarinet (non-competitive), composition (non-competitive), double bass (non-competitive), electronic music (non-competitive), flute or piccolo (non-competitive), French horn (non-competitive), harp (non-competitive), harp (non-competitive), jazz (non-competitive), oboe/English horn (non-competitive), percussion (non-competitive), piano (non-competitive), sacred music (non-competitive), saxophone (non-competitive), trombone (non-competitive), trumpet (non-competitive), tuba (non-competitive), viola (non-competitive), violin (non-competitive), violoncello (non-competitive), voice (non-competitive).

Total full-time faculty: 5. *Program contact person:* Gail McKinney.

Audition Information

No audition fee.

Facilities

Number of practice rooms and hours: 3; 7:00 am-3:00 pm (daily). *Recital hall?* no. *Concert hall?* yes. *Recording studio?* no.

SCHOOL OF THE ARTS

700 Font Boulevard, San Francisco CA 94132
Tel: 415-469-4027
Fax: 415-469-4053
Contact: Charles Roberts

General

Type of Institution: magnet-public. *Environment:* urban.

Total enrollment of institution: 410. *Degrees offered:* high school diploma.

Entrance Requirements

Audition required: live, audio. *Other requirements:* interview, recommendation, essay.

Services

Housing options: family.

Support staff: career counselor.

DANCE

Curriculum, Students, and Faculty

Required courses: African dance, anatomy, ballet, dance composition/choreography, dance writing, research and criticism, jazz, modern dance, movement techniques, rehearsal and performance, repertory, men's class (5 classes per week, 4 years to complete).

Selectivity for males: approximately 10% admitted. *Selectivity for females:* approximately 10% admitted. *Total Enrollment:* 45. *Entering class size:* 10. *Graduating class size:* 12.

Renowned alumni: Robert H. Johnson, Gabriel Trupiu, Esther Cowen.

Total full-time faculty: 1. *Total part-time faculty:* 3. *List of current faculty and past affiliations:* Enrico Labayen, Michelle Martin, Laura Bernasconi. *Program contact person:* Elvia Marta.

Audition Information

No audition fee. Audition consists of the following: ballet, modern dance, Afro-Haitian *Accompanist provided. Cassette player available; CD player available. Dress requirements for males:* leotard. *Dress requirements for females:* leotard, tights.

Audition evaluation criteria: amount of training students have (do they know the basics); what is their focus, understanding of movement and performance levels, and how fast they pick up.

Performance Information

Performance opportunities available (frequency): Fully produced concerts (1 per year), workshops (several per year), on-site performances(varies).

Performances choreographed by: faculty, students, guests. *Recent guest choreographers:* Robert H. Johnson, Cheryl Chaddick, Cecilia Marta.

Facilities

Number of studios available: 3. *Approximate studio dimensions and flooring:* Marley, wood, Marley, *Performance facilities:* SFSU McKenna's Theater; this year Cowel Theater on Fort Mason.

DRAMA

Curriculum, Students, and Faculty

Required courses: acting, audition preparation, drama criticism, improvisation, movement, playwriting, scene study, Stanislavski exercises, text analysis, voice, audition preparation.

Elective courses: directing.

Number of years required to complete program: 4. *Summer program not available. no affiliation with a professional theater company. Selectivity for males:* approximately 33% admitted. *Selectivity for females:* approximately 10% admitted. *Total enrollment:* 65. *Entering class size:* 22. *Graduating class size:* 20.

Total full-time faculty: 1. *Total part-time faculty:* 5.

Audition Information

No audition fee. Audition consists of the following: cold readings, comedic monologue, Shakespearean monologue, group warm-up. *Repertoire that students should avoid?* monologues from published plays only.

Performance Information

Performance opportunities available (frequency): fully produced performances (1-2 per year), informal performances (4 per year), workshops (2 per year) casting is assigned, auditioned.

Facilities

Type and capacity: pro arch 200.

MUSIC

Curriculum, Students, and Faculty

Unique or innovative music curriculum: Electronic music, chamber music, jazz band, music survey (master classes collaboration with professional arts organizations). *How are major teacher assignments made?* according to teacher preference. Faculty is informed of a student's teacher preference at the time of the audition. *Lessons with a teaching assistant. May a student change major teachers during the course of study?* possibly. *Study of secondary instrument or discipline is allowed.*

Selectivity for instruments or programs offered (rating): bassoon (selective), choral singing (selective), clarinet (selective), composition (selective), double bass (selective), electronic music (selective), flute or piccolo (selective), French horn (selective), guitar (highly selective), harp (selective), harpsichord (selective), jazz (selective), oboe/English horn (selective), orchestral conducting (highly selective), organ (selective), percussion (selective), piano (selective), saxophone (selective), trombone (selective), trumpet (selective), tuba (selective), viola (selective), violin (selective), violoncello (selective), voice (selective).

Total enrollment: 100. *Entering class size:* 25. *Graduating class size:* 23.

Renowned alumni: Damian Austin, Metropolitan Opera; Annie Chang, Phoenix Symphony.

Total full-time faculty: 3. *Total part-time faculty:* 10. *Program contact person:* Jerry Pannoue.

Audition Information

No audition fee. Audition consists of the following: scales, orchestral excerpts, sight reading, *Instruments provided for:* percussionists

Repertoire that students should avoid? pop music for auditions in instrumental music. *Performance opportunities available (frequency):* band, chamber music, jury examinations, orchestral concerts, recitals, chorus.

Facilities

Number of practice rooms and hours: 3; 4 hours. *Recital hall?* no. *Concert hall?* no. *Recording studio?* no.

VENICE HIGH SCHOOL

13000 Venice Boulevard, Los Angeles CA 90066
Tel: 310-306-7981 ext. 384
Fax: 310-306-3249
Email: dawnfields@aol.com
Contact: Wendy Kornbeck

General

Type of Institution: magnet-public. *Environment:* urban. *Academic education is offered on-site.*

Total enrollment of institution: 2,500. *Degrees offered:* high school diploma.

Entrance Requirements

Audition required: live, audio, video, regional. *Other requirements:* photograph.

Costs & Financial Aid

Types of scholarships and aid awarded: government aid.

Services

Housing options: off-campus housing, family.

Support staff: college advisor, financial aid advisor, foreign student advisor, physical therapist, psychological counselor, resident nurse, student affairs officer.

DANCE

Curriculum, Students, and Faculty

Required courses: music, rehearsal and performance.

Elective courses: African dance, character, ballet, dance composition/choreography, jazz, other world dance forms, Spanish, stagecraft, tap.

Selectivity for males: admit all who apply. *Selectivity for females:* admit all who apply. *Total enrollment:* 60. *Entering class size:* 30. *Graduating class size:* 30. *Percent international:* 20%. *Countries most represented:* Asian countries, South American countries. *Total part-time faculty:* 1. *Program contact person:* Francis Evans.

Audition Information

No audition fee. Audition consists of the following: ballet, improvisation. *Accompanist not provided. Cassette player available; CD player available.*

Performance Information

Performance opportunities available (frequency): Fully produced concerts (2 per year), informal concerts (2 per year).

Performances choreographed by: faculty, students, guests. *Recent guest choreographers:* Colors United, Sony Choreography Staff.

Facilities

Number of studios available: 2. *Approximate studio dimensions and flooring:* 60' x 120' wood. *Performance facilities:* full 1,500-seat auditorium.

DRAMA

Curriculum, Students, and Faculty

Required courses: acting, drama criticism, make-up, mime, scene study, speech, improvisation.

Number of years required to complete program: 3. *Summer program available. Affiliation with a professional theater company: Royal Shakespeare Company in Stratford-on-Avon.*

Selectivity for males: admit all who apply. *Selectivity for females:* admit all who apply. *Total enrollment:* 175. *Entering class size:* 90. *Graduating class size:* 30. *Percent international:* 50%. *Countries most represented:* South American countries.

Total full-time faculty: 1. *List of current faculty and past affiliations:* Cherie Smith.

Audition Information

No audition fee. Audition consists of the following: a cappella singing, cold readings, comedic monologue, improvisation, movement class, group warm-up. *Repertoire that students should avoid?* language appropriate for high school.

Performance Information

Performance opportunities available (frequency): fully produced performances (4 per year), informal performances (2 per year), workshops (daily), off-site performances (6 per year) casting is assigned, auditioned.

Facilities

Rehearsal facilities and hours: drama room with stage, full costume room, green room, 1,500-seat auditorium, lighting, stage crews, sound crew available. *Number of theaters on campus:* 2. *Type and capacity:* theater 1,500.

MUSIC

Curriculum, Students, and Faculty

Unique or innovative music curriculum: a small program that focuses on individual attention and performance. *How are major teacher assignments made?* students may choose, made by the school, according to teacher preference and teacher availability. Faculty is informed of a student's teacher preference at the time of the audition. *20 lessons with major teacher. May a student change major teachers during the course of study?* Possibly. *Study of secondary instrument or discipline is allowed.*

Selectivity for instruments or programs offered (rating): accompanying (selective), accordion (open), bagpipes (open), bassoon (open), choral conducting (highly selective), choral singing (selective), clarinet (selective), composition (selective), double bass (open), electronic music (open), flute or piccolo (selective), French horn (open), guitar (selective), harpsichord (open), jazz (competitive), oboe/English horn (competitive), orchestral conducting (highly selective), percussion (selective), piano (open), sacred music (non-competitive), saxophone (selective), trombone (selective), trumpet (selective), tuba (selective), viola (open), violin (open), violoncello (open), voice (highly selective).

Total enrollment: 500. *Entering class size:* 250. *Graduating class size:* 250. *Percent international:* 50%. *Countries most represented:* Asian countries, South American countries.

Renowned alumni: Lucas Richman, Los Angeles Philharmonic; Dr. Paul Salamunovich, Los Angeles Master Choral.

Total full-time faculty: 2. *Program contact person:* Wendy Kornbeck, Stephen Burch (instrumental).

Audition Information

No audition fee. Audition consists of the following: scales, orchestral excerpts, music theory, rhythmic dictation, arpeggios, sight reading, improvisation, melodic dictation, repertoire. *Instruments provided for:* percussionists; pianists.

Required repertoire: 1 song in a foreign language and 1 art song for voice, 10 minutes long. *Performance opportunities available (frequency):* band, chamber music, jury examinations (4 per year), orchestral concerts (2 per year), recitals (1 per year), touring (1 per year), chorus.

Facilities

Number of practice rooms and hours: 5; 8:00 am-5:30 pm. *Recital hall?* yes. *Concert hall?* yes. *Recording studio?* yes.

DENVER SCHOOL OF THE ARTS

150 Pearl Street, Denver CO 80209
Tel: 303-722-4669
Fax: 303-764-6917
Contact: Allen Balczarek

General

Type of Institution: magnet-public. *Environment:* urban.

Total enrollment of institution: 600. *Total student body from other countries:* 3%. *Degrees offered:* high school diploma.

Entrance Requirements

Audition required: live, video. *Other requirements:* interview, recommendation, essay, photograph.

Services

Support staff: financial aid advisor, resident nurse, student affairs officer.

DANCE

Curriculum, Students, and Faculty

Required courses: African dance, anatomy, character, ballet, dance composition/choreography, dance history, dance theory, dance writing, research and criticism, historical dance, jazz, Labanotation, master classes, men's class, music, nutrition, pas de deux, pointe, rehearsal and performance, repertory, Spanish, stagecraft, tap, variations.

Selectivity for males: approximately 60% admitted. *Selectivity for females:* approximately 60% admitted. *Entering class size:* 10. *Graduating class size:* 2.

Total full-time faculty: 1. *Total part-time faculty:* 1. *List of current faculty and past affiliations:* Micheal O'Banion, Mark Hase. *Program contact person:* Michael O'Banion.

Audition Information

No audition fee. Audition consists of the following: ballet, improvisation, modern dance, pointe works, prepared solo. *Accompanist provided. Cassette player available; CD player available. Dress requirements for males:* tights. *Dress requirements for females:* tights.

Performance Information

Performance opportunities available (frequency): fully produced concerts (4 per year), informal concerts (varies), workshops (6 per year), on-site performances (25 per year), touring (2 per year).

Performances choreographed by: faculty, students, guests.

Facilities

Number of studios available: 2. *Approximate studio dimensions and flooring:* 30' x 40' gym. *Performance facilities:* black box.

DRAMA

Curriculum, Students, and Faculty

Required courses: acting, Alexander technique, audition preparation, directing, drama criticism, dramaturgy, improvisation, make-up, movement, musical theater, scene study, speech, stage combat, Stanislavski exercises, text analysis, verse drama, voice.

Number of years required to complete program: 7. *Summer program available. No affiliation with a professional theater company. Selectivity for males:* approximately 60% admitted. *Selectivity for females:* approximately 60% admitted. *Total enrollment:* 80. *Entering class size:* 10. *Graduating class size:* 1.

Total full-time faculty: 1. *Total part-time faculty:* 2. *List of current faculty and past affiliations:* Stephen Nye, New York University.

Audition Information

No audition fee. Audition consists of the following: cold readings, comedic monologue, improvisation, group warm-up.

Performance Information

Performance opportunities available (frequency): fully produced performances (4 per year), informal performances (8 per year), workshops (6 per year), off-site performances (varies), casting is by audition.

Facilities

Rehearsal facilities and hours: studio space, 30'x40' studio available 7:00 am-9:00 pm. *Number of theaters on campus:* 1. *Type and capacity:* black box 400.

MUSIC

Curriculum, Students, and Faculty

Unique or innovative music curriculum: jazz workshop. *How are major teacher assignments made?* made by the school. Faculty is not informed of a student's teacher preference at the time of the audition. *May a student change major teachers during the course of study?* possibly. *Study of secondary instrument or discipline is allowed.*

Selectivity for instruments or programs offered (rating): accompanying (selective), accordion (highly selective), bagpipes (selective), bassoon (selective), choral conducting (highly selective), choral singing (highly selective), clarinet (highly selective), composition (highly selective), double bass (selective), electronic music (highly selective), flute or piccolo (highly selective), French horn (selective), guitar (selective), harp (selective), harpsichord (selective), jazz (highly selective), oboe/English horn (selective), orchestral conducting (highly selective), organ (highly selective), percussion (highly selective), piano (highly selective), sacred music (highly selective), saxophone (highly selective), trombone (highly selective), trumpet (highly selective), tuba (highly selective), viola (selective), violin (highly selective), violoncello (selective), voice (highly selective).

Total enrollment: 200. *Entering class size:* 30. *Graduating class size:* 25. *Percent international:* 0%. *Countries most represented:* Cuba, Mexico.

Total full-time faculty: 3. *Total part-time faculty:* 2. *Program contact person:* Dave Hammond, Jerry Noonan.

Audition Information

No audition fee. Audition consists of the following: scales, music theory, rhythmic dictation, sight reading, repertoire. *Instruments provided for:* percussionists; pianists.

Performance opportunities available (frequency): chamber music, orchestral concerts, recitals, chorus.

Facilities

Number of practice rooms and hours: 5; 7:00 am-9:00 pm. *Recital hall?* no. *Concert hall?* yes. *Recording studio?* yes.

CONNECTICUT

ACES/EDUCATIONAL CENTER FOR THE ARTS

55 Audubon Street, New Haven CT 06510
Tel: 203-777-5451
Email: Parker@aces.k12.ct.us
Web: www.aces.k12.ct.us/eca
Contact: Robert Parker or Louise Ross

General

Type of Institution: magnet-public. *Environment:* urban. *Academic education is offered off site.*

Total enrollment of institution: 205. *Total student body from other countries:* 1%.

Entrance Requirements

Audition required: live. *Other requirements:* interview, recommendation, essay.

Geographic restrictions: greater New Haven.

Services

Support staff: college advisor.

Comments

Our school does not exactly fit into the required catagories. Students are bussed in for programs four afternoons a week.

DANCE

Curriculum, Students, and Faculty

Required courses: anatomy, ballet, dance composition/choreography, dance history, dance theory, dance writing, research and criticism, Cunningham-based modern dance, nutrition, rehearsal and performance, repertory, modern dance partnering.

Elective courses: African dance, historical dance, jazz, master classes, pas de deux, Spanish, tap, variations, Japanese dance, Haitian dance.

Selectivity for males: approximately 60% admitted. *Selectivity for females:* approximately 60% admitted. *Total enrollment:* 35. *Graduating class size:* 5. *Total part-time faculty:* 6. *List of current faculty and past affiliations:* Susan Matheke, Viola Farber company; Willie Feuer, Viola Farber Company. *Program contact person:* Robert Parker or Louise Ross.

Audition Information

No audition fee. Audition consists of the following: improvisation, modern dance. *Accompanist provided. Cassette player available; CD player available. Dress requirements for males:* t-shirt, tights or shorts. *Dress requirements for females:* leotard, footless tights.

Performance Information

Performance opportunities available (frequency): Fully produced concerts (3-5 per year), informal concerts (3-5 per year), workshops (3-5 per year), on-site performances (3-5 per year), touring (3-5 per year).

Performances choreographed by: faculty, students, guests. *Recent guest choreographers:* Loretta Abbott, noel Nantambu Hall, Harriet Browne, Linda James, Paris Mann.

Facilities

Number of studios available: 2. *Performance facilities:* black box theater.

DRAMA

Curriculum, Students, and Faculty

Required courses: acting, audition preparation, directing, drama criticism, dramaturgy, improvisation, movement, speech, Stanislavski exercises, text analysis, verse drama, voice.

Elective courses: make-up, mime, musical theater, stage combat.

Number of years required to complete program: 1-4. *Summer program not available. Selectivity for males:* approximately 60% admitted. *Selectivity for females:* approximately 60% admitted. *Total enrollment:* 45. *Graduating class size:* 10.

Total part-time faculty: 4. *List of current faculty and past affiliations:* Linda McGuire, Yale Drama School; Ingrid Schaeffer.

Audition Information

Audition consists of the following: comedic monologue, improvisation, group warm-up. *Dress requirements for males:* loose clothing. *Dress requirements for females:* loose clothing.

Performance Information

Performance opportunities available (frequency): fully produced performances (3-4 per year), informal performances (2-3 per year), off-site performances (5 per year), casting is by audition.

Facilities

Rehearsal facilities and hours: black box theater, proscenium theater. *Number of theaters on campus:* 2.

MUSIC

Curriculum, Students, and Faculty

How are major teacher assignments made? made by the school. Faculty is informed of a student's teacher preference at the time of the audition. *May a student change major teachers during the course of study?* possibly. *Study of secondary instrument or discipline is allowed.*

Total enrollment: 40. *Graduating class size:* 14. *Percent international:* 1%. *Total part-time faculty:* 8. *Program contact person:* Robert Parker or Louise Ross.

Audition Information

No audition fee. Audition consists of the following: scales, orchestral excerpts, sight reading, improvisation. *Instruments provided for:* percussionists.

Facilities

Number of practice rooms: 5. *Recital hall?* yes. *Concert hall?* yes. *Recording studio?* no.

CHOATE ROSEMARY HALL

333 Christian Street, Wallingford CT 06492
Tel: 203-697-2252
Fax: 203-697-2380
Email: cmurphy@choate.edu
Web: www.choate.edu

General

Type of Institution: day, coed, boarding. *Environment:* suburban.

Total enrollment of institution: 850. *Degrees offered:* high school diploma.

Entrance Requirements

Audition not required. Other requirements: interview, recommendation, essay. *Standardized test requirements:* SSAT; TOEFL.

Costs & Financial Aid

Application fee: $40. *Deposit:* $1,000. *Tuition:* $16,720.

Percent of students receiving financial aid: 29%. *Types of scholarships and aid awarded:* full, partial, need-based, tuition payment plan. *Forms required for scholarships:* FAFSA, income tax return, income asset verification. *Loans available. Financial aid offered to international students.*

Services

Housing options: on-site dorms.

Support staff: college advisor, dorm parent, financial aid advisor, foreign student advisor, physical therapist, psychological counselor, resident nurse, student affairs officer.

DANCE

Curriculum, Students, and Faculty

Elective courses: African dance, ballet, jazz, pointe, rehearsal and performance, tap, Cunningham-based, Nikolais-based modern dance, modern dance.

Selectivity for males: admit all who apply. *Selectivity for females:* admit all who apply.

Total full-time faculty: 3. *List of current faculty and past affiliations:* noble Barker, New Haven Ballet. *Program contact person:* Paul Tines.

Audition Information

No audition fee.

Performance Information

Performance opportunities available (frequency): Informal concerts (1 per year), workshops (several times a year).

Performances choreographed by: faculty, students.

Facilities

Number of studios available: 1. *Approximate studio dimensions and flooring:* 30' x 30' sprung wood floor. *Performance facilities:* main stage.

DRAMA

Curriculum, Students, and Faculty

Required courses: acting, directing, movement.

Elective courses: directing, improvisation, musical theater, rehearsal and performance, speech.

Renowned alumni: Edward Albee, Michael Douglas, Jamie Lee Curtis, Paul Giamatti, Stephen Bagordus.

Total full-time faculty: 3.

Audition Information

No audition fee.

Facilities

Rehearsal facilities and hours: main stage, experimental theater, 2 hours each day (Mon-Fri). *Number of theaters on campus:* 2. *Type and capacity:* theater 800, experimental 200.

MUSIC

Curriculum, Students, and Faculty

Selectivity for instruments or programs offered (rating): clarinet, double bass, flute, piccolo, French horn, guitar, harp, harpsichord, oboe/English horn, organ, percussion, piano, saxophone, trombone, trumpet, violin, violoncello, voice, jazz piano, jazz bass guitar.

Total full-time faculty: 3. *Total part-time faculty:* 18 *Program contact person:* Paul Tines.

Audition Information

No audition fee. Audition consists of the following: orchestral excerpts, ensemble playing, sight reading.

Facilities

Recital hall? yes. *Concert hall?* yes.

COOPERATIVE ARTS AND HUMANITIES MAGNET HIGH SCHOOL

444 Orange Street, New Haven CT 06511
Tel: 203-946-5923
Fax: 203-946-5926
Contact: Keith Cunningham

General

Type of Institution: magnet-public. *Environment:* urban. *Academic education is offered on-site.*

Total enrollment of institution: 375. *Degrees offered:* high school diploma.

Entrance Requirements

Audition not required.

Geographic restrictions: no restriction but practically limited to greater New Haven region. Admission based on lottery.

Costs & Financial Aid

Tuition (in-state/out-state): $0.

Services

Support staff: college advisor.

DANCE

Curriculum, Students, and Faculty

Required courses: African dance, ballet, dance composition/choreography, dance history, dance theory, dance writing, research and criticism, jazz, Graham-based modern dance, rehearsal and performance.

Total enrollment: 60. *Entering class size:* 20. *Graduating class size:* 10. *Total part-time faculty:* 3. *List of current faculty and past affiliations:* Cheree Knight, Camara, Zenzile Dance Co.; Christine Kershaw, Paul Hall Dance Co.; Caroline Smith, Boston Conservatory, RAD Academy of Dance. *Program contact person:* Keith Cunningham.

Audition Information

No audition fee. Accompanist not provided. Cassette player available; CD player available. Dress requirements for males: leotard or unitard, dance shoes.

Performance Information

Performance opportunities available (frequency): Fully produced concerts (2 per year), informal concerts (4 per year), on-site performances (2-4 per year), touring (2-4 per year).

Performances choreographed by: faculty, students.

Facilities

Number of studios available: 4 *Approximate studio dimensions and flooring:* 20' x 40' wood. *Performance facilities:* local theaters.

DRAMA

Curriculum, Students, and Faculty

Required courses: acting, movement, voice.

Elective courses: musical theater, text analysis.

Number of years required to complete program: 4. *Summer program not available. Affiliation with a professional theater company:* partnership with Yale Drama School and Long Wharf Theater.

Total enrollment: 40. *Entering class size:* 15. *Graduating class size:* 12.

Total part-time faculty: 3. *List of current faculty and past affiliations:* Sally Kaczynski, Charlene Andrade, Dana Sachs, Renaissance Theater.

Performance Information

Performance opportunities available (frequency): fully produced performances (4 per year), informal performances (6-8 annually), off-site performances (2-4 annually), casting is by audition.

Recent guest artists: Mike Seeger, Bruce Altman, Pee Wee Love, Greg Mouning, Funkestra.

Facilities

Rehearsal facilities and hours: classroom. *Number of theaters on campus:* 1. *Type and capacity:* gymnatorium 400.

MUSIC

Curriculum, Students, and Faculty

Unique or innovative music curriculum: Partnership with Yale School of Music. *How are major teacher assignments made?* made by the school. Faculty is not informed of a student's teacher preference at the time of the audition. *70 lessons with major teacher. May a student change major teachers during the course of study?* usually. *Study of secondary instrument or discipline is allowed.*

Total enrollment: 50. *Entering class size:* 20. *Graduating class size:* 10.

Total full-time faculty: 1. *Total part-time faculty:* 2. *Program contact person:* Keith Cunningham.

Performance opportunities available (frequency): band (5 per year), chamber music (5 per year), band (5 per year), recitals (5 per year), chorus (5 per year).

Facilities

Recital hall? no. *Concert hall?* no. *Recording studio?* no.

THE ETHEL WALKER SCHOOL

230 Bushy Hill Road, Simsbury CT 06070
Tel: 860-408-4200
Fax: 860-408-4201
Web: www.ews.pvt.KIZ.US
Contact: Holly Treat

General

Type of Institution: girls school, day and boarding. *Environment:* suburban.

Total enrollment of institution: 190. *Total student body from other countries:* 13%. *Degrees offered:* high school diploma.

Entrance Requirements

Other requirements: interview, recommendation, essay. *Standardized test requirements:* SSAT; TOEFL; 500.

Costs & Financial Aid

Application fee: $40. *Deposit:* $2,000. *Tuition:* $16,000. *Other fees:* $450 student services, $600 books.

Percent of students receiving financial aid: 38% *Types of scholarships and aid awarded:* full, partial, need-based, named, institutional aid, tuition payment plan. *Forms required for scholarships:* income tax return, income asset verification, SSS form. *Loans available. Procedure for applying for loans:* outside contracts with banks recommended by school. *Percent of international students receiving scholarships:* 0%. *Other aid available to international students:* none.

Services

Housing options: on-site dorms.

Support staff: college advisor, dorm parent, financial aid advisor, foreign student advisor, housing advisor, psychological counselor, resident assistant, resident nurse, student affairs officer.

DANCE

Curriculum, Students, and Faculty

Required courses: character, ballet, dance composition/choreography, master classes, modern dance, movement techniques, nutrition, rehearsal and performance, repertory.

Elective courses: music, pointe, stagecraft, rehearsal and performance (5 classes per week).

Selectivity for males: admit all who apply. *Selectivity for females:* approximately 60% admitted. *Total enrollment:* 48. *Entering class size:* 12. *Graduating class size:* 15.

Renowned alumni: Kari Richardson, presently with Douglous Dunn Company of New York City.

Total full-time faculty: 1. *Total part-time faculty:* 1. *List of current faculty and past affiliations:* Ching Hosier, School of Hartford Ballet University of Hartford's; Dorothy Silverherz, danced with New York City Opera Ballet and on Broadway. *Program contact person:* Dorothy Silverherz.

Audition Information

No audition fee. Audition consists of the following: ballet, improvisation, modern dance, prepared solo, jazz phrase. *Accompanist not provided. Cassette player available; CD player available. Dress requirements for females:* tights, leotard, ballet shoes for ballet, bare feet for modern.

Audition evaluation criteria: presence, expression, musicality, a demonstrated personal history of respect and devotion to this art form, working knowledge of basic ballet and modern vocabulary.

Performance Information

Performance opportunities available (frequency): fully produced concerts (2 per year), musical each spring.

Performances choreographed by: faculty, students, guests. *Recent guest choreographers:* Tim Martin, New York based contemporary choreographer. Gemze DeLappe, former ballerina with Ballet Theater. Toni Davis, member of Hartford based "Out of Africa" Dance and Music Company.

Facilities

Number of studios available: 2. *Approximate studio dimensions and flooring:* 30' x 40' Marley over wood. *Performance facilities:* theater seats 400, 30' x 40' stage; student and professional performances take place in this theater on an annual basis.

DRAMA

Curriculum, Students, and Faculty

Elective courses: improvisation.

Summer program not available. No affiliation with a professional theater company. Total enrollment: 34. *Entering class size:* 5. *Graduating class size:* 10.

Renowned alumni: Sigourney Weaver.

Total part-time faculty: 3. *List of current faculty and past affiliations:* Steve Wacher, University of Hartford; Doreen Cohn, Priscilla Jackson.

Audition Information

No audition fee.

Performance Information

Performance opportunities available (frequency): fully produced performances (1 per year), informal performances (4 per year), workshops (3 per year), off-site performances (1 per year), casting is by audition.

Facilities

Type and capacity: theater 300, black box 75.

MUSIC

Curriculum, Students, and Faculty

Unique or innovative music curriculum: The school provides choir, 2 chamber choir groups, and music lessons in a variety of instruments. We have six part-time music faculty members, unusual for a high school. *How are major teacher assignments made?* made by the school. Faculty is not informed of a student's teacher preference at the time of the audition. *May a student change major teachers during the course of study?* Never. *Study of secondary instrument or discipline is allowed.*

Selectivity for instruments or programs offered (rating): accompanying (highly selective), choral singing (open), clarinet (open), electronic music (open), flute or piccolo (open), guitar (open), organ (open), piano (open), saxophone (open), viola (open), violin (open), voice (open).

Total enrollment: 74. *Entering class size:* 27. *Graduating class size:* 21.

Total full-time faculty: 1. *Total part-time faculty:* 6. *Program contact person:* Kelly McGregor.

Audition Information

No audition fee. Audition consists of the following: ensemble playing, sight reading, repertoire.

Required repertoire: 1 piece of performer's choice. *Performance opportunities available (frequency):* chorus (4 per year).

Facilities

Number of practice rooms and hours: 3; 8:00 am-7:00 pm. *Recital hall?* yes. *Concert hall?* yes. *Recording studio?* yes.

Comments

For a small, private, girls' school, we offer a wide variety of musical opportunities. Any student can choose to study music, but advanced singers do have an opportunity to audition for a selective a capella singing chamber choir. Our instrumental instructors are local performers and teachers who have extensive backgrounds in musical performance study, including degrees from the Hartt School of Music and Indiana University.

GREATER HARTFORD ACADEMY OF THE ARTS

235 Wethersfield Avenue, Hartford CT 06114
Tel: 860-522-8335
Fax: 860-522-5153
Email: Academy@crec.org
Web: www.crec.org

General

Type of Institution: magnet-public, specialized. *Environment:* urban. *Academic education is offered off-site.*

Total enrollment of institution: 152.

Entrance Requirements

Audition required: live. *Other requirements:* interview, recommendation, photograph.

Tuition: $4,587.

Services

Support staff: college advisor.

DANCE

Curriculum, Students, and Faculty

Required courses: ballet, dance composition/choreography, dance history, dance theory, dance writing, research and criticism, historical dance, master classes, modern dance, rehearsal and performance, repertory, stagecraft.

Elective courses: African dance, jazz, movement techniques, other world dance forms, tap, vernacular dance, modern dance partnering.

Selectivity for males: most admitted, but not all. *Selectivity for females:* most admitted, but not all. 23. *Entering class size:* 4. *Graduating class size:* 8. *Total part-time faculty:* 11. *List of current faculty and past affiliations:* Kim Stroud, Martha Graham Dance Company. *Program contact person:* Kim Stroud.

Audition Information

No audition fee. Audition consists of the following: ballet, improvisation, modern dance, prepared solo. *Accompanist provided. Cassette player available; CD player available.*

Audition evaluation criteria: flexibility—hips, feet, back, hamstrings; strength; alignment; weight; mental understanding of physical application; coordination; artistic merit-creativity; projection; musicality; desire.

Performance Information

Performance opportunities available (frequency): Informal concerts (2 per year), workshops (4 per year), on-site performances.

Performances choreographed by: faculty, students, guests. *Recent guest choreographers:* Monica Levy (choreographer for Hartford Ballet and Pacific northwest), Darryl Thomas (Pilobolus), Elizabeth Streb (Ringside Dance Theater).

Facilities

Number of studios available: 3. *Approximate studio dimensions and flooring:* wood and Marley. *Performance facilities:* theaters and other spaces in the Hartford community.

DRAMA

Curriculum, Students, and Faculty

Required courses: acting, audition preparation, dramaturgy, improvisation, mime, movement, musical theater, scene study, speech, Stanislavski exercises, text analysis, voice, jury examinations, commedia, puppetry, acting for camera.

Elective courses: directing, Shakespeare, comic acting.

Number of years required to complete program: 3. *Summer program not available. Affiliation with a professional theater company: Students are taught a dramaturgy class by Hartford Stage Company's senior staff and may perform in their productions.*

Selectivity for males: most admitted, but not all. *Selectivity for females:* most admitted, but not all. *Total enrollment:* 54. *Entering class size:* 9. *Graduating class size:* 13.

Renowned alumni: Bill Fennelly, Chris Erk, Lacy Hornkohl.

Total part-time faculty: 16. *List of current faculty and past affiliations:* Carolyn Kirsch, Eileen Dulen, National Theater of the Deaf; Diana Moller-Marino, Oddfellows and Capitol Classics; Jonathan Gillman.

Audition Information

No audition fee. Audition consists of the following: cold readings, required monologue, 2 mimes: washing hands 1) as self and 2) as character in their monologue.

Audition evaluation criteria: potential, focus, concentration, creativity, commitment.

Performance Information

Performance opportunities available (frequency): fully produced performances (2 per year), informal performances (2 per year), workshops (2 per year), off-site performances (2 per year), casting is by audition.

Recent guest artists: Robert Rivest, Little Theater of the Deaf, Beau Geste, Irondale Players.

Facilities

Rehearsal facilities and hours: dance studio, 20' x 12', rented space, after school and Saturday.

MUSIC

Curriculum, Students, and Faculty

Unique or innovative music curriculum: emphasis on chamber music and small group jazz playing. *How are major teacher assignments made?* according to teacher preference; no private instruction.

Selectivity for instruments or programs offered (rating): bassoon (open), choral singing (open), clarinet (open), composition (open), double bass (open), flute or piccolo (open), French horn (open), guitar (open), jazz (open), oboe/English horn (open), percussion (open), piano (open), saxophone (open), trombone (open), trumpet (open), viola (open), violin (open), violoncello (open), voice (open).

Total enrollment: 58. *Entering class size:* 9. *Graduating class size:* 16. *Countries most represented:* Russia.

Renowned alumni: Jimmy Greene, Horace Silver. *Total part-time faculty:* 18. *Program contact person:* Gene Bozzi.

Audition Information

No audition fee. Audition consists of the following: scales, music theory arpeggios, sight reading. *Instruments provided for:* percussionists; piano amplifiers provided.

Facilities

Recital hall? no. *Concert hall?* no. *Recording studio?* yes.

DISTRICT OF COLUMBIA

DUKE ELLINGTON HIGH SCHOOL OF THE ARTS

3500 R Street, NW, Washington DC 20007
Tel: 202-282-1100

General

Type of Institution: public, specialized. *Environment:* urban. *Academic education is offered on-site.*

Degrees offered: high school diploma, certificate.

Entrance Requirements

Audition required: live. *Other requirements:* interview, recommendation.

Services

Support staff: college advisor.

DANCE

Curriculum, Students, and Faculty

Required courses: character, ballet, dance composition/choreography, dance history, dance writing, research and criticism, master classes, men's class, modern dance, nutrition, pas de deux, pointe, rehearsal and performance, stagecraft, tap, variations.

Elective courses: African dance.

Selectivity for males: approximately 33% admitted. *Selectivity for females:* approximately 33% admitted. *Entering class size:* 35. *Percent international:* 1%. *Countries most represented:* Russia.

Renowned alumni: Terace Jones, Joffrey; Kim Bears, Philadanco; Kathy Smith; Don Bellamy, Alvin Ailey; Nathaniel Cooper, Tap Dogs.

Total full-time faculty: 2. *Total part-time faculty:* 6. *Program contact person:* Lynn B. Wehers.

Audition Information

No audition fee. Audition consists of the following: ballet, modern dance, orthopedic evaluation, pointe works. *Accompanist provided. Cassette player available; CD player available. Dress requirements for males:* black tights, white leotard, black slippers. *Dress requirements for females:* royal leotard, skin color tights, shoes to match.

Performance Information

Performance opportunities available (frequency): Fully produced concerts (2 per year), workshops (monthly), on-site performances(varies).

Performances choreographed by: faculty, guests. *Recent guest choreographers:* Michael Vernon, Kim Bears—Philadanco, Lisa Johnson—Alvin Ailey, Rudolph KharaTian—Kirov Ballet, Adrian Bolton.

Facilities

Number of studios available: 3. *Approximate studio dimensions and flooring:* sprung floor, Marley covering. *Performance facilities:* full stage and theater.

FLORIDA

ALEXANDER W. DREYFOOS, JR. SCHOOL OF THE ARTS

501 South Sapidilla Avenue, West Palm Beach FL 33401
Tel: 561-802-6000
Fax: 561-802-6059

General

Type of Institution: magnet-public. *Environment:* urban.

Total enrollment of institution: 1,074. *Degrees offered:* high school diploma.

Entrance Requirements

Audition required: live. *Other requirements:* interview.

Geographic restrictions: Palm Beach County resident.

Costs & Financial Aid

No Tuition. Other fees: vary by course; can be waived based on need.

Services

Support staff: college advisor, resident nurse, student affairs officer.

Comments

First graduates from colleges and conservatories this year. Program is 4 years old.

DANCE

Curriculum, Students, and Faculty

Required courses: partnering.

Selectivity for males: admit all who apply. *Selectivity for females:* approximately 10% admitted. *Total enrollment:* 176. *Entering class size:* 45. *Graduating class size:* 29.

Total full-time faculty: 4. *Total part-time faculty:* 2. *Program contact person:* Jeff Satinoff.

Audition Information

No audition fee.

Performance Information

Recent guest choreographers: Violette Verdy.

Facilities

Number of studios available: 3.

DRAMA

Curriculum, Students, and Faculty

Required courses: acting, audition preparation, costume design, drama criticism, improvisation, make-up, mime, movement, scene study, speech, stagecraft, Stanislavski exercises, text analysis, voice.

Elective courses: directing, musical theater.

Number of years required to complete program: 4. *Summer program not available. Affiliation with a professional theater company: Florida Stage (formerly the Pope Theater Company).*

Selectivity for males: approximately 60% admitted. *Selectivity for females:* approximately 10% admitted. *Total enrollment:* 195. *Entering class size:* 57. *Graduating class size:* 24.

Total full-time faculty: 4. *Total part-time faculty:* 2. *List of current faculty and past affiliations:* Beverly Blanchette, Garry Q. Lewis, Tom Robbins, Dennis Sims, Jeff Leonard.

Audition Information

No audition fee. Audition consists of the following: comedic monologue, group warm-up, 16 measures of a song (or a cold reading), interview, ability to take direction, choice of showing technical project or monologue performance. *Dress requirements for males:* interview attire, professional. *Dress requirements for females:* interview attire, professional.

Audition evaluation criteria: Desire to participate in program, positive attitude, expressive ability, commitment, characterization, focus, movement, projection, believability.

Performance Information

Performance opportunities available (frequency): fully produced performances (4 per year), informal performances (10 per year), workshops (10 per year), off-site performances (20 per year), casting is assigned, auditioned.

Recent guest artists: Loretta Swit, Ozzie Davis, Charles Nelson Reilly.

Facilities

Number of theaters on campus: 2. *Type and capacity:* black box 200, theater 600.

MUSIC

Curriculum, Students, and Faculty

How are major teacher assignments made? made by the school.

Selectivity for instruments or programs offered (rating): bassoon (selective), choral singing (selective), clarinet (selective), double bass (non-competitive), flute or piccolo (highly selective), French horn (selective), harp (non-competitive), oboe/English horn (selective), percussion (selective), piano (highly selective), saxophone (selective), trombone (selective), trumpet (selective), tuba (selective), viola (non-competitive), violin (non-competitive), violoncello (non-competitive), voice (selective).

Total enrollment: 246. *Entering class size:* 59. *Graduating class size:* 37. *Percent international:* 3%. *Countries most represented:* Germany.

Total full-time faculty: 4. *Total part-time faculty:* 7. *Program contact person:* Randy Sonntag.

Audition Information

No audition fee. Audition consists of the following: scales, music theory sight reading. *Instruments provided for:* harpists, percussionists.

Repertoire that students should avoid? popular music. *Performance opportunities available (frequency):* band (4 per year), chamber music (2-3 per year), band (several), jury examinations (2 per year), orchestral concerts (4-5 per year), recitals (several), chorus (several).

Facilities

Number of practice rooms and hours: 18; 8:00 am-5:00 pm. *Concert hall?* yes. *Recording studio?* yes.

BOOKER HIGH SCHOOL/SARASOTA VISUAL AND PERFORMING ARTS SCHOOL

3201 North Orange Avenue, Sarasota FL 33580
Tel: 941-355-2967
Fax: 941-359-5757
Contact: Don Rainone

General

Type of Institution: magnet-public. *Environment:* urban.

Total enrollment of institution: 1,450. *Degrees offered:* high school diploma, certificate.

Entrance Requirements

Audition required: live. *Other requirements:* interview, recommendation.

DANCE

Curriculum, Students, and Faculty

Required courses: anatomy, ballet (2 classes per week, 4 years to complete), dance composition/choreography (2 years to complete), dance history (1 year to complete), dance writing, research and criticism, jazz (2 classes per week, 2 years to complete), master classes, modern dance, Graham-based, Horton-based modern dance, Limon-based, music, rehearsal and performance, repertory (4 years to complete), tap (2 classes per week, 2 years to complete), modern dance partnering, releasing technique.

Elective courses: nutrition, tap.

Selectivity for males: most admitted, but not all. *Selectivity for females:* approximately 60% admitted. *Total enrollment:* 46. *Entering class size:* 24. *Graduating class size:* 5.

Total full-time faculty: 1 *Total part-time faculty:* 2. *List of current faculty and past affiliations:* Stephanie Carter, Justine Coulon, Gus Giordano, Deborah Vinton. *Program contact person:* Stephanie Carter.

Audition Information

No audition fee. Audition consists of the following: ballet, modern dance. *Accompanist not provided. Cassette player available; CD player available. Dress requirements for males:* ballet—black tights, white leotard; modern—solid color tights and leotard. *Dress requirements for females:* pink tights, black leotard.

Performance Information

Performance opportunities available (frequency): Fully produced concerts (2 per year), informal concerts (1-3 per year), workshops (5-10 per year), on-site performances(10 per year).

Performances choreographed by: faculty, students.

Facilities

Number of studios available: 4 *Approximate studio dimensions and flooring:* 30' x 34' wood. *Performance facilities:* New Theatre, state-of-the-art.

DRAMA

Curriculum, Students, and Faculty

Required courses: acting, audition preparation, directing, drama criticism, improvisation, make-up, movement, scene study, text analysis, voice.

Number of years required to complete program: 4. *Summer program not available. Affiliation with a professional theater company; lend/borrow agreement for props and costumes with many local theaters that also provide reduced ticket prices and occasional complimentary tickets.*

Selectivity for males: most admitted, but not all. *Selectivity for females:* most admitted, but not all. *Total enrollment:* 94. *Entering class size:* 32. *Graduating class size:* 12.

Total full-time faculty: 1. *Total part-time faculty:* 1. *List of current faculty and past affiliations:* Ken Wiegers, Susan Mannino.

Audition Information

Audition consists of the following: cold readings, improvisation.

Performance Information

Performance opportunities available (frequency): fully produced performances (4 per year), informal performances (4-5 per year), workshops (4 per year), off-site performances (2-3 per year), a roadshow is produced yearly, casting is by audition.

Recent guest artists: John Astin, Greg Blaken, Cary Trivanovich.

Facilities

Number of theaters on campus: 2. *Type and capacity:* proscenium 437, experimental 30.

MUSIC

Curriculum, Students, and Faculty

Unique or innovative music curriculum: College level theory and ear training taught in high school. *How are major teacher assignments made?* made by the school, according to teacher preference and teacher availability. Faculty is not informed of a student's teacher preference at the time of the audition. *May a student change major teachers during the course of study?* possibly. *Study of secondary instrument or discipline is allowed.*

Selectivity for instruments or programs offered (rating): accompanying (competitive), bassoon (competitive), choral singing (competitive), clarinet (competitive), double bass (competitive), flute or piccolo (competitive), French horn (competitive), guitar (competitive), jazz (competitive), oboe/English horn (competitive), percussion (competitive), piano (competitive), saxophone (competitive), trombone (competitive), trumpet (competitive), tuba (competitive), viola (competitive), violin (competitive), violoncello (competitive), voice (competitive).

Total enrollment: 81. *Entering class size:* 43. *Graduating class size:* 14.

Total full-time faculty: 1. *Program contact person:* Wilson Cosby.

Audition Information

No audition fee. Audition consists of the following: scales, sight reading. *Instruments provided for:* percussionists.

Repertoire that students should avoid? rock. *Performance opportunities available (frequency):* jury examinations, opera workshops, recitals.

Facilities

Number of practice rooms and hours: 4; 12:00 pm-3:00 pm. *Recital hall?* yes. *Concert hall?* yes. *Recording studio?* no.

CYPRESS LAKE CENTER FOR THE ARTS

6740 Panther Lane, Ft. Myers FL 33919
Tel: 941-481-3592
Fax: 941-481-7778
Email: hinman_j@wizard.firn.edu
Web: www.lee.kiz.fl.us/cya
Contact: James Hinman

General

Type of Institution: magnet-public. *Environment:* suburban. *Academic education is offered on-site.*

Total enrollment of institution: 308. *Degrees offered:* high school diploma, certificate.

Entrance Requirements

Audition required: live. *Other requirements:* interview, recommendation, essay.

Geographic restrictions: Lee County, FL, resident.

Costs & Financial Aid

Procedure for applying for loans: applications are available in January with a 3/1 deadline, auditions are conducted in March.

Services

Support staff: career counselor.

Comments

This school is beginning its 4th year.

DANCE

Curriculum, Students, and Faculty

Required courses: African dance, ballet, dance composition/choreography, dance history, jazz, master classes, Limon-based modern dance, rehearsal and performance, repertory, tap.

Elective courses: pointe, stagecraft, contact improvisation.

Selectivity for males: most admitted, but not all. *Selectivity for females:* approximately 60% admitted. *Entering class size:* 10. *Graduating class size:* 11.

Total full-time faculty: 2. *List of current faculty and past affiliations:* Donna Duffee Kojo, Florida State University, Ohio State University; Patty Gain, Mary Anthony Dance Theatre, SW FL Dance Theater; Alyce Bochette, Mark Morris Dance Co. *Program contact person:* Patty Gair.

Audition Information

No audition fee. Audition consists of the following: ballet, improvisation, modern dance, prepared solo. *Accompanist not provided. Cassette player available; CD player available. Dress requirements for males:* white t-shirts, black sweatpants, ballet shoes if available. *Dress requirements for females:* leotards, tights, pink, black or tan ballet shoes.

Performance Information

Performance opportunities available (frequency): Fully produced concerts (4 per year), workshops (3 per year), on-site performances (6 per year), class showings (4 per year).

Performances choreographed by: faculty, students, guests. *Recent guest choreographers:* Nia Love, Paulette Jones, Jennifer Salk, Alyce Bochette.

Facilities

Number of studios available: 2. *Approximate studio dimensions and flooring:* 42' x 28' sprung floor-tongue and groove Marley covering. *Performance facilities:* black box theater, auditorium.

DRAMA

Curriculum, Students, and Faculty

Required courses: acting, audition preparation, dance, directing, improvisation, scene study, Stanislavski exercises.

Elective courses: musical theater.

Number of years required to complete program: 4. *Summer program not available. Affiliation with a professional theater company; Broadway Palm Dinner Theater.*

Selectivity for males: approximately 60% admitted. *Selectivity for females:* approximately 33% admitted. *Entering class size:* 16. *Graduating class size:* 12.

Renowned alumni: Zack Dobbins, George Pelligrino.

Total full-time faculty: 2. *List of current faculty and past affiliations:* Diane Stewart.

Audition Information

No audition fee. Audition consists of the following: comedic monologue, improvisation, Shakespearean monologue, group warm-up. *Repertoire that students should avoid?* material should be taken from plays.

Audition evaluation criteria: characterization, use of body, use of voice, preparation, stage presence, creativity, artistic potential.

Performance Information

Performance opportunities available (frequency): fully produced performances (7-9 per year), informal performances (monthly), workshops (1-2 per year) casting is assigned, auditioned.

Recent guest artists: Jude Perry, JT Smith.

Facilities

Rehearsal facilities and hours: black box theater. *Number of theaters on campus:* 2. *Type and capacity:* auditorium 900, black box 150.

MUSIC

Curriculum, Students, and Faculty

Unique or innovative music curriculum: Focus upon individual talent and skill development with opportunity for diversity in performance. Integration of music with technology and other departments, in developing multi-media technologies, filmscoring, electronic music, etc. Faculty is not informed of a student's teacher preference at the time of the audition. *May a student change major teachers during the course of study?* possibly. *Study of secondary instrument or discipline is allowed.*

Selectivity for instruments or programs offered (rating): accompanying (highly selective), bassoon (selective), choral singing (selective), clarinet (selective), double bass (selective), flute or piccolo (selective), French horn (selective), guitar (highly selective), oboe/English horn (selective), percussion (selective), piano (highly selective), saxophone (selective), trombone (selective), trumpet (selective), tuba (selective), viola (selective), violin (selective), violoncello (selective), voice (selective).

Entering class size: 29. *Graduating class size:* 26 .

Total full-time faculty: 2. *Program contact person:* Jim Palmer.

Audition Information

Audition consists of the following: scales, orchestral excerpts, music theory arpeggios. *Instruments provided for:* percussionists.

Performance opportunities available (frequency): band (4 per year), chamber music (2 per year), jury examinations (4 per year), chorus (4 per year).

Facilities

Number of practice rooms and hours: 10; 7:00 am-4:00 pm. *Recital hall?* yes. *Concert hall?* yes. *Recording studio?* yes.

DILLARD SCHOOL OF THE ARTS

2501 Northwest 11 Street, Ft. Lauderdale FL 33311
Tel: 954-797-4838
Fax: 954-797-4857
Contact: Virginia B. Shaker

General

Type of Institution: magnet-public. *Environment:* urban. *Academic education is offered on-site.*

Degrees offered: high school diploma.

Entrance Requirements

Audition required: live. *Other requirements:* interview, essay.

Services

Support staff: financial aid advisor.

DANCE

Curriculum, Students, and Faculty

Required courses: ballet (5 classes per week), dance composition/choreography, master classes, Limon-based modern dance (5 classes per week), movement techniques, rehearsal and performance.

Elective courses: dance history, dance writing, research and criticism, jazz, men's class, Pilates, music, pas de deux, pointe, repertory, stagecraft, variations.

Selectivity for males: most admitted, but not all. *Selectivity for females:* approximately 60% admitted. *Total enrollment:* 70. *Entering class size:* 25. *Graduating class size:* 12.

Renowned alumni: April Thibeanlt and Lara Lazim.

Total full-time faculty: 1. *Total part-time faculty:* 2. *List of current faculty and past affiliations:* Adelaide Maring, Lee Hemmuel.

Audition Information

No audition fee. Audition consists of the following: ballet, modern dance. *Accompanist not provided. Cassette player available; CD player available.*

Audition evaluation criteria: alignment, placement, following directions, attention in audition class.

Performance Information

Performance opportunities available (frequency): Fully produced concerts (3 per year), workshops (2-3 per year), on-site performances (2 per month).

Performances choreographed by: faculty, students, guests. *Recent guest choreographers:* Momentum Dance Company, Miami. Gina Bantz, Ft. Lauderdale, FL. Pablo Malco, Ft. Lauderdale, FL.

Facilities

Number of studios available: 2. *Approximate studio dimensions and flooring:* 40' x 40' sprung wood, 40' x 50' sprung wood. *Performance facilities:* auditorium.

DRAMA

Curriculum, Students, and Faculty

Required courses: acting, audition preparation, drama criticism, improvisation, make-up, musical theater, scene study.

Elective courses: directing, mime, stage combat.

Number of years required to complete program: 4. *Summer program not available. Selectivity for males:* most admitted, but not all. *Selectivity for females:* approximately 60% admitted. *Total enrollment:* 70. *Entering class size:* 20. *Graduating class size:* 12.

Renowned alumni: Corey Moosa.

Total full-time faculty: 3. *List of current faculty and past affiliations:* Bruce F. Broom, Mary Beth Straute, Ft. Lauderdale Children's Theater; Floyd T. Nash.

Audition Information

No audition fee. Audition consists of the following: a capella singing, cold readings, improvisation. *Audition evaluation criteria:* volume, projection, interpretation, character development.

Performance Information

Performance opportunities available (frequency): fully produced performances (3 per year), informal performances (4 per year), workshops (2-3 per year), off-site performances (1-2 per month), casting is by audition.

Facilities

Rehearsal facilities and hours: classroom, theater, and large dance studio (40' x 60'). *Type and capacity:* auditorium 700.

MUSIC

Curriculum, Students, and Faculty

How are major teacher assignments made? made by the school, according to teacher availability. *Lessons with a teaching assistant. May a student change major teachers during the course of study?* possibly. *Study of secondary instrument or discipline is allowed.*

Selectivity for instruments or programs offered (rating): bassoon (competitive), clarinet (competitive), double bass (competitive), electronic music (competitive), flute or piccolo (competitive), French horn (competitive), guitar (competitive), harp (competitive), jazz (competitive), oboe/English horn (competitive), percussion (competitive), piano (competitive), saxophone (competitive), trombone (competitive), trumpet (competitive), tuba (competitive), viola (competitive), violin (competitive), violoncello (competitive), voice (competitive).

Total enrollment: 120. *Entering class size:* 40. *Graduating class size:* 30.

Total full-time faculty: 5. *Total part-time faculty:* 2. *Program contact person:* James F. Miles.

Audition Information

No audition fee. Audition consists of the following: scales, orchestral excerpts, music theory, sight reading. *Instruments provided for:* harpists, percussionists.

Facilities

Number of practice rooms and hours: 6; during the school day. *Recital hall?* no. *Concert hall?* no. *Recording studio?* yes.

DOUGLAS ANDERSON SCHOOL OF THE ARTS

2445 San Diego Road, Jay FL 32207
Tel: 904-346-5608
Fax: 904-346-5636
Contact: Janelle Wagoner

General

Type of Institution: magnet-public, specialized. *Environment:* suburban. *Academic education is offered on-site.*

Degrees offered: high school diploma.

Entrance Requirements

Audition required. Other requirements: interview, recommendation.

Services

Support staff: college advisor, financial aid advisor.

DANCE

Curriculum, Students, and Faculty

Required courses: anatomy, character, ballet, dance composition/choreography, dance history, dance theory, dance writing, research and criticism, jazz, master classes, men's class, modern dance, pointe, repertory, ethnic dance.

Elective courses: African dance, Spanish, stagecraft, tap, variations, folk dance.

Renowned alumni: Deanna Mullis, Complexions; Christina May, Juilliard; Davis Auburn, Joffrey Ballet. *List of current faculty and past affilia-*

tions: Anne-Marie Bouygues, April Biggs, Ashley Cunningham, Monica Macbeth, Michael Ottley, Phyllis A. Penny, Janet Dygan. ***Program contact person:*** Dr. Phyllis A. Penney.

Audition Information

No audition fee. Audition consists of the following: ballet, improvisation, modern dance, prepared solo, phrase-making. ***Accompanist provided. Cassette player available; CD player available. Dress requirements for males:*** t-shirts, warm-up pants, tights, or unitard. ***Dress requirements for females:*** leotard and tights or unitard.

Performance Information

Performance opportunities available (frequency): Fully produced concerts (5 per year), informal concerts (2 per year), workshops (2-12 per year), on-site performances (2-4 per year).

Performances choreographed by: faculty, students, guests.

Facilities

Number of studios available: 4. ***Approximate studio dimensions and flooring:*** 36' x 32' sprung Marley. ***Performance facilities:*** theater 628 seats.

DRAMA

Curriculum, Students, and Faculty

Required courses: acting, directing, Stanislavski exercises.

Elective courses: movement, musical theater, speech, voice.

DR. PHILLIPS HIGH SCHOOL

6500 Turkey Lake Road, Orlando FL 32819
Tel: 407-352-4040 ext. 245
Fax: 407-352-4040

General

Type of Institution: magnet-public. ***Environment:*** urban.

Total enrollment of institution: 4,058. ***Degrees offered:*** high school diploma.

Entrance Requirements

Audition required: live. ***Other requirements:*** interview, recommendation.

Services

Support staff: career counselor.

DANCE

Curriculum, Students, and Faculty

Required courses: ballet (2 classes per week, 4 years to complete), dance composition/choreography (1 class per week, 4 years to complete), improvisation (4 years to complete), jazz (1 class per week, 4 years to complete), modern dance (4 years to complete), pointe (1 class per week, 4 years to complete), rehearsal and performance (1 class per week, 4 years to complete), tap (1 class per week, 4 years to complete).

Elective courses: master classes (4 years to complete), dance and folk culture (1 class per week, 4 years to complete), exploratory teaching (5 classes per week, 2 years to complete), teaching internships (1 class per week, 4 years to complete), Laban Movement Studies, martial arts, Feldenkreis, anatomy, music.

Selectivity for males: most admitted, but not all. ***Selectivity for females:*** most admitted, but not all. ***Total enrollment:*** 39. ***Entering class size:*** 14. ***Graduating class size:*** 8.

Renowned alumni: Laura Reynolds at New World and apprenticing with Houlihan and Company; Valerie Barreiro, at New World School of the Arts; Autumn Weidman, full scholarship at Pointe Park; Kelli Ahearn, full scholarship at SMU.

Total full-time faculty: 1. ***Total part-time faculty:*** 3. ***Program contact person:*** Kathy Follensbee.

Audition Information

No audition fee. Audition consists of the following: ballet, pointe works, prepared solo, any style, 1 1/2-minute limit jazz and modern combinations. ***Accompanist not provided. Cassette player available; CD player available. Dress requirements for males:*** white t-shirt, dark sweatpants or tights, black ballet shoes. ***Dress requirements for females:*** pink tights, black leotard, ballet and pointe shoes, hair in a bun.

Performance Information

Performance opportunities available (frequency): Fully produced concerts (3 per year), informal concerts (12-15 per year), workshops (6 per year), on-site performances(6-8 per year).

Performances choreographed by: faculty, students, guests. ***Recent guest choreographers:*** Joey Dowdy, Kelli Neal, Heather Lundy, Laura Reynolds.

Facilities

Number of studios available: 1 *Approximate studio dimensions and flooring:* 56' x 60' floating wood floor with Timestep surface. *Performance facilities:* theater.

DRAMA

Curriculum, Students, and Faculty

Required courses: mime, acting.

Total enrollment: 128. *Entering class size:* 36. *Graduating class size:* 22.

Total full-time faculty: 3.

MUSIC

Curriculum, Students, and Faculty

Faculty is not informed of a student's teacher preference at the time of the audition. *May a student change major teachers during the course of study?* never. *Study of secondary instrument or discipline is allowed.*

Selectivity for instruments or programs offered (rating): bassoon (selective), choral singing (selective), clarinet (selective), composition (open), double bass (selective), double bass (selective), electronic music (non-competitive), flute or piccolo (selective), French horn (selective), guitar (highly selective), oboe/English horn (selective), piano (highly selective), saxophone (selective), trombone (highly selective), trumpet (selective), tuba (selective), viola (selective), violin (selective), violoncello (selective), voice (highly selective).

Total enrollment: 58. *Entering class size:* 5. *Graduating class size:* 6.

Total full-time faculty: 5. *Program contact person:* Beth Meadows.

Audition Information

No audition fee. Audition consists of the following: scales, music theory rhythmic dictation, arpeggios, sight reading, melodic dictation. *Instruments provided for:* percussionists.

Performance opportunities available (frequency): band, jury examinations, recitals, chorus.

Facilities

Recital hall? yes. *Concert hall?* yes. *Recording studio?* yes.

THE HARID CONSERVATORY

2285 Potomac Road, Boca Raton FL 33431
Tel: 561-997-2677
Fax: 561-997-8920

General

Type of Institution: private high school, college, conservatory. *Environment:* suburban

Total enrollment: 94. *Total student body from other countries:* 46%.

Entrance Requirements

Audition required: live, audio, video. *Other requirements:* interview, recommendation, essay, photograph. *Standardized test requirements:* ACT; SAT I; SAT II; TOEFL.

Costs & Financial Aid

No tuition. Deposit: $500. *Other fees:* $500.

Types of scholarships and aid awarded: need-based, institutional aid. *Procedure for applying for loans:* complete request form and submit with required supporting documents by deadline stated on form. *Financial aid offered to international students. Other aid available to international students:* All students may apply for financial assistance to help cover the costs for housing, meals, travel, books/supplies, medical insurance.

Services

Housing options: on-site dorms, off-campus housing.

Support staff: dorm parent, foreign student advisor, psychological counselor, resident nurse, student affairs officer.

Comments

Harid is committed to intensive performance training for every student which includes performance studies and extensive performance opportunity; comprehensive supporting coursework in music theory, history, solfege, ear training, conducting, and electives; a balanced selection of non- music courses for the bachelor's degree (25% of program). Direct contact with faculty is a high priority in the educational training process. Most high school students are dance majors; most actors and musicians are in conservatory.

DANCE

Curriculum, Students, and Faculty

Required courses: ballet.

Selectivity for males: approximately 10% admitted. *Selectivity for females:* approximately 10% admitted. *Total enrollment:* 32. *Entering class size:* 13. *Graduating class size:* 8. *Percent international:* 6%. *Countries most represented:* Canada.

Total full-time faculty: 6. *Total part-time faculty:* 8. *Program contact person:* Janet Martinez.

Audition Information

Audition fee: $15. *Audition consists of the following:* ballet, pointe works. *Accompanist provided. Cassette player not available; CD player not available. Dress requirements for males:* black tights, white leotard. *Dress requirements for females:* pink tights, black leotard.

Audition evaluation criteria: level and quality of training, physique, talent.

Performance Information

Performance opportunities available (frequency): Fully produced concerts (2 series of 3 performances per year), informal concerts (2 per year).

Performances choreographed by: faculty, students, guests. *Recent guest choreographers:* Robert Barnett, Mark Godden, Hans van Manen.

Facilities

Number of studios available: 3. *Approximate studio dimensions and flooring:* 80' x 400' Marley/sprung, 40' x 40'. *Performance facilities:* fully equipped 840-seat theater for all dance performances.

DRAMA

Curriculum, Students, and Faculty

Required courses: text analysis.

MUSIC

Curriculum, Students, and Faculty

Unique or innovative music curriculum: Intensive training in solo, orchestral, and chamber music studies. Chamber music scheduled 4 hrs/week for all students; orchestra scheduled for 6 hrs/week. Career development seminar required 2 semesters. Mock orchestral auditions required for graduation. *How are major teacher assignments made?* only one major teacher for each instrument offered, students generally enroll with the specific intent to work with major instrument instructor. Faculty is not informed of a student's teacher preference at the time of the audition. *Study of secondary instrument or discipline is allowed.*

Selectivity for instruments or programs offered (rating): bassoon (selective), choral singing (selective), clarinet (highly selective), composition (competitive), trumpet (open), violoncello (competitive).

Total enrollment: 62. *Entering class size:* 24. *Graduating class size:* 12. *Percent international:* 66%. *Countries most represented:* Canada, China, Romania.

Total full-time faculty: 10. *Total part-time faculty:* 15. *Program contact person:* Ms. Chantal Prosperi.

Audition Information

Audition fee? no audition fee. *Audition consists of the following:* scales, orchestral excerpts, arpeggios, repertoire. *Instruments provided for:* percussionists.

Facilities

Number of practice rooms and hours: 17; 7:30 am-11:00 pm (Mon-Fri), 8:30 am-11:00 pm (Sat-Sun). *Recital hall?* yes. *Concert hall?* yes. *Recording studio?* yes.

HARRISON SCHOOL FOR THE ARTS

750 Hollingsworth Road, Lakeland FL 33801
Tel: 941-499-2855
Contact: School Administrator

General

Type of Institution: magnet-public, specialized. *Environment:* suburban. *Academic education is offered on-site.*

Total enrollment of institution: 322. *Degrees offered:* high school diploma.

Entrance Requirements

Audition required: live. *Other requirements:* interview, recommendation.

Services

Support staff: college advisor, financial aid advisor.

DANCE

Curriculum, Students, and Faculty

Required courses: anatomy, character, ballet, dance composition/choreography, dance history, dance theory, dance writing, research and criticism, jazz, modern dance, movement techniques, music, nutrition, pas de deux, pointe, rehearsal and performance, repertory, variations, modern dance partnering.

Selectivity for males: approximately 33% admitted. *Selectivity for females:* approximately 33% admitted. *Total enrollment:* 43. *Entering class size:* 13. *Graduating class size:* 11.

Total full-time faculty: 2. *Total part-time faculty:* 1. *Program contact person:* School Administrator

Audition Information

No audition fee. Audition consists of the following: ballet, modern dance. *Accompanist not provided. Cassette player available; CD player available.*

Performance Information

Performance opportunities available (frequency): fully produced concerts (4 per year), informal concerts (6 per year), workshops (6 per year), touring (1 per year), all courses are offered as part of extra curricular program.

Performances choreographed by: faculty, students, guests.

Facilities

Approximate studio dimensions and flooring: 30' x 50' sprung loaded wood floor, 25' x 30' sprung loaded wood floor. *Performance facilities:* dance studio, performing arts auditorium.

DRAMA

Curriculum, Students, and Faculty

Required courses: acting, audition preparation, directing, drama criticism, improvisation, makeup, movement, musical theater, scene study, stage combat, voice.

Number of years required to complete program: 4. *Summer program not available. No affiliation with a professional theater company. Selectivity for males:* approximately 33% admitted. *Selectivity for females:* approximately 33% admitted. *Total enrollment:* 75. *Entering class size:* 24. *Graduating class size:* 13.

Total full-time faculty: 3. *Total part-time faculty:* 1.

Audition Information

No audition fee. Audition consists of the following: group warm-up.

Performance Information

Performance opportunities available (frequency): fully produced performances (4 per year), informal performances (6 per year), workshops (6 per year), off-site performances (1 per year), casting is by audition.

Facilities

Rehearsal facilities and hours: performance hall stage, shop, black box. *Number of theaters on campus:* 1. *Type and capacity:* auditorium 725.

MUSIC

Curriculum, Students, and Faculty

How are major teacher assignments made? made by the school. Faculty is not informed of a student's teacher preference at the time of the audition. *May a student change major teachers during the course of study?* never. *Study of secondary instrument or discipline is not allowed.*

Selectivity for instruments or programs offered (rating): bassoon (competitive), choral singing (competitive), clarinet (competitive), double bass (competitive), flute or piccolo (competitive), French horn (competitive), harp (competitive), oboe/English horn (competitive), percussion (competitive), piano (competitive), saxophone (competitive), trombone (competitive), trumpet (competitive), tuba (competitive), viola (competitive), violin (competitive), violoncello (competitive), voice (competitive).

Total enrollment: 141. *Entering class size:* 36. *Graduating class size:* 38.

Total full-time faculty: 4. *Program contact person:* School Administrator.

Audition Information

No audition fee. Audition consists of the following: scales, orchestral excerpts, music theory arpeggios, sight reading. *Instruments provided for:* percussionists.

Performance opportunities available (frequency): chamber music, band, jury examinations, orchestral concerts, recitals, touring, chorus.

Facilities

Recital hall? yes. *Concert hall?* yes. *Recording studio?* no.

NEW WORLD SCHOOL OF THE ARTS

300 Northeast Second Avenue, Miami FL 33123
Tel: 305-237-3135
Fax: 305-237-2794
Email: nwsainfo@mdcc.edu
Web: www.mdcc.edu/nwsa
Contact: Ileana Gallagher

General

Type of Institution: public, high school, college, conservatory, magnet-public. *Environment:* urban. *Academic education is offered on-site. Cross registration is available through the Miami Dade Community College, University of Florida.*

Total enrollment of institution: 467. *Degrees offered:* high school diploma.

Entrance Requirements

Audition required: live, audio, video, regional. *Other requirements:* interview, recommendation. *Standardized test requirements:* TOEFL; 550. School's own English exam required.

Costs & Financial Aid

Application fee: $15.

Percent of students receiving financial aid: 80%. *Types of scholarships and aid awarded:* full, partial, merit-based, named, institutional aid, government aid, reduced tuition, work/study. *Forms required for scholarships:* FAFSA. *Loans available. Procedure for applying for loans:* standard financial aid application procedure.

Services

Housing options: off-campus housing.

Support staff: college advisor, financial aid advisor, foreign student advisor, physical therapist, psychological counselor, student affairs officer.

DANCE

Curriculum, Students, and Faculty

Required courses: anatomy, ballet (5 classes per week, 4 years to complete), dance history, dance writing, research and criticism, historical dance, Labanotation, men's class (1 class per week, 4 years to complete), Graham-based dance, Limon-based modern dance, music, pointe (1-2 classes per week, 4 years to complete), repertory, stagecraft.

Elective courses: African dance, Pilates, pas de deux, Spanish, tap, variations, vernacular dance, Caribbean, Afro-Cuban dance.

Selectivity for males: approximately 60% admitted. *Selectivity for females:* approximately 33% admitted. *Countries most represented:* Latin America.

Renowned alumni: Shirley Sastre, Amos Mechanic, Caroline Garcia, Robert Battle, Paunika Jones, Uri Sands. *List of current faculty and past affiliations:* Gerard Ebitz, New York City Ballet; Freddick Bratcher, Alvin Ailey and Martha Graham Companies; Bambi Anderson, Limon Dance Company; Mariana Alvarey, American Ballet Theater; Gerri Houlihan, Lar Lubouitch Company; Peter Condon, Martha Graham Company. *Program contact person:* Roberta Kielgaard.

Audition Information

No audition fee. Audition consists of the following: ballet, modern dance, prepared solo, 2 minutes of any style jazz. *Accompanist provided. Cassette player available; CD player available. Dress requirements for males:* black tights, white t-shirt, appropriate footwear. *Dress requirements for females:* pink tights, black leotard, appropriate footwear.

Repertoire that students should avoid? Solos on pointe are not recommended.

Audition evaluation criteria: talent and potential as a performer, level and quality of training, musicality.

Performance Information

Performance opportunities available (frequency): Fully produced concerts (8-10 per year), informal concerts (6-8 per year), workshops (4-5 per year), onsite performances (6-8 per year), touring (3-5 per year), international touring once every other year, Florida dance festival (mid to late June) in house.

Performances choreographed by: faculty, students, guests. *Recent guest choreographers:* Michael Uthoff, Anna Sokolow, Mark Taylor, Lila York, Menaka Thakkar, Rosario Suarey.

Facilities

Number of studios available: 4. *Approximate studio dimensions and flooring:* 40' x 40' sprung floors with Marley. *Performance facilities:* inhouse 200-seat black box, off site 600-seat (Colony Theater) and 1,800-seat (Gusman Center for the Performing Arts).

DRAMA

Curriculum, Students, and Faculty

Number of years required to complete program: 2. *Summer program not available.*

Selectivity for males: approximately 10% admitted. *Selectivity for females:* approximately 10% admitted. *Countries most represented:* Latin America.

Audition Information

Audition fee; Audition consists of the following: comedic monologue, improvisation, movement class, group warm-up, voice. *Audition evaluation criteria:* High level of training and talent demonstrated throughout the audition, focus, commitment, maturity.

Performance Information

Performance opportunities available (frequency): fully produced performances (frequently), informal performances (frequently), workshops (frequently), off-site performances (frequently), casting is by audition.

Facilities

Rehearsal facilities and hours: mainstage and classrooms, capacity 120-150; 4:15 pm-10:00 pm Monday through Saturday.

MUSIC

Curriculum, Students, and Faculty

Unique or innovative music curriculum: performance opportunities. *How are major teacher assignments made?* Students may choose, made by the school. Faculty is informed of a student's teacher preference at the time of the audition. *Lessons with major teacher. May a student change major teachers during the course of study?* possibly.

Selectivity for instruments or programs offered (rating): accompanying (selective), bassoon (selective), clarinet (selective), composition (selective), double bass (selective), electronic music (selective), flute or piccolo (highly selective), French horn (selective), guitar (selective), harp (selective), harpsichord (selective), oboe/English horn (selective), orchestral conducting (selective), percussion (selective), piano (highly selective), trombone (selective), trumpet (selective), tuba (selective), viola (selective), violin (selective), violoncello (selective), voice (highly selective).

Program contact person: Joy Davidson.

Audition Information

No audition fee. Audition consists of the following: scales, orchestral excerpts, music theory, rhythmic dictation, arpeggios, sight reading, melodic dictation, repertoire. *Instruments provided for:* harpists, percussionists, pianists.

Repertoire that students should avoid? Rap, rock, gospel. *Performance opportunities available (frequency):* chamber music (frequently), band (frequently), jury examinations, opera workshops (frequently), orchestral concerts (frequently), recitals (frequently), produced operas.

Facilities

Number of practice rooms and hours: 10; 8:00 am-8:00 pm. *Recital hall?* no. *Concert hall?* no. *Recording studio?* yes.

PINE CREST SCHOOL

1501 Northeast 62nd Street, Ft. Lauderdale FL 33334
Tel: 954-492-4100
Fax: 954-492-0345

General

Type of Institution: private, coed, day and boarding.

Total enrollment of institution: 1,600. *Degrees offered:* high school diploma.

Entrance Requirements

Standardized tests: ISEE; SSAT.

Costs & Financial Aid

Application fee: $75. *Deposit:* $2,000. *Boarding tuition and fees including room:* $19,685. *Day tuition:* $9,560.

Percent of students receiving financial aid: 10%. *Types of scholarships and aid awarded:* partial, need-based. *Forms required for scholarships:* income tax return, income asset verification, SSS form, PFS. *Loans available. Procedure for applying for loans:* same as need scholarships.

Services

Housing options: on-site dorms.

Support staff: college advisor, dorm parent, foreign student advisor, resident assistant.

DANCE

Curriculum, Students, and Faculty

Required courses: dance history, dance theory, kinesiology, body conditioning (1 class per week), Pilates (1 class per week). Summer program in dance.

Elective courses: ballet (3 classes per week), jazz, pointe, rehearsal and performance (2 classes per week), tap.

Selectivity for males: admit all who apply. *Selectivity for females:* admit all who apply. *Total enrollment:* 77. *Entering class size:* 20.

Renowned alumni: Jennifer Vanuchi, Southern Ballet Co.; Kim Harrell, Indiana University, Ballet; Heather Geronemus, Trainee Joffrey Ballet; Jessica Bloomgarden, Indiana University.

Total full-time faculty: 2. *Total part-time faculty:* 1. *List of current faculty and past affiliations:* Brenda B. Gooden, Pittsburgh Ballet Theater, Assistant Director Atlantic Foundation's Academy for Performing Arts; Lori Hayward, Indiana University, Tulsa Ballet. *Program contact person:* Brenda Gooden.

Audition Information

No audition fee. Audition consists of the following: no audition. *Dress requirements for males:* black lightweight sweatpants, white t-shirt, black socks, black ballet shoes. *Dress requirements for females:* solid color leotard, pink tights, pink ballet or pointe shoe.

Performance Information

Performance opportunities available (frequency): Fully produced concerts (3 per year), informal concerts (2-3 per year), on-site performances (4-5 per year).

Performances choreographed by: faculty, students guests.

Recent guest choreographers: Penne Greenly, Southern Dance, Delray, Florida; Liz Gozalez, Atlantic High School, Delray, Florida.

Facilities

Number of studios available: 2. *Approximate studio dimensions and flooring:* 30' x 40' raised, floating, sub-floor with Marley covering. *Performance facilities:* auditorium with large wooden floor, stage.

DRAMA

Curriculum, Students, and Faculty

Summer program not available. No affiliation with a professional theater company. Selectivity for males: admit all who apply. *Selectivity for females:* admit all who apply.

Renowned alumni: Kelsey Grammar.

Total part-time faculty: 2. *List of current faculty and past affiliations:* Tad Harrington, Chris Schneider.

Audition Information

No audition fee. Audition consists of the following: cold readings.

Audition evaluation criteria: Student needs to fit the part talent-wise and physically.

Performance Information

Performance opportunities available (frequency): fully produced performances (5 per year), informal performances (5 per year), workshops (2-3 per year), off-site performances (2-4 per year), forensics, 3 tournaments per month, casting is by audition.

Facilities

Rehearsal facilities and hours: classrooms and auditorium after school, evenings, and weekends. *Number of theaters on campus:* 3. *Type and capacity:* auditorium 800, auditorium 400.

MUSIC

Curriculum, Students, and Faculty

How are major teacher assignments made? made by the school, according to teacher preference and teacher availability. *May a student change major teachers during the course of study?* possibly. *Study of secondary instrument or discipline is allowed.*

Selectivity for instruments or programs offered (rating): accompanying (highly selective), bassoon (non-competitive), choral singing (open), clarinet (non-competitive), composition (highly selective), double bass (non-competitive), electronic music (non-competitive), flute or piccolo (non-competitive), French horn (non-competitive), guitar (non-competitive), jazz (highly selective), oboe/English horn (non-competitive), percussion (non-competitive), piano (open), saxophone (non-competitive), trombone (non-competitive), trumpet (non-competitive), tuba (non-competitive), viola (non-competitive), violin (non-competitive), violoncello (non-competitive), voice (non-competitive).

Renowned alumni: John Prescott, John Medeski, Scot Evans, Brian Eckert, Jason Zenobia, Karl Rundinger.

Total full-time faculty: 2. *Program contact person:* Dale Wadman/Jim Mullen.

Audition Information

Instruments provided for: percussionists.

Performance opportunities available (frequency): orchestral concerts, chorus.

Facilities

Number of practice rooms and hours: 6; 8:00 am-5:00 pm. *Recital hall?* yes. *Concert hall?* yes. *Recording studio?* yes.

Comments

Pine Crest is a college preparatory school. Fine arts classes are available, but scheduling of honors classes and AP classes take preference and having ideal ensemble groups is not possible due to scheduling.

GEORGIA

DE KALB CENTER FOR THE PERFORMING ARTS AT AVONDALE HIGH SCHOOL

1192 Clarendon Road, Avondale Estates GA 30002
Tel: 404-289-2787
Fax: 404-284-6669
Email: avondale@rehobuth.co.dekalb.k12.ga.us
Web: rehobuth.co.dekalb.k12.ga.us:80/~avondale

General

Type of Institution: magnet-public. *Environment:* urban.

Total enrollment of institution: 200. *Degrees offered:* high school diploma.

Entrance Requirements

Audition required: live. *Other requirements:* interview, recommendation. *Standardized test requirements:* SAT I; SAT II.

Geographic restrictions: Dekalb County, GA

Services

Support staff: college advisor.

Comments

All students required to take classes in drama, vocal music, and dance. Our motto: "all the arts are brothers; one is a light to another." Voltaire.

DANCE

Curriculum, Students, and Faculty

Required courses: anatomy, ballet, dance composition/choreography, dance history, dance theory, dance writing, research and criticism, jazz (1 class per week), modern dance (2 classes per week), nutrition, tap (2 classes per week).

Elective courses: character, men's class, pas de deux, pointe, variations, Cunningham-based, jazz, Spanish.

Selectivity for males: approximately 33% admitted. *Selectivity for females:* approximately 33% admitted.

Renowned alumni: Tayo Reed, Toya Willingham, Jessi Scopp, Natalie Ridley.

Total full-time faculty: 2. *Total part-time faculty:* 4. *List of current faculty and past affiliations:* Wanda Ebright, Memphis Classical Ballet, River City Ballet; Travis Catling, Norfolk State University, Ohio State Repertory Company. *Program contact person:* Wanda Ebright.

Audition Information

No audition fee. Audition consists of the following: prepared solo, 1 minute, any style, appropriate music choice. *Accompanist provided. Cassette player available; CD player available.*

Repertoire that students should avoid? no profanity or racial slurs in music.

Performance Information

Performance opportunities available (frequency): Fully produced concerts (1 per year), informal concerts (1 per year), on-site performances(3-5 per year), touring (10-20 per year).

Performances choreographed by: faculty, students, guests. *Recent guest choreographers:* Jerylann Warner, Jayne Parsons.

Facilities

Number of studios available: 2. *Approximate studio dimensions and flooring:* 20' x 40' wood with Marley, 30' x 40' sprung floor with Marley. *Performance facilities:* on-site auditorium (seats 280), black box theater, cafeteria, and gym stages.

DRAMA

Curriculum, Students, and Faculty

Required courses: acting, Alexander technique, audition preparation, directing, drama criticism, improvisation, make-up, mime, movement, musical theater, scene study, Stanislavski exercises, voice, scene study, directing.

Elective courses: directing, stage combat.

Number of years required to complete program: 3-4. *Summer program not available. Affiliation with a professional theater company: minor affiliation with the Alliance Theatre Company, a project with Alliance and Coca-Cola which allows students the opportunity to meet various professionals (artistic directors, actors, newspaper critics, etc.).*

Selectivity for males: approximately 33% admitted. *Selectivity for females:* approximately 33% admitted.

Total full-time faculty: 3. *List of current faculty and past affiliations:* Kristy Jo Stupka, Florida State Theatre Department, Alliance Theatre Company, Young Audiences Int.

Audition Information

Audition consists of the following: comedic monologue, Shakespearean monologue. *Repertoire that students should avoid?* any "over used/done" monologue for that time period.

Performance Information

Casting is by audition.

Recent guest artists: Nancy Myer, Rob Lowe, Kathleen McManus.

Facilities

Rehearsal facilities and hours: within theater space, 4:30 pm-8:00 pm. *Number of theaters on campus:* 2. *Type and capacity:* main stage 300, black box 100.

MUSIC

Curriculum, Students, and Faculty

How are major teacher assignments made? Students may choose. Faculty is not informed of a student's teacher preference at the time of the audition. *May a student change major teachers during the course of study?* never. *Study of secondary instrument or discipline is allowed.*

Selectivity for instruments or programs offered (rating): bassoon (competitive), choral singing (competitive), clarinet (competitive), composition (competitive), electronic music (competitive), flute or piccolo (competitive), flute or piccolo (competitive), French horn (competitive), oboe/English horn (competitive), percussion (competitive), piano (competitive), sacred music (competitive), saxophone (competitive), trombone (competitive), trumpet (competitive), tuba (competitive), viola (competitive), violin (competitive), voice (competitive).

Total full-time faculty: 3. *Total part-time faculty:* 6. *Program contact person:* Jeff Biering.

Audition Information

No audition fee. Audition consists of the following: scales, sight reading, repertoire. *Instruments provided for:* percussionists; pianists.

Required repertoire: selection of student's choice on instrument of student's choice. *Performance opportunities available (frequency):* band, orchestral concerts, recitals.

Facilities

Number of practice rooms and hours: 2. *Recital hall?* yes. *Concert hall?* no. *Recording studio?* yes.

GEORGIA GOVERNOR'S HONORS PROGRAM

1770 Twin Towers East, Atlanta GA 30334-5040
Tel: 404-657-0183
Fax: 404-657-7096
Email: ssearle@doe.k12.ga.us

General

Type of Institution: governors.

Total enrollment of institution: 660.

Entrance Requirements

Audition required: live. *Other requirements:* interview, recommendation, photograph.

Services

Housing options: on-site dorms.

Support staff: housing advisor, psychological counselor, resident assistant, resident nurse.

DANCE

Curriculum, Students, and Faculty

Selectivity for males: approximately 10% admitted. *Selectivity for females:* approximately 10% admitted. *Total enrollment:* 16. *Entering class size:* 16. *Graduating class size:* 16.

Total full-time faculty: 1. *Program contact person:* Joe Searle.

Audition Information

No audition fee. Accompanist not provided. Cassette player available; CD player available.

Performance Information

Performance opportunities available (frequency): fully produced concerts, workshops.

Performances choreographed by: faculty, students, guests.

Facilities

Number of studios available: 1.

DRAMA

Curriculum, Students, and Faculty

Summer program available. no affiliation with a professional theater company. Selectivity for males: approximately 10% admitted. *Selectivity for females:* approximately 10% admitted. *Total enrollment:* 30. *Entering class size:* 30. *Graduating class size:* 30.

Total full-time faculty: 3.

Audition Information

No audition fee. Audition consists of the following: improvisation, required monologue, group warm-up.

Facilities

Number of theaters on campus: 2.

MUSIC

Curriculum, Students, and Faculty

Selectivity for instruments or programs offered (rating): bassoon (highly selective), choral singing (highly selective), clarinet (highly selective), double bass (highly selective), flute or piccolo (highly selective), French horn (highly selective), guitar (highly selective), jazz (highly selective), oboe/English horn (highly selective), percussion (highly selective), piano (highly selective), saxophone (highly selective), trombone (highly selective), trumpet (highly selective), tuba (highly selective), viola (highly selective), violin (highly selective), violoncello (highly selective), voice (highly selective).

Total enrollment: 115. *Entering class size:* 115. *Graduating class size:* 115.

Total full-time faculty: 8. *Program contact person:* Joe Searle.

Audition Information

No audition fee. Audition consists of the following: music theory, improvisation. *Instruments provided for:* percussionists.

Facilities

Recital hall? no. *Concert hall?* yes. *Recording studio?* no.

NORTH ATLANTA HIGH SCHOOL CENTER FOR THE PERFORMING ARTS

2875 Northside Drive, Atlanta GA 30305
Tel: 404-351-0895
Fax: 404-351-8763
Contact: Sebastian V. Verdis, Jr.

General

Type of Institution: magnet-public. *Environment:* urban. *Academic education is offered on-site.*

Total enrollment of institution: 324. *Degrees offered:* high school diploma.

Entrance Requirements

Audition required: live. *Other requirements:*, recommendation.

DANCE

Curriculum, Students, and Faculty

Required courses: anatomy, character, ballet, dance history, dance theory, jazz, master classes, modern dance, nutrition, pointe, rehearsal and performance, repertory.

Elective courses: movement techniques, pas de deux, vernacular dance.

Selectivity for males: admit all who apply. *Selectivity for females:* approximately 60% admitted. *Total enrollment:* 45. *Entering class size:* 13. *Graduating class size:* 14.

Renowned alumni: Jasmine Guy, Ru Paul. *Total part-time faculty:* 3. *List of current faculty and past affiliations:* Michelle Jericevich-Powell, Royal Academy of Dancing; Leonard Roberson, Delia Stuart Jazz Dance Co.; Jerylann Warner, Emory University, Georgia State University, Harvard University, Lolo Beckwith and Dancers, Marcus Schulkind, Room to Move, Chorus, Garden House. *Program contact person:* Michelle Powell/Jerylanne Warnea/Leonard Roberson.

Audition Information

No audition fee. Audition consists of the following: ballet, modern dance. *Accompanist not provided. Cassette player available; CD player available. Dress requirements for males:* white leotard, black tights. *Dress requirements for females:* leotard, skirt, tights.

Repertoire that students should avoid? vulgarity, any movements that are too suggestive or musical lyrics that are offensive.

Performance Information

Performance opportunities available (frequency): Fully produced concerts (1 per year), informal concerts (1 per year), workshops (4 per year), on-site performances(3 per year).

Performances choreographed by: faculty. *Recent guest choreographers:* Nicole Livieratos, Amy Harold, Renee Toole, Royce Zackery.

Facilities

Number of studios available: 1. *Approximate studio dimensions and flooring:* 25' x 50' wood and Marley. *Performance facilities:* professional theater.

MUSIC

Curriculum, Students, and Faculty

Unique or innovative music curriculum: electronic music, music theory, music history. *How are major teacher assignments made?* made by the school. Faculty is not informed of a student's teacher preference at the time of the audition. *30 lessons with major teacher. May a student change major teachers during the course of study?* possibly. *Study of secondary instrument or discipline is allowed.*

Selectivity for instruments or programs offered (rating): double bass (selective), electronic music (selective), viola (selective), violin (selective), violoncello (selective).

Total enrollment: 173. *Entering class size:* 59. *Graduating class size:* 40.

Renowned alumni: Jasmine Guy, Andres Diaz, Crystal Fox, Carmen Thomas, Charlie DeRamus, Joseph Wise, Davis Payne.

Total full-time faculty: 4. *Program contact person:* J. Lynn Thompson/Reginald R.Colbert/ Rushia Evans/ Ella Lewis.

Audition Information

No audition fee. Audition consists of the following: scales, orchestral excerpts, music theory arpeggios, sight reading, music history, repertoire.

Required repertoire: GMEA All State Etudes (Mazas, Wolfhart, Simandl, Schroeder). *Performance opportunities available (frequency):* jury examinations, touring.

Facilities

Number of practice rooms and hours: 7. *Recital hall?* yes. *Concert hall?* yes. *Recording studio?* no.

HAWAII

MID-PACIFIC SCHOOL OF THE ARTS AT MID-PACIFIC INSTITUTE

2445 Kaala Street, Honolulu HI 96822
Tel: 808-973-5071
Fax: 808-973-5113
Email: mpsa@lava.net
Contact: Linda Johnson

General

Type of Institution: coed conservatory, day and boarding.

Total enrollment of institution: 1,100. *Total student body from other countries:* 1%. *Degrees offered:* high school diploma, international baccalaureate.

Entrance Requirements

Audition required: live, audio, video. *Other requirements:* interview, recommendation. *Standardized test requirements:* SSAT; TOEFL, 540; school's own English exam required.

Costs & Financial Aid

Application fee: $30. *Deposit:* $700. *Tuition:* $8,900. *Other fees:* $880 per class English as second language.

Percent of students receiving financial aid: 18%. *Types of scholarships and aid awarded:* partial, merit-based, need-based, named, reduced tuition, tuition payment plan, work/study. *Forms required for scholarships:* FAFSA, income tax return. *Loans available. Procedure for applying for loans:* upon request. *Financial aid offered to international students.*

Services

Housing options: on-site dorms.

Support staff: college advisor, dorm parent, financial aid advisor, foreign student advisor, housing advisor, resident assistant, resident nurse, student affairs officer.

DANCE

Curriculum, Students, and Faculty

Required courses: anatomy, ballet, dance composition/choreography, dance history, dance writing, research and criticism, jazz, modern dance, nutrition, other world dance forms, rehearsal and performance, repertory.

Elective courses: stagecraft, tap.

Selectivity for males: most admitted, but not all. *Selectivity for females:* most admitted, but not all. *Total enrollment:* 80. *Total part-time faculty:* 5. *Program contact person:* Yukle Shiroma.

Audition Information

No audition fee. Audition consists of the following: ballet, improvisation, modern dance. *Accompanist not provided. Cassette player available; CD player available.*

Performance Information

Performance opportunities available (frequency): Fully produced concerts (2 per year), informal concerts (1-2 per year), workshops (3-5 per year), on-site performances(1-2 per year), touring (1 per year).

Performances choreographed by: faculty, guests. *Recent guest choreographers:* Marcelo Tacleb, Betty Jones / Fritz Ludin, Shapiro & Smith, Dr. Schaffer & Mr. Stern, Eve Walstrum.

Facilities

Number of studios available: 2. *Approximate studio dimensions and flooring:* 45' x 20' sprung floor with dance mat covering, 50' x 15' sprung floor with dance mat covering. *Performance facilities:* auditorium.

DRAMA

Curriculum, Students, and Faculty

Required courses: acting, Alexander technique, audition preparation, musical theater, dance, drama criticism, improvisation, movement, scene study, speech, stage combat, Stanislavski exercises, text analysis, verse drama, voice.

Number of years required to complete program: 4. *Summer program available. Affiliation with a professional theater company: Manoa Valley Theatre.*

Selectivity for males: approximately 60% admitted. *Selectivity for females:* approximately 60% admitted. *Total enrollment:* 40.

Total full-time faculty: 2. *Total part-time faculty:* 5.

Audition Information

Audition consists of the following: cold readings, comedic monologue, improvisation, group warm-up. *Dress requirements for males:* neat. *Dress requirements for females:* neat. *Audition evaluation criteria:* preparation, difficulty of material, vocal skills, passion, character, intepretation of monologue, emotional connection and commitment, ability to take direction and to work effectively with others.

Performance Information

Performance opportunities available (frequency): fully produced performances (3 per year), informal performances (4 per year), workshops (2-3 per year), off-site performances (occasionally), casting is by audition.

Recent guest artists: Jason Sott Lee, Nigel Trivet, Claire Davidson.

Facilities

Rehearsal facilities and hours: theaters in which it will be performed, 3:30 pm-8:30 pm. *Number of theaters on campus:* 3. *Type and capacity:* proscenium 650, proscenium 150.

MUSIC

Curriculum, Students, and Faculty

How are major teacher assignments made? made by the school, according to teacher preference.; Faculty is not informed of a student's teacher preference at the time of the audition. *May a student change major teachers during the course of study?* possibly. *Study of secondary instrument or discipline is allowed.*

Selectivity for instruments or programs offered (rating): bassoon (non-competitive), clarinet (non-competitive), flute or piccolo (non-competitive), French horn (non-competitive), jazz (non-competitive), oboe/English horn (non-competitive), percussion (non-competitive), saxophone (non-competitive), trombone (non-competitive), trumpet (non-competitive), tuba (non-competitive).

Total enrollment: 20.

Total full-time faculty: 2. *Program contact person:* Allen Nii.

Audition Information

No audition fee. Audition consists of the following: scales, orchestral excerpts, arpeggios, sight reading. *Instruments provided for:* percussionists; band instruments.

Performance opportunities available (frequency): jury examinations.

Facilities

Number of practice rooms and hours: 6; 1-2 hours (daily). *Recital hall?* yes. *Concert hall?* yes. *Recording studio?* no.

CHICAGO ACADEMY FOR THE ARTS

1010 West Chicago Avenue, Chicago IL 60622
Tel: 312-421-0202
Fax: 312-421-3816
Email: academy@mcs.net
Web: www.mcs.net/~academy
Contact: Stephanie Strait

General

Type of Institution: day, coed. *Environment:* urban. *Academic education is offered on-site.*

Total enrollment of institution: 143. *Total student body from other countries:* 1%. *Degrees offered:* high school diploma.

Entrance Requirements

Audition required: live. *Other requirements:* interview, recommendation.

Costs & Financial Aid

Application fee: $30. *Deposit:* $1,000. *Tuition:* $8,815. *Other fees:* $250 annual activity fee, $150 matriculation fee.

Percent of students receiving financial aid: 50%. *Types of scholarships and aid awarded:* partial, merit-based, need-based, named, tuition payment plan. *Forms required for scholarships:* income tax return, SSS form. *Financial aid offered to international students. Percent of international students receiving scholarships:* 50%. *Other aid available to international students:* none.

Services

Support staff: college advisor, psychological counselor.

DANCE

Curriculum, Students, and Faculty

Required courses: ballet, dance composition/choreography, dance history, jazz, master classes, men's class, Graham-based modern dance, rehearsal and performance.

Elective courses: pas de deux, pointe, variations.

Selectivity for males: approximately 60% admitted. *Selectivity for females:* approximately 60% admitted. *Total enrollment:* 30. *Entering class size:* 5. *Graduating class size:* 7. *Percent international:* 1%. *Countries most represented:* Korea.

Renowned alumni: Tom Gold, Ed Cox, Erika Gilfether.

Total full-time faculty: 2. *Total part-time faculty:* 2. *List of current faculty and past affiliations:* Eduardo Vilaro, Ballet Theatre of Chicago, Ballet Hispanico NY; Randy Duncan, Joseph Holmes Dance Theatre; Claire Bataille, Hubbard St. Dance Theatre; Rodney Erwin, Ruth Page Foundation. *Program contact person:* Anna Paskevska.

Audition Information

No audition fee. Audition consists of the following: ballet, modern dance. *Accompanist provided. Cassette player available; CD player available. Dress requirements for males:* tights, t-shirt, correct shoes. *Dress requirements for females:* tights, leotard, correct shoes.

Performance Information

Performance opportunities available (frequency): Fully produced concerts (2 per year), informal concerts (1-6 per year), workshops (4-6 per year), on-site performances (3-5 per year).

Performances choreographed by: faculty, students, guests. *Recent guest choreographers:* James Kelly, Ginger Farley, Eduardo Vilaro.

Facilities

Number of studios available: 3. *Approximate studio dimensions and flooring:* 28' x 22' Marley, 26' x 22', 75' x 24'. *Performance facilities:* studio is adapted.

DRAMA

Curriculum, Students, and Faculty

Required courses: acting, dramaturgy, movement, speech, text analysis, voice.

Elective courses: dance, directing, musical theater, verse drama.

Number of years required to complete program: 4. *Summer program available. no affiliation with a professional theater company. Selectivity for males:* approximately 60% admitted. *Selectivity for females:* approximately 60% admitted. *Total enrollment:* 42. *Entering class size:* 10. *Graduating class size:* 12. *Percent international:* 0%.

Renowned alumni: Lara Flynn Boyle, James Jones, Senta Moses.

Total full-time faculty: 3. *Total part-time faculty:* 2. *List of current faculty and past affiliations:* Franette Liebow, City Lit Theatre, Illinois Theatre Center, Yale University; Lindsay Jones, North Carolina School for the Arts; James Pacino Jones, Strawdog Theatre Company; Robert Barrie, NY Drama League.

Audition Information

No audition fee. Audition consists of the following: comedic monologue, Shakespearean monologue, musical theater: sing with music.

Performance Information

Performance opportunities available (frequency):, each student performs twice a year, produce about 10 productions a year, casting is assigned, auditioned.

Recent guest artists: Pyetor Tomaszuk, Roddy McDowall, Brian Dennehy.

Facilities

Rehearsal facilities and hours: 4 studios, 1 main stage. *Number of theaters on campus:* 1. *Type and capacity:* proscenium 50.

MUSIC

Curriculum, Students, and Faculty

Unique or innovative music curriculum: We have a curriculum based on college music standards. We incorporated 4 levels of music theory and ear training. 2 levels of piano lab, a music history/literature class and ensemble. *How are major teacher assignments made?* placement by level of knowledge. Faculty is not informed of a student's teacher preference at the time of the audition. *May a student change major teachers during the course of study?* possibly. *Study of secondary instrument or discipline is allowed.*

Total enrollment: 13. *Entering class size:* 5. *Graduating class size:* 4. *Percent international:* 0%.

Total full-time faculty: 1. *Total part-time faculty:* 6. *Program contact person:* Marie Cinquemani.

Audition Information

No audition fee. Audition consists of the following: repertoire. *Instruments provided for:* percussionists.

Required repertoire: required repertoire. *Performance opportunities available (frequency):* band, chamber music, band, jury examinations, opera workshops, recitals, produced operas, chorus.

Facilities

Number of practice rooms and hours: 7; 9:00 am-4:30 pm. *Recital hall?* yes. *Concert hall?* no. *Recording studio?* yes.

CURIE METROPOLITAN HIGH SCHOOL

4959 South Archer Avenue, Chicago IL 60632
Tel: 773-535-2104
Fax: 773-535-2044
Contact: Ana Espinoza

General

Type of Institution: magnet-public. *Environment:* urban.

Total enrollment of institution: 3,400. *Degrees offered:* high school diploma, international baccalaureate.

Entrance Requirements

Audition required: live. *Other requirements:* interview, recommendation.

Geographic restrictions: no restrictions, although 99.8% of students are residents of Chicago.

Services

Housing options: family.

Support staff: college advisor, foreign student advisor, psychological counselor, resident nurse.

DANCE

Curriculum, Students, and Faculty

Required courses: ballet, modern dance, rehearsal and performance, variations.

Elective courses: African dance, anatomy, character, dance composition/choreography, dance history, dance theory, dance writing, research and criticism, jazz, master classes, men's class, movement techniques, music, nutrition, pas de deux, pointe, repertory, tap, modern dance partnering.

Total enrollment: 200. *Entering class size:* 60. *Graduating class size:* 55.

Renowned alumni: Vernard Gilmore, Nkosi Kress.

Total full-time faculty: 2. *List of current faculty and past affiliations:* Joel Hall, Lake Shore, Maning; Timothy Buckley, Chicago Dance Medium. *Program contact person:* Melina Wilson.

Audition Information

No audition fee. Audition consists of the following: ballet, improvisation, modern dance, pas de deux, pointe works, *Cassette player available; CD player available. Dress requirements for males:* school uniform. *Dress requirements for females:* school uniform.

Audition evaluation criteria: criteria representations of 4 levels of dance instruction offered.

Performance Information

Performance opportunities available (frequency): Fully produced concerts (annually), informal concerts (annually), workshops (annually), on-site performances (annually).

Performances choreographed by: faculty, students.

Facilities

Number of studios available: 1. *Approximate studio dimensions and flooring:* 75' x 100' wood-suspended. *Performance facilities:* 1000-seat, state-of-the-art theater.

DRAMA

Curriculum, Students, and Faculty

Required courses: acting, audition preparation, improvisation, make-up, mime, movement, scene study, speech, Stanislavski exercises, text analysis.

Elective courses: directing, drama criticism, dramaturgy, martial arts, musical theater, stage combat, verse drama, voice.

Number of years required to complete program: 4. *Summer program available. Affiliation with a professional theater company: Goodman, Beverly Art Center.*

Selectivity for males: most admitted, but not all. *Selectivity for females:* most admitted, but not all. *Total enrollment:* 300. *Entering class size:* 70. *Graduating class size:* 65.

Renowned alumni: Sonia Scales.

Total full-time faculty: 3. *List of current faculty and past affiliations:* Sandra Meyer, DePaul; Lilian Monkus, Wendy Richards-Goodman.

Audition Information

No audition fee. Audition consists of the following: cold readings, improvisation.

Audition evaluation criteria: criteria representative of 4 levels of drama instruction offered.

Performance Information

Performance opportunities available (frequency): fully produced performances (annually), informal performances (4-5 per year), workshops (varies), off-site performances (varies), casting is by audition.

Facilities

Rehearsal facilities and hours: 2 rehearsal halls, 4:00 pm-7:00 pm. *Number of theaters on campus:* 1 *Type and capacity:* proscenium 1,000.

MUSIC

Curriculum, Students, and Faculty

Unique or innovative music curriculum: includes electronic music component featured on the Internet. *How are major teacher assignments made?* Students may choose. Faculty is informed of a student's teacher preference at the time of the audition. *80 lessons with major teacher; 20 lessons with a teaching assistant. May a student change major teachers during the course of study?* usually. *Study of secondary instrument or discipline is allowed.*

Selectivity for instruments or programs offered (rating): accompanying (non-competitive), bassoon (non-competitive), choral conducting (competitive), choral singing (non-competitive), clarinet (non-competitive), composition (non-competitive), double bass (non-competitive), electronic music (non-competitive), flute or piccolo (non-competitive), French horn (non-competitive), guitar (non-competitive), harp (non-competitive), jazz (competitive), oboe/English horn (non-competitive), orchestral conducting (competitive), percussion (non-competitive), piano (non-competitive), saxophone (non-competitive), trombone (non-competitive), trumpet (non-competitive), tuba (non-competitive), viola (non-competitive), violin (non-competitive), violoncello (non-competitive), voice (non-competitive).

Total enrollment: 500. *Entering class size:* 100. *Graduating class size:* 90.

Renowned alumni: Anthony Wonsey, Brian Rosewell.

Total full-time faculty: 10. *Program contact person:* Carole Butler.

Audition Information

No audition fee. Audition consists of the following: scales, music theory, sight reading. *Instruments provided for:* harpists, percussionists; all large string, brass, wind instruments.

Performance opportunities available (frequency): jury examinations, recitals.

Facilities

Number of practice rooms and hours: 10; throughout the school day. *Recital hall?* yes. *Concert hall?* yes. *Recording studio?* yes.

BROAD RIPPLE HIGH SCHOOL

Indianapolis Public Schools Center for Performing and Visual Arts
1115 East Broad Ripple Avenue, Indianapolis IN 46220
Tel: 317-226-3784
Fax: 317-226-3552

General

Type of Institution: magnet-public. *Environment:* urban.

Total enrollment of institution: 2,100. *Degrees offered:* high school diploma.

Entrance Requirements

Audition required. Other requirements: interview, recommendation.

Costs & Financial Aid

Other aid available to international students: We have foreign exchange students participate in our program. Their participation is the same as all IPS students.

Services

Support staff: college advisor.

Comments

The Center for Performing and Visual Arts is a magnet (9-12) program of the Indianapolis public schools. As a school-within-a-school we are small (250 students) and must draw our students from within the school system boundaries. In addition to music (80-90 students), theatre (50-60 students), and dance (40-50 students), we also offer a visual arts program with approximately 60 students participating.

DANCE

Curriculum, Students, and Faculty

Required courses: ballet (3 classes per week), dance composition/choreography, dance writing, research and criticism (4 years to complete), modern dance, Graham-based modern dance (1 class per week), jazz, African dance.

Selectivity for males: approximately 60% admitted. *Selectivity for females:* approximately 60% admitted. *Total enrollment:* 50. *Entering class size:* 25. *Graduating class size:* 10.

Renowned alumni: Yolanda Jordan.

Total full-time faculty: 1. *Total part-time faculty:* 1. *List of current faculty and past affiliations:* Melissa Ferise, Butler University, Indiana Pacers, Pacemate. *Program contact person:* Melissa Ferise.

Audition Information

No audition fee. Audition consists of the following: ballet. *Accompanist provided. Cassette player available; CD player available. Dress requirements for males:* white t-shirt, black tights, black shoes. *Dress requirements for females:* black leotard, pink tights, pink ballet slippers.

Audition evaluation criteria: general posture, muscle tone, musicality, coordination, gracefulness; theatrical projection and personality, attitude and desire to work.

Performance Information

Performance opportunities available (frequency): Fully produced concerts (1 per year), informal concerts (1 per year), on-site performances(2 per year), guest artists- 1 per month.

Performances choreographed by: faculty, students, guests.

Facilities

Number of studios available: 1. *Approximate studio dimensions and flooring:* 25' x 50' Marley over wood. *Performance facilities:* large stage and auditorium.

DRAMA

Curriculum, Students, and Faculty

Required courses: acting (4 years to complete), Alexander technique, audition preparation, improvisation, make-up, mime, movement, scene study, speech, stage combat, stagecraft, Stanislavski exercises, text analysis, theater history, topics seminar, acting, voice.

Elective courses: directing.

Number of years required to complete program: 4. *Summer program not available. Partnership agreement with The Edyvean Repertory Theatre and very close ties to Indiana Repertory Theatre. Director serves on boards of both theatres.*

Selectivity for males: most admitted, but not all. *Selectivity for females:* most admitted, but not all. *Total enrollment:* 60. *Entering class size:* 15. *Graduating class size:* 10.

Total full-time faculty: 1. *Total part-time faculty:* 1. *List of current faculty and past affiliations:* Gari L. Williams, Ball State University; Michael Moffatt, Ohio Wesleyan University.

Audition Information

No audition fee. Audition consists of the following: comedic monologue, cold readings including Shakespearean monologue.

Audition evaluation criteria: audition selections, dynamics, voice/speech projection, range, tone, resonance, articulation, pronunciation, body management, facial expression, characterization, creative demonstration of emotion, reading ability, interview.

Performance Information

Performance opportunities available (frequency): fully produced performances (2 per year), informal performances (1 per semester), workshops (4-12 per year), off-site performances (varies), one-act festival, 1 per year, auditioned. Some assigned roles for informal performances.

Facilities

Rehearsal facilities and hours: classroom, 2:45 pm-5:30 pm, auditorium, 2:45 pm-5:30 pm, 10:00 am.-4:00 pm (Sat). *Number of theaters on campus:* 1. *Type and capacity:* auditorium 900.

MUSIC

Curriculum, Students, and Faculty

Unique or innovative music curriculum: 4 years of music theory, history, and free private lessons. *How are major teacher assignments made?* made by the school. Faculty is not informed of a student's teacher preference at the time of the audition. *34 lessons with major teacher. May a student change major teachers during the course of study?* usually. *Study of secondary instrument or discipline is allowed.*

Selectivity for instruments or programs offered (rating): bassoon (non-competitive), clarinet (competitive), double bass (non-competitive), flute or piccolo (competitive), guitar (competitive), oboe/English horn (non-competitive), percussion (competitive), piano (selective), saxophone (competitive), trombone (competitive), trumpet (competitive), tuba (competitive), viola (non-competitive), violin (competitive), violoncello (non-competitive), voice (selective).

Total enrollment: 90. *Entering class size:* 30. *Graduating class size:* 12.

Renowned alumni: Richard Moll.

Total full-time faculty: 2. *Total part-time faculty:* 12. *Program contact person:* Alice Arkin.

Audition Information

No audition fee. Audition consists of the following: sight reading. *Instruments provided for:* percussionists.

Performance opportunities available (frequency): band, jury examinations, chorus.

Facilities

Number of practice rooms and hours: 8. *Recital hall?* no. *Concert hall?* yes. *Recording studio?* no.

EMERSON SCHOOL FOR THE VISUAL AND PERFORMING ARTS

716 East 7th Avenue, Gary IN 46402
Tel: 219-886-6555
Fax: 219-881-4125
Contact: Lea Larson

General

Type of Institution: magnet-public. *Environment:* urban.

Total enrollment of institution: 550. *Degrees offered:* high school diploma.

Entrance Requirements

Audition required: live. *Other requirements:* interview, recommendation, essay.

Services

Housing options: off-campus housing.

Support staff: college advisor, financial aid advisor, psychological counselor, resident nurse.

Comments

Throughout the year we have at least 50 request performances.

DANCE

Curriculum, Students, and Faculty

Required courses: ballet, dance composition/choreography, dance history, jazz, Graham-based modern dance, pointe, rehearsal and performance, tap, rehearsal and performance.

Selectivity for males: approximately 60% admitted. *Selectivity for females:* approximately 33% admitted. *Total enrollment:* 72. *Entering class size:* 18. *Graduating class size:* 3.

Total full-time faculty: 2. *Total part-time faculty:* 1. *List of current faculty and past affiliations:* Randy Grass, Joseph Holmes Theatre and School, Alvin Ailey Theater and School; Michael Davis, Indiana University dance department, Homewood Repertory Theater. *Program contact person:* Randy Grass.

Audition Information

No audition fee. Audition consists of the following: ballet. *Accompanist not provided. Cassette player available; CD player available. Dress requirements for males:* loose, comfortable clothing. *Dress requirements for females:* loose, comfortable clothing.

Repertoire that students should avoid? students are not required to have a routine prepared.

Audition evaluation criteria: body type, movement ability, turn out, flexibility, arch, movement recall, stage presence.

Performance Information

Performance opportunities available (frequency): on-site performances (varies), touring.

Performances choreographed by: faculty.

Facilities

Number of studios available: 1. *Approximate studio dimensions and flooring:* 50' x 40' oak-sprung. *Performance facilities:* studio is used for lecture demonstration, small stage in auditorium.

DRAMA

Curriculum, Students, and Faculty

Required courses: acting, audition preparation, directing, drama criticism, improvisation, makeup, mime, movement, scene study, speech, Stanislavski exercises, text analysis, verse drama, voice, musical theater, stage combat.

Elective courses: musical theater, speech, improvisation.

Number of years required to complete program: 4. *Summer program not available. no affiliation with a professional theater company. Selectivity for males:* approximately 33% admitted. *Selectivity for females:* approximately 33% admitted. *Total enrollment:* 106. *Entering class size:* 18. *Graduating class size:* 15.

Renowned alumni: Raquel (Rocki) McFerson, Chester Gregory.

Total full-time faculty: 2. *Total part-time faculty:* 1. *List of current faculty and past affiliations:* Charla Booth, Visions of the Future Arts Camp; Robert Herr, Festival Players.

Audition Information

No audition fee. Audition consists of the following: cold readings, comedic monologue, improvisation, required monologue, Shakespearean monologue. *Audition evaluation criteria:* preparation, stage presence, imagination, character development, concentration, impulse, articulation, vocal variety, movement, understanding, ability to read unfamiliar material, character contrast, spontaneity, believability.

Performance Information

Performance opportunities available (frequency): fully produced performances (2), informal performances (4-5 per year), off-site performances (frequently), casting is by audition.

Recent guest artists: Avery Brooks.

Facilities

Rehearsal facilities and hours: 1 studio is available after school for rehearsal, as well as the theater and connecting band area. *Number of theaters on campus:* 1. *Type and capacity:* proscenium 400.

MUSIC

Curriculum, Students, and Faculty

Unique or innovative music curriculum: the only school in the city of Gary that has a full string, band, piano and vocal department, as well as offering music history and music theory. *How are major teacher assignments made?* made by the school, according to teacher preference. Faculty is not informed of a student's teacher preference at the time of the audition. *45 lessons with major teacher; May a student change major teachers during the course of study?* possibly. *Study of secondary instrument or discipline is allowed.*

Selectivity for instruments or programs offered (rating): bassoon (non-competitive), choral singing (highly selective), clarinet (non-competitive), double bass (non-competitive), flute or piccolo (non-competitive), French horn (non-competitive), oboe/English horn (non-competitive), percussion (non-competitive), piano (highly selective), saxophone (non-competitive), trombone (non-competitive), trumpet (non-competitive), tuba (non-competitive), viola (non-competitive), violin (non-competitive), violoncello (non-competitive), voice (highly selective).

Total enrollment: 283. *Entering class size:* 77. *Graduating class size:* 29.

Total full-time faculty: 4 *Total part-time faculty:* 3. *Program contact person:* Lea Larson.

Audition Information

No audition fee. Audition consists of the following: scales, music theory, rhythmic dictation, sight reading. *Instruments provided for:* percussionists; string bass, cello.

Repertoire that students should avoid? nothing popular. *Performance opportunities available (frequency):* recitals (4).

Facilities

Number of practice rooms and hours: 11; 8:00 am-4:00 pm. *Recital hall?* yes. *Concert hall?* yes. *Recording studio?* no.

NORTH SIDE HIGH SCHOOL

475 East State Boulevard, Fort Wayne IN 46805
Tel: 219-425-7530
Fax: 219-425-7137
Email: ljtal@aol.com
Web: ljtal@aol.com
Contact: Ron Flickinger

General

Type of Institution: public. *Environment:* urban *Academic education is offered on-site.*

Total enrollment of institution: 1,541. *Total student body from other countries:* 1%. *Degrees offered:* high school diploma.

Services

Support staff: college advisor, psychological counselor.

DANCE

Curriculum, Students, and Faculty

Required courses: ballet, jazz, rehearsal and performance, tap.

Elective courses: dance composition/choreography, pas de deux, pointe.

Selectivity for males: admit all who apply. *Selectivity for females:* admit all who apply. *Total enrollment:* 147. *Entering class size:* 37. *Graduating class size:* 27. *Percent international:* 20% *Countries most represented:* Japan, Brazil, Germany, Finland, Sweden, France, Norway, Italy, Mexico.

Renowned alumni: Kirk Ruben.

Total full-time faculty: 1. *List of current faculty and past affiliations:* Bonnie Amburgey. *Program contact person:* Bonnie Amburgey.

Audition Information

No audition fee.

Performance Information

Performance opportunities available (frequency): Fully produced concerts (2 per year), workshops (1 per year), on-site performances(2 per year), competitions: 2 per year.

Performances choreographed by: faculty, students, guests. *Recent guest choreographers:* Micheal Tevlin, Amy Markey Holmes, Radmila Teodorovic novosel, Sara Taylor, and Lisa Root.

Facilities

Number of studios available: 2. *Approximate studio dimensions and flooring:* 36' x 43' Harlequin-cascade for jazz and ballet, 40' x 38' wood—tap studio. *Performance facilities:* 1,100-seat auditorium.

DRAMA

Curriculum, Students, and Faculty

Required courses: acting, directing, drama criticism, dramaturgy, improvisation, make-up, mime, musical theater, scene study, speech, text analysis, voice.

Number of years required to complete program: 4. *Summer program not available. Selectivity for males:* admit all who apply. *Selectivity for females:* admit all who apply. *Total enrollment:* 66. *Entering class size:* 41. *Graduating class size:* 8. *Percent international:* 10%. *Countries most represented:* France, Chile, Colombia, Mexico, Brazil.

Renowned alumni: Drake Hogestyn.

Total full-time faculty: 1. *List of current faculty and past affiliations:* Claryn Myers, Fort Wayne Arena Theatre.

Audition Information

No audition fee.

Performance Information

Performance opportunities available (frequency): fully produced performances (2 per year), informal performances (1 per year), casting is by audition.

Facilities

Rehearsal facilities and hours: 1,100 seat auditorium available after the school day.

MUSIC

Curriculum, Students, and Faculty

Unique or innovative music curriculum: We play professional big band literature. *How are major teacher assignments made?* made by the school, according to teacher preference. *Faculty is not informed of a student's teacher preference at the time of the audition. Study of secondary instrument or discipline is allowed.*

Selectivity for instruments or programs offered (rating): accompanying (non-competitive), clarinet (open), double bass (competitive), flute or piccolo (competitive), French horn (non-competitive), guitar (competitive), jazz (competitive), percussion (competitive), piano (competitive), saxophone (competitive), trombone (competitive), trumpet (competitive), tuba (non-competitive), violin (non-competitive), voice (non-competitive).

Total enrollment: 435. *Entering class size:* 143. *Graduating class size:* 76. *Percent international:* 40%. *Countries most represented:* Brazil, Germany, Finland, Italy, Mexico.

Renowned alumni: Craig Johnson.

Total full-time faculty: 3. *Program contact person:* Ed King.

Audition Information

No audition fee. Audition consists of the following: scales, music theory ensemble playing, arpeggios, sight reading, improvisation. *Instruments provided for:* harpists, percussionists; drum set, bass, bass amplifier.

Performance opportunities available (frequency): band.

Facilities

Number of practice rooms and hours: 3; 8:00 am-4:00 pm. *Recital hall?* no. *Concert hall?* yes. *Recording studio?* yes.

KENTUCKY

KENTUCKY'S GOVERNOR'S SCHOOL FOR THE ARTS

501 West Main Street
5 Riverfront Plaza, Louisville KY 40202
Tel: 502-562-0147
Fax: 502-562-0747

General

Type of Institution: governors, boarding. *Environment:* urban.

Total enrollment of institution: 160.

Entrance Requirements

Audition required: live. *Other requirements:* interview, essay, photograph.

Geographic restrictions: must be a resident of Kentucky and attend a Kentucky high school as a sophomore or junior at the time of application.

Costs & Financial Aid

No tuition.

Percent of students receiving financial aid: 100%. *Types of scholarships and aid awarded:* full.

Services

Housing options: on-site dorms.

Support staff: housing advisor, psychological counselor, resident assistant.

DANCE

Curriculum, Students, and Faculty

Required courses: African dance, anatomy, ballet, dance history, master classes, modern dance, nutrition, pointe, rehearsal and performance.

Elective courses: character, dance composition/choreography, dance theory, dance writing, research and criticism, historical dance, jazz, Labanotation, men's class, movement techniques, music, other world dance forms, pas de deux, repertory, Spanish, stagecraft, variations, vernacular dance, modern dance partnering.

DRAMA

Curriculum, Students, and Faculty

Required courses: acting, Alexander technique, audition preparation, improvisation, movement, scene study, stage combat, Stanislavski exercises, text analysis, voice.

YOUTH PERFORMING ARTS SCHOOL

1517 South Second Street, Louisville KY 40208
Tel: 502-485-8355
Fax: 502-485-8808

General

Type of Institution: magnet-public. *Environment:* urban.

Total enrollment of institution: 450. *Degrees offered:* high school diploma.

Entrance Requirements

Audition required: live. *Other requirements:* interview, recommendation, essay, photograph.

DANCE

Curriculum, Students, and Faculty

Required courses: master classes.

DRAMA

Curriculum, Students, and Faculty

Required courses: movement.

LOUISIANA

CADDO MAGNET HIGH SCHOOL

1601 Viking Drive, Shreveport LA 71101
Tel: 318-221-2501
Fax: 318-227-1393
Email: web@cmhs.com
Web: www.cmhs.com
Contact: Dr. Beatrice James

General

Type of Institution: magnet-public. *Environment:* suburban *Academic education is offered on-site.*

Total enrollment of institution: 1,265. *Total student body from other countries:* 1%. *Degrees offered:* high school diploma.

Entrance Requirements

Audition required: live, audio. *Other requirements:* interview.

Geographic restrictions: resident of Caddo Parish.

DANCE

Curriculum, Students, and Faculty

Required courses: music, repertory, dance composition/choreography, rehearsal and performance.

DRAMA

Curriculum, Students, and Faculty

Elective courses: acting, audition preparation, directing, drama criticism, improvisation, scene study, speech, Stanislavski exercises.

Number of years required to complete program: Each year is a complete program. Students may take up to four years of drama. *Summer program not available. no affiliation with a professional theater company. Selectivity for males:* admit all who apply. *Selectivity for females:* admit all who apply. *Total enrollment:* 99.

Renowned alumni: Heather Peak, Shenandoah Shakespeare Express.

Total full-time faculty: 1. *List of current faculty and past affiliations:* Anna Aslin, East Bank Theatre.

Audition Information

No audition fee. Audition consists of the following: a cappella singing, comedic monologue, Shakespearean monologue, group warm-up. *Repertoire that students should avoid?* no.

Performance Information

Performance opportunities available (frequency): fully produced performances (3 per year), informal performances (30 per year), casting is by audition.

Recent guest artists: Richard Folmer, Mary Jarvis, Dick King.

Facilities

Number of theaters on campus: 2. *Type and capacity:* proscenium 200, proscenium 612.

MUSIC

Curriculum, Students, and Faculty

How are major teacher assignments made? made by the school, according to teacher availability. Faculty is not informed of a student's teacher preference at the time of the audition. *May a student change major teachers during the course of study?* never. *Study of secondary instrument or discipline is allowed.*

Selectivity for instruments or programs offered (rating): bassoon (non-competitive), clarinet (non-competitive), double bass (non-competitive), flute or piccolo (non-competitive), French horn (non-competitive), guitar (non-competitive), jazz (non-competitive), oboe/English horn (non-competitive), orchestral conducting (non-competitive), percussion (non-competitive), piano (non-competitive), saxophone (non-competitive), trombone (non-competitive), trumpet (non-competitive), tuba (non-competitive), viola (non-competitive), violin (non-competitive), violoncello (non-competitive), voice (non-competitive).

Total enrollment: 220.

Total full-time faculty: 2. *Total part-time faculty:* 1. *Program contact person:* Johnette Parker.

Audition Information

No audition fee. Audition consists of the following: scales, orchestral excerpts, sight reading, *Instruments provided for:* percussionists.

Facilities

Number of practice rooms and hours: 2; 24 hours a day. *Recital hall?* no. *Concert hall?* yes. *Recording studio?* no.

LOUISIANA SCHOOL FOR MATH, SCIENCE, AND THE ARTS

715 College Avenue, Natchitoches LA 71457
Tel: 318-357-3174
Fax: 318-357-3299

General

Type of Institution: public, boarding. *Academic education is offered on-site.*

Total enrollment of institution: 400. *Degrees offered:* high school diploma.

Entrance Requirements

Audition required: live. *Other requirements:* interview, recommendation, essay.

Geographic restrictions: students and parents must be Louisiana residents.

Costs & Financial Aid

Other fees: $150 student activity fee/miscellaneous.

Percent of students receiving financial aid: 9%. *Types of scholarships and aid awarded:* full, partial, need-based. *Forms required for scholarships:* income tax return. *Procedure for applying for loans:* obtain application, submit completed applications and transcripts (9th and 10th grade) along with personal essay and portfolio; semifinalists come for an on-site interview and audition.

Services

Housing options: on-site dorms.

Support staff: college advisor, dorm parent, financial aid advisor, housing advisor, psychological counselor, resident assistant, student affairs officer.

DANCE

Curriculum, Students, and Faculty

Elective courses: ballet, dance composition/choreography, jazz, Cunningham-based, Limon-based modern dance, rehearsal and performance, repertory, stagecraft.

Selectivity for males: admit all who apply. *Selectivity for females:* admit all who apply. *Total enrollment:* 70.

Total full-time faculty: 1. *List of current faculty and past affiliations:* Randy Allen, Jean-Marc Matos and Co., June Finch Co., Memphis Ballet. *Program contact person:* Randy Allen.

Audition Information

No audition fee. Audition consists of the following: ballet, modern dance, jazz combination. *Accompanist not provided. Cassette player available; CD player available. Dress requirements for males:* solid color tights and leotard, jazz shoes, footless tights. *Dress requirements for females:* solid color tights, footless tights, solid leotard, jazz shoes.

Audition evaluation criteria: dynamics, personality, learning ability, technique level, overall evaluation.

Performance Information

Performance opportunities available (frequency): Fully produced concerts (1 per year), on-site performances(3-4 per year), touring (2 per year).

Performances choreographed by: faculty.

Facilities

Number of studios available: 1. *Approximate studio dimensions and flooring:* 60' x 30' Harlequin floor covering with sprung floor. *Performance facilities:* adjacent university auditorium.

DRAMA

Curriculum, Students, and Faculty

Required courses: acting, improvisation, movement, scene study.

Number of years required to complete program: 2. *Summer program available. no affiliation with a professional theater company. Selectivity for males:* approximately 33% admitted. *Selectivity for females:* approximately 33% admitted. *Total enrollment:* 70.

Renowned alumni: "Varla Jean Merman" a.k.a. Jeff Roberson, Class of 1986.

Total full-time faculty: 1.

Audition Information

Audition consists of the following: cold readings, comedic monologue. *Audition evaluation criteria:* talent, potential.

Performance Information

Performance opportunities available (frequency): fully produced performances (2 per year), informal performances (4 per year), workshops (occasionally), off-site performances (1 per year), casting is by audition.

Recent guest artists: Vince Williams.

Facilities

Rehearsal facilities and hours: 6:00 pm-7:30 pm (Mon-Thurs). *Number of theaters on campus:* 2. *Type and capacity:* black box 100, proscenium 450.

MUSIC

Curriculum, Students, and Faculty

How are major teacher assignments made? made by the school, according to teacher availability. Faculty is informed of a student's teacher preference at the time of the audition. *28 lessons with major teacher. May a student change major teachers during the course of study?* possibly. *Study of secondary instrument or discipline is allowed.*

Selectivity for instruments or programs offered (rating): accompanying (competitive), bassoon (competitive), choral singing (non-competitive), clarinet (competitive), double bass (competitive), flute or piccolo (competitive), French horn (competitive), guitar (open), harp (competitive), jazz (non-competitive), oboe/English horn (competitive), organ (competitive), percussion (competitive), piano (competitive), saxophone (competitive), trombone (competitive), trumpet (competitive), tuba (competitive), viola (competitive), violin (competitive), violoncello (competitive), voice (competitive).

Total enrollment: 165.

Total full-time faculty: 2. *Program contact person:* Charles Jones.

Audition Information

Audition consists of the following: scales, sight reading, repertoire.

Required repertoire: 2 songs of constrasting styles and tempos.

Facilities

Number of practice rooms and hours: 4; 7:00 am-9:30 pm. *Recital hall?* yes. *Concert hall?* no. *Recording studio?* no.

NEW ORLEANS CENTER FOR CREATIVE ARTS

6048 Perrier Street, New Orleans LA 70118
Tel: 504-899-0055
Fax: 504-897-2275
Contact: John Otis

General

Type of Institution: public, center-model: pre-professional arts training. *Environment:* urban.

Total enrollment of institution: 288. *Degrees offered:* certificate.

Entrance Requirements

Audition required: live. *Other requirements:* interview, essay.

Geographic restrictions: metro-region, 8 parishes of greater New Orleans, access limited only by individual transit time.

Services

Support staff: career counselor.

DANCE

Curriculum, Students, and Faculty

Required courses: character, ballet, dance composition/choreography, dance history, dance writing, research and criticism, jazz, master classes, Horton-based modern dance, music, nutrition, pointe, rehearsal and performance, repertory, tap, variations.

Elective courses: men's class, pas de deux.

DRAMA

Curriculum, Students, and Faculty

Required courses: acting, audition preparation, improvisation, mime, movement, scene study, speech, Stanislavski exercises, technical theater (5 classes per week), text analysis, voice.

MUSIC

Instruction in a variety of instruments.

SCOTLANDVILLE MAGNET HIGH SCHOOL

9870 Scotland Avenue, Baton Rouge LA 70807
Tel: 504-775-3715
Contact: Liza Milner

General

Type of Institution: magnet-public.

Total enrollment of institution: 1,100. *Degrees offered:* high school diploma.

Entrance Requirements

Audition required: live.

Geographic restrictions: East Baton Rouge residents (Baton Rouge, Baker, Zachary, Central).

Services

Support staff: college advisor, resident nurse, student affairs officer.

DANCE

Curriculum, Students, and Faculty

Elective courses: ballet, dance composition/choreography, modern dance, rehearsal and performance, combination.

Selectivity for males: admit all who apply. *Selectivity for females:* admit all who apply.

Renowned alumni: Helen Daigle; Feld Ballet, Ballet Hispanico.

Total full-time faculty: 1. *List of current faculty and past affiliations:* Molly Buchman, Baton Rouge Ballet Theatre. *Program contact person:* Molly Buchman.

Audition Information

No audition fee. Audition consists of the following: ballet, modern dance.

Audition evaluation criteria: applies only to upper-level classes: technical, proficiency, amount of training.

Performance Information

Performance opportunities available (frequency): Fully produced concerts (1 per year), informal concerts (2 per year), workshops (2 per year), onsite performances (10-15 per year).

Performances choreographed by: faculty, students.

Facilities

Number of studios available: 2. *Approximate studio dimensions and flooring:* 40' x 25' dance linoleum over suspended sub-floor, 25' x 25' dance linoleum over suspended sub-floor. *Performance facilities:* high school auditorium.

DRAMA

Curriculum, Students, and Faculty

Elective courses: acting, speech, methods and style, advanced play production.

Summer program not available. Selectivity for males: admit all who apply. *Selectivity for females:* admit all who apply. *Total enrollment:* 150.

Total full-time faculty: 1. *Total part-time faculty:* 1. *List of current faculty and past affiliations:* Claire Thames, Baker Little Theater.

Audition Information

No audition fee. Audition consists of the following: cold readings, improvisation, group warm-up. *Audition evaluation criteria:* teacher evaluation.

Performance Information

Performance opportunities available (frequency): fully produced performances (2 per year), informal performances (several), workshops (1 per year), offsite performances (2 per year), casting is by audition.

Facilities

Rehearsal facilities and hours: run throughs, 3:30-5:30 pm. *Number of theaters on campus:* 1. *Type and capacity:* proscenium.

MUSIC

Curriculum, Students, and Faculty

Elective courses: musical theater, music theory, chorus, piano, strings, band.

May a student change major teachers during the course of study? never.

Total enrollment: 350.

Total full-time faculty: 2. *Total part-time faculty:* 2. *Program contact person:* Marie Cotaya.

Recent guest artists: Louisiana State University Music Department.

Audition Information

No audition fee. Audition consists of the following: scales, arpeggios, sight reading, melodic dictation. *Instruments provided for:* percussionists.

Performance opportunities available (frequency): band (4), band (12), chorus (6).

Facilities

Recital hall? no. *Concert hall?* no. *Recording studio?* no.

MARYLAND

BALTIMORE ACTORS THEATRE CONSERVATORY

The Dumbarton House
300 Dumbarton Road, Baltimore MD 21212
Tel: 410-337-8519
Fax: 410-337-8582
Email: batpro@bcpl.md.lib_us
Contact: Walter E. Anderson

General

Type of Institution: conservatory, day coed. *Environment:* suburban. *Academic education is offered on-site.*

Degrees offered: high school diploma.

Entrance Requirements

Audition required: live. *Other requirements:* interview, recommendation, essay, photograph.

Costs & Financial Aid

Application fee: $50. *Deposit:* $100. *Tuition:* $6,900. *Other fees:* uniform (varies).

Types of scholarships and aid awarded: partial, need-based, institutional aid, reduced tuition, tuition payment plan. *Forms required for scholarships:* income tax return, income asset verification. *Loans available.*

Services

Housing options: family.

Support staff: college advisor, financial aid advisor.

DANCE

Curriculum, Students, and Faculty

Required courses: ballet, jazz, modern dance, pointe, rehearsal and performance, Spanish.

DRAMA

Curriculum, Students, and Faculty

Required courses: acting, Alexander technique, improvisation, musical theater, scene study, speech, Stanislavski exercises, voice.

Elective courses: audition preparation.

BALTIMORE SCHOOL FOR THE ARTS

712 Cathedral Street, Baltimore MD 21201
Tel: 410-396-1185
Fax: 410-539-1430
Email: srom@worldnet.att.net
Contact: Leslie Seyffert

General

Type of Institution: magnet-public, specialized. *Environment:* urban. *Academic education is offered on-site.*

Total enrollment: 300. *Total student body from other countries:* 1%. *Degrees offered:* high school diploma.

Entrance Requirements

Audition required: live. *Other requirements:* interview.

Tuition: $2,000.

Services

Housing options: family.

Support staff: college advisor, physical therapist, psychological counselor.

DANCE

Curriculum, Students, and Faculty

Required courses: African dance, ballet, dance history, men's class, modern dance, music, nutrition, pas de deux, pointe, rehearsal and performance, variations.

Elective courses: jazz.

Selectivity for males: approximately 33% admitted. *Selectivity for females:* approximately 10% admitted. *Total enrollment:* 60. *Entering class size:* 15. *Graduating class size:* 10.

Total full-time faculty: 3. *Total part-time faculty:* 12. *Program contact person:* Norma Pera.

Audition Information

No audition fee. Audition consists of the following: ballet, improvisation, modern dance, orthopedic evaluation, pas de deux, pointe works, prepared solo. *Accompanist provided. Cassette player available; CD player available.*

Performance Information

Performance opportunities available (frequency): Fully produced concerts (2 annual series), informal concerts (2 annual series), workshops (4 per year), on-site performances(2 annual series).

Performances choreographed by: faculty, guests. *Recent guest choreographers:* Hinton Battle, John Clifford, Lisa De Ribere.

Facilities

Number of studios available: 2.

DRAMA

Curriculum, Students, and Faculty

Required courses: acting, Alexander technique, audition preparation, improvisation, make-up, mime, movement, musical theater, scene study, speech, Stanislavski exercises.

Elective courses: stage combat.

Number of years required to complete program: 4. *Summer program not available. Selectivity for males:* approximately 33% admitted. *Selectivity for females:* approximately 10% admitted. *Total enrollment:* 60. *Entering class size:* 15. *Graduating class size:* 10.

Renowned alumni: Jada Pinkett, Tupac Shakur.

Total full-time faculty: 3. *Total part-time faculty:* 15.

Audition Information

Audition consists of the following: required monologue, group warm-up.

Performance Information

Performance opportunities available (frequency): fully produced performances (2 annual series), informal performances (2 annual series), workshops (2 per year), casting is by audition.

Facilities

Rehearsal facilities and hours: 2 lab theaters, 1 proscenium theater.

MUSIC

Curriculum, Students, and Faculty

Unique or innovative music curriculum: All students receive one studio lesson each week at no charge. *How are major teacher assignments made?* made by the school. Faculty is not informed of a student's teacher preference at the time of the audition. *30 lessons with major teacher. May a student change major teachers during the course of study?* possibly. *Study of secondary instrument or discipline is allowed.*

Selectivity for instruments or programs offered (rating): bassoon (selective), choral singing (highly selective), clarinet (selective), double bass (competitive), flute or piccolo (selective), French horn (competitive), guitar (selective), harp (highly selective), harpsichord (selective), jazz (selective), oboe/English horn (competitive), percussion (highly selective), piano (highly selective), saxophone (selective), trombone (competitive), trumpet (selective), tuba (selective), viola (selective), violin (highly selective), violoncello (competitive), voice (highly selective).

Total enrollment: 125. *Entering class size:* 30. *Graduating class size:* 25. *Countries most represented:* Korea, Germany.

Total full-time faculty: 3. *Total part-time faculty:* 45. *Program contact person:* Christopher Ford.

Audition Information

No audition fee. Audition consists of the following: scales, music theory. *Instruments provided for:* harpists, percussionists.

Facilities

Number of practice rooms and hours: 24; 7:30 am-7:00 pm. *Recital hall?* yes. *Concert hall?* yes. *Recording studio?* no.

CARVER CENTER FOR ARTS & TECHNOLOGY

983 York Road, Baltimore MD 21204
Tel: 410-887-2775
Fax: 410-796-9114
Contact: Patty Bond

General

Type of Institution: magnet-public. *Environment:* urban. *Academic education is offered on-site.*

Total enrollment: 800. *Degrees offered:* high school diploma.

Entrance Requirements

Audition required: live. *Other requirements:* interview.

Geographic restrictions: Baltimore County residents; others on space available basis with payment of tuition.

Tuition (out-of-county): $4,249.

Services

Support staff: college advisor, psychological counselor, resident nurse.

Comments

Carver Center for Arts and Technology is a Baltimore County public school which provides interrelated arts, technology, and academic programs for students in grades 9-12. Founded in 1993, Carver Center is a countywide magnet school offering college preparatory academic curricula and rigorous courses of study in visual arts, theater, dance, literary arts, business, carpentry, cosmetology, and culinary arts.

DANCE

Curriculum, Students, and Faculty

Required courses: ballet (3 classes per week, 4 years to complete), dance composition/choreography (3 classes per week), dance history (3 classes per week), Labanotation (3 classes per week), Limon-based modern dance (3 classes per week, 4 years to complete), movement techniques, Pilates (1 class per week, 4 years to complete), pointe (3 classes per week, 2 years to complete), eclectic (3 classes per week, 4 years to complete), rehearsal and performance.

Elective courses: rehearsal and performance (5 classes per week), variations (3 classes per week).

Selectivity for males: approximately 33% admitted. *Selectivity for females:* approximately 33% admitted. *Total enrollment:* 54. *Entering class size:* 15. *Graduating class size:* 14.

Total full-time faculty: 1. *Total part-time faculty:* 3. *List of current faculty and past affiliations:* Amanda Thom, Carver Center and Goucher College, member Surge Dance Company; Elizabeth Ahearn, Goucher College, Certified Pilates Instructor, former member Ballet Oklahoma, member Surge Dance Company; Ken Skrzesz, Surge Dance Company, former member Deborah Carr Dance Company. *Program contact person:* Amanda Thom-Woodson.

Audition Information

No audition fee. Audition consists of the following: ballet, improvisation, modern dance, individual interview. *Accompanist provided. Cassette player available; CD player available. Dress requirements for males:* solid colored leotard and tights, footless tights for modern class, soft shoes for ballet class, dance belt recommended. *Dress requirements for females:* hair should be neat and tied back if long.

Audition evaluation criteria: technical ability (modern), technical ability (ballet alignment), ability to learn quickly, directional ability, quality of movement, discipline/concentration, creativity, growth potential.

Performance Information

Performance opportunities available (frequency): Fully produced concerts (2 per year), on-site performances (4 per year).

Performances choreographed by: faculty, students, guests. *Recent guest choreographers:* Randy James, Todd Rosenlieb.

Facilities

Number of studios available: 2. *Approximate studio dimensions and flooring:* 40' x 40' Gerstung 400 base. 20' x 18' Gerstung 400 base, *Performance facilities:* theater with dance flooring.

DRAMA

Curriculum, Students, and Faculty

Required courses: acting, Alexander technique, drama criticism, dramaturgy, improvisation, make-up, mime, movement, musical theater, scene study, Stanislavski exercises, text analysis, verse drama, voice.

Elective courses: directing, speech, stage combat.

Number of years required to complete program: 4. *Summer program not available.*

Selectivity for males: approximately 60% admitted. *Selectivity for females:* approximately 60% admitted. *Total enrollment:* 122. *Entering class size:* 35. *Graduating class size:* 33.

Total full-time faculty: 3.

Audition Information

No audition fee. Audition consists of the following: improvisation, Shakespearean monologue, group warm-up. Portfolio: list of theater experiences including programs and photographs. *Audition evaluation criteria:* Group interaction (follows directions, sustains involvement, cooperative, uninhibited, initiates actions). Acting (voice: projection and range, tone and resonation, articulation/pronunciation; body/characterization: facial expression, hand expression, reading-phrasing/pausing, character, creative demonstration of emotions, and movement). Improvisation (scene development, use of dialogue and movement, imaginative situation).

Performance Information

Performance opportunities available (frequency): fully produced performances (4 per year), informal performances (4 per year), workshops (4 per year), off-site performances (6-8 per year), casting by audition.

Recent guest artists: Imagimime, Shenandoah Shakespeare Express.

Facilities

Rehearsal facilities and hours: 2 spaces used after school and on weekends. *Number of theaters on campus:* 2. *Type and capacity:* black box 100, black box 200.

SUITLAND HIGH SCHOOL CENTER FOR THE VISUAL AND PERFORMING ARTS

5200 Silver Hill Road, Forestville MD 20747
Tel: 301-817-0091
Fax: 301-817-0515
Contact: Ronald Johnson

General

Type of Institution: magnet-public. *Environment:* suburban. *Academic education is offered on-site.*

Total enrollment: 351. *Degrees offered:* high school diploma, international baccalaureate.

Entrance Requirements

Audition required: live. *Other requirements:* interview.

Geographic restrictions: student's must live in Prince George's County, MD.

Services

Support staff: college advisor, psychological counselor.

DANCE

Curriculum, Students, and Faculty

Required courses: African dance (2 classes per week, 1 year to complete), ballet (2-3 classes per week, 4 years to complete), dance composition/choreography (2 classes per week, 1 year to complete), jazz (2-3 classes per week, 2 years to complete), master classes, modern dance (2-3 classes per week, 4 years to complete), pointe (1-3 classes per week, 4 years to complete), rehearsal and performance, repertory (2-3 classes per week, 1 year to complete).

Selectivity for males: approximately 60% admitted. *Selectivity for females:* approximately 10% admitted. *Total enrollment:* 50. *Entering class size:* 16. *Graduating class size:* 13. *Percent international:* 1%. *Countries most represented:* France.

Renowned alumni: Melissa Miller, Broadway dancer; Eric Underwood, NYC Ballet top apprentice class.

Total full-time faculty: 3. *List of current faculty and past affiliations:* Heidi Miller, Graham School, Boston Conservatory; Linda Dan, Martha modern company in Pittsburgh; Barbara Marks, Myra Kiniko Co., studied with Tudor, Craske, Perry Brunson, Ballet Russe School, Johns Hopkins and Towson State University, Peabody Music Conservatory, choreographed for Balto Opera Company. *Program contact person:* Barbara Marks.

Audition Information

No audition fee. Audition consists of the following: ballet, modern dance, pas de deux, pointe works, prepared solo. *Accompanist not provided. Cassette player available; CD player available.*

Audition evaluation criteria: natural flexibility, strength, endurance, coordination, ability to pickup and remember steps and musicality.

Performance Information

Performance opportunities available (frequency): Fully produced concerts (2 per year), informal concerts (1 per year), on-site performances(2-3 per year).

Performances choreographed by: faculty, students, guests. *Recent guest choreographers:* Kathy Hardy-Gray (Limon); Christel Stevens (Kathak Dance); Kim Bears (Philadanco).

Facilities

Number of studios available: 3. *Approximate studio dimensions and flooring:* 80' x 50' sprung wood. with Marley covering, 60' x 30' sprung wood, 30' x 40' sprung wood. *Performance facilities:* small theater—seats 200; large auditorium—seats 1,000.

DRAMA

Curriculum, Students, and Faculty

Required courses: acting, audition preparation, directing, improvisation, make-up, scene study, stage combat, text analysis.

Number of years required to complete program: 3-4. *Summer program not available. Affiliation with a professional theater company: Folger Theatre.*

Selectivity for males: approximately 10% admitted. *Selectivity for females:* approximately 10% admitted. *Total enrollment:* 35. *Entering class size:* 12. *Graduating class size:* 8.

Total full-time faculty: 3.

Audition Information

No audition fee. Audition consists of the following: cold readings, improvisation. *Repertoire that students should avoid?* Selections should be appropriate for presentation in a public school setting.

Performance Information

Performance opportunities available (frequency): fully produced performances (3 per year), workshops (frequently), off-site performances (frequently), casting by audition.

Facilities

Rehearsal facilities and hours: experimental theater, school auditorium *Type and capacity:* experimental 300, auditorium 1,000.

MUSIC

Curriculum, Students, and Faculty

Unique or innovative music curriculum: Students receive music theory all four years and study with a private teacher all four years. *How are major teacher assignments made?* made by the school, according to teacher availability. Faculty is not informed of a student's teacher preference at the time of the audition. *45 lessons with major teacher. May a student change major teachers during the course of study?* possibly. *Study of secondary instrument or discipline is allowed.*

Selectivity for instruments or programs offered (rating): bassoon (highly selective), clarinet (highly selective), double bass (highly selective), flute or piccolo (highly selective), French horn (highly selective), oboe/English horn (highly selective), percussion (highly selective), piano (highly selective), saxophone (highly selective), trombone (highly selective), trumpet (highly selective), tuba (highly selective), viola (highly selective), violin (highly selective), violoncello (highly selective), voice (highly selective).

Total enrollment: 102. *Entering class size:* 30. *Graduating class size:* 22.

Total full-time faculty: 5. *Total part-time faculty:* 19. *Program contact person:* Leroy Barton.

Audition Information

No audition fee. Audition consists of the following: scales, music theory, rhythmic dictation, sight reading, melodic dictation. *Instruments provided for:* percussionists, string bass, pianists.

Performance opportunities available (frequency): band, jury examinations, opera workshops, orchestral concerts, recitals, touring, chorus.

Facilities

Number of practice rooms and hours: 18; 9 hours during school. *Recital hall?* yes. *Concert hall?* yes. *Recording studio?* no.

MASSACHUSETTS

CAMBRIDGE SCHOOL OF WESTON

Georgian Road, Weston MA 02193
Tel: 617-642-8650
Fax: 617-899-3870

General

Type of Institution: coed, day and boarding. *Environment:* suburban. *Academic education is offered on-site.*

Total enrollment: 240 *Degrees offered:* high school diploma.

Entrance Requirements

Standardized test requirements: ISEE; SSAT.

Costs & Financial Aid

Application fee: $40. *Tuition:* $17,160.

Percent of students receiving financial aid: 25%. *Types of scholarships and aid awarded:* partial, need-based, work/study. *Forms required for scholarships:* FFS, income tax return, income asset verification. *Loans available.*

Services

Housing options: on-site dorms.

Support staff: college advisor, dorm parent, psychological counselor, resident nurse.

Comments

We are a college preparatory school with a century-old tradition of innovative learning. We have extensive offerings in the performing arts.

CONCORD ACADEMY

166 Main Street, Concord MA 01742
Tel: 978-369-6080
Fax: 978-369-3452
Email: admissions@concordacademy.org
Web: www.concordacademy.org

General

Type of Institution: coed, day and boarding. *Environment:* suburban. *Academic education is offered on-site.*

Total enrollment: 330. *Total student body from other countries:* 10%. *Degrees offered:* high school diploma.

Entrance Requirements

Audition not required Other requirements: interview, recommendation, essay. *Standardized test requirements:* ISEE; SSAT; TOEFL.

Costs & Financial Aid

Application fee: $45. *Deposit:* $750. *Tuition:* $19,400.

Percent of students receiving financial aid: 20% *Types of scholarships and aid awarded:* full, partial, need-based, tuition payment plan. *Forms required for scholarships:* income tax return, PFS (school and student services for financial aid), W-2 form. *Loans available. Procedure for applying for loans:* return financial aid request form, parents financial statement, federal tax return, copies of W-2's, tax form 4506.

Services

Housing options: on-site dorms, off-campus housing.

Support staff: college advisor, dorm parent, financial aid advisor, foreign student advisor, housing advisor, physical therapist, psychological counselor, resident assistant, resident nurse, student affairs officer.

Comments

Concord Academy is primarily a college preparatory institution, but one which has an exceptionally strong arts program. All student are required to fulfill both a performing and visual art requirement, but many students go far beyond the requirement. Students do not "major" or concentrate in one area but can explore different art forms and/or focus on one if they so chose. Students sometimes come to Concord with extensive acting, dance or musical experience, but there are also opportunities available for novices to develop experience. A rigorous academic program must be maintained by all students through the end of the senior year. In addition Concord Academy has a year round theater and dance company. These are two distinct companies which have also collaborrated on dance theater productions such as Canterbury Tales and Monal/Sade. The works of Pirandello and Calvino have also been used to create an evening of dance and theater.

DANCE

Curriculum, Students, and Faculty

Elective courses: ballet (3 classes per week), dance composition/choreography (3 classes per week), jazz (1 class per week), master classes, Cunningham-based (3 classes per week), Nikolais-based dance (3 classes per week), Tharp-based modern dance (3 classes per week), rehearsal and performance (3 classes per week).

Selectivity for males: most admitted, but not all. *Selectivity for females:* most admitted, but not all. 60 *Entering class size:* 12. *Percent international:* 6%. *Countries most represented:* Japan, Thailand, France, England.

Total full-time faculty: 2 *Total part-time faculty:* 1. *List of current faculty and past affiliations:* Richard Colton, Amy Spencer *Program contact person:* Richard Colton.

Audition Information

No audition fee. Audition consists of the following: ballet, modern dance. *Accompanist provided. Cassette player available; CD player available.*

Audition evaluation criteria: a solid classic foundation with a strong individual movement sense.

Performance Information

Performance opportunities available (frequency): Fully produced concerts (3 per year), informal concerts (2 per year), on-site performances(2 per year).

Performances choreographed by: faculty, students.

Facilities

Number of studios available: 2. *Approximate studio dimensions and flooring:* 40' x 40' sprung wood. *Performance facilities:* auditorium—performing arts center.

DRAMA

Curriculum, Students, and Faculty

Elective courses: acting, directing, improvisation, make-up, mime, movement, musical theater, stage combat, text analysis.

Number of years required to complete program: 3. *Summer program available. Affiliation with a professional theater company: American Repertory Theater. We visit rehearsals and performances and have guests from there visit our school.*

Selectivity for males: most admitted, but not all. *Selectivity for females:* most admitted, but not all. *Total enrollment:* 25. *Entering class size:* 6. *Percent international:* 6%. *Countries most represented:* Thailand, Japan, Korea, France, England.

Total full-time faculty: 2. *List of current faculty and past affiliations:* David Sinaiko, Annie Elias.

Audition Information

No audition fee.

Performance Information

Performance opportunities available (frequency): fully produced performances (3 per year), informal performances (5 per year), workshops (2 per year), year round theater company plus additional shows assigned, casting is by audition.

Recent guest artists: Randal Jagnes.

Facilities

Rehearsal facilities and hours: stage, mini black box, dance studio. *Number of theaters on campus:* 1. *Type and capacity:* theater 350.

MUSIC

Curriculum, Students, and Faculty

How are major teacher assignments made? Students may choose, according to teacher availability. *30 lessons with major teacher; May a student change major teachers during the course of study?* possibly. *Study of secondary instrument or discipline is allowed.*

Selectivity for instruments or programs offered (rating): accompanying (non-competitive), bassoon (non-competitive), choral singing (non-competitive), clarinet (non-competitive), composition (non-competitive), double bass (non-competitive), electronic music (non-competitive), flute or piccolo (non-competitive), French horn (non-competitive), guitar (non-competitive), harp (non-competitive), harpsichord (non-competitive), jazz (non-competitive), oboe/English horn (non-competitive), organ (non-competitive), percussion (non-competitive), piano (non-competitive), saxophone (non-competitive), trombone (non-competitive), trumpet (non-competitive), tuba (non-competitive), viola (non-competitive), violin (non-competitive), violoncello (non-competitive), voice (non-competitive).

Total enrollment: 100. *Entering class size:* 25. *Percent international:* 15% *Countries most represented:* Japan, Korea.

Renowned alumni: Larry Goldings, Hiliary Walter.

Total full-time faculty: 1. *Total part-time faculty:* 16. *Program contact person:* Keith Daniel.

Audition Information

Instruments provided for: percussionists; double bass, alto saxophone, flute, pianos (all year).

Facilities

Number of practice rooms and hours: 10; 7:00 am-10:30 pm. *Recital hall?* yes. *Recording studio?* yes.

ROLAND HAYES DIVISION OF MUSIC

55 New Dudley Street, Roxbury MA 02119
Tel: 617-635-8973

General

Type of Institution: magnet-public. *Environment:* urban. *Academic education is offered on-site. Cross registration is available through the John O'Bryant School of Mathematics and Science.*

Total enrollment: 550. *Degrees offered:* high school diploma.

Entrance Requirements

Audition not required. Other requirements: interview.

Services

Support staff: college advisor, financial aid advisor, psychological counselor, resident nurse.

Comments

Roland Hayes Division of Music provides music programs for mainly two campus schools, John D. O'Bryant School of Mathematics and Science and Madison Park Technical and Vocational School. All music courses and ensembles meet daily. There are opportunities for a student to practice during the early morning before the classes begin, and during the afternoon and evenings following school dismissal. No auditions are required for admission.

MUSIC

Curriculum, Students, and Faculty

Unique or innovative music curriculum: Delineated standards and expectations. *How are major teacher assignments made?* Students may choose, made by the school. *May a student change major teachers during the course of study?* possibly. *Study of secondary instrument or discipline is allowed.*

Selectivity for instruments or programs offered (rating): choral singing (non-competitive), clarinet (non-competitive), composition (non-competitive), double bass (non-competitive), flute or piccolo (non-competitive), French horn (non-competitive), guitar (non-competitive), harp (non-competitive), harpsichord (non-competitive), jazz (non-competitive), organ (non-competitive), percussion (non-competitive), piano (non-competitive), sacred music (non-competitive), saxophone (non-competitive), trombone (non-competitive), trumpet (non-competitive), tuba (non-competitive), viola (non-competitive), violin (non-competitive), violoncello (non-competitive), voice (non-competitive).

STONELEIGH-BURNHAM SCHOOL

574 Bernardston Road, Greenfield MA 01301
Tel: 413-774-2711
Fax: 413-772-2602
Email: admissions@sbschool.org
Web: www.sbschool.org
Contact: Becca Coale

General

Type of Institution: day, girls, boarding.

Total enrollment: 151. *Total student body from other countries:* 19%. *Degrees offered:* high school diploma.

Entrance Requirements

Audition required: live. *Other requirements:* interview, recommendation, essay. *Standardized test requirements:* SSAT; TOEFL.

Costs & Financial Aid

Application fee: $35. *Deposit:* $1,500. *Tuition:* $22,850. *Medical fee:* $450. *Other fees:* $200 technology, $150 activity fee.

Percent of students receiving financial aid: 49% *Types of scholarships and aid awarded:* partial, need-based, named. *Forms required for scholarships:* income tax return, PFS, W-2 form. *Loans available. Procedure for applying for loans:* apply to SSS at Princeton with completed PFS, submit all income tax returns and W-2s.

Services

Housing options: on-site dorms.

Support staff: dorm parent, financial aid advisor, foreign student advisor, housing advisor, psychological counselor, resident assistant, student affairs officer.

DANCE

Curriculum, Students, and Faculty

Required courses: ballet (3 classes per week,4 years to complete), dance history, jazz, master classes, modern dance (2 classes per week,4 years to complete), movement techniques, rehearsal and performance.

Elective courses: African dance, dance composition/choreography, music, pointe, stagecraft.

Selectivity for females: approximately 33% admitted. *Total enrollment:* 51. *Countries most represented:* Korea, Japan.

Total full-time faculty: 1. *Total part-time faculty:* 3. *List of current faculty and past affiliations:* Ann Sorvino, Juilliard School, Merce Cunningham Dance; Kathleen Keillor, Smith College. *Program contact person:* Ann Sorvino.

Audition Information

No audition fee. Audition consists of the following: ballet, modern dance. *Accompanist not provided. Cassette player available; CD player available. Dress requirements for females:* leotard, tights, unitard, slippers for ballet.

Audition evaluation criteria: judged on skill, quick study, and presentation.

Performance Information

Performance opportunities available (frequency): Fully produced concerts (3 per year), informal concerts (2 per year), workshops (6 per year), on-site performances(3 per year), touring (rarely), performed in Athens, Greece, and at the London School of Contemporary Dance.

Performances choreographed by: faculty, students, guests. *Recent guest choreographers:* Eno Washington.

Facilities

Number of studios available: 1. *Approximate studio dimensions and flooring:* suspended Marley floor. *Performance facilities:* theater, fully equipped lighting system, professional dance flooring.

DRAMA

Curriculum, Students, and Faculty

Elective courses: acting, directing, musical theater, text analysis, voice, martial arts.

Number of years required to complete program: 1. *Summer program not available.*

Selectivity for females: most admitted, but not all. *Percent international:* 19%. *Countries most represented:* Korea, Japan.

Total full-time faculty: 1. *Total part-time faculty:* 3.

Audition Information

No audition fee. Audition consists of the following: a cappella singing, cold readings, group warm-up. Once students are admitted, they may audition for any performance. *Dress requirements for females:* no costumes.

Performance Information

Performance opportunities available (frequency): fully produced performances (2 per year), informal performances (3-4 per year), workshops (1-2 per year), casting is by audition.

Facilities

Rehearsal facilities and hours: full sized stage, small theater gallery, evening hours.

MUSIC

Curriculum, Students, and Faculty

How are major teacher assignments made? according to teacher availability. Faculty is not informed of a student's teacher preference at the time of the audition. *30 lessons with major teacher. May a student change major teachers during the course of study?* possibly. *Study of secondary instrument or discipline is allowed.*

Selectivity for instruments or programs offered (rating): bagpipes (competitive), choral singing (competitive), clarinet (competitive), double bass (competitive), flute or piccolo (competitive), guitar (competitive), harp (competitive), harpsichord (competitive), percussion (competitive), piano (competitive), saxophone (competitive), trumpet (competitive), viola (competitive), violin (competitive), violoncello (competitive), voice (competitive).

Countries most represented: Germany.

Total full-time faculty: 1. *Total part-time faculty:* 5. *Program contact person:* Cynthia Meese.

Audition Information

No audition fee. Audition consists of the following: scales, music theory, arpeggios, sight reading, improvisation.

Performance opportunities available (frequency): recitals, chorus.

Facilities

Number of practice rooms and hours: 2. *Recital hall?* yes. *Concert hall?* no. *Recording studio?* no.

WALNUT HILL SCHOOL

12 Highland Street, Natick MA 01760
Tel: 508-653-4312
Fax: 508-653-9593
Email: walnuthill@aol.com
Web: walnuthillarts.org
Contact: Tony Blackman

General

Type of Institution: coed, boarding and day. *Environment:* suburban. *Academic education is offered on-site.*

Total enrollment: 222 *Total student body from other countries:* 28% *Degrees offered:* high school diploma.

Entrance Requirements

Audition required: live, audio, video. *Other requirements:* interview, recommendation, essay. *Standardized test requirements:* ISEE; SSAT; TOEFL.

Costs & Financial Aid

Application fee: $35. *Deposit:* $2,000. *Medical fee:* $50.

Percent of students receiving financial aid: 35%. *Types of scholarships and aid awarded:* partial, merit-based, need-based, named, reduced tuition, tuition payment plan. *Forms required for scholarships:* income tax return, PFS. *Loans available. Procedure for applying for loans:* submit necessary form by deadline.

Services

Housing options: on-site dorms.

Support staff: college advisor, dorm parent, financial aid advisor, foreign student advisor, housing advisor, physical therapist, psychological counselor, resident nurse, student affairs officer.

DANCE

Curriculum, Students, and Faculty

Required courses: character, ballet, dance history, jazz, men's class, modern dance, nutrition, pointe, repertory, Spanish, stagecraft, variations.

Elective courses: dance composition/choreography, music, dance pedagogy, pas de deux, men's class, character.

Selectivity for males: approximately 60% admitted. *Selectivity for females:* approximately 33% admitted. *Total enrollment:* 44. *Entering class size:* 20. *Graduating class size:* 14. *Percent international:* 18%. *Countries most represented:* Japan, Canada.

Renowned alumni: Eva Nissen, Mucuy Bolles, Dylan Newcomb, Shawn Stevens, Jeremy Collins, Susanna Vennerbeck.

Total full-time faculty: 4. *Total part-time faculty:* 2. *List of current faculty and past affiliations:* Samuel Kurkjian, Boston Ballet, Dance Theatre of Harlem; Tamara King, Boston Ballet, Ballet West, Louisville Ballet; Diane Noya, Prometheus Dance, Institute Superior de Danze, Venezuela, Boston

Conservatory; Elizabeth Rising, Royal Academy of Dancing. *Program contact person:* Elizabeth Rising-Musgrave.

Audition Information

No audition fee. Audition consists of the following: ballet, orthopedic evaluation, pointe works. *Accompanist provided. Cassette player not available; CD player not available. Dress requirements for males:* tights, leotard or white t-shirt, shoes. *Dress requirements for females:* tights, leotard, pointe shoes, technique shoes, no skirts, no warm-ups, no jewelry

Repertoire that students should avoid? prepared variations/solos are not requested.

Audition evaluation criteria: physical facility, (flexibility, line, turnout) musicality, coordination, technical proficiency and strength, receptivity to instruction; expression/artistry.

Performance Information

Performance opportunities available (frequency): Fully produced concerts (2 per year), informal concerts (1 per year), workshops (several per season), on-site performances (occasionally), touring (occasionally).

Performances choreographed by: faculty, guests.

Facilities

Number of studios available: 5. Approximate studio dimensions and flooring: 40' x 40' Harlequin, 40' x 50' seamless Marley floor. *Performance facilities:* fully equipped 350-seat theater.

DRAMA

Curriculum, Students, and Faculty

Required courses: acting, dramaturgy, improvisation, movement, scene study, text analysis, masks, verse drama, make-up.

Elective courses: audition preparation, directing, jazz, musical theater, tap, stage combat.

Number of years required to complete program: 4. *Summer program available. No affiliation with a professional theater company. Selectivity for males:* approximately 60% admitted. *Selectivity for females:* approximately 60% admitted. *Total enrollment:* 57. *Entering class size:* 21. *Graduating class size:* 17. *Percent international:* 3%. *Countries most represented:* Germany, Korea.

Renowned alumni: Helen Patton, Paige Turco, Merle Perkins, Hajne Moss-Fishburne

Total full-time faculty: 4. *Total part-time faculty:* 2. *List of current faculty and past affiliations:* Joe Cabrali, Neighborhood Playhouse, Boston Conservatory; Roger Shoemaker, Trinity College, Catholic University; Kristen McKinney, Boston Conservatory.

Audition Information

No audition fee. Audition consists of the following: a cappella singing, comedic monologue, Shakespearean monologue. For the monologues, students may choose. For a cappella, only if student wants to take a musical theater class.

Audition evaluation criteria: creation of character, consistency, concentration/focus, perception of material, level of challenge and risk, enunciation, articulation, inotnation, projection, range, gesture, consistency, energy, presence, poise, intonation.

Performance Information

Performance opportunities available (frequency): fully produced performances (3 per year), informal performances (2 per year), workshops (1 per year), off-site performances (3 per year), casting is by audition.

Facilities

Rehearsal facilities and hours: 1 studio space, black box theater. *Number of theaters on campus:* 2 *Type and capacity:* proscenium 350, black box 85.

MUSIC

Curriculum, Students, and Faculty

Unique or innovative music curriculum: we are directly affiliated with the New England Conservatory. *How are major teacher assignments made?* made by the school, student requests and possible direct arrangements with teachers. Faculty is informed of a student's teacher preference at the time of the audition. *30 lessons with major teacher. May a student change major teachers during the course of study?* possibly. *Study of secondary instrument or discipline is allowed.*

Selectivity for instruments or programs offered (rating): bassoon (competitive), clarinet (selective), composition (competitive), double bass (selective), flute or piccolo (selective), French horn (competitive), harp (competitive), oboe/English horn (selective), organ (selective), percussion (competitive), piano (highly selective), saxophone (selective), trombone (selective), trumpet (selective), tuba (selective), viola (selective), violin (selective), violoncello (selective), voice (competitive).

Total enrollment: 63. *Entering class size:* 23. *Graduating class size:* 15. *Percent international:* 51%. *Countries most represented:* Korea, Taiwan.

Renowned alumni: Hae Sun Paik, Esther Bujiardo.

Total full-time faculty: 4. *Total part-time faculty:* 61. *Program contact person:* Patty Thom.

Audition Information

No audition fee. Audition consists of the following: repertoire. *Instruments provided for:* Pianos only.

Required repertoire: Varies by instrument. Please call school for repertoire information. *Repertoire that students should avoid?* no. *Performance opportunities available (frequency):* chamber music, jury examinations, opera workshops, orchestral concerts, recitals, produced operas, chorus.

Facilities

Number of practice rooms and hours: 20; 7:45 am-10:00 pm. *Recital hall?* yes. *Concert hall?* yes. *Recording studio?* no.

Comments

Music program has been running 10-15 years. Faculty affiliations: Benjamin Zander—conductor of Boston Philharmonic Orchestra and Youth Philharmonic Orchestra, Patty Thom—Boston University, Chris Malby—Brandeis University, Jean Saladino—Florida State University.

MICHIGAN

DETROIT HIGH SCHOOL FINE/PERFORMING ARTS

4333 Rosa Parks Boulevard, Detroit MI
Tel: 313-494-2357
Fax: 313-494-1506
Email: denise-davis@dpsnet.detpub.k12.mi.us

General

Type of Institution: specialized. *Environment:* urban. *Academic education is offered on-site.*

Degrees offered: high school diploma.

Entrance Requirements

Audition required: live. *Other requirements:* interview, recommendation.

Services

Support staff: psychological counselor.

DANCE

Curriculum, Students, and Faculty

Required courses: African dance, ballet, dance composition/choreography, dance history, dance theory, dance writing, research and criticism, master classes, modern dance, rehearsal and performance, repertory, vernacular dance.

Selectivity for males: most admitted, but not all. *Selectivity for females:* approximately 60% admitted. *Entering class size:* 25. *Graduating class size:* 20. *List of current faculty and past affiliations:* Carolyn Rowland, Mumford High School, WSU Workshop, Detroit Cooperative Dance Company. *Program contact person:* Caroland Rowland.

Audition Information

No audition fee. Accompanist not provided. Cassette player available; CD player available.

Repertoire that students should avoid? street dance.

Performance Information

Performance opportunities available (frequency): Fully produced concerts (2 per year), informal concerts (3-12 per year), workshops (1-2 per year), on-site performances (3-12 per year).

Performances choreographed by: faculty, students, guests.

Facilities

Number of studios available: 2.

DRAMA

Curriculum, Students, and Faculty

Elective courses: acting, dramaturgy, speech, voice.

Number of years required to complete program: 4. *Summer program not available. No affiliation with a professional theater company. Selectivity for males:* approximately 33% admitted. *Selectivity for females:* approximately 33% admitted. *Graduating class size:* 10.

Total full-time faculty: 2. *List of current faculty and past affiliations:* P. Ford, MSU.

Audition Information

No audition fee. Audition consists of the following: cold readings, comedic monologue, improvisation, movement class. *Dress requirements for males:* no costumes.

Audition evaluation criteria: poise, articulations, characterization, voice quality/reading skills good, emotion.

Performance Information

Performance opportunities available (frequency): fully produced performances (2 per year, 7 forensics), workshops (1 year), off-site performances (2 years), casting is assigned, auditioned.

Recent guest artists: Walk and Squak from South Africa.

MUSIC

Curriculum, Students, and Faculty

How are major teacher assignments made? according to teacher preference. Faculty is not informed of a student's teacher preference at the time of the audition. *May a student change major teachers during the course of study?* possibly. *Study of secondary instrument or discipline is allowed.*

Selectivity for instruments or programs offered (rating): bassoon (non-competitive), choral conducting (non-competitive), choral singing (non-competitive), clarinet (non-competitive), double bass (non-competitive), flute or piccolo (non-competitive), French horn (non-competitive), jazz (selective), oboe/English horn (non-competitive), orchestral conducting (highly selective), percussion (non-competitive), saxophone (non-competitive), trombone (non-competitive), trumpet (non-competitive), tuba (non-competitive), viola (non-competitive), violin (non-competitive), voice (non-competitive).

Entering class size: 130. *Graduating class size:* 80.

Renowned alumni: Aaliyah.

Total full-time faculty: 7.

Audition Information

No audition fee. Audition consists of the following: scales, sight reading. *Instruments provided for:* percussionists.

Performance opportunities available (frequency): band, chorus.

Facilities

Number of practice rooms and hours: 10; varies. *Recital hall?* no. *Concert hall?* no. *Recording studio?* no.

INTERLOCHEN ARTS ACADEMY

Center for the Arts
P.O. Box 199, Interlochen MI 49643
Tel: 616-276-7472
Fax: 616-276-6321
Email: admissions@interlochen.k12.mi.us
Web: www.interlochen.org

General

Type of Institution: coed, boarding. *Academic education is offered on-site.*

Total enrollment: 430. *Total student body from other countries:* 15%. *Degrees offered:* high school diploma.

Entrance Requirements

Audition required: live, audio, video. *Other requirements:* recommendation, essay, photograph.

Costs & Financial Aid

Application fee: $25 *Deposit:* $1,000

Percent of students receiving financial aid: 67%. *Types of scholarships and aid awarded:* full, partial, merit-based, need-based, institutional aid, tuition payment plan. *Forms required for scholarships:* income tax return, PFS. *Loans available. Procedure for applying for loans:* separate application. *Financial aid offered to international students. Percent of international students receiving scholarships:* 50%.

Services

Housing options: on-site dorms.

Support staff: college advisor, dorm parent, financial aid advisor, foreign student advisor, housing advisor, physical therapist, resident assistant, resident nurse, student affairs officer.

DANCE

Curriculum, Students, and Faculty

Required courses: ballet, jazz, master classes, men's class, Cunningham-based modern dance, nutrition, pas de deux, pointe, repertory, Spanish, tap, variations.

Elective courses: music, stagecraft.

Selectivity for males: approximately 33% admitted. *Selectivity for females:* approximately 33% admitted. *Graduating class size:* 13. *Percent international:* 3%. *Countries most represented:* Canada.

Renowned alumni: Peter Sparling, Victoria Marks, Todd Stickney, and Janet Eilber.

Total full-time faculty: 3. *Total part-time faculty:* 6. *List of current faculty and past affiliations:* Michael Tevlin, St. Louis Ballet, MUNY Opera, Butler Ballet; Sharon Randolph, Colorado Ballet, Alberta Ballet, DanceAspen; Wendy Masterson, DanceAspen, Bolshoi Ballet Academy at Vail. *Program contact person:* Sharon Randolph.

Audition Information

No audition fee. Audition consists of the following: ballet, pas de deux, pointe works, prepared solo, videotape and/or live on campus, spring information weekend on campus. *Accompanist provided. Cassette player available; CD player available. Dress requirements for males:* white t-shirt, black tights, white socks and shoes. *Dress requirements for females:* black leotard, pink tights, slippers, ballet shoes, hair in a bun.

Audition evaluation criteria: potential—rated 1-5.

Performance Information

Performance opportunities available (frequency): Fully produced concerts (3 per year), informal concerts (2 per year), touring (2-3 per year).

Performances choreographed by: faculty, students, guests. *Recent guest choreographers:* Kay Braden, Alan Scofield, Bettijane Sills, Janet Gary, Nan Giordano, Jacqulyn Buglisi, Martha Graham.

Facilities

Number of studios available: 5. *Approximate studio dimensions and flooring:* 24' x 30' sprung/Marley covered, 45' x 90' Marley covered/sprung. *Performance facilities:* 3 on-campus stages.

DRAMA

Curriculum, Students, and Faculty

Required courses: acting.

Elective courses: directing, make-up, movement, musical theater, stage combat, text analysis, verse drama, voice.

Summer program available. No affiliation with a professional theater company. Selectivity for males: approximately 33% admitted. *Selectivity for females:* approximately 33% admitted. *Graduating class size:* 18. *Percent international:* 3%. *Countries most represented:* Canada.

Renowned alumni: Tom Hulce, Richard Brooks, Sean Young, Meredith Baxter, Janet Eilber.

Total full-time faculty: 4. *Total part-time faculty:* 2. *List of current faculty and past affiliations:* David Montee, Arts Encounter Theatre Troupe; Everett Corum, University of Missouri; Robin Ellis.

Audition Information

Audition consists of the following: a cappella singing, comedic monologue, live or videotape. Spring information weekend on campus. *Dress requirements for males:* not too casual. *Dress requirements for females:* not too casual. *Repertoire that students should avoid?* Do not perform material beyond ability.

Audition evaluation criteria: Potential rated—1-5.

Performance Information

Performance opportunities available (frequency): fully produced performances (7+ per year), informal performances (4 per year), workshops (3 per year), casting by audition.

Recent guest artists: Nebraska Acting Caravan.

Facilities

Rehearsal facilities and hours: 4 spaces, 4 hours of classes daily minimum. *Number of theaters on campus:* 3. *Type and capacity:* proscenium 1,000, black box 250, thrust 200.

MUSIC

Curriculum, Students, and Faculty

Unique or innovative music curriculum: Top rated competitive program. *How are major teacher assignments made?* students may choose, made by the school, according to teacher preference and teacher availability. Faculty is not informed of a student's teacher preference at the time of the audition. *May a student change major teachers during the course of study?* possibly. *Study of secondary instrument or discipline is allowed.*

Selectivity for instruments or programs offered (rating): bassoon (selective), choral singing (selective), clarinet (highly selective), composition (selective), double bass (selective), flute or piccolo (highly selective), French horn (selective), guitar (selective), harp (selective), jazz (selective), oboe/English horn (highly selective), organ (selective), percussion (selective), piano (selective), saxophone (selective), trombone (selective), trumpet (highly selective), tuba (selective), viola (selective), violin (selective), violoncello (selective), voice (selective).

Graduating class size: 124. *Percent international:* 21%. *Countries most represented:* South Korea, China, Japan, Taiwan, Canada.

Renowned alumni: Lorin Maazel, Jessye Norman, Joel McNeely, Ida Kavafian, Ani Kavafian, Lisa Saffer.

Total full-time faculty: 22. *Total part-time faculty:* 8. *Program contact person:* Byron Hanson.

Audition Information

No audition fee. Audition consists of the following: scales, orchestral excerpts. *Instruments provided for:* harpists, pianists, organists.

Facilities

Recital hall? yes. *Concert hall?* yes. *Recording studio?* yes.

RENAISSANCE HIGH SCHOOL

6565 West Auter Drive, Detroit MI 48235
Tel: 313-494-7232
Contact: Delores Elswick

General

Type of Institution: public. *Environment:* urban.

Total enrollment: 850. *Total student body from other countries:* 5%. *Degrees offered:* high school diploma.

Entrance Requirements

Audition not required.

DANCE

Curriculum, Students, and Faculty

Required courses: dance composition/choreography, dance writing, research and criticism, jazz, rehearsal and performance, repertory.

Elective courses: modern dance.

Selectivity for males: admit all who apply. *Selectivity for females:* approximately 10% admitted. *Total enrollment:* 90. *Entering class size:* 35. *Graduating class size:* 20. *Countries most represented:* Spain.

Total full-time faculty: 1. *List of current faculty and past affiliations:* Gina Ellis, New York City with Louis Johnson, George Faison, and Eleo Pomare. *Program contact person:* Gina Ellis.

Audition Information

No audition fee. Audition consists of the following: ballet, modern dance. *Accompanist not provided. Cassette player available; CD player available. Dress requirements for females:* black leotard, tights.

Performance Information

Performance opportunities available (frequency): Fully produced concerts (2 per year), on-site performances (6+ per year).

Performances choreographed by: faculty, students, guests. *Recent guest choreographers:* Joi Hayes—Wayne State University Student, Charles Wallace—New York City, Heni Williams.

Facilities

Number of studios available: 1. *Approximate studio dimensions and flooring:* 40' x 40' concrete. *Performance facilities:* gym.

MINNESOTA

APPLE VALLEY HIGH SCHOOL

14450 Hayes Road, Apple Valley MN 55124
Tel: 612-431-8206
Fax: 612-431-8282
Email: wellssp@avhs.isd196.k12.mn.us
Web: www.isd196.k12.mn.us/schools/avhs/avhshome.html
Contact: Dr. Steven Wells

General

Type of Institution: public. *Environment:* suburban.

Total enrollment: 2,182. *Total student body from other countries:* 1%. *Degrees offered:* high school diploma.

Services

Housing options: family.

Support staff: college advisor, physical therapist, psychological counselor, resident nurse, student affairs officer.

DANCE

Curriculum, Students, and Faculty

Elective courses: anatomy, ballet, dance composition/choreography, jazz, master classes, modern dance: Cunningham-based, Graham-based dance, Limon-based, Nikolais-based dance, movement techniques, body conditioning, Laban Movement Studies, rehearsal and performance, repertory, historical dance, master classes.

Selectivity for males: admit all who apply. *Selectivity for females:* admit all who apply. *Total enroll-*

ment: 80. *Entering class size:* 23. *Graduating class size:* 12. *Countries most represented:* Russia.

Renowned alumni: Jill Hinrichs, Catherine Wright, Elizabeth Donahue. *Total full-time faculty:* 1. *List of current faculty and past affiliations:* Emmy Johnson, Ririe-Woodbury Dance Company, Gesel Mason Dancers with Liz Lerman. *Program contact person:* Emmy Johnson.

Audition Information

No audition fee. Accompanist not provided. Cassette player available; CD player available.

Performance Information

Performance opportunities available (frequency): Fully produced concerts (2 per year), informal concerts (3 per year), workshops (6 per year), onsite performances(5 per year), touring (1 per year).

Performances choreographed by: faculty, students, guests. *Recent guest choreographers:* Shirley Ririe, Morris Johnson, Mariusz Olszewsky.

Facilities

Number of studios available: 1. *Approximate studio dimensions and flooring:* 40' x 50' suspended stage step. *Performance facilities:* 600-seat theater.

DRAMA

Curriculum, Students, and Faculty

Required courses: speech, movement.

Elective courses: acting, Alexander technique, audition preparation, directing, drama criticism, improvisation, movement, musical theater, scene study, Stanislavski exercises, text analysis, voice, stage combat, make-up, mime.

Number of years required to complete program: 2. *Summer program not available. Selectivity for males:* approximately 60% admitted. *Selectivity for females:* approximately 33% admitted. *Total enrollment:* 100. *Entering class size:* 75. *Graduating class size:* 25.

Renowned alumni: Chris Orr.

Total full-time faculty: 1.

Audition Information

No audition fee. Audition consists of the following: cold readings, improvisation, movement class, group warm-up. *Dress requirements for males:* dressed for movement. *Dress requirements for females:* dressed for movement. *Repertoire that students should avoid?* Tunes from Disney movies (shop-worn Neil Simon/balcony scenes *Romeo and Juliet*.)

Audition evaluation criteria: vocal: tonality, expression/interpretation, musicality. Spoken: focus, clear objectives, projection, ease. Movement: energy, interpretation, ability to read combinations.

Performance Information

Performance opportunities available (frequency): fully produced performances (3 per year), informal performances (1 per year), casting is by audition.

Facilities

Rehearsal facilities and hours: shared space for early rehearsal, but generally unencumbered. *Number of theaters on campus:* 1. *Type and capacity:* 698.

MUSIC

Curriculum, Students, and Faculty

Unique or innovative music curriculum: together with 650 students in performing ensembles, we offer piano lab; music technology; music theory; history of jazz and popular music; music improvisation; private vocal instruction. *How are major teacher assignments made?* made by the school. Faculty is not informed of a student's teacher preference at the time of the audition. *28 lessons with major teacher. Study of secondary instrument or discipline is allowed.*

Selectivity for instruments or programs offered (rating): bassoon (open), choral singing (open), clarinet (open), composition (non-competitive), electronic music (non-competitive), flute or piccolo (open), French horn (open), jazz (competitive), oboe/English horn (open), percussion (open), saxophone (open), trombone (open), trumpet (open), tuba (open), voice (open).

Total enrollment: 642. *Entering class size:* 257. *Graduating class size:* 104. *Total full-time faculty:* 5. *Total part-time faculty:* 1. *Program contact person:* Bruce Becker.

Audition Information

Audition consists of the following: scales, music theory, arpeggios, sight reading, melodic dictation. *Instruments provided for:* percussionists. Any instrument is available for rental.

Performance opportunities available (frequency): recitals.

Facilities

Number of practice rooms and hours: 6; 7:00 am-5:00 pm. *Recital hall?* no. *Concert hall?* yes. *Recording studio?* yes.

LOLA AND RUDY PERPICH MINNESOTA CENTER FOR ARTS EDUCATION

6125 Olson Memorial Highway, Golden Valley MN 55422
Tel: 612-591-4700
Fax: 612-591-4747
Contact: Bev DeVos

General

Type of Institution: public, boarding, specialized. *Environment:* suburban. *Academic education is offered on-site.*

Total enrollment: 300. *Degrees offered:* high school diploma.

Entrance Requirements

Audition required: live. *Other requirements:* interview, essay.

Geographic restrictions: Minnesota residents only.

Services

Housing options: on-site dorms.

Support staff: college advisor, resident assistant, resident nurse, student affairs officer.

Comments

Public, statewide, 11th and 12th grades, Minnesota residents only.

DANCE

Curriculum, Students, and Faculty

Selectivity for males: approximately 60% admitted. *Selectivity for females:* approximately 60% admitted. *Total entollment:* 30. *Entering class size:* 15. *Graduating class size:* 15.

Renowned alumni: Jessica Muker, Stephen Petronio Co.

Total full-time faculty: 1. *Total part-time faculty:* 1. *List of current faculty and past affiliations:* Mary Harding, Zeron Dance Co., University of Minnesota; Chris Aiken, Body Logic, University of Minnesota. *Program contact person:* Mary Harding.

Audition Information

No audition fee. Audition consists of the following: improvisation, modern dance. *Accompanist provided. Cassette player available; CD player available.*

Performance Information

Performance opportunities available (frequency): fully produced concerts (4 per year), informal concerts (6 per year), on-site performances(1 per year).

Performances choreographed by: faculty, students, guests.

Facilities

Number of studios available: 1. *Approximate studio dimensions and flooring:* 60' x 45' Marley and spruce wooden floor. *Performance facilities:* black box theater.

DRAMA

Curriculum, Students, and Faculty

Number of years required to complete program: 2. *Summer program not available. Affiliation with a professional theater company: Southern Theater, use of their facility and staff.*

Selectivity for males: approximately 60% admitted. *Selectivity for females:* approximately 60% admitted. *Total enrollment:* 50. *Entering class size:* 25. *Graduating class size:* 25.

Total full-time faculty: 2. *Total part-time faculty:* 1. *List of current faculty and past affiliations:* Barbara Morin, Guthrie Theater; Tory Peterson, Arizona State.

Audition Information

No audition fee. Audition consists of the following: comedic monologue, improvisation, Shakespearean monologue, group warm-up, student can choose type of monologue (not required to perform one of each type).

Performance Information

Performance opportunities available (frequency): fully produced performances (1 per year), informal performances (2 per year), workshops (1 per year), off-site performances (1 per year), casting is assigned, by audition.

Recent guest artists: Punumbra Theater Company.

Facilities

Rehearsal facilities and hours: black box, performance classroom, 6:30 am-10:30 pm. *Number of theaters on campus:* 1. *Type and capacity:* black box 150.

MUSIC

Curriculum, Students, and Faculty

Unique or innovative music curriculum: very diverse—jazz, rock, electronic, classical. *How are major teacher assignments made?* made by the school. Faculty is not informed of a student's teacher preference at the time of the audition. ***May a student change major teachers during the course of study?*** never. ***Study of secondary instrument or discipline is allowed.***

Selectivity for instruments or programs offered (rating): accompanying (competitive), accordion (competitive), bagpipes (competitive), bassoon (competitive), choral conducting (competitive), choral singing (competitive), clarinet (competitive), composition (competitive), double bass (competitive), electronic music (competitive), flute or piccolo (competitive), French horn (competitive), guitar (competitive), harp (competitive), harpsichord (competitive), jazz (competitive), oboe/English horn (competitive), orchestral conducting (competitive), organ (competitive), percussion (competitive), piano (competitive), sacred music (competitive), saxophone (competitive), trombone (competitive), trumpet (competitive), tuba (competitive), viola (competitive), violin (competitive), violoncello (competitive), voice (competitive).

Total enrollment: 70. ***Entering class size:*** 35. ***Graduating class size:*** 35.

Total full-time faculty: 1. ***Total part-time faculty:*** 4. ***Program contact person:*** Jan Hunton.

Audition Information

No audition fee. Audition consists of the following: scales, orchestral excerpts, ensemble playing, improvisation.

Performance opportunities available (frequency): recitals.

Facilities

Number of practice rooms and hours: 12; 7:00 am-10:00 pm. ***Recital hall?*** yes. ***Recording studio?*** yes.

NEVADA

LAS VEGAS ACADEMY OF INTERNATIONAL STUDIES, PERFORMING AND VISUAL ARTS

315 South 7th, Las Vegas NV 89101
Tel: 702-799-7800
Fax: 702-799-7948

General

Type of Institution: magnet-public. ***Environment:*** urban.

Total enrollment: 1,231. ***Total student body from other countries:*** 1%. ***Degrees offered:*** high school diploma.

Entrance Requirements

Audition required: live. ***Other requirements:*** interview.

Geographic restrictions: all students in Clark County, NV.

Services

Support staff: college advisor.

DANCE

Curriculum, Students, and Faculty

Required courses: ballet, dance composition/choreography, dance theory, dance writing, research and criticism, jazz, master classes, pas de deux, variations.

Elective courses: African dance, dance history, historical dance, Spanish, tap.

Selectivity for males: approximately 60% admitted. ***Selectivity for females:*** approximately 60% admitted. ***Total entollment:*** 160. ***Entering class size:*** 36. ***Graduating class size:*** 30.

Renowned alumni: Ralph Perkins

Total full-time faculty: 4. ***Total part-time faculty:*** 6. ***List of current faculty and past affiliations:*** Jeanine Gallo, Harvard. ***Program contact person:*** Jeanine Gallo.

Audition Information

No audition fee. Audition consists of the following: ballet, modern dance. ***Accompanist not provided. Cassette player available; CD player available.***

Performance Information

Performance opportunities available (frequency): Fully produced concerts (4 per year), informal concerts (2 per year), workshops (4 per year), on-site performances(2 per year).

Performances choreographed by: faculty, students, guests.

Facilities

Number of studios available: 5. ***Approximate studio dimensions and flooring:*** 40' x 40' sprung wood with Marley. ***Performance facilities:*** 1,300-seat theater.

DRAMA

Curriculum, Students, and Faculty

Required courses: acting, audition preparation, directing, improvisation, make-up, mime, musical theater, speech, Stanislavski exercises, voice.

Number of years required to complete program: 4. *Summer program available. Selectivity for males:* approximately 60% admitted. *Selectivity for females:* approximately 60% admitted. *Total enrollment:* 300. *Entering class size:* 100. *Graduating class size:* 75.

Total full-time faculty: 5. *Total part-time faculty:* 1.

Audition Information

No audition fee. Audition consists of the following: a cappella singing, cold readings, comedic monologue, improvisation.

Performance Information

Performance opportunities available (frequency): fully produced performances (10 per year), informal performances (2 per year), workshops (2 per year), off-site performances (8 per year), casting is by audition.

Facilities

Type and capacity: proscenium 1,300.

MUSIC

Curriculum, Students, and Faculty

How are major teacher assignments made? made by the school. Faculty is not informed of a student's teacher preference at the time of the audition. *180 lessons with major teacher; 50 lessons with a teaching assistant. May a student change major teachers during the course of study?* possibly.

Total enrollment: 310. *Entering class size:* 45. *Graduating class size:* 40. *Countries most represented:* Asian.

Total full-time faculty: 6. *Total part-time faculty:* 20. *Program contact person:* Ed Jackson, Elizabeth Kamerin.

Audition Information

No audition fee. Audition consists of the following: scales, music theory, sight reading. *Instruments provided for:* percussionists.

Performance opportunities available (frequency): band (6 per year), chamber music (4 per year), opera workshops (1 per year), orchestral concerts (6 per year), touring (1 per year).

Facilities

Number of practice rooms and hours: 6; 10 hours per day. *Recital hall?* no. *Concert hall?* yes. *Recording studio?* yes.

PHILLIPS EXETER ACADEMY

20 Main Street, Exeter NH 03833
Tel: 603-777-3437
Fax: 603-777-4399
Email: admit@exeter.edu
Web: www.exeter.edu
Contact: Thomas Hassan

General

Type of Institution: coed, boarding. *Environment:* suburban.

Total enrollment: 992. *Total student body from other countries:* 12%. *Degrees offered:* high school diploma.

Entrance Requirements

Audition not required. Other requirements: interview, recommendation, essay. *Standardized test requirements:* SATI, 1100; SSAT, 85; TOEFL, 600.

Costs & Financial Aid

Percent of students receiving financial aid: 36%. *Types of scholarships and aid awarded:* need-based. *Loans available. Procedure for applying for loans:* financial aid forms. *Financial aid offered to international students.*

Services

Housing options: on-site dorms.

DANCE

Curriculum, Students, and Faculty

Required courses: dance composition/choreography, rehearsal, and performance.

DRAMA

Curriculum, Students, and Faculty

Elective courses: scene study, improvisation, musical theater, movement, verse drama.

MUSIC

Music theory, several performance ensembles.

ST. PAUL'S SCHOOL

325 Pleasant Street
Concord, NH 03301-2591
Tel: 603-229-4700
fax: 603-229-4771
Email: admissions@sps.edu
Web: www.sps.edu

General

Type of institution: coed, boarding. *Environment:* rural.

Total enrollment: 513. *Total student body from other countries:* 10%. *Degrees offered:* high school diploma.

Entrance Requirements

Audition not required. Other requirements: SSAT, interview, recommendations.

Costs & Financial Aid

Tuition, room, and board: $21,500. Tuition payment plans, merit scholarships, need-based.

Services

Housing options: on-site dorms.

Support staff: college advisor, dorm parent, psychological counselor, resident assistant, resident nurse.

DANCE/DRAMA/MUSIC

Conservatory-level preparation.

NEW JERSEY

NEW JERSEY GOVERNOR'S SCHOOL OF THE ARTS

Contact Information
The College of New Jersey
P.O. Box 7718, Ewing NJ 08628-0718
Tel: 609-771-3114
Fax: 609-637-5128
Email: NJGSA@TCNJ.edu
Contact: William A.L. Glenn

General

Environment: suburban.

Total enrollment of institution: 89. *Degrees offered:* certificate.

Entrance Requirements

Audition required: live, audio. *Other requirements:* interview, recommendation, essay.

Costs & Aid

Types of scholarships and aid awarded: full, merit-based, institutional aid.

Services

Housing options: on-site dorms.

Support staff: dorm parent.

DANCE

Curriculum, Students, and Faculty

Required courses: African dance, dance composition/choreography, dance history, jazz (5 classes per week), master classes, modern dance (5 classes per week), movement techniques, other world dance forms, rehearsal and performance, repertory (5 classes per week), Spanish, vernacular dance, modern dance partnering, dance theory, music.

Selectivity for males: approximately 10% admitted. *Selectivity for females:* approximately 10% admitted. *Total enrollment:* 12. *Entering class size:* 12. *Graduating class size:* 12.

Renowned alumni: Jody Kaplan, one female on Broadway, one male on Broadway. *Total full-time faculty:* 9. *Total part-time faculty:* 9. *List of current faculty and past affiliations:* members of Brazilian company, members of Limon Company, members of Harkness and Washington Ballet Companies; Jana Feinman, Hunter College; Kathryn Kearns, Penn State University; Lisa Twamley, Mercer County School of Performing Arts; Ernesta Corvino, Juilliard School, Metropolitan Opera Ballet, American Chamber Ballet. *Program contact person:* William A.L. Glenn.

Audition Information

No audition fee. Audition consists of the following: ballet, modern dance, prepared solo. *Accompanist not provided. Cassette player available; CD player available. Dress requirements for males:* leotards, tights or sweatpants. *Dress requirements for females:* leotard, tights.

Audition evaluation criteria: body awareness, time, space, sense of style, response to correction, performance/projection, clarity of form, preparation.

Performance Information

Performance opportunities available (frequency): Fully produced concerts (1 per week), informal concerts (1 per week), workshops (1 per week), on-site performances(1-2 per week).

Performances choreographed by: faculty, students

Facilities

Number of studios available: 1. *Performance facilities:* theater.

RED BANK REGIONAL HIGH SCHOOL PERFORMING ARTS PROGRAM

101 Ridge Road, Little Silver NJ 07739-1698
Tel: 732-842-8000
Contact: Wayne Rose

General

Type of Institution: magnet-public, specialized. *Environment:* suburban.

Total enrollment: 989. *Degrees offered:* high school diploma.

Entrance Requirements

Audition required: live. *Other requirements:* interview, recommendation.

Services

Housing options: family.

Support staff: college advisor, foreign student advisor, physical therapist, student affairs officer.

DANCE

Curriculum, Students, and Faculty

Required courses: anatomy, ballet, dance composition/choreography, dance history, dance theory, dance writing, research and criticism, historical dance, jazz, master classes, modern dance, movement techniques, nutrition, pointe, rehearsal and performance, repertory, modern dance partnering.

Elective courses: Spanish, tap.

Selectivity for males: approximately 60% admitted. *Selectivity for females:* approximately 60% admitted. *Total enrollment:* 22. *Entering class size:* 10. *Graduating class size:* 4. *Total part-time faculty:* 2. *List of current faculty and past affiliations:* T.J. Kuchon, Patricia Morton. *Program contact person:* Wayne Rose.

Audition Information

No audition fee. Audition consists of the following: ballet, modern dance, pas de deux, pointe works. *Accompanist not provided. Cassette player available; CD player available. Dress requirements for males:* black leotard, no jewelry. *Dress requirements for females:* black leotard, hair off the face, no jewelry.

Performance Information

Performance opportunities available (frequency): Fully produced concerts (2 per year), informal concerts (1 per year), workshops (2 per year), on-site performances (2 per year), touring (1 per year).

Performances choreographed by: faculty. *Recent guest choreographers:* Robin Becker, Laurie Abramson, Michael Byars.

Facilities

Number of studios available: 1. *Approximate studio dimensions and flooring:* 50' x 40' raised dance. *Performance facilities:* auditorium 120' x 80' stage.

DRAMA

Curriculum, Students, and Faculty

Required courses: acting, directing, drama criticism, dramaturgy, make-up, movement, speech, stage combat, text analysis, voice.

Number of years required to complete program: 4. *Summer program available. Affiliation with a professional theater company: internships with Count Basic Two River Theater.*

Selectivity for males: approximately 60% admitted. *Selectivity for females:* approximately 60% admitted. *Total enrollment:* 34. *Entering class size:* 11. *Graduating class size:* 4.

Renowned alumni: Brian Gaskel.

Total part-time faculty: 1. *List of current faculty and past affiliations:* Joseph Russo.

Audition Information

No audition fee. Audition consists of the following: cold readings, comedic monologue, improvisation, required monologue, movement class, Shakespearean monologue. *Dress requirements for males:* dark colors. *Dress requirements for females:* dark colors.

Performance Information

Performance opportunities available (frequency): fully produced performances (2 per year), informal performances (1 per year), workshops (2 per year), off-site performances (2 per year) casting is assigned, auditioned.

Recent guest artists: Rick Sordelet.

Facilities

Rehearsal facilities and hours: stage, available 80 minutes daily. *Number of theaters on campus:* 1. *Type and capacity:* 800.

MUSIC

Curriculum, Students, and Faculty

How are major teacher assignments made? Students may choose, made by the school. Faculty is not informed of a student's teacher preference at the time of the audition. *May a student change major teachers during the course of study?* never. *Study of secondary instrument or discipline is allowed.*

Selectivity for instruments or programs offered (rating): composition (competitive), piano (selective), voice (selective).

Total enrollment: 120. *Entering class size:* 32. *Graduating class size:* 19.

Total full-time faculty: 2. *Total part-time faculty:* 2. *Program contact person:* Wayne Rose.

Audition Information

No audition fee. Audition consists of the following: scales, music theory, rhythmic dictation, arpeggios, sight reading.

Facilities

Number of practice rooms and hours: 2. *Recital hall?* yes. *Concert hall?* yes. *Recording studio?* no.

SOMERSET COUNTY VOCATIONAL/ TECHNICAL HIGH SCHOOL

P.O. Box 6350, Bridgewater NJ 08807
Tel: 908-526-8900
Fax: 908-704-0784

General

Type of Institution: magnet-public, specialized. *Environment:* suburban.

Total enrollment of Institution: 634. *Degrees offered:* high school diploma, certificate.

Entrance Requirements

Audition required: live. *Other requirements:* interview, recommendation, photograph.

Costs & Financial Aid

Types of scholarships and aid awarded: partial, work/study.

Services

Housing options: family.

Support staff: college advisor, resident nurse.

DANCE

Curriculum, Students, and Faculty

Required courses: anatomy, ballet, dance composition/choreography, dance history, dance writing, research and criticism, historical dance, jazz, master classes, modern dance, movement techniques, nutrition, other world dance forms, rehearsal and performance, repertory, stagecraft.

Selectivity for males: most admitted, but not all. *Selectivity for females:* most admitted, but not all. *Total enrollment:* 14. *Entering class size:* 6. *Graduating class size:* 4.

Renowned alumni: Meghan Brazil, Teal Marx, Bethany Furmica, Rachel Evers, Stacey Meyers *Total part-time faculty:* 4. *List of current faculty and past affiliations:* Sheila Buttermore, Janet Danforth, Marylynn McAnally, Carol Bellis. *Program contact person:* Sheila Buttermore.

Audition Information

No audition fee. Audition consists of the following: ballet, modern dance, prepared solo, jazz phrase. *Accompanist not provided. Cassette player available; CD player available. Dress requirements for males:* solid leotard, tights. *Dress requirements for females:* solid leotard, tights.

Repertoire that students should avoid? hip-hop, funk.

Audition evaluation criteria: alignment, flexibility, vocabulary.

Performance Information

Performance opportunities available (frequency): Fully produced concerts (1 per year), informal concerts (2 per year), on-site performances(2-3 per year), touring (7-15 per year).

Performances choreographed by: faculty, students.

Facilities

Number of studios available: 2. *Approximate studio dimensions and flooring:* wood sprung with Marley floor. *Performance facilities:* dance studio w/ side and overhead lighting and wings; auditorium—full lighting, sets, etc.

DRAMA

Curriculum, Students, and Faculty

Required courses: acting, audition preparation, drama criticism, dramaturgy, improvisation, mime, movement, musical theater, scene study, speech, Stanislavski exercises, voice.

Elective courses: directing, make-up, stage combat, verse drama.

Number of years required to complete program: 2-4. *Summer program available. Selectivity for males:* approximately 33% admitted. *Selectivity for females:* approximately 10% admitted. *Total enrollment:* 31. *Entering class size:* 18. *Graduating class size:* 11.

Total full-time faculty: 1. *Total part-time faculty:* 5. *List of current faculty and past affiliations:* Art Niel, Franklin Villagers Theater; Vince DiMura, McCarthy Theater.

Audition Information

No audition fee. Audition consists of the following: cold readings, comedic monologue, improvisation, required monologue, staff/student interviews. *Dress requirements for males:* comfortable, loose-fitting clothes and sneakers. *Dress requirements for females:* comfortable, loose-fitting clothes and sneakers.

Audition evaluation criteria: Technical proficiency: knowledge of lines, volume, memorization, props, costumes, presentation, organization, enunciation. Creative Proficiency: realization of character, truth, interpretation, comprehension, emotional depth, physical choices, energy, overall quality.

Performance Information

Performance opportunities available (frequency): fully produced performances (2 per year), informal performances (3 per year), workshops (1 per marking period), off-site performances (20-30 per year), casting is by audition.

Recent guest artists: James Brennan, Louis Zorich, Tommy Re.

Facilities

Rehearsal facilities and hours: auditorium theater, studio, used evenings and weekends. *Number of theaters on campus:* 2. *Type and capacity:* theater 650, black box 75.

NEW YORK

EMMA WILLARD SCHOOL

285 Pawling Avenue, Troy NY 12180
Tel: 518-274-3478
Fax: 518-274-0923
Email: asuvm.inre@asu.edu

General

Type of Institution: day, girls day and boarding. *Environment:* suburban. *Academic education is offered on-site.*

Total enrollment: 275. *Total student body from other countries:* 15%. *Degrees offered:* high school diploma.

Entrance Requirements

Standardized test requirements: SSAT.

Costs & Financial Aid

Application fee: $25. *Tuition:* $13,900.

Percent of students receiving financial aid: 46%. *Types of scholarships and aid awarded:* full, partial, need-based. *Forms required for scholarships:* FFS, income tax return. *Loans available.*

Services

Housing options: on-site dorms.

Support staff: college advisor, dorm parent, financial aid advisor, resident assistant, resident nurse.

F.H. LAGUARDIA H.S. OF MUSIC AND THE ARTS

100 Amsterdam Avenue, New York NY 10023
Tel: 212-496-0700
Fax: 212-724-5748

General

Type of Institution: public, specialized. *Environment:* urban.

Total enrollment: 2,498. *Degrees offered:* high school diploma.

Entrance Requirements

Audition required: live.

Geographic restrictions: New York City resident.

Services

Housing options: off-campus housing.

Support staff: college advisor, financial aid advisor, foreign student advisor, psychological counselor.

DANCE

Curriculum, Students, and Faculty

Required courses: character (2 classes per week, 1 year to complete), ballet (5 classes per week, 4 years to complete), dance composition/choreography (1 class per week, 2 years to complete), historical dance (1 class per week, 1 year to complete), jazz (1 class per week, 1 year to complete), men's class (2 classes per week, 1 year to complete), Graham-based modern dance (5 classes per week, 4 years to complete), pointe, rehearsal and performance (5 classes per week, 1 year to complete), tap (1 class per week, 1 year to complete).

Selectivity for males: approximately 10% admitted. *Selectivity for females:* approximately 10% admitted. *Total enrollment:* 222. *Entering class size:* 60. *Graduating class size:* 45. *Countries most represented:* China, Korea, Russia, Taiwan.

Renowned alumni: Bruce Marks, Arthur Mitchell, Ben Vereen, Eliot Feld, Desmond Richardson.

Total full-time faculty: 12. *Total part-time faculty:* 1. *List of current faculty and past affiliations:* Elisa King; Penny Frank; Deborah Zall-Graham; Brunilda Ruiz, Joffrey; Michelle Benash, American Ballet Theatre; Joey Smith, Eliot Feld. *Program contact person:* Ms. Evelyn Rivera.

Audition Information

No audition fee. Audition consists of the following: ballet, modern dance, prepared solo, *Accompanist provided. Cassette player available; CD player available.*

Audition evaluation criteria: body structure, dance techniques, performance

Performance Information

Performance opportunities available (frequency): Fully produced concerts (8 per senior year), informal concerts (8 per year), touring (8 per year).

Performances choreographed by: faculty, students, guests. *Recent guest choreographers:* Pat Catterson, Shapiro and Smith, Septime Weber, Jacqulyn Buglisi, Eleo Pomari, Janet Rowthorn, Joe Lanteri, Luis Fuente, Eddie Shellman, James Sutton, HT Chen.

Facilities

Number of studios available: 5. *Approximate studio dimensions and flooring:* 2,000 sq.ft. sprung floor. *Performance facilities:* 1 black box-50-60 seating, 1 theater (500 seats), 1 concert hall (1,100 seats).

DRAMA

Curriculum, Students, and Faculty

Required courses: acting, audition preparation, improvisation, make-up, movement, musical theater, scene study, Stanislavski exercises, text analysis, theater history, verse drama, voice, career counseling, diction, performance on stage.

Number of years required to complete program: 3-4. *Summer program not available. Affiliation with a professional theater company: Lincoln Center Institute, National Actors Theatre, Manhattan Theatre Club.*

Selectivity for males: approximately 10% admitted. *Selectivity for females:* approximately 10% admitted. *Total enrollment:* 290. *Entering class size:* 70. *Graduating class size:* 65. *Countries most represented:* China, Korea, Russia, Taiwan.

Renowned alumni: Al Pacino, Jennifer Aniston.

Total full-time faculty: 9. *List of current faculty and past affiliations:* Marian Pearce, Vassar, Columbia, Harvard, O'Neill Foundation.

Audition Information

No audition fee. Audition consists of the following: cold readings, improvisation, group warm-up, 2 one-minute monologues. *Dress requirements for males:* loose, comfortable clothing. *Dress requirements for females:* loose, comfortable clothing. *Audition evaluation criteria:* prepared readings, unprepared reading, voice and diction, use of self, energy, intensity, imagination.

Performance Information

Performance opportunities available (frequency): fully produced performances (1), informal performances (7), workshops (3), casting is by audition.

Recent guest artists: Royal National Theatre of Great Britain; City Opera.

Facilities

Number of theaters on campus: 2. *Type and capacity:* theater 491, concert hall.

MUSIC

Curriculum, Students, and Faculty

Unique or innovative music curriculum: 2 Orchestras, 2 concert bands, 4 string ensembles, 2 jazz ensembles. Courses in: music technology, jazz improvisation, conducting, orchestration, instrumental instruction classes. *How are major teacher assignments made?* according to teacher availability.

Total enrollment: 955. *Entering class size:* 240. *Graduating class size:* 198. *Countries most represented:* China, Korea, Russia, Taiwan.

Renowned alumni: Dr. Leon Botstein; James Conlan; Murray Perahia; Shari Lewis.

Total full-time faculty: 21. *Program contact person:* Ms. Evelyn Rivera.

Audition Information

No audition fee. Audition consists of the following: sight reading. *Instruments provided for:* harpists, percussionists.

Repertoire that students should avoid? no band or orchestral parts, solo only.

Facilities

Recital hall? yes. *Concert hall?* yes. *Recording studio?* yes.

LINCOLN HIGH SCHOOL

375 Kneeland Avenue, Yonkers NY 10704
Tel: 914-376-8400
Fax: 914-376-8414

General

Environment: suburban.

Degrees offered: high school diploma.

Entrance Requirements

Audition required: live.

Services

Support staff: college advisor, student affairs officer.

Comments

Two music instructors have CDs that have made the jazz charts.

DANCE

Curriculum, Students, and Faculty

Required courses: African dance, anatomy, character, ballet, dance composition/choreography, dance history, dance theory, dance writing, research and criticism, jazz, master classes, Cunningham-based, Graham-based, Limon-based modern dance, body conditioning, nutrition, rehearsal and performance, repertory, tap.

Elective courses: Labanotation, music, pointe, Spanish, stagecraft.

Selectivity for males: most admitted, but not all. *Selectivity for females:* most admitted, but not all. *Total enrollment:* 115. *Entering class size:* 25.

Renowned alumni: Maria Alvarez, Hartford School of Ballet; Rachel Saffer, The Sky is the Limit).

Total full-time faculty: 1. *List of current faculty and past affiliations:* Karan Tribou, Arts in Education Performing Arts High School workshops at Purchase College, Logrea Dance Academy, Westchester Ballet Company; Judy Rubin, Martha Graham School, Ballet Hispanics. *Program contact person:* Karan Tribou.

Audition Information

No audition fee. Audition consists of the following: ballet, improvisation, modern dance, orthopedic evaluation, prepared solo for choreography class only completed medical forms. *Accompanist not provided. Cassette player available; CD player available. Dress requirements for males:* sport shorts, dark colored jazz pants, white t-shirt. *Dress requirements for females:* leotard, leggings, optional short dance skirt.

Repertoire that students should avoid? no, the more varied the better.

Performance Information

Performance opportunities available (frequency): Fully produced concerts (2 per year), informal concerts (2 per year), workshops (3 or more per year), on-site performances (3 or more per year), touring (2 or more), auditions (solo and ensemble) offer performance and participation in high school dance festivals (Philadelphia/Miami).

Performances choreographed by: faculty, students, guests. *Recent guest choreographers:* Reginald Yates, Joe Cavise, Mette Spaniardi.

Facilities

Number of studios available: 1. *Approximate studio dimensions and flooring:* 36' x 24' bravo coverings over suspended floor. *Performance facilities:* dance studio and large stage (auditorium).

DRAMA

Curriculum, Students, and Faculty

Number of years required to complete program: 3. *Summer program not available. No affiliation with a professional theater company.*

Selectivity for males: most admitted, but not all. *Selectivity for females:* most admitted, but not all. *Total enrollment:* 90. *Entering class size:* 30.

Renowned alumni: Robert Ruiz.

Total full-time faculty: 1. *List of current faculty and past affiliations:* Barbara Litt.

Audition Information

Audition consists of the following: cold readings, group warm-up. *Dress requirements for males:* comfortable clothes. *Dress requirements for females:* comfortable clothes.

Performance Information

Performance opportunities available (frequency): fully produced performances (2 per year), informal performances (frequently), workshops (frequently) assigned, auditioned.

Facilities

Rehearsal facilities and hours: small stage in classroom and stage in auditorium. *Number of theaters on campus:* 1. *Type and capacity:* proscenium.

THE MASTERS SCHOOL

49 Clinton Avenue, Dobbs Ferry NY 10522
Tel: 914-693-1400
Fax: 914-693-1230
Email: admissions@e-mail.themastersschool.com
Contact: Bill Andres, Susan Hendicks

General

Type of Institution: private, coed, boarding. *Environment:* suburban. *Academic education is offered on-site.*

Total enrollment: 360. *Total student body from other countries:* 35%. *Degrees offered:* high school diploma.

Entrance Requirements

Audition not required Other requirements: interview, recommendation, essay. *Standardized test requirements:* ISEE; SSAT.

Costs & Financial Aid

Application fee: $40. *Deposit:* $1,000.

Types of scholarships and aid awarded: need-based. *Forms required for scholarships:* income tax return. *Loans available. Other aid available to international students:* none.

Services

Housing options: on-site dorms.

Support staff: college advisor, dorm parent, financial aid advisor, foreign student advisor, housing advisor, psychological counselor, resident nurse.

DANCE

Curriculum, Students, and Faculty

Required courses: ballet (3 classes per week), dance composition/choreography, dance history, dance theory, dance writing, research and criticism, jazz (3 classes per week), master classes, movement techniques, rehearsal and performance (5 classes per week), Humphrey-Weidman (3 classes per week).

Selectivity for males: admit all who apply. *Selectivity for females:* admit all who apply.

Renowned alumni: We have no "renowned" dance alumni, but 6 to 12 dancers who either make their living in the professional dance world or who are dance majors in college.

Total full-time faculty: 1. *Total part-time faculty:* 1. *List of current faculty and past affiliations:* Karen Kristin, The Tamaris-Nagrin Dance Co. *Program contact person:* Karen Kristin.

Audition Information

No audition fee. Audition consists of the following: ballet, modern dance, prepared solo, jazz and tap combinations. *Accompanist not provided. Cassette player available; CD player available.*

Audition evaluation criteria: technical ability, creativity, willingness to work, love of dance.

Performance Information

Performance opportunities available (frequency): Fully produced concerts (2 per year), workshops (1 per year), on-site performances (5 in a 9 month period of time).

Performances choreographed by: faculty, students, guests. *Recent guest choreographers:* Bick Goss-NYC, Karen Atherly-NYC.

Facilities

Number of studios available: 1. *Approximate studio dimensions and flooring:* 28' x 36' sprung wood. *Performance facilities:* theater (450 seat).

DRAMA

Curriculum, Students, and Faculty

Required courses: speech.

Elective courses: acting, audition preparation, directing, improvisation, make-up, movement, musical theater, scene study.

Number of years required to complete program: 4. *Summer program not available.*

Selectivity for males: admit all who apply. *Selectivity for females:* admit all who apply.

Total full-time faculty: 2. *Total part-time faculty:* 1. *List of current faculty and past affiliations:* Mary Anne Haskin, Bruce Robbins, Jennifer Stasko.

Audition Information

No audition fee.

Audition evaluation criteria: varies from production to production.

Performance Information

Performance opportunities available (frequency): fully produced performances (3 per year), informal performances (1 per month), workshops (5 per year), off-site performances (1 per year), casting is by audition.

Recent guest artists: Sallie Sills, Darcy Gittell, Amy Miller, Jennifer von Meyenhauser.

Facilities

Type and capacity: main stage thrust 450, theater in the round 200.

MUSIC

Curriculum, Students, and Faculty

How are major teacher assignments made? Students may choose, made by the school according to teacher availability. Faculty is informed of a student's teacher preference at the time of the audition. *28 lessons with major teacher. May a student change major teachers during the course of study?* possibly. *Study of secondary instrument or discipline is allowed.*

Selectivity for instruments or programs offered (rating): bassoon (open), choral singing (open), clarinet (open), flute or piccolo (open), guitar (open), jazz (open), oboe/English horn (open), percussion (open), piano (open), saxophone (open), trumpet (open), viola (open), violin (open), violoncello (open), voice (open).

Renowned alumni: Marin Alsop.

Total full-time faculty: 2. *Total part-time faculty:* 6. *Program contact person:* Nancy Theeman.

Audition Information

Instruments provided for: percussionists. Limited number of string and woodwind instruments.

Facilities

Number of practice rooms and hours: 10; 7:00 am-9:30 pm. *Recital hall?* yes. *Concert hall?* yes. *Recording studio?* yes.

Comments

Music is an integral part of the life of our school. One-third of the students study privately and over half of them are involved in a performing group. Our philosophy is that music should be available to everyone regardless of previous experience or level. Because of the school's proximity to New York City, qualified students may also enroll in the Saturday pre-college programs at Mannes, Manhattan, and Juilliard.

NASSAU BOCES CULTURAL ARTS CENTER

239 Cold Spring Road, Syosset NY 11791
Tel: 516-364-1177
Fax: 516-364-6947
Email: afavard@mail.nasboces.org

General

Type of Institution: magnet-public, specialized. *Environment:* suburban. *Academic education is offered on-site.*

Total enrollment: 200. *Degrees offered:* certificate.

Entrance Requirements

Audition required: live. *Other requirements:* interview, recommendation, essay.

Geographic restrictions: Nassau and Suffolk County school districts.

Costs & Financial Aid

Types of scholarships and aid awarded: full. *Procedure for applying for loans:* tuition paid by home school district, all at no cost to student/parent other than school taxes.

Services

Housing options: family.

Support staff: college advisor, psychological counselor, resident nurse.

DANCE

Curriculum, Students, and Faculty

Required courses: ballet, dance history, jazz, master classes, modern dance, music, nutrition, pas de deux, pointe, tap, variations.

Elective courses: dance composition/choreography, martial arts, ethnic dance.

DRAMA

Curriculum, Students, and Faculty

Required courses: acting, audition preparation, movement, musical theater, speech, voice.

Elective courses: dramaturgy, martial arts, mime, scene study, stage combat.

PROFESSIONAL CHILDREN'S SCHOOL

132 West 60th Street, New York NY 10023
Tel: 212-582-3116
Fax: 212-956-3295
Contact: Kelye Bush

General

Type of Institution: private, day, coed. *Environment:* urban. *Academic education is offered on-site.*

Total enrollment: 200. *Total student body from other countries:* 26%. *Degrees offered:* high school diploma.

Entrance Requirements

Other requirements: interview, recommendation, essay. *Standardized test requirements:* ISEE; TOEFL.

Costs & Financial Aid

Types of scholarships and aid awarded: full, partial, need-based. *Forms required for scholarships:* FFS, income tax return. *Financial aid offered to international students. Percent of international students receiving scholarships:* 26%.

Services

Housing options: off-campus housing, family.

Support staff: college advisor, foreign student advisor.

Comments

The students at PCS are either professionals or pre-professionals receiving their specialized training in the arts at one of New York City's other institutions such as School of American Ballet (SAB), Mannes, Manhattan, or Juilliard Pre-College, for example. PCS is the only fully accredited, non-profit school in the United States to offer an academic college preparatory education specifically designed for young performers and students preparing for careers in the arts and in competitive sports. The program combines "guided study" to enable students to meet professional engagements that occur during school hours.

PROFESSIONAL PERFORMING ARTS SCHOOL

328 West 48th Street, New York NY 10036
Tel: 212-247-8652
Fax: 212-247-7514
Email: mgc@mail.conz.com
Web: ppas.dorsai.org
Contact: Kim Bruno

General

Type of Institution: public, specialized. *Environment:* urban.

Total enrollment: 330. *Degrees offered:* high school diploma.

Entrance Requirements

Audition required: live. *Other requirements:* interview, recommendation, essay.

Services

Support staff: college advisor, financial aid advisor, psychological counselor, resident nurse, student affairs officer.

DANCE

Curriculum, Students, and Faculty

Required courses: African dance, ballet, jazz, Graham-based, Horton-based modern dance, body conditioning, nutrition, rehearsal and performance, repertory, Spanish.

Selectivity for males: approximately 10% admitted. *Selectivity for females:* approximately 10% admitted. *Total enrollment:* 80. *Graduating class size:* 10.

Renowned alumni: Clyde Archer, won first place in the National Arts Recognition Talent School. *Total part-time faculty:* 8. *List of current faculty and past affiliations:* Cassandra Phifer, Dance Theater of Harlem; Nancy Turano, Ballet Hispanico; Earl Mosley, Alvin Ailey Repertory Ensemble; Derrick Minter, Alvin Ailey Repertory Ensemble. *Program contact person:* Kim Bruno.

Audition Information

Audition consists of the following: ballet, modern dance, orthopedic evaluation. *Dress requirements for males:* dance attire. *Dress requirements for females:* dance attire.

Audition evaluation criteria: applicants will be judged on their ability to dance and their ability to respond to movement vocabulary.

Performance Information

Performance opportunities available (frequency): fully produced concerts (1 per year), workshops (2 per year), on-site performances (every June).

Performances choreographed by: faculty.

Facilities

Number of studios available: 6. *Approximate studio dimensions and flooring:* 32' x 50' sprung wood with Marley covering. *Performance facilities:* studio and university theater space.

DRAMA

Curriculum, Students, and Faculty

Required courses: acting, audition preparation, drama criticism, improvisation, mime, movement, scene study, speech, Stanislavski exercises, theatrical dance, text analysis, voice.

Elective courses: directing, make-up, musical theater, stage combat.

Number of years required to complete program: 4. *Summer program not available. Affiliation with a professional theater company: partnership with The Actors Institute, New York City.*

Selectivity for males: approximately 10% admitted. *Selectivity for females:* approximately 10% admitted. *Total enrollment:* 150. *Graduating class size:* 20.

Renowned alumni: Mike Damus, Daisy Egan, Claire Danes, Gaby Hoffman.

Total part-time faculty: 10. *List of current faculty and past affiliations:* Sean Nelson.

Audition Information

Audition consists of the following: a cappella singing, cold readings, comedic monologue, required monologue. *Dress requirements for males and females:* clothing that allows free movement *Audition evaluation criteria:* Applicants will be judged on their demonstrated ability to interpret character, express emotions, and work with direction.

Performance Information

Performance opportunities available (frequency): fully produced performances (2 per year), informal performances (2 per year), workshops (all year long), touring musical theater repertory company, casting is by audition.

Facilities

Rehearsal facilities and hours: classrooms, 2 rehearsal studios, flexible hours. *Number of theaters on campus:* 1. *Type and capacity:* proscenium 600.

MUSIC

Curriculum, Students, and Faculty

Unique or innovative music curriculum: Jazz curriculum taught by professional jazz musicians. *How are major teacher assignments made?* made by the school. *May a student change major teachers during the course of study?* possibly. *Study of secondary instrument or discipline is allowed.*

Total enrollment: 100. *Graduating class size:* 15. *Total part-time faculty:* 15. *Program contact person:* Kim Bruno.

Audition Information

Audition consists of the following: scales, music theory, rhythmic dictation, ensemble playing, arpeggios, sight reading, melodic dictation. *Instruments provided for:* percussionists; pianists, amplifier.

Performance opportunities available (frequency): band (3 per year), band (3 per year), jury examinations (2 per year), orchestral concerts (3 per year), recitals (3 per year), chorus (3 per year).

Facilities

Number of practice rooms and hours: 5; 1:30 pm-3:30 pm. (after school hours to be arranged) *Recital hall?* yes. *Concert hall?* yes. *Recording studio?* no.

SAINT ANN'S SCHOOL

129 Pierrepont Street, Brooklyn NY 11201
Tel: 718-522-1660
Fax: 718-522-2599
Email: lkaufman@saintanns.k12.ny.us
Web: www.saintanns.k12.ny.us

General

Type of Institution: private, day, coed. *Environment:* urban.

Total enrollment: 298. *Degrees offered:* high school diploma.

Entrance Requirements

Audition not required. Other requirements: interview. School's own English exam required.

Costs & Financial Aid

Application fee: $100. *Deposit:* $1,500. *Tuition:* $15,400.

Percent of students receiving financial aid: 15%. *Types of scholarships and aid awarded:* full, partial, need-based. *Forms required for scholarships:* PFS from school. *Procedure for applying for loans:* through Admissions Office.

Services

Support staff: college advisor, foreign student advisor, resident nurse, student affairs officer.

DANCE

Curriculum, Students, and Faculty

Elective courses: African dance, dance composition/choreography, modern dance, stagecraft, tap, repertory, variations, Chinese dance, pointe. *Total enrollment:* 66.

Renowned alumni: Katherine Healy, Martha Enson, Leslie Yancey. *Total part-time faculty:* 12. *List of current faculty and past affiliations:* Edissa Weeks, Avila/Weeks Dance, Jane Comfort and Company, Bill T. Jones, Arnie Zane Dance Company, Elizabeth Streb, Ringside. *Program contact person:* Sharon Lamazor.

Audition Information

No audition fee.

Performance Information

Performance opportunities available (frequency): fully produced concerts (4 per year), informal concerts (several per year), workshops (several), on-site performances(1-2 per year).

Facilities

Number of studios available: 2. *Approximate studio dimensions and flooring:* 44' x 30' wood, 27' x 33' wood. *Performance facilities:* Theater—on Marley Floor.

DRAMA

Curriculum, Students, and Faculty

Elective courses: acting, character, costume design, modern dance, musical theater, playwriting, technical theater, voice, Shakespeare, puppetry, directing.

Number of years required to complete program: 4. *Summer program not available. Total enrollment:* 188.

Renowned alumni: Denis Markell, Joie Lee, Jennifer Connolly, John Cullum, Stephen Mailer, Sam Kass, Akira Goldsman, Adrienne Hurd, Mia Sara.

Total part-time faculty: 12. *List of current faculty and past affiliations:* Nancy Reardon, NYU, Shakespeare in the Park; Sharon Lamazor, Hartman Theater Company.

Performance Information

Performance opportunities available (frequency): fully produced performances (3 per year), informal performances (frequently), casting is by audition.

Recent guest artists: Ming Cho Lee.

Facilities

Rehearsal facilities and hours: school hours, evenings, weekends in theater, classrooms, dance studios. *Number of theaters on campus:* 1. *Type and capacity:* 150.

MUSIC

Curriculum, Students, and Faculty

Unique or innovative music curriculum: Starts in preschool. Depth of education increases as students get older.

Selectivity for instruments or programs offered (rating): choral singing, clarinet, composition, flute or piccolo, guitar, jazz, oboe/English horn, piano, trombone, trumpet, violin, violoncello, voice.

Total enrollment: 288.

Renowned alumni: Erika Nickrenz, Nick Eanet, Justin Chen, Wendy Chen, Ben Yarmolinsky, Dan Gilbert, Simone Dinnerstein, Joshua Kohl, Beatrice Affran, Victoria Eanet, Beth Kiper, Michael Dimond, Barbara Brousal, Sam Brody, Paul Garment. *Total part-time faculty:* 10. *Program contact person:* James Busy and Erika Nickrenz.

Facilities

Recital hall? yes. *Concert hall?* yes. *Recording studio?* no.

NORTH CAROLINA

NORTH CAROLINA SCHOOL OF THE ARTS

1533 Mail Street, Winston-Salem NC 27127-2188
Tel: 336-770-3291
Fax: 330-770-3370
Web: www.ncarts.edu
Contact: Carol Palm

General

Type of Institution: high school, college, conservatory. *Environment:* urban. *Academic education is offered on-site.*

Total enrollment: 1,034. *Total student body from other countries:* 4%. *Degrees offered:* high school diploma, college.

Entrance Requirements

Audition required: live, audio, video. *Other requirements:* interview, recommendation, essay, photograph. *Standardized test requirements:* ACT; SATI; TOEFL, 550.

Costs & Financial Aid

Application fee: $35. *Deposit:* $100. *Tuition:* $5,194. *Medical fee:* $300. *Other fees:* $989 activity and health.

Types of scholarships and aid awarded: full, partial, merit-based, need-based, named, institutional aid, government aid, work/study, gig office. *Forms required for scholarships:* FAFSA, income tax return. *Loans available.*

Services

Housing options: on-site dorms.

Support staff: college advisor, dorm parent, financial aid advisor, housing advisor, physical therapist, psychological counselor, resident assistant, resident nurse, student affairs officer.

DANCE

Curriculum, Students, and Faculty

Required courses: character, ballet, dance composition/choreography, dance history, improvisation, jazz, make-up, men's class, modern dance, movement techniques, body conditioning, Pilates, music, pas de deux, pointe, rehearsal and performance, repertory, technical theater, variations, ballet repertory.

Selectivity for males: approximately 10% admitted. *Selectivity for females:* approximately 10% admitted. *Total enrollment:* 204. *Graduating class size:* 53. *Percent international:* 7%. *Countries most represented:* Spain.

Renowned alumni: Michael Thomas, Mary Cochram, Janie Parker, Trey McIntyre, Victor Barbee, Jaime Martinez, Jeanne Ruddy, Mel A. Tomlinson, Christine Spizzo, Katita Waldo, Keith Roberts, Mark Dendy, Edward Stierle, Peter Pucci.

Total full-time faculty: 14. *List of current faculty and past affiliations:* Susan McCullough, Trish Casey, Warren Conover, Fanchon Cordell, Brenda Daniels, Nina Danilova, Melisssa Hayden, Melinda Lawrence, Dianne Markham, Lynn Messick, Gyula Pandi, Frank Smith, Gina Vidal, Duncan Noble, Karla Wolfangle. *Program contact person:* Susan McCullaugh.

Audition Information

No audition fee. Audition consists of the following: ballet, modern dance, pointe works, prepared solo, contemporary and/or students own choreography to classical music. *Accompanist provided. Cassette player available; CD player available. Dress requirements for males:* practice clothes, no jewelry *Dress requirements for females:* practice clothes, no jewelry, hair should be worn up.

Repertoire that students should avoid? no jazz.

Audition evaluation criteria: potential to pursue a professional career.

Performance Information

Performance opportunities available (frequency): Fully produced concerts (5 per year, consisting of 4-10 performances), workshops (3 per year), on-site performances (13-15 per year).

Performances choreographed by: faculty, students, guests.

Facilities

Number of studios available: 9. *Performance facilities:* Stevens Center, 1,500 seats. Agnes De Mille Theater, 200 seats.

DRAMA

Curriculum, Students, and Faculty

Required courses: acting, Alexander technique, audition preparation, improvisation, movement, musical theater, scene study, speech, Stanislavski exercises, verse drama, voice.

MUSIC

Conservatory training in all orchestral and keyboard instruments.

NORTHWEST SCHOOL OF THE ARTS

1415 Beatties Ford Road, Charlotte NC 28216
Tel: 704-343-5500
Fax: 704-343-5593
Email: laborde1@ix.netcom.com
Contact: Henry Grossek

General

Type of Institution: magnet-public. *Environment:* urban. *Academic education is offered on-site.*

Total enrollment: 1,054. *Degrees offered:* high school diploma.

Entrance Requirements

Audition not required.

Geographic restrictions: Northwest School of the Arts serves students in all parts of Charlotte, NC and Meckenburg County.

Services

Housing options: off-campus housing.

Support staff: college advisor, financial aid advisor, foreign student advisor.

DANCE

Curriculum, Students, and Faculty

Required courses: ballet, improvisation, Cunningham-based, Graham-based, Limon-based, Nikolais-based modern dance, rehearsal and performance.

Elective courses: dance composition / choreography, dance history, historical dance, jazz, pointe, repertory.

Selectivity for males: most admitted, but not all. *Selectivity for females:* approximately 60% admitted. *Total enrollment:* 564.

Total full-time faculty: 3. *List of current faculty and past affiliations:* Laura Brown, Louisville Ballet, Bay Ballet, North Carolina Dance Theater; Nicole Papciak, Brosseau Dance Works. *Program contact person:* Nicole Papciak.

Audition Information

No audition fee. Audition consists of the following: ballet, improvisation, modern dance, pointe works, prepared solo optional. *Accompanist not provided. Cassette player not available; CD player not available. Dress requirements for males:* t-shirt tucked into sweatpants, shorts, or tights. *Dress requirements for females:* black leotard, pink tights, hair pulled neatly and securely away from face.

Audition evaluation criteria: appearance, poise, technical ability, overall performance.

Performance Information

Performance opportunities available (frequency): Fully produced concerts (at least 2 per year), informal concerts (frequently), workshops (frequently), on-site performances(2-3 per year).

Performances choreographed by: faculty, students, guests. *Recent guest choreographers:* Martha Connerton.

Facilities

Number of studios available: 3. *Approximate studio dimensions and flooring:* wood sprung, wood sprung with Marley, wood sprung. *Performance facilities:* black box theater, auditorium.

DRAMA

Curriculum, Students, and Faculty

Required courses: acting, audition preparation, directing, drama criticism, improvisation, journaling, Meisner exercises, playwriting, Robert Lewis exercises, scene study, speech, Stanislavski exercises, technical theater, voice, UTA exercises.

Elective courses: dance.

Number of years required to complete program: 4. *Summer program not available. Affiliation with a professional theater company: Theatre Charlotte Children' Theatre, Blumenthal Performing Arts Center. Our school regulary collabrates with area theater companies. In the spring, we produce a full scale musical and perform at Charlotte's Booth Theatre. Collaboration with other companies is on-going.*

Selectivity for males: admit all who apply. *Selectivity for females:* admit all who apply. *Total enrollment:* 746.

Audition Information

Audition consists of the following: cold readings, comedic monologue, improvisation, 2 contrasting monologues one minute each. *Dress requirements for males:* casual slacks, dress shirt, dress shoes, no denim jeans. *Dress requirements for females:* slacks, dress, skirt, hose, dress shoes, no denim jeans. *Audition evaluation criteria:* confidence, level of selection, memorization, focus, believability.

Performance Information

Performance opportunities available (frequency): fully produced performances (frequently), informal performances (frequently), off-site performances (frequently) casting is assigned, auditioned. We attempt for each student to perform on stage at least once.

Recent guest artists: Jennifer Saylor.

Facilities

Rehearsal facilities and hours: auditorium, black box theater, choral facilities. *Number of theaters on campus:* 2. *Type and capacity:* black box 200, auditorium 650.

MUSIC

Curriculum, Students, and Faculty

Total enrollment: 996.

Total full-time faculty: 5. *Program contact person:* Linda Howard.

OHIO

FORT HAYES METROPOLITAN EDUCATION CENTER

546 Jack Gibbs Boulevard, Columbus OH 43215
Tel: 614-365-6681
Fax: 614-365-6988
Email: skriska@iwaynet.net
Web: www.fhayes.com

General

Type of Institution: magnet-public. *Environment:* urban. *Academic education is offered on-site.*

Total enrollment: 607. *Degrees offered:* high school diploma, certificate.

Entrance Requirements

Geographic restrictions: must live in school district.

Services

Support staff: career counselor.

DANCE

Curriculum, Students, and Faculty

Required courses: African dance, anatomy, ballet, dance composition/choreography, dance history, dance writing, research and criticism, jazz, Labanotation, modern dance, nutrition, other world dance forms, pointe, rehearsal and performance, tap.

Total full-time faculty: 2. *Total part-time faculty:* 1. *List of current faculty and past affiliations:* China White, Ohio State University (OSU), The Dance Theatre of Harlem; Yolanda Connor, OSU, University Dance Company; Darlene Suhay, OSU, Zivili Ohio Dance, National Dance Association. *Program contact person:* China White.

Audition Information

No audition fee. Audition consists of the following: ballet, improvisation, modern dance, warm-up. *Accompanist not provided. Cassette player available; CD player available.*

Performance Information

Performance opportunities available (frequency): Fully produced concerts, informal concerts workshops, on-site performances, touring.

Performances choreographed by: faculty, students.

Facilities

Number of studios available: 3. *Approximate studio dimensions and flooring:* 20' x 50' sprung wooden floors with Marley, 20' x 50' sprung wooden floors with Marley, 30' x 40' sprung wood floors with Marley. *Performance facilities:* one performance facility/theater—4 alternative performance spaces.

DRAMA

Curriculum, Students, and Faculty

Required courses: acting, Alexander technique, directing, drama criticism, dramaturgy, make-up, martial arts, movement, musical theater, scene study, stage combat, Stanislavski exercises, text analysis, theater history, verse drama, voice.

Elective courses: speech.

Number of years required to complete program: 2-4. *Summer program not available. Affiliation with a professional theater company: students work with professional theater companies as volunteers and interns.*

Selectivity for males: admit all who apply. *Selectivity for females:* admit all who apply. *Total enrollment:* 182.

Renowned alumni: Valerie Accetta, Doug Noe, Cheryl Gaysunas, Bill Partton, Rachael Embers, Amy Anderson, Mary Carter, Wayne Weber, Stephanie Thomas.

Total full-time faculty: 3. *List of current faculty and past affiliations:* Dr. Phillip Wilson, Ohio State University; Todd Decker, Interlochen; Barb Young.

Audition Information

No audition fee. Audition consists of the following: cold readings, improvisation, movement class, dialects, ear training, Q & A, follow directions. *Dress requirements for males:* dress professionally and be able to move. *Dress requirements for females:* dress professionally and be able to move. *Repertoire that students should avoid?* Overuse of profanity or inappropriate material for age group.

Audition evaluation criteria: follow directions, projection, articulation, desire, attitude, vocal range, movement, communication, focus, energy.

Performance Information

Performance opportunities available (frequency): fully produced performances (4 per year), informal performances (30 per year), workshops (15 per year), off-site performances (10 per year), casting is by audition.

Recent guest artists: David Cryer, David Morris, Robert Post, Stuart Paton, Jeanine Thompson.

Facilities

Rehearsal facilities and hours: 2 studio spaces, one theater space, available 180 hours total. *Number of theaters on campus:* 1. *Type and capacity:* proscenium with a thrust 300.

MUSIC

Curriculum, Students, and Faculty

How are major teacher assignments made? made by the school. Faculty is not informed of a student's teacher preference at the time of the audition. *May a student change major teachers during the course of study?* often. *Study of secondary instrument or discipline is allowed.*

Selectivity for instruments or programs offered (rating): bassoon (competitive), choral singing (open), clarinet (selective), composition (highly selective), double bass (highly selective), electronic music (highly selective), flute or piccolo (highly selective), French horn (highly selective), guitar (highly selective), jazz (highly selective), oboe/English horn (highly selective), percussion (highly selective), piano (selective), saxophone (highly selective), trombone (highly selective), trumpet (highly selective), tuba (highly selective), viola (highly selective), violin (highly selective), violoncello (highly selective), voice (highly selective).

Total enrollment: 30.

Renowned alumni: David Tolley, Kevin Turner, Andy Woodson.

Total full-time faculty: 5. *Program contact person:* David King.

Audition Information

No audition fee. Audition consists of the following: improvisation. *Instruments provided for:* percussionists; guitar amplifiers, bass amplifiers, keyboard, computers.

Repertoire that students should avoid? anything from Andrew Lloyd Weber. *Performance opportunities available (frequency):* band, jury examinations, orchestral concerts, recitals, touring, chorus.

Facilities

Number of practice rooms and hours: 6; 8:00 am-6:00 pm. *Concert hall?* yes. *Recording studio?* yes.

SCHOOL FOR CREATIVE AND PERFORMING ARTS

1310 Sycamore Street, Cincinnati OH 45210
Tel: 513-632-5900
Fax: 513-632-5969
Web: www.scpa.org
Contact: Stephen Finn

General

Type of Institution: magnet-public. *Environment:* urban.

Total enrollment: 950. *Total student body from other countries:* 1%. *Degrees offered:* high school diploma.

Entrance Requirements

Audition required: live. *Other requirements:* recommendation, essay, photograph.

Services

Support staff: career counselor.

DANCE

Curriculum, Students, and Faculty

Required courses: ballet, jazz, pointe (1 class per week), variations.

Elective courses: African dance.

Selectivity for males: approximately 60% admitted. *Selectivity for females:* approximately 60% admitted. *Total enrollment:* 75.

Renowned alumni: Heather McBride, Jeffrey Sams, Jay Goodlett.

Total full-time faculty: 3. *Total part-time faculty:* 1. *Program contact person:* Sheila Cohen.

Audition Information

No audition fee. Audition consists of the following: ballet.

Performance Information

Performance opportunities available (frequency): fully produced concerts (annually), workshops (semi annually), on-site performances (monthly).

Performances choreographed by: faculty, students, guests.

Facilities

Number of studios available: 3. *Approximate studio dimensions and flooring:* 20' x 40' hung wood. *Performance facilities:* 500-seat theater.

DRAMA

Curriculum, Students, and Faculty

Required courses: acting, speech, voice.

Elective courses: directing, martial arts, movement.

Summer program not available. No affiliation with a professional theater company. Selectivity for males: approximately 60% admitted. *Selectivity for females:* approximately 60% admitted. *Total enrollment:* 400.

Renowned alumni: Rocky Carroll.

Total full-time faculty: 4. *Total part-time faculty:* 1. *List of current faculty and past affiliations:* David White, Ensemble Theatre of Cincinnati.

Audition Information

No audition fee. Audition consists of the following: cold readings, improvisation.

Performance Information

Performance opportunities available (frequency): fully produced performances (3 per year), informal performances (3 per year), workshops (3 per year), casting is by audition.

Facilities

Number of theaters on campus: 2. *Type and capacity:* proscenium 500, black box 150.

MUSIC

Curriculum, Students, and Faculty

How are major teacher assignments made? made by the school. Faculty is not informed of a student's teacher preference at the time of the audition. *May a student change major teachers during the course of study?* usually. *Study of secondary instrument or discipline is allowed.*

Selectivity for instruments or programs offered (rating): bassoon (non-competitive), choral singing (competitive), clarinet (non-competitive), composition (competitive), double bass (non-competitive), electronic music (competitive), flute or piccolo (non-competitive), French horn (non-competitive), guitar (non-competitive), harp (non-competitive), harpsichord (non-competitive), jazz (competitive), oboe/English horn (non-competitive), organ (non-competitive), percussion (competitive), piano (non-competitive), saxophone (non-competitive), trumpet (non-competitive), tuba (non-competitive), viola (non-competitive), violin (non-competitive), violoncello (non-competitive), voice (competitive).

Total enrollment: 300.

Total full-time faculty: 8. *Total part-time faculty:* 4. *Program contact person:* John Gardner.

Audition Information

Audition consists of the following: scales, sight reading, improvisation.

Facilities

Number of practice rooms and hours: 10. *Recital hall?* yes. *Concert hall?* yes. *Recording studio?* no.

OKLAHOMA

BOOKER T. WASHINGTON HIGH SCHOOL

1631 East Woodrow Place, Tulsa OK 74105
Tel: 918-428-6000, ext. 227
Fax: 918-428-6001

General

Type of Institution: magnet-public. *Environment:* urban.

Total enrollment: 1,200. *Degrees offered:* high school diploma, international baccalaureate.

Entrance Requirements

Audition required. Other requirements: interview.

Services

Housing options: off-campus housing.

Support staff: college advisor, resident nurse.

DRAMA

Curriculum, Students, and Faculty

Elective courses: acting.

Number of years required to complete program: 2. *Summer program not available. No affiliation with a professional theater company. Selectivity for males:* approximately 60% admitted. *Selectivity for females:* approximately 60% admitted.

Total full-time faculty: 1. *List of current faculty and past affiliations:* Barbara Wilson.

Audition Information

No audition fee. Audition consists of the following: cold readings, comedic monologue. *Repertoire that students should avoid?* no.

Performance Information

Performance opportunities available (frequency): fully produced performances (2 per year), informal performances (5 per year), auditioned.

Facilities

Number of theaters on campus: 1. *Type and capacity:* auditorium 750.

CLASSEN SCHOOL OF ADVANCED STUDIES

1901 North Ellison, Oklahoma City OK 73106
Tel: 405-556-5070
Fax: 405-556-5080
Email: jtbsmb@aol.com
Contact: Brian Staples or Lois Townsend

General

Type of Institution: magnet-public. *Environment:* urban.

Total enrollment: 991. *Total student body from other countries:* 1%. *Degrees offered:* high school diploma, international baccalaureate.

Entrance Requirements

Audition required: live. *Other requirements:* interview, recommendation.

Geographic restrictions: all applicants from Oklahama County area accepted.

No tuition.

Services

Support staff: college advisor, financial aid advisor, foreign student advisor, psychological counselor.

DANCE

Curriculum, Students, and Faculty

Required courses: anatomy, ballet (2-3 classes per week), dance composition/choreography, dance history, dance theory, dance writing, research and criticism, historical dance, Labanotation, master classes, men's class (2-3 classes per week), modern dance (2-3 classes per week), Graham-based modern dance (2-3 classes per week), Limon-based modern dance (2-3 classes per week), music, nutrition, pointe (1-3 classes per week), rehearsal and performance, repertory, stagecraft.

Elective courses: African dance, jazz, Indian dance, tap, Middle Eastern dance, Native American dance, vernacular dance.

Selectivity for males: approximately 10% admitted. *Selectivity for females:* approximately 10% admitted. *Total enrollment:* 225. *Entering class size:* 15. *Graduating class size:* 8. *Countries most represented:* Germany, Brazil.

Total full-time faculty: 2. *Total part-time faculty:* 5. *List of current faculty and past affiliations:* Nancy Trait-Lira, Danni Kelly, Robyn Johnson Connors, Suze Cheever, Cynthia Bona Perry. *Program contact person:* Nancy Trait-Lira.

Audition Information

No audition fee. Audition consists of the following: ballet, improvisation, modern dance, prepared solo must be choreographed by applicant. *Accompanist not provided. Cassette player available; CD player available. Dress requirements for males:* leotard or close-fitting t-shirt, tights or shorts. *Dress requirements for females:* leotard, tights or close-fitting t-shirt and shorts.

Audition evaluation criteria: alignment, flexibility, technical skills, musicality, locomotor skills/movement coordination, improvisational skills/creativity, self discipline, motivation.

Performance Information

Performance opportunities available (frequency): Fully produced concerts (2-3 per year), informal concerts (1-2 per year), workshops (1-8 per year), on-site performances (2-3 per year), touring (9-10 per year).

Performances choreographed by: faculty, students, guests. *Recent guest choreographers:* Tina Kambour, Joe Medrano, Frank Chavez, Alvin Ailey.

Facilities

Number of studios available: 2. *Approximate studio dimensions and flooring:* 40' x 40' raised wood flooring with purchased dance floor, 24' x 40'. *Performance facilities:* auditorium.

DRAMA

Curriculum, Students, and Faculty

Required courses: acting, directing, musical theater, speech.

Elective courses: improvisation, make-up, movement, voice, text analysis, mime, acting, voice, Alexander technique.

Number of years required to complete program: 7. *Summer program not available. Selectivity for males:* approximately 33% admitted. *Selectivity for females:* approximately 33% admitted. *Total enrollment:* 455. *Entering class size:* 112. *Graduating class size:* 80.

Renowned alumni: Sarah Hoy.

Total full-time faculty: 2. *Total part-time faculty:* 1.

Audition Information

No audition fee. Repertoire that students should avoid? no poems.

Audition evaluation criteria: projection, energy, focus, reading skills.

Performance Information

Performance opportunities available (frequency): fully produced performances (5 per year), informal performances (weekly), workshops (monthly), off-site performances (4 per year), casting by audition.

Recent guest artists: Christopher Maier, Olivia Heminway, Doobie Pooter.

Facilities

Rehearsal facilities and hours: auditorium stage, classroom, classroom stage, during classtime and after school 2:30 pm-4:30 pm or 5:30 pm. *Number of theaters on campus:* 1. *Type and capacity:* auditorium 600.

MUSIC

Curriculum, Students, and Faculty

Unique or innovative music curriculum: music technology, bell choirs, ensembles. *How are major teacher assignments made?* made by the school, according to teacher preference. Faculty is informed of a student's teacher preference at the time of the audition. *May a student change major teachers during the course of study?* possibly. *Study of secondary instrument or discipline is allowed.*

Selectivity for instruments or programs offered (rating): accompanying (competitive), bassoon (highly selective), choral singing (highly selective), clarinet (highly selective), composition (highly selective), double bass (selective), electronic music (competitive), flute or piccolo (highly selective), French horn (highly selective), guitar (highly selective), harp (selective), jazz (highly selective), oboe/English horn (highly selective), orchestral conducting (competitive), organ (highly selective), percussion (highly selective), piano (selective), sacred music (competitive), saxophone (highly selective), trombone (highly selective), trumpet (highly selective), tuba (highly selective), viola (selective), violin (selective), violoncello (selective), voice (highly selective), bells (selective).

Total enrollment: 770. *Entering class size:* 97. *Graduating class size:* 40.

Total full-time faculty: 6. *Total part-time faculty:* 2. *Program contact person:* Rebecca Lindley.

Audition Information

No audition fee. Audition consists of the following: scales, orchestral excerpts, music theory, rhythmic dictation, arpeggios, sight reading, melodic dictation, repertoire. *Instruments provided for:* harpists, percussionists, bells.

Required repertoire: 1 vocal piece in a foreign language, 1 vocal Broadway piece of student's choice, memorized solo for wind and percussion instruments. *Repertoire that students should avoid?* only play from standard teaching repertory for piano, avoid rock and popular music for voice. *Performance opportunities available (frequency):* chamber music (frequently), band (frequently), jury examinations (frequently), orchestral concerts, recitals, touring (frequently).

Facilities

Recital hall? no. *Concert hall?* yes. *Recording studio?* no.

PENNSYLVANIA

ABINGTON FRIENDS SCHOOL

575 Washington Lane, Jenkintown PA 19046
Tel: 215-886-4350
Fax: 215-886-9143
Email: aps.pvt.k12.pa.us
Contact: Karen Loder

General

Type of Institution: day coed. *Religious affiliation:* Quaker. *Environment:* suburban.

Total enrollment: 680. *Total student body from other countries:* 2%. *Degrees offered:* high school diploma.

Entrance Requirements

Audition not required.

Costs & Financial Aid

Application fee: $16. *Deposit:* $725. *Tuition:* $12,000.

Percent of students receiving financial aid: 35%. *Types of scholarships and aid awarded:* full, partial, merit-based, need-based. *Forms required for scholarships:* income tax return, SSS form. *Financial aid offered to international students. Percent of international students receiving scholarships:* 80%. *Other aid available to international students:* need-based.

Services

Support staff: college advisor, financial aid advisor, housing advisor, psychological counselor, resident nurse, student affairs officer.

DRAMA

Curriculum, Students, and Faculty

Elective courses: acting, technical theater.

Summer program not available. Percent international: 1%.

List of current faculty and past affiliations: Megan Bellwoa-Hollinger, Philadelphia Drama Guild; Fran Brookes, Peoples Light & Theatre Company.

Audition Information

No audition fee.

Performance Information

Performance opportunities available (frequency): fully produced performances (2 per year), informal performances (1 per year), casting is by audition.

Facilities

Number of theaters on campus: 2. *Type and capacity:* black box 150, proscenium 400.

PENNSYLVANIA GOVERNORS SCHOOL FOR THE ARTS

519 Oaklake Road, New Kinsington PA 15068
Tel: 412-339-4443
Fax: 412-337-7161
Contact: Doug Woods

General

Type of institution: governors, public. *Environment:* suburban.

Total enrollment: 200. *Degrees offered:* certificate.

Entrance Requirements

Audition required: live, audio, video. *Other requirements:* interview, essay.

Services

Housing options: on-site dorms.

Support staff: housing advisor, physical therapist, psychological counselor, resident assistant, resident nurse, student affairs officer.

DANCE

Curriculum, Students, and Faculty

Required courses: ballet, pointe, modern dance.

THE PITTSBURGH HIGH SCHOOL FOR THE CREATIVE AND PERFORMING ARTS

925 Brushton Avenue, Pittsburgh PA 15208
Tel: 412-247-7860
Fax: 412-247-7895
Email: jvalco@pps.pgh.pa.us
Web: emma.capa.pps.pgh.pa.us
Contact: Ronald Jacobs

General

Type of Institution: magnet-public. *Environment:* urban.

Total enrollment: 300. *Total student body from other countries:* 1%. *Degrees offered:* high school diploma, certificate.

Entrance Requirements

Audition required: live. *Other requirements:* interview, recommendation.

Costs & Financial Aid

Procedure for applying for loans: audition. *Percent of international students receiving scholarships:* 1%. *Other aid available to international students:* Full tuition to exchange students.

Services

Support staff: college advisor, financial aid advisor, resident nurse.

DRAMA

Curriculum, Students, and Faculty

Required courses: acting.

Number of years required to complete program: 4. *Summer program not available. Selectivity for males:* approximately 60% admitted. *Selectivity for females:* approximately 33% admitted. *Total enrollment:* 63. *Entering class size:* 14. *Graduating class size:* 14.

Renowned alumni: Ron McClelland; Jane Swtieri, Duquesne University; Michael Fuller, Harvard.

Total full-time faculty: 1. *Total part-time faculty:* 7. *List of current faculty and past affiliations:* Billy Porter.

Audition Information

No audition fee. Audition consists of the following: cold readings, movement class. *Repertoire that students should avoid?* Shakespearean monologue.

Performance Information

Performance opportunities available (frequency): fully produced performances (2 per year), informal performances (2 per year), workshops (4 per year), off-site performances (5-6 per year), casting is by audition.

Recent guest artists: Dan Kamon, Billy Wilson, Jeff Shade.

Facilities

Number of theaters on campus: 1. *Type and capacity:* proscenium 350.

MUSIC

Curriculum, Students, and Faculty

Unique or innovative music curriculum: Computer Lab, Composer's Concert, New Music Ensemble, AP Theory. Faculty is informed of a student's teacher preference at the time of the audition. *May a student change major teachers during the course of study?* possibly. *Study of secondary instrument or discipline is allowed.*

Selectivity for instruments or programs offered (rating): accompanying (selective), composition (highly selective), electronic music (open), percussion (competitive), piano (highly selective), trombone (selective), violin (open).

Total enrollment: 104 *Entering class size:* 32. *Graduating class size:* 32. *Percent international:* 1%. *Countries most represented:* Sweden.

Renowned alumni: Billy Porter, George Russell, Mary Ann McCormick.

Total full-time faculty: 2. *Total part-time faculty:* 13. *Program contact person:* John Garrick

Audition Information

No audition fee. Audition consists of the following: scales, orchestral excerpts, music theory ensemble playing, arpeggios, improvisation, melodic dictation. *Instruments provided for:* percussionists; pianists, all wind, strings.

Facilities

Number of practice rooms and hours: 5. *Recital hall?* yes. *Concert hall?* yes. *Recording studio?* yes.

SCHOOL FOR THE PERFORMING AND VISUAL ARTS

3325 Cherry Street, Erie PA 16505
Tel: 814-871-6489
Contact: Renee Vicary

General

Type of Institution: magnet-public. *Environment:* urban.

Degrees offered: high school diploma.

Entrance Requirements

Audition required: live *Other requirements:* interview, recommendation.

Geographic restrictions: City of Erie.

Services

Support staff: physical therapist, psychological counselor, resident nurse.

DANCE

Curriculum, Students, and Faculty

Required courses: ballet (2 classes per week), dance composition/choreography, dance theory, dance writing research and criticism, jazz (2 classes per week), master classes, modern dance, Graham-based modern dance, Limon-based modern dance, pointe (1 class per week), rehearsal and performance, tap (1 class per week).

Elective courses: African dance, movement techniques, body conditioning, Pilates, music, Indian dance, Spanish, stagecraft, Middle Eastern dance, East Indian dance.

Selectivity for males: most admitted, but not all. *Selectivity for females:* most admitted, but not all. *Countries most represented:* India, Denmark.

Total full-time faculty: 1. *Total part-time faculty:* 3. *List of current faculty and past affiliations:* Carrie Burns, Lake Erie Ballet Company; Carrie Donkowski; Sharon Filon, formerly Graham Dance Company. *Program contact person:* Renee Vicary.

Audition Information

Audition consists of the following: ballet, improvisation, medical. *Accompanist provided. Cassette player available; CD player available. Dress requirements for males:* black pants, white t-shirt *Dress requirements for females:* black leotard, pink tights.

Audition evaluation criteria: physicality, flexibility, and musicality.

Performance Information

Performance opportunities available (frequency): Fully produced concerts (every other year), informal concerts (2-3 per year), workshops (1 per year), on-site performances(3-4 per year), touring (1 per year).

Performances choreographed by: faculty, students, guests. *Recent guest choreographers:* Michael Marcu, Carrie Burns Frase.

Facilities

Number of studios available: 1. *Approximate studio dimensions and flooring:* wood subflooring, Marley surface. *Performance facilities:* school stage / auditorium, seating capacity: 1,000.

DRAMA

Curriculum, Students, and Faculty

Required courses: acting, audition preparation, drama criticism, improvisation, make-up, mime, movement, scene study, Stanislavski exercises, text analysis, voice.

Elective courses: directing, verse drama.

Number of years required to complete program: 4. *Summer program not available. No affiliation with a professional theater company. Selectivity for males:* approximately 60% admitted. *Selectivity for females:* approximately 60% admitted.

Total full-time faculty: 1.

Audition Information

Audition consists of the following: cold readings, comedic monologue, improvisation, group warm-up. *Dress requirements for males:* comfortable clothing. *Dress requirements for females:* comfortable clothing. *Audition evaluation criteria:* Pantomime: appropriate movement, animation, flexibility. Improvisation: originality, realism, spontaneity. Monologue: projection, clarity, characterization. General consideration: stage presence, focus, ability to take direction. Interview: other activities, motivation, grades, technical work.

Performance Information

Performance opportunities available (frequency): fully produced performances (4 per year), informal performances (2 per year), workshops (2 per year), off-site performances (1 per year), casting is by audition.

Recent guest artists: Scottie Davis, Squonk Opera.

Facilities

Rehearsal facilities and hours: classroom, auditorium, rehearsal 2 hours daily, 3-4 hours during production week.

ROGERS HIGH SCHOOL

15 Wickham Road, Newport RI 02840
Tel: 401-847-6235

General

Type of Institution: public. *Environment:* urban.

Total enrollment: 900. *Degrees offered:* high school diploma.

Entrance Requirements

Audition required: live. *Other requirements:,* recommendation, essay.

Services

Support staff: financial aid advisor, psychological counselor.

DANCE

Curriculum, Students, and Faculty

Elective courses: African dance, dance composition / choreography, jazz, nutrition, rehearsal and performance, tap.

Selectivity for males: admit all who apply. *Selectivity for females:* approximately 60% admitted. *Total enrollment:* 150.

Total full-time faculty: 1. *List of current faculty and past affiliations:* Diana Dinsmore. *Program contact person:* Diana Dinsmore.

Audition Information

Audition consists of the following: prepared solo, combination taught. *Accompanist not provided. Cassette player available; CD player available.*

Performance Information

Performance opportunities available (frequency): Fully produced concerts (3 per year), informal concerts (1-2 per year), workshops (5 per year), on-site performances(3-5 per year), touring (3-5 per year), parades, etc.

Performances choreographed by: faculty, students, guests. *Recent guest choreographers:* Abdel Salaom, Adrienne Hawkins.

Facilities

Number of studios available: 1. *Approximate studio dimensions and flooring:* 30' x 30' stage-wood floor. *Performance facilities:* auditorium.

FINE ARTS CENTER

School District of Greenville County
1613 West Washington Street, Greensville SC 29601
Tel: 864-241-3327
Fax: 864-241-3502

General

Type of Institution: public, specialized. *Environment:* urban.

Total enrollment: 250. *Degrees offered:* high school diploma.

Entrance Requirements

Audition required: live. *Other requirements:* interview, recommendation, essay.

Services

Support staff: career counselor.

DANCE

Curriculum, Students, and Faculty

Required courses: ballet (2 classes per week), Cunningham-based, Horton-based, Limon-based modern dance.

Selectivity for males: most admitted, but not all. *Selectivity for females:* most admitted, but not all. *Total enrollment:* 29.

Renowned alumni: Kevin Boseman, Alvin Ailey, Jared Phillips, Merce Cunningham Company; Kim Sikorski, Eglevsky Ballet. *Total part-time faculty:* 2. *List of current faculty and past affiliations:* Andrew Kuharsky, Atlanta Ballet, Les Grands Ballet Canadiens, and Joffery II; Jan Woodword. *Program contact person:* Andrew Kuharsky.

Audition Information

No audition fee. Audition consists of the following: ballet, modern dance. *Cassette player available; CD player available. Dress requirements for males:* loose-fitting clothes if student does not have dance clothes. *Dress requirements for females:* loose-fitting clothes if student does not have dance clothes.

Audition evaluation criteria: rotation, alignment, flexibility, musicality, elevation, ability to learn, performance, feet, creativity, concentration.

Performance Information

Performance opportunities available (frequency): Fully produced concerts (1 per year), informal concerts (2 per year), on-site performances (2 per year).

Performances choreographed by: faculty, students, guests. *Recent guest choreographers:* Beth McNeill.

Facilities

Number of studios available: 1. *Approximate studio dimensions and flooring:* 60' x 28' Marley over wood. *Performance facilities:* small black box theater.

DRAMA

Curriculum, Students, and Faculty

Required courses: acting, Alexander technique, movement, scene study, speech, Stanislavski exercises, verse drama, voice.

Number of years required to complete program: 4. *Summer program not available. Affiliation with a professional theater company: Apprenticeship with the Warehouse Theater, South Carolina's only Equity Theatre.*

Selectivity for males: most admitted, but not all. *Selectivity for females:* approximately 60% admitted. *Total enrollment:* 35.

Total full-time faculty: 1. *List of current faculty and past affiliations:* Christine Keefe, Duke University.

Audition Information

No audition fee. Dress requirements for males: casual, but pulled together, no ripped jeans. *Dress requirements for females:* casual, but pulled together, no ripped jeans. *Audition evaluation criteria:* presence, diction, energy, commitment, risk-taking, physical connection to material.

Performance Information

Performance opportunities available (frequency): fully produced performances (2 per year), informal performances (1-2 per year) casting is assigned, auditioned. Depends on the show.

Recent guest artists: Mimi Wyche, Kimilee Bryant.

Facilities

Rehearsal facilities and hours: 9:00 am-3:00 pm for classes, as scheduled for rehearsals and other events. *Number of theaters on campus:* 1. *Type and capacity:* black box 150.

MUSIC

Curriculum, Students, and Faculty

Unique or innovative music curriculum: Curriculum is taught by professional musicians and geared toward developing students through individual and small group instruction, rather than through large ensembles. *How are major teacher assignments made?* Students may choose, according to teacher availability. *Study of secondary instrument or discipline is allowed.*

Selectivity for instruments or programs offered (rating): bassoon (non-competitive), clarinet (non-competitive), double bass (competitive), flute or piccolo (non-competitive), French horn (non-competitive), guitar (competitive), jazz (competitive), oboe/English horn (non-competitive), percussion (non-competitive), saxophone (non-competitive), trombone (non-competitive), trumpet (non-competitive), tuba (non-competitive), viola (competitive), violin (competitive), violoncello (competitive), voice (competitive).

Total enrollment: 102.

Renowned alumni: Elizabeth Bishop, Kimilee Bryant.

Total full-time faculty: 5. *Program contact person:* Gary Robinson.

Audition Information

Audition consists of the following: scales, orchestral excerpts, ensemble playing, arpeggios, sight reading. *Instruments provided for:* percussionists.

Facilities

Number of practice rooms and hours: 5; school hours. *Recital hall?* yes. *Concert hall?* no. *Recording studio?* no.

TENNESSEE

GERMANTOWN HIGH SCHOOL

Fine Arts Department
7653 Old Poplar Pike, Germantown TN 38138
Tel: 901-755-7775
Fax: 901-755-6951
Email: efblue@aol.com

General

Type of Institution: public, specialized. *Environment:* suburban. *Academic education is offered on-site.*

Total enrollment: 2,500. *Degrees offered:* high school diploma.

Entrance Requirements

Audition not required.

Services

Housing options: off-campus housing.

Support staff: college advisor.

DRAMA

Curriculum, Students, and Faculty

Elective courses: acting, speech, voice.

Summer program available. No affiliation with a professional theater company. Total enrollment: 350. *Entering class size:* 150. *Graduating class size:* 35. *Percent international:* 2%.

Renowned alumni: Ross Jolly, Steve Hayslip, Dorothea Hough Nissen, Martin Cutler, Karen Keadle, Dan McCleary, Beth Ann Steele, Jeff Webb, Kelly Griffith, Wes Day.

Total full-time faculty: 5. *List of current faculty and past affiliations:* E. Frank Bluestein, GHS-TV, Opryland USA; Leonid B. Mazok, Moscow Technology University Theatre; Elizabeth Anne Brown.

Audition Information

No audition fee.

Performance Information

Performance opportunities available (frequency): fully produced performances (4 per year), informal performances (2 per year), workshops (10 per year), off-site performances (2 per year), casting is by audition.

Recent guest artists: Charles Strosse, Jarome Lawrence, David Leosl, Kathy Bates.

Facilities

Rehearsal facilities and hours: 1 lab space. *Number of theaters on campus:* 1. *Type and capacity:* proscenium 300.

MUSIC

Curriculum, Students, and Faculty

How are major teacher assignments made? Students may choose. *10 lessons with major teacher; Study of secondary instrument or discipline is allowed.*

Total enrollment: 300. *Entering class size:* 100. *Graduating class size:* 50. *Percent international:* 2%. *Countries most represented:* Mexico, Russia.

Total full-time faculty: 2. *Program contact person:* E. Frank Bluesteis.

Audition Information

Audition fee? no audition fee.

Facilities

Number of practice rooms and hours: 8; until 5:00 pm.

GOVERNOR'S SCHOOL FOR THE ARTS

Middle Tennessee State University
P.O. Box 38, Murfreesboro TN 38132
Tel: 615-898-2223
Fax: 615-898-2223
Email: gschool@mtsu.edu

General

Type of Institution: governor's.

Total enrollment of institution: 23. *Degrees offered:* certificate.

Entrance Requirements:

Audition required: live. *Other requirements:* interview, recommendation.

Costs & Financial Aid

Types of scholarships and aid awarded: institutional aid. *Procedure for applying for loans:* recommended by school's teacher, fill out application provided by Tennessee Governor's Schools through guidance counselor (high schools), dance teacher, private music, band, drama teachers.

Services

Housing options: on-site dorms.

Support staff: college advisor, dorm parent, resident assistant, resident nurse, student affairs officer.

DANCE

Curriculum, Students, and Faculty

Required courses: character (2 classes per week), ballet (6 classes per week), dance theory, jazz (1 class per week), Graham-based dance (6 classes per week), Limon-based (6 classes per week), nutrition, pas de deux (1 class per week), pointe (6 classes per week), rehearsal and performance, Spanish (2 classes per week).

Selectivity for males: approximately 10% admitted. *Selectivity for females:* approximately 33% admitted. *Total enrollment:* 13. *Total full-time faculty:* 3. *List of current faculty and past affiliations:* Nancy Turpin, Ballet West, Chicago Opera, Memphis Ballet, Nashville Ballet; Sharyn Wood, Pennsylvania Youth Ballet, Memphis Classical Ballet, Nashville Ballet; Cathleen Cruz. *Program contact person:* James T. Brooks.

Audition Information

No audition fee. Audition consists of the following: ballet, pointe works. *Accompanist provided. Audition evaluation criteria:* consistent quality of technique through entire class—good placement, footwork, alignment, and quick learning.

Performance Information

Performance opportunities available (frequency): fully produced concerts (1 for 4 week session), informal concerts (2 for 4 week session).

Performances choreographed by: faculty, guests. *Recent guest choreographers:* Paul Vasterling—Nashville Ballet, Cathleen Cruz.

Facilities

Number of studios available: 2. *Approximate studio dimensions and flooring:* 80' x 80' wooden. *Performance facilities:* theater.

DRAMA

Curriculum, Students, and Faculty

Required courses: acting, improvisation, make-up, mime, movement, scene study, stage combat, verse drama, voice.

Number of years required to complete program: 4 weeks. *Summer program available. No affiliation with a professional theater company. Selectivity for males:* approximately 10% admitted. *Selectivity for females:* approximately 10% admitted. *Total enrollment:* 32.

Total full-time faculty: 8.

Audition Information

No audition fee. Audition consists of the following: cold readings, comedic monologue, *Repertoire that students should avoid?* contemporary/plays with characters in students' age-range.

Performance Information

Performance opportunities available (frequency): fully produced performances (1), informal performances (2), workshops (5), auditioned.

Recent guest artists: Ronun Foreman, Voices of the South.

Facilities

Rehearsal facilities and hours: proscenium theater, 8:00 am-6:00 pm. *Number of theaters on campus:* 2. *Type and capacity:* studio 180, proscenium 1,000.

MUSIC

Curriculum, Students, and Faculty

Unique or innovative music curriculum: only offered to Tennessee Students. *How are major teacher assignments made?* made by the school;

Faculty is not informed of a student's teacher preference at the time of the audition. *Study of secondary instrument or discipline is allowed.*

Selectivity for instruments or programs offered (rating): bassoon (selective), choral singing (highly selective), clarinet (highly selective), double bass (competitive), flute or piccolo (highly selective), French horn (highly selective), jazz (competitive), oboe/English horn (highly selective), percussion (selective), piano (highly selective), saxophone (highly selective), trombone (selective), trumpet (highly selective), tuba (highly selective), viola (competitive), violin (competitive), violoncello (competitive), voice (non-competitive).

Total enrollment: 134. *Total full-time faculty:* 17. *Total part-time faculty:* 10. *Program contact person:* James T. Brooks.

Audition Information

No audition fee. Audition consists of the following: scales, arpeggios, sight reading. *Instruments provided for:* no harpists.

Facilities

Recital hall? yes. *Concert hall?* yes. *Recording studio?* no.

SCHOOL OF PERFORMING AND VISUAL ARTS AT CHATTANOOGA HIGH

1331 Dallas Road, Chattanooga TN 37405
Tel: 423-209-5942
Fax: 423-209-5942
Contact: Kathy Allison

General

Type of Institution: magnet-public. *Environment:* urban. *Academic education is offered on-site.*

Total enrollment: 200. *Degrees offered:* high school diploma.

Entrance Requirements

Audition required: live. *Other requirements:* interview, recommendation, essay.

Geographic restrictions: county resident, tuition changed for out of county/state.

DANCE

Curriculum, Students, and Faculty

Required courses: ballet (2-3 classes per week), jazz (1 class per week), modern dance, pointe (1 class per week), repertory (1 class per week), variations (2 classes per week).

Selectivity for males: most admitted, but not all. *Selectivity for females:* approximately 60% admitted. *Total enrollment:* 25. *Entering class size:* 4. *Graduating class size:* 4. *Total part-time faculty:* 3. *List of current faculty and past affiliations:* Pam Andre-Miller, Chattanooga Civic Ballet, Scottish American Ballet; Joellen Wojtowicz, Chattanooga Ballet; Frank Hay, Chattanooga Ballet *Program contact person:* Pam Andre.

Audition Information

No audition fee. Audition consists of the following: ballet, modern dance, prepared solo. *Accompanist provided. Cassette player available; CD player available. Dress requirements for males:* black tights, shoes. *Dress requirements for females:* pink or black tights, black leotard, ballet shoes.

Audition evaluation criteria: participation in dance class; demonstrate technical abilities and ability to take direction; prepared solo piece; previous ballet training a plus.

Performance Information

Performance opportunities available (frequency): Fully produced concerts (2 per year), informal concerts (1+ per year), workshops (varies), on-site performances(6 per year).

Performances choreographed by: faculty. *Recent guest choreographers:* Marcus Alford, Amanda Dean, Judy Woodruff.

Facilities

Number of studios available: 2. *Approximate studio dimensions and flooring:* Marley over suspended/elevated wood. *Performance facilities:* auditorium/studio.

DRAMA

Curriculum, Students, and Faculty

Required courses: acting, directing, improvisation, movement, musical theater, voice, scene study.

Summer program not available. No affiliation with a professional theater company. Selectivity for males: approximately 60% admitted. *Selectivity for females:* approximately 60% admitted. *Total enrollment:* 24. *Entering class size:* 5. *Graduating class size:* 2.

Total part-time faculty: 1.

Audition Information

No audition fee. Audition consists of the following: cold readings, comedic monologue, improvisation, movement class, group warm-up. *Repertoire that students should avoid?* none.

Audition evaluation criteria: must demonstrate concentration, articulation, projection, discipline, commitment, self-confident communication, and self-expression.

Performance Information

Performance opportunities available (frequency): fully produced performances (2 per year), informal performances (4 per year), workshops (5 per year), off-site performances (5 per year), casting is by audition.

Recent guest artists: Shawn Kinley.

Facilities

Type and capacity: proscenium 1,068.

MUSIC

Curriculum, Students, and Faculty

Unique or innovative music curriculum: musical theater is in the music department. Classical guitar consort offered. *How are major teacher assignments made?* made by the school central office. Faculty is informed of a student's teacher preference at the time of the audition. *18 lessons with major teacher. May a student change major teachers during the course of study?* possibly. *Study of secondary instrument or discipline is allowed.*

Selectivity for instruments or programs offered (rating): bassoon (non-competitive), choral singing (competitive), clarinet (non-competitive), double bass (non-competitive), flute or piccolo (non-competitive), French horn (non-competitive), guitar (competitive), oboe/English horn (non-competitive), percussion (non-competitive), saxophone (non-competitive), trombone (non-competitive), trumpet (non-competitive), tuba (non-competitive), viola (non-competitive), violin (non-competitive), violoncello (non-competitive), voice (competitive).

Total enrollment: 114. *Entering class size:* 18. *Graduating class size:* 18.

Total full-time faculty: 1. *Total part-time faculty:* 4. *Program contact person:* Allan Ledford.

Audition Information

No audition fee. Audition consists of the following: scales, rhythmic dictation, sight reading. *Instruments provided for:* percussionists; winds, strings, brass, guitar.

Performance Information

Performance opportunities available (frequency): band (2 per year), chamber music (1 per year), band (2 per year), orchestral concerts (2 per year), touring (25 per year).

Facilities

Number of practice rooms and hours: 4; 9:00 am-4:00 pm. *Recital hall?* no. *Concert hall?* yes. *Recording studio?* no.

TEXAS

BOOKER T. WASHINGTON HIGH SCHOOL FOR THE PERFORMING AND VISUAL ARTS

2501 Flora Street, Dallas TX 75201
Tel: 214-720-7300
Fax: 214-720-7330

General

Type of Institution: magnet-public. *Environment:* urban.

Total enrollment: 700. *Total student body from other countries:* 1%. *Degrees offered:* high school diploma, certificate.

Entrance Requirements

Audition required: live. *Other requirements:* interview, recommendation, essay.

Geographic restrictions: priority given to in-district students.

Services

Housing options: off-campus housing, family.

Support staff: college advisor, financial aid advisor, psychological counselor, resident nurse.

DANCE

Curriculum, Students, and Faculty

Required courses: ballet (3 classes per week, 4 years to complete), men's class, pointe, eclectic.

Elective courses: African dance, dance composition/choreography, dance history, historical dance, jazz, Labanotation, master classes, Pilates, other world dance forms, rehearsal and performance, repertory, Spanish, tap, vernacular dance.

Selectivity for males: most admitted, but not all. *Selectivity for females:* approximately 33% admitted. *Total enrollment:* 110. *Entering class size:* 40.

Graduating class size: 27. *Countries most represented:* Israel.

Renowned alumni: Derick Brown, University of Amsterdam; Mark Morris, Griff Braun-American Ballet Theatre; and Jay Franke, Twyla Tharp.

Total full-time faculty: 6. *Total part-time faculty:* 8. *List of current faculty and past affiliations:* Anne Donavan, Royal Academy; Kevin Brown, Dallas Ballet and Chicago Ballet; Rosann Cox, College Board Arts Committee; Lily Weiss, Texas Choreographer's Award; Carla Daniels, Dallas Block Dance Theater; and Linda James, Editor of CBRD. *Program contact person:* Rosann Cox, Lily White.

Audition Information

No audition fee. Accompanist provided. Cassette player available; CD player available.

Repertoire that students should avoid? hip-hop and funky jazz.

Performance Information

Performance opportunities available (frequency): Fully produced concerts (6 per year), informal concerts (4 per year), on-site performances (20-30 per year), touring (6-8 per year).

Performances choreographed by: faculty, guests. *Recent guest choreographers:* John Mead, Stephen Mills, Luis Montero, Sherry Locey, Martha Cartis, and Art Bridgman and Myrna Packer.

Facilities

Number of studios available: 4. *Approximate studio dimensions and flooring:* 50' x 60' L'Air floor-a shock absorbent floor, 50' x 45' L'Air floor, 30' x 36' sprung oak floor. *Performance facilities:* studio theater—small school auditorium.

MUSIC

Curriculum, Students, and Faculty

How are major teacher assignments made? made by the school.

Selectivity for instruments or programs offered (rating): bassoon (non-competitive), choral singing (competitive), clarinet (competitive), double bass (competitive), flute or piccolo (competitive), French horn (competitive), guitar (selective), oboe/English horn (non-competitive), percussion (competitive), piano (competitive), saxophone (competitive), trombone (competitive), trumpet (competitive), tuba (competitive), viola (competitive), violin (competitive), violoncello (competitive).

Total enrollment: 240. *Entering class size:* 60. *Graduating class size:* 41.

Renowned alumni: Eryka Badu, Roy Hargrove, Edie Bricknell, John Koen, Aaron Comess.

Total full-time faculty: 10. *Total part-time faculty:* 5. *Program contact person:* Douglas Cornell.

Audition Information

No audition fee. Audition consists of the following: scales, sight reading. *Instruments provided for:* percussionists.

Performance opportunities available (frequency): band, chamber music, jury examinations, opera workshops, orchestral concerts, produced operas, chorus.

Facilities

Number of practice rooms and hours: 13; 9:00 am-4:30 pm. *Concert hall?* yes. *Recording studio?* yes.

EPISCOPAL HIGH SCHOOL

4650 Bissonnet, Bellaire TX 77401
Tel: 713-512-3400
Fax: 713-512-3601
Email: nkahlden@ehshouston.org
Web: andy.Ehshouston.org
Contact: Nancy Kahlden

General

Type of Institution: day coed. *Religious affiliation:* Episcopal. *Environment:* urban.

Total enrollment: 550. *Degrees offered:* high school diploma.

Costs & Financial Aid

Application fee: $50. *Deposit:* $1,000. *Other fees:* $325 student fee, $660 lunch program, $200 technology fee.

Types of scholarships and aid awarded: full, partial, need-based. *Forms required for scholarships:* FFS.

Services

Support staff: college advisor, physical therapist, psychological counselor.

DANCE

Curriculum, Students, and Faculty

Required courses: ballet, historical dance, jazz, Cunningham-based, Limon-based modern dance, repertory, tap.

Selectivity for males: admit all who apply. *Selectivity for females:* approximately 33% admitted. *Total enrollment:* 60.

Renowned alumni: Elissa Criner, Laura Kaufman. *Total part-time faculty:* 3. *List of current faculty and past affiliations:* John Truax; Evelyn Iretan; and Bonnie Busker, Weave Dance Co. *Program contact person:* John Truax.

Audition Information

No audition fee. Audition consists of the following: ballet, modern dance, jazz. *Accompanist not provided. Cassette player available; CD player available. Dress requirements for males:* leotard, tights, ballet and jazz shoes. *Dress requirements for females:* leotard, tights, ballet and jazz shoes.

Performance Information

Performance opportunities available (frequency): Fully produced concerts (2 per year), informal concerts (2 per year), on-site performances (1 per year), touring.

Performances choreographed by: faculty, students, guests. *Recent guest choreographers:* Sadra Organ, Houston Ballet; Janie Carothers, High School of Performing and Visual Arts, Houston; Rob Davidson, Faculty at Stephens College; and Juilet Hicks, Weaver Dance Co.

Facilities

Number of studios available: 2. *Approximate studio dimensions and flooring:* 30' x 40' used dance floors. *Performance facilities:* theater.

DRAMA

Curriculum, Students, and Faculty

Elective courses: audition preparation, drama criticism, improvisation, make-up, mime, movement, musical theater, scene study.

Total enrollment: 57.

Total part-time faculty: 2.

Audition Information

No audition fee. Audition consists of the following: comedic monologue, improvisation, group warm-up, oral discussion of self and reasons for auditions.

Performance Information

Performance opportunities available (frequency): fully produced performances (2-3 per year), informal performances (frequently), workshops (1-2 per year), casting is by audition.

Facilities

Rehearsal facilities and hours: full theater, proscenium, or black box, 4:00 pm-6:00 pm or 4:00 pm-8:00 pm. *Number of theaters on campus:* 2. *Type and capacity:* black box 60, proscenium 800.

MUSIC

Curriculum, Students, and Faculty

Unique or innovative music curriculum: We have a great keyboard lab and a percussion ensemble. *How are major teacher assignments made?* Students may choose, made by the school, according to teacher preference and teacher availability. *Study of secondary instrument or discipline is allowed.*

Selectivity for instruments or programs offered (rating): accompanying (highly selective), bassoon (open), choral singing (open), clarinet (open), composition (open), double bass (open), electronic music (open), flute or piccolo (open), French horn (open), guitar (open), harp (open), jazz (open), oboe/English horn (open), organ (highly selective), percussion (open), piano (selective), sacred music (open), saxophone (open), trombone (open), trumpet (open), tuba (open), viola (open), violin (open), violoncello (open), voice (open).

Total enrollment: 80.

Renowned alumni: Todd Frazier.

Total full-time faculty: 3. *Program contact person:* Kristen Fusco.

Audition Information

No audition fee. Audition consists of the following: scales, orchestral excerpts, music theory, rhythmic dictation, ensemble playing, arpeggios. *Instruments provided for:* percussionists.

Facilities

Number of practice rooms and hours: 10; 7:00 am-9:00 pm. *Recital hall?* no. *Concert hall?* yes. *Recording studio?* no.

HIGH SCHOOL FOR PERFORMING & VISUAL ARTS

4001 Stanford, Houston TX 77006
Tel: 713-942-1960
Fax: 713-942-1968

General

Type of Institution: magnet-public. *Environment:* urban.

Total enrollment: 670. *Degrees offered:* high school diploma, certificate.

Entrance Requirements

Audition required: live. *Other requirements:* interview, recommendation.

Geographic restrictions: Houston students given preference.

Costs & Financial Aid

Other fees: $50-$200 art area fees.

Services

Support staff: college advisor, psychological counselor, resident nurse.

DANCE

Curriculum, Students, and Faculty

Required courses: African dance, ballet (3 classes per week), dance composition/choreography (2 classes per week), dance history (2 classes per week), dance theory (2 classes per week), jazz (2 classes per week), master classes, modern dance (3 classes per week), movement techniques, nutrition, pointe (2 classes per week), rehearsal and performance (2 classes per week), repertory (2 classes per week), tap (2 classes per week), dance writing, research and criticism, rehearsal and performance.

Selectivity for males: approximately 33% admitted. *Selectivity for females:* approximately 10% admitted. *Total enrollment:* 99. *Entering class size:* 31. *Graduating class size:* 24.

Renowned alumni: Keith Cross, Cecelia Meimbach, Sonia Noriega, Sophia Torres, Dorrell Martin.

Total full-time faculty: 2. *Total part-time faculty:* 4. *Program contact person:* Lu Anne Carter.

Audition Information

No audition fee. Audition consists of the following: ballet, modern dance, pointe works. *Accompanist provided. Dress requirements for males:* white shirt, black tights, ballet shoes. *Dress requirements for females:* black leotard, pink or black tights, ballet and pointe shoes.

Audition evaluation criteria: body alignment and physique, coordination and flexibility, rhythmical accuracy, ability to sight read movement, evidence of natural ability and potential.

Performance Information

Performance opportunities available (frequency): Fully produced concerts (2 per year), informal concerts (4 per year), workshops (1-2 per year), on-site performances (8-12 per semester), touring (every other year).

Performances choreographed by: faculty, guests. *Recent guest choreographers:* Trey McIntyre, Nathan Montoya, Ilze Klavins Sell, Jan Stockman Simonds, Deborah Potts Quanaim.

Facilities

Number of studios available: 3 *Approximate studio dimensions and flooring:* 48' x 48' floated wood floor, 44' x 32' vinyl Rosco tap dance floor, 48' x 48' vinyl floor. *Performance facilities:* informal performances occur in the 2 dance studios. Formal concert are in the Denney theater—550 seats. Stage dimensions are 40' x 52' and meets union stage specifications.

DRAMA

Curriculum, Students, and Faculty

Required courses: acting, audition preparation, directing, drama criticism, improvisation, make-up, movement, musical theater, scene study, speech, stage combat, Stanislavski exercises, text analysis, verse drama, voice, make-up, mime.

Number of years required to complete program: 4. *Summer program not available. No affiliation with a professional theater company. Selectivity for males:* approximately 33% admitted. *Selectivity for females:* approximately 60% admitted. *Total enrollment:* 99. *Entering class size:* 25. *Graduating class size:* 22.

Renowned alumni: Tim Guinee, K1 Todd Freeman, Renee O'Connor, Lichelle Forbes, Kevin Cahoon, Mark Payne, Michael Taplay, Wendee Curtis.

Total full-time faculty: 3. *Total part-time faculty:* 3. *List of current faculty and past affiliations:* Suzanne Phillips, Houston Shakespeare Festival; Stephen Wolf, University of Texas; Robert Singleton, Oregon Shakespeare Festival.

Audition Information

No audition fee. Audition consists of the following: cold readings, improvisation, movement class, group warm-up. *Dress requirements for males:* clothing that allows free movement and sitting or lying on the floor. *Dress requirements for females:* clothing that allows free movement and sitting or lying on the floor. *Repertoire that students should avoid?* yes—however because of the limited access to good material and the inexperience of some of the applicants we do not publish an "avoid" list. Should be published and age and language appropriate.

Audition evaluation criteria: warm-up, environment, snap shots prep, snap shot performance, cold reading, introduction, visual creativity, audition behavior, monologue voice, vocal idiosyncracies, monologues, singing.

Performance Information

Performance opportunities available (frequency): fully produced performances (3-5 per year), informal performances (occasionally), workshops (2-3 per year), off-site performances (3-4 per year), casting is assigned, auditioned. Students audition, but we balance performance experience.

Facilities

Rehearsal facilities and hours: black box theater, rehearsal hall, 1:00 pm-5:30 pm (Mon, Wed, Fri), 3:30 pm-5:30 pm (Tue, Thur). *Number of theaters on campus:* 2. *Type and capacity:* proscenium 500, black box 180.

MUSIC

Curriculum, Students, and Faculty

Unique or innovative music curriculum: We have an in-school concert contest for an appearance with the HSPVA symphony. We offer chamber music (string) and composition. *How are major teacher assignments made?* made by the school for ensembles only, private lessons not offered as part of curriculum. *Study of secondary instrument or discipline is allowed.*

Selectivity for instruments or programs offered (rating): bassoon (competitive), choral singing (selective), clarinet (competitive), double bass (competitive), double bass (competitive), flute or piccolo (competitive), French horn (competitive), guitar (non-competitive), harp (highly selective), jazz (competitive), oboe/English horn (competitive), percussion (competitive), piano (selective), saxophone (competitive), trombone (competitive), trumpet (competitive), tuba (competitive), viola (competitive), violin (competitive), violin (open), violoncello (competitive), voice (competitive).

Total enrollment: 219. *Entering class size:* 55. *Graduating class size:* 57.

Renowned alumni: Everette Harp, Sara Hickman, Herman Matthews.

Total full-time faculty: 8. *Total part-time faculty:* 10. *Program contact person:* Pat Bonner.

Audition Information

No audition fee. Audition consists of the following: scales, music theory, arpeggios, sight reading. *Instruments provided for:* harpists, percussionists, (except for drum set).

Repertoire that students should avoid? Operatic or oratorio arias, very big, extended works. *Performance opportunities available (frequency):* band, orchestral concerts, recitals, chorus.

Facilities

Recital hall? yes. *Concert hall?* yes. *Recording studio?* no.

Comments

All students are required to be in large performing ensembles, and are selected by audition for small ensembles. Our curriculum includes a classical piano and harp program and a jazz guitar program. All seniors desiring the special fine arts certificate are required to present a senior recital or project.

VIRGINIA

CHURCHLAND HIGH SCHOOL

Visual and Performing Arts Magnet Program
4301 Cedar Lane, Portsmouth VA 23703
Tel: 757-686-2500
Fax: 757-686-2511
Contact: Betty Shifferly

General

Type of Institution: magnet-public. *Environment:* urban.

Total enrollment: 1,481. *Degrees offered:* high school diploma.

Entrance Requirements

Audition required: live. *Other requirements:* interview, recommendation, essay.

Geographic restrictions: City of Portsmouth, VA.

Services

Support staff: college advisor, financial aid advisor.

DANCE

Curriculum, Students, and Faculty

Required courses: anatomy, ballet, dance composition/choreography, dance history, dance theory, dance writing, research and criticism, historical dance, jazz, modern dance, music, nutrition, rehearsal and performance, tap.

Elective courses: African dance, repertory, stagecraft, vernacular dance.

Selectivity for males: approximately 60% admitted. *Selectivity for females:* approximately 60% admitted. *Total enrollment:* 25. *Entering class size:* 25. *Graduating class size:* 8. *Total part-time faculty:* 2. *Program contact person:* Betty Shifferly.

Audition Information

No audition fee. Audition consists of the following: prepared solo, student's choice of 2 selections showing alternate styles. *Accompanist not provided. Cassette player available; CD player available. Dress requirements for males:* standard dance wear. *Dress requirements for females:* standard dance wear.

Performance Information

Performance opportunities available (frequency): Fully produced concerts (2 per year), informal concerts (monthly), on-site performances(4 per year).

Performances choreographed by: faculty, students.

Facilities

Number of studios available: 1. *Approximate studio dimensions and flooring:* wood flooring. *Performance facilities:* school auditorium.

MUSIC

Curriculum, Students, and Faculty

How are major teacher assignments made? made by the school. Faculty is not informed of a student's teacher preference at the time of the audition. *30 lessons with major teacher. May a student change major teachers during the course of study?* possibly. *Study of secondary instrument or discipline is allowed.*

Selectivity for instruments or programs offered (rating): bassoon (competitive), choral singing (competitive), clarinet (competitive), flute or piccolo (competitive), French horn (competitive), oboe/English horn (competitive), percussion (competitive), piano (competitive), saxophone (competitive), trombone (competitive), trumpet (competitive), tuba (competitive), viola (competitive), violin (competitive), violoncello (competitive), voice (competitive).

Total enrollment: 48. *Entering class size:* 24. *Graduating class size:* 6.

Total full-time faculty: 2. *Total part-time faculty:* 11. *Program contact person:* Betty Shifferly.

Audition Information

No audition fee. Audition consists of the following: scales, rhythmic dictation. *Instruments provided for:* percussionists.

Facilities

Number of practice rooms and hours: 5; school hours. *Recital hall?* no. *Concert hall?* no. *Recording studio?* no.

EASTERN VIRGINIA SCHOOL FOR THE PERFORMING ARTS

P.O. Box 273
1915 Pocahontas C-6, Williamsburg VA 23187
Tel: 757-229-8535
Fax: 757-220-9091
Email: evspa@widomaker.com
Web: www.euspa.widomaker.com
Contact: Ron Boucher

General

Environment: suburban.

Entrance Requirements

Audition required: live.

Costs & Financial Aid

Forms required for scholarships: income tax return.

DANCE

Curriculum, Students, and Faculty

Required courses: ballet, pas de deux, pointe, rehearsal and performance, variations.

Elective courses: jazz, men's class, Limon-based modern dance, tap.

DRAMA

Curriculum, Students, and Faculty

Required courses: acting, audition preparation, improvisation, speech, voice.

Elective courses: dance, make-up, movement, stage combat.

THE GOVERNOR'S SCHOOL FOR THE ARTS

Old Dominion University, Norfolk VA 23529-0556
Tel: 757-451-4711
Fax: 757-451-4715
Contact: Chip Gallagher

General

Type of Institution: governor's. *Environment:* urban. *Academic education is offered off-site.*

Total enrollment: 320. *Degrees offered:* high school diploma.

Entrance Requirements

Audition required. Other requirements: recommendation.

Geographic restrictions: Norfolk City, Portsmouth City, Southampton County, Suffolk City, Virginia Beach City, Chesapeake City, Isle of Wight County, Franklin City.

DANCE

Curriculum, Students, and Faculty

Required courses: anatomy (1 class per week), ballet (5 classes per week), dance composition/choreography (2 classes per week), dance history (1 class per week), jazz (1-2 classes per week), Labanotation, modern dance (5 classes per week), movement techniques, nutrition, pas de deux (1-2 classes per week), pointe (2 classes per week), repertory (2 classes per week), variations (1-2 classes per week).

Elective courses: African dance, character, master classes, men's class, rehearsal and performance, tap (1-2 classes per week), Flamenco.

Selectivity for males: most admitted, but not all. *Selectivity for females:* approximately 33% admitted. *Total enrollment:* 61. *Entering class size:* 14. *Graduating class size:* 12.

Renowned alumni: Jeanette Hanley, Hartford Ballet; Brian Simerson, Momix.

Total full-time faculty: 1. *Total part-time faculty:* 7. *List of current faculty and past affiliations:* Deborah Thorpe, Goucher College, Colorado State University; Kathy Brenner, Ballet Met; Lorraine Graves, Dance Theatre of Harlem; Gayle Zukevich, Certified Pilates Instructor, Ballet Michigan. *Program contact person:* Deborah Thorpe.

Audition Information

No audition fee. Audition consists of the following: ballet, improvisation, modern dance, jazz. *Accompanist provided. Cassette player available; CD player available. Dress requirements for males:* solid color tights and leotard or t-shirt. *Dress requirements for females:* solid color tights and leotard.

Audition evaluation criteria: movement quality, coordination, musicality, physical appearance, flexibility: legs and upper body, control, quick study, allegro, adagio.

Performance Information

Performance opportunities available (frequency): Fully produced concerts (5 per year), informal concerts (1 per year), touring (varies).

Performances choreographed by: faculty, students, guests. *Recent guest choreographers:* Alan Arnett, Todd Rosenlieb, Shane O'Hara, Valarie Smith, Randy James.

Facilities

Number of studios available: 3. *Approximate studio dimensions and flooring:* 35' x 50' Marley, 30' x 40' Marley, 25' x 30' Marley. *Performance facilities:* University theater, seats 288; Chrysler Museum, seats 275; Wells Theatre, seats 600; Wilder auditorium, seats 1,900.

DRAMA

Curriculum, Students, and Faculty

Required courses: acting, audition preparation, drama criticism, improvisation, martial arts, movement, scene study, speech, stage combat, text analysis, voice.

Elective courses: Alexander technique, directing, make-up, mime, musical theater, verse drama.

Number of years required to complete program: 1-4. *Summer program not available. Affiliation with a professional theater company; fully affiliated with the Virginia State Company (LORTC).*

Selectivity for males: approximately 33% admitted. *Selectivity for females:* approximately 10% admitted. *Total enrollment:* 56. *Entering class size:* 5. *Graduating class size:* 15.

Total full-time faculty: 2. *Total part-time faculty:* 2. *List of current faculty and past affiliations:* Michael S. Tick, Trinity Repertory; Christopher Spiel, Santa Fe Chamber Music Festival, Santa Fe Opera.

Audition Information

No audition fee. Audition consists of the following: a cappella, comedic monologue, improvisation, Shakespearean monologue.

Audition evaluation criteria: script interpretation, believability, focus/concentration, articulation, vocal variety, movement quality.

Performance Information

Performance opportunities available (frequency): fully produced performances (3 per year), informal performances (4-6 per year), workshops (varies), all performances of the Virginia State Company (LORTC), casting is by audition.

Recent guest artists: Paula Cole, Peter Cocuzza, Lisa Baldwin, Heidi Rose Robbins, Andrew Heffernan, Tim James.

Facilities

Rehearsal facilities and hours: small rehearsal studio, 9:30 am-9:00 pm. *Type and capacity:* black box 100, proscenium 650.

MUSIC

Curriculum, Students, and Faculty

Unique or innovative music curriculum: curriculm is individualized to large degree. *How are major teacher assignments made?* students may choose, made by the school, according to teacher availability. Faculty is not informed of a student's teacher preference at the time of the audition. *36 lessons with major teacher. May a student change major teachers during the course of study?* possibly. *Study of secondary instrument or discipline is allowed.*

Selectivity for instruments or programs offered (rating): accompanying (highly selective), bassoon (selective), clarinet (competitive), composition (selective), double bass (selective), electronic music (selective), flute or piccolo (selective), French horn (selective), guitar (selective), jazz (selective), oboe/English horn (selective), percussion (selective), piano (highly selective), saxophone (selective), trombone (selective), trumpet (selective), tuba (selective), viola (selective), violin (selective), violoncello (selective).

Total enrollment: 109. *Entering class size:* 34. *Graduating class size:* 36.

Total full-time faculty: 3. *Total part-time faculty:* 28. *Program contact person:* Instrumental: Ray Pancarowicz, Vocal: Alan Fisch.

Audition Information

No audition fee. Audition consists of the following: repertoire. *Instruments provided for:* percussionists.

Required repertoire: 2 contrasting selections of student's choice. *Performance opportunities available (frequency):* chamber music (monthly), jury examinations (2 per year), orchestral concerts (2 per year), recitals (monthly).

Facilities

Number of practice rooms and hours: 10; 1:00 pm-5:00 pm. *Recital hall?* yes. *Concert hall?* yes. *Recording studio?* yes.

HENRICO HIGH SCHOOL CENTER FOR THE ARTS

302 Azalea Avenue, Richmond VA 23227
Tel: 804-228-2718
Fax: 804-228-2715
Contact: Lee Hanchey

General

Type of Institution: public. *Environment:* suburban.

Total enrollment: 118. *Degrees offered:* high school diploma, international baccalaureate.

Entrance Requirements

Audition required: live. *Other requirements:* recommendation.

Geographic restrictions: must live in Henrico County.

Costs & Financial Aid

Other fees: $8 art fee.

Services

Support staff: housing advisor, physical therapist, psychological counselor, resident assistant, resident nurse, student affairs officer.

DANCE

Curriculum, Students, and Faculty

Required courses: African dance (4 years to complete), Alexander technique, anatomy, ballet (2 classes per week, 4 years to complete), dance composition/choreography, dance history, dance theory, dance writing research and criticism, jazz (1 class per week, 4 years to complete), master classes, modern dance (1 class per week, 4 years to complete), Cunningham-based (1 class per week, 4 years to complete), Graham-based (1 class per week, 4 years to complete), Limon-based modern dance (1 class per week, 4 years to complete), movement techniques, Laban Movement Studies, music, nutrition, other world dance forms, Indian dance, Irish, rehearsal and performance, repertory, Spanish (4 years to complete), tap (4 years to complete).

Elective courses: character, vernacular dance.

Selectivity for males: most admitted, but not all. *Selectivity for females:* most admitted, but not all. *Total enrollment:* 43. *Entering class size:* 20. *Graduating class size:* 13.

Renowned alumni: Andrea Hammond.

Total full-time faculty: 1. *List of current faculty and past affiliations:* Lauren Winter Fine, University of Missouri, Towson State University. *Program contact person:* Lauren Fine.

Audition Information

No audition fee. Audition consists of the following: ballet, modern dance. *Accompanist provided. Cassette player available; CD player available. Dress requirements for males:* (ballet): black leotard, pink tights, pink slippers; (modern): black leotard, black footless tights; (jazz): purple tank leotard, black tights, black jazz shoes. *Dress requirements for females:* (ballet): black leotard, pink tights, pink slippers; (modern): black leotard, black footless tights; (jazz): purple tank leotard, black tights, black jazz shoes.

Repertoire that students should avoid? The Nutcracker.

Audition evaluation criteria: posture, musicality, form, quick learning ability, willingness to learn, grace.

Performance Information

Performance opportunities available (frequency): Fully produced concerts (2 per year), informal concerts (1 per year), workshops (frequently), on-site performances(every January).

Performances choreographed by: faculty, students, guests. *Recent guest choreographers:* Anna Ines King, Latin; Michael Kern, Paul Taylor; Melanie Richards, VCU; Ezibu Muntu, African Dance Company; Leslie Harrington; Kaye Weinstein, Richmond Ballet.

Facilities

Number of studios available: 1. *Approximate studio dimensions and flooring:* very large raised wood with permanent movable barres. *Performance facilities:* the school auditorium.

DRAMA

Curriculum, Students, and Faculty

Required courses: acting, audition preparation, directing, drama criticism, dramaturgy, improvisation, movement, scene study, Stanislavski exercises, text analysis, voice.

Elective courses: Alexander technique, dance, make-up, martial arts, mime, musical theater, stage combat, verse drama.

Number of years required to complete program: 2-4. *Summer program not available. No affiliation with a professional theater company. Selectivity for males:* admit all who apply. *Selectivity for females:* most admitted, but not all. *Total enrollment:* 40. *Entering class size:* 20. *Graduating class size:* 20.

Renowned alumni: Emma Role.

Total full-time faculty: 1. *List of current faculty and past affiliations:* Jacque Collins, Aspen Theatre.

Audition Information

No audition fee. Audition consists of the following: cold readings, comedic monologue, improvisation. *Repertoire that students should avoid?* Phenomenal Woman by Maya Angelou, poems by Langston Hughes, monologues from prepared monologue books.

Performance Information

Performance opportunities available (frequency): fully produced performances (2-3 per year), informal performances (4-6 per year), workshops (4-6 per year), off-site performances (1-2 per year) casting is assigned, auditioned.

Recent guest artists: TAKE 5-Improv Troupe.

Facilities

Number of theaters on campus: 2. *Type and capacity:* auditorium 780, studio 75.

VIRGINIA SCHOOL OF THE ARTS

2240 Rivermont Avenue, Lynchburg VA 24503
Tel: 804-847-8688
Fax: 804-847-4380
Email: Vasarts@aol.com

General

Environment: urban.

Total student body from other countries: 2%. *Degrees offered:* high school diploma, certificate.

Entrance Requirements

Audition required: live, video. *Other requirements:*, recommendation, photograph.

Costs & Financial Aid

Application fee: $30. *Deposit:* $500. *Medical fee:* $100. *Other fees:* $270 activity fee.

Percent of students receiving financial aid: 38% *Types of scholarships and aid awarded:* full, partial, merit-based, need-based, tuition payment plan. *Forms required for scholarships:* income tax return. *Loans available. Procedure for applying for loans:* audition, application, acceptance. *Financial aid offered to international students. Percent of international students receiving scholarships:* 1%.

Other aid available to international students: financial aid through same process as U.S. students.

Services

Housing options: on-site dorms.

Support staff: college advisor, dorm parent, financial aid advisor, foreign student advisor.

Comments

We also have summer programs as well as the academic year programs.

DANCE

Curriculum, Students, and Faculty

Required courses: movement techniques.

DRAMA

Curriculum, Students, and Faculty

Elective courses: audition preparation.

WISCONSIN

MILWAUKEE HIGH SCHOOL OF THE ARTS

2300 West Highland Avenue, Milwaukee WI 53233
Tel: 414-933-1500
Fax: 414-345-5786
Web: ftp.milwaukee.k12.wi.us/schools/mhsa/mhsa.html
Contact: Jeannette Van Dorn

General

Type of Institution: public, specialized. *Environment:* urban. *Academic education is offered on-site.*

Total enrollment: 952. *Total student body from other countries:* 1%. *Degrees offered:* high school diploma.

Entrance Requirements

Audition required: live. *Other requirements:* interview, recommendation, essay.

Geographic restrictions: city residents and suburban transfers.

Services

Support staff: financial aid advisor, foreign student advisor, psychological counselor, student affairs officer.

DANCE

Curriculum, Students, and Faculty

Required courses: African dance, anatomy, ballet, dance composition/choreography, dance history, dance theory, dance writing, research and criticism, historical dance, jazz, master classes, modern dance, nutrition, rehearsal and performance, repertory, Spanish, tap, variations, modern dance partnering, ballet, pedagogy.

Selectivity for males: most admitted, but not all. *Selectivity for females:* most admitted, but not all. *Total enrollment:* 171. *Entering class size:* 60. *Graduating class size:* 30. *Percent international:* 25%. *Countries most represented:* Brazil.

Renowned alumni: Valdemar Sanchez, Lombardo.

Total full-time faculty: 4. *List of current faculty and past affiliations:* Dean Drews; Sandra Jordan, Ko-thi Dance Co.; Lisa Sherman, Colt-Proart Dance Studio; Jennifer Toth. *Program contact person:* Dean Drews.

Audition Information

No audition fee. Audition consists of the following: ballet, modern dance. *Accompanist not provided. Cassette player available; CD player available. Dress requirements for males:* tights, t-shirt. *Dress requirements for females:* tights, leotard.

Performance Information

Performance opportunities available (frequency): Fully produced concerts (1 per year), informal concerts (4-6 per year), workshops (10 per year), on-site performances (2 per year), touring (10 per year), recitals (2 per year).

Performances choreographed by: faculty, students, guests. *Recent guest choreographers:* Ed Burgess, Bruce Stedman, Brian Jeffreys, Yves de Boutellier, Deb Lowen, Bob Eisen, Allison Green.

Facilities

Number of studios available: 3. *Approximate studio dimensions and flooring:* 40' x 100' sprung wood dance floor, 40' x 30' Marley covered, 40' x 30' Marley covered. *Performance facilities:* 1 main stage auditorium (Marley covered stage floor), 800 seats.

DRAMA

Curriculum, Students, and Faculty

Required courses: acting, audition preparation, directing, drama criticism, dramaturgy, improvisation, make-up, mime, scene study, stage combat, Stanislavski exercises, text analysis, verse drama, voice, speech.

Elective courses: movement, musical theater.

Number of years required to complete program: 4. *Summer program not available. No affiliation with a professional theater company. Selectivity for males:* most admitted, but not all. *Selectivity for females:* most admitted, but not all. *Total enrollment:* 175. *Entering class size:* 60. *Graduating class size:* 30. *Percent international:* 25%. *Countries most represented:* Japan.

Renowned alumni: Amy Pietz, Tom Plotkin, David Kovak, Carrie Nuezering, Cincinnati Shakespeare Company.

Total full-time faculty: 5. *Total part-time faculty:* 3. *List of current faculty and past affiliations:* David Valdes, Robert Hoyt, Steven Koehler, Rhodes Nathan, Glen Copper.

Audition Information

No audition fee. Audition consists of the following: required monologue.

Performance Information

Performance opportunities available (frequency): fully produced performances (4 per year), informal performances (12 per year), workshops (1-2 per month), casting is by audition.

Recent guest artists: Milwaukee Repertory Theatre, Milwaukee Chamber Theater.

Facilities

Rehearsal facilities and hours: 2 studio spaces, 40' x 30', 3:00 pm-6:00 pm. *Number of theaters on campus:* 2. *Type and capacity:* proscenium 800, black box 100.

MUSIC

Curriculum, Students, and Faculty

How are major teacher assignments made? made by the school. Faculty is not informed of a student's teacher preference at the time of the audition. *30 lessons with major teacher. May a student change major teachers during the course of study?* never. *Study of secondary instrument or discipline is allowed.*

Selectivity for instruments or programs offered (rating): accompanying (highly selective), bassoon (open), choral singing (competitive), clarinet (open), composition (highly selective), double bass (open), electronic music (open), flute or piccolo (open), French horn (open), guitar (open), harp (open), jazz (open), oboe/English horn (open), orchestral conducting (highly selective), percussion (competitive), piano (open), sacred music (competitive), saxophone (open), trombone (open), trumpet (open), tuba (open), viola (open), violin (open), violoncello (open), voice (open).

Total enrollment: 290. *Entering class size:* 120. *Graduating class size:* 60. *Percent international:* 25%. *Countries most represented:* Sweden, Japan.

Renowned alumni: Tarrah Reynolds, New York Groups; Ben Love, New York Groups; Erin Alrige; Leslie Cook, Chamber Music Institute University of Wisconsin.

Total full-time faculty: 5. *Total part-time faculty:* 1. *Program contact person:* Jack Watson.

Audition Information

No audition fee. Audition consists of the following: scales, orchestral excerpts, sight reading, improvisation, repertoire. *Instruments provided for:* harpists, percussionists; string bass, tuba.

Performance opportunities available (frequency): band (4 per year), jury examinations (2 per year).

Facilities

Recital hall? no. *Concert hall?* yes. *Recording studio?* no.

WYOMING

WYOMING SEMINARY COLLEGE PREPARATORY SCHOOL

201 North Sprague Avenue, Kingston PA 18707
Tel: 717-283-6000
Fax: 717-283-6099
Email: kbarilla@prolog.net
Web: www.wyoming seminary.org
Contact: Kayanne Barilla

General

Type of institution: coed, boarding, and day. *Environment:* suburban.

Total enrollment of institution: 785. *Total student body from other countries:* 15%. *Degrees offered:* high school diploma.

Entrance Requirements:

Audition not required Other requirements: interview, recommendation, essay. *Standardized test requirements:* SSAT; TOEFL.

Costs & Financial Aid

Application fee: $25. *Tuition:* $10,200.

Percent of students receiving financial aid: 40%. *Types of scholarships and aid awarded:* full, partial, merit-based, need-based, named, institutional aid, work/study. *Forms required for scholarships:* FAFSA, income tax return. *Loans available. Procedure for applying for loans:* contact Admission Office for application. *Financial aid offered to international students. Percent of international students receiving scholarships:* 40%. *Other aid available to international students:* all.

Services

Housing options: on-site dorms.

Support staff: college advisor, dorm parent, financial aid advisor, foreign student advisor.

DANCE

Curriculum, Students, and Faculty

Elective courses: historical dance, African dance.

DRAMA

Curriculum, Students, and Faculty

Required courses: directing.

MUSIC

Elective courses: touring chorus, music theory.

AUSTRALIA

VICTORIAN COLLEGE OF THE ARTS SECONDARY SCHOOL

234 Street Kilda Road, Melbourne VI 30004
Australia
Tel: 03-9685-9320
Fax: 03-9685-9463
Contact: Ema Yandall

General

Type of Institution: public, specialized. *Environment:* urban.

Total enrollment of institution: 200. *Degrees offered:* certificate, Victorian Certificate of Education (VCE)-year 12 matriculation.

Entrance Requirements

Audition required: video.

Services

Housing options: off-campus housing.

Support staff: college advisor, foreign student advisor, physical therapist, psychological counselor, resident assistant, resident nurse, student affairs officer.

DANCE

Curriculum, Students, and Faculty

Required courses: character (1 class per week, 4 years to complete), ballet (5 classes per week, 6 years to complete), dance composition/choreography (1 class per week, 4 years to complete), dance history (1 class per week, 3 years to complete), dance theory (1 class per week, 3 years to complete), jazz (1 class per week), men's class (2 classes per week, 6 years to complete), Cunningham-based (3 classes per week, 4 years to complete), Graham-based (3 classes per week, 4 years to complete), Limon-based modern dance (3 classes per week, 4 years to complete), body conditioning (3 classes per week, 3 years to complete), music (1 class per week, 6 years to complete), pas de deux (2 classes per week, 3 years to complete), pointe (2 classes per week, 5 years to complete), rehearsal and performance (3 classes per week, 6 years to complete), tap (1 class per week).

Selectivity for males: approximately 10% admitted. *Selectivity for females:* approximately 10% admitted. *Total enrollment:* 100. *Entering class size:* 33. *Graduating class size:* 18. *Countries most represented:* Taiwan.

Renowned alumni: Greg Horsman, English National Ballet; and Justine Summers, Principal Australian Ballet.

Total full-time faculty: 2. *Total part-time faculty:* 10. *List of current faculty and past affiliations:* Maggie Gorraine, Royal Ballet; Robert Ray, Australian Ballet; Valmai Roberts; and David Asolmoce. *Program contact person:* Tim Storey.

Audition Information

Audition fee: $30 fee. *Audition consists of the following:* ballet, improvisation, modern dance, orthopedic evaluation, pas de deux, pointe works, *Accompanist provided.*

Repertoire that students should avoid? no.

Performance Information

Performance opportunities available (frequency): Fully produced concerts (2 per year), informal concerts (3 per year), workshops (4 per year), on-site performances (2 per year), touring (varies).

Performances choreographed by: faculty, students, guests.

Facilities

Number of studios available: 10. *Approximate studio dimensions and flooring:* 12 m. x 12 m.

Tarkett flooring. *Performance facilities:* One small Tarkett, one studio Tarkett.

MUSIC

Curriculum, Students, and Faculty

How are major teacher assignments made? made by the school. Faculty is informed of a student's teacher preference at the time of the audition. *30 lessons with major teacher. May a student change major teachers during the course of study?* possibly. *Study of secondary instrument or discipline is allowed.*

Selectivity for instruments or programs offered (rating): bassoon (selective), clarinet (highly selective), double bass (selective), flute or piccolo (highly selective), French horn (selective), guitar (highly selective), harp (selective), jazz (highly selective), oboe/English horn (selective), organ (highly selective), percussion (highly selective), piano (highly selective), saxophone (highly selective), trombone (highly selective), trumpet (highly selective), tuba (highly selective), viola (highly selective), violin (highly selective), violoncello (highly selective), voice (highly selective).

Total enrollment: 100. *Entering class size:* 34. *Graduating class size:* 29. *Countries most represented:* China, Korea.

Total full-time faculty: 3. *Total part-time faculty:* 60. *Program contact person:* Margaret Arnold.

Audition Information

Audition fee? $30. *Audition consists of the following:* scales, rhythmic dictation, arpeggios, sight reading, *Instruments provided for:* harpists, percussionists.

Performance opportunities available (frequency): jury examinations, orchestral concerts, recitals, chorus.

Facilities

Number of practice rooms and hours: 60. *Recital hall?* yes. *Concert hall?* no. *Recording studio?* yes.

CANADA

VICTORIA SCHOOL OF PERFORMING AND VISUAL ARTS

10210-108 Avenue, Edmonton AL T5H1A8
Tel: 403-426-3010
Fax: 403-425-4626
Contact: Tami Dowler-Coltman

General

Type of Institution: magnet-public. *Environment:* urban. *Academic education is offered on-site.*

Total enrollment of institution: 1,600. *Degrees offered:* high school diploma, international baccalaureate.

Entrance Requirements

Audition not required Other requirements: interview, recommendation.

Costs & Financial Aid

Types of scholarships and aid awarded: full, partial, merit-based, need-based, named.

Services

Housing options: off-campus housing, family.

Support staff: career counselor.

DRAMA

Curriculum, Students, and Faculty

Elective courses: acting, directing, improvisation, mime, musical theater, speech.

CANTERBURY HIGH SCHOOL

Arts Canterbury
900 Canterbury Avenue, Ottawa ON K1G3A7
Tel: 613-731-1191
Fax: 613-731-5210
Email: jkirsh@obe.edu.on.ca
Web: www.schoolnet.ca/collections

General

Type of Institution: magnet-public. *Environment:* urban.

Total enrollment of institution: 741. *Degrees offered:* high school diploma.

Entrance Requirements

Audition required: live *Other requirements:* interview, recommendation, essay, photograph.

Geographic restrictions: Eastern Ontario, but in reality co-terminus boards of Ottawa-Carleton region.

Costs & Financial Aid

Other fees: $35 school fee, $25 music, $90 art, cost of theater tickets for dance and drama.

Services

Housing options: family.

Support staff: psychological counselor.

Comments

The overall arts program has 750 students in the following areas: dance, drama, literary arts, music and visual.

DANCE

Curriculum, Students, and Faculty

Required courses: ballet (4 classes per week), dance composition/choreography (1 class per week), dance history (1 class per week), dance theory (1 class per week), dance writing research and criticism (1 class per week), modern dance (1 class per week), Graham-based dance (1 class per week), rehearsal and performance (1 class per week), dance history, dance theory.

Selectivity for males: approximately 60% admitted. *Selectivity for females:* approximately 60% admitted. *Total enrollment:* 100. *Entering class size:* 30. *Graduating class size:* 20.

Total full-time faculty: 4. *List of current faculty and past affiliations:* Fabyenne Gosselin, Theatre Ballet; Connie St. Louis, Le Groupe de la Place Royal; Madeleim Demers, Les Grands Ballets Canadiens. *Program contact person:* Madeleine Demers.

Audition Information

No audition fee. Audition consists of the following: ballet, improvisation, modern dance, orthopedic evaluation. *Accompanist provided. Dress requirements for males:* t-shirt, tights, bare feet. *Dress requirements for females:* leotard, tights, bare feet.

Performance Information

Performance opportunities available (frequency): fully produced concerts (1 per year), informal concerts (1-2 per year), workshops (1-2 per year).

Performances choreographed by: faculty, students, guests. *Recent guest choreographers:* Sylvie Dos Rosiers.

Facilities

Number of studios available: 3 *Approximate studio dimensions and flooring:* 25' x 40' sprung floor covered in "approved" linoleum. *Performance facilities:* fully equipped theater space (seats 700).

DRAMA

Curriculum, Students, and Faculty

Required courses: acting, audition preparation, directing, drama criticism, dramaturgy, improvisation, mime, movement, scene study, speech, Stanislavski exercises, text analysis, voice.

Number of years required to complete program: 4. *Summer program not available. Selectivity for males:* approximately 33% admitted. *Selectivity for females:* approximately 33% admitted. *Total enrollment:* 210. *Entering class size:* 60. *Graduating class size:* 40.

Renowned alumni: Tyley Ross, Robert Parker, Releha Shah.

Total full-time faculty: 5. *List of current faculty and past affiliations:* B. Kalp, University of Toronto.

Audition Information

Audition consists of the following: cold readings, improvisation, movement class, group warm-up. *Dress requirements for males:* comfortable and suitable for movement. *Dress requirements for females:* comfortable and suitable for movement.

Performance Information

Casting is by audition.

Facilities

Rehearsal facilities and hours: 4 studios, 3 equipped as performance space with lights. *Number of theaters on campus:* 2. *Type and capacity:* theater—700 seats.

MUSIC

Curriculum, Students, and Faculty

How are major teacher assignments made? made by the school. Faculty is not informed of a student's teacher preference at the time of the audition. *Study of secondary instrument or discipline is allowed.*

Selectivity for instruments or programs offered (rating): bassoon (competitive), choral singing (competitive), clarinet (competitive), double bass (competitive), flute or piccolo (selective), French horn (competitive), oboe/English horn (competitive), percussion (selective), saxophone (selective), trombone (competitive), trumpet (selective), tuba (competitive), viola (competitive), violin (competitive), violoncello (competitive), voice (competitive).

Total enrollment: 211. *Entering class size:* 65. *Graduating class size:* 20.

Renowned alumni: Scott Tresham, Dan Chamandy.

Total full-time faculty: 4. *Total part-time faculty:* 1. *Program contact person:* Christine Hansen.

Audition Information

No audition fee. Audition consists of the following: scales, orchestral excerpts, rhythmic dictation, sight reading. *Instruments provided for:* percussionists.

Performance opportunities available (frequency): band, chamber music (2 per year), orchestral concerts (2 per year), recitals (1 per year), chorus (2 times per year).

Facilities

Number of practice rooms and hours: 25; 8:00 am-5:30 pm (Mon-Fri). *Concert hall?* yes. *Recording studio?* yes.

CENTRE D'EXCELLENCE ARTISTIQUE DE LA SALLE

Ecole Secondarire Publicque De La Salle
501 Old St. Patrick Street, Ottawa ON K1N 8R3
Tel: 613-789-0053
Fax: 613-789-1545
Web: www.cyberus.ca~delasalle
Contact: J. C. Bergeron

General

Type of Institution: public, specialized regional high school. *Environment:* urban. *Academic education is offered on-site.*

Total enrollment of institution: 1,100. *Degrees offered:* high school diploma, certificate.

Entrance Requirements

Audition required: live. *Other requirements:* interview, photograph.

Geographic restrictions: program is regional but accepts students from all of province.

Services

Housing options: off-campus housing, family.

Support staff: psychological counselor.

DANCE

Curriculum, Students, and Faculty

Required courses: Alexander technique, anatomy, character, ballet, dance composition/choreography, dance history, dance theory, dance writing research and criticism, historical dance, master classes, men's class, Cunningham-based, Graham-based, Limon-based, Nikolais-based modern dance, Laban Movement Studies, Pilates, nutrition, pointe, rehearsal and performance, stagecraft.

Selectivity for males: approximately 33% admitted. *Selectivity for females:* approximately 33% admitted. *Total enrollment:* 50. *Entering class size:* 23.

Renowned alumni: Anik Bouvrette, Michele Steinwald, Noemie LaFrance, Louise Plante, and Isabelle Poirier, O'Vertigo.

Total full-time faculty: 2. *Program contact person:* Solange Paquette.

Audition Information

Audition fee: $10 fee. *Audition consists of the following:* ballet, improvisation, modern dance, orthopedic evaluation, pointe works, interview. *Accompanist provided. Cassette player available; CD player available. Dress requirements for males:* regular dance costume or t-shirt and shorts. *Dress requirements for females:* dance costume or t-shirt and shorts.

Performance Information

Performance opportunities available (frequency): Fully produced concerts (1 per year), informal concerts (2-3 per year), workshops (3 per year), on-site performances (1-2 per year), touring (1 per year).

Performances choreographed by: faculty, students, guests. *Recent guest choreographers:* Anirk Bouvrette and Andre Laprise.

Facilities

Number of studios available: 2. *Approximate studio dimensions and flooring:* 50' x 30' Rosco floor, 60' x 40' soft floor. *Performance facilities:* barres, mirrors, sound system with CD and tape player, piano, percussion equipment.

DRAMA

Curriculum, Students, and Faculty

Required courses: acting, audition preparation, directing, drama criticism, dramaturgy, improvisation, make-up, scene study, speech, Stanislavski exercises, text analysis, verse drama.

Elective courses: Alexander technique, martial arts, mime, movement, musical theater, stage combat, voice.

Number of years required to complete program: 4. *Summer program not available. Affiliation with a professional theater company: representatives from the National Arts Centre Theratre sit on our advisory board.*

Selectivity for males: approximately 60% admitted. *Selectivity for females:* approximately 60% admitted. *Total enrollment:* 85. *Entering class size:* 25.

Renowned alumni: Noemie Godin Vigneaut.

Total full-time faculty: 2.

Audition Information

Audition fee: $10 fee. *Audition consists of the following:* cold readings, improvisation, interview. *Repertoire that students should avoid?* compostitions by students themselves.

Performance Information

Performance opportunities available (frequency): fully produced performances (2 per year), informal performances (3-4 per year), workshops (2 per year), off-site performances (3-4 per year), casting is assigned, auditioned.

Facilities

Number of theaters on campus: 2. *Type and capacity:* auditorium—732 seats, black box—80 seats.

MUSIC

Curriculum, Students, and Faculty

How are major teacher assignments made? Students may choose, made by the school according to teacher preference and teacher availability. *30 lessons with major teacher. May a student change major teachers during the course of study?* possibly. *Study of secondary instrument or discipline is allowed.*

Selectivity for instruments or programs offered (rating): bassoon (competitive), choral singing (non-competitive), clarinet (competitive), composition (competitive), double bass (competitive), electronic music (competitive), flute or piccolo (competitive), French horn (competitive), harp (competitive), harpsichord (competitive), jazz (competitive), oboe/English horn (competitive), percussion (competitive), saxophone (competitive), trombone (competitive), trumpet (competitive), tuba (competitive), viola (competitive), violin (competitive), violoncello (competitive), voice (competitive).

Total enrollment: 100. *Entering class size:* 40.

Renowned alumni: Nicolas Currie, Baltimore Orchestra.

Total full-time faculty: 3. *Total part-time faculty:* 1. *Program contact person:* J Claude Bergeron.

Audition Information

Audition fee? $10. *Audition consists of the following:* scales, orchestral excerpts, music theory, rhythmic dictation, sight reading, music history, melodic dictation. *Instruments provided for:* percussionists.

Performance opportunities available (frequency): band (2 per year), chamber music (5 per year), jury examinations (2 per year), orchestral concerts (6 per year), recitals (3 per year), touring (1 per year), chorus (2 per year).

Facilities

Number of practice rooms and hours: 18; 8:00 am-9:00 am, 11:45 am-12:35 pm, 3:15 pm-5:00 pm. *Recital hall?* yes. *Concert hall?* yes. *Recording studio?* no.

MAYFIELD SECONDARY SCHOOL

Regional Arts Program
RR #4, Brampton ON L6T351
Tel: 905-846-6060
Fax: 905-584-9823
Contact: Doreen Shackelton

General

Type of Institution: public. *Environment:* suburban. *Academic education is offered on-site.*

Total enrollment of institution: 768. *Degrees offered:* high school diploma.

Entrance Requirements

Audition required: live. *Other requirements:* interview, recommendation, photograph.

Geographic restrictions: must live in Peel County.

Costs & Financial Aid

Application fee: $10. *Tuition:* $50.

Services

Housing options: family.

Support staff: career counselor.

DANCE

Curriculum, Students, and Faculty

Required courses: African dance, anatomy, character, ballet, dance composition/choreography, dance history, dance theory, dance writing research and criticism, historical dance, jazz, modern dance, movement techniques, music, nutrition, other world dance forms, pas de deux, rehearsal and performance, stagecraft, tap, variations.

Elective courses: master classes, men's class, repertory, Spanish dance, modern dance partnering, ballet, modern dance.

Selectivity for males: most admitted, but not all. *Selectivity for females:* approximately 60% admitted. *Total enrollment:* 139. *Entering class size:* 40. *Graduating class size:* 28.

Renowned alumni: Clyde Alues, Rhett George, Natasha Lutz.

Total full-time faculty: 2. *Total part-time faculty:* 1. *List of current faculty and past affiliations:* Teresa Pennacchietti; Jeffrey Baker, Les Grand Ballet Canadiens, Cozerado Ballet, Canadian Opera Co. *Program contact person:* Jeff Baker.

Audition Information

Audition fee: $10 fee. *Audition consists of the following:* ballet, improvisation, modern dance, orthopedic evaluation, prepared solo. *Accompanist provided. Cassette player available; CD player available. Dress requirements for males:* shorts, t-shirt, tights, leotard, ballet shoes. *Dress requirements for females:* shorts, t-shirt, tights, leotard, ballet shoes.

Audition evaluation criteria: classwork, technique, flexibility, presentation, creativity, knowledge of steps.

Performance Information

Performance opportunities available (frequency): fully produced concerts informal concerts workshops on-site performances.

Performances choreographed by: faculty, students, guests. *Recent guest choreographers:* Peggy Baker, Robert Desrosier.

Facilities

Number of studios available: 2. *Performance facilities:* large stage in auditorium.

DRAMA

Curriculum, Students, and Faculty

Required courses: acting, audition preparation, directing, drama criticism, dramaturgy, improvisation, martial arts, mime, movement, musical theater, scene study, speech, Stanislavski exercises, text analysis, theater history, verse drama, voice, pedagogy, video, speech, dance.

Elective courses: make-up, stage combat, audition preparation.

Number of years required to complete program: 4. *Summer program not available. Selectivity for males:* approximately 60% admitted. *Selectivity for females:* approximately 60% admitted. *Total enrollment:* 209. *Entering class size:* 58. *Graduating class size:* 48.

Renowned alumni: Kris Lemche.

Total full-time faculty: 3. *Total part-time faculty:* 1. *List of current faculty and past affiliations:* Ken Stern, Theatre Toronto, Canadian Mime Theatre Canadian Touring Theatre.

Audition Information

Audition fee: $10 fee. *Audition consists of the following:* cold readings, improvisation, required monologue, interview. *Audition evaluation criteria:* strong interest in drama, self-discipline, talent, understanding, voice, movement, ability to take direction.

Performance Information

Performance opportunities available (frequency): fully produced performances (4 per class per year), informal performances (2-3 per year), workshops (1-2 per year) assigned, auditioned. Negotiated in collective pieces

Recent guest artists: Stephen Woodgetts, Cam MacDuffee, Steve LaFrenie.

Facilities

Rehearsal facilities and hours: one video edit suite, two drama studios, two dance studios. *Number of theaters on campus:* 1. *Type and capacity:* proscenium—350 seats.

MUSIC

Curriculum, Students, and Faculty

How are major teacher assignments made? made by the school, according to teacher preference and teacher availability. Faculty is not informed of a student's teacher preference at the time of the audition. *Study of secondary instrument or discipline is allowed.*

Selectivity for instruments or programs offered (rating): bassoon (competitive), choral singing (competitive), clarinet (competitive), double bass (competitive), flute or piccolo (competitive), French horn (competitive), guitar (competitive), oboe/English horn (competitive), percussion (competitive), piano (competitive), saxophone (competitive), trombone (competitive), trumpet (competitive), tuba (competitive).

Total enrollment: 222.

Total full-time faculty: 5. *Total part-time faculty:* 1. *Program contact person:* John Chalmers.

Audition Information

Audition fee? $10. *Audition consists of the following:* scales, sight reading, repertoire. *Instruments provided for:* percussionists.

Repertoire that students should avoid? Popular music. *Performance opportunities available (frequency):* band (frequently), jury examinations (1 per semester), chorus (2 per semester).

Facilities

Number of practice rooms and hours: 9; 7:30 am-5:00 pm. *Recital hall?* no. *Concert hall?* yes. *Recording studio?* no.

NIAGARA DISTRICT SECONDARY SHOOL

P.O. Box 1030, Niagara-on-the-Lake ON

General

Type of Institution: public.

Total enrollment of institution: 150. *Degrees offered:* high school diploma.

Entrance Requirements

Audition required: live. *Other requirements:* interview.

Services

Support staff: student affairs officer.

DANCE

Curriculum, Students, and Faculty

Required courses: character, ballet, pas de deux, pointe, variations.

Selectivity for males: most admitted, but not all. *Selectivity for females:* most admitted, but not all. *Total enrollment:* 50.

Total full-time faculty: 1. *List of current faculty and past affiliations:* Catherine Thompson, Dany Grossman Dance Company; Joyce Gauthier *Program contact person:* C. Thompson/Joyce Gautier.

Audition Information

No audition fee. Accompanist not provided. Cassette player available; CD player available.

Repertoire that students should avoid? no.

Facilities

Number of studios available: 1. *Approximate studio dimensions and flooring:* wood flooring (not sprung). *Performance facilities:* black box theater.

DRAMA

Curriculum, Students, and Faculty

Required courses: acting, audition preparation, directing, improvisation, make-up, mime, movement, musical theater, scene study, speech, stage combat, Stanislavski exercises, text analysis.

Number of years required to complete program: 4-5. *Summer program not available. Affiliation with a professional theater company: Shaw Festival in Niagara-on-the-lake.*

Selectivity for males: most admitted, but not all. *Selectivity for females:* most admitted, but not all. *Total enrollment:* 60.

Total full-time faculty: 1. *List of current faculty and past affiliations:* Javier Soyka, Ecole Internationale de Theatre; Jaques Kecog, Paris.

Audition Information

No audition fee. Audition consists of the following: presentation of prepared piece.

Performance Information

Performance opportunities available (frequency): fully produced performances (3 per year), informal performances (2 per year), off-site performances (varies), auditioned.

Recent guest artists: David Langlois.

Facilities

Rehearsal facilities and hours: fully equipped balck box theater. *Number of theaters on campus:* 1. *Type and capacity:* black box—190 seats, studio.

MUSIC

Curriculum, Students, and Faculty

May a student change major teachers during the course of study? usually. *Study of secondary instrument or discipline is allowed.*

Total enrollment: 40. *Entering class size:* 30. *Graduating class size:* 25.

Total full-time faculty: 1. *Program contact person:* T. Matic.

Audition Information

Instruments provided for: percussionists.

Performance opportunities available (frequency): band (frequently), recitals (frequently), chorus.

Facilities

Number of practice rooms and hours: 3.

SUDBURY SECONDARY SCHOOL

85 Mackenzie Street, Sudbury ON P3C 442
Tel: 705-674-7551
Fax: 705-674-5383
Email: Mantlj@sbe.sudburyp.edu.on.ca
Web: www.sudburyp.edu.on.ca/sss/sss intro.html
Contact: Sandra Siren

General

Type of Institution: magnet-public. *Environment:* urban.

Total enrollment of institution: 1,022. *Total student body from other countries:* 1%. *Degrees offered:* high school diploma, certificate.

Entrance Requirements

Audition required: live. *Other requirements:* interview, recommendation.

Services

Support staff: career counselor.

DANCE

Curriculum, Students, and Faculty

Required courses: character, ballet, dance composition/choreography, dance writing research and criticism, historical dance, jazz, modern dance, pointe, rehearsal and performance.

Selectivity for males: most admitted, but not all. *Selectivity for females:* most admitted, but not all. *Total enrollment:* 66. *Entering class size:* 8. *Graduating class size:* 8.

Total full-time faculty: 2. *List of current faculty and past affiliations:* Karen Rammul, Faburdeau, Jazzworks, Toronto Ryerson Polytechnic University; Carolle Mageau, National Ballet of Canada. *Program contact person:* Karen Rammul.

Audition Information

No audition fee. Audition consists of the following: orthopedic evaluation, prepared solo, musicality and coordination testing. *Accompanist not provided. Cassette player available; CD player available. Dress requirements for males:* dancewear, if available, otherwise loose, comfortable clothing that does not restrict movement. *Dress requirements for females:* dancewear, if available, otherwise loose comfortable clothing that does not restrict movement.

Repertoire that students should avoid? tap, acrobatics.

Performance Information

Performance opportunities available (frequency): Fully produced concerts (3 per year), informal concerts (4 per year), workshops (4 per year), on-site performances (2 per year).

Performances choreographed by: faculty, students, guests.

Facilities

Number of studios available: 2. *Approximate studio dimensions and flooring:* 70' x 35' hardwood/spring, 37' x 22.5' rubber/Marley. *Performance facilities:* Sheridan Auditorium—fully equipped in-school facility.

DRAMA

Curriculum, Students, and Faculty

Required courses: acting, audition preparation, directing, drama criticism, improvisation, mime, movement, musical theater, scene study, speech, stage combat, Stanislavski exercises, voice, movement, text analysis.

Number of years required to complete program: 4-4.5. *Summer program not available. No affiliation with a professional theater company. No formal affiliation but regular communication with Sudbury Theatre Centre.*

Selectivity for males: approximately 60% admitted. *Selectivity for females:* approximately 60% admitted. *Total enrollment:* 164. *Entering class size:* 30. *Graduating class size:* 22.

Renowned alumni: Jennifer Racicot.

Total full-time faculty: 2. *Total part-time faculty:* 1. *List of current faculty and past affiliations:* Judith Straughan, Sudbury Theatre Centre, Thorniloe Players, Theatre Ontario, Alison Witty.

Audition Information

No audition fee. Audition consists of the following: comedic monologue, improvisation. Students may choose between a dramatic or comedic monologue for their audition. An interview is also required. *Repertoire that students should avoid?* no.

Audition evaluation criteria: interview—an enthusiastic and committed personality who enjoys working with people and who is a good academic/attendance risk. Evidence of some talent in the actual audition or at least an enthusiasm and willingness to learn.

Performance Information

Performance opportunities available (frequency): fully produced performances (4-5 annually), informal performances (1 per week), workshops (2-3 per year), off-site performances (1-2 per year) assigned, auditioned. Extracurricular auditioned, in class assigned or auditioned.

Recent guest artists: John Boylan, Cal Coons.

Facilities

Rehearsal facilities and hours: one small studio with lighting, two rehearsal spaces, used as classrooms 8:30 am-2:45 pm and as rehearsal space, 3:00 pm-5:30 pm (Mon, Wed, Fri). *Number of theaters on campus:* 1. *Type and capacity:* proscenium 400.

MUSIC

Curriculum, Students, and Faculty

Unique or innovative music curriculum: vocal jazz, musical theatre, music and computers. *How are major teacher assignments made?* made by the school according to teacher preference according to teacher availability. Faculty is not informed of a student's teacher preference at the time of the audition. *May a student change major teachers during the course of study?* possibly. *Study of secondary instrument or discipline is allowed.*

Selectivity for instruments or programs offered (rating): choral singing (competitive), clarinet (non-competitive), double bass (non-competitive), electronic music (selective), flute or piccolo (non-competitive), French horn (non-competitive), guitar (highly selective), jazz (selective), oboe/English horn (non-competitive), percussion (non-competitive), piano (competitive), saxophone (non-competitive), trombone (non-competitive), trumpet (non-competitive), tuba (non-competitive), voice (competitive).

Total enrollment: 143. *Entering class size:* 18. *Graduating class size:* 13.

Total full-time faculty: 2. *Program contact person:* Ralph McIntosh.

Audition Information

No audition fee. Audition consists of the following: scales, music theory rhythmic dictation, sight reading. *Instruments provided for:* percussionists.

Repertoire that students should avoid? pop songs using karoake tapes in bad keys. *Performance opportunities available (frequency):* band (6 per year), chamber music (2 per year), jury examinations (2 per year), orchestral concerts (2 per year), recitals (4 per year), touring (2 per year), chorus (20 per year).

Facilities

Number of practice rooms and hours: 7; 8:00 am-5:00 pm. *Recital hall?* no. *Concert hall?* yes. *Recording studio?* no.

UNIONVILLE HIGH SCHOOL, ARTS YORK PROGRAMME

201 Town Centre Boulevard, Unionville ON L3R 8G5
Tel: 905-479-2787 ext. 227
Fax: 905-479-1539
Contact: Gail Harrison

General

Type of Institution: public, specialized. *Environment:* suburban. *Academic education is offered on-site.*

Total enrollment of institution: 2,000. *Degrees offered:* certificate.

Entrance Requirements

Audition required: live. *Other requirements:* interview, recommendation, photograph.

Geographic restrictions: students who reside within the region of York (north of Toronto).

Costs & Financial Aid

Application fee: $100.

Services

Support staff: college advisor, psychological counselor.

Comments

As our first graduating class was in 1990, we have not yet produced renowned alumni.

DANCE

Curriculum, Students, and Faculty

Required courses: anatomy, ballet, dance composition/choreography, dance history, dance theory, dance writing research and criticism, improvisation, master classes, modern dance, body conditioning, Pilates, nutrition, pointe, rehearsal and performance, stagecraft, composition, ballet (2 classes per week, 1 year to complete), modern dance (2 classes per week, 1 year to complete), composition.

Elective courses: jazz, repertory.

Selectivity for males: most admitted, but not all. *Selectivity for females:* approximately 60% admitted. *Total enrollment:* 77. *Entering class size:* 26. *Graduating class size:* 14.

List of current faculty and past affiliations: Gabrielle Blair, London Festival Ballet; Wendy Chiles, Toronto Dance Theatre; Deborah Radbourne, Motus 'O, Toronto; Michelle Farwell, York University (Toronto); Lauri Mark, National Ballet School (Toronto). *Program contact person:* Gabrielle Blair.

Audition Information

Audition fee: $10 fee. *Audition consists of the following:* ballet, improvisation, modern dance, orthopedic evaluation, optional interview. *Accompanist provided. Cassette player available; CD player available.*

Repertoire that students should avoid? no.

Performance Information

Performance opportunities available (frequency): Fully produced concerts (5+), on-site performances (4), touring (10-12 annually).

Performances choreographed by: faculty, students, guests. *Recent guest choreographers:* Peggy Baker, Gerrill Maquire, Pat Fraser, Kathleen Rea, Debbie Collins, Trish Armstrong, Janice Pomer, Susan McNaughton, Timothy Spain, Stelio Calagias, Laurence Gradus, Lea Creswell, Carol Anderson, Andrea Smith, Patti Ross-Milne.

Facilities

Number of studios available: 2 *Approximate studio dimensions and flooring:* 60' x 45' sprung hardwood covered with Rosco linoleum, 45' x 30' sprung hardwood covered with Rosco linoleum. *Performance facilities:* Markham Theatre (525 seats), school atrium and studio.

DRAMA

Curriculum, Students, and Faculty

Required courses: directing, drama criticism, dramaturgy, mime, movement, stage combat, text analysis, verse drama, voice, acting.

Elective courses: musical theater, speech, improvisation.

Number of years required to complete program: 4. *Summer program available. No affiliation with a professional theater company. Selectivity for males:* approximately 60% admitted. *Selectivity for females:* approximately 33% admitted. *Total enrollment:* 142. *Entering class size:* 42. *Graduating class size:* 31.

Renowned alumni: Adam Brazier, Stratford Festival; Christina Cox.

List of current faculty and past affiliations: Jeffrey Young, York University, University of Toronto; Rob Cook, Queen's University; Janette Pirie-Banff.

Audition Information

Audition fee: $10 fee. *Audition consists of the following:* movement class, group warm-up, dynamic creative drama exercise. *Dress requirements for males:* comfortable clothing. *Dress requirements for females:* comfortable clothing. *Repertoire that students should avoid?* Shakespeare, American Musical Theater, Anne of Green Gables.

Performance Information

Performance opportunities available (frequency): fully produced performances (every 8-10 weeks), informal performances (weekly), workshops (monthly), off-site performances (annually) assigned.

Recent guest artists: Daniel Brooks, Rob Trick, Peter Jarvis, Domini Blythe, Michael Burgess.

Facilities

Rehearsal facilities and hours: 3 studio spaces, one doubles as a performance space seating 75.

MUSIC

Curriculum, Students, and Faculty

How are major teacher assignments made? made by the school. Faculty is not informed of a student's teacher preference at the time of the audition. *90 lessons with major teacher. May a student change major teachers during the course of study?* possibly. *Study of secondary instrument or discipline is allowed.*

Selectivity for instruments or programs offered (rating): bassoon (selective), clarinet (selective), double bass (selective), flute or piccolo (selective), French horn (selective), guitar (highly selective), oboe/English horn (selective), percussion (selective), piano (selective), saxophone (selective), trombone (selective), trumpet (selective), tuba (selective), viola (selective), violin (selective), violoncello (selective), voice (selective).

Total enrollment: 153. *Entering class size:* 31. *Graduating class size:* 40. *Program contact person:* John Phillips.

Audition Information

Audition fee? $10. *Audition consists of the following:* scales, music theory, rhythmic dictation, sight reading, melodic dictation, repertoire. *Instruments provided for:* percussionists.

Required repertoire: vocal, piano, and strings perform selected repertoire from Royal Conservatory, school sends out technical studies to winds. *Repertoire that students should avoid?* Popular music.

Facilities

Number of practice rooms and hours: 6; all day. *Recital hall?* no. *Concert hall?* no. *Recording studio?* no.

WINDSOR CENTRE FOR THE CREATIVE ARTS

2100 Richmond Street, Windsor ON N8Y 3E9
Tel: 519-252-6514
Fax: 519-252-3404
Email: Firstname_Lastname@Fcmail.wboe.edu.on.ca
Contact: John Vacratsis

General

Type of Institution: magnet-public. *Environment:* urban. *Academic education is offered on-site.*

Total enrollment of institution: 325. *Degrees offered:* high school diploma.

Entrance Requirements

Audition required: live. *Other requirements:* interview, recommendation, essay, photograph.

Geographic restrictions: City of Windsor, County of Essex.

Costs & Financial Aid

Other fees: $40 public registration, $130 per month non-residents.

Types of scholarships and aid awarded: gig office. *Other aid available to international students:* NA.

Services

Support staff: psychological counselor.

Comments

We are a relatively new institution; we have over two dozen music graduates in post-secondary education and in the field.

DANCE

Curriculum, Students, and Faculty

Required courses: anatomy, character, ballet, dance composition/choreography, dance history, dance theory, dance writing, research and criticism, historical dance, jazz, master classes, modern dance, movement techniques, music, nutrition, rehearsal and performance, repertory, Spanish, tap, variations.

Elective courses: African dance, Labanotation, pas de deux, pointe, stagecraft, vernacular dance, modern dance partnering.

Selectivity for males: most admitted, but not all. *Selectivity for females:* approximately 60% admitted. *Total enrollment:* 110. *Entering class size:* 30. *Graduating class size:* 20.

Total full-time faculty: 1. *Total part-time faculty:* 1. *List of current faculty and past affiliations:* Janice Brode; Barb Robinson, Windsor City Ballet, National. *Program contact person:* Janice Brode.

Audition Information

No audition fee. Audition consists of the following: ballet, modern dance, pointe works. *Accompanist provided. Cassette player available; CD player available. Dress requirements for males:* leotard, ballet shoes. *Dress requirements for females:* leotard, ballet shoes.

Performance Information

Performance opportunities available (frequency): Fully produced concerts (3 per year), informal concerts (4 per year), workshops (2 per year), on-site performances (2 per year), touring (1 per year).

Performances choreographed by: faculty, students.

Facilities

Number of studios available: 3. *Approximate studio dimensions and flooring:* 50' x 100' sprung wood floors, 20' x 40' Rosco covering in ballet studio, 24' x 42' stage. *Performance facilities:* auditorium (1,600 seat—raked balcony wonderful accoustics).

DRAMA

Curriculum, Students, and Faculty

Required courses: acting, audition preparation, directing, drama criticism, improvisation, makeup, mime, movement, speech, voice.

Elective courses: musical theater, stage combat, verse drama.

Number of years required to complete program: 4. *Summer program not available. Affiliation with a professional theater company:* ***Window Light Opera.***

Selectivity for males: most admitted, but not all. *Selectivity for females:* approximately 60% admitted. *Total enrollment:* 80. *Entering class size:* 30. *Graduating class size:* 20.

Total part-time faculty: 2. *List of current faculty and past affiliations:* Jeff Marontate, J. Michael Lyons, Lynn Harris Ladd.

Audition Information

No audition fee. Audition consists of the following: cold readings, comedic monologue, improvisation, mime. *Repertoire that students should avoid?* Shakespearean, heavily accented.

Performance Information

Performance opportunities available (frequency): fully produced performances (2 per year), informal performances (monthly), workshops (2 per year), off-site performances (2 per year), casting is by audition.

Recent guest artists: Toronto Repertory Theater.

Facilities

Rehearsal facilities and hours: auditorium stage, drama music room. *Type and capacity:* balcony 600.

MUSIC

Curriculum, Students, and Faculty

How are major teacher assignments made? students may choose, made by the school according to teacher preference. Faculty is informed of a student's teacher preference at the time of the audition. *May a student change major teachers during the course of study?* possibly. *Study of secondary instrument or discipline is allowed.*

Selectivity for instruments or programs offered (rating): accompanying (selective), bassoon (competitive), choral singing (competitive), clarinet (competitive), double bass (competitive), flute or piccolo (competitive), French horn (non-competitive), oboe/English horn (competitive), percussion (non-competitive), piano (selective), saxophone (competitive), trombone (competitive), trumpet (competitive), tuba (competitive), viola (competitive), violin (competitive), violoncello (competitive), voice (selective).

Total enrollment: 120. *Entering class size:* 50. *Graduating class size:* 30.

Total full-time faculty: 2. *Total part-time faculty:* 6. *Program contact person:* Elsbeth Maynard.

Audition Information

No audition fee. Audition consists of the following: scales, orchestral excerpts, music theory, rhythmic dictation, sight reading. *Instruments provided for:* percussionists.

Repertoire that students should avoid? pop, rock. *Performance opportunities available (frequency):* band, chamber music, jury examinations, orchestral concerts, recitals.

Facilities

Number of practice rooms and hours: 8. *Recital hall?* yes. *Concert hall?* yes. *Recording studio?* no.

FRANCE

CONSERVATOIRE NATIONAL SUPERIEUR DE MUSIQUE DE LYON

3 Quai Chauveau, C.P. 120, F-69266
Cedex 09, Lyon Tel: 04-72-19-26-26
Fax: 04-72-19-26-00

General

Type of Institution: public. *Environment:* urban.

Total enrollment of institution: 550. *Degrees offered:* high school diploma.

Costs & Financial Aid

Other fees: $15 first year studies.

Types of scholarships and aid awarded: need-based.

Services

Housing options: on-site dorms, off-campus housing, sorority.

Support staff: college advisor, foreign student advisor, housing advisor, student affairs officer.

DANCE

Curriculum, Students, and Faculty

Required courses: ballet, dance composition/choreography, dance history, dance writing research and criticism, historical dance, master classes, men's class, Cunningham-based, Graham-based, Limon-based modern dance, music, pas de deux, pointe, rehearsal and performance, repertory, variations.

PHILIPPINES

PHILIPPINE HIGH SCHOOL FOR THE ARTS

National Arts Center
Mt. Makiling, Los Banos, Laguna
Tel: 049-536-2862
Fax: 049-536-2862

General

Type of Institution: public specialized.

Total enrollment of institution: 123. *Degrees offered:* high school diploma.

Entrance Requirements

Audition required: live. *Other requirements:* interview, recommendation. *Standardized test requirements:* SATI.

Geographic restrictions: admits only Filipino students but plans for international exchange are being discussed.

Costs & Financial Aid

Deposit: $300.

Types of scholarships and aid awarded: full. *Procedure for applying for loans:* entrance examination/audition.

Services

Housing options: on-site dorms.

Support staff: dorm parent, resident nurse, student affairs officer.

DANCE

Curriculum, Students, and Faculty

Required courses: ballet, dance composition/choreography, dance history, dance theory, dance writing research and criticism, modern dance, nutrition, pointe, rehearsal and performance, repertory.

Elective courses: music, stagecraft.

Selectivity for males: admit all who apply. *Selectivity for females:* approximately 33% admitted. *Total enrollment:* 28. *Entering class size:* 7. *Graduating class size:* 7.

Total full-time faculty: 2. *Total part-time faculty:* 2. *List of current faculty and past affiliations:* Agnes Locsin, Ballet Philippines; Corazon Inigo, University of the Philippines; Nonoy Froilan; Myra Beltran; Josefina Guillen, Cultural Center of the Philippines. *Program contact person:* Milwida C. Oliveros.

Audition Information

No audition fee. Audition consists of the following: ballet, improvisation, orthopedic evaluation, pointe works, prepared solo. *Dress requirements for males:* black tights, white t-shirt, ballet shoes. *Dress requirements for females:* pink tights, black leotard, ballet or toe shoes.

Performance Information

Performance opportunities available (frequency): Fully produced concerts (2 per year), informal concerts (frequently), workshops (2 per year), on-site performances (frequently), touring (1 per year).

Performances choreographed by: faculty, students. *Recent guest choreographers:* Agnes Locsin.

Facilities

Number of studios available: 1. *Approximate studio dimensions and flooring:* 150 sq. m. wood. *Performance facilities:* theater, auditorium.

DRAMA

Curriculum, Students, and Faculty

Required courses: acting, directing, drama criticism, improvisation, scene study, speech, text analysis.

Number of years required to complete program: 4. *Summer program not available. Selectivity for males:* approximately 33% admitted. *Selectivity for females:* approximately 33% admitted. *Total enrollment:* 27. *Entering class size:* 7. *Graduating class size:* 7.

Total full-time faculty: 2. *Total part-time faculty:* 2.

Audition Information

No audition fee. Audition consists of the following: improvisation, movement class, creative exercise.

Performance Information

Performance opportunities available (frequency): fully produced performances (1 per year), informal performances (varies), workshops (2 per year), off-site performances (2 per year), auditioned.

Facilities

Type and capacity: proscenium 3,000, black box 200.

MUSIC

Curriculum, Students, and Faculty

How are major teacher assignments made? Students may choose, made by the school according to teacher preference and teacher availability. Faculty is informed of a student's teacher preference at the time of the audition. *May a student change major teachers during the course of study?* possibly. *Study of secondary instrument or discipline is allowed.*

Selectivity for instruments or programs offered (rating): choral singing (competitive), clarinet (selective), flute or piccolo (selective), piano (competitive), trumpet (selective), violin (selective), violoncello (selective), voice (competitive).

Total enrollment: 22. *Entering class size:* 7. *Graduating class size:* 7.

Renowned alumni: Rowena Arrieta, Greg Zuniega, Noel Arce, Aries Caces, Zinorl Bromola.

Total full-time faculty: 1. *Total part-time faculty:* 12. *Program contact person:* Jomar B. Ferreria.

Audition Information

Audition consists of the following: scales, music theory, rhythmic dictation, arpeggios, sight reading, melodic dictation.

Repertoire that students should avoid? no. *Performance opportunities available (frequency):* recitals, chorus.

Facilities

Number of practice rooms and hours: 20; 5. *Recital hall?* yes. *Concert hall?* no. *Recording studio?* no.

SWITZERLAND

ECOLE DE DANSE DE GENEVE; BALLET JUNIOR

44 Coulouvreniere, Geneve CH-1204
Tel: 022-329-12-10
Fax: 022-329-12-11

Entrance Requirements

Audition not required.

DANCE

Curriculum, Students, and Faculty

Elective courses: repertory.

DRAMA

Curriculum, Students, and Faculty

Required courses: audition preparation.

TAIWAN

TSOYING HIGH SCHOOL

55 Hai-Kung Road
Dance Division, Tsoying, Kaohsiung Tel: 886-7-5853083
Fax: 886-7-5853083
Email: dame@mail.tyhs.edu.tw
Contact: Su-ling Chou

General

Type of Institution: magnet-public. *Environment:* suburban.

Degrees offered: high school diploma.

Entrance Requirements

Audition required: live.

Costs & Financial Aid

Other fees: $2,800 books.

Types of scholarships and aid awarded: merit-based, need-based, institutional aid, government aid, reduced tuition, work/study. *Forms required for scholarships:* income tax return. *Loans available.*

Services

Housing options: family.

Support staff: college advisor, financial aid advisor, resident nurse, student affairs officer.

DANCE

Curriculum, Students, and Faculty

Required courses: ballet, dance composition/choreography (1 year to complete), dance history (2 years to complete), modern dance, movement techniques, music, rehearsal and performance.

Selectivity for males: most admitted, but not all. *Selectivity for females:* approximately 10% admitted. *Entering class size:* 30. *Graduating class size:* 12.

Renowned alumni: Yi-fun Wu, Chun-shen Wu, Yao-chen Shu dancer of Cloud Gate Dance Company, Zoh-mei Chao, Chin-shan Haiek.

Total full-time faculty: 1. *Total part-time faculty:* 10. *List of current faculty and past affiliations:* Liang-ling Yeh, Su-wen Lin, Au-li Su. *Program contact person:* Su-ling Chou.

Audition Information

No audition fee. Audition consists of the following: ballet, modern dance, Chinese Opera, movement. *Accompanist provided. Cassette player available; CD player available.*

Repertoire that students should avoid? no.

Performance Information

Performance opportunities available (frequency): Fully produced concerts (1 per year), informal concerts (5 per year), workshops (2 per year), on-site performances (2-3 per year), touring (2).

Performances choreographed by: faculty, students, guests. *Recent guest choreographers:* Yun-yu Wang, Danna Frangione, Daniel Lewis, Susan Street, Ho-ping Kung, Hsin-hua Kao, Lisa Fusillo, Sharon Garber, Leon Koning.

Facilities

Number of studios available: 3. *Approximate studio dimensions and flooring:* 15' x 35' wood, 10' x 12'. *Performance facilities:* piano, mirrors, bars, percussion musical instrument.

9

COLLEGE PROGRAM PROFILES

ALASKA

UNIVERSITY OF ALASKA, ANCHORAGE

Department of Theatre and Dance
3211 Providence Drive, Anchorage AK 99508
Tel: 907-786-1792
Fax: 907-786-1799

General

Type of Institution: public, university. *Environment:* suburban.

Total enrollment: 18,000. *Degrees offered:* BA.

Entrance Requirements

Audition required: video. *Other requirements:* recommendation, essay, photograph. *Standardized test requirements:* ACT; SAT I.

Costs & Financial Aid

Other fees: extended site fees, distance delivery fees, etc.

Types of scholarships and aid awarded: full, partial, merit-based, need-based, named, institutional aid, government aid, reduced tuition, work/study. *Forms required for scholarships:* income tax return, income asset verification. *Loans available. Procedure for applying for loans:* write the Student Financial Aid Office. *Financial aid offered to international students.*

Services

Housing options: on-site dorms, off-campus housing.

Support staff: career counselor, financial aid advisor, foreign student advisor, physical therapist, psychological counselor, resident assistant, resident nurse, student affairs officer.

Comments

No degree in dance.

DANCE

Curriculum, Students, and Faculty

Elective courses: African dance, jazz, modern dance, tap.

Selectivity for males: admit all who apply. *Selectivity for females:* admit all who apply. *Total enrollment:* 25. *Entering class size:* 15. *Percent international:* 5%.

Total full-time faculty: 1. *Total part-time faculty:* 3. *Program contact person:* Dr. Jill Crosby.

Audition Information

No audition fee. Accompanist not provided. Cassette player available; CD player available.

Performance Information

Performance opportunities available (frequency): Fully produced concerts (2-3 per year), workshops (2 per year), on-site performances (2-3 per year).

Performances choreographed by: faculty, students, guests. *Recent guest choreographers:* Heather Carnell, Jannie Hill, Pete Carpenter, and Marianne Kim.

Facilities

Number of studios available: 1. *Approximate studio dimensions and flooring:* sprung floor with Marley.

DRAMA

Curriculum, Students, and Faculty

Required courses: acting, directing, movement.

Elective courses: audition preparation, drama criticism, improvisation, make-up, musical theater, scene study, speech, stage combat, Stanislavski exercises, text analysis, verse drama, voice, musical theater.

Number of years required to complete program: 4-6. *Summer program available. Affiliation with a professional theater company: associated with every theatre company in Anchorage (semi-professional and community), working exchanges with several professional companies in Russia and the Russian Far East; many visiting artists.*

Total enrollment: 50. *Entering class size:* 20. *Percent international:* 5%. *Countries most represented*: Japan, Russia.

Total full-time faculty: 6. *Total part-time faculty:* 1.

Audition Information

No audition fee.

Performance Information

Performance opportunities available (frequency): fully produced performances (4 per year), informal performances (frequently), workshops (frequently), off-site performances (frequently).

Facilities

Number of theaters on campus: 3. *Type and capacity:* proscenium—900, thrust—200, black box—100.

BIRMINGHAM-SOUTHERN COLLEGE

P.O. Box 509033, Birmingham AL 35254
Tel: 205-226-4950 or 800-523-5793
Fax: 205-226-3058
Email: gwood@bsc.edu
Web: www.bsc.edu
Contact: Becky Baxter

General

Type of Institution: college. *Religious Affiliation:* United Methodist. *Environment:* urban.

Total enrollment: 1,800. *Total student body from other countries:* 5%. *Degrees offered:* BA, BFA, BM, BME.

Entrance Requirements

Audition required: live, audio tape. *Other requirements:* interview, recommendation, essay. *Standardized test requirements:* ACT, 26; SAT I, 600.

Costs & Financial Aid

Application fee: $25. *Tuition:* $13,750. *Medical fee:* $214. *Other fees:* $175-$325 private music lessons, $75 graduation, $105 student activity fee, $214 student insurance.

Types of scholarships and aid awarded: full, partial, merit-based, need-based, named, institutional aid, government aid, reduced tuition, tuition payment plan, work/study. *Forms required for scholarships:* FAFSA, income tax return. *Loans available. Procedure for applying for loans:* contact Financial Aid Office.

Services

Housing options: on-site dorms, off-campus housing, fraternity, sorority.

Support staff: career counselor, dorm parent, financial aid advisor, foreign student advisor, housing advisor, psychological counselor, resident assistant, resident nurse, student affairs officer.

DANCE

Curriculum, Students, and Faculty

Required courses: anatomy, ballet, dance composition/choreography, dance history, dance theory, dance writing, research and criticism, jazz, modern dance, Cunningham-based, Graham-based dance, other modern dance, music, pas de deux, pointe, rehearsal and performance, repertory, variations, pedagogy, stagecraft.

Elective courses: African dance, master classes, movement techniques, other world dance forms, vernacular dance, modern dance partnering.

Selectivity for males: approximately 60% admitted. *Selectivity for females:* approximately 60% admitted. *Total enrollment:* 150. *Entering class size:* 20.

Renowned alumni: Phoebe Pearipeu, Gary Gaper.

Total full-time faculty: 2. *Total part-time faculty:* 3. *List of current faculty and past affiliations:* Ruth Henry; L. Popvich, National Ballet Yugoslavia; Jennifer Pontius. *Program contact person:* Mira Popovich.

Audition Information

No audition fee. Audition consists of the following: ballet. *Accompanist provided. Cassette player available; CD player available. Dress requirements for males:* black tights, white shirt, socks. *Dress requirements for females:* black leotard, pink tights.

Audition evaluation criteria: auditions are only for scholarships.

Performance Information

Performance opportunities available (frequency): Fully produced concerts (3 per year), informal concerts (2 per year), workshops (1 per year), on-site performances(1-2 per year).

Performances choreographed by: faculty, students, guests. *Recent guest choreographers:* Dany Lenies, Leisha Berkut.

Facilities

Number of studios available: 2. *Approximate studio dimensions and flooring:* 40' x 50' allegro and wood, 30' x 45' allegro and wood. *Performance facilities:* college theater.

DRAMA

Curriculum, Students, and Faculty

Required courses: acting, audition preparation, directing, make-up, movement, musical theater, scene study, stage combat, Stanislavski exercises, text analysis, voice, directing.

Elective courses: drama criticism, verse drama.

Number of years required to complete program: 4. *Summer program not available. Selectivity for males:* most admitted, but not all. *Selectivity for females:* most admitted, but not all. *Total enrollment:* 100. *Entering class size:* 5.

Total full-time faculty: 3. *Total part-time faculty:* 2.

Audition Information

No audition fee. Audition consists of the following: comedic monologue, improvisation, interview with faculty member. *Dress requirements for males:* comfortable, but nice. *Dress requirements for females:* comfortable, but nice. *Repertoire that students should avoid?* Shakespeare or any period material.

Performance Information

Performance opportunities available (frequency): fully produced performances (4-5 a year), workshops (7-10 per year), casting is by audition.

Recent guest artists: Lorrine Vozoff, Nira Pullin.

Facilities

Type and capacity: flexible—372, black box—100.

MUSIC

Curriculum, Students, and Faculty

Unique or innovative music curriculum: conservatory quality training in a liberal arts setting. *How are major teacher assignments made?* Students may choose. Faculty is not informed of a student's teacher preference at the time of the audition. *26 lessons with major teacher. May a student change major teachers during the course of study?* possibly. *Study of secondary instrument or discipline is allowed.*

Total enrollment: 500. *Entering class size:* 20.

Renowned alumni: Michael Gimenez, Cleveland Institute of Music; Tiffany Murdock, Florida State University; James Dorroh.

Total full-time faculty: 9. *Total part-time faculty:* 30. *Program contact person:* Charles Mason.

Audition Information

No audition fee. Instruments provided for: percussionists.

Performance opportunities available (frequency): jury examinations (every semester).

Facilities

Recital hall? yes. *Concert hall?* no. *Recording studio?* yes.

Comments

We are highly selective due to high required ACT or SAT scores; however, students do not formally declare a major until the end of their sophomore year. By that time, any students who is not suited for music study will be quite aware of the fact as they will have had two years of music courses. So it is quite rare that we reject anyone.

HUNTINGDON COLLEGE

1500 East Fairview Avenue, Montgomery AL 36106
Tel: 334-833-4457
Fax: 334-833-4264
Email: jwglass@huntingdon.edu
Web: www.huntingdon.edu

General

Type of Institution: college. *Religious Affiliation:* United Methodist Church. *Environment:* urban. *Cross registration is available through Auburn University—Montgomery.*

Total enrollment: 641. *Total student body from other countries:* 3%. *Degrees offered:* certificate, BA.

Entrance Requirements

Audition required: live *Other requirements:* interview, essay *Standardized test requirements:* ACT, 25; SAT I, 1123; TOEFL, 500.

Costs & Financial Aid

Application fee: $25. *Deposit:* $200. *Tuition:* $10,100. *Other fees:* $890 student activity fee.

Percent of students receiving financial aid: 90%. *Types of scholarships and aid awarded:* full, partial, merit-based, need-based, named, institutional aid, government aid, tuition payment plan, work/study. *Forms required for scholarships:* FAFSA. *Loans available. Procedure for applying for loans:* through Financial Aid Office. *Financial aid offered to international students. Percent of international students receiving scholarships:* 80%.

Services

Housing options: on-site dorms.

Support staff: career counselor, financial aid advisor, foreign student advisor, housing advisor, psychological counselor, resident assistant, resident nurse, student affairs officer.

DANCE

Curriculum, Students, and Faculty

Required courses: anatomy, ballet (3-5 classes per week, 4 years to complete), dance composition/choreography (2 years to complete), dance history, Labanotation, modern dance (2 classes per week), body conditioning, pas de deux (3 classes per week, 1 year to complete), rehearsal and performance (4 years to complete).

Elective courses: pointe (2 classes per week, 2 years to complete).

Selectivity for males: admit all who apply. *Selectivity for females:* admit all who apply. *Total enrollment:* 23.

Total full-time faculty: 2. *List of current faculty and past affiliations:* Diana F. Green, Julian Green, Washington Dance Spectrum. *Program contact person:* Diana Green.

Audition Information

No audition fee. Audition consists of the following: ballet, modern dance, pointe works, prepared solo, interview. *Accompanist provided. Cassette player available; CD player available. Dress requirements for males:* black tights, black leotard or white t-shirt. *Dress requirements for females:* black leotard, pink or black tights.

Audition evaluation criteria: alignment, knowledge of technique, ability to assimilate movement quickly, an open and flexible attitude toward movement study.

Performance Information

Performance opportunities available (frequency): Fully produced concerts (3 per year), informal concerts (2-4 per year), workshops (2 per year), on-site performances (1 per year).

Performances choreographed by: faculty, students, guests. *Recent guest choreographers:* Israel Gabriel.

Facilities

Number of studios available: 2. *Approximate studio dimensions and flooring:* 60' x 40' basket weave with permanent Marley, 30' x 20' basket weave with permanent Marley. *Performance facilities:* Dungeon Theatre—Seats 100 (stage 46' x 28'), Outdoor Stage—(64' x 40').

DRAMA

Curriculum, Students, and Faculty

Required courses: acting, directing, movement techniques, musical theater, scene study, voice.

Elective courses: audition preparation, dramaturgy, improvisation.

Number of years required to complete program: 4. *Summer program not available. Technical internships with Alabama Shakespeare Festival, performers give lectures and workshops.*

Selectivity for males: approximately 60% admitted. *Selectivity for females:* approximately 60% admitted. *Total enrollment:* 17.

Total full-time faculty: 1. *List of current faculty and past affiliations:* Fiona Macleod, Alabama Shakespeare Festival.

Audition Information

Audition consists of the following: cold readings, comedic monologue, group warm-up. *Dress requirements for males:* clothes suitable for movement, no jeans. *Dress requirements for females:* clothes suitable for movement, no jeans. *Audition evaluation criteria:* Familiarity with material, understanding of work, diversity of characterization, quality of movement, voice, ability to take direction.

Performance Information

Performance opportunities available (frequency): fully produced performances (4 per year), informal performances (3 per year), workshops (3 per year), off-site performances (occasionally), casting is by audition.

Recent guest artists: Parnassus Institute, member of Alabama Shakespeare Festival.

Facilities

Rehearsal facilities and hours: theater open until 10:00 pm with faculty members. *Number of theaters on campus:* 1. *Type and capacity:* proscenium—135.

MUSIC

Curriculum, Students, and Faculty

Unique or innovative music curriculum: Huntingdon College gives each student a PC opportunity—Vivace software. *How are major teacher assignments made?* made by the school according to teacher availability. Faculty is informed of a student's teacher preference at the time of the audition. *30 lessons with major teacher. May a student change major teachers during the course of study?* possibly. *Study of secondary instrument or discipline is allowed.*

Selectivity for instruments or programs offered (rating): bassoon (competitive), choral singing (competitive), clarinet (competitive), composition (competitive), double bass (competitive), flute or piccolo (competitive), French horn (competitive), guitar (competitive), jazz (competitive), oboe/English horn (competitive), organ (competitive), percussion (competitive), piano (competitive), sacred music, saxophone (competitive), trombone (competitive), trumpet (competitive), tuba (competitive), viola (competitive), violin (competitive), violoncello (competitive), voice (competitive).

Total enrollment: 27. *Percent international:* 2%. *Countries most represented*: Korea.

Renowned alumni: Rockland Osgood, Gene Jarvis.

Total full-time faculty: 4. *Total part-time faculty:* 8. *Program contact person:* Dr. James Glass.

Audition Information

No audition fee. Audition consists of the following: music theory, rhythmic dictation, melodic dictation. *Instruments provided for:* percussionists, organists.

Performance opportunities available (frequency): band (frequently), jury examinations (frequently), recitals (frequently), touring (frequently), chorus.

Facilities

Number of practice rooms and hours: 12; 7:00 am-10:00 pm. *Recital hall?* yes. *Concert hall?* yes.

ARIZONA

ARIZONA STATE UNIVERSITY

College of Fine Arts
P.O. Box 872102, Tempe AZ 85287-2102
Tel: 602-965-6536 or 800-252-ASU1
Fax: 602-965-9073
Email: asuvm.inre@asu.edu
Web: www.asu.edu/sfa
Contact: Gina Stephens

General

Type of Institution: university. *Environment:* urban.

Total enrollment: 44,255. *Total student body from other countries:* 6%. *Degrees offered:* BA, BFA, BM.

Entrance Requirements

Audition required: live, audio, video. *Standardized test requirements:* ACT, 24; SAT I, 1110.

Costs & Financial Aid

Application fee: $40. *Tuition:* $8,711. *Other fees:* $700 books. *Room and board:* $4,700.

Percent of students receiving financial aid: 35%. *Types of scholarships and aid awarded:* full, partial, merit-based, need-based, named, institutional aid, government aid, work/study. *Forms required for scholarships:* FASTWEB, paper forms. *Loans available. Financial aid offered to international students.*

Services

Housing options: on-site dorms, off-campus housing, fraternity, sorority.

Support staff: career counselor, financial aid advisor, foreign student advisor, housing advisor, physical therapist, psychological counselor, resident assistant, student affairs officer.

DANCE

Curriculum, Students, and Faculty

Required courses: anatomy, ballet (2 classes per week, 2 years to complete), dance composition/choreography, dance history, dance theory, dance writing, research and criticism, historical dance, movement techniques, music, nutrition, rehearsal and performance, repertory, stagecraft, variations (2 classes per week, 1 year to complete).

Elective courses: African dance, character, jazz, Labanotation, master classes, men's class, partnering, other world dance forms, pas de deux, pointe, Spanish, tap, vernacular dance.

Selectivity for males: admit all who apply. *Selectivity for females:* admit all who apply. *Total enrollment:* 135. *Entering class size:* 39. *Percent international:* 2%.

Total full-time faculty: 11. *Total part-time faculty:* 5. *Program contact person:* Rose Welch, 602-965-6807.

Audition Information

No audition fee. Audition consists of the following: ballet, improvisation, modern dance. *Accompanist provided. Cassette player available; CD player available.*

Performance Information

Performance opportunities available (frequency): Fully produced concerts (2 per-year), informal concerts (8 per-year), workshops (6-10 per-year), on-site performances (10-12 per-year), touring.

Performances choreographed by: faculty, students, guests. *Recent guest choreographers:* Bebe Miller, Kevin O' Day, Ralph Lemon, Liz Lerhman, Alvin Ailey Company.

Facilities

Number of studios available: 8. *Approximate studio dimensions and flooring:* Marley flooring. *Performance facilities:* Gammage auditorium—3,000 seats, Galvin Theater—500 seats, Dance Lab—120 seats, Dance Box—90 seats.

DRAMA

Curriculum, Students, and Faculty

Required courses: acting, directing, drama criticism, dramaturgy, make-up, martial arts, movement, speech, stage combat, text analysis, verse drama, voice.

Elective courses: mime, musical theater.

Number of years required to complete program: 4. *Summer program available. No affiliation with a professional theater company. Selectivity for males:* admit all who apply. *Selectivity for females:* admit all who apply. *Total enrollment:* 325. *Entering class size:* 61.

Total full-time faculty: 20. *Total part-time faculty:* 4.

Audition Information

No audition fee.

Performance Information

Performance opportunities available (frequency): fully produced performances (4 per year), informal performances (25-30 per year), casting is by audition.

Facilities

Rehearsal facilities and hours: variety of spaces, hours are as needed by cast and crew. *Number of theaters on campus:* 4. *Type and capacity:* proscenium—500 seats, proscenium—125 seats, proscenium—75 seats, proscenium—75 seats.

MUSIC

Curriculum, Students, and Faculty

Unique or innovative music curriculum: Music Therapy, Music Education, and Jazz. *How are major teacher assignments made?* Students may choose, made by the school, according to teacher preference and to teacher availability. Faculty is informed of a student's teacher preference at the time of the audition. *30 lessons with major teacher. May a student change major teachers during the course of study?* possibly. *Study of secondary instrument or discipline is allowed.*

Selectivity for instruments or programs offered (rating): accompanying (highly selective), bassoon (competitive), choral conducting (selective), choral singing (highly selective), clarinet (selective), composition (competitive), double bass (selective), flute or piccolo (selective), French horn (selective), guitar (selective), harp (non-competitive), harpsichord (competitive), jazz (competitive), oboe/English horn (competitive), orchestral conducting (highly selective), organ (highly selective), percussion (highly selective), piano (highly selective), saxophone (highly selective), trombone (competitive), trumpet (highly selective), tuba (highly selective), viola (selective), violin (competitive), violoncello (competitive), voice (highly selective).

Total enrollment: 771. *Entering class size:* 111. *Percent international:* 5%.

Total full-time faculty: 64. *Total part-time faculty:* 8. *Program contact person:* Karen Bryan, 602-965-5069.

Audition Information

No audition fee. Audition consists of the following: scales, arpeggios, sight reading. *Instruments provided for:* harpists, percussionists, pianists, organists.

Facilities

Recital hall? yes. *Concert hall?* yes. *Recording studio?* no.

CALIFORNIA

CALIFORNIA INSTITUTE OF THE ARTS

24700 McBean Parkway, Valencia CA 91355
Tel: 805-255-1050 or 800-292-2787
Fax: 805-254-8352
Email: admiss@musc.calarts.edu
Web: www.calarts.edu
Contact: Kenneth Young

General

Type of Institution: college, conservatory. *Environment:* suburban.

Total enrollment: 1,125. *Total student body from other countries:* 12%. *Degrees offered:* BFA.

Entrance Requirements

Audition required. Other requirements: essay. *Standardized test requirements:* TOEFL, 550.

Costs & Financial Aid

Application fee: $60. *Deposit:* $300. *Tuition:* $18,120. *Medical fee:* $325. *Other fees:* $70 student activity fee, $2,700 room.

Percent of students receiving financial aid: 75%. *Types of scholarships and aid awarded:* full, partial, merit-based, need-based, named, institutional aid, government aid, tuition payment plan, work/study, gig office. *Forms required for scholarships:* FAFSA, income tax return, income asset verification. *Loans available. Financial aid offered to international students. Percent of international students receiving scholarships:* 50%. *Other aid available to international students:* merit only.

Services

Housing options: on-site dorms.

Support staff: career counselor, financial aid advisor, foreign student advisor, housing advisor, psychological counselor, resident assistant, resident nurse, student affairs officer.

Comments

Obtain a free copy of our admissions bulletin for complete information.

DANCE

Curriculum, Students, and Faculty

Required courses: anatomy, ballet, dance composition/choreography, dance history, dance theory, dance writing, research and criticism, master classes, Cunningham-based, Graham-based dance, Limon-based modern dance, music, rehearsal and performance, repertory, stagecraft.

Elective courses: African dance, martial arts, Indonesian, Japanese dance.

Total enrollment: 59. *Entering class size:* 27.

Renowned alumni: Susan Rose, David Landis, Jacques Heim, Lisa K. Locke.

Total full-time faculty: 7. *Total part-time faculty:* 7. *Program contact person:* Cristyne Lawson.

Audition Information

No audition fee. Audition consists of the following: improvisation, modern dance. *Accompanist provided. Cassette player not available; CD player not available. Dress requirements for males:* leotard, tights. *Dress requirements for females:* leotard, tights.

Performance Information

Performance opportunities available (frequency): fully produced concerts (varies), informal concerts (varies), workshops (varies).

Performances choreographed by: faculty, students, guests. *Recent guest choreographers:* Ann Carlson, Ralph Lemon, Mary Ann Kellogg, L. Martina Young.

Facilities

Number of studios available: 5. *Approximate studio dimensions and flooring:* 36' x 50' sprung. *Performance facilities:* 2 theaters (50' x 70').

DRAMA

Curriculum, Students, and Faculty

Required courses: acting, audition preparation, directing, drama criticism, dramaturgy, make-up, martial arts, movement, scene study, speech, stage combat, text analysis, verse drama, voice.

Number of years required to complete program: 4. *Summer program not available. No affiliation with a professional theater company. Total enrollment:* 220. *Entering class size:* 94.

Renowned alumni: Ed Harris, Don Cheadly, Bill Irwin, Kathy Segel, Kathy Beker, Paul Reuben.

Total full-time faculty: 21. *Total part-time faculty:* 23.

Audition Information

No audition fee. Audition consists of the following: comedic monologue, Shakespearean monologue.

Performance Information

Performance opportunities available (frequency): fully produced performances (varies), informal performances (varies), workshops (varies), casting is by audition.

Recent guest artists: Travis Preston, August Wilson, Lee Brewer, Steven Porchas, Joseph Chaiken, Peter Selbs.

Facilities

Rehearsal facilities and hours: varies. *Number of theaters on campus:* 6. *Type and capacity:* black box—99 seats, flexible—320 seats.

MUSIC

Curriculum, Students, and Faculty

How are major teacher assignments made? students may choose, according to teacher preference and teacher availability. *30 lessons with major teacher. May a student change major teachers during the course of study?* possibly. *Study of secondary instrument or discipline is allowed.*

Total enrollment: 194. *Entering class size:* 78.

Renowned alumni: Carl Stone, Lois V. Vierk, Mike Cain, James Dunhem, Nedra Wheeler.

Total full-time faculty: 27. *Total part-time faculty:* 37. *Program contact person:* David Rosenboom.

Audition Information

Audition consists of the following: scales, orchestral excerpts, music theory, sight reading, improvisation. *Instruments provided for:* harpists, percussionists.

Performance opportunities available (frequency): chamber music (frequently), recitals (frequently), chorus.

Facilities

Number of practice rooms and hours: 25; 24 hours a day. *Recital hall?* yes. *Concert hall?* yes. *Recording studio?* yes.

CALIFORNIA STATE UNIVERSITY, HAYWARD

Theatre and Dance
25800 Carlos Bee Boulevard, Hayward CA 94542
Tel: 510-885-4813
Fax: 510-885-4748
Email: third@csnhayward.edu
Web: www.csuhayward.edu

General

Type of Institution: public university. *Environment:* urban.

Total enrollment: 12,000. *Degrees offered:* BA.

Entrance Requirements

Audition required: live, video. *Other requirements:* recommendation. *Standardized test requirements:* ACT, 20; SAT I, 900.

Costs & Financial Aid

Application fee: $55. *Tuition (in-state/out-state):* $1,800/$5,500.

Types of scholarships and aid awarded: partial, merit-based, need-based, named, government aid, reduced tuition, work/study.

Services

Housing options: on-site dorms, off-campus housing, family.

Support staff: career counselor, financial aid advisor, foreign student advisor, housing advisor, psychological counselor, resident assistant, resident nurse, student affairs officer.

DANCE

Curriculum, Students, and Faculty

Required courses: dance composition/choreography, dance history, dance theory, modern dance, rehearsal and performance, stagecraft, jazz, master classes.

Elective courses: African dance, character, ballet, dance writing, research and criticism, jazz, martial arts, movement techniques, Pilates, music, repertory, tap, variations, dance history.

Selectivity for males: most admitted, but not all. *Selectivity for females:* most admitted, but not all. *Total enrollment:* 20. *Entering class size:* 2. *Graduating class size:* 5. *Percent international:* 10%. *Countries most represented*: Brazil.

Total part-time faculty: 5. *List of current faculty and past affiliations:* Laura Ellis, Dimensions Dance; Cynthia Berfol, Shally Anderson; Laura Renaud Wilson, Mills College and University of California at Berkeley. *Program contact person:* Laura Renaud-Wilson.

Audition Information

No audition fee. Audition consists of the following: prepared solo. *Accompanist not provided. Cassette player available; CD player available.*

Performance Information

Performance opportunities available (frequency): Fully produced concerts (1-2 per year), informal concerts (1-2 per year), workshops (1-3 per year), on-site performances (10-15 per year), touring (10-15 per year).

Performances choreographed by: faculty, students, guests.

Facilities

Number of studios available: 1. *Approximate studio dimensions:* 45' x 100'. *Performance facilities:* 2 stages; proscenium—500-seat, black box—120-seat.

DRAMA

Curriculum, Students, and Faculty

Required courses: audition preparation, directing, drama criticism, make-up, text analysis.

Elective courses: acting, improvisation, movement, musical theater, scene study, verse drama, voice, stage combat.

Number of years required to complete program: 4. *Summer program available. Selectivity for males:* most admitted, but not all. *Selectivity for females:* most admitted, but not all. *Total enrollment:* 40. *Entering class size:* 10. *Graduating class size:* 12. *Percent international:* 5%. *Countries most represented*: France, United Kingdom, Japan.

Total full-time faculty: 5. *Total part-time faculty:* 1. *List of current faculty and past affiliations:* Ric Prindle, ACT; Edgardo De La Cruz, International Performance Workshops.

Audition Information

Audition consists of the following: Any 2 monologues; prefer tape of actual performance (even chorus part).

Performance Information

Performance opportunities available (frequency): fully produced performances (1-3 per quarter), informal performances (1-2 per quarter), workshops (occasionally), off-site performances (every other year), tour to Scotland, France, casting is by audition.

Recent guest artists: American Theatres Ventures.

Facilities

Rehearsal facilities and hours: acting studio, 20' x 50', 8:00 am-10:00 pm. *Number of theaters on campus:* 2. *Type and capacity:* proscenium—500 seats, studio—150 seats.

CALIFORNIA STATE UNIVERSITY, FULLERTON

P.O. Box 6850, Fullerton CA 92834-6850
Tel: 714-278-2011
Fax: 714-278-5956
Web: www.fullerton.edu

General

Type of Institution: public, university. *Environment:* urban.

Total enrollment: 22,000. *Degrees offered:* BA, BM.

Entrance Requirements

Audition required: live. *Other requirements:* essay. *Standardized test requirements:* ACT; SAT I; TOEFL, 500.

Costs & Financial Aid

Application fee: $55. *Medical fee:* $25. *Other fees:* $54 per semester parking fee.

Types of scholarships and aid awarded: full, partial, merit-based, named. *Forms required for scholarships:* FAFSA.

Services

Housing options: on-site dorms, off-campus housing.

Support staff: career counselor, financial aid advisor, foreign student advisor, housing advisor, physical therapist, psychological counselor, resident nurse, student affairs officer.

DRAMA

Curriculum, Students, and Faculty

Required courses: acting, drama criticism, movement, acting, text analysis.

MUSIC

Curriculum, Students, and Faculty

How are major teacher assignments made? students may choose, made by the school according to teacher preference, according to teacher availability. Faculty is not informed of a student's teacher preference at the time of the audition. *30 lessons with major teacher. May a student change major teachers during the course of study?* possibly. *Study of secondary instrument or discipline is allowed.*

Selectivity for instruments or programs offered (rating): accompanying (non-competitive), accordion (non-competitive), bassoon (non-competitive), choral conducting (non-competitive), choral singing (non-competitive), clarinet (non-competitive), composition (non-competitive), double bass (non-competitive), electronic music (non-competitive), flute or piccolo (non-competitive), French horn (non-competitive), guitar (non-competitive), harp (non-competitive), harpsichord (non-competitive), oboe/English horn (non-competitive), orchestral conducting (non-competitive), organ (non-competitive), percussion (non-competitive), piano (non-competitive), saxophone (non-competitive), trombone (non-competitive), trumpet (non-competitive), tuba (non-competitive), viola (non-competitive), violin (non-competitive), violoncello (non-competitive), voice (non-competitive).

Total enrollment: 300. *Entering class size:* 65. *Graduating class size:* 40. *Countries most represented*: Vietnam, Korea, Mexico, Taiwan.

Renowned alumni: Deborah Voigt, Rodney Gilfry, Jubilant Sykes, Joaquin Valdepenas, Stan Hill, Eric Alatorre, Gordon Paine, Deborah Smith, Steve Johnson, Patrick Macey, Diane Elias.

Total full-time faculty: 19. *Total part-time faculty:* 35. *Program contact person:* Gordon Paine.

Audition Information

No audition fee. Audition consists of the following: music theory, music history. *Instruments provided for:* harpists, percussionists.

Performance opportunities available (frequency): band (4-5 per year), chamber music (every semester), jury examinations (every semester), opera workshops (every semester), orchestral concerts (4-5 per year), recitals (junior and senior year), produced operas (annual), chorus (each semester).

Facilities

Recital hall? yes. *Concert hall?* yes. *Recording studio?* yes.

Comments

Most are admitted to the music program for any of the offered instruments, but are often required to do remedial work before fully admitted to the program.

CALIFORNIA STATE UNIVERSITY, LONG BEACH

1250 Bellflower Boulevard
Long Beach CA 90840-2004
Tel: 562-985-4364
Fax: 562-985-7883
Web: www.csulb.edu

CALIFORNIA STATE UNIVERSITY, LOS ANGELES

Department of Music
5151 State University Drive, Los Angeles CA 90032
Tel: 213-343-4060
Fax: 213-343-4062
Email: wbelan@calstatela.edu
Web: www.calstatela.edu
Contact: George Bachman

General

Type of Institution: public, university. *Environment:* urban.

Total enrollment: 25,000. *Degrees offered:* BA, BM.

Entrance Requirements

Audition required: live, audio, video *Other requirements:* interview. *Standardized test requirements:* ACT; SAT I; SAT II; TOEFL, 550.

Costs & Financial Aid

Application fee: $55.

Types of scholarships and aid awarded: full, partial, merit-based, need-based, named, institutional aid, government aid, tuition payment plan, work/study. *Forms required for scholarships:* FFS, FAFSA, income tax return, income asset verification. *Loans available. Procedure for applying for loans:* contact Financial Aid Office. *Financial aid offered to international students.*

Services

Housing options: on-site dorms.

Support staff: career counselor, financial aid advisor, foreign student advisor, housing advisor, psychological counselor, resident assistant, resident nurse, student affairs officer.

MUSIC

Curriculum, Students, and Faculty

Unique or innovative music curriculum: Pacific Contemporary Music Center on-site, Roger Wagner Center for Choral Studies on site. *How are major teacher assignments made?* Students may choose. Faculty is informed of a student's teacher preference at the time of the audition. *30 lessons with major teacher. May a student change major teachers during the course of study?* possibly. *Study of secondary instrument or discipline is allowed.*

Selectivity for instruments or programs offered (rating): accompanying (selective), bassoon (selective), choral conducting (highly selective), choral singing (non-competitive), clarinet (selective), composition (selective), double bass (selective), electronic music (selective), flute or piccolo (selective), French horn (selective), guitar (selective), harp (selective), harpsichord (selective), jazz (selective), oboe/English horn (selective), orchestral conducting (highly selective), organ (selective), percussion (selective), piano (selective), saxophone (selective), trombone (selective), trumpet (selective), tuba (selective), viola (selective), violin (selective), violoncello (selective), voice (selective).

Total enrollment: 250. *Entering class size:* 50. *Graduating class size:* 20. *Countries most represented:* Korea, Taiwan, China.

Renowned alumni: James Newton, Raynor Carroll.

Total full-time faculty: 17. *Total part-time faculty:* 40. *Program contact person:* H. David Caffey.

Audition Information

No audition fee. Audition consists of the following: scales, orchestral excerpts, music theory. *Instruments provided for:* harpists, percussionists.

Facilities

Recital hall? yes. *Concert hall?* yes. *Recording studio?* yes.

HUMBOLDT STATE UNIVERSITY

Arcata CA 95521
Tel: 707-826-3531
Fax: 707-826-3528

General

Type of Institution: public, university.

Degrees offered: BA.

Entrance Requirements

Audition required: audio. *Other requirements:* interview, recommendation, essay, photograph.

Costs & Financial Aid

Procedure for applying for loans: custom form, audition tape.

Services

Housing options: on-site dorms, off-campus housing, fraternity, sorority.

Support staff: career counselor, financial aid advisor, foreign student advisor, housing advisor, psychological counselor, resident assistant, resident nurse, student affairs officer.

MUSIC

Curriculum, Students, and Faculty

Unique or innovative music curriculum: One BA degree, with 3 performance tracks (vocal, instrumental, piano); credential track (music education); or general track. *How are major teacher assignments made?* students may choose, made by the school according to teacher preference and teacher availability. Faculty is not informed of a student's teacher preference at the time of the audition. *May a student change major teachers during the course of study?* possibly. *Study of secondary instrument or discipline is allowed.*

Selectivity for instruments or programs offered (rating): accompanying (non-competitive), bassoon (non-competitive), choral singing (competitive), clarinet (non-competitive), composition (non-competitive), double bass (non-competitive), electronic music (competitive), flute or piccolo (non-competitive), French horn (non-competitive), guitar (competitive), harp (open), harpsichord (non-competitive), jazz (competitive), oboe/English horn (non-competitive), organ (non-competitive), percussion (competitive), piano (non-competitive), saxophone (non-competitive), trombone (non-competitive), trumpet (non-competitive), tuba (non-competitive), viola (non-competitive), violin (open), violoncello (non-competitive), voice (competitive).

Total enrollment: 240. *Entering class size:* 25. *Graduating class size:* 18.

Renowned alumni: Christopher Breen, *Macuser Magazine*.

Total full-time faculty: 9. *Total part-time faculty:* 14. *Program contact person:* Dr. Gilbert D. Cline, (707) 826-3531.

Audition Information

No audition fee. Audition consists of the following: music theory, rhythmic dictation, melodic dictation. *Instruments provided for:* harpists, percussionists.

Performance opportunities available (frequency): band (frequently), jury examinations (frequently), orchestral concerts (frequently), recitals (frequently), chorus.

Facilities

Number of practice rooms and hours: 30; 7:00 am-12:00 am. *Recital hall?* yes. *Concert hall?* yes. *Recording studio?* no.

MOUNT ST. MARY'S COLLEGE

12001 Chalon Road, Los Angeles CA 90049
Tel: 301-954-4265
Fax: 301-954-4379
Contact: Kelly Farlnad

General

Type of Institution: college. *Religious Affiliation:* Roman Catholic. *Cross registration is available through the University of California—Los Angeles.*

Total enrollment: 1,984. *Degrees offered:* BA, BM.

Entrance Requirements

Audition required. Other requirements: interview, recommendation. *Standardized test requirements:* ACT; SAT I; SAT II; TOEFL, 550.

Costs & Financial Aid

Application fee: $32. *Deposit:* $100. *Medical fee:* $315.

Types of scholarships and aid awarded: full, partial, merit-based, need-based, named, institutional aid, tuition payment plan, work/study. *Loans available. Procedure for applying for loans:* if applying for need-based aid, students must complete a FAFSA; no FAFSA needed if student is applying for merit-based scholarship. *Other aid available to international students:* merit academic scholarship.

Services

Housing options: on-site dorms.

Support staff: career counselor, financial aid advisor, psychological counselor, resident assistant, student affairs officer.

MUSIC

Curriculum, Students, and Faculty

How are major teacher assignments made? students may choose. Faculty is informed of a student's teacher preference at the time of the audition. *May a student change major teachers during the course of study?* never. *Study of secondary instrument or discipline is allowed.*

Selectivity for instruments or programs offered (rating): guitar (competitive), organ (competitive), piano (competitive), saxophone (competitive), trumpet (competitive), viola (competitive).

Total enrollment: 25.

Renowned alumni: Paul Salmunovich, Rick Henn, Paul Gibson.

Total full-time faculty: 1. *Total part-time faculty:* 7. *Program contact person:* Sister Teresita Espinosa.

Audition Information

No audition fee. Audition consists of the following: music theory, repertoire. *Instruments provided for:* percussionists.

Required repertoire: 2 different stylistic periods. *Performance opportunities available (frequency):* chamber music (1 per semester), band (1 per semester), jury examinations (1 per semester), recitals, touring (1 per year), chorus (2 per semester).

Facilities

Number of practice rooms: 8. *Recital hall?* yes. *Concert hall?* yes. *Recording studio?* no.

POMONA COLLEGE

333 North College Way, Claremont CA 91711
Tel: 909-621-8134
Email: admissions@pomona.edu
Web: www.pomona.edu
Contact: Bruce Poch

General

Type of Institution: college. *Environment:* suburban. *Part of Claremont Colleges.*

Total enrollment: 1,420. *Degrees offered:* BA.

Entrance Requirements

Audition not required. Other requirements: essay *Standardized test requirements:* SAT I.

Costs & Financial Aid

Application fee: $50. *Deposit:* $300. *Tuition:* $20,500.

Percent of students receiving financial aid: 55%. *Types of scholarships and aid awarded:* need-based, government aid, tuition payment plan, work/study. *Forms required for scholarships:* FAFSA, income tax return, income asset verification, CSS Profile. *Loans available. Procedure for applying for loans:* complete required forms by 2/1. *Financial aid offered to international students. Percent of international students receiving scholarships:* 38%. *Other aid available to international students:* Limited to 4 freshmen each year (need-based).

Services

Housing options: on-site dorms.

Support staff: career counselor, financial aid advisor, foreign student advisor, housing advisor, psychological counselor, resident assistant, student affairs officer.

DANCE

Curriculum, Students, and Faculty

Required courses: anatomy, ballet, dance composition/choreography, dance history, dance theory, Graham-based, Limon-based modern dance, Laban Movement Studies, music, rehearsal and performance, repertory, stagecraft.

Elective courses: African dance, Alexander Technique, dance writing, research and criticism, jazz, other world dance forms, Spanish, tap.

Selectivity for males: approximately 33% admitted. *Selectivity for females:* approximately 33% admitted. *Total enrollment:* 150. *Graduating class size:* 5.

Total full-time faculty: 1. *Total part-time faculty:* 6. *List of current faculty and past affiliations:* Nicholas Gunn, Paul Taylor Co.; Victoria Koenig, Eliot Feld; John Pennington, Bella Lewitzky; Laurie Cameron, Folkwang Schule, Essen, Germany. *Program contact person:* Laurie Cameron.

Audition Information

Audition consists of the following: student should send a videotape.

Performance Information

Performance opportunities available (frequency): fully produced concerts (2 per year), informal concerts (1 per year), workshops (10 per year), on-site performances (2 per semester).

Performances choreographed by: faculty, students, guests. *Recent guest choreographers:* Ferne Ackerman, Jerry Pearson.

Facilities

Number of studios available: 2. *Approximate studio dimensions and flooring:* 50' x 75' wood, Marley. *Performance facilities:* 300-seat theater, studio theater.

DRAMA

Curriculum, Students, and Faculty

Required courses: acting, Alexander technique, audition preparation, dance, directing, improvisation, make-up, scene study, speech, Stanislavski exercises, text analysis.

Elective courses: drama criticism, martial arts, mime, musical theater.

Summer program available on an informal basis with the Santa Fe Opera and La Jolla Playhouse.

Selectivity for males: approximately 60% admitted. *Selectivity for females:* approximately 60% admitted.

Renowned alumni: Kelly Perrine, Joe Wrightman, Kris Kristofferson, Rose Portillo, Michael Addison, George Wolfe, Joel McCrae, Anthony Zerbe, Sherry Linnell, Robert Manden.

List of current faculty and past affiliations: Betty Bernhard, Tom Leabhart, Jim Taylor.

Performance Information

Performance opportunities available (frequency): fully produced performances (4 per year), off-site performances (1 per year), casting is by audition.

Facilities

Rehearsal facilities and hours: studio stage 7:00 pm-10:00 pm (Mon-Fri), 1:00 pm-5:00 pm (Sat).

MUSIC

Curriculum, Students, and Faculty

How are major teacher assignments made? made by the school, according to teacher availability. Faculty is informed of a student's teacher preference at the time of the audition. *28 lessons with major teacher. May a student change major teachers during the course of study?* possibly. *Study of secondary instrument or discipline is allowed.*

Selectivity for instruments or programs offered (rating): accompanying (selective), bassoon (competitive), choral conducting (competitive), choral singing (non-competitive), clarinet (competitive), composition (non-competitive), double bass (competitive), electronic music (open), flute or piccolo (competitive), French horn (competitive), guitar (non-competitive), harp (competitive), harpsichord (competitive), jazz (selective), oboe/English horn (competitive), orchestral conducting (selective), organ (competitive), Balanese gamelan (open), West African drum (open), percussion (competitive), piano (competitive), saxophone (competitive), trombone (competitive), trumpet (competitive), tuba (competitive), viola (competitive), violin (competitive), violoncello (competitive), voice (competitive).

Renowned alumni: Lucy Shelton, David Noon. *Program contact person:* Eric Lindholm.

Audition Information

Instruments provided for: harpists, percussionists; some instruments available on loan.

Facilities

Number of practice rooms and hours: 10; 24 hours a day. *Recital hall?* yes. *Concert hall?* yes. *Recording studio?* yes.

Comments

The music department maintains programs and facilities for students of all talent and experience levels. The more advanced students are those who participate in chamber music, larger ensembles, etc.

SAN FRANCISCO CONSERVATORY OF MUSIC

1201 Ortega Street, San Francisco CA 94122
Tel: 415-759-3422
Fax: 415-759-3499
Email: jgordon@sirius.com
Web: www.sfcm.edu
Contact: Joan Gordon

General

Type of Institution: conservatory. *Environment:* urban.

Total enrollment: 260. *Total student body from other countries:* 20%. *Degrees offered:* BM, music diploma.

Entrance Requirements

Audition required: live, video, regional. *Other requirements:* recommendation. *Standardized test requirements:* ACT; SAT I, 1152; TOEFL, 500.

Costs & Financial Aid

Application fee: $60. *Deposit:* $200. *Tuition:* $16,300. *Other fees:* $250 annual regstration fee.

Percent of students receiving financial aid: 70%. *Types of scholarships and aid awarded:* full, partial, merit-based, need-based, institutional aid, government aid, tuition payment plan, work/

study, gig office. *Forms required for scholarships:* FAFSA, school's own financial aid form. *Loans available. Procedure for applying for loans:* file FAFSA and institutional form by 3/1. *Financial aid offered to international students. Percent of international students receiving scholarships:* 35%. *Other aid available to international students:* on-campus employment.

Services

Housing options: off-campus housing.

Support staff: financial aid advisor, foreign student advisor.

Comments

Our students receive extensive performance opportunities both at the conservatory and as members of the many performing organizations in the San Francisco Bay area.

MUSIC

Curriculum, Students, and Faculty

Unique or innovative music curriculum: 86% of our classes have fewer than 20 students and 32% have fewer than 10 students. *How are major teacher assignments made?* made by the school, according to teacher preference and teacher availability. Faculty is informed of a student's teacher preference at the time of the audition. *32 lessons with major teacher. May a student change major teachers during the course of study?* possibly. *Study of secondary instrument or discipline is allowed.*

Selectivity for instruments or programs offered (rating): accompanying (selective), bassoon (selective), clarinet (selective), composition (selective), double bass (competitive), flute or piccolo (selective), French horn (highly selective), guitar (selective), harp (selective), harpsichord (selective), oboe/English horn (competitive), orchestral conducting (highly selective), organ (competitive), percussion (selective), piano (selective), trombone (highly selective), trumpet (selective), tuba (highly selective), viola (selective), violin (selective), violoncello (highly selective), voice (selective), chamber music (highly selective).

Total enrollment: 260. *Entering class size:* 100. *Graduating class size:* 85. *Countries most represented:* Korea, Taiwan, Japan, China, Canada.

Renowned alumni: Jeff Kahane, Wendy Hillhouse, Warren Jones, Michael Barrett. *Total full-time faculty:* 25. *Total part-time faculty:* 46. *Program contact person:* Joan Gordon.

Audition Information

No audition fee. Audition consists of the following: orchestral excerpts. *Instruments provided for:* harpists, percussionists.

Performance opportunities available (frequency): jury examinations, orchestral concerts, recitals.

Facilities

Number of practice rooms and hours: 55; 7:00 am-11:00 pm. *Recital hall?* yes. *Concert hall?* yes. *Recording studio?* yes.

SAN FRANCISCO STATE UNIVERSITY

College of Creative Arts
1600 Hollywood Avenue, San Francisco CA 94132
Tel: 415-338-1471
Fax: 415-338-6159

General

Type of Institution: public, university. *Environment:* urban.

Total enrollment: 21,049. *Total student body from other countries:* 13%. *Degrees offered:* BA, BM.

Entrance Requirements

Audition required: live. *Standardized test requirements:* ACT; SAT I; TOEFL.

Costs & Financial Aid

Medical fee: $130.

Percent of students receiving financial aid: 50%. *Types of scholarships and aid awarded:* partial, merit-based, need-based, tuition payment plan, work/study. *Forms required for scholarships:* FAFSA, income tax return. *Loans available. Procedure for applying for loans:* come in or call for application.

Services

Housing options: on-site dorms, off-campus housing.

Support staff: career counselor, financial aid advisor, foreign student advisor, housing advisor, physical therapist, psychological counselor, resident assistant, resident nurse, student affairs officer.

DANCE

Curriculum, Students, and Faculty

Required courses: dance composition/choreography, dance history, dance theory, Labanotation, movement techniques, music, nutrition, rehearsal and performance, stagecraft, dance history.

Elective courses: African dance, ballet, jazz, master classes, modern dance, repertory, Spanish, tap, Brazilian dance, ballroom dance, Haitian dance,

Kathak dance, master classes, variations (1 class per week, 1 year to complete).

Selectivity for males: admit all who apply. *Selectivity for females:* admit all who apply. *Total enrollment:* 93. *Entering class size:* 15. *Graduating class size:* 5.

Total full-time faculty: 6. *Total part-time faculty:* 9. *List of current faculty and past affiliations:* Nont Sizi Cayou, Wajumbe Cultural Center and International Dance Institute, panelist NEA Grants; Jerry Duke, TU Congress on Research in Dance, Khadra International Folk Ballet, panelist for NEA grants. *Program contact person:* Jerry Duke.

Audition Information

No audition fee. Accompanist provided. Cassette player available; CD player available.

Audition evaluation criteria: audition is for placement in technique class. There is no audition for acceptance into program.

Performance Information

Performance opportunities available (frequency): Fully produced concerts (1 per semester), informal concerts (1-2 per year), workshops (occasionally), on-site performances (5-6 per year), touring (occasionally).

Performances choreographed by: faculty, students, guests.

Facilities

Number of studios available: 2. *Approximate studio dimensions and flooring:* 1,700 sq. ft.-2,000 sq. ft. wood. *Performance facilities:* shared theater space—2 proscenium theaters (700 and 300 seats).

DRAMA

Curriculum, Students, and Faculty

Required courses: acting, directing, text analysis, theater history, dramatic literature, voice, speech.

Number of years required to complete program: 4. *Summer program available. Affiliation with a professional theater company: A.C.T., Berkeley Repertory, California Shakespeare, Marsh, San Francisco Mime Troupe, Santa Rosa Summer Repertory.*

Selectivity for males: most admitted, but not all. *Selectivity for females:* most admitted, but not all. *Total enrollment:* 205. *Entering class size:* 40 *Graduating class size:* 34.

Renowned alumni: Annette Benning, Johnny Mathis, Dan Sullivan, Robert Woodruff.

Total full-time faculty: 14. *Total part-time faculty:* 5. *List of current faculty and past affiliations:* Larry Eilenberg, Magic Theatre; John Wilson; York Kennedy; Camille Howard.

Audition Information

No audition fee. Audition consists of the following: required monologues.

Performance Information

Performance opportunities available (frequency): fully produced performances (varies), informal performances (varies), workshops (varies), off-site performances (varies), casting is by audition.

Recent guest artists: Geoff Hoyle, San Francisco Mime Troup, Erik Ehn.

Facilities

Rehearsal facilities and hours: classrooms and four theatres, rehearsals 6:00 or 7:00 pm-10:00 or 10:30 pm. *Type and capacity:* black box—60, proscenium—750, thrust.

MUSIC

Curriculum, Students, and Faculty

Unique or innovative music curriculum: BA in Jazz and Popular Styles, BM composition students have worked, performed and recorded professionally. *How are major teacher assignments made?* students may choose, made by the school. Faculty is not informed of a student's teacher preference at the time of the audition. *30 lessons with major teacher. May a student change major teachers during the course of study?* possibly. *Study of secondary instrument or discipline is allowed.*

Selectivity for instruments or programs offered (rating): bassoon (non-competitive), choral conducting (selective), choral singing (non-competitive), clarinet (competitive), composition (selective), double bass (competitive), electronic music (competitive), flute or piccolo (competitive), French horn (non-competitive), guitar (selective), harp (non-competitive), jazz (non-competitive), oboe/English horn (non-competitive), orchestral conducting (selective), organ (highly selective), percussion (competitive),piano (competitive), saxophone (competitive), trombone (competitive), trumpet (competitive), tuba (competitive), viola (competitive), violin (competitive), violoncello (competitive), voice (selective).

Total enrollment: 304. *Entering class size:* 150. *Graduating class size:* 150.

Renowned alumni: Paul Gemignani, NY Conductor; Weslia Whitfield; Paul Renzi; Donna Petersen, San Francisco Opera; Richard Festinger; Elinor Armer; Howard Brubeck; Richard Felciano.

Total full-time faculty: 15. *Total part-time faculty:* 30. *Program contact person:* Patricia Lee.

Audition Information

No audition fee. Audition consists of the following: scales, music theory, rhythmic dictation, sight reading, melodic dictation, repertoire. *Instruments provided for:* harpists, percussionists.

Required repertoire? yes. *Repertoire that students should avoid?* Beethoven "Fur Elise". *Performance opportunities available (frequency):* band (every semester), chamber music (every semester), jury examinations (every semester), orchestral concerts, recitals (15 per semester), chorus (each semester).

Facilities

Recital hall? yes. *Concert hall?* yes. *Recording studio?* yes.

SANTA CLARA UNIVERSITY

500 El Camino Real, Santa Clara CA 95053
Tel: 408-554-4989
Fax: 408-554-5199
Web: www.scu.edu

General

Type of Institution: university. *Religious Affiliation:* Catholic. *Environment:* suburban.

Total enrollment: 4,500. *Total student body from other countries:* 9%. *Degrees offered:* BA.

Entrance Requirements

Audition not required. Other requirements: recommendation, essay. *Standardized test requirements:* ACT, 27; SAT I, 1160; TOEFL, 550.

Costs & Financial Aid

Application fee: $40. *Deposit:* $400. *Tuition:* $16,635. *Medical fee:* $300. *Other fees:* $2,500-$2,900 books and miscellaneous expenses.

Types of scholarships and aid awarded: full, partial, need-based, government aid, reduced tuition, tuition payment plan, work/study. *Forms required for scholarships:* FAFSA, income tax return. *Loans available.*

Services

Housing options: on-site dorms, off-campus housing, fraternity, sorority.

Support staff: career counselor, financial aid advisor, foreign student advisor, psychological counselor, resident assistant, resident nurse, student affairs officer.

DANCE

Curriculum, Students, and Faculty

Required courses: ballet, dance composition/choreography, dance history, modern dance, rehearsal and performance, stagecraft.

Elective courses: African dance, jazz, master classes.

Total full-time faculty: 1. *Total part-time faculty:* 3. *List of current faculty and past affiliations:* David Popalisky. *Program contact person:* David Popalisky.

Audition Information

Accompanist not provided. Cassette player available; CD player available.

Performance Information

Performance opportunities available (frequency): Fully produced concerts (2 per year), informal concerts (9 per year), workshops (2-3 per year).

Performances choreographed by: faculty, students, guests.

Facilities

Number of studios available: 2. *Approximate studio dimensions and flooring:* sprung floors with Marley. *Performance facilities:* Full proscenium theater—floor covered with Marley.

DRAMA

Curriculum, Students, and Faculty

Required courses: acting, dramaturgy, improvisation, movement, scene study, Stanislavski exercises, text analysis, verse drama.

Elective courses: Alexander Technique, audition preparation, directing, drama criticism, make-up, musical theater, speech, stage combat, voice.

Summer program not available. Affiliation with a professional theater company: internships with San Jose Repertory Theater.

Renowned alumni: Ron Lagomarsino, Jim Houghton, Signature Theater Company; Patrick Martin, Dave Cosieu.

Total full-time faculty: 4.

Audition Information

Audition consists of the following: comedic monologue. *Dress requirements:* presentable appearance, dress may be adapted to audition piece. *Audition evaluation criteria:* Understanding of the text, authenticity, believability of emotion, and clarity.

Performance Information

Performance opportunities available (frequency): fully produced performances (4 per year), workshops (4 per year), casting is by audition.

Facilities

Number of theaters on campus: 2.

MUSIC

Curriculum, Students, and Faculty

How are major teacher assignments made? students may choose, according to teacher availability. Faculty is not informed of a student's teacher preference at the time of the audition. *30 lessons with major teacher. Study of secondary instrument or discipline is allowed.*

Selectivity for instruments or programs offered (rating): accompanying (competitive), bassoon (open), choral conducting (open), choral singing (non-competitive), clarinet (open), composition (open), double bass (open), flute or piccolo (open), French horn (open), guitar (open), harp (open), harpsichord (open), oboe/English horn (open), orchestral conducting (open), percussion (open), piano (open), sacred music (open), saxophone (open), trombone (open), trumpet (open), tuba (open), viola (open), violin (open), violoncello (open), voice (open).

Renowned alumni: Colleen Harrison, Olagalydia Urbano.

Total full-time faculty: 4. *Total part-time faculty:* 30. *Program contact person:* Hans Boepple.

Performance opportunities available (frequency): band (3 per year), jury examinations (3 per year), orchestral concerts (3 per year), chorus (3 per year).

Facilities

Number of practice rooms and hours: 6; 8:00 am-11:00 pm. *Recital hall?* yes. *Concert hall?* no. *Recording studio?* no.

SCRIPPS COLLEGE

1030 Columbia Avenue, Claremont CA 91711
Tel: 800-770-1333
Fax: 909-621-8323
Email: admofc@ad.scrippscol.edu
Web: www.scrippscol.edu
Contact: Mimi Tung

General

Type of Institution: all women's college. *Environment:* suburban. Part of Claremont Colleges.

Total enrollment: 700. *Total student body from other countries:* 5%. *Degrees offered:* BA.

Entrance Requirements

Audition not required live, audio, video. *Other requirements:* recommendation, essay. *Standardized test requirements:* ACT; SAT I, 1230; TOEFL, 550.

Costs & Financial Aid

Application fee: $40. *Deposit:* $350. *Tuition:* $19,356. *Other fees:* $124 student association fees. *Room and board:* $7,700.

Types of scholarships and aid awarded: full, partial, merit-based, need-based, named, institutional aid, government aid, tuition payment plan, work/study. *Forms required for scholarships:* FAFSA, CSS Profile. *Loans available. Procedure for applying for loans:* submit FAFSA and CSS profile by the appropriate application deadline. *Financial aid offered to international students. Percent of international students receiving scholarships:* 1%. *Other aid available to international students:* merit-based.

Services

Housing options: on-site dorms.

Support staff: career counselor, financial aid advisor, foreign student advisor, housing advisor, psychological counselor, resident assistant, resident nurse, student affairs officer.

DANCE

Curriculum, Students, and Faculty

Required courses: anatomy, character (2 classes per week, 1 year to complete), ballet (2 classes per week, 2 years to complete), dance composition/choreography, dance history, dance writing, research and criticism, senior thesis, eclectic modern dance (2 classes per week, 3 years to complete), movement techniques.

Elective courses: African dance, dance theory, jazz, movement techniques, rehearsal and performance, repertory, stagecraft, women and dance, Folklorico dance, Kabuki dance, Latin dance, world dance forms.

Selectivity for females: admit all who apply. *Graduating class size:* 1.

Total full-time faculty: 2. *Total part-time faculty:* 1. *List of current faculty and past affiliations:* Ronnie Brosterman, Boston Ballet Co. *Program contact person:* Ronnie Brosterman.

Audition Information

No audition fee. Accompanist not provided. Cassette player not available; CD player not available.

Performance Information

Performance opportunities available (frequency): Fully produced concerts (2 per year), informal concerts (2+ per year), workshops (2 per year), on-site performances (4 per year), attendance at American College Dance Festival Regional, (annual).

Performances choreographed by: faculty, students, guests. *Recent guest choreographers:* Suchi Braufman, Doris Humphrey (reconstruction) by Mary Corey, Nita Little.

Facilities

Number of studios available: 4. *Approximate studio dimensions and flooring:* 35' x 55' sprung wood or Marley over sprung wood, 20' x 36', 45' x 65', 40' x 50'. *Performance facilities:* 2 proscenium theaters, 1 studio theater.

DRAMA

Curriculum, Students, and Faculty

Required courses: acting, Alexander technique, audition preparation, drama criticism, dramaturgy, improvisation, make-up, mime, movement, scene study, speech, Stanislavski exercises, text analysis, verse drama, drama criticism.

Elective courses: directing, martial arts, musical theater, stage combat.

Number of years required to complete program: 4. *Summer program not available. Affiliation with a professional theater company: internships at Williamstown and Santa Fe Opera.*

Selectivity for males: approximately 10% admitted. *Selectivity for females:* approximately 10% admitted. *Graduating class size:* 2.

Total full-time faculty: 6. *Total part-time faculty:* 3. *List of current faculty and past affiliations:* Leonard Pronko, National Theater of Japan; Sherry Linnell, South Coast Repertory; Carol Davis, Old Globe, San Diego

Performance Information

Performance opportunities available (frequency): fully produced performances (5 per year), informal performances (2-3 per month), workshops (4 per semester), off-site performances (2 per semester), casting is by audition.

Recent guest artists: Dan Kwong, Rachel Rosenthal, Luis Alfaro, Jude Narita.

Facilities

Rehearsal facilities and hours: 2 studios, 1 black box, 1 main stage, 6:00 pm-11:00 pm. *Type and capacity:* proscenium—2,000 seats.

MUSIC

Curriculum, Students, and Faculty

Unique or innovative music curriculum: harmony, counterpoint, and college skills included in all music theory, courses. *Music electives include:* orchestra, chamber music, choir, chamber choir, American music, women in music. *How are major teacher assignments made?* according to teacher preference, according to teacher availability, by student level. Faculty is not informed of a student's teacher preference at the time of the audition. *29 lessons with major teacher. May a student change major teachers during the course of study?* possibly. *Study of secondary instrument or discipline is allowed.*

Selectivity for instruments or programs offered (rating): choral conducting (non-competitive), choral singing (non-competitive), composition (competitive), harpsichord (non-competitive), orchestral conducting (competitive), piano (non-competitive), viola (competitive), violin (competitive), voice (non-competitive).

Graduating class size: 2.

Renowned alumni: Vicki Seldon; Sharon Baker, Boston Baroque; Linda Horowitz; Marjorie Merriman, Boston University; Marsha Genensky, Anon IV, Medieval Music Group.

Total full-time faculty: 5. *Total part-time faculty:* 4. *Program contact person:* Michael Lamkin.

Audition Information

No audition fee. Audition consists of the following: repertoire. *Instruments provided for:* percussionists.

Repertoire that students should avoid? classical repertoire is preferred, but some popular repertoire is acceptable. *Performance opportunities available:* jury examinations, recitals.

Facilities

Number of practice rooms and hours: 8; 15 hours per day. *Recital hall?* yes. *Concert hall?* yes. *Recording studio?* yes.

Comments

Introduction in all orchestral instruments, organ, and guitar is available at Pomona College, a fellow member of the Claremont Colleges (of which Scripps is also a member). Scripps College offers a BA in Music (performance, music history, or composition), and the opportunity to take a music minor, or a double major. Our music curriculum is part of a liberal arts curriculum.

STANFORD UNIVERSITY

Mem. Aud. Room 144, Stanford CA 94305-5010
Tel: 650-725-2396
Fax: 650-723-0843
Email: ron.davies@forsythe.stanford.edu
Web: www-leland.stanford.edu/dept/drama
Contact: n/a

General

Type of Institution: private university. *Environment:* suburban.

Total enrollment: 6,000. *Degrees offered:* BA.

Entrance Requirements

Audition required: live, video. *Other requirements:* interview, recommendation, essay, you must be admitted to the university.

Costs & Financial Aid

Tuition: $21,300. *Medical fee:* $546. *Room and board:* $7,155.

Percent of students receiving financial aid: 61%. *Types of scholarships and aid awarded:* full, partial, need-based, named, institutional aid, government aid, work/study. *Loans available. Procedure for applying for loans:* submit FAFSA, copy of family income tax return. *Financial aid offered to international students. Other aid available to international students:* loans, in some cases.

Services

Housing options: on-site dorms, off-campus housing, fraternity, sorority, family.

Support staff: financial aid advisor, foreign student advisor.

DANCE

Elective courses: tap, repertory.

Comments

Drama at Stanford is a small program in a liberal arts setting within a major research university. About 20-25 majors active; another 20-25 drama-interested students involved daily. Lots of individual attention and opportunities for students who show initiative in creating productions both inside and outside the department. An active alumni group (Stanford Alumni in Entertainment) provides some access to the entertainment industry, where Stanford graduates work in film and television as producers, directors, screenwriters, casting directors, entertainment lawyers, actors, etc. There is also a strong music department.

UNIVERSITY OF CALIFORNIA, BERKELEY

101 Dwinelle Annex
Department of Dramatic Arts, Berkeley CA 94720-2560
Tel: 510-642-1677
Fax: 510-643-9956
Email: marniw@UCLink4.berkeley.edu
Web: www.berkeley.edu

General

Type of Institution: public university. *Environment:* urban.

Total enrollment: 31,000. *Degrees offered:* BA.

Entrance Requirements

Audition required: live. *Standardized test requirements:* SAT I, SAT II.

Costs & Financial Aid

Types of scholarships and aid awarded: full, partial, merit-based, need-based, work/study. *Loans available. Procedure for applying for loans:* file FAFSA.

Services

Housing options: on-site dorms, off-campus housing, fraternity, sorority, family.

Support staff: financial aid advisor, physical therapist, psychological counselor, resident assistant.

DANCE

Curriculum, Students, and Faculty

Required courses: dance composition/choreography, dance history, dance writing, research and criticism, modern dance, music, rehearsal and performance, stagecraft, ballet, men's class.

Elective courses: dance theory, master classes, repertory, pas de deux.

Selectivity for males: approximately 33% admitted. *Selectivity for females:* approximately 33% admitted. *Total enrollment:* 250. *Entering class size:* 70.

Renowned alumni: Danny Ezralow, Raegan Wood, soloists with Paul Taylor; Christopher Dolder, Camille Brown, Deborah Kantor, soloists with Martha Graham; Ellen Cornfield, Robert Remley, Karen Ahlix, Megan Walker, dancers in Merce Cunningham Co.

Total full-time faculty: 3. *Total part-time faculty:* 1. *List of current faculty and past affiliations:* Marnie Thomas, Graham Company; Christopher

Dolder, Graham Company; Carol Murota. *Program contact person:* Mary Ajideh, Marni Wood.

Audition Information

No audition fee. Audition consists of the following: modern dance. *Accompanist provided. Cassette player available; CD player available. Dress requirements for males:* clothing that fits the body. *Dress requirements for females:* clothing that fits the body.

Performance Information

Performance opportunities available (frequency): Fully produced concerts (2 weeks annually each spring), informal concerts (1-2 per semester (2 annually), workshops (annually), on-site performances (12-20), touring (12-20), honors projects or full evening work student choreography.

Performances choreographed by: faculty, students, guests. *Recent guest choreographers:* Margaret Jenkins, Carolyn Brown.

Facilities

Number of studios available: 2. *Approximate studio dimensions and flooring:* 60' x 30' hardwood, 40' x 25' Marley. *Performance facilities:* 453-seat playhouse theater, 148-seat Durham theater,100-seat room.

DRAMA

Curriculum, Students, and Faculty

Elective courses: acting, directing, improvisation, scene study, speech, voice, directing, musical theater, voice, improvisation.

Number of years required to complete program: 2-4. *Summer program available. Affiliation with a professional theater company: informally affiliated with Berkeley Repertory Theatre and American Conservatory Theatre (ACT).*

Selectivity for males: approximately 60% admitted. *Selectivity for females:* approximately 60% admitted. *Total enrollment:* 700. *Graduating class size:* 20.

Renowned alumni: Stacey Keach, Karen Grassle.

Total full-time faculty: 1. *Total part-time faculty:* 12. *List of current faculty and past affiliations:* Marty Berman, ACT; Lura Dolas, California Shakespeare Festival, Oregon Shakespeare Festival.

Performance Information

Performance opportunities available (frequency): fully produced performances (6-8 per year), informal performances (2-4 per year), workshops (2-4 per year), casting is by audition.

Facilities

Rehearsal facilities and hours: playhouse, studio theater, black box theater. *Number of theaters on campus:* 3. *Type and capacity:* theater—400, studio—150, black box—75.

UNIVERSITY OF CALIFORNIA, DAVIS

Department of Dramatic Art and Dance, Department of Music
1 Shields Avenue, Wright Hall Room 222, Davis CA 95616-8577
Tel: 530-752-0888
Fax: 530-752-8818
Web: www.ucdavis.edu

General

Type of Institution: public university. *Environment:* suburban.

Total enrollment: 27,000.

Entrance Requirements

You must be admitted to the University. *Audition required:* live, video. *Other requirements:* interview, recommendation, essay, photograph. *Standardized test requirements:* ACT; SAT I; SAT II; TOEFL.

Costs & Financial Aid

Tuition (in-state/out-state): $4,174/$11,872. *Other fees:* student education fee for miscellaneous association student activities. *Room and board:* $5,720.

Types of scholarships and aid awarded: full, partial, merit-based, need-based, named, institutional aid, government aid, reduced tuition, tuition payment plan, work/study, gig office. *Forms required for scholarships:* FAFSA, income tax return. *Loans available. Financial aid offered to international students.*

Services

Housing options: on-site dorms, off-campus housing, fraternity, sorority, family.

Support staff: career counselor, dorm parent, financial aid advisor, foreign student advisor, housing advisor, physical therapist, psychological counselor, resident assistant, resident nurse, student affairs officer.

DANCE

Curriculum, Students, and Faculty

Elective courses: African dance, Alexander Technique, ballet (2 classes per week), dance composition/

choreography, dance history, dance theory, dance writing, research and criticism, historical dance, jazz (2 classes per week), master classes, Cunningham-based, Graham-based, Horton-based, Limon-based modern dance, Laban Movement Studies, rehearsal and performance, stagecraft, yoga.

Selectivity for males: admit all who apply. *Selectivity for females:* admit all who apply. *Total enrollment:* 345. *Percent international:* 2%. *Countries most represented*: Germany, Japan.

Total full-time faculty: 2. *Total part-time faculty:* 5. *List of current faculty and past affiliations:* Bobbi Wynn Bolden, Dance Theater of Harlem, Ailey School; Susan Foster. *Program contact person:* Karen Shimakawa.

Performance Information

Performance opportunities available (frequency): fully produced concerts (1-2 per year), informal concerts (1-2 per year), workshops (1-2 per year), touring.

Performances choreographed by: faculty, students, guests. *Recent guest choreographers:* Marlies Yearby.

Facilities

Number of studios available: 2. *Approximate studio dimensions and flooring:* 40' x 60' hardwood, 35' x 50' Marley. *Performance facilities:* state-of-the art theater and studio theater.

DRAMA

Curriculum, Students, and Faculty

Required courses: acting, audition preparation, improvisation, make-up, martial arts, movement, scene study, speech, stage combat, Stanislavski exercises, text analysis, verse drama, voice, period dance.

Elective courses: Alexander technique, directing, drama criticism, dramaturgy, musical theater.

Number of years required to complete program: 4. *Summer program not available. Affiliation with a professional theater company: Sacramento Theater Company.*

Selectivity for males: approximately 33% admitted. *Selectivity for females:* approximately 33% admitted. *Total enrollment:* 68. *Entering class size:* 20. *Percent international:* 2%. *Countries most represented:* Japan, China.

Renowned alumni: Carol Flynt, Dottie Dartlord, Dan Vickery.

Total full-time faculty: 7. *Total part-time faculty:* 10. *List of current faculty and past affiliations:* Sara Pia Anderson, Sue Ellen Case, Barbara Sellers Young, Win Worthen, Karen Shimakawa, Janeue Reinert, Bobbie Wynn.

Audition Information

Audition consists of the following: a cappella, Shakespearean monologue. Auditions are required only for students interested in entering the MFA program. *Dress requirements for males:* no restrictive clothing. *Dress requirements for females:* no restrictive clothing.

Performance Information

Performance opportunities available (frequency): fully produced performances (5-7 per year), informal performances (3-4 per year), workshops (3-4 per year), off-site performances (1 per year), casting is assigned, auditioned.

Recent guest artists: D. Trevis, William Gaskill, Richard Cottrell, Frank Hausar, Peter Lichtenfels, Pip Simmons, Howard Brenton, Yvonne Brewster.

Facilities

Rehearsal facilities and hours: arena theater, main theater, thrust theater, two acting studios, rehearsals 6:00 pm-11:00 pm (Mon-Fri) and some weekends and evenings. *Number of theaters on campus:* 4. *Type and capacity:* proscenium—512, arena (black box)—100, theater—220, lab—60.

MUSIC

Curriculum, Students, and Faculty

30 lessons with major teacher. May a student change major teachers during the course of study? possibly. *Study of secondary instrument or discipline is allowed.*

Total enrollment: 80. *Entering class size:* 20.

Renowned alumni: Barry Kernfield; Steven Mackey, Princeton; Dennis McNeil; Carlo Scibelli; Tom Sturges, Chrysalis Records.

Total full-time faculty: 11. *Total part-time faculty:* 20. *Program contact person:* David Nulter.

Audition Information

Instruments provided for: harpists, percussionists; orchestra and band instruments are available.

Facilities

Number of practice rooms and hours: 5; 9:00 am-9:00 pm. *Recital hall?* yes. *Concert hall?* yes. *Recording studio?* yes.

Comments

For more informtion on dance/drama contact Darrell Winn, dfwinn@ucdavis.edu, fax: (530) 752-8818, phone: (530) 752-7090. Music selectivity is not applicable for study of instruments because UC Davis does not offer a degree in performance.

UNIVERSITY OF CALIFORNIA, IRVINE

School of the Arts, Irvine CA 92697
Tel: 714-824-6612
Fax: 714-824-2450
Web: www.arts.uci.edu
Contact: Cloud Hsueh

General

Type of Institution: public university. *Environment:* suburban

Total enrollment: 17,258. *Total student body from other countries:* 3%. *Degrees offered:* BA, BFA. BM.

Entrance Requirements

Other requirements: essay. *Standardized test requirements:* SAT I; SAT II; TOEFL, 550.

Costs & Financial Aid

Application fee: $40. *Deposit:* $100. *Tuition (in-state/out-state)*: $4,049/$11,748.

Percent of students receiving financial aid: 60%. *Types of scholarships and aid awarded:* full, partial, merit-based, need-based, institutional aid, government aid, reduced tuition, tuition payment plan, work/study. *Forms required for scholarships:* FAFSA. *Loans available. Procedure for applying for loans:* same as application for Federal Aid. *Financial aid offered to international students. Other aid available to international students:* merit-based.

Services

Housing options: on-site dorms, off-campus housing, fraternity, sorority.

Support staff: career counselor, financial aid advisor, foreign student advisor, psychological counselor, resident assistant, resident nurse, student affairs officer.

DANCE

Curriculum, Students, and Faculty

Required courses: anatomy, ballet, dance composition/choreography, dance history, dance writing, research and criticism, jazz, Labanotation, modern dance, music, nutrition, pas de deux, rehearsal and performance, stagecraft.

Elective courses: African dance, character, master classes, men's class, pointe, repertory, Spanish, tap, variations.

Selectivity for males: approximately 33% admitted. *Selectivity for females:* approximately 33% admitted. *Total enrollment:* 130. *Entering class size:* 36. *Graduating class size:* 25.

Renowned alumni: our alumni have entered several companies, including the Martha Graham Dance Ensemble, Limon West, the Bella Lewitzky Dance Company, Garth Fagin Dance Company national/international tours of several shows including "Phantom of the Opera," " Will Roger's "Follies," and "West Side Story," Asia tour; ballet companies film, and television.

Total full-time faculty: 8. *List of current faculty and past affiliations:* David Allen, National Ballet of Canada; Dr. Jill Beck, City University of New York, Professor of Dance; Don Bradburn, former dancer/choreographer for CBS television. *Program contact person:* Mary Corey.

Audition Information

No audition fee. Audition consists of the following: ballet, modern dance, jazz. *Accompanist provided. Dress requirements for males:* leotard, tights, ballet slippers, jazz shoes. *Dress requirements for females:* leotard, tights, ballet slippers, jazz shoes.

Audition evaluation criteria: technical proficiency.

Performance Information

Performance opportunities available (frequency): Fully produced concerts (5 per year), informal concerts (occasionally), workshops (3 per year).

Performances choreographed by: faculty, students, guests.

Facilities

Number of studios available: 4. *Approximate studio dimensions and flooring:* 40' x 60' wood dance floor, 45' x 50' wood dance floor, 31' x 39.5' wood dance floor. *Performance facilities:* Irvine Barclay Theatre, Village Theatre, Concert Hall.

DRAMA

Curriculum, Students, and Faculty

Required courses: acting, scene study.

Elective courses: audition preparation, directing, musical theater, speech, voice.

Number of years required to complete program: 4. *Summer program not available. Informal affiliation with Utah Shakeapeare Festival and South Coast Repertory.*

Selectivity for males: approximately 60% admitted. *Selectivity for females:* approximately 60% admitted. *Total enrollment:* 183. *Entering class size:* 58. *Graduating class size:* 38.

Renowned alumni: Bob Gunton, Jeff Greenberg, Jon Lovitz, Greg Louganis, Cam Harvey, Kelly Perine, Thomas Ruzika, Michael Gras.

Total full-time faculty: 13. *Total part-time faculty:* 15. *List of current faculty and past affiliations:* Robert Cohan, Yale University; Dudley Knight, Yale University; Robert Weimann, Humboldt University; Stephen Barker, University of Arizona; Madeline Kozlowski, Brandeis University.

Performance Information

Performance opportunities available (frequency): fully produced performances (quarterly), informal performances (quarterly), workshops (quarterly), auditioned.

Recent guest artists: David Wheeler, G.L. Shoup, Sylvia Turner, Chon Bribiestas, Radha Carman.

Facilities

Rehearsal facilities and hours: rehearsals in theater facilities, could be available 24 hours per day. *Number of theaters on campus:* 6. *Type and capacity:* concert hall—217, theater—165, studio—80.

MUSIC

Curriculum, Students, and Faculty

Unique or innovative music curriculum: jazz, composition, performance, technology in music. *How are major teacher assignments made?* students may choose, made by the school, according to teacher preference and teacher availability. Faculty is informed of a student's teacher preference at the time of the audition. *30 lessons with major teacher. May a student change major teachers during the course of study?* possibly. *Study of secondary instrument or discipline is not allowed.*

Selectivity for instruments or programs offered (rating): bassoon (selective), clarinet (selective), composition (selective), double bass (selective), electronic music (selective), flute or piccolo (selective), French horn (selective), guitar (selective), jazz (selective), oboe/English horn (selective), percussion (selective), piano (highly selective), saxophone (selective), trombone (selective), trumpet (selective), tuba (selective), viola (selective), violin (selective), violoncello (selective), voice (selective).

Total enrollment: 123. *Entering class size:* 53. *Graduating class size:* 21.

Renowned alumni: Angel Liu violinist, Pacific Symphony; J.R. Raganas Miss Saigon, Broadway; Laurel Boud, Metropolitan Opera; Jennifer Bodenweber, New York City Opera.

Total full-time faculty: 11. *Total part-time faculty:* 23. *Program contact person:* Bernard Gilmore.

Audition Information

Audition consists of the following: scales, orchestral excerpts, arpeggios. *Instruments provided for:* percussionists.

Performance opportunities available (frequency): jury examinations (1 per year), orchestral concerts (quarterly), recitals, chorus (quarterly).

Facilities

Number of practice rooms and hours: 17; 24 hours a day. *Recital hall?* yes. *Concert hall?* yes. *Recording studio?* yes.

UNIVERSITY OF CALIFORNIA, LOS ANGELES

405 Hilgard Avenue, Los Angeles CA 90095
Tel: 310-825-3101
Fax: 310-206-1206
Web: www.ucla.edu

Entrance Requirements

Audition not required. You must be admitted to the university.

Services

Support staff: housing advisor, resident assistant, resident nurse, student affairs officer.

DANCE

Curriculum, Students, and Faculty

Required courses: pointe, character, modern dance, dance theory.

DRAMA

Curriculum, Students, and Faculty

Required courses: voice, speech, drama criticism, acting.

UNIVERSITY OF CALIFORNIA, SAN DIEGO

Department of Theatre and Dance
9500 Gilman Drive, La Jolla CA 92093-0344
Tel: 619-534-3619
Fax: 619-534-1080
Email: sferneyhough@uscd.edu
Web: www.ucsd.edu/music

General

Type of Institution: public university. *Environment:* urban.

Total enrollment: 18,424. *Degrees offered:* BA.

Entrance Requirements

Audition not required. You must be admitted to the University.

Services

Housing options: on-site dorms, off-campus housing.

Support staff: foreign student advisor, psychological counselor, resident assistant, student affairs officer.

DANCE

Curriculum, Students, and Faculty

Elective courses: ballet, dance composition/choreography, dance history, modern dance, movement techniques, tap.

DRAMA

Curriculum, Students, and Faculty

Required courses: acting, design for the performing arts, directing, playwriting, stage management, theater history, practicum.

Elective courses: dance, movement, scene study, speech, text analysis, voice.

MUSIC

Curriculum, Students, and Faculty

Unique or innovative music curriculum: study of avant garde, experimental 20th-century music is the main focus. *How are major teacher assignments made?* made by the school. Faculty is not informed of a student's teacher preference at the time of the audition. *30 lessons with major teacher. May a student change major teachers during the course of study?* possibly.

Selectivity for instruments or programs offered (rating): bassoon (competitive), choral singing (competitive), clarinet (competitive), composition (open), double bass (competitive), electronic music (open), flute or piccolo (competitive), French horn (competitive), guitar (competitive), harp (competitive), harpsichord (competitive), jazz (competitive), oboe/English horn (competitive), organ (competitive), percussion (competitive), piano (competitive), sacred music (open), saxophone (competitive), trombone (competitive), trumpet (competitive), tuba (competitive), viola (competitive), violin (competitive), violoncello (competitive), voice (competitive).

Entering class size: 20. *Graduating class size:* 25.

Renowned alumni: Nathan East, Diamanda Galas. *Program contact person:* Stephanie Ferneyhough.

Audition Information

Audition consists of the following: rhythmic dictation, melodic dictation, repertoire. *Instruments provided for:* harpists, percussionists, pianists.

Repertoire that students should avoid? no nonclassical music, such as show tunes or popular music.

Facilities

Number of practice rooms and hours: 12; 24 hours a day. *Recital hall?* yes. *Concert hall?* yes. *Recording studio?* yes.

UNIVERSITY OF CALIFORNIA, SANTA CRUZ

Music Department, Santa Cruz CA 95064
Tel: 408-459-2292
Fax: 408-459-3535
Email: music@cats.ucsc.edu
Web: www.arts.ucsc.edu/divarts/boards/music

General

Type of Institution: public university.

Total enrollment: 10,000. *Degrees offered:* BA, BM.

Entrance Requirements

Audition not required. You must be admitted to the university.

Costs & Financial Aid

Tuition (in-state/out-state): $4,181/$8,984.

Percent of students receiving financial aid: 50%. *Types of scholarships and aid awarded:* partial, need-based, institutional aid, government aid, work/study. *Forms required for scholarships:* FAFSA, California state form.

Services

Housing options: on-site dorms, off-campus housing.

Support staff: career counselor, dorm parent, financial aid advisor, foreign student advisor, housing advisor, physical therapist, psychological counselor, resident assistant, resident nurse, student affairs officer.

UNIVERSITY OF SOUTHERN CALIFORNIA

School of Music
University Park, Los Angeles CA 90089-0851
Tel: 800-872-2213
Fax: 213-740-8995
Email: uscmusic@mizar.usc.edu
Web: www.usc.edu

General

Type of Institution: private university. *Environment:* urban.

Total enrollment: 30,000. *Degrees offered:* BA, BS in music industry/recording arts.

Entrance Requirements

Audition required: live, audio, video. *Other requirements:* recommendation, essay. *Standardized test requirements:* ACT; SAT I, 1250; TOEFL; school's own English exam required.

Costs & Financial Aid

Application fee: $55. *Deposit:* $250. *Tuition and fees:* $20,516. *Room and board:* $6,832.

Percent of students receiving financial aid: 65%. *Types of scholarships and aid awarded:* full, partial, merit-based, need-based, named, institutional aid, government aid, tuition payment plan, work/study, gig office. *Forms required for scholarships:* FAFSA, income tax return, income asset verification, CSS Profile. *Loans available. Procedure for applying for loans:* meet deadline of 2/15. *Financial aid offered to international students. Other aid available to international students:* merit only.

Services

Housing options: on-site dorms, off-campus housing, fraternity, sorority.

Support staff: financial aid advisor, foreign student advisor, housing advisor, physical therapist, psychological counselor, resident assistant, resident nurse, student affairs officer.

MUSIC

Curriculum, Students, and Faculty

Unique or innovative music curriculum: music industry, recording arts, composition with film scoring emphasis, minors in music theater, composition, performance, and jazz. *How are major teacher assignments made?* students may choose, made by the school, according to teacher preference and teacher availability. Faculty is informed of a student's teacher preference at the time of the audition. ***30 lessons with major teacher. May a student change major teachers during the course of study?*** possibly. ***Study of secondary instrument or discipline is allowed.***

Total enrollment: 970. *Entering class size:* 301. *Percent international:* 30%.

Total full-time faculty: 52. *Total part-time faculty:* 100. *Program contact person:* Christopher Sampson.

Audition Information

No audition fee. Audition consists of the following: repertoire. *Instruments provided for:* harpists, percussionists, pianists.

Required repertoire: varies by instrument. Please call school for repertoire information. *Performance opportunities available (frequency):* band (2-3 per semester), chamber music (2-3 per semester), jury examinations (1 per semester), opera workshops (2-3 per semester), orchestral concerts (2-3 per semester), recitals (1 per year), produced operas (1 per semester), chorus (2-3 per semester).

Facilities

Recital hall? yes. *Concert hall?* yes. *Recording studio?* yes.

COLORADO

COLORADO STATE UNIVERSITY

Department of Music,Theater, and Dance, Fort Collins CO 80523-1778
Tel: 970-491-5529
Fax: 970-491-7541
Email: wrunyan@vines.colostate.edu
Web: www.colostate.edu/depts/music

General

Type of Institution: public university. *Environment:* suburban.

Total enrollment: 22,344. *Total student body from other countries:* 4%. *Degrees offered:* BA, BM.

Entrance Requirements

Audition required: live, audio, video. *Other requirements:* interview, recommendation. *Standardized test requirements:* ACT, SAT I, SAT II.

Costs & Financial Aid

Application fee: $30. *Tuition (in-state/out-state)*: $2,933/$10,155. *Room and board:* $4,976.

Types of scholarships and aid awarded: partial, merit-based, institutional aid, government aid, work/study. *Forms required for scholarships:* creative and performing arts scholarship form.

Services

Housing options: on-site dorms, off-campus housing, fraternity, sorority.

Support staff: career counselor, financial aid advisor, foreign student advisor, psychological counselor, resident assistant, resident nurse, student affairs officer.

DANCE

Curriculum, Students, and Faculty

Required courses: anatomy, ballet, dance composition/choreography, dance history, jazz, master classes, modern dance, Limon-based modern dance, music, rehearsal and performance, repertory, stagecraft.

Elective courses: African dance, historical dance, pas de deux, pointe, tap.

Selectivity for males: admit all who apply. *Selectivity for females:* admit all who apply. *Total enrollment:* 14. *Entering class size:* 5. *Graduating class size:* 5.

Total full-time faculty: 1. *Total part-time faculty:* 6. *Program contact person:* Jane Slusarski-Harris.

Audition Information

No audition fee. Audition consists of the following: ballet, improvisation, modern dance, jazz. *Accompanist not provided. Cassette player available; CD player available.*

Audition evaluation criteria: versatility, intermediate/advanced levels.

Performance Information

Performance opportunities available (frequency): Fully produced concerts (2 per year), informal concerts (4 per year), workshops (2 per year), on-site performances (2 per year).

Performances choreographed by: faculty, students, guests.

Facilities

Number of studios available: 3. *Approximate studio dimensions and flooring:* 60' x 40' sprung floor, 60' x 40' Marley surface, 10' x 20'. *Performance facilities:* informal theater and proscenium.

DRAMA

Curriculum, Students, and Faculty

Required courses: acting, make-up, speech, text analysis.

Elective courses: audition preparation, directing, drama criticism, dramaturgy, improvisation, movement, musical theater, scene study, Stanislavski exercises, verse drama.

Number of years required to complete program: 4. *Summer program available. Selectivity for males:* most admitted, but not all. *Selectivity for females:* most admitted, but not all. *Total enrollment:* 38. *Entering class size:* 6. *Graduating class size:* 8.

Total full-time faculty: 5. *Total part-time faculty:* 3.

Audition Information

No audition fee. Audition evaluation criteria: there are no auditions for entry.

Performance Information

Performance opportunities available (frequency): fully produced performances (6 per year), informal performances (frequently), workshops (2-3 per year), off-site performances (rarely), casting is by audition.

Facilities

Rehearsal facilities and hours: 2 acting studio spaces and mainstage theatre, 6:00 am-11:00 pm (6 days per week), 6:00 am-1:00 pm (1 day a week). *Number of theaters on campus:* 2. *Type and capacity:* experimental—100, main stage—314.

MUSIC

Curriculum, Students, and Faculty

How are major teacher assignments made? according to teacher availability. Faculty is not informed of a student's teacher preference at the time of the audition. *30 lessons with major teacher. May a student change major teachers during the course of study?* possibly.

Selectivity for instruments or programs offered (rating): accompanying (non-competitive), bassoon (non-competitive), choral singing (non-competitive), clarinet (non-competitive), composition (non-competitive), double bass (non-competitive), flute or piccolo (non-competitive), French horn (non-competitive), guitar (competitive), harp (competitive), harpsichord (non-competitive), jazz (non-competitive), oboe/English horn (non-competitive), organ (non-competitive), percussion (non-competitive), piano (non-competitive), saxophone (non-competitive), trombone (non-competitive), trumpet (non-competitive), tuba (non-competitive), viola (non-competitive), violin (non-competitive), violoncello (non-competitive), voice (non-competitive).

Total enrollment: 197. *Entering class size:* 40. *Graduating class size:* 59.

Renowned alumni: Joseph Jennings.

Total full-time faculty: 20. *Total part-time faculty:* 13. *Program contact person:* William E. Runyan.

Audition Information

No audition fee. Audition consists of the following: scales, rhythmic dictation, arpeggios, sight reading, melodic dictation. *Instruments provided for:* harpists, percussionists.

Repertoire that students should avoid? popular music.

Facilities

Number of practice rooms and hours: 20. *Recital hall?* yes. *Concert hall?* yes. *Recording studio?* no.

UNIVERSITY OF COLORADO, BOULDER

College of Music, Campus Box 301, Boulder CO 80309-0301
Tel: 303-492-6352
Fax: 303-492-5619
Email: ugradmus@colorado.edu
Web: www.colorado.edu

General

Type of Institution: public university. *Environment:* suburban.

Total enrollment: 25,000. *Total student body from other countries:* 4%. *Degrees offered:* certificate, BA, BM, BME.

Entrance Requirements

Audition required: live, audio, video. *Other requirements:* essay. *Standardized test requirements:* ACT, 25; SAT I, 1165; TOEFL, 500.

Costs & Financial Aid

Application fee: $40. *Deposit:* $200. *Tuition (in-state/out-state):* $2,877/$14,927. *Medical fee:* $585. *Room and board:* $4,670.

Types of scholarships and aid awarded: full, partial, merit-based, need-based, named, institutional aid, government aid, reduced tuition, work/study. *Forms required for scholarships:* FAFSA, income tax return, income asset verification. *Loans available. Procedure for applying for loans:* student must complete FAFSA and submit tax forms by 3/1. *Financial aid offered to international students. Percent of international students receiving scholarships:* 80%. *Other aid available to international students:* gift funds and adopt-a-student scholarships (based on audition).

Services

Housing options: on-site dorms, off-campus housing.

Support staff: career counselor, financial aid advisor, foreign student advisor, housing advisor, physical therapist, psychological counselor, resident assistant, resident nurse, student affairs officer.

MUSIC

Curriculum, Students, and Faculty

Unique or innovative music curriculum: The BM and BME programs require a small number of credits outside of music, and no specific general education courses are required, therefore, music majors can also major in other areas, completing double major in 4-5 years. *How are major teacher assignments made?* according to teacher availability, students may express preference. Faculty is informed of a student's teacher preference at the time of the audition. *32 lessons with major teacher. May a student change major teachers during the course of study?* possibly. *Study of secondary instrument or discipline is allowed.*

Selectivity for instruments or programs offered (rating): accompanying (competitive), bassoon (competitive), choral conducting (competitive), clarinet (competitive), composition (highly selective), double bass (competitive), flute or piccolo (highly selective), French horn (competitive), guitar (highly selective), harp (competitive), harpsichord (competitive), jazz (highly selective), oboe/English horn (competitive), orchestral conducting (highly selective), organ (competitive), percussion (highly selective), piano (highly selective), sacred music (competitive), saxophone (highly selective), trombone (competitive), trumpet (competitive), tuba (competitive), viola (competitive), violin (competitive), violoncello (competitive), voice (highly selective).

Total enrollment: 300. *Entering class size:* 102. *Graduating class size:* 36. *Percent international:* 8%. *Countries most represented*: Hong Kong.

Renowned alumni: Dave Grusin, Cynthia Lawrence, Scot Weir, Tim Cooper.

Total full-time faculty: 53. *Total part-time faculty:* 2. *Program contact person:* Office of Undergraduate Dean, (303) 492-6352.

Audition Information

No audition fee. Audition consists of the following: repertoire. *Instruments provided for:* percussionists, pianists.

Required repertoire: varies by instrument. Please call school for repertoire information. *Performance opportunities available (frequency):* band, jury examinations, orchestral concerts, recitals, chorus.

Facilities

Number of practice rooms and hours: 86; 7:00 am-11:00 pm. *Recital hall?* yes. *Concert hall?* yes. *Recording studio?* yes.

Comments

The College of Music is a small college within a large university. This means we are autonomous, and allowed to set standards for admission through graduation. In addition, we enjoy a spectacular mountain setting and a full range of cultural opportunities is available in the area of Boulder and Denver.

UNIVERSITY OF DENVER, LAMONT SCHOOL OF MUSIC

7111 Montview, Denver CO 80220
Tel: 303-871-6952 or 800-525-9495
Fax: 303-871-3118
Email: jdocksey@du.edu
Web: www.du.edu.lamont
Contact: Roger Campbell

General

Type of Institution: university, conservatory. *Environment:* urban.

Total enrollment: 9,000. *Total student body from other countries:* 10%. *Degrees offered:* certificate, BA, BM, artist diploma.

Entrance Requirements

Audition required: live, audio. *Other requirements:* interview, recommendation. *Standardized test requirements:* ACT; TOEFL, 550.

Costs & Financial Aid

Application fee: $25. *Deposit:* $200. *Tuition:* $17,000. *Medical fee:* $60. *Room and board:* $6,010.

Types of scholarships and aid awarded: full, partial, merit-based, need-based, named, institutional aid, government aid, reduced tuition, tuition payment plan, work/study. *Forms required for scholarships:* FAFSA, income tax return. *Loans available. Procedure for applying for loans:* application for University of Denver undergraduate admissions, application for Lamont School of Music, audition for Lamont School of Music faculty. *Financial aid offered to international students. Percent of international students receiving scholarships:* 75%.

Services

Housing options: on-site dorms, off-campus housing, fraternity, sorority.

Support staff: dorm parent, financial aid advisor, foreign student advisor, housing advisor, psychological counselor, resident assistant, student affairs officer.

MUSIC

Curriculum, Students, and Faculty

How are major teacher assignments made? students may choose, made by the school according to teacher availability. Faculty is informed of a student's teacher preference at the time of the audition. *30 lessons with major teacher. May a student change major teachers during the course of study?* possibly. *Study of secondary instrument or discipline is allowed.*

Selectivity for instruments or programs offered (rating): accordion (selective), bassoon (competitive), choral conducting (selective), choral singing (competitive), clarinet (competitive), composition (competitive), double bass (competitive), electronic music (competitive), flute or piccolo (competitive), French horn (competitive), guitar (highly selective), harp (competitive), jazz (selective), oboe/English horn (competitive), orchestral conducting (selective), organ (competitive), percussion (competitive), piano (competitive), saxophone (selective), trombone (competitive), trumpet (competitive), tuba (competitive), viola (competitive), violin (competitive), violoncello (competitive), voice (competitive).

Total enrollment: 200. *Entering class size:* 50. *Graduating class size:* 40. *Percent international:* 10%.

Renowned alumni: Hao Tien, New York Metropolitan Opera.

Total full-time faculty: 22. *Total part-time faculty:* 17. *Program contact person:* Malcolm Lynn Baker.

Audition Information

No audition fee. Audition consists of the following: scales, sight reading, improvisation, repertoire. *Instruments provided for:* harpists, percussionists, pianists.

Required repertoire: varies by instrument. Please call school for repertoire information. Improvisation for jazz studies candidates only.

Facilities

Number of practice rooms and hours: 26; 7:00 am-12:00 am. *Recital hall?* yes. *Concert hall?* yes. *Recording studio?* yes.

CONNECTICUT

CONNECTICUT COLLEGE

270 Mohegan Avenue, New London CT 06320
Tel: 860-447-1911
Fax: 860-439-2700
Web: camel.conncoll.edu

General

Type of Institution: private college. *Environment:* suburban.

Total enrollment: 1,857. *Total student body from other countries:* 7%. *Degrees offered:* BA.

Entrance Requirements

You must be admitted to the college. *Other requirements:* interview, recommendation, essay. *Standardized test requirements:* ACT; SAT II; TOEFL, 600.

Costs & Financial Aid

Application fee: $45. *Deposit:* $250. *Tuition and fees:* $29,175.

Percent of students receiving financial aid: 54% *Types of scholarships and aid awarded:* need-based, tuition payment plan, work/study. *Forms required for scholarships:* FAFSA, income tax return, income asset verification, CSS Profile, divorce/separated statement, business/farm supplement. *Loans available. Financial aid offered to international students. Percent of international students receiving scholarships:* 1%. *Other aid available to international students:* institutional aid.

Services

Housing options: on-site dorms.

Support staff: career counselor, financial aid advisor, foreign student advisor, housing advisor, psychological counselor, resident assistant, resident nurse, student affairs officer.

DANCE

Curriculum, Students, and Faculty

Required courses: anatomy, ballet (2 classes per week, 4 years to complete), dance composition/choreography, dance history, master classes, modern dance, music, rehearsal and performance, repertory, stagecraft.

Elective courses: African dance, dance writing, research and criticism, jazz, Labanotation, other world dance forms, repertory stagecraft, nutrition.

Selectivity for males: most admitted, but not all. *Selectivity for females:* approximately 33% admitted. *Total enrollment:* 413. *Graduating class size:* 5.

Renowned alumni: David Dorfman, Nick Lecliter.

Total full-time faculty: 4. *List of current faculty and past affiliations:* Lan-Lan Wang, London Contemporary Dance; Dan Wagoner, Paul Taylor, Martha Graham Companies; George de la Pena, American Ballet Theatre. *Program contact person:* Lan-Lan Wang.

Audition Information

No audition fee. Audition consists of the following: ballet, modern dance, prepared solo. *Accompanist provided. Cassette player available; CD player available.*

Audition evaluation criteria: technical ability, creativity, performance quality, and academic excellence; intelligence, preparation, aptitude in liberal arts.

Performance Information

Performance opportunities available (frequency): Fully produced concerts (2 per year), informal concerts (3-4 per year), workshops (all year).

Performances choreographed by: faculty, students, guests. *Recent guest choreographers:* Eddie Taketa for Doug Varone, Joy Kellman, Ross Parkes, Doug Nielsen, Sara Rudner, and Heidi Latsky.

Facilities

Number of studios available: 3. *Approximate studio dimensions and flooring:* 100' x 51' Marley, 51' x 24' Marley, 45' x 45' Marley. *Performance facilities:* Plamer auditorium—formal performing, Myers Studio—informal Performing.

DRAMA

Curriculum, Students, and Faculty

Required courses: acting, directing, improvisation, make-up, scene study, text analysis, verse drama.

Elective courses: Alexander technique, audition preparation, drama criticism, dramaturgy, martial arts, mime, movement, musical theater, speech, stage combat, Stanislavski exercises, voice.

Summer program not available. Affiliation with a professional theater company: Long Wharf Internship. Summer employment with Eugene O'Neill Theater.

Selectivity for males: most admitted, but not all. *Selectivity for females:* most admitted, but not all. *Total enrollment:* 137. *Graduating class size:* 10. *Percent international:* 1%.

Renowned alumni: Estelle Parsons, Jessica Hecht, Susan St. James, Ted Chapin.

Total full-time faculty: 3. *Total part-time faculty:* 6. *List of current faculty and past affiliations:* Linda Herr, Stevenson Carlebach, David Jaffe.

Audition Information

No audition fee. Audition consists of the following: Shakespearean monologue.

Audition evaluation criteria: intelligence, preparation, aptitude in the liberal arts.

Performance Information

Performance opportunities available (frequency): fully produced performances (4 per year), informal performances (8-10 per year), workshops (3-4 per year), off-site performances (6-8 per year), casting is by audition.

Recent guest artists: Estelle Parsons.

Facilities

Rehearsal facilities and hours: 1 rehearsal hall, 1,300-seat theater, 1 black box being built. *Number of theaters on campus:* 2. *Type and capacity:* music hall 500, technology auditorium 200.

MUSIC

Curriculum, Students, and Faculty

How are major teacher assignments made? made by the school. Faculty is not informed of a student's teacher preference at the time of the audition. *27 lessons with major teacher; May a student change major teachers during the course of study?* possibly. *Study of secondary instrument or discipline is allowed.*

Selectivity for instruments or programs offered (rating): bassoon (non-competitive), choral singing (competitive), clarinet (non-competitive), composition (competitive), double bass (non-competitive), electronic music (competitive), flute or piccolo (non-competitive), French horn (non-competitive), guitar (non-competitive), harp (non-competitive), harpsichord (non-competitive), jazz (competitive), oboe/English horn (non-competitive), orchestral conducting (non-competitive), organ (non-competitive), percussion (non-competitive), piano (competitive), saxophone (non-competitive), trombone (non-competitive), trumpet (non-competitive), tuba (non-competitive), viola (non-competitive), violin (non-competitive), violoncello (non-competitive), voice (non-competitive).

Total enrollment: 390. *Graduating class size:* 3. *Percent international:* 1%.

Total full-time faculty: 6. *Total part-time faculty:* 8. *Program contact person:* Thomas Stoner.

Audition Information

No audition fee. Audition consists of the following: scales, arpeggios, sight reading, repertoire. *Instruments provided for:* percussionists; the department lends a few selected instruments to students (specific requests should be made to the chair of the department).

Performance opportunities available (frequency): jury examinations (1 per semester), recitals (4 per semester).

Facilities

Number of practice rooms and hours: 14; 6:30 am-12:00 am. *Recital hall?* yes. *Concert hall?* yes. *Recording studio?* yes.

THE HARTT SCHOOL

University of Hartford
200 Bloomfield Avenue, West Hartford CT 06117-1599
Tel: 860-768-4115
Fax: 860-768-4441
Email: hawken@uhavax.hartford.edu
Contact: James Jacobs

General

Type of Institution: university, conservatory. *Environment:* suburban. *Academic education is offered on-site.*

Total enrollment: 450. *Total student body from other countries:* 10%. *Degrees offered:* BA, BFA, BM.

Entrance Requirements

Audition required: live, audio. *Other requirements:* interview, recommendation, essay. *Standardized test requirements:* ACT; SAT I; TOEFL, 550.

Costs & Financial Aid

Application fee: $40. *Deposit:* $150. *Tuition:* $16,380. *Medical fee:* $295. *Other fees:* $75 per semester technology fee.

Percent of students receiving financial aid: 85%. *Types of scholarships and aid awarded:* full, partial, merit-based, need-based, tuition payment plan, work/study, gig office. *Forms required for scholarships:* FAFSA, income tax return, income asset verification. *Financial aid offered to international students.*

Services

Housing options: on-site dorms, off-campus housing, fraternity, sorority.

Support staff: career counselor, financial aid advisor, foreign student advisor, housing advisor, psychological counselor, resident assistant, resident nurse, student affairs officer.

DANCE

Curriculum, Students, and Faculty

Required courses: anatomy, character, ballet (5 classes per week, 4 years to complete), dance composition/choreography, dance history, dance theory, jazz, Labanotation, master classes, men's class (2 classes per week, 4 years to complete), modern dance (4 classes per week, 4 years to complete), music, pas de deux (1 class per week, 4 years to complete), pointe (2 classes per week, 4 years to complete), rehearsal and performance, repertory, stagecraft, variations (1 class per week, 4 years to complete), modern dance.

Elective courses: tap.

Selectivity for males: approximately 60% admitted. *Selectivity for females:* approximately 60% admitted.*Total enrollment:* 70. *Entering class size:* 25. *Countries most represented:* Russia, Taiwan. *List of current faculty and past affiliations:* Peggy Lyman, Martha Graham Dance Co.; Alla Osipenko, Kirov Ballet; Elaine Werner Hutchison, founder Royal Winnipeg Ballet's Teacher Course. *Program contact person:* Enid Lynn, (860) 525-9396

Audition Information

Audition fee: $30. *Audition consists of the following:* ballet, modern dance, pointe works. *Accompanist provided.*

Performance Information

Performance opportunities available (frequency): Fully produced concerts (3 per year), on-site performances (2 per year), touring (10 per year).

Performances choreographed by: faculty, students, guests. *Recent guest choreographers:* Jean Grand-Maitre, Vicki Simon.

Facilities

Number of studios available: 5. *Approximate studio dimensions and flooring:* 1,000 sq. ft. basketweave construction, 1,600 sq. ft. Forbo surface. *Performance facilities:* use of two theaters for main-stage concerts.

DRAMA

Curriculum, Students, and Faculty

Required courses: acting, audition preparation, movement, scene study, speech, stage combat, text analysis, verse drama, voice, verse drama.

Number of years required to complete program: 4. *Summer program not available. No affiliation with a professional theater company. Selectivity for males:* approximately 10% admitted. *Selectivity for females:* approximately 10% admitted. *Total enrollment:* 30. *Entering class size:* 19.

List of current faculty and past affiliations: Jeanne Ruskin, Roundabout Theatre, Felix Ivanov, Russia; Rebecca Lazier, Royal Winnipeg Ballet; Greg Leaming, The Hartford Stage; Malcom Morrison, World Theatre Training Institute National Theatre Conference.

Audition Information

Audition fee: $30. *Audition consists of the following:* a cappella singing, comedic monologue.

Performance Information

Performance opportunities available (frequency): fully produced performances (3rd and 4th year), informal performances (2nd year) casting is assigned.

Facilities

Rehearsal facilities and hours: a variety of flexible facilities and time. *Number of theaters on campus:* 3.

MUSIC

Curriculum, Students, and Faculty

Unique or innovative music curriculum: programs in music and performing arts management, music production and technology, jazz studies, performance 20/20 an honors chamber music program which is tuition-free. *How are major teacher assignments made?* students may choose, made by the school. Faculty is informed of a student's teacher preference at the time of the audition. *28 lessons with major teacher. May a student change major teachers during the course of study?* possibly. *Study of secondary instrument or discipline is allowed.*

Selectivity for instruments or programs offered (rating): bassoon (competitive), choral singing (selective), clarinet (competitive), composition (selective), double bass (competitive), flute or piccolo (highly selective), French horn (selective), guitar (selective), harp (competitive), jazz (highly selective), oboe/English horn (selective), organ (selective), percussion (selective), piano (highly selective), saxophone (selective), trombone (selective), trumpet (selective), tuba (competitive), viola (selective), violin (highly selective), violoncello (highly selective), voice (selective).

Total enrollment: 350. *Entering class size:* 157. *Graduating class size:* 1. *Percent international:* 10%. *Countries most represented:* Korea, Taiwan, Japan. *Program contact person:* James Jacobs.

Audition Information

Audition fee? $30. *Audition consists of the following:* scales, orchestral excerpts, music theory, melodic dictation, repertoire. *Instruments provided for:* harpists, percussionists.

Required repertoire: 2-3 contrasting works from standard literature. P*erformance opportunities available (frequency):* jury examinations.

Facilities

Recital hall? yes. *Concert hall?* yes. *Recording studio?* yes.

TRINITY COLLEGE (CT)

300 Summit Street, Hartford CT 06106-3100
Tel: 860-297-2180
Fax: 860-297-2287
Email: admissions.office@trincoll.edu
Web: www.trincoll.edu
Contact: Nathalie Perez

General

Type of Institution: college. *Environment:* urban.

Total enrollment: 2,043. *Total student body from other countries:* 4%. *Degrees offered:* BA.

Entrance Requirements

You must be admitted to the college. *Audition not required. Other requirements:* recommendation, essay *Standardized test requirements:* ACT, 27; SAT I, 621; SAT II, 625; TOEFL, 550.

Costs & Financial Aid

Application fee: $50. *Deposit:* $250. *Tuition:* $21,710. *Other fees:* $785 general, activity and transcript fees. *Room and board:* $6,330.

Percent of students receiving financial aid: 47%. *Types of scholarships and aid awarded:* full, partial, need-based, named, institutional aid, government aid, reduced tuition, work/study. *Forms required for scholarships:* FAFSA, income tax return, income asset verification, CSS Profile, business/ farm supplement, divorced/separated parents statement. *Loans available. Procedure for applying for loans:* complete the admission process and file the FAFSA and CSS profile. *Financial aid offered to international students. Percent of international students receiving scholarships:* 16%. *Other aid available to international students:* Trinity loans; Trinity grants.

Services

Housing options: on-site dorms, fraternity, sorority.

Support staff: career counselor, financial aid advisor, foreign student advisor, housing advisor, psychological counselor, resident assistant, resident nurse, student affairs officer.

DANCE

Curriculum, Students, and Faculty

Required courses: dance history (2 classes per week), dance theory, dance writing, research and criticism, stagecraft, Asian movement forms.

Elective courses: anatomy (2 classes per week), ballet (2 classes per week), dance composition/ choreography, improvisation, jazz (2 classes per week), master classes, modern dance (2 classes per week), movement techniques (2 classes per week), body conditioning, music, rehearsal and performance, repertory (2 classes per week), contact improvisation, meditation.

Selectivity for males: admit all who apply. *Selectivity for females:* admit all who apply. *Total enrollment:* 158. *Graduating class size:* 2.

Renowned alumni: Tim Martin.

Total full-time faculty: 3. *Total part-time faculty:* 7. *List of current faculty:* Judy Dworin, Karen Bacon. *Program contact person:* Judy Dworin and Katharine Power.

Audition Information

Accompanist not provided. Cassette player not available; CD player not available.

Performance Information

Performance opportunities available (frequency): Fully produced concerts (2 per year), informal concerts (1-2 per year), workshops (intermittently), on-site performances(1 per year), touring.

Performances choreographed by: faculty, students, guests. *Recent guest choreographers:* Tiffany Mills.

Facilities

Number of studios available: 3. *Approximate studio dimensions and flooring:* 30' x 30' Marley, *Performance facilities:* proscenium stage, black box theater, lighting and sound equipped studio.

DRAMA

Curriculum, Students, and Faculty

Elective courses: acting, directing, drama criticism, dramaturgy, improvisation, mime, movement, speech, Stanislavski exercises, voice.

Number of years required to complete program: 4. *Summer program available. Affiliation with a professional theater company: Hartford Stage. Many of their artists teach here; students do internships at Hartford Stage; a faculty member at Trinity is the Resident Dramaturg at Hartford Stage. La Ma Ma in New York City. Hartford Ballet: internships and classes in which Trinity students may participate.*

Selectivity for males: admit all who apply. *Selectivity for females:* admit all who apply. *Total enrollment:* 108. *Graduating class size:* 5. *Percent international:* 1%. *Countries most represented*: Venezuela.

Renowned alumni: Edward Albee, Michael Countryman, Amy McPherson.

Total full-time faculty: 2. *Total part-time faculty:* 5. *List of current faculty and past affiliations:* Arthur Feinsod, Hartford Stage; M. Joshua Karter, Nikitsky Gates Theater in Moscow; Bartlett Shev, Hartford Stage & Portland Stage Company.

Performance Information

Performance opportunities available (frequency): fully produced performances (2 per year), informal performances (2-3 per year), workshops (2-3 per year), off-site performances (occasionally), casting is by audition. As part of course work, class members participate in end-of-course productions.

Recent guest artists: Anna Deveare Smith, Spiderwoman Theater Collective, Irish Repertory Theatre.

Facilities

Rehearsal facilities and hours: one rehearsal studio, available at all hours. *Number of theaters on campus:* 3. *Type and capacity:* proscenium—380, black box—80, lab 40.

MUSIC

Curriculum, Students, and Faculty

How are major teacher assignments made? according to teacher preference and teacher availability. *May a student change major teachers during the course of study?* usually. *Study of secondary instrument or discipline is allowed.*

Selectivity for instruments or programs offered (rating): accompanying (open), accordion, bagpipes (open), bassoon (open), choral conducting (open), choral singing (open), clarinet (open), composition (open), double bass (open), electronic music (open), flute or piccolo (open), French horn (open), guitar (open), harp (open), harpsichord (open), jazz (open), oboe / English horn (open), orchestral conducting (open), organ (open), percussion (open), piano (open), sacred music (open), saxophone (open), trombone (open), trumpet (open), tuba (open), viola (open), violin (open), violoncello (open), voice (open).

Total enrollment: 210. *Graduating class size:* 4.

Renowned alumni: Liesl Odenweller, John Cockrell.

Total full-time faculty: 5. *Total part-time faculty:* 3. *Program contact person:* Douglas B. Johnson, Gerald Moshell.

Audition Information

No audition fee. Audition consists of the following: orchestral excerpts, music theory, foreign language, rhythmic dictation, ensemble playing, *Instruments provided for:* percussionists.

Facilities

Number of practice rooms and hours: 8; 86 hours per week. *Recital hall?* no. *Concert hall?* no. *Recording studio?* no.

UNIVERSITY OF CONNECTICUT

Music Department U-12
876 Coventry Road, Storrs CT 06269-1012
Tel: 860-486-3728
Fax: 860-486-3796
Web: www.sfa.uconn.edu/music.html

General

Type of Institution: public university.

Total enrollment: 15,541. *Degrees offered:* BA, BM, BS in music education.

Entrance Requirements

Audition required: live, audio. *Other requirements:* interview.

Costs & Financial Aid

Tuition (in-state/out-state): $5,342/$14,676. *Other fees:* $725 books, $1,084 university and student fee. *Room and board:* $5,862.

Types of scholarships and aid awarded: partial, named.

Services

Housing options: on-site dorms, off-campus housing, fraternity, sorority.

MUSIC

Curriculum, Students, and Faculty

How are major teacher assignments made? made by the school. Faculty is not informed of a student's teacher preference at the time of the audition. *May a student change major teachers during the course of study?* Never. *Study of secondary instrument or discipline is allowed.*

Selectivity for instruments or programs offered (rating): bassoon (competitive), choral conducting (competitive), choral singing (competitive), clarinet (competitive), double bass (competitive), flute or piccolo (competitive), French horn (competitive), guitar (competitive), jazz (competitive), oboe/English horn (competitive), orchestral conducting (competitive), organ (competitive), percussion (competitive), piano (competitive), saxophone (competitive), trombone (competitive), trumpet (competitive), tuba (competitive), viola (competitive), violin (competitive), voice (competitive).

Total enrollment: 282. *Entering class size:* 56. *Graduating class size:* 15. *Percent international:* 4%. *Countries most represented*: Asian countries.

Total full-time faculty: 20. *Total part-time faculty:* 25. *Program contact person:* Deborah Trahan.

Audition Information

No audition fee. Audition consists of the following: scales, music theory, sight reading, repertoire.

Required repertoire: varies by instrument. Please call school for repertoire information. *Performance opportunities available (frequency):* band, chamber music, jury examinations, opera workshops, orchestral concerts, recitals, produced operas, chorus.

Facilities

Number of practice rooms and hours: 20; 6:00 am-12:00 am *Recital hall?* yes. *Recording studio?* no.

WESLEYAN UNIVERSITY

Middletown CT 06459
Tel: 860-685-3000
Fax: 860-685-3001
Web: www.wesleyan.edu
Contact: Diana Ip

General

Type of Institution: private college. *Environment:* suburban.

Total enrollment: 2,700. *Total student body from other countries:* 6%. *Degrees offered:* BA.

Entrance Requirements

Audition not required. You must be admitted to the university. *Other requirements:* recommendation, essay *Standardized test requirements:* ACT, 29; SAT I, 1350; SAT II; TOEFL, 600.

Costs & Financial Aid

Application fee: $55. *Deposit:* $250. *Tuition:* $23,000. *Room and board:* $5,960.

Percent of students receiving financial aid: 45%. *Types of scholarships and aid awarded:* full, need-based, named, institutional aid, government aid, work/study. *Forms required for scholarships:* FAFSA, income tax return. *Loans available. Financial aid offered to international students. Percent of international students receiving scholarships:* 25%.

Services

Housing options: on-site dorms, off-campus housing, fraternity, sorority.

Support staff: career counselor, financial aid advisor, foreign student advisor, housing advisor, physical therapist, psychological counselor, resident assistant, resident nurse, student affairs officer.

YALE UNIVERSITY

New Haven CT 06511
Tel: 203-432-9300
Web: www.yale.edu/yaleinfo

General

Type of Institution: private university. *Environment:* urban.

Total enrollment: 11,000. *Degrees offered:* BA.

Entrance Requirements

You must be admitted to the university. *Audition required:* live, audio, visual. *Other requirements:* interview, recommendations, essays. *Standardized test requirements:* SAT I, SAT II, TOEFL.

Costs & Financial Aid

Tuition and fees: $25,150. *Room and board* $6,910.

Percent of students receiving financial aid: 47%. *Forms required for scholarships:* FAFSA, income tax return.

Services

Housing options: on-site dorms, off-campus housing.

Comments

Outstanding courses in music and theater studies, and the Yale School of Music is world renowned. Although primarily a graduate school, some qualified undergraduates may take lessons with the faculty at the School of Music.

DELAWARE

UNIVERSITY OF DELAWARE

Newark DE 19716-6210
Tel: 302-831-8123
Email: admissions@udel.edu
Web: www.udel.edu

General

Type of Institution: public university. *Environment:* suburban.

Total enrollment: 21,000. *Degrees offered:* BA.

Entrance Requirements

You must be admitted to the university. *Audition required:* for Professional Theater Training Program, live. *Other requirements:* interview, recommendations, essays. *Standardized test requirements:* ACT, SAT I, TOEFL.

Costs & Financial Aid

Tuition and fees (in-state/out-state): $4,630/$12,690. *Room and board* $4,990.

Percent of students receiving financial aid: 61%. *Forms required for scholarships:* FAFSA.

Services

Housing options: on-site dorms, off-campus housing, fratenity, sorority.

DRAMA

Curriculum, Students, Faculty

Required courses: acting, improvisation, scene study, speech, Stanislavski exercises, voice. *Elective courses:* directing, drama criticism, make-up, audition preparation.

DISTRICT OF COLUMBIA

AMERICAN UNIVERSITY

4400 Massachusetts Avenue, NW, Washington DC 20016
Tel: 202-885-6000
Fax: 202-885-3420
Email: afa@american.edu
Web: www.american.edu
Contact: Dr. Naima Prevots

General

Type of Institution: private university. *Religious Affiliation:* Methodist. *Environment:* urban.

Total student body from other countries: 14%. *Degrees offered:* BA, BFA.

Entrance Requirements

Audition not required. Other requirements: recommendation, essay. *Standardized test requirements:* ACT, 26; SAT I, 1050; TOEFL.

Costs & Financial Aid

Application fee: $45. *Deposit:* $600. *Tuition and fees:* $19,575. *Room and board:* $7,650.

Percent of students receiving financial aid: 60%. *Types of scholarships and aid awarded:* full, partial, merit-based, need-based, named, institutional aid, tuition payment plan, work/study. *Forms required for scholarships:* FAFSA, school's own financial aid form. *Loans available. Procedure for applying for loans:* submit FAFSA and institutional form by 3/1 of application year. *Financial aid offered to international students. Other aid available to international students:* none.

Services

Housing options: on-site dorms, off-campus housing, fraternity, sorority, family.

Support staff: career counselor, financial aid advisor, foreign student advisor, housing advisor, psychological counselor, resident assistant, resident nurse, student affairs officer.

DANCE

Curriculum, Students, and Faculty

Elective courses: African dance, ballet, dance composition/choreography, dance history, dance theory, dance writing, research and criticism, jazz, Labanotation, martial arts, master classes, modern dance, body conditioning, Feldenkreis, music, nutrition, Indian dance, pas de deux, pointe, rehearsal and performance, repertory, stagecraft, tap, variations, vernacular dance, Japanese dance.

DRAMA

Curriculum, Students, and Faculty

Required courses: acting, audition preparation, directing, improvisation, make-up, movement, scene study, speech, Stanislavski exercises, voice.

Elective courses: mime, musical theater.

MUSIC

Comments

The music division is housed within a department of performing arts which contains a department of dance, theatre, music theatre, music and arts management. It is easy to take courses in any of the other disciplines. We produce 2 musical staged productions a year, 2 large choral works with orchestra, 2-4 orchestral concerts, a madrigal dinner and 3-6 additional choral programs as well as opera workshop performances.

THE CATHOLIC UNIVERSITY OF AMERICA

620 Michigan Avenue, NE, Washington DC 20064
Tel: 202-319-5305
Fax: 202-319-6533
Email: CUA-Admissions@CUA.edu
Web: www.CUA.edu

General

Type of Institution: private university. *Religious Affiliation:* Roman Catholic. *Environment:* urban. *Cross registration is available through the Consortium of Universities of the Washington Metropolitan Area.*

Total enrollment: 2,400. *Total student body from other countries:* 11%. *Degrees offered:* BA, BM.

Entrance Requirements

Audition required: live, audio, video. *Other requirements:* recommendation, essay. *Standardized test requirements:* ACT, 24; SAT I, 1100; TOEFL, 550. School's own English exam required.

Costs & Financial Aid

Application fee: $50. *Deposit:* $200. *Tuition:* $16,500. *Medical fee:* $610. *Other fees:* $100 activities, $400 university services, $160 orientation, $110 student technology fee, $115 student records fee. *Room and board:* $6,608.

Percent of students receiving financial aid: 53%. *Types of scholarships and aid awarded:* full, partial, merit-based, need-based, named, institutional aid, government aid, reduced tuition, tuition payment plan, work/study, gig office. *Forms required for scholarships:* FAFSA, income tax return, income asset verification. *Loans available. Procedure for applying for loans:* application form. *Financial aid offered to international students.*

Services

Housing options: on-site dorms, off-campus housing.

Support staff: career counselor, dorm parent, financial aid advisor, foreign student advisor, housing advisor, psychological counselor, resident assistant, resident nurse, student affairs officer.

DANCE

Curriculum, Students, and Faculty

Required courses: ballet, jazz, rehearsal and performance, tap, movement techniques.

DRAMA

Curriculum, Students, and Faculty

Required courses: directing, scene study.

Elective courses: Alexander technique, speech.

Number of years required to complete program: 4. *Summer program not available. Affiliation with a professional theater company: flexible arrangement with Washington area theaters.*

Total enrollment: 51. *Entering class size:* 20. *Graduating class size:* 20.

Renowned alumni: Walter Bobbie, Philip Bosco, Allen Lee Hughes, Joseph V. Mellilo, Susan Sarandon, Jon Voight, Paula Vogel, Stan Wojewodski, Jr.

List of current faculty and past affiliations: Gitta Honegger, Yale; Gary J. Williams, Yale University, Folger Shakespeare Library Senior Fellow; Jackson Phippin, William Foeller, Thomas F. Donahue, Roland Reed, Caroline McGee.

Performance Information

Performance opportunities available (frequency): fully produced performances (4-8 per year), informal performances (3 per semester), workshops (2-3 per semester), casting is by audition.

Recent guest artists: Joshua Sobol, Monica Raya, Edna Sobol, Nancy Thun.

Facilities

Type and capacity: proscenium—590, 3/4 round—120, black box—80.

MUSIC

Curriculum, Students, and Faculty

Unique or innovative music curriculum: Conservatory training within a liberal arts setting. *How are major teacher assignments made?* students may choose, made by the school according to teacher preference and teacher availability. Faculty is informed of a student's teacher preference at the time of the audition. *28 lessons with major teacher.*

Selectivity for instruments or programs offered (rating): bassoon (selective), clarinet (selective), composition (selective), double bass (selective), flute or piccolo (selective), French horn (selective), guitar (competitive), harp (selective), oboe/English horn (selective), organ (selective), percussion (selective), piano (selective), saxophone (selective), trombone (selective), trumpet (selective), viola (selective), violin (selective), violoncello (selective), voice (selective), music education (selective), musical theater (selective), music history and literature (selective).

Total enrollment: 150. *Entering class size:* 40. *Graduating class size:* 40.

Renowned alumni: John Aler, Harolyn Blackwell, Myra Merritt, Carmen Barthrop, Helen Bickers, Jung Ah Lee.

Total full-time faculty: 18. *Total part-time faculty:* 120. *Program contact person:* Dr. Amy Antonelli.

Audition Information

No audition fee. Audition consists of the following: scales, sight reading, repertoire. *Instruments provided for:* harpists, percussionists.

Required repertoire: 3 pieces in contrasting styles. *Performance opportunities available (frequency):* jury examinations (frequently), recitals (frequently).

Facilities

Number of practice rooms and hours: 48; 7:00 am-11:00 pm. *Recital hall?* yes. *Concert hall?* yes. *Recording studio?* yes.

GEORGE WASHINGTON UNIVERSITY

Office of Admissions
2121 I Street, NW, Washington DC 20052
Tel: 202-994-6040
Fax: 202-994-0325
Email: gwadm@gwis2.circ.gwu.edu
Web: www.gwu.edu/go2gw
Contact: Tish Peterson

General

Type of Institution: private university. *Environment:* urban.

Total enrollment: 6,600. *Total student body from other countries:* 12%. *Degrees offered:* BA, BM.

Entrance Requirements

Audition required: live, audio, video *Other requirements:* interview, recommendation, essay *Standardized test requirements:* ACT, 26; SAT I, 1250; TOEFL.

Costs & Financial Aid

Application fee: $55. *Deposit:* $650. *Tuition:* $20,400. *Other fees:* $825 books, personal expenses. *Room and board:* $6,970.

Percent of students receiving financial aid: 67%. *Types of scholarships and aid awarded:* partial, merit-based, need-based, named, institutional aid. *Forms required for scholarships:* FAFSA, income tax return, income asset verification, CSS Profile. *Loans available. Procedure for applying for loans:* through lenders, merit scholarships. *Other aid available to international students:* 6 total merit scholarships per year for international students.

Services

Housing options: on-site dorms, off-campus housing, fraternity.

Support staff: career counselor, financial aid advisor, foreign student advisor, physical therapist, psychological counselor, resident assistant, resident nurse, student affairs officer.

DANCE

Curriculum, Students, and Faculty

Required courses: dance composition/choreography, dance history, dance theory, modern dance, movement techniques, rehearsal and performance, dance history, dance theory, modern dance (1 class per week), dance writing, research and criticism, rehearsal and performance.

Elective courses: African dance, ballet, Labanotation, master classes, Indian dance, pointe, repertory, Spanish, Brazilian dance.

Selectivity for males: admit all who apply. *Selectivity for females:* admit all who apply. *Total enrollment:* 200.

Total full-time faculty: 3. *Total part-time faculty:* 4. *List of current faculty and past affiliations:* Joseph Mills, Pilobolus; Maida Withers. *Program contact person:* Pam Bentley.

Audition Information

No audition fee. Audition consists of the following: modern dance, prepared solo. *Accompanist not provided. Cassette player available; CD player not available. Dress requirements for males:* appropriate dance clothing. *Dress requirements for females:* appropriate dance clothing.

Repertoire that students should avoid? prefer no tap dance.

Audition evaluation criteria: evaluated by faculty—subjective.

Performance Information

Performance opportunities available (frequency): Fully produced concerts (2 per year), informal concerts (3 per year), workshops (2-3 per year).

Performances choreographed by: faculty, students, guests. *Recent guest choreographers:* Ann Carlson.

Facilities

Number of studios available: 3. *Approximate studio dimensions and flooring:* Marley, Marley, wood. *Performance facilities:* theater, small studio.

DRAMA

Curriculum, Students, and Faculty

Required courses: acting, improvisation, scene study, speech, Stanislavski exercises, voice, musical theater.

Elective courses: directing, drama criticism, make-up, audition preparation.

Number of years required to complete program: 4. *Summer program not available. Selectivity for males:* admit all who apply. *Selectivity for females:* admit all who apply. *Total enrollment:* 400.

Total full-time faculty: 7. *Total part-time faculty:* 4. *List of current faculty and past affiliations:* Leslie Jacobson, Horizons Theatre; Alan Wade, National Theater.

Audition Information

No audition fee. Audition consists of the following: interview. *Audition evaluation criteria:* subjective; by faculty.

Performance Information

Performance opportunities available (frequency): fully produced performances (4 per year), informal performances (6-10 per year), workshops (2-3 per year), casting is by audition.

Recent guest artists: Arthur Joseph, Jerry Lewis.

Facilities

Rehearsal facilities and hours: studio, theater stage, black box. *Number of theaters on campus:* 4. *Type and capacity:* thrust—400, black box—50, proscenium—50, auditorium—1200.

MUSIC

Curriculum, Students, and Faculty

How are major teacher assignments made? students may choose, according to teacher availability, scheduling, and compatability. Faculty is not informed of a student's teacher preference at the time of the audition. *28 lessons with major teacher. Study of secondary instrument or discipline is allowed.*

Selectivity for instruments or programs offered (rating): accompanying (open), bassoon (open), choral singing (competitive), clarinet (open), composition (open), double bass (open), electronic music (open), flute or piccolo (open), French horn (open), guitar (open), harp (open), harpsichord (open), jazz (open), oboe/English horn (open), orchestral conducting (open), organ (non-competitive), percussion (open), piano (open), sacred music (open), saxophone (open), trombone (open), trombone (selective), trumpet (open), tuba (open), viola (open), violin (open), violoncello (open), voice (open).

Total enrollment: 950.

Total full-time faculty: 5. *Total part-time faculty:* 48. *Program contact person:* Jessica Fyles.

Audition Information

No audition fee. Audition consists of the following: scales, orchestral excerpts, sight reading, improvisation. *Instruments provided for:* harpists, percussionists, pianists; harpsichord, pipe organ.

Repertoire that students should avoid? no more than one pop/show tune.

Facilities

Number of practice rooms and hours: 15; 7:00 am-12:00 am (Mon-Fri), 8:00 am-11:00 pm (Sat-Sun). *Recital hall?* yes. *Concert hall?* no. *Recording studio?* no.

Comments

No audition required for BA in Music, minor in Music or minor in Jazz Studies. Audition required for presidential arts scholarships (5 selected per year, $7500 per year for 4 yrs) and for BM in Performance. Other students can participate in Music Department offerings and performing groups; no need to major or minor in Music.

HOWARD UNIVERSITY

College of Fine Arts
2400 Sixth Street, NW, Washington DC 20059
Tel: 202-806-2755
Fax: 202-806-6503
Email: admissions@howard.edu
Web: www.howard.edu

General

Type of Institution: private university, historically African-American. *Environment:* urban.

Total enrollment: 12,510. *Degrees offered:* BFA, BM.

Entrance Requirements

Audition required: live, audio, video. *Other requirements:* interview. *Standardized test requirements:* ACT; SAT I.

Costs & Financial Aid

Tuition: $8,530. *Other fees:* $40. *Room and board:* $5,420.

Types of scholarships and aid awarded: full, partial, merit-based, need-based, work/study. *Forms required for scholarships:* FAFSA, income tax return. *Loans available.*

Services

Housing options: on-site dorms, off-campus housing.

Support staff: career counselor, financial aid advisor, foreign student advisor, housing advisor, psychological counselor, resident assistant, resident nurse, student affairs officer.

FLORIDA

ECKERD COLLEGE

4200 54th Avenue South, St. Petersburg FL 33711
Tel: 813-864-8279
Fax: 813-864-7800
Email: tottenc@acasun.eckerd.edu
Web: www.eckard.edu/academics/cra/theatre
Contact: Dick Hallin

General

Type of Institution: private college. *Religious Affiliation:* Presbyterian. *Environment:* suburban.

Total enrollment: 1,475. *Degrees offered:* BA.

Entrance Requirements

Audition not required Other requirements: recommendation, essay. *Standardized test requirements:* ACT, 25; SAT I, 1165.

Costs & Financial Aid

Tuition: $16,975. *Other fees:* $180 student fees.

Percent of students receiving financial aid: 85%. *Types of scholarships and aid awarded:* merit-based, named, institutional aid, government aid, tuition payment plan, work/study. *Forms required for scholarships:* FAFSA. *Loans available. Procedure for applying for loans:* upon acceptance to college all students are considered for scholarships. *Financial aid offered to international students. Percent of international students receiving scholarships:* 1%. *Other aid available to international students:* 1 (merit-based, 2) international loans (harder to get).

Services

Housing options: on-site dorms, off-campus housing.

Support staff: career counselor, financial aid advisor, foreign student advisor, housing advisor, psychological counselor, resident assistant, resident nurse, student affairs officer.

DANCE

Curriculum, Students, and Faculty

Total part-time faculty: 1. *Program contact person:* Cindy Henessy.

DRAMA

Curriculum, Students, and Faculty

Required courses: acting, directing, movement.

Elective courses: audition preparation, improvisation, musical theater, scene study, speech, voice.

Number of years required to complete program: 4. ***Summer program not available. Internships available at various professional companies.***

Selectivity for males: admit all who apply. *Selectivity for females:* admit all who apply. *Graduating class size:* 6.

Renowned alumni: Tyler Bunch, Pina De Rosa, Stephanie Fisher, Bill Munoz.

Total full-time faculty: 3. *Total part-time faculty:* 1. *List of current faculty and past affiliations:* Rich Rice, Tom Bunch, Cynthia Totter.

Audition Information

No audition fee. Audition consists of the following: cold readings, comedic monologue, improvisation, group warm-up. Open auditions for all plays but no audition requirements to get into the program.

Performance Information

Performance opportunities available (frequency): fully produced performances (2-6 per year), workshops (1 per year), casting is by audition.

Recent guest artists: Joan Darling, Kevin Kling, Patrick Tovatt, Chuck Kartali, Cathey Sawyer, Ethan Phillips, Len Berkman, Kimberly Scott, Tony Campisi, Bill Mondy, David Kranes.

Facilities

Rehearsal facilities and hours: 350-seat proscenium theater, flexible black box studio theater. *Number of theaters on campus:* 2.

MUSIC

Curriculum, Students, and Faculty

How are major teacher assignments made? made by the school. ***25 lessons with major teacher. May a student change major teachers during the course of study?*** possibly. ***Study of secondary instrument or discipline is allowed.***

Renowned alumni: Christopher Trakas, Antonia Brown.

Total full-time faculty: 2. *Program contact person:* Joan Epstein.

Audition Information

No audition fee.

Performance opportunities available (frequency): jury examinations, touring.

Facilities

Number of practice rooms and hours: 5; 24 hours a day. *Recital hall?* yes. *Concert hall?* no. *Recording studio?* no.

Comments

As a liberal arts college, we allow all students to study voice or an instrument. Majors are required to reach a high level of academic musical achievement and to make significant progress as performers while enrolled.

FLORIDA A&M UNIVERSITY

1500 Martin Luther King, Jr. Boulevard, Tallahassee FL 32307
Tel: 850-599-3334
Fax: 850-599-8753

General

Type of Institution: public, university. *Environment:* suburban.

Total enrollment: 11,000. *Degrees offered:* BA.

Entrance Requirements

Audition required: live, audio, video. *Other requirements:* recommendation, essay, photograph. *Standardized test requirements:* ACT, 21; SAT I, 900.

Costs & Financial Aid

Application fee: $20. *Deposit:* $350. *Medical fee:* $48. *Tuition and fees (in-state/out-state):* $2,079/ $7,724. *Room and board:* $2,078.

Percent of students receiving financial aid: 55%. *Types of scholarships and aid awarded:* full, partial, merit-based, need-based, named, institutional aid, government aid, tuition payment plan, work/ study. *Forms required for scholarships:* FFS, FAFSA, income tax return. ***Loans available. Procedure for applying for loans:*** write to the Office of Financial Aid which will supply appropriate forms. ***Financial aid offered to international students. Percent of international students receiving scholarships:*** 100%. *Other aid available to international students:* loans.

Services

Housing options: on-site dorms, off-campus housing, fraternity, sorority, family.

Support staff: career counselor, financial aid advisor, foreign student advisor, housing advisor, physical therapist, psychological counselor, resident assistant, resident nurse, student affairs officer.

MUSIC

Curriculum, Students, and Faculty

Unique or innovative music curriculum: Majors are offered in instrumental and choral music, in addition to jazz and commercial music. *How are major teacher assignments made?* students may choose, made by the school. Faculty is not informed of a student's teacher preference at the time of the audition. *May a student change major teachers during the course of study?* possibly. *Study of secondary instrument or discipline is allowed.*

Selectivity for instruments or programs offered (rating): accompanying (non-competitive), bassoon (non-competitive), choral singing (non-competitive), clarinet (non-competitive), double bass (non-competitive), electronic music (non-competitive), flute or piccolo (non-competitive), French horn (non-competitive), jazz (selective), oboe/English horn (non-competitive), organ (non-competitive), percussion (non-competitive), piano (non-competitive), sacred music (non-competitive), saxophone (non-competitive), trombone (non-competitive), trumpet (non-competitive), tuba (non-competitive), voice (non-competitive).

Total enrollment: 153. *Entering class size:* 40. *Graduating class size:* 25. *Percent international:* 3%. *Countries most represented*: Virgin Islands.

Renowned Alumni: Julian Adderly, Nat Adderly, Lucious Wyatt, Lenard Bowie, Julian White, Lindsey Sarjeant, Shaylor James, Wallace Clark, John Daneils, Dennine Mathis, Linoel Moore.

Total full-time faculty: 19. *Total part-time faculty:* 2. *Program contact person:* Dr. William P. Foster

Audition Information

No audition fee. Audition consists of the following: scales, orchestral excerpts, music theory, rhythmic dictation, ensemble playing, arpeggios, sight reading, music history, improvisation, melodic dictation. *Instruments provided for:* percussionists.

Performance opportunities available (frequency): band (frequently), chamber music (frequently), jury examinations (frequently), opera workshops (frequently), recitals (frequently), touring (frequently), chorus.

Facilities

Number of practice rooms and hours: 40; 7:00 am-11:00 pm. *Recital hall?* yes. *Concert hall?* yes. *Recording studio?* yes.

FLORIDA ATLANTIC UNIVERSITY

777 Glades Road, Boca Raton FL 33431
Tel: 561-367-3000
Fax: 561-367-2758
Contact: Anissa Zanino

General

Type of Institution: private university. *Environment:* suburban.

Total enrollment: 19,000. *Degrees offered:* BA, BFA, BM.

Entrance Requirements

Audition required: live, audio, video. *Other requirements:* interview, recommendation, photograph. *Standardized test requirements:* SAT I, SAT II, TOEFL.

Costs & Financial Aid

Application fee: $20. *Other fees:* $5 Identification, $30 parking.

Percent of students receiving financial aid: 80%. *Types of scholarships and aid awarded:* partial, merit-based, need-based, named, institutional aid, government aid, work/study. *Loans available. Procedure for applying for loans:* contact Office of Financial Aid. *Financial aid offered to international students. Percent of international students receiving scholarships:* 50%.

Services

Housing options: on-site dorms, off-campus housing.

Support staff: financial aid advisor, foreign student advisor, psychological counselor, resident assistant, resident nurse, student affairs officer.

DRAMA

Curriculum, Students, and Faculty

Required courses: acting, Alexander technique, audition preparation, directing, dramaturgy, improvisation, make-up, movement, scene study, speech, stage combat, text analysis, verse drama, voice.

Elective courses: drama criticism, martial arts.

Number of years required to complete program: 2-4. *Summer program available. Affiliation with a professional theater company: Pope Theatre, New Theatre, Caldwell Theatre.*

Selectivity for males: approximately 60% admitted. *Selectivity for females:* approximately 60%

admitted. *Total enrollment:* 130. *Entering class size:* 30. *Percent international:* 5%. *Countries most represented*: Canada, Bahamas.

Renowned Alumni: Marc Kudish, Joanne Camp.

Total full-time faculty: 9. *Total part-time faculty:* 5. *List of current faculty and past affiliations:* Jean-Louis Baldet, Tom Atkins, Matthew Wright, University of San Diego, Jana Tift, Florida State University.

Audition Information

No audition fee. Audition consists of the following: comedic monologue, Shakespearean monologue. *Dress requirements for males:* clothing that shows clean body line. *Dress requirements for females:* clothing that shows clean body line.

Performance Information

Performance opportunities available (frequency): fully produced performances (5-8 per year), off-site performances (summers), casting is by audition.

Recent guest artists: Patricia Conolly, Bill Homewood, Estelle Kohler, Zoe Caldwell.

Facilities

Rehearsal facilities and hours: 3 rehearsal studios, 1 dance studio, 7:00 am-11:00 pm. *Number of theaters on campus:* 3. *Type and capacity:* proscenium—548, thrust—175, black box—125.

MUSIC

Curriculum, Students, and Faculty

How are major teacher assignments made? made by the school. Faculty is not informed of a student's teacher preference at the time of the audition. *24 lessons with major teacher; May a student change major teachers during the course of study?* possibly. *Study of secondary instrument or discipline is allowed.*

Selectivity for instruments or programs offered (rating): bassoon (competitive), choral conducting (competitive), choral singing (competitive), clarinet (competitive), composition (competitive), double bass (competitive), flute or piccolo (competitive), French horn (competitive), guitar (competitive), jazz (competitive), oboe/English horn (competitive), organ (competitive), percussion (competitive), piano (competitive), saxophone (competitive), trombone (competitive), trumpet (competitive), tuba (competitive), viola (competitive), violin (competitive), violoncello (competitive), voice (competitive).

Total enrollment: 125. *Entering class size:* 30. *Percent international:* 3%. *Countries most represented*: Israel, Haiti, Bahamas.

Total full-time faculty: 8. *Total part-time faculty:* 40. *Program contact person:* Stuart Glazer.

Audition Information

No audition fee. Audition consists of the following: scales, orchestral excerpts, arpeggios. *Instruments provided for:* percussionists.

Performance opportunities available (frequency): band, jury examinations, orchestral concerts, recitals, chorus.

Facilities

Number of practice rooms and hours: 15; 8:00 am-10:00 pm. *Recital hall?* no. *Concert hall?* yes. *Recording studio?* no.

FLORIDA STATE UNIVERSITY

Office of Admissions, Tallahassee FL 32306
Tel: 850-644-6200
Fax: 850-644-0197
Email: admissions@admin.fsu.edu
Web: www.fsu.edu

General

Type of Institution: public university. *Environment:* urban.

Total enrollment: 30,000. *Total student body from other countries:* 6%. *Degrees offered:* BA.

Entrance Requirements

Audition required: live, audio. *Other requirements:* recommendation, photograph. *Standardized test requirements:* ACT, 24; SAT I, 1100; TOEFL, 550.

Costs & Financial Aid

Application fee: $20. *Other fees:* $700. *Tuition and fees (in-state/out-state):* $2,082/$7,727. *Room and board:* $4,772.

Percent of students receiving financial aid: 66%. *Types of scholarships and aid awarded:* full, partial, merit-based, need-based, named, institutional aid, government aid, reduced tuition, tuition payment plan, work/study. *Forms required for scholarships:* FAFSA. *Loans available. Procedure for applying for loans:* submit FAFSA, gain admission to the university, audition in specific area. *Financial aid offered to international students. Percent of international students receiving scholarships:* 30%. *Other aid available to international students:* partial tuition waivers, stipends.

Services

Housing options: on-site dorms, off-campus housing, fraternity, sorority.

Support staff: career counselor, financial aid advisor, foreign student advisor.

DANCE

Curriculum, Students, and Faculty

Elective courses: dance composition/choreography.

DRAMA

Curriculum, Students, and Faculty

Elective courses: directing.

Number of years required to complete program: 4. *Summer program available. Total enrollment:* 400. *Entering class size:* 150. *Graduating class size:* 62. *Percent international:* 1%. *Countries most represented*: Costa Rica.

Renowned Alumni: Davis Gaines, Steve Sears, Faye Dunaway, Burt Reynolds, Robin Swicord, Tina Gallegos, Tomi Stewart, Dan Carter, Dan Markely, Carrie Warsaw, Chip Chalmers, Steve Rothman.

Total full-time faculty: 30. *Total part-time faculty:* 1. *List of current faculty and past affiliations:* Stuart Baker: Co-Manager Washington Players Studio Theatre, William Byrnes, Fred Chappell: Artistic Director of the Alliance Theatre; George Judy: Utah Shakespeare Festival Director of New Play Development, Brant Pope: Associate Artistic Director, Asolo Theatre Company, Jose Quintero: Member of Theatre Hall of Fame, Jim Wise: Principal Acting Teacher and Consultant for Florida Professional Theatre Association, Michael Zelenak: Assistant and Associate Professor of Theatre and Dramaturgy at Yale Univ.

Audition Information

Audition consists of the following: movement class, Shakespearean monologue.

Performance Information

Performance opportunities available (frequency): fully produced performances (6 or more per year), informal performances (5-10 per year), casting is by audition. Cast all shows from general auditions at start of semester.

Recent guest artists: Lynn McNutt, Henry Polic III.

Facilities

Number of theaters on campus: 4. *Type and capacity:* proscenium—500, black box—250.

MUSIC

Curriculum, Students, and Faculty

Unique or innovative music curriculum: Broad-based with many world music and early music ensemblees, as well as traditional ones. *How are major teacher assignments made?* made by the school. Faculty is informed of a student's teacher preference at the time of the audition. *30 lessons with major teacher. May a student change major teachers during the course of study?* possibly. *Study of secondary instrument or discipline is allowed.*

Total enrollment: 681. *Entering class size:* 200. *Graduating class size:* 95. *Percent international:* 3%. *Countries most represented*: Russia.

Renowned Alumni: Ellen Taofee Zwilich, Charles Rex, Bob Duke, Cliff Colnot.

Total full-time faculty: 80. *Total part-time faculty:* 85. *Program contact person:* Mr. Ben Edener, (850) 644-6102.

Audition Information

Audition consists of the following: scales, arpeggios, *Instruments provided for:* percussionists

Facilities

Number of practice rooms and hours: 130; 7:00 am-12:30 am. *Recital hall?* yes. *Concert hall?* yes. *Recording studio?* yes.

THE HARID CONSERVATORY

2285 Potomac Road, Boca Raton FL 33431
Tel: 561-997-2677
Fax: 561-997-8920

General

Type of Institution: high school, college, conservatory. *Environment:* suburban

Total enrollment: 94. *Total student body from other countries:* 46%.

Entrance Requirements

Audition required: live, audio, video. *Other requirements:* interview, recommendation, essay, photograph. *Standardized test requirements:* ACT; SAT I; SAT II; TOEFL.

Costs & Financial Aid

No tuition. Deposit: $500. *Other fees:* $500.

Types of scholarships and aid awarded: need-based, institutional aid. *Procedure for applying for loans:* complete request form and submit with required supporting documents by deadline stated on form. *Financial aid offered to international students. Other aid available to international students:* All students may apply for financial assistance to help cover the costs for housing, meals, travel, books/supplies, medical insurance.

Services

Housing options: on-site dorms, off-campus housing.

Support staff: career counselor, dorm parent, foreign student advisor, psychological counselor, resident nurse, student affairs officer.

Comments

Harid is committed to intensive performance training for every student which includes performance studies and extensive performance opportunity; comprehensive supporting coursework in music theory, history, solfege, ear training, conducting, and electives; a balanced selection of non- music courses for the bachelor's degree (25% of program). Direct contact with faculty is a high priority in the educational training process. Most high school students are dance majors; most actors and musicians are in conservatory.

DANCE

Curriculum, Students, and Faculty

Required courses: ballet.

Selectivity for males: approximately 10% admitted. *Selectivity for females:* approximately 10% admitted. *Total enrollment:* 32. *Entering class size:* 13. *Graduating class size:* 8. *Percent international:* 6%. *Countries most represented:* Canada.

Total full-time faculty: 6. *Total part-time faculty:* 8. *Program contact person:* Janet Martinez.

Audition Information

Audition fee: $15. *Audition consists of the following:* ballet, pointe works. *Accompanist provided. Cassette player not available; CD player not available. Dress requirements for males:* black tights, white leotard. *Dress requirements for females:* pink tights, black leotard.

Audition evaluation criteria: level and quality of training, physique, talent.

Performance Information

Performance opportunities available (frequency): Fully produced concerts (2 series of 3 performances per year), informal concerts (2 per year).

Performances choreographed by: faculty, students, guests. *Recent guest choreographers:* Robert Barnett, Mark Godden, Hans van Manen.

Facilities

Number of studios available: 3. *Approximate studio dimensions and flooring:* 80' x 400' Marley/sprung, 40' x 40'. *Performance facilities:* fully equipped 840-seat theater for all dance performances.

DRAMA

Curriculum, Students, and Faculty

Required courses: text analysis.

MUSIC

Curriculum, Students, and Faculty

Unique or innovative music curriculum: Intensive training in solo, orchestral, and chamber music studies. Chamber music scheduled 4 hrs/week for all students; orchestra scheduled for 6 hrs/week. Career development seminar required 2 semesters. Mock orchestral auditions required for graduation. *How are major teacher assignments made?* only one major teacher for each instrument offered, students generally enroll with the specific intent to work with major instrument instructor. Faculty is not informed of a student's teacher preference at the time of the audition. *Study of secondary instrument or discipline is allowed.*

Selectivity for instruments or programs offered (rating): bassoon (selective), choral singing (selective), clarinet (highly selective), composition (competitive), flute (competitive), trumpet (open), violoncello (competitive).

Total enrollment: 62. *Entering class size:* 24. *Graduating class size:* 12. *Percent international:* 66%. *Countries most represented:* Canada, China, Romania.

Total full-time faculty: 10. *Total part-time faculty:* 15. *Program contact person:* Ms. Chantal Prosperi.

Audition Information

Audition fee? no audition fee. *Audition consists of the following:* scales, orchestral excerpts, arpeggios, repertoire. *Instruments provided for:* percussionists.

Facilities

Number of practice rooms and hours: 17; 7:30 am-11:00 pm (Mon-Fri), 8:30 am-11:00 pm (Sat-Sun). *Recital hall?* yes. *Concert hall?* yes. *Recording studio?* yes.

NEW WORLD SCHOOL OF THE ARTS

300 Northeast Second Avenue, Miami FL 33123
Tel: 305-237-3135
Fax: 305-237-2794
Email: nwsainfo@mdcc.edu
Web: www.mdcc.edu/nwsa
Contact: Ileana Gallagher

General

Type of Institution: public, college, conservatory, magnet-public. *Environment:* urban. *Cross registration is available through the Miami Dade Community College, University of Florida.*

Total enrollment: 467.

Entrance Requirements

Audition required: live, audio, video. *Other requirements:* interview, recommendation. *Standardized test requirements:* TOEFL, 550. School's own English exam required.

Costs & Financial Aid

Application fee: $15.

Percent of students receiving financial aid: 80%. *Types of scholarships and aid awarded:* full, partial, merit-based, named, institutional aid, government aid, reduced tuition, work/study. *Forms required for scholarships:* FAFSA. *Loans available. Procedure for applying for loans:* standard finacial aid application procedure .

Services

Housing options: off-campus housing.

Support staff: career counselor, financial aid advisor, foreign student advisor, physical therapist, psychological counselor, student affairs officer.

DANCE

Curriculum, Students, and Faculty

Required courses: anatomy, ballet (5 classes per week, 4 years to complete), dance history, dance writing, research and criticism, historical dance, Labanotation, men's class (1 class per week, 4 years to complete), Graham-based dance, Limon-based modern dance, music, pointe (1-2 classes per week, 4 years to complete), repertory, stagecraft.

Elective courses: African dance, Pilates, pas de deux, Spanish, tap, variations, vernacular dance, Caribbean, Afro-Cuban dance.

Selectivity for males: approximately 60% admitted. *Selectivity for females:* approximately 33% admitted. *Countries most represented:* Latin America.

Renowned alumni: Shirley Sastre, Amos Mechanic, Caroline Garcia, Robert Battle, Paunika Jones, Uri Sands. *List of current faculty and past affiliations:* Gerard Ebitz, New York City Ballet; Freddick Bratcher, Alvin Ailey and Martha Graham Companies; Bambi Anderson, Limon Dance Company; Mariana Alvarey, American Ballet Theater; Gerri Houlihan, Lar Lubouitch Company; Peter Condon, Martha Graham Company. *Program contact person:* Roberta Kielgaard.

Audition Information

No audition fee. Audition consists of the following: ballet, modern dance, prepared solo, 2 minutes of any style jazz. *Accompanist provided. Cassette player available; CD player available. Dress requirements for males:* black tights, white t-shirt, appropriate footwear. *Dress requirements for females:* pink tights, black leotard, appropriate footwear.

Repertoire that students should avoid? Solos on pointe are not recommended

Audition evaluation criteria: talent and potenial as a performer, level and quality of training, musicality.

Performance Information

Performance opportunities available (frequency): Fully produced concerts (8-10 per year), informal concerts (6-8 per year), workshops (4-5 per year), on-site performances (6-8 per year), touring (3-5 per year), international touring once every other year, Florida Dance Festival (mid to late June) in house.

Performances choreographed by: faculty, students, guests. *Recent guest choreographers:* Michael Uthoff, Anna Sokolow, Mark Taylor, Lila York, Menaka Thakkar, Rosario Suarey.

Facilities

Number of studios available: 4. *Approximate studio dimensions and flooring:* 40' x 40' sprung floors with Marley. *Performance facilities:* inhouse 200-seat black box, off site 600-seat (Colony Theater) and 1,800-seat (Gusman Center for the Performing Arts).

DRAMA

Curriculum, Students, and Faculty

Number of years required to complete program: 2. *Summer program not available.*

Selectivity for males: approximately 10% admitted. *Selectivity for females:* approximately 10% admitted. *Countries most represented:* Latin America.

Audition Information

Audition fee; Audition consists of the following: comedic monologue, improvisation, movement class, group warm-up, voice. *Audition evaluation criteria:* High level of training and talent demonstrated throughout the audition, focus, commitment, maturity.

Performance Information

Performance opportunities available (frequency): fully produced performances (frequently)fully produced performances (frequently), informal performances (frequently), workshops (frequently), off-site performances (frequently), casting is by audition.

Facilities

Rehearsal facilities and hours: mainstage and classrooms, capacity 120-150; 4:15 pm-10:00 pm Monday through Saturday.

MUSIC

Curriculum, Students, and Faculty

Unique or innovative music curriculum: performance opportunities. *How are major teacher assignments made?* students may choose, made by the school. Faculty is informed of a student's teacher preference at the time of the audition. *Lessons with major teacher; May a student change major teachers during the course of study?* possibly.

Selectivity for instruments or programs offered (rating): accompanying (selective), bassoon (selective), clarinet (selective), composition (selective), double bass (selective), electronic music (selective), flute or piccolo (highly selective), French horn (selective), guitar (selective), harp (selective), harpsichord (selective), oboe/English horn (selective), orchestral conducting (selective), percussion (selective), piano (highly selective), trombone (selective), trumpet (selective), tuba (selective), viola (selective), violin (selective), violoncello (selective), voice (highly selective).

Countries most represented: Latin America. *Program contact person:* Joy Davidson.

Audition Information

No audition fee. Audition consists of the following: scales, orchestral excerpts, music theory, rhythmic dictation, arpeggios, sight reading, melodic dictation, repertoire. *Instruments provided for:* harpists, percussionists.

Repertoire that students should avoid? rap, rock, gospel. *Performance opportunities available (frequency):* chamber music (frequently), band (frequently), jury examinations, opera workshops (frequently), orchestral concerts (frequently), recitals (frequently), produced operas.

Facilities

Number of practice rooms and hours: 10; 8:00 am-8:00 pm. *Recital hall?* no. *Concert hall?* no. *Recording studio?* yes.

ROLLINS COLLEGE

1000 Holt Avenue, Winter Park FL 32789-4499
Tel: 407-646-2161
Fax: 407-646-1502
Email: admission@rollins.edu
Web: www.rollins.edu
Contact: Dave Erdmann

General

Type of Institution: college.

Total enrollment: 1,480. *Total student body from other countries:* 5%. *Degrees offered:* BA.

Entrance Requirements

Audition not required. Other requirements: recommendation, essay. *Standardized test requirements:* SAT I; TOEFL.

Costs & Financial Aid

Application fee: $40. *Deposit:* $500. *Tuition:* $19,450. *Other fees:* $560. *Room and board:* $6,740.

Percent of students receiving financial aid: 62%. *Types of scholarships and aid awarded:* merit-based, need-based, named, institutional aid, government aid, tuition payment plan, work/study. *Forms required for scholarships:* FAFSA, forms for Florida state residents. *Loans available. Financial aid offered to international students.*

Services

Housing options: on-site dorms, off-campus housing, fraternity, sorority.

Support staff: career counselor, financial aid advisor, foreign student advisor, housing advisor, psychological counselor, resident assistant, resident nurse, student affairs officer.

DANCE

Curriculum, Students, and Faculty

Required courses: ballet, dance composition/choreography, dance history, jazz, Graham-based dance, Horton-based modern dance.

Elective courses: African dance, Labanotation, master classes, rehearsal and performance, stagecraft, tap.

Selectivity for males: admit all who apply. *Selectivity for females:* admit all who apply.

Total full-time faculty: 1. *Total part-time faculty:* 3. *List of current faculty and past affiliations:* W. Robert Sherry, Lesley Brasseux, Suzanne Salapa, Russell Sultzbach. *Program contact person:* Robert Sherry.

Performance Information

Performance opportunities available (frequency): Fully produced concerts (1 per year), informal concerts (1-2 per year), workshops (2 per year), on-site performances (1-2 per year).

Performances choreographed by: guests. *Recent guest choreographers:* Russell Sultzbach—Joffrey Ballet, Robbie Mackey—Walt Disney World.

Facilities

Number of studios available: 1. *Approximate studio dimensions and flooring:* sprung floor-Marley. *Performance facilities:* Annie Russell Theatre, Fred Stone Theatre.

DRAMA

Curriculum, Students, and Faculty

Required courses: acting, directing, drama criticism, dramaturgy, text analysis, voice.

Elective courses: audition preparation, make-up, movement, musical theater, scene study.

Summer program not available. no affiliation with a professional theater company. Total enrollment: 36. *Entering class size:* 16. *Graduating class size:* 13.

Renowned alumni: Tony Perkins, Dana Ivey, Buddy Ebsen.

Total full-time faculty: 8. *Total part-time faculty:* 2. *List of current faculty and past affiliations:* S. Joseph Nassif, W. Robert Sherry, Charles Rodgers, Steve Neilson, Lisa Cody-Rapport, James Prescott, Thomas Ouellette, James Fulton.

Audition Information

Audition consists of the following: a cappella singing, comedic monologue, movement class, group warm-up. Audition required for special scholarship consideration.

Performance Information

Performance opportunities available (frequency): fully produced performances (4 per year), informal performances (frequently), workshops (2 per year), off-site performances (1 per year), casting is by audition.

Recent guest artists: Olympia Dukakis, Wendy Wasserstein, Janis Hirsch.

Facilities

Number of theaters on campus: 2. *Type and capacity:* proscenium—377, experimental—70.

MUSIC

Curriculum, Students, and Faculty

How are major teacher assignments made? made by the school. *May a student change major teachers during the course of study?* possibly. *Study of secondary instrument or discipline is allowed.*

Selectivity for instruments or programs offered (rating): bassoon (open), choral conducting (open), choral singing (open), clarinet (open), composition (open), double bass (open), electronic music (open), flute or piccolo (open), French horn (open), guitar (open), harp (open), harpsichord (open), jazz (open), oboe/English horn (open), orchestral conducting (open), organ (open), percussion (open), piano (open), saxophone (open), trombone (open), trumpet (open), tuba (open), viola (open), violin (open), violoncello (open), voice (open).

Total enrollment: 36. *Entering class size:* 5. *Graduating class size:* 8.

Renowned alumni: Fred Rogers, Joanne Byrd Rogers, Chrissy Chauncey.

Total full-time faculty: 4. *Total part-time faculty:* 7. *Program contact person:* John Sinclair.

Audition Information

Audition consists of the following: repertoire, *Instruments provided for:* percussionists; strings, tuba, flute, guitar.

Repertoire that students should avoid? Broadway shows. *Performance opportunities available (frequency):* chamber music, jury examinations (1 per semester), orchestral concerts, recitals, chorus (2 per week).

Facilities

Number of practice rooms and hours: 18; 7:00 am-12:00 am. *Recital hall?* yes.

UNIVERSITY OF MIAMI SCHOOL OF MUSIC

P.O. Box 248165, Coral Gables FL 33124
Tel: 305-284-2245
Fax: 305-284-6475
Email: kmoses@miami.edu
Web: www.music.miami.edu
Contact: Kenneth J. Moses

General

Type of Institution: private university.

Total enrollment: 13,000. *Degrees offered:* BA, BM.

Entrance Requirements

Audition required: live, audio, video. *Other requirements:* recommendation, essay. *Standardized test requirements:* ACT; SAT I; TOEFL, 550.

Costs & Financial Aid

Application fee: $40. *Deposit:* $200. *Tuition:* $19,000. *Room and board:* $7,852.

Percent of students receiving financial aid: 85%. *Types of scholarships and aid awarded:* full, partial, merit-based, need-based, named, institutional aid, government aid, tuition payment plan, work/study. *Forms required for scholarships:* FAFSA. *Loans available. Financial aid offered to international students. Other aid available to international students:* private scholarships.

Services

Housing options: on-site dorms, off-campus housing, fraternity, sorority.

Support staff: career counselor, financial aid advisor, foreign student advisor, psychological counselor, resident assistant, resident nurse, student affairs officer.

MUSIC

Curriculum, Students, and Faculty

How are major teacher assignments made? students may choose. Faculty is not informed of a student's teacher preference at the time of the audition. *May a student change major teachers during the course of study?* possibly. *Study of secondary instrument or discipline is allowed.*

Selectivity for instruments or programs offered (rating): bassoon (selective), clarinet (selective), composition (selective), double bass (selective), flute or piccolo (selective), French horn (selective), guitar (selective), harp (selective), jazz (selective), oboe/English horn (selective), percussion (selective), piano (selective), saxophone (selective), trombone (selective), trumpet (selective), tuba (selective), viola (selective), violin (selective), violoncello (selective), voice (selective).

Total enrollment: 700. *Entering class size:* 150. *Percent international:* 10%.

Total full-time faculty: 58. *Total part-time faculty:* 56. *Program contact person:* Kenneth J. Moses.

Audition Information

Audition fee: $50. *Instruments provided for:* harpists, percussionists.

Facilities

Recital hall? yes. *Concert hall?* yes. *Recording studio?* yes.

GEORGIA

AUGUSTA STATE UNIVERSITY

2500 Walton Way, Augusta GA 30904
Tel: 706-737-1453
Fax: 706-737-1773
Email: cshotwel@aug.edu

General

Type of Institution: public university. *Environment:* urban.

Total enrollment: 5,700. *Total student body from other countries:* 5%. *Degrees offered:* BA, BM.

Entrance Requirements

Audition required: live, audio. *Other requirements:* recommendation. *Standardized test requirements:* SAT I, 950.

Costs & Financial Aid

Types of scholarships and aid awarded: full, partial, merit-based, need-based, work/study.

Services

Housing options: off-campus housing.

Support staff: financial aid advisor, foreign student advisor, student affairs officer.

MUSIC

Curriculum, Students, and Faculty

How are major teacher assignments made? according to teacher availability. Faculty is not informed of a student's teacher preference at the time of the audition. *30 lessons with major teacher. May a student change major teachers during the course of study?* possibly. *Study of secondary instrument or discipline is allowed.*

Selectivity for instruments or programs offered (rating): accompanying (competitive), bassoon (non-competitive), choral singing (non-competitive), clarinet (non-competitive), composition (competitive), double bass (non-competitive), flute or piccolo (non-competitive), French horn (non-competitive), guitar (non-competitive), jazz (non-competitive), oboe/English horn (non-competitive), orchestral conducting (non-competitive), organ (non-competitive), percussion (non-competitive), piano (non-competitive), saxophone (non-competitive), trombone (non-competitive), trumpet (non-competitive), tuba (non-competitive), viola (non-competitive), violin (non-competitive), violoncello (non-competitive), voice (non-competitive).

Total enrollment: 90. *Entering class size:* 15.

Total full-time faculty: 9. *Total part-time faculty:* 25. *Program contact person:* Dr. Clayton Shotwell.

Audition Information

No audition fee? Audition consists of the following: scales, music theory, arpeggios. *Instruments provided for:* percussionists.

Repertoire that students should avoid? popular music. *Performance opportunities available (frequency):* band (frequently), jury examinations, opera workshops, orchestral concerts, recitals (frequently), chorus.

Facilities

Number of practice rooms and hours: 9; open. *Recital hall?* no. *Concert hall?* yes. *Recording studio?* yes.

BRENAU UNIVERSITY

One Centennial Circle, Gainesville GA 30501
Tel: 770-534-6299
Fax: 770-538-4306
Email: upchurch@lib.brenau.edu
Web: www.brenau.edu

General

Type of Institution: private university. *Environment:* suburban.

Total enrollment: 2,500. *Total student body from other countries:* 5%. *Degrees offered:* BA, BFA, BM.

Entrance Requirements

Audition required: live, video. *Other requirements:* recommendation. *Standardized test requirements:* ACT, 22; SAT I, 1069; TOEFL, 500.

Costs & Financial Aid

Application fee: $30. *Deposit:* $350. *Tuition:* $10,740.

Percent of students receiving financial aid: 45%. *Types of scholarships and aid awarded:* partial, merit-based, need-based, named, institutional aid, government aid, tuition payment plan, work/study. *Forms required for scholarships:* FAFSA, income tax return, income asset verification, school's own financial aid form. *Loans available. Procedure for applying for loans:* contact Financial Aid Office. *Financial aid offered to international students. Percent of international students receiving scholarships:* 50%. *Other aid available to international students:* student worker.

Services

Housing options: on-site dorms, sorority.

Support staff: career counselor, foreign student advisor, housing advisor, psychological counselor, resident assistant, resident nurse, student affairs officer.

DANCE

Curriculum, Students, and Faculty

Required courses: anatomy (1/2 years to complete), ballet (4 classes per week, 2-4 years to complete), dance composition/choreography (1-2 years to complete), dance history (2 classes per week, 1 year to complete), jazz (1 class per week, 2-4 years to complete), modern dance, Cunningham-based (4 classes per week, 2-4 years to complete), music, pointe (5 classes per week, 2 years to complete), rehearsal and performance (1/2-3 years to complete), stagecraft (1/2 years to complete), ballet technique.

Elective courses: tap (2 classes per week, 1/2 years to complete), variations (4 classes per week, 1 year to complete).

Selectivity for males: approximately 60% admitted. *Selectivity for females:* approximately 60% admitted. *Entering class size:* 12. *Graduating class size:* 6. *Percent international:* 6%. *Countries most represented*: Japan.

Renowned alumni: Carol McCoy, Ballet House; Lisa Garick Michaels, creator of Tempo, Level, Energy and Shapes Syllabus for Ages 3-6.

Total full-time faculty: 2. *Total part-time faculty:* 3. *List of current faculty and past affiliations:* Diane Callahan, Atlanta Ballet, San Francisco Ballet, Ballet de Cuba; Vincas Greene, California Institute of the Arts, Mark Morris Dance Group; Carol Smiarowski, Florida State University, Mobile Ballet, Ruth Mitchell Dance Theatre (Atlanta). *Program contact person:* Dr. Carol Smiarowski.

Audition Information

No audition fee. Audition consists of the following: ballet, modern dance, pointe works, modern dance class, center combination at the end of ballet class, pointe work where applicable. *Accompanist provided. Cassette player available; CD player available. Dress requirements for males:* white t-shirt, white or grey tights, ballet shoes. *Dress requirements for females:* solid color leotard, pink tights and shoes, hair in bun or twist.

Audition evaluation criteria: technical proficiency, performance qualities, body type, attitude, work habits.

Performance Information

Performance opportunities available (frequency): Fully produced concerts (2 per year), informal concerts (2-4 per year), workshops (1 per year), on-site performances (1 per month).

Performances choreographed by: faculty, students, guests. *Recent guest choreographers:* Cornelius Carter, Robin Williams, Kris Cangelosi, Veta Goler.

Facilities

Number of studios available: 4. *Approximate studio dimensions and flooring:* 37' x 21' wooden overlaid with Marley type flooring. *Performance facilities:* on campus-full size theater with 750-seat houses, black box—seating 50.

DRAMA

Curriculum, Students, and Faculty

Required courses: acting, design for the performing arts, directing, movement, musical theater, speech, stagecraft, theater history, theater arts management, voice.

Elective courses: audition preparation.

Number of years required to complete program: 4. *Summer program available. Affiliation with a professional theater companies: Gainesville Theatre Alliance is a semi-professional company composed of professionals, students, and faculty from Brenau Univesity and Gainesville College and community members all of whom are involved in production.*

Selectivity for males: most admitted, but not all. *Selectivity for females:* most admitted, but not all. *Total enrollment:* 33. *Entering class size:* 16 *Graduating class size:* 6. *Percent international:* 6%.

Renowned alumni: Sandra Williams.

Total full-time faculty: 1. *Total part-time faculty:* 3. *List of current faculty and past affiliations:* Jim Hammond, Ann Demling, Sandy Blankenship, Stuart Beaman.

Audition Information

No audition fee. Audition consists of the following: Shakespeare, required for BFA Musical theatre: may sing if BA theatre candidates: 30-second selection from musical with accompaniment on cassette tape. *Dress requirements for males:* avoid very casual. *Dress requirements for females:* avoid very casual.

Audition evaluation criteria: understanding and ability to convey understanding of material, projection, vocal physical flexibility, ability to take direction/suggestions.

Performance Information

Performance opportunities available (frequency): fully produced performances (4-5 per year), informal performances (1-2 per semester), workshops (1-2 per semester), off-site performances (3 per week), casting is by audition.

Recent guest artists: Liz Lee, Chris Kayser, Gene Ruyle.

Facilities

Rehearsal facilities and hours: proscenium also used for reherasals, 7:00 pm-11:00 pm (Mon-Fri), black box used for studio/student directed scenes, various mornings and evenings, rehearsal hall, variuos hours. *Number of theaters on campus:* 3. *Type and capacity:* proscenium—750, black box—50, rehearsal hall.

MUSIC

Curriculum, Students, and Faculty

Unique or innovative music curriculum: BM in Piano Accompanying. *How are major teacher assignments made?* students may choose, made by the school. Faculty is not informed of a student's teacher preference at the time of the audition. *May a student change major teachers during the course of study?* possibly. *Study of secondary instrument or discipline is allowed.*

Selectivity for instruments or programs offered (rating): accompanying (competitive), choral conducting (competitive), choral singing (competitive), harp (competitive), piano (competitive), voice (competitive), music education.

Total enrollment: 17. *Entering class size:* 12. *Graduating class size:* 1. *Percent international:* 6%. *Countries most represented*: Japan.

Renowned alumni: Kristin Clayton, San Francisco Opera.

Total full-time faculty: 1. *Total part-time faculty:* 6. *Program contact person:* Dr. Michelle Roueche.

Audition Information

No audition fee. Audition consists of the following: music theory, sight reading. *Instruments provided for:* harpists, pianists, organists.

Repertoire that students should avoid? Popular music and show tunes. *Performance opportunities available (frequency):* chamber music (4-6 per year), band (4-6 per year), jury examinations (2 per year), opera workshops (2 per year), orchestral concerts, recitals (4-6 per year), touring (2 per year), produced operas, chorus (4-6 per year).

Facilities

Number of practice rooms and hours: 9; 8:00 am-11:00 pm. *Recital hall?* no. *Concert hall?* yes. *Recording studio?* no.

Comments

We have had 100% employment rate of our music education grads for the past several years.

SPELMAN COLLEGE

350 Spelman Lane, SW, Atlanta GA 30314
Tel: 800-982-2411
Fax: 404-215-7788

General

Type of Institution: Historically African-American.

Entrance Requirements

Audition not required.

Services

Support staff: housing advisor, physical therapist, psychological counselor, resident assistant, resident nurse, student affairs officer.

DRAMA

Curriculum, Students, and Faculty

Required courses: drama criticism.

UNIVERSITY OF GEORGIA

School of Music
250 River Road, Athens GA 30602
Tel: 706-542-3737
Fax: 706-542-2773
Email: rmgrahm@uga.cc.uga.edu ; esandor@uga.cc.uga.edu; ugmusic@uga
Web: uga.edu/-music
Contact: Rita Free

General

Type of Institution: university. *Environment:* urban.

Total enrollment: 30,000. *Degrees offered:* BA, BM.

Entrance Requirements

Audition required: live, audio. *Other requirements:* interview, recommendation. *Standardized test requirements:* ACT; SAT I.

Costs & Financial Aid

Percent of students receiving financial aid: 25%. *Types of scholarships and aid awarded:* partial, merit-based, need-based, institutional aid, government aid, work/study. *Loans available. Procedure for applying for loans:* available on internet.

Services

Housing options: on-site dorms, off-campus housing, fraternity, sorority.

Support staff: housing advisor, physical therapist, psychological counselor, resident assistant, student affairs officer.

Comments

The School of Music is now housed in the university's new performing and visual arts complex. The music instruction building offers state-of-the-art facilities for studio and classroom teaching, a 5,000 square feet band rehearsal room, a choral music rehearsal suite and a 180-seat performance hall. The adjacent performance building includes an 1,100-seat concert hall and a 360-seat recital hall as well as an orchestra rehearsal room. These new facilities afford our students the opportunity to learn and perform in an environment second to none.

MUSIC

Curriculum, Students, and Faculty

How are major teacher assignments made? Students may choose, made by the school, according to teacher preference and according to teacher availability. Faculty is not informed of a student's teacher preference at the time of the audition. ***30 lessons with major teacher. May a student change major teachers during the course of study?*** possibly. ***Study of secondary instrument or discipline is allowed.***

Selectivity for instruments or programs offered (rating): accompanying (selective), bassoon (non-competitive), choral conducting (highly selective), choral singing (non-competitive), clarinet (non-competitive), composition (competitive), double bass (competitive), electronic music (competitive), flute or piccolo (competitive), French horn (non-competitive), guitar (competitive), harp (non-competitive), harpsichord (competitive), jazz (non-competitive), oboe/English horn (non-competitive), orchestral conducting (highly selective), organ (competitive), percussion (non-competitive), piano (competitive), saxophone (competitive), trombone (non-competitive), trumpet (competitive), tuba (non-competitive), viola (non-competitive), violin (non-competitive), violoncello (non-competitive), voice (non-competitive).

Total enrollment: 450. ***Entering class size:*** 150.

Renowned alumni: Steve Norrell, Metropolitan Opera; Gretchen Lund.

Total full-time faculty: 50. ***Total part-time faculty:*** 8. ***Program contact person:*** John N. Culvahouse.

Audition Information

No audition fee. Audition consists of the following: scales, arpeggios, sight reading, repertoire. ***Instruments provided for:*** harpists, percussionists; large "color" instruments.

Required repertoire: selections from varied periods, not titles.

Facilities

Number of practice rooms and hours: 60; 8:00 am-11:00 pm. ***Recital hall?*** yes. ***Concert hall?*** yes. ***Recording studio?*** yes.

HAWAII

UNIVERSITY OF HAWAII, MANOA

Department of Theatre and Dance/Music Department
1770 East-West Road, Honolulu HI 96822
Tel: 808-956-7756
Fax: 808-956-9657

General

Type of Institution: public, university. ***Environment:*** urban.

Total enrollment: 1,900. ***Degrees offered:*** BA, BFA, BM, BME.

Entrance Requirements

Audition required: live, audio, video. ***Other requirements:*** recommendation, essay. ***Standardized test requirements:*** SAT, 1020; TOEFL, 600.

Costs & Financial Aid

Application fee: $25. ***Other fees:*** $84 student fee, $59 student activity fee.

Types of scholarships and aid awarded: full, partial, merit-based, need-based, named, reduced tuition, work/study. ***Forms required for scholarships:*** FAFSA. ***Loans available. Procedure for applying for loans:*** contact University of Hawaii at Manoa Financial Aid Office, 2600 Campus Road Room 112, Honolulu, HI 96822. ***Financial aid offered to international students.***

Services

Housing options: on-site dorms, off-campus housing, fraternity, sorority.

Support staff: financial aid advisor, foreign student advisor.

Comments

For room and board contact: student housing office, 2555 Dole St., Honolulu, HI 96822.

DANCE

Curriculum, Students, and Faculty

Required courses: anatomy, ballet (3 classes per week, 4 years to complete), dance composition/choreography, dance history, dance writing, research and criticism, Labanotation, modern dance, Limon-based (3 classes per week, 4 years to complete), music, nutrition, rehearsal and performance, stagecraft, rehearsal and performance.

Elective courses: jazz, repertory, tap.

Selectivity for males: most admitted, but not all. ***Selectivity for females:*** most admitted, but not all. ***Total Enrollment:*** 380. ***Countries most represented***: United Kingdom, Germany, Japan, China, Korea.

Renowned alumni: Eddie Taketa, Darryl Thomas.

Total full-time faculty: 4. ***Total part-time faculty:*** 11. ***List of current faculty and past affiliations:*** Betsy Fisher, Gregg Lizenbery, Peggy Hunt, Meridith Monk. ***Program contact person:*** Gregg Lizenbery/Caren Shiroma.

Audition Information

No audition fee. Audition consists of the following: ballet, modern dance. *Accompanist provided.*

Performance Information

Performance opportunities available (frequency): Fully produced concerts (3 per year), informal concerts (1-2 per year), workshops (varies), on-site performances (varies), touring (varies).

Performances choreographed by: faculty, students, guests. *Recent guest choreographers:* Joe Goode, Jeff Slayton, Claudia Jeshke, Donald McKaye, Mary Corey, Liu Yolan, Vickie Takamine, Wayne Mendoza, Chung Won Meyer.

Facilities

Number of studios available: 3. *Approximate studio dimensions and flooring*: 40' x 70' L'Air flooring with vinyl covering, 35' x 60' hardwood, 22' x 60' hardwood with vinyl covering. *Performance facilities:* Kennedy Theatre Mainstage—630 Seats, Fly Space, computerized lighting, Earle Ernsy Lab Theatre—150 seats, black box, flexible set-up.

DRAMA

Curriculum, Students, and Faculty

Required courses: acting, drama criticism, movement, text analysis, voice.

Elective courses: directing, dramaturgy, make-up, musical theater, speech, stage combat.

Number of years required to complete program: 4. *Summer program available. Affiliation with a professional theater company: training regularly provided by professional performers from China and Japan.*

Selectivity for males: most admitted, but not all. *Selectivity for females:* most admitted, but not all. *Total enrollment:* 680. *Percent international:* 25%. *Countries most represented*: China, Malaysia, Indonesia, Japan, India, Germany.

Renowned alumni: Randal Duk Kim, Georgia Engels, Bette Midler.

Total full-time faculty: 14. *Total part-time faculty:* 14. *List of current faculty and past affiliations:* Terence Knapp, Royal Academy of Dramatic Art; James Brandon, National Theatre of Japan; Elizabeth Wizhwann, Jiangsu and Shanghai Beijing Opera Companies.

Audition Information

No audition fee.

Performance Information

Performance opportunities available (frequency): fully produced performances (10 per year), informal performances (varies), workshops (varies), off-site performances (varies), casting is by audition.

Recent guest artists: Jiangsu Province Beijing Opera Company.

Facilities.

Number of theaters on campus: 2.

MUSIC

Curriculum, Students, and Faculty

Unique or innovative music curriculum: A recognized ethnomusicology component. *How are major teacher assignments made?* students may choose according to teacher preference and teacher availability. Faculty is informed of a student's teacher preference at the time of the audition. *29 lessons with major teacher. May a student change major teachers during the course of study?* possibly. *Study of secondary instrument or discipline is allowed.*

Selectivity for instruments or programs offered (rating): bassoon (selective), clarinet (selective), composition (selective), double bass (selective), flute or piccolo (selective), French horn (selective), guitar (selective), harp (selective), oboe/English horn (selective), percussion (selective), piano (selective), saxophone (selective), trombone (selective), trumpet (selective), tuba (selective), viola (selective), violin (selective), violoncello (selective), voice (selective).

Total enrollment: 184. *Entering class size:* 50. *Graduating class size:* 5. *Countries most represented*: Japan.

Total full-time faculty: 23. *Total part-time faculty:* 25. *Program contact person:* Dr. Dale Hall.

Audition Information

No audition fee. Audition consists of the following: scales, music theory, sight reading, melodic dictation. *Instruments provided for:* harpists, percussionists.

Performance opportunities available (frequency): band (frequently), chamber music (frequently), jury examinations (frequently), opera workshops (frequently), orchestral concerts (frequently), recitals (frequently), chorus.

Facilities

Number of practice rooms and hours: 18; 8:00 am-9:00 pm. *Recital hall?* yes. *Concert hall?* no. *Recording studio?* no.

COE COLLEGE

1220 First Avanue, Cedar Rapids IA 52402
Tel: 319-399-8521
Fax: 319-399-8521
Email: mmarrs@coe.edu
Contact: John Sullivan

General

Type of Institution: college. *Religious Affiliation:* Presbyterian Covenant Relationship. *Environment:* urban.

Total enrollment: 1,050. *Total student body from other countries:* 4%. *Degrees offered:* BA, BM.

Entrance Requirements

Audition not required Other requirements: recommendation, essay. *Standardized test requirements:* ACT.

Costs & Financial Aid

Deposit: $150. *Tuition:* $16,170. *Other fees:* $150 general.

Percent of students receiving financial aid: 95%. *Types of scholarships and aid awarded:* full, partial, merit-based, need-based, institutional aid, government aid, tuition payment plan, work/study, gig office. *Forms required for scholarships:* FAFSA. *Loans available. Procedure for applying for loans:* completed FAFSA and application for admission. *Financial aid offered to international students. Percent of international students receiving scholarships:* 72%. *Other aid available to international students:* work/study (college).

Services

Housing options: on-site dorms, fraternity, sorority.

Support staff: career counselor, financial aid advisor, foreign student advisor, housing advisor, resident assistant, resident nurse, student affairs officer.

DRAMA

Curriculum, Students, and Faculty

Number of years required to complete program: 4. *Summer program not available. No affiliation with a professional theater company. Selectivity for males:* most admitted, but not all. *Selectivity for females:* most admitted, but not all.

Renowned alumni: Holly Hynes.

Total full-time faculty: 3. *Total part-time faculty:* 1. *List of current faculty and past affiliations:* Michael Pufall, Susan Wolverton, Candace Pufall.

Audition Information

No audition fee. Audition consists of the following: cold readings, comedic monologue, improvisation. *Repertoire that students should avoid?* Shakespeare.

Performance Information

Performance opportunities available (frequency): fully produced performances (3 per year), workshops (2-3 per year), casting is by audition.

Facilities

Rehearsal facilities and hours: Dows Stage or Mills Black Box theatre, 7:00 pm-10:00 pm (Mon-Fri). *Type and capacity:* proscenium—1,150, thrust/arena—300, black box—90.

MUSIC

Curriculum, Students, and Faculty

How are major teacher assignments made? Students may choose, made by the school according to teacher preference, according to teacher availability; assignments vary per curriculum/major. Faculty is not informed of a student's teacher preference at the time of the audition. *26 lessons with major teacher. May a student change major teachers during the course of study?* possibly.

Selectivity for instruments or programs offered (rating): accompanying (non-competitive), bassoon (non-competitive), choral conducting (non-competitive), choral singing (non-competitive), clarinet (non-competitive), composition (non-competitive), double bass (non-competitive), electronic music (non-competitive), flute or piccolo (non-competitive), French horn (non-competitive), guitar (non-competitive), harpsichord (non-competitive), oboe/English horn (non-competitive), organ (non-competitive), percussion (non-competitive), piano (non-competitive), saxophone (non-competitive), trombone (non-competitive), trumpet (non-competitive), tuba (non-competitive), viola (non-competitive), violin (non-competitive), violoncello (non-competitive), voice (non-competitive).

Total enrollment: 65. *Entering class size:* 25 *Graduating class size:* 10.

Renowned alumni: Michael Boddicker, Dan Haerle.

Total full-time faculty: 6. *Total part-time faculty:* 18. *Program contact person:* Sharon Kay Stang.

Audition Information

No audition fee. Instruments provided for: percussionists.

Performance opportunities available (frequency): band (1 per term), jury examinations (1 per term), orchestral concerts (1 per term), chorus (1 per term).

Facilities

Number of practice rooms and hours: 12; 7:00 am-12:00 am. *Recital hall?* yes. *Concert hall?* yes. *Recording studio?* yes.

Comments

Students accepted by the college may enter the music curriculum. Students hoping to pursue a BM degree must pass an evaluation at the end of their sophomore year. Evaluation consists of performance, review of academic work, and interview.

ILLINOIS

BARAT COLLEGE CONSERVATORY OF DANCE

700 East Westleigh Road, Lake Forest IL 60045
Tel: 847-604-6264
Fax: 847-234-1084
Contact: Diana Knight

General

Type of Institution: college, conservatory. *Environment:* suburban.

Total enrollment: 800. *Total student body from other countries:* 7%. *Degrees offered:* BA, BFA.

Entrance Requirements

Audition required: live, video. *Other requirements:* recommendation, essay. *Standardized test requirements:* ACT, 21; SAT I, 1000; TOEFL, 550.

Costs & Financial Aid

Application fee: $20. *Deposit:* $250. *Tuition:* $12,570. *Other fees:* $500 per semester optional room, $500 per year books, $450 per semester private room.

Percent of students receiving financial aid: 70%. *Types of scholarships and aid awarded:* partial, merit-based, need-based, named, institutional aid, government aid, tuition payment plan, work/study. *Forms required for scholarships:* FAFSA, Barat internal application. *Loans available. Procedure for applying for loans:* performing arts scholarships are available through auditions, merit-based scholarships are issued at the completion of the admission application process. *Financial aid offered to international students. Other aid available to international students:* scholarships and grants.

Services

Housing options: on-site dorms, off-campus housing.

Support staff: career counselor, financial aid advisor, foreign student advisor, housing advisor, psychological counselor, resident assistant, student affairs officer.

DANCE

Curriculum, Students, and Faculty

Required courses: anatomy, character, ballet, dance composition/choreography, dance history, historical dance, improvisation, jazz, master classes, Graham-based modern dance, Pilates, music, nutrition, rehearsal and performance, repertory, stagecraft, tap, pedagogy, Astanga yoga.

Elective courses: dance writing, research and criticism, pas de deux, pointe, variations.

Selectivity for males: approximately 60% admitted. *Selectivity for females:* approximately 33% admitted. *Total enrollment:* 50. *Entering class size:* 23. *Graduating class size:* 9.

Renowned alumni: Venus Hall, Vernard Gilmore, Alvin Ailey American Dance Theatre; DeShona Pepper, Dayton Contemporary Dance Company; Julie MacDuffy, Lexington Ballet.

Total full-time faculty: 2. *Total part-time faculty:* 12. *List of current faculty and past affiliations:* Rory Foster, American Ballet Theatre; Pamela Johnson, Joffrey Ballet; Eileen Cropley, Paul Taylor Dance Company; Linda Spriggs, Alvin Ailey American Dance Theatre. *Program contact person:* Rory Foster.

Audition Information

No audition fee. Audition consists of the following: ballet, modern dance. *Accompanist provided. Cassette player not available; CD player not available. Dress requirements for males:* tights, t-shirt or unitard, ballet shoes. *Dress requirements for females:* pink tights, dark solid colored leotard, ballet shoes.

Audition evaluation criteria: strength, flexibility, coordination, weight, receptivity to taking direction, and facility for applying corrections; adequate amount of pre-collegiate dance training in ballet and modern.

Performance Information

Performance opportunities available (frequency): Fully produced concerts (4-5 per semester), informal concerts (regularly), workshops (regularly), on-site performances (varies).

Performances choreographed by: faculty, students, guests.

Facilities

Number of studios available: 3. *Approximate studio dimensions and flooring:* 65' x 28' Harlequin and Tarkett. *Performance facilities:* Drake Theatre—630 seats, Hilton Theatre—175 seats.

BRADLEY UNIVERSITY

Costance Hall, Peoria IL 61625
Tel: 309-677-2595
Fax: 309-677-3871
Email: dvroman@bradley.edu
Web: www.bradley.edu
Contact: Tom Richmond

General

Environment: urban.

Total enrollment: 6,000. *Degrees offered:* BA, BM.

Entrance Requirements

Audition required: live, audio, video. *Other requirements:* interview, recommendation. *Standardized test requirements:* ACT, 25; SAT I; SAT II; TOEFL.

Costs & Financial Aid

Application fee: $35. *Deposit:* $100. *Tuition:* $12,610. *Other fees:* $80.

Percent of students receiving financial aid: 85%. *Types of scholarships and aid awarded:* full, partial, merit-based, need-based, named, institutional aid, government aid, tuition payment plan, work/study. *Forms required for scholarships:* FAFSA. *Loans available. Procedure for applying for loans:* by filing FAFSA.

Services

Housing options: on-site dorms, off-campus housing, fraternity, sorority.

Support staff: financial aid advisor, resident assistant, student affairs officer.

DANCE

Curriculum, Students, and Faculty

Required courses: variations (2 classes per week, 2 years to complete), pas de deux (2 classes per week, 2 years to complete).

MUSIC

Curriculum, Students, and Faculty

Unique or innovative music curriculum: good technology resources—innovative program to combine music with another major. *How are major teacher assignments made?* made by the school. Faculty is not informed of a student's teacher preference at the time of the audition. *30 lessons with major teacher. May a student change major teachers during the course of study?* possibly. *Study of secondary instrument or discipline is allowed.*

Selectivity for instruments or programs offered (rating): accompanying (non-competitive), bassoon (non-competitive), choral conducting (non-competitive), choral singing (non-competitive), clarinet (non-competitive), composition (non-competitive), double bass (non-competitive), flute or piccolo (non-competitive), French horn (non-competitive), guitar (non-competitive), harp (non-competitive), harpsichord (non-competitive), jazz (non-competitive), oboe/English horn (non-competitive), orchestral conducting (non-competitive), percussion (non-competitive), piano (non-competitive), saxophone (non-competitive), trombone (non-competitive), trumpet (non-competitive), tuba (non-competitive), viola (non-competitive), violin (non-competitive), violoncello (non-competitive), voice (non-competitive), Chinese instruments (non-competitive).

Total enrollment: 70. *Entering class size:* 25.

Renowned alumni: Jerry Hadley, Kevin Maynor.

Total full-time faculty: 10. *Total part-time faculty:* 17. *Program contact person:* David Vroman.

Audition Information

No audition fee. Audition consists of the following: music theory, repertoire. *Instruments provided for:* percussionists.

Required repertoire: repertoire of student's choice. *Repertoire that students should avoid?* no. *Performance opportunities available (frequency):* band, jury examinations, opera workshops, orchestral concerts, recitals, chorus.

Facilities

Number of practice rooms and hours: 16; 7:00 am-11:00 pm. *Recital hall?* yes. *Concert hall?* yes. *Recording studio?* no.

COLUMBIA COLLEGE, CHICAGO
THE DANCE CENTER

4730 N Sheridan Road, Chicago IL 60640
Tel: 773-989-3310
Fax: 773-271-7046

General

Type of Institution: college. *Environment:* urban. *Total enrollment:* 8,000. *Degrees offered:* BA.

Entrance Requirements

Audition not required. Other requirements: essay. *Standardized test requirements:* TOEFL.

Costs & Financial Aid

Tuition: $8,000.

Types of scholarships and aid awarded: full, partial, merit-based, need-based, tuition payment plan, work/study. *Loans available. Procedure for applying for loans:* contact Financial Aid Office. *Other aid available to international students:* no special programs.

Services

Housing options: on-site dorms, off-campus housing.

Support staff: career counselor, financial aid advisor, foreign student advisor, housing advisor, resident assistant, student affairs officer.

DANCE

Curriculum, Students, and Faculty

Required courses: anatomy, ballet, dance composition/choreography, dance history, dance theory, master classes, modern dance, music, rehearsal and performance, stagecraft.

Elective courses: African dance, historical dance, jazz, martial arts, body conditioning, Pilates, other world dance forms, Spanish, tap, vernacular dance.

Selectivity for males: admit all who apply. *Selectivity for females:* admit all who apply. *Total enrollment*: 80. *Entering class size:* 25. *Graduating class size:* 12. *Percent international:* 1%. *Countries most represented*: Japan, Korea, Sweden.

Renowned alumni: Shirley Modine, Chair; Artistic Director: Mordine and Co. Dance Theatre; Jan Erkert, Jan Erkert and Dancers.

Total full-time faculty: 4. *Total part-time faculty:* 20. *Program contact person:* Keri Kurlinski.

Audition Information

No audition fee. Accompanist provided. Cassette player available; CD player available. Dress requirements for males: ballet only—black and white, form fitting. *Dress requirements for females:* ballet only—black and white, form fitting.

Performance Information

Performance opportunities available (frequency): Fully produced concerts (3-7 per year), informal concerts (2-5 per year), workshops (2-5 per year), on-site performances.

Performances choreographed by: faculty, students, guests.

Facilities

Number of studios available: 5.

DEPAUL UNIVERSITY

School of Music
804 West Belden Avenue, Chicago IL 60614
Tel: 773-325-7444
Fax: 773-325-7429
Email: rbeacrat@wppost.depaul.edu
Web: www.depaul.edu

General

Type of Institution: private university. *Environment:* urban.

Total enrollment: 19,000. *Degrees offered:* BA, BM.

Entrance Requirements

Audition required: live, audio, video. *Other requirements:* interview. *Standardized test requirements:* ACT, 22; SAT I, 1140; TOEFL, 550.

Costs & Financial Aid

Application fee: $25. *Tuition:* $15,000.

Types of scholarships and aid awarded: partial, merit-based, need-based, government aid, reduced tuition. *Forms required for scholarships:* FAFSA, income tax return. *Loans available. Procedure for applying for loans:* file single application. *Financial aid offered to international students. Percent of international students receiving scholarships:* 50%.

Services

Housing options: on-site dorms.

Support staff: career counselor, financial aid advisor, foreign student advisor, housing advisor, psychological counselor, resident assistant, resident nurse, student affairs officer.

DRAMA

Curriculum, Students, and Faculty

Theater school offers comprehensive training.

MUSIC

Curriculum, Students, and Faculty

How are major teacher assignments made? students may choose, made by the school according to teacher availability. Faculty is not informed of a student's teacher preference at the time of the audition. *27 lessons with major teacher. May a student change major teachers during the course of study?* possibly. *Study of secondary instrument or discipline is allowed.*

Selectivity for instruments or programs offered (rating): bassoon (selective), clarinet (highly selective), composition (highly selective), double bass (selective), flute or piccolo (highly selective), French horn (selective), guitar (highly selective), harp (highly selective), jazz (highly selective), oboe/English horn (selective), percussion (highly selective), piano (highly selective), saxophone (highly selective), trombone (highly selective), trumpet (highly selective), tuba (highly selective), viola (selective), violin (selective), violoncello (selective), voice (highly selective).

Total enrollment: 400. *Entering class size:* 130. *Graduating class size:* 100. *Percent international:* 9%. *Countries most represented*: Korea, Australia, Colombia, Japan.

Renowned alumni: Loren Levee, Los Angeles Symphony; Sam Magad—concertmaster, Chicago Symphony; Jeff Mattsey—Metropolitan Opera, Lyric Opera; Victor Faraci—Senior Vice President, Warner Bros. Records.; George Perle—Pulitzer Prize winning composer.

Total full-time faculty: 23. *Total part-time faculty:* 95. *Program contact person:* Ross Beacratt.

Audition Information

No audition fee. Audition consists of the following: scales, arpeggios, sight reading, improvisation, repertoire. *Instruments provided for:* harpists, percussionists.

Facilities

Number of practice rooms and hours: 75; *Recital hall?* yes. *Concert hall?* yes. *Recording studio?* yes.

ILLINOIS STATE UNIVERSITY

Normal IL 61790
Tel: 309-438-8284
Fax: 309-438-3932
Web: orathost.cfa.ilstu.edu

General

Type of Institution: public, university. *Environment:* urban.

Total enrollment: 17,366. *Total student body from other countries:* 1%. *Degrees offered:* BA, BS, BME.

Entrance Requirements

Audition not required Standardized test requirements: ACT, 17; SAT I, 810; TOEFL, 550.

Costs & Financial Aid

Tuition (in-state/out-state): \$3,970/\$9,870.

Percent of students receiving financial aid: 75%. *Types of scholarships and aid awarded:* full, partial, merit-based, need-based, named, institutional aid, government aid, reduced tuition, work/study. *Forms required for scholarships:* FAFSA. *Loans available. Procedure for applying for loans:* submit FAFSA by 3/1. *Other aid available to international students:* scholarships for academically talented students.

Services

Housing options: on-site dorms, off-campus housing, fraternity, sorority.

Support staff: career counselor, financial aid advisor, foreign student advisor, housing advisor, physical therapist, psychological counselor, resident assistant, resident nurse, student affairs officer.

DANCE

Curriculum, Students, and Faculty

Required courses: anatomy, ballet (1.5 minimum years to complete), dance composition/choreography, dance history (1 year to complete), dance theory (1 year to complete), dance writing, research and criticism, historical dance, jazz (2 classes per week, 1.5 years to complete), master classes, Cunningham-based (2 classes per week,1.5 years to complete), Graham-based (2 classes per week, 1.5 years to complete), Limon-based modern dance (2 classes per week, 1.5 years to complete), music, rehearsal and performance, repertory, stagecraft, tap, character.

Elective courses: character, men's class, movement techniques, body conditioning, nutrition, other world dance forms, pas de deux, pointe, variations (2 classes per week), modern dance partnering, pas de deux.

Selectivity for males: admit all who apply. *Selectivity for females:* admit all who apply.

Renowned alumni: Patrick Mullaney, Randy Duncan, Jeanette Buell, Douglas E. Woods, Jackie Conrad.

Total full-time faculty: 3. *List of current faculty and past affiliations:* Philip Johnston, Laurie Merriman, Kim Nofsinger *Program contact person:* Laurie Merriman.

Audition Information

No audition fee. Audition consists of the following: prepared solo. *Accompanist not provided. Cassette player available; CD player available. Dress requirements for males:* tights, t-shirt, appropriate footwear for solo. *Dress requirements for females:* solid color leotards, tights, appropriate footwear for solo.

Audition evaluation criteria: technical performance and artistic performance, choreographic promise.

Performance Information

Performance opportunities available (frequency): Fully produced concerts (2 per year), informal concerts (3-4 per year), workshops (3-4 per year), on-site performances (3-4 per year), touring (1-2 per year).

Performances choreographed by: faculty, students, guests. *Recent guest choreographers:* Jeannie Hill, Amy Schwartz, Randy Duncan, Dwight Roden, Pat Catterson, Tom Evert, Heisha Folkes, Steve Rooks.

Facilities

Number of studios available: 2. *Approximate studio dimensions and flooring:* large studio Marley, small studio wood. *Performance facilities:* 2 theaters and one studio theater space—performing arts center in process of being built.

DRAMA

Curriculum, Students, and Faculty

Required courses: acting, directing, make-up, movement, scene study, text analysis, verse drama, voice and speech, Stanislavski exercises, directing, musical theater, text analysis.

Elective courses: audition preparation, drama criticism, improvisation, musical theater.

Number of years required to complete program: 4. *Summer program available. Affiliation with a professional theater company: internships with Steppenwolf and other more informal arrangements.*

Selectivity for males: admit all who apply. *Selectivity for females:* admit all who apply. *Total enrollment:* 244. *Entering class size:* 83. *Graduating class size:* 33.

Renowned alumni: Juith Ivey, John Malkovich, Laurie Metcalf, Gary Cole.

Total full-time faculty: 21. *List of current faculty and past affiliations:* Jack McLaughlin-Gray, Marian Hampton, Connie DeVeer.

Audition Information

No audition fee. Audition consists of the following: auditions required only for scholarship; no entry audition required.

Audition evaluation criteria: talent, taste.

Performance Information

Performance opportunities available (frequency): fully produced performances (10 per year), informal performances (unlimited), workshops (1-2 per semester), off-site performances (several), casting is by audition.

Recent guest artists: Jeff Corey, Joanne Akalaitis, Arne Zaslov.

Facilities

Rehearsal facilities and hours: 2 theaters, studio and classrooms, 7:00 pm-11:00 pm. *Number of theaters on campus:* 4. *Type and capacity:* proscenium—550, thrust stage—200, proscenium—1,200, studio 100.

MUSIC

Curriculum, Students, and Faculty

How are major teacher assignments made? made by the school, according to teacher availability. Faculty is not informed of a student's teacher preference at the time of the audition. *May a student change major teachers during the course of study?* possibly. *Study of secondary instrument or discipline is allowed.*

Selectivity for instruments or programs offered (rating): accompanying (competitive), bassoon (non-competitive), choral conducting (selective), choral singing (non-competitive), clarinet (competitive), composition (selective), double bass (competitive), electronic music (selective), flute or piccolo (competitive), French horn (selective), guitar (competitive), harp (competitive), harpsichord (competitive), jazz (competitive), oboe/English horn (non-competitive), orchestral conducting (selective), organ (competitive), percussion (competitive), piano (competitive), saxophone (competitive), trombone (competitive), trumpet (competitive), tuba (competitive), viola (non-competitive), violin (competitive), violoncello (competitive), voice (competitive).

Total enrollment: 258. *Entering class size:* 82. *Graduating class size:* 35.

Renowned alumni: Keith Mehlan, United States Navy Band; Angela Harkenrider, Chicago Civic Orchestra; Steven Brinkman, Disneyworld; Rex Martin, Chicago Symphony; Gregory Kunded, Chicago Lyric, La Scala Opera Companies; Ray Roderick; Christine Cauleton; Robert Shaw.

Total full-time faculty: 32. *Total part-time faculty:* 3. *Program contact person:* Judy Thomas.

Audition Information

No audition fee. Audition consists of the following: scales, music theory, sight reading, repertoire. *Instruments provided for:* harpists, percussionists.

Required repertoire: varies by instrument. Please call school for repertoire information. *Performance opportunities available (frequency):* band (4 per semester), jury examinations (1 per semester), orchestral concerts (3-4 per semester), recitals (50-70 per semester), chorus (6 per semester).

Facilities

Number of practice rooms and hours: 30. *Recital hall?* yes. *Concert hall?* yes. *Recording studio?* yes.

ILLINOIS WESLEYAN UNIVERSITY

P.O. Box 2900, Bloomington IL 61702
Tel: 309-556-3031
Fax: 309-556-3411

General

Type of Institution: university. *Environment:* suburban.

Total enrollment: 1,855. *Total student body from other countries:* 5%. *Degrees offered:* BA, BFA, BM.

Entrance Requirements

Audition required: live, audio, video. *Other requirements:* recommendation, essay. *Standardized test requirements:* ACT; SAT I.

Costs & Financial Aid

Tuition: $17,320.

Types of scholarships and aid awarded: full, partial, merit-based, need-based. *Forms required for scholarships:* FAFSA. *Loans available.*

Services

Housing options: on-site dorms.

DRAMA

Curriculum, Students, and Faculty

Total enrollment: 90.

Renowned alumni: Frankie Faison, Stephanie Faracy.

Total full-time faculty: 12.

MUSIC

Curriculum, Students, and Faculty

Unique or innovative music curriculum: BM in sacred music is offered.

Total enrollment: 147.

Renowned alumni: Susan Quittmeyer, Dawn Upshaw

Total full-time faculty: 33. *Program contact person:* Laura Dolan, (309)-556-3063.

MILLIKIN UNIVERSITY

College of Fine Arts
1184 West Main Street, Decatur IL 62522-2084
Tel: 800-373-7733
Fax: 217-424-3993
Email: sfiol@mail.millikin.edu
Contact: Brian Toberman

General

Type of Institution: university. *Environment:* urban.

Total enrollment: 2,000. *Degrees offered:* BA, BFA, BM, BS in music business administration.

Entrance Requirements

Audition required: live, audio, video *Other requirements:* interview. *Standardized test requirements:* ACT; SAT I; TOEFL, 550.

Costs & Financial Aid

Deposit: $150. *Tuition:* $13,988. *Other fees:* $150.

Percent of students receiving financial aid: 94%. *Types of scholarships and aid awarded:* merit-based, need-based, named, institutional aid, government aid, tuition payment plan, work/study. *Forms required for scholarships:* FAFSA, income tax return, income asset verification, MAFA. *Loans available. Procedure for applying for loans:* file MAFA and FAFSA after January. *Financial aid offered to international students. Percent of international students receiving scholarships:* 96%. *Other aid available to international students:* institutional grants.

Services

Housing options: on-site dorms, off-campus housing, fraternity, sorority.

Support staff: career counselor, financial aid advisor, foreign student advisor, housing advisor, physical therapist, psychological counselor, resident assistant, resident nurse, student affairs officer.

DANCE

Curriculum, Students, and Faculty

Required courses: ballet, dance composition/ choreography, jazz, rehearsal and performance, tap, theatrical dance.

Elective courses: master classes, modern dance, movement techniques, music, nutrition, stagecraft, modern dance partnering.

Selectivity for males: approximately 60% admitted. *Selectivity for females:* approximately 60% admitted. *Total enrollment*: 75.

Renowned alumni: Several students working in national tours, Broadway, and regionally.

Total full-time faculty: 1. *Total part-time faculty:* 4. *List of current faculty and past affiliations:* Kevin T. Halpin, Marie Jagger-Taylor, Darlene Harsbarger; Gary Shull; Cindy Halpin. *Program contact person:* Kevin Halpin.

Audition Information

No audition fee. Audition consists of the following: prepared solo. *Accompanist not provided. Cassette player available; CD player available.*

Repertoire that students should avoid? Selecting from "show choir" repertoire should be avoided.

Audition evaluation criteria: center, extension, flexibility, line, phrase, pulse (proficiency and potential).

Performance Information

Performance opportunities available (frequency): Fully produced concerts (1 per semester), informal concerts (varies), workshops (1 per semester), on-site performances (occasionally).

Performances choreographed by: faculty, students.

Facilities

Number of studios available: 3. *Approximate studio dimensions and flooring:* 1,900 sq. ft. Marley stage step-sprung, 2,400 sq. ft. Marley stage step-sprung, 1,200 sq. ft. wood sprung. *Performance facilities:* 2 theaters, 2,000-seat and 300-seat.

DRAMA

Curriculum, Students, and Faculty

Required courses: acting, directing, drama criticism, dramaturgy, make-up, martial arts, musical theater, scene study, speech, Stanislavski exercises, text analysis, verse drama, voice, Tai Chi, stage combat.

Elective courses: Alexander technique, audition preparation, improvisation, stage combat.

Number of years required to complete program: 4. *Summer program available. Affiliation with a professional theater company: design/tech internship at The Center for the Visual and Performing Arts, Munster, IN.*

Total enrollment: 180. *Entering class size:* 75. *Graduating class size:* 32.

Renowned alumni: Karl Wahl, Jodi Bensen, Heather Buress, Scott Rollison.

Total full-time faculty: 11. *Total part-time faculty:* 2. *List of current faculty and past affiliations:* Barry Pearson, David A. Golden, Kevin Halpin, Laura Ledford-Pearson.

Audition Information

No audition fee. Audition evaluation criteria: believability, character, intentionality, involvement, physicality, voice.

Performance Information

Performance opportunities available (frequency): fully produced performances (6 per year), informal performances (1-4 per week), off-site performances (1 per year), 2 dance concerts, 3-5 vocal ensembles, student run studio, casting is by audition.

Facilities

Rehearsal facilities and hours: 2 black box spaces, 2 large classrooms, 8:00 am-12:00 am. *Number of theaters on campus:* 3. *Type and capacity:* proscenium—2,000, proscenium—300, experimental—60.

MUSIC

Curriculum, Students, and Faculty

How are major teacher assignments made? students may choose, made by the school according to teacher preference and teacher availability. Faculty is informed of a student's teacher preference at the time of the audition. *May a student change major teachers during the course of study?* possibly. *Study of secondary instrument or discipline is allowed.*

Selectivity for instruments or programs offered (rating): accompanying (non-competitive), bassoon (non-competitive), choral singing (non-competitive), clarinet (competitive), composition (selective), double bass (non-competitive), electronic music (competitive), flute or piccolo (competitive), French horn (non-competitive), guitar (competitive), jazz (competitive), oboe/English horn (non-competitive), organ (competitive), percussion (competitive), piano (selective), sacred music (non-competitive), saxophone (competitive), trombone (non-competitive), trumpet (competitive), tuba (non-competitive), viola (non-competitive), violin (non-competitive), violoncello (non-competitive), voice (competitive).

Total enrollment: 275. *Entering class size:* 110. *Graduating class size:* 48.

Total full-time faculty: 21. *Total part-time faculty:* 29. *Program contact person:* Mary Ellen Poole.

Audition Information

No audition fee. Audition consists of the following: scales, sight reading, repertoire. *Instruments provided for:* percussionists; string bass, tuba.

Required repertoire: varies by instrument. Please call school for repertoire information. *Performance opportunities available (frequency):* band (4 per year), recitals (130 per year), touring (every year), chorus (4 per year).

Facilities

Number of practice rooms and hours: 23; 7:00 am-12:00 pm. *Recital hall?* yes. *Concert hall?* yes. *Recording studio?* yes.

NORTHERN ILLINOIS UNIVERSITY

School of Music, DeKalb IL 60115
Tel: 815-753-1546
Fax: 815-753-1759
Email: lslater@niv.edu
Web: www.vpa.niv.edu/music

General

Type of Institution: public, university. *Environment:* suburban.

Total enrollment: 22,000. *Total student body from other countries:* 5%. *Degrees offered:* BA, BM.

Entrance Requirements

Audition required: live, video. *Other requirements:* interview. *Standardized test requirements:* ACT; TOEFL, 500.

Costs & Financial Aid

Tuition (in-state/out-state): $3,000/$9,000. *Medical fee:* $280. *Other fees:* $825 activity and athletic fee.

Percent of students receiving financial aid: 50%. *Types of scholarships and aid awarded:* full, partial, merit-based, named, tuition payment plan, work/study. *Forms required for scholarships:* FFS, FAFSA, income tax return. *Loans available. Procedure for applying for loans:* audition for music scholarship, for. *Other aid* contact Financial Aid Office. *Financial aid offered to international students. Percent of international students receiving scholarships:* 90%. *Other aid available to international students:* none.

Services

Housing options: on-site dorms, off-campus housing, fraternity, sorority.

Support staff: career counselor, financial aid advisor, foreign student advisor, housing advisor, psychological counselor, resident assistant, resident nurse, student affairs officer.

MUSIC

Curriculum, Students, and Faculty

How are major teacher assignments made? students may choose, according to teacher availability. Faculty is informed of a student's teacher preference at the time of the audition. *May a student change major teachers during the course of study?* possibly. *Study of secondary instrument or discipline is allowed.*

Selectivity for instruments or programs offered (rating): accompanying (selective), bassoon (competitive), clarinet (competitive), composition (highly selective), double bass (selective), electronic music (selective), flute or piccolo (competitive), French horn (competitive), guitar (highly selective), harp (competitive), harpsichord (competitive), jazz (selective), oboe/English horn (competitive), organ (competitive), percussion (highly selective), piano (selective), saxophone (highly selective), trombone (selective), trumpet (selective), tuba (selective), viola (highly selective), violin (highly selective), violoncello (highly selective), voice (competitive).

Total enrollment: 375. *Entering class size:* 80. *Graduating class size:* 60. *Percent international:* 5%. *Countries most represented*: Germany, England, Holland, Taiwan.

Renowned alumni: James Ross, Chicago Symphony Orchestra, The Shanghai Quartet; Melissa Dye.

Total full-time faculty: 32. *Total part-time faculty:* 28. *Program contact person:* Lynn Slater.

Audition Information

No audition fee. Instruments provided for: harpists, percussionists, pianists.

Performance opportunities available (frequency): chamber music (frequently), band (frequently), jury examinations (every semester), opera workshops (2 per year), orchestral concerts (9 per year), recitals (200 per year), produced operas (2 per year), chorus (12 per year).

Facilities

Number of practice rooms and hours: 120; 6:00 am-12:00 am. *Recital hall?* yes. *Concert hall?* yes. *Recording studio?* yes.

NORTHWESTERN UNIVERSITY

1979 South Campus Drive, Evanston IL 60208
Tel: 847-491-3147
Fax: 847-467-2019
Email: ug-admissions@nwu.edu
Web: www.nwu.edu

General

Type of Institution: university. *Environment:* suburban.

Degrees offered: BS, BA, BM

Entrance Requirements

Audition not required. Other requirements: recommendation, essay. *Standardized test requirements:* ACT, 30; SAT I, 1350.

Costs & Financial Aid

Application fee: $55. *Deposit:* $200. *Tuition:* $22,392. *Room and board*: $6,554.

Percent of students receiving financial aid: 60%. *Types of scholarships and aid awarded:* need-based, government aid, tuition payment plan, work/study. *Forms required for scholarships:* FAFSA, CSS Profile. *Loans available. Procedure for applying for loans:* indicate need on application for admissions, complete FAFSA and CSS profile, request a copy of your need analysis from these to be sent to Northwestern. *Other aid available to international students:* none.

Services

Housing options: on-site dorms, off-campus housing, fraternity, sorority.

Support staff: career counselor, financial aid advisor, foreign student advisor, housing advisor, physical therapist, psychological counselor, resident assistant, resident nurse, student affairs officer.

DANCE

Curriculum, Students, and Faculty

Required courses: dance composition/choreography, dance writing, research and criticism, rehearsal and performance.

Elective courses: African dance, ballet, dance history, dance theory, historical dance, jazz, Labanotation, men's class, modern dance, nutrition, other world dance forms, repertory, stagecraft, tap, vernacular dance.

Total enrollment: 40. *Entering class size:* 20.

Renowned alumni: Judi Sheppard Missett, Kevin Wore, Dereck Clifford.

Total full-time faculty: 5. *Total part-time faculty:* 5. *List of current faculty and past affiliations:* Billy Siegenfeld, Jump Rhythm Jazz, Hunter College; Robin Lakes, Rush Dance; Brian Jeffrey, Xsight, University of Wisconsin—Milwaukee. *Program contact person:* Terri Ganer.

Audition Information

No audition fee.

Performance Information

Performance opportunities available (frequency): Fully produced concerts (2 per year), informal concerts (1 per month), workshops (1 per quarter), on-site performances (regularly).

Performances choreographed by: faculty, students, guests. *Recent guest choreographers:* Thea Nerissa Barnes, Jeannie Hill.

Facilities

Number of studios available: 3. Performance facilities: loft type space, proscenium theater.

DRAMA

Curriculum, Students, and Faculty

Comprehensive training offered through School of Speech.

MUSIC

Curriculum, Students, and Faculty

Many faculty are principal players in the Chicago Symphony.

UNIVERSITY OF CHICAGO

1116 East 59th Street, Chicago IL 60637
Tel: 773-702-8650
Fax: 773-702-4199
Email: college-admissions@uchicago.edu

General

Type of Institution: private university. *Environment:* urban.

Total enrollment: 12,000.

Costs & Financial Aid

Tuition and fees: $21,485. *Room and board*: $7,375.

Entrance Requirements

Audition not required.

Services

Support staff: psychological counselor, resident nurse, career counselor, financial aid advisor, student affairs advisor.

DRAMA

Curriculum, Students, and Faculty

Required courses: text analysis, musical theater.

MUSIC

Curriculum, Students, and Faculty

Taught within the context of a liberal arts education.

UNIVERSITY OF ILLINOIS, URBANA-CHAMPAIGN

506 South Wright Street, Urbana IL 61801
Tel: 217-333-1000
Web: www.illinois.edu
Contact: Randy Dickerson

General

Type of Institution: public university. *Environment:* small city.

Total enrollment: 26,464. *Degrees offered:* BA, BM, BME.

Entrance Requirements

Audition required: live, audio, video. *Other requirements:* interview. *Standardized test requirements:* ACT, 29; TOEFL, 550.

Costs & Financial Aid

Application fee: $40. *Tuition (in-state/out-state):* $3,308/$9,924. *Medical fee:* $135. *Other fees:* $136 service fee, $93 general fee, $25 transportation. *Room and board*: $5,778.

Types of scholarships and aid awarded: full, partial, merit-based, need-based, named, institutional aid, tuition payment plan, work/study. *Loans available. Financial aid offered to international students.*

Services

Housing options: on-site dorms, off-campus housing, fraternity, sorority.

Support staff: career counselor, financial aid advisor, foreign student advisor, housing advisor, psychological counselor, resident assistant, student affairs officer.

DANCE

Curriculum, Students, and Faculty

Required courses: anatomy, ballet (2 years to complete), dance composition/choreography, dance history, master classes, modern dance (3 years to complete), music, rehearsal and performance, repertory, stagecraft, ballet, pointe, men's class, pas de deux.

Elective courses: Labanotation, movement techniques, pointe (1 year to complete), tap, variations.

Selectivity for males: approximately 60% admitted. *Selectivity for females:* approximately 60% admitted. *Total enrollment*: 54. *Entering class size:* 20. *Graduating class size:* 9. *Percent international:* 1%. *Countries most represented*: El Salvador, Colombia, Japan.

Renowned alumni: Kathleen Fisher, Ming-Lung Yang, both dancers in Trisha Brown Co.; Kathleen Hermesdorf, Stuart Gold, Ming-Shen Ku.

Total full-time faculty: 7. *Total part-time faculty:* 4. *List of current faculty and past affiliations:* Sean Sullivan, Jose Limon Dance Co.; Renee Wadleigh, Paul Taylor, Dan Wagoner and Mel Wong Companies; Walter Kennedy, Bella

Leuntzky Co.; Rebecca Nettl-Fiol, Ohio State University, SUNY at Potsdam, Certified teacher of Labanotation and Alexander Technique; John Perpener, Hartford Ballet, Maryland Dance Theater, DC Repertory Co. ***Program contact person:*** Becky Nettl-Fiol.

Audition Information

No audition fee. Audition consists of the following: ballet, modern dance, prepared solo, modern, ballet or jazz, preferably choreographed by the student. ***Accompanist provided. Cassette player available; CD player available. Dress requirements for males:*** tights and tight fitting t-shirt. ***Dress requirements for females:*** leotards, tights.

Repertoire that students should avoid? no.

Audition evaluation criteria: technical, creative, and performing ability; body structure and weight; musicality; movement perception; and dance potential in general.

Performance Information

Performance opportunities available (frequency): Fully produced concerts (4 per year), informal concerts (4-5 per year), workshops (2 per year), on-site performances (4-10 per year).

Performances choreographed by: faculty, students, guests. ***Recent guest choreographers:*** Joe Goode, Beverly Blossom, Bill Young, Bebe Miller, Stephen Koester, Lynn Dally, Jeff Slayton, Ralph Lemon.

Facilities

Number of studios available: 5. ***Approximate studio dimensions and flooring:*** 3,168 sq. ft. wood (sprung), 2,800 sq. ft. Harlequin floors, 1,700 sq. ft. linoleum, 1,240 sq. ft. ***Performance facilities:*** Krannert Center for the Performing Arts—theaters and an informal studio space.

DRAMA

Curriculum, Students, and Faculty

Required courses: acting, drama criticism, improvisation, make-up, movement, musical theater, scene study, speech, stage combat, Stanislavski exercises, verse drama, voice.

Elective courses: audition preparation, dance, directing, voice, speech, Alexander technique, drama criticism.

Number of years required to complete program: 4. ***Summer program not available. No affiliation with a professional theater company. Selectivity for males:*** approximately 33% admitted. ***Selectivity for females:*** approximately 33% admitted. ***Total enrollment:*** 139. ***Entering class size:*** 65. ***Graduating class size:*** 30.

Renowned alumni: Lynne Thigpen, Bob Falls, Alan Ruck, Scott Bradley, Ang Lee.

Total full-time faculty: 16. ***Total part-time faculty:*** 15. ***List of current faculty and past affiliations:*** Bruce Halverson, Robin McFargahar, Goodman Theatre, Steppenwolf and Shakespeare Repertory Theaters; James Berton Harris; Tom Mitchell, Nancy Hovasse, Christine Sevec-Johnson, San Diego Old Globe Theatre; Michael Franklin-White, Arena Stage, Seattle Rep.

Audition Information

No audition fee. Audition consists of the following: comedic monologue, improvisation, group warm-up, interview.

Audition evaluation criteria: truthful, dynamic acting; voice, speech, and movement free of serious impairment.

Performance Information

Performance opportunities available (frequency): fully produced performances (7 per year), informal performances (11 per semester), workshops (4-6 per year), auditioned.

Recent guest artists: Meredith Monk, Timothy Douglas, Rachel Lampert, Scott Bradley.

Facilities

Rehearsal facilities and hours: four large rehearsal halls, 7:00 pm-11:00 pm (Mon-Fri), 1:00 pm-5:00 pm (Sun). ***Number of theaters on campus:*** 4. ***Type and capacity:*** proscenium—700, proscenium—900, studio 200, black box—150.

MUSIC

Curriculum, Students, and Faculty

Total enrollment: 450. ***Entering class size:*** 100. ***Graduating class size:*** 117. ***Percent international:*** 2%. ***Countries most represented***: Spain, Yugoslavia, Romania, Austria, Canada, Australia.

Total full-time faculty: 80. ***Total part-time faculty:*** 10. ***Program contact person:*** Mark Rabideau. ***Contact***: School of Music 217-244-2676. ***Unique or innovative music curriculum:*** Highly selective University and School of Music specialize in Performance, Music education, Composition-Theory and Musicology. Open Studies allows student-assigned curriculum in a variety of areas. ***How are major teacher assignments made?*** students may choose, made by the school, according to teacher preference and teacher availability. Faculty is not informed of a student's teacher preference at the time of the audition. ***30 lessons with major teacher. May a student change major teachers***

during the course of study? possibly. *Study of secondary instrument or discipline is allowed.*

Selectivity for instruments or programs offered (rating): bassoon (selective), choral conducting (selective), clarinet (selective), composition (selective), double bass (selective), electronic music (selective), flute or piccolo (selective), French horn (selective), harp (selective), harpsichord (selective), jazz (selective), jazz (highly selective), oboe/English horn (highly selective), orchestral conducting (selective), organ (selective), percussion (selective), piano (selective), saxophone (highly selective), trombone (highly selective), trumpet (selective), tuba (selective), viola (selective), violin (selective), violoncello (selective), voice (highly selective).

Renowned alumni: Malcom Bilson, George Crumb, Jerry Hadley, Michael Colgrass, Eric Mills, Eric Halfvarson.

Audition Information

No audition fee. Audition consists of the following: scales, arpeggios, sight reading, repertoire. *Instruments provided for:* harpists, percussionists.

Repertoire that students should avoid? depends upon each area. *Performance opportunities available (frequency):* band (4-6 per year), jury examinations (every semester), orchestral concerts (6 or more per year), recitals, touring (varies), produced operas (2-3 per year), chorus (4-6 per year).

Facilities

Number of practice rooms and hours: 120; 17 hours (daily). *Recital hall?* yes. *Concert hall?* yes. *Recording studio?* yes.

WESTERN ILLINOIS UNIVERSITY

1 University Circle
Department of Music, Brown Hall 122, Macomb IL 61455
Tel: 309-298-1544
Fax: 309-298-1968
Email: claudia_mccain@ccmail.wiu.edu
Web: www.win.edu

General

Type of Institution: public, university.

Total enrollment: 12,000. *Total student body from other countries:* 4%. *Degrees offered:* BA.

Entrance Requirements

Audition required: live. *Other requirements:* recommendation. *Standardized test requirements:* ACT, 22; TOEFL.

Costs & Financial Aid

Percent of students receiving financial aid: 70%. *Types of scholarships and aid awarded:* full, partial, merit-based, need-based, named, reduced tuition, work/study. *Loans available. Procedure for applying for loans:* contact Financial Aid Office.

Services

Housing options: on-site dorms, off-campus housing, fraternity, sorority, family.

Support staff: career counselor, financial aid advisor, foreign student advisor, psychological counselor, resident assistant, resident nurse, student affairs officer.

MUSIC

Curriculum, Students, and Faculty

Unique or innovative music curriculum: degrees offered in applied studies, music education, music business, music therapy. *How are major teacher assignments made?* Students may choose, made by the school, according to teacher preference and teacher availability. Faculty is not informed of a student's teacher preference at the time of the audition. *30 lessons with major teacher. May a student change major teachers during the course of study?* possibly. *Study of secondary instrument or discipline is allowed.*

Selectivity for instruments or programs offered (rating): bassoon (competitive), clarinet (competitive), double bass (competitive), flute or piccolo (competitive), French horn (competitive), jazz (competitive), oboe/English horn (competitive), organ (competitive), percussion (competitive), piano (competitive), saxophone (competitive), trombone (competitive), trumpet (competitive), tuba (competitive), viola (competitive), violin (competitive), violoncello (competitive), voice (competitive).

Total enrollment: 230. *Entering class size:* 50. *Graduating class size:* 30. *Countries most represented*: Malaysia, Korea.

Total full-time faculty: 37. *Total part-time faculty:* 2. *Program contact person:* Lorena Saxton.

Audition Information

No audition fee. Audition consists of the following: scales, music theory, sight reading, repertoire. *Instruments provided for:* percussionists.

Required repertoire: an audition repertoire is suggested. *Performance opportunities available (frequency):* jury examinations (frequently), recitals (frequently).

Facilities

Number of practice rooms and hours: 22. *Recital hall?* yes. *Concert hall?* yes. *Recording studio?* yes.

WHEATON COLLEGE CONSERVATORY OF MUSIC

501 East College Avenue, Wheaton IL 60187
Tel: 630-752-5097
Fax: 630-752-5341
Email: deborah.a.rodgers@wheaton.edu

General

Type of Institution: college, conservatory. *Religious Affiliation*: Christian, non-denominational. *Environment:* suburban.

Total enrollment: 2,300. *Total student body from other countries:* 8%. *Degrees offered:* BM, BME.

Entrance Requirements

Audition required: live, audio, video. *Other requirements:* interview, recommendation, essay. *Standardized test requirements:* ACT, 29; SAT I, 1300; TOEFL.

Costs & Financial Aid

Application fee: $35. *Deposit:* $200. *Tuition:* $14,360. *Other fees:* $190 per semester music lesson fee, $16 per credit hour music course fee.

Percent of students receiving financial aid: 75%. *Types of scholarships and aid awarded:* partial, merit-based, need-based, named, institutional aid, government aid, tuition payment plan, work/study. *Forms required for scholarships:* FAFSA, income tax return, income asset verification. *Loans available. Procedure for applying for loans:* FAFSA form and Wheaton College form.

Services

Housing options: on-site dorms.

Support staff: career counselor, dorm parent, financial aid advisor, foreign student advisor, housing advisor, psychological counselor, resident assistant, resident nurse, student affairs officer.

MUSIC

Curriculum, Students, and Faculty

How are major teacher assignments made? by chair of area. Faculty is not informed of a student's teacher preference at the time of the audition. *May a student change major teachers during the course of study?* possibly. *Study of secondary instrument or discipline is allowed.*

Selectivity for instruments or programs offered (rating): bassoon (competitive), clarinet (competitive), composition (competitive), double bass (competitive), flute or piccolo (selective), French horn (competitive), guitar (competitive), harp (competitive), oboe/English horn (competitive), organ (competitive), percussion (competitive), piano (selective), saxophone (competitive), trombone (competitive), trumpet (competitive), tuba (competitive), viola (competitive), violin (selective), violoncello (competitive), voice (selective).

Total enrollment: 200. *Entering class size:* 50. *Graduating class size:* 40.

Renowned alumni: Sylvia McNair, Wendy White, Doug Yeo, John Nelson.

Total full-time faculty: 19. *Total part-time faculty:* 16. *Program contact person:* Deborah Rodgers.

Audition Information

No audition fee. Audition consists of the following: scales, orchestral excerpts, arpeggios, sight reading, repertoire. *Instruments provided for:* percussionists.

Repertoire that students should avoid? no arias for voice.

Facilities

Number of practice rooms and hours: 40; 6:00 am-12:00 am. *Recital hall?* yes. *Concert hall?* yes. *Recording studio?* yes.

INDIANA

BUTLER UNIVERSITY

Jordan College of Fine Arts
4600 Sunset Avenue, Indianapolis IN 46208
Tel: 317-940-9231
Fax: 317-940-9658
Contact: Maggie Hayworth

General

Type of Institution: university. *Environment:* urban.

Total enrollment: 3,911. *Total student body from other countries:* 3%. *Degrees offered:* BA, BFA, BM, BS in arts administration, BS in music business.

Entrance Requirements

Audition required: live. *Other requirements:* interview, recommendation, essay, photograph. *Standardized test requirements:* ACT, 25; SAT I, 1145; TOEFL, 550.

Costs & Financial Aid

Application fee: $25. *Deposit:* $200. *Tuition:* $7,785. *Other fees:* $60.

Percent of students receiving financial aid: 84%. *Types of scholarships and aid awarded:* full, partial, merit-based, need-based, named, institutional aid, government aid, tuition payment plan, work/study. *Forms required for scholarships:* FAFSA. *Loans available. Procedure for applying for loans:* FAFSA and university form. *Financial aid offered to international students.*

Services

Housing options: on-site dorms, fraternity, sorority.

Support staff: career counselor, dorm parent, financial aid advisor, foreign student advisor, housing advisor, physical therapist, psychological counselor, resident assistant, resident nurse, student affairs officer.

DANCE

Curriculum, Students, and Faculty

Required courses: character (2 classes per week, 1 year to complete), ballet (5 classes per week, 4 years to complete), dance composition/choreography (2 classes per week, 2 years to complete), dance history (3 classes per week, 1 year to complete), dance theory (1 class per week, 1 year to complete), jazz (2 classes per week, 1-2 years to complete), men's class (5 classes per week, 4 years to complete), Graham-based modern dance (2-3 classes per week, 3 years to complete), movement techniques, body conditioning (2 classes per week, 1 year to complete), Feldenkreis (2 classes per week, 1 year to complete), Laban Movement Studies (3 classes per week, 1 year to complete), Pilates (2 classes per week, 1 year to complete), music (2 classes per week, 1 year to complete), pas de deux (2 classes per week, 3 years to complete), pointe (2 classes per week, 3 years to complete), rehearsal and performance (4 classes per week, 4 years to complete), Spanish (2 classes per week, 1/2 years to complete), tap (3 classes per week, 1/2 year to complete).

Elective courses: master classes, other world dance forms, variations (1 class per week, 1 year to complete).

Selectivity for males: approximately 60% admitted. *Selectivity for females:* approximately 33% admitted. *Total enrollment:* 75. *Entering class size:* 26. *Graduating class size:* 12. *Percent international:* 2%.

Renowned alumni: refer to catalog.

Total full-time faculty: 6. *Total part-time faculty:* 6. *List of current faculty and past affiliations:* refer to catalog. *Program contact person:* Stephan Laurent.

Audition Information

No audition fee. Audition consists of the following: ballet, 2 ballet classes. *Accompanist provided. Cassette player not available; CD player not available. Dress requirements for males:* black tights, white t-shirts or leotard, white socks, white ballet shoes. *Dress requirements for females:* pink tights, black leotard, pink ballet shoes (no pointe required).

Audition evaluation criteria: technical proficiency, phrasing, and quality and flow of movement; weight and bone structure.

Performance Information

Performance opportunities available (frequency): Fully produced concerts (13-15 per year), touring (1-2 weeks per year), informal (fully produced).

Performances choreographed by: faculty, guests. *Recent guest choreographers:* Donald Byrd.

Facilities

Number of studios available: 4. *Approximate studio dimensions and flooring:* 44' x 28' L'Air pneumatic floor and Marley, 44' x 22' L'Air pneumatic floor and Marley, 36' x 36' L'Air pneumatic floor and Marley, 25' x 20' L'Air pneumatic floor and Marley. *Performance facilities:* Clowes Memorial Hall—2,000-seat major auditorium, Lilly Hall studio theater—120 seat black box theater.

DRAMA

Curriculum, Students, and Faculty

Required courses: acting, audition preparation, directing, make-up, movement, scene study, speech, text analysis, voice, Stanislavski exercises, improvisation, audition preparation.

Elective courses: ballet, jazz, musical theater.

Number of years required to complete program: 4. *Summer program not available. Affiliation with a professional theater company: Informal affiliation with Indiana Repertory Theatre in Indianapolis. Students are occasionally placed in internships and artistic personnel do occasional class visits.*

Selectivity for males: approximately 60% admitted. *Selectivity for females:* approximately 60% admitted. *Total enrollment:* 48. *Entering class size:* 15. *Graduating class size:* 13.

Renowned alumni: Zan Sawyer-Dailey, Actors Theatre of Louisville; R.K. Little Kelley.

Total full-time faculty: 5. *Total part-time faculty:* 2. *List of current faculty and past affiliations:* Daniel Pugh, The Theatre School/Goodman Theatre; Owen W. Schaub, Indiana University, Kent State University, Westbury Music Fair; Diane Timmerman, Indiana University, Indiana Repertory Theatre.

Audition Information

Audition consists of the following: 2 memorized, contrasting monologues. *Dress requirements for males:* clothing comfortable for sitting and moving. *Dress requirements for females:* clothing comfortable for sitting and moving.

Audition evaluation criteria: preparation (memorization, research); concentration; bodily expression (facial and physical movement); voice (pitch, volume, rate, projection); interpretation of character/screenplay.

Performance Information

Performance opportunities available (frequency): fully produced performances (5-6 per semester), informal performances (varies), workshops (varies), casting is by audition.

Facilities

Rehearsal facilities and hours: Except during scheduled classes, the studio classroom is available for rehearsal 7:00 am-11:00 pm (Mon-Sat). *Number of theaters on campus:* 3. *Type and capacity:* studio—50, flexible—150, proscenium—2,080.

MUSIC

Curriculum, Students, and Faculty

How are major teacher assignments made? students may choose, according to teacher availability. Faculty is not informed of a student's teacher preference at the time of the audition. *14 lessons with major teacher. May a student change major teachers during the course of study?* possibly. *Study of secondary instrument or discipline is allowed.*

Selectivity for instruments or programs offered (rating): bassoon (competitive), choral conducting (selective), choral singing (selective), clarinet (competitive), composition (selective), double bass (competitive), flute or piccolo (selective), French horn (competitive), guitar (open), harp (selective), oboe/English horn (competitive), orchestral conducting (selective), organ (noncompetitive), percussion (competitive), piano (competitive), saxophone (selective), trombone (competitive), trumpet (competitive), tuba (competitive), viola (competitive), violin (competitive), violoncello (competitive), voice (selective).

Total enrollment: 251. *Entering class size:* 84. *Graduating class size:* 45. *Percent international:* 2%.

Renowned alumni: Al Savia.

Total full-time faculty: 25. *Total part-time faculty:* 35. *Program contact person:* Dan Bolin.

Audition Information

No audition fee. Audition consists of the following: scales, music theory, sight reading. *Instruments provided for:* harpists, percussionists.

Performance opportunities available (frequency): band, chamber music, jury examinations (1 per semester), opera workshops, orchestral concerts, recitals, chorus.

Facilities

Recital hall? yes. *Concert hall?* yes. *Recording studio?* no.

INDIANA STATE UNIVERSITY

Department of Music, Terre Haute IN 47802
Tel: 812-237-2771
Fax: 812-237-3009
Web: www.indstate.edu/music

General

Type of Institution: public university. *Environment:* urban.

Total enrollment: 11,000. *Total student body from other countries:* 10%. *Degrees offered:* certificate, BA, BM, BME, BS in music business.

Entrance Requirements

Audition required: live, audio, video.

Costs & Financial Aid

Types of scholarships and aid awarded: full, partial, merit-based, named, institutional aid, work/study. *Procedure for applying for loans:* audition.

Services

Housing options: on-site dorms.

MUSIC

Curriculum, Students, and Faculty

How are major teacher assignments made? according to teacher availability. Faculty is informed of a student's teacher preference at the time of the audition. *30 lessons with major teacher. May a student change major teachers during the course of study?* possibly. *Study of secondary instrument or discipline is allowed.*

Selectivity for instruments or programs offered (rating): accompanying (competitive), bassoon (competitive), choral conducting (competitive), choral singing (competitive), clarinet (competitive), composition (competitive), double bass (competitive), electronic music (competitive), flute or piccolo (competitive), French horn (competitive), harp (competitive), jazz (competitive), oboe/English horn (competitive), orchestral conducting (competitive), percussion (competitive), piano (competitive), saxophone (competitive), trombone (competitive), trumpet (competitive), tuba (competitive), viola (competitive), violin (competitive), violoncello (competitive), voice (competitive).

Total enrollment: 240. *Entering class size:* 80. *Graduating class size:* 20. *Percent international:* 10%.

Total full-time faculty: 27. *Total part-time faculty:* 10. *Program contact person:* Dr. James O'Donnell.

Audition Information

No audition fee. Instruments provided for: harpists, percussionists; pianists.

Performance opportunities available (frequency): jury examinations (frequently), orchestral concerts (frequently).

Facilities

Number of practice rooms and hours: 37. *Recital hall?* yes. *Concert hall?* yes. *Recording studio?* yes.

INDIANA UNIVERSITY

Hope School of Fine Arts & School of Music
300 North Jordan Avenue, Bloomington IN 47405
Tel: 812-855-0661
Email: iuadmit@indiana.edu
Web: www.indiana.edu

General

Type of Institution: public university. *Environment:* suburban.

Total enrollment: 35,594. *Degrees offered:* BA, BFA, BM, artist diploma.

Entrance Requirements

Audition required: live, audio, video. *Other requirements:* recommendation, essay. *Standardized test requirements:* ACT; SAT I.

Costs & Financial Aid

Application fee: $40. *Tuition (in-state/out-state):* $4,582/$12,770. *Other fees:* $30-$45. recital program printing, $35 recital recording, $132 applied music fee, $32 instrument rental. *Room and board:* $4,660.

Percent of students receiving financial aid: 62%. *Types of scholarships and aid awarded:* full, partial, merit-based, need-based, institutional aid. *Forms required for scholarships:* FAFSA, income tax return. *Loans available.*

Services

Housing options: on-site dorms, off-campus housing, fraternity, sorority.

Support staff: career counselor, financial aid advisor, foreign student advisor, housing advisor, psychological counselor, resident assistant, resident nurse, student affairs officer.

DRAMA

Curriculum, Students, and Faculty

Total enrollment: 200.

Renowned alumni: Kevin Kline, Stephen Macht.

MUSIC

Curriculum, Students, and Faculty

Total enrollment: 743.

Renowned alumni: Joshua Bel, Sylvia McNair, Timothy Noble.

Total full-time faculty: 137. *Total part-time faculty:* 15. *Program contact person:* Gwyn Richards, (812) 855-7998.

VALPARAISO UNIVERSITY

Office of Admissions
Kretzmann Hall, Valparaiso IN 46383-6493
Tel: 800-GO-VALPO
Fax: 219-464-5244
Email: Undergrad_admissions@valpo.edu
Web: www.valpo.edu
Contact: Andi Jones

General

Type of Institution: private college. *Environment:* suburban.

Total enrollment: 2,750. *Total student body from other countries:* 4%. *Degrees offered:* BA, BME.

Entrance Requirements

Audition required: live, video. *Other requirements:* interview. *Standardized test requirements:* ACT; SAT I.

Costs & Financial Aid

Application fee: $30. *Deposit:* $200. *Other fees:* $500.

Percent of students receiving financial aid: 80%. *Types of scholarships and aid awarded:* full, partial, merit-based, need-based, named, institutional aid, government aid, tuition payment plan, work/study. *Loans available. Procedure for applying for loans:* complete FAFSA and include Valparaiso University's school code of 001842. *Financial aid offered to international students. Other aid available to international students:* very limited.

Services

Housing options: on-site dorms, off-campus housing, fraternity, sorority.

Support staff: career counselor, financial aid advisor.

DANCE

Curriculum, Students, and Faculty

Required courses: music, dance composition/choreography.

DRAMA

Curriculum, Students, and Faculty

Elective courses: dramaturgy, Alexander technique, Stanislavski exercises.

MUSIC

Curriculum, Students, and Faculty

How are major teacher assignments made? students may choose made by the school according to teacher preference according to teacher availability. Faculty is not informed of a student's teacher preference at the time of the audition. *28 lessons with major teacher; May a student change major teachers during the course of study?* possibly. *Study of secondary instrument or discipline is allowed.*

Selectivity for instruments or programs offered (rating): clarinet (highly selective), tuba (competitive).

Total enrollment: 97. *Entering class size:* 31. *Graduating class size:* 20. *Percent international:* 1%.

Renowned alumni: Martin Jean, Thomas Schmidt, Frank Ferko, Marilyn Schmeige.

Total full-time faculty: 8. *Total part-time faculty:* 24. *Program contact person:* Linda Ferguson.

Audition Information

Audition consists of the following: music theory, music history. *Instruments provided for:* percussionists.

Facilities

Number of practice rooms and hours: 14; 8:00 am-11:00 pm. *Recital hall?* yes. *Concert hall?* no. *Recording studio?* yes.

KANSAS

WICHITA STATE UNIVERSITY

1845 Fairmount
School of Performing Arts-Dance, Wichita KS 67260-0101
Tel: 316-978-3530
Contact: Jennifer Chapman

General

Type of Institution: university. *Environment:* urban.

Degrees offered: BFA.

Entrance Requirements

Audition required: live, video.

Costs & Financial Aid

Application fee: $20.

Percent of students receiving financial aid: 80%. *Types of scholarships and aid awarded:* partial, merit-based, need-based, government aid, reduced tuition, tuition payment plan, work/study. *Procedure for applying for loans:* apply through admissions for academic scholarship, for dance scholarship by audition. *Financial aid offered to international students. Percent of international students receiving scholarships:* 70%.

Services

Housing options: on-site dorms, off-campus housing.

Support staff: career counselor, dorm parent, financial aid advisor, foreign student advisor, housing advisor, physical therapist, psychological counselor, resident assistant, resident nurse, student affairs officer.

DANCE

Curriculum, Students, and Faculty

Required courses: anatomy, ballet (3 classes per week), dance composition/choreography, dance history, dance theory, modern dance (4 classes per week), music, rehearsal and performance (2 classes per week).

Elective courses: African dance, jazz, master classes, stagecraft, tap.

Selectivity for males: most admitted, but not all. *Selectivity for females:* approximately 60% admitted. *Total enrollment:* 230. *Entering class size:* 7. *Percent international:* 2%. *Countries most represented*: Malaysia.

Renowned alumni: Eddie Martinez, Pina Bausch; Dawn Di Psasquale.

Total full-time faculty: 3. *Total part-time faculty:* 4. *List of current faculty and past affiliations:* C. Nicholas Johnson, Ruth Page Foundation/Chicago, Goldston and Johnson mimes, Invisible People Mime Theater; Teresa Wylie McWilliams, National tours of Broadway musicals; Solomons Company/dance and Carol Fonda; Denise Celestin, Ballet Met, Columbus Ohio, Fifth USA International Ballet Competition. *Program contact person:* C. Nicholas Johnson, ext. 3645.

Audition Information

No audition fee. Audition consists of the following: ballet, modern dance, jazz. *Accompanist provided. Cassette player available; CD player available.*

Repertoire that students should avoid? no hip-hop preferably.

Audition evaluation criteria: open admissions currently; however, placement is through auditions.

Performance Information

Performance opportunities available (frequency): Fully produced concerts (2 per year), informal concerts (4 per year), workshops (2 per year), on-site performances (20 per year).

Performances choreographed by: faculty, students, guests. *Recent guest choreographers:* Anita Lemon, Therese Hembruch, Joey Hancock, Melissa Lowe, David Norwood.

Facilities

Number of studios available: 2. *Approximate studio dimensions and flooring:* 40' x 51' wooden covered with Marley type flooring, 39' x 69' sprung floors. *Performance facilities:* Milles Hall—seats 532, proscenium theater. Litwin theater—studio space with lighting for workshops and undergraduate choreography.

KENTUCKY

UNIVERSITY OF LOUISVILLE

School of Music, Louisville KY 40292
Tel: 508-852-6907
Fax: 502-852-0520

General

Type of Institution: public, university. *Environment:* urban.

Total enrollment: 300. *Total student body from other countries:* 5%. *Degrees offered:* BA, BM.

Entrance Requirements

Audition required: live. *Other requirements:* interview, recommendation. *Standardized test requirements:* ACT; TOEFL.

Costs & Financial Aid

Application fee: $25. *Tuition (in-state/out-state)*: $2,630/$7,430.

Percent of students receiving financial aid: 80%. *Types of scholarships and aid awarded:* full, partial, merit-based, need-based, named, work/study. *Financial aid offered to international students. Percent of international students receiving scholarships:* 100%.

Services

Housing options: on-site dorms, off-campus housing.

Support staff: housing advisor, physical therapist, psychological counselor, resident assistant, resident nurse, student affairs officer.

MUSIC

Curriculum, Students, and Faculty

How are major teacher assignments made? Students may choose according to teacher availability. Faculty is not informed of a student's teacher preference at the time of the audition. *30 lessons with major teacher. May a student change major teachers during the course of study?* possibly. *Study of secondary instrument or discipline is allowed.*

Selectivity for instruments or programs offered (rating): bassoon (competitive), clarinet (competitive), composition (competitive), double bass (competitive), flute or piccolo (competitive), French horn (competitive), guitar (competitive), harp (non-competitive), oboe/English horn (competitive), organ (competitive), percussion (competitive), percussion (highly selective), piano (competitive), saxophone (competitive), trombone (competitive), trumpet (competitive), tuba (competitive), viola (competitive), violin (competitive), violoncello (competitive), voice (competitive), voice (competitive).

Total enrollment: 300. *Entering class size:* 90. *Graduating class size:* 20. *Percent international:* 5%. *Countries most represented*: Ecuador.

Renowned alumni: William Schwann, James Walker, Stacy Blair, Cliff Blackburn, Edith Davis Tidwell.

Total full-time faculty: 31. *Total part-time faculty:* 15. *Program contact person:* Linda Wheeler.

Audition Information

No audition fee. Instruments provided for: percussionists.

Performance opportunities available (frequency): band, jury examinations, chorus.

Facilities

Number of practice rooms and hours: 76; 7:00 am-11:00 pm. *Recital hall?* yes.

LOUISIANA STATE UNIVERSITY AND A&M COLLEGE

Baton Rouge LA 70803
Tel: 504-388-3202
Fax: 504-388-4433
Web: www.lsu.edu

General

Type of Institution: public, university. *Environment:* urban.

Total enrollment: 22,725. *Total student body from other countries:* 3%. *Degrees offered:* BA, BM.

Entrance Requirements

Audition not required. Standardized test requirements: ACT; SAT I; TOEFL.

Costs & Financial Aid

Application fee: $25. *Tuition (in-state/out-state)*: $2,711/$6,311.

Percent of students receiving financial aid: 62%. *Types of scholarships and aid awarded:* full, partial, merit-based, need-based, institutional aid, government aid, work/study. *Forms required for scholarships:* FAFSA. *Loans available. Procedure for applying for loans:* contact Financial Aid Office by 2/1, various scholarships have different application procedures. *Financial aid offered to international students. Percent of international students receiving scholarships:* 27%.

Services

Housing options: on-site dorms, fraternity, sorority.

Support staff: career counselor, financial aid advisor, foreign student advisor, housing advisor, resident assistant, resident nurse, student affairs officer.

DRAMA

Curriculum, Students, and Faculty

Required courses: acting, directing, dramaturgy, movement, scene study, text analysis, theater technology.

Elective courses: audition preparation, dance, drama criticism, improvisation, make-up, musical theater, voice.

Number of years required to complete program: 4. *Summer program available. Affiliation with a professional theater company: Swine Palace Productions, an Equity non-profit company formed in affiliation with the LSU Department of Theatre, was established in 1991. Since its inception, Swine Palace Productions has evolved from a producing organization housed within the Theatre Department towards a nationally recognized professional theatre for the state of Louisiana. The plan was conceived by Artistic Director, Barry Kyle, Professor in the Department of Theatre, and the original Board of Directors, many of whom are still actively involved with the company.*

Selectivity for males: admit all who apply. *Selectivity for females:* admit all who apply. *Total enrollment:* 77. *Entering class size:* 9. *Graduating class size:* 11.

Renowned alumni: John McConnell, Chris Boneau, Joe Chrest, Joanne Woodward, Rebecca Wells.

Total full-time faculty: 12. *List of current faculty and past affiliations:* Barry Kyle, Royal Shakespeare Company; Nels Anderson, Singapore Repertory; Steve Woods, Jose Limon Dance Company; John Dennis, Mark Taper Forum; Annmarie Davis-Monomy Theatre, Cape Cod.

Audition Information

No audition fee. Audition consists of the following: Auditions are for productions only, not for becoming part of an undergraduate acting program. *Repertoire that students should avoid?* no.

Audition evaluation criteria: audition requirements for individual productions are posted prior to audition dates.

Performance Information

Performance opportunities available (frequency): fully produced performances (9 per year), informal performances (3-4 per year), auditioned.

Recent guest artists: Kevin Coleman.

Facilities

Number of theaters on campus: 3. *Type and capacity:* proscenium—400, proscenium—90, black box—100.

MUSIC

Curriculum, Students, and Faculty

How are major teacher assignments made? Students may choose according to teacher availability. Faculty is not informed of a student's teacher preference at the time of the audition. *30 lessons with major teacher. May a student change major teachers during the course of study?* possibly. *Study of secondary instrument or discipline is allowed.*

Selectivity for instruments or programs offered (rating): bassoon (highly selective), clarinet (selective), composition (selective), double bass (selective), electronic music (highly selective), flute or piccolo (highly selective), French horn (highly selective), French horn (non-competitive), harp (selective), oboe/English horn (highly selective), organ (selective), percussion (selective), piano (selective), saxophone (highly selective), trombone (highly selective), trumpet (selective), tuba (highly selective), viola (selective), violin (highly selective), violoncello (highly selective), voice (selective).

Total enrollment: 292. *Entering class size:* 88. *Graduating class size:* 60. *Percent international:* 8%. *Countries most represented*: Bulgaria, Malaysia, Georgia.

Renowned alumni: Bill Conti, James King, Carl Fontana, Travis Paul Groves.

Total full-time faculty: 40. *Total part-time faculty:* 5. *Program contact person:* William Grimes.

Audition Information

No audition fee. Audition consists of the following: scales, orchestral excerpts, sight reading. *Instruments provided for:* harpists, percussionists.

Performance opportunities available (frequency): band (2), chamber music, jury examinations (1 per semester), orchestral concerts, recitals, chorus.

Facilities

Number of practice rooms and hours: 50; 7:00 am-11:00 pm. *Recital hall?* yes. *Concert hall?* yes. *Recording studio?* yes.

LOYOLA UNIVERSITY, NEW ORLEANS

6363 St. Charles Avenue, New Orleans LA 70118
Tel: 504-865-2011
Web: www.loyno.edu
Contact: Eli Clarke

General

Type of Institution: college, university. *Religious Affiliation:* Jesuit, Roman Catholic. *Environment:* urban.

Total enrollment: 5,499. *Total student body from other countries:* 6%. *Degrees offered:* BA, BM, BAM, BME, BMT.

Entrance Requirements

Audition required: live, audio, video. *Other requirements:* recommendation, essay, photograph. *Standardized test requirements:* ACT; SAT I; SAT II; TOEFL, 500.

Costs & Financial Aid

Application fee: $20. *Deposit:* $200. *Other fees:* $385 student fee.

Percent of students receiving financial aid: 75%. *Types of scholarships and aid awarded:* full, partial, merit-based, need-based, named, institutional aid, government aid, reduced tuition, tuition payment plan, work/study. *Loans available. Procedure for applying for loans:* file FAFSA. *Percent of international students receiving scholarships:* 1%. *Other aid available to international students:* Monroe Foundation Scholarships for specifically recruited Costa Rican students.

Services

Housing options: on-site dorms, off-campus housing, fraternity, sorority.

Support staff: career counselor, financial aid advisor, foreign student advisor, psychological counselor, resident assistant, resident nurse, student affairs officer.

DANCE

Curriculum, Students, and Faculty

Required courses: ballet, dance composition/choreography, dance history, dance theory, men's class, music, pointe, rehearsal and performance, repertory, variations, theatrical dance, ethnic dance, folk dance, arts management.

Elective courses: character, master classes, pas de deux, Spanish, anatomy, dance history.

Selectivity for males: most admitted, but not all. *Selectivity for females:* most admitted, but not all.

Renowned alumni: Laura Zambrano, ballet mistress, Ballet Iowa; Paul Varterling, Choreographer Nashville Ballet; Diane Lala, faculty Musical Theatre Dept. Cincinnati Conservatory; Greg Bonin featured ice skater performing in Europe.

Total full-time faculty: 1. *List of current faculty and past affiliations:* Gayle Parmelee, certified to teach Vaganova syllabus, Russia formerly directed Savannah Ballet, Jackson Ballet, and Louisiana Ballet. Performed professionally on Broadway, National Ballet and opera companies. *Program contact person:* Gayle L. Parmelee.

Audition Information

No audition fee. Audition consists of the following: ballet, pas de deux, pointe works. *Accompanist provided. Cassette player available; CD player available. Dress requirements for males:* black tights, t-shirt, dance belt, socks, ballet shoes. *Dress requirements for females:* pink tights, colored leotard, pink shoes, pointe shoes.

Audition evaluation criteria: musicality, technique, artistry, experience.

Performance Information

Performance opportunities available (frequency): Fully produced concerts (fall and spring concerts), informal concerts (varies), workshops (every summer), on-site performances(occasionally), touring (occasionally).

Performances choreographed by: faculty, students, guests. *Recent guest choreographers:* Svetlana Al Neyadi, Liza Gennaro.

Facilities

Number of studios available: 1. *Approximate studio dimensions and flooring:* 40' x 30' Harlequin-cascade over basket weave flooring. *Performance facilities:* 600-seat theater stage 40 x 50, wood, Rosco covering.

DRAMA

Curriculum, Students, and Faculty

Required courses: acting, directing, dramaturgy, movement techniques, text analysis, voice, audition preparation.

Elective courses: audition preparation, make-up, scene study, stage combat, directing.

Number of years required to complete program: 4. *Summer program not available. Affiliation with a professional theater company: internships can be established by individual students with regional theatres; Southern Repertory New Orleans is a Loyola affiliate.*

Selectivity for males: approximately 60% admitted. *Selectivity for females:* approximately 60% admitted. *Total enrollment:* 76. *Entering class size:* 29. *Graduating class size:* 7. *Percent international:* 3%.

Renowned alumni: Paul Amend, Actor's Warehouse Theatre; Ryan Blanchard, Dean Cochran, Kiel Junius, Tom Keynton.

Total full-time faculty: 5. *Total part-time faculty:* 8.

Audition Information

No audition fee. Audition consists of the following: comedic monologue. Shakespearean monologue, 2-minute monologue of student's choice. *Dress requirements for males:* neat. *Dress requirements for females:* neat. *Audition evaluation criteria:* vocal qualities, movement/physical, character choices.

Performance Information

Performance opportunities available (frequency): fully produced performances (7-22), informal performances (1-3 per year), auditioned.

Recent guest artists: Paula Vogel, Eric Overmyer, Susan Sarandon.

Facilities

Rehearsal facilities and hours: large acting studio, 8:00 am-10:00 pm, black box, 3:00 pm-10:00 pm, proscenium theater, 6:00 pm-10:00 pm. *Number of theaters on campus:* 2. *Type and capacity:* 150, black box—70.

MUSIC

Curriculum, Students, and Faculty

How are major teacher assignments made? made by the school according to teacher preference according to teacher availability. Faculty is informed of a student's teacher preference at the time of the audition. *May a student change major teachers during the course of study?* possibly. *Study of secondary instrument or discipline is allowed.*

Selectivity for instruments or programs offered (rating): bassoon (competitive), clarinet (competitive), composition (competitive), double bass (competitive), flute or piccolo (competitive), French horn (competitive), guitar (competitive), harp (competitive), harpsichord (competitive), jazz (competitive), oboe/English horn (competitive), organ (competitive), percussion (competitive), piano (competitive), saxophone (competitive), trombone (competitive), trumpet (competitive), tuba (competitive), viola (competitive), violin (competitive), violoncello (competitive), voice (competitive).

Total enrollment: 266. *Entering class size:* 88. *Graduating class size:* 24. *Percent international:* 4%.

Renowned alumni: Charles Anthony, Al Belletto, Charlie Brent, Brett Duggan, Mchael Geneuay, Quincy Jones, Anthony Laciura, Ellis Marsalis, Cheryl Maranto, Natalie Rom, Steven Spooner, Norman Treigle, Alfred Walker, Logan Skelton.

Total full-time faculty: 21. *Total part-time faculty:* 33. *Program contact person:* Dr. Anthony A. Decuir.

Audition Information

No audition fee. Audition consists of the following: music theory, rhythmic dictation, sight reading, improvisation, melodic dictation, repertoire. *Instruments provided for:* percussionists.

Required repertoire: minimum of 2 contrasting selections from the standard repertoire. *Repertoire that students should avoid?* no. *Performance opportunities available (frequency):* band (4 per year), jury examinations (2 per year), orchestral concerts (4 per year), recitals (varies), chorus (6 times a year).

Facilities

Number of practice rooms and hours: 25; 6:00 am-2:00 am. *Recital hall?* yes. *Concert hall?* yes. *Recording studio?* yes.

Contact: H. Jac McCracken, interim Associate Dean, Tel: (504) 865-3037; Fax: (504) 865-2852 Email: mcracken@beta.loyno.edu

NORTHEAST LOUISIANA UNIVERSITY

School of Music, Monroe LA 71209-0250
Tel: 318-342-1570
Fax: 318-342-1369
Email: Muedwards@alpha.nlu.edu

General

Type of Institution: public, university. *Environment:* urban.

Total enrollment: 11,000. *Degrees offered:* BA, BM, BME.

Entrance Requirements

Audition required: live, audio, video. *Standardized test requirements:* ACT; TOEFL.

Costs & Financial Aid

Application fee: $15. *Tuition (in-state/out-state):* $1,926/$4,325. *Other fees:* $25 vehicle registration.

Percent of students receiving financial aid: 75%. *Types of scholarships and aid awarded:* full, partial, merit-based, need-based, named, institutional aid, reduced tuition, work/study. *Loans available. Financial aid offered to international students.*

Services

Housing options: on-site dorms, fraternity, sorority.

Support staff: financial aid advisor, foreign student advisor, housing advisor, resident assistant, resident nurse, student affairs officer.

MUSIC

Curriculum, Students, and Faculty

How are major teacher assignments made? students may choose made by the school according to teacher availability. Faculty is informed of a student's teacher preference at the time of the audition. ***28 lessons with major teacher. May a student change major teachers during the course of study?*** possibly. ***Study of secondary instrument or discipline is allowed.***

Selectivity for instruments or programs offered (rating): accompanying (competitive), bassoon (competitive), choral conducting (competitive), choral singing (competitive), clarinet (competitive), composition (open), double bass (competitive), electronic music (competitive), flute or piccolo (competitive), French horn (competitive), guitar (competitive), jazz (competitive), oboe/English horn (competitive), orchestral conducting (open), organ (competitive), percussion (competitive), piano (competitive), saxophone (competitive), trombone (competitive), trumpet (competitive), tuba (open), viola (competitive), violin (competitive), violoncello (competitive), voice (competitive), band conducting (competitive).

Total enrollment: 115. ***Entering class size:*** 25. ***Graduating class size:*** 10. ***Percent international:*** 7%. ***Countries most represented***: People's Republic of China.

Total full-time faculty: 22. ***Total part-time faculty:*** 6. ***Program contact person:*** Dr. Larry W. Edwards.

Audition Information

No audition fee. Audition consists of the following: scales, orchestral excerpts, music theory, rhythmic dictation, arpeggios, sight reading. ***Instruments provided for:*** percussionists.

Performance opportunities available (frequency): jury examinations (2).

Facilities

Number of practice rooms and hours: 18; 65 hours per week. ***Recital hall?*** yes. ***Concert hall?*** yes. ***Recording studio?*** no.

SOUTHEASTERN LOUISIANA UNIVERSITY

Department of Music
SLU 815, Hammond LA 70402
Tel: 504-549-2184
Fax: 504-549-2892

General

Type of Institution: university.

Total student body from other countries: 12%. ***Degrees offered:*** BM, BME.

Entrance Requirements

Audition required: live, audio ***Standardized test requirements:*** ACT; TOEFL, 500.

Costs & Financial Aid

Application fee: $10.

Percent of students receiving financial aid: 70%. ***Types of scholarships and aid awarded:*** full, partial, merit-based, work/study. ***Financial aid offered to international students. Percent of international students receiving scholarships:*** 100%.

Services

Housing options: on-site dorms, fraternity, sorority.

Support staff: career counselor, financial aid advisor, foreign student advisor, housing advisor, resident assistant, student affairs officer.

MUSIC

Curriculum, Students, and Faculty

Unique or innovative music curriculum: Computer Labs, Electronic Music. ***How are major teacher assignments made?*** Students may choose. Faculty is informed of a student's teacher preference at the time of the audition. ***20 lessons with major teacher. May a student change major teachers during the course of study?*** possibly. ***Study of secondary instrument or discipline is allowed.***

Selectivity for instruments or programs offered (rating): bassoon (non-competitive), choral singing (non-competitive), clarinet (non-competitive), composition (non-competitive), double bass (non-competitive), electronic music (non-competitive), flute or piccolo (non-competitive), French horn (non-competitive), guitar (non-competitive), jazz (non-competitive), oboe/English horn (non-competitive), percussion (non-competitive), piano (non-competitive), saxophone (non-competitive), trombone (non-competitive), trumpet (non-competitive), tuba (non-competitive), viola (non-competitive), violin (non-competitive), violoncello (non-competitive), voice (non-competitive).

Total enrollment: 120. *Percent international:* 12%. *Countries most represented*: Moldavia, Honduras, Bulgaria.

Renowned alumni: Bill Evans.

Total full-time faculty: 13. *Total part-time faculty:* 18. *Program contact person:* Dr. David Evenson.

Audition Information

No audition fee.

Performance opportunities available (frequency): recitals.

Facilities

Recital hall? yes. *Concert hall?* yes.

TULANE UNIVERSITY

6823 St. Charles, New Orleans LA 70118-5680
Tel: 504-865-5731
Fax: 504-862-8715

Entrance Requirements

Audition not required.

Services

Support staff: housing advisor, physical therapist, psychological counselor, resident assistant, student affairs officer.

DANCE

Curriculum, Students, and Faculty

Required courses: music, nutrition, dance composition/choreography.

DRAMA

Curriculum, Students, and Faculty

Elective courses: directing, musical theater.

MAINE

BATES COLLEGE

23 Campus Avenue, Lewiston ME 04240-9917
Tel: 207-786-6000
Fax: 207-786-6060

Entrance Requirements:

Audition not required.

Services

Support staff: physical therapist.

DANCE

Curriculum, Students, and Faculty

Elective courses: dance writing, research and criticism.

DRAMA

Curriculum, Students, and Faculty

Required courses: movement, text analysis, verse drama.

BOWDOIN COLLEGE

500 College Station, Brunswick ME 04011
Tel: 207-725-3100
Fax: 207-725-3101
Email: admissions-lit@polar.bowdoin.edu
Web: www.bowdoin.edu

General

Type of Institution: private college. *Environment:* suburban.

Total enrollment: 1,605. *Total student body from other countries:* 3%. *Degrees offered:* BA.

Costs & Financial Aid

Application fee: $55. *Deposit:* $300. *Tuition:* $22,460. *Other fees:* $235 health insurance, $210 student activity fee. *Room and board:* $6,215.

Percent of students receiving financial aid: 38%. *Types of scholarships and aid awarded:* full, partial, need-based, named, institutional aid, government aid, workstudy. *Forms required for scholarships:* FAFSA, income tax return, income asset verification, school's own financial aid form. ***Loans available. Procedure for applying for loans:*** information comes with application. ***Financial aid offered to international students. Percent of international students receiving scholarships:*** 56%.

Services

Housing options: on-site dorms, off-campus housing.

Support staff: career counselor, financial aid advisor, foreign student advisor, housing advisor, physical therapist, psychological counselor, resident assistant, resident nurse, student affairs officer.

DANCE

Curriculum, Students, and Faculty

Elective courses: dance composition or choreography, dance writing, research and criticism, master classes, modern dance, rehearsal and performance.

Selectivity for males: admit all who apply. *Selectivity for females:* admit all who apply. *Total enrollment:* 75.

Renowned alumni: Sharon Hayes, Martha Enson, and Trisha Bauman.

Total full-time faculty: 2. *Total part-time faculty:* 5. *List of current faculty and past affiliations:* June Vail, dance writer for Maine Times; Gwyneth Jones, formerly of David Wagonier and Dancers; Paul Sarvis, formerly of Liz Lehman's Dance Exchange. *Program contact person:* June Vail.

Performance Information

Performance opportunities available (frequency): Fully produced concerts (1 per year), informal concerts (2-4 per year), workshops (1 per year).

Performances choreographed by: faculty, students, guests. *Recent guest choreographers:* Dan Hurlin, Freedman and Coleman.

Facilities

Number of studios available: 1. *Approximate studio dimensions and flooring:* 20' x 60' wood. *Performance facilities:* one studio, one full proscenium stage.

DRAMA

Curriculum, Students, and Faculty

Elective courses: acting, design for the performing arts, directing, performance arts, theater history.

Summer program not available. No affiliation with a professional theater company. Selectivity for males: admit all who apply. *Selectivity for females:* admit all who apply. *Total enrollment:* 83. *Renowned alumni:* Ray Rutan, Louis Frederick.

Total full-time faculty: 2. *Total part-time faculty:* 5. *List of current faculty and past affiliations:* Daniel Kramer, Simone Federman.

Audition Information

Bowdoin does not audition theater students.

Performance Information

Performance opportunities available (frequency): fully produced performances (2 per year), informal performances (4-10 per year), workshops (2-4 per year) casting is assigned, auditioned.

Recent guest artists: Elizabeth Wong, Dan Hurlin, Spaulding Gray, Aquila Theater Company.

Facilities

Rehearsal facilities and hours: one black box theater, one converted classroom, 7:00 am-midnight daily. *Type and capacity:* black box—100, proscenium—600.

MUSIC

Curriculum, Students, and Faculty

Unique or innovative music curriculum: Intergration of history and theory; American music is a requirement for majors. *How are major teacher assignments made?* according to teacher availability. ***28 lessons with major teacher;***

Selectivity for instruments or programs offered (rating): bassoon (open), clarinet (open), composition (open), double bass (open), flute or piccolo (open), French horn (open), guitar (open), harpsichord (open), jazz (open), oboe/English horn (open), organ (open), percussion (open), piano (open), saxophone (open), trombone (open), trumpet (open), tuba (open), viola (open), violin (open), violoncello (open), voice (open).

Total enrollment: 260. *Renowned alumni:* Kurt Ollman, David Sherman. *Total full-time faculty:* 4 *Total part-time faculty:* 3. *Program contact person:* Maty Hunter.

Audition Information

No audition fee.

Performance opportunities available (frequency): jury examinations.

Facilities

Number of practice rooms and hours: 7; 7:00 am-12:00 am. *Recital hall?* yes. *Concert hall?* no. *Recording studio?* no.

GOUCHER COLLEGE

1021 Dulaney Valley Road, Baltimore MD 21204
Tel: 410-337-6000
Fax: 410-337-6123
Email: admission@goucher.edu
Web: www.goucher.edu

General

Type of Institution: private, coed college. *Environment:* suburban.

Total enrollment: 1,085. *Total student body from other countries:* 5%. *Degrees offered:* BA.

Entrance Requirements

Audition not required Other requirements: interview, recommendation, essay. *Standardized test requirements:* ACT; SAT I, 1175.

Costs & Financial Aid

Application fee: $40. *Deposit:* $500. *Tuition:* $18,525. *Medical fee:* $130. *Other fees:* $100 room deposit, $4,600 for 2 semesters. *Room and board:* $6,800.

Types of scholarships and aid awarded: full, partial, merit-based, need-based, named, institutional aid, government aid, work/study. *Forms required for scholarships:* FAFSA, income asset verification, school's own financial aid form. *Loans available. Procedure for applying for loans:* contact Student Administrative Services (410-337-6500), forms must be in by 2/15.

Services

Housing options: on-site dorms.

Support staff: career counselor, financial aid advisor, psychological counselor, resident assistant, resident nurse, student affairs officer.

DANCE

Curriculum, Students, and Faculty

Required courses: ballet (5 classes per week), dance composition/choreography (3 classes per week), dance history (3 classes per week), dance theory (2 classes per week), dance writing, research and criticism (2 classes per week), Labanotation (2 classes per week), modern dance (5 classes per week), music (2 classes per week), rehearsal and performance (6 classes per week), stagecraft (2 classes per week).

Elective courses: anatomy (2 classes per week), historical dance (2 classes per week), jazz (3 classes per week), men's class (2 classes per week), Pilates (3 classes per week), pas de deux (2 classes per week), pointe (4 classes per week).

Selectivity for males: approximately 33% admitted. *Selectivity for females:* approximately 33% admitted. *Total enrollment:* 17. *Graduating class size:* 5.

Renowned alumni: Robin Shavitz, Amy Marshall, Dina Macline.

Total full-time faculty: 4. *Total part-time faculty:* 6. *List of current faculty and past affiliations:* Chrystelle Bond, Juliet Forrest, Elizabeth Ahearn, Amanda Thom Woodson. *Program contact person:* Amanda Woodson.

Audition Information

No audition fee.

Performance Information

Performance opportunities available (frequency): Fully produced concerts (2 per year), informal concerts (4 per year), touring (6 per year).

Performances choreographed by: faculty, students, guests. *Recent guest choreographers:* John Clifford, Ib Anderson, Miriam Madhaviawi, Joe Chuala, Doug Varone, Pat Graney.

Facilities

Number of studios available: 4. *Approximate studio dimensions and flooring:* 70' x 70' Gerstung spring floor, 70' x 60' Gerstung spring floor, 40' x 20' Gerstung spring floor, 20' x 20' Gerstung sprung floor. *Performance facilities:* auditorium (998), informal studio/theater space.

DRAMA

Curriculum, Students, and Faculty

Required courses: acting, drama criticism, dramaturgy.

Elective courses: directing, movement, speech, voice.

Number of years required to complete program: 4. *Summer program not available. Affiliation with a professional theater company: Action Theatre Residency.*

Selectivity for males: admit all who apply. *Selectivity for females:* admit all who apply. *Total enrollment:* 10. *Graduating class size:* 8.

Renowned alumni: Mildred Dunnock.

Total full-time faculty: 2. *Total part-time faculty:* 2.

Audition Information

Audition consists of the following: Open auditions required for productions, but no auditions are required for entry into the program.

Performance Information

Performance opportunities available (frequency): fully produced performances (2-6 per year), informal performances (4-10 per year), workshops (2-3 per year), auditioned.

Recent guest artists: Action Theatre Residency, Theatre of Yuger.

Facilities

Rehearsal facilities and hours: black box theater, confrence rooms. *Number of theaters on campus:* 3. *Type and capacity:* black box—150, 998, 405.

MUSIC

Curriculum, Students, and Faculty

Unique or innovative music curriculum: advanced computer music studio, African drum and dance ensemble. *How are major teacher assignments made?* Students may choose according to teacher availability. *28 lessons with major teacher. May a student change major teachers during the course of study?* possibly.

Selectivity for instruments or programs offered (rating): accompanying (open), accordion (open), bagpipes (open), bassoon (open), choral conducting (open), choral singing (open), clarinet (open), composition (open), double bass (open), electronic music (open), flute or piccolo (open), French horn (open), guitar (open), harp (open), harpsichord (open), jazz (open), oboe/English horn (open), orchestral conducting (open), organ (open), piano (open), sacred music (open), saxophone (open), trombone (open), trumpet (open), tuba (open), viola (open), violin (open), violoncello (open), voice (open).

Total enrollment: 8. *Graduating class size:* 6.

Total full-time faculty: 3. *Total part-time faculty:* 9. *Program contact person:* Fred Mauk.

Audition Information

No audition fee.

Facilities

Recital hall? yes. *Concert hall?* yes. *Recording studio?* no.

PEABODY CONSERVATORY

1 East Mount Vernon Place, Baltimore MD 21202
Tel: 410-659-8110
Fax: 410-659-8102

General

Type of Institution: conservatory. *Environment:* urban.

Total student body from other countries: 24%. *Degrees offered:* BM.

Entrance Requirements

Audition required: live, audio, video, regional. *Other requirements:* essay.

Costs & Financial Aid

Application fee: $50. *Tuition:* $21,700. *Other fees:* $500.

Types of scholarships and aid awarded: full, partial, merit-based, need-based, work/study, gig office. *Forms required for scholarships:* FAFSA, income tax return. *Loans available.*

Services

Housing options: on-site dorms, off-campus housing.

Support staff: career counselor, financial aid advisor, foreign student advisor, housing advisor, psychological counselor, resident assistant, resident nurse, student affairs officer.

MUSIC

Curriculum, Students, and Faculty

How are major teacher assignments made? students may choose, according to teacher availability.

Total enrollment: 375. *Percent international:* 24%. *Countries most represented*: Korea, Japan.

Renowned alumni: Dominick Argento, James Morris, Andre Watts.

Total full-time faculty: 76. *Total part-time faculty:* 77. *Program contact person:* David Lane.

Audition Information

Audition consists of the following: orchestral excerpts, repertoire. *Instruments provided for:* harpists, percussionists, pianists, organists.

Repertoire that students should avoid? no jazz, popular music, or musical theater.

Facilities

Recital hall? yes. *Concert hall?* yes. *Recording studio?* yes.

TOWSON STATE UNIVERSITY

Towson MD 21204-7097
Tel: 410-830-2112

General

Type of Institution: public, university. *Environment:* suburban. *Cross registration is available through the Exchange Program with Leningrad State Conservatory.*

Total enrollment: 10,000. *Total student body from other countries:* 5%. *Degrees offered:* BFA, BM.

Entrance Requirements

Audition required: live, audio, video. *Other requirements:* recommendation, essay. *Standardized test requirements:* ACT; SAT I; TOEFL.

Costs & Financial Aid

Tuition (in-state/out-state): $5,122/$7,624.

Types of scholarships and aid awarded: work/study, gig office. *Forms required for scholarships:* FAFSA, income tax return. *Loans available.*

Services

Housing options: on-site dorms, off-campus housing.

Support staff: financial aid advisor, foreign student advisor, housing advisor, psychological counselor, resident assistant, resident nurse, student affairs officer.

Curriculum, Students, and Faculty

Total enrollment: 60.

Renowned alumni: Mino Nicholas.

Total full-time faculty: 5. *Total part-time faculty:* 4. *Contact:* (410)-830-2760.

Facilities

Number of studios available: 2. *Approximate studio dimensions and flooring:* sprung flooring.

DRAMA

Curriculum, Students, and Faculty

Number of years required to complete program: 4.

Total full-time faculty: 10. *Total part-time faculty:* 6.

Audition Information

Audition consists of the following: comedic monologue.

Facilities

Number of theaters on campus: 1.

MUSIC

Curriculum, Students, and Faculty

Total enrollment: 255.

Renowned alumni: Spiro Malas.

Total full-time faculty: 27. *Contact:* 410-830-2143.

Audition Information

Audition consists of the following: orchestral excerpts, repertoire.

Facilities

Recital hall? yes. *Concert hall?* yes. *Recording studio?* yes.

UNIVERSITY OF MARYLAND

2114 Tawes Fine Arts Building, College Park MD 20742
Tel: 301-405-5549
Fax: 301-314-9504
Email: knicely@deans.umd.edu
Web: www.umd.edu
Contact: Kathleen Nicely

General

Type of Institution: public university. *Environment:* suburban. *Academic education is offered on-site.*

Total enrollment: 33,000. *Degrees offered:* BA, BFA, BM.

Entrance Requirements

Audition required: live, video. *Other requirements:* interview, recommendation, essay. *Standardized test requirements:* SAT I; TOEFL, 575.

Costs & Financial Aid

Application fee: $45. *Deposit:* $100. *Tuition (in-state/out-state)*: $4,460/$10,589. *Other fees:* $200 per semester applied music fee. *Room and board:* $5,807.

Percent of students receiving financial aid: 25%. *Types of scholarships and aid awarded:* full, partial, merit-based, need-based, named, institutional aid, government aid, reduced tuition, tuition payment plan, work/study. *Forms required for scholarships:* FAFSA, income tax return, income asset verification. *Loans available. Procedure for applying for loans:* contact the Financial Aid Department (301-314-9000). *Financial aid offered to international students.*

Services

Housing options: on-site dorms, off-campus housing, fraternity, sorority.

Support staff: career counselor, financial aid advisor, foreign student advisor, housing advisor, physical therapist, psychological counselor, resident assistant, resident nurse, student affairs officer.

Comments

The School of Music, Department of Dance, and Department of Theater will be moving into the $107 million Maryland Center of the Performing Arts in 1999. This new center will have six performance spaces and will be an exciting village for the performing arts.

DANCE

Curriculum, Students, and Faculty

Required courses: anatomy, ballet, dance composition/choreography, dance history, dance theory, dance writing, research and criticism, Cunningham-based, Limon-based, Laban Movement Studies, music, rehearsal and performance, stagecraft.

Elective courses: African dance, jazz, Labanotation, master classes, repertory, Spanish, tap.

Countries most represented: India, China, Korea, Taiwan, countries of the former USSR. *Program contact person:* Alane Wiltz.

Audition Information

No audition fee. Audition consists of the following: improvisation, modern dance, prepared solo; audition required only for scholarship. *Accompanist provided. Cassette player available; CD player available. Dress requirements for males:* fitted attire. *Dress requirements for females:* fitted attire.

Performance Information

Performance opportunities available (frequency): Fully produced concerts (5 per semester), informal concerts (2 per semester), workshops (2-3 per semester), on-site performances(1 per semester), touring (rarely).

Performances choreographed by: faculty, students, guests. *Recent guest choreographers:* Garth Fagan, Don Redlich, Christalyn Wright, and Mark Dandy.

DRAMA

Curriculum, Students, and Faculty

Required courses: acting, directing, speech, verse drama, voice.

Elective courses: drama criticism, dramaturgy, make-up, movement, musical theater, scene study.

Number of years required to complete program: 4. *Summer program not available. Selectivity for males:* admit all who apply. *Selectivity for females:* admit all who apply. *Countries most represented*: India, China, Korea, Taiwan, countries of the former USSR.

Performance Information

Performance opportunities available (frequency): fully produced performances (5 per year), informal performances (10-15 per year), auditioned.

Facilities

Rehearsal facilities and hours: 2 classrooms, 24 hours. *Number of theaters on campus:* 3. *Type and capacity:* proscenium—1,300, thrust—100, experimental, black box—60.

MUSIC

Curriculum, Students, and Faculty

How are major teacher assignments made? students may choose, made by the school according to teacher preference and teacher availability. Faculty is informed of a student's teacher preference at the time of the audition. *May a student change major teachers during the course of study?* possibly. *Study of secondary instrument or discipline is allowed.*

Selectivity for instruments or programs offered (rating): accompanying (selective), bassoon (competitive), choral conducting (highly selective), choral singing (competitive), clarinet (selective), composition (selective), double bass (competitive), electronic music (selective), flute or piccolo (highly selective), French horn (selective), harp (selective), jazz (selective), oboe/English horn (competitive), orchestral conducting (highly selective), percussion (selective), piano (highly selective), saxophone (selective), trombone (selective), trumpet (selective), tuba (selective), viola (competitive), violin (selective), violoncello (selective), voice (highly selective).

Total enrollment: 200. *Entering class size:* 60. *Graduating class size:* 50. *Countries most represented:* India, China, Korea, Taiwan, countries of the former USSR.

Renowned alumni: Gordon Hawkins, Cedric Dent, Peter Bay, Carmen Balthrop. *Program contact person:* Kathleen Nicely.

Audition Information

Audition consists of the following: orchestral excerpts, music theory, rhythmic dictation, sight reading, music history, melodic dictation. *Instruments provided for:* harpists, percussionists, pianists, organists.

Repertoire that students should avoid? no show tunes. *Performance opportunities available (frequency):* band, band, jury examinations (1 per semester), opera workshops, orchestral concerts, recitals, produced operas, chorus.

Facilities

Number of practice rooms and hours: 50; 24 hours a day (seven days a week). *Recital hall?* yes. *Concert hall?* yes. *Recording studio?* yes.

MASSACHUSETTS

AMHERST COLLEGE

P.O. Box 5000, Amherst MA 01002-500
Tel: 413-542-2328
Fax: 413-542-2040
Email: admissions@amherst.edu
Web: www.amherst.edu
Contact: Will Dix

General

Type of Institution: private college. *Environment:* suburban.

Total enrollment: 1,642. *Total student body from other countries:* 4%. *Degrees offered:* BA.

Entrance Requirements

Audition not required Other requirements: recommendation, essay. *Standardized test requirements:* ACT; SAT I; SAT II; TOEFL, 600.

Costs & Financial Aid

Application fee: $55. *Deposit:* $400. *Tuition:* $22,680.

Percent of students receiving financial aid: 44%. *Types of scholarships and aid awarded:* need-based. *Forms required for scholarships:* FAFSA, income tax return, CSS Profile, school's own finacial aid form. *Loans available. Financial aid offered to international students.*

Services

Housing options: on-site dorms.

Support staff: career counselor, financial aid advisor, foreign student advisor, housing advisor, psychological counselor, resident assistant, student affairs officer.

Comments

Our focus is upon personal attention for the individual student and for creating an environment in which performance, creativity, and intellectual pursuits interact and flourish.

DANCE

Curriculum, Students, and Faculty

Required courses: dance composition/choreography, dance history, dance theory, dance writing, research and criticism, rehearsal and performance.

Elective courses: African dance, Alexander Technique, anatomy, ballet, improvisation, jazz, Labanotation, martial arts, master classes, movement techniques, Feldenkreis, Laban Movement Studies, music, nutrition, other world dance forms, pointe, repertory, Spanish, stagecraft, tap.

DRAMA

Curriculum, Students, and Faculty

Required courses: acting, directing, movement.

Elective courses: mime, text analysis.

MUSIC

Curriculum, Students, and Faculty

Unique or innovative music curriculum: mixture of pop, classical, jazz, rock, and world music in our curriculum. We give credit for performance study in all styles of music. *How are major teacher assignments made?* students may choose; made by the school according to teacher preference and to teacher availability. Faculty is informed of a student's teacher preference at the time of the audition. *14 lessons with major teacher. May a student change major teachers during the course of study?* possibly. *Study of secondary instrument or discipline is allowed.*

Selectivity for instruments or programs offered (rating): bassoon (highly selective), choral conducting (highly selective), choral singing (highly selective), clarinet (highly selective), composition (highly selective), double bass (highly selective), electronic music (highly selective), flute or piccolo (highly selective), French horn (highly selective), guitar (highly selective), harp (highly selective), harpsichord (highly selective), jazz (highly selective), oboe/English horn (highly selective), orchestral conducting (highly selective), organ (highly selective), percussion (highly selective), piano (highly selective), saxophone (highly selective), trombone (highly selective), trumpet (highly selective), tuba (highly selective), viola (highly selective), violin (highly selective), violoncello (highly selective), voice (highly selective).

Graduating class size: 9.

Renowned alumni: Philip Gosset, Theodore Levine.

Total full-time faculty: 6. *Program contact person:* Prof. Reck.

Audition Information

No audition fee. Instruments provided for: percussionists; Instruments for study of South India's classical music: Javanese gamelan.

Repertoire that students should avoid? no.

Facilities

Number of practice rooms and hours: 14; 7:00 am-1:00 am. *Recital hall?* yes. *Concert hall?* yes. *Recording studio?* yes.

ANNA MARIA COLLEGE

50 Sunset Lane, Paxton MA 01612
Tel: 508-849-3450
Fax: 508-849-3334
Email: rgreene@anna-maria.edu
Web: www.anna-maria.edu
Contact: Christine Soverow

General

Type of Institution: college.

Total enrollment: 1,200. *Degrees offered:* BA, BM.

Entrance Requirements

Audition required: live, audio, video. *Other requirements:* interview, recommendation, essay. *Standardized test requirements:* SAT I; TOEFL.

Costs & Financial Aid

Application fee: $35. *Deposit:* $200. *Tuition:* $11,230.

Percent of students receiving financial aid: 85%. *Types of scholarships and aid awarded:* partial, merit-based, need-based, institutional aid, tuition payment plan, work/study. *Loans available. Financial aid offered to international students.*

Services

Housing options: on-site dorms.

MUSIC

Curriculum, Students, and Faculty

Unique or innovative music curriculum: large music therapy program; one of only two in New England. *How are major teacher assignments made?* made by the school according to teacher availability. Faculty is not informed of a student's teacher preference at the time of the audition. *28 lessons with major teacher. May a student change major teachers during the course of study?* possibly. *Study of secondary instrument or discipline is allowed.*

Selectivity for instruments or programs offered (rating): bassoon (competitive), clarinet (competitive), double bass (competitive), flute or piccolo (competitive), French horn (competitive), guitar (competitive), harp (competitive), harpsichord (competitive), oboe/English horn (competitive), percussion (competitive), piano (competitive), saxophone (competitive), trombone (competitive), trumpet (competitive), tuba (competitive), viola (competitive), violin (competitive), violoncello (competitive), voice (competitive).

Total enrollment: 80. *Entering class size:* 30. *Graduating class size:* 15.

Total full-time faculty: 5. *Total part-time faculty:* 12. *Program contact person:* Roger W. Greene.

Audition Information

No audition fee. Audition consists of the following: scales, rhythmic dictation, melodic dictation. *Instruments provided for:* percussionists.

Repertoire that students should avoid? must be classical piece, not pop, jazz. *Performance opportunities available (frequency):* band (frequently), jury examinations, chorus.

Facilities

Number of practice rooms and hours: 12. *Recital hall?* yes. *Concert hall?* yes. *Recording studio?* no.

BERKLEE COLLEGE OF MUSIC

1140 Boylston Street, Boston MA 02215
Tel: 617-266-1400
Fax: 617-747-2047
Web: www.berklee.edu

General

Type of Institution: college. *Environment:* urban.

Total enrollment: 2,933. ***Total student body from other countries:*** 39%. ***Degrees offered:*** BM.

Entrance Requirements

Audition required. Other requirements: recommendation, essay. ***Standardized test requirements:*** ACT; SAT I; TOEFL. School's own English exam required.

Costs & Financial Aid

Application fee: $65. ***Deposit:*** $250. ***Tuition:*** $14,950. ***Medical fee:*** $535. ***Other fees:*** $75 registration and accident insurance, optional medical fee.

Percent of students receiving financial aid: 60%. ***Types of scholarships and aid awarded:*** full, partial, merit-based, need-based, named, institutional aid, government aid, tuition payment plan, work/study, gig office. ***Financial aid offered to international students. Percent of international students receiving scholarships:*** 44%. ***Other aid available to international students:*** Merit-based, scholarships via tape or live audition.

Services

Housing options: on-site dorms.

Support staff: career counselor, financial aid advisor, foreign student advisor, housing advisor, resident assistant, student affairs officer.

THE BOSTON CONSERVATORY

8 The Fenway, Boston MA 02215
Tel: 617-536-6340
Fax: 617-536-3176
Email: admissions@bostonconservatory.edu
Web: www.bostonconservatory.edu
Contact: Richard Wallace

General

Type of Institution: college, conservatory. ***Environment:*** urban. ***Cross registration is available through the Pro Arts Consortium, Berklee College of Music, Emerson College, Massachusetts College of Art, Boston Architectural Center, School of the Museum of Fine Arts.***

Total enrollment: 500. ***Total student body from other countries:*** 28%. ***Degrees offered:*** certificate, BFA, BM.

Entrance Requirements

Audition required: live, audio, video. ***Other requirements:*** recommendation, essay. ***Standardized test requirements:*** ACT, 24; SAT I, 1050.

Costs & Financial Aid

Application fee: $60. ***Deposit:*** $500. ***Tuition:*** $15,300. ***Medical fee:*** $95.

Percent of students receiving financial aid: 82%. ***Types of scholarships and aid awarded:*** full, partial, merit-based, need-based, institutional aid, government aid, reduced tuition, tuition payment plan, work/study, gig office. ***Forms required for scholarships:*** FAFSA, school's own financial aid form. ***Loans available. Procedure for applying for loans:*** contact Financial Aid Office ***Financial aid offered to international students. Percent of international students receiving scholarships:*** 69%. ***Other aid available to international students:*** Conservatory employment. Student Loans.

Services

Housing options: on-site dorms, off-campus housing.

Support staff: financial aid advisor, foreign student advisor, housing advisor, resident assistant, student affairs officer.

DANCE

Curriculum, Students, and Faculty

Required courses: anatomy, ballet (5 classes per week, 4 years to complete), dance composition/choreography, dance history, Labanotation, master classes, men's class (2 classes per week, 4 years to complete), modern dance (5 classes per week, 4 years to complete), movement techniques, music, pointe (4 classes per week, 4 years to complete), rehearsal and performance, repertory (1 class per week, 4 years to complete), stagecraft.

Elective courses: jazz (4 classes per week, 4 years to complete), nutrition, pas de deux (1 class per week, 4 years to complete), tap (4 classes per week, 4 years to complete), variations (4 classes per week, 4 years to complete), Flamenco (4 classes per week, 4 years to complete).

Selectivity for males: approximately 60% admitted. *Selectivity for females:* approximately 60% admitted. *Entering class size:* 26. *Graduating class size:* 15. *Percent International:* 15%. *Countries most represented:* Japan.

Renowned alumni: Andrew Lebeau, Josie Coyoc, Jack Noseworthy, Tommy Walch, Tina Paul. *List of current faculty and past affiliations:* Omara Amaya, Ruth Sandholm Ambrose, Diane Arvanites-Noya. *Program contact person:* Richard Wallace.

Audition Information

No audition fee. Audition consists of the following: ballet, modern dance, prepared solo. *Accompanist provided. Cassette player available; CD player not available. Dress requirements for males:* black or white t-shirt, black or grey tights, black ballet slippers. *Dress requirements for females:* black or colored leotard, pink tights, pink ballet slippers.

Audition evaluation criteria: suitable body for dance. Ballet: barre work, adagio, turns, petit allegro, grand allegro, port de bras; Modern: dynamics, use of weight, use of space, falls, level changes, transitions, alignment, facility, musicality, potential, attitude, performance quality.

Performance Information

Performance opportunities available (frequency): Fully produced concerts (5 per year), informal concerts (1 per year), workshops (1 per year), on-site performances (3 per year), touring (15 per year).

Performances choreographed by: faculty, students, guests. *Recent guest choreographers:* Monica Levy, Sean Curran, Spencer Cotton, Lance Westgard, Kathryn Posin, Karla Wolfangle.

Facilities

Number of studios available: 7. *Approximate studio dimensions and flooring:* 30' x 40' sprung floor with Marley covering. *Performance facilities:* full theater.

DRAMA

Curriculum, Students, and Faculty

Required courses: acting, audition preparation, directing, drama criticism, improvisation, make-up, movement, musical theater, scene study, Stanislavski exercises, text analysis, verse drama, voice.

Number of years required to complete program: 4. *Summer program not available. No affiliation with a professional theater company. Selectivity for males:* approximately 33% admitted. *Selectivity for females:* approximately 33% admitted. *Total enrollment:* 170. *Entering class size:* 64. *Graduating class size:* 32. *Percent International:* 7%. *Countries most represented:* Canada.

Renowned alumni: Jack Noseworthy, Cloe Webb, Peter Reckel.

Total full-time faculty: 11. *Total part-time faculty:* 5. *List of current faculty and past affiliations:* Michael Allosso, Chiswick Park Theatre, Sudbury, Chatham Repertory Theatre; Erika Batdorf, Brandeis University, University of Alaska; Robert J. Bouffier, University of Dayton, Boston College; Jane Baldwin.

Audition Information

No audition fee. Audition consists of the following: a cappella singing, comedic monologue, Shakespearean monologue, group warm-up. *Repertoire that students should avoid?* monologue book excerpts.

Audition evaluation criteria: integrity, commitment to choices, relationship, adjustments, throughline/progression, physicality.

Performance Information

Performance opportunities available (frequency): fully produced performances (3 per year), informal performances (14 per year), workshops (occasionally), off-site performances (1 per year), casting by audition.

Recent guest artists: Eddie Korbich, Maryanne Plunkett, Sally Mayes, Joan Morris, Maureen Brennan.

Facilities

Number of theaters on campus: 2. *Type and capacity:* proscenium—400, flexible—75.

MUSIC

Curriculum, Students, and Faculty

How are major teacher assignments made? students may choose, made by the school according to teacher preference and teacher availability. Faculty is not informed of a student's teacher preference at the time of the audition. *May a student change major teachers during the course of study?* possibly. *Study of secondary instrument or discipline is allowed.*

Selectivity for instruments or programs offered (rating): bassoon (competitive), choral conducting (competitive), clarinet (competitive), composition (selective), double bass (competitive), flute or piccolo (selective), French horn (selective), guitar (competitive), harp (competitive), harpsichord (competitive), jazz (competitive), oboe/English horn (competitive), organ (competitive), percussion (competitive), piano (selective), saxophone (competitive), trombone (competitive), trumpet (competitive), tuba (competitive), viola (competitive), violin (competitive), violoncello (competitive), voice (competitive).

Total enrollment: 250. *Entering class size:* 117. *Graduating class size:* 87. *Percent International:* 43%. *Countries most represented:* Korea.

Renowned alumni: Kathy Lame, Victoria Livengood, Robert Laws, Sondra Kelly, Albert Tiu. *Program contact person:* Richard Wallace.

Audition Information

No audition fee. Audition consists of the following: repertoire. *Instruments provided for:* harpists, percussionists, pianists, organists.

Required repertoire: varies by instrument. Please call school for repertoire information.

Facilities

Recital hall? yes. *Concert hall?* yes. *Recording studio?* no.

BOSTON UNIVERSITY

School of the Arts
855 Commonwealth Avenue, Boston MA 02215
Tel: 617-353-3350
Fax: 617-353-5331
Email: arts@bu.edu
Web: www.bu.edu/SFA
Contact: Jen Lundgren-Gilliman

General

Type of Institution: private university; conservatory. *Environment:* urban.

Total enrollment: 15,414. *Degrees offered:* certificate, BFA, BM, degree is offered in music administration, artist diploma.

Entrance Requirements

Audition required: live, audio, video. *Other requirements:* recommendation, essay, photograph. *Standardized test requirements:* ACT; SAT I.

Costs & Financial Aid

Application fee: $50. *Deposit:* $400. *Tuition:* $21,970. *Medical fee:* $540. *Other fees:* $308 undergraduate student fee. *Room and board:* $7,750.

Types of scholarships and aid awarded: full, partial, merit-based, need-based, named, institutional aid, tuition payment plan, work/study. *Forms required for scholarships:* FAFSA, income tax return, income asset verification, CSS Profile. *Loans available. Procedure for applying for loans:* complete the CSS profile and the FAFSA on the admissions application, check "yes" on the financial aid question, send Boston University recommended supporting documents. *Financial aid offered to international students. Percent of international students receiving scholarships:* 50%.

Services

Housing options: on-site dorms, off-campus housing.

Support staff: career counselor, financial aid advisor, foreign student advisor, housing advisor, physical therapist, psychological counselor, resident assistant, resident nurse, student affairs officer.

DANCE

Curriculum, Students, and Faculty

Elective courses: African dance, ballet (2-3 classes per week, 4 years to complete), dance composition/choreography, jazz, modern dance other, rehearsal and performance, repertory, tap, vernacular dance.

Selectivity for males: admit all who apply. *Selectivity for females:* admit all who apply. *Percent international:* 33%. *List of current faculty and past affiliations:* Ann Brown Allen, Danny Sloan Dance Company; Margot Parsons, Yoriko, Pearl Lang; Micki Taylor-Pinney, Dance Collective; Helen Costa *Program contact person:* Micki Taylor Pinney, 617-353-2748.

Audition Information

Audition consists of the following: ballet, improvisation, modern dance, teaching a short phrase to others. *Accompanist provided. Cassette player available; CD player available. Dress requirements for males:* leotard, tights. *Dress requirements for females:* leotard, tights.

Audition evaluation criteria: articulate verbal communication, strong technical base, creative, intelligent.

Performance Information

Performance opportunities available (frequency): Fully produced concerts (2 per year), informal concerts (3 per year), workshops (2 per year), on-site performances(occasionally).

Performances choreographed by: faculty, students, guests. *Recent guest choreographers:* Sean Curran, Simone Forti, Michael Foley

Facilities

Number of studios available: 3. *Approximate studio dimensions and flooring:* 75' x 35' sprung wood floor, 30' x 50' sprung wood. *Performance facilities:* studio theater, proscenium theater.

DRAMA

Curriculum, Students, and Faculty

Required courses: acting, audition preparation, drama criticism, improvisation, martial arts, movement, scene study, speech, stage combat, Stanislavski exercises, text analysis, verse drama, voice.

Elective courses: Alexander technique, directing, dramaturgy, musical theater.

Number of years required to complete program: 4. *Summer program available. Affiliation with a professional theater company: The Huntington Theater Company has been the professional theater in residence since 1982. This relationship provides theater arts students with an exceptional range of participation in professional work. During an average season, approximately 25 advanced acting, directing, design, and technical production students serve on professional productions.*

Selectivity for males: approximately 10% admitted. *Selectivity for females:* approximately 10% admitted. *Total enrollment:* 250. *Entering class size:* 78. *Graduating class size:* 33. *Percent international:* 9%.

Renowned alumni: Jason Alexander, Olympia Dukakis, Faye Dunaway, Julianne Moore, Geena Davis.

Total full-time faculty: 16. *Total part-time faculty:* 4. *List of current faculty and past affiliations:* Peter Altman, Jacques Cartier, Claudia Catania, Ben Emerson, Caroline Errington, Sidney Friedman, Karin Hartman, Caroline Eves, Jonathan Lipsky, Roger Meeker, Robert Morgan, Sharon Perlmutter, Nina Pleasance, Patricia Quinlan, Davis Robinson, Tom Sturgo, Elaine Van Hogue, Mariann Verheyan, Denise Wallace, Robert Walsh.

Audition Information

No audition fee. Audition consists of the following: Shakespearean monologue, contemporary. *Audition evaluation criteria:* applicants aptitude for theatre and commitment to professional training.

Performance Information

Performance opportunities available (frequency): fully produced performances (5 per season), informal performances (40-50 per season), workshops (40-50 per season) assigned.

Recent guest artists: William Hurt, Campbell Scott, Caroline Eves, Ralph Finicello, Pat McCorkie.

Facilities

Rehearsal facilities and hours: Rehearsal facilities are available at the School for the Arts and Boston University Theater. The Boston University Theater is available 7:00 am-11:00 pm daily. There is a wide variety of theaters on campus.

MUSIC

Curriculum, Students, and Faculty

Unique or innovative music curriculum: professional training in a major university with curricular options including dual degrees and double majors. *How are major teacher assignments made?* students may choose, made by the school, according to teacher preference and teacher availability. Faculty is informed of a student's teacher preference at the time of the audition. *28 lessons with major teacher. May a student change major teachers during the course of study?* possibly. *Study of secondary instrument or discipline is allowed.*

Selectivity for instruments or programs offered (rating): accompanying (highly selective), bassoon (selective), choral conducting (highly selective), clarinet (selective), composition (highly selective), double bass (highly selective), flute or piccolo (highly selective), French horn (highly selective), harp (highly selective), oboe/English horn (selective), orchestral conducting (highly selective), organ (selective), percussion (selective), piano (highly selective), saxophone (selective), trombone (selective), trumpet (highly selective), tuba (selective), viola (highly selective), violin (highly selective), violoncello (highly selective), voice (highly selective).

Total enrollment: 500. *Entering class size:* 83. *Graduating class size:* 44. *Percent international:* 38%.

Renowned alumni: Grace Bumbry, Jamie Rogers, Dominque LaBelle, Sanford Sylvan, Anthony Tommasini.

Total full-time faculty: 37. *Total part-time faculty:* 64. *Program contact person:* Halley Shefler, 617-353-3341.

Audition Information

No audition fee. Audition consists of the following: scales, orchestral excerpts, arpeggios, sight reading. *Instruments provided for:* percussionists, pianists, organists.

Repertoire that students should avoid? popular music. *Performance opportunities available (frequency):* jury examinations, orchestral concerts (frequently), recitals (frequently), chorus.

Facilities

Number of practice rooms and hours: 100; 7:00 am-11:00 pm. *Recital hall?* yes. *Concert hall?* yes. *Recording studio?* yes.

EMERSON COLLEGE

100 Beacon Street, Boston MA 02116-1596
Tel: 617-824-8600
Fax: 617-824-8609
Email: admission@emerson.edu
Web: www.emerson.edu/admiss

General

Type of Institution: private college. *Environment:* urban.

Total enrollment: 2,300. *Total student body from other countries:* 15%. *Degrees offered:* BA, BFA.

Entrance Requirements

Audition required. Other requirements: recommendation, essay. *Standardized test requirements:* ACT, 24; SAT I, 1150; TOEFL.

Costs & Financial Aid

Application fee: $45. *Deposit:* $500. *Tuition:* $17,376. *Medical fee:* $210. *Other fees:* $152 student government fee, $24 activity, $70 orientation fee.

Percent of students receiving financial aid: 75%. *Types of scholarships and aid awarded:* partial, merit-based, need-based, named, institutional aid, government aid, tuition payment plan, work/study. *Forms required for scholarships:* FAFSA, income tax return, CSS Profile, school's own financial aid form. *Loans available. Procedure for applying for loans:* completion of all of the above forms and any other requested documentation. *Other aid available to international students:* administrative assistantships.

Services

Housing options: on-site dorms, off-campus housing.

Support staff: career counselor, foreign student advisor, psychological counselor, resident assistant, resident nurse, student affairs officer.

DRAMA

Curriculum, Students, and Faculty

Required courses: acting, dramaturgy, improvisation, movement, musical theater, scene study, speech, Stanislavski exercises, text analysis, voice.

Elective courses: audition preparation, directing, make-up, stage combat.

HAMPSHIRE COLLEGE

Admissions Office
893 West Street, Amherst MA 01002
Tel: 413-559-5471
Fax: 413-559-5631
Email: admissions@hampshire.edu
Web: www.hampshire.edu

Entrance Requirements

Audition not required.

Costs & Financial Aid

Tuition and fees: $24,780. *Room and board:* $6,525.

DRAMA

Curriculum, Students, and Faculty

Required courses: speech, Alexander technique, scene study, Stanislavski exercises, improvisation, audition preparation.

HARVARD AND RADCLIFFE COLLEGES

Byerly Hall
8 Garden Street, Cambridge MA 02138
Tel: 617-495-1551
Fax: 617-495-8821
Web: www.harvard.edu
Contact: Director of Admissions

General

Type of Institution: private university. *Environment:* urban.

Total enrollment: 6,400. *Total student body from other countries:* 10%. *Degrees offered:* BA.

Entrance Requirements

Other requirements: interview, recommendation, essay. *Standardized test requirements:* ACT; SAT I; SAT II.

Costs & Financial Aid

Application fee: $60. *Tuition:* $23,618. *Other fees:* $2,118 medical, books, etc. *Room and board:* $6,810.

Percent of students receiving financial aid: 70%. *Types of scholarships and aid awarded:* need-based, work/study. *Forms required for scholarships:* FAFSA, income tax return, CSS Profile, school's own financial aid form. ***Loans available. Procedure for applying for loans:*** fill out forms, need-based aid. ***Financial aid offered to international students.***

Services

Housing options: on-site dorms, off-campus housing.

Support staff: career counselor, financial aid advisor, foreign student advisor, housing advisor, psychological counselor, resident assistant, resident nurse, student affairs officer.

Comments

All dance and almost all drama courses are offered as extracurricular programs. Please request brochure which details classes. The music department is within a liberal arts curriculum. Renowned alumni include Leonard Bernstein and Yo-Yo Ma.

LONGY SCHOOL OF MUSIC

One Follen Street, Cambridge MA 02138
Tel: 617-876-0956
Fax: 617-876-9326
Email: music@longy.edu
Web: www.longy.edu

General

Type of Institution: conservatory. *Environment:* urban.

Total enrollment: 130. *Total student body from other countries:* 57%. *Degrees offered:* diploma.

Entrance Requirements

Audition required: live, audio, video. *Other requirements:* interview, recommendation, essay. *Standardized test requirements:* TOEFL, 550.

Costs & Aid

Application fee: $75. *Deposit:* $300. *Tuition:* $11,500. *Other fees:* $200 activity, registration, practice room.

Percent of students receiving financial aid: 70%. *Types of scholarships and aid awarded:* full, partial, merit-based, need-based, named, institutional aid, government aid, work/study, gig office. *Forms required for scholarships:* FFS, FAFSA, income tax return, school's own financial aid form. ***Loans available. Financial aid offered to international students.*** *Percent of international students receiving scholarships:* 70%.

Services

Housing options: on-site dorms, off-campus housing.

Support staff: financial aid advisor, foreign student advisor, student affairs officer.

Comments

Longy is a small, selective conservatory of music in the European-American tradition, with a strong emphasis on overall musicianship as well as technical accomplishment. The school's strong emphasis on chamber music, piano accompanying, Dalcroze Eurhythmics, and early music complement its traditional strengths in string, wind, voice, piano, and opera performance.

MUSIC

Curriculum, Students, and Faculty

Unique or innovative music curriculum: French solfege system and Dalcroze Eurhythmics are central to our undergraduate program. *How are major teacher assignments made?* Students may choose, made by the school, according to teacher availability. Faculty is informed of a student's teacher preference at the time of the audition. ***30 lessons with major teacher. May a student change major teachers during the course of study?*** possibly. ***Study of secondary instrument or discipline is allowed.***

Selectivity for instruments or programs offered (rating): accompanying (selective), bassoon (selective), clarinet (selective), composition (competitive), double bass (selective), flute or piccolo (selective), French horn (competitive), guitar (competitive), harpsichord (highly selective), jazz (competitive), oboe/English horn (selective), orchestral conducting (selective), organ (selective), percussion (selective), piano (selective), saxophone (selective), trombone (competitive), trumpet (competitive), viola (highly selective), violin (highly selective), violoncello (highly selective), voice (selective).

Total enrollment: 130. *Entering class size:* 50. *Graduating class size:* 30. *Percent International:* 57%. *Countries most represented:* Japan, Russia, Israel.

Renowned alumni: Elliot Carter, Eunice Alberts, Schuyler Chapin.

Total full-time faculty: 3. *Total part-time faculty:* 120. *Program contact person:* Kurt Piemonte.

Audition Information

No audition fee. Audition consists of the following: orchestral excerpts, repertoire. *Instruments provided for:* percussionists.

Performance opportunities available (frequency): chamber music (2 years), band (every semester), jury examinations (every year), orchestral concerts (every semester), recitals (1), chorus (1 year).

Facilities

Number of practice rooms and hours: 25; 7:30 am-11:00 pm. *Recital hall?* yes. *Concert hall?* yes. *Recording studio?* yes.

NEW ENGLAND CONSERVATORY

290 Huntington Avenue, Boston MA 02115
Tel: 617-262-1120
Fax: 617-262-0500
Web: copernicus.bbn.com/nec
Contact: Allison Ball

General

Type of Institution: conservatory. *Environment:* urban. *Cross registration is available through the Tufts University, Simmons College, Northeastern University.*

Total enrollment: 823. *Total student body from other countries:* 37%. *Degrees offered:* BM, diploma.

Entrance Requirements

Audition required: live, audio, video, regional *Other requirements:* recommendation, essay. *Standardized test requirements:* SAT I, 1163; TOEFL.

Costs & Financial Aid

Application fee: $75. *Deposit:* $500. *Tuition:* $17,900. *Medical fee:* $1,145.

Types of scholarships and aid awarded: full, partial, need-based, named, institutional aid, government aid, tuition payment plan, work/study, gig office. *Forms required for scholarships:* FAFSA, income tax return, income asset verification. *Loans available. Procedure for applying for loans:* contact Financial Aid Office. *Financial aid offered to international students. Percent of international students receiving scholarships:* 15%. *Other aid available to international students:* none.

Services

Housing options: on-site dorms, off-campus housing.

Support staff: financial aid advisor, foreign student advisor, physical therapist, psychological counselor, resident assistant, student affairs officer.

SMITH COLLEGE

Elm Street, Northampton MA 01063
Tel: 413-585-2500
Fax: 413-585-2527
Email: admissions@smith.smith.edu
Web: www.smith.edu

General

Type of Institution: private womens' college.

Entrance Requirements

Audition not required. Standardized test requirements: SAT I; SAT II; TOEFL.

Costs & Financial Aid

Tuition and fees: $22,360. *Room and board:* $7,450.

DRAMA

Curriculum, Students, and Faculty

Required courses: acting.

TUFTS UNIVERSITY

Department of Drama and Dance, Medford MA 02155
Tel: 617-627-3524
Fax: 617-627-3803
Contact: Sally O'Leary

General

Type of Institution: university. *Environment:* urban.

Total enrollment: 4,200. *Degrees offered:* BA.

Entrance Requirements

Audition not required.

Costs & Financial Aid

Application fee: $55. *Deposit:* $600. *Tuition:* $22,230. *Medical fee:* $415. *Room and board:* $5,968.

Percent of students receiving financial aid: 45%. *Types of scholarships and aid awarded:* full, partial, need-based, named, institutional aid, government aid, tuition payment plan, work/study. *Forms required for scholarships:* income tax return, income asset verification, FAFSA. *Loans available. Procedure for applying for loans:* fill out forms.

Services

Housing options: on-site dorms, off-campus housing, fraternity, sorority.

Support staff: career counselor, financial aid advisor, foreign student advisor, psychological counselor, resident assistant, resident nurse, student affairs officer.

DANCE

Curriculum, Students, and Faculty

Elective courses: dance composition/choreography, modern dance, rehearsal and performance, Afro-Brazilian dance.

Renowned alumni: Donald Byrd, Harry Streep, Mitchell Rose, Art Bridgeman.

Total full-time faculty: 1. *Total part-time faculty:* 3. *List of current faculty and past affiliations:* Alice E. Trexler, Lynn Fredericksen. *Program contact person:* Downing Cless.

Performance Information

Performance opportunities available (frequency): Informal concerts (2 per year), workshops (3 annually), student organizations (2 of them) have about 3 concerts annually, plus others by culturally-based groups.

Performances choreographed by: faculty, students.

Facilities

Number of studios available: 2. *Approximate studio dimensions and flooring:* 45' x 50' Marley, 18' x 35' Marley. *Performance facilities:* 45' x 50' studio doubles as informal performance lab space.

DRAMA

Curriculum, Students, and Faculty

Required courses: acting, drama criticism, theater history, theater technology, movement.

Elective courses: directing.

Summer program not available. No affiliation with a professional theater company. Selectivity for males: approximately 10% admitted. *Selectivity for females:* approximately 10% admitted. *Total enrollment:* 30. *Graduating class size:* 15.

Renowned alumni: William Hurt, Hank Azaria, Peter Roth, Dorothy Marshall, Oliver Platt, Kristen Lee Kelly, Barry Edelstein, Robert O' Hara, Megan Cole, Peter Gallagher.

Total full-time faculty: 10. *Total part-time faculty:* 2. *List of current faculty and past affiliations:* Anthony Cornish, Barbara W. Grossman, Laurence Senelick.

Performance Information

Performance opportunities available (frequency): fully produced performances (3 per year), informal performances (5 annually), workshops (2 annually), about 10 productions annually by 5 student organizations, auditioned.

Facilities

Rehearsal facilities and hours: 2-3 25' x 35' rooms. *Number of theaters on campus:* 1. *Type and capacity:* arena—215.

MUSIC

Music, including much world music, is taught within the context of a liberal arts education. There is also cross-registration with New England Conservatory.

UNIVERSITY OF MASSACHUSETTS, AMHERST

University Admissions Center, Amherst MA 01003
Tel: 413-545-0222
Fax: 413-545-4312

General

Type of institution: public university. *Environment:* suburban.

Total enrollment of institution: 24,300.

Entrance Requirements

Audition not required.

Services

Support staff: housing advisor, psychological counselor, resident assistant, resident nurse, student affairs officer.

DANCE

Curriculum, Students, and Faculty

Required courses: ballet, modern dance, jazz.

DRAMA

Curriculum, Students, and Faculty

Required courses: directing.

MUSIC

Curriculum, Students, and Faculty

Required courses: music theory, music history, private lessons.

MICHIGAN

CENTRAL MICHIGAN UNIVERSITY SCHOOL OF MUSIC

Mt. Pleasant MI 48859
Tel: 517-774-3281
Fax: 517-774-3766
Email: edward.kvet@cmich.edu
Web: www.cst.cmich.edu/units/mus

General

Type of Institution: public university. *Environment:* suburban.

Total enrollment of institution: 14,640. *Total student body from other countries:* 1%. *Degrees offered:* BA, BM, BME, BS.

Entrance Requirements

Audition required: live, audio. *Standardized test requirements:* SAT I; SAT II.

Costs & Financial Aid

Types of scholarships and aid awarded: full, partial, merit-based, need-based, named. *Loans available. Financial aid offered to international students. Other aid available to international students:* music scholarships.

Services

Housing options: on-site dorms, off-campus housing, fraternity, sorority.

Support staff: career counselor, financial aid advisor, foreign student advisor, housing advisor, physical therapist, psychological counselor, resident assistant, student affairs officer.

MUSIC

Curriculum, Students, and Faculty

Unique or innovative music curriculum: technology-based curriculum in music. *How are major teacher assignments made?* students may choose, made by the school. Faculty is informed of a student's teacher preference at the time of the audition. *15 lessons with major teacher. May a student change major teachers during the course of study?* possibly. *Study of secondary instrument or discipline is allowed.*

Selectivity for instruments or programs offered (rating): accompanying (competitive), bassoon (competitive), clarinet (selective), composition (selective), double bass (competitive), electronic music (selective), flute or piccolo (selective), French horn (selective), oboe/English horn (selective), organ (competitive), percussion (selective), piano (competitive), saxophone (selective), trombone (selective), trumpet (selective), tuba (selective), viola (competitive), violin (competitive), violoncello (competitive), voice (competitive).

Total enrollment: 348. *Entering class size:* 100. *Graduating class size:* 75.

Total part-time faculty: 32. *Total part-time faculty:* 5. *Program contact person:* Edward Kvet.

Audition Information

Audition consists of the following: scales, music theory, rhythmic dictation, melodic dictation. *Instruments provided for:* harpists, percussionists.

Performance opportunities available (frequency): band (frequently), band (frequently), jury examinations (frequently), opera workshops (frequently), orchestral concerts (frequently), recitals (frequently), chorus.

Facilities

Number of practice rooms and hours: 68; 7:00 am-12:00 am. *Recital hall?* yes. *Concert hall?* yes. *Recording studio?* yes.

HOPE COLLEGE

P.O. Box 9000, Holland MI 49422-9000
Tel: 616-395-7000
Fax: 616-395-7922
Email: Admissions@hope.edu
Web: www.hope.edu
Contact: Stu Post

General

Type of Institution: college. *Religious Affiliation:* Reformed Church in America. *Environment:* suburban.

Total enrollment of institution: 2,911. *Total student body from other countries:* 8%. *Degrees offered:* BA, BM.

Entrance Requirements

Audition required: live, audio, video. *Other requirements:* interview, essay. *Standardized test requirements:* ACT, 29; SAT I, 1100; TOEFL.

Costs & Financial Aid

Application fee: $25. *Deposit:* $300. *Tuition:* $14,788. *Other fees:* $90 per year activity fee.

Percent of students receiving financial aid: 65%. *Types of scholarships and aid awarded:* partial, merit-based, need-based, named, institutional aid, government aid, tuition payment plan, work/study. *Forms required for scholarships:* FASA, CSS Profile. *Loans available. Procedure for applying for loans:* file FAFSA and CSS profile before 2/15.

Services

Housing options: on-site dorms, off-campus housing, fraternity, sorority.

Support staff: career counselor, financial aid advisor, foreign student advisor, housing advisor, psychological counselor, resident assistant, resident nurse, student affairs officer.

Comments

All four arts departments (visual arts, dance, music, theatre) are accredited by their national associations. There are a varity of no-need artistic awards with highly competitive auditions on all instruments and voice.

DANCE

Curriculum, Students, and Faculty

Required courses: anatomy, character, ballet, dance composition or choreography, dance history, dance theory, dance writing research and criticism, jazz, Labanotation, master classes, modern dance, movement techniques, music, pointe, rehearsal and performance, repertory, stagecraft, tap, dance history.

Elective courses: historical dance, vernacular dance.

Selectivity for females: approximately 60% admitted. *Total enrollment*: 45. *Entering class size:* 20. *Graduating class size:* 10. *Percent International*: 2%.

Renowned alumni: Elizabeth Gormly, Lisa Nojonen Dance Co, Pori, Finland, Kate Faller, Ruth Rosenberg Dance Ensemble.

Total part-time faculty: 3. *Total part-time faculty:* 3. *List of current faculty and past affiliations:* Maxine DeBruyn, NASD, "Little Footsteps to Go"; Julio Rivera, Contemporary Motions Co., Primary Choreo. *Program contact person:* Maxine Debruyn.

Audition Information

No audition fee. Audition consists of the following: ballet, improvisation, modern dance, interview. *Accompanist not provided. Cassette player available; CD player available.*

Performance Information

Performance opportunities available (frequency): Fully produced concerts (1), informal concerts (2), workshops (2), on-site performances(12+ per year), touring (12+ per year).

Performances choreographed by: faculty, students, guests.

Facilities

Number of studios available: 5. *Performance facilities:* 2 major theaters.

DRAMA

Curriculum, Students, and Faculty

Required courses: acting, audition preparation, improvisation, make-up, movement, scene study, voice.

Elective courses: directing, drama criticism, musical theater, speech, stage combat, text analysis, make-up.

Number of years required to complete program: 4. *Summer program available. Affiliation with a professional theater company: Hope Summer Repertory Theatre operates as an Equity Guest Artist theater.*

Selectivity for males: most admitted, but not all. *Selectivity for females:* most admitted, but not all. *Total enrollment:* 30. *Entering class size:* 10.

Renowned alumni: Kim Zimmer, Sara Murphy, Mark Dittmar, Amy Gaipa, Jim Gray.

Total full-time faculty: 6. *Total part-time faculty:* 2. *List of current faculty and past affiliations:* Daina Robins, John Tammi.

Audition Information

No audition fee. Audition consists of the following: a cappella, comedic monologue, improvisation, movement class, Shakespearean monologue, group warm-up, interview; accompanist provided for singing. *Dress requirements for males:* comfortable. *Dress requirements for females:* comfortable.

Performance Information

Performance opportunities available (frequency): fully produced performances (4 per year), informal performances (8 per year), workshops (4 per year), off-site performances (2 per year), casting is by audition.

Recent guest artists: Tom Stechschulte, David Colacci.

Facilities

Rehearsal facilities and hours: variety of spaces, from dance rehearsal room to converted warehouses. *Number of theaters on campus:* 2 *Type and capacity:* black box 100, convertible thrust/proscenium 480.

MUSIC

Curriculum, Students, and Faculty

Unique or innovative music curriculum: A conservatory style of teaching within the context of a liberal arts education. *How are major teacher assignments made?* students may choose, according to teacher availability, by audition. Faculty is informed of a student's teacher preference at the time of the audition. *30 lessons with major teacher. May a student change major teachers during the course of study?* possibly. *Study of secondary instrument or discipline is allowed.*

Selectivity for instruments or programs offered (rating): accompanying (competitive), bassoon (non-competitive), choral conducting (non-competitive), choral singing (competitive), clarinet (non-competitive), composition (non-competitive), double bass (non-competitive), electronic music (non-competitive), flute or piccolo (competitive), French horn (non-competitive), guitar (non-competitive), harp (non-competitive), harpsichord (non-competitive), jazz (competitive), oboe/English horn (non-competitive), orchestral conducting (non-competitive), organ (non-competitive), percussion (non-competitive), piano (competitive), sacred music (non-competitive), saxophone (non-competitive), trombone (non-competitive), trumpet (non-competitive), tuba (non-competitive), viola (non-competitive), violin (competitive), violoncello (competitive), voice (competitive).

Total enrollment: 85. *Entering class size:* 35. *Graduating class size:* 15.

Renowned alumni: Bill Kuipers, New York Philharmonic; Al Fedak; Thomas Barthal, Zurich Opera.

Total part-time faculty: 11. *Total part-time faculty:* 24. *Program contact person:* Wesley Ball.

Audition Information

No audition fee. Audition consists of the following: music theory. *Instruments provided for:* harpists, percussionists; double bass.

Performance opportunities available (frequency): band (3 per year), chamber music (6 per year), jury examinations (2 per year), orchestral concerts (3 per year), recitals (12 per year), chorus (3 per year).

Facilities

Number of practice rooms and hours: 19; 24 hours a day (with access card). *Recital hall?* yes. *Concert hall?* no. *Recording studio?* no.

UNIVERSITY OF MICHIGAN, ANN ARBOR

1220 Student Activities Building, Ann Arbor MI 48109
Tel: 734-764-7433
Fax: 734-936-0740
Email: ugadmiss@mich.edu
Web: www.umich.edu

Services

Support staff: housing advisor, psychological counselor, resident assistant, resident nurse, student affairs officer.

DANCE

Curriculum, Students, and Faculty

Elective courses: pas de deux, pointe.

DRAMA

Curriculum, Students, and Faculty

Elective courses: musical theater, movement.

MUSIC

Conservatory training within large, public university.

WAYNE STATE UNIVERSITY

5451 Cass Avenue
Music Department, Detroit MI 48202
Tel: 313-577-1795
Fax: 313-577-5420

General

Type of Institution: university. *Environment:* urban.

Total enrollment of institution: 35,000. *Total student body from other countries:* 10%.

Entrance Requirements

Audition required: live, audio, video. *Other requirements:* interview.

Costs & Financial Aid

Application fee: $20. *Deposit:* $489. *Other fees:* $350 per month and up room, $69 registration fee.

Types of scholarships and aid awarded: full, partial, merit-based, need-based, named, government aid, work/study, gig office. *Forms required for scholarships:* FFS, FAFSA, income tax return, income asset verification. *Loans available. Procedure for applying for loans:* contact university financial aid. *Financial aid offered to international students. Percent of international students receiving scholarships:* 90%.

Services

Housing options: on-site dorms.

Support staff: college advisor, financial aid advisor, psychological counselor.

MUSIC

Curriculum, Students, and Faculty

How are major teacher assignments made? Students may choose, made by the school according to teacher availability. Faculty is informed of a student's teacher preference at the time of the audition. *24 lessons with major teacher. May a student change major teachers during the course of study?* possibly. *Study of secondary instrument or discipline is allowed.*

Selectivity for instruments or programs offered (rating): accompanying (competitive), accordion (competitive), bagpipes (competitive), bassoon (competitive), choral conducting (competitive), choral singing (competitive), clarinet (competitive), composition (competitive), double bass (competitive), electronic music (competitive), flute or piccolo (competitive), French horn (competitive), guitar (competitive), harp (competitive), harpsichord (competitive), jazz (competitive), oboe/English horn (competitive), orchestral conducting (competitive), organ (competitive), percussion (competitive), piano (competitive), sacred music (competitive), saxophone (competitive), trombone (competitive), trumpet (competitive), tuba (competitive), viola (competitive), violin (competitive), violoncello (competitive), voice (competitive).

Total enrollment: 375. *Entering class size:* 80. *Percent International*: 10%. *Countries most represented*: Canada.

Renowned alumni: Kenny Burrell; Joe LoDuca; George Shirley, Metropolitan Opera.

Total full-time faculty: 18. *Total part-time faculty:* 75. *Program contact person:* James Lentini.

Audition Information

No audition fee. Audition consists of the following: scales, music theory, arpeggios, sight reading, music history, repertoire, *Instruments provided for:* harpists, percussionists.

Performance opportunities available (frequency): band (every semester), chamber music (every semester), jury examinations (every semester), opera workshops (every semester), recitals (every semester), produced operas (1 per year), chorus (each semester).

Facilities

Number of practice rooms and hours: 40; 8:30 am-7:00 pm. *Recital hall?* yes. *Concert hall?* yes. *Recording studio?* yes.

WESTERN MICHIGAN UNIVERSITY

1201 Oliver Street, Kalamazoo MI 49008
Tel: 616-387-5830
Fax: 616-387-5809
Email: jane.baas@wmich.edu
Web: www.wmich.edu/dance

General

Type of Institution: public, university. *Environment:* urban.

Total enrollment of institution: 22,000. *Degrees offered:* BA, BFA.

Entrance Requirements

Audition required: live. *Other requirements:* interview, recommendation, essay. *Standardized test requirements:* ACT; SAT I; SAT II; TOEFL.

Costs & Financial Aid

Application fee: $25. *Deposit:* $50. *Other fees:* $8 activity fee, $219 enrollment.

Percent of students receiving financial aid: 70%. *Types of scholarships and aid awarded:* full, partial, merit-based, need-based, named, institutional aid, government aid, tuition payment plan, work/study. *Forms required for scholarships:* FAFSA, income tax return, income asset verification. *Loans available. Procedure for applying for loans:* varies, depending on type of loan. *Other aid available to international students:* dance has only rarely had international students.

Services

Housing options: on-site dorms, off-campus housing, fraternity, sorority.

Support staff: career counselor, financial aid advisor, foreign student advisor, housing advisor, physical therapist, psychological counselor, resident assistant, resident nurse, student affairs officer.

DANCE

Curriculum, Students, and Faculty

Required courses: ballet (3 classes per week), dance composition or choreography, dance history, dance theory, dance writing research and criticism, improvisation, jazz (3 classes per week), kinesiology, music, rehearsal and performance, stagecraft, eclectic (3 classes per week).

Elective courses: African dance (2 classes per week), anatomy, Labanotation, master classes, men's class (2 classes per week), pas de deux (2 classes per week), pointe (3 classes per week), repertory (2 classes per week), tap (2 classes per week), vernacular dance.

Selectivity for males: most admitted, but not all. *Selectivity for females:* approximately 33% admitted. 70. *Entering class size:* 25. *Graduating class size:* 15.

Renowned alumni: Kathleen Hermesdorf, Margaret Jenkins; Derrick Evans, Giordano, MTV choreographer.

Total full-time faculty: 7. *Total part-time faculty:* 6. *List of current faculty and past affiliations:* Sharon Garber, Maryland, Iowa, Dallas/Ft Worth Ballet; David Carwen, Maryland, Hartford, Milwaukee, Ft. Worth/Dallas Ballet. *Program contact person:* Wendy Cornish.

Audition Information

No audition fee. Audition consists of the following: ballet, improvisation, modern dance, jazz dance class. *Accompanist provided. Cassette player available; CD player available. Dress requirements for males:* black tights, slippers, white t-shirt, jazz shoes. *Dress requirements for females:* pink tight, solid color leotard, slippers, jazz shoes.

Audition evaluation criteria: students must place into majors level 1 technique or above in at least 2 of the 3 dance idioms.

Performance Information

Performance opportunities available (frequency): Fully produced concerts (1+ per semester), informal concerts (4-6 per semester), on-site performances (15 per year), 2 student-produced concerts, university operas and musicals, occasional collaborative events.

Performances choreographed by: faculty, students, guests. *Recent guest choreographers:* Victoria Simon, John Dayger.

Facilities

Number of studios available: 4. *Approximate studio dimensions and flooring:* 70' x 50' floating, 60' x 40' floating, 20' x 40' floating, 18' x 30' floating. *Performance facilities:* 1 studio theater, 570-proscenium theater, 200-seat proscenium theater, 1 round multi-form theater (seats 196 in thrust configuration) 3,500 proscenium theater.

MINNESOTA

CONCORDIA COLLEGE

901 South Eighth Street, Moorhead MN 56562
Tel: 218-299-4414
Fax: 218-299-3058
Email: childs@cord.edu
Web: www1.cord.edu/music
Contact: James Hausemar

General

Type of Institution: college. *Religious Affiliation:* Evangelical Lutheran Church in America. *Environment:* urban.

Total enrollment of institution: 2,950. *Degrees offered:* BA, BM.

Entrance Requirements

Audition not required. Other requirements: interview, recommendation, essay. *Standardized test requirements:* ACT.

Costs & Financial Aid

Types of scholarships and aid awarded: partial, merit-based, need-based, named, institutional aid, government aid, work/study. *Forms required for scholarships:* FFS, FAFSA. *Loans available. Procedure for applying for loans:* write to the Admissions Office or use the Internet. *Financial aid offered to international students.*

Services

Housing options: on-site dorms, off-campus housing.

Support staff: career counselor, dorm parent, financial aid advisor, foreign student advisor, housing advisor, psychological counselor, resident assistant, resident nurse, student affairs officer.

DANCE

Curriculum, Students, and Faculty

Elective courses: dance theory.

DRAMA

Curriculum, Students, and Faculty

Elective courses: audition preparation.

MUSIC

Curriculum, Students, and Faculty

How are major teacher assignments made? Students may choose, according to teacher availability. Faculty is not informed of a student's teacher preference at the time of the audition. ***30 lessons with major teacher. May a student change major teachers during the course of study?*** possibly.

Total enrollment: 160. ***Entering class size:*** 50. ***Graduating class size:*** 30. ***Percent international:*** 5%. ***Countries most represented:*** Norway.

Total part-time faculty: 18. ***Total part-time faculty:*** 20. ***Program contact person:*** David Childs.

Audition Information

No audition fee. ***Instruments provided for:*** percussionists.

Performance opportunities available (frequency): jury examinations (2 per year), recitals (50 per year).

Facilities

Number of practice rooms and hours: 35; 7:00 am-11:00 pm. ***Recital hall?*** yes. ***Concert hall?*** no. ***Recording studio?*** no.

MACALESTER COLLEGE

1600 Grand Avenue, St. Paul MN 55105
Tel: 612-696-6382
Fax: 612-696-6785
Email: macy@macalester.edu
Web: www.macalester.edu

General

Type of Institution: private college. ***Environment:*** urban.

Total enrollment of institution: 1,700. ***Degrees offered:*** BA.

Entrance Requirements

Audition not required. Other requirements: recommendation, essay. ***Standardized test requirements:*** ACT; SAT I; SAT II, school's own English exam.

Costs & Financial Aid

Tuition: $20,000. ***Room and board:*** $5,530.

Percent of students receiving financial aid: 76%. ***Types of scholarships and aid awarded:*** full, partial, merit-based, need-based, named, institutional aid, government aid, work/study. ***Forms required for scholarships:*** FAFSA. ***Loans available. Financial aid offered to international students.***

Services

Housing options: on-site dorms, off-campus housing.

Support staff: career counselor, financial aid advisor, foreign student advisor, psychological counselor, resident assistant, resident nurse, student affairs officer.

MUSIC

Curriculum, Students, and Faculty

Unique or innovative music curriculum: African music. ***How are major teacher assignments made?*** Students may choose made by the school according to teacher availability. ***24 lessons with major teacher. May a student change major teachers during the course of study?*** possibly.

Selectivity for instruments or programs offered (rating): accompanying (open), accordion (open), bagpipes (open), bassoon (open), choral conducting (open), choral singing (open), clarinet (open), composition (open), double bass (open), electronic music (open), flute or piccolo (open), French horn (open), guitar (open), harp (open), harpsichord (open), jazz (open), oboe/English horn (open), orchestral conducting (open), organ (open), percussion (open), piano (open), sacred music (open), saxophone (open), trombone (open), trumpet (open), tuba (open), viola (open), violin (open), violoncello (open), voice (open).

Total enrollment: 250. ***Entering class size:*** 35. ***Graduating class size:*** 10. ***Percent International:*** 10%. ***Countries most represented:*** Turkey, Finland, Japan, China.

Renowned alumni: James De Mars, Cary John Franklin, Tom Morgan.

Total part-time faculty: 2. ***Total part-time faculty:*** 25. ***Program contact person:*** Carleton Macy.

Audition Information

Instruments provided for: percussionists.

Performance opportunities available (frequency): jury examinations.

Facilities

Number of practice rooms and hours: 15; 8:00 am-12:00 am. *Recital hall?* yes. *Concert hall?* yes. *Recording studio?* yes.

MANKATO STATE UNIVERSITY

Performing Arts Center
P.O. Box 5, Mankato MN 56002-8400
Tel: 507-389-2118
Fax: 507-389-2922

General

Type of Institution: public university.

Degrees offered: BA, BS in music education, BS in music management, BS in theatre arts.

Entrance Requirements

Audition required: live, audio, video. *Other requirements:* interview, recommendation.

Costs & Financial Aid

Application fee: $342. *Tuition (in-state/out-state):* $2,363/ $5,423. *Other fees:* $465 books.

Types of scholarships and aid awarded: partial, merit-based, need-based, institutional aid, work/study. *Forms required for scholarships:* FAFSA, income tax return. *Loans available. Procedure for applying for loans:* contact Financial Aid Office. *Financial aid offered to international students. Other aid available to international students:* special grants, scholarships.

Services

Housing options: on-site dorms, off-campus housing, fraternity, sorority.

Support staff: career counselor, dorm parent, financial aid advisor, foreign student advisor, housing advisor, physical therapist, psychological counselor, resident assistant, resident nurse, student affairs officer.

DRAMA

Curriculum, Students, and Faculty

Required courses: acting, audition preparation, directing, improvisation, make-up, scene study, speech, Stanislavski exercises, text analysis, voice, text analysis, stage combat.

Elective courses: drama criticism, martial arts, musical theater, stage combat.

Number of years required to complete program: 4. *Summer program available. Affiliation with a professional theater company: produce Highland Summer Theatre, a non-equity professional summer-stock now in its 32nd season.*

Selectivity for males: admit all who apply. *Selectivity for females:* admit all who apply. *Total enrollment:* 100. *Entering class size:* 25. *Graduating class size:* 8. *Percent International*: 5%. *Countries most represented*: Japan.

Renowned alumni: Duke Durfee, Dudley Riggs, Dudley Riggs Theatre; Lou Bellamy.

List of current faculty and past affiliations: Paul Hustoles, American College Theatre Festival; Lewis E. Whitlock, Tom Blese, United States Institute for Theatre Technology.

Audition Information

No audition fee. Audition consists of the following: a cappella, comedic monologue.

Performance Information

Performance opportunities available (frequency): fully produced performances (15 per year), informal performances (60 per year), off-site performances (20-30 per year), auditioned.

Recent guest artists: Tony Nation.

Facilities

Rehearsal facilities and hours: several, open 24 hours a day. *Number of theaters on campus:* 3. *Type and capacity:* proscenium 529, black box 70.

MUSIC

Curriculum, Students, and Faculty

Unique or innovative music curriculum: BA-liberal arts, BS-Music Education (choral, instrumental), BS-Music Management. *How are major teacher assignments made?* made by the school, according to teacher preference according to teacher availability. Faculty is informed of a student's teacher preference at the time of the audition. *May a student change major teachers during the course of study?* possibly. *Study of secondary instrument or discipline is allowed.*

Selectivity for instruments or programs offered (rating): accompanying (selective), bassoon (selective), bassoon (competitive), choral conducting (selective), choral singing (competitive), clarinet (selective), composition (selective), double bass (competitive), electronic music (selective), flute or piccolo (selective), French horn (selective), guitar (selective), harpsichord (selective), jazz (competitive), oboe/English horn (selective), orchestral conducting (selective), organ (selective), percussion (selective), piano (selective), sacred music (competitive), saxophone (selective), trombone (selective), trombone (non-competitive), trumpet (selective), tuba (competitive), tuba (non-competitive), viola (competitive), violin (competitive), violoncello (competitive), voice (selective).

Total enrollment: 120. *Entering class size:* 30. *Graduating class size:* 15. *Percent International*: 5%. *Countries most represented*: Taiwan, Mexico. *Program contact person:* Dr. Linda Duckett.

Audition Information

No audition fee. Instruments provided for: percussionists.

Repertoire that students should avoid? no. *Performance opportunities available (frequency):* band, band, jury examinations, orchestral concerts, recitals, chorus.

Facilities

Recital hall? yes. *Concert hall?* yes. *Recording studio?* yes.

ST. OLAF COLLEGE

1520 St. Olaf Avenue, Northfield MN 55057
Tel: 507-646-3832
Email: music@stolaf.edu
Web: www.stolaf.edu

General

Type of Institution: private college. *Religious Affiliation*: Lutheran.

Total enrollment of institution: 2,900. *Degrees offered:* BA, BM.

Entrance Requirements

Audition not required.

Costs & Financial Aid

Deposit: $500.

Types of scholarships and aid awarded: partial, merit-based, need-based, institutional aid, government aid, tuition payment plan. ***Loans available.***

Services

Housing options: on-site dorms.

Support staff: career counselor, dorm parent, financial aid advisor, foreign student advisor, psychological counselor, resident assistant, resident nurse, student affairs officer.

DRAMA

Curriculum, Students, and Faculty

Required courses: acting, costume design, directing, intro to theater, scene design, technical theater, theater history, topics seminar, scenery and costume design.

Elective courses: martial arts, movement, musical theater, speech, stage combat, voice.

MUSIC

Curriculum, Students, and Faculty

Selectivity for instruments or programs offered (rating): voice (highly selective), choral singing (highly selective).

Total enrollment: 281. *Entering class size:* 87. *Graduating class size:* 59. *Program contact person:* Dan Dressen.

Audition Information

Audition consists of the following: music theory sight reading, repertoire.

UNIVERSITY OF MINNESOTA

240 Williamson Hall
281 Pillsbury Drive, SE
Minneapolis, MN 55455
Tel:800-752-1000 or 612-625-2800
Email:admissions@tc.umn.edu
Web:www.admissions.tc.umn.edu

General

Type of institution: public university. *Environment:* urban.

Total enrollment: 37,000. *Degrees offered:* BA, BM.

Entrance Requirements

Audition required: live, audio, video. *Standardized tests*: SAT I, ACT, TOEFL.

Costs & Financial Aid

Tuition (in/out): $3,960/$10,545. *Room and board*: $4,385.

Services

Housing options: Limited on-site dorms, off-campus housing. *Support staff*: career counselor, financial aid advisor, psychological couselor, resident assistant, student affairs officer.

MUSIC

All instruments offered. Conservatory-level training within a liberal arts university.

MISSOURI

SAINT LOUIS UNIVERSITY

221 North Grand Boulevard, St. Louis MO 63103
Tel: 314-977-2222
Fax: 314-977-3874
Email: admitme@slu.edu
Web: www.slu.edu
Contact: Scott Belobrajdic

General

Type of Institution: university. *Religious Affiliation*: Jesuit Roman Catholic. *Environment:* urban.

Total enrollment of institution: 11,038. *Degrees offered:* BA, BS.

Entrance Requirements

Audition required: live. *Other requirements:* interview, recommendation, essay, photograph. *Standardized test requirements:* ACT; TOEFL.

Costs & Financial Aid

Percent of students receiving financial aid: 66%. *Types of scholarships and aid awarded:* full, partial, merit-based, need-based, named, institutional aid, government aid, reduced tuition, tuition payment plan, work/study. *Forms required for scholarships:* FAFSA. *Loans available*.

Services

Housing options: on-site dorms, fraternity. *Support staff:* career counselor, financial aid advisor, foreign student advisor, housing advisor, physical therapist, psychological counselor, resident assistant, resident nurse, student affairs officer.

DANCE

Curriculum, Students, and Faculty

Required courses: Alexander technique, movement techniques, Laban Movement Studies.

Elective courses: jazz, modern dance, rehearsal and performance.

Total Enrollment: 3. *Entering class size:* 3. *Graduating class size:* 6. *Total part-time faculty:* 2. *List of current faculty and past affiliations:* Susan Gash, Gash/Voigt Dance Theater; Suzanne Celentano, University of Alabama. *Program contact person:* Mark Landis.

Audition Information

Audition consists of the following: auditions are recommended and required for certain scholarships. *Accompanist provided. Cassette player available; CD player available. Dress requirements for males:* dance shoes, tights, standard dancewear. *Dress requirements for females:* leotard, tights, ballet slippers.

Performance Information

Performance opportunities available (frequency): fully produced concerts (1 per year).

Performances choreographed by: faculty. *Recent guest choreographers:* Susan Gash.

Facilities

Number of studios available: 1. *Approximate studio dimensions and flooring:* 35' x 20' wood suspended. *Performance facilities:* theater.

DRAMA

Curriculum, Students, and Faculty

Required courses: acting, Alexander technique, dramaturgy, improvisation, movement, scene study, Stanislavski exercises, text analysis, voice.

Elective courses: audition preparation, directing, drama criticism, make-up, musical theater, speech, stage combat, verse drama.

Number of years required to complete program: 4. *Summer program not available. Selectivity for males:* approximately 60% admitted. *Selectivity for females:* approximately 60% admitted. *Total enrollment:* 17. *Entering class size:* 9. *Graduating class size:* 4.

Renowned alumni: Andreas Katsulas, Jerry Becker.

Total full-time faculty: 3. *Total part-time faculty:* 4.

Audition Information

No audition fee. Audition consists of the following: comedic monologue. Auditions are recommended and required for certain scholarships. *Audition evaluation criteria:* sincere portrayals of material within the student's age range.

Performance Information

Performance opportunities available (frequency): fully produced performances (4 per year), informal performances (2 or more per year), casting is by audition.

Recent guest artists: Chris Limberr, Ron Himes, Susan Gash.

Facilities

Rehearsal facilities and hours: 3 available from early morning until late night. *Number of theaters on campus:* 2. *Type and capacity:* proscenium 400, flexible 170.

MUSIC

Curriculum, Students, and Faculty

290 *How are major teacher assignments made?* Students may choose, according to teacher preference. Faculty is informed of a student's teacher preference at the time of the audition. *28 lessons with major teacher. May a student change major teachers during the course of study?* possibly. *Study of secondary instrument or discipline is allowed.*

Selectivity for instruments or programs offered (rating): accompanying (competitive), accordion (competitive), bagpipes (competitive), bassoon (competitive), choral conducting (competitive), choral singing (competitive), clarinet (competitive), composition (open), double bass (competitive), electronic music (open), flute or piccolo (competitive), French horn (competitive), guitar (competitive), harp (competitive), harpsichord (open), jazz (competitive), oboe/English horn (competitive), orchestral conducting (competitive), organ (competitive), percussion (competitive), piano (competitive), sacred music (competitive), saxophone (competitive), trombone (competitive), trumpet (competitive), tuba (competitive), viola (competitive), violin (competitive), violoncello (competitive), voice (competitive).

Total enrollment: 13. *Entering class size:* 3. *Graduating class size:* 1.

Total part-time faculty: 3. *Total part-time faculty:* 1. *Program contact person:* Jeny Troxell.

Audition Information

Audition consists of the following: orchestral excerpts. *Instruments provided for:* harpists.

Performance opportunities available (frequency): band, jury examinations, orchestral concerts, recitals, chorus.

Facilities

Number of practice rooms and hours: 5; 24 hours a day. *Recital hall?* yes. *Concert hall?* no. *Recording studio?* no.

TRUMAN STATE UNIVERSITY

100 East Normal
Division of Fine Arts, Kirksville MO 63501
Tel: 816-785-4417
Fax: 816-785-7463
Email: finearts@truman.edu
Web: www.truman.edu
Contact: Elaine DeJovin

General

Type of Institution: public university. *Academic education is offered on-site.*

Total enrollment of institution: 6,000. *Total student body from other countries:* 3%. *Degrees offered:* BA, BFA, BM.

Entrance Requirements

Audition required: live, audio, video. *Other requirements:* interview, essay, photograph. *Standardized test requirements:* ACT; TOEFL.

Costs & Financial Aid

Tuition (in-state/out-state): $3,256/$5,736. *Medical fee:* $12. *Other fees:* $9 per semester student activities fee, $100 freshman orientation fee.

Types of scholarships and aid awarded: full, partial, merit-based, need-based, named, institutional aid, government aid, reduced tuition, tuition payment plan, work/study. *Forms required for scholarships:* FAFSA, income tax return. *Loans available. Procedure for applying for loans:* see Financial Aid Office. *Percent of international students receiving scholarships:* 0%. *Other aid available to international students:* none.

Services

Housing options: on-site dorms, off-campus housing, fraternity, sorority.

Support staff: career counselor, college advisor, financial aid advisor, foreign student advisor, psychological counselor, resident assistant, resident nurse, student affairs officer.

Facilities

DRAMA

Curriculum, Students, and Faculty

Required courses: acting, audition preparation, directing, dramaturgy, make-up, scene study, Stanislavski exercises, text analysis, verse drama.

Elective courses: musical theater.

Number of years required to complete program: 4. *Summer program available. Selectivity for males:* approximately 33% admitted. *Selectivity for females:* approximately 33% admitted. *Total enrollment:* 46. *Entering class size:* 10. *Graduating class size:* 14. *Percent International*: 0%.

Renowned alumni: Steven Rose, Darwin Harris.

Total full-time faculty: 4. *List of current faculty and past affiliations:* Dr. Lee Orchard, Dr. John Schmor, Ron Rybkowski.

Audition Information

No audition fee. Audition consists of the following: cold readings, comedic monologue, improvisation, Shakespearean monologue, group warm-up, for musicals, prepared song with taped accompaniment. *Dress requirements for males:* dress comfortably for movement, but in clothes that are flattering. *Dress requirements for females:* dress comfortably for movement, but in clothes that are flattering. *Repertoire that students should avoid?* Durang plays; "A My Name is Alice;" Songs from "Les Miserables" or "Miss Saigon."

Performance Information

Performance opportunities available (frequency): fully produced performances (6 per year), informal performances (2 per year), workshops (2-3 per year), auditioned.

Facilities

Number of theaters on campus: 3. *Type and capacity:* proscenium 220, black box 50, auditorium 1,350.

MUSIC

Curriculum, Students, and Faculty

Unique or innovative music curriculum: Frequent master classes and appearences by performing artists. *How are major teacher assignments made?* according to teacher availability. Faculty is informed of a student's teacher preference at the time of the audition. *32 lessons with major teacher. May a student change major teachers during the course of study?* usually. *Study of secondary instrument or discipline is allowed.*

Selectivity for instruments or programs offered (rating): accompanying (competitive), bassoon (competitive), choral conducting (competitive), choral singing (competitive), clarinet (competitive), composition (non-competitive), double bass (competitive), electronic music (competitive), flute or piccolo (competitive), French horn (competitive), harpsichord (competitive), jazz (competitive), oboe/English horn (competitive), orchestral conducting (competitive), organ (competitive), percussion (competitive), piano (competitive), saxophone (competitive), trombone (competitive), trumpet (competitive), tuba (competitive), viola (competitive), violin (competitive), violoncello (competitive), voice (competitive).

Total enrollment: 130. *Entering class size:* 25. *Graduating class size:* 20.

Renowned alumni: Michael Metheny.

Total part-time faculty: 18. *Total part-time faculty:* 5. *Program contact person:* Dan Peterson.

Audition Information

No audition fee. Audition consists of the following: scales, orchestral excerpts, sight reading, repertoire. *Instruments provided for:* percussionists.

Repertoire that students should avoid? no. *Performance opportunities available (frequency):* band, orchestral concerts.

Facilities

Number of practice rooms and hours: 20; varies, usually 18 hrs per day. *Recital hall?* yes. *Concert hall?* yes. *Recording studio?* yes.

UNIVERSITY OF MISSOURI, COLUMBIA

School of Fine Arts
140 Fine Arts Building, Columbia MO 65211
Tel: 573-882-2606
Fax: 573-884-7444
Email: musicap@shoeme.missouri.edu
Web: www.missouri.edu~music
Contact: Kelly Crockett

General

Type of Institution: public university. *Environment:* urban.

Total enrollment of institution: 22,500. *Total student body from other countries:* 6%. *Degrees offered:* BA, BFA, BM.

Entrance Requirements

Audition required: live, audio. *Standardized test requirements:* ACT, 25; TOEFL, 550. school's own English exam required.

Costs & Financial Aid

Application fee: $25. *Deposit:* $300. *Medical fee:* $55. *Other fees:* $107. undergraduate activities, $123 per semester applied music. *Tuition (in state/out-of-state)* $9,475. *Room and board:* $4,560.

Types of scholarships and aid awarded: full, partial, merit-based, need-based, named, institutional aid, government aid, reduced tuition, tuition payment plan, work/study, gig office. *Forms required for scholarships:* FAFSA, income tax return, income asset verification, school's own financial aid form. *Loans available. Procedure for applying for loans:* fill out FAFSA.

Services

Housing options: on-site dorms, off-campus housing, fraternity, sorority, family.

Support staff: career counselor, dorm parent, financial aid advisor, foreign student advisor, housing advisor, physical therapist, psychological counselor, resident assistant, resident nurse, student affairs officer.

DRAMA

Curriculum, Students, and Faculty

Required courses: acting, audition preparation, improvisation, make-up, movement, scene study, speech.

Elective courses: dance, directing, musical theater, stage combat, Stanislavski exercises, verse drama, voice, stage combat, verse drama, make-up.

Number of years required to complete program: 4. *Summer program available. No affiliation with a professional theater company. Selectivity for males:* approximately 33% admitted. *Selectivity for females:* approximately 33% admitted. *Total enrollment:* 72. *Entering class size:* 75. *Graduating class size:* 13. *Percent International*: 3%.

Renowned alumni: George C. Scott, Tom Berenger, Robert Loggia, Brent Briscoe.

Total full-time faculty: 9. *List of current faculty and past affiliations:* Jim Miller, Tulane; Clyde Ruffin, Webster College, Metro Theatre, St. Louis; Pat Atkins.

Audition Information

Audition consists of the following: a cappella, cold readings, comedic monologue, improvisation, movement class, musical presentation. *Repertoire that students should avoid?* no.

Performance Information

Performance opportunities available (frequency): fully produced performances (8 per year), informal performances (2 per year), workshops (1 per year), off-site performances (occasionally), auditioned.

Recent guest artists: Charles "Mississippi" Beuel, Von Washington, Black Theatre Workshop.

Facilities

Rehearsal hours: 8:00 am-5:00 pm. *Number of theaters on campus:* 2. *Type and capacity:* black box 100, proscenium 284.

MUSIC

Curriculum, Students, and Faculty

How are major teacher assignments made? Students may choose, according to teacher availability. Faculty is informed of a student's teacher preference at the time of the audition. *30 lessons with major teacher; 30 lessons with a teaching assistant. May a student change major teachers during the course of study?* possibly. *Study of secondary instrument or discipline is allowed.*

Selectivity for instruments or programs offered (rating): accompanying (highly selective), bassoon (selective), choral conducting (highly selective), choral singing (selective), clarinet (selective), composition (highly selective), double bass (highly selective), electronic music (highly selective), flute or piccolo (highly selective), French horn (non-competitive), jazz (selective), oboe/English horn (selective), orchestral conducting (selective), percussion (competitive), piano (highly selective), saxophone (highly selective), trombone (competitive), trumpet (selective), tuba (selective), viola (selective), violin (competitive), violoncello (competitive), violoncello (selective), voice (competitive).

Total enrollment: 180. *Entering class size:* 90. *Graduating class size:* 20. *Percent International:* 3%.

Renowned alumni: Cheryl Crowe, Gene Watts, Gary Kendall.

Total part-time faculty: 31. *Total part-time faculty:* 7. *Program contact person:* Alex Pickard.

Audition Information

No audition fee. Audition consists of the following: scales, music theory, rhythmic dictation, sight reading, music history, repertoire. *Instruments provided for:* percussionists.

Required repertoire: music suitable for district and state contest. P*erformance opportunities available (frequency):* band (frequently), chamber music (frequently), jury examinations, orchestral concerts (frequently), recitals (frequently), chorus.

Facilities

Number of practice rooms and hours: 25; 8:00 am-10:00 pm. *Recital hall?* yes. *Concert hall?* yes. *Recording studio?* yes.

WASHINGTON UNIVERSITY IN ST. LOUIS

One Brookings Drive
Campus Box 1089, St. Louis MO 63130-4899
Tel: 314-935-6000
Fax: 314-935-4290
Email: admission@wustl.edu
Web: www.wustl.edu
Contact: Mary Anne Modzelewski

General

Type of Institution: university. *Environment:* suburban.

Total enrollment of institution: 5,190. *Total student body from other countries:* 7%. *Degrees offered:* BA.

Entrance Requirements

Audition not required. Other requirements: recommendation, essay. *Standardized test requirements:* ACT; SAT I; TOEFL.

Costs & Financial Aid

Application fee: $55. *Deposit:* $450. *Tuition:* $22,200. *Other fees:* $222 miscellaneous fee. *Room and board:* $6,893.

Percent of students receiving financial aid: 60% *Types of scholarships and aid awarded:* full, partial, merit-based, need-based, named, institutional aid, government aid, tuition payment plan, work/study. *Forms required for scholarships:* FAFSA, income tax return, CSS Profile. *Loans available.*

Services

Housing options: on-site dorms, off-campus housing, fraternity, sorority.

Support staff: career counselor, financial aid advisor, foreign student advisor, housing advisor, psychological counselor, resident assistant, resident nurse, student affairs officer.

DANCE

Curriculum, Students, and Faculty

Required courses: ballet, dance composition or choreography, dance history, dance theory, dance writing research and criticism, master classes, Cunningham-based, Limon-based, pointe, rehearsal and performance, stagecraft, variations.

Elective courses: African dance, Alexander technique, jazz, Pilates, Indian dance, repertory, West African.

DRAMA

Curriculum, Students, and Faculty

Required courses: acting, audition preparation, directing, drama criticism, improvisation, makeup, movement, scene study, speech, Stanislavski exercises.

Elective courses: Alexander technique, dramaturgy, musical theater.

MUSIC

Curriculum, Students, and Faculty

How are major teacher assignments made? made by the school. Faculty is informed of a student's teacher preference at the time of the audition. *28 lessons with major teacher. May a student change major teachers during the course of study?* possibly. *Study of secondary instrument or discipline is allowed.*

Selectivity for instruments or programs offered (rating): accompanying (highly selective), bassoon (open), choral conducting (highly selective), choral singing (selective), clarinet (open), composition (selective), double bass (open), electronic music (non-competitive), flute or piccolo (open), French horn (open), guitar (open), harp (open), harpsichord (open), jazz (selective), oboe/English horn (open), orchestral conducting (highly selective), organ (open), percussion (open), piano (open), saxophone (open), trombone (open), trumpet (open), tuba (open), viola (open), violin (open), violoncello (open), voice (open).

Renowned alumni: Professor Olly Wilson, Oliver Nelson, Ronald Stein, Janice Myerson. *Program contact person:* Henry I. Schvey.

Audition Information

Instruments provided for: harpists, percussionists.

Performance opportunities available (frequency): jury examinations.

Facilities

Number of practice rooms and hours: 27; 7:00 am-12:00 am. *Recital hall?* no. *Concert hall?* no. *Recording studio?* yes.

WEBSTER UNIVERSITY

470 East Lockwood Avenue, St. Louis MO 63119-3194
Tel: 314-968-6991
Fax: 314-968-7115
Email: lauear@websteruniv.edu
Web: www.websteruniv.edu
Contact: Bethany Wood

General

Type of Institution: university. *Environment:* suburban.

Total enrollment of institution: 1,600. *Degrees offered:* BA, BFA, BM.

Entrance Requirements

Audition required: live, audio, video. *Other requirements:* interview, recommendation, essay. *Standardized test requirements:* ACT, 24; SAT I, 1100; TOEFL.

Costs & Financial Aid

Application fee: $45. *Deposit:* $200. *Other fees:* applied music fees.

Percent of students receiving financial aid: 85%. *Types of scholarships and aid awarded:* full, partial, merit-based, need-based, named, institutional aid, government aid, tuition payment plan, work/study, gig office. *Forms required for scholarships:* FAFSA, income tax return, income asset verification, school's own financial aid form. *Loans available. Procedure for applying for loans:* standard procedure. *Financial aid offered to international students.*

Services

Housing options: on-site dorms, off-campus housing.

Support staff: career counselor, financial aid advisor, foreign student advisor, housing advisor, physical therapist, psychological counselor, resident assistant, resident nurse, student affairs officer.

DANCE

Curriculum, Students, and Faculty

Required courses: anatomy, ballet (5 classes per week, 4 years to complete), dance composition or choreography (3 years to complete), dance history, jazz (4 classes per week, 2 years to complete), music, rehearsal and performance (2 years to complete), eclectic (4 classes per week, 3 years to complete).

Elective courses: master classes, pas de deux, pointe, repertory, tap.

Selectivity for males: approximately 60% admitted. *Selectivity for females:* approximately 60% admitted. *Total enrollment:* 33. *Entering class size:* 12.

Renowned alumni: Melanie Stewart, William Thomas.

Total part-time faculty: 2. *Total part-time faculty:* 5. *List of current faculty and past affiliations:* Gary Hobler, Webster Dance Theatre and America Dance Network, Dance St. Louis; Belkah Noist, Gash/Voiet Dance Theatre. *Program contact person:* Gary Hubler.

Audition Information

Audition fee; $20 fee. Audition consists of the following: ballet. *Accompanist provided. Cassette player available; CD player available.*

Performance Information

Performance opportunities available (frequency): Fully produced concerts (3 per year), on-site performances (2 per year), outreach lecture/demos.

Performances choreographed by: faculty, students, guests. *Recent guest choreographers:*

William Thomas, John Mario, Fred Matthews, Michael Simms, Kay Henderson, Suzanne Grace, Christine O'Neil.

Facilities

Number of studios available: 2. *Approximate studio dimensions and flooring:* 1,800 sq. ft. sprung floor with Harlequin cover, 2,400 sq. ft. sprung floor with Harlequin cover. *Performance facilities:* Loretto-Hilton center of the arts—1 concert; stage III—2 concerts.

DRAMA

Curriculum, Students, and Faculty

Required courses: acting, Alexander technique, audition preparation, directing, drama criticism, improvisation, make-up, martial arts, movement, musical theater, scene study, speech, stage combat, Stanislavski exercises, text analysis, voice.

Number of years required to complete program: 4. *Summer program not available. Affiliation with a professional theater company: The Repertory Theatre of St. Louis is located on campus. Students work with the company on a regular basis and staff are faculty members. The relationship is over 30 years and is used as a model for training institutions. Also, Opera Theatre of St. Louis.*

Selectivity for males: approximately 10% admitted. *Selectivity for females:* approximately 10% admitted. *Total enrollment:* 150. *Entering class size:* 47. *Graduating class size:* 28.

Renowned alumni: Marsha Mason, Rockey Carroll, Jeff Sams, Jenifer Lewis, Ron Bohmer, Mary Alice Dwyer Dobbins, Phyllis Huffman, William Daugherty, Randy Donaldson.

Total full-time faculty: 12. *Total part-time faculty:* 17. *List of current faculty and past affiliations:* Byron Grant, Marion Woodruff, Bruce Loneworth, Bill Lynch, Theresa Mitchell, Gary Glasson, Steven Woolf, Kim Bozark, Kathryn Mitchaell, Doraty Marshall, Donsi Dai, Peter Sarsent, Joan Wylle, Carole Tucker, Mark Willson.

Audition Information

Audition fee: $20 fee. *Audition consists of the following:* group warm-up, 2 monologues of contrasting nature, not more than 2 minutes each; 2 songs for musical theatre. *Dress requirements for males:* comfortable to permit freedom of movement. *Dress requirements for females:* comfortable to permit freedom of movement. *Repertoire that students should avoid?* no extreme characterizations of body, voice, or speech; no dialect or accent.

Performance Information

Performance opportunities available (frequency): fully produced performances (6 per year), workshops (20) assigned, auditioned.

Recent guest artists: Pam Hunt, Gary Griffin, Philip Boehan.

Facilities

Rehearsal facilities and hours: 5 classroom spaces available, 8:00 am-12:00 am. *Number of theaters on campus:* 3. *Type and capacity:* thrust 720, flexible 125, proscenium 150.

MUSIC

Curriculum, Students, and Faculty

Unique or innovative music curriculum: Orchestral activities are in connection with professional players and in cooperative partnership with the St. Louis Symphony Orchestra. *How are major teacher assignments made?* made by the school according to teacher availability. Faculty is not informed of a student's teacher preference at the time of the audition. *30 lessons with major teacher. May a student change major teachers during the course of study?* possibly. *Study of secondary instrument or discipline is allowed.*

Selectivity for instruments or programs offered (rating): bassoon (selective), choral singing (selective), clarinet (selective), composition (selective), double bass (selective), flute or piccolo (selective), French horn (selective), guitar (selective), jazz (selective), oboe/English horn (selective), percussion (selective), piano (selective), sacred music (competitive), saxophone (selective), trumpet (selective), tuba (selective), viola (selective), violin (competitive), violoncello (selective), voice (selective).

Total enrollment: 101. *Entering class size:* 25. *Graduating class size:* 20.

Total part-time faculty: 10. *Total part-time faculty:* 20. *Program contact person:* Michael Parkinson.

Audition Information

Audition fee? $20. *Audition consists of the following:* orchestral excerpts, sight reading. *Instruments provided for:* percussionists.

Repertoire that students should avoid? no. *Performance opportunities available (frequency):* band (frequently), jury examinations, chorus.

Facilities

Number of practice rooms and hours: 16; 8:00 am-11:30 pm. *Recital hall?* yes. *Concert hall?* no. *Recording studio?* yes.

WILLIAM JEWELL COLLEGE

500 College Hill, Liberty MO 64068
Tel: 816-781-7700
Fax: 816-415-5027
Email: brownd@william.jewell.edu

MISSISSIPPI

MISSISSIPPI COLLEGE

Department of Music
P.O. Box 4206, Clinton MS 39058
Tel: 601-925-3440
Fax: 601-925-3945
Email: joiner@mc.edu
Contact: Chad Phillips

General

Type of Institution: college. *Religious Affiliation:* Baptist. *Environment:* suburban. *Academic education is offered on-site.*

Total enrollment of institution: 3,500. *Total student body from other countries:* 3%. *Degrees offered:* BA, BM, BME.

Entrance Requirements

Audition required: live, audio, video. *Other requirements:* interview, recommendation, essay, photograph. *Standardized test requirements:* ACT, 18; TOEFL.

Costs & Financial Aid

Percent of students receiving financial aid: 85%. *Types of scholarships and aid awarded:* full, partial, merit-based, need-based, named, institutional aid, tuition payment plan, work/study. *Forms required for scholarships:* FAFSA, income tax return. *Loans available. Procedure for applying for loans:* complete application form for scholarship from Admission Office.

Services

Housing options: on-site dorms, off-campus housing.

Support staff: career counselor, dorm parent, financial aid advisor, foreign student advisor, housing advisor, physical therapist, psychological counselor, resident assistant, resident nurse, student affairs officer.

MUSIC

Curriculum, Students, and Faculty

How are major teacher assignments made? Students may choose, made by the school according to teacher availability. Faculty is not informed of a student's teacher preference at the time of the audition. *50 lessons with major teacher. May a student change major teachers during the course of study?* possibly. *Study of secondary instrument or discipline is allowed.*

Selectivity for instruments or programs offered (rating): choral singing (non-competitive), clarinet (non-competitive), composition (non-competitive), double bass (non-competitive), flute or piccolo (non-competitive), French horn (non-competitive), guitar (non-competitive), harp (non-competitive), oboe/English horn (non-competitive), organ (non-competitive), percussion (non-competitive), piano (non-competitive), sacred music (non-competitive), saxophone (non-competitive), trombone (non-competitive), trumpet (non-competitive), viola (non-competitive), violin (non-competitive), violoncello (non-competitive), voice (non-competitive).

Total enrollment: 90. *Entering class size:* 36. *Graduating class size:* 20.

Renowned alumni: Kathleen Striegler; Barbara Sutton- Adam; Al Anderson, Capitol University.

Total part-time faculty: 11. *Total part-time faculty:* 8. *Program contact person:* James Richard Joiner.

Audition Information

No audition fee. Audition consists of the following: scales, orchestral excerpts, repertoire. *Instruments provided for:* harpists, percussionists.

Required repertoire: English and Italian song literature. *Repertoire that students should avoid?* pop or gospel. *Performance opportunities available (frequency):* band, chamber music, band, jury examinations, opera workshops, orchestral concerts, recitals, touring, produced operas, chorus.

Facilities

Recital hall? yes. *Concert hall?* yes. *Recording studio?* yes.

THE UNIVERSITY OF NEBRASKA, OMAHA

Department of Music, Omaha NE 68182-0245
Tel: 402-554-2251
Fax: 402-554-2252
Email: jimsaker@unomaha.edu

General

Type of Institution: public university. *Environment:* urban.

Total enrollment: 16,000.

Entrance Requirements

Audition required: live, audio. *Other requirements:* interview, recommendation. *Standardized test requirements:* ACT; TOEFL, 450.

Costs & Financial Aid

Application fee: $25. *Other fees:* $100 student fee.

Percent of students receiving financial aid: 60%. *Types of scholarships and aid awarded:* full, partial, merit-based, need-based, named, institutional aid, government aid, work/study. *Forms required for scholarships:* FFS. *Loans available. Procedure for applying for loans:* submit request in writing to Financial Aid Department scholarship application directly to the department. *Financial aid offered to international students. Percent of international students receiving scholarships:* 100%. *Other aid available to international students:* through International Studies.

Services

Housing options: on-site dorms, off-campus housing, fraternity, sorority, family.

Support staff: career counselor, financial aid advisor, foreign student advisor, psychological counselor, resident assistant, resident nurse, student affairs officer.

DANCE

Curriculum, Students, and Faculty

Total full-time faculty: 1. *Program contact person:* Josie Metal-Corbin.

Audition Information

No audition fee. Audition consists of the following: modern dance. *Accompanist not provided. Cassette player available; CD player available.*

Performance Information

Performance opportunities available (frequency): fully produced concerts (1 per semester), informal concerts workshops.

Performances choreographed by: faculty, students, guests.

Facilities

Number of studios available: 1. *Approximate studio dimensions and flooring:* 60' x 60' hard surfaces. *Performance facilities:* 2 theaters.

DRAMA

Curriculum, Students, and Faculty

Required courses: acting, directing, make-up, movement, speech.

Elective courses: improvisation, musical theater, stage combat, verse drama, voice.

Number of years required to complete program: 4. *Summer program available. Selectivity for males:* most admitted, but not all. *Selectivity for females:* most admitted, but not all. *Total enrollment:* 80. *Entering class size:* 15.

Total full-time faculty: 6. *Total part-time faculty:* 4.

Audition Information

No audition fee.

Performance Information

Performance opportunities available (frequency): fully produced performances (4 per year), auditioned.

Facilities

Rehearsal facilities and hours: excellent, brand new. *Number of theaters on campus:* 2. *Type and capacity:* concert hall 500, black box 200.

MUSIC

Curriculum, Students, and Faculty

Unique or innovative music curriculum: nearly 100% placement of graduates, progressive innovative undergraduate program, exceptional faculty of artists/teachers. *How are major teacher assignments made?* made by the school according to teacher availability. Faculty is informed of a student's teacher preference at the time of the audition. *30 lessons with major teacher. May a student change major teachers during the course of study?* possibly. *Study of secondary instrument or discipline is allowed.*

Selectivity for instruments or programs offered (rating): accompanying (non-competitive), bassoon (non-competitive), choral conducting (non-competitive), choral singing (non-competitive), clarinet (non-competitive), composition (non-competitive), double bass (non-competitive), flute or piccolo (non-competitive), French horn (non-competitive), guitar (non-competitive), harp (non-competitive), jazz (non-competitive), oboe/English horn (non-competitive), orchestral conducting (non-competitive), organ (non-competitive), percussion (non-competitive), piano (non-competitive), saxophone (non-competitive), trombone (non-competitive), trumpet (non-competitive), tuba (non-competitive), viola (non-competitive), violin (non-competitive), violoncello (non-competitive), voice (non-competitive).

Total enrollment: 200. *Entering class size:* 65. *Graduating class size:* 25. *Percent International*: 3%. *Countries most represented*: Korea, Japan, Malaysia.

Renowned alumni: Karrin Allyson, Cecil Adkins, Mark Schultze, Roberts Jespusen, James Sheperd, Janet Carlsen Campbell, Doug Keiser.

Total part-time faculty: 15. *Total part-time faculty:* 20. *Program contact person:* James Saker.

Audition Information

No audition fee. Instruments provided for: harpists, percussionists; all wind, string instruments, piano, organ.

Performance opportunities available (frequency): recitals (frequently).

Facilities

Number of practice rooms and hours: 20; 6:00 am-11:00 pm. *Recital hall?* yes. *Recording studio?* yes.

NEW HAMPSHIRE

DARTMOUTH COLLEGE

Drama Department
6204 Hopkins Center, Hanover NH 03755
Tel: 603-646-3104
Fax: 603-646-1757
Email: drama@dartmouth.edu
Web: www.dartmouth.edu/~drama

General

Type of Institution: private college. *Total enrollment of institution:* 4,285. *Total student body from other countries:* 5%. *Degrees offered:* BA.

Entrance Requirements

Audition not required. You must be admitted to the college.

Costs & Financial Aid

Application fee: $60. *Tuition:* $22,896. *Other fees:* $115.

Procedure for applying for loans: contact Financial Aid Office. *Financial aid offered to international students. Other aid available to international students:* contact Financial Aid.

Services

Housing options: on-site dorms, off-campus housing, fraternity, sorority.

Support staff: career counselor, financial aid advisor, foreign student advisor, housing advisor, physical therapist, psychological counselor, resident assistant, resident nurse, student affairs officer.

Comments

Drama department requirements for entrance: all students submit the same required components of the application, regardless of intended major. Some choose to send additional materials, such as videotapes of performances.

DANCE

Curriculum, Students, and Faculty

Required courses: dance history.

Elective courses: ballet, jazz, master classes, movement techniques, pas de deux, pointe, repertory, variations, modern dance partnering, eclectic.

Selectivity for males: approximately 60% admitted. *Selectivity for females:* approximately 33% admitted. *Total enrollment*: 34.

Renowned alumni: Andrew Asnes, Paul Taylor; Melinda DeChiazza, Boston Ballet/Twyla Tharp; Gino Grenek, Desrossier Ballet; Wilmore Coleman, Washington Ballet; Pilobolus was created at Dartmouth.

Total part-time faculty: 1. *List of current faculty and past affiliations:* Joseph Pepe DeChiazza, Lester Horton Co., Eugene Loring School of Dance; Vicki Mansfield, Pacific Ballet, San Francisco; Donald McKayle Series, A.B.T. School. *Program contact person:* Pepe DeChiazza or Fran Goldsmith.

Audition Information

No audition fee. Audition consists of the following: ballet, improvisation, modern dance. *Dress requirements for males:* non-baggy clothing. *Dress requirements for females:* non-baggy clothing.

Audition evaluation criteria: technique and artistry.

Performance Information

Performance opportunities available (frequency): Fully produced concerts (annually), informal concerts (occasionally), workshops (frequently).

Performances choreographed by: faculty, students, guests.

Facilities

Number of studios available: 1. *Approximate studio dimensions and flooring:* 40' x 40' sprung covered floor. *Performance facilities:* good theater space and floor.

DRAMA

Curriculum, Students, and Faculty

Required courses: technology, history of Western theater.

Elective courses: acting, directing, drama criticism, movement, speech, text analysis, voice.

Number of years required to complete program: 4. *Summer program available. No affiliation with a professional theater company. New York Theater Workshop, annual summer residencies collaborate with summer term drama courses.*

Selectivity for males: approximately 10% admitted. *Selectivity for females:* approximately 10% admitted. *Total enrollment:* 521. *Graduating class size:* 18. *Percent International*: 1%.

Renowned alumni: Jerry Zaks, John Hart, David Birney, Julie Davis.

Total full-time faculty: 11. *Total part-time faculty:* 3. *List of current faculty and past affiliations:* August Wilson, Mara Sabinson, San Francisco Mime Troupé.

Audition Information

Audition consists of the following: no audition.

Performance Information

Performance opportunities available (frequency): fully produced performances (12 per year), informal performances (varies), workshops (6), auditioned.

Recent guest artists: Spalding Gray, Mikhail Barishnikov, Donald Byrd, Jerry Zaks, Sam West.

Facilities

Number of theaters on campus: 2. *Type and capacity:* proscenium 480, black box 180.

MUSIC

Curriculum, Students, and Faculty

Selectivity for instruments or programs offered (rating): clarinet (selective), tuba (non-competitive), violin (open).

Program contact person: Jean Knight.

NEW JERSEY

MONTCLAIR STATE UNIVERSITY

Calcia Hall, Upper Montclair NJ 07043
Tel: 973-655-4000
Fax: 973-655-5366
Web: www.montclair.edu

General

Type of Institution: public university. *Environment:* suburban.

Total enrollment of institution: 9,300. *Degrees offered:* high school diploma, BA, BFA, BM.

Entrance Requirements

Audition required: live, audio. *Other requirements:* interview, recommendation, essay. *Standardized test requirements:* SAT I, 1050; TOEFL.

Costs & Financial Aid

Application fee: $40. *Other fees:* $821 student fee.

Percent of students receiving financial aid: 70%. *Types of scholarships and aid awarded:* full, partial, merit-based, need-based, named, government aid, tuition payment plan, work/study. *Forms required for scholarships:* FAFSA. *Loans available. Procedure for applying for loans:* contact Financial Aid Office, complete FAFSA.

Services

Housing options: on-site dorms.

Support staff: career counselor, college advisor, financial aid advisor, foreign student advisor, psychological counselor, resident assistant, resident nurse, student affairs officer.

DANCE

Curriculum, Students, and Faculty

Required courses: anatomy, ballet, dance composition or choreography, dance history, jazz (2 classes per week), modern dance, movement techniques, music, pointe (1class per week), rehearsal and performance, repertory, modern dance.

Selectivity for males: approximately 60% admitted. *Selectivity for females:* approximately 60% admitted. 60. *Entering class size:* 20.

Renowned alumni: Sebastian Smeureann, Pilobolus; Gaspard Louis, Pilobolus; Joelle Van Sickle, Nikolais; Donna Siro Gentile, Nikolais Soundance; Toya Lewis, Chuck Davis, African American Dance Ensemble.

Total part-time faculty: 2. *Total part-time faculty:* 11. *List of current faculty and past affiliations:* Lori Katterhenry, Florida State Univ.; Linda Roberts, performed with Janet Soares; Paul Sutherland, NJ Ballet; Sara Pearson, performed with Murray Louis. *Program contact person:* Lori Katterhenry.

Audition Information

No audition fee. Audition consists of the following: ballet, modern dance. *Accompanist provided. Cassette player available; CD player available. Dress requirements for males:* ballet shoes, tights, leotard or shirt, bare feet for modern dance. *Dress requirements for females:* tights, leotard, ballet shoes, bare feet for modern.

Repertoire that students should avoid? no.

Performance Information

Performance opportunities available (frequency): Fully produced concerts (3 per year), informal concerts (2 per year), workshops (1-2 per year), on-site performances(1-2 per year), touring.

Performances choreographed by: faculty, students, guests. *Recent guest choreographers:* Shapiro and Smith, Sara Pearson/Patrik Widrig, Claire Porter, Joanne Mendl/Shaw, Art Bridgeman/Myrna Packer, Kelly Drummond of Shapiro and Smith.

Facilities

Number of studios available: 2. *Approximate studio dimensions and flooring:* 25' x 40' spring with Marley, 30' x 40' spring with Marley. *Performance facilities:* 1 dance studio theater—80 seats, 1 large auditorium—1,000 seats.

DRAMA

Curriculum, Students, and Faculty

Required courses: acting, audition preparation, directing, drama criticism, improvisation, makeup, movement, scene study, speech, Stanislavski exercises, text analysis, voice, Stanislavski exercises.

Number of years required to complete program: 4. *Summer program not available. Affiliation with a professional theater company; Summer Theatre: Theatrefest, Equity Summer Theatre on campus.*

Total enrollment: 135. *Entering class size:* 50. *Percent International*: 2%. *Countries most represented*: England, Australia.

Renowned alumni: Steve Biensleie, Bruce Willis, Gerry McIntyre.

Total full-time faculty: 8. *Total part-time faculty:* 8. *List of current faculty and past affiliations:* Ramon L. Delgado, William R. DeLuca.

Audition Information

No audition fee. Audition consists of the following: comedic monologue, group warm-up. *Audition evaluation criteria:* versatility, vocal control, physical control, internal technique.

Performance Information

Performance opportunities available (frequency): fully produced performances (3 per year), informal performances (4-6 per semester), auditioned.

Facilities

Rehearsal facilities and hours: theaters, rehearsal halls, 6:00 pm-10:00 pm. *Number of theaters on campus:* 2. *Type and capacity:* auditorium 1,000, black box 120.

MUSIC

Curriculum, Students, and Faculty

How are major teacher assignments made? made by the school according to teacher availability. Faculty is not informed of a student's teacher preference at the time of the audition. *30 lessons with major teacher. May a student change major teachers during the course of study?* possibly. *Study of secondary instrument or discipline is allowed.*

Selectivity for instruments or programs offered (rating): accompanying (competitive), bassoon (open), choral conducting (competitive), choral singing (competitive), clarinet (competitive), composition (competitive), double bass (competitive), electronic music (competitive), flute or piccolo (competitive), French horn (competitive), guitar (competitive), harp (competitive), harpsichord (competitive), jazz (competitive), oboe/English horn (competitive), orchestral conducting (competitive), organ (competitive), percussion (competitive), piano (competitive), saxophone (competitive), trombone (competitive), trumpet (competitive), tuba (competitive), viola (competitive), violin (competitive), violoncello (competitive), voice (competitive).

Total enrollment: 217. *Entering class size:* 65. *Graduating class size:* 40. *Percent International:* 7%. *Countries most represented:* Korea.

Renowned alumni: Paul Plishka, George Rochberg.

Total part-time faculty: 16. *Total part-time faculty:* 44. *Program contact person:* Ruth Rendleman or Gina Balestracci: 973-655-7219.

Audition Information

No audition fee. Audition consists of the following: scales, orchestral excerpts, music theory, arpeggios, sight reading, repertoire. *Instruments provided for:* percussionists.

Required repertoire: varies by instrument. Please call school for repertoire information. *Repertoire that students should avoid?* no.

Facilities

Number of practice rooms and hours: 15. *Recital hall?* yes. *Concert hall?* yes. *Recording studio?* yes.

PRINCETON UNIVERSITY

P.O. Box 430, Princeton NJ 08544
Tel: 609-258-3060
Web: www.princeton.edu

General

Type of Institution: private university. *Environment:* suburban.

Total enrollment of institution: 4,500. *Degrees offered:* BA.

Entrance Requirements

Audition not required, audio, video. *Other requirements:* interview, recommendation, essay. *Standardized test requirements:* SAT I; SAT II; TOEFL.

Costs & Financial Aid

Tuition: $20,940. *Room and board*: $5,910.

Percent of students receiving financial aid: 42%. *Types of scholarships and aid awarded:* full, partial, need-based, work/study. *Forms required for scholarships:* FAFSA, income tax return.

Services

Housing options: on-site dorms.

Support staff: career counselor, financial aid advisor, foreign student advisor, housing advisor, psychological counselor, resident assistant, resident nurse, student affairs officer.

MUSIC

Curriculum, Students, and Faculty

Music is offered as a major within the context of a liberal arts education.

Total enrollment: 10.

Renowned alumni: Milton Babbitt, Roger Sessions.

Total part-time faculty: 12. *Total part-time faculty:* 1. *Contact*: 609-258-4241.

ROWAN UNIVERSITY

Department of Music
201 Mullica Hill Road, Glassboro NJ 08028
Tel: 609-256-4555
Email: depeasquale@heroes.rowan.edu
Web: www.rowan.edu

General

Type of Institution: public university. *Environment:* suburban.

Total enrollment of institution: 9,000. *Degrees offered:* BA, BM.

Entrance Requirements

Audition required: live, audio. *Other requirements:* interview, essay. *Standardized test requirements:* SAT I, 1100; TOEFL, 550.

Costs & Financial Aid

Application fee: $50. *Deposit:* $100. *Tuition:* $2,740. *Medical fee:* $110. *Other fees:* $50-$105 per semester.

Percent of students receiving financial aid: 80%. *Types of scholarships and aid awarded:* full, partial, merit-based, need-based, named, institutional aid, government aid, tuition payment plan, work/study. *Forms required for scholarships:* FAFSA, income tax return, income asset verification. *Loans available. Procedure for applying for loans:* contact Financial Aid Office. *Financial aid offered to international students. Percent of international students receiving scholarships:* 0%. *Other aid available to international students:* tuition waivers, college-awarded scholarships after attendance of one-and-a-half semesters.

Services

Housing options: on-site dorms, off-campus housing, fraternity, sorority, family.

Support staff: career counselor, college advisor, financial aid advisor, foreign student advisor, housing advisor, psychological counselor, resident assistant, resident nurse, student affairs officer.

MUSIC

Curriculum, Students, and Faculty

Unique or innovative music curriculum: Ensemble participation required each semester in attendance. *How are major teacher assignments made?* Students may choose, according to teacher availability. Faculty is not informed of a student's teacher preference at the time of the audition. *May a student change major teachers during the course of study?* possibly. *Study of secondary instrument or discipline is allowed.*

Selectivity for instruments or programs offered (rating): accordion (non-competitive), bassoon (non-competitive), clarinet (non-competitive), composition (non-competitive), double bass (non-competitive), electronic music (non-competitive), flute or piccolo (non-competitive), French horn (non-competitive), guitar (non-competitive), harp (non-competitive), jazz (non-competitive), oboe/English horn (non-competitive), orchestral conducting (non-competitive), organ (non-competitive), percussion (non-competitive), piano (non-competitive), saxophone (non-competitive), trombone (non-competitive), trumpet (non-competitive), tuba (non-competitive), viola (non-competitive), violin (non-competitive), violoncello (non-competitive), voice (non-competitive).

Total enrollment: 170. *Entering class size:* 40. *Graduating class size:* 12. *Percent International*: 3%. *Countries most represented*: Far East, South America.

Renowned alumni: Eugene Grier, Mary D'arcy, Donald Lang. *Total part-time faculty:* 42. *Program contact person:* Lawrence DePasquale.

Audition Information

No audition fee. Audition consists of the following: scales, orchestral excerpts, music theory, rhythmic dictation, sight reading, melodic dictation, repertoire. *Instruments provided for:* percussionists; organ.

Required repertoire: suggested list is sent to all applicants. *Repertoire that students should avoid?* no.

Facilities

Number of practice rooms and hours: 80; 7:00 am-12:00 am. *Recital hall?* yes. *Concert hall?* yes. *Recording studio?* yes.

RUTGERS, THE STATE UNIVERSITY OF NEW JERSEY

Mason Gross School of the Arts
P.O. Box 2101, New Brunswick NJ 08903-2101
Tel: 732-932-INFO
Fax: 732-445-0237
Email: admissions@asbugadm.rutgers.edu
Web: www.rutgers.edu

General

Type of Institution: public university. *Environment:* suburban.

Total enrollment of institution: 47,850. *Total student body from other countries:* 10%. *Degrees offered:* BA, BFA, BM.

Entrance Requirements

Audition required: live, audio, video. *Other requirements:* interview. *Standardized test requirements:* SAT I, 555; TOEFL, 550.

Costs & Financial Aid

Application fee: $50. *Deposit:* $125. *Tuition (in-state/out-state):* $4,262/ $8,676. *Other fees:* $1,104 per year college fee.

Percent of students receiving financial aid: 71%. *Types of scholarships and aid awarded:* partial, merit-based, named, institutional aid, government aid, tuition payment plan, work/study. *Forms required for scholarships:* FAFSA, income tax return. *Loans available.*

Services

Housing options: on-site dorms, off-campus housing, fraternity, sorority.

Support staff: career counselor, financial aid advisor, foreign student advisor, housing advisor, physical therapist, psychological counselor, resident assistant, resident nurse, student affairs officer.

DANCE

Curriculum, Students, and Faculty

Required courses: anatomy, ballet (3 classes per week), dance composition or choreography (3.5 years to complete), dance history (1year to complete), Labanotation, modern dance (5 classes per week, 4 years to complete), music, stagecraft (1year to complete), ballet, modern dance, Cunningham-based.

Elective courses: African dance, jazz, master classes, repertory (2 years to complete), Spanish.

Selectivity for males: approximately 33% admitted. *Selectivity for females:* approximately 33% admitted. *Total enrollment*: 71. *Entering class size:* 25. *Graduating class size:* 8.

Renowned alumni: Raguel Horsford, Stomp; Bethany Formica, Michael Foley Dance Company; Lorinda Santos, Broadway cast, Gentlemen Prefer Blondes, 1995.

Total part-time faculty: 7. *Total part-time faculty:* 3. *List of current faculty and past affiliations:* Sherry Alban, charter member of Princeton Ballet, American Repertory Ballet; Robert "Tigger" Benford, Paul Winter Consort, American Dance Festival. *Program contact person:* Pat Mayer.

Audition Information

No audition fee. Audition consists of the following: modern dance, prepared solo, 1-minute of original choreography created by auditioner, required only for students transfering from a program where they studied choreography. *Accompanist provided. Cassette player available; CD player available. Dress requirements for males:* must be able to observe body; no baggy clothing. *Dress requirements for females:* must be able to observe body, no baggy clothing.

Audition evaluation criteria: body structure, movement facility, performance quality, willingness to explore movement.

Performance Information

Performance opportunities available (frequency): Fully produced concerts (2-3 per term), informal concerts (2 per semester), workshops (1-2 per year), on-site performances (2-3 per term), touring (1 per week for 4 weeks).

Performances choreographed by: faculty, students, guests. *Recent guest choreographers:* David Grenke, Murray Lewis, Claire Porter.

Facilities

Number of studios available: 4. *Approximate studio dimensions and flooring:* 40' x 60' sprung wood, 40' x 90' sprung wood. *Performance facilities:* 1 studio theater, 1 proscenium theater, 1 concert hall.

DRAMA

Curriculum, Students, and Faculty

Required courses: acting, audition preparation, make-up, movement, singing, speech, text analysis, verse drama, voice, acting/directing workshop, Stanislavski exercises, improvisation, drama criticism, musical theater.

Number of years required to complete program: 4. *Summer program not available. No affiliation with a professional theater company. Selectivity for males:* approximately 10% admitted. *Selectivity for females:* approximately 10% admitted. *Total enrollment:* 90. *Entering class size:* 25. *Graduating class size:* 12.

Renowned alumni: Avery Brooks, Calista Flockhart, William Mastrosimine, Neil Cuthbert, Sheryl Lee Ralph, Riccardo Kahn, Matthew Mulbern, Dina Spybey, Tim DeKay.

Total full-time faculty: 13. *Total part-time faculty:* 13. *List of current faculty and past affiliations:* Maggie Flanigan, Mai Laughran, Nancy Magans, Yale, Carnegie Mellon, Trinity Repertory Conservatory; Patricia Noreia Edwards, Leonard Petit.

Audition Information

No audition fee. Audition consists of the following: 2 memorized monologues: 1 classical, 1 contemporary combined not to exceed 5 minutes. *Repertoire that students should avoid?* no.

Performance Information

Performance opportunities available (frequency): fully produced performances (3 tiers, 15-18 per year), workshops (3-4), auditioned.

Facilities

Type and capacity: black box 330.

MUSIC

Curriculum, Students, and Faculty

How are major teacher assignments made? according to teacher preference and teacher availability. Faculty is informed of a student's teacher preference at the time of the audition. *May a student change major teachers during the course of study?* possibly. *Study of secondary instrument or discipline is allowed.*

Selectivity for instruments or programs offered (rating): bassoon (competitive), clarinet (selective), double bass (non-competitive), flute or piccolo (selective), French horn (competitive), guitar (highly selective), harp (non-competitive), harpsichord (non-competitive), jazz (competitive), oboe/English horn (selective), percussion (selective), piano (selective), saxophone (selective), trombone (competitive), trumpet (selective), tuba (competitive), tuba (highly selective), viola (competitive), violin (non-competitive), violoncello (competitive), voice (selective).

Total enrollment: 140. *Entering class size:* 65. *Graduating class size:* 9. *Percent International*: 10%. *Countries most represented*: Taiwan.

Renowned alumni: Qiang Tu, New York Philharmonic; Terrence Blanchard; Regine Bell; Susan Kynkor, Bogota Symphony; Yi- Wen Jiang, Shanghai Quartet.

Total part-time faculty: 43. *Total part-time faculty:* 17. *Program contact person:* Lois Fromer.

Audition Information

No audition fee. Audition consists of the following: scales, music theory, arpeggios, repertoire. *Instruments provided for:* harpists, percussionists; amplifiers.

Required repertoire: Varies by instrument. Please call school for repertoire information. *Repertoire that students should avoid?* Show tunes for voice. *Performance opportunities available (frequency):* chamber music, jury examinations (2 per year), orchestral concerts, recitals, touring, chorus.

Facilities

Number of practice rooms and hours: 20; 7:30 am-12:00 am. *Recital hall?* yes. *Concert hall?* yes.

THE RICHARD STOCKTON COLLEGE OF NEW JERSEY

P.O. Box 195, Pomona NJ 08240-0195
Tel: 609-652-4505
Fax: 609-652-4550
Contact: Alison Henry

General

Type of Institution: college. *Environment:* suburban. *Total enrollment of institution:* 6,203. *Total student body from other countries:* 4%. *Degrees offered:* BA.

Entrance Requirements

Audition required: live, video. *Standardized test requirements:* ACT, 24; SAT I, 1136; TOEFL, 525.

Costs & Financial Aid

Application fee: $35. *Deposit:* $100.

Percent of students receiving financial aid: 55%. *Types of scholarships and aid awarded:* full, partial, merit-based, need-based, named, institutional aid, government aid, reduced tuition, tuition payment plan, work/study. *Forms required for scholarships:* FAFSA, income tax return, income asset verification. *Loans available. Procedure for applying for loans:* complete FAFSA by 3/1 for fall term and 8/15 for spring term. *Other aid available to international students:* Richard Stockton Foundation Scholarships.

Services

Housing options: on-site dorms, off-campus housing.

Support staff: career counselor, financial aid advisor, foreign student advisor, housing advisor, physical therapist, psychological counselor, resident assistant, resident nurse, student affairs officer.

DANCE

Curriculum, Students, and Faculty

Required courses: acting, anatomy, ballet (2 classes per week), costume design, improvisation, jazz, master classes, modern dance (3 classes per week), Laban Movement Studies, rehearsal and performance, repertory, stagecraft, topics seminar, social dance, dance internship.

Selectivity for males: approximately 60% admitted. *Selectivity for females:* approximately 60% admitted. *Total enrollment*: 15. *Entering class size:* 3. *Graduating class size:* 3. *Countries most represented*: Kenya, Canada.

Renowned alumni: Jason Nelson, Danish Dance Theater.

Total part-time faculty: 2. *Total part-time faculty:* 2. *List of current faculty and past affiliations:* Nancy Lanier, Bella Lewitzky Dance Company; Henry Van Kuiken, choreographed over 40 works which were performed in New York City. *Program contact person:* Henry Van Kuiken.

Audition Information

No audition fee. Audition consists of the following: ballet, modern dance. *Accompanist provided. Cassette player available; CD player available.*

Dress requirements for males: tights and leotard, t-shirt, or unitard. *Dress requirements for females:* tights and leotard or unitard.

Audition evaluation criteria: observation and assessment of prospective students in technique classes.

Performance Information

Performance opportunities available (frequency): Fully produced concerts (1 per year), informal concerts (2 per year), workshops (1 per year), on-site performances (1 per year).

Performances choreographed by: faculty, students, guests. *Recent guest choreographers:* Jim Clinton, the Jose Limon Dance Company; Carolyn Dorfman, Carolyn Dorfman Dance Company; Sally Hess, Dancetales Dance Company; Francine Landes-formerly of the Louis Falco Dance Company; Janet Soares-formerly of the Jose Limon Dance Company; Chair of the dance program at Barnard College, Columbia University.

Facilities

Approximate studio dimensions and flooring: 30' x 60' sprung wood flooring. *Performance facilities:* Performing Arts Center—500-seat semi-thrust proscenium theater; experimental theater—70-seat black box.

WESTMISTER CHOIR COLLEGE OF RIDER UNIVERSITY

101 Walnut Lane, Princeton NJ 08540-3899
Tel: 609-921-7144
Fax: 609-921-2538
Email: wcc.admission.edu
Contact: Heather J. Sano

General

Type of Institution: college, conservatory. *Environment:* suburban. *Cross registration is available through Rider University and Princeton University.*

Total enrollment of institution: 415. *Total student body from other countries:* 19%. *Degrees offered:* BA, BM.

Entrance Requirements

Audition required: live, audio, video. *Other requirements:* interview, recommendation, essay. *Standardized test requirements:* ACT; SAT I; TOEFL, 550.

Costs & Financial Aid

Application fee: $40. *Deposit:* $400. *Tuition:* $15,120. *Medical fee:* $140. *Other fees:* $700 books, supplies, $425 school fees.

Percent of students receiving financial aid: 80%. *Types of scholarships and aid awarded:* partial, merit-based, need-based, named, institutional aid, government aid, tuition payment plan, work/study. *Loans available. Procedure for applying for loans:* submit FAFSA form. *Financial aid offered to international students. Percent of international students receiving scholarships:* 85%. *Other aid available to international students:* grants.

Services

Housing options: on-site dorms.

Support staff: financial aid advisor, foreign student advisor, housing advisor, psychological counselor, resident assistant, resident nurse, student affairs officer.

Comments

All students perform in professional concerts each year. The 200-voice Westminster Symphonic Choir sings and records on a regular basis with the New York Philharmoic and the Philadelphia Orchestra under world-class conductors at Lincoln Center, Carnegie Hall and the Philadelphia Academy of Music. Students may also perform in six additional choirs. Wesminster has the largest organ department in the United States (including 21 pipe organs). The faculty at Westminster are published and world-renowned.

MUSIC

Curriculum, Students, and Faculty

Unique or innovative music curriculum: only school of its kind in the world; all students sing in choral ensemble every year. *How are major teacher assignments made?* made by the school according to teacher preference according to teacher availability. Faculty is not informed of a student's teacher preference at the time of the audition. *24 lessons with major teacher. May a student change major teachers during the course of study?* possibly. *Study of secondary instrument or discipline is allowed.*

Selectivity for instruments or programs offered (rating): composition (competitive), organ (competitive), piano (competitive), sacred music (competitive), voice (selective), music education (competitive).

Total enrollment: 415. *Entering class size:* 80. *Graduating class size:* 40. *Percent International:*

19%. *Countries most represented*: Korea, Taiwan, Canada, Japan.

Renowned alumni: Jennifer Larmore, Daniel Beckwith, Joan Lippincott, Diane Curry.

Total part-time faculty: 38. *Total part-time faculty:* 40. *Program contact person:* Heather J. Sano.

Audition Information

No audition fee. Audition consists of the following: repertoire.

Required repertoire: varies by instrument. Please call school for repertoire information. *Performance opportunities available (frequency):* jury examinations (frequently), recitals (frequently), touring (frequently), chorus.

Facilities

Number of practice rooms and hours: 61; 7:00 am-12:00 am. *Recital hall?* yes. *Concert hall?* yes. *Recording studio?* no.

NEW YORK

ADELPHI UNIVERSITY

South Avenue
Post Hall Room 4, Garden City NY 11530
Tel: 516-877-3000
Fax: 516-877-3039
Email: petron@adlibv.adelphi.edu
Web: www.adelphi.edu
Contact: Rosemarie Burnett

General

Type of Institution: private university. *Environment:* suburban.

Degrees offered: BA, BFA.

Entrance Requirements

Audition required: live, video. *Other requirements:* interview. *Standardized test requirements:* ACT; SAT I, 1000; TOEFL.

Costs & Financial Aid

Application fee: $35. *Deposit:* $250. *Tuition:* $14,000. *Other fees:* $170 student activity fee, optional medical fee. *Room and board*: $6,560.

Percent of students receiving financial aid: 75%. *Types of scholarships and aid awarded:* full, partial, merit-based, need-based, named, institutional aid, government aid, reduced tuition, tuition payment plan, work/study. *Forms required for scholarships:* FAFSA, income tax return, income asset verification. *Loans available. Financial aid offered to international students. Percent of international students receiving scholarships:* 15%. *Other aid available to international students:* merit scholarship.

Services

Housing options: on-site dorms, off-campus housing.

Support staff: career counselor, dorm parent, financial aid advisor, foreign student advisor, housing advisor, physical therapist, psychological counselor, resident assistant, resident nurse, student affairs officer.

DANCE

Curriculum, Students, and Faculty

Elective courses: pas de deux, other world dance forms.

Selectivity for males: approximately 60% admitted. *Selectivity for females:* approximately 60% admitted. *Percent International*: 25%. *List of current faculty and past affiliations:* Carmen De Lavallade, Rebecca Wright, Regina Larkin. *Program contact person:* Rebecca Wright.

Audition Information

No audition fee. Audition consists of the following: ballet, modern dance, prepared solo. *Accompanist provided. Cassette player available; CD player available.*

Repertoire that students should avoid? tap.

Audition evaluation criteria: form, potential.

Performance Information

Performance opportunities available (frequency): Fully produced concerts (2), informal concerts (4), workshops (2).

Performances choreographed by: faculty, guests. *Recent guest choreographers:* Janice Brenner, Gregory Hines.

Facilities

Number of studios available: 4. *Approximate studio dimensions and flooring: Performance facilities:* Olmsted Theater.

DRAMA

Curriculum, Students, and Faculty

Required courses: acting, dramaturgy, Alexander technique, audition preparation, directing, improvisation, make-up, movement, scene study,

Stanislavski exercises, text analysis, verse drama, voice. *Elective courses:* drama criticism.

Number of years required to complete program: 4. *Summer program available. No affiliation with a professional theater company. Selectivity for males:* approximately 60% admitted. *Selectivity for females:* approximately 60% admitted. *Percent International*: 15%.

Renowned alumni: Jonathan Larson.

List of current faculty and past affiliations: Nicholas Petron, Nancy Miller.

Audition Information

No audition fee. Audition consists of the following: cold readings, Shakespearean monologue. *Repertoire that students should avoid?* no.

Audition evaluation criteria: potential, knowledge, poise, talent.

Performance Information

Performance opportunities available (frequency): fully produced performances (3), informal performances (4), workshops (6) assigned, auditioned. Auditioned for mainstages, assigned for minor productions.

Facilities

Rehearsal facilities and hours: large studio, Olmsted Theater, weekday evenings, Friday and Saturday. *Number of theaters on campus:* 1.

MUSIC

Curriculum, Students, and Faculty

How are major teacher assignments made? made by the school. Faculty is not informed of a student's teacher preference at the time of the audition. *May a student change major teachers during the course of study?* possibly.

Percent international: 25%. *Program contact person:* Latty Newland.

Audition Information

Audition fee? yes. *Audition consists of the following:* scales, orchestral excerpts, melodic dictation. *Instruments provided for:* percussionists.

Repertoire that students should avoid? no.

Facilities

Number of practice rooms and hours: 4. *Recital hall?* no. *Concert hall?* yes. *Recording studio?* yes.

BARD COLLEGE

Annandale-on-Hudson NY 12504
Tel: 914-758-6822
Fax: 914-758-5208
Email: admission@bard.edu
Web: www.bard.edu

General

Type of Institution: private college.

Total enrollment of institution: 1,000. *Degrees offered:* BA.

Entrance Requirements

Audition not required. Other requirements: recommendation, essay. *Standardized test requirements:* TOEFL, 550.

Costs & Financial Aid

Application fee: $40. *Deposit:* $350. *Tuition:* $21,700. *Medical fee:* $380. *Other fees:* $140 student activity fee. *Room and board*: $6,720.

Percent of students receiving financial aid: 67%. *Types of scholarships and aid awarded:* partial, merit-based, need-based, institutional aid, government aid, tuition payment plan, work/study. *Forms required for scholarships:* FAFSA, CSS profile, TAP form for New York State residents. *Loans available. Procedure for applying for loans:* international students only must write letter to Financial Aid Office requesting loan. *Financial aid offered to international students. Percent of international students receiving scholarships:* 75%. *Other aid available to international students:* Bard Scholarship, Bard Foreign Loan.

Services

Housing options: on-site dorms, off-campus housing.

Support staff: career counselor, financial aid advisor, foreign student advisor, housing advisor, physical therapist, psychological counselor, resident assistant, resident nurse, student affairs officer.

DANCE

Curriculum, Students, and Faculty

Required courses: dance composition or choreography, modern dance (4 classes per week), Cunningham-based (4 classes per week), Limon-based (4 classes per week), modern dance other (4 classes per week), rehearsal and performance, stagecraft, introduction to acting, ballet for modern dancers, dance composition or choreography, rehearsal and performance, repertory.

Elective courses: anatomy, ballet, dance history, dance theory, dance writing research and criticism, Laban Movement Studies, movement techniques other, music, repertory, Spanish.

Selectivity for males: admit all who apply. *Selectivity for females:* admit all who apply. *Total enrollment*: 15.

Renowned alumni: Arthur Aviles, Joanna Hygood, Ann Bogart, Blythe Danner.

Total part-time faculty: 2. *Total part-time faculty:* 3. *List of current faculty and past affiliations:* Albert Reid, Cunningham Company; Jean Churchill, Boston Ballet; Susan Osbey, Lucinda Childs Company; Aileen Passloff, James Waring. *Program contact person:* Jean Churchill.

Performance Information

Performance opportunities available (frequency): Fully produced concerts (2 per semester), informal concerts (weekly), workshops (1-2 per semester), on-site performances(1-2 per semester).

Performances choreographed by: faculty, students.

Facilities

Number of studios available: 2. *Approximate studio dimensions and flooring:* 40' x 160' linoleum on wood, 30' x 40' linoleum on wood. *Performance facilities:* studio converted to theater—with full lighting, sound, scrim, wings.

DRAMA

Curriculum, Students, and Faculty

Required courses: directing, drama criticism.

MUSIC

Music is taught within the context of a liberal arts college.

BARNARD COLLEGE

3009 Broadway
New York, NY 10027
Telephone: 212-854-2014
Email: admissions@barnard.columbia.edu
Web: barnard.columbia.edu

General

Type of Institution: all women, private college. *Environment*: urban. *Degrees offered*: BA. Cross registration is available through Columbia University, Teacher's College, Jewish Theological Seminary, Manhattan School of Music, and Juilliard. *Total enrollment:* 2,300.

Entrance Requirements

Audition not required. *Other requirements*: recommendations, essays, interview. *Standardized test requirements*: SAT I, SAT II, TOEFL.

Costs & Financial Aid

Tuition and fees: $20,424. *Room and board:* $8,474. *Percentage of students receiving financial aid*: 60%.

Services

Housing options: on-site dorms, off-campus housing. *Support staff*: career counselor, financial aid advisor, housing advisor, foreign student advisor, psychological counselor, resident assistant, resident nurse, student affairs officer.

DANCE

Comprehensive program offered with many performance opportunities. Some electives may also be taken at Juilliard.

DRAMA

Joint department with Columbia.

MUSIC

Music is taught within the context of a liberal arts education. Private lessons are available and students may audition for Manhattan School of Music or Juilliard. *Renowned alumni:* Twyla Tharp, Suzanne Vega, Rita Shane, Joan Rivers.

COLUMBIA UNIVERSITY

2960 Broadway, New York NY 10027
Tel: 212-854-1257
Fax: 212-854-8191
Web: www.columbia.edu

General

Type of Institution: private university. *Environment:* urban. *Cross registration is available through Barnard College, Teacher's College, Jewish Theological Seminary and Juilliard.*

Total enrollment of institution: 20,000. *Total student body from other countries:* 19%.

Entrance Requirements

Audition not required. Other requirements: recommendation, essay. *Standardized test requirements:* ACT; SAT I, 1403; SAT II; TOEFL, 600, school's own English exam required.

Costs & Financial Aid

Application fee: $50. *Tuition:* $22,072. *Medical fee:* $516. *Room and board:* $8,474.

Percent of students receiving financial aid: 50% *Types of scholarships and aid awarded:* partial, need-based, institutional aid, government aid, tuition payment plan, work/study. *Forms required for scholarships:* FAFSA, income tax return, income asset verification, CSS Profile form, school's own financial aid form. *Loans available. Procedure for applying for loans:* apply with application for admission. *Financial aid offered to international students.*

Services

Housing options: on-site dorms, off-campus housing, fraternity, sorority, family.

Support staff: career counselor, financial aid advisor, foreign student advisor, housing advisor, psychological counselor, resident assistant, resident nurse, student affairs officer.

MUSIC

Curriculum, Students, and Faculty

Music is taught within the context of a liberal arts education. Private lessons available. Auditions are required for joint program with Juilliard.

Total full-time faculty: 4. *Total part-time faculty:* 36. *Program contact person:* George Rothman, 212-854-5409.

Audition Information

No audition fee. Audition consists of the following: scales, orchestral excerpts, sight reading. *Instruments provided for:* percussionists.

CORNELL UNIVERSITY

Center for Theatre Arts
430 College Avenue, Ithaca NY 14850-4696
Tel: 607-254-2700
Fax: 607-254-2733
Email: theatre@cornell.edu
Web: www.arts.cornell.edu/theatrearts
Contact: Bonnielyn Jones

General

Type of Institution: private university. *Environment:* suburban.

Total enrollment of institution: 13,000. *Total student body from other countries:* 19%. *Degrees offered:* BA.

Entrance Requirements

Audition not required. Other requirements: essay. *Standardized test requirements:* ACT; SAT I, 1500; SAT II; TOEFL, 550, school's own English exam required.

Costs & Financial Aid

Application fee: $65. *Tuition:* $21,914. *Other fees:* books and personal expenses. *Room and board:* $6,962.

Percent of students receiving financial aid: 50%. *Types of scholarships and aid awarded:* full, partial, need-based, named, institutional aid, government aid, tuition payment plan, work/study. *Forms required for scholarships:* FAFSA, income tax return, income asset verification, CSS Profile. *Loans available. Procedure for applying for loans:* contact Financial Aid Office. *Financial aid offered to international students. Other aid available to international students:* same as other students.

Services

Housing options: on-site dorms, off-campus housing, fraternity, sorority, family.

Support staff: career counselor, dorm parent, financial aid advisor, foreign student advisor, housing advisor, physical therapist, psychological counselor, resident assistant, resident nurse, student affairs officer.

DANCE

Curriculum, Students, and Faculty

Required courses: anatomy, ballet (2 classes per week, 1 year to complete), dance composition or choreography, dance history, Cunningham-based (2 classes per week, 1 year to complete), music, rehearsal and performance, stagecraft, dance improvisation.

Elective courses: African dance, master classes, Indian dance, film and performance, exploration in movement and performance.

DRAMA

Curriculum, Students, and Faculty

Required courses: acting, drama criticism, scene study, text analysis.

Elective courses: audition preparation, directing, dramaturgy, make-up, speech, voice.

EASTMAN SCHOOL OF MUSIC

University of Rochester
26 Gibbs Street, Rochester NY 14604-2599
Tel: 800-388-9695 (US)
Contact: Charles Krusenstjerna

General

Type of Institution: conservatory, coed. *Environment:* urban. *Cross registration is available through the University of Rochester.*

Total enrollment of institution: 800. *Degrees offered:* BM.

Entrance Requirements

Audition required: live, audio, video. *Standardized test requirements:* TOEFL.

Costs & Financial Aid

Deposit: $200. *Tuition:* $18,700. *Medical fee:* $320. *Other fees:* $95 undergraduate activity fee, $600 books and supplies. *Room and board*: $6,930.

Percent of students receiving financial aid: 50%. *Types of scholarships and aid awarded:* full, partial, merit-based, need-based, named, institutional aid, work/study, gig office. *Forms required for scholarships:* FAFSA, income tax return. *Loans available. Procedure for applying for loans:* financial aid information is included with the application, no financial aid offers will be made to students until the Federal Student Aid Report (SAR) is received. *Financial aid offered to international students.*

Services

Housing options: on-site dorms, off-campus housing.

Support staff: financial aid advisor, foreign student advisor, housing advisor.

FORDHAM UNIVERSITY AT LINCOLN CENTER

113 West 60th Street, New York NY 10023
Tel: 212-636-6303
Fax: 212-636-6788
Web: www.fordham.edu
Contact: Joe Korevec

General

Type of Institution: private university. *Religious Affiliation*: Jesuit Roman Catholic. *Environment:* urban.

Degrees offered: BA.

Entrance Requirements

Audition required: live, video. *Other requirements:* interview, recommendation, essay. *Standardized test requirements:* SAT I, 1150.

Costs & Financial Aid

Tuition: $13,600.

Types of scholarships and aid awarded: full, partial, merit-based, need-based, work/study. *Forms required for scholarships:* FFS, FAFSA, income tax return. *Loans available. Procedure for applying for loans:* check with Financial Aid Office (212) 636-6700. *Financial aid offered to international students.*

Services

Housing options: on-site dorms, off-campus housing.

Support staff: career counselor, financial aid advisor, housing advisor, psychological counselor, resident assistant, resident nurse, student affairs officer.

DRAMA

Curriculum, Students, and Faculty

Required courses: acting, movement, scene study, speech, Stanislavski exercises, voice, Suzuki.

Elective courses: directing, make-up, musical theater, stage combat, text analysis, verse drama.

Number of years required to complete program: 4. *Summer program not available. Affiliation with a professional theater company: small AEA summer company using Fordham graduates.*

Selectivity for males: approximately 33% admitted. *Selectivity for females:* approximately 33% admitted. *Total enrollment:* 100. *Entering class size:* 40. *Percent International*: 20%.

Renowned alumni: Denzel Washington, Dylan McDermott, Patricia Clarkson.

Total full-time faculty: 7. *Total part-time faculty:* 7. *List of current faculty and past affiliations:* Diane Carter, Yolanda King, Joan MacIntosh, Lawrence Sacharow, Michael Massee, Matthew Maguire, Eva Patton, Elizabeth Margid.

Audition Information

No audition fee. Audition consists of the following: Shakespearean monologue. *Repertoire that students should avoid?* none from monologue books.

Audition evaluation criteria: imagination, understanding of text, motivation, maturity, potential for growth, interest in Fordham College.

Performance Information

Performance opportunities available (frequency): fully produced performances (14-19 per year), workshops (4 per year), auditioned.

Recent guest artists: Julie Taymore, Denzel Washington, Harvey Keitel, Anne Bogart.

Facilities

Rehearsal facilities and hours: Pope Auditorium, available 24 hours, "White Box" black box studio. *Number of theaters on campus:* 2. *Type and capacity:* mainstage 175, black box 70.

HOFSTRA UNIVERSITY

J.C. Adams Playhouse
118 Hofstra University, Hempstead NY 11549-1180
Tel: 516-463-5444
Fax: 516-463-4001
Email: DRMADN@hofstra.edu
Web: www.hofstra.edu

General

Type of Institution: private university. *Environment:* suburban.

Total enrollment of institution: 7,157. *Degrees offered:* BA, BFA.

Entrance Requirements

Audition not required Standardized test requirements: ACT, 23; SAT I, 1000; TOEFL, 550.

Costs & Financial Aid

Application fee: $50. *Deposit:* $250. *Tuition:* $13,966. *Medical fee:* $46. *Other fees:* $72 university fee, $10 activity fee. *Room and board:* $6,750.

Types of scholarships and aid awarded: full, partial, merit-based, need-based, named, institutional aid, government aid, reduced tuition, tuition payment plan, work/study. *Forms required for scholarships:* FFS, FAFSA, income tax return, income asset verification. *Loans available. Procedure for applying for loans:* contact Financial Aid Office (516) 463-6680. *Financial aid offered to international students. Other aid available to international students:* Contact Financial Aid office (516) 463-6680.

Services

Housing options: on-site dorms, off-campus housing, family.

Support staff: career counselor, financial aid advisor, foreign student advisor, psychological counselor, resident assistant, resident nurse, student affairs officer.

DANCE

Curriculum, Students, and Faculty

Required courses: anatomy, ballet, dance composition/choreography, dance history, dance writing research and criticism, jazz, master classes, Cunningham-based, Graham-based dance, Limon-based modern dance, rehearsal and performance, repertory, stagecraft.

Elective courses: music, nutrition, modern dance partnering.

Selectivity for males: admit all who apply. *Selectivity for females:* admit all who apply. *Total enrollment*: 50. *Entering class size:* 16. *Graduating class size:* 9. *Percent International*: 2%. *Countries most represented*: Japan, Holland, China.

Renowned alumni: Larry Keigwin.

Total part-time faculty: 3. *Total part-time faculty:* 6. *List of current faculty and past affiliations:* Stormy Brandenberger, Lance

Westergard. *Program contact person:* Stormy Brandenberger.

Audition Information

No audition fee. Audition consists of the following: ballet, modern dance, prepared solo, preferably choreographed by student. *Accompanist provided. Cassette player available; CD player available. Dress requirements for males:* leotard, tights. *Dress requirements for females:* leotard, tights.

Repertoire that students should avoid? no tap dancing.

Audition evaluation criteria: strong ballet training is important.

Performance Information

Performance opportunities available (frequency): Fully produced concerts (4 per year), informal concerts (5 per year), workshops (4 per year), onsite performances (2 per year), American College Dance Festival.

Performances choreographed by: faculty, students, guests. *Recent guest choreographers:* Eleo Pomare, Blondell Cummings, Claire Porter, Janis Brenner, Colin Conner, Sara Rudner, Kathryn Posin, Remy Charlip, Rosalind Newman, David Malamut, Cathy McCann, Tyrone Brooks, Liza Genarro.

Facilities

Number of studios available: 3. *Approximate studio dimensions and flooring:* 40' x 60' sprung wooden floor, 20' x 40' sprung wooden floor. *Performance facilities:* J.C. Adams Playouse (proscenium—seats 1,134), Spiegel Theater (proscenium—seats 99), West End Theater (black box—seats 125).

DRAMA

Curriculum, Students, and Faculty

Number of years required to complete program: 4. *Summer program not available. Selectivity for males:* approximately 33% admitted. *Selectivity for females:* approximately 33% admitted. *Total enrollment:* 91. *Entering class size:* 32. *Graduating class size:* 27. *Percent International*: 2%. *Countries most represented*: Japan, Holland, Greece.

Renowned alumni: Francis Ford Coppola, Thom Bray, Robert Davi, Elizabeth Dennehy, Peter Friedman, Dan Ingram, Madeline Kahn, Ray Klausen, Ken Kraft, Irene Lewis, Charles Ludlam, Joe Morton, Joel Oliansky, Arturo Porazzi, Kevin Schinick, James Barbour, Philip Rosenthal, Charles Repole, Susan Schulman, Joan See, Susan Sullivan, Frank Von Zerneck, Tom McGowan.

Total full-time faculty: 7. *Total part-time faculty:* 5.

Audition Information

Audition consists of the following: a cappella, comedic monologue, singing with a tape; contemporary monologue, classical monologue. *Dress requirements for males:* shirt, tie, slacks. *Dress requirements for females:* dress skirt and blouse, suit. *Audition evaluation criteria:* individual evaluation varies.

Performance Information

Performance opportunities available (frequency): fully produced performances (6 per year), informal performances (varies), workshops (varies), extracurricular groups, 2 shows per year, auditioned.

Recent guest artists: Lainie Kazan, Gloria Foster, Charles Repole, Larry Arrick, Kenneth Mitchell, David Holdgrive, Clay Fullum.

Facilities

Rehearsal facilities and hours: J.C. Adams Playhouse, Spiegel Theater, West End Theater, Emily Lowe Rehearsal Studio. *Number of theaters on campus:* 3 *Type and capacity:* proscenium 1,134, proscenium 99, black box 125.

ITHACA COLLEGE

Office of Admissions
100 Job Hall, Ithaca NY 14850
Tel: 607-274-3124
Fax: 607-274-1990
Email: admission@ithaca.edu
Web: www.ithaca.edu

General

Type of Institution: private college. *Environment:* suburban. *Cross registration is available through the Cornell University.*

Total enrollment of institution: 5,629. *Total student body from other countries:* 2%. *Degrees offered:* BA, BFA, BS.

Entrance Requirements

Audition required: live, video. *Other requirements:* interview, recommendation, essay. *Standardized test requirements:* ACT; SAT I; TOEFL, 550.

Costs & Financial Aid

Application fee: $40. *Deposit:* $250. *Tuition:* $16,900.

Percent of students receiving financial aid: 78%. *Types of scholarships and aid awarded:* full, partial, merit-based, need-based, named, institutional aid, government aid, reduced tuition, tuition payment plan, work/study. *Forms required for scholarships:* FAFSA, income tax return, income asset verification. *Loans available. Procedure for applying for loans:* part of financial aid package. *Financial aid offered to international students. Other aid available to international students:* institutional scholarships, institutional work study.

Services

Housing options: on-site dorms, fraternity, sorority.

Support staff: career counselor, financial aid advisor, foreign student advisor, housing advisor, physical therapist, psychological counselor, resident assistant, resident nurse, student affairs officer.

Comments

Ithaca offers a competitive, performance-oriented program within a liberal art college setting. It focuses on undergraduate education (450 undergraduates, 40 graduates), offers a respected music education curriculum as well as majors in performance, performance/music education (4.5 years), music with an outside field, jazz studies, composition, theory, and musical theatre.

Ithaca College does not offer a major in dance but has a dance minor. It also offers a major in musical theater, which includes both dance and drama.

DANCE

Curriculum, Students, and Faculty

Elective courses: ballet, dance composition or choreography, dance history, jazz, modern dance, stagecraft, tap.

Total enrollment: 49. *Entering class size:* 13. *Graduating class size:* 12.

Total part-time faculty: 3. *Total part-time faculty:* 1. *List of current faculty and past affiliations:* Eugenia Wacker-Hoeflin, Metropolitan Opera, Les Grandes Ballet Canadiens; Mary Corsaro, New York University, Indiana University; Jean McGregor, University of Michigan.

Performance Information

Performance opportunities available (frequency): Fully produced concerts (varies), informal concerts (varies).

Performances choreographed by: faculty, students.

Facilities

Number of studios available: 2. *Approximate studio dimensions and flooring:* 34' x 45' Timestep Marley-like surface, neoprene insolators, 35.6' x 48.4' Timestep Marley-like surface, neoprene insolators.

DRAMA

Curriculum, Students, and Faculty

Number of years required to complete program: 4. *Summer program not available. No affiliation with a professional theater company. Selectivity for males:* approximately 10% admitted. *Selectivity for females:* approximately 10% admitted. *Total enrollment:* 184. *Entering class size:* 44. *Graduating class size:* 29. *Percent International*: 3%. *Countries most represented*: Finland, Japan, Mexico, Turkey.

Renowned alumni: Tim Jerome, Aaron Lusting, Matt Fox, Sal Mistretta, Kenny Butler, Daniel McDonald, Amanda Naughton.

Total full-time faculty: 18. *Total part-time faculty:* 5. *List of current faculty and past affiliations:* Barbara Anger, Susannah Berryman, Gerg Bostwick, Diane Claussen, John L. Bracewell, Mary Corsaro, Nancy Gaspar, Norman Johnson, Earl McCarroll, Beverly Pattan, Fean McGregor.

Audition Information

No audition fee. Audition consists of the following: cold readings, comedic monologue, group warm-up. *Repertoire that students should avoid?* Do not perform comic monologues written for particular performers, ie., Irma Bombeck, Richard Pryor, George Carlin, etc. Avoid monologues that are not from plays but simply contained in books of monologues. Don't try to play both characters in a scene by talking to and answering yourself. Avoid elaborate introductions; we are probably familiar with the piece you have chosen.

Audition evaluation criteria: overall talent.

Performance Information

Performance opportunities available (frequency): fully produced performances (2 per year), informal performances (4-5), workshops (1 per acting class a year), off-site performances (6-8)fully produced performances (6 per year), informal performances (8-17 per year), auditioned.

Facilities

Rehearsal facilities and hours: studios, classrooms, 7:00 pm-1:00 am. *Number of theaters on campus:* 2. *Type and capacity:* proscenium 535, arena 280.

MUSIC

Curriculum, Students, and Faculty

How are major teacher assignments made? students may choose. Most student requests are honored after 6/1. Faculty is not informed of a student's teacher preference at the time of the audition. *May a student change major teachers during the course of study?* possibly. *Study of secondary instrument or discipline is allowed.*

Selectivity for instruments or programs offered (rating): accompanying (selective), bassoon, clarinet (competitive), composition (competitive), double bass (competitive), electronic music (competitive), flute or piccolo (selective), French horn, guitar (competitive), jazz (competitive), oboe/English horn (competitive), organ, percussion (selective), piano, saxophone (selective), trombone (competitive), trumpet (selective), tuba (competitive), viola (non-competitive), violin, violoncello, voice (highly selective).

Total enrollment: 172. *Entering class size:* 39. *Graduating class size:* 41. *Percent International*: 6%. *Countries most represented*: Japan, Brazil, Bulgaria, Canada, Colombia, England, Malaysia.

Renowned alumni: Amald Gabriel; Sharon Sweet, Metropolitan Opera, New York Voices; Gail Williams, Chicago Orchestra.

Total part-time faculty: 50. *Total part-time faculty:* 19. *Program contact person:* Graham Stewart, (607) 274-3366.

Audition Information

No audition fee. Audition consists of the following: scales, arpeggios, sight reading, repertoire. *Instruments provided for:* percussionists.

Required repertoire: 2-3 contrasting solos. *Performance opportunities available (frequency):* band, chamber music, jury examinations, opera workshops, orchestral concerts, recitals, produced operas, chorus.

Facilities

Number of practice rooms and hours: 90; 7:00 am-1:00 am. *Recital hall?* yes. *Concert hall?* yes.

JUILLIARD SCHOOL

60 Lincoln Center Plaza, New York NY 10023
Tel: 212-799-5000
Fax: 212-769-6420
Web: www.juilliard.edu
Contact: Mary K. Gray

General

Type of Institution: conservatory, coed. *Environment:* urban. *Cross registration is available through Columbia University and Barnard College.*

Total enrollment of institution: 768. *Total student body from other countries:* 30%. *Degrees offered:* certificate, BFA, BM.

Entrance Requirements

Audition required: live. *Other requirements:* recommendation, essay. *Standardized test requirements:* TOEFL, 526.

Costs & Financial Aid

Application fee: $85. *Deposit:* $250. *Tuition:* $15,200. *Other fees:* $600 comprehensive fee (includes medical).

Percent of students receiving financial aid: 85%. *Types of scholarships and aid awarded:* full, partial, merit-based, need-based, named, institutional aid, government aid, reduced tuition, work/study. *Forms required for scholarships:* FAFSA, income tax return, school's own financial aid form. *Loans available. Procedure for applying for loans:* through Financial Aid Office. *Financial aid offered to international students. Percent of international students receiving scholarships:* 65%. *Other aid available to international students:* work/study.

Services

Housing options: on-site dorms.

Support staff: career counselor, financial aid advisor, foreign student advisor, housing advisor, physical therapist, psychological counselor, resident assistant, resident nurse, student affairs officer.

DANCE

Curriculum, Students, and Faculty

Required courses: ballet, dance composition/choreography, dance history, men's class, Graham-based, Limon-based, Taylor-based modern dance, music, pas de deux, rehearsal and performance, repertory, stagecraft, modern dance partnering.

Elective courses: anatomy, jazz, Indian dance, pointe, tap.

Selectivity for males: approximately 60% admitted. *Selectivity for females:* approximately 10% admitted. *Total enrollment:* 84. *Entering class size:* 23. *Graduating class size:* 18. *Percent International*: 10%. *Countries most represented*: Taiwan, Japan, Brazil, Canada.

Renowned alumni: Paul Taylor, Lar Lubovitch, Bruce Marks, Daniel Lewis, Martha Clarke, Dennis Nahat.

Total part-time faculty: 17. *Total part-time faculty:* 13. *List of current faculty and past affiliations:* Ethel Winter; Christine Dakin, Martha Graham Dance Company; Sue Bernhard; Laura Glenn; Stephen Pier, Jose Limon Dance Company; Carolyn Adams; Linda Kent; Jane Kosminsky; Elizabeth Keen, Paul Taylor Dance Company; Stephen Pier, Royal Danish Ballet; Andra Corvino, Metropolitan Opera Ballet Company. *Program contact person:* Diana Feingold.

Audition Information

Audition consists of the following: ballet, modern dance, prepared solo. *Cassette player available; CD player available. Dress requirements for males:* white t-shirt, black tights, white socks, ballet shoes. *Dress requirements for females:* black leotard, pink tights, ballet shoes.

Audition evaluation criteria: technique, musicality, performance.

Performance Information

Performance opportunities available (frequency): Fully produced concerts (2 per year), workshops (8 per year).

Performances choreographed by: faculty, students, guests. *Recent guest choreographers:* Igal Perry, Jiri Kylian, Lila York, Glen Tetley.

Facilities

Number of studios available: 6. *Approximate studio dimensions and flooring:* wood, Marley. *Performance facilities:* The Juilliard Theater—seats 933; Clark Studio Theater.

DRAMA

Curriculum, Students, and Faculty

Required courses: acting, Alexander technique, audition preparation, improvisation, make-up, mime, movement, scene study, singing, speech, stage combat, Stanislavski exercises, text analysis, verse drama, voice.

Number of years required to complete program: 4. *Summer program not available. No affiliation with a professional theater company. Michael Kahn, Director of Drama Division, is the Artistic Director of the Shakespeare Theatre in Washington, D.C. Many alumni are hired as company members.*

Selectivity for males: approximately 5% admitted. *Selectivity for females:* approximately 3% admitted. *Total enrollment:* 72. *Entering class size:* 20. *Graduating class size:* 16. *Percent International*: 1%.

Renowned alumni: Kevin Kline, Patti Lupone, Christopher Reeve, Kevin Spacey, Robin Williams.

Total full-time faculty: 24. *Total part-time faculty:* 10. *List of current faculty and past affiliations:* Garland Wright, the Guthrie Theatre; Eve Shapiro, Royal Academy of Dramatic Art; John Stix, Circle in the Square.

Audition Information

Audition consists of the following: a cappella, cold readings, improvisation, group warm-up. *Dress requirements for males:* comfortable clothing that permits freedom of movement. *Dress requirements for females:* comfortable clothing that permits freedom of movement.

Performance Information

Performance opportunities available (frequency): fully produced performances (12-16 per year), informal performances (10-15 per year), workshops (4-8 per year) assigned.

Facilities

Rehearsal facilities and hours: 7 rehearsal spaces on site, hours vary according to specific productions. *Number of theaters on campus:* 2. *Type and capacity:* thrust 206, black box 70.

MUSIC

Curriculum, Students, and Faculty

Unique or innovative music curriculum: A music theory curriculum "Literature and Materials of music" required for all four years. *How are major teacher assignments made?* Students may choose, made by the school, according to teacher preference and teacher availability. Faculty is not informed of a student's teacher preference at the time of the audition. *30 lessons with major teacher. May a student change major teachers during the course of study?* possibly. *Study of secondary instrument or discipline is allowed.*

Selectivity for instruments or programs offered (rating): accompanying (highly selective), bassoon (highly selective), clarinet (highly selective), composition (highly selective), double bass (highly selective), flute or piccolo (highly selective), French horn (highly selective), guitar (highly selective), harp (highly selective), oboe/ English horn (highly selective), orchestral conducting (highly selective), organ (highly selective), percussion (highly selective), piano (highly selective), trombone (highly selective), trumpet (highly selective), tuba (highly selective), viola (highly selective), violin (highly selective), violoncello (highly selective), voice (highly selective).

Total enrollment: 616. *Entering class size:* 75. *Graduating class size:* 75. *Percent International*: 36%. *Countries most represented*: Korea, Canada, Japan, Taiwan.

Total part-time faculty: 50. *Total part-time faculty:* 100. *Program contact person:* Mary K. Gray.

Audition Information

Audition consists of the following: scales, orchestral excerpts, music theory, arpeggios, sight reading, call for required repertoire. *Instruments provided for:* harpists, percussionists.

Performance opportunities available (frequency): chamber music, band, jury examinations, opera workshops, orchestral concerts, recitals, produced operas, chorus.

Facilities

Number of practice rooms and hours: 106; 8:00 am-10:00 pm. *Recital hall?* yes. *Concert hall?* yes. *Recording studio?* yes.

MANHATTAN SCHOOL OF MUSIC

120 Claremont Avenue, New York NY 10027
Tel: 212-749-2802
Fax: 212-749-5471
Email: admission@msmnyc.edu
Contact: Lee Cioppa

General

Type of Institution: conservatory. *Environment:* urban.

Total student body from other countries: 41%. *Degrees offered:* BM.

Entrance Requirements

Audition required: live, video. *Other requirements:* essay. *Standardized test requirements:* TOEFL.

Costs & Financial Aid

Application fee: $90. *Deposit:* $300. *Tuition:* $18,200. *Medical fee:* $150.

Percent of students receiving financial aid: 75%. *Types of scholarships and aid awarded:* full, partial, merit-based, institutional aid, government aid, work/study, gig office. *Forms required for scholarships:* FAFSA, income tax return, income asset verification. *Loans available. Financial aid offered to international students. Percent of international students receiving scholarships:* 35%.

Services

Housing options: on-site dorms.

Support staff: career counselor, financial aid advisor, foreign student advisor, housing advisor, resident assistant, student affairs officer.

MANHATTANVILLE COLLEGE

2900 Purchase Street, Purchase NY 10577
Tel: 800-32-VILLE
Fax: 914-694-4408
Web: www.manhattanville.edu
Contact: Jose Flores

General

Type of Institution: private college. *Environment:* suburban. *Cross registration is available through the State University of New York-Purchase.*

Total enrollment of institution: 975. *Degrees offered:* BA, BM.

Entrance Requirements

Audition required: live, audio. *Other requirements:* interview.

Services

Housing options: on-site dorms.

Support staff: financial aid advisor, foreign student advisor, housing advisor, psychological counselor, resident assistant, resident nurse, student affairs officer.

DANCE

Curriculum, Students, and Faculty

Required courses: dance composition or choreography, dance history, dance writing research and criticism, Labanotation, modern dance, movement techniques, repertory, stagecraft, stagecraft, dance composition or choreography, rehearsal and performance.

Elective courses: African dance, ballet, jazz, other world dance forms, dance writing research and criticism.

DRAMA

Curriculum, Students, and Faculty

Required courses: acting, improvisation, speech, voice.

Elective courses: audition preparation, directing, drama criticism, movement techniques, musical theater, stage combat, text analysis.

Performance Information

Performance opportunities available (frequency): fully produced performances (3 per year), informal performances (2 per year), workshops (6 per year), off-site performances (4 per year), 4-8 senior thesis project performances per year.

MUSIC

Curriculum, Students, and Faculty

Unique or innovative music curriculum: part of college-portfolio system. Music curriculum strongly integrated with liberal arts requirements. *How are major teacher assignments made?* students may choose according to teacher availability. Faculty is not informed of a student's teacher preference at the time of the audition. 29 lessons with major teacher. *May a student change major teachers during the course of study?* possibly. *Study of secondary instrument or discipline is allowed.*

Selectivity for instruments or programs offered (rating): bassoon (selective), clarinet (selective), double bass (selective), flute or piccolo (selective), French horn (selective), guitar (selective), harp (selective), oboe/English horn (selective), organ (selective), piano (selective), saxophone (selective), trombone (selective), trumpet (selective), tuba (selective), viola (selective), violin (selective), violoncello (selective), voice (selective).

Total enrollment: 382. *Entering class size:* 25. *Graduating class size:* 12.

Renowned alumni: Brian Hilt, John Curtis, Charles Pistoner, Joan Kennedy, Carol Crawford, Tamara Brooks.

Total full-time faculty: 3. *Total part-time faculty:* 17. *Program contact person:* Dr. Anthony Lamagra.

Audition Information

No audition fee. Audition consists of the following: scales, music theory, rhythmic, dictation, arpeggios, melodic dictation, repertoire.

Required repertoire: 3 varied compositions. *Repertoire that students should avoid?* no. *Performance opportunities available (frequency):* chamber music, band (frequently), jury examinations (frequently), recitals (frequently), chorus.

Facilities

Number of practice rooms and hours: 14; 8:00 am-11:00 pm. *Recital hall?* yes. *Concert hall?* yes. *Recording studio?* no.

MANNES COLLEGE OF MUSIC

150 West 85th Street, New York NY 10024
Tel: 212-580-0210
Fax: 212-580-1738
Contact: Lisa Crissman Wright

General

Type of Institution: college, conservatory. *Environment:* urban. *Cross registration is available through the New School of Social Research.*

Total enrollment of institution: 289. *Total student body from other countries:* 50%. *Degrees offered:* BFA, BM.

Entrance Requirements

Audition required: live. *Other requirements:* recommendation. *Standardized test requirements:* TOEFL, 550, school's own English exam required.

Costs & Financial Aid

Application fee: $100. *Deposit:* $500. *Tuition:* $15,580. *Other fees:* $6,500-$8,000 room.

Types of scholarships and aid awarded: full, partial, merit-based, tuition payment plan, work/study, gig office. *Forms required for scholarships:* FAFSA, income tax return, income asset verification. *Loans available. Procedure for applying for loans:* contact Financial Aid Office. *Financial aid offered to international students.*

Services

Housing options: on-site dorms.

Support staff: financial aid advisor, foreign student advisor, housing advisor, physical therapist, psychological counselor, resident assistant, student affairs officer.

NEW YORK UNIVERSITY

School of Education, Department of Music and Peforming Arts
35 West 4th, Room 777, New York NY 10012
Tel: 212-998-5424
Fax: 212-995-4043
Email: nyuadmit@uccum.edu
Web: www.nyu.edu

General

Type of Institution: university. *Environment:* urban.

Total enrollment of institution: 36,306. *Total student body from other countries:* 20%. *Degrees offered:* BM, BS.

Entrance Requirements

Audition required: live, audio, video. *Other requirements:* interview, recommendation, essay *Standardized test requirements:* SAT I, 1200; TOEFL, 600.

Costs & Financial Aid

Application fee: $50. *Deposit:* $200. *Tuition:* $23,000. *Room and board*: $8,056.

Percent of students receiving financial aid: 65% *Types of scholarships and aid awarded:* full, partial, merit-based, need-based, named, institutional aid, government aid, reduced tuition, tuition payment plan, work/study, gig office. *Forms required for scholarships:* FFS, FAFSA, income tax return, income asset verification. *Loans available. Procedure for applying for loans:* contact admissions. *Percent of international students receiving scholarships:* 0%.

Services

Housing options: on-site dorms, off-campus housing, fraternity, sorority.

Support staff: career counselor, financial aid advisor, foreign student advisor, housing advisor, physical therapist, psychological counselor, resident assistant, resident nurse, student affairs officer.

DANCE

Curriculum, Students, and Faculty

Required courses: anatomy, character, ballet, dance composition or choreography, dance history, dance theory, jazz, Labanotation, men's class, music, pas de deux, pointe, rehearsal and performance, repertory, tap, variations, dance writing research and criticism, rehearsal and performance, ballet (2 classes per week, 4 years to complete).

Elective courses: African dance, dance writing research and criticism, historical dance, master classes, movement techniques, nutrition, other world dance forms, Spanish, stagecraft, vernacular dance, modern dance partnering.

Selectivity for males: approximately 60% admitted. *Selectivity for females:* approximately 60% admitted. *Total enrollment*: 100. *Entering class size:* 10. *Graduating class size:* 5. *Percent International*: 10%. *Countries most represented*: Taiwan, Korea.

Total full-time faculty: 2. *Total part-time faculty:* 22. *List of current faculty and past affiliations:* Gregory Scott, M. Roskin Berger. *Program contact person:* M. Roskin-Berger.

Audition Information

No audition fee. Audition consists of the following: ballet, prepared solo. *Accompanist provided. Cassette player available; CD player available.*

Performance Information

Performance opportunities available (frequency): Fully produced concerts (3 per year), informal concerts (3 per year), workshops (10 per year).

Performances choreographed by: faculty, students, guests.

Facilities

Number of studios available: 10. *Approximate studio dimensions and flooring: Performance facilities:* large studio theaters on campus. *Contact*: Nicole Scrotani or Anne Wennerstrand, (212) 998-5407.

DRAMA

Curriculum, Students, and Faculty

Required courses: acting, directing, improvisation, movement, scene study, speech, voice, Stanislavski exercises.

Elective courses: Alexander technique, audition preparation, drama criticism, make-up, martial arts, mime, musical theater, stage combat, Stanislavski exercises, text analysis, verse drama, voice, speech.

Number of years required to complete program: 4. *Summer program available. Total enrollment:* 100. *Entering class size:* 12. *Graduating class size:* 4. *Percent International*: 10%. *Countries most represented*: Taiwan, Korea.

Audition Information

Audition consists of the following: comedic monologue, improvisation, group warm-up.

MUSIC

Curriculum, Students, and Faculty

How are major teacher assignments made? students may choose. Faculty is not informed of a student's teacher preference at the time of the audition. 30 lessons with major teacher. *May a student change major teachers during the course of study?* possibly. *Study of secondary instrument or discipline is allowed.*

Selectivity for instruments or programs offered (rating): accompanying (competitive), bagpipes (competitive), bassoon (competitive), choral singing (competitive), clarinet (competitive), composition (competitive), double bass (competitive), electronic music (competitive), flute or piccolo (competitive), French horn (competitive), guitar (competitive), harp (competitive), jazz (competitive), oboe/English horn (competitive), organ (competitive), percussion (competitive), piano (competitive), saxophone (competitive), trombone (competitive), trumpet (competitive), tuba (competitive), viola (competitive), violin, violoncello (competitive).

Total enrollment: 600. *Entering class size:* 140. *Graduating class size:* 55. *Percent International*: 20%. *Countries most represented*: Taiwan, Korea.

Renowned alumni: L. Ferrara, M. Steinberg, Mari Kimura.

Total full-time faculty: 17. *Total part-time faculty:* 220. *Program contact person:* L. Ferrara.

Audition Information

No audition fee. Audition consists of the following: music theory, rhythmic dictation, music history, melodic dictation. *Instruments provided for:* percussionists.

Performance opportunities available (frequency): chamber music, jury examinations, orchestral concerts, recitals, chorus.

Facilities

Number of practice rooms and hours: 55; 8:00 am-11:00 pm. *Recital hall?* yes. *Concert hall?* yes. *Recording studio?* yes.

ROBERTS WESLEYAN COLLEGE

2301 Westside Drive, Rochester NY 14624
Tel: 716-594-6000
Fax: 716-594-6534
Email: mageen@roberts.edu
Web: www.roberts.edu
Contact: Linda Kurtz

General

Type of Institution: private college. *Religious Affiliation*: Free Methodist Church. *Environment:* suburban.

Total enrollment of institution: 1,350. *Total student body from other countries:* 5%. *Degrees offered:* BA, BS in music performance, BS in music education.

Entrance Requirements

Audition required: live. *Other requirements:* interview, recommendation, essay. *Standardized test requirements:* ACT, 23; SAT I, 1066; TOEFL, 550.

Costs & Financial Aid

Application fee: $35. *Deposit:* $200. *Tuition:* $11,390. *Medical fee:* $110. *Other fees:* $540 returning students, $575 new students.

Types of scholarships and aid awarded: partial, merit-based, need-based, named, institutional aid, government aid, tuition payment plan, work/study. *Forms required for scholarships:* FAFSA, income tax return. *Loans available. Procedure for applying for loans:* Supplemental Aid Form through Financial Aid Office. *Financial aid offered to international students. Other aid available to international students:* institutional.

Services

Housing options: on-site dorms, off-campus housing.

Support staff: career counselor, financial aid advisor, foreign student advisor, housing advisor, psychological counselor, resident assistant, resident nurse, student affairs officer.

MUSIC

Curriculum, Students, and Faculty

Unique or innovative music curriculum: Piano Pedagogy Certification, which can be combined with music education. *How are major teacher assignments made?* Students may choose, made by the school according to teacher preference and teacher availability. Faculty is not informed of a student's teacher preference at the time of the audition. *May a student change major teachers during the course of study?* possibly. *Study of secondary instrument or discipline is allowed.*

Selectivity for instruments or programs offered (rating): accompanying (non-competitive), accordion (non-competitive), bagpipes (non-competitive), bassoon (non-competitive), choral conducting (non-competitive), choral singing (non-competitive), clarinet (non-competitive), composition (non-competitive), double bass (non-competitive), electronic music, flute or piccolo (non-competitive), French horn, guitar (non-competitive), harp, harpsichord (non-competitive), jazz (non-competitive), oboe/English horn (non-competitive), orchestral conducting (non-competitive), organ (non-competitive), percussion (non-competitive), piano (non-competitive), sacred music (non-competitive), saxophone (non-competitive), trombone (non-competitive), trumpet (non-competitive), tuba (non-competitive), viola (non-competitive), violin (non-competitive), violoncello (non-competitive), voice (non-competitive).

Total enrollment: 92. *Entering class size:* 40. *Countries most represented*: Japan.

Renowned alumni: Sharon Sweet, Metropolitan Opera.

Total full-time faculty: 6. *Total part-time faculty:* 25. *Program contact person:* Dr. Noel Magee.

Audition Information

Audition consists of the following: music theory repertoire. *Instruments provided for:* percussionists.

Required repertoire: 2 contrasting compositions. *Performance opportunities available (frequency):* band (frequently), jury examinations (frequently), orchestral concerts (frequently), recitals (frequently).

Facilities

Number of practice rooms and hours: 20; 6 hours per week for 1 credit (based on credit). *Recital hall?* yes. *Concert hall?* yes. *Recording studio?* no.

SARAH LAWRENCE COLLEGE

1 Mead Way, Bronxville NY 10708-5999
Tel: 914-395-2510
Fax: 914-395-2668
Email: slcadmit@mail.slc.edu
Web: www.slc.edu
Contact: Thyra Briggs

General

Type of Institution: private college. *Environment:* suburban.

Total enrollment of institution: 1,388. *Total student body from other countries:* 4%. *Degrees offered:* BA.

Entrance Requirements

Audition not required. Other requirements: recommendation, essay. *Standardized test requirements:* ACT, 27; SAT I, 1260; SAT II; TOEFL.

Costs & Financial Aid

Deposit: $400. *Tuition:* $22,530. *Other fees:* $546 technology, activity. *Room and board*: $6,902.

Percent of students receiving financial aid: 66%. *Types of scholarships and aid awarded:* partial, need-based, named, institutional aid, government aid, tuition payment plan, work/study. *Forms required for scholarships:* FAFSA, income tax return, income asset verification, CSS Profile. *Loans available. Procedure for applying for loans:* complete FAFSA and CSS profile.

Services

Housing options: on-site dorms, off-campus housing.

Support staff: career counselor, financial aid advisor, foreign student advisor, housing advisor, psychological counselor, resident assistant, resident nurse, student affairs officer.

DANCE

Curriculum, Students, and Faculty

Required courses: dance composition or choreography, dance writing research and criticism, modern dance, rehearsal and performance.

Elective courses: Alexander technique, ballet, jazz, movement techniques, body conditioning, pointe.

Selectivity for males: admit all who apply. *Selectivity for females:* admit all who apply. *Total enrollment*: 83.

Renowned alumni: Meredith Monk, Lucinda Childs, Alison Easter, Carolyn Adams, Adele Myers.

Total full-time faculty: 7. ***List of current faculty and past affiliations:*** Emmy Devine, Dan Wagoner Dance Co.; Lanee Westergard, Kathryn Posin Dance Co.; Cassandra Phifer, Dance Theater of Harlem; Roseanne Thorn, *Dance Magazine*. ***Program contact person:*** Viola Farber.

Performance Information

Performance opportunities available (frequency): fully produced concerts (6 per year), informal concerts (varies), workshops (2 per year), on-site performances(1 per year).

Performances choreographed by: faculty, students, guests.

Facilities

Number of studios available: 2. ***Approximate studio dimensions and flooring:*** 40' x 50' Harlequin, 30' x 50'. ***Performance facilities:*** studio transforms into performance space, lights in place, risers and chairs for audience.

DRAMA

Curriculum, Students, and Faculty

Elective courses: acting, Alexander technique, audition preparation, dance, directing, drama criticism, dramaturgy, improvisation, movement, musical theater, scene study, speech, Stanislavski exercises, text analysis, verse drama, voice.

Number of years required to complete program: 4. ***Summer program not available. Affiliation with a professional theater company: Ensemble Studio Theater, All Seasons Theater, and internships through the NYC Theaters.***

Selectivity for males: most admitted, but not all. ***Selectivity for females:*** most admitted, but not all. ***Total enrollment:*** 198. ***Percent International***: 2%. ***Countries most represented***: Canada, England, France, Japan.

Renowned alumni: Jane Alexander, Joanne Woodward, Tovah Feldshuh, Juliana Marqulies.

Audition Information

Audition consists of the following: no formal auditions.

Facilities

Number of theaters on campus: 5. ***Type and capacity:*** proscenium 175, experimental 150, black box 75, black box 50, recital hall 350.

MUSIC

Curriculum, Students, and Faculty

Unique or innovative music curriculum: SLC music program is especially structured to integrate theory and practice and offers conservatory-level studies for students aspiring to professional careers as well as superb instruction for those who love music and want to study it within the context of a liberal arts program. All programs are individually designed based on a core of private tutorials. We have study progams in jazz, world music, and electronic music. ***How are major teacher assignments made?*** Students may choose, made by the school, according to teacher preference and teacher availability. Faculty is informed of a student's teacher preference at the time of the audition. ***30 lessons with major teacher. May a student change major teachers during the course of study?*** possibly. ***Study of secondary instrument or discipline is allowed.***

Selectivity for instruments or programs offered (rating): accompanying (selective), accordion (selective), bassoon (non-competitive), choral conducting (selective), choral singing (open), clarinet (non-competitive), composition (non-competitive), double bass (non-competitive), electronic music (non-competitive), flute or piccolo (non-competitive), French horn (non-competitive), guitar (non-competitive), harp (non-competitive), harpsichord (non-competitive), jazz (non-competitive), oboe/English horn (non-competitive), orchestral conducting (selective), organ (non-competitive), percussion (non-competitive), piano (non-competitive), saxophone (non-competitive), trombone (non-competitive), trumpet (non-competitive), tuba (non-competitive), viola (non-competitive), violin (non-competitive), violoncello (non-competitive), voice (non-competitive).

Total enrollment: 165.

Renowned alumni: Meredith Monk, Yoko Ono, Carol Hall. ***Program contact person:*** Chester Biscardi.

Performance opportunities available (frequency): orchestral concerts (frequently), chorus.

Facilities

Number of practice rooms and hours: 15; 6:00 am-2:00 am. ***Recital hall?*** yes. ***Concert hall?*** yes. ***Recording studio?*** yes.

Comments

SLC believes in the commitment to the development of the total self, as a literate, disciplined and inspired musician and human being. This is the reason that we feel it so important that music be part of a liberal arts education.

SKIDMORE COLLEGE

815 North Broadway, Saratoga Springs NY 12866
Web: www.skidmore.edu
Contact: Mary Lou Bates

General

Type of Institution: private college. *Environment:* suburban. *Cross registration is available through the Hudson-Mohawk Association of Colleges and Universities.*

Total enrollment of institution: 2,191. *Total student body from other countries:* 3%. *Degrees offered:* BA, BS in theater, BS in dance.

Entrance Requirements

Audition not required. Other requirements: interview, recommendation, essay. *Standardized test requirements:* ACT, 25; SAT I, 1178; TOEFL, 570.

Costs & Financial Aid

Application fee: $45. *Deposit:* $300. *Tuition:* $21,750. *Other fees:* $225 student activity fee. *Room and board:* $5,990.

Percent of students receiving financial aid: 35%. *Types of scholarships and aid awarded:* partial, merit-based, need-based, named, institutional aid, government aid, tuition payment plan, work/study. *Forms required for scholarships:* FAFSA, CSS Profile, divorced/separated parents statement. *Loans available. Procedure for applying for loans:* file FAFSA and profile by 2/1 of year of entrance.

Services

Housing options: on-site dorms, off-campus housing.

Support staff: career counselor, financial aid advisor, foreign student advisor, housing advisor, psychological counselor, resident assistant, resident nurse, student affairs officer.

DANCE

Curriculum, Students, and Faculty

Required courses: dance composition or choreography, dance history, rehearsal and performance.

Elective courses: African dance, character, ballet, dance theory, dance writing research and criticism, jazz, modern dance, Graham-based dance, Limon-based, music, Bharata Natyam, pas de deux, pointe, repertory, stagecraft, tap, variations.

Graduating class size: 10.

Renowned alumni: Kenneth Topping, Graham Company; Elizabeth Czerepak, Boston Ballet; Julie Stahd, Twyla Tharp.

Total full-time faculty: 5. *Total part-time faculty:* 1. *Program contact person:* Dr. Mary DiSanto-Rose.

Performance Information

Performance opportunities available (frequency): Fully produced concerts (4 per semester), informal concerts (1 per semester), workshops (2 per semster), on-site performances(1-2 per semester), touring (occasionally).

Performances choreographed by: faculty, students, guests. *Recent guest choreographers:* Kenneth Topping, Doug Varone, Dwight Rhoden, Katherine Kramer, Yacub Addy, Kirston Simone.

Facilities

Number of studios available: 3. *Approximate studio dimensions and flooring:* 50' x 50' sprung wood. *Performance facilities:* dance theater. Sprung floor: stage 40' x 25'; seating 200.

DRAMA

Curriculum, Students, and Faculty

Required courses: directing.

Elective courses: acting, improvisation, movement, scene study, Stanislavski exercises, voice.

Summer program not available. No affiliation with a professional theater company. Graduating class size: 21.

Total full-time faculty: 8. *Total part-time faculty:* 3.

Performance Information

Performance opportunities available (frequency): fully produced performances (2 per term), workshops (4 per term). Open auditions.

Facilities

Rehearsal facilities and hours: 2 rehearsal studios, open availability evenings and weekends *Number of theaters on campus:* 2. *Type and capacity:* black box 100, thrust 345.

MUSIC

Curriculum, Students, and Faculty

Unique or innovative music curriculum: Combined music and history theory sequence. *26 lessons with major teacher. Study of secondary instrument or discipline is allowed.*

Graduating class size: 7.

Total part-time faculty: 13. *Total part-time faculty:* 17. *Program contact person:* Dr. Gordon Thompson.

Performance opportunities available (frequency): jury examinations.

Facilities

Number of practice rooms and hours: 8; 18 hours per day. *Recital hall?* yes. *Concert hall?* no. *Recording studio?* yes.

STATE UNIVERSITY OF NEW YORK, BINGHAMTON

P.O. Box 6001, Binghamton NY 13902-6001
Tel: 607-777-2171
Fax: 607-777-4445
Email: admit@binghamton.edu
Web: www.binghamton.edu
Contact: Jim Fowler

General

Type of Institution: public university. *Environment:* suburban.

Total enrollment of institution: 12,000. *Total student body from other countries:* 2%. *Degrees offered:* BA, BFA.

Entrance Requirements

Audition required: live, video. *Other requirements:* recommendation, essay. *Standardized test requirements:* ACT, 24; SAT I, 1220.

Costs & Financial Aid

Application fee: $30. *Deposit:* $250. *Tuition (in-state/out-state):* $3,400/$8,400. *Other fees:* $700.

Types of scholarships and aid awarded: full, partial, merit-based, need-based, tuition payment plan, work/study. *Forms required for scholarships:* FAFSA. *Loans available. Procedure for applying for loans:* FAFSA. *Financial aid offered to international students.*

Services

Housing options: on-site dorms, off-campus housing.

Support staff: career counselor, financial aid advisor, foreign student advisor, resident assistant, resident nurse, student affairs officer.

Comments

Binghamton University offers a wide variety of opportunities for both majors and non-majors in the performing arts. Lessons are free and available to non-majors. In addition to departmental groups there are many extracurricular opportunities for students in dance, theatre, and music.

DANCE

Curriculum, Students, and Faculty

Required courses: ballet, jazz, modern dance, music, rehearsal and performance, stagecraft.

Elective courses: African dance, dance composition or choreography, dance theory, master classes, movement techniques, tap.

Selectivity for males: admit all who apply. *Selectivity for females:* admit all who apply.

Renowned alumni: Second Hand Dance Company.

Total full-time faculty: 2. *List of current faculty and past affiliations:* Fred Weiss, Rhae Ann Busch. *Program contact person:* Diana Webb.

Audition Information

No audition fee. Audition consists of the following: prepared solo, send videotape. *Accompanist not provided. Cassette player not available; CD player not available.*

Repertoire that students should avoid? no.

Audition evaluation criteria: overall ability and potential.

Performance Information

Performance opportunities available (frequency): Fully produced concerts (varies), informal concerts (varies), workshops (varies), on-site performances(varies), touring (varies).

Performances choreographed by: faculty, students, guests. *Recent guest choreographers:* Bill T. Jones.

Facilities

Number of studios available: 4. *Approximate studio dimensions and flooring:* wood. *Performance facilities:* three large theaters and two studios.

DRAMA

Curriculum, Students, and Faculty

Required courses: acting, drama criticism.

Elective courses: Alexander technique, directing, improvisation, make-up, mime, movement, musical theater, scene study, speech, stage combat, Stanislavski exercises, text analysis, verse drama, voice.

Number of years required to complete program: 4. *Summer program not available. Affiliation with a professional theater company: The Cider Mill Playhouse, Endicott, NY.*

Selectivity for males: admit all who apply. *Selectivity for females:* admit all who apply.

Renowned alumni: Ruben Santiago-Hudson, Paul Reiser, William Baldwin.

Total full-time faculty: 9. *Total part-time faculty:* 5. *List of current faculty and past affiliations:* Don Boror, Tom Kremer, Gene Lesser.

Audition Information

No audition fee. Audition consists of the following: a cappella, submit videotape. *Repertoire that students should avoid?* no.

Audition evaluation criteria: overall ability and potential.

Performance Information

Performance opportunities available (frequency): fully produced performances (varies), informal performances (varies), workshops (varies), off-site performances (varies), auditioned.

Facilities

Rehearsal facilities and hours: many rehearsal rooms available, 8:00 am-11:00 pm. *Type and capacity:* theater 1,200, chamber hall 450, 650, studio 150, studio 150.

MUSIC

Curriculum, Students, and Faculty

Unique or innovative music curriculum: available BA or BFA. *How are major teacher assignments made?* made by the school according to teacher preference. Faculty is informed of a student's teacher preference at the time of the audition. *May a student change major teachers during the course of study?* possibly. *Study of secondary instrument or discipline is allowed.*

Selectivity for instruments or programs offered (rating): accompanying (open), bassoon (open), choral conducting (open), clarinet (open), composition (open), double bass (open), electronic music (open), flute or piccolo (open), French horn (open), jazz (open), oboe/English horn (open), orchestral conducting (open), organ (open), percussion (open), piano (open), saxophone (open), trombone (open), trumpet (open), tuba (open), viola (open), violin (open), violoncello (open), voice (open).

Total enrollment: 50. *Entering class size:* 15. *Graduating class size:* 10.

Renowned alumni: Paul Reiser, Michael Convertino, Marietta Simpson.

Total full-time faculty: 21. *Total part-time faculty:* 14. *Program contact person:* Jane Zuckerman.

Audition Information

No audition fee. Audition consists of the following: scales, sight reading, repertoire.

Required repertoire: 1-2 prepared pieces, refers to NYSSMA list. *Performance opportunities available (frequency):* band (varies), jury examinations (varies), orchestral concerts (varies), chorus (varies).

Facilities

Number of practice rooms and hours: 30; 8:00 am-11:00 pm. *Recital hall?* yes. *Concert hall?* yes. *Recording studio?* yes.

STATE UNIVERSITY OF NEW YORK, BROCKPORT COLLEGE

Department of Dance, Brockport NY 14420
Tel: 716-395-2153
Fax: 716-395-5134

General

Type of Institution: public college.

Degrees offered: BA, BFA.

Entrance Requirements

Audition required: live, video. *Other requirements:* essay, photograph.

Costs & Financial Aid

Tuition (in-state/out-state): \$1,700/\$4,150 *Medical fee:* \$75. *Other fees:* \$12.50 college fee, \$75.50 BSG fee, \$50 athletic fee, \$60 technology fee.

Percent of students receiving financial aid: 30%. *Types of scholarships and aid awarded:* partial, merit-based, institutional aid, tuition payment plan, work/study. *Loans available. Procedure for applying for loans:* through financial aid.

Services

Housing options: on-site dorms, off-campus housing, fraternity, sorority, family.

Support staff: career counselor, dorm parent, financial aid advisor, foreign student advisor, housing advisor, physical therapist, psychological counselor, resident assistant, resident nurse, student affairs officer.

DANCE

Curriculum, Students, and Faculty

Required courses: anatomy, dance composition or choreography, dance history, historical dance, master classes, modern dance, music, nutrition, rehearsal and performance, repertory, stagecraft, dance theory.

Elective courses: African dance, ballet, dance theory, dance writing research and criticism, jazz, Labanotation, movement techniques, tap, vernacular dance, modern dance partnering, music.

Selectivity for males: most admitted, but not all. *Selectivity for females:* most admitted, but not all. *Total enrollment*: 85. *Entering class size:* 40. *Graduating class size:* 30. *Percent International*: 2%. *Countries most represented*: Jamaica.

Renowned alumni: Elizabeth Streb, modern dance choreographer, McArthur foundation award; Wayne Cilento, Broadway; Teresa Maldanado, Graham soloist.

Total full-time faculty: 9. *Total part-time faculty:* 6. *List of current faculty and past affiliations:* Sondra Fraleigh, noted author; Mary Wigman, Alwin Nickolais, guest teacher in Japan, certified in Feldenkrais; Jim Payton, Jose Limon; Susannah Newman, Viola Farber, Graham; Clyde Morgan, African specialist, Limon dancer; Santo Giglio, UCLA graduate, Broadway musical specialist. *Program contact person:* Sandra Fraleigh.

Audition Information

No audition fee. Audition consists of the following: improvisation, modern dance. *Accompanist provided. Cassette player available; CD player available.*

Repertoire that students should avoid? no.

Performance Information

Performance opportunities available (frequency): fully produced concerts (2 per year), informal concerts (2 per semester), workshops (frequently), on-site performances (occasionally), touring (frequently), performing ensemble, African company.

Performances choreographed by: faculty, students, guests. *Recent guest choreographers:* Chen and Dancers, Doug Elkins.

Facilities

Performance facilities: As of 1999—new facilities, state-of-the art, best of everything including jacuzzi baths.

STATE UNIVERSITY OF NEW YORK, BUFFALO

Admissions
17 Capen Hall, Buffalo NY 14260
Tel: 716-645-6900
Fax: 716-645-6498
Email: ub-admissions@admissions.buffalo.edu
Web: www.buffalo.edu
Contact: Kathy Glaser, Don McGuire

General

Type of Institution: public university. *Environment:* urban.

Total enrollment of institution: 23,000. *Total student body from other countries:* 8%. *Degrees offered:* BA, BFA, BM.

Entrance Requirements

Audition required: live, video. *Other requirements:* interview. *Standardized test requirements:* ACT, 25; SAT I, 1171; TOEFL, 550.

Costs & Financial Aid

Application fee: $30. *Deposit:* $150. *Tuition:* $3,400. *Other fees:* $940.

Percent of students receiving financial aid: 60%. *Types of scholarships and aid awarded:* full, partial, merit-based, need-based, tuition payment plan, work/study. *Forms required for scholarships:* FAFSA, income tax return. *Loans available. Procedure for applying for loans:* file FAFSA.

Services

Housing options: on-site dorms, off-campus housing, fraternity, sorority.

Support staff: career counselor, financial aid advisor, foreign student advisor, housing advisor, physical therapist, psychological counselor, resident assistant, resident nurse, student affairs officer.

DANCE

Curriculum, Students, and Faculty

Required courses: anatomy, ballet, dance composition or choreography, dance history, dance theory, dance writing research and criticism, jazz, men's class, modern dance, movement techniques, music, pas de deux, pointe, stagecraft, vernacular dance, modern dance partnering.

Elective courses: master classes, rehearsal and performance.

Selectivity for males: approximately 60% admitted. *Selectivity for females:* approximately 60% admitted. *Total enrollment*: 135. *Entering class size:* 21. *Graduating class size:* 20.

Renowned alumni: Sam Viuerito, Jeffery Denman, Marie Jo Ralabate, Katty Jo Wolosyn, Anne Marie Biancofiore, Joyce Dara, Jon Lehner, Jennifer Howard, Steve Hunnesagen.

Total part-time faculty: 4. *Total part-time faculty:* 6. *List of current faculty and past affiliations:* Affiliations include National and Pageant Faculties, Professional Adjudications, Arts in Education Institute, Young Audiences Incorporation, Disney Enterprises, and Universal Studios. *Program contact person:* Linda Swiniuch.

Audition Information

No audition fee. Audition consists of the following: ballet, improvisation, modern dance. *Accompanist not provided. Cassette player available; CD player available. Dress requirements for males:* no color requirements, close fitting, non-patterned clothes, no bare midriff. *Dress requirements for females:* close fitting, non-patterned clothes, no bare midriff.

Audition evaluation criteria: potential as performers, scholars, or interest in health/recreation related dance professions.

Performance Information

Performance opportunities available (frequency): Fully produced concerts (2 per year), workshops (3 per year), on-site performances (3-5 per year), music theatre: 2 productions yearly.

Performances choreographed by: faculty, students. *Recent guest choreographers:* David Parsons Company, Taylor II Company, Gus Giordano Company, Kiddutz Dance Company, Cleo Laine and John Dankworth.

Facilities

Number of studios available: 2. *Approximate studio dimensions and flooring:* 48' x 50' cushioned hard maple, 50' x 60' cushioned white pine. *Performance facilities:* 2 proscenium theaters, 1 thrust theater, 2 black box theaters.

DRAMA

Curriculum, Students, and Faculty

Required courses: acting, audition preparation, improvisation, movement, musical theater, scene study, text analysis, verse drama, voice.

Elective courses: Alexander technique, ballet, directing, drama criticism, dramaturgy, jazz, make-up, martial arts, mime, stage combat, tap, creative movement.

Number of years required to complete program: 4. *Summer program not available. Affiliation with a professional theater company: LORT House, Irish Classical Theater, Shakespeare in Delaware Park.*

Selectivity for males: approximately 60% admitted. *Selectivity for females:* approximately 60% admitted. *Total enrollment:* 130. *Entering class size:* 26. *Graduating class size:* 28.

Renowned alumni: Martin Takel, Arthur Oliner, Chris Dunford, Joyce Dara.

Total full-time faculty: 9. *Total part-time faculty:* 5. *List of current faculty and past affiliations:* Kazimierz Braun, Gary Casarella; Jerry Finnegan, Anna Kay France, Stephen Henderson, Maria Horne, Richard Mennen, Catherine Norgren.

Audition Information

No audition fee. Audition consists of the following: auditions are not required to be accepted into the department.

Performance Information

Performance opportunities available (frequency): fully produced performances (2 per year), informal performances (2 per year), workshops (2 per year), music theater, usually 2 per year, auditioned.

Recent guest artists: Carol Burnett, Kitty Carlisle Hart, Gregory Peck, Cleo Laine, John Dankworth, Francisco Ortuno.

Facilities

Rehearsal facilities and hours: rehearsal workshop, 2 acting clasrooms. *Number of theaters on campus:* 8. *Type and capacity:* proscenium 1,800, proscenium 1,800, proscenium 1,800, proscenium 1800, proscenium 1,800, black box 350.

MUSIC

Curriculum, Students, and Faculty

Unique or innovative music curriculum: All courses taught by graduate faculty. *How are major teacher assignments made?* students may choose, made by the school according to teacher preference and teacher availability. Faculty is informed of a student's teacher preference at the time of the audition. *15 lessons with major teacher. May a student change major teachers during the course of study?* possibly. *Study of secondary instrument or discipline is allowed.*

Selectivity for instruments or programs offered (rating): accompanying (selective), bassoon (competitive), clarinet (highly selective), composition (highly selective), double bass (competitive), flute or piccolo (highly selective), French horn (competitive), guitar (highly selective), harp (competitive), harpsichord (highly selective), oboe/English horn (competitive), organ (selective), percussion (highly selective), piano (selective), saxophone (selective), trombone (competitive), trumpet (selective), tuba (competitive), viola (competitive), violoncello (competitive), voice (selective).

Total enrollment: 110. *Entering class size:* 27. *Graduating class size:* 17. *Percent International*: 1%. *Countries most represented*: Argentina, Korea.

Renowned alumni: Anthony DeMare; Laura Aikin; Ellen Lang; Kirk Brundage; Anthony Miranda; Joanne Castellani; Michael Andriaccio, Amherst Saxophone Quartet.

Total part-time faculty: 20. *Total part-time faculty:* 24. *Program contact person:* Michael Burke.

Audition Information

No audition fee. Audition consists of the following: scales, orchestral excerpts, music theory, rhythmic dictation, sight reading, melodic dictation, repertoire. *Instruments provided for:* harpists, percussionists; double bass.

Performance opportunities available (frequency): jury examinations (2 per year).

Facilities

Number of practice rooms and hours: 65; 16 hours per day. *Recital hall?* yes. *Concert hall?* yes. *Recording studio?* yes.

STATE UNIVERSITY OF NEW YORK, POTSDAM

The Crane School of Music
44 Pierrepont Avenue, Postdam NY 13676
Tel: 315-267-2415
Fax: 315-267-2413
Email: stoltijm@potsdam.edu

General

Type of Institution: public college.

Total enrollment of institution: 4,500. *Degrees offered:* BA.

Entrance Requirements

Audition required: live, audio. *Other requirements:* interview, recommendation. *Standardized test requirements:* ACT, 20; SAT I, 1050; TOEFL, 500.

Costs & Financial Aid

Deposit: $50. *Tuition (in-state/out-state):* $3,400/$8,300. *Medical fee:* $120. *Other fees:* $319 student fees.

Percent of students receiving financial aid: 70%. *Types of scholarships and aid awarded:* partial, merit-based, need-based, named, institutional aid, government aid, tuition payment plan, work/study, gig office. *Forms required for scholarships:* FAFSA, income tax return. *Loans available. Financial aid offered to international students. Other aid available to international students:* standard campus academic or music scholarships.

Services

Housing options: on-site dorms, off-campus housing.

Support staff: career counselor, financial aid advisor, foreign student advisor, psychological counselor.

Comments

Crane School of Music is based in a modern 5-building complex with 450-seat music theate and 1400-seat concert hall. Crane provided all the music for 1980 Winter Olympics at Lake Placid and the Crane Chorus provided music for the dedication of the Statue of Liberty, same years of history, 1886-1996 and also performed with the NY Philharmonic on that occasion.

MUSIC

Curriculum, Students, and Faculty

Unique or innovative music curriculum: oldest and largest undergraduate music education school in the country. Studios follow a conservatory model; all students have one-on-one lessons with full time resident faculty. Over 50% of music teachers in New York State are Crane graduates. *How are major teacher assignments made?* students may choose, made by the school according to teacher preference and teacher availability. Faculty is not informed of a student's teacher preference at the time of the audition. *May a student change major teachers during the course of study?* possibly. *Study of secondary instrument or discipline is allowed.*

Selectivity for instruments or programs offered (rating): accompanying, bassoon (selective), choral conducting, choral singing (selective), clarinet (selective), composition (highly selective), double bass (highly selective), electronic music, flute or piccolo (highly selective), French horn (highly selective), guitar (highly selective), harp (highly selective), harpsichord (highly selective), jazz (selective), oboe/English horn (highly selective), orchestral conducting, organ (highly selective), percussion (highly selective), piano (highly selective), saxophone (highly selective), trombone (highly selective), trumpet (highly selective), tuba (highly selective), viola (highly selective), violin (highly selective), violoncello (highly selective), voice (selective).

Total enrollment: 600. *Entering class size:* 135. *Graduating class size:* 100. *Percent International*: 1%.

Renowned alumni: Renee Fleming, Metropolitan Opera Company; Alan Goodman, Los Angeles Philharmonic; Stephanie Blythe, Metropolitan Young Artist; Margaret Latimore, Metropolitan Young Artist; Stephen Gerko, Dallas Symphony.

Total full-time faculty: 48. *Total part-time faculty:* 16. *Program contact person:* James M. Stoltie.

Audition Information

Audition fee? $25. *Audition consists of the following:* orchestral excerpts, music theory, rhythmic dictation, sight reading. *Instruments provided for:* percussionists; tuba, string bass (upon request).

Performance opportunities available (frequency): band, jury examinations, opera workshops (frequently), orchestral concerts, recitals (frequently), produced operas, chorus.

Facilities

Number of practice rooms and hours: 75; 7:00 am-11:00 pm. *Recital hall?* yes. *Concert hall?* yes. *Recording studio?* no.

STATE UNIVERSITY OF NEW YORK, PURCHASE COLLEGE

735 Anderson Hill Road, Purchase NY 10577-1400
Tel: 914-251-6300
Fax: 914-251-6314
Contact: Janicemarie Hamm

General

Type of Institution: public, college, conservatory. *Environment:* suburban.

Total enrollment of institution: 3,500. *Degrees offered:* BFA.

Entrance Requirements

Audition required: live, audio, video. *Other requirements:* interview, recommendation, essay, photograph. *Standardized test requirements:* ACT; SAT I; TOEFL, 550.

Costs & Financial Aid

Application fee: $30. *Deposit:* $150. *Tuition (in-state/out-state):* $3,400/$8,300. *Medical fee:* $150.

Types of scholarships and aid awarded: partial, merit-based, need-based, named, institutional aid, government aid, tuition payment plan, work/study. *Forms required for scholarships:* FAFSA, income tax return. *Loans available. Procedure for applying for loans:* admitted students are automatically considered for scholarships and will be notified if additional documents are needed, scholarships are awarded based upon need and/or talent. *Percent of international students receiving scholarships:* 1%.

Services

Housing options: on-site dorms, off-campus housing.

Support staff: career counselor, financial aid advisor, housing advisor, psychological counselor, resident assistant, resident nurse, student affairs officer.

DANCE

Curriculum, Students, and Faculty

Required courses: anatomy, ballet (5 classes per week, 4 years to complete), dance composition or choreography (4 years to complete), dance history (2 years to complete), men's class (1 class per week, 4 years to complete), modern dance (5 classes per week, 4 years to complete), music (3 years to complete), pas de deux (1class per week, 4 years to complete), pointe (2 classes per week, 4 years to complete), rehearsal and performance, repertory, stagecraft (1year to complete), modern dance partnering (4 classes per week), ballet.

Elective courses: nutrition, variations, pointe.

Selectivity for males: approximately 10% admitted. *Selectivity for females:* approximately 10% admitted. *Total enrollment*: 140. *Graduating class size:* 32. *Percent International*: 10%. *Countries most represented*: Taiwan, Mexico, South Africa, Europe, Japan, Korea.

Renowned alumni: Noele Rose, Alaska Dance Theatre; Denise Frey, Columbia City Ballet, South Carolina; Elizabeth Koeppen, David Parsons Dance Company.

Total full-time faculty: 7. *Total part-time faculty:* 8. *List of current faculty and past affiliations:* Gayle Young, ABT; Michael Owen, ABT; Rosanna Seravalli, ABT; Kevin Wynn, Limon Company; Bettijane Sills, New York City Ballet; Cathy Kerr, Cunningham Company; Kim Stroud, Graham Company; Neil Greenberg, Cunningham Company. *Program contact person:* Carol Walker, Kathy Wolfe.

Audition Information

Audition fee: $50. *Audition consists of the following:* ballet, modern dance, pas de deux, pointe works, prepared solo. *Accompanist provided. Cassette player available; CD player available. Dress requirements for males:* white t-shirt, dance support, black tights, white socks or bare feet, black or white shoes. *Dress requirements for females:* black leotard, white, tan, or pink tights, ballet shoes, hair neatly secured (no pony tails), no jewelry.

Repertoire that students should avoid? no.

Audition evaluation criteria: talent and potential as a performer, prior training and ability to demonstrate a knowledge of modern and/or classical ballet techniques, musicality, good physical proportions in a healthy body that is injury free.

Performance Information

Performance opportunities available (frequency): Fully produced concerts (3 per year), informal concerts (7 per year), on-site performances (14 per year), touring (varies).

Performances choreographed by: faculty, students, guests. *Recent guest choreographers:* Kenneth MacMillan, Lois Bewley, Doug Varone, Kevin Wynn, Tera O'Conner.

Facilities

Number of studios available: 10. *Approximate studio dimensions and flooring:* Marley. *Performance facilities:* Performing Arts Center—3 theaters, fully equipped dance theater lab, studio B—in dance building.

DRAMA

Curriculum, Students, and Faculty

Required courses: acting, Alexander technique, audition preparation, drama criticism, improvisation, make-up, mime, movement, speech, stage combat, Stanislavski exercises, text analysis, verse drama, voice, make-up.

Number of years required to complete program: 4. *Summer program available. Affiliation with a professional theater company: Denver Theater Center, Arena stage, Hartford Stage, Crossroad Theater, Longwharf Theater Company, Alabama Shakespeare Company.*

Selectivity for males: approximately 10% admitted. *Selectivity for females:* approximately 10% admitted. *Total enrollment:* 232. *Graduating class size:* 32. *Countries most represented*: Israel, China, Switzerland.

Renowned alumni: Sherry Stringfield, Wesley Snipes, Stanley Tucci, Jay O. Sanders, Steven Webber, Brian McDevitt, Ken Posner, David Grill, David Finley, Karen Silas, Hal Hartley, Nick Gomez.

Total full-time faculty: 10. *Total part-time faculty:* 29.

Audition Information

Audition fee: $35. *Audition consists of the following:* 2 contrasting monologues, 2 minutes each. *Repertoire that students should avoid?* no.

Performance Information

Performance opportunities available (frequency): fully produced performances (6 per year), workshops (frequently), off-site performances (occasionally), auditioned.

Recent guest artists: Hal Hartley, Sherry Stringfield, Arthur Penn, Daniel Rish, (The guest artists do not perform with the students. They supervise, provide lectures and workshops).

Facilities

Rehearsal facilities and hours: 3:00 pm-6:00 pm, 7:00 pm-11:00 pm (Mon, Tue, Wed, Thur), 7:00 pm-11:00 pm (Wed), up to 5 hours on Sat, up to 10 hours during tech week. *Number of theaters on campus:* 4. *Type and capacity:* theater 1,400, black box.

MUSIC

Curriculum, Students, and Faculty

How are major teacher assignments made? Students may choose, made by the school according to teacher preference and teacher availability. Faculty is not informed of a student's teacher preference at the time of the audition. *26 lessons with major teacher. May a student change major teachers during the course of study?* possibly. *Study of secondary instrument or discipline is allowed.*

Selectivity for instruments or programs offered (rating): accompanying (highly selective), bassoon (highly selective), clarinet (highly selective), composition (highly selective), double bass (highly selective), electronic music (highly selective), flute or piccolo (highly selective), French horn (highly selective), guitar (highly selective), harp (highly selective), harpsichord (competitive), jazz, oboe/English horn, orchestral conducting (highly selective), organ, percussion, piano (highly selective), saxophone (highly selective), trombone, trumpet, tuba, viola (highly selective), violin, violoncello (highly selective), voice (highly selective).

Total enrollment: 300. *Graduating class size:* 50. *Percent International*: 17%.

Renowned alumni: Dwayne Croft, Metropolitan Opera; Eric Ralske, New York Philharmonic.

Total full-time faculty: 8. *Total part-time faculty:* 40. *Program contact person:* Karl Krammer, Fred Griffen.

Audition Information

Audition fee? $50. *Instruments provided for:* harpists, percussionists.

Performance opportunities available (frequency): chamber music, jury examinations, opera workshops, orchestral concerts, recitals.

Facilities

Number of practice rooms and hours: 72; daily. *Recital hall?* yes. *Concert hall?* yes. *Recording studio?* yes.

STATE UNIVERSITY OF NEW YORK, STONY BROOK

Office of Admissions, Stony Brook NY 11794-1901
Tel: 516-632-6868
Fax: 516-632-9898
Email: admiss@mail.vpsa.sunysb.edu
Web: www.sunysb.edu

Entrance Requirements

Audition not required.

DRAMA

Curriculum, Students, and Faculty

Elective courses: speech.

MUSIC

Conservatory-level training.

SYRACUSE UNIVERSITY

College of Visual and Performing Arts
202 Crouse College, Syracuse NY 13244-1010
Tel: 315-443-2769
Fax: 315-443-1935
Email: Jimccumb@vpa.syr.edu
Web: www.syr.edu

General

Type of Institution: private university. *Environment:* urban.

Total enrollment of institution: 10,344. *Total student body from other countries:* 10%. *Degrees offered:* BFA, BM, BID, BS.

Entrance Requirements

Audition required: live, audio, video. *Other requirements:* recommendation, essay. *Standardized test requirements:* SAT I, 1170; TOEFL, 550.

Costs & Financial Aid

Application fee: $40. *Deposit:* $500. *Tuition:* $17,550. *Medical fee:* $294. *Other fees:* $156 music practice rooms, lessons. *Room and board:* $7,960.

Percent of students receiving financial aid: 80%. *Types of scholarships and aid awarded:* full, partial, merit-based, need-based, institutional aid, government aid, tuition payment plan, work/study. *Forms required for scholarships:* FAFSA, income tax return, income asset verification. *Loans available. Procedure for applying for loans:* file FAFSA by 2/15; academic merit scholarships do not require an application: talent scholarships based on audition. *Percent of international students receiving scholarships:* 10%. *Other aid available to international students:* only academic merit scholarships available.

Services

Housing options: on-site dorms, off-campus housing, fraternity, sorority.

Support staff: career counselor, college advisor, financial aid advisor, foreign student advisor, housing advisor, psychological counselor, resident assistant, resident nurse, student affairs officer.

DRAMA

Curriculum, Students, and Faculty

Required courses: acting, improvisation, movement, musical theater, scene study, text analysis, verse drama, voice.

Elective courses: audition preparation, directing, drama criticism, dramaturgy, make-up, martial arts, stage combat.

Number of years required to complete program: 4. *Summer program available. Affiliation with a professional theater company: Syracuse Stage, professional theater.*

Selectivity for males: approximately 33% admitted. *Selectivity for females:* approximately 33% admitted. *Total enrollment:* 237. *Entering class size:* 75. *Graduating class size:* 60. *Percent International*: 1%. *Countries most represented*: Korea.

Renowned alumni: Vanessa Williams, Aaron Sorkin, Tom Scott, Frank Langella, Denise Dillon, Jose Abady, Jim Clow, Taye Diggs, Jerry Stiller, Vera Farmiga, Sam Lloyd, Kristin Wilson, Amelia Campbell.

Total full-time faculty: 14. *Total part-time faculty:* 19. *List of current faculty and past affiliations:* Bob Moss, Playwrights Horizon; Rodney Hudson, American Repertory Theatre; Geraldine Clark, Indiana Repertory Theatre; Jim Clark.

Audition Information

No audition fee. Audition consists of the following: improvisation, group warm-up, singing with accompaniment and dance combination for musical theater applicants. *Repertoire that students should avoid?* verse drama.

Audition evaluation criteria: emotional connection to character, ability to make adjustments in audition, ability to relax body and voice.

Performance Information

Performance opportunities available (frequency): fully produced performances (20), informal performances (all the time), auditioned.

Recent guest artists: John Cullum, Steve Lang, Jean Stapleton, Aaron Sorkin, Joe Regabuto, Roma Downy, Alan Rosenberg.

Facilities

Rehearsal facilities and hours: 5 acting rooms, 2 dance studios, 4 practice rooms, 8:00 am-11:00 pm. *Number of theaters on campus:* 4. *Type and capacity:* stage 200, cabaret 70, black box 100, main stage 500.

MUSIC

Curriculum, Students, and Faculty

How are major teacher assignments made? made by the school according to teacher availability. Faculty is informed of a student's teacher preference at the time of the audition. *28 lessons with major teacher. May a student change major teachers during the course of study?* possibly. *Study of secondary instrument or discipline is allowed.*

Selectivity for instruments or programs offered (rating): accompanying (selective), bassoon (selective), clarinet (selective), composition (selective), double bass (selective), flute or piccolo (selective), French horn (selective), guitar (selective), oboe/English horn (selective), organ (selective), percussion (selective), piano (selective), saxophone (selective), trombone (selective), trumpet (selective), tuba (selective), viola (selective), violin (selective), violoncello (selective), voice (selective).

Total enrollment: 145. *Entering class size:* 40. *Graduating class size:* 35. *Percent International*: 1%. *Countries most represented*: China, Korea.

Renowned alumni: Phyllis Bryn-Julsone, Donald Sutherland, Carlisle Floyd, Donald Martino.

Total full-time faculty: 13. *Total part-time faculty:* 53. *Program contact person:* Judy McCumber.

Audition Information

No audition fee. Audition consists of the following: scales, orchestral excerpts, ensemble playing, arpeggios, sight reading. *Instruments provided for:* harpists, percussionists; organ, harpsichord, piano.

Performance opportunities available (frequency): jury examinations, recitals.

Facilities

Number of practice rooms and hours: 30; 24 hours a day. *Recital hall?* no. *Concert hall?* yes. *Recording studio?* yes.

Comments

Harpsichord, organ and harp majors may be accepted under certain circumstances. Call for information.

VASSAR COLLEGE

124 Raymond Avenue
P.O. Box 18, Poughkeepsie NY 12604-0018
Tel: 914-437-7319
Fax: 914-437-7114
Email: riwilson@vassar.edu
Web: www.vassar.edu/music/index/html
Contact: David Borus

General

Type of Institution: private college, coed. *Environment:* suburban.

Entrance Requirements

Other requirements: essay.

Costs & Financial Aid

Application fee: $60. *Deposit:* $200. *Tuition:* $21,780. *Medical fee:* $130. *Room and board:* $6,510.

Percent of students receiving financial aid: 64%. *Types of scholarships and aid awarded:* merit-based, need-based. *Forms required for scholarships:* CSS Profile. *Loans available. Financial aid offered to international students.*

Services

Housing options: on-site dorms.

Support staff: career counselor, dorm parent, financial aid advisor, foreign student advisor, housing advisor, physical therapist, psychological counselor, resident assistant, resident nurse.

DRAMA

Comprehensive curriculum within liberal arts. Many performance opportunities.

Renowned alumni: Meryl Streep.

MUSIC

Curriculum, Students, and Faculty

How are major teacher assignments made? Students may choose, made by the school according to teacher preference and teacher availability. Faculty is informed of a student's teacher preference at the time of the audition. *26 lessons with major teacher. May a student change major teachers during the course of study?* possibly. *Study of secondary instrument or discipline is allowed.*

Total enrollment: 200.

Renowned alumni: Phoebe Legere; Ellen Rosand, Yale; Sandra Brown.

Total full-time faculty: 25. *Program contact person:* Richard Wilson.

Audition Information

Audition consists of the following: scales, orchestral excerpts, sight reading. *Instruments provided for:* harpists.

Repertoire that students should avoid? no.

Facilities

Number of practice rooms and hours: 20; 24 hours a day. *Recital hall?* yes. *Concert hall?* yes. *Recording studio?* yes.

CATAWBA COLLEGE

Theatre Arts Department
2300 West Innes Street, Salisbury, NC 28144
Tel: 704-637-4440
Fax: 704-637-4207
Email: jepperso@catawba.edu
Web: www.catawba.edu/infoindx/infoindx.htm
Contact: Elaine Holden

General

Type of Institution: college. *Religious Affiliation*: United Church of Christ. *Environment:* suburban. *Academic education is offered on-site.*

Total enrollment of institution: 1,250. *Total student body from other countries:* 1%. *Degrees offered:* BA, BFA, BS in theatre arts administration.

Entrance Requirements

Audition not required. Standardized test requirements: SAT I, 1100; TOEFL, 500.

Costs & Financial Aid

Application fee: $25. *Deposit:* $400. *Tuition:* $11,352. *Medical fee:* $142. *Other fees:* $275 regular new student fee; $100 refundable dorm damage deposit.

Percent of students receiving financial aid: 90%. *Types of scholarships and aid awarded:* partial, merit-based, need-based, named, institutional aid, government aid, reduced tuition, tuition payment plan, work/study. *Forms required for scholarships:* income tax return. *Loans available. Procedure for applying for loans:* file FAFSA, will send application, tax return needed if applicant is selected for verification. *Financial aid offered to international students. Percent of international students receiving scholarships:* 95%. *Other aid available to international students:* institutional, based on merit.

Services

Housing options: on-site dorms.

Support staff: career counselor, financial aid advisor, housing advisor, physical therapist, psychological counselor, resident assistant, resident nurse, student affairs officer.

DANCE

Curriculum, Students, and Faculty

Required courses: Alexander technique, dance history, Laban Movement Studies, Irish, rehearsal and performance, repertory, stagecraft.

Elective courses: anatomy, character, ballet, dance composition or choreography, jazz, Limon-based, pointe, tap.

Total full-time faculty: 1. *Total part-time faculty:* 1. *List of current faculty and past affiliations:* Nancy Kane, Ph.D.; Pamela Janas, professional dancer for 30 years; danced and worked with Gene Kelly, Peter Genero, Deborah Mitchell, Germaine Goodson. *Program contact person:* James R. Epperson.

Performance Information

Performance opportunities available (frequency): Fully produced concerts (2 per year), on-site performances (3 per year).

Performances choreographed by: faculty, students.

Facilities

Number of studios available: 1. *Approximate studio dimensions and flooring:* 40' x 40' tongue and grove sprung dance floor. *Performance facilities:* 1,500-seat pricenium auditorium, 250-seat thrust theater.

DRAMA

Curriculum, Students, and Faculty

Required courses: acting, Alexander technique, audition preparation, directing, dramaturgy, improvisation, make-up, movement, musical theater, scene study, speech, stage combat, Stanislavski exercises, voice.

Elective courses: drama criticism, martial arts, mime, verse drama.

Number of years required to complete program: 4. *Summer program not available. No affiliation with a professional theater company. However, many of our students work professionally with various companies during the summer.*

Selectivity for males: approximately 33% admitted. *Selectivity for females:* approximately 33% admitted. *Total enrollment:* 80. *Entering class size:* 35.

Renowned alumni: Fred Inkley, Scott Holms, Veronica Worts.

Total full-time faculty: 6. *Total part-time faculty:* 2. *List of current faculty and past affiliations:* James Parker, Dayne Anderson.

Audition Information

No audition fee. Audition consists of the following: a cappella, comedic monologue, Shakespearean monologue, B.F.A. Musical theatre requires audition selections in dance, voice, and drama. All require an interview. *Repertoire that students should avoid?* Since audition does not occur until the second semester of the freshman year, this information is received after enrollment.

Audition evaluation criteria: Professional promise plus academic achievement, commitment, skill achievement.

Performance Information

Performance opportunities available (frequency): fully produced performances (9 per year), informal performances (9-12 per year), workshops (6 per year), off-site performances (5 per year), American College Theatre Festival assigned. B.F.A. Acting roles may be assigned for thesis, all others are by audition.

Recent guest artists: Shakespeare Express, Junebug/Jack Company.

Facilities

Rehearsal facilities and hours: 2 rehearsal halls for theater, use as reserved by faculty and students. *Number of theaters on campus:* 5. *Type and capacity:* proscenium 1,500, thrust 250, black box 100, recital hall 100, dinner theater 150.

Comments

The theater arts program at Catawba College is unique. The facilities, faculty, courses offered, degrees offered, productions realized, reputation, etc. make it one of the strongest undergraduate programs in the nation. One hundred percent of its graduates each year either work professionally or go to graduate school. All of this in a small liberal arts college. Theater is considered at Catawba to be a premiere major. The theater program has been honored by the North Carolina Theater Conference. It is a yearly finalist in the State American College Theater Festival, which it has hosted for the past eight years. It has had regional finalists at the Regional American College Theater Festival 3 out of the last 6 years (including this year). Its playwrights, directors, actors, etc. yearly achieve recognition from the regional competition. No other college in the southeast can boast of these accomplishments.

MUSIC

Curriculum, Students, and Faculty

Unique or innovative music curriculum: a special freshman music skills, music history, and technology overview course. *How are major teacher assignments made?* students may choose. Faculty is not informed of a student's teacher preference at the time of the audition. *30 lessons with major teacher. May a student change major teachers during the course of study?* possibly. *Study of secondary instrument or discipline is allowed.*

Selectivity for instruments or programs offered (rating): accompanying (competitive), bassoon (non-competitive), choral singing (selective), clarinet (non-competitive), double bass (non-competitive), flute or piccolo (non-competitive), French horn (non-competitive), jazz (competitive), oboe/English horn (non-competitive), organ (competitive), piano (non-competitive), sacred music (competitive), saxophone (non-competitive), trombone (non-competitive), trumpet (non-competitive), tuba (non-competitive), viola (non-competitive), violin (non-competitive), violoncello (non-competitive), voice (competitive).

Total full-time faculty: 3. *Total part-time faculty:* 2. *Program contact person:* James R. Epperson.

Audition Information

No audition fee. Audition consists of the following: scales, music theory. *Instruments provided for:* percussionists.

Repertoire that students should avoid? no.

Facilities

Recital hall? yes. *Concert hall?* yes. *Recording studio?* no.

DAVIDSON COLLEGE

Theater Department
P.O. Box 340, Davidson, NC 28036
Tel: 704-892-2361
Fax: 704-892-2593
Email: jogardner@davidson.edu
Contact: Warren Buford

General

Type of Institution: private college. *Religious Affiliation*: Presbyterian. *Environment:* suburban.

Total enrollment of institution: 1,600. *Degrees offered:* BA.

Entrance Requirements

Audition not required. Other requirements: recommendation, essay. *Standardized test requirements:* SAT I, 1325.

Costs & Financial Aid

Application fee: $45. *Deposit:* $300. *Tuition:* $20,595. *Other fees:* $95 freshman orientation fee. *Room and Board*: $6,018.

Percent of students receiving financial aid: 35%. *Types of scholarships and aid awarded:* full, partial, merit-based, need-based, institutional aid, government aid, tuition payment plan, work/study. *Forms required for scholarships:* FAFSA, income tax return, CSS Profile. *Loans available. Procedure for applying for loans:* submit FAFSA. *Financial aid offered to international students.*

Services

Housing options: on-site dorms, fraternities.

Support staff: career counselor, financial aid advisor, foreign student advisor, housing advisor, psychological counselor, resident assistant, resident nurse, student affairs officer.

Comments

As a liberal arts institution, Davidson College does not hold special entrance criteria for any choice of major study. Majors must meet certain criteria for graduation.

DRAMA

Curriculum, Students, and Faculty

Required courses: acting, design for the performing arts, directing, drama criticism, theater history.

Elective courses: movement, scene study, voice, oral interpretation.

Number of years required to complete program: 4. *Summer program not available. No affiliation with a professional theater company. Internships are available to qualified students.*

Renowned alumni: Ellen Schlaefe, Frazier Marsh, Actors Theatre-Louisville, Graham Smith.

Total full-time faculty: 3. *List of current faculty and past affiliations:* Joe Gardner, Charlotte Repertory Theatre; Alex Pinkston, San Diego State, Ann Marie Costa, Berkshire Theatre Festival, Charlotte Repertory Theatre.

Performance Information

Performance opportunities available (frequency): fully produced performances (4 per year), workshops (10 per year), auditioned.

Facilities

Number of theaters on campus: 2. *Type and capacity:* proscenium 290, black box 100.

MUSIC

Curriculum, Students, and Faculty

How are major teacher assignments made? Students may choose, made by the school, according to teacher preference. Faculty is not informed of a student's teacher preference at the time of the audition. 28 lessons with major teacher. *May a student change major teachers during the course of study?* possibly. *Study of secondary instrument or discipline is allowed.*

Selectivity for instruments or programs offered (rating): accompanying (non-competitive), accordion (non-competitive), bagpipes (non-competitive), bassoon (non-competitive), choral conducting (non-competitive), choral singing (non-competitive), clarinet (non-competitive), composition (non-competitive), double bass (non-competitive), electronic music (non-competitive), flute or piccolo (non-competitive), French horn (non-competitive), guitar (non-competitive), harp (non-competitive), harpsichord (non-competitive), jazz (non-competitive), oboe/English horn (non-competitive), orchestral conducting (non-competitive), organ (non-competitive), percussion (non-competitive), piano (non-competitive), sacred music (non-competitive), saxophone (non-competitive), trombone (non-competitive), trumpet (non-competitive), tuba (non-competitive), viola (non-competitive), violin (non-competitive), violoncello (non-competitive), voice (non-competitive).

Renowned alumni: William Workman, Hamburg Opera; Joseph Robinson, New York Philharmonic; Paul Yarborough, Alexander Quartet.

Total full-time faculty: 6. *Total part-time faculty:* 5. *Program contact person:* Bill Lawing.

Audition Information

No audition fee. Instruments provided for: percussionists.

Repertoire that students should avoid? no.

Facilities

Number of practice rooms and hours: 6; 24 hours a day. *Recital hall?* yes. *Concert hall?* yes. *Recording studio?* yes.

DUKE UNIVERSITY

Undergraduate Admissions
2138 Campus Drive, P.O. Box 90586, Durham, NC 27708
Tel: 919-684-3214
Fax: 919-681-8941
Email: askduke@admiss.duke.edu
Web: www.duke.edu

General

Type of Institution: private university. *Religious Affiliation*: United Methodist Church. *Environment:* suburban.

Total enrollment of institution: 11,589. *Total student body from other countries:* 5%. *Degrees offered:* certificate, BA.

Entrance Requirements

Audition not required.

Costs & Financial Aid

Application fee: $60. *Deposit:* $500. *Tuition:* $21,550. *Other fees:* $416 student health; $100 recreation; $107 student government. *Room and board*: $6,970.

Percent of students receiving financial aid: 43% *Types of scholarships and aid awarded:* full, partial, merit-based, need-based, named, institutional aid, government aid, tuition payment plan, work/study. *Forms required for scholarships:* FAFSA, income tax return, CSS Profile, non-custodial parents statement, business /farm supplement. *Loans available. Procedure for applying for loans:* submit application concurrently with admissions application, 11/1 deadline.

Services

Housing options: on-site dorms, fraternity.

Support staff: career counselor, financial aid advisor, foreign student advisor, housing advisor, psychological counselor, resident assistant, student affairs officer.

Comments

Dance is not a major at Duke University.

DANCE

Curriculum, Students, and Faculty

Elective courses: African dance, anatomy, ballet, dance composition or choreography, dance history, dance theory, dance writing research and criticism, jazz, modern dance, Cunningham-based, Limon-based, pointe, rehearsal and performance, repertory, stagecraft, variations.

Selectivity for males: admit all who apply. *Selectivity for females:* admit all who apply.

Renowned alumni: Holly Brubach, Sandy Chase, MOMIX.

Total full-time faculty: 5 *List of current faculty and past affiliations:* Barbara Dickinson, Ways and Means Dance Company; Clay Taliaferro, Jose Limon Dance Company; Carol Childs, Jose Limon Dance Company; M'Liss Dorranice, National Ballet, Eliot Feld; Sally Sommer, dance historian, critic, author; Tyler Walteus, Joffrey Ballet. *Program contact person:* Barbara Dickinson.

Performance Information

Performance opportunities available (frequency): Fully produced concerts (1-2 per year), informal concerts (2-4 per year), workshops (varies).

Performances choreographed by: faculty, students, guests. *Recent guest choreographers:* Shapiro and Smith, Blondell Cummings, Melissa Hayden.

Facilities

Number of studios available: 3. *Approximate studio dimensions and flooring:* 60' x 40' Marley, 25' x 18' Marley, 25' x 30' wood. *Performance facilities:* 1 state of the art theater, 1 large theater (1,200 seated), Ark Dance Studio.

DRAMA

Curriculum, Students, and Faculty

Required courses: acting, audition preparation, directing, drama criticism, improvisation, scene study, Stanislavski exercises, text analysis.

Elective courses: Alexander technique, dramaturgy, make-up, martial arts, movement, musical theater, stage combat, verse drama, voice.

Number of years required to complete program: 4. *Summer program available. Affiliation with a professional theater company. Continuing informal relationship with two local professional theater companies run by drama faculty members —Manbites Dog Theater and Archipelago Theater. Co-production relationship with Ford's Theater (Washington, DC).*

Selectivity for males: approximately 10% admitted. *Selectivity for females:* approximately 10% admitted. *Total enrollment:* 44. *Graduating class size:* 12.

Renowned alumni: Kevin Gray, Jayne Brook, Rene Echevarria, Spencer Garrett.

Total full-time faculty: 8. *List of current faculty and past affiliations:* Emanuel Azenberg, Neil Blackadder, Charles Catotti, Triangle Opera Theater; John Clum, Sarah Froeber, Jelly Educational Theater; Ellen Hemphill, Archipelago Theatre Company; Rafael Lopez-Barrantes, Roy Hunt Theatre; Wenhai Ma.

Audition Information

Audition consists of the following: since applicants do not apply directly to the Drama Program but must be admitted to Duke University there is no audition process as such. Applicants with an interest in drama are invited to submit additional materials with their university application.

Performance Information

Performance opportunities available (frequency): fully produced performances (8-12 per year), informal performances (4-6 per year), workshops (3-6 per year), off-site performances (1 per year), auditioned.

Recent guest artists: Jayne Brook.

Facilities

Rehearsal facilities and hours: Rehearsals are scheduled in the various theater facilities across campus. Rehearsal must be scheduled no earlier than 7:00 pm for first year students and must end by 11:00 pm for all students. *Number of theaters on campus:* 4.

MUSIC

Curriculum, Students, and Faculty

Unique or innovative music curriculum: The undergraduate curriculum is designed for the student who wishes to pursue a broad range of musical interests within context of a liberal arts education. *How are major teacher assignments made?* made by the school. Faculty is not informed of a student's teacher preference at the time of the audition. *28 lessons with major teacher. May a student change major teachers during the course of study?* possibly. *Study of secondary instrument or discipline is allowed.*

Total enrollment: 54. *Graduating class size:* 5.

Renowned alumni: Michael Best, Steven Kimbrough, Les Brown, William Stone, Patrick Williams.

Total part-time faculty: 22. *Program contact person:* Larry Todd.

Audition Information

No audition fee. Instruments provided for: percussionists.

Facilities

Number of practice rooms and hours: 22; 24 hours a day. *Recital hall?* yes. *Concert hall?* yes.

EAST CAROLINA UNIVERSITY

Greenville NC 27858-4353
Tel: 919-328-6851
Fax: 919-328-6258
Email: foleyc@mail.ecu.edu
Web: www.music.ecu.edu

General

Type of Institution: college, university. *Academic education is offered on-site.*

Total enrollment of institution: 17,500. *Degrees offered:* certificate, BA, BM.

Entrance Requirements

Audition required: live, audio, video. *Other requirements:* recommendation. *Standardized test requirements:* SAT I; TOEFL.

Costs & Financial Aid

Percent of students receiving financial aid: 25%. *Types of scholarships and aid awarded:* full, partial, merit-based, need-based, named, government aid, reduced tuition, work/study. *Financial aid offered to international students. Percent of international students receiving scholarships:* 1%.

Services

Housing options: on-site dorms, off-campus housing, fraternity, sorority.

Support staff: career counselor, financial aid advisor, foreign student advisor, housing advisor, physical therapist, psychological counselor, resident assistant, resident nurse, student affairs officer.

DRAMA

Curriculum, Students, and Faculty

Required courses: dramaturgy, Stanislavski exercises.

MUSIC

Curriculum, Students, and Faculty

How are major teacher assignments made? Students may choose, made by the school. Faculty is not informed of a student's teacher preference at the time of the audition. *32 lessons with major teacher. May a student change major teachers during the course of study?* possibly. *Study of secondary instrument or discipline is allowed.*

Selectivity for instruments or programs offered (rating): bassoon (competitive), choral conducting (non-competitive), clarinet (competitive), composition (competitive), double bass (competitive), electronic music (competitive), flute or piccolo (selective), French horn (competitive), guitar (selective), harp (competitive), harpsichord (competitive), jazz (competitive), oboe/English horn (competitive), orchestral conducting (competitive), organ (competitive), percussion (competitive), piano (competitive), sacred music (competitive), saxophone (competitive), trombone (competitive), trumpet (competitive), tuba (competitive), viola (competitive), violin (competitive), violoncello (competitive), voice (competitive).

Total enrollment: 350. *Entering class size:* 100. *Graduating class size:* 45. *Percent International*: 2%. *Countries most represented*: Iceland, Korea, China.

Renowned alumni: Dr. Thomas, Northwestern School of Music; Jeanne Piland, LaScala, Kennedy Center, Santa Fe Opera; Ray Bunch.

Total full-time faculty: 47. *Total part-time faculty:* 6. *Program contact person:* George Knight.

Audition Information

No audition fee. Audition consists of the following: scales, music theory sight reading, repertoire. *Instruments provided for:* harpists, percussionists.

Performance opportunities available (frequency): band (frequently), jury examinations (2 per year), opera workshops (1 per year), orchestral concerts (3 per year), recitals (frequently), touring (annually), produced operas (rare), chorus (frequently).

Facilities

Number of practice rooms and hours: 85; 7:00 am-11:00 pm. *Recital hall?* yes. *Concert hall?* yes. *Recording studio?* yes.

NORTH CAROLINA SCHOOL OF THE ARTS

1533 South Main Street, Winston-Salem NC 27127-2188
Tel: 336-770-3291
Fax: 330-770-3370
Web: www.ncarts.edu
Contact: Carol Palm

General

Type of Institution: high school, college, conservatory. *Environment:* urban. *Academic education is offered on-site.*

Total enrollment: 1,034. *Total student body from other countries:* 4%. *Degrees offered:* high school diploma, college.

Entrance Requirements

Audition required: live, audio, video. *Other requirements:* interview, recommendation, essay, photograph. *Standardized test requirements:* ACT; SATI; TOEFL, 550.

Costs & Financial Aid

Application fee: $35. *Deposit:* $100. *Tuition:* $5,194. *Medical fee:* $300. *Other fees:* $989 activity and health.

Types of scholarships and aid awarded: full, partial, merit-based, need-based, named, institutional aid, government aid, work/study, gig office. *Forms required for scholarships:* FAFSA, income tax return. *Loans available.*

Services

Housing options: on-site dorms.

Support staff: career counselor, dorm parent, financial aid advisor, housing advisor, physical therapist, psychological counselor, resident assistant, resident nurse, student affairs officer.

DANCE

Curriculum, Students, and Faculty

Required courses: character, ballet, dance composition/choreography, dance history, improvisation, jazz, make-up, men's class, modern dance, movement techniques, body conditioning, Pilates, music, pas de deux, pointe, rehearsal and performance, repertory, technical theater, variations, ballet repertory.

Selectivity for males: approximately 10% admitted. *Selectivity for females:* approximately 10% admitted. *Total enrollment:* 204. *Graduating class size:* 53. *Percent international:* 7%. *Countries most represented:* Spain.

Renowned alumni: Michael Thomas, Mary Cochram, Janie Parker, Trey McIntyre, Victor Barbee, Jaime Martinez, Jeanne Ruddy, Mel A. Tomlinson, Christine Spizzo, Katita Waldo, Keith Roberts, Mark Dendy, Edward Stierle, Peter Pucci.

Total full-time faculty: 14. *List of current faculty and past affiliations:* Susan McCullough, Trish Casey, Warren Conover, Fanchon Cordell, Brenda Daniels, Nina Danilova, Melisssa Hayden, Melinda Lawrence, Dianne Markham, Lynn Messick, Gyula Pandi, Frank Smith, Gina Vidal, Duncan Noble, Karla Wolfangle. *Program contact person:* Susan McCullaugh.

Audition Information

No audition fee. Audition consists of the following: ballet, modern dance, pointe works, prepared solo, contemporary and/or students own choreography to classical music. *Accompanist provided. Cassette player available; CD player available. Dress requirements for males:* practice clothes, no jewelry *Dress requirements for females:* practice clothes, no jewelry, hair should be worn up.

Repertoire that students should avoid? no jazz.

Audition evaluation criteria: potential to pursue a professional career.

Performance Information

Performance opportunities available (frequency): Fully produced concerts (5 per year, consisting of 4-10 performances), workshops (3 per year), on-site performances (13-15 per year).

Performances choreographed by: faculty, students, guests.

Facilities

Number of studios available: 9. *Performance facilities:* Stevens Center, 1,500 seats. Agnes De Mille Theater, 200 seats.

DRAMA

Curriculum, Students, and Faculty

Required courses: acting, Alexander technique, audition preparation, improvisation, movement, musical theater, scene study, speech, Stanislavski exercises, verse drama, voice.

MUSIC

Conservatory training in all orchestral and keyboard instruments.

UNIVERSITY OF NORTH CAROLINA, CHAPEL HILL

Chapel Hill NC 27599
Tel: 919-966-3621
Fax: 919-962-3045

General

Type of Institution: public university. *Environment:* suburban.

Total enrollment of institution: 25,000. *Degrees offered:* BA.

Entrance Requirements

Audition not required. Other requirements: recommendation *Standardized test requirements:* SAT I, 800; TOEFL.

Costs & Financial Aid

Application fee: $55. *Deposit:* $150. *Tuition (in-state/out-state):* $2,225/$11,210. *Other fees:* $600 books and supplies, $1,650 personal expenses. *Room and board:* $4,650.

Types of scholarships and aid awarded: full, partial, merit-based, need-based, named, institutional aid, tuition payment plan, work/study. *Forms required for scholarships:* FAFSA, income tax return. *Loans available. Procedure for applying for loans:* contact Financial Aid Office (919-962-8396).

Services

Housing options: on-site dorms, off-campus housing, fraternity, sorority, family.

Support staff: career counselor, financial aid advisor, foreign student advisor, housing advisor, physical therapist, psychological counselor, resident assistant, resident nurse, student affairs officer.

DRAMA

Curriculum, Students, and Faculty

Required courses: text analysis, theater practicum.

Elective courses: audition preparation, directing, movement, speech, stage combat, verse drama, voice.

Number of years required to complete program: 4. *Summer program not available. Affiliation with a professional theater company: Playmakers Repertory Company, 5 show season plus holiday show. Graduate students and a few undergraduates appear in professional shows. Undergraduates crew and stage manage.*

Selectivity for males: approximately 10% admitted. *Selectivity for females:* approximately 10% admitted. *Entering class size:* 17. *Countries most represented*: England, Taiwan, South Africa.

Renowned alumni: George Grizzard, Andy Griffith, Michael Wilson, Louise Fletcher, John Forsythe, William Ivey Cong, Robert Long, Reed Diamond.

Total full-time faculty: 15. *Total part-time faculty:* 6. *List of current faculty and past affiliations:* Ray Dooley, Yale Repertory, Hartford Stage; David Hammond, Juilliard, Yale Drama School; Christopher Baker, American Repertory Theatre, Alley Theatre; Adam Versenyi, Yale Repertory Theatre, Yale School of Drama.

Performance Information

Performance opportunities available (frequency): fully produced performances (4-6), informal performances (10-12), workshops (3-5), auditioned.

Recent guest artists: Matthew Broderick, Ellen Burstyn, Polly Holliday, Kathleen Widdoes, Frank Converse, Elizabeth Ashley, Keir Dullea, Tazewell Thompson, Eva Marie Saint, Judd Hirsh, Paul Benedict, Jan Maxwell.

Facilities

Rehearsal facilities and hours: rehearsal hall and studio in New Center for Dramatic Art, 2:00 pm-6:00 pm, 7:00 pm-11:00 pm. *Type and capacity:* proscenium 1,200, proscenium 250, 3/4 thrust 500, studio 285, theater 200.

UNIVERSITY OF NORTH CAROLINA, GREENSBORO

Dance UNCG
P.O. Box 26169, Greensboro NC 27402-6169
Tel: 336-334-5570
Fax: 336-334-3238
Email: Dance@UNCG
Web: www.uncg.edu/dce

General

Type of Institution: public, university. *Environment:* urban. *Academic education is offered on-site.*

Total enrollment of institution: 12,000. *Total student body from other countries:* 2%. *Degrees offered:* BA, BFA, BS.

Entrance Requirements

Audition not required Standardized test requirements: SAT I, 1027; TOEFL, 550.

Costs & Financial Aid

Medical fee: $94. *Other fees:* $400 per semester.

Percent of students receiving financial aid: 60%. *Types of scholarships and aid awarded:* full, partial, merit-based, need-based, named, institutional aid, government aid, tuition payment plan, work/study. *Forms required for scholarships:* FAFSA,

RFAFSA. *Procedure for applying for loans:* UNCG Financial Aid Office.

Services

Housing options: on-site dorms, off-campus housing, fraternity, sorority.

Support staff: career counselor, financial aid advisor, foreign student advisor, physical therapist, psychological counselor, resident assistant, resident nurse, student affairs officer.

DANCE

Curriculum, Students, and Faculty

Required courses: African dance (2 classes per week), anatomy, ballet (2 classes per week), dance composition or choreography, dance history, jazz, modern dance, music, repertory, stagecraft, vernacular dance (2 classes per week), dance composition or choreography.

Elective courses: dance theory, dance writing research and criticism, master classes, movement techniques, rehearsal and performance, ballet.

Selectivity for males: admit all who apply. *Selectivity for females:* admit all who apply. *Total enrollment*: 135. *Entering class size:* 35. *Graduating class size:* 10.

340 *Renowned alumni:* Jack Arnold, Chrystelle Trump Bond, Rick McCullough, Sherone Price.

Total part-time faculty: 10. *Total part-time faculty:* 5. *List of current faculty and past affiliations:* John Gamble, Temple U.; Rick McCullough, Nederlands Dance Theatre; Jan Van Dyke, Jan Van Dyke Dance Theatre; Eluza Santos. *Program contact person:* Dr. Susan Stinson.

Audition Information

No audition fee. Audition consists of the following: ballet, modern dance. *Accompanist provided.*

Performance Information

Performance opportunities available (frequency): fully produced concerts (14 per year), informal concerts (2 per year).

Performances choreographed by: faculty, students, guests. *Recent guest choreographers:* Carol Richards, Leslie Dworkin, Jack Arnold.

Facilities

Number of studios available: 5. *Approximate studio dimensions and flooring:* wood, black vinyl. *Performance facilities:* 180-seat fully equipped theater.

OHIO

BALDWIN-WALLACE COLLEGE

275 Eastland Road, Berea OH 44017
Tel: 440-826-2368
Fax: 440-826-3239
Email: thecon@bw.edu
Web: www.bw.edu
Contact: Anita S. Evans

General

Type of Institution: college, conservatory. *Religious Affiliation*: Methodist. *Environment:* suburban.

Total enrollment of institution: 2,800. *Total student body from other countries:* 6%. *Degrees offered:* BA, BME.

Entrance Requirements

Audition required: live, video. *Other requirements:* recommendation, essay. *Standardized test requirements:* ACT, 23; SAT I, 1060; TOEFL, 500.

Costs & Financial Aid

Application fee: $15. *Deposit:* $200.

Percent of students receiving financial aid: 71%. *Types of scholarships and aid awarded:* merit-based, need-based, named, institutional aid, government aid, work/study. *Forms required for scholarships:* FAFSA. *Loans available. Procedure for applying for loans:* regular application to the College. *Other aid available to international students:* talent scholarships.

Services

Housing options: on-site dorms, off-campus housing, fraternity, sorority.

Support staff: career counselor, financial aid advisor, housing advisor, resident assistant, resident nurse, student affairs officer.

DRAMA

Curriculum, Students, and Faculty

Required courses: acting, audition preparation, drama criticism, make-up, movement, musical theater, scene study, text analysis, voice.

Elective courses: directing, improvisation, martial arts, speech, stage combat.

Performance Information

Performance opportunities available (frequency): fully produced performances (5 per year), informal performances (5 per year), workshops (2-4 per year), professional theater assignments with Great Lakes Theatre Festival, Cleveland Playhouse Music.

Curriculum, Students, and Faculty

Conservatory of Music on campus.

Total enrollment: 285. *Entering class size:* 86. *Percent International*: 4%.

Total full-time faculty: 22. *Total part-time faculty:* 32. *Program contact person:* Anita S. Evans.

CASE WESTERN RESERVE UNIVERSITY

Eldred Theater
10900 Euclid Avenue, Cleveland OH 44106-7077
Tel: 216-368-2858
Fax: 216-368-5184
Email: claz@po.cwru.edu

General

Type of Institution: college, university. *Environment:* urban. *Academic education is offered on-site.*

Total enrollment of institution: 3,500. *Degrees offered:* BA.

Entrance Requirements

Audition required: live. *Other requirements:* interview. *Standardized test requirements:* ACT, 29; SAT I, 1340.

Costs & Financial Aid

Tuition: $17,800. *Medical fee:* $142. *Room and board*: $5,560.

Types of scholarships and aid awarded: full, partial, merit-based, need-based, named, institutional aid, government aid, tuition payment plan, work/study. *Forms required for scholarships:* FFS, FAFSA, income tax return. *Loans available. Procedure for applying for loans:* contact Financial Aid Office.

Services

Housing options: on-site dorms, off-campus housing, fraternity, sorority.

Support staff: career counselor, dorm parent, financial aid advisor, foreign student advisor, housing advisor, psychological counselor, resident assistant, student affairs officer.

DANCE

Curriculum, Students, and Faculty

Total enrollment: 40. *Entering class size:* 12. *Graduating class size:* 7.

Total full-time faculty: 2. *Total part-time faculty:* 1. *Program contact person:* Kelly Holt.

Audition Information

No audition fee. Audition consists of the following: improvisation, modern dance, orthopedic evaluation. *Accompanist not provided. Cassette player available; CD player available.*

Performance Information

Performance opportunities available (frequency): Fully produced concerts (4 per year), informal concerts (several), workshops (every month).

Performances choreographed by: faculty, students, guests.

Facilities

Number of studios available: 3.

DRAMA

Curriculum, Students, and Faculty

Required courses: acting, audition preparation, directing, drama criticism, improvisation, movement, scene study, speech, Stanislavski exercises, text analysis, voice, theater history.

Elective courses: Alexander technique, dramaturgy, mime, stage combat.

Number of years required to complete program: 4. *Summer program not available. Affiliation with a professional theater company: The Cleveland Playhouse for MFA actors, but some opportunities for undergraduates.*

Selectivity for males: approximately 10% admitted. *Selectivity for females:* approximately 10% admitted.

Renowned alumni: Ross Humter, Alan Rosenberg, Gordon Davidson.

Total full-time faculty: 8. *List of current faculty and past affiliations:* John Orlock, Catherine Albers, Beth Mcgee.

Audition Information

Audition consists of the following: Shakespearean monologue. *Repertoire that students should avoid?* no.

Audition evaluation criteria: preparedness, creativity, potential.

Performance Information

Performance opportunities available (frequency): fully produced performances (5 per year), workshops (2-4 per year), off-site performances (2 per year), auditioned.

Recent guest artists: Ed Call, Richard Termine, Tanya Belov.

Facilities

Number of theaters on campus: 2. *Type and capacity:* proscenium 160, lab 50.

UNIVERSITY OF CINCINNATI COLLEGE-CONSERVATORY OF MUSIC

University of Cincinnati
PO Box 210003
Cincinatti, OH 45221-0003
Tel: 513-556-5463
Fax: 513-556-1028
Email: angela.vauble@uc.edu
Web: www.uc.edu/www/ccm/
Contact: Angela Vaubel

CLEVELAND INSTITUTE OF MUSIC

11021 East Boulevard, Cleveland OH 44106
Tel: 216-791-5000
Fax: 216-791-1530
Email: ewf3@po.cwru.edu

General

Type of Institution: conservatory, coed. *Environment:* urban. *Cross registration is available through Case Western Reserve.*

Total enrollment of institution: 271. *Total student body from other countries:* 25%. *Degrees offered:* BM.

Entrance Requirements

Audition required: live, audio, video. *Other requirements:* recommendation, essay. *Standardized test requirements:* ACT; SAT I; TOEFL.

Costs & Financial Aid

Tuition: $16,500. *Other fees:* $500.

Types of scholarships and aid awarded: full, partial, merit-based, need-based, named, tuition payment plan, work/study, gig office. *Forms required for scholarships:* FAFSA, income tax return. *Loans available. Financial aid offered to international students.*

Services

Housing options: on-site dorms, off-campus housing.

Support staff: financial aid advisor, foreign student advisor, housing advisor, student affairs officer.

MUSIC

Curriculum, Students, and Faculty

How are major teacher assignments made? Students may choose, according to teacher availability. Faculty is not informed of a student's teacher preference at the time of the audition. *May a student change major teachers during the course of study?* possibly. *Study of secondary instrument or discipline is allowed.*

Total enrollment: 271.

Renowned alumni: Maria Ewing, Sydney Harth, Lyndon Woodside.

Total part-time faculty: 40. *Total part-time faculty:* 72. *Program contact person:* William Fay.

Audition Information

Audition consists of the following: orchestral excerpts, music theory, music history, repertoire, *Instruments provided for:* harpists, percussionists.

Performance opportunities available (frequency): jury examinations, orchestral concerts, recitals.

Facilities

Recital hall? yes. *Concert hall?* yes. *Recording studio?* yes.

COLLEGE OF WOOSTER

1189 Beall Avenue, Wooster OH 44691
Tel: 330-263-2000
Fax: 330-263-2621
Email: admissions@acs.wooster.edu
Web: www.wooster.edu
Contact: Valerie Baldwin

General

Type of Institution: college. *Religious Affiliation*: Presbyterian.

Total enrollment of institution: 1,714. *Total student body from other countries:* 6%. *Degrees offered:* BA, BM, BME, BME in music therapy.

Entrance Requirements

Other requirements: interview, recommendation, essay. *Standardized test requirements:* ACT, 26; SAT I, 1180; TOEFL, 550.

Costs & Financial Aid

Application fee: $35. *Deposit:* $250. *Tuition:* $19,230. *Medical fee:* $74. *Other fees:* $63 campus council.

Types of scholarships and aid awarded: full, partial, merit-based, need-based, named, institutional aid, government aid, reduced tuition, tuition payment plan, work/study. *Forms required for scholarships:* FAFSA, income tax return, income asset verification. *Loans available. Financial aid offered to international students*.

Services

Housing options: on-site dorms, fraternity, sorority.

Support staff: career counselor, financial aid advisor, foreign student advisor, housing advisor, psychological counselor, resident assistant, resident nurse.

DANCE

Curriculum, Students, and Faculty

Required courses: ballet, dance composition or choreography, rehearsal and performance.

DRAMA

Curriculum, Students, and Faculty

Required courses: acting, directing, drama criticism, improvisation, movement techniques, technology.

Elective courses: lighting design, make-up, scene design, voice.

Number of years required to complete program: 4. *Summer program available. Affiliation with a professional theater company: The Ohio Light Opera.*

Selectivity for males: admit all who apply. *Selectivity for females:* admit all who apply. *Percent International*: 1%.

Total full-time faculty: 4. *Total part-time faculty:* 1. *List of current faculty and past affiliations:* Dale Seeds, Ohio Light Opera, Abbey Theatre of Dublin, Ireland; Alexander Brietzke, Lehigh University, New York Shakespeare Festival; Raymond McCall, Ohio Light Opera; Dale Shields, Actor's Studio.

Audition Information

Audition consists of the following: comedic monologue. Auditions are required only for students interested in scholarships. *Repertoire that students should avoid?* high school monologues, such as competition pieces.

Audition evaluation criteria: potential and commitment.

Performance Information

Performance opportunities available (frequency): fully produced performances (3-5), informal performances (2-3), workshops (1), auditioned.

Facilities

Number of theaters on campus: 2. *Type and capacity:* proscenium 396, black box 100.

MUSIC

Curriculum, Students, and Faculty

Unique or innovative music curriculum: For a small, liberal arts college, the College of Wooster has a more diverse group of course offerings than most, including two courses in African American music, one in jazz history, and one in women's contribution to music. *How are major teacher assignments made?* Students may choose, according to teacher preference and teacher availability. *28 lessons with major teacher. May a student change major teachers during the course of study?* possibly. *Study of secondary instrument or discipline is allowed.*

Selectivity for instruments or programs offered (rating): bagpipes (open), bassoon (open), clarinet (open), composition (non-competitive), double bass (open), electronic music (open), flute or piccolo (open), French horn (open), guitar (open), jazz (competitive), oboe/English horn (open), organ (open), percussion (open), piano (open), saxophone (open), trombone (open), trumpet (open), tuba (open), viola (open), violin (open), violoncello (open), voice (open).

Total enrollment: 43.

Renowned alumni: Erie Mills, Metropolitan Opera.

Total part-time faculty: 8. *Total part-time faculty:* 12. *Program contact person:* Brian Dykstra.

Performance opportunities available (frequency): jury examinations, touring.

Facilities

Number of practice rooms and hours: 24. *Recital hall?* yes. *Concert hall?* yes. *Recording studio?* yes.

DENISON UNIVERSITY

Granville OH 43023
Tel: 740-587-0810
Fax: 740-587-6750
Email: ruess@denison.edu
Web: www.denison.edu

General

Type of Institution: coed university.

Total enrollment of institution: 2,000. *Total student body from other countries:* 13%. *Degrees offered:* BA, BFA.

Entrance Requirements

Other requirements: interview, recommendation, essay *Standardized test requirements:* ACT, 26; SAT I, 1178; TOEFL, 550.

Costs & Financial Aid

Application fee: $35. *Deposit:* $300. *Tuition:* $19,310. *Medical fee:* $230. *Other fees:* $710 activity fee. *Room and board:* $5,670.

Percent of students receiving financial aid: 35%. *Types of scholarships and aid awarded:* full, partial, merit-based, need-based, named, institutional aid, government aid, tuition payment plan, work/study. *Forms required for scholarships:* FAFSA, income tax return. *Loans available. Financial aid offered to international students. Other aid available to international students:* full, partial, merit-based, need-based, named, institutional aid, government, tuition payment plan, work/study.

Services

Housing options: on-site dorms, off-campus housing.

Support staff: career counselor, financial aid advisor, foreign student advisor, housing advisor, psychological counselor, resident assistant, resident nurse, student affairs officer.

DANCE

Curriculum, Students, and Faculty

Required courses: anatomy, ballet, dance composition or choreography, dance history, dance theory, dance writing research and criticism, Labanotation, Cunningham-based, kinesiology, Laban Movement Studies, rehearsal and performance, repertory, variations.

Elective courses: African dance, jazz, master classes, other world dance forms, pointe, tap.

Total enrollment: 280. *Entering class size:* 15. *Graduating class size:* 10. *Countries most represented*: Vietnam, East India, Germany.

Renowned alumni: Molly Shanahan, Madshak Dance Company/Chicago.

Total part-time faculty: 3. *Total part-time faculty:* 1. *List of current faculty and past affiliations:* Gill Wright Miller; Sandy Matthern; April Berry, Alvin Ailey Company; Robert Cole, National Dance Company of Canada. *Program contact person:* Gill Wright Miller.

Audition Information

No audition fee. Audition consists of the following: ballet, improvisation, modern dance, audition required for BFA only. *Accompanist provided. Cassette player available; CD player available.*

Performance Information

Performance opportunities available (frequency): Fully produced concerts (2 per year), informal concerts (2 per year), workshops (4 per year), on-site performances(occasionally).

Performances choreographed by: faculty, students, guests. *Recent guest choreographers:* Dwight Rhoden, Trisha Bauman, Tom Evert, Susan Van Pelt.

Facilities

Number of studios available: 3. *Approximate studio dimensions and flooring:* 44' x 60' 5 layer, sprung loaded wood, 44' x 60' 5 layer, sprung loaded wood, 25' x 50' 5 layer, sprung loaded wood. *Performance facilities:* studio theater in dance building, proscenium in theater building.

DRAMA

Curriculum, Students, and Faculty

Required courses: acting, improvisation, scene study, Stanislavski exercises, text analysis.

Elective courses: audition preparation, drama criticism, make-up, martial arts, musical theater, voice.

Number of years required to complete program: 4. *Summer program not available. No affiliation with a professional theater company. Selectivity for males:* approximately 33% admitted. *Selectivity for females:* approximately 33% admitted. *Total enrollment:* 770. *Entering class size:* 25. *Graduating class size:* 14.

Renowned alumni: Hal Holbrook, John Davidson, John Schuck.

Total full-time faculty: 6. *List of current faculty and past affiliations:* Jon Farris, Peter Pauze; Cynthia Turnbull, Texas Shakespeare Festival.

Audition Information

No audition fee. Audition consists of the following: individual interviews. *Dress requirements for males:* comfortable attire, neutral. *Dress requirements for females:* comfortable attire, neutral. *Repertoire that students should avoid?* anything inappropriate for age and experience.

Audition evaluation criteria: this is for the program, not for a part. Therefore we are looking at the person's ability to speak a line that makes sense. Life, intelligence, inventiveness, passion, etc. Find the reality of a piece and enjoy it!

Performance Information

Performance opportunities available (frequency): fully produced performances (4 per year), informal performances (4 per year), auditioned.

Facilities

Rehearsal facilities and hours: on set of given play, 7:00 pm-11:00 pm, 5-6 rehearsals per week *Number of theaters on campus:* 2. *Type and capacity:* proscenium 195, black box 150.

MUSIC

Curriculum, Students, and Faculty

Unique or innovative music curriculum: our Music Technology program is exceptional. *How are major teacher assignments made?* students may choose. *May a student change major teachers during the course of study?* possibly. *Study of secondary instrument or discipline is allowed.*

Total enrollment: 825. *Entering class size:* 5. *Graduating class size:* 2.

Renowned alumni: Debra Vanderlinde.

Total part-time faculty: 5. *Total part-time faculty:* 17. *Program contact person:* Rick Brunetto.

Audition Information

No audition fee.

Facilities

Recital hall? yes. *Concert hall?* yes. *Recording studio?* yes.

KENYON COLLEGE

Admissions Office
Ransom Hall, Gambier OH 43022
Tel: 740-427-5776
Fax: 740-427-2634
Email: admissions@Kenyon.edu
Web: www.Keyon.edu

Entrance Requirements

Audition not required.

DANCE

Curriculum, Students, and Faculty

Required courses: historical dance, master classes, anatomy, dance history.

DRAMA

Curriculum, Students, and Faculty

Required courses: voice, scene study, improvisation, audition preparation.

Renowned alumnus: Paul Newman.

MUSKINGUM COLLEGE

Department of Music, New Concord OH 43762
Tel: 614-826-8182
Fax: 614-826-8404
Email: wschlacks@muskingum.edu
Web: www.muskingum.edu
Contact: J.C. White

General

Type of Institution: college. *Religious Affiliation:* Presbyterian.

Total enrollment of institution: 1,200. *Total student body from other countries:* 3%. *Degrees offered:* BA, BS in music education.

Entrance Requirements

Audition required: live, audio, video. *Other requirements:* interview, recommendation, essay. *Standardized test requirements:* ACT, 18; SAT I, 950; TOEFL, 550.

Costs & Financial Aid

Application fee: $20. *Deposit:* $150. *Tuition:* $10,450. *Other fees:* $435 student activity fee, telecommunications.

Types of scholarships and aid awarded: full, partial, merit-based, need-based, named, institutional aid, government aid, reduced tuition, tuition payment plan, work/study, gig office. *Forms required for scholarships:* FAFSA, income tax return, income asset verification. *Loans available. Financial aid offered to international students. Percent of international students receiving scholarships:* 70%. *Other aid available to international students:* none.

Services

Housing options: on-site dorms, off-campus housing, fraternity, sorority.

Support staff: financial aid advisor, foreign student advisor, housing advisor, psychological counselor, resident assistant, resident nurse, student affairs officer.

DRAMA

Curriculum, Students, and Faculty

Required courses: acting, directing, drama criticism, speech, technical theater, theater history, make-up.

Number of years required to complete program: 4. *Summer program not available. No affiliation with a professional theater company. Selectivity for males:* admit all who apply. *Selectivity for females:* admit all who apply. *Entering class size:* 15. *Graduating class size:* 5.

Renowned alumni: Agnes Moorehead.

Audition Information

No audition fee. Audition consists of the following: comedic monologue. *Audition evaluation criteria:* talent and observed potential.

Performance Information

Performance opportunities available (frequency): fully produced performances (4), informal performances (2), auditioned.

Recent guest artists: CATCO, Bob Belfance, Sandra Perlman.

Facilities

Number of theaters on campus: 2. *Type and capacity:* proscenium 160, flexible 100.

MUSIC

Curriculum, Students, and Faculty

Unique or innovative music curriculum: At Muskingum, music students may double major with any other major/discipline. *How are major teacher assignments made?* made by the school according to teacher preference and teacher availability. Faculty is informed of a student's teacher preference at the time of the audition. *26 lessons with major teacher. May a student change major teachers during the course of study?* possibly.

Selectivity for instruments or programs offered (rating): accompanying (non-competitive), bassoon (non-competitive), clarinet (non-competitive), double bass (non-competitive), electronic music (non-competitive), flute or piccolo (non-competitive), French horn (non-competitive), guitar (non-competitive), harpsichord (non-competitive), jazz (non-competitive), oboe/English horn (non-competitive), organ (non-competitive), percussion (non-competitive), piano (non-competitive), saxophone (non-competitive), trombone (non-competitive), trumpet (non-competitive), tuba (non-competitive), viola (non-competitive), violin (non-competitive), violoncello (non-competitive), voice (non-competitive).

Total enrollment: 40. *Entering class size:* 18. *Graduating class size:* 5.

Total part-time faculty: 4. *Total part-time faculty:* 20. *Program contact person:* W. Schlacks.

Audition Information

No audition fee. Audition consists of the following: scales, music theory repertoire. *Instruments provided for:* percussionists.

Required repertoire: prepared solo. *Performance opportunities available (frequency):* orchestral concerts, touring, chorus.

Facilities

Number of practice rooms and hours: 8; 8:00 am-11:00 pm. *Concert hall?* yes. *Recording studio?* no.

OBERLIN COLLEGE

Carnegie Building
Admissions Office, Oberlin OH 44074
Tel: 440-775-8411
Fax: 440-775-6905
Email: college.admissions@oberlin.edu
Web: www.oberlin.edu

General

Type of Institution: college, conservatory, coed.

Total enrollment of institution: 2,861. *Total student body from other countries:* 5%. *Degrees offered:* BA, BM.

Entrance Requirements

Audition required: live, audio, video. *Other requirements:* recommendation, essay. *Standardized test requirements:* ACT, 28; SAT I, 1300; TOEFL, 550.

Costs & Financial Aid

Application fee: $45. *Deposit:* $200. *Tuition:* $22,282. *Other fees:* $156 activity fee. *Room and board*: $6,658.

Percent of students receiving financial aid: 65%. *Types of scholarships and aid awarded:* merit-based, need-based, work/study. *Forms required for scholarships:* FAFSA, CSS Profile. *Loans available. Procedure for applying for loans:* submit FAFSA and profile. *Financial aid offered to international students. Percent of international students receiving scholarships:* 35%. *Other aid available to international students:* none.

Services

Housing options: on-site dorms, off-campus housing.

Support staff: career counselor, financial aid advisor, foreign student advisor, housing advisor, physical therapist, psychological counselor, resident assistant, resident nurse, student affairs officer.

DANCE

Curriculum, Students, and Faculty

Required courses: anatomy, dance composition or choreography, dance history, dance theory, dance writing research and criticism, historical dance, master classes, modern dance, rehearsal and performance, repertory, tap (2 classes per week, 2 years to complete), repertory (4 years to complete).

Elective courses: African dance.

Total enrollment: 5. *Entering class size:* 5.

Renowned alumni: Brenda Way, Susan Van Delt, Nancy Stark Smith.

Total part-time faculty: 4. *Total part-time faculty:* 1. *List of current faculty and past affiliations:* Carolyn Husted, Oberlin; Elesa Rosasco, University of Michigan; Carter McAdams, New York University, Partner's Dance Company (founder).

Performance Information

Performance opportunities available (frequency): Fully produced concerts (2 per year), informal concerts (6-7 per year), workshops (2 per year).

Performances choreographed by: faculty, students, guests.

Facilities

Number of studios available: 2. *Performance facilities:* Hall Auditorium at Warner Center.

DRAMA

Curriculum, Students, and Faculty

Required courses: acting, audition preparation, directing, improvisation, movement, scene study, speech, text analysis, verse drama, voice, movement, text analysis.

Elective courses: Alexander technique, drama criticism, dramaturgy, make-up, martial arts, mime, musical theater, stage combat, Stanislavski exercises.

Number of years required to complete program: 4. *Summer program not available. Total enrollment:* 15. *Graduating class size:* 15.

Renowned alumni: Bill Irwin, Eric Bogosian, Jim Burrows, John Kandor, Ramulus Linneil, Avery Brook, Julie Taymor, Judy Kuhn, Tom Kline, Tony Musante.

Total full-time faculty: 4. *Total part-time faculty:* 1. *List of current faculty and past affiliations:* Roger Copeland, Chris Flaharty, Jane Armitage, Paul Moser .

Facilities

Rehearsal facilities and hours: Warner Center, 8:00 am-11:00 pm.

MUSIC

Curriculum, Students, and Faculty

Total enrollment: 591. *Entering class size:* 140. *Graduating class size:* 120. *Percent International*: 10%.

Total full-time faculty: 70. *Program contact person:* Michael Manderen.

OHIO NORTHERN UNIVERSITY

525 South Main Street, Ada OH 45810
Tel: 419-772-2150
Fax: 419-772-1932
Email: e-williams@onu.edu
Web: www.onu.edu
Contact: Julie Bianci

General

Type of Institution: university. *Religious Affiliation*: United Methodist.

Total enrollment of institution: 2,900. *Degrees offered:* BA, BFA, BM.

Entrance Requirements

Audition required: live. *Other requirements:* interview. *Standardized test requirements:* ACT; SAT I; TOEFL.

Costs & Financial Aid

Application fee: $30. *Deposit:* $200. *Tuition:* $18,870. *Other fees:* $50 applied music fee.

Types of scholarships and aid awarded: full, partial, merit-based, need-based, named, institutional aid, government aid, reduced tuition, tuition payment plan, work/study. *Forms required for scholarships:* FAFSA. *Loans available. Procedure for applying for loans:* call Admissons Office and request an admissions packet. *Financial aid offered to international students. Other aid available to international students:* aid is determined on an individual basis.

Services

Housing options: on-site dorms, off-campus housing, fraternity, sorority.

Support staff: career counselor, financial aid advisor, foreign student advisor, psychological counselor, resident assistant, resident nurse, student affairs officer.

DANCE

Curriculum, Students, and Faculty

Required courses: ballet, dance composition or choreography, dance history, historical dance, jazz, master classes, modern dance, Pilates, music, rehearsal and performance, stagecraft, tap, modern dance partnering.

Elective courses: movement techniques.

Selectivity for males: approximately 60% admitted. *Selectivity for females:* approximately 60% admitted. *Total enrollment:* 15. *Entering class size:* 5. *Graduating class size:* 4.

Total full-time faculty: 1 *List of current faculty and past affiliations:* Laurie Bell, Brenda Hoyt. *Program contact person:* Laurie Bell.

Audition Information

No audition fee. Audition consists of the following: applicants are taught a routine when they arrive. *Accompanist provided. Cassette player available; CD player available.*

Repertoire that students should avoid? no.

Audition evaluation criteria: potential for development.

Performance Information

Performance opportunities available (frequency): Fully produced concerts (1-2), informal concerts (1-2), workshops (3-5).

Performances choreographed by: faculty, guests.

Facilities

Number of studios available: 2. *Approximate studio dimensions and flooring:* 20' x 30' sprung floor, 40' x 60' sprung floor. *Performance facilities:* large concert hall, experimental theater.

DRAMA

Curriculum, Students, and Faculty

Required courses: acting, audition preparation, directing, drama criticism, improvisation, makeup, movement, musical theater, scene study, speech, stage combat, Stanislavski exercises, text analysis, voice, verse drama.

Number of years required to complete program: 4. *Summer program available. No affiliation with a professional theater company. Selectivity for males:* approximately 60% admitted. *Selectivity for females:* approximately 60% admitted. *Total enrollment:* 50. *Entering class size:* 20. *Graduating class size:* 15.

Total full-time faculty: 2. *Total part-time faculty:* 1. *List of current faculty and past affiliations:* Nilo Riess, Renee Dobson, Burt Reynolds Theatre.

Audition Information

No audition fee. Audition consists of the following: a cappella, comedic monologue, movement class, Shakespearean monologue. ***Repertoire that students should avoid?*** no.

Audition evaluation criteria: potential for development.

Performance Information

Performance opportunities available (frequency): fully produced performances (3-5 per year), informal performances (1-2 per year), off-site performances (3-5 per year), auditioned.

Facilities

Number of theaters on campus: 2.

MUSIC

Curriculum, Students, and Faculty

Unique or innovative music curriculum: We are designing a curriculum to include elective studies in business for students pursuing a BM degree. ***How are major teacher assignments made?*** Students may choose, according to teacher preference and teacher availability. Faculty is informed of a student's teacher preference at the time of the audition. 30 lessons with major teacher. ***May a student change major teachers during the course of study?*** possibly. ***Study of secondary instrument or discipline is allowed.***

Selectivity for instruments or programs offered (rating): bassoon (competitive), choral singing (competitive), clarinet (competitive), composition (competitive), double bass (competitive), electronic music (competitive), flute or piccolo (competitive), French horn (competitive), harpsichord (competitive), oboe/English horn (competitive), organ (competitive), percussion (competitive), piano (competitive), saxophone (competitive), trombone (competitive), trombone (open), trumpet (competitive), tuba (competitive), viola (competitive), violin (competitive), violoncello (competitive), voice (competitive).

Total enrollment: 75. ***Entering class size:*** 25. ***Graduating class size:*** 15.

Renowned alumni: Robert Klotman, American String Teachers Association.

Total full-time faculty: 7. ***Total part-time faculty:*** 15. ***Program contact person:*** Dr. Edwin L. Williams.

Audition Information

No audition fee. Instruments provided for: percussionists.

Required repertoire: repertoire is established with the auditionee before arrival on campus. ***Repertoire that students should avoid?*** popular music. ***Performance opportunities available (frequency):*** band (all year), jury examinations (3), recitals (25-35), touring, chorus (all year).

Facilities

Number of practice rooms and hours: 19; always open. ***Recital hall?*** yes. ***Concert hall?*** yes. ***Recording studio?*** no.

OHIO STATE UNIVERSITY

College of the Arts
128 North Oval Mall, Columbus OH 43210-1363
Tel: 614-292-3980
Email: admissions@osu.edu

General

Type of Institution: public university.

Degrees offered: BA, BM.

MUSIC

Curriculum, Students, and Faculty

Unique or innovative music curriculum: all freshmen take a computer music technology course during the first year. ***How are major teacher assignments made?*** students may choose, according to teacher availability. Faculty is not informed of a student's teacher preference at the time of the audition. ***May a student change major teachers during the course of study?*** possibly. ***Study of secondary instrument or discipline is allowed.***

Total enrollment: 550.

Renowned alumni: Richard Stoltzman, Barbara Daniels, Diane Kesling, Jack Renner, Stephen Montague.

Total full-time faculty: 60. ***Total part-time faculty:*** 11. ***Program contact person:*** Judith Delzell.

Audition Information

Audition consists of the following: scales, music theory, arpeggios, sight reading, improvisation. ***Instruments provided for:*** harpists, percussionists.

Performance opportunities available (frequency): jury examinations (1-2 per year).

Facilities

Number of practice rooms and hours: 57; 7:00 am - 11:00 pm (daily). ***Recital hall?*** yes. ***Concert hall?*** yes. ***Recording studio?*** yes.

OHIO UNIVERSITY

Athens OH 45701
Tel: 614-593-1826
Fax: 614-593-0749
Email: Dancedept@Ohiou.edu
Web: www.dance/ohiou.edu
Contact: Jerry Reese

General

Type of Institution: public university.

Total enrollment of institution: 19,000. *Degrees offered:* BFA, BA.

Entrance Requirements

Audition required: live. *Other requirements:* interview, recommendation, essay, photograph. *Standardized test requirements:* ACT; SAT I; TOEFL.

Costs & Financial Aid

Application fee: $30. *Tuition (in-state/out-state):* $4,080/ $8,574. *Medical fee:* $448. *Other fees:* $70 testing fee, $65 recreational fee.

Types of scholarships and aid awarded: full, partial, merit-based, named, government aid, tuition payment plan, work/study. *Forms required for scholarships:* FAFSA. *Loans available. Procedure for applying for loans:* contact Financial Aid Office.

Services

Housing options: on-site dorms, off-campus housing, fraternity, sorority.

Support staff: career counselor, college advisor, financial aid advisor, foreign student advisor, housing advisor, physical therapist, psychological counselor, resident assistant, resident nurse, student affairs officer.

DANCE

Curriculum, Students, and Faculty

Required courses: anatomy, ballet (2 classes per week, 4 years to complete), dance composition or choreography, dance history, dance theory, Labanotation, master classes, modern dance, movement techniques, music, Indian dance, rehearsal and performance, stagecraft.

Elective courses: dance writing research and criticism, jazz, body conditioning, Laban Movement Studies, Pilates, nutrition, other world dance forms, repertory, modern dance partnering.

Selectivity for males: approximately 60% admitted. *Selectivity for females:* approximately 60% admitted. *Total enrollment:* 60. *Entering class size:* 30. *Graduating class size:* 7. *Percent International*: 3%. *Countries most represented*: Japan.

Renowned alumni: Linda Bell Calloway, Sarah Gomblin, Linda Sohl Donnell, Tom Evert. *List of current faculty and past affiliations:* SusanVan Pelt, Sara Rudner Dance Company; Lisa Ford Moulton, Rire Woodbury Dance Company; Madeleine Scott Douglas, Nielsen Dances. *Program contact person:* Madeleine Scott.

Audition Information

No audition fee. Audition consists of the following: ballet, improvisation, modern dance. *Accompanist provided. Dress requirements for males:* barefoot, leotards, tights. *Dress requirements for females:* barefoot, leotard, tights.

Performance Information

Performance opportunities available (frequency): Fully produced concerts (3 per year), informal concerts (2 per year), workshops (12 per year), on-site performances (3 per year), touring (1 per year).

Performances choreographed by: faculty, students, guests. *Recent guest choreographers:* Patt Catterson, Nusha Mortynuk, Chris Aiken, Douglas Nielsen.

Facilities

Number of studios available: 6. *Approximate studio dimensions and flooring:* 15' x 30' 3 sprung floors, 30' x 30' 2 with tarkette, wood. *Performance facilities:* studio theater, proscenium theater.

DRAMA

Curriculum, Students, and Faculty

Required courses: acting, directing, drama criticism, make-up, movement, speech, Stanislavski exercises, text analysis, voice.

Elective courses: audition preparation, dramaturgy, improvisation, martial arts, mime, scene study, stage combat, verse drama.

Number of years required to complete program: 4. *Summer program available. Affiliation with a professional theater company: Cincinatti Playhouse in the Park is affiliated formally with our MFA acting programs. Monomoy Theater in Cape Cod is owned by Ohio University and is a 40-year old summer stock theater.*

Selectivity for males: approximately 33% admitted. *Selectivity for females:* approximately 33% admitted. *Total enrollment:* 160. *Entering class size:* 60. *Graduating class size:* 40.

Renowned alumni: Chuck Cooper, Betty Thomas, Jonathan Freeman, Scott McPherson, Edward Pierce, Gann Cameron Webb.

Total full-time faculty: 19. ***List of current faculty and past affiliations:*** Charles Smith, Goodman and Victory Gardens/Northwestern; Ulsula Belder.

Audition Information

No audition fee. Audition consists of the following: comedic monologue, group warm-up, audition for scholarship not for entrance. ***Repertoire that students should avoid?*** Barefoot in the Park.

Audition evaluation criteria: immediacy, range, truth.

Performance Information

Performance opportunities available (frequency): fully produced performances (8 per season), informal performances (30 per season), workshops (4 per year), auditioned. Open casting, supervised by faculty advisors with final responsibility given to the director of the school.

Recent guest artists: Jonathan Freeman, Darko Lukic.

Facilities

Number of theaters on campus: 3. ***Type and capacity:*** proscenium 260, thrust 260, black box 90.

MUSIC

Comments

BM degrees offered in music performance, music education, music therapy, composition, theory, history and literature, piano pedagogy.

OHIO WESLEYAN UNIVERSITY

61 South Sandusky Street, Delaware OH 43015
Tel: 614-368-3700
Fax: 614-368-3723
Email: musicd@cc.owu.edu
Contact: Mr.Stephen R. O'Connell

General

Type of Institution: college. ***Religious Affiliation:*** United Methodist. ***Environment:*** suburban.

Total enrollment of institution: 1,854. ***Total student body from other countries:*** 10%. ***Degrees offered:*** BA, BM.

Entrance Requirements

Audition required: live, audio, video. ***Other requirements:*** interview, recommendation, essay. ***Standardized test requirements:*** ACT, 24; SAT I, 1100; TOEFL, 550.

Costs & Financial Aid

Application fee: $35. ***Deposit:*** $300. ***Tuition:*** $19,140. ***Room and board:*** $6,680.

Percent of students receiving financial aid: 67%. ***Types of scholarships and aid awarded:*** full, partial, merit-based, need-based, named, institutional aid, government aid, tuition payment plan, work/study. ***Forms required for scholarships:*** FAFSA, income tax return, school's own financial aid form. ***Loans available. Procedure for applying for loans:*** file FAFSA and request loan consideration. ***Financial aid offered to international students. Percent of international students receiving scholarships:*** 90%.

Services

Housing options: on-site dorms, fraternity.

Support staff: career counselor, financial aid advisor, foreign student advisor, housing advisor, psychological counselor, resident assistant, resident nurse, student affairs officer.

DANCE

Curriculum, Students, and Faculty

Required courses: dance composition or choreography, dance writing research and criticism, master classes, modern dance, movement techniques, rehearsal and performance, stagecraft.

Audition Information

No audition fee. Audition consists of the following: prepared solo. ***Accompanist not provided. Cassette player available; CD player available.***

Performance Information

Performance opportunities available (frequency): Fully produced concerts (1 per year), informal concerts (1- 2 per year), workshops (2-3 per year), on-site performances (2-3 per year), touring (1-2 per year).

Performances choreographed by: faculty, students, guests.

Facilities

Number of studios available: 1. ***Approximate studio dimensions and flooring:*** wood sprung. ***Performance facilities:*** 1 studio, 1 proscenium.

DRAMA

Curriculum, Students, and Faculty

Required courses: acting, directing, drama criticism, text analysis.

Elective courses: Alexander technique, audition preparation, movement, musical theater, scene study, verse drama, voice.

Number of years required to complete program: 4. *Summer program not available. No affiliation with a professional theater company. Selectivity for males:* approximately 33% admitted. *Selectivity for females:* approximately 33% admitted. *Total enrollment:* 9. *Entering class size:* 9. *Graduating class size:* 9.

Renowned alumni: Robert E. Lee, Ron Liebman.

Total full-time faculty: 4. *Total part-time faculty:* 2. *List of current faculty and past affiliations:* L.B. Rabby, D.V. Vanderbilt, Bonnie Milne Gardner, Elane Denny.

Audition Information

No audition fee. Audition consists of the following: comedic monologue, *Dress requirements for males and females:* comfortable, generic clothing. *Audition evaluation criteria:* technique, intellect, a willingness to learn, believability.

Performance Information

Performance opportunities available (frequency): fully produced performances (4-6 per year), informal performances (2-3 per year), workshops (2-3 per year), off-site performances (2-3 per year), auditioned.

Recent guest artists: Bread & Puppet Theatre, Robert Post, Cleveland Signstage Theater.

Facilities

Rehearsal facilities and hours: rehearsal room, 2 theaters, open 7 days per week. *Number of theaters on campus:* 2. *Type and capacity:* proscenium 375, flexible 120.

MUSIC

Curriculum, Students, and Faculty

How are major teacher assignments made? made by the school. Faculty is informed of a student's teacher preference at the time of the audition. *28 lessons with major teacher. May a student change major teachers during the course of study?* possibly. *Study of secondary instrument or discipline is allowed.*

Selectivity for instruments or programs offered (rating): bassoon (non-competitive), clarinet (non-competitive), double bass (non-competitive), flute or piccolo (non-competitive), French horn (non-competitive), oboe/English horn (non-competitive), organ (non-competitive), piano (non-competitive), saxophone (non-competitive), trombone (non-competitive), trumpet (non-competitive), tuba (non-competitive), viola (non-competitive), violin (non-competitive), violoncello (non-competitive), voice (non-competitive).

Total enrollment: 41. *Entering class size:* 12. *Graduating class size:* 10.

Total part-time faculty: 7. *Total part-time faculty:* 9. *Program contact person:* Robert Griffith.

Audition Information

No audition fee. Audition consists of the following: scales, repertoire. *Instruments provided for:* percussionists.

Required repertoire: varies by instrument. Please call school for repertoire information. *Performance opportunities available (frequency):* band (frequently), jury examinations (frequently), orchestral concerts (frequently), recitals (frequently), touring, chorus.

Facilities

Number of practice rooms and hours: 25; 7:30 am-10:30 pm. *Recital hall?* yes. *Concert hall?* yes. *Recording studio?* yes.

OTTERBEIN COLLEGE

Office of Admission
One Otterbein College, Westerville OH 43081-2006
Tel: 800-488-8144
Fax: 614-823-1200
Email: uotterb@otterbein.edu
Web: www.otterbein.edu
Contact: Lavona See

General

Type of Institution: college. *Religious Affiliation:* Methodist. *Environment:* suburban *Cross registration is available through the several central Ohio colleges and universities.*

Total enrollment of institution: 2,550. *Degrees offered:* BA, BFA, BME.

Entrance Requirements

Audition required: live, audio, video. *Other requirements:* interview, recommendation, photograph. *Standardized test requirements:* ACT, 23. SAT I, 1090; TOEFL, 500.

Costs & Financial Aid

Application fee: $20. *Deposit:* $100. *Tuition:* $14,997. *Other fees:* varies.

Percent of students receiving financial aid: 95%. *Types of scholarships and aid awarded:* merit-based, need-based, named, institutional aid, government aid, tuition payment plan, work/study. *Forms required for scholarships:* FAFSA, income tax return. *Loans available. Procedure for applying for loans:* completed admission application and acceptance to the college. *Financial aid offered to international students.*

Services

Housing options: on-site dorms, fraternity, sorority.

Support staff: career counselor, foreign student advisor, housing advisor, physical therapist, psychological counselor, resident assistant, resident nurse, student affairs officer.

DANCE

Curriculum, Students, and Faculty

Total enrollment: 37. *Entering class size:* 3. *Graduating class size:* 4.

Total full-time faculty: 1. *Total part-time faculty:* 6. *Program contact person:* Stells Kane.

DRAMA

Curriculum, Students, and Faculty

Elective courses: improvisation.

Summer program not available. Total enrollment: 130. *Entering class size:* 35. *Graduating class size:* 40. *Percent International:* 1%.

Total full-time faculty: 8. *Total part-time faculty:* 2.

MUSIC

Curriculum, Students, and Faculty

How are major teacher assignments made? students may choose according to teacher availability. Faculty is not informed of a student's teacher preference at the time of the audition. *30 lessons with major teacher. May a student change major teachers during the course of study?* possibly. *Study of secondary instrument or discipline is allowed.*

Selectivity for instruments or programs offered (rating): accompanying (competitive), accordion (competitive), bagpipes (competitive), bassoon (competitive), choral conducting (competitive), choral singing (competitive), clarinet (competitive), composition (competitive), double bass (competitive), electronic music (competitive), flute or piccolo (competitive), French horn (competitive), guitar (competitive), harp (competitive), harpsichord (competitive), jazz (competitive), oboe/English horn (competitive), orchestral conducting (competitive), organ (competitive), percussion (competitive), piano (competitive), sacred music (competitive), saxophone (competitive), trombone (competitive), trumpet (competitive), tuba (competitive), viola (competitive), violin (competitive), violoncello (competitive), voice (competitive).

Total enrollment: 100. *Entering class size:* 30. *Graduating class size:* 30. *Percent International:* 1%.

Total full-time faculty: 8. *Total part-time faculty:* 28. *Program contact person:* Dr. Morton Achter.

Audition Information

Audition consists of the following: scales, arpeggios, sight reading. *Instruments provided for:* percussionists.

Repertoire that students should avoid? no.

Facilities

Number of practice rooms and hours: 17; all times. *Recital hall?* yes. *Concert hall?* yes. *Recording studio?* yes.

THE UNIVERSITY OF AKRON SCHOOL OF DANCE, THEATRE, AND ARTS ADMINISTRATION

354 East Market Street, Akron OH 44325-2502
Tel: 330-972-7948
Fax: 330-972-7902

General

Type of Institution: university. *Environment:* suburban.

Total enrollment of institution: 23,500. *Degrees offered:* BA, BFA, BM.

Entrance Requirements

Audition required: live, video. *Other requirements:* photograph. *Standardized test requirements:* ACT; SAT I.

Costs & Financial Aid

Application fee: $25. *Other fees:* $14.45 per credit hour general fee, $60 parking fee.

Types of scholarships and aid awarded: partial, merit-based, need-based, named, institutional aid, government aid, reduced tuition, tuition payment plan, work/study. *Procedure for applying for loans:* file FAFSA.

Services

Housing options: on-site dorms, off-campus housing, fraternity, sorority.

Support staff: career counselor, financial aid advisor, foreign student advisor, housing advisor, physical therapist, psychological counselor, resident assistant, resident nurse, student affairs officer.

DANCE

Curriculum, Students, and Faculty

Required courses: ballet (5 classes per week), dance composition or choreography, dance history, jazz (2 classes per week), modern dance, Graham-based dance (3 classes per week), Limon-based (3 classes per week), rehearsal and performance, repertory (2 classes per week), tap (2 classes per week).

Elective courses: character (1class per week), movement techniques, music, nutrition, pas de deux, pointe (2 classes per week), variations (2 classes per week).

DRAMA

Curriculum, Students, and Faculty

Required courses: acting, costume design, directing, make-up, movement, musical theater, theater history, voice, dramatic literature.

MUSIC

Total enrollment: 490.

Major opera in spring with orchestra. 2 summer musical theatre productions in conjunction with school of theater/dance.

UNIVERSITY OF DAYTON

Department of Music
300 College Park, Dayton OH 45469-0290
Tel: 937-229-3936
Fax: 937-229-3916
Email: mus_adms@yar.udayton.edu
Web: www.udayton/2music
Contact: Myron Achbach

General

Type of Institution: university. *Environment:* small city.

Total enrollment of institution: 7,500. *Degrees offered:* BA, BM.

Entrance Requirements

Audition required: live, audio, video. *Other requirements:* recommendation. *Standardized test requirements:* ACT, 24; SAT I, 1144; TOEFL, 525.

Costs & Financial Aid

Application fee: $30. *Deposit:* $200. *Other fees:* $490 university fee.

Types of scholarships and aid awarded: full, partial, merit-based, need-based, named, institutional aid, government aid, tuition payment plan, work/study. *Forms required for scholarships:* FAFSA, form for academic scholarships and leadership awards. *Loans available. Procedure for applying for loans:* contact. Office of Financial Aid (937) 229-4311.

Services

Housing options: on-site dorms, off-campus housing, fraternity, sorority.

Support staff: financial aid advisor, foreign student advisor, housing advisor, physical therapist, psychological counselor, resident assistant, resident nurse, student affairs officer.

MUSIC

Curriculum, Students, and Faculty

How are major teacher assignments made? made by the school according to teacher preference and teacher availability. Faculty is not informed of a student's teacher preference at the time of the audition. *28 lessons with major teacher. May a student change major teachers during the course of study?* possibly. *Study of secondary instrument or discipline is allowed.*

Selectivity for instruments or programs offered (rating): accompanying (competitive), bassoon (competitive), clarinet (competitive), composition (competitive), double bass (competitive), flute or piccolo (competitive), French horn (competitive), guitar (competitive), harp (competitive), harpsichord (competitive), jazz (competitive), oboe/ English horn (competitive), organ (competitive), percussion (competitive), piano (competitive), saxophone (competitive), trombone (competitive), trumpet (competitive), tuba (competitive), viola (competitive), violin (competitive), violoncello (competitive), voice (competitive).

Total enrollment: 110. *Entering class size:* 35. *Graduating class size:* 25. *Percent International*: 4%.

Total full-time faculty: 13. *Total part-time faculty:* 27. *Program contact person:* Richard Benedum.

Audition Information

No audition fee. Audition consists of the following: scales, sight reading. *Instruments provided for:* harpists, percussionists.

Performance opportunities available (frequency): band, band, jury examinations, recitals, chorus.

Facilities

Number of practice rooms and hours: 13; 7:30 am-11:00 pm. *Recital hall?* yes. *Concert hall?* yes. *Recording studio?* yes.

WRIGHT STATE UNIVERSITY

3640 Colonel Glenn Highway, Dayton OH 45435-0001
Tel: 937-775-5740
Fax: 937-775-3301
Web: www.wright.edu

General

Type of Institution: university. *Environment:* small city.

Total enrollment of institution: 16,000. *Degrees offered:* BFA.

Entrance Requirements

Audition required: live. *Other requirements:* interview, photograph. *Standardized test requirements:* ACT; SAT I; SAT II.

Costs & Financial Aid

Application fee: $30. *Tuition (in-state/out-state):* $11,508/$14,500.

Types of scholarships and aid awarded: full, partial, merit-based, named, government aid, work/ study. *Financial aid offered to international students.*

Services

Housing options: on-site dorms, off-campus housing.

Support staff: career counselor, financial aid advisor, foreign student advisor, physical therapist, psychological counselor, resident assistant, resident nurse.

DANCE

Curriculum, Students, and Faculty

Required courses: anatomy, ballet (5 classes per week, 4 years to complete), dance composition or choreography, dance history, jazz (2 classes per week, 4 years to complete), master classes, men's class (1 class per week), modern dance (3 classes per week, 4 years to complete), music, pas de deux (1 class per week, 4 years to complete), pointe (1 class per week, 4 years to complete), rehearsal and performance, variations (1 class per week, 4 years to complete).

Elective courses: stagecraft.

Selectivity for males: approximately 60% admitted. *Selectivity for females:* approximately 33% admitted. *Total enrollment:* 50. *Entering class size:* 28. *Graduating class size:* 8. *Percent International*: 1%. *Countries most represented*: Denmark.

Total full-time faculty: 3. *Total part-time faculty:* 3. *List of current faculty and past affiliations:* Jon Rodriguez, Advisory Board of Regional Dance America; Suzanne Walker, Awarded the Virginia Sebastian Choreographic Award; Patricia White. *Program contact person:* Victoria Oleen or Jon Rodriguez.

Audition Information

No audition fee. Audition consists of the following: ballet, modern dance. *Accompanist provided. Cassette player available; CD player available.*

Audition evaluation criteria: technical strength and artistic potential for a performing career.

Performance Information

Performance opportunities available (frequency): Fully produced concerts (1 season), informal concerts (1 season), on-site performances (frequently), touring (2-3 per season), musicals (2 per season).

Performances choreographed by: faculty, students, guests. *Recent guest choreographers:* Douglas Nielson, Mark Diamond, Kevin Ward, Bess Saylor.

Facilities

Number of studios available: 3. *Approximate studio dimensions and flooring:* 50' x 60', 45' x 50' sprung wood floors, 35' x 40' covered w/Marley. *Performance facilities:* procenium, flexible (black box), studio.

DRAMA

Curriculum, Students, and Faculty

Required courses: acting, audition preparation, improvisation, make-up, movement, musical theater, scene study, speech, stage combat, Stanislavski exercises, text analysis, verse drama, voice.

Elective courses: directing, drama criticism, martial arts, musical theater.

Number of years required to complete program: 4. *Summer program not available. Selectivity for males:* approximately 10% admitted. *Selectivity for females:* approximately 10% admitted. *Total enrollment:* 87. *Entering class size:* 53. *Graduating class size:* 12.

Total full-time faculty: 6. *Total part-time faculty:* 4. *List of current faculty and past affiliations:* Bruce Cromel, Santa Fe Stage; Sandra Crews-University of Florida; Mary Donahoe, Pomona College; Joe Deer, Carnegie Mellon; Rocco Dal Vera, Denver Center for Performing Arts.

Audition Information

Audition consists of the following: comedic monologue, movement class, Shakespearean monologue, group warm-up. *Dress requirements for males:* dance clothes for musical theatre majors. *Dress requirements for females:* dance clothes for musical theatre majors.

Performance Information

Performance opportunities available (frequency): fully produced performances (9 per year), informal performances (12 per year), auditioned.

Recent guest artists: Martin Sheen, Samantha Longeum.

Facilities

Number of theaters on campus: 3. *Type and capacity:* proscenium 376, black box 120, proscenium 92.

OKLAHOMA

OKLAHOMA BAPTIST UNIVERSITY

500 West University
Box 61276, Shawnee OK 74801-2590
Tel: 405-878-2305
Fax: 405-878-2328
Email: paul_hammond@mail.okbu.edu
Web: www.okbu.edu

General

Type of Institution: university. *Religious Affiliation*: Southern Baptist. *Environment:* suburban. *Cross registration is available through St. Gregory's University.*

Total enrollment of institution: 2,360. *Total student body from other countries:* 3%. *Degrees offered:* BA, BM, BMA (Bachelor of Musical Arts).

Entrance Requirements

Audition required: live, audio, video. *Other requirements:* photograph. *Standardized test requirements:* ACT, 24; SAT II, 950.

Costs & Financial Aid

Application fee: $25. *Other fees:* $133 general fees, $600 applied music.

Types of scholarships and aid awarded: full, partial, merit-based, need-based, named, institutional aid, government aid, reduced tuition, tuition payment plan, work/study. *Loans available. Procedure for applying for loans:* contact admissions (405-878-2033 or 800-654-3285). *Financial aid offered to international students. Other aid available to international students:* college work; accompanying; private piano teaching in preparatory department.

Services

Housing options: on-site dorms, off-campus housing.

Support staff: financial aid advisor, foreign student advisor, housing advisor, resident assistant, student affairs officer.

DRAMA

Curriculum, Students, and Faculty

Required courses: acting, audition preparation, directing, drama criticism, speech, voice.

Elective courses: dramaturgy, make-up, musical theater.

Number of years required to complete program: 4. *Summer program not available. No affiliation with a professional theater company. Selectivity for males:* approximately 60% admitted. *Selectivity for females:* approximately 60% admitted. *Total enrollment:* 27. *Entering class size:* 10.

Total full-time faculty: 2 *List of current faculty and past affiliations:* Dr. Marion Castleberry; Laura Byland.

Audition Information

No audition fee. Audition consists of the following: comedic monologue. *Repertoire that students should avoid?* no

Performance Information

Performance opportunities available (frequency): fully produced performances (3 per year), informal performances (1-2 per year), auditioned.

Facilities

Rehearsal facilities and hours: black box, available evenings. *Number of theaters on campus:* 1. *Type and capacity:* black box 150.

MUSIC

Curriculum, Students, and Faculty

Unique or innovative music curriculum: BMA degree allows for a non-music minor of student's choosing. *How are major teacher assignments made?* according to teacher preference and teacher availability. Faculty is not informed of a student's teacher preference at the time of the audition. 30 lessons with major teacher. *May a student change major teachers during the course of study?* possibly. *Study of secondary instrument or discipline is allowed.*

Selectivity for instruments or programs offered (rating): accompanying (selective), bassoon (open), choral singing (competitive), clarinet (open), composition (open), electronic music (open), flute or piccolo (open), French horn (open), guitar (open), harp (open), jazz (open), oboe/English horn (open), organ (open), percussion (open), piano (competitive), sacred music (open), saxophone (open), trombone (open), trumpet (open), tuba (open), viola (open), violin (open), violoncello (open), voice (open).

Total enrollment: 145. *Entering class size:* 35. *Percent International*: 1%. *Countries most represented*: Malaysia.

Renowned alumni: Ray Ferguson, Bruce Fowler, Michael Rees Davis, Al Travis, Michael Cox, Nancy Hill Cobb.

Total full-time faculty: 22. *Total part-time faculty:* 7. *Program contact person:* Dr. Paul Hammond.

Audition Information

No audition fee. Audition consists of the following: scales, arpeggios, sight reading. *Instruments provided for:* percussionists.

Performance opportunities available (frequency): band (frequently), jury examinations (frequently), opera workshops (frequently), recitals (frequently), touring (frequently), chorus.

Facilities

Number of practice rooms and hours: 30; 7:00 am-11:00 pm. *Recital hall?* yes. *Concert hall?* no. *Recording studio?* no.

OKLAHOMA CITY UNIVERSITY

2501 North Blackwelder, Oklahoma City OK 73106
Tel: 405-521-5050
Fax: 405-521-5916
Email: uadmissions@frodo.oku.edu
Web: www.oklu.edu

General

Type of Institution: university. *Religious Affiliation*: United Methodist. *Environment:* small city. *Academic education is offered on-site.*

Total enrollment of institution: 4,680. *Degrees offered:* BA, BM, BPA in dance, BS in Dance Management, BS in Technical Theater.

Entrance Requirements

Audition required: live, audio, video. *Other requirements:* recommendation, essay, photograph. *Standardized test requirements:* ACT, 20; SAT I, 940; TOEFL, 550.

Costs & Financial Aid

Application fee: $20. *Deposit:* $100. *Tuition:* $8,380. *Medical fee:* $4. *Other fees:* $20 per semester registration, $25 yearbook, $1 per credit hour student senate, $50 graduation, $40 per semester applied music, $140-$165 accompanist, $12 per year parking permits.

Percent of students receiving financial aid: 81%. *Types of scholarships and aid awarded:* partial, merit-based, need-based, named, institutional aid, government aid, reduced tuition, tuition payment plan, work/study. *Forms required for scholar-*

ships: FAFSA, income tax return, income asset verification, financial aid transcripts. ***Loans available. Financial aid offered to international students. Percent of international students receiving scholarships:*** 1%.

Services

Housing options: on-site dorms, off-campus housing, fraternity.

Support staff: career counselor, financial aid advisor, foreign student advisor, housing advisor, physical therapist, psychological counselor, resident assistant, resident nurse, student affairs officer.

DANCE

Curriculum, Students, and Faculty

Required courses: anatomy, ballet (5 classes per week, 4 years to complete), dance composition or choreography, musical theater dance (2 classes per week, 2 years to complete), dance history, dance theory, jazz (3 classes per week, 4 years to complete), music, nutrition, stagecraft, tap (3 classes per week, 3 years to complete).

Elective courses: pas de deux, pointe.

Selectivity for males: approximately 60% admitted. ***Selectivity for females:*** approximately 33% admitted. ***Total enrollment:*** 170. ***Entering class size:*** 55. ***Graduating class size:*** 27. ***Percent International***: 1%. ***Countries most represented***: Canada.

Renowned alumni: Rhonda Miller, Clarence Brooks, Marie Lawrence Danviers.

Total full-time faculty: 5. ***Total part-time faculty:*** 4. ***List of current faculty and past affiliations:*** Jo Rowan, School of American Ballet; Liz Reiter, Giordano Dance Company; Kay Sandel, Chicago Lyric Opera Ballet. ***Program contact person:*** Angela Cumpton.

Audition Information

Audition fee; $21. ***Audition consists of the following:*** ballet, prepared solo, tap class, jazz class ***Accompanist not provided. Cassette player available; CD player available. Dress requirements for males:*** depends on technique. ***Dress requirements for females:*** depends on technique.

Audition evaluation criteria: technical proficiency in tap, jazz, and ballet; professional appearance consistant with "A Broadway Line;" performance personality; ability to project.

Performance Information

Performance opportunities available (frequency): Fully produced concerts (1), workshops (2), on-site performances (12), touring (2), 2 fully produced operas, 2 fully produced musicals, student choreography show, one Christmas holiday extravaganza with the Oklahoma City Philharmonic and Oklahoma City Cant.

Performances choreographed by: faculty, students, guests.

Facilities

Number of studios available: 5. ***Approximate studio dimensions and flooring:*** 28' x 56' suspended floors with tap resistant vinyl covering, 35' x 48' suspended floors with tap resistant vinyl covering, 30' x 40' suspended floors with tap resistant vinyl covering, 25' x 30' suspended floors with tap resistant vinyl covering. ***Performance facilities:*** Oklahoma Civic Center Music Hall—3,200 seats professional venue, Kirkpatrick auditorium, Oklahoma University—1,100-seat proscenium, Burg Theater—256-seat three quarters round.

DRAMA

Curriculum, Students, and Faculty

Required courses: acting, audition preparation, children's theater, creative drama, directing, drama criticism, improvisation, movement, scene study, speech, Stanislavski exercises, technical theater, text analysis, TV/film acting class, voice.

Elective courses: Alexander technique, make-up, martial arts, mime, musical theater, stage combat, verse drama.

Number of years required to complete program: 4. ***Affiliation with a professional theater company: Carpenter Square Theater.***

Selectivity for males: approximately 60% admitted. ***Selectivity for females:*** approximately 60% admitted. ***Total enrollment:*** 50. ***Entering class size:*** 14. ***Graduating class size:*** 5. ***Percent International***: 5%. ***Countries most represented***: Taiwan, Singapore, China.

Total full-time faculty: 4. ***Total part-time faculty:*** 3.

Audition Information

Audition consists of the following: 2 contrasting monologues and an interview. ***Repertoire that students should avoid?*** Audition must consist of monologues from plays only; forensics or interpreted pieces from prose, poetry, or any non-play sources, will not be considered.

Audition evaluation criteria: memorization, projection, diction, rate, gesture, tone, resonance-both technical, and characterization elements of physical and vocal life, consistancy, sincerity, honesty of characterization, avoidance of stereotypes, absence of nervous mannerisms, depth and breadth of contrast, and choice of monologues.

Performance Information

Performance opportunities available (frequency): fully produced performances (6 per year), off-site performances (1 per year), graduating student productions, directing projects, number varies, auditioned. Cold readings and/or prepared monologues, separate auditions for each show.

Facilities

Rehearsal facilities and hours: classrooms, Burg Theater, Kirkpatrick Theater are all by reservation only, Children's Center for the Arts. *Type and capacity:* thrust—256, proscenium—1,089.

MUSIC

Curriculum, Students, and Faculty

Unique or innovative music curriculum: OCU offers a variety of degrees, most of which are very strong in practical application, including 4 major opera and music theater productions. *How are major teacher assignments made?* Students may choose, according to teacher availability. Faculty is not informed of a student's teacher preference at the time of the audition. *May a student change major teachers during the course of study?* possibly. *Study of secondary instrument or discipline is allowed.*

Selectivity for instruments or programs offered (rating): accompanying (selective), bassoon (selective), choral singing (competitive), clarinet (selective), composition (selective), double bass (selective), electronic music (competitive), flute or piccolo (selective), French horn (selective), guitar (selective), harp (selective), harpsichord (selective), jazz (competitive), oboe/English horn (selective), organ (selective), percussion (selective), piano (selective), sacred music (competitive), saxophone (selective), trombone (selective), trumpet (selective), tuba (selective), viola (selective), violin (selective), violoncello (selective), voice (selective).

Total enrollment: 220. *Entering class size:* 75. *Graduating class size:* 24. *Percent International*: 5%. *Countries most represented*: Taiwan, China, Korea, Israel, Sweden, Malaysia.

Renowned alumni: Ron Raines, Kristin Chenowith, Mason Williams, Stacey Logan.

Total full-time faculty: 19. *Total part-time faculty:* 42. *Program contact person:* Mark Blakeman.

Audition Information

Audition consists of the following: scales, sight reading, repertoire. *Instruments provided for:* harpists, percussionists; most wind and string instruments can be provided for use.

Required repertoire: varies by instrument. Please call school for repertoire information. *Performance opportunities available (frequency):* band, jury examinations, opera workshops, orchestral concerts, recitals, produced operas, chorus.

Facilities

Number of practice rooms and hours: 19; 8:00 am-12:00 am. *Recital hall?* yes. *Concert hall?* yes. *Recording studio?* yes.

Comments

OCU is a liberal arts university, and has one of the oldest opera and music theater companies, now in its 46th season. The Margaret E. Petre School of Music and Performing Arts hosts more than 200 performances each year.

OKLAHOMA STATE UNIVERSITY MUSIC DEPARTMENT

132 Seretean Center for the Performing Arts,
Stillwater OK 74078-4077
Tel: 405-744-6133
Fax: 405-744-9324
Email: musica@okway.okstate.edu

General

Type of Institution: university. *Environment:* suburban.

Total enrollment of institution: 20,000. *Degrees offered:* BA, BM, BME.

Entrance Requirements

Audition required: live, audio, video. *Other requirements:* recommendation *Standardized test requirements:* ACT, 22; SAT I; TOEFL.

Costs & Financial Aid

Application fee: $15. *Medical fee:* $46. *Other fees:* $2 per semester college paper fee, $5 per semester records fee, $25 per credit hours. Music instruction fees: individual lessons, $15 per credit hours beginning music class, $10 per credit hours organ practice, $75 maximum semester fee.

Types of scholarships and aid awarded: partial, merit-based, need-based, named, institutional aid, government aid, reduced tuition, tuition payment plan, work/study. *Forms required for scholarships:* FAFSA, income tax return, income asset verification. *Loans available. Procedure for applying for loans:* complete and return FAFSA 1/1-

3/1 for financial aid, complete and return Freshman Scholarship Application by 1/31 for all scholarships. ***Financial aid offered to international students.***

Services

Housing options: on-site dorms, off-campus housing, fraternity, sorority.

Support staff: career counselor, financial aid advisor, foreign student advisor, housing advisor, psychological counselor, resident assistant, resident nurse, student affairs officer.

MUSIC

Curriculum, Students, and Faculty

How are major teacher assignments made? Students may choose, made by the school according to teacher preference and teacher availability. Faculty is not informed of a student's teacher preference at the time of the audition. ***26 lessons with major teacher. May a student change major teachers during the course of study?*** possibly. ***Study of secondary instrument or discipline is allowed.***

Selectivity for instruments or programs offered (rating): accompanying (non-competitive), bassoon (non-competitive), choral conducting (non-competitive), choral singing (non-competitive), clarinet (non-competitive), double bass (non-competitive), flute or piccolo (non-competitive), French horn (non-competitive), harp (competitive), harpsichord (competitive), jazz (non-competitive), oboe/English horn (non-competitive), organ (competitive), percussion (non-competitive), piano (competitive), saxophone (non-competitive), trombone (non-competitive), trumpet (non-competitive), tuba (non-competitive), viola (non-competitive), violin (non-competitive), violoncello (non-competitive), voice (non-competitive).

Total enrollment: 143. ***Entering class size:*** 60. ***Graduating class size:*** 15.

Total full-time faculty: 19. ***Total part-time faculty:*** 5. ***Program contact person:*** William L. Ballenger.

Audition Information

No audition fee. Audition consists of the following: scales. ***Instruments provided for:*** percussionists; large brass.

Repertoire that students should avoid? gospel, popular, or Christian contemporary music for vocalists. ***Performance opportunities available (frequency):*** band, jury examinations, orchestral concerts, recitals, chorus.

Facilities

Number of practice rooms and hours: 20; 24 hours a day (accessibe by key). ***Recital hall?*** yes. ***Concert hall?*** yes. ***Recording studio?*** yes.

UNIVERSITY OF OKLAHOMA

College of Fine Arts
540 Parrington Oval, Room 122, Norman OK 73019-3021
Tel: 405-325-7370
Fax: 405-325-1667
Email: cinelson@ou.edu
Web: cinelson@ou.edu

General

Type of Institution: public university. ***Environment:*** suburban.

Total enrollment of institution: 20,026. ***Total student body from other countries:*** 6%. ***Degrees offered:*** BFA, BM, BME, BMA.

Entrance Requirements

Audition required: live, audio, video. ***Other requirements:*** interview, recommendation, essay ***Standardized test requirements:*** ACT, 23; SAT I, 1127.

Costs & Financial Aid

Application fee: $25. ***Deposit:*** $25. ***Tuition (in-state/out-state):*** $1,745/$5,785. ***Other fees:*** $566 includes medical fee. ***Room and board:*** $4,024.

Percent of students receiving financial aid: 66%. ***Types of scholarships and aid awarded:*** full, partial, merit-based, need-based, named, institutional aid, government aid, reduced tuition, tuition payment plan, work/study. ***Forms required for scholarships:*** FAFSA, income tax return, income asset verification. ***Loans available. Procedure for applying for loans:*** FAFSA.

Services

Housing options: on-site dorms, off-campus housing, fraternity, sorority.

Support staff: career counselor, financial aid advisor, foreign student advisor, housing advisor, physical therapist, psychological counselor, resident assistant, resident nurse, student affairs officer.

DANCE

Curriculum, Students, and Faculty

Required courses: character, ballet, dance composition or choreography, dance history, dance theory, dance writing research and criticism, modern dance, music, stagecraft, variations, stage make-up, pedagogy, teaching practicum.

Elective courses: jazz, men's class, movement techniques, body conditioning, pas de deux, pointe, repertory, tap, survival for dancers, jazz.

Selectivity for males: approximately 60% admitted. *Selectivity for females:* approximately 33% admitted. *Total enrollment:* 75. *Entering class size:* 31. *Graduating class size:* 15. *Percent International*: 10%. *Countries most represented*: Korea, China, Taiwan, Mexico, Peru, Malaysia.

Renowned alumni: Donn Edwards, Derrick Minter, Tiffany Klier, Susan Intille, Crystal Allen, Astrit Zejnati, Justin Flores, Jeffrey Sodowsky, Jena Sager, Shane Patton, Elizabeth Jimenez, Ricardo Sarcos, James Scott Salmon, Randi Ulevog, Natalie Winston, Kelly Burnette, and Cynthia Crews.

Total full-time faculty: 6. *Total part-time faculty:* 3. *List of current faculty and past affiliations:* Mary Margaret Holt, San Francisco Ballet, NY City Ballet, Houston Ballet; Donn Edwards, Joffrey Ballet, Frankfurt Ballet, Boston Ballet; Allan Kinzie, Ballet du Nord, Boston Ballet; Denise Vale, Martha Graham Ballet; Anna Sokolow; Derrick Minter, Ailey Rep, Ensemble, Graham, Broadway; Julie Stadler, American Dance Festival. *Program contact person:* Donn Edwards.

Audition Information

No audition fee. Audition consists of the following: modern dance, pas de deux, pointe works. *Accompanist provided. Cassette player available; CD player available. Dress requirements for males:* ballet prefers white t-shirt, black tights. *Dress requirements for females:* ballet prefers black leotard, pink tights.

Audition evaluation criteria: placement, musicality, technique level, and potential.

Performance Information

Performance opportunities available (frequency): Fully produced concerts (3 per year), informal concerts (2 per year), workshops (1 per year), on-site performances (5 per year), touring (3-5 per year), opera and musical theater opportuities.

Performances choreographed by: faculty, students, guests. *Recent guest choreographers:* Dennis Poole, Earl Mosley, James Clouser, Michael Job, Takako Asakawska, Richard Shi, Miquel Terekov.

Facilities

Number of studios available: 4. *Approximate studio dimensions and flooring:* 40' x 50' sprung/ Marley.

DRAMA

Curriculum, Students, and Faculty

Required courses: acting, audition preparation, directing, drama criticism, dramaturgy, improvisation, make-up, movement, scene study, Stanislavski exercises, text analysis, verse drama, voice.

Elective courses: Alexander technique, musical theater, stage combat.

Number of years required to complete program: 4. *Summer program available. No affiliation with a professional theater company. Selectivity for males:* approximately 60% admitted. *Selectivity for females:* approximately 60% admitted. *Total enrollment:* 140. *Entering class size:* 50. *Graduating class size:* 30.

Renowned alumni: Max Weitzenhoffer, Van Heflin, James Garner, Dennis Weaver.

Total full-time faculty: 12. *Total part-time faculty:* 5. *List of current faculty and past affiliations:* Steve Wallace, OK Summer Stage.

Audition Information

No audition fee. Audition consists of the following: comedic monologue. *Repertoire that students should avoid?* no.

Performance Information

Performance opportunities available (frequency): fully produced performances (12 per year), informal performances (10 per year), workshops (10 per year), auditioned.

Recent guest artists: John Cullum, Mark Medoff.

Facilities

Rehearsal facilities and hours: 4 rehearsal halls, 6:00 am-12:00 am. *Number of theaters on campus:* 3. *Type and capacity:* proscenium 650, black box 206, proscenium 99.

MUSIC

Curriculum, Students, and Faculty

Unique or innovative music curriculum: Bachelor of Musical Arts Degree—Music plus a second major, BME-instrumental methods and conducting combined and team taught. *How are major teacher assignments made?* Students may choose, made by the school, according to teacher preference according to teacher availability. Faculty is informed of a student's teacher preference at the time of the audition. 30 lessons with major teacher. *May a student change major teachers during the course of study?* possibly. *Study of secondary instrument or discipline is allowed.*

Selectivity for instruments or programs offered (rating): bassoon (competitive), choral conducting (competitive), choral singing (competitive), clarinet (competitive), composition (competitive), double bass (competitive), flute or piccolo (competitive), French horn (competitive), guitar (competitive), harpsichord (competitive), jazz (competitive), oboe/English horn (competitive), orchestral conducting (competitive), organ (competitive), percussion (competitive), piano (competitive), saxophone (competitive), trombone (competitive), trumpet (competitive), tuba (competitive), viola (competitive), violin (competitive), violoncello (competitive), voice (competitive).

Total enrollment: 296. *Entering class size:* 69. *Graduating class size:* 40.

Renowned alumni: Tom Paxton, David Pittman Jennings, Robert W. Hale, James Croft.

Total full-time faculty: 37. *Total part-time faculty:* 14. *Program contact person:* Sally Faulconer.

Audition Information

No audition fee. Audition consists of the following: scales, sight reading, melodic dictation. *Instruments provided for:* harpists, percussionists.

Performance opportunities available (frequency): band (frequently), jury examinations (every semester), orchestral concerts (6 per year), recitals (2 per year), touring (rarely), chorus (4-5 per year).

Facilities

Number of practice rooms and hours: 40; 6:00 am-12:00 am. *Recital hall?* yes. *Concert hall?* yes. *Recording studio?* no.

PORTLAND STATE UNIVERSITY

P.O. Box 751, Portland OR 97207
Tel: 503-725-3011
Fax: 503-725-8215
Email: fpa@1h.pdx.edu
Web: www.fpa.pdx.edu/depts/fpa

General

Type of Institution: public, university. *Environment:* urban.

Total enrollment of institution: 14,000. *Total student body from other countries:* 5%. *Degrees offered:* BA, BM, BS.

Entrance Requirements

Audition required: live, audio, video. *Other requirements:* recommendation *Standardized test requirements:* SAT I; TOEFL.

Costs & Financial Aid

Application fee: $25.

Percent of students receiving financial aid: 60%. *Types of scholarships and aid awarded:* full, partial, merit-based, need-based, named, institutional aid, government aid, reduced tuition, tuition payment plan, work/study, gig office. *Forms required for scholarships:* FAFSA. *Loans available. Procedure for applying for loans:* contact Admissions Department. *Financial aid offered to international students.*

Services

Housing options: on-site dorms, off-campus housing, fraternity, sorority.

Support staff: career counselor, financial aid advisor, foreign student advisor, housing advisor, psychological counselor, resident nurse, student affairs officer.

MUSIC

Curriculum, Students, and Faculty

Unique or innovative music curriculum: urban connection with professional groups (symphony, opera). *How are major teacher assignments made?* made by the school according to teacher preference. Faculty is informed of a student's teacher preference at the time of the audition. *30 lessons with major teacher. Study of secondary instrument or discipline is allowed.*

Selectivity for instruments or programs offered (rating): accompanying (competitive), bassoon (competitive), choral conducting (highly selective), choral singing (competitive), clarinet (competitive), composition (selective), double bass (competitive), flute or piccolo (competitive), French horn (competitive), guitar (competitive), harp (competitive), harpsichord (competitive), jazz (competitive), oboe/English horn (competitive), orchestral conducting (highly selective), organ (competitive), percussion (competitive), piano (competitive), saxophone (competitive), trombone (competitive), trumpet (competitive), tuba (competitive), viola (competitive), violin (competitive), violoncello (competitive), voice (competitive).

Total enrollment: 250. *Entering class size:* 75. *Graduating class size:* 45. *Percent International*: 2%. *Countries most represented*: Japan, Korea, Europe.

Total part-time faculty: 14. *Total part-time faculty:* 8. *Program contact person:* Stan Stanford.

Audition Information

No audition fee. Audition consists of the following: scales, arpeggios, repertoire. *Instruments provided for:* harpists, percussionists

Required repertoire: specified by student. *Performance opportunities available (frequency):* band (frequently), jury examinations (frequently), orchestral concerts (frequently), recitals (frequently), touring, chorus.

Facilities

Number of practice rooms and hours: 30; 7:00 am-11:00 pm. *Recital hall?* yes. *Concert hall?* yes. *Recording studio?* no.

REED COLLEGE

3203 SE Woodstock Boulevard, Portland OR 97202
Tel: 503-777-7511
Fax: 503-777-7553
Email: admission@reed.edu
Web: www.reed.edu

General

Type of Institution: private college. *Environment:* urban.

Total enrollment of institution: 1,250. *Total student body from other countries:* 8%. *Degrees offered:* BA.

Entrance Requirements

Audition not required. Other requirements: recommendation, essay. *Standardized test requirements:* ACT, 29; SAT I, 1340; TOEFL, 600.

Costs & Financial Aid

Application fee: $40. *Deposit:* $300. *Tuition:* $22,180. *Other fees:* $160 student body fee. *Room and board:* $6,400.

Percent of students receiving financial aid: 50%. *Types of scholarships and aid awarded:* full, partial, need-based, named, institutional aid, government aid, tuition payment plan, work/study. *Forms required for scholarships:* FAFSA, CSS Profile. *Loans available. Procedure for applying for loans:* file FAFSA. *Financial aid offered to international students.*

Services

Housing options: on-site dorms, off-campus housing.

Support staff: foreign student advisor, psychological counselor, resident assistant, student affairs officer.

DANCE

Curriculum, Students, and Faculty

Required courses: dance composition or choreography, dance history, dance theory, dance writing research and criticism, modern dance, partnering, rehearsal and performance, jazz, anatomy, dance history, stagecraft, ballet, modern dance, dance composition or choreography.

Elective courses: African dance, tap.

List of current faculty and past affiliations: Judy Mossee, Director of Dance Department, Martha Graham School; Patricia Wong, founding member of Portland Dance Theater; Carla Mann. *Program contact person:* Patricia Wong.

Performance Information

Performance opportunities available (frequency): Fully produced concerts (2 per year), informal concerts (2-3 per year), workshops (2-3 per year).

Performances choreographed by: faculty, students, guests. *Recent guest choreographers:* Armgard Von Bardleben, Viola Farber, Raymond Johnson, Bryan Hayes, Benny Bell, Nina Weiner, Trisha Brown.

Facilities

Number of studios available: 1. *Performance facilities:* The Reed Theater—main stage (160 seats), black box (60 seats), The Kaul Auditorium (800 seats).

DRAMA

Curriculum, Students, and Faculty

Required courses: acting, directing, scene study, theater history, dramatic literature, directing.

Elective courses: audition preparation, drama criticism, improvisation, make-up, martial arts, playwriting, stage combat, Stanislavski exercises, text analysis.

Number of years required to complete program: 4. *Summer program not available. No affiliation with a professional theater company. Selectivity for males:* admit all who apply. *Selectivity for females:* admit all who apply. *Total enrollment:* 16.

Renowned alumni: Lee Blessing, Eric Overmeyer, Mark Worthington.

Total full-time faculty: 2. *Total part-time faculty:* 2. *List of current faculty and past affiliations:* Craig Clinton, Carnegie Mellon, Yale; Carolyn Carr, University of Utah, Idaho State; Stephan Simek, University of Washington, Academy of Dramatic Arts; Cathleen Warley, Pomona College, American Conservatory Theatre.

Performance Information

Performance opportunities available (frequency): fully produced performances (4-7 per year), informal performances (3-4 per year), auditioned.

Recent guest artists: Seth Ulman, Lee Blessing.

Facilities

Number of theaters on campus: 3. *Type and capacity:* auditorium 800, theater 160, black box 70.

MUSIC

Curriculum, Students, and Faculty

Faculty is not informed of a student's teacher preference at the time of the audition.

Total enrollment: 15.

Renowned alumni: Jon Appleton, Dartmouth College; Barnet Hansen; Peter Child, Massachusetts Institute of Technology; Jan Chciuk-Celt, Flying Heart Records; Johnathan Waldron, Interleaf Inc.

Total full-time faculty: 2. *Total part-time faculty:* 2. *Program contact person:* David Schiff.

Facilities

Number of practice rooms and hours: 20; 7:00 am-12:00 am. (includes 16 private music rooms). *Recital hall?* yes. *Concert hall?* yes. *Recording studio?* yes.

Comments

Visiting artists and scholars: Raphael Trio; the Early Music Quatermaria; musicologists Richard Taruskin, William Ashbrook, Philip Gossett, Harold Powers and Michael Beckerman; ethnomusicologists Christopher Waterman and David Wessel.

UNIVERSITY OF OREGON

1225 University of Oregon, Eugene OR 97403-1225
Tel: 541-346-3761
Fax: 541-346-0723
Email: mbradeti@oregon.uoregon.edu
Web: www.music1.uoregon.edu

General

Type of Institution: public, university. *Environment:* urban.

Total enrollment of institution: 17,207. *Total student body from other countries:* 10%. *Degrees offered:* BA, BM, BS.

Entrance Requirements

Audition required: live, audio, video. *Other requirements:* recommendation, essay. *Standardized test requirements:* ACT; SAT I; TOEFL.

Costs & Financial Aid

Application fee: $50. *Deposit:* $200 *Tuition (in-state/out-state):* $3,648/$12,099. *Other fees:* $25 per term music major fee, $25 per term dance major fee. *Room and board:* $4,846.

Percent of students receiving financial aid: 23%. *Types of scholarships and aid awarded:* full, partial, merit-based, need-based, named, institutional aid, government aid, reduced tuition, tuition payment plan, work/study. *Forms required for scholarships:* FAFSA, income tax return. *Loans available. Procedure for applying for loans:* contact University Financial Aid Office; specific music scholarships by application and audition; specific dance scholarships by application. *Financial aid offered to international students. Percent of international students receiving scholarships:* 6%. *Other aid available to international students:* International cultural service program.

Services

Housing options: on-site dorms, off-campus housing, fraternity, sorority, family.

Support staff: career counselor, financial aid advisor, foreign student advisor, housing advisor, physical therapist, psychological counselor, resident assistant, resident nurse, student affairs officer.

DANCE

Curriculum, Students, and Faculty

Required courses: ballet, dance composition or choreography, dance history, historical dance, Labanotation, modern dance, music, dance and folk culture, rehearsal and performance, stagecraft, internship, looking for dance, senior project.

Elective courses: African dance, Alexander technique, dance theory, dance writing research and criticism, jazz, master classes, other world dance forms, repertory, dance in Asia, tap, Balkan and East European dance, Near and Middle East, scientific aspects, theoretical foundations of dance, Chinese dance, dance kinesiology.

Selectivity for males: admit all who apply. *Selectivity for females:* admit all who apply. *Total enrollment:* 40. *Entering class size:* 10. *Graduating class size:* 9. *Percent International*: 2%. *Countries most represented*: China.

Renowned alumni: Barry McNabb, Tiffany Mills, Diane Markham, Heidi Bunting, Maria Basile.

Total full-time faculty: 5. *Total part-time faculty:* 7 *List of current faculty and past affiliations:* Sherrie Barr, Steven Chatfield, Jenifer Craig, Janet W. Descutner. *Program contact person:* Jenifer Craig, (541) 346-3386.

Audition Information

No audition fee. Audition consists of the following: ballet, modern dance. *Accompanist provided. Dress requirements for males:* appropriate dance wear. *Dress requirements for females:* appropriate dance wear.

Audition evaluation criteria: The audition is to place students at the appropriate technical levels. It is given as a class and evaluated by faculty observing.

Performance Information

Performance opportunities available (frequency): fully produced concerts (1 per term), informal concerts (1 per term), workshops (varies), on-site performances(rarely), touring (spring term).

Performances choreographed by: faculty, students, guests. *Recent guest choreographers:* Claire Porter, Mae Chesney, Janet Towner, Kay Bardsley, Bryan Hayes.

Facilities

Number of studios available: 3. *Approximate studio dimensions and flooring:* 39' x 79' L'Air system, 49' x 64' L'Air system, 20' x 50' L'Air system. *Performance facilities:* studio-theater.

MUSIC

Curriculum, Students, and Faculty

How are major teacher assignments made? students may choose, made by the school according to teacher preference and teacher availability. Faculty is informed of a student's teacher preference at the time of the audition. *30 lessons with major teacher. May a student change major teachers during the course of study?* possibly. *Study of secondary instrument or discipline is allowed.*

Selectivity for instruments or programs offered (rating): accompanying (competitive), bassoon (competitive), choral conducting (competitive), clarinet (competitive), composition (selective), double bass (competitive), electronic music (competitive), flute or piccolo (competitive), French horn (competitive), guitar (competitive), harp (competitive), harpsichord (competitive), jazz (selective), oboe/English horn (competitive), orchestral conducting (competitive), organ (competitive), percussion (competitive), piano (competitive), saxophone (competitive), trombone (competitive), trumpet (competitive), viola (competitive), violin (competitive), violoncello (competitive), voice (selective).

Total enrollment: 287. *Entering class size:* 86. *Graduating class size:* 32. *Percent International*: 3%. *Countries most represented*: Germany, Japan, Korea, Taiwan, Hong Kong, Canada, Cypress.

Renowned alumni: Jon Appleton; Jerold Ottley, Mormon Tabernacle Choir; Richard Fuller; Pamela Kuhn; Candace Burrows.

Total full-time faculty: 38. *Total part-time faculty:* 21. *Program contact person:* Marilyn Bradetich, (541) 346-5664.

Audition Information

Audition fee? yes. *Audition consists of the following:* scales, orchestral excerpts, music theory, arpeggios, sight reading, music history, improvisation, repertoire. *Instruments provided for:* percussionists; many rental intruments available, 7 concert grands for piano majors (only in practice rooms).

Required repertoire: Varies by instrument. Please call school for repertoire information. *Performance opportunities available (frequency):* band, chamber music, jury examinations, opera workshops, orchestral concerts, recitals, chorus.

Facilities

Number of practice rooms and hours: 30. *Recital hall?* yes. *Concert hall?* yes. *Recording studio?* yes.

UNIVERSITY OF PORTLAND

5000 North Willamette Boulevard, Portland OR 97203
Tel: 503-283-7228
Fax: 503-283-7399
Email: doyle@uofport.edu
Web: www.uofport.edu

General

Type of Institution: university. *Religious Affiliation:* Roman Catholic. *Environment:* urban.

Total enrollment of institution: 2,800. *Total student body from other countries:* 12%. *Degrees offered:* BA, BME.

Entrance Requirements

Audition required: live, audio, video. *Other requirements:* recommendation. *Standardized test requirements:* ACT; SSAT; TOEFL, 550.

Costs & Financial Aid

Application fee: $40. *Tuition:* $7,710. *Medical fee:* $218. *Other fees:* $50 student government.

Percent of students receiving financial aid: 60%. *Types of scholarships and aid awarded:* full, partial, merit-based, need-based, named, institutional aid, government aid, reduced tuition, tuition payment plan, work/study, gig office. *Forms required for scholarships:* FFS, FAFSA, income tax return, income asset verification. *Loans available. Procedure for applying for loans:* see application material for full details. *Financial aid offered to international students. Other aid available to international students:* see University Director of Financial Aid.

Services

Housing options: on-site dorms, off-campus housing.

Support staff: career counselor, dorm parent, financial aid advisor, foreign student advisor, housing advisor, physical therapist, psychological counselor, resident assistant, resident nurse, student affairs officer.

Comments

Our music programs are fully accredited by the National Association of Schools of Music (NASM).

DRAMA

Curriculum, Students, and Faculty

Required courses: acting, directing, make-up, movement, musical theater, scene study, voice, speech.

Elective courses: audition preparation, drama criticism, scene study, Stanislavski exercises, improvisation, costume design, musical theater, movement, verse drama.

Number of years required to complete program: 4-5. *Summer program available. Affiliation with a professional theater company: Summer resident company, Mock's Crest Festival Production.*

Selectivity for males: approximately 60% admitted. *Selectivity for females:* approximately 60% admitted. *Total enrollment:* 30. *Entering class size:* 10. *Graduating class size:* 5. *Percent International*: 5%.

Renowned alumni: Paul Winfield.

Total full-time faculty: 3. *Total part-time faculty:* 3. *List of current faculty and past affiliations:* Dr. Ed Bowen, Lawrence Laisen, Jill Hoddick, Caren Ceraham.

Audition Information

No audition fee. Audition consists of the following: comedic monologue, monologues are suggested but not required. *Repertoire that students should avoid?* no.

Audition evaluation criteria: imagination, stage intuition, evidence of experience.

Performance Information

Performance opportunities available (frequency): fully produced performances (4 per year), informal performances (2-3 per term), workshops (2-3 per year), off-site performances (rarely), auditioned.

Recent guest artists: Anne Blythe, Mercedes McCambridge, Will Gneer.

Facilities

Rehearsal facilities and hours: black box, dance studio. *Number of theaters on campus:* 2. *Type and capacity:* thrust/proscenium 290, outdoor amphitheater.

MUSIC

Curriculum, Students, and Faculty

Unique or innovative music curriculum: highly flexible so program can be geared to student needs and interests. *How are major teacher assignments made?* students may choose according to teacher availability. Faculty is not informed of a student's teacher preference at the time of the audition. *25 lessons with major teacher. May a student change major teachers during the course of study?* possibly. *Study of secondary instrument or discipline is allowed.*

Selectivity for instruments or programs offered (rating): bassoon (competitive), choral conducting (selective), choral singing (competitive), clarinet (competitive), composition (selective), double bass (competitive), electronic music (selective), flute or piccolo (competitive), French horn (competitive), guitar (competitive), harp (competitive), harpsichord (competitive), jazz (competitive), oboe/English horn (competitive), orchestral conducting (selective), organ (competitive), percussion (competitive), piano (competitive), sacred music (selective), saxophone (competitive), trombone (competitive), trumpet (competitive), tuba (competitive), viola (competitive), violin (selective), violoncello (competitive), voice (selective).

Total enrollment: 35. *Entering class size:* 12. *Graduating class size:* 7. *Percent International*: 5%.

Total full-time faculty: 5. *Total part-time faculty:* 8. *Program contact person:* Dr. Kenneth Kleszynski.

Audition Information

No audition fee. Audition consists of the following: scales. *Instruments provided for:* harpists, percussionists.

Repertoire that students should avoid? Popular songs and rock repertoire are not encouraged. *Performance opportunities available (frequency):* band, jury examinations, recitals.

Facilities

Number of practice rooms and hours: 10; 14 hours per day. *Recital hall?* yes. *Concert hall?* yes. *Recording studio?* yes.

WESTERN OREGON UNIVERSITY

Division of Creative Arts
345 North Monmouth Avenue, Monmouth OR 97361
Tel: 503-838-8462
Fax: 503-838-8474
Email: kregert@fsa.wou.edu
Web: www.wou.edu
Contact: Alison Marshall

General

Type of Institution: public university.

Total enrollment of institution: 3,889. *Total student body from other countries:* 4%. *Degrees offered:* BA, BS in music.

Entrance Requirements

Audition required: live, audio, video. *Other requirements:* recommendation. *Standardized test requirements:* ACT, 21; SAT I, 1000; TOEFL, 500.

Costs & Financial Aid

Application fee: $50. *Deposit:* $25 *Tuition:* $3,153. *Medical fee:* $158. *Other fees:* various class and lab fees.

Percent of students receiving financial aid: 50%. *Types of scholarships and aid awarded:* full, partial, merit-based, need-based, named, institutional aid, government aid, reduced tuition, tuition payment plan, work/study. *Loans available. Procedure for applying for loans:* contact Financial Aid Office (503) 838-8475. *Financial aid offered to international students. Percent of international students receiving scholarships:* 12%. *Other aid available to international students:* International Cultural Service program.

Services

Housing options: on-site dorms, off-campus housing.

Support staff: career counselor, financial aid advisor, foreign student advisor, housing advisor, psychological counselor, resident assistant, resident nurse, student affairs officer.

DANCE

Curriculum, Students, and Faculty

Required courses: dance composition or choreography, dance history, modern dance, rehearsal and performance, ballet.

Elective courses: African dance, anatomy, dance theory, historical dance, jazz, Labanotation, master classes, music, pointe, repertory, stagecraft, tap, vernacular dance, Butbla, Hula.

Selectivity for males: admit all who apply. *Selectivity for females:* admit all who apply. *Total enrollment:* 10.

Total full-time faculty: 3. *Total part-time faculty:* 2. *List of current faculty and past affiliations:* Deborah Jones-Peterson, UC—Berkeley, Mills College; Sharon Oberst, University of Oregon, Houston Ballet Academy; Darryl Thomas, University of Hawaii, Pilobolus. *Program contact person:* Sharon Oberst.

Audition Information

No audition fee. Accompanist not provided. Cassette player available; CD player available.

Performance Information

Performance opportunities available (frequency): fully produced concerts (1 per year), informal concerts (2 per year), workshops (5 per year).

Performances choreographed by: faculty, students, guests. *Recent guest choreographers:* Doris Humphrey reconstructions.

Facilities

Number of studios available: 1. *Approximate studio dimensions and flooring:* 1,260 sq. ft. maple sprung. *Performance facilities:* large theater.

DRAMA

Curriculum, Students, and Faculty

Required courses: acting, audition preparation, directing, drama criticism, improvisation, makeup, movement, scene study, Stanislavski exercises, text analysis, voice.

Elective courses: martial arts, mime, musical theater, speech, stage combat.

Number of years required to complete program: 4. *Summer program available. Students may intern with local community theaters and have sometimes interned with regional theaters.*

Selectivity for males: most admitted, but not all. *Selectivity for females:* most admitted, but not all. *Total enrollment:* 25. *Entering class size:* 5. *Graduating class size:* 4. *Percent International*: 3%. *Countries most represented*: Japan.

Renowned alumni: David Nickelson, Rex Rabold.

Total full-time faculty: 3. *Total part-time faculty:* 2. *List of current faculty and past affiliations:* Richard Davis, Robert L. Page, Dean Bourland.

Audition Information

No audition fee. Audition consists of the following: cold readings, improvisation. There is an audition for each production but not for admission to the program. Prepared pieces are sometimes used depending on the director. *Repertoire that students should avoid?* no.

Performance Information

Performance opportunities available (frequency): fully produced performances (6-9), informal performances (frequently), workshops (occasionally), off-site performances (occasionally), auditioned.

Recent guest artists: Patrick Page.

Facilities

Number of theaters on campus: 2. *Type and capacity:* 659, studio 52.

MUSIC

Curriculum, Students, and Faculty

Unique or innovative music curriculum: strength in vocal and choral music, jazz, and electronic music. *How are major teacher assignments made?* Students may choose, made by the school according to teacher preference and teacher availability. Faculty is informed of a student's teacher preference at the time of the audition. *30 lessons with major teacher. May a student change major teachers during the course of study?* possibly. *Study of secondary instrument or discipline is allowed.*

Selectivity for instruments or programs offered (rating): accompanying (non-competitive), bassoon (non-competitive), choral conducting (non-competitive), choral singing (non-competitive), clarinet (non-competitive), composition (non-competitive), double bass (non-competitive), electronic music (competitive), flute or piccolo (non-competitive), French horn (non-competitive), guitar (non-competitive), jazz (non-competitive), oboe/English horn (non-competitive), percussion (non-competitive), piano (non-competitive), saxophone (non-competitive), trombone (non-competitive), trombone (selective), trumpet (non-competitive), tuba (non-competitive), voice (non-competitive).

Total enrollment: 40. *Countries most represented*: Japan.

Renowned alumni: Nancy Emrick, Solveig Holmquist, Lane Shetterly, Kerry French, Russ Christensen, James Taylor.

Total full-time faculty: 8. *Total part-time faculty:* 2. *Program contact person:* Richard Sorenson.

Audition Information

No audition fee. Audition consists of the following: scales, rhythmic dictation, sight reading, melodic dictation. *Instruments provided for:* percussionists.

Facilities

Number of practice rooms and hours: 11; 7:30 am-10:00 pm (Mon-Fri), 1:00 pm-4:00 pm (Sat), 6:30 pm-10:00 pm (Sun). *Recital hall?* yes. *Concert hall?* yes. *Recording studio?* no.

WILLAMETTE UNIVERSITY

900 State Street, Salem OR 97301-3931
Tel: 503-370-6255
Fax: 503-370-6260
Email: wumusic@willamette.edu
Web: www.willamette.edu
Contact: Teresa Hukins

General

Type of Institution: private university. *Religious affiliation:* United Methodist. *Environment:* urban.

Total enrollment of institution: 2,400. *Degrees offered:* BA, BM, BS in music.

Entrance Requirements

Audition required: live, audio. *Other requirements:* interview, recommendation, essay. *Standardized test requirements:* ACT; SAT I.

Costs & Financial Aid

Application fee: $35. *Deposit:* $200. *Tuition:* $18,300. *Medical fee:* $220. *Other fees:* $90 student body fee, $200 half hour music lesson per semester.

Percent of students receiving financial aid: 75%. *Types of scholarships and aid awarded:* full, partial, merit-based, need-based, named, institutional aid, government aid, tuition payment plan, work/study. *Forms required for scholarships:* FAFSA. *Loans available. Financial aid offered to international students.*

Services

Housing options: on-site dorms, off-campus housing, fraternity, sorority.

Support staff: career counselor, financial aid advisor, foreign student advisor, housing advisor, psychological counselor, resident assistant, resident nurse, student affairs officer.

MUSIC

Curriculum, Students, and Faculty

How are major teacher assignments made? students may choose, made by the school according to teacher preference and teacher availability. Faculty is informed of a student's teacher preference at the time of the audition. *28 lessons with major teacher. May a student change major teachers during the course of study?* possibly. *Study of secondary instrument or discipline is allowed.*

Selectivity for instruments or programs offered (rating): accompanying (competitive), bassoon (non-competitive), choral singing (competitive), clarinet (competitive), composition (competitive), double bass (non-competitive), flute or piccolo (non-competitive), French horn (open), guitar (non-competitive), harp (open), jazz (competitive), oboe/English horn (competitive), organ (open), percussion (competitive), piano (competitive), saxophone (non-competitive), trombone (non-competitive), trumpet (non-competitive), tuba (non-competitive), viola (non-competitive), violin (non-competitive), violoncello (non-competitive), voice (competitive).

Total enrollment: 50.

Renowned alumni: John Doan, Reid Shelton.

Total full-time faculty: 9. *Total part-time faculty:* 26. *Program contact person:* Linda Unrein.

Audition Information

No audition fee. Audition consists of the following: orchestral excerpts, sight reading, improvisation, repertoire. *Instruments provided for:* harpists, percussionists; some band instruments, horn, clarinet, tuba, saxophone.

Performance opportunities available (frequency): band (frequently), chamber music (frequently), band (frequently), jury examinations (frequently), opera workshops (frequently), orchestral concerts (frequently), recitals (frequently), touring (frequently), produced operas, chorus.

Facilities

Recital hall? yes. *Concert hall?* yes. *Recording studio?* no.

PENNSYLVANIA

BUCKNELL UNIVERSITY

Lewisburg PA 17837
Tel: 717-524-1101
Fax: 717-524-3760
Email: admissions@bucknell.edu
Web: www.bucknell.edu
Contact: Judy Ellis

General

Type of Institution: private university.

Total enrollment of institution: 3,269. *Total student body from other countries:* 2%. *Degrees offered:* BA.

Entrance Requirements

Audition required: live, audio, video. *Other requirements:* recommendation, essay. *Standardized test requirements:* SAT I, 1240; TOEFL, 550.

Costs & Financial Aid

Application fee: $45. *Deposit:* $200. *Tuition:* $21,080. *Other fees:* $130. *Room and board:* $5,400.

Percent of students receiving financial aid: 60%. *Types of scholarships and aid awarded:* full, partial, need-based, institutional aid, government aid, tuition payment plan, work/study. *Forms required for scholarships:* FAFSA, income asset verification, CSS Profile. *Loans available. Financial aid offered to international students. Percent of international students receiving scholarships:* 10%. *Other aid available to international students:* need-based grants.

Services

Housing options: on-site dorms.

Support staff: career counselor, foreign student advisor, housing advisor, psychological counselor, resident assistant, resident nurse, student affairs officer.

DANCE

Curriculum, Students, and Faculty

Required courses: ballet, dance composition or choreography, dance history, modern dance, Cunningham-based, rehearsal and performance.

Elective courses: jazz, master classes, movement techniques, body conditioning, Pilates, pointe, repertory, variations, Chinese dance.

Selectivity for males: admit all who apply. *Selectivity for females:* most admitted, but not all. *Percent International*: 2%.

Renowned alumni: Danny Buraczeski, Todd Rosenlieb.

Total full-time faculty: 2. *List of current faculty and past affiliations:* Er-Dong Hu, Dayton Ballet, Beijing Dance Academy. *Program contact person:* Danna Frangione.

Audition Information

No audition fee. Accompanist not provided. Cassette player not available; CD player not available.

Performance Information

Performance opportunities available (frequency): fully produced concerts (2 per year), informal concerts (2 per year), workshops (4-6 per year).

Performances choreographed by: faculty, students, guests. *Recent guest choreographers:* Robert Atwood, Yun-Yu Wang, Ze' Eva Choen, Allyson Green, Kevin Wynn, Li-Chou Cheng, Gabriel Masson, Graciela Daniele.

Facilities

Number of studios available: 1. *Approximate studio dimensions and flooring:* Marley over sprung wood. *Performance facilities:* 3 theaters.

DRAMA

Curriculum, Students, and Faculty

Required courses: acting, drama criticism, dramaturgy, make-up, movement, scene study, speech, Stanislavski exercises, text analysis, verse drama.

Elective courses: audition preparation, directing, improvisation, stage combat, voice.

Number of years required to complete program: 4. *Summer program not available. Members of the Bloomsburg Theatre Ensemble teach in the curriculum; students participate in a year-long post-baccalaureate internship in acting; performance and design faculty produce on the BTE stage; Bucknell and BTE have co-produced productions.*

Selectivity for males: admit all who apply. *Selectivity for females:* admit all who apply.

Renowned alumni: Edward Herrmann, John Bolger, David Ackroyd, Les Moonves, Mary McGlynn, Ralph Waite.

Total full-time faculty: 5. *List of current faculty and past affiliations:* Gary Grant, Elaine Williams, Bob Gainer.

Audition Information

No audition fee.

Performance Information

Performance opportunities available (frequency): fully produced performances (6 per season), informal performances (weekly), workshops (3-day residency each term with guest artist), auditioned.

Recent guest artists: Mabou Mines, Ping Chong, Meredith Monk, Bernardo Solano, Ed Hermann, John Bolger, Ron Jenkins, Nyoman Catro, Daniel Stein, Mark Olson.

Facilities

Rehearsal facilities and hours: rehearsals in two acting studios and 2 theaters, 7:00 am-10:30 pm (Mon-Sat). *Type and capacity:* proscenium 480, black box 150.

MUSIC

Curriculum, Students, and Faculty

How are major teacher assignments made? according to teacher preference and teacher availability. Faculty is informed of a student's teacher preference at the time of the audition. *26 lessons with major teacher. May a student change major teachers during the course of study?* possibly.

Selectivity for instruments or programs offered (rating): accompanying (selective), bassoon (highly selective), choral conducting (highly selective), choral singing (highly selective), clarinet (highly selective), composition (highly selective), double bass (highly selective), electronic music (highly selective), flute or piccolo (highly selective), French horn (highly selective), guitar (highly selective), harp (highly selective), harpsichord (highly selective), jazz (highly selective), oboe/English horn (highly selective), orchestral conducting (highly selective), organ (highly selective), percussion (highly selective), piano (highly selective), saxophone (highly selective), trombone (highly selective), trumpet (highly selective), tuba (highly selective), viola (highly selective), violin (highly selective), violoncello (highly selective), voice (highly selective).

Total enrollment: 28. *Percent International*: 1%.

Renowned alumni: Rudolph Palmer, D'Anna Fortunato, Brian Nedvin, Lynn Eastis.

Total full-time faculty: 10. *Program contact person:* William Payne.

Audition Information

No audition fee. Audition consists of the following: scales, music theory, rhythmic dictation, arpeggios, sight reading, repertoire. *Instruments provided for:* percussionists; strings.

Facilities

Number of practice rooms and hours: 20. *Recital hall?* yes. *Concert hall?* yes. *Recording studio?* yes.

CARNEGIE MELLON UNIVERSITY

500 Forbes Avenue, Pittsburgh PA 15213
Tel: 412-268-2372
Fax: 412-268-1431
Email: undergraduate-admissions@andrew.cmu.edu
Web: www.cmu.edu/cfa/music

General

Type of Institution: private university. *Environment:* urban. *Cross registration is available through the Pittsburgh Council on Higher Education.*

Degrees offered: BFA.

Entrance Requirements

Audition required: live, audio, video. *Other requirements:* recommendation, essay. *Standardized test requirements:* SAT I; TOEFL, 600.

Costs & Financial Aid

Application fee: $40. *Deposit:* $400 *Tuition:* $20,275/. *Other fees:* $100 activity fee, $160 orientation. *Room and board:* $6,425.

Types of scholarships and aid awarded: full, partial, merit-based, need-based, named, institutional aid, government aid, tuition payment plan, work/study, gig office. *Other aid available to international students:* Merit-based aid.

Services

Housing options: on-site dorms, off-campus housing, fraternity, sorority.

Support staff: career counselor, financial aid advisor, foreign student advisor, housing advisor, psychological counselor, resident assistant, resident nurse, student affairs officer.

DRAMA

Comprehensive drama program.

Renowned alumni: Holly Hunter, Ted Danson, Blair Underwood.

MUSIC

Curriculum, Students, and Faculty

Unique or innovative music curriculum: Conservatory level instruction in a university setting. ***How are major teacher assignments made?*** students may choose, made by the school. Faculty is not informed of a student's teacher preference at the time of the audition. ***28 lessons with major teacher. May a student change major teachers during the course of study?*** possibly. ***Study of secondary instrument or discipline is allowed.***

Selectivity for instruments or programs offered (rating): bagpipes (highly selective), bassoon (selective), choral conducting (highly selective), clarinet (selective), composition (selective), double bass (selective), flute or piccolo (highly selective), French horn (selective), guitar (selective), harp (selective), orchestral conducting (highly selective), organ (selective), percussion (selective), piano (selective), saxophone (selective), trombone (selective), trumpet (selective), tuba (selective), viola (selective), violin (selective), violoncello (selective), voice (highly selective).

Total enrollment: 225. ***Entering class size:*** 40. ***Graduating class size:*** 35. ***Percent International***: 20%. ***Countries most represented***: Chile, Taiwan.

Renowned alumni: Donald Ashworth; Keith Lockhort, The Boston Pops; Dale Clevenger, Chicago Symphony; Earl Wild, pianist.

372

Total full-time faculty: 20. ***Total part-time faculty:*** 70. ***Program contact person:*** Annette Valenti. Email: musicschool@andrew.cmu.edu.

Audition Information

Audition fee? $45. ***Audition consists of the following:*** scales, music theory rhythmic dictation, sight reading, melodic dictation, repertoire. ***Instruments provided for:*** harpists, percussionists.

Required repertoire: varies by instrument. Please call school for repertoire information. P*erformance opportunities available (frequency):* band (1 per month), chamber music (varies), jury examinations (2 per year), opera workshops (4 per year), orchestral concerts (1 per month), recitals (2 per year), touring (varies), produced operas (2 per year), chorus (4 per year).

Facilities

Number of practice rooms and hours: 40; 24 hours a day. ***Recital hall?*** yes. ***Concert hall?*** yes. ***Recording studio?*** yes.

THE CURTIS INSTITUTE OF MUSIC

1716 Locust Street, Philadelphia PA 19103
Tel: 215-893-5252
Fax: 215-893-9065

General

Type of Institution: conservatory. ***Environment:*** urban.

Total enrollment of institution: 163. ***Total student body from other countries:*** 49%. ***Degrees offered:*** certificate, BM.

Entrance Requirements:

Audition required: live. ***Other requirements:*** recommendation, essay. ***Standardized test requirements:*** SAT II; TOEFL.

Costs & Aid

Application fee: $60. ***Medical fee:*** $1,100. ***Other fees:*** $695 comprehensive fee.

Types of scholarships and aid awarded: full, partial, need-based, work/study, gig office. ***Forms required for scholarships:*** income tax return, income asset verification. ***Loans available. Financial aid offered to international students. Percent of international students receiving scholarships:*** 33%.

Services

Housing options: off-campus housing.

Support staff: career counselor, financial aid advisor, foreign student advisor, housing advisor, psychological counselor, student affairs officer.

MUSIC

Curriculum, Students, and Faculty

How are major teacher assignments made? made by the school. Faculty is not informed of a student's teacher preference at the time of the audition. ***30 lessons with major teacher. May a student change major teachers during the course of study?*** possibly. ***Study of secondary instrument or discipline is allowed.***

Selectivity for instruments or programs offered (rating): bassoon (highly selective), clarinet (highly selective), composition (highly selective), double bass (highly selective), flute or piccolo (highly selective), French horn (highly selective), harp (highly selective), harpsichord (highly selective), oboe/English horn (highly selective), orchestral conducting (highly selective), organ (highly selective), percussion (highly selective), piano (highly selective), trombone (highly selective), trumpet (highly selective), tuba (highly selective), viola (highly selective), violin (highly selective), violoncello (highly selective), voice (highly selective).

Entering class size: 37. *Graduating class size:* 37. *Percent international:* 49%.

Renowned alumni: Jaime Laredo, Peter Serkin, Robert Spano, Benita Valente, Michael Schade, Aaron Rosand, Julius Baker, Richard Woodhams, Gary Graffman, Richard Goode, Lynn Harrell.

Total part-time faculty: 80. *Program contact person:* Christopher Hodges.

Audition Information

Audition fee: $85. *Audition consists of the following:* repertoire. *Instruments provided for:* harpists, percussionists, pianists.

Required repertoire: varies by instrument. Please call school for repertoire information. *Performance opportunities available (frequency):* chamber music (frequently), band (frequently), opera workshops (frequently), orchestral concerts (frequently), recitals (frequently), produced operas.

Facilities

Recital hall? yes. *Recording studio?* yes.

DICKINSON COLLEGE

Box 1773, Carlisle PA 17013-2896
Tel: 717-245-1568
Fax: 717-245-1937
Email: bullardt@dickinson.edu
Contact: R.Russell Shunk

General

Type of Institution: private college. *Environment:* suburban.

Total enrollment of institution: 1,800. *Degrees offered:* BA.

Entrance Requirements

Audition not required. Other requirements: recommendation.

Costs & Financial Aid

Application fee: $35. *Deposit:* $200 *Tuition:* $21,450. *Other fees:* $760 per semester for 1 credit applied music, $380 per semester for a half credit. *Room and board:* $5,980.

Loans available. Financial aid offered to international students.

Services

Housing options: on-site dorms, off-campus housing, fraternity, sorority.

Support staff: career counselor, financial aid advisor, foreign student advisor, housing advisor, psychological counselor, resident assistant, resident nurse, student affairs officer.

DANCE

Curriculum, Students, and Faculty

Required courses: Laban Movement Studies.

Elective courses: African dance, jazz, master classes, rehearsal and performance.

Selectivity for males: admit all who apply. *Selectivity for females:* admit all who apply. *Total enrollment:* 3. *Graduating class size:* 2. *Countries most represented*: Latin America, France.

Renowned alumni: Amy Filbin and Lee Shopley, currently dancing in NY, freelance and as members of Mary Seidman Dance Co.; Bliss Kohlmyer, currently performing with modern company in San Francisco.

Total full-time faculty: 1. *Total part-time faculty:* 2 *List of current faculty and past affiliations:* Amy Ginsburg, Temple University; Ann Vachar, Dance Conduct (Philadelphia), guest with Deborah Riley Dance Projects (Washington, D.C.). *Program contact person:* Amy Ginsburg.

Audition Information

No audition fee. Audition consists of the following: no formal audition required for general participation in dance program. *Accompanist not provided. Cassette player available; CD player available. Dress requirements for males:* leotards, tights, t-shirt for some classes and rehearsals, appropriate shoes (jazz or ballet) or barefoot. *Dress requirements for females:* leotards and tights for some classes and rehearsals, appropriate shoes (jazz or ballet) or barefoot.

Repertoire that students should avoid? no.

Performance Information

Performance opportunities available (frequency): Fully produced concerts (1-2 per year), informal concerts (1-2 per year), workshops (3 per semester), regular participation in American College Dance Festival.

Performances choreographed by: faculty, students, guests. *Recent guest choreographers:* Jo Anne Mendl Shaw (NYC), Mark Taylor (Pittsburgh Dance Alley, Artistic Director).

Facilities

Number of studios available: 2. *Approximate studio dimensions and flooring:* 27' x 38' sprung floor with Marley surface, 20' x 30' sprung floor with Marley surface. *Performance facilities:* mainstage theater is proscenium style—house seats 245; black box theater may be arranged any way.

DRAMA

Curriculum, Students, and Faculty

Required courses: acting, directing, drama criticism, movement, scene study.

Elective courses: speech, text analysis, verse drama, voice.

Number of years required to complete program: 4. *Summer program not available. We enjoy a very close relationship with the Jean Cocteau Repertory in New York City. We have done joint productions, residencies, and student internships in New York.*

Selectivity for males: admit all who apply. *Selectivity for females:* admit all who apply. *Total enrollment:* 12. *Graduating class size:* 6. *Countries most represented*: Germany.

Renowned alumni: Vince Patterson, Rich Fisher, Francis Conroy, Stuart Pankin.

Total full-time faculty: 4. *List of current faculty and past affiliations:* Todd Wronski, Guthrie Theater; Robert Hupp, Jean Cocteau Repertory, National Shakespeare Conservatory; Polly Boersig, Ashland Shakespeare Festival, Children's Theater Company.

Audition Information

No audition fee.

Performance Information

Performance opportunities available (frequency): fully produced performances (3), informal performances (3-4), off-site performances (6 per year), auditioned.

Recent guest artists: Fred Morsell, Jean Cocteau Repertory.

Facilities

Rehearsal facilities and hours: studio theater, mainstage theater, 15 hours weekly, evenings. *Number of theaters on campus:* 2. *Type and capacity:* proscenium 244, flexible 700.

MUSIC

Curriculum, Students, and Faculty

Unique or innovative music curriculum: stresses international exchange studying in Europe. *How are major teacher assignments made?* made by the school. Faculty is not informed of a student's teacher preference at the time of the audition. *28 lessons with major teacher. May a student change major teachers during the course of study?* never. *Study of secondary instrument or discipline is allowed.*

Selectivity for instruments or programs offered (rating): bassoon (open), choral conducting (selective), clarinet (open), composition (selective), double bass (open), electronic music (selective), flute or piccolo (open), French horn (open), guitar (open), jazz (open), oboe/English horn (open), orchestral conducting (selective), percussion (open), piano (selective), saxophone (open), trombone (open), trumpet (open), tuba (open), viola (open), violin (selective), violoncello (open), voice (selective).

Total enrollment: 150. *Entering class size:* 50. *Graduating class size:* 30.

Renowned alumni: William Kinderman; David Metzer; David Hildebrant; Virginia Hildebrant; William Jenks; Richard Amoroso, Philadelphia Orchestra; Rebecca Anstine.

Total full-time faculty: 6. *Program contact person:* Dr. Truman Bullard.

Audition Information

No audition fee. Instruments provided for: percussionists; oboe, bassoon, classical guitar, all saxophones, trombone, tuba.

Performance opportunities available (frequency): jury examinations.

Facilities

Number of practice rooms and hours: 10; 24 hours a day. *Recital hall?* yes. *Concert hall?* yes. *Recording studio?* yes.

DUQUESNE UNIVERSITY SCHOOL OF MUSIC

600 Forbes Avenue, Pittsburgh PA 15282
Tel: 412-396-6080
Fax: 412-396-5479
Email: jordanof@duq2.cc.duq.edu
Web: www.duq.edu

General

Type of Institution: university. *Religious Affiliation*: Catholic. *Environment:* urban.

Total enrollment of institution: 9,500. *Total student body from other countries:* 5%. *Degrees offered:* BM, BS in Music Education BS in music therapy.

Entrance Requirements

Audition required: live, audio, video. *Other requirements:* recommendation, essay *Standardized test requirements:* ACT; SAT I, school's own English exam required.

Costs & Financial Aid

Application fee: $40. *Deposit:* $500. *Tuition:* $17,323.

Percent of students receiving financial aid: 78%. *Types of scholarships and aid awarded:* full, partial, merit-based, need-based, named, institutional aid, government aid, reduced tuition, tuition payment plan, work/study, gig office. *Forms required for scholarships:* FAFSA. *Loans available. Procedure for applying for loans:* deadline for academic scholarship is 1/15, deadline for music scholarship is 3/15. *Financial aid offered to international students. Percent of international students receiving scholarships:* 90%. *Other aid available to international students:* talent based scholarships.

Services

Housing options: on-site dorms, off-campus housing.

Support staff: career counselor, financial aid advisor, foreign student advisor, housing advisor, psychological counselor, resident assistant, resident nurse, student affairs officer.

MUSIC

Curriculum, Students, and Faculty

Unique or innovative music curriculum: Performance majors receive extensive career counseling as part of their required curriculum. *How are major teacher assignments made?* made by the school; most student requests honored. Faculty is not informed of a student's teacher preference at the time of the audition. *May a student change major teachers during the course of study?* possibly. *Study of secondary instrument or discipline is allowed.*

Selectivity for instruments or programs offered (rating): bassoon (competitive), clarinet (selective), composition (selective), double bass (competitive), electronic music (competitive), flute or piccolo (selective), French horn (selective), guitar (competitive), harp (highly selective), jazz (competitive), oboe/English horn (competitive), organ (competitive), percussion (selective), piano (competitive), saxophone (selective), trombone (competitive), trumpet (selective), tuba (competitive), viola (competitive), violin (competitive), violin (competitive), violoncello (competitive), voice (competitive).

Total enrollment: 350. *Entering class size:* 80. *Graduating class size:* 80. *Percent International*: 5%. *Countries most represented*: Venezuela.

Renowned alumni: Jason Brooks, Marianna Christos, Marianne Cornetti, Micah Howard, Sammy Nestico, Bobby Vinton, Rossen Milanov.

Total full-time faculty: 26. *Total part-time faculty:* 60. *Program contact person:* Nicholas Jordanoff.

Audition Information

No audition fee. Audition consists of the following: scales, music theory, arpeggios, sight reading, repertoire. *Instruments provided for:* harpists, percussionists; organ, piano.

Required repertoire: varies by instrument. Please call school for repertoire information. *Performance opportunities available (frequency):* jury examinations.

Facilities

Number of practice rooms and hours: 46; 24 hours per day. *Recital hall?* yes. *Recording studio?* yes.

Comments

The School of Music places a special emphasis on technology and the music of our time. Virtually all performances include literature from the second half of the 20th century. The faculty includes over 20 members of the Pittsburgh Symphony Orchestra.

FRANKLIN & MARSHALL COLLEGE

P.O. Box 3003, Lancaster PA 17604
Tel: 717-291-3985
Fax: 717-399-4455
Email: G_Rosenstein@ACAD.FANDM.EDU
Contact: Julio Sanchez

General

Type of Institution: private college. *Environment:* small city.

Total enrollment of institution: 1,840. *Total student body from other countries:* 9%. *Degrees offered:* BA.

Entrance Requirements

Audition not required. Other requirements: recommendation, essay *Standardized test requirements:* ACT; SAT I; SAT II; TOEFL.

Costs & Financial Aid

Application fee: $50. *Deposit:* $400 *Tuition:* $22,664. *Room and board:* $5,830.

Percent of students receiving financial aid: 50%. *Types of scholarships and aid awarded:* merit-based, need-based, institutional aid, government aid, tuition payment plan, work/study. *Forms required for scholarships:* FAFSA, income tax return, CSS Profile. *Loans available. Financial aid offered to international students. Percent of international students receiving scholarships:* 50%.

Services

Housing options: on-site dorms, off-campus housing, fraternity, sorority.

Support staff: career counselor, financial aid advisor, foreign student advisor, housing advisor, physical therapist, psychological counselor, resident assistant, resident nurse, student affairs officer.

DANCE

Curriculum, Students, and Faculty

Required courses: master classes, modern dance, rehearsal and performance, repertory.

Elective courses: dance composition or choreography, dance history, dance theory, historical dance, kinesiology, movement techniques other, Spanish, stagecraft, repertory.

Selectivity for males: most admitted, but not all. *Selectivity for females:* most admitted, but not all.

Renowned alumni: Glen Tetley.

Total full-time faculty: 2. *Total part-time faculty:* 1. *List of current faculty and past affiliations:* Jose Greco, Jose Greco Dance Company; Lynn Brooks, Temple University, Laban/Bartenieff Institute of Movement Studies. *Program contact person:* Dr. Lynn Brooks.

Audition Information

No audition fee. Audition consists of the following: ballet, improvisation, modern dance. *Accompanist not provided. Cassette player available; CD player available.*

Audition evaluation criteria: movement skills, movement potential, approach to the work presented.

Performance Information

Performance opportunities available (frequency): Fully produced concerts (2 per year), workshops (6 per year), on-site performances(1-2 per year).

Performances choreographed by: faculty, students, guests. *Recent guest choreographers:* Ze'eva Cohen, Lori Belilore.

Facilities

Number of studios available: 1. *Approximate studio dimensions and flooring:* 40' x 62' sprung with an old Marley over it. *Performance facilities:* 1 studio theater (seats 80-100), 1 mainstage proscenium theater (seats 200).

DRAMA

Curriculum, Students, and Faculty

Required courses: acting, text analysis.

Elective courses: directing.

Number of years required to complete program: 3-4. *Summer program not available. No affiliation with a professional theater company. Selectivity for males:* approximately 33% admitted. *Selectivity for females:* approximately 33% admitted. *Graduating class size:* 2.

Renowned alumni: Treat Williams, Roy Scheider, James Lapine.

Total full-time faculty: 5. *Total part-time faculty:* 1. *List of current faculty and past affiliations:* Dorothy Louise, Stanford University; John Austin, University of Illinois, National Jewish Theatre.

Audition Information

No audition fee. Audition consists of the following: cold readings, comedic monologue, improvisation, Shakespearean monologue, group warm-up. *Dress requirements for males:* comfortable, able to move. *Dress requirements for females:* comfortable, able to move, heels and short skirts not recommended. *Repertoire that students should avoid?* no.

Audition evaluation criteria: Auditions open for productions open to any student enrolled at Franklin and Marshall.

Performance Information

Performance opportunities available (frequency): fully produced performances (3 per year), informal performances (4-8 per year), workshops (2 per year), auditioned.

Recent guest artists: Penn and Teller.

Facilities

Number of theaters on campus: 2. *Type and capacity:* proscenium and warehouse 200, black box 100.

MUSIC

Curriculum, Students, and Faculty

Unique or innovative music curriculum: strong composition program, many chamber music opportunities. *How are major teacher assignments made?* made by the school. *Study of secondary instrument or discipline is allowed.*

Selectivity for instruments or programs offered (rating): double bass (highly selective), violin (competitive).

Graduating class size: 2.

Renowned alumni: Bruce Sussman.

Total full-time faculty: 4. *Total part-time faculty:* 8. *Program contact person:* Dr. Bruce Gustafson.

Audition Information

No audition fee. Instruments provided for: percussionists.

Repertoire that students should avoid? no. *Performance opportunities available (frequency):* jury examinations.

Facilities

Number of practice rooms and hours: 8; some are 24 hours. *Recital hall?* yes. *Concert hall?* yes. *Recording studio?* no.

MUHLENBERG COLLEGE

2400 West Chew Street, Allentown PA 18104
Tel: 610-821-3100
Fax: 610-821-3633
Web: www.muhlenberg.edu

General

Type of Institution: private college. *Religious Affiliation:* Lutheran. *Cross registration is available through Lehigh University, Allentown College, Cedar Crest College, Lafayette College.*

Total enrollment of institution: 1,800. *Total student body from other countries:* 2%. *Degrees offered:* BA.

Entrance Requirements

Other requirements: recommendation, essay. *Standardized test requirements:* ACT, 24; SAT I, 1074; TOEFL, 550.

Costs & Financial Aid

Application fee: $40. *Deposit:* $400. *Tuition:* $18,660. *Room and Board:* $5,325.

Percent of students receiving financial aid: 65%. *Types of scholarships and aid awarded:* full, partial, merit-based, need-based, named, institutional aid, government aid, tuition payment plan, work/study. *Forms required for scholarships:* FAFSA, income tax return, income asset verification, CSS Profile. *Loans available. Procedure for applying for loans:* through FAFSA or bank.

Services

Housing options: on-site dorms, off-campus housing, fraternity, sorority.

Support staff: career counselor, financial aid advisor, foreign student advisor, housing advisor, psychological counselor, resident assistant, resident nurse, student affairs officer.

DANCE

Curriculum, Students, and Faculty

Required courses: dance composition/choreography, dance history, music, stagecraft.

Elective courses: ballet, dance writing research and criticism, jazz, master classes, modern dance, pointe, tap, other world dance forms, movement techniques.

Selectivity for males: admit all who apply. *Selectivity for females:* admit all who apply. *Total enrollment:* 18. *Entering class size:* 6. *Graduating class size:* 5.

Total full-time faculty: 1. *Total part-time faculty:* 5. *List of current faculty and past affiliations:* Karen Dearborn, Connecticut College, Mount Holyoke College, and University of Massachusettes; Karen Carlson, Dance Fusion in Philadelphia; Susan Creitz, University of Michigan; Kim Maniscalco, Pittsburgh Ballet Theatre School *Program contact person:* Karen Dearborn, (610) 821-3335.

Audition Information

No audition fee. Audition consists of the following: ballet, prepared solo, no special requirements. *Accompanist provided. Cassette player available; CD player available.*

Repertoire that students should avoid? no.

Audition evaluation criteria: talent, physical potential, creative and intellectual abilities.

Performance Information

Performance opportunities available (frequency): Fully produced concerts (1-2 per year), informal concerts (1-2 per year), workshops (1-4 per year), on-site performances (1-8 per year).

Performances choreographed by: faculty, students, guests. *Recent guest choreographers:* Nicholas Leichter, David Dortman, Clare Byrne, Judith Moss.

Facilities

Number of studios available: 2. *Approximate studio dimensions and flooring:* 70' x 35' sprung wood-Marley overlay, 30' x 30' sprung wood-Marley overlay. *Performance facilities:* proscenium theater—400-seat, studio theater—100-seat.

DRAMA

Curriculum, Students, and Faculty

Required courses: acting, directing, improvisation, scene study, Stanislavski exercises, text analysis.

Elective courses: make-up, movement, musical theater, speech..

Number of years required to complete program: 4. *Summer program available. Affiliation with a professional theater company: Muhlenberg Summer Music Theatre produces two large musicals each semester for extended runs. All positions are paid. Major New York designers, directors, and equity actors are used and students are involved at all levels of the theater, both as actors and technical staff.*

Selectivity for males: approximately 60% admitted. *Selectivity for females:* approximately 60% admitted. *Total enrollment:* 80. *Entering class size:* 30. *Graduating class size:* 30. *Percent international:* 2%. *Countries most represented:* Japan.

Renowned alumni: David Masenheimer, Alison Lowey, John Speredakos, Kam Chang.

Total full-time faculty: 5. *Total part-time faculty:* 3. *List of current faculty and past affiliations:* Charles Richter, Pennsylvania Stage Company; Ensemble Studio Theatre, New York City Opera Education Department; Devon Allen, The Brecht Company, LaJolla Playhose; Tim Averill, Pennsylvania Stage Company. *Contact:* Charles Richter (610) 821-3330.

Audition Information

No audition fee. Audition consists of the following: comedic monologue. *Audition evaluation criteria:* We look for basic ability to make active choices in the monologue. Level of physical and vocal relaxation are also factors. Ability to work "in the moment."

Facilities

Rehearsal facilities and hours: black box, rehearsal hall, 5:30 pm-11:00 pm, used for classes during the day. *Number of theaters on campus:* 2. *Type and capacity:* proscenium 392, black box 40.

MUSIC

Curriculum, Students, and Faculty

Unique or innovative music curriculum: classical and jazz studies are available. Elaborate Midi studio. *How are major teacher assignments made?* students may choose. Faculty is informed of a student's teacher preference at the time of the audition. *26 lessons with major teacher. May a student change major teachers during the course of study?* possibly. *Study of secondary instrument or discipline is allowed.*

Selectivity for instruments or programs offered (rating): bassoon (open), choral singing (open), clarinet (open), composition (selective), double bass (open), electronic music (open), flute or piccolo (open), French horn (open), guitar (open), oboe/English horn (open), organ (open), percussion (open), piano (non-competitive), saxophone (open), trombone (open), trumpet (open), tuba (open), viola (open), violin (open), violoncello (open), voice (open).

Total enrollment: 12. *Entering class size:* 6. *Graduating class size:* 6.

Total full-time faculty: 3. *Total part-time faculty:* 10. *Program contact person:* Douglas Ovens (610) 821-3365.

Audition Information

Audition consists of the following: scales, arpeggios, sight reading, repertoire. *Instruments provided for:* percussionists.

Required repertoire: prepared repertoire of student's choice, call for more information. *Performance opportunities available (frequency):* jury examinations (every semester).

Facilities

Number of practice rooms and hours: 8; 8:00 am-11:00 pm. *Recital hall?* yes. *Concert hall?* yes. *Recording studio?* no.

PHILADELPHIA COLLEGE OF BIBLE

200 Manor Avenue, Langhorne PA 19047
Tel: 215-702-4329
Fax: 215-702-4342
Email: Music@pcb.edu
Web: www.pcb.edu

General

Type of Institution: college. *Religious Affiliation:* non-denominational. *Environment:* suburban.

Total enrollment of institution: 1,500. *Total student body from other countries:* 6%. *Degrees offered:* BM.

Entrance Requirements

Audition required: live, audio, video. *Other requirements:* interview, essay. *Standardized test requirements:* ACT, 19; SAT I; TOEFL, 550.

Costs & Financial Aid

Application fee: $15. *Deposit:* $100.

Percent of students receiving financial aid: 68% *Types of scholarships and aid awarded:* partial, merit-based, need-based, institutional aid, government aid, reduced tuition, tuition payment plan, work/study. *Forms required for scholarships:* FAFSA, income tax return. *Loans available. Procedure for applying for loans:* file FAFSA and loan application B-4 5-1. *Financial aid offered to international students. Percent of international students receiving scholarships:* 24%. *Other aid available to international students:* deserving and needy can receive 100% tuition and work/study to pay room and board.

Services

Housing options: on-site dorms, off-campus housing.

Support staff: career counselor, financial aid advisor, foreign student advisor, physical therapist, psychological counselor, resident assistant, resident nurse, student affairs officer.

MUSIC

Curriculum, Students, and Faculty

Unique or innovative music curriculum: students receive both a bachelor's in music and Bachelors of Science in Bible at the end of 5 years. *How are major teacher assignments made?* made by the school according to teacher availability. Faculty is informed of a student's teacher preference at the time of the audition. *24 lessons with major teacher. May a student change major teachers during the course of study?* possibly. *Study of secondary instrument or discipline is allowed.*

Selectivity for instruments or programs offered (rating): bassoon (non-competitive), clarinet (non-competitive), composition (selective), double bass (non-competitive), flute or piccolo (non-competitive), French horn (non-competitive), guitar (non-competitive), harp (selective), oboe/English horn (non-competitive), organ (non-competitive), percussion (non-competitive), piano (non-competitive), sacred music (non-competitive), saxophone (non-competitive), trombone (non-competitive), trumpet (non-competitive), tuba (non-competitive), viola (non-competitive), violin (non-competitive), violoncello (non-competitive), voice (non-competitive).

Total enrollment: 70. *Entering class size:* 25. *Graduating class size:* 15.

Renowned alumni: Samuel Hsu, Don Hart, Paul Jones, William Brandstein, Dean Christman, conductor, Cynthia Rasmussen.

Total full-time faculty: 7. *Total part-time faculty:* 19. *Program contact person:* Dr. Al Lunde.

Audition Information

Audition consists of the following: scales, music theory, rhythmic dictation, sight reading, melodic dictation, repertoire. *Instruments provided for:* percussionists.

Required repertoire: 2 classical pieces, 1 sacred piece at level 6 or higher. *Performance opportunities available (frequency):* band (frequently), jury examinations, opera workshops, touring, chorus.

Facilities

Recital hall? yes. *Concert hall?* yes. *Recording studio?* yes.

POINT PARK COLLEGE

201 Wood Street, Pittsburgh PA 15222
Tel: 412-392-3454
Fax: 412-391-2424

General

Type of Institution: college. *Environment:* urban.

Total enrollment of institution: 2,400. *Degrees offered:* BA.

Entrance Requirements

Audition required: live, video. *Other requirements:* interview, recommendation, essay, photograph. *Standardized test requirements:* ACT; SAT I, 950.

Costs & Financial Aid

Application fee: $20. *Deposit:* $150.

Types of scholarships and aid awarded: full, partial, merit-based, need-based, named, institutional aid, government aid, tuition payment plan, work/study. *Forms required for scholarships:* FFS, FAFSA, income tax return. *Loans available. Procedure for applying for loans:* prospective students must contact the Office of Enrollment. *Financial aid offered to international students.*

Services

Housing options: on-site dorms.

Support staff: career counselor, financial aid advisor, foreign student advisor.

Comments

Please note that we do not offer a music degree. Our music department serves our musical theatre program and offers a general music appreciation course to other college majors.

DANCE

Curriculum, Students, and Faculty

Selectivity for males: most admitted, but not all. *Selectivity for females:* approximately 33% admitted. *Total enrollment:* 159. *Entering class size:* 63. *Graduating class size:* 25. *Percent international:* 3%. *Countries most represented:* Japan.

Total full-time faculty: 9. *Total part-time faculty:* 11. *Program contact person:* Ron Tassone.

Audition Information

No audition fee. Audition consists of the following: ballet, modern dance, pas de deux, pointe works. *Accompanist provided. Cassette player available; CD player available. Dress requirements for males:* black tights, white t-shirts, ballet slippers, jazz shoes. *Dress requirements for females:* black leotard, pink tights, ballet slippers, jazz shoes.

Performance Information

Performance opportunities available (frequency): fully produced concerts (5), informal concerts (2), workshops (4), on-site performances(6), touring (11).

Performances choreographed by: faculty, students, guests. *Recent guest choreographers:* Howard Richard, Ginger Farley, Claire Batai, Maxine Sherman, Bel Miler; Duncan Nobel; Jennifer Muller; Lar Lubovitch; Richard Levi, and Mikhail Koro.

Facilities

Number of studios available: 9. *Approximate studio dimensions and flooring:* sprung with Marley. *Performance facilities:* 430-seat procenium theater.

DRAMA

Curriculum, Students, and Faculty

Required courses: audition preparation.

TEMPLE UNIVERSITY

Office of Undergraduate Admissions, Conwell Hall
1801 North Broad Street, Philadelphia PA 19122
Tel: 888-340-2222
Email: TUADM@vm.temple.edu
Web: www.temple.edu

General

Type of Institution: university. *Environment:* urban.

Total enrollment of institution: 29,300. *Total student body from other countries:* 5%. *Degrees offered:* BA, BFA, BS in music.

Entrance Requirements

Audition required: live *Other requirements:* essay. *Standardized test requirements:* ACT; SAT I; TOEFL, 500. School's own English exam required.

Costs & Financial Aid

Application fee: $35. *Deposit:* $350. *Tuition (in-state/out-state):* $5,870/$10,752. *Medical fee:* $70. *Other fees:* $210. *Room and Board:* $5,912.

Types of scholarships and aid awarded: full, partial, merit-based, need-based, named, institutional aid, government aid, reduced tuition, tuition payment plan, work/study, gig office. *Forms required for scholarships:* FAFSA. *Loans available. Procedure for applying for loans:* complete and return FAFSA form by 3/31. *Financial aid offered to international students. Percent of international students receiving scholarships:* 5%. *Other aid available to international students:* for music Boyer scholarships, performance grants, grants in aid.

Services

Housing options: on-site dorms, off-campus housing, fraternity, sorority.

Support staff: career counselor, college advisor, financial aid advisor, foreign student advisor, housing advisor, physical therapist, psychological counselor, resident assistant, resident nurse, student affairs officer.

DANCE

Curriculum, Students, and Faculty

Required courses: anatomy, dance composition/choreography, dance history, dance theory, dance writing research and criticism, Labanotation, modern dance, Laban Movement Studies, music, nutrition, rehearsal and performance, repertory, stagecraft.

Elective courses: African dance, ballet, jazz, master classes, body conditioning, Pilates, tap.

Total enrollment: 135. *Entering class size:* 20. *Percent international:* 5%. *Countries most represented:* Caribbean, Brazil, Taiwan.

Renowned alumni: Dr. Jane Boubright, Executive Director, National Dance Association.

Total full-time faculty: 9. *Total part-time faculty:* 7. *List of current faculty and past affiliations:* Ann Vachon, Jose Limon Dance Company; Dr. Brenda Dixon Gottschild, Mary Anthony Dance Company, author of "Digging the Africanist Presence;" Dr. Sarah Hilsendayer. *Program contact person:* Luke Kahlich.

Audition Information

No audition fee. Audition consists of the following: ballet, modern dance. *Accompanist provided. Cassette player available; CD player available. Dress requirements for males:* no loose fitting clothing. *Dress requirements for females:* no loose fitting clothing.

Audition evaluation criteria: technical ability, interview, creative ability.

Performance Information

Performance opportunities available (frequency): Fully produced concerts (2 per year), workshops (1-2 per year), on-site performances (2-4 per year).

Performances choreographed by: faculty, students, guests.

Facilities

Number of studios available: 4. *Approximate studio dimensions and flooring:* sprung wood. *Performance facilities:* Conwell Dance Theater, Tomlinson Theater.

DRAMA

Curriculum, Students, and Faculty

Required courses: acting, directing, drama criticism, improvisation, Stanislavski exercises.

Elective courses: Alexander technique, audition preparation, make-up, martial arts, movement, musical theater, scene study, speech, stage combat, text analysis, verse drama, voice, mime.

Number of years required to complete program: 4. *Summer program not available. Affiliation with a professional theater company. Every other year we do a play with Venture Theater, a professional theater, with which we share directors and actors. Undergraduates perform with professionals. Venture is a multi-cultural theater.*

Entering class size: 45. *Graduating class size:* 146. *Percent international:* 3%. *Countries most represented:* Japan.

Renowned alumni: Tom Sizemore, Jude Ciccolelli, Danielle Perna, John Connolly, Jason George, Eric Stuart, Kim Rhodes.

Total full-time faculty: 11. *Total part-time faculty:* 9. *List of current faculty and past affiliations:* Donna Snow, American Conservatory Theater; David Hale, Curt Seni, Kevin Cotter, Neil Bierbower, Robert Hedley, Dan Boylen, Jan Silverma, Kathy Garvinella, Joe Leonardo, Carnegie Mellon, Michael Barne, Denver Theater Center.

Audition Information

No audition fee.

Performance Information

Performance opportunities available (frequency): fully produced performances (6 per year), informal performances (1), workshops (8 per semester), one-act play festival (spring), auditioned.

Recent guest artists: Monique Fowler, Jacqueline Rowen, Jed Diamond, Peter Francis James, Irene Baird.

Facilities

Rehearsal facilities and hours: classrooms, rehearsal hall, black box theater, all equipped with rehearsal furniture. *Type and capacity:* black box 100.

MUSIC

Curriculum, Students, and Faculty

Unique or innovative music curriculum: Temple University's Esther Boyer College of Music offers comprehensive professional education in music, baccalaureate through doctorate, for performers, educators, therapists, and scholars. Students enjoy a 10-to-1 student to faculty ratio. Our world- renowned faculty includes many members of The Philadelphia Orchestra, as well as many other noted recording and performing artists. The Esther Boyer College of Music is home to Rock Hall, Philadelphia's premier chamber music facility and state-of-the-art computer laboratories. In conjunction with the rich cultural resources offered by the city of Philadelphia, the Esther Boyer College of Music provides its students with the competitive edge in the professional world of music. *How are major teacher assignments made?* students may choose, made by the school according to teacher preference and teacher availability. Faculty is informed of a student's teacher preference at the time of the audition. *May a student change major teachers during the course of study?* possibly. *Study of secondary instrument or discipline is allowed.*

Selectivity for instruments or programs offered (rating): accompanying (selective), accordion (selective), bagpipes (selective), bassoon (selective), choral singing (selective), clarinet (selective), composition (selective), double bass (selective), electronic music (selective), flute or piccolo (selective), French horn (selective), guitar (selective), harp (selective), harpsichord (selective), jazz (selective), oboe/English horn (selective), orchestral conducting (selective), organ (selective), percussion (selective), piano (selective), sacred music (selective), saxophone (selective), trombone (selective), trumpet (selective), tuba (selective), viola (selective), violin (selective), violoncello (selective), voice (selective).

Total enrollment: 600. *Entering class size:* 160. *Graduating class size:* 110. *Percent international:* 20%. *Countries most represented:* The Americas, Asia, Europe.

Renowned alumni: Laurie Bloom, Chicago Symphony; Donald Luizzi, Philadelphia Orchestra; Cynthia DeAlmeida, Pittsburgh Symphony; Judith Dines, Houston Symphony; Cathy Cahill, New York Philharmonic; Nico Castel, Metropolitan Opera.

Total full-time faculty: 44. *Total part-time faculty:* 78. *Program contact person:* Ms. Catherine Grudzinski.

Audition Information

No audition fee. Audition consists of the following: repertoire. *Instruments provided for:* harpists, percussionists.

Required repertoire: varies by instrument and program. Please call school for repertoire information.

Facilities

Number of practice rooms and hours: 45; 7:00 am-11:00 pm (Mon-Sat). *Recital hall?* yes. *Concert hall?* yes. *Recording studio?* yes.

UNIVERSITY OF PENNSYLVANIA

34th and Spruce Street, Philadelphia PA 19104
Tel: 215-898-7507
Fax: 215-898-9670
Web: www.upenn.edu

Entrance Requirements

Audition not required. Cross-registration available with Curtis School of Music.

DANCE

Curriculum, Students, and Faculty

Elective courses: tap, African dance.

MUSIC

Music is taught within the context of a liberal arts education.

UNIVERSITY OF THE ARTS

320 South Broad Street, Philadelphia PA 19102
Tel: 215-875-4808
Fax: 215-875-5458

General

Type of Institution: conservatory.

Total enrollment of institution: 1,300. *Total student body from other countries:* 5%. *Degrees offered:* certificate, BFA, BM, certificate, artisit diploma.

Entrance Requirements

Audition required: live, audio, video. *Standardized test requirements:* ACT; SAT I; TOEFL.

Costs & Financial Aid

Tuition: $13,900. *Other fees:* $500.

Types of scholarships and aid awarded: need-based. *Forms required for scholarships:* FAFSA, income tax return. *Loans available. Financial aid offered to international students.*

Services

Housing options: on-site dorms, off-campus housing.

Support staff: career counselor, financial aid advisor, foreign student advisor, housing advisor, psychological counselor, resident assistant, resident nurse, student affairs officer.

RHODE ISLAND

BROWN UNIVERSITY

Box 1876, 45 Prospect Street
Providence, RI 02912
Tel: 401-863-2378
Web: www.brown.edu

General

Type of institution: university. *Environment:* small city.

Total enrollment: 7,650. *Degrees offered:* BA.

Entrance Requirements

You must be admitted to the university. *No audition required. Standardized test requirements:* SAT I; SAT II; TOEFL.

Costs and Financial Aid

Tuition and fees: $22,280. *Room and board:* $6,840.

Types of scholarships and aid awarded: need-based. *Forms required for scholarships:* FAFSA.

Services

Housing options: on-site dormitories.

Support staff: career counselor, financial aid advisor, foreign student advisor, housing advisor, psychological counselor, resident assistant, resident nurse.

DRAMA

Taught within the context of a liberal arts university.

Renowned alumni: Alfred Uhry, Laura Linney.

SOUTH CAROLINA

COLUMBIA COLLEGE OF SOUTH CAROLINA

1301 Columbia College Drive, Columbia SC 29203
Tel: 803-786-3012
Fax: 803-786-3674
Email: jmitchell@colcoll.edu
Contact: Ms. Charlotte Broome

General

Type of Institution: college. *Religious Affiliation:* United Methodist Church (South Carolina Conference). *Environment:* urban.

Total enrollment of institution: 1,317. *Total student body from other countries:* 1%. *Degrees offered:* BA, BFA, BM.

Entrance Requirements

Audition required: live, video. *Other requirements:* interview, recommendation. *Standardized test requirements:* SAT I, 1030; TOEFL, 550, school's own English exam required.

Costs & Financial Aid

Application fee: $20. *Deposit:* $100. *Tuition:* $12,050. *Other fees:* $100 per semester music majors, art studio, fees vary, $50 technological fee.

Percent of students receiving financial aid: 89%. *Types of scholarships and aid awarded:* partial, merit-based, need-based, named, institutional aid, government aid, reduced tuition, tuition payment plan, work/study. *Forms required for scholarships:* FAFSA. *Loans available. Procedure for applying for loans:* apply for admission and complete the FAFSA as soon as possible after 1/1 of each year. *Percent of international students receiving scholarships:* 100%.

Services

Housing options: on-site dorms.

Support staff: career counselor, financial aid advisor, psychological counselor, resident assistant, resident nurse, student affairs officer.

DANCE

Curriculum, Students, and Faculty

Required courses: anatomy, ballet (2-4 classes per week, 4 years to complete), dance composition/choreography (2-3 classes per week), dance history, jazz (2 classes per week), modern dance (2-4 classes per week, 4 years to complete), music, other world dance forms, rehearsal and performance.

Elective courses: pointe, repertory, tap, dance history.

Selectivity for females: most admitted, but not all. *Total enrollment:* 42. *Entering class size:* 15. *Graduating class size:* 8.

Total full-time faculty: 5. *Total part-time faculty:* 3. *List of current faculty and past affiliations:* Martha Brim, Patty Graham, Brenda McCutchen, Allison Tipton, Chase Angier. *Program contact person:* Ms. Martha Brim, (803) 786-3825.

Audition Information

No audition fee. Audition consists of the following: ballet, modern dance, prepared solo. *Accompanist provided. Cassette player available; CD player available. Dress requirements for females:* hair pulled back and away from face, leotard, tights without toes for modern dance, leotard, tights, ballet slippers.

Performance Information

Performance opportunities available (frequency): Fully produced concerts (2 per semester), informal concerts (2 per semester), workshops (varies), on-site performances (2 per year), touring (2 per year).

Performances choreographed by: faculty, students, guests. *Recent guest choreographers:* Sean Curran, Randy James, Shapiro and Smith, Laura Dean.

Facilities

Number of studios available: 3. *Approximate studio dimensions and flooring:* 62' x 41' sprung floor, 41' x 29' Marley covering, 33.5' x 24'. *Performance facilities:* Cottingham Theater is a proscenium stage with Marley over wood floor. House seat: 376.

DRAMA

Curriculum, Students, and Faculty

Required courses: speech.

Elective courses: acting, introduction to theater, voice, improvisation.

Summer program not available. No affiliation with a professional theater company. Total enrollment: 2. *Graduating class size:* 5.

Renowned alumni: Donna Drake, Clarence Felder.

Total full-time faculty: 2. *Total part-time faculty:* 1. *List of current faculty and past affiliations:* Sara Nalley, University of Florida; Wayne Bradley, University of South Carolina, Patchwork Players.

Performance Information

Performance opportunities available (frequency): informal performances (2-3 per year), workshops (1-2 per year), auditioned.

Recent guest artists: South Carolina Shakespeare Company, South Carolina Actors' Theater, Gigi Grizzard, Southeastern Theatrical Productions.

Facilities

Rehearsal facilities and hours: rehearsals scheduled in campus theaters as needed. *Number of theaters on campus:* 3. *Type and capacity:* proscenium 376, 88, lab 40.

MUSIC

Curriculum, Students, and Faculty

Unique or innovative music curriculum: Both the BA and BM degrees are offered. Additionally, we have a Center for Contractual Studies where a student may work out a curriculum under faculty supervision which is unique to her needs. *How are major teacher assignments made?* Students may choose according to teacher availability. Faculty is not informed of a student's teacher preference at the time of the audition. *28 lessons with major teacher. May a student change major teachers during the course of study?* possibly. *Study of secondary instrument or discipline is allowed.*

Selectivity for instruments or programs offered (rating): accompanying (competitive), bassoon (competitive), choral conducting (competitive), choral singing (competitive), clarinet (competitive), composition (competitive), double bass (competitive), electronic music (competitive), flute or piccolo (competitive), French horn (competitive), guitar (competitive), harp (competitive), harpsichord (competitive), jazz (competitive), oboe/English horn (competitive), orchestral conducting (competitive), organ (competitive), percussion (competitive), piano (competitive), sacred music, saxophone (competitive), trombone (competitive), trumpet (competitive), tuba (competitive), viola (competitive), violin (competitive), violoncello (competitive), voice (competitive).

Total enrollment: 60. *Entering class size:* 18. *Graduating class size:* 7. *Percent international:* 1%. *Countries most represented:* Korea.

Renowned alumni: Sylvia Plyler, Ann Berson, Lanny Palmer, Virgina Houser, Fern Coldwell, Dawn Smith Jordan, Dana Russell, Danna Drake.

Total full-time faculty: 8. *Total part-time faculty:* 15. *Program contact person:* Dr. James Caldwell, 803-786-3761.

Audition Information

Audition consists of the following: scales, melodic dictation. *Instruments provided for:* percussionists.

Repertoire that students should avoid? no taped accompaniments. *Performance opportunities available (frequency):* opera workshops, touring, produced operas.

Facilities

Number of practice rooms and hours: 16; 7:00 am-11:00 pm. *Recital hall?* yes. *Concert hall?* yes. *Recording studio?* yes.

WINTHROP UNIVERSITY

College of Visual and Performing Arts, Rock Hill SC 29733
Tel: 803-323-2323
Fax: 803-323-2333

General

Type of Institution: university. *Environment:* urban.

Total student body from other countries: 2%. *Degrees offered:* BA, BM, BME.

Entrance Requirements

Audition required: live. *Standardized test requirements:* ACT; SAT I; TOEFL, 520.

Costs & Financial Aid

Application fee: $10. *Deposit:* $150. *Tuition (in-state/out-state):* $1,882/$3,523.

Types of scholarships and aid awarded: full, partial, merit-based, need-based, named, institutional aid, tuition payment plan, work/study. *Forms required for scholarships:* FAFSA, school's own financial aid form. *Procedure for applying for loans:* contact Offices of Financial Resource Center at 119 Tillman Hall. *Financial aid offered to international students. Other aid available to international students:* dean's merit scholarships based on artistic talent for visual and performing arts majors only.

Services

Housing options: on-site dorms, off-campus housing, fraternity, sorority, family.

Support staff: career counselor, financial aid advisor, foreign student advisor, housing advisor, psychological counselor, resident assistant, resident nurse, student affairs officer.

DANCE

Curriculum, Students, and Faculty

Required courses: anatomy (1 class per week), dance composition/choreography (4 classes per week), dance history (2 classes per week), dance theory (1 class per week), dance writing research and criticism (1 class per week), modern dance (2 classes per week, 3 years to complete), music (1 class per week), other world dance forms, rehearsal and performance (8 classes per week), stagecraft (1 class per week).

Elective courses: jazz (2 classes per week), tap (1 class per week).

Selectivity for males: most admitted, but not all. *Selectivity for females:* most admitted, but not all. *Total enrollment:* 30. *Entering class size:* 8. *Graduating class size:* 4.

List of current faculty and past affiliations: Sandra Neels, Merce Cunningham; Joanne Lurt; Mary Beth Thompson. *Program contact person:* Marc Powers, (803) 323-2287.

Audition Information

No audition fee. Audition consists of the following: ballet, modern dance. *Accompanist provided. Cassette player available; CD player available.*

Audition evaluation criteria: basic proficiency in ballet and modern.

Performance Information

Performance opportunities available (frequency): Fully produced concerts (1 per year), informal concerts (1 per year), workshops (2 per year), on-site performances (2 per year), touring (2-6).

Performances choreographed by: faculty, students, guests. *Recent guest choreographers:* Mickie Geller, Alain Charvan.

Facilities

Number of studios available: 3. *Approximate studio dimensions and flooring:* 40' x 80' sprung with Marley covering, 40' x 60', 20' x 30'. *Performance facilities:* 330-seat proscenium theater shared with theater program.

DRAMA

Curriculum, Students, and Faculty

Required courses: make-up, stagecraft, stage management, theater history.

Elective courses: acting, audition preparation, costume design, martial arts, movement, scene design, scene study, sound design, stage combat, Stanislavski exercises, text analysis, verse drama, voice, history of design, drafting.

Number of years required to complete program: 4. *Summer program not available. Affiliation with a professional theater company: internship with Charlotte Repertory Theatre.*

Selectivity for males: most admitted, but not all. *Selectivity for females:* most admitted, but not all. *Total enrollment:* 80. *Entering class size:* 28. *Graduating class size:* 16.

List of current faculty and past affiliations: Marc Powers, Blair Beasley, Anne Fletcher, Anna Sartin, Jeannie Woods.

Audition Information

No audition fee. Audition consists of the following: comedic monologue, Shakespearean monologue, 2 contrasting monologues. *Repertoire that students should avoid?* no.

Audition evaluation criteria: vocal clarity, physical and vocal expressiveness, stage presence, acting (clear objectives and motivation), creativity (interesting choices made).

Performance Information

Performance opportunities available (frequency): fully produced performances (6 per year), informal performances (2-8 per year), workshops (2-8 per year), off-site performances (0-8 per year), auditioned. Primarily cold readings, open calls.

Facilities

Rehearsal facilities and hours: theater, studio theater, acting studio, most rehearsals 7:00 pm-10:00 pm (Sun-Fri). *Number of theaters on campus:* 2. *Type and capacity:* proscenium 330, black box 100, proscenium 3,500, proscenium 700, proscenium 250.

MUSIC

Curriculum, Students, and Faculty

Unique or innovative music curriculum: newly revised music education curriculum. *How are major teacher assignments made?* students may choose made by the school according to teacher availability. Faculty is informed of a student's teacher preference at the time of the audition. *May a student change major teachers during the course of study?* possibly. *Study of secondary instrument or discipline is allowed.*

Selectivity for instruments or programs offered (rating): bassoon (open), choral singing (open), clarinet (open), flute or piccolo (open), French horn (open), guitar (open), harpsichord (open), jazz (open), oboe/English horn (open), organ (open), percussion (open), percussion (competitive), piano (open), saxophone (open), trombone (open), trumpet (open), tuba (open), tuba (open), voice (open), voice (competitive).

Total enrollment: 150. *Entering class size:* 50. *Graduating class size:* 25. *Percent international:* 3%. *Countries most represented:* China, Korea, Japan.

Renowned alumni: Cassandra Riddle, Craig Estep, John Fowler.

Total full-time faculty: 17. *Total part-time faculty:* 16. *Program contact person:* Don Rogers, (803) 323-2255.

Audition Information

No audition fee. Audition consists of the following: scales. *Instruments provided for:* percussionists.

Repertoire that students should avoid? no. *Performance opportunities available (frequency):* band (8 per semester), jury examinations (2 per year), recitals (80 per year).

Facilities

Number of practice rooms and hours: 24; 7:00 am-1:00 am. *Recital hall?* yes. *Concert hall?* yes. *Recording studio?* yes.

Comments

The Department of Music will provide opportunities for students to develop their creative and musical potentials, prepare students for careers in music, continue its historic leadership role in music education, serve the campus community by offering musical experiences and the opportunity to develop musical knowledge and skills, serve the larger community through programs of national distinction, and be responsive to change and committed to on-going self-evaluation.

BELMONT UNIVERSITY SCHOOL OF MUSIC

1900 Belmont Boulevard, Nashville TN 37212-3757
Tel: 615-460-6408
Fax: 615-386-0239
Email: Belmont music@Belmont.edu
Web: www.belmont.edu/music/musichome.html
Contact: Angie Shedd

General

Type of Institution: university. *Religious Affiliation:* Tennessee Baptist Convention. *Environment:* urban.

Total enrollment of institution: 2,996. *Total student body from other countries:* 4%. *Degrees offered:* BM.

Entrance Requirements

Audition required: live, audio, video. *Other requirements:* recommendation. *Standardized test requirements:* ACT, 20; SAT I, 1000.

Costs & Financial Aid

Application fee: $25. *Deposit:* $250. *Tuition:* $10,500. *Other fees:* $100 enrichment fee, $15 activity fee.

Types of scholarships and aid awarded: full, partial, merit-based, need-based, named, institutional aid, government aid, reduced tuition, tuition payment plan, work/study. *Forms required for scholarships:* FAFSA, income tax return. *Loans available. Procedure for applying for loans:* contact Financial Aid Office to request financial aid form. *Financial aid offered to international students. Percent of international students receiving scholarships:* 75%. Russians receive 100% of tuition, room and board without book allowance. Germans and French receive full tuition.

Services

Housing options: on-site dorms, off-campus housing.

Support staff: career counselor, financial aid advisor, foreign student advisor, housing advisor, psychological counselor, resident assistant, resident nurse, student affairs officer.

MUSIC

Curriculum, Students, and Faculty

Unique or innovative music curriculum: commercial music degree offers opportunity to study jazz, rock, country, and other contemporary styles. *How are major teacher assignments made?* Students may choose made by the school; Faculty is not informed of a student's teacher preference at the time of the audition. *30 lessons with major teacher. May a student change major teachers during the course of study?* possibly. *Study of secondary instrument or discipline is allowed.*

Selectivity for instruments or programs offered (rating): accompanying (competitive), bassoon (competitive), choral singing (competitive), clarinet (competitive), composition (competitive), double bass (competitive), electronic music (competitive), flute or piccolo (competitive), French horn (competitive), guitar (competitive), harp (competitive), harpsichord (competitive), jazz (competitive), oboe/English horn (competitive), organ (competitive), percussion (competitive), piano (competitive), sacred music (competitive), saxophone (competitive), trombone (competitive), trumpet (competitive), tuba (competitive), viola (competitive), violin (competitive), violoncello (competitive), voice (competitive).

Total enrollment: 350. *Entering class size:* 120. *Graduating class size:* 55. *Percent international:* 4%. *Countries most represented:* Germany, Russia.

Renowned alumni: Tammy Rogers; Chris Rodriguez; Hugh Clifton Forbis, Metropolitan Opera.

Total full-time faculty: 26. *Total part-time faculty:* 50. *Program contact person:* Dr. Jean Fallis.

Audition Information

No audition fee. Audition consists of the following: scales, orchestral excerpts, music theory, ensemble playing, arpeggios, *Instruments provided for:* percussionists

Facilities

Recital hall? yes. *Concert hall?* yes. *Recording studio?* yes.

EAST TENNESSEE STATE UNIVERSITY

P.O. Box 70661, Johnson City TN 37601
Tel: 423-439-4270
Fax: 423-439-7088
Email: blackman@etsu-tn.edu

General

Type of Institution: public, university. *Environment:* urban.

Total enrollment of institution: 12,000. *Degrees offered:* BM.

Entrance Requirements

Audition not required.

Costs & Financial Aid

Application fee: $15. *Tuition:* $890. *Other fees:* $70 campus access.

Types of scholarships and aid awarded: full, partial, merit-based, need-based, named, reduced tuition, work/study. *Forms required for scholarships:* FAFSA, income tax return. *Loans available.*

Services

Housing options: on-site dorms, off-campus housing, fraternity, sorority.

Support staff: career counselor, financial aid advisor, housing advisor, physical therapist, psychological counselor, resident assistant, resident nurse, student affairs officer.

MUSIC

Curriculum, Students, and Faculty

Unique or innovative music curriculum: bluegrass and country music programs, Suzuki flute program. *How are major teacher assignments made?* students may choose, according to teacher preference and teacher availability. Faculty is not informed of a student's teacher preference at the time of the audition. *29 lessons with major teacher. May a student change major teachers during the course of study?* possibly. *Study of secondary instrument or discipline is allowed.*

Selectivity for instruments or programs offered (rating): bassoon (non-competitive), choral singing (non-competitive), clarinet (non-competitive), double bass (open), flute or piccolo (non-competitive), French horn (non-competitive), guitar (non-competitive), oboe/English horn (non-competitive), percussion (non-competitive), piano (non-competitive), saxophone (non-competitive), trombone (non-competitive), trumpet (non-competitive), tuba (non-competitive), viola (open), violin (open), violoncello (open), voice (non-competitive).

Total enrollment: 300. *Entering class size:* 50. *Graduating class size:* 10.

Renowned alumni: Tim Stafford, Teresa Bowers, Mark Jacoby, Frank Little, Earl Henry, Kenny Chesney.

Total full-time faculty: 17. *Total part-time faculty:* 10. *Program contact person:* Kathy Martin.

Audition Information

No audition fee. Audition consists of the following: scales, orchestral excerpts, music theory sight reading. *Instruments provided for:* percussionists.

Performance opportunities available (frequency): band (all semester), jury examinations (every semester), chorus (all semester).

Facilities

Recital hall? yes. *Concert hall?* yes. *Recording studio?* no.

UNION UNIVERSITY

1050 Union University Drive, Jackson TN 38305
Tel: 800-33UNION
Fax: 901-661-5175
Web: www.uu.edu
Contact: Trent Presley

General

Type of Institution: university. *Religious Affiliation:* Tennessee Baptist Convention. *Environment:* suburban. *Cross registration is available through the Lambuth University, Freed-Hardemann University.*

Total enrollment of institution: 2,000. *Degrees offered:* BA, BM.

Entrance Requirements

Audition required: live, audio, video. *Other requirements:* interview. *Standardized test requirements:* ACT.

Costs & Financial Aid

Application fee: $25. *Deposit:* $200. *Tuition:* $7,990. *Other fees:* $190 per year student service fee (includes medical, computing, activity), $450 per year music application fee.

Percent of students receiving financial aid: 90%. *Types of scholarships and aid awarded:* full, partial, merit-based, need-based, named, institutional aid, government aid, tuition payment plan, work/study. *Forms required for scholarships:* FAFSA, school's own financial aid form. *Loans available. Procedure for applying for loans:* varies with type of loan. *Financial aid offered to international students.*

Services

Housing options: on-site dorms.

Support staff: career counselor, dorm parent, financial aid advisor, foreign student advisor, housing advisor, psychological counselor, resident assistant, resident nurse, student affairs officer.

DRAMA

Curriculum, Students, and Faculty

Required courses: acting, directing, speech.

Elective courses: scene study, verse drama, voice.

Number of years required to complete program: 4. *Summer program not available. No affiliation with a professional theater company. Selectivity for males:* admit all who apply. *Selectivity for females:* admit all who apply. *Total enrollment:* 15.

Total full-time faculty: 2. *Total part-time faculty:* 0. *List of current faculty and past affiliations:* Wayne Johnson, Pasadena Playhouse, Purdue University, David Burke, University of Houston; Julian Williamson, University of Memphis.

Audition Information

No audition fee. Audition consists of the following: comedic monologue. *Audition evaluation criteria:* enthusiasm, energy, connection with character, directability, openness, inhibitions level.

Performance Information

Performance opportunities available (frequency): fully produced performances (4 per season), informal performances (4 per season), workshops (occasionally), off-site performances (periodically), auditioned.

Recent guest artists: Bruce Kuhn, Curt Cloninger, Parnassus Theatre Company, Ruth and Charlie Jones, A.D. Players, George Fischott.

Facilities

Rehearsal facilities and hours: 3/4 thrust and chapel, 2-4 hours, 4-5 days per week. *Number of theaters on campus:* 3. *Type and capacity:* 3/4 thrust—200, proscenium—250, proscenium—1,200.

MUSIC

Curriculum, Students, and Faculty

Unique or innovative music curriculum: many opportunities for music internships and performance experience in the community. *How are major teacher assignments made?* students may choose, according to teacher availability. Faculty is not informed of a student's teacher preference at the time of the audition. *May a student change major teachers during the course of study?* possibly. *Study of secondary instrument or discipline is allowed.*

Selectivity for instruments or programs offered (rating): bassoon (non-competitive), choral singing (competitive), clarinet (non-competitive), flute or piccolo (non-competitive), French horn (non-competitive), guitar (competitive), jazz (competitive), jazz (non-competitive), oboe/English horn (non-competitive), organ (competitive), percussion (competitive), piano (competitive), sacred music (non-competitive), saxophone (non-competitive), trombone (non-competitive), trumpet (non-competitive), tuba (competitive), voice (competitive).

Total enrollment: 100. *Entering class size:* 43. *Graduating class size:* 20.

Renowned alumni: Julie Freeman, New York City Opera; Mark Ring, Notre Dame University.

Total full-time faculty: 10. *Total part-time faculty:* 8. *Program contact person:* Dr. Andrew Roby.

Audition Information

No audition fee. Audition consists of the following: scales, music theory, arpeggios, sight reading, repertoire. *Instruments provided for:* percussionists.

Facilities

Number of practice rooms and hours: 14; 6:00 am-12:00 am. *Recital hall?* yes. *Concert hall?* yes. *Recording studio?* no.

Comments

Greatest strengths are in sacred music and music education. Placement rates and graduate school rates for our graduates are excellent.

VANDERBILT UNIVERSITY

2400 Blakemore Avenue
Blair School of Music, Nashville TN 37212
Tel: 615-322-7651
Fax: 615-343-0324
Email: dwayne.p.sagen@vanderbilt.edu
Web: www.vanderbilt.edu
Contact: Dean Dwayne Sagen

General

Type of Institution: private university. *Environment:* urban.

Total enrollment of institution: 5,400. *Total student body from other countries:* 5%. *Degrees offered:* certificate, BM, BME.

Entrance Requirements

Audition required: live, audio, video. *Other requirements:* recommendation, essay. *Standardized test requirements:* ACT; SAT I; SAT II; TOEFL.

Costs & Financial Aid

Application fee: $50. *Deposit:* $250. *Tuition:* $20,900. *Other fees:* $578 activity fee. *Room and board:* $7,588.

Percent of students receiving financial aid: 70%. *Types of scholarships and aid awarded:* full, partial, merit-based, need-based, named, institutional aid, government aid, work/study, gig office. *Forms required for scholarships:* FFS, FAFSA, income tax return, CSS Profile. *Loans available. Procedure for applying for loans:* audition and written application to Financial Aid Office.

Services

Housing options: on-site dorms, off-campus housing, fraternity, sorority.

Support staff: career counselor, financial aid advisor, foreign student advisor, housing advisor, psychological counselor, resident assistant, resident nurse, student affairs officer.

MUSIC

Curriculum, Students, and Faculty

Unique or innovative music curriculum: 5 year Bachelor of Music/Master of Education leads to Music Teacher licensure in public schools. *How are major teacher assignments made?* students may choose; made by the school according to teacher preference, according to teacher availability. Faculty is not informed of a student's teacher preference at the time of the audition. *30 lessons with major teacher. May a student change major teachers during the course of study?* possibly. *Study of secondary instrument or discipline is allowed.*

Selectivity for instruments or programs offered (rating): bassoon (highly selective), choral singing (highly selective), clarinet (highly selective), composition (highly selective), double bass (highly selective), flute or piccolo (highly selective), French horn (highly selective), guitar (highly selective), harp (highly selective), oboe/English horn (highly selective), organ (highly selective), percussion (highly selective), piano (highly selective), saxophone (highly selective), trombone (highly selective), trumpet (highly selective), tuba (highly selective), viola (highly selective), violin (highly selective), violoncello (highly selective), voice (highly selective).

Total enrollment: 154. *Entering class size:* 51. *Graduating class size:* 25. *Percent international:* 2%. *Countries most represented:* China, Japan.

Total full-time faculty: 30. *Total part-time faculty:* 39. *Program contact person:* Dwayne Sagen.

Audition Information

No audition fee. Audition consists of the following: scales, orchestral excerpts, music theory, sight reading, repertoire. *Instruments provided for:* harpists, percussionists.

Required repertoire: varies by instrument. Please call school for repertoire information. *Performance opportunities available (frequency):* jury examinations.

Facilities

Number of practice rooms and hours: 18; 6:00 am-12:00 am. *Recital hall?* yes. *Concert hall?* yes. *Recording studio?* no.

TEXAS

BAYLOR UNIVERSITY

P.O. Box 97032, Waco TX 76798-7032
Tel: 254-710-2061
Tel: 800-BAYLORU
Fax: 254-710-2062

General

Type of Institution: private university. *Religious Affiliation:* Baptist. *Environment:* urban.

Total enrollment of institution: 10,597. *Degrees offered:* BA, BFA, BM, BME.

Entrance Requirements

Audition required: Other requirements: essay *Standardized test requirements:* ACT; SAT I; TOEFL, 540.

Costs & Financial Aid

Application fee: $35. *Deposit:* $100. *Tuition and Fees:* $10,478. *Room and board:* $4,533.

Percent of students receiving financial aid: 70%. *Types of scholarships and aid awarded:* full, partial, merit-based, need-based, named, institutional aid, tuition payment plan, work/study. *Forms required for scholarships:* FAFSA. *Loans available.*

Services

Housing options: on-site dorms, off-campus housing.

Support staff: career counselor, dorm parent, financial aid advisor, foreign student advisor, housing advisor, psychological counselor, resident assistant, resident nurse, student affairs officer.

DRAMA

Curriculum, Students, and Faculty

Required courses: acting, Alexander technique, audition preparation, dance, directing, improvisation, make-up, movement, scene study, Stanislavski exercises, text analysis, verse drama, voice.

Number of years required to complete program: 4-5. *Summer program available. No affiliation with a professional theater company. Selectivity for males:* approximately 60% admitted. *Selectivity for females:* approximately 60% admitted. *Total enrollment:* 43. *Entering class size:* 8.

Renowned alumni: Sherri Parker Lee, Beau Gravett, Greg Holt.

Total full-time faculty: 8. *Total part-time faculty:* 1 *List of current faculty and past affiliations:* Steven Peters, Terry Price.

Audition Information

No audition fee. Audition consists of the following: singing with accompaniment optional.

Performance Information

Performance opportunities available (frequency): fully produced performances (5-6 per year), informal performances (5-6 per year), workshops (10-12 per semester), historical pageant assigned, auditioned. Worshops are assigned, main stage are by audition.

Recent guest artists: Rick Hamilton, Fredi Olster.

Facilities

Number of theaters on campus: 3. *Type and capacity:* proscenium 350, thrust 250, black box 90.

MUSIC

Curriculum, Students, and Faculty

Unique or innovative music curriculum: music technology central to the curriculum. Also, opera program. *How are major teacher assignments made?* students may choose, made by the school according to teacher preference and teacher availability. Faculty is not informed of a student's teacher preference at the time of the audition.

Selectivity for instruments or programs offered (rating): accompanying (competitive), bassoon (competitive), choral conducting (highly selective), choral singing (non-competitive), clarinet (competitive), composition (highly selective), double bass (competitive), electronic music (highly selective), flute or piccolo (competitive), French horn (competitive), harp (selective), harpsichord (highly selective), jazz (selective), oboe/English horn (competitive), orchestral conducting (highly selective), organ (selective), percussion (competitive), piano (competitive), sacred music (competitive), saxophone (competitive), trombone (competitive), trumpet (competitive), tuba (competitive), viola (competitive), violin (competitive), violoncello (competitive), voice (competitive).

Total enrollment: 308. *Entering class size:* 81.

Renowned alumni: Steven Stucky, Thomas Stewart, Alan Smith, Kathryn Alexander.

Total full-time faculty: 54. *Total part-time faculty:* 13. *Program contact person:* Marvin Lamb, Dean.

Audition Information

No audition fee. Audition consists of the following: scales, arpeggios, sight reading. *Instruments provided for:* harpists, percussionists.

RICE UNIVERSITY

Shepherd School of Music
P.O. Box 1892, Houston TX 77251
Tel: 800-527-OWLS
Web: www.rice.edu

General

Type of Institution: private university. *Environment:* urban. *Academic education is offered on-site.*

Total enrollment of institution: 4,100. *Degrees offered:* BA, BM.

Entrance Requirements

Audition required: live, audio, video. *Other requirements:* interview, recommendation, essay. *Standardized test requirements:* SAT I; SAT II; TOEFL.

Costs & Financial Aid

Tuition: $11,300. *Room and board:* $5,700.

Percent of students receiving financial aid: 75%. *Types of scholarships and aid awarded:* full, partial, merit-based, need-based, work/study, gig office. *Forms required for scholarships:* FAFSA, income tax return.

Services

Housing options: on-site dorms, off-campus housing.

Support staff: career counselor, financial aid advisor, foreign student advisor, psychological counselor, resident assistant, resident nurse, student affairs officer.

MUSIC

Curriculum, Students, and Faculty

Total enrollment: 250.

Total full-time faculty: 34. *Total part-time faculty:* 16. *Program contact person:* Gary Smith, (713) 527-4047.

Audition Information

Audition consists of the following: orchestral excerpts, repertoire.

SAM HOUSTON STATE UNIVERSITY—DANCE PROGRAM

P.O. Box 2269, Huntsville TX 77341-2269
Tel: 409-294-1875
Fax: 407-294-3954
Web: www.shsu.edu/~drm_www/dance

General

Type of Institution: university. *Environment:* suburban.

Total enrollment of institution: 12,500. *Degrees offered:* BA, BFA.

Entrance Requirements

Audition not required.

Costs & Financial Aid

Percent of students receiving financial aid: 54%. *Types of scholarships and aid awarded:* full, partial, merit-based, need-based, institutional aid, government aid, tuition payment plan, work/study. *Forms required for scholarships:* FAFSA, income tax return, income asset verification. *Loans available. Procedure for applying for loans:* FAFSA or through Financial Aid Office.

Services

Housing options: on-site dorms, off-campus housing, fraternity, sorority.

DANCE

Curriculum, Students, and Faculty

Required courses: ballet, dance composition/choreography, dance history, dance theory, dance writing research and criticism, Labanotation, master classes, modern dance, music, pointe, rehearsal and performance, repertory, stagecraft.

Elective courses: jazz, nutrition, tap, vernacular dance, movement techniques.

Selectivity for males: admit all who apply. *Selectivity for females:* admit all who apply. *Total enrollment:* 400. *Entering class size:* 50. *Graduating class size:* 9.

Renowned alumni: James Clouser, Roseanne Cox, Scott Bodily, Luis Narvaez.

Total full-time faculty: 3. *Total part-time faculty:* 7. *List of current faculty and past affiliations:* Dana E. Nicolay, Royal Winnipeg Ballet, Houston Ballet, Contemporary Dancers Canada; Dr.Cindy Gratz, NYU, UCLA; Teresa Walshak Trum,

Florida State University. *Program contact person:* Sissy Johnson.

Audition Information

No audition fee. Audition consists of the following: ballet, improvisation, modern dance. *Accompanist provided. Cassette player available; CD player available. Dress requirements for males:* white t-shirt, black tights, white ballet shoes and socks. *Dress requirements for females:* black leotard, tights.

Performance Information

Performance opportunities available (frequency): Fully produced concerts (1 per semester), informal concerts (4 per semester), workshops (1 per semester), on-site performances (3-4 per semester).

Performances choreographed by: faculty, students, guests. *Recent guest choreographers:* Donald McKayle, Gus Solomons Jr., Mark Taylor, Bridgman/Packer, Creach/Koester.

Facilities

Number of studios available: 6. *Approximate studio dimensions and flooring:* 40' x 60' Harlequin, 40' x 50' Rosco, 50' x 70' wood, 50' x 50', 25' x 50'. *Performance facilities:* proscenium—140 seats, university theater main stage—490 seats.

SOUTHERN METHODIST UNIVERSITY

Meadows School of the Arts
P.O. Box 750356, Dallas TX 75275-0356
Tel: 214-768-3217
Fax: 214-768-3272
Email: hmccowen@mail.smu.edu
Web: www.smu.edu/~meadows
Contact: Heather Viles

General

Type of Institution: university. *Religious affiliation:* Methodist. *Environment:* urban.

Total enrollment of institution: 8,000. *Degrees offered:* BA, BFA, BM.

Entrance Requirements

Audition required: live, audio, video. *Other requirements:* interview, photograph. *Standardized test requirements:* ACT, 24; SAT I, 1000; TOEFL, 550.

Costs & Financial Aid

Types of scholarships and aid awarded: merit-based, need-based, named, institutional aid, government aid, work/study. *Forms required for scholarships:* FAFSA. *Loans available.*

Services

Housing options: on-site dorms, fraternity, sorority.

Support staff: career counselor, financial aid advisor, foreign student advisor, housing advisor, psychological counselor, resident assistant, resident nurse.

DANCE

Curriculum, Students, and Faculty

Required courses: ballet, dance composition/choreography, dance history, jazz, Labanotation, modern dance, pointe, stagecraft.

Selectivity for males: approximately 33% admitted. *Selectivity for females:* approximately 10%. admitted. *Total enrollment:* 125. *Entering class size:* 24. *List of current faculty and past affiliations:* Dr. Shelley C. Berg, London Festival Ballet; Karen Kriete, Harkness Ballet; Nathan Montoya, The Alvin Ailey American Dance Center. *Program contact person:* Joe Orlando.

Audition Information

Audition consists of the following: ballet, modern dance, pointe works, prepared solo. *Accompanist not provided. Cassette player not available; CD player not available. Dress requirements for males:* solid color leotard. *Dress requirements for females:* solid color leotard.

Performance Information

Performance opportunities available (frequency): fully produced concerts (2 per year), informal concerts (every semester), workshops (every semester), on-site performances (every few years).

Performances choreographed by: faculty, students, guests.

Facilities

Number of studios available: 4. *Approximate studio dimensions and flooring:* sprung floor. *Performance facilities:* Bob Hope Theatre, Sharp Studio, Meadow Lobby.

DRAMA

Curriculum, Students, and Faculty

Required courses: acting, dramaturgy, improvisation, movement, stage management, theater history, voice.

Elective courses: directing.

Selectivity for males: approximately 33% admitted. *Selectivity for females:* approximately 33% admitted. *Total enrollment:* 150. *Entering class size:* 30.

List of current faculty and past affiliations: Rhonda Blair, Melia Bensussen, Oregon Shakespeare Festival; Michael Connolly, Pennsylvania State University.

Audition Information

Audition consists of the following: a cappella, 2 contemporary monologues.

Performance Information

Performance opportunities available (frequency): fully produced performances (4 per year), informal performances (4 per year), numerous independent projects.

Facilities

Number of theaters on campus: 3. *Type and capacity:* proscenium, black box, classical thrust stage.

MUSIC

Curriculum, Students, and Faculty

How are major teacher assignments made? students may choose, according to teacher preference and teacher availability. Faculty is not informed of a student's teacher preference at the time of the audition. *May a student change major teachers during the course of study?* possibly. *Study of secondary instrument or discipline is allowed.*

Selectivity for instruments or programs offered (rating): bassoon (highly selective), choral conducting (selective), choral singing (open), clarinet (selective), composition (competitive), double bass (competitive), flute or piccolo (selective), French horn (highly selective), guitar (selective), harp (competitive), harpsichord (competitive), oboe/English horn (highly selective), orchestral conducting (highly selective), organ (competitive), percussion (selective), piano (competitive), sacred music (competitive), saxophone (competitive), trombone (highly selective), trumpet (selective), tuba (highly selective), viola (selective), violin (selective), violoncello (selective), voice (highly selective).

Total enrollment: 350. *Entering class size:* 55. *Graduating class size:* 50.

Total full-time faculty: 24. *Total part-time faculty:* 50. *Program contact person:* Tom Booth.

Audition Information

Audition consists of the following: orchestral excerpts, music theory, sight reading. *Instruments provided for:* harpists, percussionists.

Performance opportunities available (frequency): band (every week), chamber music (2 per semester), jury examinations (1 per semester), recitals (2), produced operas (1 per year), chorus (every week).

Facilities

Number of practice rooms and hours: 45. *Recital hall?* yes. *Concert hall?* yes. *Recording studio?* yes.

SOUTHWEST TEXAS STATE UNIVERSITY

601 University, San Marcos TX 78666
Tel: 512-245-2111
Fax: 512-245-8044
Email: admissions@swt.edu
Web: www.swt.edu

General

Type of Institution: public, university. *Environment:* urban.

Total enrollment of institution: 20,702. *Total student body from other countries:* 1%. *Degrees offered:* certificate, BA, BFA, BM.

Entrance Requirements

Audition required: live. *Standardized test requirements:* ACT, 23; SAT I, 1050.

Costs & Financial Aid

Application fee: $25. *Medical fee:* $28. *Other fees:* $312 general, $139 student service, $50 student center, $29 bus, $72 computer, $6 student publication, $38 recreational sports, $24 library, $670 total, room ranges from $738 to $1,627.

Percent of students receiving financial aid: 49%. *Types of scholarships and aid awarded:* full, partial, merit-based, need-based, named, institutional aid. *Forms required for scholarships:* FAFSA, income tax return, income asset verification. *Loans available. Financial aid offered to international students. Percent of international students receiving scholarships:* 11%. *Other aid available to international students:* grants, loans, employment; 49% receive financial aid of some nature.

Services

Housing options: on-site dorms, off-campus housing, fraternity, sorority.

Support staff: career counselor, financial aid advisor, foreign student advisor, housing advisor, physical therapist, psychological counselor, resident assistant, resident nurse, student affairs officer.

DANCE

Curriculum, Students, and Faculty

Required courses: ballet (2 classes per week, 1 year to complete), dance composition/choreography, dance history, dance theory, historical dance, Labanotation, modern dance (5 classes per week, 3 years to complete), music, nutrition, rehearsal and performance, stagecraft, Hawkins-based dance.

Elective courses: jazz, master classes.

Selectivity for males: most admitted, but not all. *Selectivity for females:* most admitted, but not all. *Total enrollment:* 100. *Entering class size:* 35.

Renowned alumni: Connie Webb Brown, Le Anne Stedmann, Vaness Dudney, Cherie Carson.

Total full-time faculty: 3. *Total part-time faculty:* 2. *Program contact person:* Joan Hays.

Audition Information

Accompanist not provided. Cassette player available; CD player available.

Repertoire that students should avoid? poor alignment.

Performance Information

Performance opportunities available (frequency): Fully produced concerts (3 per year), informal concerts (3 per year), workshops (2-3 per year), on-site performances (1-2 per year), touring.

Performances choreographed by: faculty, students, guests. *Recent guest choreographers:* Louis Kavouras.

Facilities

Number of studios available: 2. *Approximate studio dimensions and flooring:* 45' x 50' red oak. *Performance facilities:* 1 studio stage.

DRAMA

Curriculum, Students, and Faculty

Required courses: acting, Alexander technique, directing, drama criticism, movement, scene study, speech, text analysis, TV/film acting class, voice.

Elective courses: audition preparation, improvisation, make-up, martial arts, mime, musical theater, stage combat, Stanislavski exercises.

Number of years required to complete program: 4-4.5. *Summer program available. No affiliation with a professional theater company. Selectivity for males:* admit all who apply. *Selectivity for females:* admit all who apply. *Total enrollment:* 385. *Entering class size:* 62. *Percent international:* 1% *Countries most represented:* Mexico, Germany.

Renowned alumni: Powers Boothe, G.W. Baily, Thomas Carter, Chelcie Ross.

Total full-time faculty: 13. *Total part-time faculty:* 1. *List of current faculty and past affiliations:* Dr. Richard Sodders, LSU, NYU; Dr. Ed Simone.

Audition Information

Audition consists of the following: comedic monologue, Shakespearean monologue. Auditions are not required for program admission but for productions. *Audition evaluation criteria:* director's notes.

Performance Information

Performance opportunities available (frequency): fully produced performances (5 per year), informal performances (50-60 per year), workshops (2-3 per year), off-site performances (1 per year), auditioned.

Recent guest artists: G.W. Bailey, Bill Cobbs, Loretta Devine.

Facilities

Rehearsal facilities and hours: 350 seat modified proscenium university theater, 6:00 pm-11:00 pm. *Number of theaters on campus:* 2. *Type and capacity:* studio 100, proscenium 350.

MUSIC

Curriculum, Students, and Faculty

Unique or innovative music curriculum: We have an award-winning jazz and sound recording technology program. *How are major teacher assignments made?* students may choose according to teacher preference and teacher availability. Faculty is informed of a student's teacher preference at the time of the audition. *May a student change major teachers during the course of study?* possibly.

Selectivity for instruments or programs offered (rating): accompanying (non-competitive), bassoon (non-competitive), choral conducting (non-competitive), choral singing (open), clarinet (non-competitive), composition (competitive), double bass (non-competitive), electronic music (non-competitive), flute or piccolo (competitive), French horn (non-competitive), guitar (non-competitive), harpsichord (non-competitive), jazz (competitive), oboe/English horn (non-competitive), orchestral conducting (non-competitive), organ (non-competitive), percussion (competitive), piano (non-competitive), saxophone (competitive), trombone (non-competitive), trumpet (competitive), tuba (non-competitive), viola (non-competitive), violin (non-competitive), violoncello (non-competitive), voice (competitive).

Total enrollment: 450. *Entering class size:* 150. *Percent international:* 1%. *Countries most represented:* Hong Kong, Mexico.

Renowned alumni: Janet Ellis, Vernon Hartman, Don Boomgaarden.

Total full-time faculty: 33. *Total part-time faculty:* 15. *Program contact person:* Kathy Hunt.

Audition Information

Audition consists of the following: music theory. *Instruments provided for:* percussionists, some instruments are available for lease.

Required repertoire: prepared repertoire varies by area. *Performance opportunities available (frequency):* band (frequently), jury examinations (frequently), orchestral concerts (frequently), recitals (frequently), touring (frequently), chorus.

Facilities

Recital hall? yes. *Concert hall?* yes. *Recording studio?* yes.

Comments

The SWT Music Department has grown steadily over the past several years (from 270 enrolled in 1994 to nearly 500 this year). In order to maintain professor-only studio lessons, we are implementing an admission by audition policy. Auditioning in a timely manner is, therefore, very important. International exchange and touring programs are in place with England, Poland, Russia as well as other countries. The SRT and Jazz programs have won numerous Downbeat awards.

TEXAS CHRISTIAN UNIVERSITY

College of Fine Arts and Communication
P.O. Box 298000, Fort Worth TX 76129
Tel: 817-921-7601
Fax: 817-921-7703
Email: frogmail@tcu.edu
Web: www.tcu.edu

General

Type of Institution: private university. *Environment:* urban.

Total enrollment of institution: 7,273. *Total student body from other countries:* 5%. *Degrees offered:* certificate, BA, BFA, BM, artist diploma.

Entrance Requirements

Audition required: live. *Standardized test requirements:* ACT, 25; SAT I, 1190; TOEFL, 550.

Costs & Financial Aid

Application fee: $30. *Medical fee:* $292. *Other fees:* $595. *Tuition and fees:* $10,400. *Room and board:* $4,000.

Types of scholarships and aid awarded: full, partial, merit-based, need-based, named, institutional aid, government aid, reduced tuition, tuition payment plan, work/study. *Forms required for scholarships:* FAFSA. *Loans available. Procedure for applying for loans:* submit FAFSA. *Financial aid offered to international students. Percent of international students receiving scholarships:* 25%. *Other aid available to international students:* loans (with U.S. co-signer), grants, athletic aid, small institutional loans.

Services

Housing options: on-site dorms, fraternity, sorority.

Support staff: career counselor, financial aid advisor, foreign student advisor, housing advisor, psychological counselor, resident assistant, resident nurse, student affairs officer.

DANCE

Curriculum, Students, and Faculty

Required courses: anatomy, character, ballet (5 classes per week, 4 years to complete), dance composition/choreography, dance history, dance theory, jazz, modern dance (5 classes per week, 4 years to complete), movement techniques, music, other world dance forms, pas de deux (5 classes per week, 4 years to complete), pointe, rehearsal and performance, repertory, stagecraft, variations (5 classes per week, 4 years to complete).

Selectivity for males: most admitted, but not all. *Selectivity for females:* approximately 33% admitted. *Total enrollment:* 61.

Renowned alumni: Caryn Heilman, Paul Taylor Company; General Hambrick, Broadway (Cats, Miss Saigon)

Total full-time faculty: 5. *Total part-time faculty:* 2. *Program contact person:* Ellen Garrison.

Audition Information

No audition fee. Audition consists of the following: ballet, modern dance, pointe works. *Accompanist provided. Dress requirements for males:* leotard or t-shirt, tights, barefoot for modern. *Dress requirements for females:* pink tights, solid color leotard for ballet, bare feet for modern.

Audition evaluation criteria: technical skills, performance skills, potential.

Performance Information

Performance opportunities available (frequency): Fully produced concerts (2-4 per year), informal concerts (4-6 annually), workshops (2-3 annually), on-site performances (6-8 annually), touring (1-2 annually).

Performances choreographed by: faculty, students, guests. *Recent guest choreographers:* Fernando Bijoms, Sunny Savoy, Yunya Wang.

Facilities

Number of studios available: 3. *Approximate studio dimensions and flooring:* 40' x 80' spring floors with linoleum. *Performance facilities:* 1,200-seat proscenium theater, 250-seat proscenium theater, 200 black box "Flex" theater.

DRAMA

Curriculum, Students, and Faculty

Required courses: acting, directing, make-up, text analysis.

Elective courses: audition preparation, drama criticism, martial arts, movement, musical theater, scene study, stage combat, Stanislavski exercises, verse drama, voice.

Number of years required to complete program: 4. *Summer program not available. Affiliation with a professional theater company: internship for students with Casa Manana, Stage West, Circle Theater, Fort Worth.*

Selectivity for males: approximately 33% admitted. *Selectivity for females:* approximately 33% admitted. *Total enrollment:* 77.

Renowned alumni: Betty Buckley, Gayle Hunicutt, Frederick Forrest.

Total full-time faculty: 4. *Total part-time faculty:* 4. *List of current faculty and past affiliations:* Margaret Loft.

Audition Information

No audition fee. Audition consists of the following: comedic monologue.

Performance Information

Performance opportunities available (frequency): fully produced performances (4-6 annually), informal performances (12-16 annually), auditioned.

Recent guest artists: Russian State Theater Kaleso.

Facilities

Number of theaters on campus: 3. *Type and capacity:* proscenium 1,200, proscenium 220, thrust 240.

MUSIC

Curriculum, Students, and Faculty

Unique or innovative music curriculum: Piano-artist diploma and undergraduate performer's certificate. *How are major teacher assignments made?* Students may choose according to teacher availability. Faculty is informed of a student's teacher preference at the time of the audition. *May a student change major teachers during the course of study?* possibly. *Study of secondary instrument or discipline is allowed.*

Selectivity for instruments or programs offered (rating): accompanying (selective), bassoon (selective), choral conducting (selective), choral singing (highly selective), clarinet (selective), composition (selective), double bass (selective), electronic music (selective), flute or piccolo (selective), French horn (selective), guitar (selective), harp (competitive), harpsichord (selective), jazz (competitive), oboe/English horn (selective), orchestral conducting (selective), organ (selective), percussion (selective), piano (highly selective), sacred music (selective), saxophone (selective), trombone (selective), trumpet (selective), tuba (selective), viola (selective), violin (selective), violoncello (selective), voice (selective).

Total enrollment: 191.

Renowned alumni: John Giordano, Betty Buckley.

Total full-time faculty: 24. *Total part-time faculty:* 26. *Program contact person:* Dr. Kenneth Raessler.

Audition Information

No audition fee. Audition consists of the following: scales, orchestral excerpts, arpeggios, sight reading. *Instruments provided for:* percussionists.

Repertoire that students should avoid? no. *Performance opportunities available (frequency):* band (frequently), chamber music (frequently), jury examinations (frequently), orchestral concerts (frequently), recitals (frequently), touring (frequently), chorus.

Facilities

Number of practice rooms and hours: 25; 7:00 am-2:00 am. *Recital hall?* yes. *Concert hall?* yes. *Recording studio?* yes.

TEXAS WOMAN'S UNIVERSITY

304 Administration Drive
Clock Tower, Denton TX 76201
Tel: 940-898-2000
Web: www.twu.edu

General

Type of Institution: all women, university. *Environment:* urban.

Total enrollment of institution: 10,000. *Degrees offered:* BA.

Entrance Requirements

Audition required: live, video. *Other requirements:* interview. *Standardized test requirements:* ACT; SAT I; TOEFL, 550.

Costs & Financial Aid

Application fee: $25. *Medical fee:* $25.

Percent of students receiving financial aid: 45%. *Types of scholarships and aid awarded:* partial, merit-based, need-based, named, institutional aid, government aid, reduced tuition, tuition payment plan, work/study. *Financial aid offered to international students. Other aid available to international students:* tuition waivers, departmental scholarships. Percent of students receiving scholarships varies from department to department.

Services

Housing options: on-site dorms, off-campus housing.

Support staff: career counselor, financial aid advisor, foreign student advisor, housing advisor, physical therapist, psychological counselor, resident assistant, resident nurse, student affairs officer.

DANCE

Curriculum, Students, and Faculty

Required courses: anatomy, ballet (2 classes per week, 4 years to complete), dance composition/choreography, dance history, dance theory, dance writing research and criticism, jazz (2 classes per week, 1 year to complete), Labanotation, master classes, modern dance (3 classes per week, 4 years to complete), music, nutrition, rehearsal and performance, repertory (2 classes per week), tap (2 classes per week, 1 year to complete).

Elective courses: African dance, historical dance, other world dance forms, Spanish, vernacular dance.

Selectivity for males: admit all who apply. *Selectivity for females:* admit all who apply. *Total enrollment:* 90. *Entering class size:* 25. *Graduating class size:* 12. *Percent international:* 5%. *Countries most represented:* Asian countries.

Total full-time faculty: 8. *Total part-time faculty:* 11. *List of current faculty and past affiliations:* Mary Wilford, Mark Taylor and Friends; Penelope Hanstein, National Dance Association Scholar of the Year; Gladys Keeton, Texas Higher Education Dance Educator of the Year 1996; Adrienne Fisk, American College Theatre Festival Award-Winning Choreographer; Janice La Pointe-Grump, Dance Scholar. *Contact:* (940) 898-2085.

Audition Information*Faculty is informed of a student's teacher preference at the time of the audition.*

No audition fee. Audition consists of the following: improvisation, modern dance, interviews. *Accompanist provided. Cassette player available; CD player available.*

Repertoire that students should avoid? no.

Audition evaluation criteria: potential for artistic and academic success.

Performance Information

Performance opportunities available (frequency): Fully produced concerts (1-2 per semester), informal concerts (2-3 per semester), workshops (1-5 per year), on-site performances (1-2 per year), touring (several per year), also participation in ACDA.

Performances choreographed by: faculty, students, guests. *Recent guest choreographers:* Claire Porter, Sean Curran, Michael Foley, Art Bridgman, Myrna Packer, Kariamu Welsh-Asante, Bebe Miller, Steve Koester, David Dorfman, Oakland Ballet, Mark Taylor.

Facilities

Number of studios available: 4. *Approximate studio dimensions and flooring:* 40' x 60' L'Air Pneumatic Flooring. *Performance facilities:* 1150-seat theater with current technology, 330-seat theater, studio theater setting.

DRAMA

Curriculum, Students, and Faculty

Required courses: acting, directing, make-up, movement, Stanislavski exercises.

Elective courses: audition preparation, improvisation, musical theater, scene study, speech, text analysis, verse drama, voice.

Number of years required to complete program: 4 years with 1 summer session. *Summer program available. No affiliation with a professional theater company. Selectivity for males:* most admitted, but not all. *Selectivity for females:* most admitted, but not all. *Total enrollment:* 50. *Percent international:* 2%.

Total full-time faculty: 4. *Total part-time faculty:* 2. *List of current faculty and past affiliations:* Rhonda Weller-Stilson, Oklahoma Shakespearean Festival, Alabama Shakespearean Festival, Dr. Mary Lou Hoyle, Trinity University, Charles Harrill.

Audition Information

No audition fee. Audition consists of the following: comedic monologue, 2 contrasting pieces, one may be musical (accompanist will be provided); personal interview. *Dress requirements for males:* professional attire. *Dress requirements for females:* professional attire. *Repertoire that students should avoid?* no.

Performance Information

Performance opportunities available (frequency): fully produced performances (6 per year), informal performances (2 per year), auditioned. All roles filled by open auditions.

Facilities

Rehearsal facilities and hours: proscenium theaters, two classroom spaces, 8:00 am-10:00 pm. *Number of theaters on campus:* 2. *Type and capacity:* proscenium 1,200, proscenium 332.

MUSIC

Curriculum, Students, and Faculty

Unique or innovative music curriculum: Music Therapy emphasis, BS. *How are major teacher assignments made?* according to teacher availability. Faculty is informed of a student's teacher preference at the time of the audition. 28 *lessons with major teacher. May a student change major teachers during the course of study?* possibly. *Study of secondary instrument or discipline is allowed.*

Selectivity for instruments or programs offered (rating): clarinet (non-competitive), French horn (non-competitive), guitar (non-competitive), organ (non-competitive), piano (non-competitive), saxophone (non-competitive), trombone (non-competitive), trumpet (non-competitive), voice (competitive).

Total enrollment: 120. *Percent international:* 8%.

Renowned alumni: Emily Crocker, Cheryl Allison, Robert Caldwell.

Total full-time faculty: 12. *Contact:* 940-898-2509.

Audition Information

No audition fee. Audition consists of the following: music theory, repertoire. *Instruments provided for:* harpists, percussionists.

Repertoire that students should avoid? no. *Performance opportunities available (frequency):* band (frequently), chamber music (frequently), jury examinations (frequently), recitals (weekly), touring (annually).

Facilities

Number of practice rooms and hours: 11; 7:00 am-10:00 pm. *Recital hall?* yes. *Concert hall?* yes.

Comments

The music program highlights programs in music therapy, vocal performance, and piano pedagogy. The integrated music/drama/dance opportunities provide unique options for music theatre and cross-discipline studies.

TRINITY UNIVERSITY

715 Stadium Drive, San Antonio TX 78212
Web: www.trinity.edu

General

Type of Institution: university. *Environment:* urban.

Total enrollment of institution: 2,400. *Degrees offered:* BA, BM.

Entrance Requirements

Audition required: live, audio, video. *Standardized test requirements:* ACT; SAT I.

Costs & Financial Aid

Application fee: $25. *Tuition:* $13,000. *Room and board:* $5,965.

Percent of students receiving financial aid: 75%. *Types of scholarships and aid awarded:* full, partial, merit-based, need-based, named, institutional aid. *Forms required for scholarships:* FAFSA, income tax return.

Services

Housing options: on-site dorms, off-campus housing.

Support staff: career counselor, financial aid advisor, foreign student advisor, housing advisor, psychological counselor, resident assistant, resident nurse, student affairs officer.

MUSIC

Curriculum, Students, and Faculty

How are major teacher assignments made? according to teacher availability. Faculty is informed of a student's teacher preference at the time of the audition. *30 lessons with major teacher. May a student change major teachers during the course of study?* possibly. *Study of secondary instrument or discipline is allowed.*

Selectivity for instruments or programs offered (rating): accompanying (selective), bassoon (selective), choral singing (competitive), clarinet (selective), composition (selective), double bass (selective), electronic music (selective), flute or piccolo (selective), French horn (selective), guitar (competitive), harp (selective), harpsichord (selective), oboe/English horn (selective), organ (selective), percussion (selective), piano (selective), saxophone (selective), trombone (selective), trumpet (selective), tuba (selective), viola (selective), violin (selective), violoncello (selective), voice (selective).

Total enrollment: 250.

Total full-time faculty: 10. *Total part-time faculty:* 16. *Program contact person:* Ken Greene.

Audition Information

No audition fee. Audition consists of the following: scales, orchestral excerpts, arpeggios, sight reading. *Instruments provided for:* harpists, percussionists, tuba, bass.

Performance opportunities available (frequency): jury examinations.

Facilities

Number of practice rooms and hours: 18; 7:00 am-12:00 am. *Recital hall?* yes. *Concert hall?* yes. *Recording studio?* no.

UNIVERSITY OF NORTH TEXAS COLLEGE OF MUSIC

P.O. Box 311367, Denton TX 76203-1367
Tel: 940-565-2791
Fax: 940-565-2002
Email: May@music.unt.edu
Web: www.music.unt.edu

General

Type of Institution: public, university. *Environment:* suburban. *Total enrollment of institution:* 26,000. *Total student body from other countries:* 11%. *Degrees offered:* certificate, BA, BM.

Entrance Requirements

Audition required: live, audio, video. *Other requirements:* recommendation. *Standardized test requirements:* ACT; SAT I; SAT II; TOEFL, 550.

Costs & Financial Aid

Application fee: $25. *Deposit:* $100. *Tuition (in-state/out-state):* $1,800/$9,000. *Medical fee:* $25. *Other fees:* $1,500, variety of special services.

Percent of students receiving financial aid: 30%. *Types of scholarships and aid awarded:* full, partial, merit-based, named, institutional aid, government aid, work/study, gig office. *Loans available. Procedure for applying for loans:* contact Cindy Andrews, College of Music. *Financial aid offered to international students. Other aid available to international students:* work/study; grants.

Services

Housing options: on-site dorms, off-campus housing, fraternity, sorority, family.

Support staff: career counselor, financial aid advisor, foreign student advisor, housing advisor, physical therapist, psychological counselor, resident assistant, resident nurse, student affairs officer.

MUSIC

Curriculum, Students, and Faculty

Unique or innovative music curriculum: leading program in Jazz Studies (*U.S. News and World Report*) and in percussion. *How are major teacher assignments made?* students may choose, made by the school according to teacher preference and teacher availability. Faculty is informed of a student's teacher preference at the time of the audition. *32 lessons with major teacher. May a student change major teachers during the course of study?* possibly. *Study of secondary instrument or discipline is allowed.*

Selectivity for instruments or programs offered (rating): accompanying (selective), bassoon (selective), choral conducting (highly selective), choral singing (competitive), clarinet (selective), composition (selective), double bass (selective), electronic music (selective), flute or piccolo (selective), French horn (selective), guitar (highly selective), harp (selective), harpsichord (selective), jazz (highly selective), oboe/English horn (selective), orchestral conducting (highly selective), organ (selective), percussion (highly selective), piano (selective), saxophone (selective), trombone (selective), trumpet (selective), tuba (selective), viola (selective), violin (selective), violoncello (selective), voice (selective).

Total enrollment: 1,400. *Entering class size:* 300. *Graduating class size:* 195. *Percent international:* 18%. *Countries most represented:* Mexico, Canada, Taiwan.

Renowned alumni: Lou Marini, Herb Ellis, Pat Racette, Tim Jenkins.

Total full-time faculty: 90. *Total part-time faculty:* 120. *Program contact person:* William V. May.

Audition Information

No audition fee. Audition consists of the following: scales, music theory, arpeggios, sight reading, repertoire. *Instruments provided for:* harpists, percussionists

Required repertoire: requirements differ with instrument. *Performance opportunities available (frequency):* jury examinations.

Facilities

Number of practice rooms and hours: 300; 24 hours a day. *Recital hall?* yes. *Concert hall?* yes. *Recording studio?* yes.

UNIVERSITY OF TEXAS, AUSTIN

College of Fine Arts, Austin TX 78712
Tel: 512-471-7764, 512-471-5793 (music)
Fax: 512-471-2333, 512-471-0824 (music)
Email: utmusic@www.utexas.edu, svasquez@mail.utexas.edu
Web: www.utexas.edu
Contact: Karen Payne

General

Type of Institution: public, university. *Environment:* urban.

Total enrollment of institution: 48,000. *Degrees offered:* BA, BFA.

Entrance Requirements

Audition required: live, audio, video. *Other requirements:* recommendation, essay *Standardized test requirements:* ACT; SAT I; TOEFL.

Costs & Financial Aid

Application fee: $40. *Deposit:* $200. *Tuition (in-state/out-of-state:* $2,842/$10,032. *Other fees:* $1,878 personal fees, $720 transportation fees, $670 books. *Room and board:* $3,051.

Percent of students receiving financial aid: 60%. *Types of scholarships and aid awarded:* full, partial, merit-based, need-based, named, institutional aid, government aid, reduced tuition, tuition payment plan, work/study, gig office. *Forms required for scholarships:* FFS, FAFSA. *Loans available. Procedure for applying for loans:* complete FAFSA and send to Federal processor *Financial aid offered to international students. Other aid available to international students:* some grants and loan programs are available to international students on a limited basis.

Services

Housing options: on-site dorms, off-campus housing, fraternity, sorority, family.

Support staff: career counselor, dorm parent, financial aid advisor, foreign student advisor, housing advisor, physical therapist, psychological counselor, resident assistant, resident nurse, student affairs officer.

DANCE

Curriculum, Students, and Faculty

Required courses: ballet (3 classes per week, 4 years to complete), dance composition/choreography, dance history, dance writing research and criticism, modern dance (5 classes per week, 4 years to complete), Cunningham-based (5 classes per week, 4 years to complete), Horton-based dance (5 classes per week, 4 years to complete), Limon-based (5 classes per week, 4 years to complete), rehearsal and performance, repertory.

Elective courses: anatomy, dance theory, historical dance, jazz, master classes, movement techniques, Laban Movement Studies, music, nutrition, other world dance forms, Spanish, stagecraft, tap.

Selectivity for males: approximately 60% admitted. *Selectivity for females:* approximately 60% admitted. *Total enrollment:* 60. *Entering class size:* 20. *Graduating class size:* 5.

Renowned alumni: Richard Gonzales, Toni Bravo, Jose Bustamente, Charles Santos.

Total full-time faculty: 7. *Total part-time faculty:* 4. *List of current faculty and past affiliations:* Yacov Sharir, Sondra Lomax, Andrea Beckham, Jeffery Bullock, Lyn Elam, Holly Williams, Mark Morris, Sharon Vasquez. *Program contact person:* Holly Williams.

Audition Information

No audition fee. Audition consists of the following: ballet, improvisation, modern dance, dance scholarships are available. *Accompanist provided. Cassette player available; CD player available.*

Dress requirements for males: standard dance attire. *Dress requirements for females:* standard dance attire.

Repertoire that students should avoid? no.

Audition evaluation criteria: student is reviewed by entire dance faculty and ranked by number.

Performance Information

Performance opportunities available (frequency): Fully produced concerts (1 per year), informal concerts (1 per semester), workshops (frequently), on-site performances (occasionally), touring (some).

Performances choreographed by: faculty, students, guests. *Recent guest choreographers:* Jose Bustamante, Kraig Patterson, Mark Morris.

Facilities

Number of studios available: 5. *Approximate studio dimensions and flooring:* 40' x 30' Marley. *Performance facilities:* several.

DRAMA

Curriculum, Students, and Faculty

Elective courses: acting, Alexander technique, directing, drama criticism, dramaturgy, improvisation, make-up, movement, scene study, speech, stage combat, text analysis, verse drama, voice.

Number of years required to complete program: 4. ***Summer program available. Affiliation with a professional theater company: there are affiliations with the Alley Theater and Texas Under The Stars. Both theaters are in Houston, Texas.***

Total enrollment: 320. *Entering class size:* 130. *Graduating class size:* 30.

Renowned alumni: Robert Schenklan, Tommy Tune, Pat Hingle, Marcia Gay Harden, Barbara Barrie, Tom Jones, Amanda McBroom, and Zachary Scott.

Total full-time faculty: 24. *Total part-time faculty:* 10.

Performance Information

Performance opportunities available (frequency): fully produced performances (6-8 per year), informal performances (10-15 per year), workshops (1-5 per semester) assigned, auditioned.

Recent guest artists: Mabou Mines.

Facilities

Rehearsal facilities and hours: most rehearsals occur in the Winship Drama Building which includes a 500-seat proscenium theater and a 200-seat black box space. We also use a smaller proscenium space called the Lab Theater. Other rehearsal spaces are available in the building. *Type and capacity:* 3,000, 500, 200, 125, 420.

MUSIC

Curriculum, Students, and Faculty

How are major teacher assignments made? Students may choose. Faculty is informed of a student's teacher preference at the time of the audition. ***50 lessons with major teacher. Study of secondary instrument or discipline is allowed.***

Selectivity for instruments or programs offered (rating): accompanying (selective), accordion (selective), bassoon (selective), choral conducting (highly selective), choral singing (highly selective), clarinet (highly selective), composition (highly selective), double bass (selective), electronic music (highly selective), flute or piccolo (highly selective), French horn (selective), guitar (highly selective), harp (selective), harpsichord (selective), jazz (highly selective), oboe/English horn (selective), orchestral conducting (highly selective), organ (selective), percussion (highly selective), piano (highly selective), sacred music (selective), saxophone (highly selective), trombone (highly selective), trumpet (highly selective), tuba (selective), viola (selective), violin (highly selective), violoncello (highly selective), voice (highly selective).

Total enrollment: 725. *Entering class size:* 100. *Graduating class size:* 65. *Percent international:* 1%.

Renowned alumni: Barbara Conrad; Lewis Lane; Carl St. Clair.

Total full-time faculty: 70. *Total part-time faculty:* 14. *Program contact person:* Matt Orem.

Audition Information

No audition fee. Instruments provided for: harpists, percussionists.

Performance opportunities available (frequency): band, jury examinations, chorus.

Facilities

Recital hall? yes. *Concert hall?* yes. *Recording studio?* yes.

UTAH

BRIGHAM YOUNG UNIVERSITY

P.O. Box 26410
C550 HFAC, Provo UT 84602
Tel: 801-378-3083
Fax: 801-378-5973
Email: musicrec@byugate.byu.edu
Web: www.byu.edu/music

General

Type of Institution: university. *Religious Affiliation:* Church of Jesus Christ of Latter Day Saints. *Environment:* urban.

Total enrollment of institution: 31,249. *Total student body from other countries:* 6%. *Degrees offered:* BA, BFA, BM.

Entrance Requirements

Audition required: live, video. *Other requirements:* recommendation.

Costs & Financial Aid

Application fee: $25. *Medical fee:* $118. *Other fees:* $182 married students insurance. *Tuition:* $1,765. *Room and board:* $2,065.

Percent of students receiving financial aid: 67%. *Types of scholarships and aid awarded:* full, partial, merit-based, need-based, named, government aid, reduced tuition, tuition payment plan, work/study. *Forms required for scholarships:* FAFSA, income tax return. *Loans available. Procedure for applying for loans:* fill out FAFSA and talk to financial aid officer. *Financial aid offered to international students. Other aid available to international students:* sponsors, money from their government.

Services

Housing options: on-site dorms, off-campus housing, family.

Support staff: career counselor, financial aid advisor, foreign student advisor, housing advisor, physical therapist, psychological counselor, resident assistant, resident nurse, student affairs officer.

MUSIC

Curriculum, Students, and Faculty

How are major teacher assignments made? students may choose according to teacher preference according to teacher availability. Faculty is informed of a student's teacher preference at the time of the audition. *24 lessons with major teacher. May a student change major teachers during the course of study?* possibly. *Study of secondary instrument or discipline is allowed.*

Selectivity for instruments or programs offered (rating): bassoon (non-competitive), clarinet (competitive), composition (selective), double bass (competitive), flute or piccolo (highly selective), French horn (competitive), guitar (competitive), harp (competitive), oboe/English horn (competitive), organ (competitive), percussion (competitive), piano (selective), saxophone (competitive), trombone (competitive), trumpet (competitive), tuba (competitive), viola (selective), violin (selective), violoncello (competitive), voice (highly selective).

Total enrollment: 673. *Entering class size:* 227. *Graduating class size:* 112. *Percent international:* 6%. *Countries most represented:* Canada.

Renowned alumni: Kurt Bestor, Lawrence Vincent, Mack Wilberg, Ariel Bybee, Sam Cardon, James Thatcher

Total full-time faculty: 48. *Total part-time faculty:* 38. *Program contact person:* Walt Birkedahl, (801) 378-3294

Audition Information

No audition fee. Audition consists of the following: scales, music theory, arpeggios. *Instruments provided for:* harpists, percussionists.

Repertoire that students should avoid? no.

Facilities

Number of practice rooms and hours: 46; 6:00 am-11:00 pm. *Recital hall?* yes. *Concert hall?* yes. *Recording studio?* yes.

UNIVERSITY OF UTAH, DEPARTMENT OF BALLET

300 South 1500 East
Room 110, Salt Lake City UT 84112-0280
Tel: 801-581-8231
Fax: 801-581-5442
Email: B.Hamblin@m.cc.utah.edu
Web: www.dance.utah.edu

General

Type of Institution: public, university. *Environment:* urban. *Academic education is offered on-site.*

Total enrollment of institution: 25,000. *Degrees offered:* certificate, BA, BFA, BM.

Entrance Requirements

Audition required: live, video. *Other requirements:* photograph. *Standardized test requirements:* ACT; SAT I; TOEFL, 500.

Costs & Financial Aid

Application fee: $30. *Tuition (in-state/out-state):* $2,500/$7,500. *Other fees:* $45 optional linen fee, computer fees assessed by credit hours total.

Percent of students receiving financial aid: 60%. *Types of scholarships and aid awarded:* full, partial, merit-based, need-based, named, institutional aid, government aid, reduced tuition, work/study. *Forms required for scholarships:* FAFSA. *Loans available. Procedure for applying for loans:* contact Financial Aid and Scholarships Office (801-581-6211). *Percent of international students receiving scholarships:* 50%.

Services

Housing options: on-site dorms, off-campus housing, fraternity, sorority, family.

Support staff: career counselor, financial aid advisor, foreign student advisor, housing advisor, psychological counselor, resident assistant, resident nurse, student affairs officer.

Comments

Numerous graduates placed in higher education.

DANCE

Curriculum, Students, and Faculty

Required courses: anatomy, character (2 classes per week, 1 year to complete), ballet (5 classes per week, 4 years to complete), dance composition/choreography (1 year to complete), dance history, dance writing research and criticism, jazz (2 classes per week, 1 year to complete), men's class (2 classes per week, 4 years to complete), Graham-based dance (3 classes per week, 1 year to complete), music, pas de deux (1-2 classes per week, 1-2 years to complete), pointe (3 classes per week, 4 years to complete), repertory, Spanish, variations, injury prevention, modern dance, body conditioning, Pilates.

Elective courses: body conditioning, Laban Movement Studies, rehearsal and performance.

Selectivity for males: most admitted, but not all. *Selectivity for females:* approximately 60% admitted. *Total enrollment:* 200. *Entering class size:* 45. *Percent international:* 5%. *Countries most represented:* Canada, Mexico, China.

Total full-time faculty: 6. *Total part-time faculty:* 6. *List of current faculty and past affiliations:* Bene Arnold, San Francisco Ballet, Mistress for Ballet West; Attila Ficzere, Royal Winnipeg, San Francisco Ballet; Conrad Ludlow, New York City Ballet, San Francisco Ballet; Barbara Hamblin, Ballet West. *Program contact person:* Valerie Horton. Modern: Scott Marsh.

Audition Information

No audition fee. Audition consists of the following: ballet, pointe works, modern. Videotape for international. *Accompanist provided. Dress requirements for males:* white t-shirt, black tights, black or white shoes. *Dress requirements for females:* pink tights and shoes, black leotard (choice of style). Barefoot for modern.

Repertoire that students should avoid? no.

Audition evaluation criteria: body type, proportions; suppleness of joints in feet, hips, back; strength in torso, legs, feet (arms for males).

Performance Information

Performance opportunities available (frequency): Fully produced concerts (5 per year), informal concerts (1-2 per year), workshops (every summer), on-site performances (10-15), touring (2-3 per year).

Performances choreographed by: faculty, students, guests. *Recent guest choreographers:* Violette Verdy, Derryl Yeager, Victoria Morgan, Mark Lanham, Jacques d'Amboise.

Facilities

Number of studios available: 3. *Approximate studio dimensions and flooring:* 40' x 60' Harlequin over oak with basket weave foundation, 40' x 70' Harlequin over oak with basket weave foundation. *Performance facilities:* The Alice Sheets Marriott Center for Dance has a 310-seat theater. Performances also take place in Kingsbury Hall, seats 2,000.

VERMONT

BENNINGTON COLLEGE

Bennington VT 05201
Tel: 800-833-6845
Fax: 802-440-4320
Email: admissions@bennington.edu
Web: www.bennington.edu
Contact: John Caron

General

Type of Institution: private college.

Total enrollment of institution: 500. *Total student body from other countries:* 17%. *Degrees offered:* BA.

Entrance Requirements

Audition not required. Other requirements: interview, recommendation, essay. *Standardized test requirements:* ACT; SAT I; TOEFL, 550.

Costs & Financial Aid

Application fee: $45. *Deposit:* $400. *Tuition and Fees:* $26,100.

Types of scholarships and aid awarded: merit-based, need-based, work/study. *Forms required for scholarships:* FAFSA, income tax return. *Loans available. Procedure for applying for loans:* financial aid form. *Financial aid offered to international students.*

Services

Housing options: on-site dorms.

Support staff: career counselor, financial aid advisor, foreign student advisor, housing advisor, psychological counselor, resident assistant, resident nurse, student affairs officer.

Comments

Faculty: Allen Shawn, Tobias Picker, Milyord Graves, Charles Gate, Ida Faiella.

DANCE

Curriculum, Students, and Faculty

Elective courses: African dance, anatomy, dance composition/choreography, dance history, dance writing research and criticism, modern dance, movement techniques, rehearsal and performance.

DRAMA

Curriculum, Students, and Faculty

Elective courses: acting, directing, drama criticism, movement, musical theater, voice.

MUSIC

Comprehensive curriculum.

MIDDLEBURY COLLEGE

The Emma Willard House, Middlebury VT 05753-6002
Tel: 802-443-3000
Fax: 802-443-2056
Email: admissions@middlebury.edu
Web: www.middlebury.edu

General

Degrees offered: BA.

Entrance Requirements

Audition not required.

Costs & Financial Aid

Loans available. Tuition and fees: $29,740.

DANCE

Curriculum, Students, and Faculty

Elective courses: jazz.

DRAMA

Curriculum, Students, and Faculty

Required courses: theater history.

MUSIC

Comprehensive curriculum. All performing arts in new state-of-the-art center.

VIRGINIA

COLLEGE OF WILLIAM & MARY

P.O. Box 8795, Williamsburg VA 23187-8795
Tel: 757-221-2660
Fax: 757-221-2507
Email: rxpalm@facstaff.wm.edu
Web: www.wm.edu

General

Type of Institution: public college. *Environment:* suburban.

Total enrollment of institution: 5,500. *Total student body from other countries:* 3%. *Degrees offered:* BA.

Entrance Requirements

Audition not required Other requirements: essay. *Standardized test requirements:* SAT I, 1200; TOEFL.

Costs & Financial Aid

Application fee: $40. *Deposit:* $350. Tuition *(in-state/out-of-state):* $5,106/$15,616. *Room and board:* $4,670.

Percent of students receiving financial aid: 35%. *Types of scholarships and aid awarded:* need-based, named, work/study. *Forms required for scholarships:* FAFSA, income tax return. *Loans available.*

Services

Housing options: on-site dorms, off-campus housing, fraternity, sorority.

Support staff: career counselor, financial aid advisor, foreign student advisor, housing advisor, physical therapist, psychological counselor, resident assistant, resident nurse, student affairs officer.

DANCE

Curriculum, Students, and Faculty

Elective courses: Alexander technique, ballet, dance composition/choreography, dance history, jazz, master classes, modern dance, Cunningham-based, Graham-based dance, Limon-based, rehearsal and performance.

Selectivity for males: admit all who apply. *Selectivity for females:* admit all who apply.

Renowned alumni: John Taylor, Diversions Dance Company; Cardift Wales; Kathryn Westwater, Gowanus Arts, NYC; Emily Crews; Deborah Wiley, Dance Projects and City Dance Ensemble, D.C.

Total full-time faculty: 3. *List of current faculty and past affiliations:* Joan Gavaler, The Moving Arts Company; Carol Wallace Sherman, Pauline Koner Company and Jeff Duncan Company (NYC). *Program contact person:* Carol Sherman.

Audition Information

No audition fee.

Performance Information

Performance opportunities available (frequency): Fully produced concerts (4 per semester), informal concerts (2 per semester, 3 perfomances).

Performances choreographed by: faculty, students.

Facilities

Number of studios available: 1. *Approximate studio dimensions and flooring:* 46' x 66' sprung wood (Northern kiln-dried maple). *Performance facilities:* lab theater in studio and large (750-seat) fully equipped college theater.

DRAMA

Curriculum, Students, and Faculty

Required courses: acting, directing, text analysis, drama criticism.

Elective courses: Alexander technique, audition preparation, drama criticism, improvisation, make-up, martial arts, scene study, speech, Stanislavski exercises, voice.

Number of years required to complete program: 4. *Summer program available. No affiliation with a professional theater company. Selectivity for males:* approximately 10% admitted. *Selectivity for females:* approximately 10% admitted. *Total enrollment:* 530.

Renowned alumni: Glenn Close, Linda Lavin, Scot Glen.

Total full-time faculty: 13.

Audition Information

No audition fee.

Performance Information

Performance opportunities available (frequency): fully produced performances (6 per year), informal performances (50 per year), workshops (6 per year), off-site performances (15 per year), casting is by audition.

Recent guest artists: Lois Weaver.

Facilities

Number of theaters on campus: 6. *Type and capacity:* proscenium 800, proscenium 300, proscenium 150, proscenium 100, black box 150, black box 100.

GEORGE MASON UNIVERSITY

Department of Music
MS 3E3, Fairfax VA 22030-4444
Tel: 703-993-1380
Fax: 703-993-4661
Email: jshirk1@osf1.gmu.edu
Web: www.admissions.gmu.edu
Contact: Patricia Riordan

General

Type of Institution: public university. *Environment:* suburban.

Total enrollment of institution: 26,000. *Degrees offered:* BA, BM, BME.

Entrance Requirements

Audition required: live, audio. *Standardized test requirements:* SAT I; TOEFL, 570.

Costs & Financial Aid

Application fee: $30. *Tuition (in-state/out-state):* $4,848/$12,952. *Medical fee:* $666. *Room and board:* $5,580.

Types of scholarships and aid awarded: partial, named, institutional aid, work/study. *Forms required for scholarships:* FAFSA, income tax return. *Loans available. Procedure for applying for loans:* fill out FAFSA and submit by deadline.

Services

Housing options: on-site dorms, off-campus housing.

Support staff: career counselor, financial aid advisor, foreign student advisor, housing advisor.

MUSIC

Curriculum, Students, and Faculty

Unique or innovative music curriculum: all students receive some training in the art of teaching music. Internship program. *How are major teacher assignments made?* Students may choose, made by the school. Faculty is informed of a student's teacher preference at the time of the audition. *28 lessons with major teacher. May a student change major teachers during the course of study?* possibly. *Study of secondary instrument or discipline is allowed.*

Selectivity for instruments or programs offered (rating): accompanying (selective), bassoon (competitive), choral conducting (selective), choral singing (competitive), clarinet (competitive), composition (selective), double bass (competitive), flute or piccolo (competitive), French horn (competitive), guitar (competitive), harp (competitive), harpsichord (competitive), oboe/English horn (competitive), orchestral conducting (highly selective), organ (competitive), percussion (competitive), piano (competitive), saxophone (competitive), trombone (competitive), trumpet (competitive), tuba (competitive), viola (competitive), violin (competitive), violoncello (competitive), voice (competitive).

Total enrollment: 210. *Entering class size:* 55. *Graduating class size:* 38.

Total full-time faculty: 12. *Total part-time faculty:* 50. *Program contact person:* Joseph Shirk.

Audition Information

No audition fee. Audition consists of the following: scales, sight reading. *Instruments provided for:* harpists, percussionists.

Performance opportunities available (frequency): band, jury examinations, orchestral concerts, recitals, chorus.

Facilities

Number of practice rooms and hours: 24; 24 hours a day. *Recital hall?* yes. *Concert hall?* yes. *Recording studio?* no.

HOLLINS COLLEGE

7916 Williamson Road
P.O. Box 9707, Roanoke VA 24020
Tel: 540-362-6401
Fax: 540-362-6218
Email: huadm@hollins.edu
Web: www.hollins.edu

General

Type of Institution: all women's college. *Environment:* suburban.

Total enrollment of institution: 867. *Total student body from other countries:* 3%. *Degrees offered:* BA.

Entrance Requirements

Audition not required. Other requirements: interview, recommendation, essay. *Standardized test requirements:* ACT, 24; SAT I, 1127; TOEFL, 550.

Costs & Financial Aid

Application fee: $25. *Deposit:* $400. *Tuition:* $15,600. *Other fees:* $250 student government fee. *Room and board:* $6,075.

Percent of students receiving financial aid: 58% *Types of scholarships and aid awarded:* partial, merit-based, need-based, named, institutional aid, government aid, tuition payment plan, work/study. *Forms required for scholarships:* FAFSA, income tax return. *Loans available. Procedure for applying for loans:* contact Financial Aid Office to request appliction forms, application must be completed by 2/15. *Financial aid offered to international students. Percent of international students receiving scholarships:* 67%. *Other aid available to international students:* work/study.

Services

Housing options: on-site dorms.

Support staff: career counselor, financial aid advisor, foreign student advisor, housing advisor, psychological counselor, resident assistant, resident nurse, student affairs officer.

Comments

In recent years Hollins graduates have been admitted to and have excelled in highly selective graduate programs as performers and scholars.

DANCE

Curriculum, Students, and Faculty

Required courses: Alexander Technique, dance composition/choreography, dance history, dance theory, dance writing research and criticism, historical dance, master classes, modern dance, body conditioning, music, nutrition, rehearsal and performance, repertory, stagecraft, internship.

Elective courses: African dance, anatomy, character, ballet, jazz, martial arts, Feldenkreis, Laban Movement Studies, movement techniques other, Pilates, other world dance forms, pointe, Spanish, tap, variations, modern dance partnering, BMC.

Selectivity for females: approximately 60% admitted.

Renowned alumna: Joan Mischo, assistant to the editor-in-chief of *Dance Magazine.*

Total full-time faculty: 1. *Total part-time faculty:* 6. *List of current faculty and past affiliations:* Donna Faye Burchfield, American Dance Festival; Shen Wei, performs with Martha Clark and former company member of Guongdong Modern Dance company of China. *Program contact person:* Donna Faye Burchfield.

Audition Information

No audition fee. Audition consists of the following: modern dance, tapes of choreographic work accepted but not required, evidence of other expressions of creativity such as writing and drawing helpful. *Accompanist provided. Cassette player available; CD player available.*

Repertoire that students should avoid? no.

Audition evaluation criteria: talent and desire.

Performance Information

Performance opportunities available (frequency): Fully produced concerts (6 evenings for 3 fully produced concerts), informal concerts (2-4), workshops (4-6), on-site performances (2-4), participation at American College Dance Festival as well as ADF/Duke University and New York City as well as Internat.

Performances choreographed by: faculty, students, guests. *Recent guest choreographers:* Mark Haim, Shen Wei, Doug Varone, Nathan Trice, Nicholas Leichter, Jack Arnold/Carol Parker, Lakey Evens, and Byron Suber, Gerri Houlihan and Dancers.

Facilities

Number of studios available: 3. *Approximate studio dimensions and flooring:* 27' x 50' professionally sprung wood supported flooring, 27' x 50' Marley covered supported floor. *Performance facilities:* Hollins Theater (seats 568).

DRAMA

Curriculum, Students, and Faculty

Required courses: acting, text analysis.

Elective courses: directing, make-up, movement, scene study, stage combat, verse drama.

Number of years required to complete program: 4. *Summer program not available. Affiliation with a professional theater company: Mill Mountain (LOA) Regional Internships.*

Selectivity for females: admit all who apply.

Total full-time faculty: 2 *Total part-time faculty:* 1. *List of current faculty and past affiliations:* David Dvorscak, Mill Moutain Theater; Allison Campbell, Paper Bag Players.

Performance Information

Performance opportunities available (frequency): fully produced performances (2 per year), informal performances (4 per year), workshops (2 per year), off-site performances (varies), auditioned.

Recent guest artists: Sean Bridges.

Facilities

Rehearsal facilities and hours: 1 rehearsal space, all hours. *Number of theaters on campus:* 1. *Type and capacity:* proscenium 568.

MUSIC

Curriculum, Students, and Faculty

Unique or innovative music curriculum: high quality music instruction in the context, flexibility and breadth of a liberal arts education. *24 lessons with major teacher. Study of secondary instrument or discipline is allowed.*

Selectivity for instruments or programs offered (rating): organ (non-competitive), piano (non-competitive), voice (non-competitive).

Entering class size: 203.

Renowned alumni: Martha Anna Dorminy Verbit.

Total full-time faculty: 3. *Total part-time faculty:* 8. *Program contact person:* Michael Sitton.

Performance opportunities available (frequency): jury examinations (1 per semester), recitals (1 per senior year).

Facilities

Number of practice rooms and hours: 12; 7:00 am-10:00 pm. *Recital hall?* yes. *Concert hall?* no. *Recording studio?* no.

SHENANDOAH UNIVERSITY AND CONSERVATORY

1460 University Drive, Winchester VA 22601-5195
Tel: 540-665-4581
Fax: 540-665-4627
Email: admit@su.edu

General

Type of Institution: conservatory.

Total enrollment of institution: 1,652. *Total student body from other countries:* 5%. *Degrees offered:* BM.

Entrance Requirements

Audition required: live, audio, video. *Other requirements:* interview, recommendation *Standardized test requirements:* ACT; SAT I.

Costs & Financial Aid

Application fee: $30. *Tuition:* $13,470. *Other fees:* $350 private music lessons for majors.

Types of scholarships and aid awarded: full, partial, merit-based, need-based, work/study. *Forms required for scholarships:* FAFSA. *Loans available.*

Services

Housing options: on-site dorms.

MUSIC

Curriculum, Students, and Faculty

Total enrollment: 253.

Total full-time faculty: 31. *Total part-time faculty:* 26. *Program contact person:* Michael Carpenter.

Audition Information

Audition consists of the following: repertoire. *Instruments provided for:* harpists, percussionists.

Facilities

Recital hall? yes. *Concert hall?* yes. *Recording studio?* yes.

UNIVERSITY OF VIRGINIA

P.O. Box 9017
Office of Admission, Charlottesville VA 22906
Tel: 804-982-3200
Fax: 804-924-3587
Email: undergrad-admission@virginia.edu
Web: www.virginia.edu
Contact: Amy Garrou

General

Type of Institution: public, university. *Environment:* suburban.

Total enrollment of institution: 18,000. *Total student body from other countries:* 4%. *Degrees offered:* BA.

Entrance Requirements

Audition not required Other requirements: recommendation, essay. *Standardized test requirements:* ACT; SAT I, 1300; SAT II; TOEFL, 600.

Costs & Financial Aid

Application fee: $40. *Deposit:* $250. *Tuition (in-state/out-state):* $4,790/$15,040. *Other fees:* $700 books. *Room and board:* $3,970.

Percent of students receiving financial aid: 35%. *Types of scholarships and aid awarded:* full, partial, merit-based, need-based, institutional aid, government aid, tuition payment plan, work/study. *Forms required for scholarships:* FAFSA, income tax return, school's own financial aid form. *Loans available. Procedure for applying for loans:* complete FAFSA and University's financial aid form by 3/1. *Other aid available to international students:* Jefferson Scholars, full merit scholarship program.

Services

Housing options: on-site dorms, off-campus housing, fraternity, sorority.

Support staff: career counselor, financial aid advisor, foreign student advisor, housing advisor, physical therapist, psychological counselor, resident assistant, resident nurse, student affairs officer.

DRAMA

Curriculum, Students, and Faculty

Required courses: movement.

Elective courses: Alexander technique, audition preparation, directing, improvisation, make-up, martial arts, musical theater, scene study, stage combat, Stanislavski exercises, text analysis, verse drama, voice, acting.

Number of years required to complete program: 4. *Summer program available. Affiliation with a professional theater company: Heritage Repertory Theatre, professional summer theater.*

Selectivity for males: approximately 33% admitted. *Selectivity for females:* approximately 10% admitted. *Total enrollment:* 80. *Entering class size:* 25.

Renowned alumni: Paul Witt, Mark Johnson, Lewis Allen, Jason George, Van Zeiler.

Total full-time faculty: 15. *Total part-time faculty:* 4. *List of current faculty and past affiliations:* Richard Warner, Rubert Chapel, Gweneth Westa, Tom Bloom, Lee Kennedy, Jeff Award, Colleen Kelly.

Audition Information

No audition fee. Audition consists of the following: a cappella, comedic monologue. *Repertoire that students should avoid?* no.

Audition evaluation criteria: presence, vocal and physical technique, immediacy in presenting the character, sense of preparedness.

Performance Information

Performance opportunities available (frequency): fully produced performances (6 per year), informal performances (5-10 per year), workshops (2-3 per semester), auditioned.

Recent guest artists: Bill Irwin, Cherry Morris, Ann Bogart, Ann Hould-Ward, Tina Shepard, JoAnne Akalaitis.

Facilities

Rehearsal facilities and hours: 3 rehearsal rooms, always available when not used formally for classes. *Number of theaters on campus:* 2. *Type and capacity:* proscenium 595, black box 200.

MUSIC

Curriculum, Students, and Faculty

Unique or innovative music curriculum: classes not only in classical music but also in jazz and ethnomusicology. We also offer electronic music and composition. *How are major teacher assignments made?* students may choose, according to teacher preference and teacher availability. Faculty is not informed of a student's teacher preference at the time of the audition. *28 lessons with major teacher. May a student change major teachers during the course of study?* possibly. *Study of secondary instrument or discipline is allowed.*

Selectivity for instruments or programs offered (rating): bassoon, choral conducting, choral singing, clarinet, composition, double bass, electronic music, flute or piccolo, French horn, guitar, harp, harpsichord, jazz, oboe/English horn, orchestral conducting, organ, percussion, piano, saxophone, trombone, trombone (selective), trumpet, tuba, viola, violin, violin (competitive), violoncello, voice.

Total enrollment: 30. *Entering class size:* 15.

Total full-time faculty: 12. *Total part-time faculty:* 36. *Program contact person:* Fred Maus.

Audition Information

No audition fee. Instruments provided for: harpists, percussionists.

Facilities

Number of practice rooms and hours: 12; 9:00 am-11:00 pm. *Recital hall?* yes. *Concert hall?* yes. *Recording studio?* no.

VIRGINIA COMMONWEALTH UNIVERSITY

1315 Floyd Avenue
Department of Dance and Choreography, Richmond VA 23284-3007
Tel: 804-828-1711
Fax: 804-828-7356
Email: mmcurtis@vcu.edu

General

Type of Institution: public, university. *Environment:* urban. *Academic education is offered on-site.*

Total enrollment of institution: 22,000. *Degrees offered:* BFA.

Entrance Requirements

Audition required: live. *Other requirements:* recommendation, essay. *Standardized test requirements:* SAT I, 800; SAT II.

Costs & Financial Aid

Tuition (in-state/out-state): $4,111/$12,279. *Medical fee:* $68. *Other fees:* $300 school of the arts.

Types of scholarships and aid awarded: full, partial, merit-based, need-based, named, institutional aid. *Forms required for scholarships:* FFS, FAFSA, income tax return, income asset verification. *Loans available.*

Services

Housing options: on-site dorms, off-campus housing, fraternity, sorority.

Support staff: career counselor, dorm parent, financial aid advisor, foreign student advisor, housing advisor, physical therapist, psychological counselor, resident assistant, resident nurse, student affairs officer.

DANCE

Curriculum, Students, and Faculty

Required courses: ballet, dance composition/choreography, dance history, master classes, modern dance, music, other world dance forms, rehearsal and performance, stagecraft.

Elective courses: African dance, historical dance, jazz, movement techniques, nutrition, repertory, Spanish, tap, vernacular dance, modern dance partnering.

Selectivity for males: most admitted, but not all. *Selectivity for females:* approximately 60% admitted. *Total enrollment:* 80. *Entering class size:* 80. *Graduating class size:* 10.

Renowned alumni: students dancing with Bella Lewitzky Pittsburgh Dance Alley, Liz Lerman, and others.

Total full-time faculty: 7. *Total part-time faculty:* 12. *List of current faculty and past affiliations:* Chris Burnside, Melanie Richards, Audrey Jung, Judy Steel, Martha Curtis. *Program contact person:* Martha Curtis.

Audition Information

No audition fee. Audition consists of the following: ballet, improvisation, modern dance. *Accompanist provided.*

Audition evaluation criteria: talent, creativity, open mind.

Performance Information

Performance opportunities available (frequency): Fully produced concerts (5 per year), informal concerts (2 per year), on-site performances (3 per year).

Performances choreographed by: faculty, students, guests. *Recent guest choreographers:* Barb Grubel, Doug Nielson, Doug Varone.

Facilities

Number of studios available: 7. *Approximate studio dimensions and flooring:* 70' x 50' sprung wood, 25' x 30' sprung wood. *Performance facilities:* Grace Street Theatre sprung floor, designed for dance.

VIRGINIA INTERMONT COLLEGE

1013 Moore Street, Bristol VA 24201
Tel: 800-451-1842
Fax: 540-669-5763
Email: viadmit@uic.edu
Web: viadmit@vic.edu

General

Type of Institution: college. *Religious Affiliation:* Southern Baptist. *Environment:* suburban.

Total enrollment of institution: 491. *Total student body from other countries:* 3%. *Degrees offered:* BA, BFA.

Entrance Requirements

Audition required: live. *Other requirements:* recommendation.

Costs & Financial Aid

Application fee: $15. *Deposit:* $200. *Tuition:* $10,450. *Other fees:* $100 tech fee, $450 cable phone.

Types of scholarships and aid awarded: full, partial, merit-based, need-based, named, institutional aid. *Forms required for scholarships:* FAFSA, income tax return, income asset verification. *Loans available. Procedure for applying for loans:* contact Financial Aid Office. *Other aid available to international students:* none.

Services

Housing options: on-site dorms.

Support staff: career counselor, financial aid advisor, foreign student advisor, psychological counselor, resident assistant, student affairs officer.

DANCE

Curriculum, Students, and Faculty

Required courses: anatomy, ballet, dance composition/choreography, dance history, dance theory, modern dance, Graham-based dance, Horton-based dance, Limon-based, music, pointe, rehearsal and performance.

Elective courses: character, men's class, pas de deux, repertory, stagecraft, variations, ballet, variations.

Selectivity for males: most admitted, but not all. *Selectivity for females:* most admitted, but not all. *Total enrollment:* 17.

Total full-time faculty: 2. *Total part-time faculty:* 1. *List of current faculty and past affiliations:* D. Harolyn Gaudette, University of California—Santa Barbara; Judith Casavechia, Compania Nacionalede Danza Clasico, Mexico City; Carloee Watts-Hacker, featured dancer, Opryland USA. *Program contact person:* D. Harolyn Gaudette.

Audition Information

No audition fee. Audition consists of the following: ballet, modern dance. *Accompanist not provided.*

Audition evaluation criteria: coordination, previous training, creativity, artistry, dance goals, desire to perfect technique, history of medical problems or injuries.

Performance Information

Performance opportunities available (frequency): Fully produced concerts (2 per year), informal concerts (1-2 per year), workshops (1 or more per year), on-site performances (1 per year), touring (occasionally).

Performances choreographed by: faculty, students, guests. *Recent guest choreographers:* Rob Scoggins, Randy Allen, Jonathan Kane, Margaret Faust.

Facilities

Number of studios available: 3. *Performance facilities:* 1,200-seat auditorium, large studio, 160-seat theater.

DRAMA

Curriculum, Students, and Faculty

Required courses: acting, audition preparation, directing, make-up, movement, scene study, speech, Stanislavski exercises, text analysis, voice.

Elective courses: drama criticism, musical theater, stage combat, musical theater, movement, martial arts.

Number of years required to complete program: 4. *Summer program not available. Affiliation with a professional theater company: internships available at Barter Theatre, Abingdon, VA.*

Selectivity for males: most admitted, but not all. *Selectivity for females:* most admitted, but not all. *Total enrollment:* 11. *Entering class size:* 4. *Percent international:* 10%. *Countries most represented:* Japan.

Total full-time faculty: 2. *Total part-time faculty:* 1. *List of current faculty and past affiliations:* Glenn Patterson, Emory College; Dmitri Gurkweitz; Ken Cornett, Barter Theatre.

Audition Information

No audition fee. Audition consists of the following: comedic monologue, vocal and dance auditions optional. *Audition evaluation criteria:* previous experience, ability to show range of emotion, focused interest in theater.

Performance Information

Performance opportunities available (frequency): fully produced performances (4 per year), informal performances (occasionally), workshops (1 per year), off-site performances (occasionally), auditioned.

Facilities

Rehearsal facilities and hours: recital hall for vocal work. *Number of theaters on campus:* 3. *Type and capacity:* proscenium 160, proscenium 900, amphitheater 1,000.

WASHINGTON

CENTRAL WASHINGTON UNIVERSITY

400 East 8th Avenue, Ellensburg WA 98926
Tel: 509-963-1111
Fax: 509-963-1241
Web: www.cwu.edu

General

Type of Institution: public, university. *Academic education is offered on-site.*

Total enrollment of institution: 7,000. *Total student body from other countries:* 2%. *Degrees offered:* BA, BM.

Entrance Requirements

Audition required: live.

Costs & Financial Aid

Application fee: $35. *Tuition (in-state/out-state):* $781/$2,763. *Medical fee:* $25. *Other fees:* $25-$47 graduation, $150 international studies, $18 computer use.

Percent of students receiving financial aid: 65%. *Types of scholarships and aid awarded:* full, partial, merit-based, need-based, named, government aid, work/study. *Forms required for scholarships:* FAFSA. *Loans available.*

Services

Housing options: on-site dorms, off-campus housing.

Support staff: career counselor, financial aid advisor, foreign student advisor, housing advisor, psychological counselor, resident assistant, student affairs officer.

DANCE

Curriculum, Students, and Faculty

Required courses: ballet (2 classes per week, 1 year to complete), dance composition/choreography, dance history, modern dance (2 classes per week, 1 year to complete).

Elective courses: anatomy, jazz, tap.

Selectivity for males: admit all who apply. *Selectivity for females:* admit all who apply. *Total enrollment:* 166. *Countries most represented:* Japan.

Total full-time faculty: 22. *Total part-time faculty:* 5. *List of current faculty and past affiliations:* Lana Jo Sharpe, University of Utah; Therese Young, Texas Womens University. *Program contact person:* Lana Jo Shape, (509) 963-1937.

Audition Information

No audition fee. Audition consists of the following: no auditions required.

Performance Information

Performance opportunities available (frequency): Informal concerts (2).

Performances choreographed by: faculty, students.

Facilities

Number of studios available: 1. *Approximate studio dimensions and flooring:* 96' x 65' Robbins Hardwood. *Performance facilities:* dance studio.

DRAMA

Curriculum, Students, and Faculty

Required courses: acting, audition preparation, directing, drama criticism, dramaturgy, improvisation, movement, scene study, Stanislavski exercises, text analysis, verse drama, voice.

Elective courses: Alexander technique, make-up, martial arts, mime, musical theater, speech, stage combat.

Performance Information

Performance opportunities available (frequency): fully produced performances (6 per year), informal performances (2-4 per year), workshops (12-15 per year), off-site performances (at least 2 per year), original student plays, (12-15 per year).

MUSIC

Curriculum, Students, and Faculty

How are major teacher assignments made? made by the school, according to teacher preference and teacher availability. *30 lessons with major teacher. May a student change major teachers during the course of study?* possibly. *Study of secondary instrument or discipline is allowed.*

Selectivity for instruments or programs offered (rating): bassoon (non-competitive), choral conducting (competitive), choral singing (non-competitive), clarinet (non-competitive), composition (non-competitive), flute or piccolo (non-competitive), French horn (non-competitive), guitar (non-competitive), harpsichord (non-competitive), jazz (non-competitive), oboe/English horn (non-competitive), orchestral conducting (competitive), organ (non-competitive), percussion (non-competitive), piano (non-competitive), saxophone (non-competitive), trombone (non-competitive), trumpet (non-competitive), tuba (non-competitive), viola (non-competitive), violin (non-competitive), violoncello (non-competitive), voice (non-competitive).

Total enrollment: 300. *Graduating class size:* 27.

Total full-time faculty: 22. *Total part-time faculty:* 5. *Program contact person:* Russ Schultz, (509) 963-1216.

Audition Information

No audition fee. Audition consists of the following: scales, improvisation. *Instruments provided for:* percussionists.

Performance opportunities available (frequency): band (3 per year), jury examinations (3 per year), orchestral concerts (3 per year), chorus (3 per year).

Facilities

Number of practice rooms and hours: 17. *Recital hall?* yes. *Concert hall?* no. *Recording studio?* no.

EASTERN WASHINGTON UNIVERSITY

MS 100, Cheney WA 99004
Tel: 509-359-2241
Fax: 509-359-7028

General

Type of Institution: public, university. *Environment:* suburban.

Total enrollment of institution: 6,700. *Degrees offered:* BA, BFA, BM.

Entrance Requirements

Audition required: live, video. *Other requirements:* interview. *Standardized test requirements:* ACT; SAT I.

Costs & Financial Aid

Loans available.

Services

Housing options: on-site dorms, off-campus housing, fraternity, sorority, family.

Support staff: career counselor, financial aid advisor, foreign student advisor, housing advisor, psychological counselor, resident assistant, resident nurse, student affairs officer.

MUSIC

Curriculum, Students, and Faculty

How are major teacher assignments made? students may choose, according to teacher preference and teacher availability. Faculty is informed of a student's teacher preference at the time of the audition. *30 lessons with major teacher. May a student change major teachers during the course of study?* possibly. *Study of secondary instrument or discipline is allowed.*

Selectivity for instruments or programs offered (rating): accompanying (non-competitive), bassoon (non-competitive), bassoon (competitive), choral conducting (competitive), choral singing (competitive), clarinet (competitive), composition (competitive), double bass (competitive), electronic music (competitive), flute or piccolo (competitive), French horn (competitive), jazz (competitive), oboe/English horn (non-competitive), orchestral conducting (competitive), percussion (competitive), piano (competitive), sacred music (competitive), saxophone (competitive), trombone (competitive), trumpet (competitive), tuba (competitive), viola (competitive), violin (competitive), violoncello (competitive), violoncello (selective), voice (competitive).

Total enrollment: 125. *Entering class size:* 40. *Graduating class size:* 20.

Renowned alumni: Robert Gillespie, Thomas Hampson. *Program contact person:* Lynn Brinckmeyer.

Audition Information

No audition fee. Audition consists of the following: scales, orchestral excerpts, music theory, rhythmic dictation, sight reading. *Instruments provided for:* percussionists.

Performance opportunities available (frequency): band (frequently), band, jury examinations (frequently), orchestral concerts (frequently), recitals, touring, chorus.

Facilities

Recital hall? yes. *Concert hall?* yes. *Recording studio?* yes.

UNIVERSITY OF PUGET SOUND

School of Music
1500 North Warner, Tacoma WA 98416
Tel: 253-756-3730
Fax: 253-756-3500
Email: pgjording@ups.edu
Web: www.ups.edu/music

General

Type of Institution: private university. *Environment:* small city.

Total enrollment of institution: 2,700. *Total student body from other countries:* 1%. *Degrees offered:* BA, BM.

Entrance Requirements

Audition required: live, audio, video.

Costs & Financial Aid

Application fee: $35. *Deposit:* $200. *Tuition:* $18,790. *Other fees:* $150. *Room and board:* $5,020.

Percent of students receiving financial aid: 70%. *Types of scholarships and aid awarded:* full, partial, merit-based, need-based, named, institutional aid, government aid, work/study. *Forms required for scholarships:* FAFSA, CSS Profile. *Loans available. Procedure for applying for loans:* submit required forms to Office of Financial Aid and Scholarships; audition for music scholarships. *Financial aid offered to international students. Other aid available to international students:* institutional aid.

Services

Housing options: on-site dorms, off-campus housing, fraternity, sorority.

Support staff: career counselor, college advisor, financial aid advisor, resident nurse.

MUSIC

Curriculum, Students, and Faculty

How are major teacher assignments made? students may choose according to teacher preference according to teacher availability. Faculty is not informed of a student's teacher preference at the time of the audition. *May a student change major teachers during the course of study?* possibly. *Study of secondary instrument or discipline is allowed.*

Selectivity for instruments or programs offered (rating): bassoon (competitive), choral conducting (competitive), choral singing (competitive), clarinet (competitive), composition (competitive), double bass (competitive), flute or piccolo (competitive), French horn (competitive), guitar (competitive), harp (competitive), harpsichord (competitive), oboe/English horn (competitive), orchestral conducting (competitive), organ (competitive), percussion (competitive), piano (competitive), saxophone (competitive), trombone (competitive), trumpet (competitive), tuba (competitive), viola (competitive), violin (competitive), violoncello (competitive), voice (competitive).

Total enrollment: 300. *Entering class size:* 80. *Graduating class size:* 70.

Renowned alumni: Phil Cutlip, Rob McPherson.

Total full-time faculty: 12. *Total part-time faculty:* 20. *Program contact person:* Paul Gjording.

Audition Information

Audition consists of the following: sight reading, *Instruments provided for:* harpists, percussionists.

Facilities

Number of practice rooms and hours: 20. *Recital hall?* no. *Concert hall?* yes. *Recording studio?* yes.

UNIVERSITY OF WASHINGTON

School of Music
P.O. Box 353450, Seattle WA 98195
Tel: 206-543-1201
Fax: 206-685-9499
Email: musicadv@u.washington.edu
Web: www.weber.u.washington.edu/~musicweb
Contact: Jan Kammert

General

Type of Institution: public university. *Environment:* urban.

Total enrollment of institution: 40,000. *Degrees offered:* certificate, BA, BM, BA/BM (concurrent double degree).

Entrance Requirements

Audition required: live, audio, video. *Other requirements:* essay. *Standardized test requirements:* ACT; SAT I; SAT II; TOEFL.

Costs & Financial Aid

Deposit: $100. *Tuition (in-state/out-state):* $3,366/$10,656. *Room and board:* $4,729.

Types of scholarships and aid awarded: full, partial, merit-based, need-based, institutional aid, government aid, work/study. *Forms required for scholarships:* FFS, FAFSA, income tax return, income asset verification. *Loans available. Other aid available to international students:* none that is government funded, but merit-based which is through the School of Music.

Services

Housing options: on-site dorms, off-campus housing, fraternity, sorority.

Support staff: career counselor, financial aid advisor, foreign student advisor, housing advisor, psychological counselor, resident assistant, student affairs officer.

MUSIC

Curriculum, Students, and Faculty

10 lessons with major teacher. May a student change major teachers during the course of study? possibly. *Study of secondary instrument or discipline is allowed.*

Selectivity for instruments or programs offered (rating): accompanying (highly selective), bassoon (selective), choral singing (competitive), clarinet (selective), composition (selective), double bass (selective), flute or piccolo (selective), French horn (selective), guitar (selective), harp (selective), harpsichord (selective), jazz (selective), oboe/English horn (selective), organ (selective), percussion (selective), piano (highly selective), saxophone (selective), trombone (selective), trumpet (selective), tuba (selective), viola (selective), violin (selective), voice (highly selective).

Total enrollment: 520. *Entering class size:* 55.

Renowned alumni: Robin McCabe, William Bolcom, Marcia Bellamy, Fredrick Dockweld, Paul Elliott Cobbs, George Shangrow, Richard Spark, Dennis Coleman, Kenny G.

Total full-time faculty: 45. *Total part-time faculty:* 20. *Program contact person:* Beth Miguel Alipio.

Performance opportunities available (frequency): chamber music, opera workshops, recitals, produced operas.

Facilities

Recital hall? yes. *Concert hall?* yes. *Recording studio?* no.

BELOIT COLLEGE

700 College Street, Beloit WI 53511
Tel: 608-363-2000
Fax: 608-363-2717
Email: admiss@beloit.edu
Web: www.beloit.edu

General

Type of Institution: private college. *Environment:* small city.

Total enrollment of institution: 1,200. *Total student body from other countries:* 11%. *Degrees offered:* BA.

Entrance Requirements

Audition not required Other requirements: recommendation, essay. *Standardized test requirements:* ACT, 27; SAT I, 1240; TOEFL, 525.

Costs & Financial Aid

Application fee: $25. *Deposit:* $200. *Tuition:* $19,050. *Room and board:* $4,540.

Percent of students receiving financial aid: 69%. *Types of scholarships and aid awarded:* full, partial, merit-based, need-based, named, institutional aid, government aid, tuition payment plan, work/study. *Forms required for scholarships:* FAFSA, income tax return. *Loans available. Financial aid offered to international students.*

Services

Housing options: on-site dorms, fraternity, sorority.

Support staff: career counselor, financial aid advisor, foreign student advisor, psychological counselor, resident assistant, student affairs officer.

DANCE

Curriculum, Students, and Faculty

Required courses: dance composition/choreography, rehearsal and performance, master classes, Labanotation, dance history.

Elective courses: ballet, jazz, modern dance, anatomy.

Selectivity for males: admit all who apply. *Selectivity for females:* admit all who apply.

Total full-time faculty: 2. *Program contact person:* Rod Umlas.

Audition Information

No audition fee.

Performance Information

Performance opportunities available (frequency): Fully produced concerts (1 per year), informal concerts (2 per year), workshops (2 per year), touring (occasionally).

Performances choreographed by: faculty, students, guests.

Facilities

Number of studios available: 1. *Approximate studio dimensions and flooring:* 30' x 40' sprung hardwood covered with Marley. *Performance facilities:* 2 theaters, Neese—Thrust, Wilson—proscenium.

DRAMA

Curriculum, Students, and Faculty

Required courses: acting, text analysis, theater history, acting, speech, scene study, improvisation.

Elective courses: audition preparation, directing, drama criticism, dramaturgy, improvisation, make-up, movement, performance arts, scene study, speech, Stanislavski exercises, voice.

Number of years required to complete program: 4. *Summer program not available. Connections with American Players Theater (Spring Green, WI) and New American Theater (Rockford, IL).*

Selectivity for males: admit all who apply. *Selectivity for females:* admit all who apply.

Total full-time faculty: 7.

Performance Information

Performance opportunities available (frequency): fully produced performances (5 per year), informal performances (2-3 per year), workshops (1-2 per year), off-site performances (occasionally), auditioned.

Facilities

Rehearsal facilities and hours: two excellent theaters and shops housed in Neese Theatre Complex *Number of theaters on campus:* 3. *Type and capacity:* Guthrie type thrust 300, black box 200, proscenium 400.

LAWRENCE UNIVERSITY

P.O. Box 599, Appleton WI 54912-0599
Tel: 800-227-0982
Fax: 920-832-6782
Email: excel@lawrence.edu
Web: www.lawrence.edu
Contact: David Stull

General

Type of Institution: university, conservatory. *Environment:* small city.

Total enrollment of institution: 1,250. *Total student body from other countries:* 10%. *Degrees offered:* BA, BM.

Entrance Requirements

Audition required: live, audio, video. *Other requirements:* recommendation, essay. *Standardized test requirements:* ACT, 28; SAT I, 1280; TOEFL, 575.

Costs & Financial Aid

Application fee: $30. *Deposit:* $200. *Tuition:* $19,494. *Other fees:* $125 activity fee. *Room and board:* $4,741.

Types of scholarships and aid awarded: partial, merit-based, need-based, named, institutional aid, government aid, tuition payment plan, work/study. *Forms required for scholarships:* FAFSA, income tax return, income asset verification. *Loans available. Procedure for applying for loans:* Lawrence financial aid application *Financial aid offered to international students. Other aid available to international students:* Lawrence grants.

Services

Housing options: on-site dorms, off-campus housing, fraternity, sorority.

Support staff: career counselor, financial aid advisor, foreign student advisor, housing advisor, psychological counselor, resident assistant, resident nurse, student affairs officer.

DANCE

Curriculum, Students, and Faculty

Required courses: stagecraft, ballet for modern dancers, modern dance.

DRAMA

Curriculum, Students, and Faculty

Elective courses: directing, make-up, stage combat, Stanislavski exercises, verse drama.

Summer program not available. Affiliation with a professional theater company: internship with theatres across the country, such as Guthrie in Minneapolis.

Selectivity for males: admit all who apply. *Selectivity for females:* admit all who apply. *Total enrollment:* 20. *Percent international:* 10%.

Renowned alumni: Jeff Jones, Campbell Scott.

Total full-time faculty: 4.

Audition Information

No audition fee.

Performance Information

Performance opportunities available (frequency): fully produced performances (9-13 per year), informal performances (frequently), workshops (frequently), auditioned.

Recent guest artists: Campbell Scott.

Facilities

Number of theaters on campus: 2. *Type and capacity:* main stage 600, black box 200.

MUSIC

Curriculum, Students, and Faculty

Unique or innovative music curriculum: double degree program. *How are major teacher assignments made?* students may choose made by the school. Faculty is not informed of a student's teacher preference at the time of the audition. *May a student change major teachers during the course of study?* possibly. *Study of secondary instrument or discipline is allowed.*

Selectivity for instruments or programs offered (rating): bassoon (competitive), clarinet (competitive), composition (selective), double bass (competitive), flute or piccolo (highly selective), French horn (competitive), guitar (competitive), harpsichord (competitive), jazz (highly selective), oboe/English horn (competitive), organ (noncompetitive), percussion (competitive), piano (competitive), saxophone (highly selective), trombone (competitive), trumpet (competitive), tuba (competitive), viola (competitive), violin (competitive), violoncello (competitive), voice (highly selective).

Total enrollment: 300. *Entering class size:* 125. *Graduating class size:* 65. *Percent international:* 10%.

Renowned alumni: Ed Hoffman, Baltimore Symphony; Larry Strieby, St. Louis Symphony; Dale Duesing, William Sharp singers.

Total full-time faculty: 40. *Total part-time faculty:* 6. *Program contact person:* David Stull.

Audition Information

No audition fee. Audition consists of the following: scales, orchestral excerpts, music theory, rhythmic dictation, arpeggios, sight reading, repertoire. *Instruments provided for:* percussionists.

Repertoire that students should avoid? no. *Performance opportunities available (frequency):* band, chamber music, band, jury examinations, opera workshops, orchestral concerts, recitals, produced operas, chorus.

Facilities

Number of practice rooms and hours: Recital hall? yes. *Concert hall?* yes. *Recording studio?* yes.

Comments

Recent competition winners: National Met Opera, National NATS, Carmel Chamber Competition (first prize), MTNA National Solo and Chamber Music, Vamos Competition (first prize). *Downbeat* magazine outstanding soloist, and numerous others.

UNIVERSITY OF WISCONSIN, MADISON

Undergraduate Admissions
140 Peterson Building, 750 University Avenue, Madison WI 53706
Tel: 608-263-3961
Fax: 608-262-1429
Web: polyglot.lss.wisc.edu/tnd/theatre/html

General

Type of Institution: public university. *Environment:* urban.

Total enrollment of institution: 26,910. *Degrees offered:* BA, BS.

Costs & Financial Aid

Forms required for scholarships: FFS, FAFSA, income tax return.

Services

Housing options: on-site dorms, off-campus housing, fraternity, sorority.

Support staff: career counselor, financial aid advisor, foreign student advisor, psychological counselor, resident assistant, resident nurse, student affairs officer.

DANCE

Curriculum, Students, and Faculty

Required courses: anatomy, ballet, dance composition/choreography, dance history, dance theory, dance writing research and criticism, master classes, modern dance, movement techniques, Laban Movement Studies, music, rehearsal and performance, repertory, stagecraft, dance theory.

Elective courses: African dance, jazz, ballroom dance, Asian American dance.

DRAMA

Curriculum, Students, and Faculty

Number of years required to complete program: 4. *Summer program available. Affiliation with a professional theater company: Madison Repertory Theatre and American Players Theater provide internships of all kinds.*

Selectivity for females: admit all who apply. *Total enrollment:* 83. *Entering class size:* 14. *Graduating class size:* 16.

Renowned alumni: Shirly Lauro, Daniel J. Travanti, Uta Hagen.

Total full-time faculty: 13. *Total part-time faculty:* 3. *List of current faculty and past affiliations:* Patricia Boyette; Karen Ryker; Phillip Zarrilli, Asian Theatre.

Audition Information

No audition fee. Audition consists of the following: a cappella, comedic monologue, improvisation. *Repertoire that students should avoid?* anything out of their range.

Audition evaluation criteria: are they interesting, believable, and engaging—if so why, if not why? Also students should dress appropriately; no costumes, but wear something that does not contradict the characters they are performing—something that shows them off at their best in the situation.

Performance Information

Performance opportunities available (frequency): fully produced performances (6 per year, 3 per summer), informal performances (varies), workshops (2 per year), off-site performances (several) assigned, auditioned. Depends on situation, most by open casting.

Recent guest artists: Billie Whitelaw, Geoffrey Beevers, Spaulding Gray, Gomez Pena, Meredith Monk.

Facilities

Rehearsal facilities and hours: 4 studio spaces used for performance classes and rehearsals, in constant use. *Type and capacity:* proscenium—1,300, thrust—350, black box—150.

UNIVERSITY OF WISCONSIN, WHITEWATER

College of Arts and Communication
800 West Main Street, Whitewater WI 53190
Tel: 414-472-1221
Fax: 414-472-1436
Email: townsenp@uwwvax.uww.edu

General

Type of Institution: university.

Total enrollment of institution: 9,585. *Total student body from other countries:* 2%. *Degrees offered:* BA, BFA, BM.

Entrance Requirements

Standardized test requirements: ACT; SAT I; TOEFL.

Costs & Financial Aid

Application fee: $35. *Deposit:* $100. *Tuition (in-state/out-state):* $4,600/$10,500.

Percent of students receiving financial aid: 60%. *Types of scholarships and aid awarded:* partial, merit-based, need-based, named, institutional aid, government aid, reduced tuition, tuition payment plan, work/study. *Forms required for scholarships:* FFS, FAFSA, income tax return, income asset verification. *Loans available. Procedure for applying for loans:* fill out FFS and FAS, work with Financial Aid Office. *Percent of international students receiving scholarships:* 11%. *Other aid available to international students:* work/study, campus work.

Services

Housing options: on-site dorms, off-campus housing, fraternity, sorority.

Support staff: career counselor, financial aid advisor, foreign student advisor, housing advisor, physical therapist, psychological counselor, resident assistant, resident nurse, student affairs officer.

DANCE

Curriculum, Students, and Faculty

Required courses: anatomy, ballet, dance composition/choreography, dance history, Cunningham-based, Limon-based, rehearsal and performance, repertory, eclectic.

Selectivity for males: admit all who apply. *Selectivity for females:* admit all who apply. *Total enrollment:* 28. *Entering class size:* 4. *Graduating class size:* 4.

Renowned alumni: Pamela Huggins.

Total full-time faculty: 2. *Total part-time faculty:* 1. *List of current faculty and past affiliations:* Mark Kotz formerly with Lar Lubovitch and Hartford Ballet Comapny; Robin Pettersen, Alfred University, Alfred New York. *Program contact person:* Robin Petterson.

Audition Information

No audition fee.

Performance Information

Performance opportunities available (frequency): Fully produced concerts (1 per year), informal concerts (1 per semester), workshops (2+ per year), on-site performances (1+ per year).

Performances choreographed by: faculty, students, guests. *Recent guest choreographers:* Janet Lilly (formerly of Bill T. Jones), Brian Jeffery (Exsight of Chicago), Julia Mayer (Chicago).

Facilities

Number of studios available: 2. *Performance facilities:* mainstage and black box theaters.

DRAMA

Curriculum, Students, and Faculty

Required courses: acting, directing, drama criticism, make-up, movement, acting.

Number of years required to complete program: 4. *Summer program available. No affiliation with a professional theater company. Selectivity for males:* admit all who apply. *Selectivity for females:* admit all who apply. *Total enrollment:* 72. *Entering class size:* 11. *Graduating class size:* 8.

Total full-time faculty: 4. *Total part-time faculty:* 4.

Audition Information

Audition consists of the following: cold readings, comedic monologue, 2 contrasting pieces. *Audition evaluation criteria:* each director uses his/her own criteria

Performance Information

Performance opportunities available (frequency): fully produced performances (7), informal performances (every semester), workshops (4 per year), auditioned.

Recent guest artists: Lee Meriwether.

Facilities

Number of theaters on campus: 3 *Type and capacity:* proscenium—450, proscenium—1300, black box—160.

MUSIC

Curriculum, Students, and Faculty

How are major teacher assignments made? made by the school. Faculty is informed of a student's teacher preference at the time of the audition. *30 lessons with major teacher. May a student change major teachers during the course of study?* possibly. *Study of secondary instrument or discipline is allowed.*

Selectivity for instruments or programs offered (rating): accompanying (competitive), bassoon (competitive), clarinet (competitive), double bass (competitive), flute or piccolo (competitive), French horn (competitive), harp (selective), jazz (competitive), oboe/English horn (competitive), organ (selective), percussion (competitive), piano (competitive), trombone (competitive), trumpet (competitive), tuba (competitive), viola (competitive), violin (competitive), violoncello (competitive), voice (competitive).

Total enrollment: 132. *Entering class size:* 32. *Graduating class size:* 16.

Total full-time faculty: 17. *Total part-time faculty:* 11. *Program contact person:* John Webb.

Audition Information

Audition consists of the following: scales, music theory. *Instruments provided for:* harpists, percussionists.

Repertoire that students should avoid? no. *Performance opportunities available (frequency):* band (frequently), jury examinations, orchestral concerts, recitals (frequently), touring, chorus.

Facilities

Recital hall? yes. *Concert hall?* yes. *Recording studio?* yes.

UNIVERSITY OF WISCONSIN, SUPERIOR MUSIC DEPARTMENT

1800 Grand Avenue, Superior WI 54880-2898
Tel: 715-394-8115
Fax: 715-394-8404
Email: abumgard@staff.uwsuper.edu
Web: www.uwsuper.edu/music

General

Type of Institution: public university. *Environment:* suburban. *Academic education is offered on-site.*

Total enrollment of institution: 2,600. *Total student body from other countries:* 1%. *Degrees offered:* BA, BM.

Entrance Requirements

Audition required: live, audio. *Standardized test requirements:* ACT, 20.

Costs & Financial Aid

Application fee: $28. *Deposit:* $30. *Tuition (in-state/out-state):* $2,334/$7,740.

Types of scholarships and aid awarded: full, partial, merit-based, need-based, named, institutional aid, government aid, reduced tuition, tuition payment plan, work/study. *Forms required for scholarships:* FFS, income tax return. *Loans available. Procedure for applying for loans:* obtain necessary forms from Financial Aid Office. *Financial aid offered to international students.*

Services

Housing options: on-site dorms, off-campus housing.

Support staff: career counselor, financial aid advisor, foreign student advisor, housing advisor, psychological counselor, resident assistant, resident nurse, student affairs officer.

MUSIC

Curriculum, Students, and Faculty

How are major teacher assignments made? students may choose, made by the school, according to teacher availability. Faculty is informed of a student's teacher preference at the time of the audition. *32 lessons with major teacher. May a student change major teachers during the course of study?* possibly. *Study of secondary instrument or discipline is allowed.*

Selectivity for instruments or programs offered (rating): accompanying (competitive), bassoon (competitive), choral conducting (competitive), choral singing (competitive), clarinet (competitive), composition (competitive), double bass (competitive), flute or piccolo (competitive), French horn (competitive), guitar (competitive), harp (competitive), harpsichord (competitive), jazz (competitive), oboe/English horn (competitive), organ (competitive), percussion (competitive), piano (competitive), saxophone (competitive), trombone (competitive), trombone (competitive), trumpet (competitive), tuba (competitive), viola (competitive), violin (competitive), violoncello (competitive), voice (competitive).

Total enrollment: 50. *Entering class size:* 20. *Graduating class size:* 10. *Percent international:* 1%. *Countries most represented:* Japan.

Renowned alumni: Dr. Michale Corzine; David Sabee, Cellist-Seattle Symphony; Frank McGinnis, MTNA.

Total full-time faculty: 7. *Total part-time faculty:* 13. *Program contact person:* Dr. T.A. Bumgardner.

Audition Information

No audition fee. Audition consists of the following: repertoire. *Instruments provided for:* harpists, percussionists.

Required repertoire: class A solo from State High School League List. *Performance opportunities available (frequency):* band (frequently), band (frequently), jury examinations (frequently), orchestral concerts (frequently), recitals (frequently), chorus.

Facilities

Number of practice rooms and hours: 30; 24 hours a day. *Recital hall?* yes. *Concert hall?* yes. *Recording studio?* yes.

WEST VIRGINIA

WEST VIRGINIA UNIVERSITY

College of Creative Arts
P.O. Box 6111, Morgantown WV 26506-6111
Tel: 304-293-4617
Fax: 304-293-7491
Email: jmlewis@wvu.edu
Web: www.wvu.edu
Contact: Catherine Thieme

General

Type of Institution: public.

Total enrollment of institution: 22,000. *Total student body from other countries:* 10%. *Degrees offered:* BM.

Entrance Requirements

Audition required: live, audio.

Costs & Financial Aid

Financial aid offered to international students.

Services

Housing options: on-site dorms, off-campus housing, fraternity, sorority, family.

Support staff: career counselor, financial aid advisor, foreign student advisor, housing advisor, physical therapist, psychological counselor, resident assistant, resident nurse, student affairs officer.

MUSIC

Curriculum, Students, and Faculty

Unique or innovative music curriculum: World Music program featuring performance ensembles in Taiko Drums, Steel Drums and African Music and Dance. Also studies on forte piano and harpsichord. ***How are major teacher assignments made?*** according to teacher availability. Faculty is informed of a student's teacher preference at the time of the audition. ***30 lessons with major teacher. May a student change major teachers during the course of study?*** possibly. ***Study of secondary instrument or discipline is allowed.***

Selectivity for instruments or programs offered (rating): accompanying (competitive), bassoon (competitive), choral conducting (competitive), choral singing (competitive), clarinet (competitive), composition (competitive), double bass (competitive), flute or piccolo (competitive), French horn (competitive), guitar (competitive), harpsichord (competitive), jazz (competitive), oboe/English horn (competitive), orchestral conducting (competitive), organ (competitive), percussion (competitive), piano (competitive), saxophone (competitive), trombone (competitive), trumpet (competitive), tuba (competitive), viola (competitive), violin (competitive), violoncello (competitive), voice (competitive).

Total enrollment: 318. ***Entering class size:*** 70. ***Graduating class size:*** 63. ***Percent international:*** 10%. ***Countries most represented:*** Malaysia.

Renowned alumni: John Blake; David Booth, Philadelphia Orchestra; Jay Chattaway; Paul MacDowell, Scottish National Orchestra; Philip J. Faini, College of Creative Arts at West Virginia University; Carol Jean Ross, University of Kansas; William Winstead, Cincinnati Symphony, Cincinnati Conservatory.

Total full-time faculty: 34. ***Total part-time faculty:*** 14. ***Program contact person:*** Jodie Lewis.

Audition Information

No audition fee. Audition consists of the following: scales. ***Instruments provided for:*** percussionists.

Repertoire that students should avoid? no. ***Performance opportunities available (frequency):*** jury examinations (every semester).

Facilities

Number of practice rooms and hours: 35; all day. ***Recital hall?*** yes. ***Concert hall?*** yes. ***Recording studio?*** yes.

Comments

Degrees offered at the doctoral level in performance, composition and music education. Nearly 100% of our music education students are placed in jobs or graduate programs.

CANADA

MCGILL UNIVERSITY

845 Sherbrooke Street West, Montreal QU H3A 2T5
Tel: 514-398-3910
Fax: 514-398-8939
Email: admissions@aro.lan.mcgill.ca
Web: www.mcgill.ca
Contact: Veronica Slobodian

General

Type of Institution: university. ***Environment:*** urban.

Total enrollment of institution: 29,948. ***Degrees offered:*** BM, artist diploma, licentiate in music.

Entrance Requirements

Audition not required.

Services

Housing options: on-site dorms, off-campus housing.

MUSIC

Curriculum, Students, and Faculty

How are major teacher assignments made? students may choose, made by the school according to teacher preference and teacher availability. Faculty is not informed of a student's teacher preference at the time of the audition. ***13 lessons with major teacher. May a student change major teachers during the course of study?*** often. ***Study of secondary instrument or discipline is allowed.***

Selectivity for instruments or programs offered (rating): accompanying (highly selective), bassoon (competitive), choral conducting (highly selective), clarinet (selective), composition (competitive), double bass (selective), flute or piccolo (highly selective), French horn (selective), guitar (competitive), harp (open), harpsichord (open), jazz (competitive), oboe/English horn (selective), orchestral conducting (highly selective), organ (open), percussion (selective), piano (highly selective), saxophone (competitive), trombone (selective), trombone (competitive), trumpet (selective), tuba (selective), viola (open), violin (highly selective), violoncello (highly selective), voice (selective).

Total enrollment: 524. *Entering class size:* 150.

Renowned alumni: Benjamin Butterfield, Jens Lindemann. ***Program contact person:*** Veronica Slobodian.

Audition Information

Audition fee? $25. ***Audition consists of the following:*** scales, orchestral excerpts, rhythmic dictation, arpeggios, sight reading, music history, improvisation, melodic dictation, repertoire. ***Instruments provided for:*** harpists, percussionists.

Facilities

Recital hall? yes. ***Concert hall?*** yes. ***Recording studio?*** yes.

ROYAL CONSERVATORY OF MUSIC THE GLENN GOULD PROFESSIONAL SCHOOL

273 Bloor Street West, Toronto ON M55 1W2
Tel: 416-408-2824
Fax: 416-408-3096
Email: Professional_school@rcmusic.ca
Web: www.rcmusic.ca
Contact: Colleen Dideer

General

Type of Institution: college, conservatory. ***Environment:*** urban. ***Cross registration is available through the University of British Columbia.***

Total enrollment of institution: 160. ***Total student body from other countries:*** 60%. ***Degrees offered:*** BM, artist diploma.

Entrance Requirements

Audition required: live, audio, video. ***Other requirements:*** interview, recommendation. ***Standardized test requirements:*** TOEFL, 300.

Costs & Financial Aid

Application fee: $75. ***Deposit:*** $500.

Percent of students receiving financial aid: 95%. ***Types of scholarships and aid awarded:*** full, partial, merit-based, named, institutional aid, reduced tuition, tuition payment plan, work/study, gig office. ***Financial aid offered to international students. Percent of international students receiving scholarships:*** 50%.

Services

Housing options: off-campus housing.

Support staff: career counselor, financial aid advisor, foreign student advisor.

MUSIC

Curriculum, Students, and Faculty

Unique or innovative music curriculum: 1) technology component, 2) artist in the schools component, 3) professional-level orchestra, 4), master classes with international artists. ***How are major teacher assignments made?*** students may choose, made by the school. Faculty is informed of a student's teacher preference at the time of the audition. ***28 lessons with major teachers. May a student change major teachers during the course of study?*** possibly. ***Study of secondary instrument or discipline is allowed.***

Total enrollment: 160. ***Entering class size:*** 30. ***Graduating class size:*** 25. ***Percent international:*** 60%. ***Countries most represented:*** Eastern Europe, England, Asia.

Renowned alumni: Teresa Stratas; Glenn Gould; John Vicors; Martin Beaver; Jamie Parker, St. Lawrence String Quartet. ***Program contact person:*** Shannon Paterson.

Audition Information

Audition fee? $75. ***Audition consists of the following:*** orchestral excerpts, music theory rhythmic dictation, music history, melodic dictation. ***Instruments provided for:*** harpists, percussionists, organ, pianists.

Performance opportunities available (frequency): chamber music (frequently), jury examinations, opera workshops, orchestral concerts (frequently), recitals (frequently), produced operas, chorus.

Facilities

Number of practice rooms and hours: 90; 8:00 am-11:00 pm (Mon-Fri), 8:00 am-6:00 pm (Sat), 12:00 am-6:00 pm (Sun). ***Recital hall?*** yes. ***Concert hall?*** yes. ***Recording studio?*** no.

UNIVERSITY OF WATERLOO

Waterloo ON N2L 3GI
Tel: 519-888-4567
Fax: 519-746-2882
Email: registrar@uwaterloo.ca
Web: www.uwaterloo.ca

General

Type of Institution: public university. *Environment:* suburban. *Cross registration is available through Wilfred Laurier University.*

Total enrollment of institution: 21,903. *Total student body from other countries:* 6%. *Degrees offered:* BA.

Entrance Requirements

Standardized test requirements: SAT I; TOEFL, 600.

Costs & Financial Aid

Application fee: $80. *Tuition (in-state/out-state):* $3,350/$14,500. *Medical fee:* $400. *Other fees:* $240-$1,100.

Percent of students receiving financial aid: 33%. *Types of scholarships and aid awarded:* partial, merit-based, need-based, institutional aid, work/study. *Forms required for scholarships:* FAFSA. *Loans available. Procedure for applying for loans:* application. *Other aid available to international students:* International students may be considered for entrance. Scholarships based on academic standing.

Services

Housing options: on-site dorms, off-campus housing.

Support staff: career counselor, financial aid advisor, foreign student advisor, housing advisor, physical therapist, psychological counselor, resident assistant, resident nurse, student affairs officer.

DRAMA

Curriculum, Students, and Faculty

Required courses: drama criticism, theater history, theater production, dramatic literature.

Elective courses: acting, audition preparation, directing, movement, musical theater, scene study, speech, stage combat, voice.

Number of years required to complete program: 3 for a general Bachelor of Arts, 4 for honors Bachelor of Arts. *Summer program not available. No affiliation with a professional theater company. Selectivity for males:* most admitted, but not all. *Selectivity for females:* most admitted, but not all. *Total enrollment:* 49. *Graduating class size:* 10. *Percent international:* 4%.

Renowned alumni: Rebecca Jenkins

List of current faculty and past affiliations: Joel Greenberg, Theatre Aquarius (Hamilton), Marlene Smith Productions, Centaur Theatre William Chadwick- Playwright, Bill Chesney- Freelance designer; recent- Manitoba Theatre for young people, Centaur.

Audition Information

No audition fee. Audition consists of the following: comedic monologue, Shakespearean monologue, auditions are for senior course.

Performance Information

Performance opportunities available (frequency): fully produced performances (4 per year), informal performances (1-2 per semester), auditioned.

Facilities

Number of theaters on campus: 3. *Type and capacity:* proscenium—750 seats, thrust—498 seats, studio—65 seats.

MUSIC

Curriculum, Students, and Faculty

Unique or innovative music curriculum: emphasis on a liberal arts approach. Options in music and society (pop, world, women and music, jazz, etc.); arts administration and church music and worship options. *How are major teacher assignments made?* made by the school. Faculty is not informed of a student's teacher preference at the time of the audition. *12 lessons with major teacher. May a student change major teachers during the course of study?* possibly. *Study of secondary instrument or discipline is not allowed.*

Selectivity for instruments or programs offered (rating): accordion (non-competitive), bassoon (non-competitive), choral conducting (non-competitive), choral singing (non-competitive), clarinet (non-competitive), composition (non-competitive), double bass (non-competitive), flute or piccolo (non-competitive), French horn (non-competitive), guitar (non-competitive), harp (non-competitive), harpsichord (non-competitive), oboe/English horn (non-competitive), organ (non-competitive), percussion (non-competitive), piano (non-competitive), sacred music (non-competitive), saxophone (non-competitive), trombone (non-competitive), trumpet (non-competitive), tuba (non-competitive), viola (non-competitive), violin (non-competitive), violoncello (non-competitive), voice (non-competitive).

Program contact person: Carol Anne Weaver.

Audition Information

No audition fee. Audition consists of the following: sight reading, repertoire.

Required repertoire: 2 contrasting pieces at roughly Toronto Conservatory Grade 8 level or beyond. *Performance opportunities available (frequency):* jury examinations, recitals.

Facilities

Number of practice rooms and hours: 6; 12 hours per week. *Recital hall?* yes. *Concert hall?* no. *Recording studio?* no.

ENGLAND

GUILDHALL SCHOOL OF MUSIC & DRAMA

Barbican, London EC2Y 8 DT
Tel: 441-71-628-2571

General

Type of Institution: conservatory, coed.

Total enrollment of institution: 1,300. *Degrees offered:* BFA, BM.

Entrance Requirements

Audition required: live, audio.

Costs & Financial Aid

Tuition (in-state/out-state): $7,000/$11,000.

Types of scholarships and aid awarded: full, partial, merit-based, need-based, named. *Procedure for applying for loans:* limited scholarships available, apply by 6/1. *Financial aid offered to international students.*

ROYAL ACADEMY OF MUSIC

Marlebone Road, London NW15HT
Tel: 44-71-935-5461
Fax: 44-71-487-3342

General

Type of Institution: conservatory.

Total student body from other countries: 30%. *Degrees offered:* BM, artist diploma.

Entrance Requirements

Audition required: live, audio, video.

Costs & Financial Aid

Percent of international students receiving scholarships: 30%.

Services

Housing options: on-site dorms, off-campus housing.

FRANCE

CONSERVATOIRE NATIONAL SUPERIEUR DE DANSE DE PARIS

209 Avenue Jean James
7 Sorg, Paris
Tel: 0033140404633
Fax: 0033140404602
Email: danse@cusmdp.jr

General

Type of Institution: conservatory. *Environment:* urban.

Degrees offered: certificate, BA..

Entrance Requirements

Audition required: Other requirements: interview.

Costs & Financial Aid

Percent of students receiving financial aid: 20%. *Financial aid offered to international students.*

Services

Housing options: on-site dorms.

Support staff: career counselor, financial aid advisor, housing advisor, physical therapist, resident assistant, student affairs officer.

DANCE

Curriculum, Students, and Faculty

Required courses: anatomy, character, ballet, dance composition/choreography, master classes, men's class, modern dance, pas de deux, repertory, variations, melting pot.

Selectivity for males: approximately 33% admitted. *Selectivity for females:* approximately 10% admitted. *Percent international:* 2%. *Countries most represented:* France. *Program contact person:* Gicquel Christine.

Audition Information

Audition fee; Audition consists of the following: ballet, modern dance, pointe works, prepared solo. *Accompanist provided. Cassette player available; CD player available.*

Performance Information

Performance opportunities available (frequency): Fully produced concerts (8 per year), informal concerts (6 per year), workshops (4 per year), on-site performances (8 per year), touring (4 per year).

Performances choreographed by: students, guests.

Facilities

Number of studios available: 6. *Approximate studio dimensions and flooring:* 200 sq. m. Tapis. *Performance facilities:* 2 theaters, 1 studio.

MUSIC

Program contact person: Anussen Gretchen.

ECOLE SUPERIEUR DE DANSE DE CANNES

5 Rue de Colmar
06400 Cannes, France
Tel: 04-93-06-79-75
Fax: 04-93-06-79-78
Contact: Stephane Panaras
Rosella Hightower

GERMANY

ABTEILUNG CHOREOGRAPHIE DER THEATERHOCHSCHULE ERNST BUSCH

Hauptstrasse 2, Berlin D-10317
Tel: 030-636-22-61

Entrance Requirements

Audition not required.

Services

Support staff: housing advisor, psychological counselor, resident assistant.

DRAMA

Curriculum, Students, and Faculty

Elective courses: technical theater.

AKADEMIE DES TANZES DER STAATLICHEN HOCHSCHULE

Kunste, N7,18, Mannheim D-68161
Tel: 0621-292-35-15

Entrance Requirements

Audition not required.

DANCE

Curriculum, Students, and Faculty

Required courses: modern dance.

DRAMA

Curriculum, Students, and Faculty

Required courses: voice.

BALLETTAKADEMIE DES FREISTAATES BAYERN

Heinz-Bosl Stiftung
Wilhelmstrasse 19b, Munchen D-80801
Tel: 089-33-77-63

Entrance Requirements

Audition not required.

Costs & Financial Aid

Forms required for scholarships: FAFSA, income tax return, income asset verification.

Services

Support staff: psychological counselor, resident assistant, student affairs officer.

DANCE

Curriculum, Students, and Faculty

Required courses: variations.

BALLETGYMNASIUM ESSEN-WERDEN

Grafenstrasse 9, Essen D-45239
Tel: 0201 49 946

Entrance Requirements
Audition not required.

DANCE

Curriculum, Students, and Faculty
Elective courses: Spanish.

DRAMA

Curriculum, Students, and Faculty
Required courses: make-up.

BALLETTSCHULE DER HAMBURGISCHEN STAATSOPER; BALLETTZENTRUM

Caspar-Voght-Strasse 54, Hamburg D-20535
Tel: 4021118831
Fax: 40 211188-88

Entrance Requirements
Audition not required.

Services
Support staff: housing advisor, physical therapist, psychological counselor, resident assistant, resident nurse.

DANCE

Curriculum, Students, and Faculty
Required courses: pas de deux.

BALLETTSCHULE DER OPER LEIPZIG

Wilhelm-Seyfferth-Strasse 6, Leipzig D-04004
Tel: 341 2132632
Fax: 341 132691

Entrance Requirements
Audition not required.

Services
Support staff: psychological counselor, resident assistant, resident nurse, student affairs officer.

DANCE

Curriculum, Students, and Faculty
Required courses: pointe.

DRAMA

Curriculum, Students, and Faculty
Required courses: Alexander technique.

BALLETTSCHULE HAMBURG BALLETT

Ballett-Zentrum Hamburg
Caspar-Voght-Strasse 64, Hamburg D-20535
Tel: 040 21 11 88-31
Fax: 040 21 11 88 88

Entrance Requirements
Audition not required.

Services
Support staff: resident assistant, resident nurse.

DANCE

Curriculum, Students, and Faculty
Elective courses: men's class.

DRAMA

Curriculum, Students, and Faculty
Required courses: scene study.

DIE WERSTATT E.V. -EDDC

Bornestrasse 10, Dusseldorf D-40211
Tel: 0211-172-700

Entrance Requirements
Audition not required.

DANCE
Curriculum, Students, and Faculty
Elective courses: other world dance forms.

DRAMA
Curriculum, Students, and Faculty
Required courses: movement.

FACHGRUPPE BALLETT DER HOCHSCHULE FUR MUSIK UND DARSTELLENDE

Eschersheimer-Landstrasse 29-39, Frankfurt am Main 60322
Tel: 069-15-40-07-33 03 3

Entrance Requirements
Audition not required.

DANCE
Curriculum, Students, and Faculty
Elective courses: Limon-based modern dance.

DRAMA
Curriculum, Students, and Faculty
Required courses: mime, acting.

FOLKWANG-HOCHSCHULE ESSEN

Postfach 4428, Essen D-45224
Tel: 201-4903-0
Fax: 221-491-1618

Entrance Requirements
Audition not required.

DANCE
Curriculum, Students, and Faculty
Elective courses: rehearsal and performance, movement techniques

DRAMA
Curriculum, Students, and Faculty
Required courses: drama criticism, scene study.

HEINZ-BOSL-STIFTUNG BALLETTAKADEMIE DES FREISTAATES BAYERN

Wilhelmstrasse 19b, Munchen D-80801
Tel: 89337763
Fax: 89 344221

Entrance Requirements
Audition not required.

DANCE
Curriculum, Students, and Faculty
Required courses: stagecraft, nutrition.

DRAMA
Curriculum, Students, and Faculty
Required courses: musical theater, movement.

HOCHSCHULE DER KUNSTE

Darstellende Kunst Fasanen Strasse 1B, Berlin 10623
Tel: 49 30 3185 2334
Fax: 49 30 3185 2689
Email: presse@hak-berlin.de
Web: presse@hdk-berlin.de
Contact: Ursala Stephen-Rechenmacher

General
Type of Institution: public, university, conservatory. *Environment:* urban. *Academic education is offered on-site. Cross registration is available through the Free University, Technical University, Humboldt University.*

Total enrollment of institution: 4,600. *Total student body from other countries:* 15%. *Degrees offered:* diploma.

Entrance Requirements

Audition required: live. *Other requirements:* essay, photograph.

Costs & Financial Aid

Other fees: DM300 per month room, DM100 per month medical, DM40 per semester student welfare contribution, DM15 per semester student union fees, DM100 per semester administrative fee.

Types of scholarships and aid awarded: full, merit-based. *Procedure for applying for loans:* request application form from Ms. Ursula Stephan-Rechenmacher. *Other aid available to international students:* German Academic Exchange Service (DAAD) in Bonn offers scholarships for study in Germany.

Services

Housing options: off-campus housing.

Support staff: college advisor, foreign student advisor, psychological counselor, student affairs officer.

DANCE

Curriculum, Students, and Faculty

Required courses: ballet, dance composition/choreography, jazz, modern dance, movement techniques, rehearsal and performance, tap, vernacular dance.

Selectivity for males: approximately 10% admitted. *Selectivity for females:* approximately 10% admitted. *Total enrollment:* 28. *Entering class size:* 12. *Graduating class size:* 9. *Percent international:* 3%. *Total part-time faculty:* 12. *Program contact person:* Ursula Stephan-Rechenmacher.

Audition Information

Audition consists of the following: ballet, improvisation, modern dance, orthopedic evaluation, prepared solo. *Accompanist provided. Cassette player available; CD player available. Dress requirements for males:* tights, ballet slippers, jazz shoes. *Dress requirements for females:* leotard, ballet slippers, jazz shoes.

Performance Information

Performance opportunities available (frequency): Informal concerts workshops.

Performances choreographed by: faculty.

Facilities

Number of studios available: 4. *Approximate studio dimensions and flooring:* wood.

HOCHSCHULE DES SAARLANDES FUR MUSIK UND THEATER

Bismarckstrasse 1, Saarbrucken D-66111
Tel: 681 96731-0
Fax: 681 96731-30

Entrance Requirements

Audition not required.

HOCHSCHULE FUR KUNSTE BREMEN

Am Wandrahm 23, Bermen D-28195
Tel: 421 3019-0
Fax: 421 3019 119

Entrance Requirements

Audition not required.

HOCHSCHULE FUR MUSIK CARL MARIA VON WEBER

Wettiner Platz 13
PF120039, Dresden 01001
Tel: 49351492360
Fax: 493514923657
Contact: Frau Geidel

General

Environment: urban.

Total enrollment of institution: 750. *Total student body from other countries:* 8%. *Degrees offered:* German diploma.

Entrance Requirements

Audition required: live.

Services

Housing options: off-campus housing.

Support staff: college advisor, foreign student advisor, student affairs officer.

MUSIC

Curriculum, Students, and Faculty

How are major teacher assignments made? students may choose, according to teacher preference and teacher availability. Faculty is not informed of a student's teacher preference at the time of the audition. *32 lessons with major teacher. May a student change major teachers during the course of study?* possibly. *Study of secondary instrument or discipline is allowed.*

Selectivity for instruments or programs offered (rating): accompanying (selective), bassoon (selective), choral conducting (selective), clarinet (selective), composition (selective), flute or piccolo (highly selective), guitar (selective), jazz (selective), oboe/English horn (selective), orchestral conducting (highly selective), piano (highly selective), saxophone (highly selective), trombone (highly selective), trumpet (selective), tuba (highly selective), viola (selective), violin (selective), violoncello (selective), voice (highly selective).

Total enrollment: 750. *Entering class size:* 103. *Graduating class size:* 85 *Percent international:* 8%. *Countries most represented:* Japan. *Program contact person:* Frau Geidel.

Audition Information

Audition consists of the following: music theory, rhythmic dictation, sight reading, melodic dictation, repertoire. *Instruments provided for:* harpists, percussionists.

Repertoire that students should avoid? no.

Facilities

Recital hall? yes. *Recording studio?* yes.

HOCHSCHULE FUR MUSIK DETMOLD

Neustandt 22
Tel: 5231 975 5
Fax: 5231 975 972

Entrance Requirements

Audition not required.

DANCE

Curriculum, Students, and Faculty

Required courses: modern dance.

HOCHSCHULE FUR MUSIK "FRANZ LISZT" WEIMAR

Postfach 552, Weimar D-99423
Tel: 3643 555-0
Fax: 3643 61865

Entrance Requirements

Audition not required.

DANCE

Curriculum, Students, and Faculty

Required courses: ballet.

HOCHSCHULE FUR MUSIK "HANNS EISLER" BERLIN

Postfach 1 47, Berlin D-10104
Tel: 30 20209-2411
Fax: 30 20309-2408

Entrance Requirements

Audition not required.

DANCE

Curriculum, Students, and Faculty

Required courses: pointe.

HOCHSCHULE FUR MUSIK IN MUNCHEN

Arcisstrasse 12, Munchen 80333
Tel: 49-89-28901
Fax: 49-89-28927419
Web: www.musikhochschule.muenchen.mhn.d
Contact: Dr. Alexander Krause

General

Type of Institution: university. *Environment:* urban.

Degrees offered: German diploma.

Entrance Requirements
Audition required: live. *Other requirements:* essay, photograph, school's own English exam required.

Services
Housing options: off-campus housing.

Support staff: career counselor, financial aid advisor, foreign student advisor, housing advisor, physical therapist, psychological counselor, resident assistant, resident nurse, student affairs officer.

HOCHSCHULE FUR MUSIK KOLN-TANZ

Dagobert Strasse 38, Koln D-50668
Tel: 49-221-725031
Fax: 49-221-131204
Web: www.mhs-koeln.de

General
Type of Institution: university. *Environment:* urban

Total student body from other countries: 25%. *Degrees offered:* German diploma.

Entrance Requirements
Audition required. Other requirements: interview.

Costs & Financial Aid
Other fees: DM 186.50 registration.

Loans available.

Services
Housing options: off-campus housing.

Support staff: career counselor, college advisor, dorm parent, financial aid advisor, foreign student advisor, housing advisor, physical therapist, psychological counselor, resident assistant, resident nurse, student affairs officer.

HOCHSCHULE FUR MUSIK UND DARSTELLENDE KUNST FRANFURT AM MAIN

Eschersheimer Landstrasse 29-39, Frankfurt am Main D-60322
Tel: 69 154007-0
Fax: 69 154007-108

Entrance Requirements
Audition not required.

DANCE
Curriculum, Students, and Faculty
Required courses: Alexander Technique.

DRAMA
Curriculum, Students, and Faculty
Elective courses: voice.

HOCHSCHULE FUR MUSIK UND THEATER "FELIX MENDELSSOHN BARTHOLDY"

Postfach 100809, Leipzig 04008
Tel: 49-341-2144-620
Fax: 49-341-2144-624
Email: breich@rz.uni-leipzig.de
Contact: Dr. Sabine Witzel

General
Type of Institution: public college. *Environment:* urban.

Total enrollment of institution: 811. *Total student body from other countries:* 15%. *Degrees offered:* German diploma.

Entrance Requirements
Audition required: live, audio. *Other requirements:* photograph, school's own English exam required.

Costs & Financial Aid
Application fee: $6. *Other fees:* DM 200 per month room.

Services
Housing options: off-campus housing.

Support staff: college advisor, foreign student advisor, housing advisor, student affairs officer.

DANCE
Curriculum, Students, and Faculty
Required courses: rehearsal and performance.

DRAMA
Curriculum, Students, and Faculty
Elective courses: speech.

MUSIC

Curriculum, Students, and Faculty

Unique or innovative music curriculum: applied lessons are 90 minutes. *How are major teacher assignments made?* Students may choose. Faculty is informed of a student's teacher preference at the time of the audition. *32 lessons with major teacher. May a student change major teachers during the course of study?* possibly. *Study of secondary instrument or discipline is allowed.*

Selectivity for instruments or programs offered (rating): accompanying (competitive), bassoon (non-competitive), choral conducting (non-competitive), clarinet (competitive), composition (competitive), double bass (non-competitive), flute or piccolo (selective), French horn (selective), guitar (non-competitive), harp (non-competitive), harpsichord (non-competitive), jazz (selective), oboe/English horn (competitive), orchestral conducting (selective), organ (competitive), percussion (non-competitive), piano (highly selective), sacred music (competitive), saxophone (non-competitive), trombone (competitive), trumpet (competitive), tuba (non-competitive), viola (competitive), violin (highly selective), violoncello (competitive), voice (highly selective).

Total enrollment: 691. *Entering class size:* 120. *Graduating class size:* 70. *Percent international:* 15%.

Total full-time faculty: 81. *Total part-time faculty:* 60. *Program contact person:* Dr. Sabine Witzel.

Audition Information

No audition fee. Audition consists of the following: repertoire. *Instruments provided for:* harpists, percussionists.

Required repertoire: information available from the Admissions Office. *Performance opportunities available (frequency):* chamber music, orchestral concerts, recitals.

Facilities

Number of practice rooms and hours: 70; 8:00 am-9:45 pm. *Recital hall?* yes. *Recording studio?* yes.

HOCHSCHULE FUR MUSIK UND THEATER HAMBURG

Harvestehuder Weg 12, Hamburg D-20148
Tel: 40 44195-0
Fax: 40 44295-666

Entrance Requirements

Audition not required.

Services

Support staff: housing advisor, resident assistant, student affairs officer.

DANCE

Curriculum, Students, and Faculty

Required courses: ballet.

DRAMA

Curriculum, Students, and Faculty

Elective courses: scene study.

HOCHSCHULE FUR MUSIK UND THEATER HANNOVER

Emmichplatz 1, Hannover D-30175
Tel: 511-3100-1
Fax: 511-3100-200

Entrance Requirements

Audition not required.

DANCE

Curriculum, Students, and Faculty

Required courses: variations.

DRAMA

Curriculum, Students, and Faculty

Elective courses: Stanislavski exercises.

HOCHSCHULE FUR MUSIK UND THEATER ROSTOCK

Am Bussebart 11, Rostock D-18055
Tel: 381 2020-621
Fax: 381 2020-625

Entrance Requirements
Audition not required.

Services
Support staff: housing advisor, physical therapist, psychological counselor, resident assistant, resident nurse, student affairs officer.

DANCE
Curriculum, Students, and Faculty
Required courses: pas de deux.

DRAMA
Curriculum, Students, and Faculty
Elective courses: improvisation.

HOCHSCHULE FUR MUSIK WURZBURG

Hofstallstrasse 6-8, Wurzburg D-97070
Tel: 931 32187-0
Fax: 931 14408

Entrance Requirements
Audition not required.

DANCE
Curriculum, Students, and Faculty
Required courses: pointe, men's class, modern dance.

DRAMA
Curriculum, Students, and Faculty
Elective courses: audition preparation, directing.

INSTITUT FUR BUHNENTANZ DER MUSIK HOCHSCHULE KOLN

Dagoberstrasse 38, Koln D-50668
Tel: 0221 912 81 80

Entrance Requirements
Audition not required.

DANCE
Curriculum, Students, and Faculty
Required courses: Graham-based modern dance, Pilates, dance writing research and criticism.

DRAMA
Curriculum, Students, and Faculty
Elective courses: audition preparation.

JOHN CRANKO SCHULE; BALLETTSCHULE DES WURTEMBERGISCHEN STAAT

Urbanstrasse 94, Stuttgart D-70190
Tel: 0711 28 53 90
Fax: 0711 28 53 934

Entrance Requirements
Audition not required.

DANCE
Curriculum, Students, and Faculty
Required courses: rehearsal and performance.

DRAMA
Curriculum, Students, and Faculty
Required courses: stage combat, make-up, acting.

MUSIK HOCHSCHULE LUBECK

Grosse Petersgrube 17-28, Lubeck 23552
Tel: 49-451-15050
Fax: 49-451-1505300
Email: info@mh-luebeck.de
Web: www.mh-luebeck.de

General

Type of Institution: public, conservatory. *Environment:* urban.

Total student body from other countries: 25%. *Degrees offered:* German diploma.

Entrance Requirements

Audition required: live. *Other requirements:* photograph.

Costs & Financial Aid

Other fees: students' welfare board, students' union, transportation.

Other aid available to international students: private grants.

Services

Housing options: off-campus housing, family.

Support staff: student affairs officer.

Comments

Our general acceptance average is 20-25% of applicants.

DRAMA

Curriculum, Students, and Faculty

Required courses: movement.

MUSIC

Curriculum, Students, and Faculty

How are major teacher assignments made? students may choose, made by the school according to teacher preference and teacher availability. Faculty is informed of a student's teacher preference at the time of the audition. *33 lessons with major teacher. May a student change major teachers during the course of study?* possibly. *Study of secondary instrument or discipline is allowed.*

Selectivity for instruments or programs offered (rating): accordion (competitive), bassoon (selective), clarinet (selective), composition (highly selective), double bass (selective), flute or piccolo (selective), French horn (selective), guitar (selective), harp (selective), oboe/English horn (selective), orchestral conducting (highly selective), organ (selective), percussion (highly selective), piano (selective), sacred music (competitive), trumpet (selective), viola (highly selective), violin (highly selective), violoncello (highly selective), voice (highly selective).

Total enrollment: 480. *Entering class size:* 85. *Graduating class size:* 50. *Percent international:* 25%. *Countries most represented:* Japan, Korea, Russia.

Total full-time faculty: 36. *Total part-time faculty:* 150. *Program contact person:* Achim Stenzel.

Audition Information

Audition consists of the following: orchestral excerpts, music theory, rhythmic dictation, arpeggios, sight reading, music history. *Instruments provided for:* harpists, percussionists.

Performance opportunities available (frequency): band, orchestral concerts, recitals, produced operas, chorus.

Facilities

Number of practice rooms and hours: 46. *Recital hall?* yes. *Concert hall?* yes. *Recording studio?* yes.

PALUCCA SCHULE DRESDEN

Basteiplate 4, Dresden D-01277
Tel: 49-351-259-060
Fax: 49-351-259-06-11
Contact: Mrs. Golker

General

Type of Institution: college, university, boarding. *Environment:* urban. *Academic education is offered on-site.*

Total student body from other countries: 10% *Degrees offered:* diploma for professional dance.

Entrance Requirements

Audition required: live, video. *Other requirements:* recommendation, photograph.

Costs & Financial Aid

Tuition: $1,500. *Other fees:* medical insurance fee.

Percent of students receiving financial aid: 5%. *Types of scholarships and aid awarded:* full, partial, merit-based, need-based, reduced tuition. *Percent of international students receiving scholarships:* 10%. *Other aid available to international students:* partial scholarships for students from abroad under special circumstances.

Services

Housing options: off-campus housing.

Support staff: foreign student advisor, housing advisor, physical therapist, psychological counselor, student affairs officer.

DANCE

Curriculum, Students, and Faculty

Required courses: anatomy, character, ballet, dance composition/choreography, dance history, dance theory, jazz, Labanotation, master classes, men's class, modern dance, Limon-based modern dance, movement techniques, Laban Movement Studies, music, nutrition, pas de deux, pointe, rehearsal and performance, repertory, Spanish, variations.

Selectivity for males: approximately 33% admitted. *Selectivity for females:* approximately 10% admitted. *Total enrollment:* 185. *Entering class size:* 30. *Graduating class size:* 20. *Percent international:* 10%. *Countries most represented:* Austria, Korea.

Renowned alumni: Raymond Hilbert, Birgit Scherzer, Hannelore Bey, Stephan Thob.

Total full-time faculty: 18. *Total part-time faculty:* 15. *List of current faculty and past affiliations:* dancers from well-renowned European dance companies with teacher training diplomas. *Program contact person:* Mrs. Wandthe/Mr. Tappendorff.

Audition Information

No audition fee. Audition consists of the following: ballet, improvisation, modern dance, orthopedic evaluation, pointe works. *Accompanist provided. Cassette player available; CD player available. Dress requirements for males:* leotard, tights. *Dress requirements for females:* leotard, tights.

Performance Information

Performance opportunities available (frequency): fully produced concerts (6-8 per year), workshops (40 per year), on-site performances (15-20 per year), touring (1-2 per year).

Performances choreographed by: faculty, students, guests. *Recent guest choreographers:* Brigitta Luisa Merki, Dietmar Seyffort, Alan Danielson.

Facilities

Number of studios available: 7. *Approximate studio dimensions and flooring:* 12 m. x 24 m. swinging wooden floor with standard dance mats. 10m. x 16m. swing wooden floor with standard dance mats. *Performance facilities:* 2 large studios.

ROBERT-SCHUMANN-HOCHSCHULE DUSSELDORF

Fisherstrasse 110, Dusseldorf D-40476
Tel: 211 4918-0
Fax: 211 4911618

General

Type of Institution: college. *Environment:* suburban

Total enrollment of institution: 1,350. *Degrees offered:* BA, BS in music performance, BS in music education.

Entrance Requirements

Audition not required.

Costs & Financial Aid

Loans available.

DRAMA

Curriculum, Students, and Faculty

Elective courses: make-up, speech.

STAATLICHE BALLETTSCHULE BERLIN UND SCHULE FUR ARTISTIK-FACHRICHTUNG BUHNENTANZ

Erich-Weinert-Strasse 103, Berlin D-10409
Tel: 49-30-424-4028
Fax: 49-30-424-5987

General

Type of Institution: public conservatory. *Environment:* urban. *Academic education is offered on-site.*

Total enrollment of institution: 175. *Total student body from other countries:* 24%. *Degrees offered:* dance diploma.

Entrance Requirements

Audition required: live. *Other requirements:* interview, photograph.

Costs & Financial Aid

Other fees: accident insurance.

Loans available. Procedure for applying for loans: only for Germans. *Other aid available to international students:* if foreign students take full education, for example, practice and theory, education is free. They must be fluent in German.

Services

Housing options: on-site dorms.

Support staff: foreign student advisor, physical therapist, resident assistant, student affairs officer.

Comments

All international students are required to take a German language proficieny exam. If foreign students take full education such as practice and theory, education is free. They must be fluent in German.

DANCE

Curriculum, Students, and Faculty

Required courses: anatomy, character, ballet, dance history, dance theory, historical dance, jazz, men's class, modern dance, music, pas de deux, pointe, rehearsal and performance, repertory, variations.

Elective courses: Benesh notation.

Selectivity for males: approximately 60% admitted. *Selectivity for females:* approximately 33% admitted. *Total enrollment:* 175. *Entering class size:* 29. *Graduating class size:* 29. *Percent international:* 24%. *Countries most represented:* Switzerland, Russia.

Renowned alumni: Oliver Matz, Raimondo Rebeck, Gregor Seyffert, Steffi Scherzer, Angela Reinhardt

Total full-time faculty: 16. *Total part-time faculty:* 2. *List of current faculty and past affiliations:* Tamar Ben-Ami, Marc Bogaerts, Astrid Erlach, Emilia Gabriel, Kelvin Hardy, Barbara Harendt, Jaako Helkavaara Olaf Hofer, Anita Iden, Ursula Leesch, Stefan Lux, Harry Muller, Angelina Nikiforowa, Karin Sandner, Elena Shemtschushina, Gyorgyike Seilkopf, Margot Weschke-Leupold, Christel Wirsching. *Program contact person:* Jaako Helkavaara.

Audition Information

Audition consists of the following: ballet, improvisation, modern dance, orthopedic evaluation. *Accompanist provided.*

Audition evaluation criteria: musicality, technical standard, suitability.

Performance Information

Performance opportunities available (frequency): fully produced concerts (3), on-site performances (14), regular participation in repertory of local opera houses.

Performances choreographed by: faculty.

Facilities

Number of studios available: 9. *Approximate studio dimensions and flooring:* 65 sq. m.-400 sq. m. linoleum and wood. *Performance facilities:* a studio with lighting.

DRAMA

Curriculum, Students, and Faculty

Required courses: text analysis, acting.

STAATILCHE HOCHSCHULE FUR MUSIK FREIBURG I. BR.

Postfach, Freiburg I, Berlin D-79095

Entrance Requirements

Audition not required.

DRAMA

Curriculum, Students, and Faculty

Required courses: movement.

STAATLICHE HOCHSCHULE FUR MUSIK KARLSRUHE

Wolfartsweierer Strasse 7a, Karlsruhe D-76131
Tel: 721 6629 0
Fax: 721 6629 66

Entrance Requirements

Audition not required.

DANCE

Curriculum, Students, and Faculty

Elective courses: variations.

DRAMA

Curriculum, Students, and Faculty

Elective courses: stage combat.

STAATLICHE HOCHSCHULE FUR MUSIK TROSSINGEN

Schultheiss-Koch-Platz 3, Trossingen D-78647
Tel: 49-7425-94910
Fax: 49-7425-949148

General

Type of Institution: public, university, conservatory.

Total enrollment of institution: 495. *Total student body from other countries:* 30%. *Degrees offered:* Diplom Musikleherin Diplom Orchestermusikerlin.

Entrance Requirements

Audition required: live. *Other requirements:* interview.

Services

Housing options: on-site dorms.

Support staff: foreign student advisor, student affairs officer.

MUSIC

Curriculum, Students, and Faculty

How are major teacher assignments made? students may choose according to teacher availability. Faculty is informed of a student's teacher preference at the time of the audition. *May a student change major teachers during the course of study?* possibly.

Selectivity for instruments or programs offered (rating): accompanying (highly selective), accordion (competitive), bassoon (competitive), choral conducting (highly selective), choral singing (competitive), clarinet (competitive), composition (non-competitive), double bass (competitive), flute or piccolo (competitive), French horn (competitive), guitar (competitive), harpsichord (competitive), jazz (competitive), oboe/English horn (competitive), orchestral conducting (selective), organ (competitive), percussion (competitive), piano (highly selective), sacred music (competitive), trombone (competitive), trumpet (selective), tuba (competitive), viola (competitive), violin (competitive), violoncello (competitive), voice (competitive).

Total enrollment: 495. *Entering class size:* 88. *Percent international:* 30%. *Countries most represented:* Korea, Japan.

Total full-time faculty: 47. *Total part-time faculty:* 113. *Program contact person:* Fran Weissen.

Audition Information

Audition consists of the following: scales, orchestral excerpts, music theory, rhythmic dictation, sight reading, improvisation, melodic dictation, repertoire. *Instruments provided for:* percussionists.

Facilities

Recital hall? yes. *Concert hall?* yes.

STAATLICHE HOCHSCHULE FUR MUSIK UND DARSTELLENDE KUNST

N7,18, Mannhiem D-68161
Tel: 621-292-3514
Fax: 612-292-2072

Entrance Requirements

Audition not required.

DANCE

Curriculum, Students, and Faculty

Elective courses: character.

DRAMA

Curriculum, Students, and Faculty

Elective courses: verse drama.

STAATLICHE HOCHSCHULE FUR MUSIK UND DARSTELLENDE KUNST

Urbansplatz 2, Stuttgart D-70182
Tel: 711 212-0
Fax: 711 212-4639

Entrance Requirements

Audition not required.

DANCE

Curriculum, Students, and Faculty

Required courses: modern dance.

DRAMA

Curriculum, Students, and Faculty

Elective courses: make-up.

STUDIENGANG TANZ DER HOCHSCHULE

Emmichplatz 1, Hannover 30175
Tel: 0511 31 00 237

Entrance Requirements

Audition not required.

DANCE

Curriculum, Students, and Faculty

Required courses: dance composition/choreography.

DRAMA

Curriculum, Students, and Faculty

Required courses: drama criticism.

DANCE

Curriculum, Students, and Faculty

Required courses: ballet (5 classes per week, 4 years to complete), dance composition/choreography (1-2 classes per week, 4 years to complete), dance history (1 class per week, 4 years to complete), Labanotation (1 class per week, 4 years to complete), men's class (2 classes per week, 4 years to complete), Graham-based modern dance (5 classes per week, 4 years to complete), Limon-based modern dance (5 classes per week, 4 years to complete), Pilates (3 classes per week, 4 years to complete), music (1 class per week, 3 years to complete), pas de deux (1 class per week, 2 years to complete), pointe (2-4 classes per week, 4 years to complete), variations (2 classes per week, 3 years to complete).

Selectivity for males: approximately 60% admitted. *Selectivity for females:* approximately 33% admitted. *Graduating class size:* 10. *Percent international:* 50%. *Countries most represented:* France, Spain, Italy, Turkey.

Renowned alumni: Jochen Ulrich, Tanz forum Koln; Bernd Schindowski, Ballet director Gelsenkirchen; Heide Tegeder, Hannover.

Total full-time faculty: 8. *Total part-time faculty:* 5. *List of current faculty and past affiliations:* Paul Melis, Ballet de XXieme Siecle, Tanzforum/Koln, Rambert Dance Company; Armgard ron Bardeleben, Martha Graham Company; Ursula Borrmann, Palucca School. *Program contact person:* Paul Melis/Armgard von Bardeleben.

Audition Information

No audition fee. Audition consists of the following: ballet, modern dance, pointe works. *Accompanist provided. Cassette player available; CD player available. Dress requirements for males:* tight fitting dance clothing. *Dress requirements for females:* tight fitting dance clothing.

Audition evaluation criteria: appearance, classical training, musicality, physicality, coordination, response to corrections.

Performance Information

Performance opportunities available (frequency): Fully produced concerts (2 per year), informal concerts (1-3 per semster), workshops (2 per semster).

Performances choreographed by: faculty, students, guests. *Recent guest choreographers:* Vera Sander; Christina Sommerlade; Michael Hall.

Facilities

Number of studios available: 4. *Approximate studio dimensions and flooring:* 36' x 51' sprung floor

Harlequin, 21' x 21' sprung floor, Harlequin, 45' x 45' sprung floor, Harlequin, 45' x 45' sprung floor, Harlequin. *Performance facilities:* Konzert Halle at Hochschule, Koln; Studio I and II can be made into a theater to seat 146 people. Fully equipped stage.

HONG KONG

THE HONG KONG ACADEMY FOR PERFORMING ARTS

1 Gloucester Road, Wanchai
Tel: 852-2584-8500
Fax: 852-2802-4372
Email: aso@mail.hkapa.edu
Web: www.hkapa.edu

General

Type of Institution: public college. *Environment:* urban.

Total enrollment of institution: 697. *Total student body from other countries:* 12%. *Degrees offered:* certificate, BFA, BM, advanced diploma, professional diploma, advanced certificate, professional certificate.

Entrance Requirements

Audition required: live, video. *Other requirements:* interview, photograph. *Standardized test requirements:* TOEFL, school's own English exam required.

Costs & Financial Aid

Other fees: HK$250 new student caution money, HK$70 student union membership, HK$100 annual union fees.

Types of scholarships and aid awarded: full, partial, merit-based, need-based, gig office. *Forms required for scholarships:* income tax return. *Loans available. Financial aid offered to international students. Percent of international students receiving scholarships:* 62%.

Services

Housing options: off-campus housing.

Support staff: physical therapist, psychological counselor, resident nurse, student affairs officer.

DANCE

Curriculum, Students, and Faculty

Required courses: acting (1-2 classes per week, 4 years to complete), anatomy, character (1 class per week, 5 years to complete), ballet (5 classes per week, 5 years to complete), dance composition/choreography, musical theater dance (1-4 classes per week, 4 years to complete), dance history, dance theory, dance writing research and criticism, improvisation (2 classes per week, 5 years to complete), jazz (2 classes per week, 3 years to complete), Labanotation, master classes, men's class (2 classes per week, 5 years to complete), modern dance (2 classes per week, 3 years to complete), body conditioning (1 class per week, 4 years to complete), music, pas de deux (1-2 classes per week, 4 years to complete), pointe (2 classes per week, 5 years to complete), repertory (1-4 classes per week, 5 years to complete), singing (1-2 classes per week, 4 years to complete), stagecraft, tap (2 classes per week, 4 years to complete), variations (1-2 classes per week, 4 years to complete), contact improvisation (2 classes per week, 1 year to complete), coaching (1 class per week, 2 years to complete), acrobatics (2 classes per week, 2 years to complete), Chinese classical dance (5 classes per week, 5 years to complete), shen yun (2 classes per week, 5 years to complete), Chinese folk dance (4 classes per week, 5 years to complete), Chinese dance repertory (1-3 classes per week, 5 years to complete), Chinese dance (2 classes per week, 3 years to complete).

Selectivity for males: approximately 60% admitted. *Selectivity for females:* approximately 60% admitted. *Total enrollment:* 147. *Entering class size:* 37. *Graduating class size:* 11. *Percent international:* 29%. *Countries most represented:* Taiwan.

Renowned alumni: Tran Thuc Hahn, Broadway revival the King and I; William Yong, Adventures in Motion Pictures; L-e Mai Linh, Cleveland/San Jose Ballet; Stella Lay, Pasha Umer, Xaio Ming, Mike Wong, Tso Po-Lin, Anthony Meh, Mikey Lee, Stanley Chu.

Total full-time faculty: 17. *Total part-time faculty:* 28. *List of current faculty and past affiliations:* Margaret Carlson, Cleveland Ballet, Univeristy of Akron; Tom Brown; Rudy Perez; Danny Lewis; Cheung Yuen-Chiu, Central Ballet; Geta Constantinescy, Romanian State Opera Ballet; Graeme Collins, Heat Ballet-Australian Ballet; Rosalind Newman, Wesleyan, Rotterdam, London Contemporary. *Program contact person:* Winnie Wong.

Audition Information

No audition fee. Audition consists of the following: ballet, improvisation, modern dance, orthopedic evaluation, pointe works, prepared solo, music test for all, musical theater class and Chinese dance class for Chinese applicants, singing test for musical theater applicants. *Accompanist provided. Cassette player available; CD player available. Dress requirements for males:* proper dance attire, no leg or body warmers. *Dress requirements for females:* proper dance attire with no leg or body warmers.

Audition evaluation criteria: physique; coordination; rhythmic understanding.

Performance Information

Performance opportunities available (frequency): Fully produced concerts (5 per year), informal concerts (2 per year), workshops (frequently), on-site performances (5 per year), touring (2-4 per year), interships with Hong Kong professional companies.

Performances choreographed by: faculty, students, guests. *Recent guest choreographers:* Jeffery Hughes, Lin Hwai-min, Yuri Ng, Helen Lai, Isabella Fokine, Bettijane Sills, Tom Evert.

Facilities

Number of studios available: 10. *Approximate studio dimensions and flooring:* 50 sq. m.-480 sq. m. sprung wooden floors, some with Marley covering. *Performance facilities:* 5 theaters of various sizes from 120-1,171 seats.

DRAMA

Curriculum, Students, and Faculty

Required courses: acting, audition preparation, directing, drama criticism, dramaturgy, improvisation, make-up, martial arts, mime, movement, scene study, speech, stage combat, Stanislavski exercises, text analysis, verse drama, voice.

Number of years required to complete program: 2-3. *Summer program not available. Selectivity for males:* approximately 10% admitted. *Selectivity for females:* approximately 10% admitted. *Total enrollment:* 111. *Entering class size:* 26. *Graduating class size:* 15. *Percent international:* 2%.

Total full-time faculty: 8. *Total part-time faculty:* 8.

Audition Information

No audition fee. Audition consists of the following: a cappella singing, comedic monologue, required monologue, movement class, Shakespearean monologue.

Performance Information

Performance opportunities available (frequency): fully produced performances (7 per year), informal performances (1-2 per year), workshops (1 per week), off-site performances (occasionally) assigned, auditioned.

Recent guest artists: Gao Xing-jian, Travis Preston.

Facilities

Rehearsal facilities and hours: drama rehearsal rooms. *Number of theaters on campus:* 3. *Type and capacity:* studio.

MUSIC

Curriculum, Students, and Faculty

Unique or innovative music curriculum: Many performance opportunities including opera, orchestra, choral, solo and chamber concerts, both within and outside the Academy. Over 90 visiting artists come and give master classes, workshops, lectures, etc. each year. *How are major teacher assignments made?* students may choose, made by the school according to teacher preference. Faculty is not informed of a student's teacher preference at the time of the audition. *32 lessons with major teacher. May a student change major teachers during the course of study?* possibly. *Study of secondary instrument or discipline is allowed.*

Selectivity for instruments or programs offered (rating): accompanying (highly selective), bassoon (non-competitive), clarinet (non-competitive), composition (selective), double bass (non-competitive), electronic music (selective), flute or piccolo (competitive), French horn (non-competitive), guitar (selective), harp (non-competitive), harpsichord (selective), oboe/English horn (competitive), organ (competitive), percussion (competitive), piano (highly selective), saxophone (non-competitive), trombone (non-competitive), trumpet (non-competitive), tuba (non-competitive), viola (selective), violin (selective), violoncello (selective), voice (selective), Chinese instruments (competitive).

Total enrollment: 181. *Entering class size:* 41. *Graduating class size:* 21. *Percent international:* 19%. *Countries most represented:* Mainland China.

Total full-time faculty: 17. *Total part-time faculty:* 100. *Program contact person:* Lisa Tzeng.

Audition Information

No audition fee. Audition consists of the following: scales, music theory, rhythmic dictation, arpeggios, sight reading, music history, melodic dictation. *Instruments provided for:* harpists, percussionists.

Required repertoire: no required repertoire but need contrasting works demonstrating level of ability. *Repertoire that students should avoid?* no. *Performance opportunities available (frequency):*

band, jury examinations, produced operas, chorus.

Facilities

Number of practice rooms and hours: 20; 8:00 am-11:00 pm. *Recital hall?* yes. *Concert hall?* yes. *Recording studio?* yes.

JAPAN

TOHO GAKUEN SCHOOL OF MUSIC

1-41-1 Wakaba-Cho
Chofu-Shi, Tokyo 182
Tel: 81-03-3307-4401 ext. 4401
Fax: 81-03-3326-8844

General

Type of Institution: public conservatory. *Environment:* urban.

Degrees offered: BM, diploma, soloist diploma, ensemble diploma.

Entrance Requirements

Audition required: live, audio, video.

Costs & Financial Aid

Types of scholarships and aid awarded: full, partial, merit-based, need-based. *Procedure for applying for loans:* scholarships are available, file school form by 2/1. ***Financial aid offered to international students.***

Services

Housing options: on-site dorms, off-campus housing.

SWITZERLAND

STIFTUNG SCHWEIZERISCHE BALLETTBERUFSSCHULE

Seefeldstrasse 225, Zurich CH-8008
Tel: 01 422 46 86
Fax: 01 42 47 77

Entrance Requirements

Audition not required.

DANCE

Curriculum, Students, and Faculty

Required courses: stagecraft.

DRAMA

Curriculum, Students, and Faculty

Required courses: audition preparation.

10

SUMMER PROGRAM PROFILES—DANCE

ALABAMA

LATE DAY OF LATE SUMMER/SUMMER SEMINAR

Winter Contact Information
Alabama Dance Theatre at the Armory Learning Arts Center, 1018 Madison Avenue, Montgomery AL 36104
Tel: 334-241-2590
Fax: 334-241-2504
Contact: Kitty Seale

Summer Contact Information
Alabama Dance Theatre at the Armory Learning Arts Center, 1018 Madison Avenue, Montgomery AL 36104
Tel: 334-241-2590
Fax: 334-241-2504
Contact: Kitty Seale

General

Minimum age or age range: 10. *Level of program:* intermediate, advanced.

High school credit available? no. *College credit available?* no.

Application Information

Program dates: first 2 weeks of August. *Application deadline:* early July. *Application fee:* none. *Requirements:* recommendation, photograph. *Acceptance notification:* early July.

Audition Information

No audition fee. Audition consists of the following: recommendation from current dance teacher.

Audition evaluation criteria: based on recommendation from current dance teacher.

Costs & Financial Aid

Tuition (full): $150. *Room & board:* $50.

Financial aid available? full scholarship, partial scholarship. *Students receiving financial aid:* 5%. *Procedure for applying for financial aid:* by written request, based on need and talent.

Curriculum, Students, and Faculty

Required courses: character, ballet, dance composition/choreography, jazz, modern dance, pointe. *Specific curriculum information:* curriculum fixed.

Selectivity for males: most admitted, but not all. *Selectivity for females:* approximately 60% admitted.

Renowned alumni: Wendy White, Alvin Ailey Repertory Ensemble; Kate Seale, Alabama Ballet.

Full-time faculty: 3. *Guest faculty:* 3. *List of some faculty:* Dame Sonia Arova, Thom Clower, Doug Nielsen, Leslie Jane Pessemier, Francesca Corkle, Larissa Skylanskya, Magda Aunon.

Performance Information

Performance opportunities and frequency: Workshop performance(s): 2. *Performances choreographed by:* faculty, students, guests. *Number of studios (description):* 3 (30' x 40' Marleys) *Performance facilities:* workshop performance done in a large rehearsal hall.

Affiliations

Summer program is affiliated with a pre-professional company: future company members are recruited from this program; company apprentices are recruited from this program.

ARIZONA

HIGH SCHOOL INTENSIVE AT ARIZONA STATE UNIVERSITY

Winter Contact Information
Department of Dance, P.O. Box 870304, Tempe AZ 85287
Tel: 602-965-1208
Fax: 602-965-2247
Email: asuaj@asuvm.inre.asu.edu
Contact: Valerie Jeremijenko

Summer Contact Information
Department of Dance, Main Campus, PO Box 870304, Tempe AZ 85287-0304
Tel: 602-965-1208
Fax: 602-965-2247
Email: asuaj@asuvm.inre.asu.edu
Contact: Valerie Jeremijenko

General

Minimum age or age range: 14 to 18.

High school credit available? no. *College credit available?* no.

Application Information

Program dates: first week of August. *Enrollment full by:* 6/30.

Audition Information

No audition fee.

Costs & Financial Aid

Tuition (full): $95. *Procedure for applying for financial aid:* most scholorships are granted by the students' own schools.

Curriculum, Students, and Faculty

Required courses: African dance, ballet, Cunningham-based, Graham-based, Limon-based, Nikolais-based modern dance, repertory, Spanish. *Specific curriculum information:* curriculum fixed.

Selectivity for males: admit all who apply. *Selectivity for females:* admit all who apply.

Full-time faculty: 2. *Guest faculty:* 2. *List of some faculty:* C.K. Ganyo, Fred Darsow

Performance Information

Performances choreographed by: faculty, students, guests, faculty. *Number of studios (description):* 6 (63' x 100' Marley, 73' x 33' Marley, 53' x 96' Marley, 73' x 33' Marley, 53' x 53' Marley, 44' x 80' Marley,). *Performance facilities:* 2 venues, 1 presently under renovation.

Affiliations

Summer program is affiliated with other program(s): future students are often recruited from this program.

THE SCHOOL OF BALLET ARIZONA SUMMER INTENSIVE PROGRAM

Winter Contact Information

3645 East Indian School Road, Pheonix AZ 85016
Tel: 602-381-0184
Fax: 602-381-0189

Summer Contact Information

3645 East Indian School Road, Pheonix AZ 85016
Tel: 602-381-0184
Fax: 602-381-0189

General

Minimum age or age range: 4 to 25. *Level of program:* beginning, intermediate, advanced.

High school credit available? yes. *College credit available?* no.

Application Information

Application fee: $50.

Audition Information

No audition fee. Audition consists of the following: ballet, *accompanist provided, cassette player available.*

Dress requirements for females: yes.

Costs & Financial Aid

Tuition (full): $78-$80

Financial aid available? partial scholarship. *Students receiving financial aid:* 5%. *Procedure for applying for financial aid:* talented students who have been in school for at least one year will be considered.

Curriculum, Students, and Faculty

Required courses: character, ballet, dance composition/choreography, dance history, historical dance, jazz, make-up, men's class, Pilates, music, pas de deux, pointe, repertory, Spanish, variations, Bill Evans, Chinese dance. *Specific curriculum information:* curriculum fixed.

Selectivity for males: admit all who apply. *Selectivity for females:* admit all who apply.

Renowned alumni: Tamara Barden, American Ballet Theatre; Kendra Mitchell, Ballet Arizona; Kelly Robinson, American Ballet Theatre; Holly Crueshank.

Full-time faculty: 3. *Guest faculty:* 5. *List of some faculty:* Kee Juan Han, Nadya Zubkov, Sibylle Acatos, Arthur Leeth.

Performance Information

Performance opportunities and frequency: Workshop performance(s); open class: 1. *Performances choreographed by:* faculty.

Number of studios (description): 3 (40' x 40' sprung wood floor with Marley, 40' x 40' sprung wood floor with Marley, 30' x 30' sprung wood floor with Marley). *Performance facilities:* high school auditorium or cultural center.

Affiliations

Summer program is affiliated with a professional company: future company members are recruited from this program; company apprentices are recruited from this program.

CALIFORNIA

BALLET PACIFICA SUMMER INTENSIVE PROGRAM

Winter Contact Information

Summer Intensive Program, 1824 Kaiser Avenue, Irvine CA 92614
Tel: 714-851-9930
Fax: 714-851-9974
Contact: Gillian Finley

Summer Contact Information

1825 Kaiser Avenue, Irvine CA 92614
Tel: 714-851-9930
Fax: 714-851-9974
Contact: Gillian Finley

General

Total enrollment: 60-75. *Minimum age or age range:* 11 and up. *Level of program:* intermediate, advanced.

High school credit available? no. *College credit available?* no.

Services

Housing options: off-campus housing.

Application Information

Program dates: 4 weeks in August. *Application deadline:* 7/1. *Application fee:* $10. *Requirements:* recommendation, photograph (optional for out of town students who cannot attend audition).

Audition Information

Audition fee: $10. *Audition consists of the following:* ballet, pointe work; *Accompanist provided, cassette player available, CD player available*

Dress requirements for females: yes. *Special dress requirements:* black leotard, pink tights for intermediate, solid leotards, pink or black tights for advanced.

Costs & Financial Aid

Room & board: $1,200.

Financial aid available? partial scholarship. *Students receiving financial aid:* 30%. *Procedure for applying for financial aid:* send essay explaining financial situation.

Curriculum, Students, and Faculty

Required courses: character, ballet, dance history, jazz, Cunningham-based, Graham-based, Limon-based modern dance, body conditioning, music, nutrition, pointe, repertory, variations, injury prevention. *Specific curriculum information:* curriculum fixed.

Selectivity for males: approximately 60% admitted. *Selectivity for females:* approximately 60% admitted.

Full-time faculty: 12. *Guest faculty:* 4-5. *List of some faculty and their affiliations:* David Allan, National Ballet of Canada; Tina Le Blanc, San Francisco Ballet; Robert Sund, San Francisco Ballet.

Performance Information

Performances choreographed by: faculty, guests. *Number of studios (description):* 3 (46' x 53' basket-weave sprung floors with Marley overlay, 46' x 53' basket-weave sprung floors with Marley overlay, 46' x 53' basket-weave sprung floors with Marley overlay). *Performance facilities:* 450-seat theater at University of California, Irvine.

Affiliations

Summer program is affiliated with a professional company: future Ballet Pacifica company members are never recruited from this program; company apprentices are never recruited from this program.

BAROQUE DANCE SUMMER WORKSHOP

Winter Contact Information

Department of Music, Stanford University, Stanford CA 94303
Tel: 650-723-3811
Fax: 650-725-2686
Contact: Melinda McGee

Summer Contact Information

Department of Music, Stanford University, Stanford CA 94303
Tel: 650-723-3811
Fax: 650-725-2686
Contact: Melinda McGee

General

Minimum age or age range: 16 and up. *Level of program:* beginning, intermediate, advanced.

High school credit available? no. *College credit available?* no.

Services

Housing options: on-site housing.

Application Information

Program dates: late July to early August. *Application fee:* $15.

Audition Information

No audition fee.

Costs & Financial Aid

Tuition (full): $475. *Room & board:* $37.

Financial aid available? no.

Curriculum, Students, and Faculty

Required courses: dance history, historical dance, music, Feuillet Notation, early notation. *Specific curriculum information:* curriculum fixed.

Selectivity for males: admit all who apply. *Selectivity for females:* admit all who apply.

Full-time faculty: 5. *List of some faculty and their affiliations:* Wendy Hilton, Juilliard School; Linda Tomko, UC Riverside; Paige Whitley-Baugess, Craven Historical Dancers; Thomas Baird, Early Dance Alliance.

Performance Information

Performances choreographed by: faculty, advanced students. *Number of studios (description):* 4 (size varies, wood). *Performance facilities:* dance studios.

Affiliations

Summer program is affiliated with other program(s): future students are not recruited from this program.

Additional Comments

The Baroque Dance Summer Workshop at Stanford University offers intensive study in the style, technique, and notation of French court and theater dance at beginning, intermediate, and advanced levels. Daily activities include two technique classes, a dance notation class, a music class or lecture-demonstration, and time to use the music library with its extensive dance collection and the Lully Archives.

BERKELEY BALLET THEATER, SUMMER INTENSIVE WORKSHOP; NON-WORKSHOP CONTINUING CLASSES

Winter Contact Information

2640 College Avenue, Berkeley CA 94704
Tel: 510-843-4687
Fax: 510-843-2606
Contact: Office Manager

Summer Contact Information

2640 College Avenue, Berkeley CA 94704
Tel: 510-843-4687
Fax: 510-843-2606
Contact: Office Manager

General

Minimum age or age range: 4 to 18. *Level of program:* beginning, intermediate, advanced.

High school credit available? no. *College credit available?* no.

Application Information

Program dates: 7/7-8/16. *Application deadline:* 6/1. *Application fee:* $10.

Audition Information

No audition fee. Accompanist provided, cassette player available, CD player available

Dress requirements for females: yes.

Costs & Financial Aid

Financial aid available? no.

Curriculum, Students, and Faculty

Courses offered: African dance, character, ballet, dance composition/choreography, dance history, jazz, men's class, Graham-based modern dance, movement techniques, body conditioning, Pilates, pas de deux, pointe, repertory, variations. *Specific curriculum information:* curricula choices.

Selectivity for males: admit all who apply. *Selectivity for females:* most admitted, but not all.

Renowned alumni: Kyra Nichols, Arch Higgins.

Performance Information

Performance opportunities and frequency: final performance. *Performances choreographed by:* faculty, guests. *Number of studios (description):* 4 (Marley, Marley, Marley, Marley). *Performance facilities:* theater in building, summer performances are done in studio.

CALIFORNIA STATE SUMMER SCHOOL FOR THE ARTS

Winter Contact Information

4825 J Street Suite 120, Sacramento CA 95819
Tel: 916-227-9320
Fax: 916-227-9455
Email: alameida@csssa.org
Contact: Joseph Alameida

Summer Contact Information

24700 McBean Parkway, Valencia CA 91355
Tel: 805-225-1050
Fax: 805-254-8352
Email: alameida@csssa.org
Contact: Joseph Alameida

General

Total enrollment: 40-50. *Minimum age or age range:* 13 to 18. *Level of program:* beginning, intermediate, advanced.

High school credit available? no. *College credit available?* yes.

Services

Housing options: on-site housing.

Application Information

Program dates: 7/11-8/8. *Application deadline:* 2/27. *Application fee:* $20. *Enrollment full by:* May. *Requirements:* essay, recommendation. *Acceptance notification:* 5/1.

Audition Information

Audition fee: $20. *Audition consists of the following:* pointe work, prepared solo, warm-up and introduction. *accompanist provided, cassette player available, CD player available*

Dress requirements: no.

Costs & Financial Aid

Tuition (full): $1,300. *Other fees:* $90 for optional field trips.

Financial aid available? full scholarship, partial scholarship. *Students receiving financial aid:* 50%. *Procedure for applying for financial aid:* included with application.

Curriculum, Students, and Faculty

Courses Offered: African dance, ballet, dance composition/choreography, dance history, jazz, Cunningham-based, Graham-based modern dance, body conditioning, Pilates, pointe, repertory, Spanish, variations, Chinese dance. *Specific curriculum information:* Curricula choices.

Selectivity for males: approximately 60% admitted. *Selectivity for females:* approximately 60% admitted.

Full-time faculty: 4. *Guest faculty:* 6. *List of some faculty:* Cynthia Young, Claire Duncan, Sylvia Palmer, Gail Chodera.

Performance Information

Performance opportunities and frequency: informal showings; 1 per week. *Performances choreographed by:* faculty, students, guests. *Number of studios (description):* 3 (40' x 50' Marley-dance flooring, 40' x 50' Marley-dance flooring, 40' x 50' Marley-dance flooring). *Performance facilities:* theater space.

DANCE WORKSHOP

Winter Contact Information

Dance Workshop, UCSB Summer Sessions,
Department of Public Relations,
Santa Barbara CA 93106
Tel: 805-893-8950
Fax: 805-893-7306
Email: su01mort@ucsbuxa.ucsb.edu
Contact: Beth Burleson

Summer Contact Information

Dance Workshop, Santa Barbara CA 93106
Tel: 805-893-8950
Fax: 805-893-7306
Email: su01mort@ucsbuxa.ucsb.edu
Contact: Beth Burleson

General

Total enrollment: 30-50. *Minimum age or age range:* 18 and up. *Level of program:* advanced.

High school credit available? no. *College credit available?* yes.

Services

Housing options: off-campus housing.

Application Information

Program dates: 6/22-7/31. *Application deadline:* 5/1. *Application fee:* $35. *Requirements:* recommendation.

Audition Information

No audition fee. Audition consists of the following: modern dance, prepared solo.

Costs & Financial Aid

Tuition (full): $250-$900

Financial aid available? no.

Curriculum, Students, and Faculty

Courses offered: dance composition/choreography, modern dance, repertory. *Specific curriculum information:* curricula choices.

Selectivity for males: approximately 60% admitted. *Selectivity for females:* approximately 60% admitted.

Full-time faculty: 0. *Guest faculty:* 3-5.

Performance Information

Performances choreographed by: faculty, varies.

Number of studios (description): 3 (40' x 60' and larger basketweave, 40' x 60' and larger basketweave, 40' x 60' and larger basketweave). *Performance facilities:* proscenium, black box.

Affiliations

Summer program is affiliated with other program(s): future students are sometimes recruited from this program.

DANCERS' GROUP STUDIO THEATER

Winter Contact Information

3221 22nd Street, San Francisco CA 94110
Tel: 415-824-5044
Fax: 415-824-2873
Email: dg@dancersgroup.org
Contact: Wayne Hazzard

Summer Contact Information

3221 22nd Street, San Francisco CA 94110
Tel: 415-824-5044
Fax: 415-824-2873
Email: dg@dancersgroup.org
Contact: Wayne Hazzard

General

Minimum age or age range: 18. *Level of program:* beginning, intermediate, advanced.

High school credit available? no. *College credit available?* no.

Application Information
Program dates: June-August. *Application fee:* $50.

Audition Information
No audition fee. Accompanist provided, cassette player available, CD player available

Dress requirements: no.

Costs & Financial Aid
Tuition (full): $175-$350

Financial aid available? no.

Curriculum, Students, and Faculty
Required courses: dance composition/choreography, master classes, modern dance, other. *Specific curriculum information:* curriculum fixed.

Selectivity for males: admit all who apply. *Selectivity for females:* admit all who apply.

Full-time faculty: 0. *Guest faculty:* 6-8. *List of some faculty and their affiliations:* Joe Goode Performance Group

Performance Information
Performances choreographed by: students.

Number of studios (description): 1 (40' x 60' wood). *Performance facilities:* studio setting.

JARVIS CONSERVATORY, BAROQUE BALLET WORKSHOP & FESTIVAL

Winter Contact Information
1711 Main Street, Napa CA 94559
Tel: 707-255-5445
Fax: 707-255-5482
Contact: Jay Goetting

Summer Contact Information
1711 Main Street, Napa CA 94559
Tel: 707-255-5445
Fax: 707-255-5482
Contact: Jay Goetting

General
Minimum age or age range: 18 to 40. *Level of program:* intermediate, advanced.

High school credit available? no. *College credit available?* yes.

Application Information
Program dates: 7/20-8/9. *Application fee:* none. *Enrollment full by:* first day of workshop. *Requirements:* recommendation. *Acceptance notification:* within 2 weeks.

Audition Information
No audition fee. Audition consists of the following: prepared solo or ensemble.

Costs & Financial Aid
Tuition (full): $200-$500 *Room:* $35.

Financial aid available? full scholarship, partial scholarship. *Students receiving financial aid:* 50%. *Procedure for applying for financial aid:* fill out application, send videotape, phone interview with artistic director.

Curriculum, Students, and Faculty
Required courses: dance composition/choreography, dance history, historical dance, master classes, music. *Specific curriculum information:* curriculum fixed.

Selectivity for males: most admitted, but not all. *Selectivity for females:* most admitted, but not all.

Renowned alumni: Deda Christina Colonna, Yoro Jehise, Letizia Dradi, Deborah Ford.

Full-time faculty: 5. *Guest faculty:* 3. *List of some faculty:* Catherine Turocy, Patrick Boustiha, Deda Christina Colonna, Carlos Fittante, James Richman, Ani Udovicki.

Performance Information
Performances choreographed by: faculty.

Number of studios (description): 8 (40' x 40' sprung, 40' x 40' sprung, 40' x 40' sprung,, 40' x 40' sprung, 40' x 40' sprung). *Performance facilities:* 221-seat theater.

Affiliations
Summer program is affiliated with other program(s): future students are recruited from this program.

LIMON WEST DANCE PROJECT

Winter Contact Information
SJSU/Washington Square Hall #104E, San Jose CA 95125
Tel: 408-924-5046
Fax: 408-924-4365
Contact: Gary Masters

Summer Contact Information
SJSU/Washigton Square Hall #104E, San Jose CA 95125
Tel: 408-924-5046
Fax: 408-924-4365
Contact: Gary Masters

General

Total enrollment: 50-60. *Minimum age or age range:* 15. *Level of program:* intermediate, advanced.

High school credit available? no. *College credit available?* no.

Services

Housing options: on-site housing, off-campus housing.

Application Information

Program dates: first 2 weeks of August. *Application deadline:* 6/1. *Enrollment full by:* June. *Requirements:* recommendation.

Audition Information

No audition fee. Accompanist provided.

Dress requirements: no.

Costs & Financial Aid

Financial aid available? partial scholarship. *Students receiving financial aid:* 20%. *Procedure for applying for financial aid:* send recommendation, a videotape of performance or classroom work; aid based on talent and need.

Curriculum, Students, and Faculty

Courses offered: Alexander technique, dance composition/choreography, dance history, master classes, Limon-based modern dance, body conditioning, repertory, Mexican folklorica, Flamenco, Humphrey-Weidman. *Specific curriculum information:* Curricula choices.

Selectivity for males: most admitted, but not all. *Selectivity for females:* most admitted, but not all.

Full-time faculty: 4. *Guest faculty:* 1. *List of some faculty:* Libby Nye, Fred Mathews, Gary Masters.

Performance Information

Performances choreographed by: taken from the repertory and dance composition classes. *Number of studios (description):* 4 (30' X 50' Marley, 30' x 50' Marley, 30' x 50' Marley, 30' x 50' Marley). *Performance facilities:* studio/theater, 120 seats.

Affiliations

Summer program is affiliated with other program(s): future students are sometimes recruited from this program.

ODC SUMMER INTENSIVE

Winter Contact Information
3153 17th Street, San Francisco CA 94110
Tel: 415-863-6606
Fax: 415-863-9833
Email: ktnelson@odcdance.org
Contact: KT Nelson

Summer Contact Information
3153 17th Street, San Francisco CA 94110
Tel: 415-863-6606
Fax: 415-863-9833
Email: ktnelson@odcdance.org
Contact: KT Nelson

General

Minimum age or age range: 18. *Level of program:* intermediate, advanced.

High school credit available? no. *College credit available?* no.

Application Information

Program dates: two one-week programs. *Application fee:* $30. *Enrollment full by:* May. *Requirements:* essay, recommendation, photograph. *Acceptance notification:* 5/15.

Audition Information

Audition consists of the following: ballet, modern dance, (some problem solving). *Accompanist provided.*

Special dress requirements: jazz shoes.

Costs & Financial Aid

Financial aid available? partial scholarship. *Students receiving financial aid:* 5%. *Procedure for applying for financial aid:* Call KT Nelson (415-863-6606), scholarships are work exchange.

Curriculum, Students, and Faculty

Required courses: dance composition/choreography, repertory, dance aesthetics, ODC style modern dance, floor barre, rhythm. *Specific curriculum information:* curriculum fixed.

Selectivity for males: most admitted, but not all. *Selectivity for females:* approximately 60% admitted.

Renowned alumni: Robert Moses, Liz Gravell, Mae Chesney, Frank Everett, Daniel Sanchez, Arturo Fernandez, Ney Fonseca, Liz Ann McAdams.

Full-time faculty: 3. *Guest faculty:* 5. *List of some faculty and their affiliations:* Brenda Way, KT Nelson, Kimi Okada.

Performance Information

Performances choreographed by: faculty, guests, *Number of studios (description):* 2 (50' x 75', 25' x 30'). *Performance facilities:* small, 200-seat theater.

Affiliations

Summer program is affiliated with a professional company: future company members are sometimes recruited from this program; company apprentices are sometimes recruited from this program.

ODC/SAN FRANCISCO

Winter Contact Information

3153 17th Street, San Francisco CA 94110
Tel: 415-863-6606
Fax: 415-863-9833
Contact: KT Nelson

Summer Contact Information

3153 17th Street, San Francisco CA 94110
Tel: 415-863-6606
Fax: 415-863-9833
Contact: KT Nelson

General

Minimum age or age range: 17 to 39. *Level of program:* intermediate, advanced.

High school credit available? no. *College credit available?* no.

Services

Housing options: off-campus housing.

Application Information

Program dates: June or July. *Enrollment full by:* May. *Requirements:* essay, recommendation. *Acceptance notification:* 5/15.

Audition Information

No audition fee. Audition consists of the following: videotape, must be able to see dance well, present 2 types of work, no longer than 3 minutes.

Dress requirements: no.

Audition evaluation criteria: personality, intelligence, type of movement, type of experience, type of training.

Costs & Financial Aid

Financial aid available? partial scholarship. *Students receiving financial aid:* 6%. *Procedure for applying for financial aid:* submit standard forms, may include phone conversation and recommendations if decision is difficult.

Curriculum, Students, and Faculty

Required courses: dance composition/choreography, music, repertory, tap, contact improvisation, ODC style modern dance, stomp class. *Specific curriculum information:* curriculum fixed.

Selectivity for males: approximately 60% admitted. *Selectivity for females:* approximately 60% admitted.

Full-time faculty: 3. *Guest faculty:* 3. *List of some faculty:* Brenda Way, KT Nelson, Kevin Okada, Daniel Lui, Kevin Wear, Shannon Michell.

Performance Information

Performance opportunities and frequency: Informal showings, end of session. *Performances choreographed by:* faculty, students, guests. *Number of studios (description):* 2 (Marley, wood). *Performance facilities:* 250-seat theater, ODC performance gallery.

Affiliations

Summer program is affiliated with a professional company: future company members are recruited from this program; company apprentices are recruited from this program.

ORANGE COAST COLLEGE SUMMER DANCE PROGRAM

Winter Contact Information

2701 Fairview Road, P.O. Box 5005, Costa Mesa CA 92628
Tel: 714-432-5506
Fax: 714-432-5934
Contact: Karen Shanley

Summer Contact Information

2701 Fairview Road, P.O. Box 5005, Costa Mesa CA 92628
Tel: 714-432-5506
Fax: 714-432-5934
Contact: Karen Shanley

General

Minimum age or age range: 16. *Level of program:* beginning, intermediate, advanced.

High school credit available? no. *College credit available?* yes.

Services

Housing options: off-campus housing.

Application Information

Program dates: 2 weeks in June, 5-6 weeks until end of July. *Application fee:* none.

Audition Information

No audition fee.

Dress requirements: no.

Costs & Financial Aid

Tuition (full): $13-$126 *Other fees:* $40 incidental health, parking, college service fee.

Financial aid available? yes. *Procedure for applying for financial aid:* call Financial Aid Office for information or to obtain applications (714-432-5508).

Curriculum, Students, and Faculty

Courses offered: African dance, ballet, jazz, master classes, Cunningham-based modern dance, body conditioning, Pilates, tap, Near and Middle East, Flamenco. *Specific curriculum information:* Curricula choices.

Selectivity for males: admit all who apply. *Selectivity for females:* admit all who apply.

Renowned alumni: Donna Uchizono.

Full-time faculty: 2. *Guest faculty:* 2. *List of some faculty:* Linda Sohl-Donnell, Rama Bharadvaj, Lilia Llorens, Karen Shanley.

Performance Information

Number of studios (description): 2 (60' x 40' wood-sprung-Marley over wood, 50' x 40' wood-sprung-Marley over wood). *Performance facilities:* studio theater, main stage.

Affiliations

Summer program is affiliated with a pre-professional company: future company members are recruited from this program. *Summer program is affiliated with other program(s).* future students are recruited from this program.

Additional Comments

Every other year a tap festival is sponsored. OCC also offers 2 vocational certificate programs. Students can do their internship or take classes toward these certificates in the summer.

PENINSULA DANCE CAMP

Winter Contact Information
734 Sicuer Spur Road #105, Rolling Hills Estates CA 90274
Tel: 310-541-1293
Fax: 310-541-6279
Email: pavlova2@aol.com
Contact: Chris Paltin

Summer Contact Information
734 Sicuer Spur Road #105, Rolling Hills Estates CA 90274
Tel: 310-541-1293
Fax: 310-541-6279
Email: pavlova2@aol.com
Contact: Chris Paltin

General

Minimum age or age range: 8 and up. *Level of program:* beginning, intermediate, advanced.

High school credit available? no. *College credit available?* no.

Services

Housing options: on-site housing.

Application Information

Program dates: first 2 weeks in August. *Enrollment full by:* summer. *Requirements:* recommendation.

Audition Information

Accompanist provided, cassette player available, CD player available.

Dress requirements: no.

Costs & Financial Aid

Tuition (full): $450.

Financial aid available? full scholarship, partial scholarship. *Students receiving financial aid:* 10%.

Curriculum, Students, and Faculty

Courses offered: ballet, dance history, jazz, master classes, Graham-based modern dance, body conditioning, tap, hip-hop. *Specific curriculum information:* Curricula choices.

Selectivity for males: admit all who apply. *Selectivity for females:* admit all who apply.

Renowned alumni: Jill Matson, Matt Shaffer, Gus Giordano Company.

Full-time faculty: 5. *Guest faculty:* 4. *List of some faculty:* Keith Clifton, Frank and Janina Bove, Jason Myhre.

Performance Information

Performance opportunities and frequency: final performance. *Performances choreographed by:* faculty. *Number of studios (description):* 3 (60' x 30' Rarseo, 30' x 40' Rarseo, 30' x 40' Rarseo). *Performance facilities:* stage, gym.

Affiliations

Summer program is affiliated with a pre-professional company: future company members are not recruited from this program; company apprentices are not recruited from this program. *Summer program is affiliated with other program(s):* future students are not recruited from this program.

SAN DIEGO BALLET SUMMER PROGRAM

Winter Contact Information
5304-B Metro Street, San Diego CA 92110
Tel: 619-294-7378
Fax: 619-294-7378
Contact: Gail Mackler

Summer Contact Information
5304-B Metro Street, San Diego CA 92110
Tel: 619-294-7378
Fax: 619-294-7378
Contact: Gail Mackler

General

Total enrollment: 30-40. *Minimum age or age range:* 12 to 20. *Level of program:* beginning, intermediate, advanced.

High school credit available? no. *College credit available?* no.

Services

Housing options: on-site housing.

Application Information

Program dates: TBA. *Application deadline:* 6/1. *Application fee:* $20. *Requirements:* interview, recommendation, photograph. *Acceptance notification:* 2 weeks after audition.

Audition Information

Audition fee: $10. *Audition consists of the following:* ballet, pointe work. *Accompanist provided.*

Dress requirements for females: leotard, tights, pointe shoes.

Audition evaluation criteria: subjective.

Costs & Financial Aid

Tuition (full): $450. *Room & board:* $675.

Financial aid available? partial scholarship. *Students receiving financial aid:* 10%. *Procedure for applying for financial aid:* letter and interview.

Curriculum, Students, and Faculty

Required courses: character, ballet, dance composition/choreography, men's class, modern dance, Pilates, pas de deux, pointe, variations, Alvin Ailey style modern dance. *Specific curriculum information:* curriculum fixed.

Selectivity for males: most admitted, but not all. *Selectivity for females:* most admitted, but not all.

Full-time faculty: 5. *List of some faculty and their affiliations:* Jock Soto, NYC Ballet; Christopher Wheeldon, NYC Ballet; Stephanie Saland, NYC Ballet; Zoe Mackler, NYC Ballet; Anita Ardalan, Paris Opera; Anne Christian Daly, NYC Ballet; Robin Sheretz Morgan, NYC Ballet.

Performance Information

Performance opportunities and frequency: Final performance. *Performances choreographed by:* faculty, students. *Number of studios (description):* 3 (50' x 40' sprung, 30' x 40' sprung, 60' x 20' sprung). *Performance facilities:* studio, theater.

Affiliations

Summer program is affiliated with a professional company: future company members are often recruited from this program; company apprentices are often recruited from this program. *Summer program is affiliated with a pre-professional company:* future company members are often recruited from this program; company apprentices are often recruited from this program.

SAN FRANCISCO BALLET SCHOOL SUMMER SESSION

Winter Contact Information
455 Franklin Street, San Francisco CA 94102
Tel: 415-553-4642
Fax: 415-861-2684
Contact: Andrea Yannone

Summer Contact Information
455 Franklin Street, San Francisco CA 94102
Tel: 415-553-4642
Fax: 415-861-2684
Contact: Andrea Yannone

General

Level of program: intermediate, advanced.

High school credit available? no. *College credit available?* no.

Services

Housing options: off-campus housing.

Application Information

Program dates: 6/22-7/24. *Requirements:* essay, photograph.

Audition Information

Audition fee: $15. *Audition consists of the following:* ballet, pointe work, batterie for men. *Accompanist provided.*

Special dress requirements: leotard, tights for girls, tights and snug white t-shirt for boys.

Costs & Financial Aid

Tuition (full): $700-$800 *Room & board:* $1,295. *Other fees:* $75 chaperone fee if staying in dorms, $60 registration fee.

Financial aid available? full scholarship, partial scholarship. *Procedure for applying for financial aid:* fill out an application.

Curriculum, Students, and Faculty

Required courses: character, ballet, dance history, men's class, modern dance, music, pas de deux, pointe, repertory, variations. *Specific curriculum information:* curriculum fixed.

Selectivity for males: approximately 10% admitted. *Selectivity for females:* approximately 10% admitted.

Renowned alumni: Catherine Batcheller, Ricardo Bustamante, Evelyn Cisneros, Val Caniparoli, Christina Fagundes, Cynthia Gregory, Elizabeth Loscavio, John McFall, Terry Orr, Katita Waldo, Stanton Welch.

Full-time faculty: 10. *Guest faculty:* 6. *List of some faculty:* Lola de Avila, Ricardo Bustamante, Antonio Castilla, Kristi DeCaminada, Jorge Esquivel, Irina Jacobson, Pascale Leroy, Kathleen Mitchell, Jocelyn Vollmar, Noemi Nargizian, Ingrid Nemeckova, Margaret Jenkins, Ellie Klopp, Claire Sheridan, Richard Gibbs

Performance Information

Performances choreographed by: students, guests; open class; end of session.

Number of studios (description): 8. *Performance facilities:* studios of professional quality shared with San Francisco Ballet Company, San Francisco Opera House, Palace of Fine Arts Theater.

Affiliations

Summer program is affiliated with a professional company: future company members are recruited from this program; company apprentices are recruited from this program.

SUMMER INTENSIVE TRAINING PROGRAM

Winter Contact Information

Contra Costa Ballet Centre, 2040 North Broadway, Walnut Creek CA 94596
Tel: 510-935-7984
Fax: 510-932-3221
Contact: Richard Cammack

Summer Contact Information

Contra Costa Ballet Centre, 2040 North Broadway, Walnut Creek CA 94596
Tel: 510-935-7984
Fax: 510-932-3221
Contact: Richard Cammack

General

Minimum age or age range: 12 to 19.

High school credit available? no. *College credit available?* no.

Application Information

Program dates: July, first week in August. *Application deadline:* 3/30. *Application fee:* $15. *Enrollment full by:* 3/30. *Requirements:* photograph. *Acceptance notification:* as soon as possible.

Audition Information

Audition fee: $15. *Audition consists of the following:* ballet.

Costs & Financial Aid

Tuition (full): $975.

Financial aid available? partial scholarship. *Procedure for applying for financial aid:* fill out application.

Curriculum, Students, and Faculty

Required courses: character, ballet, modern dance, pas de deux, variations. *Specific curriculum information:* curriculum fixed. *List of some faculty:* Charles Anderson, Alexi Badrak, Johanna Berman, Evelyn Cisneros, Pascale Leroy, Xinge Lin, Suki Schorer, Michael Smuin.

Performance Information

Performances choreographed by: faculty, guests. *Number of studios (description):* 3 (Harlequin). *Performance facilities:* local theater.

Additional Comments

Tuition includes room

YOUNG DANCERS INSTITUTE

Winter Contact Information

University of California, Santa Barbra Summer Sessions, Department PR, Santa Barbara CA 93106
Tel: 805-893-8950
Fax: 805-893-7306
Email: su01mort@ucsbuxa.ucsb.edu
Contact: Beth Burleson

Summer Contact Information

UCSB Summer Sessions, Department PR, Santa Barbara CA 93106
Tel: 805-893-8950
Fax: 805-893-7306
Email: su01mort@ucsbuxa.ucsb.edu
Contact: Beth Burleson

General

Minimum age or age range: 15 to 18.

High school credit available? yes. *College credit available?* yes.

Services

Housing options: on-site housing.

Application Information

Program dates: 6/21-7/31. *Application deadline:* 5/1. *Application fee:* $35. *Requirements:* essay, recommendation, photograph. *Acceptance notification:* within 2 weeks after application is received.

Audition Information

No audition fee. Audition consists of the following: ballet, modern dance, prepared solo.

Costs & Financial Aid

Tuition (full): $1,200. *Room & board:* $1,200.

Financial aid available? partial scholarship. *Students receiving financial aid:* 30%. *Procedure for applying for financial aid:* request application for scholarship, deadline 3/31.

Curriculum, Students, and Faculty

Courses offered: ballet, dance composition/choreography, jazz, modern dance, pointe, repertory, dance orientation. *Specific curriculum information:* Curricula choices.

Selectivity for males: most admitted, but not all. *Selectivity for females:* most admitted, but not all.

Full-time faculty: 5. *List of some faculty:* Jerry Pearson, Delila Moseley, Christina McCarthy, Valerie Uston, Nancy Colahan, Beth Burleson.

Performance Information

Performances choreographed by: faculty, students. Open class. *Number of studios (description):* 3 (40' x 60' basketweave). *Performance facilities:* proscenium, black box.

Affiliations

Summer program is affiliated with a conservatory: future students are sometimes recruited from this program.

COLORADO

ACADEMY OF COLORADO BALLET SUMMER INTENSIVE PROGRAM

Winter Contact Information

1278 Lincoln Street, Denver CO 80203
Fax: 303-861-7174
Contact: Patricia Renzetti

Summer Contact Information

1278 Lincoln Street, Denver CO 80203
Fax: 303-861-7174
Contact: Patricia Renzetti

General

Minimum age or age range: 12 to 25. *Level of program:* beginning, intermediate, advanced.

High school credit available? no. *College credit available?* no.

Application Information

Program dates: 6/29-7/24. *Application deadline:* 5/1. *Application fee:* none. *Requirements:* photograph (an 8 x 10 in arabesque). *Acceptance notification:* within 2 weeks of audition.

Audition Information

Audition fee: $15. *Audition consists of the following:* ballet, pointe work. *Accompanist provided.*

Costs & Financial Aid

Tuition (full): $950. *Room & board:* $600.

Financial aid available? full scholarship, partial scholarship.

Curriculum, Students, and Faculty

Required courses: anatomy, character, ballet, dance history, historical dance, master classes, men's class, modern dance, music, pas de deux, pointe, variations. *Specific curriculum information:* curriculum fixed.

Selectivity for males: most admitted, but not all. *Selectivity for females:* approximately 60% admitted.

Full-time faculty: 3. *Guest faculty:* 2. *List of some faculty:* Zhanna Dubrovskaya, Inessa Pakin, Yuri Chatal.

Performance Information

Performances choreographed by: faculty. *Number of studios (description):* 6 (Marley on sprung wood). *Performance facilities:* large studio.

Affiliations

Summer program is affiliated with a professional company: future company members are recruited from this program; company apprentices are recruited from this program. *Summer program is affiliated with a pre-professional company:* future company members are recruited from this program; company apprentices are recruited from this program.

BOLSHOL BALLET ACADEMY AT VAIL

Winter Contact Information

P.O. Box 309, Vail CO 81658
Tel: 970-949-1999
Fax: 970-949-9265
Email: vvfsales@vail.net
Contact: Katherine Kersten

Summer Contact Information

P.O. Box 309, Vail CO 81658
Tel: 970-949-1999
Fax: 970-949-9265
Email: vvfsales@vail.net
Contact: Katherine Kersten

General

Application Information

Requirements: recommendation, photograph.

Audition Information

Audition consists of the following: ballet, pointe work.

Curriculum, Students, and Faculty

Required courses: repertory, Russian culture lectures.

Performance Information

Performances choreographed by: faculty, *Number of studios (description):* 2 (40' x 50' suspended).

COLORADO COLLEGE SUMMER BALLET INTENSIVE

Winter Contact Information

Colorado College, 14 East Cache la Poudre,
Colorado Springs CO 80903
Tel: 719-389-6656
Fax: 719-397-6955
Email: ballet@ce.colrado.edu
Contact: Kalah Fuller

Summer Contact Information

Colorado College, 14 East Cache la Poudre,
Colorado Springs CO 80903
Tel: 719-389-6656
Fax: 719-397-6955
Email: ballet@ce.colrado.edu
Contact: Kalah Fuller

General

Minimum age or age range: 12 and up. *Level of program:* beginning, intermediate, advanced.

High school credit available? yes. *College credit available?* yes.

Services

Housing options: on-site housing.

Application Information

Program dates: June. *Application deadline:* 4/15. *Application fee:* $25. *Requirements:* essay, recommendation, photograph.

Audition Information

No audition fee. Audition consists of the following: ballet, prepared solo. *Accompanist provided, cassette player available, CD player available.*

Special dress requirements: black tights, white t-shirts for men; pink tights, black leotard, short skirts at advanced levels for women.

Costs & Financial Aid

Tuition (full): $675. *Room & board:* $700.

Financial aid available? full scholarship, partial scholarship. *Students receiving financial aid:* 80%. *Procedure for applying for financial aid:* provided with application material.

Curriculum, Students, and Faculty

Required courses: character, ballet, men's class, body conditioning, Pilates, music, pointe, Spanish, variations. *Specific curriculum information:* curriculum fixed.

Selectivity for males: approximately 33% admitted. *Selectivity for females:* approximately 33% admitted.

Full-time faculty: 4. *Guest faculty*: 2. *List of some faculty*: Anne Adam Wilkens, Lindsay Fischer, Mandy Jayne Richardson, Johnny Eliason.

Performance Information

Performance opportunities and frequency: Informal showings; 1. *Performances choreographed by:* faculty, guests, open class. *Number of studios (description):* 4 (57' x 76' wood covered with Marley, 28' x 57' wood covered with Marley, 30' x 55' wood covered with Marley, 28' x 48' wood covered with Marley). *Performance facilities:* performance hall, large studio.

Affiliations

Summer program is affiliated with other program(s): future students are often recruited from this program.

COLORADO DANCE FESTIVAL

Winter Contact Information

P.O. Box 356, Boulder CO 80306
Tel: 303-442-7666
Fax: 303-449-7732
Email: cdfest@concentric.net

Summer Contact Information

P.O. Box 356, Boulder CO 80306
Tel: 303-442-7666
Fax: 303-449-7732
Email: cdfest@concentric.net

General

Level of program: beginning, intermediate, advanced.

High school credit available? no. *College credit available?* no.

Services

Housing options: on-site housing.

Application Information

Program dates: 4 weeks in July. *Application deadline:* 6/27. *Application fee:* none. *Enrollment full by:* 6/1.

Audition Information

No audition fee.

Costs & Financial Aid

Financial aid available? full scholarship.

Curriculum, Students, and Faculty

Courses offered: African dance, Alexander technique, anatomy, dance composition/choreography, historical dance, master classes, modern dance, Pilates, other world dance forms, repertory, tap, injury prevention, Caribbean, Afro-Cuban dance, Mexican folkloria, Salsa, Merengue, Bolero, Afro-Brazilian dance, Orixas, Mexican folk dance, Near and Middle Eastern dance, Folklorico dance, Caribbean dance, Tango. *Specific curriculum information:* Curricula choices.

Selectivity for males: admit all who apply. *Selectivity for females:* admit all who apply. *Guest faculty:* 33. *List of some faculty and their affiliations:* Ralph Lemon, Chuck Davis, Sarah Skaggs, Rosangela Silvestre.

Performance Information

Performance opportunities and frequency: Informal showings; end of session. *Performances choreographed by:* students. *Number of studios (description):* 4 (30' x 60' wood or Marley, 30' x 60' wood or Marley, 30' x 60' wood or Marley, 30' x 60' wood or Marley). *Performance facilities:* black box theater, proscenium theater.

COLORADO DANCE THEATRE SUMMER INTENSIVE PROGRAM

Winter Contact Information

Colorado Dance Theatre Inc., 813 8th Street, Greeley CO 80631
Tel: 970-356-7104
Fax: 970-351-1923
Email: Jmrockl@Bentley.UnivNorthCo.edu
Contact: Jeffrey Marc Rockland

Summer Contact Information

Colorado Dance Theatre Inc., 813 8th Street, Greeley CO 80631
Tel: 970-356-7104
Fax: 970-351-1923
Email: Jmrockl@Bentley.UnivNorthCo.edu
Contact: Jeffrey Marc Rockland

General

Services

Housing options: off-campus housing.

Application Information

Requirements: recommendation, photograph.

Audition Information

Audition consists of the following: ballet.

Curriculum, Students, and Faculty

Courses offered: African dance, character, ballet, jazz, men's class, modern dance, pas de deux, pointe, repertory, Spanish, variations.

Performance Information

Performances choreographed by: faculty, students, guests. *Number of studios (description):* 3 (25' x 50' sprung wood floors and Marley).

Affiliations

Summer program is affiliated with a professional company: future company members are not recruited from this program; company apprentices are recruited from this program. *Summer program is affiliated with a pre-professional company:* company apprentices are often recruited from this program.

DAVID TAYLOR DANCE THEATRE, SUMMER INTENSIVE PROGRAM

Winter Contact Information
2539 West Main Street, Littleton CO 80120
Tel: 303-797-6944
Fax: 303-797-6944
Contact: David Taylor

Summer Contact Information
2539 West Main Street, Littleton CO 80120
Tel: 303-797-6944
Fax: 303-797-6944
Contact: David Taylor

General

Total enrollment: 35-55. *Minimum age or age range:* 11 to mid 20s. *Level of program:* intermediate, advanced.

High school credit available? no. *College credit available?* no.

Application Information

Program dates: 6/9-7/5. *Application fee:* $25. *Enrollment full by:* 5/26. *Requirements:* recommendation, photograph. *Acceptance notification:* March-April.

Audition Information

Audition consists of the following: ballet, pointe work. *Accompanist provided, cassette player available, CD player available.*

Dress requirements for females: yes. *Special dress requirements:* black leotard, pink tights.

Audition evaluation criteria: basic intermediate level of ballet required.

Costs & Financial Aid

Tuition (full): $700. *Room & board:* $500.

Financial aid available? full scholarship, partial scholarship. *Students receiving financial aid:* 10%. *Procedure for applying for financial aid:* letter, phone call requesting information.

Curriculum, Students, and Faculty

Required courses: character, ballet, dance history, historical dance, jazz, make-up, Horton-based, Limon-based modern dance, body conditioning, music, pas de deux, pointe, variations, injury prevention, foot care and pointe shoe workshop. *Specific curriculum information:* curriculum fixed.

Selectivity for males: most admitted, but not all. *Selectivity for females:* most admitted, but not all.

Renowned alumni: James Clouser, Paul Sutherland, Arturo Fernandez, Anna Donovan, Milton Myers, Hannah Kahn, Tricia Steurcke, Ronnie Whittaker, Tauna Hunter.

Full-time faculty: 4. *Guest faculty:* 7. *List of some faculty and their affiliations:* James Clouser, American Ballet Theatre, Royal Winnipeg; Milton Myers, Philadanco; Tauna Hunter, Ballet West.

Performance Information

Performances choreographed by: faculty. *Number of studios (description):* 3 (40' x 30' suspended wood, Marley covered, 40' x 30' suspended wood, Marley covered, 40' x 30' suspended wood, Marley covered). *Performance facilities:* small theater across the street.

Affiliations

Summer program is affiliated with a professional company: future company members are sometimes recruited from this program; company apprentices are recruited from this program.

PERRY-MANSFIELD PERFORMING ARTS SCHOOL & CAMP

Winter Contact Information
40755 RCR 36, Steamboat Spring CO 80487
Tel: 970-879-7125
Fax: 970-879-5823
Contact: Tami Thurston

Summer Contact Information
40755 RCR 36, Steamboat Spring CO 80487
Tel: 970-879-7125
Fax: 970-879-5823
Contact: Tami Thurston

General

Minimum age or age range: 9 to mid 20s. *Level of program:* beginning, intermediate, advanced.

High school credit available? no. *College credit available?* yes.

Services

Housing options: on-site housing.

Application Information

Program dates: 6/14-8/23. *Application fee:* $50. *Enrollment full by:* March. *Requirements:* recommendation, photograph.

Audition Information

Audition fee: $10. *Audition consists of the following:* ballet, modern dance, jazz. *Accompanist provided, cassette player available, CD player available.*

Dress requirements: no.

Costs & Financial Aid

Tuition (full): $2,280-$2,780 *Other fees:* private voice lessons, rafting, equestrian.

Financial aid available? full scholarship, partial scholarship. *Students receiving financial aid:* 5%. *Procedure for applying for financial aid:* ask for application.

Curriculum, Students, and Faculty

Courses offered: African dance, ballet, dance composition/choreography, dance history, jazz, master classes, modern dance, music, tap. *Specific curriculum information:* Curricula choices.

Selectivity for males: admit all who apply. *Selectivity for females:* admit all who apply.

Renowned alumni: Lauren Miville, Ozzie Rand, Barbara Morganstern, Roberta Marshall, Cynthia Rand, Peggy Lawler, Dick Caram, Rob Schiffman, Nina Cochran, Randy Cochran, Cynthia Dufault, Rusty de Lucia, Dee Covington, Lindsey Smith, Britni Smith, Claire Gardenhire.

Full-time faculty: 9. *List of some faculty*: Robert Bailis, Todd Breaugh, Rusty Delucia, Dick Caram, Melinda McCrary, Jill Meyers, Bruce Roach, Jon Rothstein, Rob Schiffmann, Gina Buntz, Jane Delay, Cindy Dufault, Glen Eddy, Jennifer Glaws, Elizabeth Mischler, Walter White, Mary E. Poore, Jay Majernik, Jacek Sobieraj, Kristin Atwell, John Fleming, Ashley Benton, Emil Schlee, Tina Schmeisser.

Performance Information

Performances choreographed by: faculty.

Number of studios (description): 4 (wood).

Affiliations

Summer program is affiliated with a pre-professional company: future company members are recruited from this program; company apprentices are recruited from this program.

Additional Comments

Rustic cabins with electric, bathooms within walking distance; auditions for scholarship only; range of tuition $2,280-$2,750 for 1997—include room and board; additional fees for private voice, rafting, and equestrian lessons.

VAIL INTERNATIONAL WORKSHOP

Winter Contact Information

P.O. Box 309, Vail CO 81658
Tel: 970-949-1999
Fax: 970-949-9265
Email: vvfsales@vail.net
Contact: Katherine Kersten

Summer Contact Information

P.O. Box 309, Vail CO 81658
Tel: 970-949-1999
Fax: 970-949-9265
Email: vvfsales@vail.net
Contact: Katherine Kersten

General

Minimum age or age range: 11 to 14.

High school credit available? no. *College credit available?* no.

Application Information

Application fee: $25. *Requirements:* recommendation, photograph. *Acceptance notification:* 3/15.

Audition Information

Audition fee: $15.

Costs & Financial Aid

Tuition (full): $685. *Room & board:* $725.

Financial aid available? full scholarship.

Curriculum, Students, and Faculty

Required courses: choreography, nutrition, pointe, variations. *Specific curriculum information:* curriculum fixed.

List of some faculty: Michael Ho, Julia Walsh, Denise Briner, Annegret Howe, Teresa Luba.

Performance Information

Performance facilities: Colorado Mountain College, Meadow Mountain Elementary School.

Affiliations

Additional Comments

If commuting, there will be an addition activity fee of $150.

CONNECTICUT

CONNECTICUT BALLET CENTER SUMMER DANCE

Winter Contact Information

20 Acosta Street, Stamford CT 06902
Tel: 203-978-0771
Fax: 203-961-1928
Contact: Brett Raphael

Summer Contact Information

20 Acosta Street, Stamford CT 06902
Tel: 203-978-0771
Fax: 203-961-1928
Contact: Brett Raphael

General

Minimum age or age range: 7 to 18. *Level of program:* beginning, intermediate, advanced.

High school credit available? no. *College credit available?* no.

Services

Housing options: off-campus housing.

Application Information

Program dates: July-August. *Requirements:* recommendation.

Audition Information

No audition fee. Audition consists of the following: ballet. *Cassette player available, CD player available.*

Dress requirements: no.

Costs & Financial Aid

Financial aid available? full scholarship, partial scholarship. *Students receiving financial aid:* 50%. *Procedure for applying for financial aid:* request application.

Curriculum, Students, and Faculty

Required courses: African dance, character, ballet, dance composition/choreography, dance history, jazz, Horton-based modern dance, movement techniques, Pilates, music, pas de deux, pointe, Spanish, tap, variations. *Specific curriculum information:* curriculum fixed.

Selectivity for males: approximately 60% admitted. *Selectivity for females:* approximately 60% admitted.

Full-time faculty: 10. *Guest faculty:* 2-3. *List of some faculty and their affiliations:* Corin Hollifield, All Nations Dance Company; Tatiana Litvinova, Kiev Opera Ballet; Barbara Sandonato, Pennsylvania Ballet, National Ballet of Canada.

Performance Information

Performances choreographed by: faculty, students, *Number of studios (description):* 3 (48' x 34' sprung floor with Rosco dance flooring). *Performance facilities:* studio.

Affiliations

Summer program is affiliated with a professional company: future company members are recruited from this program; company apprentices are recruited from this program.

SCHOOL OF HARTFORD BALLET

Winter Contact Information

228 Farmington Avenue, Hartford CT 06105
Tel: 860-525-9396
Fax: 860-249-8116
Contact: Enid Lynn

Summer Contact Information

228 Farmington Avenue, Hartford CT 06105
Tel: 860-525-9396
Fax: 860-249-8116
Contact: Enid Lynn

General

Minimum age or age range: 9 to mid 20s. *Level of program:* beginning, intermediate, advanced.

High school credit available? no. *College credit available?* yes.

Services

Housing options: on-site housing.

Application Information

Program dates: 6/22-7/31. *Enrollment full by:* 4/30. *Acceptance notification:* 2 weeks after audition.

Audition Information

Audition fee: $10. *Audition consists of the following:* ballet, pointe work. *Accompanist provided.*

Dress requirements for males: yes. *Dress requirements for females:* yes. *Special dress requirements:* appropriate dance attire.

Costs & Financial Aid

Tuition: $700 (3 wks) $ 1100 (6 wks) Room: $615 (3 wks) $935 (6 wks) Board: $225 (3 wks) $450 (6 wks).

Financial aid available? full scholarship, partial scholarship. *Students receiving financial aid:* 30%. *Procedure for applying for financial aid:* merit scholarship determined through audition; work study, or need based.

Curriculum, Students, and Faculty

Required courses: African dance, character, ballet, dance composition/choreography, dance history, jazz, men's class, Cunningham-based, Graham-based, Limon-based modern dance, body conditioning, pas de deux, pointe, repertory, tap, variations. *Specific curriculum information:* curriculum fixed.

Selectivity for males: approximately 60% admitted. *Selectivity for females:* approximately 60% admitted.

Renowned alumni: Rena Robinson, Bill Parton, Emily Gresh, Peter Hanson, Henry Seth, Alberto Flores, Melissa Wishinuki, Charmaine Hunter.

Full-time faculty: 10. *Guest faculty:* 5. *List of some faculty*: Franco De Vita, Alla Osipenko, Wang Shao-Pen, Elaine Werner Hutchison, Peggy Lyman, Ambre Emory-Maier, Patrick Nollet, Ching Hosier.

Performance Information

Performances choreographed by: faculty. *Number of studios (description)*: 5 (10' x 10' sprung, 80' x 80', 120' x 120'). *Performance facilities:* not on-site.

Affiliations

Summer program is affiliated with a professional company: future company members are often recruited from this program; company apprentices are recruited from this program. *Summer program is affiliated with a conservatory:* future students are often recruited from this program.

Additional Comments

Other fees: $25 registration fee.

DISTRICT OF COLUMBIA

THE KIROV ACADEMY SUMMER PROGRAM

Winter Contact Information

Registrar, 4301 Harewood Road, NE, Washington DC 20017
Tel: 202-832-1087
Fax: 202-526-9274
Contact: Laura Hampton

Summer Contact Information

Registrar, 4301 Harewood Road, NE, Washington DC 20017
Tel: 202-832-1087
Fax: 202-526-9274
Contact: Laura Hampton

General

Total enrollment: 10-20. *Minimum age or age range:* 10 to 20. *Level of program:* beginning, intermediate, advanced.

High school credit available? no. *College credit available?* no.

Services

Housing options: on-site housing.

Application Information

Program dates: 4 weeks in July. *Application deadline:* January-February. *Application fee:* $25. *Enrollment full by:* 3/15. *Requirements:* photograph. *Acceptance notification:* 1-2 weeks after audition.

Audition Information

Audition fee: $15. *Audition consists of the following:* ballet. *Accompanist provided.*

Dress requirements for females: yes.

Costs & Financial Aid

Tuition (full): $1,000. *Room & board:* $975.

Financial aid available? partial scholarship. *Students receiving financial aid:* 9%. *Procedure for applying for financial aid:* no application; merit-based only.

Curriculum, Students, and Faculty

Required courses: African dance, character, ballet, historical dance, jazz, men's class, modern dance, pointe, Spanish, variations. *Specific curriculum information:* curriculum fixed.

Selectivity for males: most admitted, but not all. *Selectivity for females:* approximately 33% admitted.

Full-time faculty: 7. *Guest faculty:* 4.

Performance Information

Performances choreographed by: faculty, guests, open class. *Number of studios (description)*: 4 (60' x 40' suspended). *Performance facilities:* studio lighting, seating risers.

Affiliations

Summer program is affiliated with other program(s): future students are often recruited from this program.

FLORIDA

ACADEMY OF BALLET FLORIDA SUMMER DANCE WORKSHOP

Winter Contact Information

500 Fern Street, West Palm Beach FL 33401
Tel: 561-659-1212
Fax: 561-659-2222
Contact: Francia Kulchar

Summer Contact Information

500 Fern Street, West Palm Beach FL 33401
Tel: 561-659-1212
Fax: 561-659-2222
Contact: Francia Kulchar

General

Minimum age or age range: 9 to 19. *Level of program:* beginning, intermediate, advanced.

High school credit available? yes. *College credit available?* yes.

Services

Housing options: off-campus housing.

Application Information

Program dates: 6/15-7/10. *Application deadline:* 5/15. *Application fee:* $20. *Acceptance notification:* 2-3 weeks after audition.

Audition Information

Audition fee: $10. *Audition consists of the following:* ballet, pointe work. *Accompanist provided, cassette player available, CD player available.*

Dress requirements for females: yes. *Special dress requirements:* plain leotard, pink tights, ballet shoes, pointe shoes.

Costs & Financial Aid

Tuition (full): $800.

Financial aid available? full scholarship, partial scholarship. *Students receiving financial aid:* 25%. *Procedure for applying for financial aid:* fill out application with most recent 1040 and W-2.

Curriculum, Students, and Faculty

Required courses: anatomy, character, ballet, dance history, jazz, make-up, Graham-based modern dance, movement techniques, body conditioning, music, pas de deux, pointe, stagecraft, tap, variations, sports medicine. *Specific curriculum information:* curriculum fixed.

Selectivity for males: most admitted, but not all. *Selectivity for females*: most admitted, but not all.

Renowned alumni: Amy Brogan, Julie Gumbinner, Kim Wagman, Glenn Tuggle, Stephanie Hyde, Victor Trevina.

Full-time faculty: 1. *Guest faculty:* 15. *List of some faculty*: Marie Hale, Claudia Cravey, Steve Caras, Francia Kulchar, Jessica Benton, Eric Midgley.

Performance Information

Performances choreographed by: faculty. *Number of studios (description):* 4 (48' x 35' L'Air wooden floor, 46' x 35', 42' x 20', 30' x 27').

Affiliations

Summer program is affiliated with a professional company: future company members are not recruited from this program; company apprentices are recruited from this program. *Summer program is affiliated with a pre-professional company:* company apprentices are recruited from this program. *Summer program is affiliated with a conservatory:* future students are recruited from this program.

THE HARID CONSERVATORY, DANCE DIVISION SUMMER SCHOOL

Winter Contact Information

2285 Potomac Road, Boca Raton FL 33431
Tel: 561-997-2677
Fax: 561-997-8920
Contact: Gordan Wright

Summer Contact Information

2285 Potomac Road, Boca Raton FL 33431
Tel: 561-997-2677
Fax: 561-997-8920
Contact: Gordan Wright

General

Minimum age or age range: 13 to 16.

High school credit available? no. *College credit available?* no.

Services

Housing options: on-site housing.

Application Information

Program dates: last week of June. *Application deadline:* 4/30. *Application fee:* none. *Requirements:* recommendation. *Acceptance notification:* 2 weeks after audition.

Audition Information

Audition fee: $15. *Audition consists of the following:* ballet, pointe work.

Audition evaluation criteria: age, physique, prior training, talent, work habits/deportment, health.

Costs & Financial Aid

Tuition (full): $650. *Room & board:* $820.

Financial aid available? full scholarship, partial scholarship. *Students receiving financial aid:* 50%. *Procedure for applying for financial aid:* submit financial aid application form.

Curriculum, Students, and Faculty

Required courses: acting, anatomy, character, dance composition/choreography, historical dance, jazz, men's class, modern dance, music, nutrition, pas de deux, pointe, repertory, variations. *Specific curriculum information:* curriculum fixed.

Selectivity for males: approximately 10% admitted. *Selectivity for females:* approximately 10% admitted.

Renowned alumni: Pollana Robeoro, Boston Ballet; Riocama Corenzo, New York City Ballet; Marelo Gomes, American Ballet Theatre.

Full-time faculty: 3. *Guest faculty:* 5. *List of some faculty*: Gordan Wright, Oliver Pardina, Victoria Rockhill Schneider, Galina Yordanova, Michael Lazzaro, Marina Stolyar, Haydee Steeves, Tara Mitton Catao, Bertha Valentin, Deborah Rodensky, Kim Smith, Christine Cargill O'Shea, Pedro Hernandez, Olivia Shelley, Richard Patton.

Performance Information

Performances choreographed by: faculty. Open class. *Number of studios (description):* 3 (80' x 40' Marley on spring floor, 40' x 40', 40' x 40'). *Performance facilities:* large studio.

GEORGIA

ATLANTA BALLET CENTRE FOR DANCE EDUCATION

Winter Contact Information

1400 West Peachtree Street, Atlanta GA 30309
Tel: 404-873-5811
Fax: 404-874-7905
Contact: Sharon Story

Summer Contact Information

1400 West Peachtree Street, Atlanta GA 30309
Tel: 404-873-5811
Fax: 404-874-7905
Contact: Sharon Story

General

Minimum age or age range: 11 to 20. *Level of program:* intermediate, advanced.

High school credit available? no. *College credit available?* no.

Services

Housing options: on-site housing.

Application Information

Program dates: 6/14-7/4 at Western Carolina University, 7/13-8/9 in Atlanta. *Application deadline:* 5/1. *Requirements:* recommendation, photograph (two body positions).

Audition Information

Audition fee: $10. *Audition consists of the following:* ballet, pointe work, pas de deux. *Accompanist provided, cassette player available, CD player available.*

Dress requirements for females: Yes, *Special dress requirements:* black leotard, pink tights.

Audition evaluation criteria: level of technique.

Costs & Financial Aid

Financial aid available? full scholarship, partial scholarship. *Procedure for applying for financial aid:* scholarship application based on need not merit.

Curriculum, Students, and Faculty

Required courses: ballet, dance history, jazz, men's class, body conditioning, Pilates, music, pas de deux, pointe, variations, Orixas, David Parsons-Paul Taylor style modern dance. *Specific curriculum information:* curriculum fixed.

Selectivity for males: most admitted, but not all. *Selectivity for females:* approximately 60% admitted.

Full-time faculty: 4. *Guest faculty:* 5. *List of some faculty*: John Mcfall, Sharon Caplin, Timothy Cronin, Armando Luna, Mara Maldonado, Rosemary Miles, Sharon Story.

Performance Information

Performance opportunities and frequency: workshop performance(s); 1 per week. *Performances choreographed by:* faculty, guests. *Number of studios (description):* 6 (Marley). *Performance facilities:* studios.

Affiliations

Summer program is affiliated with a professional company: future company members are recruited from this program; company apprentices are recruited from this program. *Summer program is affiliated with a pre-professional company:* future company members are recruited from this program; company apprentices are recruited from this program. *Summer program is affiliated with other program(s):* future students are not recruited from this program.

HAWAII

WEST HAWAII DANCE THEATRE SUMMER SESSION

Winter Contact Information

74-5626 Alapa Street, Kailua-Kona HI 96740
Tel: 808-329-8876
Fax: 808-329-1033
Email: uh2dns4@ilhavaii.net

Summer Contact Information

74-5626 Alapa Street, Kailua-Kona HI 96740
Tel: 808-329-8876
Fax: 808-329-1033
Email: uh2dns4@ilhavaii.net

General

Minimum age or age range: 12 and up. *Level of program:* intermediate, advanced.

High school credit available? no. *College credit available?* no.

Services

Housing options: off-campus housing.

Application Information

Program dates: 7/27-8/15. *Application deadline:* 4/30. *Application fee:* $100. *Enrollment full by:* 4/30. *Requirements:* interview, essay, recommendation, photograph. *Acceptance notification:* 5/1.

Audition Information

No audition fee. Audition consists of the following: ballet, pointe work (short barre and center with pointe work). *Accompanist provided, cassette player available, CD player available.*

Special dress requirements: black leotard, pink tights, slippers, skirts, no baggy shirts or sweatpants.

Audition evaluation criteria: teacher recommendation is sufficient, 3-4 years prior training preferred.

Costs & Financial Aid

Tuition (full): $600.

Financial aid available? no.

Curriculum, Students, and Faculty

Required courses: character, ballet, jazz, men's class, modern dance, body conditioning, Pilates, pas de deux, pointe, repertory, variations. *Specific curriculum information:* curriculum fixed.

Selectivity for males: admit all who apply. *Selectivity for females:* admit all who apply.

Renowned alumni: Miho Morinove, Maki Morinove, Blossom Monarpaac, Becky Stephens, Glen-Bobby Newbeck.

Performance Information

Performance opportunities and frequency: final performance; end of session. *Performances choreographed by:* faculty, students, guests, students choreograph only in improvisation classes. *Number of studios (description):* 1 (1,200-sq. ft. Marley). *Performance facilities:* Aloha Theatre with Marley floor.

Affiliations

Summer program is affiliated with a professional company: future company members are recruited from this program; company apprentices are recruited from this program. *Summer program is affiliated with a pre-professional company:* future company members are recruited from this program; company apprentices are recruited from this program.

Additional Comments

Deposit of $100 will be applied towards tuition. There is a $25 discount if tuition is paid by April 15.

ILLINOIS

ACADEMY OF MOVEMENT AND MUSIC, DANCERS' PRODUCTION WORKSHOP

Winter Contact Information
605 Lake Street, Oak Park IL 60302
Tel: 708-848-2329
Fax: 708-848-2391
Contact: Stephanie Clemens

Summer Contact Information
605 Lake Street, Oak Park IL 60302
Tel: 708-848-2329
Fax: 708-848-2391
Contact: Stephanie Clemens

General

Minimum age or age range: 13 to 18. *Level of program:* beginning, intermediate, advanced.

High school credit available? no. *College credit available?* no.

Application Information

Program dates: mid June to late July. *Application deadline:* mid June. *Application fee:* none. *Enrollment full by:* mid June.

Audition Information

No audition fee. Audition consists of the following: ballet.

Dress requirements for females: Yes. *Special dress requirements:* black tank leotard, pink tights, pink ballet shoes.

Audition evaluation criteria: place students in level appropriate to skill level.

Costs & Financial Aid

Tuition (full): $250-$400

Financial aid available? partial scholarship. *Students receiving financial aid:* 5%. *Procedure for applying for financial aid:* request form and submit it with financial disclosure (tax forms) and letters of recommendation.

Curriculum, Students, and Faculty

Required courses: anatomy, character, ballet, dance composition/choreography, dance history, jazz, Graham-based modern dance, nutrition, pointe, Spanish, variations, Humphrey and Denishawn style modern dance. *Specific curriculum information:* curriculum fixed.

Selectivity for males: most admitted, but not all. *Selectivity for females:* most admitted, but not all.

Renowned alumni: Sandra Kaufman, Martha Graham Company; Tanya Wideman, Dance Theatre of Harlem; Ayisha McMillan, Houston Ballet; Ron DeJesus, Hubbard Street; Judith Chitwood, Northern Illinois University.

Full-time faculty: 6. *Guest faculty:* 2. *List of some faculty:* Valeri Dolgallo, Carla Graham-White, Stephanie Clemens

Performance Information

Performance opportunities and frequency: workshop performance(s); end of session. *Performances choreographed by:* faculty, students, guests. Open class; parents may observe by appointment.

Number of studios (description): 5 (20' x 30', 20' x 30', 20' x 55', 50' x 50', 50' x 30'). *Performance facilities:* black box stage, 50' x 30', with dance floor, curtains, wings, lights, sound system.

Affiliations

Summer program is affiliated with a pre-professional company: future company members are often recruited from this program; company apprentices are often recruited from this program.

DAVID HOWARD SUMMER WORKSHOP FOR TEACHERS

Winter Contact Information

Mary Price Boday, 719 West Moss, Peoria IL 61606
Tel: 309-672-2114
Fax: 309-672-2031
Email: pavlova2@aol.com
Contact: Mary Price Boday

Summer Contact Information

Mary Price Boday, 719 West Moss, Peoria IL 61606
Tel: 309-672-2114
Fax: 309-672-2031
Email: pavlova2@aol.com
Contact: Mary Price Boday

General

Level of program: beginning, intermediate, advanced.

High school credit available? no. *College credit available?* yes.

Services

Housing options: on-site housing, off-campus housing.

Application Information

Program dates: last week of June, second week of August. *Application fee:* $35. *Enrollment full by:* 6/1.

Audition Information

No audition fee. Accompanist provided, cassette player available, CD player available.

Dress requirements for females: no.

Costs & Financial Aid

Room & board: $200.

Financial aid available? full scholarship, partial scholarship. *Students receiving financial aid:* 10%. *Procedure for applying for financial aid:* contact Mary Price Boday.

Curriculum, Students, and Faculty

Required courses: ballet, jazz, master classes, men's class, Graham-based modern dance, movement techniques, body conditioning, music, pas de deux, pointe, variations, special classes for teachers. *Specific curriculum information:* curriculum fixed.

Selectivity for males: admit all who apply. *Selectivity for females:* admit all who apply.

Full-time faculty: 6. *Guest faculty:* 3. *List of some faculty:* David Howard, Mark Jelks, Dr. Daniel White, Dr. Barbara Phillips, Mary Price Boday, Douglas Corbin, Dr. Alan Woodle, Peter Schabel, Michael Owens.

Performance Information

Performances choreographed by: none. *Number of studios (description)*: 3 (40' x 40' basket weave, 40' x 40' basket weave, 30' x 40' basket weave).

Affiliations

Summer program is affiliated with a pre-professional company: future company members are recruited from this program; company apprentices are not recruited from this program. *Summer program is affiliated with other program(s):* future students are recruited from this program.

GUS GIORDANO DANCE CENTER

Winter Contact Information
614 Davis Street, Evanston IL 60201
Tel: 847-866-9442
Fax: 847-866-9228

Summer Contact Information
614 Davis Street, Evanston IL 60201
Tel: 847-866-9442
Fax: 847-866-9228

General

Minimum age or age range: 4 and up. *Level of program:* beginning, intermediate, advanced.

High school credit available? no. *College credit available?* no.

Services

Housing options: off-campus housing.

Application Information

Program dates: 6/8-7/25. *Application deadline:* rolling.

Audition Information

No audition fee.

Costs & Financial Aid

Financial aid available? full scholarship, *Procedure for applying for financial aid:* annual audition held at the end of each summer for the following year.

Curriculum, Students, and Faculty

Courses offered: ballet, jazz, modern dance, tap. *Specific curriculum information:* Curricula choices.

Selectivity for males: admit all who apply. *Selectivity for females:* admit all who apply.

Renowned alumni: Gus Giordano, Nan Giordano.

Performance Information

Performances choreographed by: faculty: *Number of studios (description):* 4 (30' x 30'-40' x 80' 3 Marley). *Performance facilities:* 2 venues, 1 presently under renovation.

Affiliations

Summer program is affiliated with a professional company: future company members are often recruited from this program; company apprentices are often recruited from this program. *Summer program is affiliated with a pre-professional company:* future company members are often recruited from this program; company apprentices are often recruited from this program.

NORTHERN ILLINOIS UNIVERSITY DANCE CAMP

Winter Contact Information
D. Booth, External Programs, Dekalb IL 60115
Tel: 815-753-1450
Fax: 815-753-8372
Email: dbooth@niu.edu
Contact: Deborah Booth

Summer Contact Information
40 D. Booth, External Programs, Dekalb IL 60115
Tel: 815-753-1450
Fax: 815-753-8372
Email: dbooth@niu.edu
Contact: Deborah Booth

General

Minimum age or age range: 12 and up.

High school credit available? no. *College credit available?* no.

Application Information

Application deadline: 1 month prior to camp. *Application fee:* none. *Enrollment full by:* 1 month prior to camp.

Audition Information

No audition fee.

Costs & Financial Aid

Financial aid available? Yes. full scholarship, *Students receiving financial aid:* 25%. *Procedure for applying for financial aid:* external to the University.

Curriculum, Students, and Faculty

Required courses: ballet, dance composition/choreography, improvisation, jazz, modern dance, pointe, repertory, tap. *Specific curriculum information:* curriculum fixed.

Selectivity for males: admit all who apply. *Selectivity for females:* admit all who apply.

Full-time faculty: 2. *Guest faculty:* 3. *List of some faculty*: Judith Chitword, Paula Fransz.

Performance Information

Performance opportunities and frequency: workshop performance(s); 1 per week. *Performances choreographed by:* faculty. *Number of studios (description):* 2 (wood).

Affiliations

Summer program is affiliated with a conservatory: future students are often recruited from this program.

NORTHWESTERN UNIVERSITY, NATIONAL HIGH SCHOOL INSTITUTE DANCE DIVISION

Winter Contact Information
617 Noyes, Evanston IL 60208
Tel: 847-491-3026
Fax: 847-467-1057
Email: nhsi@nwu.edu
Contact: Robin Lakes

Summer Contact Information
1979 South Campus Drive, Evanston IL 60208-2430
Tel: 847-491-3947
Email: nhsi@nwu.edu
Contact: Robin Lakes

General
Total enrollment: 20-30. *Minimum age or age range:* 15 to 18. *Level of program:* beginning, intermediate, advanced.

High school credit available? no. *College credit available?* no.

Services
Housing options: on-site housing.

Application Information
Program dates: 6/29-8/2. *Application deadline:* 3/28, 4/25. *Application fee:* none. *Enrollment full by:* 5/15. *Requirements:* essay, recommendation, photograph. *Acceptance notification:* 4/25 for early admissions, 5/25 for regular admissions.

Audition Information
No audition fee. Audition consists of the following: 2 minutes of dancing on videotape showcasing applicant's strengths .

Dress requirements: no.

Audition evaluation criteria: current skills, potenial growth.

Costs & Financial Aid
Tuition (full): $2,775.

Financial aid available? partial scholarship. *Students receiving financial aid:* 25%. *Procedure for applying for financial aid:* submit tax return and a financial aid form.

Curriculum, Students, and Faculty
Courses offered: African dance, ballet, dance composition/choreography, improvisation, jazz, master classes, Pilates, repertory, vernacular dance, dance aesthetics, contemporary dance, Latin dance. *Specific curriculum information:* Curricula choices.

Selectivity for males: approximately 60% admitted. *Selectivity for females:* approximately 60% admitted.

Full-time faculty: 6. *Guest faculty:* 2.

Performance Information
Performance opportunities and frequency: final performance. *Performances choreographed by:* faculty, guests. *Number of studios (description):* 3 (40' x 30' wood (sprung)). *Performance facilities:* fully equipped studio theater, seats 80.

Affiliations
Summer program is affiliated with other program(s): future students are often recruited from this program.

NORTHWESTERN UNIVERSITY SUMMER DANCE INSTITUTE

Winter Contact Information
1979 South Campus Drive, Murjurie Ward Marshall Dance Center, Evanston IL 60208
Tel: 847-491-3147
Fax: 847-467-2019
Contact: Susan Lee

Summer Contact Information
1979 South Campus Drive, Murjurie Ward Marshall Dance Center, Evanston IL 60208
Tel: 847-491-3147
Fax: 847-467-2019
Contact: Susan Lee

General
Minimum age or age range: 16 and up. *Level of program:* intermediate, advanced.

High school credit available? yes. *College credit available?* yes.

Services
Housing options: on-site housing, off-campus housing.

Application Information
Application deadline: varies.

Audition Information
No audition fee.

Dress requirements: no.

Costs & Financial Aid
Financial aid available? no.

Curriculum, Students, and Faculty

Courses offered: dance composition/choreography, historical dance, jazz, modern dance, Feldenkreis, Pilates, repertory, tap, vernacular dance. *Specific curriculum information:* Curricula choices.

Selectivity for males: most admitted, but not all. *Selectivity for females:* most admitted, but not all.

List of some faculty and their affiliations: Billy Siegenfeld, Brian Jeffery.

Performance Information

Performance opportunities and frequency: workshop performance(s); 1. Open class. *Number of studios (description):* 3 (sprung wood). *Performance facilities:* loft-style proscenium.

Affiliations

Summer program is affiliated with a professional company: future company members are sometimes recruited from this program; company apprentices are sometimes recruited from this program. *Summer program is affiliated with a pre-professional company:* company apprentices are sometimes recruited from this program.

Additional Comments

Financial information depends on credit or non-credit enrollment.

SUMMER DANCE CHICAGO

Winter Contact Information

Dance Center of Columbia College, 4730 North Sheridan Road, Chicago IL 60640
Tel: 773-989-3310
Fax: 773-271-7046
Contact: Recruitment Coordinator

Summer Contact Information

Dance Center of Columbia College, 4730 North Sheridan Road, Chicago IL 60640
Tel: 773-989-3310
Fax: 773-271-7046
Contact: Recruitment Coordinator

General

Minimum age or age range: 18.

High school credit available? no. *College credit available?* yes.

Services

Housing options: off-campus housing.

Application Information

Application deadline: 6/9. *Application fee:* $10. *Enrollment full by:* 5/31.

Audition Information

No audition fee.

Costs & Financial Aid

Financial aid available? full scholarship, partial scholarship. *Students receiving financial aid:* 10%. *Procedure for applying for financial aid:* send application and audition in April.

Curriculum, Students, and Faculty

Courses offered: ballet, dance composition/choreography, modern dance, performance arts. *Specific curriculum information:* Curricula choices.

Selectivity for males: admit all who apply. *Selectivity for females:* admit all who apply.

Full-time faculty: 7. *Guest faculty:* 2. *List of some faculty:* Shieley Mordine, Jan Erkert.

Performance Information

Performances choreographed by: faculty, students, guests; *Number of studios (description):* 3 (40' x 40' Marley, 48' x 27', 48' x 22'). *Performance facilities:* black box theater, stage, 40' x 40'.

Affiliations

Summer program is affiliated with a conservatory: future students are recruited from this program.

Additional Comments

Tuition ranges from $108 to $247; per class basis.

KENTUCKY

JAZZART TECHNIQUE AND CHOREOGRAPHY WORKSHOP

Winter Contact Information

Western Kentucky University Department of Theatre and Dance, 1 Big Red Way, Bowling Green KY 42101
Tel: 502-745-5832
Fax: 502-745-5832
Email: bob.boross@wku.edu
Contact: Bob Boross

Summer Contact Information

Western Kentucky University Department of Theater and Dance, 1 Big Red Way, Bowling Green KY 42101
Tel: 502-745-5832
Fax: 502-745-5879
Email: bob.boross@wku.edu
Contact: Bob Boross

General

Minimum age or age range: 15 to adult; planning an 11-15 level for 1999. *Level of program:* advanced.

High school credit available? no. *College credit available?* no.

Services

Housing options: on-site housing.

Application Information

Program dates: 6/30-7/8. *Application deadline:* 6/1. *Application fee:* none. *Enrollment full by:* 6/1. *Acceptance notification:* 6/1, 4/1.

Audition Information

No audition fee. Audition consists of the following: prepared solo (jazz solo on video).

Dress requirements: no.

Costs & Financial Aid

Room & board: $280. *Room:* $140. *Board:* $140.

Financial aid available? yes. partial scholarship.

Curriculum, Students, and Faculty

Required courses: ballet, jazz, tap, theatrical dance, vernacular dance. *Specific curriculum information:* curriculum fixed.

Selectivity for males: admit all who apply. *Selectivity for females:* admit all who apply.

Guest faculty: 7. *List of some faculty*: Matt Mattox, Martine Mattox, Billy Siegenfeld, Jeannie Hill, Gail Benedict, Bob Boross, Rosemary Boross.

Performance Information

Performances choreographed by: faculty.

Number of studios (description): 3 (50' x 30' Marley and sprung floors). *Performance facilities:* university theater.

Affiliations

Summer program is affiliated with a university: future students are recruited from this program.

MAINE

BATES DANCE FESTIVAL

Winter Contact Information

163 Wood Street, Bates College, Lewiston ME 04240
Tel: 207-786-6381
Fax: 207-786-8282
Email: dancefest@bates.edu

Summer Contact Information

164 Wood Street, Bates College, Lewiston ME 04240
Tel: 207-786-6381
Fax: 207-786-8282
Email: dancefest@bates.edu

General

Minimum age or age range: 18 and up. *Level of program:* intermediate, advanced.

High school credit available? no. *College credit available?* yes.

Services

Housing options: on-site housing.

Application Information

Program dates: 7/26-8/17. *Application fee:* $75. *Enrollment full by:* 4/15. *Requirements:* essay, recommendation.

Audition Information

No audition fee. Accompanist provided.

Dress requirements: no.

Costs & Financial Aid

Tuition (full): $650.

Financial aid available? full scholarship, partial scholarship. *Students receiving financial aid:* 20%. *Procedure for applying for financial aid:* fill out form, include IRS forms, résumé, recommendations.

Curriculum, Students, and Faculty

Courses offered: African dance, Alexander technique, anatomy, dance composition/choreography, dance history, modern dance, movement techniques, Feldenkreis, Laban Movement Studies, Pilates, music, Indian dance, repertory, Spanish, tap, vernacular dance, contemporary jazz techniques, Asian dance, Caribbean dance. *Specific curriculum information:* Curricula choices.

Selectivity for males: most admitted, but not all. *Selectivity for females:* most admitted, but not all.

Renowned alumni: Michael Foley, Min-Lung Yang, John Canafa, Scott Wells.

Full-time faculty: 20. *Guest faculty:* 1. *List of some faculty*: Bebe Miller, Doug Varone, David Dorfman, Rennie Harris, Danny Buraczeski, Liz Lerman.

Performance Information

Performances choreographed by: faculty, students, guests. *Number of studios (description):* 9 (varies wood and Marley). *Performance facilities:* 300-seat proscenium, 800-seat proscenium.

Affiliations

Summer program is affiliated with a professional company: company apprentices are often recruited from this program. *Summer program is affiliated with a pre-professional company:* future company members are recruited from this program; company apprentices are recruited from this program. *Summer program is affiliated with other program(s):* future students are not recruited from this program.

YOUNG DANCER WORKSHOP

Winter Contact Information

163 Wood Street, Bates College, Lewiston ME 04240
Tel: 207-786-6381
Fax: 207-786-8282
Email: dancefest@bates.edu
Contact: Laura Faure

Summer Contact Information

163 Wood Street, Bates College, Lewiston ME 04240
Tel: 207-786-6381
Fax: 207-786-8282
Email: dancefest@bates.edu
Contact: Laura Faure

Services

Housing options: on-site housing.

Application Information

Requirements: recommendation.

Curriculum, Students, and Faculty

Required courses: anatomy, ballet, dance composition/choreography, dance history, historical dance, improvisation, jazz, Labanotation, master classes, modern dance, music, repertory, Spanish, tap, vernacular dance.

Performance Information

Performance opportunities and frequency: Final performance; 1. Informal showings; frequently. *Performances choreographed by:* faculty, students, guests. *Number of studios (description):* 8 (wood and Marley).

Affiliations

Summer program is affiliated with a professional company: future company members are not recruited from this program; company apprentices are recruited from this program. *Summer program is affiliated with a pre-professional company:* company apprentices are recruited from this program.

MARYLAND

GOUCHER SUMMER DANCE WORKSHOP

Winter Contact Information

Goucher College, Department of Dance, 1021 Dulaney Valley Road, Baltimore MD 21204
Tel: 410-337-6390
Fax: 410-337-6123
Email: awoodson@goucher.edu
Contact: Amanda Thom Woodson

Summer Contact Information

Goucher College, Department of Dance, 1021 Dulaney Valley Road, Baltimore MD 21204
Tel: 410-337-6390
Fax: 410-337-6123
Email: awoodson@goucher.edu
Contact: Amanda Thom Woodson

General

Minimum age or age range: 10 to 18. *Level of program:* beginning, intermediate, advanced.

High school credit available? no. *College credit available?* no.

Services

Housing options: on-site housing.

Application Information

Program dates: 7/20-8/1. *Application deadline:* early June. *Application fee:* $50. *Enrollment full by:* June.

Audition Information

No audition fee. Accompanist provided.

Dress requirements for females: Yes. *Special dress requirements:* solid color leotard, tights.

Costs & Financial Aid

Tuition (full): $420. *Room & board:* $370.

Financial aid available? no.

Curriculum, Students, and Faculty

Required courses: African dance, ballet, dance composition/choreography, jazz, Limon-based modern dance, Pilates, pointe, repertory, tap. *Specific curriculum information:* curriculum fixed.

Selectivity for males: admit all who apply. *Selectivity for females:* admit all who apply.

Full-time faculty: 6. *Guest faculty:* 1. *List of some faculty and their affiliations:* Elizabeth Lowe Ahearn, Goucher College, Pilates, Oklahoma Ballet; Ken Skrzesz, Carver Center, Surge Dance Company

Performance Information

Performance opportunities and frequency: Informal showings; 1. *Performances choreographed by:* faculty, guests. *Number of studios (description):* 5 (Gerstung sprung floor). *Performance facilities:* auditorium.

Affiliations

Summer program is affiliated with other program(s): future students are recruited from this program.

MASSACHUSETTS

BELVOIR TERRACE

Winter Contact Information

101 West 79th Street, Apartment 15B, New York NY 10024
Tel: 212-580-3398
Fax: 212-579-7282
Email: BelvoirT@aol.com
Contact: Nancy Goldberg and Diane Goldberg

Summer Contact Information

Lenox MA 01240
Tel: 413-637-0555
Fax: 413-637-4651
Email: BelvoirT@aol.com
Contact: Nancy Goldberg and Diane Goldberg

General

Minimum age or age range: 10 to 18. *Level of program:* beginning, intermediate, advanced.

High school credit available? yes. *College credit available?* no.

Services

Housing options: on-site housing.

Application Information

Program dates: 6/25-8/14. *Application fee:* none. *Enrollment full by:* March. *Requirements:* interview.

Audition Information

No audition fee.

Costs & Financial Aid

Tuition (full): $6,100.

Financial aid available? partial scholarship. *Students receiving financial aid:* 10%. *Procedure for applying for financial aid:* application.

Curriculum, Students, and Faculty

Courses offered: character, ballet, dance composition/choreography, jazz, master classes, Graham-based modern dance, Horton-based modern dance, music, pointe, tap, variations. *Specific curriculum information:* Curricula choices. *Selectivity for females:* approximately 33% admitted.

Renowned alumni: Nannette Glushak, Susan Pilarre.

Full-time faculty: 8. *Guest faculty:* 8. *List of some faculty*: Nancy Raffa, Carolyn Lanfredi, Sheri Little, Michelle Benash, Chris Lee.

Performance Information

Performances choreographed by: faculty, students, guests. Open class. *Number of studios (description):* 4 (40' x 60' Marley). *Performance facilities:* Koussevitsky Theatre, 450-seat professional theater.

BOSTON BALLET SUMMER DANCE PROGRAM

Winter Contact Information

19 Clarendon Street, Boston MA 02116
Tel: 617-695-6950
Fax: 617-695-6955
Contact: Kate Edan

Summer Contact Information

19 Clarendon Street, Boston MA 02116
Tel: 617-695-6950
Fax: 617-695-6955
Contact: Kate Edan

General

Minimum age or age range: 13 to mid 20s. *Level of program:* intermediate, advanced.

High school credit available? no. *College credit available?* no.

Services

Housing options: off-campus housing.

Application Information

Program dates: 6/28-8/9. *Application fee:* $225. *Enrollment full by:* February. *Requirements:* recommendation, photograph. *Acceptance notification:* 2/28.

Audition Information

Audition fee: $15. *Audition consists of the following:* ballet, pointe work.

Dress requirements: Yes. *Special dress requirements:* leotards, tights, pointe shoes for women.

Costs & Financial Aid

Financial aid available? full scholarship, partial scholarship. *Procedure for applying for financial aid:* application.

Curriculum, Students, and Faculty

Required courses: character, ballet, jazz, men's class, modern dance, pas de deux, pointe, Spanish, variations. *Specific curriculum information:* curriculum fixed.

Selectivity for males: approximately 60% admitted. *Selectivity for females:* approximately 60% admitted.

Performance Information

Performances choreographed by: faculty. *Number of studios (description):* 7 (50' x 60' Marley). *Performance facilities:* grand studio, approximately 170' x 70'.

Affiliations

Summer program is affiliated with a professional company: future company members are exclusively recruited from this program; company apprentices are often recruited from this program. *Summer program is affiliated with a pre-professional company:* future company members are often recruited from this program; company apprentices are often recruited from this program. *Summer program is affiliated with other program(s):* future students are not recruited from this program.

JACOB'S PILLOW DANCE FESTIVAL AND SCHOOL

Winter Contact Information
P.O. Box 287, Lee MA 02138
Tel: 413-637-1322
Fax: 413-243-4744
Contact: J.R. Glover

Summer Contact Information
P.O. Box 287, Lee MA 02138
Tel: 413-637-1322
Fax: 413-243-4744
Contact: J.R. Glover

General

Minimum age or age range: 16. *Level of program:* advanced.

High school credit available? no. *College credit available?* yes.

Services

Housing options: on-site housing.

Application Information

Program dates: June-August. *Application fee:* $25. *Requirements:* interview, essay, recommendation, *Acceptance notification:* April.

Audition Information

Audition fee: $10. *Audition consists of the following:* modern dance, prepared solo (prepared solo for choreography workshop). *Accompanist provided, cassette player available, CD player available.*

Dress requirements: no.

Audition evaluation criteria: technique, understanding of alignment and movement fundamentals, expression, aritstry, focus.

Costs & Financial Aid

Tuition (full): $350. *Room & board:* $150. *Other fees:* $20 damage deposit.

Financial aid available? full scholarship, partial scholarship. *Students receiving financial aid:* 48%. *Procedure for applying for financial aid:* submit application form and latest tax return.

Curriculum, Students, and Faculty

Required courses: African dance, Alexander technique, ballet, dance composition/choreography, dance history, historical dance, jazz, master classes, modern dance, body conditioning, Feldenkreis, Laban Movement Studies, Pilates, music, repertory, Spanish, tap, vernacular dance, Butoh. *Specific curriculum information:* curriculum fixed.

Selectivity for males: approximately 33% admitted. *Selectivity for females:* approximately 33% admitted.

Renowned alumni: Betty Jones, Meredith Monk, Linda Kent, Chris Komar, Nikolaj Hubbe, Nina Weiner, Terese Capucilli.

Full-time faculty: 5. *Guest faculty:* 1-3. *List of some faculty and their affiliations:* Elizabeth Keen, Juilliard; Milton Myers, Alvin Ailey American Dance Theater; Danny Buraczeski, Meg Harper, Celeste Miller, Billy Siegenfeld, Jump Rhythm Dance Project; Gary Masters, Limon; David Dorfman.

Performance Information

Performance opportunities and frequency: Informal showings; 2-3. *Performances choreographed by:* faculty, students, guests. Open class. *Number of studios (description):* 4 (20' x 50' wood and Marley). *Performance facilities:* 2 theaters, 1 outdoor stage.

Affiliations

Summer program is affiliated with a professional company: company apprentices are recruited from this program. *Summer program is affiliated with a pre-professional company:* company apprentices are recruited from this program.

SUMMER INTENSIVE FOCUSING ON TEACHINGS OF GEORGE BALANCHINE

Winter Contact Information
P.O. Box 391898, Cambridge MA 02139
Tel: 617-491-8615
Fax: 617-491-8617
Email: BSTNDNC@aol.com
Contact: Ajay Bhandaram

Summer Contact Information
P.O. Box 391898, Cambridge MA 02139
Tel: 617-491-8615
Fax: 617-491-8617
Email: BSTNDNC@aol.com
Contact: Ajay Bhandaram

General
Minimum age or age range: 12 to 25.

High school credit available? no. *College credit available?* no.

Services
Housing options: on-site housing.

Application Information
Program dates: 7/7-8/15. *Application fee:* $50. *Requirements:* recommendation, photograph. *Acceptance notification:* immediately.

Audition Information
Audition fee: $10. *Audition consists of the following:* ballet, pointe work.

Costs & Financial Aid
Tuition (full): $1,500. *Room & board:* $1,650.

Financial aid available? partial scholarship. *Students receiving financial aid:* 25%. *Procedure for applying for financial aid:* talk to director.

Curriculum, Students, and Faculty
Required courses: ballet, men's class, pointe, repertory, variations. *Specific curriculum information:* curriculum fixed.

Selectivity for males: most admitted, but not all. *Selectivity for females:* approximately 33% admitted.

Renowned alumni: Andrew Drost, Miami City Ballet; Tiffany Kanet, Ballet Met; Kerry Revtensk, Chicago Ballet.

Full-time faculty: 2. *Guest faculty:* 6. *List of some faculty and their affiliations:* Deborah Wingert, Bart Cook, Maria Calegari, NYC Ballet.

Performance Information
Performances choreographed by: guests, 1 per week. *Number of studios (description):* 2 (50' x 30', 35' x 30' wood).

Affiliations
Summer program is affiliated with a professional company: future company members are recruited from this program; company apprentices are recruited from this program.

SUMMER STAGES: THE SUMMER DANCE PROJECT AT CONCORD ACADEMY

Winter Contact Information
Summer Stages, Concord Academy, 166 Main Street, Concord MA 01742
Tel: 508-369-6081
Fax: 508-369-3452
Contact: Richard Colton

Summer Contact Information
Summer Stages, Concord Academy, 166 Main Street, Concord MA 01742
Tel: 508-369-6081
Fax: 508-369-3452
Contact: Richard Colton

General
Total enrollment: 20-30. *Minimum age or age range:* 16 and up. *Level of program:* intermediate, advanced.

High school credit available? yes. *College credit available?* yes.

Services
Housing options: on-site housing.

Application Information
Program dates: 6/28-7/25. *Application deadline:* rolling. *Enrollment full by:* early June. *Requirements:* recommendation. *Acceptance notification:* rolling.

Audition Information
No audition fee. Audition consists of the following: ballet, modern dance.

Costs & Financial Aid
Tuition (full): $1,200. *Room & board:* $1,000.

Financial aid available? partial scholarship. *Procedure for applying for financial aid:* request financial aid application form.

Curriculum, Students, and Faculty
Required courses: anatomy, ballet, dance composition/choreography, modern dance, body condi-

tioning, Pilates, music, repertory, Iyengar yoga. *Specific curriculum information:* curriculum fixed.

Selectivity for males: approximately 60% admitted. *Selectivity for females:* approximately 60% admitted.

Full-time faculty: 6. *Guest faculty:* 6. *List of some faculty and their affiliations:* Richard Colton, Concord Academy, Joffrey Ballet, American Ballet Theater, White Oak; Amy Spencer, Concord Academy, American Repertory Theatre.

Performance Information

Performance opportunities and frequency: workshop performance(s); 1 per session. *Performances choreographed by:* faculty, students. *Number of studios (description):* 2 (45' x 45' Marley). *Performance facilities:* Performing Arts Center, thrust stage.

Affiliations

Summer program is affiliated with other program(s): future students are recruited from this program.

WHITE MOUNTAIN SUMMER DANCE FESTIVAL

Winter Contact Information
162 West 21st Street, New York NY 10011
Tel: 212-929-5733
Fax: 212-255-9479

Summer Contact Information
Simon's Rock College, 84 Alford Road, Great Barrington MA 01230
Tel: 413-528-7648

General

Minimum age or age range: 14 and up.

High school credit available? no. *College credit available?* yes.

Services

Housing options: on-site housing.

Application Information

Program dates: last 2 weeks of July, first week of August. *Application fee:* $75.

Audition Information

No audition fee.

Costs & Financial Aid

Tuition (full): $620. *Room & board:* $275. *Financial aid available?* partial scholarship. *Procedure for applying for financial aid:* application, questionnaire, statement of need, recommendation by an employer.

Curriculum, Students, and Faculty

Courses offered: Alexander technique, anatomy, ballet, dance composition/choreography, modern dance, body conditioning, Laban Movement Studies, repertory, yoga, Bartenieff fundamentals. *Specific curriculum information:* Curricula choices.

Selectivity for males: admit all who apply. *Selectivity for females:* admit all who apply.

Renowned alumni: John Heginbothem, Susan Marshell, Mark Morris.

Full-time faculty: 6. *Guest faculty:* 0. *List of some faculty and their affiliations:* Jim Lepore; James Martin, New York University Tisch School of the Arts; Regina Wray.

Performance Information

Performance opportunities and frequency: final performance; weekly. *Performances choreographed by:* faculty, students, guests, open class. *Performance facilities:* Simon's Rock College's ARC Theatre.

Affiliations

Summer program is affiliated with a professional company: future company members are often recruited from this program; company apprentices are often recruited from this program.

Additional Comments

Additional costs for key depost, linens, and anatomy text.

MICHIGAN

INTERLOCHEN ARTS CAMP

Winter Contact Information
P.O. Box 199, Interlochen MI 49643-0199
Tel: 616-276-7415
Fax: 616-276-6321
Email: ica@interlochen.k12.MI.US
Contact: Sharon Randolph

Summer Contact Information
P.O. Box 199, Interlochen MI 49643-0199
Tel: 616-276-7472
Fax: 616-276-6321
Contact: Krista K. Maxson

General

Minimum age or age range: 12 to 18. *Level of program:* beginning, intermediate, advanced.

High school credit available? no. *College credit available?* no.

Services

Housing options: on-site housing.

Application Information

Program dates: 6/21-8/17. *Application deadline:* 2/15. *Application fee:* $35. *Enrollment full by:* 5/1. *Requirements:* photograph. *Acceptance notification:* 4/15.

Audition Information

No audition fee. Audition consists of the following: pointe work, prepared solo. *Accompanist provided, cassette player available, CD player available.*

Dress requirements: yes.

Costs & Financial Aid

Tuition (full): $3,990.

Financial aid available? partial scholarship. *Students receiving financial aid:* 30%. *Procedure for applying for financial aid:* submit videotape, financial information, and IRS form 1040 with application.

Curriculum, Students, and Faculty

Required courses: ballet, dance composition/choreography, jazz, master classes, modern dance, pas de deux, pointe, repertory, variations. *Specific curriculum information:* curriculum fixed.

Selectivity for males: most admitted, but not all. *Selectivity for females:* approximately 60% admitted.

Renowned alumni: Janet Eilber, Peter Sparling, Terese Freedom Coleman, Jill Moffitt Nicklaus, Todd Stickney.

Full-time faculty: 10. *Guest faculty:* 1. *List of some faculty and their affiliations:* Stephanie Rand, Texas Christian University; Gay Delanghe, University of Michigan; Mauree Janson, Tom Morris, Sharon Randolph.

Performance Information

Performance opportunities and frequency: Informal showings; 2-4. Workshop performance(s); 2-4. *Performances choreographed by:* faculty, guests, open class. *Number of studios (description):* 5 (sprung floor). *Performance facilities:* Corson Auditorium, 1000 seats indoors, Interlochen Bowl, 4,000 seats outdoors, studio, 100 informal seats.

Affiliations

Summer program is affiliated with a pre-professional company: future company members are not recruited from this program; company apprentices are not recruited from this program. *Summer program is affiliated with other program(s):* future students are not recruited from this program.

JOFFREY MIDWEST WORKSHOP

Winter Contact Information

1241 East Kearsley Street, Flint MI 48503
Tel: 810-760-5017
Fax: 810-760-5016
Contact: Jennifer Ramsdell

Summer Contact Information

1241 East Kearsley Street, Flint MI 48503
Tel: 810-760-5017
Fax: 810-760-5016
Contact: Jennifer Ramsdell

General

Total enrollment: 100-120. *Minimum age or age range:* 12 and up. *Level of program:* intermediate, advanced.

High school credit available? no. *College credit available?* no.

Services

Housing options: on-site housing.

Application Information

Application fee: none. *Enrollment full by:* 5/1. *Requirements:* photograph. *Acceptance notification:* 2 weeks after audition.

Audition Information

Audition fee: $15. *Audition consists of the following:* ballet, pointe work, pas de deux. *Accompanist provided, cassette player available, CD player available.*

Special dress requirements: black, pink.

Audition evaluation criteria: technique level.

Costs & Financial Aid

Tuition (full): $2,500.

Financial aid available? full scholarship, partial scholarship. *Students receiving financial aid:* 12%. *Procedure for applying for financial aid:* merit-based, based on audition.

Curriculum, Students, and Faculty

Required courses: anatomy, character, ballet, dance history, jazz, men's class, modern dance, pas de deux, pointe, variations. *Specific curriculum information:* curriculum fixed.

Selectivity for males: approximately 33% admitted. *Selectivity for females:* approximately 33% admitted.

Full-time faculty: 5. *Guest faculty:* 2. *List of some faculty and their affiliations:* John Magnus, Joffrey Ballet School; Judy Rice, University of Iowa, Joffrey Ballet School; Francoise Martinet, University of Iowa, Joffrey Ballet School.

Performance Information

Performances choreographed by: faculty, guests. *Number of studios (description):* 6 (40' x 60' portable sprung). *Performance facilities:* 2000-seat auditorium.

Affiliations

Summer program is affiliated with a professional company: future company members are recruited from this program; company apprentices are recruited from this program. *Summer program is affiliated with a pre-professional company:* future company members are recruited from this program; company apprentices are recruited from this program.

Additional Comments

We are expanding our program and should have more information available by August 1998.

MINNESOTA

MODERN DANCE INTENSIVES AND CROSS CULTURAL DANCE CAMPS

Winter Contact Information

Nancy Hauser Dance School, 1940 Hennepin Avenue, Minneapolis MN 55403
Tel: 612-871-9077
Fax: 612-870-0764
Contact: Heidi Hauser Jasmin

Summer Contact Information

Nancy Hauser Dance School, 1940 Hennepin Avenue, Minneapolis MN 55403
Tel: 612-871-9077
Fax: 612-870-0764
Contact: Heidi Hauser Jasmin

General

Minimum age or age range: 6 to 45. *Level of program:* beginning, intermediate, advanced.

High school credit available? no. *College credit available?* no.

Services

Housing options: off-campus housing.

Application Information

Program dates: 6/9-8/30. *Application fee:* $50. *Enrollment full by:* 5/30. *Requirements:* essay, recommendation. *Acceptance notification:* 5/30.

Audition Information

No audition fee.

Costs & Financial Aid

Tuition (full): $165-$725

Financial aid available? no.

Curriculum, Students, and Faculty

Required courses: dance composition/choreography, improvisation, master classes, Nikolais-based modern dance, music, repertory, composition. *Specific curriculum information:* curriculum fixed.

Selectivity for males: approximately 60% admitted. *Selectivity for females:* approximately 60% admitted.

Renowned alumni: Jerry Pearson, Sara Pearson, Ralph Lemon, Gary Lund, Charles Moulton, Gail Turner, Maria Chang.

Full-time faculty: 3. *Guest faculty:* 1.

Performance Information

Performance opportunities and frequency: Workshop performance(s); 1-3. *Performances choreographed by:* faculty, students, guests.

Number of studios (description): 3 (40' x 80' wood sprung floor). *Performance facilities:* 100-seat theater.

Affiliations

Summer program is affiliated with a professional company: future company members are not recruited from this program; company apprentices are often recruited from this program. *Summer program is affiliated with a pre-professional company:* future company members are not recruited from this program; company apprentices are often recruited from this program.

NEW JERSEY

GOVERNOR'S SCHOOL OF ARTS

Winter Contact Information
The College of New Jersey, PO Box 7718, Ewing NJ 08608-0718
Tel: 609-771-3114
Fax: 609-637-5128
Contact: Angela Warren

Summer Contact Information
The College of New Jersey, PO Box 7718, Ewing NJ 08628-0718
Tel: 609-771-3114
Fax: 609-637-5128
Contact: Angela Warren

General
Minimum age or age range: 16 to 18. *Level of program:* advanced.

High school credit available? yes. *College credit available?* no.

Services
Housing options: on-site housing.

Application Information
Application deadline: fall of junior year. *Application fee:* none. *Requirements:* essay. *Acceptance notification:* 5/12.

Audition Information
No audition fee. Audition consists of the following: ballet, modern dance, prepared solo, (jazz). *Cassette player available, CD player available.*

Dress requirements for females: Yes. *Special dress requirements:* leotard.

Costs & Financial Aid
Financial aid available? Yes. full scholarship.

Curriculum, Students, and Faculty
Courses offered: African dance, anatomy, character, ballet, dance composition/choreography, dance history, historical dance, jazz, Labanotation, martial arts, master classes, modern dance, body conditioning, pas de deux, pointe, repertory, Spanish, tap, variations, vernacular dance. *Specific curriculum information:* curriculum fixed. *Selectivity for females:* approximately 10% admitted.

Full-time faculty: 1. *Guest faculty:* 7-10.

Performance Information
Performances choreographed by: faculty, students. *Number of studios (description):* 1 (25' x 25' wood). *Performance facilities:* main stage concert hall.

Affiliations
Summer program is affiliated with other program(s): future students are recruited from this program.

PRINCETON BALLET SCHOOL'S SUMMER WORKSHOP

Winter Contact Information
301 North Harrison Street, Princeton NJ 08540
Tel: 609-921-7758
Fax: 609-921-3249
Contact: Mary Pat Robertson

Summer Contact Information
301 North Harrison Street, Princeton NJ 08540
Tel: 609-921-7758
Fax: 609-921-3249
Contact: Mary Pat Robertson

General
Minimum age or age range: 13 and up. *Level of program:* intermediate, advanced.

High school credit available? no. *College credit available?* no.

Application Information
Program dates: last week of June-July (5 weeks). *Application deadline:* accept applications until classes are full. *Enrollment full by:* mid April. *Requirements:* recommendation (if not participating in an audition), two photographs. *Acceptance notification:* 2 weeks after audition.

Audition Information
Audition fee: $15. *Audition consists of the following:* ballet, pointe work. *Accompanist provided.*

Dress requirements: no.

Audition evaluation criteria: strong technique, good work habits, quick learners, open to corrections and new ideas.

Costs & Financial Aid
Tuition (full): $1,100. *Room & board:* $1,550. *Other fees:* $100 activities fee for dorm students, $65 optional NY performance (bus trip to Lincoln Center Theater), $25 optional purchase video of final performance.

Financial aid available? full scholarship, partial scholarship. *Students receiving financial aid:* 20%. *Procedure for applying for financial aid:* all students are automatically considered, scholarships are merit-based.

Curriculum, Students, and Faculty

Courses offered: Alexander technique, ballet, dance composition/choreography, dance history, jazz, make-up, master classes, men's class, modern dance, Pilates, nutrition, pas de deux, pointe, repertory, Spanish, variations, yoga. *Specific curriculum information:* Curricula choices.

Selectivity for males: approximately 60% admitted. *Selectivity for females:* approximately 33% admitted.

Renowned alumni: Elizabeth Guenin, Pacific Northwest Ballet, Washington Ballet; Cheryl Sladkin, Washington Ballet; Suzanne Trorano, Julie Stahl, Feld Company; Charles Pope, Boston Ballet; Julie Caprio, American Ballet Theatre; Diane Partington, Joffrey Ballet, Sarasota Ballet; Bebe Neuwirth, Douglas Dunn, Kraig Paterson, Mark Morris Company; Amy Spencer, Julie Stahl, Twyla Tharp Company.

Full-time faculty: 6. *Guest faculty:* 8. *List of some faculty and their affiliations:* Kyra Nichols, NYC Ballet; Paul Boos, NYC Ballet; Joan Goades, Joffrey Ballet, Princeton Ballet; Sandra Jennings, NYC Ballet, The National Ballet of Mozambique; Alexandre Proia, Princeton Ballet, NYC Ballet; Elizabeth Carroll, Laurie Abramson, Sherry Alban, Carol Bellis, Janell Ryrne, Alma Concepcion, Theresa Purcell Cone, Lisa de Ravel, Annie Ditmars, Kate Glasner, Elizabeth Shaff Goldblatt, Anne Woodside Gribbins, Nancy Hutchinas, Tracey Katona, Noel Kinney, Nora Orphanides, Anthony Rabara, Jennifer Reis, Mary Pat Robertson, Joy Vrooman Sayen, Susan Tenney, EV Therrien, Dr. Kim Chandler Vaccaro, Septime Webre, Katarina Wester-O'Rourke, Cheryl Whitney- Marcuard, Kasia Worrell.

Performance Information

Performances choreographed by: faculty, students, guests. *Number of studios (description):* 4 (45' x 50' sprung floor covered with Marley, 30' x 40' sprung floor covered with Marley, 30' x 35' sprung floor covered with Marley, 30' x 35' sprung floor covered with Marley). *Performance facilities:* gym at Princeton University.

Affiliations

Summer program is affiliated with a professional company: future company members are rarely recruited from this program; company apprentices are recruited from this program. *Summer program is affiliated with a pre-professional company:* future company members are often recruited from this program.

NEW YORK

ALVIN AILEY AMERICAN DANCE CENTER SUMMER INTENSIVE PROGRAM

Winter Contact Information

Alvin Ailey American Dance Center, 211 West 61st Street, 3rd Floor, New York NY 10023
Tel: 212-767-0590
Fax: 212-767-0625
Contact: JoAnne Ruggeri

Summer Contact Information

Alvin Ailey American Dance Center, 211 West 61st Street 3rd Floor, New York NY 10023
Tel: 212-767-0590
Fax: 212-767-0625
Contact: JoAnne Ruggeri

General

Minimum age or age range: 15 to 24.

High school credit available? no. *College credit available?* yes.

Services

Housing options: on-site housing, off-campus housing.

Application Information

Program dates: July-August (7 weeks). *Application deadline:* 6/1. *Application fee:* none. *Enrollment full by:* 7/1. *Requirements:* photograph. *Acceptance notification:* 2-3 weeks after application or audition.

Audition Information

No audition fee. Audition consists of the following: ballet, modern dance.

Audition evaluation criteria: strong technical training in ballet and modern dance, musicality, physical structure appropriate for several dance techniques.

Costs & Financial Aid

Financial aid available? full scholarship. *Students receiving financial aid:* 25%. *Procedure for applying for financial aid:* pass an audition.

Curriculum, Students, and Faculty

Courses offered: African dance, ballet, dance composition/choreography, jazz, master classes, men's class, Graham-based, Horton-based modern dance, body conditioning, pointe, repertory, Spanish, tap. *Specific curriculum information:* Curricula choices.

Selectivity for males: approximately 60% admitted. *Selectivity for females:* approximately 33% admitted.

Renowned alumni: Alan Barnes, Francesca Harper, Donald Byrd, Jasmine Guy, Desmond Richardson.

Full-time faculty: 35. *Guest faculty:* 0. *List of some faculty:* Jacqulyn Buglisi, Kazuko Hirabayashi, Celia Marino, Katie Langdon, Kevin Santee.

Performance Information

Performance opportunities and frequency: Final performance; 2 evenings at end of session. *Performances choreographed by:* faculty, guests, open class. *Number of studios (description):* 6 (28' x 48', 32' x 94' sprung linoleum flooring). *Performance facilities:* 2 large studios, 32'x92' and 33'x68'.

Affiliations

Summer program is affiliated with a professional company: future company members are not recruited from this program; company apprentices are not recruited from this program. *Summer program is affiliated with a pre-professional company:* company apprentices are recruited from this program. *Summer program is affiliated with a conservatory:* future students are recruited from this program.

AMERICAN ACADEMY OF BALLET AT VASSAR COLLEGE

Winter Contact Information

250 West 90th Street #3A, New York NY 10024
Tel: 212-787-9500
Fax: 212-787-8636
Contact: Mignon Furman

Summer Contact Information

Summer Programs, Poughkeepsie NY 12601
Tel: 914-437-5901
Fax: 914-437-7209
Contact: Mignon Furman

General

Minimum age or age range: 11 to 20.

High school credit available? no. *College credit available?* no.

Services

Housing options: on-site housing.

Application Information

Program dates: 7/5-7/19, 7/19-8/9, 7/5-7/9. *Application deadline:* 4/25-5/24. *Application fee:* none. *Requirements:* photograph. *Acceptance notification:* 2 weeks after audition.

Audition Information

Audition fee: $15. *Audition consists of the following:* ballet, pointe work. *Accompanist provided.*

Special dress requirements for females: black leotard, pink tights, ballet shoes.

Audition evaluation criteria: level of technique.

Costs & Financial Aid

Room & board: $1,880. *Other fees:* transportation fee.

Financial aid available? full scholarship, partial scholarship. *Students receiving financial aid:* 20%. *Procedure for applying for financial aid:* submit letter of recommendation, video tape, letter.

Curriculum, Students, and Faculty

Required courses: character, ballet, dance composition/choreography, dance history, jazz, men's class, mime, modern dance, music, Irish, pas de deux, pointe, repertory, Spanish, variations, Brazilian dance, lecture by dance professionals, acting for dancers, lecture on dance injury prevention. *Specific curriculum information:* curriculum fixed.

Selectivity for males: approximately 60% admitted. *Selectivity for females:* approximately 60% admitted.

Renowned alumni: Stelli Abrera, American Ballet Theatre.

Full-time faculty: 12. *Guest faculty:* 10. *List of some faculty and their affiliations:* Violette Verdy, NYC Ballet, Paris Opera Ballet; Antony Dowell, Royal Ballet, English National Ballet School; Sandra Jennings, NYC Ballet, Pennsylvania Ballet Company; Arcadio Carbonel, National Ballet School Madrid.

Performance Information

Performance opportunities and frequency: informal showings; 2-3. Workshop performance(s); 1-2. *Performances choreographed by:* faculty. *Number of studios (description):* 6 (1000 sq.ft.-1500 sq.ft. Marley. *Performance facilities:* studio, high school auditorium.

Affiliations

Summer program is affiliated with other program(s): future students are never recruited from this program.

Additional Comments

American Academy of Ballet has been in existence since 1995 and therefore does not yet have a list of alumni. The students are very well supervised. Classes are held 6 days a week and field trips and evening activities are part of the program. The focus is on classical ballet with a two hour technique class daily. Classes are kept small so that individual attention is given. Regional auditions are held.

AMERICAN BALLET THEATRE SUMMER INTENSIVE 1997

Winter Contact Information
890 Broadway, New York NY 10003
Tel: 212-477-3030
Fax: 212-254-5938
Email: abt@abt.org
Contact: Lynn Fenwick

Summer Contact Information
890 Broadway, New York NY 10003
Tel: 212-477-3030
Fax: 212-254-5938
Email: abt@abt.org
Contact: Lynn Fenwick

General

Minimum age or age range: 13 to 19. *Level of program:* intermediate, advanced.

High school credit available? no. *College credit available?* no.

Services

Housing options: on-site housing, off-campus housing.

Application Information

Program dates: 6/23-8/1. *Application deadline:* 3/1. *Application fee:* $30. *Enrollment full by:* 4/15. *Requirements:* recommendation, photograph. *Acceptance notification:* late March.

Audition Information

Audition fee: $30. *Audition consists of the following:* ballet, pointe work. *Accompanist provided.*

Dress requirements: yes.

Costs & Financial Aid

Tuition (full): $1,250.

Financial aid available? full scholarship, partial scholarship. *Students receiving financial aid:* 10-15%. *Procedure for applying for financial aid:* send written request, scholarship based on merit and need.

Curriculum, Students, and Faculty

Required courses: anatomy, character, choreography, ballet, dance history, jazz, men's class, modern dance, movement techniques, music, pas de deux, pointe, repertory, Spanish, variations, yoga.

Specific curriculum information: curriculum fixed.

Selectivity for males: approximately 33% admitted. *Selectivity for females:* approximately 10% admitted.

Full-time faculty: 5. *Guest faculty:* 25. *List of some faculty:* Cynthia Harvey, Rebecca Wright, Christine Spizzo, Kristine Elliott, Martine Van Hamel, Ricardo Bustamante, Danilo Radajevec, Lupe Serrano, Susan Jones, Magali Messac, Bonnie Mathis, Alaine Haubert, Diana Cartier.

Performance Information

Performances choreographed by: faculty, guests. *Number of studios (description):* 6 (30' x 60' sprung floor with linoleum). *Performance facilities:* the Pace University downtown theater.

Affiliations

Summer program is affiliated with a professional company: future company members are recruited from this program; company apprentices are recruited from this program. *Summer program is affiliated with a pre-professional company:* future company members are recruited from this program; company apprentices are not recruited from this program.

AMERICAN THEATER DANCE WORKSHOP SUMMER

Winter Contact Information
999 Herricks Road, New Hyde Park NY 11040
Tel: 516-248-6420
Fax: 516-248-6461
Contact: Madeline Dempster

Summer Contact Information
999 Herricks Road, New Hyde Park NY 11040
Tel: 516-248-6420
Fax: 516-248-6461
Contact: Madeline Dempster

General

Minimum age or age range: 14 to 20. *Level of program:* intermediate, advanced.

High school credit available? no. *College credit available?* no.

Services

Housing options: on-site housing.

Application Information

Program dates: 7/25-8/7. *Application fee:* $100. *Enrollment full by:* 5/1. *Requirements:* recommendation. *Acceptance notification:* 1-2 weeks after audition.

Audition Information

Audition fee: $15. *Audition consists of the following:* ballet, Broadway theater dance styles and combination. *Accompanist provided, cassette player available, CD player available.*

Dress requirements for females: no.

Audition evaluation criteria: directors and instructors select students based on technique, ability to pick up combinations, energy, and enthusiasm.

Costs & Financial Aid

Tuition (full): $1,000. *Room & board:* $425. *Other fees:* $100 for NYC trip, Broadway show, lunch, transportation to and from JFK and LaGuardia, $20 each way.

Financial aid available? partial scholarship. *Students receiving financial aid:* 15-20%. *Procedure for applying for financial aid:* discussion with directors.

Curriculum, Students, and Faculty

Required courses: ballet, musical theater, repertory, tap, Broadway dance. *Specific curriculum information:* curriculum fixed.

Selectivity for males: approximately 60% admitted. *Selectivity for females:* approximately 33% admitted.

Renowned alumni: Melissa Errico, Natalie Portman.

Full-time faculty: 11. *Guest faculty:* 0. *List of some faculty*: David Storey, Bruce Anthony Davis, Bill Hastings, Lynn Glauber, Fleur Israel, Scott Evans, Karin Baker, Mary Brienza, Liza Gennaro, Judy Greenhut, Bill Holland, Debbie Litwak.

Performance Information

Performance opportunities and frequency: Informal showings; 1. *Performances choreographed by:* faculty, students. *Number of studios (description):* 4 (30' x 50' Marley, 20' x 30' Marley, 15' x 30' Marley, 35' x 40' Marley). *Performance facilities:* large dance studio for informal performances.

Additional Comments

Although the program is not affiliated with a professional company, our faculty members are actively engaged in projects—summer stock, Broadway shows, workshops—which open many possibilities for our students.

BRIANSKY SARATOGA BALLET CENTER, INC.

Winter Contact Information

220 West 93 Street Suite 9D, New York NY 10025-7446
Tel: 212-799-0341
Fax: 212-799-0341
Contact: Oleg Briansky

Summer Contact Information

Skidmore College, Saratoga Springs NY 12866
Tel: 518-581-6837
Fax: 518-584-3023
Contact: Oleg Briansky

General

Minimum age or age range: 10 to 18. *Level of program:* advanced.

High school credit available? no. *College credit available?* no.

Services

Housing options: off-campus housing.

Application Information

Program dates: 6/28-7/26. *Application fee:* $300. *Enrollment full by:* 5/10. *Requirements:* recommendation, photograph.

Audition Information

Audition fee: $15. *Audition consists of the following:* ballet, pointe work. *Accompanist provided, cassette player available, CD player available.*

Dress requirements for females: yes.

Costs & Financial Aid

Financial aid available? partial scholarship.

Curriculum, Students, and Faculty

Required courses: ballet, dance history, jazz, master classes, pointe, repertory, variations. *Specific curriculum information:* curriculum fixed.

Renowned alumni: Marianne Tcherkassky, American Ballet Theatre; Pascale Leroy, San Francisco Ballet; Rob Besserer, Teresa Reyes, Michael Byars, Michaela Cerna, Prague Opera Ballet.

Full-time faculty: 5. *Guest faculty:* 5. *List of some faculty and their affiliations:* Oleg Briansky, Mireille Briane, Paris Opera Ballet, School of American Ballet; Robert Maiorano, David Keary, New York City Ballet; Ginger Tidwell, Juilliard School.

Performance Information

Performance opportunities and frequency: Workshop performance(s); 1. *Performances choreographed by:* faculty, open class. *Number of studios (description):* 4 (resilient). *Performance facilities:* dance theater.

CHAUTAUQUA-INSTITUTION SCHOOL OF DANCE

Winter Contact Information

P.O. Box 1098, Chautauqua NY 14722
Tel: 716-357-6233
Fax: 716-357-9014
Contact: Janice Wells

Summer Contact Information

P.O. Box 1098, Chautauqua NY 14722
Tel: 716-357-6298
Fax: 716-357-9014
Contact: Janice Wells

General

Minimum age or age range: 11 to 17. *Level of program:* intermediate, advanced.

High school credit available? no. *College credit available?* no.

Services

Housing options: on-site housing.

Application Information

Program dates: 6/23-8/10. *Application deadline:* 1/15. *Application fee:* $25. *Requirements:* recommendation. *Acceptance notification:* 3/15.

Audition Information

Audition fee: $25. *Audition consists of the following:* ballet, pointe work. *Accompanist provided.*

Dress requirements: Yes, *Special dress requirements:* appropriate dance attire.

Costs & Financial Aid

Tuition (full): $1,725. *Room:* $545. *Board:* $665. *Other fees:* $100 caution deposit.

Financial aid available? full scholarship, partial scholarship. *Students receiving financial aid:* 80%. *Procedure for applying for financial aid:* submit forms with application materials.

Curriculum, Students, and Faculty

Required courses: character, ballet, jazz, men's class, Limon-based modern dance, pas de deux, pointe, variations. *Specific curriculum information:* curriculum fixed.

Selectivity for males: approximately 60% admitted. *Selectivity for females:* approximately 10% admitted.

Full-time faculty: 10. *Guest faculty:* 8. *List of some faculty:* Jean Pierre Bonnefoux, Violette Verdy, Patricia McBride, John Clifford, Jerri Kumery, Donlin Foreman, Nicolas Petrov.

Performance Information

Performance opportunities and frequency: final performance; 2. Informal showings; 2-3. Workshop performance(s); 2. *Performances choreographed by:* faculty, students, guests.

Number of studios (description): 4 (40' x 55' Marley, 40' x 55' Marley, 30' x 45' Marley, 30' x 45' Marley). *Performance facilities:* open amphitheater.

Affiliations

Summer program is affiliated with a pre-professional company: future company members are recruited from this program; company apprentices are recruited from this program.

CHAUTAUQUA SUMMER SCHOOLS OF FINE AND PERFORMING ARTS

Contact Information

P.O. Box 1098, Department PR, Chautauqua NY 14722
Tel: 716-357-6233
Fax: 716-357-9014
Email: www.chautauqua-inst.org
Web: www.chautauqua-inst.org
Contact: Anne Jackson

General

Type of Institution: conservatory.

Total enrollment of institution: 300.

Entrance Requirements

Audition required: live, audio, video. *Other requirements:,* recommendation.

Costs & Aid

Application fee: $25. *Deposit:* $500. *Other fees:* $85 parking.

Percent of students receiving financial aid: 75%. *Types of scholarships and aid awarded:* partial, merit-based, need-based, institutional aid, reduced tuition. *Forms required for scholarships:* income asset verification. *Procedure for applying for loans:* audition and application. *Financial aid offered to international students. Percent of international students receiving scholarships:* 90%.

Services

Housing options: on-site dorms, off-campus housing

Support staff: financial aid advisor, foreign student advisor, housing advisor, psychological counselor, resident assistant, resident nurse, student affairs officer.

DANCE

Curriculum, Students, and Faculty

Elective courses: modern dance.

DANCE THEATER OF HARLEM SUMMER INTENSIVE

Winter Contact Information

466 West 152nd Street, New York NY 10031
Tel: 212-690-2800
Fax: 212-690-8736
Email: dnceharlem@aol.com
Contact: Robert Garland

Summer Contact Information

466 West 152nd Street, New York NY 10031
Tel: 212-690-2800
Fax: 212-690-8736
Email: dnceharlem@aol.com
Contact: Robert Garland

General

Minimum age or age range: 8 to 24. *Level of program:* beginning, intermediate, advanced.

High school credit available? no. *College credit available?* yes.

Services

Housing options: off-campus housing.

Application Information

Program dates: June-August. *Enrollment full by:* second week of June. *Requirements:* recommendation, photograph. *Acceptance notification:* 2-3 weeks after audition.

Audition Information

No audition fee. Audition consists of the following: ballet, pointe work. *Accompanist provided.*

Dress requirements: Yes. *Special dress requirements:* leotards, tights, slippers, dance belt for men.

Audition evaluation criteria: technical ability, musicality, flexibility, personality.

Costs & Financial Aid

Tuition (full): \$102-\$755 *Other fees:* \$15 registration fee.

Financial aid available? full scholarship, partial scholarship. *Students receiving financial aid:* 50%. *Procedure for applying for financial aid:* must request application after acceptance and return by due date.

Curriculum, Students, and Faculty

Required courses: anatomy, character, ballet, dance composition/choreography, dance history, jazz, men's class, music, pas de deux, pointe, tap, variations. *Specific curriculum information:* curriculum fixed.

Selectivity for males: approximately 60% admitted. *Selectivity for females:* approximately 60% admitted.

Renowned alumni: Hinton Battle.

Full-time faculty: 7. *Guest faculty:* 1-2. *List of some faculty:* Aluetina Lisina, Valerie Taylor, Jenny Chiang, Robert Garland, Rachel Afi Seky, Herman Jie Samfock, Laveen Naidu.

Number of studios (description): 4 (sprung dance floors). *Performance facilities:* largest studio converts into a performing space with lights.

Affiliations

Summer program is affiliated with a professional company: future company members are exclusively recruited from this program; company apprentices are exclusively recruited from this program. *Summer program is affiliated with a pre-professional company:* future company members are recruited from this program; company apprentices are recruited from this program.

MARTHA GRAHAM SCHOOL OF CONTEMPORARY DANCE, SUMMER INTENSIVE WORKSHOP

Winter Contact Information

316 East 63rd Street, New York NY 10021
Tel: 212-838-5886
Fax: 212-223-0351
Contact: School Director

Summer Contact Information

316 East 63rd Street, New York NY 10021
Tel: 212-838-5886
Fax: 212-223-0351
Contact: School Director

General

Minimum age or age range: 15 and up.

High school credit available? no. *College credit available?* yes.

Application Information

Program dates: 7/7-8/15. *Application deadline:* 6/9. *Application fee:* none. *Enrollment full by:* 7/1.

Audition Information

No audition fee.

Costs & Financial Aid

Tuition (full): $350-$850 *Other fees:* $25 registration fee

Financial aid available? no.

Curriculum, Students, and Faculty

Courses offered: dance composition/choreography, Graham-based modern dance, repertory. *Specific curriculum information:* Curricula choices.

Selectivity for males: admit all who apply. *Selectivity for females:* admit all who apply.

Renowned alumni: Paul Taylor, Merce Cunningham, Twyla Tharp.

List of some faculty: David Hochoy, Marnie Thomas, Elizabeth Auclair, Sandra Kauffman, Kenneth Topping, Rika Okamoto, Miki Orihara, Katherine Crockett.

Performance Information

Performance opportunities and frequency: workshop performance(s); end of session. *Performances choreographed by:* faculty, students.

Number of studios (description): 3 (wood).

Affiliations

Summer program is affiliated with a pre-professional company: future company members are sometimes recruited from this program;

NEW YORK THEATRE BALLET SUMMER INTENSIVE

Winter Contact Information

New York Theatre Ballet, 30 East 31st Street, New York NY 10016
Tel: 212-679-0401
Fax: 212-679-8171
Email: balletfore@aol.com
Contact: Diana Byer

Summer Contact Information

30 East 31st Street, New York NY 10016
Tel: 212-679-0401
Fax: 212-679-8171
Email: balletfore@aol.com
Contact: Diana Byer

General

Minimum age or age range: 12. *Level of program:* intermediate, advanced.

High school credit available? no. *College credit available?* no.

Application Information

Program dates: last week of July to first week of August. *Application deadline*: 6/1. *Application fee:* none. *Requirements:* photograph. *Acceptance notification:* immediately.

Audition Information

No audition fee. Audition consists of the following: ballet, pointe work. *Accompanist provided, cassette player available, CD player available.*

Dress requirements for females: Yes. *Special dress requirements:* pink tights, black leotard, pink ballet slippers, white head band.

Costs & Financial Aid

Financial aid available? Yes.

Curriculum, Students, and Faculty

Required courses: ballet, make-up, men's class, pas de deux, pointe, theatrical dance, variations. *Specific curriculum information:* curriculum fixed.

Selectivity for males: most admitted, but not all. *Selectivity for females:* most admitted, but not all.

Full-time faculty: 4. *Guest faculty:* 3. *List of some faculty:* Daina Byer, Sallie Wilson, Francois Perron.

Performance Information

Performances choreographed by: faculty, guests. *Number of studios (description)*: 1 (35' x 55' Marley). *Performance facilities:* The Dance Gallery.

Affiliations

Summer program is affiliated with a professional company: future company members are recruited from this program; company apprentices are recruited from this program.

NEW YORK UNIVERSITY DANCE EDUCATION

Winter Contact Information

35 West 4th Street, New York NY 10012
Tel: 212-998-5400
Fax: 212-995-4560
Email: bergermi@is.nyu.edu
Contact: Miriam R. Berger

Summer Contact Information

35 West 4th Street, New York NY 10012
Tel: 212-998-5400
Fax: 212-995-4560
Email: bergermi@is.nyu.edu
Contact: Miriam R. Berger

General

Minimum age or age range: 17 and up. *Level of program:* beginning, intermediate, advanced.

High school credit available? yes. *College credit available?* yes.

Services

Housing options: on-site housing.

Application Information

Program dates: 6/9-6/26, 6/30-7/17, 7/21-8/7. *Application deadline:* 5/1.

Audition Information

No audition fee. Audition consists of the following: ballet, modern dance. *Accompanist provided, cassette player available, CD player available.*

Dress requirements: no.

Costs & Financial Aid

Financial aid available? Yes.

Curriculum, Students, and Faculty

Courses offered: ballet, dance composition/choreography, modern dance, repertory, variations, dance therapy, dance study and performance in Pisa, Italy, dance criticism. *Specific curriculum information:* Curricula choices.

Selectivity for males: approximately 60% admitted. *Selectivity for females:* approximately 60% admitted.

Full-time faculty: 5. *Guest faculty:* 6. *List of some faculty and their affiliations:* Claude Bessy, Serge Golovine, Paris Opera; Jennifer Dunning, New York University Tisch School of the Arts; Sara Rudner.

Performance Information

Number of studios (description): 3 (wood, wood, Marley). *Performance facilities:* theater.

Affiliations

Summer program is affiliated with other program(s): future students are often recruited from this program.

Additional Comments

Financial aid only to matriculating NYU students.

PERIDANCE SUMMER PROGRAM

Winter Contact Information

132 Fourth Avenue, Second Floor, New York NY 10003
Tel: 212-505-0880
Fax: 212-674-2239
Email: peridance@earthlink.net
Contact: Igal Perry

Summer Contact Information

132 Fourth Avenue, Second Floor, New York NY 10003
Tel: 212-505-0880
Fax: 212-674-2239
Email: peridance@earthlink.net
Contact: Igal Perry

General

Minimum age or age range: 14. *Level of program:* beginning, intermediate, advanced.

High school credit available? no. *College credit available?* no.

Services

Housing options: off-campus housing.

Application Information

Program dates: 5/20-8/30. *Application deadline:* 1 week prior to individual workshop. *Application fee:* $50.

Audition Information

No audition fee. Audition consists of the following: ballet, dancer's own video showing class and/or performance. *Accompanist provided.*

Dress requirements for females: no.

Audition evaluation criteria: evaluated on talent, potential, level.

Costs & Financial Aid

Tuition (full): $200.

Financial aid available? partial scholarship. *Procedure for applying for financial aid:* interview.

Curriculum, Students, and Faculty

Courses offered: Benesh notation, ballet, jazz, master classes, men's class, Graham-based modern dance, Limon-based modern dance, body conditioning, music, pas de deux, pointe, repertory, tap, variations, contemporary dance, ballet conditioning. *Specific curriculum information:* Curricula choices.

Selectivity for males: admit all who apply. *Selectivity for females:* admit all who apply.

Renowned alumni: Mayra Rodriguez, Frankfurt Ballet; Riuji Yamamoto, Japan National Ballet.

Full-time faculty: 17. *Guest faculty:* 20. *List of some faculty and their affiliations:* Igal Perry, Peridance Ensemble; Jennifer Muller, Jennifer Muller/The Works; Donald Byrd, Sean Curran, Kevin Wynn, Elisa Monte, Dwight Rhoden.

Performance Information

Performance opportunities and frequency: every other week. *Performances choreographed by:* faculty, students, guests. *Number of studios (description):* 5 (33' x 50' raised wooden floor covered in Marley, 30' x 40' raised wood floor covered in Marley, 30' x 40' raised wooden floor covered in Marley, 30' x 40' raised wooden floor covered in Marley, 30' x 40' raised wood floor covered in Marley). *Performance facilities:* studio theater with minimal lighting, 120 seats.

Affiliations

Summer program is affiliated with a professional company: future company members are recruited from this program; company apprentices are recruited from this program.

SCHOOL OF AMERICAN BALLET SUMMER COURSE

Winter Contact Information

70 Lincoln Center Plaza, New York NY 10023-6592
Tel: 212-877-0600
Fax: 212-769-4897
Contact: Carol DelCorso

Summer Contact Information

70 Lincoln Center Plaza, New York NY 10023-6592
Tel: 212-877-0600
Fax: 212-769-4897
Contact: Carol DelCorso

General

Minimum age or age range: 12 to 18. *Level of program:* intermediate, advanced.

High school credit available? no. *College credit available?* no.

Services

Housing options: on-site housing, off-campus housing.

Application Information

Program dates: 6/22-7/24. *Application deadline:* 4/1. *Acceptance notification:* 3/14, for those auditioning nationally.

Audition Information

Audition fee: $10. *Audition consists of the following:* ballet, pointe work. *Accompanist provided.*

Dress requirements: no.

Audition evaluation criteria: classical technical accomplishment and body conforming to the classical style.

Costs & Financial Aid

Tuition (full): $675. *Room & board:* $1,225.

Financial aid available? full scholarship, partial scholarship. *Students receiving financial aid:* 20%. *Procedure for applying for financial aid:* application forms supplied to students who are judged at audition to be exceptional.

Curriculum, Students, and Faculty

Required courses: character, ballet, men's class, pas de deux, pointe, variations, weight training. *Specific curriculum information:* curriculum fixed.

Selectivity for males: approximately 33% admitted. *Selectivity for females:* approximately 10% admitted.

Renowned alumni: Edward Villella, Suzanne Farrell, Kay Mazzo, Jacques D'Amboise, Darci Kistler, Wendy Whelan, Peter Boal, Fernando Bujones.

Full-time faculty: 8. *Guest faculty:* 2. *List of some faculty:* Suki Schorer, Peter Boal, Susan Pilarre, Andrei Kramarevsky, Sheryl Ware, Peter Frame, Antonina Tumkovsky.

Performance Information

Number of studios (description): 5 (40' x 50' vinyl over woven hardwood). *Performance facilities:* none for summer.

Affiliations

Summer program is affiliated with a professional company: future company members are often recruited from this program; company apprentices are often recruited from this program.

SKIDMORE COLLEGE SUMMER DANCE WORKSHOP

Winter Contact Information

Office of the Dean of Special Programs, Saratoga Springs NY 12866
Tel: 518-580-5590
Fax: 518-584-7963
Email: mmccoll@skidmore.edu
Contact: Maria McColl

Summer Contact Information

Office of the Dean of Special Programs, Saratoga Springs NY 12866
Tel: 518-580-5590
Fax: 518-584-7963
Email: mmccoll@skidmore.edu
Contact: Maria McColl

General

Minimum age or age range: 16 and up.

High school credit available? no. *College credit available?* yes.

Services

Housing options: on-site housing.

Application Information

Program dates: June (3 weeks). *Application deadline:* none. *Application fee:* $30. *Enrollment full by:* 5/30. *Requirements:* essay. *Acceptance notification:* within 3 weeks after application is received.

Audition Information

No audition fee. Audition consists of the following: resume or narrative.

Audition evaluation criteria: dancers having intermediate/advanced experience.

Costs & Financial Aid

Tuition (full): $880. *Room & board:* $720.

Financial aid available? partial scholarship. *Procedure for applying for financial aid:* application procedure.

Curriculum, Students, and Faculty

Required courses: dance composition/choreography, master classes, modern dance, movement techniques, music, repertory. *Specific curriculum information:* curriculum fixed.

Selectivity for males: most admitted, but not all. *Selectivity for females:* most admitted, but not all.

Performance Information

Performances choreographed by: guests, open class. *Number of studios (description):* (47.5' x 49' springwood—some with Marley overleaf). *Performance facilities:* 2 theaters on campus.

Affiliations

Summer program is affiliated with a conservatory: future students are recruited from this program.

Additional Comments

Tuition rates subject to change annually.

SUMMER DANCE PROGRAM AT JUILLIARD

Winter Contact Information

60 Lincoln Center Plaza, New York NY 10023
Tel: 212-799-5000
Fax: 212-724-0263
Contact: Ernesta Corvino

Summer Contact Information

60 Lincoln Center Plaza, New York NY 10023
Tel: 212-799-5000
Fax: 212-724-0263
Contact: Ernesta Corvino

General

Minimum age or age range: 15 to 17.

High school credit available? no. *College credit available?* no.

Application Information

Program dates: last week of July to first 2 weeks of August (3 weeks). *Application deadline:* first week of April. *Application fee:* $25. *Requirements:* recommendation.

Audition Information

Audition fee: $25. *Audition consists of the following:* ballet, prepared solo.

Audition evaluation criteria: good solid ballet technique at a high intermediate or advanced level, ability to move well.

Costs & Financial Aid

Tuition (full): $6,500. *Room & board:* $650.

Financial aid available? full scholarship, partial scholarship. *Procedure for applying for financial aid:* see application.

Curriculum, Students, and Faculty

Required courses: anatomy, ballet, dance history, men's class, Taylor-based modern dance, pas de deux, pointe, music for dancers, ballroom dance. *Specific curriculum information:* curriculum fixed.

Selectivity for males: approximately 33% admitted. *Selectivity for females:* approximately 33% admitted.

Renowned alumni: Bruce Marks, Dennis Nahat, Carla Maxwell.

Full-time faculty: 7. *Guest faculty:* 0. *List of some faculty:* Benjiamin Harkarvy, Linda Kent, Kenneth Tosti, Yvonne Marceau, Irene Dowd, Jon Magnussen.

Performance Information

Performances choreographed by: students, open class. *Number of studios (description):* 5 (57' x 44' battleship linoleum). *Performance facilities:* studio.

Affiliations

Summer program is affiliated with a conservatory: future students are recruited from this program.

TISCH DANCE SUMMER RESIDENCY PROGRAM

Winter Contact Information
New York University, Tisch School of the Arts, Dept. of Dance, 111 Second Avenue, 3rd Floor, New York NY 10003
Tel: 212-998-1980
Fax: 212-505-6931
Email: cummingsk@is.nyu.edu
Contact: Kay Cummings or Maria Myers

Summer Contact Information
New York University, Tisch School of the Arts, Dept of Dance, 111 Second Avenue Room 304, New York NY 10003
Tel: 212-998-1980
Fax: 212-505-6931
Email: cummingsk@is.nyu.edu
Contact: Kay Cummings or Maria Myers

General
Minimum age or age range: 17 and up. *Level of program:* intermediate, advanced.

High school credit available? no. *College credit available?* yes.

Services
Housing options: on-site housing.

Application Information
Program dates: third week in May-late June (two 3-week sessions). *Application deadline:* 5/1 (for mail application). *Application fee:* none. *Enrollment full by:* 5/10.

Audition Information
No audition fee.

Costs & Financial Aid
Tuition (full): $995-$2,468. *Other fees:* students taking the workshop for credit pay an additional $48 Health Services fee.

Financial aid available? no.

Curriculum, Students, and Faculty
Required courses: ballet, modern dance, repertory. *Specific curriculum information:* curriculum fixed.

Selectivity for males: most admitted, but not all. *Selectivity for females:* most admitted, but not all.

Renowned alumni: Ken Tosti, Sean Curran, Anna Thereas de Keersmacher, Clarice Marshall, Mark Morris, Les Grands Ballet; Trisha Brown, Momix.

Performance Information
Performances choreographed by: guests.

Number of studios (description): 6 (40' x 60' sprung with Marley). *Performance facilities:* proscenium theater, 200 seats.

Affiliations
Summer program is affiliated with a professional company: future company members are sometimes recruited from this program; company apprentices are sometimes recruited from this program.

NORTH CAROLINA

AMERICAN DANCE FESTIVAL, SIX-WEEK SCHOOL & YOUNG DANCER'S SCHOOL

Winter Contact Information
P.O. Box 90772, Durham NC 27708
Tel: 919-684-6402
Fax: 919-684-5459
Email: adfnc@acpub.duke.edu
Contact: Joseph Fedrowitz

Summer Contact Information
P.O. Box 90772, Durham NC 27708
Tel: 919-684-6402
Fax: 919-684-5459
Contact: Joseph Fedrowitz

General
Level of program: beginning, intermediate, advanced.

High school credit available? no. *College credit available?* yes.

Services
Housing options: on-site housing, off-campus housing.

Application Information
Program dates: June, July. *Application deadline:* 5/1. *Application fee:* $30. *Enrollment full by:* 4/15. *Requirements:* recommendation.

Audition Information
No audition fee. Audition consists of the following: modern dance, improvisation, prepared solo, (no longer than 1.5 minutes). *Cassette player available, CD player available.*

Dress requirements: no.

Audition evaluation criteria: technical ability, creative potential, desire, financial need.

Costs & Financial Aid
Tuition (full): $1,450.

Financial aid available? full scholarship, partial scholarship. *Students receiving financial aid:* 40%. *Procedure for applying for financial aid:* audition and submit financial information.

Curriculum, Students, and Faculty

Courses offered: African dance, dance composition/choreography, jazz, master classes, modern dance, movement techniques, body conditioning, Pilates, repertory. *Specific curriculum information:* Curricula choices.

Selectivity for males: most admitted, but not all. *Selectivity for females:* most admitted, but not all.

Renowned alumni: Paul Taylor, Merce Cunningham, Donald McKayle, Twyla Tharp.

Full-time faculty: 40. *List of some faculty*: Carolyn Adams, Jack Arnold, Ronald K. Brown, Cornelius Carter, Sean Curran, Laura Dean, David Dorfman, Amie Dowling, Doug Elkins, Molissa Fenley, David Ferri, Eric Franklin, Barbara Grubel, Mark Haim, Ellen Hemphill, Myriam Herve-Gil, Gerri Houlihan, Lynn Jackson, Heidi Latsky.

Performance Information

Performances choreographed by: faculty, students. *Number of studios (description)*: 12 (varies, most are suspended). *Performance facilities:* varies, many venues used.

Affiliations

Summer program is affiliated with other program(s): future students are not recruited from this program.

OHIO

BALLET MET DANCE ACADEMY

Winter Contact Information
322 Mt. Vernon Avenue, Columbus OH 43220
Tel: 614-224-1672
Fax: 614-224-3697
Contact: Xandra Anderhalt

Summer Contact Information
322 Mt. Vernon Avenue, Columbus OH 43220
Tel: 614-224-1672
Fax: 614-224-3697
Contact: Xandra Anderhalt

General

Level of program: intermediate, advanced.

High school credit available? no. *College credit available?* no.

Application Information

Program dates: 6/29-8/7. *Application deadline:* 4/22. *Requirements:* photograph. *Acceptance notification: 3/15.*

Audition Information

Audition fee: $10. *Audition consists of the following:* ballet, pointe work. *Accompanist provided.* *Dress requirements for females:* yes.

Costs & Financial Aid

Tuition (full): $1,100. *Room & board:* $1,000.

Financial aid available? full scholarship, partial scholarship. *Students receiving financial aid:* 25%. *Procedure for applying for financial aid:* application.

Curriculum, Students, and Faculty

Required courses: character, ballet, dance history, jazz, men's class, modern dance, movement techniques, body conditioning, Pilates, music, pas de deux, pointe, variations. *Specific curriculum information:* curriculum fixed.

Selectivity for males: approximately 60% admitted. *Selectivity for females:* approximately 33% admitted.

Renowned alumni: John Welker, Bridget Breiner, Sonia Welker.

Full-time faculty: 8. *Guest faculty:* 3. *List of some faculty*: Yoko Ichino, David Nixon.

Performance Information

Performances choreographed by: faculty, guests, *Number of studios (description)*: 7 (60' x 120' Harlequin, 60' x 60', 20' x 20', 40' x 17'). *Performance facilities:* studio.

Affiliations

Summer program is affiliated with a professional company: future company members are recruited from this program; company apprentices are recruited from this program. *Summer program is affiliated with a pre-professional company:* company apprentices are recruited from this program.

OKLAHOMA

POINTE TO THE FUTURE

Winter Contact Information
Tulsa Ballet, 4512 South Peoria, Tulsa OK 74105
Tel: 918-749-6030
Fax: 918-749-0532
Email: sudavis@mail.webtek.com
Contact: Su Davis

Summer Contact Information
Tulsa Ballet, 4512 South Peoria, Tulsa OK 74105
Tel: 918-749-6030
Fax: 918-749-0532
Email: sudavis@mail.webtek.com
Contact: Su Davis

General
Minimum age or age range: 10 and up. *Level of program:* beginning, intermediate, advanced.

High school credit available? no. *College credit available?* no.

Services
Housing options: off-campus housing.

Application Information
Program dates: late July to early August.

Costs & Financial Aid
Financial aid available? partial scholarship. *Procedure for applying for financial aid:* send personal letter.

Curriculum, Students, and Faculty
Required courses: character, ballet, jazz, Pilates, nutrition, pointe, yoga, injury prevention. *Specific curriculum information:* curriculum fixed.

Selectivity for males: admit all who apply. *Selectivity for females:* admit all who apply.

Performance Information
Number of studios (description): 3 (sprung).

Affiliations
Summer program is affiliated with a professional company: future company members are never recruited from this program; company apprentices are never recruited from this program. *Summer program is affiliated with a pre-professional company:* future company members are never recruited from this program; company apprentices are never recruited from this program.

PENNSYLVANIA

CENTRAL PENNSYLVANIA YOUTH BALLET (CPYB), SUMMER BALLET PROGRAM (SBP)

Winter Contact Information
107 Meetinghouse Road, Carlisle PA 17013
Tel: 717-249-8723
Contact: Sandra Lee Weary

Summer Contact Information
107 Meetinghouse Road, Carlisle PA 17013
Tel: 717-249-8723
Contact: Sandra Lee Weary

General
Minimum age or age range: 4 to 60. *Level of program:* beginning, intermediate, advanced.

College credit available? yes.

Services
Housing options: on-site housing.

Application Information
Program dates: 6/21-7/26, 8/4-8/15. *Application fee:* none. *Requirements*: photograph. *Acceptance notification:* several weeks after application is received.

Audition Information
No audition fee. Audition consists of the following: ballet. *Cassette player available, CD player available.*

Dress requirements: Yes. *Special dress requirements:* dance belt, white t-shirt tucked in tights for men, black tights in levels E3 and E4, tights of other conservative colors may also be worn if student has not missed any classes, white socks, black or white ballet shoes Females: level A, B, C, D—black leotard, bra, pink tights with feet, pink or black ballet shoes, levels E1 and E2—black or blue leotard, bra, pink tights with feet, pink ballet shoes with ribbons, levels E3 and E4—black or colored leotards of any one color, bra, pink tights with feet, pink ballet shoes with ribbons.

Costs & Financial Aid
Tuition (full): \$875. *Room:* \$390. *Board:* \$525. *Other fees:* \$590 required facilities use, \$28 linen rental service, \$75 drama fee.

Financial aid available? partial scholarship. *Students receiving financial aid:* 9%. *Procedure for applying for financial aid:* complete application for scholarship aid and attach a copy of appropriate income tax form.

Curriculum, Students, and Faculty
Required courses: character, ballet, men's class, pas de deux, pointe. *Specific curriculum information:* curriculum fixed.

Selectivity for males: most admitted, but not all. *Selectivity for females:* most admitted, but not all.

Renowned alumni: Sean Lavery, New York City Ballet; Lisa De Ribieres, New York City Ballet, American Ballet Theatre; Michael Owens, American Ballet Theatre; Deborah Wingert, New York City Ballet; Darla Hoover, New York City Ballet;

Tina LeBlanc, San Fransisco Ballet; Katrina Killian, New York City Ballet; Jennifer Miller, Milwaukee Ballet.

Full-time faculty: 16. *List of some faculty:* Marcia Dale Weary, Patricia Sorrall, Darla Hoover, Deborah Wingert, Tina LeBlanc, Hilda Moralas, Robert Steele, Marian Tanner, Wes Chapman, G. Vostripov.

Performance Information

Number of studios (description): 10 (15' x 33'-40' x 50' Marley over wood). *Performance facilities:* small theater.

Affiliations

Summer program is affiliated with a pre-professional company: future company members are not recruited from this program; company apprentices are not recruited from this program. *Summer program is affiliated with other program(s):* future students are not recruited from this program.

DANCE ALLOY A SUMMER INTENSIVE WORKSHOPS

Winter Contact Information

Dance Alloy, 5530 Penn Avenue, Pittsburgh PA 15206
Tel: 412-363-4321
Fax: 412-363-4320
Contact: Tracey Maxwell

Summer Contact Information

Dance Alloy, 5530 Penn Avenue, Pittsburgh PA 15206
Tel: 412-363-4321
Fax: 412-363-4320
Contact: Tracey Maxwell

General

Level of program: intermediate, advanced.

High school credit available? yes. *College credit available?* yes.

Services

Housing options: on-site housing, off-campus housing.

Application Information

Program dates: 6/16-6/27, 7/22-8/8. *Application deadline:* first day of workshop. *Application fee:* none. *Enrollment full by:* 6/1.

Audition Information

No audition fee.

Costs & Financial Aid

Financial aid available? full scholarship, partial scholarship. *Students receiving financial aid:* 30%. *Procedure for applying for financial aid:* scholarship form stating financial need.

Curriculum, Students, and Faculty

Courses offered: Alexander technique, movement techniques, Feldenkreis, repertory, contact improvisation, Bartenieff fundamentals, developmental movement, eclectic modern dance. *Specific curriculum information:* Curricula choices.

Selectivity for males: admit all who apply. *Selectivity for females:* admit all who apply.

Full-time faculty: 8. *List of some faculty and their affiliations:* Mark Taylor, Dance Alloy; Sean Feldman, Siovan Davies Dance Company; Karen Allgire, Oberlin College, Cleveland State University.

Performance Information

Performance opportunities and frequency: Informal showings; 2. Performance opportunities and frequency: Workshop performance(s); 2. *Performances choreographed by:* faculty, students, guests. Open class. *Number of studios (description):* 2 (50' x 60' wooden sprung floor covered with Marley). *Performance facilities:* studio.

Affiliations

Summer program is affiliated with a professional company: future company members are recruited from this program; company apprentices are recruited from this program. *Summer program is affiliated with a pre-professional company:* future company members are recruited from this program; company apprentices are recruited from this program. *Summer program is affiliated with other program(s):* future students are not recruited from this program.

MUHLENBERG SUMMER DANCE INTENSIVE

Winter Contact Information

Muhlenberg College, Karen Dearborn Dance, Allentown PA 18104
Tel: 610-821-3335
Fax: 610-821-3633
Email: dearborn@muhlenberg.edu
Contact: Karen Dearborn

Summer Contact Information

Karen Dearborn Dance, Allentown PA 18104
Tel: 610-821-3335
Fax: 610-821-3633
Email: dearborn@muhlenberg.edu
Contact: Karen Dearborn

General

Minimum age or age range: 13 to 18. *Level of program:* intermediate, advanced.

High school credit available? no. *College credit available?* no.

Services

Housing options: on-site housing.

Application Information

Program dates: last week of June. *Application deadline:* 6/1. *Application fee:* $25.

Audition Information

No audition fee.

Costs & Financial Aid

Tuition (full): $110. *Room & board:* $75.

Financial aid available? full scholarship, partial scholarship. *Students receiving financial aid:* 10%. *Procedure for applying for financial aid:* audition, video, application, letters of recommendation.

Curriculum, Students, and Faculty

Required courses: ballet, dance composition/choreography, jazz, modern dance, tap. *Specific curriculum information:* curriculum fixed.

Selectivity for males: admit all who apply. *Selectivity for females:* admit all who apply.

Full-time faculty: 4. *List of some faculty:* Karen Dearborn, Shelley Oliver, Robert Torres, Clare Byrne.

Performance Information

Number of studios (description): (sprung wood, Marley overlay).

SUMMER WORLD OF DANCE

Winter Contact Information

The University of the Arts, 320 South Broad Street, Philadelphia PA 19102
Tel: 215-875-2270
Fax: 215-875-5114
Email: sglazer@op.net
Contact: Susan B. Glazer

Summer Contact Information

The University of the Arts, 320 South Broad Street, Philadelphia PA 19102
Tel: 215-875-2269
Fax: 215-875-5114
Email: sglazer@op.net
Contact: Susan B. Glazer

General

Minimum age or age range: 15 and up. *Level of program:* beginning, intermediate, advanced.

High school credit available? no. *College credit available?* yes.

Services

Housing options: on-site housing.

Application Information

Program dates: 7/8-8/1. *Application deadline:* 6/20. *Application fee:* $50.

Audition Information

No audition fee.

Costs & Financial Aid

Tuition (full): $750-$1,200 *Room:* $135. *Other fees:* $100 refundable dorm damage deposit, meal cards available in $25 denominations.

Financial aid available? partial scholarship. *Students receiving financial aid:* 25-40%. *Procedure for applying for financial aid:* send letter of need and videotape.

Curriculum, Students, and Faculty

Courses Offered: African dance, character, ballet, dance composition/choreography, jazz, master classes, men's class, Graham-based modern dance, Horton-based modern dance, Pilates, pas de deux, pointe, repertory, Spanish, tap, variations, yoga, Brazilian dance. *Specific curriculum information:* Curricula choices.

Selectivity for males: admit all who apply. *Selectivity for females:* admit all who apply.

Renowned alumni: Yu Fen Kung, Nai Ni Chen, Erin Elliott, Lisa Johnston, Carlos Anprio Scott, Johnathan Pheleps.

Full-time faculty: 5. *Guest faculty:* 2-3. *List of some faculty*: Peter Bertini, Manfre Fischbeck, Ronen Koresh, Jeannine Lee Osayande, Andrew Pap, La Vaughn Robinson, Robb Sapienza, Wayne St. David, Pat Thomas.

Performance Information

Performance opportunities and frequency: informal showings; end of session; workshop performance(s); 2. *Performances choreographed by:* faculty, students, open class.

Number of studios (description): 7 (30' x 60' Marley-wood). *Performance facilities:* dance theater.

Affiliations

Summer program is affiliated with other program(s): future students are often recruited from this program.

Additional Comments
Tuition is $1,200 for 4 weeks, $750 for 2 weeks.

SOUTH CAROLINA

CHARLESTON BALLET THEATRE INTENSIVE WORKSHOP

Winter Contact Information
477 King Street, Charleston SC 29403
Tel: 803-723-7334
Fax: 803-723-9099
Email: Tdominey@CharlstonBallet.com
Contact: Patricia Cantwell

Summer Contact Information
477 King Street, Charleston SC 29403
Tel: 803-723-7334
Fax: 803-723-9099
Email: Tdominey@CharlstonBallet.com
Contact: Patricia Cantwell

General
Minimum age or age range: 11 to mid 20s. *Level of program:* intermediate, advanced.

High school credit available? no. *College credit available?* no.

Services
Housing options: on-site housing, off-campus housing.

Application Information
Program dates: 7/5-8/1. *Application deadline:* 4/1. *Application fee:* $200. *Enrollment full by:* 4/15. *Requirements:* recommendation, photograph. *Acceptance notification:* within 2 weeks.

Audition Information
No audition fee. Audition consists of the following: ballet, pointe work. *Accompanist provided, cassette player available, CD player available.*

Costs & Financial Aid
Tuition (full): $1,100. *Room & board:* $1,200.

Financial aid available? full scholarship, partial scholarship. *Students receiving financial aid:* 15%. *Procedure for applying for financial aid:* on-site audition and interview.

Curriculum, Students, and Faculty
Required courses: character, ballet, dance composition/choreography, jazz, men's class, Cunningham-based modern dance, pointe, repertory, variations. *Specific curriculum information:* curriculum fixed.

Selectivity for males: most admitted, but not all. *Selectivity for females:* approximately 60% admitted.

Full-time faculty: 4. *List of some faculty*: Arthur Leeth, Mel Tomlinson, Jill Eathorne Bahr.

Performance Information
Performances choreographed by: faculty, guests, open class. *Number of studios (description):* 3 (wood with Marley-sprung). *Performance facilities:* 250 seat black box theater.

Affiliations
Summer program is affiliated with a professional company: future company members are recruited from this program; company apprentices are exclusively recruited from this program.

Additional Comments
$200 application fee refundable if not accepted. Full scholarships available for males. Partial scholarships available for apprentice level females.

MYRTLE BEACH SUMMER DANCE EXPERIENCE

Winter Contact Information
P.O. Box 11898, Columbia SC 29211
Tel: 803-799-7605
Fax: 803-799-7928
Email: columcityballet@mindspring.com
Contact: Sherry Horton or Sydney Miller

Summer Contact Information
P.O.Box 11898, Columbia SC 29211
Tel: 803-799-7605
Fax: 803-799-7928
Email: columcityballet@mindspring.com
Contact: Sherry Horton or Sydney Miller

General
Minimum age or age range: 13 and up. *Level of program:* beginning, intermediate, advanced.

High school credit available? no. *College credit available?* yes.

Services
Housing options: on-site housing.

Application Information
Program dates: mid July to first of August. *Application deadline:* 5/1. *Application fee:* none. *Enrollment full by:* 5/15. *Acceptance notification:* within 2 weeks of audition.

Audition Information

Audition consists of the following: ballet, pointe work, prepared solo, (prepared solo if auditioning by videotape, jazz class if seeking entry into jazz division). *Cassette player available, CD player available.*

Dress requirements: no.

Costs & Financial Aid

Tuition (full): $850. *Room & board:* $830. *Other fees:* $50-$75 activities fee.

Financial aid available? full scholarship, *Students receiving financial aid:* 10%. *Procedure for applying for financial aid:* application and recommendation.

Curriculum, Students, and Faculty

Required courses: character, ballet, jazz, men's class, pas de deux, pointe, variations. *Specific curriculum information:* curriculum fixed.

Selectivity for males: approximately 60% admitted. *Selectivity for females:* approximately 60% admitted.

Renowned alumni: Mariclare Miranda, Columbia City Ballet; Peter Kozak, Cleveland Ballet, San Jose Ballet.

Full-time faculty: 5. *List of some faculty and their affiliations:* Karena Brock, American Ballet Theatre; Hilton Head Dance Theater; Joe Lanteri, NYC Dance Alliance; William Starrett, Joffrey Ballet, American Ballet Theatre, Columbia City Ballet; Lynne Charles; Patricia Miller, Joffrey Ballet, Columbia City Ballet.

Performance Information

Performances choreographed by: faculty, guests. *Number of studios (description):* 5 (sprung floor with Marley). *Performance facilities:* college theater.

Affiliations

Summer program is affiliated with a professional company: future company members are often recruited from this program; company apprentices are not recruited from this program.

SC SUMMER DANCE CONSERVATORY

Winter Contact Information
Longstreet Theatre, Cola SC 29208
Contact: Susan Anderson, Linda Carnes

Summer Contact Information
Longstreet Dance Conservatory, Cola SC 29208
Tel: 803-777-5636
Fax: 803-777-6669
Contact: Susan Anderson, Linda Carnes

General

Minimum age or age range: 10 and up. *Level of program:* intermediate, advanced.

High school credit available? yes. *College credit available?* yes.

Services

Housing options: on-site housing.

Application Information

Application deadline: 6/30. *Application fee:* $100. *Enrollment full by:* 6/30.

Audition Information

Audition fee: $10. *Audition consists of the following:* ballet, pointe work. *Accompanist provided, cassette player available, CD player available.*

Special dress requirements: black leotard, pink tights.

Costs & Financial Aid

Tuition (full): $850. *Room & board:* $800.

Financial aid available? partial scholarship. *Students receiving financial aid:* 10%. *Procedure for applying for financial aid:* audition.

Curriculum, Students, and Faculty

Required courses: character, ballet, jazz, master classes, men's class, Graham-based modern dance, musical theater, pas de deux, pointe, repertory, variations. *Specific curriculum information:* curriculum fixed.

Selectivity for males: most admitted, but not all. *Selectivity for females:* approximately 60% admitted. *List of some faculty*: Susan Anderson, Edward Villella, Marianna Tcherkassky, Stanislav Issaev, Anne-Marie Holmes, Robin Becker, Nan Giordano, Anne Brodie, Marcus Bugler, Kyra Strasberg, Jose Traba.

Performance Information

Performances choreographed by: faculty. *Number of studios (description):* 6 (34' x 20' sprung Marley, 27' x 15'). *Performance facilities:* Koger Center for Performing Arts.

Affiliations

Summer program is affiliated with a pre-professional company: future company members are recruited from this program; company apprentices are recruited from this program. *Summer program is affiliated with a conservatory:* future students are recruited from this program.

Additional Comments

There is an additional two-week Jazz workshop that has been schedule to meet popular demand. Write for information.

TENNESSEE

GOVERNOR'S SCHOOL FOR THE ARTS

Winter Contact Information
Middle Tennessee State University
P.O. Box 38, Murfreesboro TN 37132
Tel: 615-898-2223
Fax: 615-898-2223
Email: tdecker@mtsu.edu
Contact: Trish Decker, Tom Naylor

Summer Contact Information
MTSU P.O. Box 38, Murfreesboro TN 37132
Tel: 615-898-2223
Fax: 615-898-2223
Email: tdecker@mtsu.edu
Contact: Trish Decker, Tom Naylor

General
Minimum age or age range: 16 to 18.

High school credit available? no. *College credit available?* no.

Services
Housing options: on-site housing.

Application Information
Program dates: 6/15-7/12. *Application deadline:* 12/15. *Application fee:* none. *Enrollment full by:* 3/15 (after auditions). *Requirements:* interview, essay, recommendation. *Acceptance notification:* 3/15.

Audition Information
No audition fee. Audition consists of the following: ballet, modern dance, pointe work, improvisation, (jazz). *Accompanist provided.*

Dress requirements for females: yes.

Curriculum, Students, and Faculty
Required courses: ballet, jazz, modern dance, pointe. *Specific curriculum information:* curriculum fixed.

Selectivity for males: approximately 10% admitted. *Selectivity for females:* approximately 10% admitted.

Full-time faculty: 4. *Guest faculty:* 0. *List of some faculty*: Gifford Booth, Madeline Lee Gilford, Teri Gindi, Jason Heller, Wayne Kennedy, David Leidholdt, Brooke Lieb, Alex McCord, Achim Nowak, Jeff O'Malley, Allen Schoer, Dabid Seymour, Twila Thompson.

Performance Information
Performances choreographed by: faculty. *Number of studios (description):* 1. *Performance facilities:* Middle Tennessee State University Tucker Theatre stage.

TEXAS

HOUSTON BALLET ACADEMY

Winter Contact Information
1912 West Bell, Houston TX 77219
Tel: 713-523-6300
Fax: 713-523-4038
Email: admissions@interlocken.K12.mi.us
Contact: Clara Cravey

Summer Contact Information
1912 West Bell, Houston TX 77219
Tel: 713-523-6300
Fax: 713-523-4038
Email: admissions@interlocken.K12.mi.us
Contact: Clara Cravey

General
Total enrollment: 400-500. *Level of program:* beginning, intermediate, advanced.

High school credit available? no. *College credit available?* no.

Services
Housing options: on-site housing.

Application Information
Requirements: photograph.

Audition Information
Audition fee: $15. *Audition consists of the following:* ballet, pointe work. *Accompanist provided.*

Dress requirements for females: yes.

Audition evaluation criteria: full class with several teachers.

Costs & Financial Aid
Financial aid available? full scholarship, partial scholarship. *Students receiving financial aid:* 10% *Procedure for applying for financial aid:* submit parents' W-2 forms, merit scholarships awarded by faculty.

Curriculum, Students, and Faculty
Required courses: anatomy, character, ballet, dance composition/choreography, jazz, men's class, Graham-based modern dance, Limon-based modern dance, body conditioning, Pilates, music, pas de deux, pointe, repertory, variations. *Specific curriculum information:* curriculum fixed.

Selectivity for males: approximately 60% admitted. *Selectivity for females:* approximately 10% admitted.

Renowned alumni: Lauren Anderson, Houston Ballet; Martha Butler, American Ballet Theatre, Houston Ballet; Li Cuxin, Australia Ballet; Phillip Broomhad, Houston Ballet.

Full-time faculty: 4. *Guest faculty:* 2. *List of some faculty*: Clara Cravey, Steve Brule, Prisella Natan Murphy, Bridget Payne.

Performance Information

Performance opportunities and frequency: Informal showings; 2 per year. Workshop performance(s); 1 per year. *Performances choreographed by:* faculty, students, guests, open class. *Number of studios (description):* 6 (75' x 80' Marley, 60' x 33' Marley, 60' x 50' Marley, 60' x 50' Marley, 60' x 50' Marley, 90' x 80' Marley). *Performance facilities:* Worthern Center, large studio.

Affiliations

Summer program is affiliated with a professional company: future company members are recruited from this program; company apprentices are recruited from this program.

TCU SUMMER DANCE WORSHIP

Winter Contact Information

PO Box 297910, Fort Worth TX 76129
Tel: 817-921-7615
Fax: 817-921-7675
Email: l.garrson@tcu.edu
Contact: Ellew Page Garrison

Summer Contact Information

PO Box 297910, Fort Worth TX 76129
Tel: 817-921-7615
Fax: 817-921-7675
Email: l.garrson@tcu.edu
Contact: Ellew Page Garrison

General

Total enrollment: 70-80. *Minimum age or age range:* 13. *Level of program:* intermediate, advanced.

High school credit available? no. *College credit available?* no.

Services

Housing options: on-site housing, off-campus housing.

Application Information

Program dates: 7/5-7/17. *Application deadline:* 7/1. *Application fee:* none. *Enrollment full by:* 6/15.

Audition Information

No audition fee.

Costs & Financial Aid

Tuition (full): $440. *Room:* $200. *Board:* $130. *Other fees:* approximately $100-$150 for weekend meals off campus, extra curricular activities, and shopping.

Financial aid available? no.

Curriculum, Students, and Faculty

Required courses: ballet, dance composition/choreography, jazz, master classes, Limon-based modern dance, pointe, tap, variations. *Specific curriculum information:* curriculum fixed.

Selectivity for males: approximately 60% admitted. *Selectivity for females:* approximately 60% admitted.

Renowned alumni: Cargn Heelman, Paul Taylor.

Full-time faculty: 5. *Guest faculty:* 0. *List of some faculty*: Li Chou Cheng, Susan Haigler-Robles, Elizabeth Gillasph, Ellen Page Garrison, Diane West.

Performance Information

Performance opportunities and frequency: Informal showings; end of session. *Performances choreographed by:* students.

Number of studios (description): 3 (40' x 80' sprung floor with Marley overlay). *Performance facilities:* studio performance.

Affiliations

Summer program is affiliated with other program(s): future students are recruited from this program.

THE JOEFFREY WORKSHOP

Winter Contact Information

University of the Incarnate Word, 4301 Broadway Box 57, San Antonio TX 78209
Tel: 210-829-3811
Fax: 210-829-3813
Email: uiw_ballet@juno.com
Contact: Buddy and Susan Trevino

Summer Contact Information

University of the Incarnate Word, 4301 Broadway Box 57, San Antonio TX 78209
Tel: 210-829-3811
Fax: 210-829-3813
Email: uiw_ballet@juno.com
Contact: Buddy and Susan Trevino

General

Total enrollment: 100-110. *Minimum age or age range:* 11 to 20. *Level of program:* advanced.

High school credit available? no. *College credit available?* no.

Services

Housing options: on-site housing.

Application Information

Program dates: 6/15-7/5. *Application deadline:* 4/8. *Application fee:* $500. *Enrollment full by:* 4/8. *Acceptance notification:* immediately.

Audition Information

Audition fee: $15. *Audition consists of the following:* ballet, pointe work. *Accompanist provided, cassette player available, CD player available.*

Special dress requirements: black and white for men. Women: black / pink.

Costs & Financial Aid

Tuition (full): $1,050. *Room & board:* $806. *Room:* $415. *Board:* $391.

Financial aid available? yes. *Students receiving financial aid:* 8%. *Procedure for applying for financial aid:* letter of request.

Curriculum, Students, and Faculty

Required courses: character, ballet, men's class, modern dance, body conditioning, music, nutrition, pas de deux, pointe, repertory, variations, yoga. *Specific curriculum information:* curriculum fixed.

Selectivity for males: approximately 10% admitted. *Selectivity for females:* approximately 10% admitted.

Full-time faculty: 5. *List of some faculty and their affiliations:* Jonathan Watts, Joffrey Ballet; Eleanor D' Antuono, American Ballet Theatre; Paul Sutherland, Joffrey Ballet; Brunilda Ruiz, Joffrey Ballet; Rachel Lampert, Rachel Lampert and Dances NYC.

Performance Information

Performances choreographed by: faculty, students.

Number of studios (description): 4 (45' x 35' sprung). *Performance facilities:* university Fine Arts Auditorium, 1000 seats.

Affiliations

Summer program is affiliated with a professional company: future company members are often recruited from this program; company apprentices are often recruited from this program. *Summer program is affiliated with other program(s):* future students are often recruited from this program.

UTAH

BALLET WEST CONSERVATORY SUMMER SESSION

Winter Contact Information

University of Utah, 330 South 1500 E Room 110, Salt Lake City UT 84112-0280
Tel: 801-581-6324
Fax: 801-581-5442
Email: melmcgee@leland.stanford.edu
Contact: Sharee Lane or Janette Boyd

Summer Contact Information

Salt Lake City UT 84112
Tel: 801-581-5442
Fax: 801-581-5442
Email: melmcgee@leland.stanford.edu
Contact: Sharee Lane or Janette Boyd

General

Minimum age or age range: 12. *Level of program:* beginning, intermediate, advanced.

High school credit available? yes. *College credit available?* no.

Services

Housing options: on-site housing.

Application Information

Program dates: 6/23-8/11. *Application deadline:* 5/12. *Application fee:* $25. *Enrollment full by:* 4/30. *Requirements:* recommendation, photograph. *Acceptance notification:* within 1 week of audition.

Audition Information

No audition fee. Audition consists of the following: ballet, pointe work. *Accompanist provided, cassette player available, CD player available.*

Dress requirements for females: yes.

Audition evaluation criteria: alignment, placement, vocabulary, knowledge, musicality, presentation, natural abilities, strength.

Costs & Financial Aid

Tuition (full): $800. *Room:* $460. *Board:* $400.

Financial aid available? full scholarship, partial scholarship. *Students receiving financial aid:* 2%.

Curriculum, Students, and Faculty

Required courses: character, ballet, dance history, jazz, men's class, Graham-based modern dance, Limon-based modern dance, body conditioning, music, pointe, repertory, variations. *Specific curriculum information:* curriculum fixed.

Selectivity for males: approximately 33% admitted. *Selectivity for females:* approximately 33% admitted.

Renowned alumni: Rachel Viselli, Ballet West; Heather Thackeray, Ballet West; Ashley Solomon, Ballet West; Andrea Shaw, Berlin State Opera; Miriam Wenger, Miami City Ballet; Becky Johnston, Greg Schoenwolf, Pacific Northwest Ballet.

Full-time faculty: 7. *Guest faculty:* 5. *List of some faculty:* Sharee Lane, Olaf Hofer, Sandra Sugai, Gilles Maidon, Jiang Qi, Angela Banchero-Kelleher, Janet Gray, Bene Arnold, Maureen Laird, Jean-Philippe Malatz, Janette Boyd, Bruce Caldwell, Tom Welsh, Craig Berman, Sherri Hutten.

Performance Information

Performance opportunities and frequency: final performance; end of session. *Performances choreographed by:* faculty, guests.

Number of studios (description): 4 (wood, very large Marley). *Performance facilities:* 330-seat theater.

Affiliations

Summer program is affiliated with a professional company: future company members are often recruited from this program; company apprentices are often recruited from this program. *Summer program is affiliated with a pre-professional company:* future company members are often recruited from this program; company apprentices are often recruited from this program. *Summer program is affiliated with other program(s):* future students are often recruited from this program.

BRIGHAM YOUNG UNIVERSITY SUMMER BALLET WORKSHOP-ADVANCED INTENSIVE

Winter Contact Information

Conferences and Workshops, 147 Harman Building, Provo UT 84602
Tel: 801-378-4489
Fax: 801-378-8112
Email: sandra_allen@byu.edu or denae_anderson@byu.edu
Contact: Sandra Allen or DeNae Anderson

Summer Contact Information

Conferences and Workshops, 147 Harman Building, Provo UT 84602
Tel: 801-378-8112
Fax: 801-378-8112
Email: sandra_allen@byu.edu or denae_anderson@byu.edu
Contact: Sandra Allen or DeNae Anderson

General

Total enrollment: 50-60. *Minimum age or age range:* 12 to 18. *Level of program:* advanced.

High school credit available? yes. *College credit available?* no.

Services

Housing options: on-site housing, off-campus housing.

Application Information

Program dates: 8/4-8/14. *Application deadline:* 8/4 (if space available). *Application fee: none. Acceptance notification: immediately.*

Audition Information

Audition fee: $10. *Audition consists of the following:* ballet, pointe work. *Accompanist provided, cassette player available, CD player available.*

Special dress requirements: classical attire for men. Girls: pink tights and shoes, modest black leotard without low backs or spaghetti straps.

Costs & Financial Aid

Tuition (full): $350. *Room & board:* $200.

Financial aid available? partial scholarship. *Students receiving financial aid:* 10%. *Procedure for applying for financial aid:* application form for the audition simply has a box to check, scholarships are based on talent, not on need.

Curriculum, Students, and Faculty

Required courses: character, ballet, men's class, modern dance, body conditioning, Pilates, pas de deux, pointe, repertory, variations, injury prevention, ballet as a profession. *Specific curriculum information:* curriculum fixed.

Selectivity for males: approximately 60% admitted. *Selectivity for females:* approximately 33% admitted.

Renowned alumni: Linda Jewell, Stacy Barney, Joffrey Ballet; Carrie Williams, Sarah Skelton.

Full-time faculty: 1. *Guest faculty:* 2.

Performance Information

Performance opportunities and frequency: workshop performance(s); 1. *Performances choreographed by:* faculty, students, guests, students help with modern section. *Number of studios (description):* 2 (60' x 60' raised wood and Marley, 30' x 50' raised wood). *Performance facilities:* studio theater.

Affiliations

Summer program is affiliated with a pre-professional company: future company members are often recruited from this program; company apprentices are often recruited from this program. *Summer program is affiliated with other program(s):* future students are often recruited from this program.

BRIGHAM YOUNG UNIVERSITY SUMMER BALLET WORKSHOP-INTERMEDIATE

Winter Contact Information
Conferences and Workshops, 148 Harman Building, Provo UT 84602
Tel: 801-378-4489
Fax: 801-378-8112
Email: sandra_allen@byu.edu or denal_anderson@byu.edu
Contact: Sandra Allen or DeNae Anderson

Summer Contact Information
Conferences and Workshops, 148 Harman Building, Provo UT 84602
Tel: 801-378-4489
Fax: 801-378-8112
Email: sandra_allen@byu.edu or denal_anderson@byu.edu
Contact: Sandra Allen or DeNae Anderson

General
Minimum age or age range: 11 to 18.

High school credit available? no. *College credit available?* no.

Services
Housing options: on-site housing.

Application Information
Program dates: 6/23-7/3. *Application deadline:* 4/30-6/24. *Application fee:* none. *Acceptance notification:* immediately.

Audition Information
Audition fee: $10. *Audition consists of the following:* ballet, pointe work.

Costs & Financial Aid
Tuition (full): $350. *Room & board:* $200.

Financial aid available? no.

Curriculum, Students, and Faculty
Required courses: character, ballet, dance history, jazz, men's class, modern dance, body conditioning, pointe, repertory, variations, injury prevention, ballet as a profession. *Specific curriculum information:* curriculum fixed.

Selectivity for males: most admitted, but not all. *Selectivity for females:* most admitted, but not all.

Full-time faculty: 1. *Guest faculty:* 2. *List of some faculty*: Sandra Allen, Marianne Hatton.

Performance Information
Number of studios (description): 2 (60' x 60' raised wood, 50' x 30'). *Performance facilities:* studio theater, dance production theater.

BRIGHAM YOUNG UNIVERSITY YOUTH ARTISTS

Winter Contact Information
Conferences and Workshops, 149 Harman Building, Provo UT 84602
Tel: 801-378-4489
Fax: 801-378-8112
Email: sandra_allen@byu.edu
Contact: Sandra Allen or Michele Kennedy

Summer Contact Information
Conferences and Workshops, 149 Harman Building, Provo UT 84602
Tel: 801-378-4489
Fax: 801-378-8112
Email: sandra_allen@byu.edu
Contact: Sandra Allen or Michele Kennedy

General
Minimum age or age range: 12 to 18.

High school credit available? yes. *College credit available?* no.

Application Information
Program dates: 4/26-6/6. *Application fee:* none. *Enrollment full by:* space usually available. *Acceptance notification:* 1 week to 1 month after audition.

Audition Information
Audition fee: $10. *Audition consists of the following:* ballet, pointe work.

Costs & Financial Aid
Tuition (full): $350.

Financial aid available? partial scholarship. *Procedure for applying for financial aid:* discuss with director.

Curriculum, Students, and Faculty
Required courses: ballet, men's class, pas de deux, pointe, repertory, variations. *Specific curriculum information:* curriculum fixed.

Selectivity for males: approximately 33% admitted. *Selectivity for females:* approximately 10% admitted.

Renowned alumni: Jennie Creer, Candice Taylor, Bringham Young University Principal Ballet, San Francisco Ballet; Laura Burton, Ballet Theatre of New Mexico; Tess Hopley, Nevada Dance Theatre, BYU Theatre Ballet; Rebecca Thomas, Rhodes Scholar, William F. Christ.

List of some faculty and their affiliations: Jennie Creer, Ballet West, Burklyn Ballet.

Performance Information

Performance opportunities and frequency: Informal showings. *Performances choreographed by:* faculty, guests. *Number of studios (description):* 1 (50' x 30' raised wood). *Performance facilities:* studio theater with graduated seating, traditional 166RB dance production theatre.

Affiliations

Summer program is affiliated with a professional company: future company members are often recruited from this program; company apprentices are often recruited from this program. *Summer program is affiliated with a pre-professional company:* company apprentices are recruited from this program. *Summer program is affiliated with a conservatory:* future students are recruited from this program.

BRIGHAM YOUNG UNIVERSITY-SPRING AND SUMMER TERM

Winter Contact Information

Ballet Division, 289 RB BYU, Provo UT 84602
Tel: 801-378-4489
Fax: 801-378-8112
Email: sandra_allen@byu.edu or denae_anderson@byu.edu
Contact: Sandra Allen

Summer Contact Information

289 RB, Brigham Young University, Provo UT 84602
Tel: 801-378-4489
Fax: 801-378-8112
Email: sandra_allen@byu.edu or denae_anderson@byu.edu
Contact: Sandra Allen

General

Total enrollment: 34-50. *Minimum age or age range:* 1 to 45. *Level of program:* beginning, intermediate, advanced.

High school credit available? no. *College credit available?* yes.

Services

Housing options: on-site housing, off-campus housing.

Application Information

Program dates: 6/23-8/14. *Application deadline:* 9/15-2/15. *Application fee:* $25. *Enrollment full by:* space usually available. *Requirements:* interview, recommendation. *Acceptance notification:* 3/31.

Audition Information

No audition fee. Audition consists of the following: ballet. *Accompanist provided, cassette player available, CD player available.*

Special dress requirements: classical attire or solid biking shorts for men, modest attire. Women: pink tights and shoes, modest solid leotard without low back or spaghetti straps.

Costs & Financial Aid

Room & board: $760. *Other fees:* class attire and $75 syllabus.

Financial aid available? full scholarship, *Students receiving financial aid:* 25%. *Procedure for applying for financial aid:* forms available through the Dance Department Scholarship Committee.

Curriculum, Students, and Faculty

Required courses: anatomy, character, ballet, dance composition/choreography, jazz, master classes, modern dance, music, pas de deux, pointe, repertory, tap, variations, folklore, ethnic dance, ballroom dance, social dance, aerobic. *Specific curriculum information:* curriculum fixed.

Selectivity for males: approximately 10% admitted. *Selectivity for females:* approximately 10% admitted.

Renowned alumni: Hugh Bigney, Pacific Northwest Ballet; Tess Hooley, Nevada Dance Theatre; Andrew Bayne, Oakland Ballet. *List of some faculty*: Sandra Allen, Mark Lanham, YiQi Cheng, Marianne Hatton, Connie Burton.

Performance Information

Performance opportunities and frequency: Final performance; 1. Informal showings; 1. *Performances choreographed by:* faculty, students, guests, students help with modern section, guests help with jazz and character. *Number of studios (description):* 2 (60' x 60' Marley, 50' x 30' raised wood). *Performance facilities:* studio theater for spring and summer.

Affiliations

Summer program is affiliated with a pre-professional company: future company members are recruited from this program; company apprentices are recruited from this program. *Summer program is affiliated with other program(s):* future students are recruited from this program.

MODERN DANCE AND JAZZ DANCE CAMP

Winter Contact Information
Brigham Young University Conferences and Workshops, 147 Harman Building, Provo UT 84602
Tel: 801-378-4851
Fax: 801-378-6361
Email: steve_trost@byu.edu
Contact: De Nae Anderson

Summer Contact Information
Brigham Young University Conferences and Workshops, 147 Harman Building, Provo UT 84602
Tel: 801-378-4851
Fax: 801-378-6361
Email: steve_trost@byu.edu
Contact: De Nae Anderson

General
Level of program: beginning, intermediate, advanced.

High school credit available? no.

Services
Housing options: on-site housing.

Application Information
Application deadline: first day of workshop. *Enrollment full by:* first day of workshop.

Costs & Financial Aid
Financial aid available? no.

Curriculum, Students, and Faculty
Courses offered: African dance, ballet, dance composition/choreography, improvisation, jazz, master classes, modern dance, body conditioning, repertory, tap, eclectic. *Specific curriculum information:* Curricula choices.

Selectivity for males: admit all who apply. *Selectivity for females:* admit all who apply.

Full-time faculty: 3. *Guest faculty:* 10. *List of some faculty and their affiliations:* Marilyn Berrett.

Performance Information
Performance opportunities and frequency: Informal showings; 3-4. Workshop performance(s); 1 per week. *Performances choreographed by:* faculty, students, guests. *Number of studios (description):* 4 (52' x 35', 52' x 32' sprung hardwood one with Marley, 60' x 30' sprung hardwood one with Marley, 40' x 30' sprung hardwood one with Marley). *Performance facilities:* studio theater with seating capacity of 396.

MODERN DANCE WORKSHOPS

Winter Contact Information
Brigham Young University Conferences and Workshops, Provo UT 84602
Tel: 801-378-4851
Fax: 801-378-6361
Email: dearborn@muhlberg.edu
Contact: De Nae Anderson

Summer Contact Information
Brigham Young University Conferences and Workshops, Provo UT 84602
Tel: 801-378-4851
Fax: 801-378-6361
Email: dearborn@muhlberg.edu
Contact: De Nae Anderson

General
Minimum age or age range: 18.

High school credit available? no. *College credit available?* yes.

Services
Housing options: on-site housing.

Application Information
Program dates: third week of July-first week of August. *Application deadline:* first day of workshop. *Application fee:* none. *Enrollment full by:* first day of workshop.

Audition Information
No audition fee.

Costs & Financial Aid
Tuition (full): $290. *Room & board:* $10.

Financial aid available? no.

Curriculum, Students, and Faculty
Required courses: dance composition/choreography, improvisation, modern dance. *Specific curriculum information:* curriculum fixed.

Selectivity for males: admit all who apply. *Selectivity for females:* admit all who apply.

List of some faculty and their affiliations: Garry Rugenhorn, Lucinda Childs Dance Company; Scott Rink, Lar Lubovitch Dance Company; David Grenhe, Paul Taylor Dance Company.

Performance Information
Performance opportunities and frequency: workshop performance(s); 1 per week. *Performances choreographed by:* students, guests. *Number of studios (description):* 3 (52' x 35' sprung hardwood, 53' x 32', 60' x 30'). *Performance facilities:* studios, theater with seating capacity of 396.

Additional Comments

The above tuition is for technique only. The above amounts for room and board are nightly and daily rates.

VERMONT

BURKLYN BALLET THEATRE

Winter Contact Information
P.O. Box 907, Island Heights NJ 08732
Tel: 732-288-2660
Fax: 732-288-2663
Email: Burklyn@aol.com
Contact: Angela E. Whitehill

Summer Contact Information
90 Johnson State College, Johnson VT 05656
Tel: 802-635-2356
Fax: 802-635-1248
Email: Burklyn@aol.com
Contact: Angela E. Whitehill

General

Level of program: intermediate, advanced.

High school credit available? yes. *College credit available?* no.

Services

Housing options: on-site housing.

Application Information

Program dates: 6/22-8/3. *Application deadline:* June. *Application fee:* $250. *Enrollment full by:* March. *Acceptance notification:* 3/1.

Audition Information

Audition fee: $15. *Audition consists of the following:* ballet, pointe work. *Accompanist provided.*

Audition evaluation criteria: talent.

Costs & Financial Aid

Tuition (full): $1,350-$3,000. *Other fees:* $45 accident insurance, airport pickup charge.

Financial aid available? partial scholarship. *Procedure for applying for financial aid:* audition.

Curriculum, Students, and Faculty

Required courses: character, ballet, dance composition/choreography, jazz, master classes, men's class, Horton-based modern dance, pas de deux, pointe, variations, career counseling, pointe shoe seminar. *Specific curriculum information:* curriculum fixed.

Selectivity for males: approximately 60% admitted. *Selectivity for females:* approximately 33% admitted.

Renowned alumni: Peter Morrison, American Ballet Theatre; Rebecca Metzger, New York City Ballet; Natalie Burr, Ballet Austin; Amy Rodgers, Joanne Goldberg, Atlanta Ballet; Frank Dellapolla, Metropolitan Opera Company; Floyd Flyn, Martha Graham Company.

Full-time faculty: 4. *Guest faculty:* 12-16. *List of some faculty:* David Howard, Cherie Noble, Doreen Caferella, Arthur Leeth, Robert Barnett, Alexander Bennett, Lorraine Neal, Nicolas Pacana.

Performance Information

Performances choreographed by: faculty, students, guests; there is a fully produced performance every Saturday; week 5 is completely student choreographed, costumed, and produced with faculty guidance.

Number of studios (description): 3 (48' x 40' sprung wooden floor with Rosco). *Performance facilities:* 600 seat state-of-the-art proscenium theater.

Affiliations

Summer program is affiliated with a pre-professional company: future company members are recruited from this program; company apprentices are recruited from this program.

Additional Comments

Burklyn Youth Ballet chooses 20 dancers to travel to and to perform at the Edinburgh Festival Fringe, August 9-18th.

VIRGINIA

EASTERN VIRGINIA SCHOOL FOR THE PERFORMING ARTS

Winter Contact Information
P.O. Box 273, Williamsburg VA 23187
Tel: 757-229-8535
Fax: 757-220-9091
Email: EVSPA@Widowmaker.com
Contact: Ron Boucher

Summer Contact Information
P.O. Box 273, Williamsburg VA 23187
Tel: 757-229-8535
Fax: 757-220-9091
Email: EVSPA@Widowmaker.com
Contact: Ron Boucher

General

Level of program: beginning, intermediate.

High school credit available? no. *College credit available?* no.

Services

Housing options: on-site housing, off-campus housing.

Application Information

Requirements: recommendation, photograph.

Audition Information

Audition fee: Audition consists of the following: ballet, pointe work. *Accompanist provided, cassette player available, CD player available.*

Dress requirements for females: Yes. *Special dress requirements:* traditional black leotard, pink tights.

Curriculum, Students, and Faculty

Required courses: ballet, jazz, men's class, Limon-based modern dance, pas de deux, pointe, variations. *Specific curriculum information:* curriculum fixed.

Selectivity for males: approximately 33% admitted. *Selectivity for females:* approximately 10% admitted. *Guest faculty:* 0.

Performance Information

Performances choreographed by: faculty. *Number of studios (description):* 3 (30' x 40' free floating wood floor-professional standards). *Performance facilities:* university theater.

Affiliations

Summer program is affiliated with a professional company: future company members are recruited from this program; company apprentices are recruited from this program. *Summer program is affiliated with a pre-professional company:* future company members are recruited from this program; company apprentices are recruited from this program.

SHENANDOAH PERFORMING ARTS CAMP

Winter Contact Information

Shenandoah University-Dance Department, 1460 University Drive, Winchester VA 22601
Tel: 540-665-4602
Fax: 540-665-5402
Contact: Sharon Pollard

Summer Contact Information

Shenandoah University-Dance Department, 1460 University Drive, Winchester VA 22601
Tel: 540-665-4565
Fax: 540-665-5402
Contact: Sharon Pollard

General

Minimum age or age range: 14 to 18. *Level of program:* intermediate, advanced.

High school credit available? no. *College credit available?* no.

Services

Housing options: on-site housing.

Application Information

Program dates: first 2 weeks in July. *Application deadline:* 6/20. *Application fee:* $50. *Enrollment full by:* 6/20. *Requirements:* recommendation, photograph. *Acceptance notification:* rolling.

Audition Information

No audition fee. Audition consists of the following: ballet, modern dance, improvisation (ballet, modern or jazz style, no tap), ballet exercise required. *Accompanist provided, cassette player available, CD player available.*

Dress requirements for females: yes. *Special dress requirements:* leotard, tights.

Costs & Financial Aid

Tuition (full): $535.

Financial aid available? partial scholarship. *Procedure for applying for financial aid:* submit form with application.

Curriculum, Students, and Faculty

Required courses: ballet, dance composition/choreography, dance history, historical dance, jazz, Cunningham-based, Graham-based dance, Limon-based, Nikolais-based modern dance, other world dance forms, repertory. *Specific curriculum information:* curriculum fixed.

Selectivity for males: approximately 60% admitted. *Selectivity for females:* approximately 60% admitted.

Full-time faculty: 2. *Guest faculty:* 1. *List of some faculty:* Erica Helm, Alan Arnett, Rochelle Morello.

Performance Information

Performance opportunities and frequency: Final performance; 2. Informal showings; weekly. *Performances choreographed by:* faculty, students, guests. *Number of studios (description):* 2 (70' x 40' wood and Marley, 30' x 25' wood and Marley). *Performance facilities:* gymnasium, theater.

Affiliations

Summer program is affiliated with a conservatory: future students are recruited from this program.

Additional Comments

Excellent first camp experience.

WASHINGTON

CORNISH SUMMER DANCE

Winter Contact Information

710 East Roy Street, Seattle WA 98102
Tel: 206-726-5034
Contact: Christine Juarez

Summer Contact Information

710 East Roy Street, Seattle WA 98102
Tel: 206-323-1400
Contact: Christine Juarez, Ann Coombes

General

Minimum age or age range: 4 and up. *Level of program:* beginning, intermediate, advanced.

High school credit available? no. *College credit available?* yes.

Application Information

Program dates: last week of June, 4 weeks in July (5 weeks). *Application deadline:* 6/1. *Application fee:* none. *Enrollment full by:* 6/20.

Audition Information

No audition fee. Audition consists of the following: Accompanist provided, cassette player available, CD player available.

Dress requirements: Yes. *Special dress requirements:* clean, classical look, baggy clothing not accepted.

Costs & Financial Aid

Tuition (full): $550-$650

Financial aid available? Yes. partial scholarship. *Students receiving financial aid:* 1%. *Procedure for applying for financial aid:* personal call or letter to summer director requesting information on work scholarships.

Curriculum, Students, and Faculty

Required courses: character, ballet, jazz, modern dance, Graham-based modern dance, pointe, Spanish, tap, variations. *Specific curriculum information:* curriculum fixed.

Selectivity for males: most admitted, but not all. *Selectivity for females:* most admitted, but not all.

Renowned alumni: Merce Cunningham, Martha Graham.

Full-time faculty: 5. *Guest faculty:* 5. *List of some faculty and their affiliations:* Pat Hon, Cornish College, Graham Company; Frank Bays, Joffrey Ballet, Marin Ballet; Terry Sparks, Ballet Mistress Tharp Company; Lucia Kuimova, Dannul Dailey.

Performance Information

Number of studios (description): 3

Affiliations

Summer program is affiliated with other program(s): future students are recruited from this program.

FLAMENCO IN CONCERT MORCA DANCE FESTIVAL

Winter Contact Information

1349 Franklin, Bellingham WA 98225
Tel: 360-676-7776
Fax: 360-733-9031
Email: morca@pacificrim.net
Contact: Teodoro Morca

Summer Contact Information

1349 Franklin, Bellingham WA 98225
Tel: 360-676-7776
Fax: 360-733-9031
Email: morca@pacificrim.net
Contact: Teodoro Morca

General

Minimum age or age range: 14. *Level of program:* beginning, intermediate, advanced.

High school credit available? no. *College credit available?* no.

Services

Housing options: on-site housing, off-campus housing.

Application Information

Program dates: August. *Application fee:* $495. *Enrollment full by:* 6/15. *Requirements:* essay.

Audition Information

No audition fee. Audition consists of the following: Accompanist provided.

Costs & Financial Aid

Financial aid available? no.

Curriculum, Students, and Faculty

Required courses: dance history, music, Spanish, Flamenco. *Specific curriculum information:* curriculum fixed.

Selectivity for males: admit all who apply. *Selectivity for females:* admit all who apply.

Full-time faculty: 2. *Guest faculty:* 4. *List of some faculty:* Teo Morca.

Performance Information

Performances choreographed by: Teo Morca and faculty. *Number of studios (description):* 2 (40' x 40' resilient wood). *Performance facilities:* theaters, studio.

Affiliations

Summer program is affiliated with a professional company: future company members are not recruited from this program; company apprentices are not recruited from this program. *Summer program is affiliated with a pre-professional company:* future company members are not recruited from this program; company apprentices are not recruited from this program. *Summer program is affiliated with other program(s):* future students are not recruited from this program.

Additional Comments

I give the only all flamenco workshop in the USA and the oldest, celebrating 20 years. People come from all over the world.

PACIFIC NORTHWEST BALLET SCHOOL SUMMER COURSE

Winter Contact Information

301 Mercer Street, Seattle WA 98109
Tel: 206-441-2435
Fax: 206-441-2430
Email: Marsha@pnb.org
Contact: Denise Bolstad

Summer Contact Information

301 Mercer Street, Seattle WA 98109
Tel: 206-441-2435
Fax: 206-441-2430
Email: Marsha@pnb.org
Contact: Denise Bolstad

General

Minimum age or age range: 12 to 18. *Level of program:* intermediate, advanced.

Services

Housing options: on-site housing, off-campus housing.

Application Information

Program dates: July-mid August (6 weeks). *Enrollment full by:* 6/1. *Acceptance notification:* 1 month after audition.

Audition Information

Audition fee: $15. *Audition consists of the following:* ballet, pointe work. *Accompanist provided.*

Dress requirements for females: Yes. *Special dress requirements:* solid color leotard, pink tights, pointe shoes.

Costs & Financial Aid

Tuition (full): $215-$880 *Room:* $1,250. *Other fees:* bus fare.

Financial aid available? full scholarship, partial scholarship. *Students receiving financial aid:* 66%. *Procedure for applying for financial aid:* generally granted/decided at the audition, additional requests may be directed to the school office.

Curriculum, Students, and Faculty

Required courses: character, ballet, dance history, jazz, men's class, Horton-based modern dance, body conditioning, music, nutrition, pas de deux, pointe, repertory, Spanish, variations, podiatry. *Specific curriculum information:* curriculum fixed.

Selectivity for males: approximately 33% admitted. *Selectivity for females:* approximately 10% admitted.

Full-time faculty: 9. *Guest faculty:* 4. *List of some faculty:* Francia Russell, Paula Prewett, Denise Bolstad, Victoria Pulkkinen, Sara deLuis, Truman Finney, Flemming Halby, Lucia Kuimova, Phillip Otto, Lisa Peterson, Alan Pietsch, Stephanie Saland, Lynne Short, Abbie Siegel, Marjorie Thompson, Alice Yearsly, Dan Vollema.

Performance Information

Open class parents may observe.

Number of studios (description): 6 (40' x 50' Marley on sprung floor).

Affiliations

Summer program is affiliated with a professional company: future company members are often recruited from this program; company apprentices are often recruited from this program.

WISCONSIN

MILWAUKEE BALLET SCHOOL PRE-PROFESSIONAL DANCE PROGRAM

Winter Contact Information

504 West National Avenue, Milwaukee WI 53204
Tel: 414-649-4077
Fax: 414-649-4066
Contact: Bobby G. Ball

Summer Contact Information
504 West National Avenue, Milwaukee WI 53204
Tel: 414-649-4077
Fax: 414-649-4066
Contact: Bobby G. Ball

General
Minimum age or age range: 11 to 20. *Level of program:* intermediate, advanced.

High school credit available? no. *College credit available?* no.

Services
Housing options: on-site housing, off-campus housing.

Application Information
Program dates: 6/22-7/31. *Application fee:* $15. *Requirements:* photograph. *Acceptance notification:* within 1 month of audition.

Audition Information
Audition fee: $20. *Audition consists of the following:* ballet. *Accompanist provided.*

Dress requirements for females: no.

Audition evaluation criteria: adequate technique.

Costs & Financial Aid
Tuition (full): $1,400. *Room & board:* $1,460-$1,660.

Financial aid available? full scholarship, partial scholarship. *Students receiving financial aid:* 40%. *Procedure for applying for financial aid:* merit-based.

Curriculum, Students, and Faculty
Required courses: African dance, character, ballet, dance history, jazz, men's class, modern dance, body conditioning, music, pas de deux, pointe, Spanish, variations. *Specific curriculum information:* curriculum fixed.

Selectivity for males: most admitted, but not all. *Selectivity for females:* approximately 60% admitted.

Full-time faculty: 1. *Guest faculty:* 19. *List of some faculty*: Susan Clark, Phyllis Coffey, Fiona Fuerstner, Jeannine Granger, Dwight Hutton, Margo Kuehn, Elizabeth Leggett, Peggy Lozier, Nancy McCloud, Mary McPhail, Carla Rodriguez, Lori Romito, Cynthia Schowalter, Karen Smith-English, Shenlee Sires, Karl Von Rabenau, Judith Warren, Rolando Yanes, David Mackinson, Jeanette Makaroff.

Performance Information
Performance opportunities and frequency: workshop performance(s); 2 per year. *Performances choreographed by:* faculty, guests, open class. *Number of studios (description):* 4 (40' x 60' Harlequin dance floor over sprung plywood floor, 30' x 35' Harlequin dance floor over sprung plywood floor, 30' x 40' Harlequin dance floor over sprung plywood floor, 30' x 40' Harlequin dance floor over sprung plywood floor). *Performance facilities:* no performing facility at studio workshop showcase, final performance is held at the historic Pabst Theater.

POINT ARTS CAMPS, MUSICAL THEATRE & DANCE

Winter Contact Information
A200 Fine Arts Center, UW-Stevens Point, Stevens Point WI 54481
Tel: 715-346-3956
Fax: 715-346-2718
Email: jkarlen@uwsp.edu
Contact: Joan Karlen, Kathy Gruna

Summer Contact Information
A200 Fine Arts Center, UW-Stevens Point, Stevens Point WI 54481
Tel: 715-346-3956
Fax: 715-346-2718
Email: jkarlen@uwsp.edu
Contact: Joan Karlen, Kathy Gruna

General
Minimum age or age range: 12 to 19. *Level of program:* beginning, intermediate, advanced.

High school credit available? no. *College credit available?* no.

Services
Housing options: on-site housing.

Application Information
Application deadline: 7/1. *Application fee:* $50. *Enrollment full by:* 7/1. *Requirements:* recommendation, photograph. *Acceptance notification:* upon receipt of application.

Audition Information
No audition fee. Audition consists of the following: ballet, modern dance, repertory movement combinations. *Accompanist provided.*

Dress requirements: yes. *Special dress requirements:* leotard, tights with convertible feet, ballet slippers, bare feet, jazz shoes, hair must be worn up, away from neck and face, no jewelry.

Costs & Financial Aid
Tuition (full): $395.

Financial aid available? no. *Procedure for applying for financial aid:* Department of Public Instruction assists eligible students.

Curriculum, Students, and Faculty

Required courses: acting, ballet, jazz, repertory, scene study, tap, monologues. *Specific curriculum information:* Curricula choices.

Renowned alumni: Adrianne Fang.

Full-time faculty: 3. *Guest faculty:* 7. *List of some faculty:* Mike Dashn, Shana Edmunson, Mary Martin-Fehrenbach, Karen Horwitz, Jessica Hussin, Joan Karlen, Jessica Lanius, James Moore, Linda Martin Moore, Ann Mosey, Tom Nevins, Patrick Strong, Suzy Beckman, Amy Grumann.

Performance Information

Performances choreographed by: faculty, students. *Number of studios (description):* 5 (40' x 50' sprung wood floor). *Performance facilities:* multipurpose studio theater, formal concert hall.

Additional Comments

Tuition is $395 for resident, and $275 for commutor.

CANADA

GENERAL PROGRAM, AUGUST SUMMER INTENSIVE

Winter Contact Information

Professional Program of Contemporary Dancers' May Intensive, Manitoba, Canada
Tel: 204-452-1239
Fax: 204-287-8618
Email: tdecker@mtsu.edu
Contact: Christina Medina

Summer Contact Information

Professional Program of Contemporary Dancers' May Intensive, Manitoba, Canada
Tel: 204-452-1239
Fax: 204-287-8618
Email: tdecker@mtsu.edu
Contact: Christina Medina

General

Minimum age or age range: 12 to 18.

High school credit available? no. *College credit available?* no.

Application Information

Program dates: first week of August. *Application fee:* none. *Enrollment full by:* 7/30. *Acceptance notification:* 2 weeks after application is received.

Audition Information

No audition fee.

Costs & Financial Aid

Financial aid available? no.

Curriculum, Students, and Faculty

Courses offered: African dance, Alexander technique, ballet, Limon-based modern dance, body conditioning, Pilates, pointe. *Specific curriculum information:* Curricula choices.

Selectivity for males: most admitted, but not all. *Selectivity for females:* most admitted, but not all.

Renowned alumni: Stephanie Ballard, Gaile Petursson-Hiley, Ruth Cansfield.

Full-time faculty: 4. *Guest faculty:* 2.

Performance Information

Performance opportunities and frequency: Informal showings; 1. *Performances choreographed by:* faculty, guests. *Number of studios (description):* 3 (sprung). *Performance facilities:* studio theater.

Affiliations

Summer program is affiliated with a conservatory: future students are recruited from this program.

Additional Comments

Tuition: $300-$395; Room and Board is up to the billeting family.

SUMMER SCHOOL 1997, TORONTO DANCE THEATRE

Winter Contact Information

The School of Toronto Dance Theatre, 80 Winchester Street, Toronto ON M4X1BZ Canada
Tel: 416-967-6887
Fax: 416-967-4379
Contact: Receptionist

Summer Contact Information

The School of Toronto Dance Theatre, 80 Winchester Street, Toronto ON M4X1BZCanada
Tel: 416-967-6887
Fax: 416-967-4379
Contact: Receptionist

General

Minimum age or age range: 16. *Level of program:* beginning, intermediate, advanced.

High school credit available? no. *College credit available?* no.

Services

Housing options: off-campus housing.

Application Information

Program dates: 7/6-7/31. *Application deadline:* accept applications until classes are full. *Enrollment full by:* late June.

Audition Information

No audition fee.

Dress requirements: no.

Costs & Financial Aid

Tuition (full): $781. *Room & board:* $600. *Room:* $400. *Board:* $200.

Financial aid available? no.

Curriculum, Students, and Faculty

Required courses: dance composition/choreography, Graham-based modern dance, repertory, modern barre. *Specific curriculum information:* curriculum fixed.

Selectivity for males: most admitted, but not all. *Selectivity for females:* most admitted, but not all.

Renowned alumni: Patricia Mines, Coralee McLaren.

Full-time faculty: 1. *Guest faculty:* 7. *List of some faculty:* Patricia Fraser, Patricia Beatty, Christopher House.

Performance Information

Performances choreographed by: faculty.

Number of studios (description): 3 (20' x 40' matted). *Performance facilities:* theater, seats over 100.

Affiliations

Summer program is affiliated with a professional company: future company members are not recruited from this program; company apprentices are not recruited from this program. *Summer program is affiliated with other program(s):* future students are recruited from this program.

Additional Comments

Tuition includes tax

DANCE TRAINING THE BANFF CENTRE FOR THE ARTS

Winter Contact Information

Banff AB TOL OCO Canada
Tel: 403-762-6345
Email: arts_info@banffcentre.ab.ca
Contact: Office of the Registrar-Enquiries Officer

Summer Contact Information

Banff AB TOL OCO Canada
Tel: 403-762-6345
Email: arts_info@banffcentre.ab.ca
Contact: Office of the Registrar-Enquiries Officer

General

Minimum age or age range: 13 and up. *Level of program:* intermediate, advanced.

High school credit available? yes. *College credit available?* yes.

Services

Housing options: on-site housing.

Application Information

Application deadline: 1/15. *Application fee:* $49. *Enrollment full by:* 1/30. *Requirements:* recommendation, photograph. *Acceptance notification:* 2/28.

Audition Information

No audition fee. Audition consists of the following: ballet, pointe work. *Accompanist provided.*

Costs & Financial Aid

Tuition (full): $1,628. *Room & board:* $1,015.

Financial aid available? partial scholarship. *Students receiving financial aid:* 60%. *Procedure for applying for financial aid:* application form.

Curriculum, Students, and Faculty

Required courses: character, ballet, jazz, men's class, Graham-based modern dance, pas de deux, pointe, variations. *Specific curriculum information:* curriculum fixed.

Selectivity for males: approximately 60% admitted. *Selectivity for females:* approximately 60% admitted.

Full-time faculty: 7. *Guest faculty:* 1. *List of some faculty*: Michael Byers, Michele Fronce Cloutier, Maureen Eastick.

Performance Information

Performance opportunities and frequency: Workshop performance(s); 4. *Performances choreographed by:* faculty. *Number of studios (description):* 5 (30' x 50' sprung floors). *Performance facilities:* Margaret Greenham Theatre, 246 seats.

Affiliations

Summer program is affiliated with a professional company: future company members are often recruited from this program; company apprentices are often recruited from this program. *Summer program is affiliated with a pre-professional company:* future company members are not recruited from this program; company apprentices are often recruited from this program. *Summer program is affiliated with a conservatory:* future students are not recruited from this program.

Additional Comments

All fees are quoted in Canadian dollars; application fee is $42 U.S.

DANCE INTENSIVE '98

Winter Contact Information

Royal Winnipeg Ballet School, 380 Graham Avenue, Winnipeg MT R3C4K2 Canada
Tel: 204-956-0183
Fax: 204-943-1994
Contact: Marni Wakefield

Summer Contact Information

Royal Winnipeg Ballet School, 380 Graham Avenue, Winnipeg, Winnipeg MT R3C4K2 Canada
Tel: 204-946-0183
Fax: 204-943-1994
Contact: Marni Wakefield

General

Minimum age or age range: 9 and up. *Level of program:* intermediate, advanced.

High school credit available? no. *College credit available?* no.

Services

Housing options: on-site housing.

Application Information

Program dates: 7/5-7/24. *Application deadline:* 5/15. *Application fee:* none. *Enrollment full by:* 5/1.

Audition Information

No audition fee.

Costs & Financial Aid

Tuition (full): $400 (Canadian dollars). *Room & board:* $775. *Other fees:* activities are scheduled for "non-dance" hours and are priced individually.

Financial aid available? no.

Curriculum, Students, and Faculty

Required courses: character, ballet, historical dance, jazz, Limon-based modern dance, music, pointe, repertory, variations. *Specific curriculum information:* curriculum fixed.

Selectivity for males: admit all who apply. *Selectivity for females:* admit all who apply.

Renowned alumni: Dr. Arnold Spohr.

Full-time faculty: 12.

Performance Information

Performance opportunities and frequency: Informal showings; 1. *Performances choreographed by:* faculty. *Number of studios (description):* 12 (40' x 30' Harlequin). *Performance facilities:* performance studio with lighting board, sound board, black box, 150 seats.

Affiliations

Summer program is affiliated with a pre-professional company: future company members are often recruited from this program.

Additional Comments

The Royal Winnepeg Ballet has 3 major components: 1-Internationally recognized tour company-travelled to over 40 countries and over 500 cities around the world. 2-Professional Division-A training school for dance students wishing to make dance a career (most of our company members come through this division school). 3-Recreational Program-Open to everyone from the age of 3 to 93. The RWB was founded in 1939 and chartered by Queen Elizabeth in 1953. We are the Oldest Canadian Dance School and we are housed in the largest facility. I have only given you information on our recreational program as the audition tour information is not solidified yet. We have been doing an audition tour every season for over 10 years but things are a little crazy this summer!

PROFESSIONAL PROGRAM OF CONTEMPORARY DANCERS' MAY INTENSIVE

Winter Contact Information

The School of Contemporary Dancers Inc., 109 Pulford Street, Winnipeg MT R3L 1X8 Canada
Tel: 204-452-1239
Fax: 204-287-8618
Contact: De Tomkins

Summer Contact Information

The School of Contemporary Dancers Inc., 109 Pulford Street, Winnipeg MT R3L 1X8 Canada
Tel: 204-452-1239
Fax: 204-287-8618
Contact: De Tomkins

General

Minimum age or age range: 18 and up. *Level of program:* advanced.

High school credit available? no. *College credit available?* no.

Services

Housing options: off-campus housing.

Application Information

Program dates: last week of May, first week of June (2 weeks). *Application deadline:* 3/15. *Application fee:* none. *Enrollment full by:* 4/30. *Acceptance notification:* late April.

Audition Information

No audition fee. Audition consists of the following: modern dance, prepared solo.

Dress requirements: no.

Audition evaluation criteria: applicants must be at, or deemed capable of achieving, professional level in modern dance performance, most will be attending the program currently.

Costs & Financial Aid

Tuition (full): $350.

Financial aid available? no.

Curriculum, Students, and Faculty

Required courses: ballet, Limon-based modern dance, kinesiology, Bill Evans, modern repertory. *Specific curriculum information:* curriculum fixed.

Selectivity for males: approximately 33% admitted. *Selectivity for females:* approximately 33% admitted.

Renowned alumni: Stephanie Ballard, Gaile Petursson-Hiley, Ruth Cansfield.

Full-time faculty: 2. *Guest faculty:* 3. *List of some faculty and their affiliations:* Peter Bingham; Tedd Robinson, LeGroupe de la Place Royale; Peggy Baker, National Ballet School of Toronto; Bill Evans, University of New Mexico; Marc Boivin, Rachel Browne, Gail Petursson-Hiley, Patricia Fraser.

Performance Information

Performance opportunities and frequency: Informal showings; 1. *Performances choreographed by:* guests. *Number of studios (description):* 2 (25' x 25' sprung, linoleum dance floor, 25' x 15' sprung, linoleum dance floor). *Performance facilities:* studio performance, no lighting.

Affiliations

Summer program is affiliated with a university: future students are often recruited from this program.

ALBERTA BALLET SCHOOL OF DANCE

Winter Contact Information

906 12th Avenue, NW, 2nd Floor, West Annex, Southwest Calgary
G2R1K7 Canada
Tel: 403-245-2274
Fax: 403-245-2293

Summer Contact Information

906 12th Avenue, NW, 2nd Floor, West Annex, Southwest Calgary
G2R1K7 Canada
Tel: 403-245-2274
Fax: 403-245-2293

General

Minimum age or age range: 9 to 19. *Level of program:* advanced.

High school credit available? no. *College credit available?* no.

Application Information

Program dates: August. *Application deadline:* 3/31. *Application fee:* $35. *Requirements:* essay, recommendation, photograph.

Audition Information

No audition fee.

Costs & Financial Aid

Tuition (full): $625-$850, Canadian. *Room & board:* $110-$140.

Financial aid available? partial scholarship. *Students receiving financial aid:* 5-10%. *Procedure for applying for financial aid:* complete appropriate documents, financial aid is available for Canadian citizens.

Curriculum, Students, and Faculty

Required courses: character, ballet, dance composition/choreography, master classes, men's class, modern dance, pas de deux, pointe, repertory, Spanish, variations. *Specific curriculum information:* curriculum fixed.

Selectivity for males: approximately 60% admitted. *Selectivity for females:* approximately 60% admitted.

Full-time faculty: 12. *Guest faculty:* 3-4.

Performance Information

Performances choreographed by: faculty, guests.

Number of studios (description): 4 (40' x 40' Harlequin dance floor). *Performance facilities:* varies from year to year.

Affiliations

Summer program is affiliated with a professional company: future company members are recruited from this program; company apprentices are recruited from this program. *Summer program is affiliated with a pre-professional company:* company apprentices are recruited from this program.

DENMARK

BARTHOLIN INTERNATIONAL BALLET SEMINAR

Winter Contact Information
P.O. Box 3018, St. Strandstrede 21, 1021 Copenhagen K-Denmark
Tel: 45-39900436
Fax: 45-39900436
Contact: Vivi Flindt

Summer Contact Information
P.O. Box 3018, St. Strandstrede 21, 1021 Copenhagen K-Denmark
Tel: 45-39900436
Fax: 45-39900436
Contact: Vivi Flindt

General

Total enrollment: 90-100. *Level of program:* intermediate, advanced.

High school credit available? no. *College credit available?* no.

Services

Housing options: off-campus housing.

Application Information

Program dates: 3 weeks in early July. *Application deadline:* none. *Application fee:* none. *Requirements:* photograph.

Audition Information

No audition fee. Audition consists of the following: Accompanist provided, cassette player available, CD player available.

Dress requirements: no.

Costs & Financial Aid

Financial aid available? no.

Curriculum, Students, and Faculty

Required courses: ballet, jazz, men's class, Graham-based, Limon-based modern dance, pas de deux, pointe, repertory, variations, Bournoville dance. *Specific curriculum information:* curriculum fixed.

Full-time faculty: 0. *Guest faculty:* 6-12.

Performance Information

Number of studios (description): 2 (dance floor).

Affiliations

Company apprentices are sometimes recruited from this program.

ENGLAND

THE ROYAL BALLET SCHOOL

Winter Contact Information
155 Talgarth Road, London W14 9DE England
Tel: 44-181-237-7128
Fax: 44-181-237-7127
Email: rbsaud@aol.com

Summer Contact Information
155 Talgarth Road, London W14 9DE England
Tel: 44-181-237-7128
Fax: 44-181-237-7127
Email: rbsaud@aol.com

General

Minimum age or age range: 10 to 11 juniors, 15 to 16 seniors. *Level of program:* intermediate, advanced.

High school credit available? no. *College credit available?* no.

Services

Housing options: on-site housing.

Application Information

Program dates: 7/19-8/1. *Application deadline:* 2/28. *Application fee:* none. *Enrollment full by:* 3/31. *Requirements:* photograph. *Acceptance notification:* mid April.

Audition Information

No audition fee. Audition consists of the following: ballet, pointe work for seniors.

Audition evaluation criteria: dance quality, technical facility and ability, physical suitability for classical ballet.

Costs & Financial Aid

Financial aid available? partial scholarship. *Procedure for applying for financial aid:* letter of declaration of income form.

Curriculum, Students, and Faculty

Required courses: character, ballet, men's class, partnering, pas de deux, pointe, repertory. *Specific curriculum information:* curriculum fixed.

Selectivity for males: approximately 33% admitted. *Selectivity for females:* approximately 10% admitted.

Performance Information

Performances choreographed by: faculty, students. *Number of studios (description):* (sprung-some wood). *Performance facilities:* studio theater.

Affiliations

Summer program is affiliated with a professional company: future company members are not recruited from this program; company apprentices are not recruited from this program. *Summer program is affiliated with a pre-professional company:* future company members are not recruited from this program; company apprentices are not recruited from this program. *Summer program is affiliated with a conservatory:* future students are recruited from this program.

FRANCE

STAGES INTERNATIONAUX

Winter Contact Information

Centre de Danse International, Rosella Hightower
Tel: 069-306-7979
Fax: 069-306-7978
Contact: Stephane Panaras; Rosella Hightower

Summer Contact Information

Centre de Danse International, Rosella Hightower
Tel: 069-306-7979
Fax: 069-306-7978
Contact: Stephane Panaras, Rosella Hightower

General

High school credit available? no. *College credit available?* no.

Services

Housing options: on-site housing.

Application Information

Program dates: 6/26-8/27. *Application deadline:* as soon as possible. *Requirements:* interview, photograph.

Audition Information

No audition fee.

Costs & Financial Aid

Financial aid available? no.

Curriculum, Students, and Faculty

Courses offered: ballet, jazz, men's class, modern dance, pas de deux, pointe, repertory, variations, dance therapy. *Specific curriculum information:* Curricula choices.

Selectivity for males: admit all who apply. *Selectivity for females:* admit all who apply.

Performance Information

Performances choreographed by: faculty, students, guests. *Number of studios (description):* 6 (pine). *Performance facilities:* theater.

Affiliations

Summer program is affiliated with a professional company: future company members are not recruited from this program; company apprentices are not recruited from this program. *Summer program is affiliated with a pre-professional company:* company apprentices are not recruited from this program. *Summer program is affiliated with a conservatory:* future students are not recruited from this program.

GREECE

GREEK DANCE AND FOLK CULTURE

Winter Contact Information

Greek Dance Theatre, 8 Scholion Street, Plaka, Athens 10558 Greece
Tel: 30-1-324-4395
Fax: 30-1-324-6921
Email: gzdence@hol.gr
Contact: Adamantia Angeli

Summer Contact Information

Greek Dances Theater, 8 Scholion Street, Plaka, Athens 10558Greece
Tel: 301-324-4395
Fax: 301-324-6921
Email: gzdence@hol.gr
Contact: Adamantia Angeli

General

Minimum age or age range: None. *Level of program:* beginning, intermediate, advanced.

High school credit available? no. *College credit available?* no.

Application Information

Program dates: summer. *Application fee:* none.

Audition Information

No audition fee.

Costs & Financial Aid

Tuition (full): $200.

Financial aid available? no.

Curriculum, Students, and Faculty

Required courses: dance history, historical dance, music, Greek dance, costuming. *Specific curriculum information:* curriculum fixed.

Selectivity for males: admit all who apply. *Selectivity for females:* admit all who apply.

Full-time faculty: 10. *Guest faculty:* 10.

HUNGARY

MAGYAR TANMUVESZETI FOISKOLA HUNGARIAN DANCE ACADEMY

Winter Contact Information
H-1372, P.O. Box 439, Budapest Hungary
Tel: 361-267-8646
Fax: 361-268-0828
Contact: Zsuzsa Szabo

Summer Contact Information
H-lo61, Andrassy ut 25, Budapest Hungary
Tel: 361-352-8443 or 844
Fax: 361-352-8443
Contact: Zsuzsa Szabo

General

Minimum age or age range: 13 to 27.

High school credit available? no. *College credit available?* no.

Services

Housing options: on-site housing.

Application Information

Program dates: 8/3-8/15. *Application deadline:* 5/31. *Application fee:* $30.

Audition Information

No audition fee.

Costs & Financial Aid

Tuition (full): $540. *Room & board:* $280.

Financial aid available? no.

Curriculum, Students, and Faculty

Required courses: ballet, jazz, pointe, repertory, Hungarian folk dance. *Specific curriculum information:* curriculum fixed.

Selectivity for males: admit all who apply. *Selectivity for females:* admit all who apply.

Renowned alumni: Victor Rona, Adel Orosz, Gabor Kevehazi, Ildiko Pongor, Katalin Csarnoy, Ivan Marko, Katalin Wolf, Katalin Hagai, Jeno LocseiI, Sandor Nemethey, Ferenc Barbay, Zoltan Solymosi, Gyorgy Szakaly, Zoltan Nagi, Jr..

Full-time faculty: 3. *Guest faculty:* 3.

Performance Information

Performances choreographed by: faculty, open class. *Number of studios (description):* 8 (9 m. x 12 m. PVC, 18 m. x 12 m., 11.5 m. x 11.5 m.).

Affiliations

Summer program is affiliated with a conservatory: future students are recruited from this program.

Additional Comments

Tuition rates valid in 1997, for 1998 might be changed due to inflation. And there are additional fees for travel pass for local transport and culture activities.

IRELAND

BLAS INTERNATIONAL SUMMER SCHOOL OF IRISH TRADITIONAL MUSIC AND DANCE

Winter Contact Information
Irish World Music Centre, University of Limerick, Ireland
Tel: 353-61-202565
Fax: 353-61-202589
Email: Sandra.Joyce@ul.ie
Contact: Sandra Joyce

Summer Contact Information
Irish World Music Centre, University of Limerick, Ireland
Tel: 353-61-202565
Fax: 353-61-202589
Email: Sandra.Joyce@ul.ie
Contact: Sandra Joyce

General

Minimum age or age range: 16 and up. *Level of program:* beginning, intermediate, advanced.

High school credit available? yes. *College credit available?* yes.

Services

Housing options: on-site housing.

Application Information

Program dates: July. *Application deadline:* June. *Application fee:* none. *Enrollment full by:* June. *Acceptance notification:* as soon as possible.

Audition Information

No audition fee. Accompanist provided, cassette player available, CD player available.

Dress requirements: no.

Costs & Financial Aid

Financial aid available? no.

Curriculum, Students, and Faculty

Courses offered: dance history, music, Irish: traditional dance, Irish: sean nos (old style), Irish: step dance, Irish: contemporary step dance, Irish: set (group) dance, Irish: ceili (group) dance. *Specific curriculum information:* Curricula choices.

Selectivity for males: admit all who apply. *Selectivity for females:* admit all who apply.

Full-time faculty: 1. *Guest faculty:* 12. *List of some faculty and their affiliations:* Dr. Catherine Foley, University of Limerick

Performance Information

Performance opportunities and frequency: Informal showings; daily. *Performances choreographed by:* faculty, students, guests, *Number of studios (description):* 3 (varies wooden, varies wooden, varies wooden). *Performance facilities:* concert hall, many other performance venues.

Affiliations

Summer program is affiliated with other program(s): future students are often recruited from this program.

ITALY

URBINO DANCE STUDY ABROAD PROGRAM

Winter Contact Information

Office of International Education, HAB 33 SUNY—The College at New Paltz, New Paltz NY 12561
Tel: 914-257-3125
Fax: 914-257-3125
Email: international@new paltz.edu
Contact: Joan Fever or Lynn Barr

Summer Contact Information

University of Urbino, Italy
Email: international@new paltz.edu
Contact: Joan Fever or Lynn Barr

General

Minimum age or age range: 18.

High school credit available? no. *College credit available?* yes.

Application Information

Program dates: 7/1-7/30. *Application deadline:* 4/15. *Application fee:* $25. *Enrollment full by:* 4/15. *Requirements:* recommendation, photograph. *Acceptance notification:* upon receipt of completed forms.

Audition Information

No audition fee.

Costs & Financial Aid

Tuition (full): $414. *Room & board:* $600.

Financial aid available? Yes. *Students receiving financial aid:* 3%. *Procedure for applying for financial aid:* apply at home school, not all schools offer aid for a program through another school.

Curriculum, Students, and Faculty

Courses offered: Graham-based modern dance, movement techniques, performance arts, Spanish. *Specific curriculum information:* curriculum fixed.

Selectivity for males: most admitted, but not all. *Selectivity for females:* most admitted, but not all.

Renowned alumni: Anne Marie Zanchetti, Paul Sanasrdo Company; Morris Gaines, Philadanco Company; Ricardo Viviani, Weimar Tanztheatre.

Full-time faculty: 1. *Guest faculty:* 2. *List of some faculty:* Lynn Barr.

Performance Information

Performances choreographed by: faculty, guests. *Number of studios (description):* 1 (45' x 65' gym floor). *Performance facilities:* 16th century facility with natural lighting.

Affiliations

Summer program is affiliated with a professional company: future company members are often recruited from this program; company apprentices are often recruited from this program. *Summer program is affiliated with a conservatory:* future students are not recruited from this program.

11

SUMMER PROGRAM PROFILES—DRAMA

CALIFORNIA

AMERICAN ACADEMY OF DRAMATIC ARTS

Contact Information
2250 Paloma Street, Pasadena CA 91107
Tel: 818-798-0777

AMERICAN CONSERVATORY THEATER SUMMER TRAINING CONGRESS

Winter Contact Information
American Conservatory Theater, 30 Grant Avenue, San Francisco CA 94108-5800
Tel: 415-439-2350
Fax: 415- 834-3326
Contact: Bruce Williams

Summer Contact Information
American Conservatory Theater,
30 Grant Avenue, San Francisco CA 94105800
Tel: 415- 439-2350
Fax: 415-834-3326
Contact: Bruce Williams

General

Total enrollment: 135. *Minimum age or age range:* 19 and older. *Level of program:* intermediate, advanced.

High school credit available? no. *College credit available?* yes.

Services

Housing options: off-campus housing.

Application Information

Requirements: essay, recommendation, photo. *Program dates:* mid June-late August. *Application deadline:* 5/1. *Application fee:* $60. *Enrollment full by:* 5/1. *Acceptance notification:* mid May.

Audition Information

Audition required: live, on-site. *Audition fee:* $60. *Special dress requirements:* casual.

Audition evaluation criteria: We are auditioning to create groups of students from diverse backgrounds and with different levels of training and ability.

Costs & Financial Aid

Tuition (full): $2,750.

Financial aid available? partial scholarship. *Students receiving financial aid:* 18%. *Procedure for applying for financial aid:* Contact the financial aid office for scholarship application (415-439-2411).

Curriculum, Students, and Faculty

Offered courses: acting, Alexander technique, audition preparation, improvisation, master classes, movement, singing, speech, vocal technique, multicultural theater. Curricula choices.

Selectivity for males: approximately 60% admitted. *Selectivity for females:* approximately 60% admitted.

Renowned alumni: Winona Ryder, Annette Bening, Denzel Washigton, Benjamin Bratt, Delroy Lindo.

Full-time faculty: 22. *Guest faculty:* 5.

Performance Information

Performance opportunities and frequency: 1. *Specific performance opportunities:* in-house performance of final scenes. *Performance casting:* placement interview/audition during orientation week. *Performances by visiting artists?* yes. *Recent guests:* Phillip Walker.

Rehearsal facilities and hours: evenings, weekends, modern studios located on the top four floors of a nine story downtown building. *Performance facilities:* Hastings Studio, small, flexible black box performance space.

Affiliations

Summer program is affiliated with other program(s): future students are recruited from the program.

PROFESSIONAL SCHOOL FOR THE ARTS SUMMER CONSERVATORY

Winter Contact Information
1321 Sartori Avenue, Torrance CA 90501
Tel: 310-328-7664
Fax: 310-782-2072
Email: lisamatsko@worldnet.att.net
Contact: Lisa Matsko Hamilton

Summer Contact Information
1321 Sartori Avenue, Torrance CA 90501
Tel: 310-328-7664
Fax: 310-782-2072
Email: lisamatsko@worldnet.att.net
Contact: Lisa Matsko Hamilton

General

Total enrollment: 75-100. *Minimum age or age range:* 10 to 18. *Level of program:* beginning, intermediate, advanced.

High school credit available? no. *College credit available?* no.

Housing options: none. This is a day program.

Application Information

Program dates: late June to early August. *Enrollment full by:* 6/1.

Audition Information

No audition fee.

Costs & Financial Aid

Financial aid available? full scholarship, partial scholarship. *Students receiving financial aid:* 5-8. *Procedure for applying for financial aid:* request application, live, on-site audition.

Curriculum, Students, and Faculty

Offered courses: acting, dance, improvisation, master classes, musical theater, singing, music theory, seminar on the business of music. Curricula choices.

Selectivity for males: admit all who apply. *Selectivity for females:* admit all who apply.

Renowned alumni: Ai Goeku, Scott Watanabe, Holly Bosil.

Full-time faculty: 8. *Guest faculty:* 8. *List of some faculty and their affiliations:* Mark Erson, Chris Zirbel.

Performance Information

Performance opportunities and frequency: 1 per program. *Specific performance opportunities:* mock audition showcase at the end of the program. *Performances by visiting artists?* no. *Recent guests:* Comedy Sportz™; Irv Kimber, CLO South Bay Cities; Jon Engstrom.

Rehearsal facilities and hours: 2 large studios, open 1:00 pm-10:00 pm. *Performance facilities:* on-site stage.

Additional Comments

The Professional School for the Arts takes pride in training the triple-threat performer. Equal emphasis is given to acting, dancing, singing, and music theater.

STELLA ADLER ACADEMY OF ACTING, SUMMER SESSION

Winter Contact Information

6773 Hollywood Boulevard, Hollywood CA 90028
Tel: 213-465-4446
Fax: 213-469-6049
Email: stelladler@aol.com
Contact: Irene Gilbert

Summer Contact Information

6773 Hollywood Boulevard, Hollywood CA 90028
Tel: 213-465-4446
Fax: 213-469-6049
Email: stelladler@aol.com
Contact: Irene Gilbert

General

Total enrollment: 100. *Level of program:* beginning, intermediate, advanced.

High school credit available? no. *College credit available?* no.

Services

Housing options: off-campus housing.

Requirements: interview, photo.

Audition Information

No audition fee.

Costs & Financial Aid

Tuition (full): $1,650.

Financial aid available? partial scholarship. *Students receiving financial aid:* 5%. *Procedure for applying for financial aid:* interview.

Curriculum, Students, and Faculty

Offered courses: acting, audition preparation, directing, improvisation, movement, musical theater, speech, stage combat, Shakespeare, vocal technique, Chekhov. Curricula choices.

Selectivity for males: admit all who apply. *Selectivity for females:* admit all who apply.

Renowned alumni: Marlon Brando, Melanie Griffith, Robert DeNiro.

Full-time faculty: 9. *List of some faculty and their affiliations:* Irene Gilbert, Stella Adler Theater; Margie Bowman.

Performance Information

Specific performance opportunities: culmination of the program is play production. *Recent guests:* Ken Howard, John Randolph.

Rehearsal facilities and hours: scheduled at the Academy. *Performance facilities:* 67-seat Stella Adler Studio Theater.

DISTRICT OF COLUMBIA

CLASSICAL ACTING WORKSHOP, SUMMER

Winter Contact Information
301 East Capitol Street SE, Washington DC 20003-3808
Tel: 202-547-3230 ext. 3108
Fax: 202-547-0226
Email: Ed@shakespearedc.org
Contact: Felicia Wilson

Summer Contact Information
301 East Capitol Street SE, Washington DC 20003-3808
Tel: 202-547-3230 ext. 3108
Fax: 202-547-0226
Email: Ed@shakespearedc.org
Contact: Felicia Wilson

General
Total enrollment: 32. *Minimum age or age range:* 16 and older, mostly college students. *Level of program:* intermediate, advanced.

Services
Housing options: Shakespeare Theater actor housing, program housing usually limited to 10-12 students.

Application Information
Requirements: interview, recommendation, photo. *Application fee:* $25. *Enrollment full by:* 6/1. *Acceptance notification:* 5/26.

Audition Information
Audition required: live, video, on-site, off-site. *Audition fee:* $25. *Special dress requirements:* varies.

Audition evaluation criteria: commitment, openness, clarity of acting choices, good speech.

Costs & Financial Aid
Tuition (full): $2,000. *Room:* $500.

Financial aid available? partial scholarship. *Students receiving financial aid:* 10%. *Procedure for applying for financial aid:* send written request.

Curriculum, Students, and Faculty
Offered courses: acting, Alexander technique, audition preparation, master classes, movement, speech, stage combat, text analysis, vocal technique. Curriculum fixed.

Selectivity for males: approximately 60% admitted. *Selectivity for females:* approximately 60% admitted.

Full-time faculty: 8. *Guest faculty:* 2. *List of some faculty and their affiliations:* Michael Kahn, Shakespeare Theater; Philip Goodwin, Shakespeare Theater; Sarah Felder, NYU Tisch School of the Arts.

Performance Information
Performance opportunities and frequency: 1. *Specific performance opportunities:* final performance project at the Shakespeare Theater. *Performance casting:* at the discretion of the director. *Performances by visiting artists?* no. *Recent guests:* Mark Redanty, Bauman-Hiller New York

Rehearsal facilities and hours: Shakespeare Theater rehearsal hall, classes, 9:00 am-5:00 pm, rehearsals, .6:00 pm-10:00 pm. *Performance facilities:* 449-seat Shakespeare Theater.

ILLINOIS

ACTING AS A CRAFT

Winter Contact Information
Chicago Actors Studio, Box 10941, Chicago IL 60610-0941
Tel: 773-645-0222
Fax: 773-271-2045
Contact: Edward Dennis Fogell

Summer Contact Information
Chicago Actors Studio, Box 10941, Chicago IL 60610-0941
Tel: 773-645-0222
Fax: 773-645-0040
Contact: Edward Dennis Fogell

General
Minimum age or age range: 12 to 60. *Level of program:* beginning, intermediate, advanced..

High school credit available? no. *College credit available?* yes.

Housing options: none. This is a day program.

Application Information
Requirements: interview. *Program dates:* 4/15-9/15. *Application deadline:* 4/14-7/15. *Enrollment full by:* 7/15. *Acceptance notification:* 5 days after interview.

Audition Information
No audition fee.

Audition evaluation criteria: average intelligence, strong desire to be dedicated to studies and interest in making the performing and dramatic arts a lifelong career, not a hobby.

Costs & Financial Aid
Tuition (individual): $240.

Financial aid available? partial scholarship. *Students receiving financial aid:* 25%. *Procedure for applying for financial aid:* application.

Curriculum, Students, and Faculty

Offered courses: acting, audition preparation, directing, improvisation, master classes, movement, musical theater, scene study, speech, stagecraft, Stanislavski exercises, Shakespeare, vocal technique, industrial film technique, marketing skills, cold reading, Michael Achontloff technique, on-camera techniques, trade show, commercial techniques, characterization, film technique. Curricula choices.

Selectivity for males: approximately 33% admitted. *Selectivity for females:* approximately 33% admitted.

Renowned alumni: Lois Nettelton, J.J. Johnson, Bill Campbell, Virginia Madsen, Robert Yourk, Tom Bosley, Tim Conway, Edward Dennis, Mike Nassaum, Geraldine Page.

Full-time faculty: 8. *Guest faculty:* 2.

Performance Information

Performance opportunities and frequency: quarterly. *Specific performance opportunities:* student performance showcases. *Performance casting:* by faculty. *Performances by visiting artists?* yes. *Recent guests:* Michael Nestbaum, Bill Cambell, Virginia Madsen, Edward Dennis.

Rehearsal facilities and hours: in-house rehearsal rooms, open 24 hours. *Performance facilities:* program's 250-seat, in-house theater.

Affiliations

Summer program is affiliated with other program(s): future students are recruited from the program.

Additional Comments

This school is a spin-off of the Ted Liss School of Drama, Chicago, IL. We also have an affiliate in San Diego, CA, The Screen Actors Academy.

ACTORS WORKSHOP

Winter Contact Information
1350 North Wells, #A300, Chicago IL 60610
Tel: 312-337-6602
Fax: 312- 337-6604
Contact: Michael Colucci

Summer Contact Information
1350 North Wells, #A300, Chicago IL 60610
Tel: 312-337-6602
Fax: 312-337-6604
Contact: Michael Colucci

General

Total enrollment: 24. *Minimum age or age range:* 18 to 70. *Level of program:* beginning, intermediate, advanced.

High school credit available? no. *College credit available?* no.

Application Information

Requirements: interview. *Program dates:* month by month year round.

Audition Information

No audition fee.

Costs & Financial Aid

Financial aid available? no.

Curriculum, Students, and Faculty

Offered courses: acting, audition preparation, vocal technique. Curriculum fixed.

Selectivity for males: approximately 60% admitted. *Selectivity for females:* approximately 60% admitted.

Full-time faculty: 2.

Performance Information

Performance opportunities and frequency: 5 per year. *Specific performance opportunities:* workshop theater. *Performance casting:* ensemble for shows chosen from classes. *Performances by visiting artists?* yes.

Rehearsal facilities and hours: 20'x30' studio loft, available 5 days per week. *Performance facilities:* Victory Gardens Studio.

NORTHERN ILLINOIS UNIVERSITY THEATER ARTS CAMP

Winter Contact Information
c/o D. Booth, Office of External Programs, College of Visual & Performing Arts, Northern Illinois University, Dekalb IL 60115
Tel: 815-753-1450
Fax: 815-753-8372
Email: dbooth@niu.edu
Contact: Deborah Booth

Summer Contact Information
c/o D. Booth, Office of External Programs, College of Visual & Performing Arts, Northern Illinois University, Dekalb IL 60115
Tel: 815-753-1450
Fax: 815-753-8372
Email: dbooth@niu.edu
Contact: Deborah Booth

General
Total enrollment: 80. *Minimum age or age range:* 14 to 17. *Level of program:* beginning, intermediate, advanced.

High school credit available? no. *College credit available?* no.

Services
Housing options: on-campus hotels.

Application Information
Program dates: 1 week in July. *Application deadline:* 1 month prior to camp. *Enrollment full by:* 1 month prior to camp.

Audition Information
No audition fee.

Costs & Financial Aid
Tuition (full): $435.

Financial aid available? no. *Students receiving financial aid:* 25%. *Procedure for applying for financial aid:* external sources.

Curriculum, Students, and Faculty
Offered courses: acting, directing, improvisation, make-up, movement, musical theater, technical theater. Curriculum fixed.

Selectivity for males: admit all who apply. *Selectivity for females:* admit all who apply.

Full-time faculty: 4. *Guest faculty:* 8.

Performance Information
Performance opportunities and frequency: end of the week. *Performance casting:* auditioned. *Performances by visiting artists?* yes. *Recent guests:* local story tellers.

Rehearsal facilities and hours: 3 stages. *Performance facilities:* O'Connell Theater, main stage.

Affiliations
Summer program is affiliated with a conservatory: future students are often recruited from the program.

BELVOIR TERRACE

Winter Contact Information
101 West 79th Street, New York NY 10024
Tel: 212-580-3398
Fax: 212-579-7282
Email: BelvoirT@aol.com
Contact: Nancy, Diane Goldberg

Summer Contact Information
Lenox MA 01240
Tel: 413-637-0555
Fax: 413-637-4651
Email: BelvoirT@aol.com
Contact: Nancy, Diane Goldberg

General
Total enrollment: 200. *Minimum age or age range:* 10 to 18. *Level of program:* beginning, intermediate, advanced.

High school credit available? yes.

Services
Housing options: supervised, on-campus dorms.

Application Information
Requirements: interview, recommendation, photo. *Program dates:* late June-mid August. *Enrollment full by:* February. *Acceptance notification:* immediately.

Audition Information
Audition required: live, video. *No audition fee.*

Audition evaluation criteria: potential, interest.

Costs & Financial Aid
Tuition (full): $6,000.

Financial aid available? partial scholarship. *Students receiving financial aid:* 15%. *Procedure for applying for financial aid:* application.

Curriculum, Students, and Faculty
Offered courses: acting, audition preparation, ballet, costume design, directing, improvisation, make-up, master classes, modern dance, movement, musical theater, speech, stagecraft, tap, technical theater, voice, vocal technique, opera workshop, instrumental music. Curricula choices.

Selectivity for females: approximately 33% admitted.

Renowned alumni: Jamie Gertz, Natasaa Diaz.

Full-time faculty: 4. *Guest faculty:* 5. *List of some faculty and their affiliations:* Kim Luke, Tommy Tare, Bryce Hill.

Performance Information

Performance opportunities and frequency: more than 30 quality performances, most students perform in 3 shows straight, Shakespeare, musical. *Specific performance opportunities:* many. *Performance casting:* inclusive by class. *Performances by visiting artists?* yes. *Recent guests:* Jenny Zaks, Ann Reinleug, Marge Champion, Chip Zien.

Rehearsal facilities and hours: classes, 5 hours per day, 6 days per week. *Performance facilities:* 3 fully equipped theaters, technical shop, costume shop, dance studios, music studios, classrooms.

CAMP TACONIC

Winter Contact Information

66 Chestnut Hill Lane, Briarcliff Manor NY 10510
Tel: 914-762-2820
Fax: 914-762-4437
Email: Ctaconic@aol.com
Contact: Robert Ezrol

Summer Contact Information

770 New Windsor Road, Hinsdale MA 01235
Tel: 413-665-2717
Fax: 413-655-2707
Email: Ctaconic@aol.com
Contact: Robert Ezrol

General

Total enrollment: 250. *Level of program:* beginning, intermediate.

High school credit available? no. *College credit available?* no.

Services

Housing options: on-campus cabins.

Application Information

Requirements: interview. *Program dates:* 6/27-8/19. *Application deadline:* rolling. *Enrollment full by:* 1/1.

Audition Information

No audition fee.

Costs & Financial Aid

Tuition (full): $5,800.

Financial aid available? no.

Curriculum, Students, and Faculty

Offered courses: acting, costume design, musical theater, stagecraft, technical theater. Curricula choices.

Selectivity for males: most admitted, but not all. *Selectivity for females:* most admitted, but not all.

Full-time faculty: 14.

Performance Information

Performance casting: auditioned. *Performance facilities:* program's playhouse.

PHILLIPS ACADEMY SUMMER SESSION

Winter Contact Information

180 Main Street, Andover MA 01810
Tel: 978-749-4436
Fax: 978-749-4526
Email: Mefinger@andover.edu
Contact: Mark E. Efinger

Summer Contact Information

180 Main Street, Andover MA 01810
Tel: 978-749-4436
Fax: 974-749-4526
Email: Mefinger@andover.edu
Contact: Mark E. Efinger

General

Total enrollment: 8-15. *Minimum age or age range:* 14 to 18. *Level of program:* beginning, intermediate, advanced.

High school credit available? yes. *College credit available?* no.

Services

Housing options: on-campus dorms, boarding program.

Application Information

Requirements: interview, essay, recommendation. *Program dates:* 6/28-8/13. *Application deadline:* rolling. *Application fee:* $35. *Enrollment full by:* 6/1. *Acceptance notification:* rolling.

Audition Information

Audition required: live, video. *No audition fee. Special dress requirements:* no special outfits please.

Audition evaluation criteria: vocal and physical connection to the material.

Costs & Financial Aid

Financial aid available? full scholarship, partial scholarship. *Students receiving financial aid:* 14%. *Procedure for applying for financial aid:* call for form.

Curriculum, Students, and Faculty

Offered courses: acting. Curriculum fixed.

Selectivity for males: approximately 60% admitted. *Selectivity for females:* approximately 33% admitted.

Renowned alumni: Tyrone Burton, Phung Dong.

Full-time faculty: 4.

Performance Information

Performance opportunities and frequency: 3 play dates, 1 or 2 film dates. *Specific performance opportunities:* 1 play, 1 film. *Performance casting:* director's committee.

Rehearsal facilities and hours: black box theater, 40' x 50', available all day. *Performance facilities:* black box theater, 40' x 50'.

Additional Comments

This program has been in existence for 7 years, but last year was the initial year of the Theater Enterprise, the new format described above. The two distinguished alumni of the program, Tyrone Burton and Phung Doung, attended in the summer of 1997, following their debut in the Miramax film "Squeeze" and prior to Tyrone's casting in "Parenthood."

MICHIGAN

INTERLOCHEN ARTS CAMP

Winter Contact Information
P.O. Box 199, Interlochen MI 49643-0199
Tel: 616-276-7472
Fax: 616-276-6321
Email: admissions@interlochen.k12.mi.us
Contact: Krista Maxson

Summer Contact Information
P.O. Box 199, Interlochen MI 49643-0199
Tel: 616-276-7472
Fax: 616-276-6321
Email: admissions@interlochen.k12.mi.us
Contact: Krista Maxson

General

Total enrollment: 85. *Minimum age or age range:* 15 to 18. *Level of program:* advanced.

High school credit available? no. *College credit available?* no.

Services

Housing options: on-campus cabins.

Application Information

Program dates: 6/20-8/17. *Application deadline:* 2/15. *Application fee:* $35. *Enrollment full by:* April. *Acceptance notification:* 4/15.

Audition Information

Audition required: video. *Audition fee:* $35.

Costs & Financial Aid

Tuition (full): $3,840.

Financial aid available? partial scholarship. *Students receiving financial aid:* 27%. *Procedure for applying for financial aid:* fill out section of application, submit parent's tax forms and financial information.

Curriculum, Students, and Faculty

Offered courses: acting, Alexander technique, costume design, improvisation, make-up, movement, musical theater, playwriting, technical theater, vocal technique. Curricula choices.

Selectivity for males: approximately 60% admitted. *Selectivity for females:* approximately 33% admitted.

Renowned alumni: Mike Wallace, Tom Hulce, Sara Gilbert, Tovah Feldshuh, Rain Pryor.

Full-time faculty: 35. *Guest faculty:* 4. *List of some faculty and their affiliations:* Daniel J. Stolper, Mary Creswell, Katherine Eberle Fink, Tom Owen Mitchell, Cynthia Barrett.

Performance Information

Performance opportunities and frequency: each show is performed 4 or 5 times. *Specific performance opportunities:* musical, Shakespeare, contemporary. *Performance casting:* auditioned. *Performances by visiting artists?* yes. *Recent guests:* cast of Jesus Christ Superstar.

Rehearsal facilities and hours: some students rehearse on the set of their productions. *Performance facilities:* Corsen Auditorium, seats 1,000, Kresge, open air auditorium, seats 4,000.

WAYNE STATE UNIVERSITY DEPARTMENT OF THEATER

Winter Contact Information
Old Main Building, 4841 Cass Avenue, Suite 3225,
Detroit MI 48202
Tel: 313-577-3508
Fax: 313-577-0935
Email: theater@gopher.chem.wayne.edu
Contact: James Thomas

Summer Contact Information
Old Main Building, 4841 Cass Avenue, Suite 3225,
Detroit MI 48202
Tel: 313-577-3508
Fax: 313-577-0935
Email: theater@gopher.chem.wayne.edu
Contact: James Thomas

General
Total enrollment: 20. *Minimum age or age range:* 18 to 30.

High school credit available? no. *College credit available?* yes.

Application Information
Requirements: interview, recommendation, photo. *Program dates:* rehearsals: 6/1-6/22, performance: 6/23-7/12. *Enrollment full by:* 5/1. *Acceptance notification:* 1 week after auditions.

Audition Information
Audition required: on-site. *No audition fee. Special dress requirements:* casual.

Costs & Financial Aid
Tuition (full): $1,000.

Financial aid available? no.

Curriculum, Students, and Faculty
Curriculum fixed.

Selectivity for males: admit all who apply. *Selectivity for females:* admit all who apply.

NEW HAMPSHIRE

PHILLPS EXETER ACADEMY SUMMER SCHOOL

Winter Contact Information
Phillips Exeter Academy Summer School,
20 Main Street, Exeter NH 03833-2460
Tel: 603-778-3488
Fax: 603-778-4385
Email: peasummer@aol.com
Contact: Richard "Hobart" Hardy

Summer Contact Information
Phillips Exeter Academy Summer School,
20 Main Street, Exeter NH 03833-2460
Tel: 603-778-3488
Fax: 603-778-4385
Email: peasummer@aol.com
Contact: Richard "Hobart" Hardy

General
Total enrollment: 75. *Minimum age or age range:* 14 to 19. *Level of program:* beginning, intermediate, advanced.

High school credit available? no. *College credit available?* no.

Services
Housing options: on-campus dorms, some off-campus apartments.

Application Information
Requirements: essay, recommendation, photo. *Program dates:* 6/28-8/8. *Enrollment full by:* April.

Audition Information
No audition fee. Special dress requirements: casual.

Costs & Financial Aid
Tuition (full): $3,750.

Financial aid available? full scholarship, partial scholarship. *Procedure for applying for financial aid:* request financial aid application to be submitted with the entire application.

Curriculum, Students, and Faculty
Offered courses: acting, Alexander technique, audition preparation, costume design, directing, improvisation, make-up, movement, speech, stagecraft, technical theater, vocal technique. Curricula choices.

Selectivity for males: approximately 60% admitted. *Selectivity for females:* approximately 60% admitted.

Renowned alumni: Tod Cerveris, Michael Cerveris, Adam Arkin.

Guest faculty: 2. *List of some faculty and their affiliations:* Carol Philips, Northwestern University, Ohio State University.

Performance Information
Performance opportunities and frequency: 3 performances mainstage, 3 one act plays. *Specific performance opportunities:* workshop, 1 production. *Performance casting:* open casting. *Performances by visiting artists?* yes.

Additional Comments
We are a summer enrichment program offering approximately 100 courses, including Basic Acting, Stagecraft, Scene Study, Speechmaking, Music and Arts. The new Music Center is the centerpiece of our Performing Arts component. There is a major theater production each summer as well as class

workshops. See information in the catalog on Fisher Theater. Recent plays performed during summer school were "The Taming of the Shrew," "Once Upon a Mattress," "Jesus Christ Superstar," "Grease," "Noises Off," "Greater Tuna," and "The Night of January 16th." Guests at assemblies have included poets, actors, and jugglers.

NEW JERSEY

ACTORS TRAINING INSTITUTE

Winter Contact Information
P.O. Box 2096, 91 Monmouth Street, Red Bank NJ 07701
Tel: 908-219-0055
Contact: John Eyd

Summer Contact Information
P.O. Box 2096, 91 Monmouth Street, Red Bank NJ 07701
Tel: 908-219-0055
Contact: John Eyd

General
Minimum age or age range: 6 to 60. *Level of program:* beginning, intermediate, advanced.

Housing options: none. This is a day program.

Application Information
Requirements: interview, recommendation. *Program dates:* summer months. *Application deadline:* June.

Audition Information
Audition required: live, on-site. *No audition fee.*

Costs & Financial Aid
Financial aid available? no.

Curriculum, Students, and Faculty
Offered courses: acting, Alexander technique, audition preparation, improvisation, master classes, movement, musical theater, speech, Stanislavski exercises, monologues, vocal technique, method, foreign dialects, radio/TV voice techniques, Meisner. Curriculum fixed.

Selectivity for males: most admitted, but not all. *Selectivity for females:* most admitted, but not all.

Full-time faculty: 1. *Guest faculty:* 2.

Performance Information
Specific performance opportunities: none.

NEW JERSEY GOVERNOR'S SCHOOL OF THE ARTS

The College of New Jersey
P.O. Box 7718, Ewing NJ 08628-0718
Tel: 609-771-3114
Fax: 609-637-5128
Email: NJGSA@TCNJ.edu
Contact: William A.L. Glenn

General
Environment: suburban.

Total enrollment of institution: 89. *Degrees offered:* certificate.

Entrance Requirements
Audition required: live, audio. *Other requirements:* interview, recommendation, essay.

Costs & Aid
Types of scholarships and aid awarded: full, merit-based, institutional aid.

Services
Housing options: on-site dorms.

Support staff: dorm parent.

DRAMA

Curriculum, Students, and Faculty
Required courses: acting, audition preparation, dramaturgy, improvisation, martial arts, scene study, speech, stage combat, text analysis, verse drama, voice, acting.

Number of years required to complete program: 1 month. *Summer program available. Affiliation with a professional theater company; McCarter Theatre (Princeton, NJ) provides original scripts and guest artists, New York University and members of the Atlantic Theatre Company, George Street Playhouse (New Brunswick, NJ).*

Selectivity for males: approximately 10% admitted. *Selectivity for females:* approximately 10% admitted. *Total enrollment:* 10. *Entering class size:* 10. *Graduating class size:* 10.

Total full-time faculty: 7. *Total part-time faculty:* 7. *List of current faculty and past affiliations:* Karen Kohlhaas, Atlantic Theater Company of New York University; John Pietrowski, Playwright's Theater of New Jersey; Jack Waddell, Mark Murphy, McCarter Theater, Princeton, NJ.

Audition Information
No audition fee. Audition consists of the following: improvisation, required monologue, movement class, group warm-up, discussion. *Dress*

requirements for males: clothes that are suggestive of the character or very basic. *Dress requirements for females:* clothes that are suggestive of the character or very basic. *Repertoire that students should avoid?* using songs for monologues.

Audition evaluation criteria: vocal ability, bodily skill, perception, stage presence.

Performance Information

Performance opportunities available (frequency):, final performance for one month of study assigned.

Recent guest artists: Susan Kerner, George Street Playhouse, Evangeline Morphas.

Facilities

Rehearsal facilities and hours: black box, students rehearse in the evenings five nights. *Number of theaters on campus:* 2. *Type and capacity:* main stage 850, black box 150.

NEW YORK

ACTEEN SUMMER ACADEMY

Winter Contact Information
35 West 45th Street, New York NY 10036
Tel: 212-391-5915
Fax: 212-768-8918
Contact: Rita Litton

Summer Contact Information
35 West 45th Street, New York NY 10036
Tel: 212-391-5915
Fax: 212-768-8918
Contact: Rita Litton

General

Total enrollment: 50. *Minimum age or age range:* 13 to 20. *Level of program:* beginning, intermediate, advanced.

High school credit available? no. *College credit available?* no.

Services

Housing options: off-campus housing

Application Information

Requirements: interview, essay, recommendation, photo. *Program dates:* 7/6-7/30, 8/3-8/19. *Application deadline:* 5/1. *Application fee:* $25. *Enrollment full by:* 6/15. *Acceptance notification:* 6/1.

Audition Information

Audition required: live, video, on-site, off-site. *No audition fee. Special dress requirements:* casual, comfortable.

Audition evaluation criteria: presentation, preparation, knowledge of material, talent.

Costs & Financial Aid

Tuition (full): $1,300-$1,800

Financial aid available? no.

Curriculum, Students, and Faculty

Offered courses: acting, audition preparation, improvisation, movement, musical theater, speech, stage combat, film and performance, Shakespeare, vocal technique, script writing, soap scene study, commercial technique. Curricula choices.

Full-time faculty: 13. *Guest faculty:* 5-6.

Performance Information

Performance opportunities and frequency: daily. *Specific performance opportunities:* scene study, film theater workshops. *Performance casting:* fairly, all roles must challenge. *Performances by visiting artists?* yes. *Recent guests:* Jon Seda, Jordana Brewster, Barry Shapiro.

THE ACTORS INSTITUTE/THE ACTORS CRAFT SUMMER

Winter Contact Information
159 West 25th Street, New York NY 10016
Tel: 212-924-8888
Fax: 212-627-5045
Email: taires@concentric.net
Contact: Judy Shack

Summer Contact Information
159 West 25th Street, New York NY 10016
Tel: 212-924-8888
Fax: 212-627-5045
Email: taires@concentric.net
Contact: Judy Shack

General

Total enrollment: 10. *Minimum age or age range:* 16 to 25. *Level of program:* beginning, intermediate.

High school credit available? no. *College credit available?* no.

Application Information

Requirements: interview, essay. *Program dates:* 6/23-8/18. *Application deadline:* 6/15. *Enrollment full by:* 6/15.

Audition Information

Audition required: live, video. *No audition fee. Special dress requirements:* street clothes.

Audition evaluation criteria: preparation, understanding of character and material, flexibility in taking direction.

Costs & Financial Aid

Tuition (full): $2,000.

Financial aid available? partial scholarship. *Students receiving financial aid:* 25%. *Procedure for applying for financial aid:* Speak to executive directors.

Curriculum, Students, and Faculty

Offered courses: acting, audition preparation, improvisation, master classes, movement, musical theater, speech, vocal technique. Curriculum fixed.

Selectivity for males: approximately 33% admitted. *Selectivity for females:* approximately 33% admitted.

Renowned alumni: Ted Danson, Sigourney Weaver, Holland Taylor.

Full-time faculty: 3. *Guest faculty:* 10.

Performance Information

Performance casting: auditioned. *Performances by visiting artists?* no. *Performance facilities:* Tai Space.

AMERICAN ACADEMY OF DRAMATIC ARTS, SIX WEEK SUMMER ACTING CONSERVATORY

Winter Contact Information
120 Madison Avenue, New York NY 10016
Tel: 212-686-9244
Contact: Director of Admissions

Summer Contact Information
120 Madison Avenue, New York NY 10016
Tel: 212-686-9244
Contact: Director of Admissions

General

Total enrollment: 100. *Minimum age or age range:* 14 to 60. *Level of program:* beginning, intermediate, advanced.

High school credit available? yes. *College credit available?* yes.

Services

Housing options: Students under 18 must arrange to stay with family or friends. This is a day program.

Application Information

Requirements: interview, essay, photo. *Program dates:* early July-mid August. *Application deadline:* 5/30. *Application fee:* $35. *Enrollment full by:* 6/1. *Acceptance notification:* within 4 weeks of audition.

Audition Information

Audition required: live, on-site, off-site. *Special dress requirements:* appropriate, comfortable, professional.

Audition evaluation criteria: readiness to benefit from the program as evidenced by dramatic instinct, physical fitness, ability to relax.

Costs & Financial Aid

Tuition (full): $800.

Financial aid available? no.

Curriculum, Students, and Faculty

Offered courses: acting, make-up, mime, movement, musical theater, speech, vocal technique, fencing. Curricula choices.

Selectivity for males: approximately 60% admitted. *Selectivity for females:* approximately 60% admitted.

Renowned alumni: Robert Redford, Danny DeVito, Anne Bancroft, Jason Robards.

Performance Information

Performance opportunities and frequency: 1 per program. *Specific performance opportunities:* presentation of final scenes at end of program. *Performance casting:* in class. *Performances by visiting artists?* no. *Performance facilities:* theater.

Affiliations

Summer program is affiliated with other program(s): future students recruited from the program.

Additional Comments

The summer program is based on the approach and philosophy of the world-famous American Academy of Dramatic Arts, America's first conservatory for actors. The Academy's summer program offers the high school student an opportunity to test educational goals and the choice of a profession in an environment of professional training. The program is also offered in Pasadena California, 2550 Paloma Street, Pasadena, CA 91107. (818) 798-0777.

AMERICAN GLOBE THEATER CONSERVATORY, PLAYING SHAKESPEARE SERIES

Winter Contact Information
145 West 46th Street, New York NY 10036
Tel: 212-869-9809
Fax: 212- 869-9807
Contact: John Basil

Summer Contact Information
145 West 46th Street, New York NY 10036
Tel: 212- 869-9809
Fax: 212-869-9807
Contact: John Basil

General

Total enrollment: 32. *Minimum age or age range:* 25 to 50. *Level of program:* intermediate.

High school credit available? no. *College credit available?* no.

Housing options: none. This is a day program.

Application Information

Requirements: interview. *Program dates:* June-August. *Application deadline:* 6 weeks prior to first class. *Enrollment full by:* mid-May.

Audition Information

No audition fee. Special dress requirements: professional, neat.

Audition evaluation criteria: interview, how well an actor handles the text.

Costs & Financial Aid

Tuition (full): $375.

Financial aid available? no.

Curriculum, Students, and Faculty

Offered courses: playing Shakespeare series, speaking from the text, staging from the text, techniques in practice, monologue/audition workshop.

Selectivity for males: approximately 60% admitted. *Selectivity for females:* approximately 60% admitted.

List of some faculty and their affiliations: John Basil, American Globe Theater.

Performance Information

Specific performance opportunities: outstanding students are asked to audition for the mainstage productions done with mostly Equity Artists.

Rehearsal facilities and hours: evening (Mon-Fri), day times (Sat-Sun). *Performance facilities:* 85-seat black box theater.

Additional Comments

The Conservatory is a branch of the Theater. Classes are usually Sunday, Monday, and Tuesday evenings. Guest teachers are brought in periodically for intensive workshops.

ATLANTIC THEATER COMPANY ACTING SCHOOL

Winter Contact Information
336 West 20th Street, New York NY 10011
Tel: 212-645-8015
Fax: 212- 645-8755
Contact: Kate Blumberg

Summer Contact Information
336 West 20th Street, New York NY 10011
Tel: 212-645-8015
Fax: 212-645-8755
Contact: Kate Blumberg

General

Total enrollment: 32. *Minimum age or age range:* all ages.

High school credit available? no. *College credit available?* yes.

Services

Housing options: on-campus dorms.

Application Information

Requirements: interview. *Program dates:* 6/1-8/9. *Application fee:* $25. *Enrollment full by:* 5/15.

Audition Information

No audition fee.

Costs & Financial Aid

Tuition (full): $1,300. *Room:* $588. *Board:* $705.

Financial aid available? partial scholarship. *Students receiving financial aid:* 8%. *Procedure for applying for financial aid:* send letter of request.

Curriculum, Students, and Faculty

Offered courses: acting, Alexander technique, improvisation, master classes, movement, speech, vocal technique. Curriculum fixed.

Selectivity for males: approximately 33% admitted. *Selectivity for females:* approximately 60% admitted.

Renowned alumni: David Mamet, Williams H. Macy, Kristen Johnston, Matthew Fox, Skeet Ulrich.

Full-time faculty: 6. *Guest faculty:* 5. *List of some faculty and their affiliations:* Robert Bella, Lee Cohn, Margaret Eginton, Susan Finch, Hilary Hinckle, Felicity Huffman, Karen Kohlhass, William H. Macy, Mary McCann, Susan Milani, John Pais, Carlo Dennis Patella, Paul Urcioli.

Performance Information

Specific performance opportunities: no performances in this particular program.

Rehearsal facilities and hours: 3 large open rooms with ventilation.

Affiliations

Summer program is affiliated with other program(s): future students are often recruited from the program.

CHAUTAUQUA SUMMER SCHOOLS OF FINE AND PERFORMING ARTS

Winter Contact Information

P.O. Box 1098, Dept PR, Chautauqua NY 14722
Tel: 716-357-6233
Fax: 716-357-9014
Contact: Anne N. Jackson

Summer Contact Information

P.O. Box 1098, Department PR, Chautauqua NY 14722
Tel: 716-357-6233
Fax: 716-357-9014
Web: www.chautauqua-inst.org
Contact: Anne N. Jackson

General

Type of Institution: conservatory.

Total enrollment: 300. *Minimum age or age range:* 19 to 30. *Level of program:* advanced.

High school credit available? no. *College credit available?* yes.

Services

Housing options: on-site dorms, off-campus housing

Support staff: financial aid advisor, foreign student advisor, housing advisor, psychological counselor, resident assistant, resident nurse, student affairs officer.

Entrance Requirements

Audition required: live, audio, video. *Other requirements:*, recommendation.

Application Information

Requirements: interview, photo. *Application deadline:* 4/1. *Application fee:* $25. *Enrollment full by:* 4/30. *Acceptance notification:* after 4/1

Audition Information

Audition required: live, video, on-site, off-site. *Audition fee:* $25. *Special dress requirements:* casual but nice.

Audition evaluation criteria: subjective.

Costs & Financial Aid

Tuition (full): $1,675. *Room:* $620. *Board:* $760.

Application fee: $25. *Deposit:* $500. *Other fees:* $85 parking.

Percent of students receiving financial aid: 75%. *Types of scholarships and aid awarded:* partial, merit-based, need-based, institutional aid, reduced tuition. *Forms required for scholarships:* income asset verification. *Procedure for applying for loans:* audition and application. *Financial aid offered to international students. Percent of international students receiving scholarships:* 90%.

Curriculum, Students, and Faculty

Offered courses: acting, Alexander technique, movement, speech, vocal technique, masks. Curriculum fixed.

Selectivity for males: approximately 33% admitted. *Selectivity for females:* approximately 33% admitted.

Full-time faculty: 6.

Performance Information

Performance opportunities and frequency: 8 performances per production. *Specific performance opportunities:* four plays. *Performance casting:* auditioned. *Performances by visiting artists?* yes. *Recent guests:* Karen Grassle, Ellen McLaughlin, Pamela Payton-Wright.

Rehearsal facilities and hours: classes, 9:00 am-12:00 pm, rehearsals, 1:30 pm-10:00 pm. *Performance facilities:* theater.

CHICAGO CITY LIMITS IMPROVISATIONAL THEATRE SUMMER INTERNSHIP

Winter Contact Information

1105 First Avenue, New York NY 10021
Tel: 212-888-5233
Fax: 212-888-0810
Email: CCLComedy@aol.com
Contact: Linda Gelman

Summer Contact Information
1105 First Avenue, New York NY 10021
Tel: 212- 888-5233
Fax: 212-888-0810
Email: CCLComedy@aol.com
Contact: Linda Gelman

General
Total enrollment: 100. *Minimum age or age range:* adolescent and up. *Level of program:* beginning, intermediate, advanced.

High school credit available? yes. *College credit available?* yes.

Services
Housing options: school can help with sublets. This is a day program.

Application Information
Requirements: interview, essay, recommendation, (send if available). *Enrollment full by:* 6/1. *Acceptance notification:* 1 week prior to beginning of classes.

Audition Information
Audition required: live. *No audition fee. Special dress requirements:* comfortable but well dressed.

Audition evaluation criteria: demonstrating solid improvisation technique, the ability to work in an ensemble.

Costs & Financial Aid
Financial aid available? full scholarship, partial scholarship. *Students receiving financial aid:* 10%. *Procedure for applying for financial aid:* contact office.

Curriculum, Students, and Faculty
Offered courses: improvisation. Curricula choices.

Selectivity for males: admit all who apply. *Selectivity for females:* admit all who apply.

Full-time faculty: 6. *List of some faculty and their affiliations:* Denny Siegel, Sean Conroy, John Cameron Telfer, Joe DeGise, Sue Murray.

Performance Information
Specific performance opportunities: performance class, for advanced students, culminates in a performance in our theater. *Performance facilities:* Chicago City Limits Theater.

CIRCLE IN THE SQUARE THEATRE SCHOOL INTENSIVE (SUMMER)

Winter Contact Information
1633 Broadway, New York NY 10019
Tel: 212-307-0388
Fax: 212-307-0257
Email: circleinthesquare@juno.com
Contact: E. Colin O'Leary

Summer Contact Information
1633 Broadway, New York NY 10019
Tel: 212-307-0388
Fax: 212-307-0257
Email: circleinthesquare@juno.com
Contact: E. Colin O'Leary

General
Total enrollment: 75-100. *Level of program:* beginning, intermediate, advanced.

High school credit available? no. *College credit available?* no.

Services
Housing options: off-campus housing

Application Information
Requirements: interview, recommendation, photo. *Program dates:* July-August. *Application fee:* $25. *Enrollment full by:* 6/1. *Acceptance notification:* within three weeks of audition.

Audition Information
Audition required: live, video, on-site, off-site. *Audition fee:* $25. *Special dress requirements:* depends on material being auditioned.

Costs & Financial Aid
Tuition (full): $1,550.

Financial aid available? no.

Curriculum, Students, and Faculty
Offered courses: acting, movement, scene study, speech, vocal technique, techniques, dance for actors, singing interpretation, Shakespeare text. Curriculum fixed.

Selectivity for males: approximately 60% admitted. *Selectivity for females:* approximately 60% admitted.

Renowned alumni: Robert Picardo, Ken Olin, Linda Fiorentino, Kevin Bacon, Matthew Lillard, Michael E. Knight.

Guest faculty: 8. *List of some faculty and their affiliations:* E. Colin O'Leary, David F. Eliet, Eva Barnes, B.H. Barry, Edward Berkeley, Jaqueline Brookes, Leigh Dillon, Carol Harris, Terese

Hayden, Nora Kasarda, Alan Langdon, K.C. Ligon, Lynne Meadow, Elizabeth Parrish, John Stix, Naomi Thornton, Maria Tucci, Mina Yakim, Moni Yakim.

Performance Information

Specific performance opportunities: none.

Rehearsal facilities and hours: classrooms during class hours, 9:00 am-6:00 pm (Mon-Fri).

Affiliations

Summer program is affiliated with other program(s): future students are recruited from the program.

COLLABORATIVE ARTS PROJECT 21 (CAP21)

Winter Contact Information

18 West 18th Street, 6th Floor, New York NY 10011
Tel: 212-807-0202
Fax: 212- 807-0166
Contact: Jennifer Camp

Summer Contact Information

18 West 18th Street, 6th Floor, New York NY 10011
Tel: 212-807-0202
Fax: 212-807-0166
Contact: Jennifer Camp

General

Total enrollment: 60. *Minimum age or age range:* 18 to 29. *Level of program:* beginning, intermediate, advanced.

High school credit available? no. *College credit available?* yes.

Services

Housing options: off-campus dorms through New York University or Educational Housing Services.

Application Information

Requirements: interview, recommendation, photo. *Program dates:* first 4 weeks of July, 2 weeks in August. *Application deadline:* rolling. *Enrollment full by:* 1 week prior to summer session.

Audition Information

No audition fee.

Costs & Financial Aid

Tuition (full): $1,800.

Financial aid available? no.

Curriculum, Students, and Faculty

Offered courses: acting, Alexander technique, audition preparation, ballet, jazz, master classes, tap, vocal technique, music theory, body alignment, vocal performance, musical scene study. Curriculum fixed.

Selectivity for males: approximately 60% admitted. *Selectivity for females:* approximately 60% admitted.

Renowned alumni: Meg Gillentine, Dahiell Eaves, Frances Calma, Kelly Swaim, John Simeone, Jenn Tulsa, Dan Maceyak.

Guest faculty: 15. *List of some faculty and their affiliations:* Alix Korey, Dough Moston, Actor's Studio; Mona Allen, Larry Avancio, Evalyn Baron, Madeline Doherty, Kira Guzikova, Bruce Heath, Sharon Heller, Deborah Kampmeier, Mary Kate Law, Jeanette Miller, Lonne Moretton, Bob Rizzo, Christopher Scott, Wendy Waterman, Frederick Willard.

Performance Information

Specific performance opportunities: program is not performance oriented; six-weeks of intensive training and skill building. *Performance casting: Recent guests:* Linda Lavin, Thommie Walsh, Bill Irwin, Stephen Schwartz.

Rehearsal facilities and hours: classes, 10:00 am-6:00 pm (Mon-Fri).

Affiliations

Summer program is affiliated with other program(s): future students are never recruited from the program.

Additional Comments

CAP 21 is also the musical theater training conservatory for New York University's Tisch School of the Arts undergraduate drama program. Frank Ventura is the Artistic Director. During the school year CAP 21 works exclusively for NYU in training.

FRENCH WOODS FESTIVAL OF THE PERFORMING ARTS

Winter Contact Information

P.O. Box 770086, Coral Springs FL 33077
Tel: 800-634-1703
Fax: 954-346-7564
Email: frenchwood@aol.com
Contact: Ronald Schaefer

Summer Contact Information

RR 1 Box 228
Hancock, NY 13783
Tel: 914-887-5600
Fax: 914-887-5075
Email: frenchwood@aol.com
Contact: Ronald Schaefer

General

Total enrollment: 400. *Minimum age or age range:* 7 to 17. *Level of program:* beginning, intermediate, advanced.

High school credit available? no. *College credit available?* no.

Services

Housing options: on-campus cabins.

Application Information

Program dates: 6/25-8/24. *Application deadline:* none. *Application fee:* $30. *Enrollment full by:* March.

Audition Information

Audition not required.

Audition evaluation criteria: ability to play standard chamber music repertoire.

Costs & Financial Aid

Financial aid available? partial scholarship. *Scholarship notification:* after applying. *Students receiving financial aid:* 15%. *Procedure for applying for financial aid:* submit scholarship form.

Curriculum, Students, and Faculty

Offered courses: audition preparation, master classes, movement, musical theater. Curriculum fixed. *Program concentration:* instrumental (band, orchestra, jazz) vocal (musical theatre).

Selectivity for males: approximately 60% admitted. *Selectivity for females:* approximately 60% admitted.

Full-time faculty: 8. *List of some faculty and their affiliations:* Darrell Rosenbluth, Min Young Song; Florence Altenburger, London Symphony; David Wallace, NY Philharmonic.

Performance Information

Performance opportunities and frequency: each week. *Specific performance opportunities:* many chamber performances, some solo performances.

Rehearsal facilities and hours: cabins, outdoors. *Performance facilities:* on campus and in surrounding community concert halls.

LUCY MOSES SCHOOL SUMMER MUSICAL THEATER WORKSHOP

Winter Contact Information
129 West 67 Street, New York NY 10023
Tel: 212-501-3360
Fax: 212-874-7865
Contact: Urmila Jithoo, Sean Hartley

Summer Contact Information
129 West 67 Street, New York NY 10023
Tel: 212-501-3360
Fax: 212-874-7865
Contact: Urmila Jithoo, Sean Hartley

General

Total enrollment: 130. *Minimum age or age range:* 5 to 17. *Level of program:* beginning, intermediate, advanced.

High school credit available? no. *College credit available?* no.

Application Information

Program dates: 6/30-7/31. *Application fee:* $30. *Enrollment full by:* 4/1.

Audition Information

No audition fee.

Costs & Financial Aid

Tuition (full): $770.

Financial aid available? full scholarship, partial scholarship. *Students receiving financial aid:* 15%. *Procedure for applying for financial aid:* submit application by 3/1.

Curriculum, Students, and Faculty

Offered courses: acting, Alexander technique, movement, musical theater, speech, vocal technique. Curriculum fixed.

Selectivity for males: admit all who apply. *Selectivity for females:* admit all who apply.

Full-time faculty: 2. *Guest faculty:* 4.

Performance Information

Specific performance opportunities: 2 performances at end of session. *Performance casting:* by directors. *Performances by visiting artists?* no.

Rehearsal facilities and hours: Abraham Goodman House, 10:00 am-4:30 pm. *Performance facilities:* Merken Concert Hall.

NATIONAL SHAKESPEARE CONSERVATORY

Winter Contact Information
P.O. Box 2007, New York NY 10013
Tel: 800-472-6667
Fax: 212-717-8061
Email: shkespeare@aol.com

Summer Contact Information
P.O. Box 2007, New York NY 10013
Tel: 800-472-6667
Fax: 212-717-8061
Email: shkespeare@aol.com

General

Minimum age or age range: 17 to 50. *Level of program:* intermediate, advanced.

High school credit available? no.

Services

Housing options: on-site housing.

Application Information

Requirements: recommendation, photo. *Application deadline:* rolling. *Application fee:* $25. *Acceptance notification:* rolling.

Audition Information

Audition required: live, video, on-site, off-site. *No audition fee. Special dress requirements:* comfortable clothes.

Costs & Financial Aid

Tuition (full): $2,750.

Financial aid available? partial scholarship. *Students receiving financial aid:* 20%. *Procedure for applying for financial aid:* information about financial aid is sent with acceptances.

Curriculum, Students, and Faculty

Offered courses: acting, Alexander technique, improvisation, master classes, movement, speech, vocal technique, masks. Curriculum fixed.

Selectivity for males: approximately 60% admitted. *Selectivity for females:* approximately 60% admitted.

Renowned alumni: Annabelle Gurwitch, Park Overall, Phil Hernandez, Angela Vitale, Joe Menino, Elise Sotne, Wil Leckie, Christopher Black, Monique Vukovic, Kennedy Brown, Chris Bayes, Robert Hupp, Thomas Oppenheim, Ben Donenberg, Lane Anderson, Joanne Zipay.

Guest faculty: 6-8. *List of some faculty and their affiliations:* Pamela Hare, James Tripp, Mark Zeller, Joan Evans, Sue Lawless, Fay Simpson, Shelly Wyant, Christopher Bayes, John Kane.

Performance Information

Performance opportunities and frequency: 1. *Specific performance opportunities:* Catskill Shakespeare Performance Project, an outdoor public performance staged at the end of the program. *Performance casting:* auditioned.

Additional Comments

Established in 1974, the National Shakespeare Summer Conservatory demands commitment from the actor, and in return provides a fundamental realignment of the actor's life to the art and demands of the theater. An independent theater school, the National Shakespeare Conservatory trains and encourages its actors to develop their craft to a level to work as professional theater artists.

NEIGHBORHOOD PLAYHOUSE, THE AMERICAN MEISNER TECHNIQUE SUMMER WORKSHOP

Winter Contact Information

346 East 54th Street, New York NY 10022
Tel: 212-688-3770
Fax: 212-906-9051
Contact: H. Baldridge

Summer Contact Information

346 East 54th Street, New York NY 10022
Tel: 212-688-3770
Fax: 212-906-9051
Contact: H. Baldridge

General

Total enrollment: 75-120. *Level of program:* beginning, intermediate, advanced.

High school credit available? no. *College credit available?* no.

Application Information

Requirements: interview, recommendation, photo. *Program dates:* 6/15-7/24. *Application fee:* $15. *Enrollment full by:* 6/1.

Audition Information

Special dress requirements: casual.

Costs & Financial Aid

Tuition (full): $1,500.

Financial aid available? no.

Curriculum, Students, and Faculty

Offered courses: acting, improvisation, movement, speech. Curriculum fixed.

Renowned alumni: Leslie Nielsen, Suzanne Pleshette, Jennifer Grey, Robert Duvall, Mary Steenburgen, Wayne Rogers, Christopher Lloyd, Gregory Peck, James Caan, Diane Keaton.

List of some faculty and their affiliations: Richard Pinter, Gary Ramsey, Ron Stetson.

Performance Information

Specific performance opportunities: none.

Additional Comments

The program also offers a two-week intensive workshop, The British Classic Theater Workshop, with teachers and coaches selected from London's foremost training academies and professional theater companies. The program focuses on the appreciation and practice of classical theater and Shakespeare, which are fundamental to the actor's training for modern theater, film, and television.

PLAYWRIGHTS HORIZONS THEATER SCHOOL

Winter Contact Information
440 Lafayette Street, 3rd Floor, New York NY 10003
Tel: 212-529-8720
Fax: 212-529-8762
Email: phtschool@aol.com
Contact: Michael Lonergan

Summer Contact Information
440 Lafayette Street, 3rd Floor, New York NY 10003
Tel: 212-529-8720
Fax: 212-529-8762
Email: phtschool@aol.com
Contact: Michael Lonergan

General
Total enrollment: 25. *Level of program:* intermediate, advanced.

High school credit available? no. *College credit available?* yes.

Services
Housing options: off-campus housing.

Application Information
Requirements: essay, photo. *Program dates:* May-August. *Application deadline:* 4/15. *Application fee:* $10. *Enrollment full by:* 5/1.

Audition Information
No audition fee.

Costs & Financial Aid
Tuition (full): $1,700. *Room:* $1,000. *Board:* $500.

Financial aid available? no.

Curriculum, Students, and Faculty
Offered courses: acting, directing, master classes, movement, speech. Curricula choices.

Selectivity for males: approximately 60% admitted. *Selectivity for females:* approximately 60% admitted.

Renowned alumni: Gina Gershin, Shannon Burkett, Jessica Hecht.

Guest faculty: 6. *List of some faculty and their affiliations:* Marleen Pennison, Steven Sparugen, AEA.

Performance Information
Specific performance opportunities: final presentation. *Performance casting:* ensemble work. *Performances by visiting artists?* no.

Rehearsal facilities and hours: clean wood floors with mirrors in Greenwich Village. *Performance facilities:* program's theater, 60-seat black box, computer board, dressing rooms.

Affiliations
Summer program is affiliated with other program(s): future students are recruited from the program.

TADA! HERE WE ARE

Winter Contact Information
120 West 28th Street, New York NY 10001
Tel: 212-627-1732
Fax: 212-243-6736
Email: tada@ziplink.net
Contact: Tobe Arons Seuush

Summer Contact Information
120 West 28th Street, New York NY 10001
Tel: 212-627-1732
Fax: 212-243-6736
Email: tada@ziplink.net
Contact: Tobe Arons Seuush

General
Total enrollment: 80. *Minimum age or age range:* 8- 17. *Level of program:* beginning, intermediate, advanced.

High school credit available? no. *College credit available?* yes.

Housing options: none. This is a day program.

Application Information
Program dates: varies. *Application deadline:* none. *Enrollment full by:* week.

Audition Information
No audition fee.

Costs & Financial Aid
Financial aid available? full scholarship, partial scholarship. *Students receiving financial aid:* 20-25. *Procedure for applying for financial aid:* fill out form and speak with administration.

Curriculum, Students, and Faculty
Offered courses: acting, improvisation, movement, musical theater, technical theater, vocal technique. Curricula choices.

Selectivity for males: admit all who apply. *Selectivity for females:* admit all who apply.

Renowned alumni: Ricki Lake, Willie Hernandez, Sean Nelson, Victoria Gabrielle Platt.

Performance Information

Performances by visiting artists? no.

Rehearsal facilities and hours: 1 rehearsal room, 9:30 am-2:30 pm. *Performance facilities:* 100-seat theater.

Additional Comments

TADA! Has a week-long intensive program and a program for interns. Price, size, and enrollment requirements vary for both. Listed above is the information about the week-long program only. Contact TADA! about the intern program.

TISCH SUMMER DRAMA FOR HIGH SCHOOL STUDENTS

Winter Contact Information

721 Broadway, Room 310, New York NY 10003
Tel: 212-998-1847
Fax: 212-998-1855
Contact: Kevin Kennison

Summer Contact Information

721 Broadway, Room 310, New York NY 10003
Tel: 212-998-1847
Fax: 212-998-1855
Contact: Kevin Kennison

General

Total enrollment: 32. *Minimum age or age range:* 16-17. *Level of program:* intermediate, advanced.

High school credit available? no. *College credit available?* yes.

Services

Housing options: dormitory.

Application Information

Requirements: essay, recommendation. *Program dates:* 7/6-8/2. *Application deadline:* 4/1. *Application fee:* $35. *Enrollment full by:* 5/1. *Acceptance notification:* 5/1.

Audition Information

No audition fee.

Costs & Financial Aid

Tuition (full): $2,740. *Room & board:* $700.

Financial aid available? partial scholarship. *Students receiving financial aid:* 25%. *Procedure for applying for financial aid:* application.

Curriculum, Students, and Faculty

Offered courses: acting, audition preparation, improvisation, master classes, movement, musical theater, speech, theater history, vocal technique. Curriculum fixed.

Selectivity for males: approximately 10% admitted. *Selectivity for females:* approximately 10% admitted.

Renowned alumni: Alec Baldwin, Donna Murphy, Bridget Fonda, Skeet Ulrich, Adam Sandler, Molly Shannon, Jessica Hecht, John Leguizamo.

Full-time faculty: 12. *Guest faculty:* 6.

Performance Information

Specific performance opportunities: none. *Performances by visiting artists?* yes. *Recent guests:* Alec Baldwin, Cast of *Rent*, Cast of *Angels in America*.

Rehearsal facilities and hours: dorm has mini-theater, music and vocal rooms, dance floor in gym, study/rehearsal rooms for class preparation.

Affiliations

Summer program is affiliated with other program(s): future students are often recruited from the program.

Additional Comments

Process-oriented training program for mature and focused high school Juniors. Run as an ensemble. Full-time day classes and night/weekend trips to explore entire New York theater community, cultural events, lectures, and workshops. Four week intensive explores New York, New York University, and the cultural diversity that is the New York theater community. Training presently is at the Lee Strasberg Theater Institute, and the Collaborative Arts Project, 21 (for Musical Theater), and the Drama Department, undergraduate.

NORTH CAROLINA

NORTH CAROLINA SCHOOL OF THE ARTS

Winter Contact Information

Summer Session, P.O. Box 12189,
Winston-Salem NC 27117-2189
Tel: 910-770-3204
Fax: 910-770-3375
Contact: Bill Rainey

Summer Contact Information

Summer Session, P.O. Box 12189,
Winston-Salem NC 27117-2189
Tel: 910-770-3204
Fax: 910-770-3375
Contact: Bill Rainey

General

Total enrollment: 90. *Minimum age or age range:* 15 and up. *Level of program:* beginning, intermediate, advanced.

High school credit available? yes. *College credit available?* yes.

Services

Housing options: on-campus dorms.

Application Information

Requirements: essay, recommendation. *Program dates:* 6/21-7/24. *Application deadline:* 6/1. *Application fee:* $35. *Enrollment full by:* 5/15.

Audition Information

No audition fee.

Costs & Financial Aid

Room & board: $660.

Financial aid available? no.

Curriculum, Students, and Faculty

Offered courses: acting, improvisation, master classes, movement, speech, vocal technique. Curriculum fixed.

Selectivity for males: approximately 60% admitted. *Selectivity for females:* approximately 33% admitted.

Renowned alumni: Terence Mann, Mary Louis Parker, Tim Guinee, Richard Ellis, Matt Ashford, Joe Mantello, Gary Beach, Cassandra Creach, Joyce Rahling.

Full-time faculty: 11. *Guest faculty:* 3. *List of some faculty and their affiliations:* Lesley Hunt, Tanya Belov, State Academy School of Circus and Variety Arts in Russia; Yury Belov, Lunacharsky State University of Theater and Arts; Dikki Ellis, clown for the Big Apple Circus in New York.

Performance Information

Specific performance opportunities: none. *Performances by visiting artists?* no.

PENNSYLVANIA

PRE-COLLEGE SUMMER INSTITUTE

Winter Contact Information

The University of the Arts, 320 South Broad Street,
Philadelphia PA 19102
Tel: 215-875-3355
Fax: 215-875-3374
Email: pcuarts@netaxs.com
Contact: Erin Elman

Summer Contact Information

The University of the Arts, 320 South Broad Street,
Philadelphia PA 19102
Tel: 215-875-3355
Fax: 215-875-3374
Email: pcuarts@netaxs.com
Contact: Erin Elman

General

Total enrollment: 40. *Minimum age or age range:* 15 to 18. *Level of program:* beginning, intermediate, advanced.

High school credit available? no. *College credit available?* no.

Services

Housing options: dorm.

Application Information

Program dates: 7/7-8/1. *Application deadline:* 5/2. *Application fee:* $200. *Enrollment full by:* 5/15.

Costs & Financial Aid

Tuition (full): $1,400. *Room:* $540.

Curriculum, Students, and Faculty

Offered courses: acting, dance, movement, stage combat, voice.

Selectivity for males: most admitted, but not all. *Selectivity for females:* most admitted, but not all.

Full-time faculty: 4. *Guest faculty:* 3. *List of some faculty and their affiliations:* Johnnie Hobbs, Chuck Conwell, Academy of Vocal Arts, The Shaw Festival.

Performance Information

Performance opportunities and frequency: 1 per summer. *Specific performance opportunities:* summer showcase. *Performance casting:* ensemble featuring all program participants. *Performances by visiting artists?* no.

Rehearsal facilities and hours: 2 buildings housing myriad studios, black box theaters, professional rehearsal halls, performance space. *Performance facilities:* Arts Bank, a 200-seat performance space.

Affiliations

Summer program is affiliated with other program(s): future students are recruited from the program.

WASHINGTON

PULLMAN SUMMER PALACE

Winter Contact Information
School of Music and Theater Arts, Washington State University,
Pullman WA 99164-2432
Tel: 509-335-7447
Fax: 509-335-4255
Contact: George Caldwelll

Summer Contact Information
School of Music and Theater Arts, Washington State University,
Pullman WA 99164-2432
Tel: 509-335-7447
Fax: 509-335-4255
Contact: George Caldwell

General
Total enrollment: 15. *Minimum age or age range:* 16 to 30. *Level of program:* beginning, intermediate.

High school credit available? no. *College credit available?* yes.

Services
Housing options: off-campus local apartments.

Application Information
Requirements: recommendation, photo. *Application deadline:* April. *Enrollment full by:* April. *Acceptance notification:* 5/15.

Audition Information
Audition required: video. *No audition fee. Special dress requirements:* street clothes.

Audition evaluation criteria: background, skill, recommendations.

Costs & Financial Aid
Financial aid available? no.

Curriculum, Students, and Faculty
Offered courses: acting, production. Curriculum fixed.

Selectivity for males: approximately 60% admitted. *Selectivity for females:* approximately 33% admitted.

Full-time faculty: 2. *Guest faculty:* 1.

Performance Information
Performance opportunities and frequency: 6 performances each session. *Specific performance opportunities:* 2 comedies, 1 musical. *Performance casting:* auditioned. *Performances by visiting artists?* no.

Rehearsal facilities and hours: black box, rehearsal and performance, 9:30 am-12:30 pm, 1:30 pm-4:30 pm, 7:00 pm-10:00 pm, 6 days a week, June and July. *Performance facilities:* 400-seat thrust/proscenium.

GREAT BRITAIN

SHAKESPEAREAN ACTING

Winter Contact Information
The Church, 2 Effie Road, Fulham, London SW6ITB England
Tel: 171-736-0121
Fax: 171-371-5624
Contact: Brian Parsonage Kelly

Summer Contact Information
The Church, 2 Effie Road, Fulham, London SW6ITB England
Tel: 171-736-0121
Fax: 171-371-5624
Contact: Brian Parsonage Kelly

General
Total enrollment: 20. *Minimum age or age range:* 16 to 50.

High school credit available? yes. *College credit available?* yes.

Services
Housing options: off-campus housing.

Application Information
Requirements: recommendation, photo. *Program dates:* 4 weeks in July, August. *Application deadline:* June. *Enrollment full by:* June. *Acceptance notification:* 2 weeks after receipt of application.

Audition Information
No audition fee.

Costs & Financial Aid
Tuition (full): $850.

Financial aid available? no.

Curriculum, Students, and Faculty
Offered courses: acting, improvisation, master classes, movement, speech, stage combat, theater history, vocal technique. Curriculum fixed.

Selectivity for males: admit all who apply. *Selectivity for females:* admit all who apply.

Guest faculty: 6.

Performance Information
Performance opportunities and frequency: 1 per year. *Specific performance opportunities:* at the

end of the program. *Performance casting:* on merit. *Performances by visiting artists?* no.

Rehearsal facilities and hours: own building, 30 hours. *Performance facilities:* theater.

Additional Comments

The school is 16 years old and in that time has become internationally renowned for the quality of our classical training, particularly in the graduate programs and summer schools.

SUMMER COURSE IN ACTING AND THEATRE

Winter Contact Information

30 Clareville Street, London SW75AP England
Tel: 011-171-370-4154
Fax: 011-171-373-5639
Contact: Maren Dalemann

Summer Contact Information

30 Clareville Street, London SW75AP England
Tel: 011-171-370-4154
Fax: 011-171-373-5639
Contact: Maren Dalemann

General

Total enrollment: 60. *Minimum age or age range:* 17 to 36. *Level of program:* beginning, intermediate, advanced.

High school credit available? no. *College credit available?* no.

Housing options: none. This is a day program.

Application Information

Requirements: recommendation, photo. *Program dates:* mid July-mid August. *Application deadline:* 6/1. *Application fee:* $100. *Enrollment full by:* 6/1. *Acceptance notification:* upon receipt of application.

Audition Information

No audition fee.

Costs & Financial Aid

Tuition (full): $814.

Financial aid available? no.

Curriculum, Students, and Faculty

Offered courses: acting, audition preparation, improvisation, make-up, movement, rehearsal and performance, speech, vocal technique. Curriculum fixed.

Selectivity for males: most admitted, but not all. *Selectivity for females:* most admitted, but not all.

Performance Information

Specific performance opportunities: last day of course. *Performance casting:* by the director. *Performances by visiting artists?* no.

Rehearsal facilities and hours: rehearsal studios, 2 hours per day. *Performance facilities:* Academy's theater.

12

SUMMER PROGRAM PROFILES—MUSIC

ALABAMA

TROY STATE UNIVERSITY SUMMER BAND CAMP AND DIRECTOR'S CLINIC

Winter Contact Information
Long Hall, Troy AL 36082
Tel: 334-670-3281
Fax: 334-670-3858
Email: rford@newfrontiermedia.com
Contact: Ralph Ford

Summer Contact Information
Long Hall - TSU, Troy AL 36082
Tel: 334-670-3281 Fax: 334-670-3858
Email: rford@newfrontiermedia.com
Contact: Ralph Ford

General

Total enrollment: 550. *Level of program:* beginning, intermediate, advanced.

High school credit available? no. *College credit available?* no.

Services

Housing options: On-site housing, off-campus housing.

Application Information

Program dates: 7/1-7/18. *Application deadline:* none. *Application fee:* $30. *Enrollment full by:* first day of class.

Audition Information

Audition not required.

Audition evaluation criteria: intermediate/advanced, musical proficiency.

Costs & Financial Aid

Tuition (full): $850. *Lessons:* $250. *Room:* $230.

Financial aid available? full scholarship, partial scholarship. *Scholarship notification:* acceptance date. *Students receiving financial aid:* 30%. *Procedure for applying for financial aid:* Written application.

Curriculum, Students, and Faculty

Offered courses: master classes. Curriculum fixed. *Program concentration:* Instrumental performance, large and small ensembles.

Selectivity for males: approximately 33% admitted. *Selectivity for females:* approximately 33% admitted.

List of some faculty: Milt Hintou, Ed Shaughnessy, Jacki McLeau, Ray Brown.

Performance Information

Performance opportunities and frequency: 1 per week. *Specific performance opportunities:* 2 student performances. *Performances by visiting artists?* yes. *Recent guests:* Jackie McLeau, Ray Brown, Benny Green.

Rehearsal facilities and hours: state-of-the-art facilities in small liberal arts college, open daily 8:00 am-11:00 pm. *Performance facilities:* campus recital hall, theater.

Affiliations

Summer program is affiliated with a conservatory: future students are recruited from the program.

ALASKA

UNIVERSITY OF ALASKA SUMMER FINE ARTS CAMP

Winter Contact Information
Music Department, Fairbanks AK 99775-5660
Tel: 907-474-6837
Fax: 907-474-6420
Email: fymus@aurora.alaska.edu
Contact: Dr. Theodore DeCorso

Summer Contact Information
Music Department, Fairbanks AK 99775-5660
Tel: 907-474-6837 Fax: 907-474-6420
Email: fymus@aurora.alaska.edu
Contact: Dr. Theodore DeCorso

General

Total enrollment: 225. *Level of program:* intermediate, advanced.

High school credit available? no. *College credit available?* yes.

Services

Housing options: on-campus dorms.

Application Information

Requirements: recommendation. *Program dates:* 6/19-7/18. *Application deadline:* 6/12. *Application fee:* $100. *Enrollment full by:* 6/1. *Acceptance notification:* upon receipt of completed application.

Audition Information

Audition not required.

Costs & Financial Aid

Tuition (full): $695. *Lessons:* $40 per hour. *Room & board:* $695.

Financial aid available? full scholarship, partial scholarship. *Scholarship notification:* 4/15. *Students receiving financial aid:* 10%. *Procedure for applying for financial aid:* Submit application, tape, and recommendations.

Curriculum, Students, and Faculty

Offered courses: acting for singers, arranging, band, chamber ensemble, chorus, combination, composition, conducting, creative writing, dance, diction, improvisation, jazz bands, master classes, movement, music theory, musical theater, orchestra, private lessons, theater. Curricula choices. *Program concentration:* orchestras, wind ensemble, choirs, jazz solo, chamber performance.

Selectivity for males: most admitted, but not all. *Selectivity for females:* most admitted, but not all.

Renowned alumni: Bryan Dickerson, Glen Miller Band; Richard Tremanello.

Full-time faculty: 8. *Guest faculty:* 1.

Performance Information

Performance opportunities and frequency: 11 mainstage concerts/recitals, 12 noon recitals. *Orchestra seating:* by audition. *Seat rotation:* not rotated. *Performance casting:* auditioned. *Performances by visiting artists?* yes. *Recent guests:* Marylin McDonald, Juilliard, Oberlin Conservatory; Dan Goble, University of Western Connecticut; Linda Larson, New York City Opera Touring Company. *Performance facilities:* mainstage in the Charles David Concert Hall, seats 950, noon recitals in Great Hall, seats 150.

Affiliations

Summer program is affiliated with other program(s): future students recruited from the program.

ARIZONA

RAFAEL MENDEZ BRASS INSTITUTE

Winter Contact Information

c/o Summit Brass, P.O. Box 26850, Tempe AZ 85285
Tel: 602-496-9486
Fax: 602-965-8233
Email: david.hickman@ASU.edu
Contact: David Hickman

Summer Contact Information

c/o Summit Brass,
P.O. Box 26850, Tempe AZ 85285
Tel: 602-496-9486
Fax: 602-965-8233
Email: david.hickman@ASU.edu
Contact: David Hickman

General

Total enrollment: 200. *Minimum age or age range:* 15 and up. *Level of program:* intermediate, advanced.

High school credit available? no. *College credit available?* yes.

Services

Housing options: on-campus dorms, hotels.

Application Information

Program dates: mid-June (1 week). *Application deadline:* 6/1. *Application fee:* $35. *Enrollment full by:* 6/1. *Acceptance notification:* immediately.

Audition Information

Audition not required. Audition includes: 15-minute cassette tape of applicant's choice of music.

Costs & Financial Aid

Lessons: $90 per hour. *Room:* $150.

Financial aid available? partial scholarship. *Scholarship notification:* 6/1. *Students receiving financial aid:* 10%. *Procedure for applying for financial aid:* Application letter with tape and materials required.

Curriculum, Students, and Faculty

Offered courses: audition preparation, chamber ensemble, coaching, master classes, private lessons, seminar on the business of music. Curriculum fixed. *Program concentration:* brass only.

Selectivity for males: admit all who apply. *Selectivity for females:* admit all who apply.

Performance Information

Performance opportunities and frequency: 2 per week. *Specific performance opportunities:* each student performs twice in ensemble. *Performances by visiting artists?* yes. *Recent guests:* Summit Brass, Allen Vizzutti, Doc Severinsen, Harvey Phillips, Canadian Brass.

Rehearsal facilities and hours: major music conservatory, varies each year. *Performance facilities:* major recital halls at conservatory or university.

Affiliations

Summer program is affiliated with other program(s): future students recruited from the program.

CALIFORNIA SUMMER MUSIC

Winter Contact Information
236 West Portal Avenue, No.104, San Francisco CA 94127
Tel: 415-753-8920
Fax: 415-753-8934
Email: csm@dnai.com
Contact: May Kurka

Summer Contact Information
Robert Louis Stevenson School
P.O. Box 657, Pebble Beach CA 93953
Tel: 415-753-8920
Contact: May Kurka

General
Total enrollment: 65. *Minimum age or age range:* 12 to 22. *Level of program:* advanced.

High school credit available? no. *College credit available?* no.

Services
Housing options: on-campus dorms.

Application Information
Requirements: interview, recommendation. *Program dates:* late June to mid July (3-4 weeks). *Application deadline:* first week of April. *Application fee:* $50. *Enrollment full by:* May. *Acceptance notification:* late May.

Audition Information
Audition fee: $50. *Audition includes:* 2 contrasting movements from standard current solo repertoire, 1 piece with piano. *Accompanist provided?* no.

Audition evaluation criteria: solid intonation and rhythm, good tone, facility, musicality.

Costs & Financial Aid
Tuition (full): $1,900.

Financial aid available? partial scholarship. *Procedure for applying for financial aid:* Submit CSM form and income tax return, 2 recommendations with application notification.

Curriculum, Students, and Faculty
Offered courses: coaching, composition, master classes, music history, music theory, other, private lessons. Curricula choices. *Program concentration:* Lessons and chamber music, composition for strings and piano.

Selectivity for males: approximately 60% admitted. *Selectivity for females:* approximately 60% admitted.

Full-time faculty: 11. *Guest faculty:* 5. *List of some faculty and their affiliations:* Susan Bates, San Francisco Conservatory; Wendy Sharp, Yale University; Andy Luchansky, Sacramento State University.

Performance Information
Performance opportunities and frequency: at least 3 performances by each student. *Specific performance opportunities:* solo and chamber music recitals, master classes. *Performances by visiting artists?* yes. *Recent guests:* Rostislov Dubrinsky, Luba Edlina, Donald Weilenstein.

Rehearsal facilities: Fine Arts Complex. *Performance facilities:* auditorium—450 seats, chapel—200 seats.

Additional Comments
Irene Sharp, Artistic Director, Susan Bates, Program Director, and May Kurka, Administrative Director head the list of local and national artist teachers who founded the program in 1995. CSM students are coached by gifted master teachers from the Bay Area, across the nation, and abroad.

HOLY NAME COLLEGE SUMMER SUZUKI INSTITUTE: PIANO & RECORDER

Winter Contact Information
Music Department, 3500 Mountain Boulevard, Oakland CA 94619
Tel: 510-436-1330
Fax: 510-436-1438
Contact: Robin Lee

Summer Contact Information
Holy Names College Music Department, 3500 Mountain Boulevard, Oakland CA 94619
Tel: 510-436-1330
Fax: 510-436-1438
Contact: Robin Lee

General
Minimum age or age range: 18 and up. *Level of program:* advanced.

High school credit available? yes. *College credit available?* yes.

Services
Housing options: On-campus residence hall.

Application Information
Program dates: last 3 weeks of July. *Application deadline:* 6/14. *Application fee:* $75. *Enrollment full by:* 7/1. *Acceptance notification:* 7/1.

Audition Information

Audition required. No audition fee. Audition includes: specified Suzuki repertoire. *Accompanist provided?* no.

Audition evaluation criteria: fluency, accuracy, musicality.

Costs & Financial Aid

Financial aid available? no.

Curriculum, Students, and Faculty

Offered courses: general piano pedagogy, master classes, piano literature, repertory, Suzuki piano/recorder pedagody, general piano pedogogy course and literature courses change every summer. Curricula choices. *Program concentration:* Piano and recorder Suzuki pedagogy.

Selectivity for males: approximately 33% admitted. *Selectivity for females:* approximately 33% admitted.

Full-time faculty: 1. *Guest faculty:* 4. *List of some faculty*: Carline Fraser, Doris Koppelman, Beverly Fest, Doris Harrel, Katherine White.

Performance Information

Specific performance opportunities: repertoire performance is required of all participants.

Rehearsal facilities and hours: 8 practice rooms. *Performance facilities:* 125-seat theater.

IDYLLWILD ARTS SUMMER PROGRAM

Winter Contact Information

P.O. Box 38, Idyllwild CA 92549
Tel: 909-659-2171, ext. 365
Fax: 909-659-5463
Contact: Diane Dennis

Summer Contact Information

P.O. Box 38, Idyllwild CA 92549
Tel: 909-659-2171, 365
Fax: 909-659-5463
Contact: Diane Dennis

General

Total enrollment: 600. *Minimum age or age range:* 9 to mid-20's. *Level of program:* intermediate, advanced.

High school credit available? yes. *College credit available?* no.

Services

Housing options: on-campus dorms.

Application Information

Requirements: recommendation. *Program dates:* 7/6-8/17 (2-week sessions). *Application deadline:* rolling. *Application fee:* $25. *Enrollment full by:* piano—March, others—May. *Acceptance notification:* within two weeks after tape has been received.

Audition Information

Audition required. No audition fee. Audition includes: 3-5 selections, contrasting styles.

Costs & Financial Aid

Tuition (full): $1,090.

Financial aid available? full scholarship, partial scholarship. *Scholarship notification:* First-come first-served, mid-April. *Students receiving financial aid:* 30%. *Procedure for applying for financial aid:* submit tax return, scholarship application, and recommendations.

Curriculum, Students, and Faculty

Offered courses: audition preparation, band, chamber ensemble, chorus, coaching, diction, foreign language study, master classes, movement, music theory, musical theater, orchestra, private lessons, repertory. *Specific curriculum information*: students are strongly encouraged but not required to take private lessons. Curriculum fixed. *Program concentration:* band, chamber music, choir, jazz, orchestra, piano.

Selectivity for males: admit all who apply. *Selectivity for females:* admit all who apply.

Renowned alumni: Michael Tilson Thomas, San Francisco Symphony.

Full-time faculty: 100. *List of some faculty and their affiliations:* Larry Livingston, USC; Igor Gruppman, London Symphony Orchestra; Alice Schoenfeld, Eleanor Schoenfeld, USC; Doris Lederer, Clyde Shaw, Audubon Quartet; Richard Giangiulio, Dallas Symphony, Mark Zinger, DePaul University.

Performance Information

Specific performance opportunities: 1 large ensemble performance per week, 2-3 recitals weekly. *Orchestra seating:* by first day audition. *Seat rotation:* young orchestra rotates daily.

Rehearsal facilities and hours: 30 practice rooms, all with pianos, under 18 open—7:00 am-10:00 pm, over 18 open—7:30 am-12:00 am. *Performance facilities:* main concert hall on campus, seats 300.

Affiliations

Summer program is affiliated with other program(s): future students recruited from the program.

Additional Comments

For piano and chamber music, entrance is highly selective. Open enrollment for all other programs.

MUSIC ACADEMY OF THE WEST SUMMER SCHOOL AND FESTIVAL

Winter Contact Information

1070 Fairway Road, Santa Barbara CA 93108-2899
Tel: 805-969-4726
Fax: 805-969-0686
Email: sbmaw@callamer.com
Contact: Diane Eagle, Carleen Landes

Summer Contact Information

1070 Fairway Road, Santa Barbara CA 93108-2899
Tel: 805-969-4726
Fax: 805-969-0686
Email: sbmaw@callamer.com
Contact: Diane Eagle, Carleen Landes

General

Total enrollment: 132. *Minimum age or age range:* 16 to 30. *Level of program:* advanced.

High school credit available? no. *College credit available?* yes.

Services

Housing options: on-campus dorms.

Application Information

Requirements: recommendation. *Program dates:* 6/23-8/16 (8 weeks). *Application deadline:* 1/15-3/15 (varies by department). *Application fee:* $40. *Enrollment full by:* 2/15.

Audition Information

Audition required. Audition fee: $40. *Audition includes:* several contrasting pieces, varies by department. *Accompanist provided?* yes.

Costs & Financial Aid

Financial aid available? full scholarship.

Curriculum, Students, and Faculty

Offered courses: acting for singers, audition preparation, chamber ensemble, coaching, diction, foreign language study, master classes, movement, musical theater, opera workshop, orchestra, private lessons, repertory, seminar on the business of music. Curriculum fixed. *Program concentration:* Chamber, orchestra, opera, art song.

Selectivity for males: approximately 33% admitted. *Selectivity for females:* approximately 33% admitted.

Renowned alumni: Thomas Hampson, Grace Bumbry, Marilyn Horne, Jennifer Larmore.

Full-time faculty: 23. *Guest faculty:* 9. *List of some faculty:* Nico Abondolo, Randall Behr, Timothy Day, Bruce Donnell, Marilyn Horne, Linda Jones, Jerome Lowenthal.

Performance Information

Specific performance opportunities: weekly master classes, 7 recitals, 4 orchestra performances, 2 operas, numerous chamber ensembles. *Seat rotation:* rotated by faculty for each concert and each work for winds/brass. *Performance casting:* Vocal audition committee. *Performances by visiting artists?* yes. *Recent guests:* Thomas Hampson, Benita Valente.

Rehearsal facilities and hours: private room assigned, pianists, 5 hous per day, instruments, 2 hours per day, vocal as needed. *Performance facilities:* Abravanel Hall on Music Academy campus, Lobero Theatre in downtown Santa Barbara, Lehman Hall on Music Academy campus.

A NEW APPROACH TO VIOLIN PLAYING

Winter Contact Information

Music Department, Pacific Union College, 100 Howell Mountain Road, Angwin CA 94508-9797
Tel: 707-965-6201
Fax: 707-965-6390
Email: lwheeler@puc.edu
Contact: Ivylyn Traver

Summer Contact Information

Music Department, Pacific Union College, 100 Howell Mountain Road, Angwin CA 94508-9797
Tel: 707-965-6201
Fax: 707 965 6390
Email: lwheeler@puc.edu
Contact: Ivylyn Traver

General

Minimum age or age range: 6 to 90. *Level of program:* beginning, intermediate, advanced.

College credit available? yes.

Services

Housing options: on-campus dorms, off-campus motels in St. Helena or Napa.

Application Information

Program dates: July to August. *Application deadline:* 1 week prior to classes. *Enrollment full by:* 7/15.

Audition Information
Audition not required.

Costs & Financial Aid
Lessons: $135 per hour.

Financial aid available? no.

Curriculum, Students, and Faculty
Offered courses: coaching, private lessons. Curriculum fixed. *Program concentration:* Relaxation techniques for violin playing.

Selectivity for males: most admitted, but not all.

Guest faculty: 1. *List of some faculty and their affiliations:* Kato Havas, Ysaye Foundation.

Performance Information
Performance opportunities and frequency: 1 performance. *Specific performance opportunities:* ensemble performance during workshop. *Orchestra seating:* informally by participants. *Performances by visiting artists?* no.

Rehearsal facilities and hours: 15 practice rooms, concert hall, 3 lecture rooms, 7:00 am-11:00 pm. *Performance facilities:* concert hall, 495 seats.

PIATIGORSKY SEMINAR FOR CELLISTS

Winter Contact Information
USC Music School, Mus 311, Los Angeles CA 90089-0851
Tel: 213-740-3131
Fax: 213-740-3217
Contact: Barrie Tucker

Summer Contact Information
USC Music School, Mus 311, Los Angeles CA 90089-0851
Tel: 213-740-3131
Fax: 213-740-3217
Contact: Barrie Tucker

General
Total enrollment: 12. *Minimum age or age range:* up to 26. *Level of program:* advanced.

High school credit available? no. *College credit available?* no.

Services
Housing options: on-campus dorms.

Application Information
Program dates: second week every other June. *Application deadline:* 2/1. *Enrollment full by:* 2/1.

Audition Information
Audition required; live, on-site, off-site. *No audition fee. Audition includes:* 20 minutes of required repertoire. *Accompanist provided?* no.

Curriculum, Students, and Faculty
Offered courses: chamber ensemble, master classes, repertory. Curriculum fixed.

Selectivity for males: approximately 10% admitted. *Selectivity for females:* approximately 10% admitted.

Renowned alumni: Nathaniel Rosen.

Full-time faculty: 3. *List of some faculty:* Denis Brott, David Geringas, Bernard Greenhouse.

Performance Information
Specific performance opportunities: 3 recital. *Recent guests:* Claus Adam, Erling Bengtsson, Raya Garbousova, Louis Garcia-Renart, Gary Hoffman, Yo-Yo Ma, Andre Navarra, William Pleeth, Paul Tobias.

Rehearsal facilities and hours: USC music studios, 8:00 am-11:00 pm. *Performance facilities:* USC Music Hall.

Affiliations
Summer program is affiliated with other program(s): future students recruited from the program.

THE SAN FRANCISCO EARLY MUSIC SOCIETY SUMMER WORKSHOPS

Winter Contact Information
P.O. Box 9313, Berkeley CA 94709
Tel: 510-549-9799
Fax: 510-540-6558
Email: AGSugden@aol.com
Contact: Alisa Gould Sugden

Summer Contact Information
P.O. Box 9313, Berkeley CA 94709
Tel: 511-549-9799
Fax: 511-540-6558
Email: AGSugden@aol.com
Contact: Alisa Gould Sugden

General
Minimum age or age range: 14 and up. *Level of program*: intermediate, advanced.

High school credit available? no. *College credit available?* yes.

Services
Housing options: on-campus dorms, off-campus motel.

Application Information

Program dates: 6/21-7/8 (four different weeks). *Application deadline:* tuition discount if apply by 5/1. *Application fee:* $50.

Audition Information

Audition not required.

Costs & Financial Aid

Tuition (full): $320. *Room:* $370.

Financial aid available? full scholarship, partial scholarship. *Scholarship notification:* May-June. *Students receiving financial aid:* 2%. *Procedure for applying for financial aid:* contact director.

Curriculum, Students, and Faculty

Offered courses: chamber ensemble, chorus, coaching, conducting, dance, Feldenkreis, master classes, orchestra, recorder, repertory. Curricula choices. *Program concentration:* Early music: baroque (6/21-7/4), renaissance/medieval (7/5-7/11), recorder (7/12-7/18).

Selectivity for males: most admitted, but not all. *Selectivity for females:* most admitted, but not all.

List of some faculty: Marion Verbruggen, Mary Springfels, Arthur Haas.

Performance Information

Performance opportunities and frequency: 1 per week. *Specific performance opportunities:* end of workshop performances.

Rehearsal facilities and hours: Angelico Hall and accompanying practice rooms also in dorm building, normal practice hours subject to any music department needs. *Performance facilities:* Angelico Hall, recital hall, Meadowlands Assembly Hall, informal, small.

SEQUOIA CHAMBER MUSIC WORKSHOP

Winter Contact Information
Department of Music, Arcata CA 95521
Tel: 707-826-3529
Fax: 707-826-3528
Email: dclasquin@humboldt.edu
Contact: Dr. Deborah Clasqin

Summer Contact Information
Department of Music, Arcata CA 95521
Tel: 708-826-3529
Fax: 708-826-3528
Email: dclasquin@humboldt.edu
Contact: Dr. Deborah Clasqin

General

Minimum age or age range: 12 to 20. *Level of program:* intermediate, advanced.

High school credit available? no. *College credit available?* no.

Services

Housing options: on-campus dorms.

Application Information

Requirements: recommendation. *Program dates:* last 2 weeks of June. *Application deadline:* 4/15. *Application fee:* $32. *Enrollment full by:* 3/15. *Acceptance notification:* 5/1.

Audition Information

Audition required; video. *No audition fee. Audition includes:* 2 solo scales. *Accompanist provided?* no.

Audition evaluation criteria: intonation, rhythm, note accuracy, style, level of repertoire, years of study, age of student.

Costs & Financial Aid

Tuition (full): $245. *Room:* $250.

Financial aid available? full scholarship, partial scholarship. *Scholarship notification:* 5/20. *Students receiving financial aid:* 40%. *Procedure for applying for financial aid:* Submit tax return.

Curriculum, Students, and Faculty

Offered courses: chamber ensemble, master classes, music theory, repertory. Curricula choices. *Program concentration:* Chamber music.

Selectivity for males: approximately 33% admitted. *Selectivity for females:* approximately 33% admitted.

Renowned alumni: Karen Bentley, David Filner, James Freeman.

Full-time faculty: 13. *List of some faculty*: Deborah Clasquin, Carol Jacobson, Terrie Baune, John Brecher, David Filner, Nicholas Marlowe, Cindy Moyer, Laurette Goldberg, Lisa Byrnes, Armand Ambrosini, Tom Nugent, Jerri Taylor, William Harrington.

Performance Information

Performance opportunities and frequency: 5 concerts in 6 days. *Specific performance opportunities:* daily evening concerts. *Seat rotation:* chamber assignments change daily.

Rehearsal facilities and hours: 25 practice rooms, 20 classrooms, most with grand pianos, 300-seat recital hall. *Performance facilities:* Fulkerson Recital Hall on Humboldt State University campus.

Affiliations

Summer program is affiliated with other program(s): future students recruited from the program.

STANFORD JAZZ WORKSHOP JAZZ CAMP AND JAZZ RESIDENCY

Winter Contact Information

Jazz Camp and Jazz Residency, Box 11291, Stanford CA 94309
Tel: 415-327-0778
Fax: 650-725-2686
Email: sjazzw@netcom.com
Contact: Jim Nadel

Summer Contact Information

Jazz Camp and Jazz Residency, Box 11291, Stanford CA 94309
Tel: 650-723-0816
Fax: 650- 725-2686
Email: sjazzw@netcom.com
Contact: Jim Nadel

General

Total enrollment: 550. *Minimum age or age range:* 16 to 80 (Jazz Residency), 12 to 17 (Jazz Camp). *Level of program:* intermediate, advanced.

High school credit available? no. *College credit available?* no.

Services

Housing options: on-campus dorms.

Application Information

Requirements: recommendation. *Program dates:* 7/19-8/8. *Application deadline:* 6/15. *Application fee:* $50. *Enrollment full by:* 6/1. *Acceptance notification:* 6/1-6/30.

Audition Information

Audition required. No audition fee. Accompanist provided? no.

Costs & Financial Aid

Tuition (individual): $470. *Room:* $340.

Financial aid available? full scholarship, partial scholarship. *Scholarship notification:* 6/1-6/30. *Students receiving financial aid:* 30%. *Procedure for applying for financial aid:* Submit scholarship application form.

Curriculum, Students, and Faculty

Offered courses: band, master classes, music history, music theory, private lessons, repertory, small ensemble. Curricula choices. *Program concentration:* jazz: theory, master classes, tradition.

Selectivity for males: approximately 60% admitted. *Selectivity for females:* approximately 60% admitted.

Renowned alumni: Joshua Redman, Larry Grenadier, Phil Grenadier, Benny Green.

Full-time faculty: 50. *Guest faculty:* 75. *List of some faculty:* Ray Brown, Jim Cullum, Peter Apfelbaum, Geoff Keezar, Conrad Herwig, Louie Bellson, Madeline Eastman.

Performance Information

Specific performance opportunities: student concerts on Friday of each week. *Performances by visiting artists?* yes. *Recent guests:* Joe Williams, Ray Brown, McCoy Tyner, Horace Silver, Joe Henderson, James Moody.

Rehearsal facilities: Stanford University Music Department. *Performance facilities:* Couthell Concert Hall, Garham Performing Arts Center.

SUMMER MUSIC WEST

Winter Contact Information

San Francisco Conservatory of Music, San Francisco CA 94122
Tel: 415-759-3454
Fax: 415-759-3499
Contact: Laura Reynolds Chrisp

Summer Contact Information

San Francisco Conservatory of Music, San Francisco CA 94122
Tel: 415-759-3409
Fax: 415-759-3499
Contact: Laura Reynolds Chrisp

General

Total enrollment: 100. *Minimum age or age range:* 8 to 20. *Level of program:* beginning, intermediate, advanced.

High school credit available? no. *College credit available?* no.

Services

Housing options: most students commute or arrange for housing themselves.

Application Information

Program dates: June-July. *Application deadline:* voice 3/15, other 6/1. *Application fee:* $100. *Enrollment full by:* 6/1. *Acceptance notification:* within 2 weeks of application deadline.

Audition Information

Audition required. *Audition fee:* $50. *Audition includes:* 2 contrasting pieces, sight-reading. *Accompanist provided?* no.

Costs & Financial Aid

Tuition (full): $745. *Lessons:* private lessons on one instrument included in tuition for music majors, additional instruments and non-music majors are $75.

Financial aid available? no.

Curriculum, Students, and Faculty

Offered courses: master classes, movement, musical theater. Curriculum fixed. *Program concentration:* chamber music, composition, opera, musical theater.

Selectivity for males: most admitted, but not all. *Selectivity for females:* most admitted, but not all.

Renowned alumni: Jonah Hooper, Atlanta Ballet; David B. Thompson, Barcelona Symphony.

Full-time faculty: 5. *List of some faculty:* David Applebaum, R. Garry Glenn, Frank Owenby, Carol Smiarowski, Bill Jones, Jerry Orr, Sandy Scozzari, Kee Strong, Ken Strong, Ed Wagenseller, Mary Wooten, Louis Applebaum, David Thomas, Dr. Michelle Roueche, Dr. Raymond Gotko, Dorothy Knowles.

Performance Information

Specific performance opportunities: music night, talent show with various performances, final program. *Performances by visiting artists?* no.

Rehearsal facilities and hours: college music building with private and class practice rooms, 8:00 am-11:00 pm. *Performance facilities:* Pearce Auditorium, large pipe organ and Steinway Concert grand.

Affiliations

Summer program is affiliated with a conservatory: future students are recruited from the program.

THE STACY SEMINAR
THE THOMAS STACY INTERNATIONAL ENGLISH HORN SEMINAR

Winter Contact Information

292 Granville Court, Marietta GA 30064
Tel: 770-427-8196
Fax: 770-427-8196
Contact: Barbera Secrist

Summer Contact Information

The Hidden Valley Music Seminars
P.O. Box 116, Carmel Valley CA 93924
Tel: 408-659-3155
Fax: 408-659-7442
Contact: Barbera Secrist

General

Minimum age or age range: 14 and up. *Level of program:* advanced.

High school credit available? no. *College credit available?* no.

Services

Housing options: On-site housing.

Application Information

Program dates: 8/8-8/14. *Application deadline:* 7/15.

Audition Information

Audition not required.

Costs & Financial Aid

Financial aid available? partial scholarship. *Scholarship notification:* March-April. *Students receiving financial aid:* 30%. *Procedure for applying for financial aid:* Request information from office.

Curriculum, Students, and Faculty

Offered courses: audition preparation, master classes. Curriculum fixed.

Selectivity for males: approximately 60% admitted. *Selectivity for females:* approximately 60% admitted.

Performance Information

Specific performance opportunities: orchestra and every chamber group perform weekly. *Seat rotation:* rotated.

Rehearsal facilities and hours: every student is assigned to a practice room. *Performance facilities:* concert hall on the grounds.

COLORADO

ASPEN MUSIC FESTIVAL AND SCHOOL

Winter Contact Information

2 Music School Road, Aspen CO 81611
Tel: 970-925-3254
Fax: 970-920-1643
Email: school@aspenmusic.org
Contact: Matt Tomatz

Summer Contact Information

2 Music School Road, Aspen CO 81611
Tel: 970-925-3262
Fax: 970-920-1643
Email: school@aspenmusic.org
Contact: Matt Tomatz

General

Total enrollment: 931. *Minimum age or age range:* 15 to 35. *Level of program:* advanced.

High school credit available? no. *College credit available?* yes.

Services

Housing options: on-campus dorms, off-campus paid lodging with family, hotels, rooms for rent.

Application Information

Requirements: 2 letters of recommendation. *Program dates:* 6/15-8/16. *Application deadline:* 2/27. *Enrollment full by:* deadline. *Acceptance notification:* 3/15

Audition Information

Audition required; live. *No audition fee. Audition includes:* generally 5 minutes in length to demonstrate advancement in a variety of musical styles. *Accompanist provided?* yes.

Costs & Financial Aid

Tuition (full): $2,100. *Lessons:* extra lessons $55. *Room & board:* $2,250.

Financial aid available? full scholarship, partial scholarship. *Scholarship notification:* ASAP. *Students receiving financial aid:* 75%. *Procedure for applying for financial aid:* Submit application form, audition in some cases.

Curriculum, Students, and Faculty

Offered courses: acting for singers, Alexander technique, audio recording institute, audition preparation, chamber ensemble, chorus, coaching, competition series, center for advanced quartet studies, composition studies program, concerto, conducting, diction, master classes, movement, music theory, opera workshop, orchestra, private lessons, repertory, seminar on the business of music. Curricula choices. *Program concentration:* all instruments, voice, 5 orchestras, opera, compostion, conducting, audio recording, quartet studies.

Selectivity for males: approximately 60% admitted.

Renowned alumni: Dawn Upshaw, Nadja Salerno-Sonnenberg, Robert McDuffie, Orli Shaham, Gil Shaham, Sarah Chang, James Conlon, Midori.

Full-time faculty: 150. *Guest faculty:* 25. *List of some faculty and their affiliations:* Many are prominent faculty members of the Juilliard School, Eastman School of Music, New England Conservatory, Cincinnati College Conservatory of Music.

Performance Information

Performance opportunities and frequency: more than 1 event daily for 9 weeks. *Specific performance opportunities:* many young artist concerts, master classes, 5 orchestras. *Orchestra seating:* by audition on arrival. *Seat rotation:* rotated weekly. *Performances by visiting artists?* yes. *Recent guests:* Sarah Chang, Nadja Salerno-Sonnenberg, Robert Levin, Edgar Meyer, Gil Shaham, Orli Shaham, David Finckel, Wo Han, Jon Nakamatsu, Stephen Hough, Bela Fleck.

Rehearsal facilities and hours: on-site practice rooms, 8:00 am-11:00 pm daily, larger on-site ensemble rooms. *Performance facilities:* Bayer-Benedict Music Tent, Wheeler Opera House, Harris Concert Hall, various local churches, and on campus.

NATIONAL REPERTORY ORCHESTRA

Winter Contact Information

P.O. Box 6336, Breckenridge CO 80424
Tel: 970-453-9142
Fax: 970-453-9143
Email: nro@csn.net
Contact: Susanna Tomann

Summer Contact Information

P.O. Box 6336, Breckenridge CO 80424
Tel: 970-453-9143
Fax: 970-453-9144
Email: nro@csn.net
Contact: Susanna Tomann

General

Total enrollment: 87. *Minimum age or age range:* 18 to 28. *Level of program:* advanced.

High school credit available? no. *College credit available?* no.

Services

Housing options: on-campus shared condo.

Application Information

Program dates: 6/27-8/15. *Application deadline:* 2 weeks prior to city audition date. *Application fee:* $35. *Enrollment full by:* March. *Acceptance notification:* late May

Audition Information

Audition not required. Audition fee: $45. *Audition includes:* approximately 10 minutes of playing. *Accompanist provided?* no.

Costs & Financial Aid

Financial aid available? partial scholarship. *Scholarship notification:* 4/10.

Curriculum, Students, and Faculty

Offered courses: master classes. Curriculum fixed. *Program concentration:* Classical, orchestral, master classes, coaching.

Selectivity for males: approximately 10% admitted. *Selectivity for females:* approximately 10% admitted.

Renowned alumni: Marin Alsop, Misha Amory, Martha Curtis, Carmen Dominic, Theodore Kuchar, Diane Monroe, Mitchell Stern, Mary Ellen Woodside.

List of some faculty: Charles Castleman.

Performance Information

Performance opportunities and frequency: 2 each week, including 1 off-site. *Specific performance opportunities:* each participant performs 2 complete string quartets and one 15-minute solo work learned at the program. *Performances by visiting artists?* yes. *Recent guests:* Amernet, Emerson, New Zealand String Quartets.

Rehearsal facilities and hours: practice in own room, at least 3 hours solo daily, at least 3 hours quartet daily. *Performance facilities*: Bucknell Hall.

CONNECTICUT

FAIRFIELD UNIVERSITY SUMMER JAZZ CAMP

Winter Contact Information

School of Continuing Education, North Benson Road, Fairfield CT 06430
Tel: 203-254-4220
Fax: 203-254-4106
Email: fair1.fairfield.edu
Contact: Janice Miles Dunn

Summer Contact Information

School of Continuing Education, Fairfield CT 06430
Tel: 203-254-4221
Fax: 203-254-4107
Email: fair1.fairfield.edu
Contact: Janice Miles Dunn

General

Total enrollment: 25.

High school credit available? no. *College credit available?* no.

Services

Housing options: on-campus dorms, off-campus option to commute.

Audition Information

Audition not required.

Costs & Financial Aid

Tuition (full): $625.

Financial aid available? no.

Curriculum, Students, and Faculty

Curriculum fixed.

Selectivity for males: most admitted, but not all. *Selectivity for females:* most admitted, but not all.

Full-time faculty: 2. *Guest faculty:* 4.

Performance Information

Specific performance opportunities: jazz camp weekend with a recital/concert.

Rehearsal facilities: Quick Center. *Performance facilities:* final concert held in the Levee (student social hall).

NATIONAL GUITAR SUMMER WORKSHOP

Winter Contact Information

P.O. Box 222, Lakeside CT 06758
Tel: 860-567-3736
Fax: 860-567-0347
Email: ngsw@esslink.com
Contact: Paula Dutton

Summer Contact Information

P.O. Box 222, Lakeside CT 06758
Tel: 800-234-6479Fax: 860-567-0347
Email: ngsw@esslink.com
Contact: Paula Dutton

General

Minimum age or age range: 11 to 85. *Level of program:* beginning, intermediate, advanced.

High school credit available? no. *College credit available?* yes.

Services

Housing options: on-campus dorms.

Application Information

Program dates: June-August. *Application deadline:* rolling. *Application fee:* $15. *Enrollment full by:* mid-June. *Acceptance notification:* rolling.

Audition Information

Audition not required.

Costs & Financial Aid

Tuition (full): $575.

Financial aid available? partial scholarship. *Scholarship notification:* 6/10. *Students receiving financial aid:* 7%. *Procedure for applying for financial aid:* Send in an application, tape, and a personal letter of recommendation.

Curriculum, Students, and Faculty
Offered courses: master classes, music theory. Curricula choices. *Program concentration:* Guitar, bass, drums, vocals-rock, blues, jazz, acoustic, fingerstyle, classical.

Selectivity for males: admit all who apply. *Selectivity for females:* admit all who apply.

Renowned alumni: Trey Anastwain, Mike Gordon.

Full-time faculty: 35. *Guest faculty:* 30. *List of some faculty and their affiliations:* Mark Dziuba, SUNY; Susan Mazer, Hartt Conservatory; Amanda Monaco, New School; Tom Dempsey, SUNY.

Performance Information
Performance opportunities and frequency: at least 2 opportunities to perform each week. *Specific performance opportunities:* on- and off-campus performances. *Performances by visiting artists?* yes. *Recent guests:* Manuel Barrueco, John Slofield, Pierre Bergeron, Ronnie Earl, LAGQ, Tal Farlow, Martin Simpson, John Jorgenson, Pat Martino. *Performance facilities:* on-site auditorium, off site venue (bar, coffee house, etc.).

FLORIDA

HONORS CHAMBER WINDS FLORIDA STATE UNIVERSITY SUMMER MUSIC CAMPS

Winter Contact Information
School of Music, Tallahassee FL 32306-1180
Tel: 850-644-2508
Fax: 850-644-6100
Email: griordan@mailer.fsu.edu
Contact: George T. Riordan

Summer Contact Information
School of Music, Tallahassee FL 32306-1180
Tel: 850-644-2508
Fax: 850-644-6100
Email: griordan@mailer.fsu.edu
Contact: George T. Riordan

General
Total enrollment: 15. *Minimum age or age range:* 14 to 18. *Level of program:* advanced. *High school credit available?* no. *College credit available?* no.

Services
Housing options: on-campus dorms.

Application Information
Program dates: June, July (2 weeks). *Application deadline:* mid April. *Enrollment full by:* audition deadline. *Acceptance notification:* 5/5.

Audition Information
Audition required: live, on-site. *No audition fee. Audition includes:* 2 pieces in contrasting styles, 2 scales. *Accompanist provided?* no.

Audition evaluation criteria: proficiency on instrument, orchestral experience.

Costs & Financial Aid
Tuition (full): $100.

Financial aid available? partial scholarship.

Curriculum, Students, and Faculty
Curriculum fixed. *Program concentration:* small wind ensemble, orchestra, quintets.

Selectivity for males: approximately 60% admitted. *Selectivity for females:* approximately 60% admitted.

Performance Information
Specific performance opportunities: 1 solo and 1 chamber in-camp concert, 1 finale orchestral concert. *Orchestra seating:* by audition. *Performances by visiting artists?* yes. *Recent guests:* Dr. Elmer Thomas, Cincinatti Conservatory of Music; Dr. Louis Bergonzi, Eastman School of Music; Mr. Li Fang-fang, China Armed Police Band; Mr. Qu Chunquan, Singapore Chinese Orchestra.

Rehearsal hours: 9:00 am-9:00 pm. *Performance facilities:* assembly hall at camp site, final concerts at concert hall managed by the Provisional Urban and Regional Councils.

HONORS PIANO CAMP FLORIDA STATE UNIVERSITY SUMMER MUSIC CAMPS

Winter Contact Information
School of Music, Tallahassee FL 32306-1180
Tel: 850-644-2508
Fax: 850-644-6100
Email: griordan@mailer.fsu.edu
Contact: George T. Riordan

Summer Contact Information
School of Music, Tallahassee FL 32306-1180
Tel: 850-644-2508
Fax: 850-644-6100
Email: griordan@mailer.fsu.edu
Contact: George T. Riordan

General
Total enrollment: 30.

Services
Housing options: on-campus dorms.

Audition Information
Audition required: live, on-site. *Audition includes:* 2 pieces in contrasting styles. *Accompanist provided?* no.

Curriculum, Students, and Faculty
Offered courses: audition preparation, master classes. *Program concentration:* piano performance, literature, theory.

Performance Information
Performance opportunities and frequency: weekly. *Specific performance opportunities:* master classes, recitals, orchestra, opera, chamber ensembles. *Seat rotation:* rotated by faculty for each concert and each work for winds/brass. *Performances by visiting artists?* yes. *Recent guests:* Thomas Hampson, Benita Valente.

SARASOTA MUSIC FESTIVAL

Winter Contact Information
709 North Tamiami Trail, Sarasota FL 34236
Tel: 941-952-9634
Fax: 941-953-3059
Contact: Travor Cramer

Summer Contact Information
709 North Tamiami Trail, Sarasota FL 34236
Tel: 941-952-9634
Fax: 941-953-3059
Contact: Travor Cramer

General
Total enrollment: 100.

Services
Housing options: optional on-campus housing at the Hyatt/Sarasota.

Audition Information
Audition not required. Audition includes: varies. *Accompanist provided?* no.

Curriculum, Students, and Faculty
Offered courses: audition preparation, master classes, movement. *Program concentration:* chamber music, master classes.

Performance Information
Specific performance opportunities: weekly orchestral and chamber performances. *Orchestra seating:* by faculty. *Seat rotation:* rotated for every work.

Rehearsal facilities and hours: 35 individual studios, 6 ensemble studios, one concert hall, 8:00 am-12:00 am.

STETSON UNIVERSITY DOUBLE REED WORKSHOP

Winter Contact Information
Double Reed Workshop, Unit 8399, Deland FL 32720
Tel: 904-822-8981
Ashley Heintzen, Ann Adams

Summer Contact Information
Double Reed Workshop, Unit 8399, Deland FL 32720
Tel: 904-822-8981
Contact: Ashley Heintzen, Ann Adams.

General
Level of program: intermediate.

High school credit available? no. *College credit available?* no.

Services
Housing options: on-campus dorms.

Application Information
Program dates: first, second week of June. *Application deadline:* 6/1. *Application fee:* $25.

Audition Information
Audition not required.

Costs & Financial Aid
Tuition (full): $280.

Financial aid available? partial scholarship. *Students receiving financial aid:* 5%.

Curriculum, Students, and Faculty
Offered courses: audition preparation, band, chamber ensemble, master classes, reed making. Curriculum fixed. *Program concentration:* Ensembles, master class, reed making, double reed band.

Selectivity for males: admit all who apply. *Selectivity for females:* admit all who apply.

Full-time faculty: 2. *Guest faculty:* 2. *List of some faculty and their affiliations:* Ashley Heintzen, Ann Adams, Stetson University.

Performance Information

Specific performance opportunities: faculty performance, student performance at the end of the week.

Rehearsal facilities and hours: Stetson University School of Music facilities, 8:00 am-10:00 pm. *Performance facilities:* Elizabeth Hall.

Affiliations

Summer program is affiliated with other program(s): future students recruited from the program.

STRING ORCHESTRA CAMP FLORIDA STATE UNIVERSITY SUMMER MUSIC CAMPS

Winter Contact Information

School of Music, Tallahassee FL 32306-1180
Tel: 850-644-1180
Fax: 850-644-6100
Email: griordan@mailer.fsu.edu
Contact: George T. Riordan

Summer Contact Information

School of Music, Tallahassee FL 32306-1180
Tel: 850-644-1181
Fax: 850-644-6101
Email: griordan@mailer.fsu.edu
Contact: George T. Riordan

General

Total enrollment: 111. *Minimum age or age range:* 12 to 18. *Level of program:* intermediate, advanced.

High school credit available? no. *College credit available?* no.

Services

Housing options: on-site housing.

Application Information

Program dates: June, July (2 weeks). *Application deadline:* 3 weeks prior to camp (early June).

Audition Information

Audition not required.

Costs & Financial Aid

Tuition (full): $700.

Financial aid available? no.

Curriculum, Students, and Faculty

Offered courses: audition preparation, master classes. Curriculum fixed. *Program concentration:* string, orchestral, and chamber music.

Selectivity for males: approximately 33% admitted. *Selectivity for females:* approximately 33% admitted.

Renowned alumni: Chip Owne, Alan Smith, Peter de Wit, Chris Weait, Stefan Weidenauer.

Performance Information

Specific performance opportunities: sometimes play with church ensemble for fun.

Rehearsal hours: 9:00 am-12:00 pm, 2:00 pm-5:00 pm, and evenings with playing.

Affiliations

Summer program is affiliated with a conservatory: future students are recruited from the program.

Additional Comments

Other Programs Offered: Honors Choral Ensemble Camp, Junior High Concert Band Camp, Marching Band Leadership Camp, Double Reed Workshop, Elementary String Orchestra Camp, Honors Vocal Camp, Symphonic Band Camp.

SYMPHONIC BAND CAMP FLORIDA STATE UNIVERSITY SUMMER MUSIC CAMPS

Winter Contact Information

School of Music, Tallahassee FL 32306-1180
Tel: 850-644-2508
Fax: 850-644-6100
Email: griordan@mailer.fsu.edu
Contact: George T. Riordan

Summer Contact Information

School of Music, Tallahassee FL 32306-1180
Tel: 850-644-2509
Fax: 850-644-6101
Email: griordan@mailer.fsu.edu
Contact: George T. Riordan

General

Total enrollment: 262. *Minimum age or age range:* 14 to 18. *Level of program:* intermediate, advanced.

High school credit available? no. *College credit available?* no.

Services

Housing options: on-campus dorms.

Application Information

Program dates: June, July (2 weeks). *Application deadline:* 3 weeks prior to start of camp (early June). *Application fee:* $250. *Enrollment full by:* 2 weeks prior to classes.

Audition Information

Audition not required.

Costs & Financial Aid

Tuition (full): $2,580. *Lessons:* included in the tuition.

Financial aid available? no.

Curriculum, Students, and Faculty

Offered courses: audition preparation, improvisation, master classes. Curriculum fixed. *Program concentration:* wind and percussion instruments.

GEORGIA

FIRESPARK!

Winter Contact Information

Brenau University, One Centennial Circle, Gainseville GA 30501
Tel: 770-534-6190
Fax: 770-534-6194
Email: mccord@lib.brenau.edu
Contact: Dawn H. McCord

Summer Contact Information

Brenau University, One Centennial Circle, Gainseville GA 30501
Tel: 770-534-6191
Fax: 770-534-6195
Email: mccord@lib.brenau.edu
Contact: Dawn H. McCord

General

Minimum age or age range: 13 to 18. *Level of program:* beginning, intermediate, advanced

High school credit available? no. *College credit available?* no.

Services

Housing options: on-campus dorms.

Application Information

Requirements: essay, recommendation. *Program dates:* first 2 weeks of July. *Application fee:* $100. *Enrollment full by:* May.

Audition Information

Audition not required.

Costs & Financial Aid

Tuition (full): $745.

Financial aid available? no.

Curriculum, Students, and Faculty

Offered courses: chorus, composition, conducting, master classes, movement, music theory, private lessons, world music. Curricula choices. *Program concentration:* piano, voice, organ, upper strings, brass, woodwinds.

Selectivity for males: most admitted, but not all. *Selectivity for females:* most admitted, but not all.

Renowned alumni: Jonah Hooper, Atlanta Ballet; David B. Thompson, Barcelona Symphony.

Full-time faculty: 5. *Guest faculty:* 5. *List of some faculty:* Louis Applebaum, David Thomas, Dr. Michelle Roueche, Dr. Raymond Gotko, Dorothy Knowles.

Performance Information

Performance opportunities and frequency: selective. *Specific performance opportunities:* Music Night, talent show, final program *Performances by visiting artists?* yes.

Rehearsal facilities and hours: college music building with private and class practice rooms, 8:00 am-11:00 pm. *Performance facilities:* Pierce Auditorium at Brenau University, large pipe organ and Steinway concert grand.

Affiliations

Summer program is affiliated with other program(s): future students recruited from the program.

MIDSUMMER MACON

Winter Contact Information

4760 Forsyth Road, Macon GA 31210-4462
Tel: 912-757-5174
Fax: 912-757-4030
Email: jeanette_shackelford@post.wesleyan-college.edu
Contact: Jeanette Shackelford

Summer Contact Information

4760 Forsyth Road, Macon GA 31210-4462
Tel: 912-757-5175
Fax: 912-757-4031
Email: jeanette_shackelford@post.wesleyan-college.edu
Contact: Jeanette Shackelford

General

Minimum age or age range: 14 and up. *Level of program:* beginning, intermediate, advanced.

High school credit available? no. *College credit available?* no.

Services

Housing options: on-campus dorms.

Application Information

Application deadline: 5/1. *Application fee:* $75. *Enrollment full by:* 5/31.

Audition Information

Audition required. No audition fee.

Costs & Financial Aid

Tuition (full): $465. *Room:* $405.

Financial aid available? partial scholarship. *Scholarship notification:* 6/1. *Students receiving financial aid:* 50%. *Procedure for applying for financial aid:* File form.

Curriculum, Students, and Faculty

Offered courses: audition preparation, chorus, master classes, movement, music theory, musical theater, private lessons. Curriculum fixed. *Program concentration:* piano, voice, harp.

Selectivity for males: most admitted, but not all. *Selectivity for females:* most admitted, but not all.

Renowned alumni: Caroline Thomas, Nadine Jurgensen, Jeanelle Brown.

Full-time faculty: 3. *Guest faculty:* 6. *List of some faculty and their affiliations:* Edward Eikner, Wesleyan College; Susan McDuffie, Monica Hargrave.

Performance Information

Specific performance opportunities: participants perform each other in music camp. *Performances by visiting artists?* yes. *Recent guests:* Margery McDuffie, Lisa Asher, Edward Eikner, Theodotia Hartmen, Marvin Blickenstaff. *Performance facilities:* Porter Memorial Auditorium.

IDAHO

HAMPTON YOUTH MUSIC SCHOOL

Winter Contact Information
University of Idaho, Moscow ID 83844-4015
Tel: 208-885-6231
Fax: 208-855-7254
Email: alang@uidaho.edu
Contact: Alan Gemberling

Summer Contact Information
University of Idaho, Moscow ID 83844-4015
Tel: 208-885-6231
Fax: 208-855-7254
Email: alang@uidaho.edu
Contact: Alan Gemberling

General

Total enrollment: 150. *Level of program:* beginning, intermediate, advanced.

High school credit available? no. *College credit available?* no.

Services

Housing options: on-campus dorms.

Application Information

Program dates: 6/20-6/27. *Application deadline:* first day of camp. *Application fee:* $25.

Audition Information

Audition not required.

Costs & Financial Aid

Tuition (full): $125. *Lessons:* $10 per half hour. *Room & board:* $185.

Financial aid available? partial scholarship. *Scholarship notification:* 5/20. *Students receiving financial aid:* 15%. *Procedure for applying for financial aid:* contact director.

Curriculum, Students, and Faculty

Offered courses: acting for singers, chamber ensemble, chorus, composition, computer/MIDI techniques, conducting, jazz bands, jazz improvisation, master classes, movement, music manuscript techniques, music theory, musical theater, opera workshop, orchestra, private lessons, symphonic band. Curricula choices. *Program concentration:* instrumental, choral, strings, chamber, jazz, classical piano, classical guitar.

Selectivity for males: admit all who apply. *Selectivity for females:* admit all who apply.

List of some faculty and their affiliations: Jay Mauchley, Sandy Mauchley, Alan Gamberling, Mike Russel, Daniel Bukvich, Robert McCurdy, Jerry Yonkman, University of Idaho.

Performance Information

Performance opportunities and frequency: 2 performances by student groups, finale concert of large groups. *Specific performance opportunities:* student chamber ensembles, solos, large groups. *Orchestra seating:* By audition. *Performances by visiting artists?* yes. *Recent guests:* University of Idaho Wind Ensemble, Cross Current Jazz Ensemble, Univesity of Idaho Jazz Band, University of Idaho Jazz Choir.

Rehearsal facilities and hours: building with 15 practice rooms, 7:00 am-11:00 pm. *Performance facilities:* music building recital hall for chamber groups, seats 250, university auditorium for large groups, seats 500.

THE SCHWEITZER INSTITUTE OF MUSIC

Winter Contact Information
Gunther Schuller, Artistic Director
c/o the festival at San, P.O. Box 695, Sandpoint ID 83864
Tel: 208-265-4554
Fax: 208-263-6858
Email: festival@tsmicro.com

Summer Contact Information
Email: festival@tsmicro.com

General

High school credit available? no. *College credit available?* no.

Services

Housing options: on-site housing.

Application Information

Application fee: $40.

Audition Information

Audition not required.

Audition evaluation criteria: tape sent to faculty.

Costs & Financial Aid

Tuition (full): $500.

Financial aid available? full scholarship, partial scholarship. *Scholarship notification:* 2 months prior to camp. *Procedure for applying for financial aid:* application form, audiotape.

Curriculum, Students, and Faculty

Curriculum fixed.

Selectivity for males: most admitted, but not all. *Selectivity for females:* most admitted, but not all.

Full-time faculty: 48. *Guest faculty:* 4.

Performance Information

Orchestra seating: By placement audition. *Performance casting:* Audition upon arrival. *Performances by visiting artists?* yes. *Recent guests:* Martin Bearer, Ifor James, Eiji Hashimoto, Douglas McNabney.

ILLINOIS

NATIONAL HIGH SCHOOL MUSIC INSTITUTE

Winter Contact Information
Northwestern University School of Music, 711 Elgin Road,
Evanston IL 60208-1200
Tel: 847-491-3141
Fax: 847-491-5260
Email: musiclife@nwu.edu
Contact: Heather Landes

Summer Contact Information
Northwestern University School of Music, 711 Elgin Road,
Evanston IL 60208-1200
Tel: 847-491-3141
Fax: 847-491-5260
Email: musiclife@nwu.edu
Contact: Heather Landes

General

Total enrollment: 180. *Level of program:* advanced.

High school credit available? no. *College credit available?* no.

Services

Housing options: dorm required.

Application Information

Requirements: essay, recommendation. *Program dates:* 6/29-8/1. *Application deadline:* 5/1. *Enrollment full by:* 5/15. *Acceptance notification:* 5/15.

Audition Information

Audition required; live, on-site, off-site. *No audition fee. Audition includes:* 2-3 contrasting pieces. *Accompanist provided?* no.

Audition evaluation criteria: tone, technique, phrasing, rhythmic accuracy, overall musicianship.

Costs & Financial Aid

Tuition (full): $2,775.

Financial aid available? partial scholarship. *Scholarship notification:* 5/15. *Students receiving financial aid:* 65%. *Procedure for applying for financial aid:* complete institute's application and submit tax forms.

Curriculum, Students, and Faculty

Offered courses: acting for singers, audition preparation, aural skills, band, chamber ensemble, chorus, coaching, composition, conducting, jazz improvisation, master classes, music history, music theory, musical theater, opera workshop, orchestra, private lessons, repertory. Curricula choices. *Program concentration:* performance in voice, jazz studies, piano, winds and percussion, strings and classical guitar, composition, music education.

Selectivity for males: approximately 33% admitted. *Selectivity for females:* approximately 33% admitted.

Renowned alumni: John Hagstrom, Maty Alice Stollak, Michael Vopp, Timothy Weiss.

Full-time faculty: 60. *Guest faculty:* 10.

Performance Information

Performance opportunities and frequency: 2-3 performances weekly. *Specific performance opportunities:* weekly solo and chamber music recitals, honors recitals, terminal recitals, large ensemble concerts. *Orchestra seating:* by audition. *Seat rotation:* rotated after each concert and for each piece. *Performance casting:* no productions. *Performances by visiting artists?* yes. *Recent guests:* Ravinia Steans Institute, Gerardo Ribeiro, Blair Milton.

Rehearsal facilities and hours: over 100 rooms in 2 buildings, 7:00 am-10:00 pm. *Performance facilities:* Pick-Staiger Concert Hall, seats 1,003, Lutkin Hall seats 300, Regentstein Hall, seats 200.

Affiliations

Summer program is affiliated with other program(s): future students recruited from the program.

NORTHERN ILLINOIS UNIVERSITY SUMMER IN THE ARTS CAMPS

Winter Contact Information

Office of External Programs, College of Visual and Performing Arts, Dekalb IL 60115
Tel: 815-753-1450
Fax: 815-753-8372
Email: dbooth@niu.edu
Contact: Deborah Booth

Summer Contact Information

Deborah Booth, c/o Office of External Programs College of Visual and Performing Arts, Dekalb IL 60115
Tel: 815-753-1450
Fax: 815-753-8372
Email: dbooth@niu.edu
Contact: Deborah Booth

General

Total enrollment: 70. *Minimum age or age range:* 13 to 17.

High school credit available? no. *College credit available?* no.

Services

Housing options: on-campus dorms.

Application Information

Program dates: late June (1 week). *Application deadline:* one month prior to camp. *Enrollment full by:* application deadline. *Acceptance notification:* return mail from application.

Audition Information

Audition required; live, on-site. *No audition fee. Audition includes:* sight reading. *Accompanist provided?* no.

Audition evaluation criteria: auditions for campers for placement, not to get into camp, which is open to all interested players.

Costs & Financial Aid

Lessons: $12 per half hour.

Procedure for applying for financial aid: financial aid available from other sources.

Curriculum, Students, and Faculty

Offered courses: jazz bands, jazz combo, master classes, music theory, private lessons, seminar on the business of music. Curriculum fixed. *Program concentration*: jazz.

Selectivity for males: admit all who apply. *Selectivity for females:* admit all who apply.

Full-time faculty: 4. *Guest faculty:* 5. *List of some faculty*: Rick Holly, Ron Carter, Robert Chappell.

Performance Information

Performance opportunities and frequency: 1 performance. *Specific performance opportunities:* end of week performance. *Orchestra seating:* by audition. *Performances by visiting artists?* yes. *Recent guests:* Shades of Blue Jazz Ensemble of the Air Force. *Performance facilities:* Concert Hall, NIU Music Building.

Affiliations

Summer program is affiliated with other program(s): future students Y recruited from the program.

Additional Comments

We have other programs in the arts during the summer. Please call the school for more information.

STEAN'S INSTITUTE FOR YOUNG ARTISTS

Winter Contact Information

Ravinia Festival, 400 Iris Lane, Highland Park IL 60035
Tel: 847-266-5106
Fax: 847-266-5063
Contact: Diane P. Dorn

Summer Contact Information

Ravinia Festival, 400 Iris Lane, Highland Park IL 60035
Tel: 847-266-5107Fax: 847- 266-5064
Contact: Diane P. Dorn

General

Minimum age or age range: 15 to 35. *Level of program*: advanced.

High school credit available? no. *College credit available?* no.

Services

Housing options: Dorms in nearby college.

Application Information

Requirements: recommendation. *Program dates:* 6/27-8/23. *Application deadline:* Program for singers, 12/1, program for piano & strings, TBA. *Application fee:* $50. *Acceptance notification:* as soon as possible.

Audition Information

Audition required; live, on-site, off-site. *Audition fee*: $50. *Audition includes:* singing for the chairman of the faculty. *Accompanist provided?* yes.

Audition evaluation criteria: highly developed technique, excellent voice, musicality, the potential for a career as a performing artist.

Costs & Financial Aid

Tuition (full): $2,000.

Financial aid available? full scholarship, partial scholarship. *Scholarship notification:* same time as acceptance. *Procedure for applying for financial aid:* Piano and strings submit a financial statement, all singers receive a full scholarship.

Curriculum, Students, and Faculty

Offered courses: chamber ensemble, coaching, foreign language study, master classes, private lessons. Curriculum fixed. *Program concentration:* Program for piano and strings (5 weeks) program for singers (3 weeks).

Selectivity for males: approximately 10% admitted. *Selectivity for females:* approximately 10% admitted.

Renowned alumni: Camellia Johnson, Michelle DeYoung, Awadagin Pratt, Hai-Ye Ni, Amernet Quartet; Pekka Kuosisto.

List of some faculty: Miriam Fried, Paul Biss, Michael Tree, Peter Oundjian, David Geringas, Gary Hoffman, David Owen Norris, Margo Garret, Christa Ludwig, Peter Schreier, Thomas Hampson, Thomas Allen.

Performance Information

Performance opportunities and frequency: several recitals. *Orchestra seating:* Different for each course. *Performance casting:* auditioned. *Performances by visiting artists?* yes. *Recent guests:* at the Ravinia Festival, Alicia DeLarrocha, Pinchas Zukerman, Jon Kimura Parker, Itzhak Perlman, Samuel Ramey, Peter Serkin, Gil Shaham, Frederica Von Stade.

Rehearsal facilities and hours: 15 practice rooms with Yamaha grand pianos, 8:00 am-11:00 pm. *Performance facilities:* Bennett-Gordon Hall, 450-seat auditorium, air-conditioned, excellent acoustics.

IOWA

ORPHEUS FESTIVAL

Winter Contact Information

Department of Music, Simpson College, 701 North C Street, Indianola IA 50125
Tel: 515-961-1637
Fax: 515-961-1498
Email: dipalma@storm.simpson.edu
Contact: Dr. Maria Dipalma

Summer Contact Information

Department of Music, Simpson College, 701 North C Street, Indianola IA 50125
Tel: 515-961-1637
Fax: 515-961-1498
Email: dipalma@storm.simpson.edu
Contact: Dr. Maria Dipalma

General

Total enrollment: 65. *Minimum age or age range:* 14 to 18. *Level of program*: intermediate, advanced.

High school credit available? no. *College credit available?* no.

Services

Housing options: on-campus dorms.

Application Information

Program dates: 7/12-7/20. *Application deadline:* 5/15. *Enrollment full by:* 6/15. *Acceptance notification:* 6/5.

Audition Information

Audition required. No audition fee. Audition includes: 2 solo selections in contrasting styles from each area in which student plans to take lessons. *Accompanist provided?* no.

Costs & Financial Aid

Tuition (full): $400.

Financial aid available? partial scholarship. *Scholarship notification:* 6/5. *Students receiving financial aid:* 80%.

Curriculum, Students, and Faculty

Offered courses: acting for singers, band, chamber ensemble, chorus, coaching, movement, music history, music theory, musical theater, opera workshop, private lessons. Curricula choices. *Program concentration*: piano, voice, organ, wind instruments, percussion, guitar (with ensemble and class experience).

Selectivity for males: most admitted, but not all. *Selectivity for females:* most admitted, but not all.

Full-time faculty: 13. *Guest faculty:* 7. *List of some faculty*: Dr. Robert L. Larson, Dr. Maria DiPolma, Ross A. Leeper.

Performance Information

Specific performance opportunities: recital, ensemble, musical theater, opera excerpt performance *Performance casting:* audition on the first night of the festival.

Rehearsal facilities and hours: 28 practice rooms with windows and pianos. *Performance facilities:* Lerberg Recital hall, seats 220, Duncan Rehearsal Hall, seats 150.

LOUISIANA

INTENSIVE ARTS CAMP

Winter Contact Information

The Music Academy, LSU School of Music
Baton Rouge LA 70803-2504
Tel: 504-388-3230
Fax: 504-388-2562
Contact: Robert Halbruner

Summer Contact Information

The Music Academy, LSU School of Music,
Baton Rouge LA 70803-2504
Tel: 504-388-3230
Fax: 504-388-2562
Contact: Robert Halbruner

General

Total enrollment: 90. *Minimum age or age range:* 6 to 14. *Level of program:* beginning, intermediate, advanced.

High school credit available? no. *College credit available?* no.

Application Information

Requirements: recommendation. *Program dates:* June. *Application fee:* $20.

Audition Information

Audition not required.

Costs & Financial Aid

Tuition (full): $145.

Financial aid available? no.

Curriculum, Students, and Faculty

Offered courses: chamber ensemble, chorus, music history, music theory, composition. Curriculum fixed. *Program concentration*: composition, theory, rhythm, keyboard ensemble, choral (general music).

Selectivity for males: most admitted, but not all. *Selectivity for females:* most admitted, but not all.

Full-time faculty: 4.

Performance Information

Performance opportunities and frequency: 1 per week. *Specific performance opportunities:* each camp session culminates in a group recital that presents camp activites and compositions. *Performances by visiting artists?* no.

Rehearsal facilities and hours: LSU School of Music. *Performance facilities:* 300-seat recital.

LSU HONORS CHAMBER WINDS CAMP

Winter Contact Information

Email: fwickes@unixl.sncc.lsu.edu

Summer Contact Information

292 Band Hall, Louisiana State University, Baton Rouge LA 70803
Tel: 504-388-2384
Fax: 504-388-4693
Email: fwickes@unixl.sncc.lsu.edu

General

Total enrollment: 60. *Minimum age or age range:* 15 to 18. *Level of program:* advanced.

High school credit available? no. *College credit available?* no.

Services

Housing options: on-campus dorms, off-campus independent housing for commuters.

Application Information

Program dates: last week of June. *Application deadline:* 6/1. *Enrollment full by:* 6/1. *Acceptance notification:* 6/10.

Audition Information

Audition required. No audition fee. Audition includes: major and chromatic scales, 2 prepared selections. *Accompanist provided?* no.

Costs & Financial Aid

Tuition (full): $425. *Lessons:* $40 (optional).

Financial aid available? full scholarship, partial scholarship. *Scholarship notification:* varies depending on date of applcation. *Students receiving financial aid:* 8%. *Procedure for applying for financial aid:* contact camp director.

Curriculum, Students, and Faculty

Offered courses: master classes. Curriculum fixed. *Program concentration:* chamber music for winds and percussion, wind ensemble, solo playing, master classes, private lessons.

Selectivity for males: most admitted, but not all. *Selectivity for females:* most admitted, but not all.

Full-time faculty: 12. *List of some faculty:* Steve Amundson, Mary Auge, Gerry Casper, David Carter, Dan Dressen, Lynn Erickson, Alison Feldt, Charles Forsberg, Kenneth Graber, Charles Gray, Peter Hamlin, Sheila Hanford, Tony Holt.

MAINE

KNEISEL HALL

Winter Contact Information

P.O. Box 648, Blue Hill ME 04614
Tel: 207-374-2811
Fax: 207-374-2811
Email: kneisel@hypernet.com
Contact: Tonu Kalam

Summer Contact Information

P.O. Box 648, Blue Hill ME 04614
Tel: 207-374-2812
Fax: 207-374-2173
Email: kneisel@hypernet.com
Contact: Tonu Kalam

General

Total enrollment: 50.

Services

Housing options: on-campus dorms. *Level of program:* advanced.

Audition Information

Audition required: live. *Audition includes:* 15-20 minutes taped repertoire of applicant's choice. *Accompanist provided?* no.

Scholarship notification: upon acceptance.

Curriculum, Students, and Faculty

Offered courses: master classes. *Program concentration:* chamber music for strings and piano.

Performance Information

Performance opportunities and frequency: at least 3 per week. *Specific performance opportunities:* at least 3 concerts per week as well as many other options. *Orchestra seating:* by faculty. *Performances by visiting artists?* yes. *Recent guests:* James Buswell, Joseph Silverstein, Sheryl Staples, Heidi Castleman.

Rehearsal facilities and hours: Beatrice Friedman Symphony Center, 7:00 am-11:00 pm daily.

SOUTHERN MAINE MUSIC ACADEMY

Winter Contact Information

Peter Martine
c/o Music Department University of Southern Maine, Gorham ME
Tel: 207-780-5267
Contact: Peter Martine

Summer Contact Information

Music Department, University of Southern Maine, Gorham ME
Tel: 207-780-5267
Contact: Peter Martine

General

Total enrollment: 80. *Level of program:* intermediate, advanced.

High school credit available? no. *College credit available?* no.

Services

Housing options: on-campus dorms.

Application Information

Program dates: first Saturday after 7/4 (9 days).

Audition Information

Audition not required.

Costs & Financial Aid

Lessons: $25 per half hour.

Financial aid available? partial scholarship.

Curriculum, Students, and Faculty

Offered courses: audition preparation, band, chamber ensemble, coaching, conducting, master classes, perspective in music class, private lessons. Curriculum fixed. *Program concentration:* Concert band, jazz ensemble, chamber music.

Full-time faculty: 20.

Performance Information

Specific performance opportunities: solo recitals, chamber music recitals, jazz ensemble, concert band. *Performances by visiting artists?* yes.

Rehearsal facilities and hours: 8:00 am-10:00 pm. *Performance facilities:* Corthell Concert Hall and Gorham Performing Arts Center.

Affiliations

Summer program is affiliated with other program(s): future students recruited from the program.

MARYLAND

FRENCH PIANO INSTITUTE PIANO FESTIVAL

Winter Contact Information

9908 Old Spring Road, Kensington MD 20895
Tel: 301-929-8433
Fax: 301-929-0254
Email: gdelente@msn.com
Contact: Gail Delente

Summer Contact Information

9908 Old Spring Road, Kensington MD 20895
Tel: 301-929-8433
Fax: 301-929-0254
Email: gdelente@msn.com
Contact: Gail Delente

General

Total enrollment: 50. *Minimum age or age range:* 18 to 60. *Level of program:* advanced.

High school credit available? no. *College credit available?* no.

Services

Housing options: on-campus dorms, off-campus hotel.

Application Information

Requirements: recommendation. *Program dates:* 7/3-7/20. *Application deadline:* 4/15. *Application fee:* $35. *Enrollment full by:* performers 3/15. *Acceptance notification:* rolling, 7-10 days.

Audition Information

Audition required: live, on-site, off-site. *Audition fee:* $35. *Audition includes:* recently-recorded audio cassette, performance of 1 substantial piano work and 2 other works from different periods, CV with reviews if possible, teacher letter of recommendation if college education is incomplete.

Audition evaluation criteria: level of performance.

Costs & Financial Aid

Lessons: $100.

Financial aid available? partial scholarship. *Scholarship notification:* soon after acceptance as a performer. *Students receiving financial aid:* 10%. *Procedure for applying for financial aid:* Written request, evidence of financial need.

Curriculum, Students, and Faculty

Offered courses: coaching, French language study, master classes, private lessons, repertory, interpretation, performance, Frenchnique, pedal. Curriculum fixed. *Program concentration:* master classes, lectures, recitals in piano.

Selectivity for males: approximately 33% admitted. *Selectivity for females:* approximately 33% admitted.

Renowned alumni: Richard Dowling, Golda Tutz, Nicholas Zumbro, Angela Kim, Dejan Sinadinovic.

Full-time faculty: 2. *Guest faculty:* 4. *List of some faculty and their affiliations:* Gail Delente, George Washington University; Roy Hobat.

Performance Information

Performance opportunities and frequency: 2-3 per week. *Specific performance opportunities:* performances in master classes, on musical soirees, at final public recitals, at Schola Cantorum in Paris, France. *Performances by visiting artists?* yes. *Recent guests:* Dominique Merlet, Parcal Deboyon, Cecile Ousset, Noil Lee, David Lively.

Rehearsal facilities and hours: La Schola Cantorum, 269 Mue Saint Jacques, 75005 Paris, France. *Performance facilities:* Concert Hall at Schola.

NATIONAL ORCHESTRAL INSTITUTE

Winter Contact Information

Rossborough Festival, University of Maryland,
College Park MD 20740
Tel: 301-403-8370
Fax: 301-403-8375
Email: noi@umdacc.umd.edu
Contact: Donald Reinhold

Summer Contact Information

Rossborough Festival, University of Maryland,
College Park MD 20740
Tel: 301-403-8371
Fax: 301-403-8376
Email: noi@umdacc.umd.edu
Contact: Donald Reinhold

General

Minimum age or age range: 18 to 28. *Level of program*: advanced.

High school credit available? no. *College credit available?* no.

Services

Housing options: On-site housing.

Application Information

Program dates: 3 weeks in June. *Application deadline:* must be prior to live auditions. *Application fee:* $50. *Acceptance notification:* 4/1.

Audition Information

Audition required: live, on-site, off-site. *No audition fee. Audition includes:* brief concerto solo, three contrasting orchestral excerpts of student's choice. *Accompanist provided?* no.

Audition evaluation criteria: committee review of taped audition.

Costs & Financial Aid

Tuition (full): $500. *Lessons:* $75.

Financial aid available? partial scholarship. *Scholarship notification:* 5/1. *Students receiving financial aid:* 10%. *Procedure for applying for financial aid:* preliminary written request, scholarship application.

Curriculum, Students, and Faculty

Offered courses: audition preparation. Curriculum fixed. *Program concentration:* orchestral performance and professional training for careers.

Selectivity for males: approximately 60% admitted. *Selectivity for females:* approximately 60% admitted.

Full-time faculty: 10. *List of some faculty and their affiliations:* William Bennett, English Chamber Orchestra, Royal Academy of Music; Stephen Preston, Academy of Ancient Music, Royal College of Music.

Performance Information

Specific performance opportunities: afternoon recitals in master classes.

MASSACHUSETTS

AMHERST EARLY MUSIC FESTIVAL

Winter Contact Information

65 West 95th Street, Suite 1A, New York NY 10025
Tel: 212-222-3351
Fax: 212-222-1898
Email: amherst@compuserve.com
Contact: Valerie Horst

Summer Contact Information

65 West 95th Street, Suite 1A, New York NY 10025
Tel: 212-222-3351
Fax: 212-222-1898
Email: amherst@compuserve.com
Contact: Valerie Horst

General

Minimum age or age range: 14 to 80. *Level of program:* beginning, intermediate, advanced.

High school credit available? yes. *College credit available?* no.

Services

Housing options: on-site housing.

Application Information

Program dates: 8/2-8/9, 8/9-8/16.

Audition Information

Audition not required.

Audition evaluation criteria: rehearsal technique, ability to hear and correct problems.

Costs & Financial Aid

Tuition (full): $950. *Room:* $725.

Financial aid available? no.

Curriculum, Students, and Faculty

Offered courses: dance history, historical dance, music. Curriculum fixed.

Selectivity for males: approximately 33% admitted. *Selectivity for females:* approximately 33% admitted.

Full-time faculty: 5. *Guest faculty:* 5. *List of some faculty and their affiliations:* Helmuth Rilling, Dr. Thomas Somerville, Occidental College; Kathy Romey, University of Minnesota; Gordan Paine, California State University at Fullerton.

BELVOIR TERRACE

Winter Contact Information

101 West 79th Street, New York NY 10024
Tel: 212-580-3398
Fax: 212-579-7282
Email: BelvoirT@aol.com
Contact: Nancy S. Goldberg, Diane Goldberg

Summer Contact Information

Lenox MA 01240
Tel: 413-637-0555
Fax: 413-637-4651
Email: BelvoirT@aol.com
Contact: Nancy S. Goldberg, Diane Goldberg

General

Total enrollment: 200. *Minimum age or age range:* 10 to 18. *Level of program:* beginning, intermediate, advanced.

High school credit available? no. *College credit available?* no.

Services

Housing options: on-campus dorms-supervised bunk living.

Application Information

Program dates: 6/25-8/15. *Enrollment full by:* February.

Audition Information

Audition required; live, video. *No audition fee. Audition includes:* interview, playing pieces. *Accompanist provided?* no.

Costs & Financial Aid

Financial aid available? no.

Curriculum, Students, and Faculty

Offered courses: audition preparation, master classes, movement. Curriculum fixed. *Program concentration:* instrumental, chamber music, orchestra piano, voice, opera, musical theater.

BOSTON UNIVERSITY TANGLEWOOD INSTITUTE

Winter Contact Information

855 Commonwealth Avenue, Boston MA 02215
Tel: 800-643-4796
Fax: 617-353-7455
Email: tanglewood@bu.edu
Contact: Cynthia Plumb

Summer Contact Information

Tanglewood Main Grounds
Lenox MA 01240
Tel: 413-637-1430
Fax: 413-637-2130
Email: tanglewood@bu.edu
Contact: Cynthia Plumb

General

Total enrollment: 360. *Minimum age or age range:* 15 to 30. *Level of program:* beginning, intermediate, advanced.

High school credit available? no. *College credit available?* yes.

Services

Housing options: on-campus dorms, off-site independent housing for students 21 and older.

Application Information

Program dates: 6/23-8/16. *Application deadline:* 3/1. *Application fee:* $50. *Enrollment full by:* 4/30. *Acceptance notification:* 4/1.

Audition Information

Audition required. No audition fee. Audition includes: depends on instrument. Call for information. *Accompanist provided?* no.

Costs & Financial Aid

Tuition (full): $825-$1,960. *Room & board:* $600-$1,990.

Financial aid available? full scholarship, partial scholarship. *Scholarship notification:* 4/1. *Students receiving financial aid:* 40%. *Procedure for applying for financial aid:* application and audition.

Curriculum, Students, and Faculty

Offered courses: audition preparation, chamber ensemble, chorus, coaching, diction, foreign language study, master classes, movement, music theory, opera workshop, orchestra, private lessons, repertory. Curriculum fixed. *Program concentration:* chamber music, orchestral music, vocal/choral music, brass quintet, composition.

Selectivity for males: approximately 33% admitted.

Renowned alumni: Todd Seeber, Boston Symphony Orchestra; Timothy Genis, Boston Symphony Orchestra.

Full-time faculty: 2. *Guest faculty:* 20. *List of some faculty:* Richard Cornell, Andres Diaz, Doriot Anthony Dwyer, Ralph Gomberg, Scott Hartman, Ann Howard Jones.

Performance Information

Specific performance opportunities: full concert every 2 weeks; students are often invited to perform in the Festival of Contemporary Music and other TMC events. *Orchestra seating*: by audition. *Seat rotation:* rotated at least for each concert. *Performances by visiting artists?* yes.

Rehearsal facilities and hours: practice sheds and cabins, 8:00 am-10:00 pm. *Performance facilities:* Seiji Ozawa Hall, Tanglewood Main Grounds, BUTI West Street Theater.

Affiliations

Summer program is affiliated with other program(s): future students recruited from the program.

COLLEGE LIGHT OPERA COMPANY

Winter Contact Information
162 South Cedar Street, Oberlin OH 44024
Tel: 440-774-8485
Fax: 440-775-8642
Contact: Robert and Ursula Haslun

Summer Contact Information
P.O. Drawer F
Falmouth MA 02541
Tel: 508-548-2211
Contact: Robert and Ursula Haslun

General

Total enrollment: 75. *Minimum age or age range:* 19 to 23. *Level of program:* advanced.

College credit available? yes.

Services

Housing options: on-campus dorms.

Application Information

Requirements: interview, recommendation. *Program dates:* 6/10-8/30. *Application deadline:* rolling, admissions begin March 15. *Enrollment full by:* 4/15. *Acceptance notification:* rolling.

Audition Information

Audition required. No audition fee. Audition includes: 4 selections of 1 verse each for singers; recital tape or student's choice for orchestra. *Accompanist provided?* no.

Costs & Financial Aid

Financial aid available? no.

Curriculum, Students, and Faculty

Specific curriculum information: production of and rehearsal for 9 musicals and operettas each summer. Curriculum fixed. *Program concentration:* Summer stock music theatre.

Selectivity for males: approximately 33% admitted. *Selectivity for females:* approximately 10% admitted.

Renowned alumni: Richard White, Maryanne Telese, John Lee Blatty, Nacy Anderson, Lee Merrill.

Full-time faculty: 20. *List of some faculty and their affiliations:* Kimberly Crigsby, Elizabeth Hastings, Sarasota Opera, Washington Opera; Michael Sennola, Metropolitan Opera.

Performance Information

Performance opportunities and frequency: performances each week Tuesday through Saturday. *Specific performance opportunities:* 9 fully staged and costumed productions with full orchestra, 54 total performances. *Orchestra seating:* decided by conductor. *Seat rotation:* rotated weekly. *Performance casting:* auditioned.

Rehearsal facilities and hours: Highfield Theater, 10:00 am-12:30 pm, 2:00 pm-5:00 pm daily. *Performance facilities:* 300-seat air conditioned Highfield Theater in Falmouth, Massachussetts.

MERRIMACK VALLEY MUSIC CENTER

Winter Contact Information
P.O. Box 20388, Grecley Square Station, New York NY 10001
Tel: 719-632-9534
Fax: 719-632-9534
Email: donjeri@lex.net
Contact: Jeri Jorgensen

Summer Contact Information
Merrimack College, North Andover MA 01845
Tel: 508-837-5735
Fax: 508-837-5735
Email: donjeri@lex.net
Contact: Jeri Jorgensen

General

Minimum age or age range: 18 and up. *Level of program:* beginning, intermediate, advanced.

High school credit available? no. *College credit available?* no.

Services

Housing options: air-conditioned apartment.

Application Information

Requirements: essay, recommendation. *Program dates:* 7/13-7/27. *Application deadline:* 5/15. *Application fee:* $50. *Acceptance notification:* 6/1.

Audition Information

Audition required. No audition fee. Audition includes: short solo and/or chamber music excerpt. *Accompanist provided?* no.

Costs & Financial Aid

Financial aid available? full scholarship. *Students receiving financial aid:* 1%. *Procedure for applying for financial aid:* call for information.

Curriculum, Students, and Faculty

Offered courses: chamber ensemble. Curriculum fixed. *Program concentration:* string and wind chamber music.

Full-time faculty: 8. *Guest faculty:* 1. *List of some faculty and their affiliations:* Jeri Jorgensen, Margaret Miller, Katharine Knight, DaVinci Quartet; Henry Gronnier, Thomas Diener, Rosetti Quartet;

Gerard Reuter, Dorian Quartet; Richard Slavich, University of Denver.

Performance Information

Specific performance opportunities: weekly participant to perform one movement of coached work. *Rehearsal facilities and hours:* in apartments, 8:00 am-10:00 pm. *Performance facilities:* Casica Hall, a renovated church on the grounds of Merrimack College.

Additional Comments

Merrimack Valley Center is primarily a program for adult amateurs, which utilizes advanced school and college students to fill gaps in instrumentation and round out and solidify the groups. Students gain valuable exposures to the repertoire, are coached by artists of international reputation, and gain teaching experience of their own in uncoached groups.

MOUNT HOLYOKE CONCERT GUITAR MASTER CLASSES

Winter Contact Information

c/o Phillip de Fremery, Music Department, Mount Holyoke College, South Hadley MA 01075
Tel: 413-538-2306
Fax: 413-538-2547

Summer Contact Information

c/o Phillip de Fremery, Music Department, Mount Holyoke College, South Hadley MA 01075
Tel: 413-538-2306
Fax: 413-538-2547

General

Total enrollment: 12. *Level of program:* beginning, intermediate, advanced.

High school credit available? no. *College credit available?* yes.

Services

Housing options: on-campus dorms.

Application Information

Program dates: two 2-week sessions. *Application deadline:* as soon as possible. *Enrollment full by:* April.

Audition Information

Audition not required.

Costs & Financial Aid

Tuition (full): $400. *Room:* $225.

Financial aid available? no.

Curriculum, Students, and Faculty

Offered courses: master classes. Curriculum fixed. *Program concentration:* Basically aimed at professional concert preparation, however all levels are accepted; first-come, first-served.

Selectivity for males: admit all who apply. *Selectivity for females:* admit all who apply.

Renowned alumni: Andrew Leonard, Freddie Bryant.

Full-time faculty: 2. *List of some faculty:* Phillip de Farmery, Benjamin Verdery.

Performance Information

Specific performance opportunities: class recital at end of session. *Performance casting: Performances by visiting artists?* no.

Rehearsal facilities and hours: can use dorm rooms, unlimited hours. *Performance facilities:* concert hall, chapel.

Affiliations

Summer program is affiliated with other program(s): future students recruited from the program.

MUSICORDA SUMMER STRING PROGRAM

Winter Contact Information

Musicorda, P.O. Box 557, South Hadley MA 01075
Tel: 413-538-2590
Fax: 413-538-3021
Contact: Jacqueline Melnick

Summer Contact Information

Musicorda, P.O. Box 557, South Hadley MA 01075
Tel: 413-538-2590
Fax: 413-538-3021
Contact: Jacqueline Melnick

General

Minimum age or age range: 12 to graduate school. *Level of program:* advanced.

High school credit available? no. *College credit available?* no.

Services

Housing options: on-campus dorms at Mount Holyoke College.

Application Information

Requirements: recommendation. *Program dates:* 6/27-8/8. *Application deadline:* 4/1. *Application fee:* $50. *Enrollment full by:* 3/15. *Acceptance notification:* after audition or tape evaluation.

Audition Information

Audition required; live, video. ***No audition fee.*** *Audition includes:* 2 compositions of contrasting styles and periods. *Accompanist provided?* no.

Audition evaluation criteria: level of advancement, musicianship, technical facility.

Costs & Financial Aid

Tuition (full): $3,350.

Financial aid available? full scholarship, partial scholarship. *Scholarship notification:* 4/1. *Students receiving financial aid:* 60%. *Procedure for applying for financial aid:* Submission of FAFSA and financial disclosure.

Curriculum, Students, and Faculty

Offered courses: chamber ensemble, master classes, private lessons, repertory. *Program concentration:* stringed instruments, string quartets.

Selectivity for males: approximately 10% admitted. *Selectivity for females:* approximately 10% admitted.

Renowned alumni: Rachel Barton, Jennifer Koh, Awadagin Pratt, Joji Hattori, Wilhelmina Smith.

Full-time faculty: 15.

Performance Information

Specific performance opportunities: 5 Young Artist series concerts, 6 student recitals, 20 outreach programs.

Rehearsal facilities and hours: dormitory rooms. *Performance facilities:* Chapin Auditorium, Mount Holyoke Colllege, 800-seat auditorium.

MICHIGAN

INTERLOCHEN ARTS CAMP

Winter Contact Information

P.O. Box 199, Interlochen MI 49643
Tel: 616-276-7472
Fax: 616-276-6321
Email: admissions@interlochen.k12.mi.us
Contact: Tom Bewley, Director of Admissions

Summer Contact Information

P.O. Box 199, Interlochen MI 49643
Tel: 616-276-7472
Fax: 616-276-6321
Email: admissions@interlochen.k12.mi.us
Contact: Tom Bewley, Director of Admissions

General

Total enrollment: 2,000.

Services

Housing options: on-campus cabins.

Audition Information

Audition required: live, video, on-site. *Accompanist provided?* no.

Lessons: included in the tuition.

Curriculum, Students, and Faculty

Offered courses: Alexander technique, master classes, movement, musical theater. *Program concentration:* visual arts, theatre, music, dance, creative writing.

Performance Information

Performance opportunities and frequency: 5 concerts, 1 each week. *Specific performance opportunities:* student concerts. *Performances by visiting artists?* yes. *Recent guests:* Jerome Hines, Jaime Laredo, Michael Tree, Mignon Dunn, Sharon Robinson, Eugenia Zukerman, Bernard Greenhouse, Ruth Laredo.

MINNESOTA

MINNESOTA INSTITUTE FOR TALENTED YOUTH

Winter Contact Information

Macalester College
1600 Grand Avenue
St. Paul MN 55105
Tel: 612-696-6590
Fax: 612-696-6591
Contact: Lucienne Taylor

Summer Contact Information

Macalester College
1600 Grand Avenue, St. Paul MN 55105
Tel: 612-696-6590
Fax: 612-696-6591
Contact: Lucienne Taylor

General

Minimum age or age range: 12 to 18. *Level of program:* beginning, intermediate, advanced.

High school credit available? no. *College credit available?* no.

Services

Housing options: on-campus dorms.

Application Information

Requirements: essay, recommendation. *Program dates:* 6/17-7/18. *Application deadline:* 4/23. *Enrollment full by:* 5/15. *Acceptance notification:* 5/10.

Audition Information

Audition required; live, video, off-site. *No audition fee. Audition includes:* sight-reading, scales, performance and improvisation skills. *Accompanist provided?* no.

Costs & Financial Aid

Financial aid available? full scholarship, partial scholarship. *Scholarship notification:* 5/10. *Students receiving financial aid:* 33%. *Procedure for applying for financial aid:* call or write for financial aid form.

Curriculum, Students, and Faculty

Offered courses: jazz bands, opera workshop. Curricula choices. *Program concentration:* Jazz band and opera.

Selectivity for males: approximately 33% admitted. *Selectivity for females:* approximately 33% admitted.

Renowned alumni: Michel Bland.

Full-time faculty: 6. *Guest faculty:* 2. *List of some faculty and their affiliations:* Dennis Malmber, Scott Carlei, Jim McKeel, St. Olaf College.

Performance Information

Performance opportunities and frequency: daily during last two weeks of Institute. *Specific performance opportunities:* final opera performance, 7-9 jazz band performances on campus and outside. *Performances by visiting artists?* yes. *Recent guests:* Greg Lewis.

Rehearsal facilities: music building at Macalester College. *Performance facilities:* Janet Wallace Concert Hall at Macalester College.

ST. OLAF SUMMER MUSIC CAMP

Winter Contact Information
St. Olaf College, 1520 St. Olaf Avenue,
Northfield MN 55057
Tel: 507-646-3043
Fax: 507-646-3690
Email: events@stolaf.edu
Contact: Pat Anfinson

Summer Contact Information
St. Olaf College, 1520 St. Olaf Avenue
Northfield MN 55057
Tel: 507-646-3043
Fax: 507-646-3690
Email: events@stolaf.edu
Contact: Pat Anfinson

General

Minimum age or age range: 14 to 18. *Level of program:* advanced.

High school credit available? no. *College credit available?* no.

Services

Housing options: on-campus dorms.

Application Information

Requirements: recommendation. *Enrollment full by:* 5/15.

Audition Information

Audition required; on-site. *No audition fee. Audition includes:* 5-10 minute solo. *Accompanist provided?* yes.

Costs & Financial Aid

Tuition (full): $425. *Lessons:* $40.

Financial aid available? full scholarship, partial scholarship. *Scholarship notification:* varies depending on date of application. *Students receiving financial aid:* 8%. *Procedure for applying for financial aid:* contact camp director.

Curriculum, Students, and Faculty

Offered courses: band, chamber ensemble, chorus, conducting, jazz, music history, music theory, musical theater, orchestra, private lessons. Curricula choices. *Program concentration:* band, choir, orchestra.

Selectivity for males: most admitted, but not all. *Selectivity for females:* most admitted, but not all.

Renowned alumni: Anton Armstrong, Timothy Mahr, Donna Paulsen, Gloria Kiester, Judith Nelson, Kay Sahlin, Malin Fritz, Margo Losey, Robert Scholz, Robert Smith, Steve Sandberg, Steven Snell, Sylvia Munsen.

Full-time faculty: 12. *Guest faculty:* 23. *List of some faculty:* Robert Adney, Steve Amundson, Mary Auge, Gerry Casper, David Carter, Dan Dressen, Lynn Erickson, Charles Gray, Peter Hamlin, Tony Holt, Lucinda Marvin, Jill Mahr, Priscilla McAffee, James McGuire, Harriet McCleary, James McKeel, David Miller, Sue Roberts, Steve Sandberg, Theo Wee.

Performance Information

Specific performance opportunities: small and large ensemble, solo and group recital. *Orchestra seating:* by audition. *Seat rotation:* varies. *Performance casting:* auditioned. *Performances by visiting artists?* yes. *Recent guests:* Tom Prin, Bobby Llama.

Rehearsal facilities and hours: practice rooms with piano, classrooms, 5-6 practice rooms, 5 practice modules, 1 V room, available dawn-11:00 pm. *Performance facilities:* recital hall, theater, large ensembles in the gymnasium.

Affiliations

Summer program is affiliated with other program(s): future students recruited from the program.

MISSOURI

MISSOURI SUMMER MUSIC INSTITUTE (MSMI)

Winter Contact Information
202 Loeb Hall, Columbia MO 65211
Tel: 573-882-3438
Fax: 573-884-5515
Email: musictp@showme.missouri.edu
Contact: Tina Price

Summer Contact Information
202 Loeb Hall, Columbia MO 65211
Tel: 573-882-3438
Fax: 573-884-5515
Email: musictp@showme.missouri.edu
Contact: Tina Price

General

Total enrollment: 300. *Minimum age or age range:* 12 to 18. *Level of program*: beginning, intermediate, advanced.

High school credit available? no. *College credit available?* no.

Services

Housing options: on-campus dorms.

Application Information

Requirements: essay, recommendation. *Application deadline:* 6/1. *Application fee:* $30. *Enrollment full by:* 5/1.

Audition Information

Audition required; live, video, on-site. *Audition fee:* $25. *Audition includes:* sight-reading, prepared solo, etude, scales. *Accompanist provided?* no.

Costs & Financial Aid

Lessons: $10 per hour.

Financial aid available? no.

Curriculum, Students, and Faculty

Offered courses: band, chamber ensemble, chorus, conducting, master classes, music history, music theory, private lessons. Curricula choices. *Program concentration:* band, choir, strings, theory/composition, computer, conducting, jazz improvisation, music appreciation.

Selectivity for males: most admitted, but not all. *Selectivity for females:* most admitted, but not all.

Full-time faculty: 15. *Guest faculty:* 2.

Performance Information

Performance opportunities and frequency: 1 recital, 1 full band concert. *Specific performance opportunities:* camp recitals, concerts, master classes.

Rehearsal facilities and hours: instruction from 8:30 am-5:00 pm, daily rehearsals held on campus in band facility. *Performance facilities:* concerts on campus in Memorial Union, recitals in band rehearsal hall.

Affiliations

Summer program is affiliated with other program(s): future students recruited from the program.

MONTANA

RED LODGE MUSIC FESTIVAL

Winter Contact Information
3406 Green Terrace Drive, Billings MT 59102
Tel: 406-252-4599
Fax: 406-655-4289
Email: rlmf@men.net
Contact: Eloise R. Kirk

Summer Contact Information
3206 Green Terrace Drive, Billings MT 59102
Tel: 406-252-4599Fax: 406-655-4289
Email: rlmf@men.net
Contact: Eloise R. Kirk

General

Total enrollment: 200. *Level of program:* intermediate, advanced.

High school credit available? no. *College credit available?* no.

Services

Housing options: on-campus motels and cabins, off-campus housing with friends or families.

Application Information

Application deadline: 6/10. *Application fee:* $20. *Enrollment full by:* 6/10. *Acceptance notification:* early June.

Audition Information

Audition required. No audition fee. Audition includes: an etude and a solo. *Accompanist provided?* no.

Costs & Financial Aid

Tuition (full): $150. *Lessons:* $12 per half hour. *Room:* $145.

Financial aid available? partial scholarship. *Scholarship notification:* 5/30. *Students receiving financial aid:* 10%. *Procedure for applying for financial aid:* Contact Eloise R. Kirk, 3406 Green Terrance Drive, Billings, MT 59102.

Curriculum, Students, and Faculty

Offered courses: band, chamber ensemble, jazz improvisation, master classes, orchestra, private lessons. Curricula choices.

Selectivity for males: admit all who apply. *Selectivity for females:* admit all who apply.

Renowned alumni: Maria Lambros, Len Garrison, Michael Reynolds.

Full-time faculty: 30. *List of some faculty and their affiliations:* Gowy Behm, Billings Symphony; June Huang-Elias, Levine School of Music; Leonard Garrison, John Harmon, Gary Lewis, Bernard McWilliams, Angela Mitchell, Spokane Symphony.

Performance Information

Performance opportunities and frequency: 4 performances during 9 days. *Specific performance opportunities:* 2 orchestra performances, 2 band performances, 2 jazz band performances, chamber emsembles, jazz improvisations. *Orchestra seating:* by audition. *Seat rotation:* not rotated except for winds and brass.

Rehearsal facilities and hours: practice rooms available at high school and elementary school each afternoon. *Performance facilities:* all concerts are held at the Civic Auditorium, seats 500.

NEW HAMPSHIRE

APPLE HILL CENTER FOR CHAMBER MUSIC SUMMER FESTIVAL

Winter Contact Information

P.O. Box 217, Apple Hill Road, East Sullivan NH 03445
Tel: 603-847-3371
Fax: 603-847-9734
Email: applehill@top.monad.net
Contact: Kathleen Stumacher

Summer Contact Information

P.O. Box 217, Apple Hill Road, East Sullivan NH 03445
Tel: 603-847-3371
Fax: 603-847-9734
Email: applehill@top.monad.net
Contact: Kathleen Stumacher

General

Minimum age or age range: 12 to 90. *Level of program:* intermediate, advanced.

Services

Housing options: on-campus rustic cabins, off-campus optional bed and breakfast in the area.

Application Information

Requirements: recommendation. *Program dates:* five 10-day sessions from June-August. *Application deadline:* accept applications until classes are full. *Enrollment full by:* 5/1.

Audition Information

Audition required. Audition includes: 1 chamber work, one work recently learned. *Accompanist provided?* yes.

Audition evaluation criteria: Apple Hill's Director listens to audio tapes and forms ensembles based on levels of playing and need for instruments.

Costs & Financial Aid

Room & board: $825.

Financial aid available? full scholarship, partial scholarship. *Scholarship notification:* after receipt of FA form. *Procedure for applying for financial aid:* fill out form.

Curriculum, Students, and Faculty

Offered courses: chamber ensemble, coaching, master classes. Curriculum fixed. *Program concentration:* Traditional and comtemporary chamber music.

Selectivity for males: most admitted, but not all. *Selectivity for females:* most admitted, but not all.

Renowned alumni: Eric Stumacher, Richard Hartshorne.

Full-time faculty: 2. *Guest faculty:* 7. *List of some faculty:* Emi Ohi Resnick, Lars Frandsen, Rohan Gregory, Yossi Reshef, Troy Stuart.

Performance Information

Performance opportunities and frequency: daily. *Specific performance opportunities:* daily-students are encouraged to perform as soon as they are ready. *Performance casting:* auditioned. *Performances by visiting artists?* yes.

Rehearsal facilities: rustic New England farm converted into concert hall and rehearsal space. *Performance facilities:* Louise Shank Kelly concert barn.

SUNAPEE ARTS CAMP

Winter Contact Information

P.O. Box 177, Goerges Mills NH 03751
Tel: 603-763-5111
Fax: 603-763-5111
Email: bcharp@kear.tds.net
Contact: Bruce Charpentien

Summer Contact Information

P.O. Box 177, Georges Mills NH 03751
Tel: 603-763-5111
Fax: 603-763-5111
Email: bcharp@kear.tds.net
Contact: Bruce Charpentien

General

Minimum age or age range: 8 to 15. *Level of program:* beginning, intermediate.

High school credit available? no. *College credit available?* no.

Services

Housing options: on-campus cabins.

Application Information

Program dates: 6/28 - 8/16. *Application deadline:* 5/15. *Enrollment full by:* 5/15.

Audition Information

Audition not required.

Costs & Financial Aid

Financial aid available? partial scholarship. *Students receiving financial aid:* 10%.

Curriculum, Students, and Faculty

Offered courses: band, chamber ensemble, chorus, musical theater. Curricula choices.

Performance Information

Performance opportunities and frequency: weekly. *Performances by visiting artists?* yes.

Additional Comments

This is basically a traditional children's resident camp with an emphasis in music.

NEW JERSEY

INSTITUTE FOR ARTS AND HUMANITIES EDUCATION—NEW JERSEY SUMMER ARTS INSTITUTE

Winter Contact Information

New Jersey Summer Arts Institute, 100 Jersey Avenue, Suite B-104, New Brunswick NJ 08901
Tel: 908-220-1600
Fax: 908-220-1515
Contact: Rina Shere

Summer Contact Information

New Jersey Summer Arts Institute, 100 Jersey Avenue, Suite B-104, New Brunswick NJ 08901
Tel: 908-220-1600
Fax: 908-220-1515
Contact: Rina Shere

General

Minimum age or age range: 14 to 19. *Level of program:* intermediate, advanced.

High school credit available? yes. *College credit available?* no.

Services

Housing options: on-campus dorms.

Application Information

Requirements: interview, essay, recommendation. *Program dates:* 6/28-7/31. *Application deadline:* 5/31. *Application fee:* $25. *Enrollment full by:* May.

Audition Information

Audition required. Audition includes: group arts activity, personal interview.

Costs & Financial Aid

Tuition (full): $3,200.

Financial aid available? full scholarship, partial scholarship. *Scholarship notification:* May-June. *Students receiving financial aid:* 50%. *Procedure for applying for financial aid:* income eligibility.

Curriculum, Students, and Faculty

Offered courses: movement, Curricula choices.

Selectivity for males: approximately 60% admitted. *Selectivity for females:* approximately 60% admitted.

Renowned alumni: Tisha Cambell, Kraig Paterson, Mark Morris Dance.

Full-time faculty: 2. *Guest faculty:* 8.

Performance Information

Performance opportunities and frequency: 10 performances. *Performances by visiting artists?* no. *Recent guests:* Anita Gonzanles, Catherine Doty. *Performance facilities:* New Jersey, New York, Toronto, Montreal.

Affiliations

Summer program is affiliated with other program(s): future students recruited from the program.

NEW JERSEY GOVERNOR'S SCHOOL OF THE ARTS

The College of New Jersey
P.O. Box 7718, Ewing NJ 08628-0718
Tel: 609-771-3114
Fax: 609-637-5128
Email: NJGSA@TCNJ.edu
Contact: William A.L. Glenn

General

Environment: suburban.

Total enrollment of institution: 89. *Degrees offered:* certificate.

Entrance Requirements

Audition required: live, audio. *Other requirements:* interview, recommendation, essay.

Costs & Aid

Types of scholarships and aid awarded: full, merit-based, institutional aid.

Services

Housing options: on-site dorms.

Support staff: dorm parent.

MUSIC

Curriculum, Students, and Faculty

Unique or innovative music curriculum: Considerable small (chamber) ensemble performance. *How are major teacher assignments made?* made by the school.

Selectivity for instruments or programs offered (rating): bassoon (highly selective), bassoon (competitive), clarinet (highly selective), flute or piccolo (highly selective), French horn (highly selective), French horn (open), oboe/English horn (highly selective), percussion (highly selective), percussion (non-competitive), piano (highly selective), saxophone (highly selective), saxophone (open), trombone (highly selective), trumpet (highly selective), trumpet (open), tuba (highly selective), viola (highly selective), viola (open), violin (highly selective), violoncello (highly selective), voice (highly selective), voice (competitive).

Total enrollment: 42. *Entering class size:* 42. *Graduating class size:* 42. *Total full-time faculty:* 10. *Total part-time faculty:* 10. *Program contact person:* William A.L. Glenn.

Audition Information

Audition fee? no audition fee. *Audition consists of the following:* scales, sight reading, melodic dictation, repertoire., *Instruments provided for:* percussionists.

Performance opportunities available (frequency): band.

Facilities

Recital hall? yes. *Concert hall?* yes. *Recording studio?* yes.

NEW MEXICO

TAOS SCHOOL OF MUSIC SUMMER CHAMBER MUSIC

Winter Contact Information

P.O. Box 1879, Taos NM 87571
Tel: 505-776-2388
Contact: Chilton Anderson

Summer Contact Information

P.O. Box 1879, Taos NM 87571
Tel: 505-776-2388
Contact: Chilton Anderson

General

Total enrollment: 19. *Minimum age or age range:* 18 to 30. *Level of program:* advanced.

High school credit available? no. *College credit available?* no.

Services

Housing options: motel.

Application Information

Requirements: recommendation. *Program dates:* 6/7-8/2. *Application fee:* $50. *Acceptance notification:* 4/15.

Audition Information

Audition required: live, video. *Audition fee*: $50. *Audition includes:* chamber music excerpts, solo material. *Accompanist provided?* no.

Audition evaluation criteria: faculty evaluation of technical ability, musicality, personality.

Costs & Financial Aid

Tuition (full): $600.

Financial aid available? everyone is automatically on a large partial scholarship.

Curriculum, Students, and Faculty

Offered courses: chamber ensemble, Feldenkreis. Curriculum fixed. *Program concentration:* Chamber music for strings and piano.

Selectivity for males: approximately 10% admitted. *Selectivity for females:* approximately 10% admitted.

Full-time faculty: 5. *Guest faculty:* 1. *List of some faculty and their affiliations:* Robert McDonald, Peabody Conservatory.

Performance Information

Performance opportunities and frequency: 8 concerts in 8 weeks. *Performances by visiting artists?* yes. *Recent guests:* Michael Tree, Guarneri Quartet; Steven Geber, Cleveland Symphony; Arnold Steinhart, Guarneri Quartet.

Rehearsal facilities: dorm rooms and practice rooms, some with piano. *Performance facilities:* Taos Community Auditorium, Motel St. Bernos.

NEW YORK

CHAUTAUQUA SUMMER SCHOOLS

Winter Contact Information
P.O. Box 1098, Department PR, Chautauqua NY 14722
Tel: 716-357-6233
Fax: 716-357-9014
Contact: Anne N. Jackson

Summer Contact Information
P.O. Box 1098, Department PR, Chautauqua NY 14722
Tel: 716-357-6233
Fax: 716-357-9014
Contact: Anne N. Jackson

General

Total enrollment: 150. *Minimum age or age range:* 16 to 26. *Level of program:* advanced.

High school credit available? no. *College credit available?* yes.

Services

Housing options: on-campus dorms.

Application Information

Requirements: recommendation. *Program dates:* 6/27-8/18. *Application deadline:* 3/1. *Application fee:* $25. *Enrollment full by:* 4/1. *Acceptance notification:* 3/15.

Audition Information

Audition required; live, video, on-site, off-site. *Audition fee*: $25. *Audition includes:* 2-3 suggested pieces for instrumental; an aria from an Oratorio or opera for vocal (song in English, song in German); 3 memorized selections from different style periods for piano. *Accompanist provided?* no.

Costs & Financial Aid

Room: $545.

Financial aid available? full scholarship, partial scholarship. *Scholarship notification:* 3/15. *Students receiving financial aid:* 75%. *Procedure for applying for financial aid:* audition and application.

Curriculum, Students, and Faculty

Offered courses: chamber ensemble, coaching, conducting, diction, foreign language study, master classes, movement, musical theater, opera workshop, orchestra, private lessons. Curriculum fixed. *Program concentration:* instrumental (orchestra, chamber ensembles, private instruction), vocal/opera, piano, conducting fellowship.

Renowned alumni: Modechai Kaston, Ai-Lan Zhu, Guipeng Deng, Angelina Reaux, Jon Villais, Olivia Gorra Ramon, Marie Plette, Michael Dean.

Full-time faculty: 40. *Guest faculty:* 23. *List of some faculty*: Timothy Muffitt, Ron Barnett, Jan Eberle, Thompson Hanks, Rebecca Root, William Scribner, Richard Sherman, Marlena Malas, Spiro Malas.

Performance Information

Performance opportunities and frequency: weekly. *Specific performance opportunities:* 5-concert series for orchestra, weekly instrumental chamber and solo recitals, weekly voice and piano recitals/concerts. *Orchestra seating*: decided by conductor. *Seat rotation:* rotated for every concert. *Performances by visiting artists?* yes. *Recent guests:* Elmar Oliveira, Benita Valente, Gabriel Chodos.

Rehearsal facilities: sound-proof rooms in dormitory, small practice huts. *Performance facilities:* orchestral concerts in the 5,000-seat amphitheater, chamber and solo concerts/recitals in modern, acoustically sound recital hall, seats 500, small open-aired amphitheater.

EASTERN U.S. MUSIC CAMP—COLGATE UNIVERSITY

Winter Contact Information
Dr. Thomas A. Brown, 7 Brook Hollow Road
Ballston Lake NY 12019
Tel: 518-877-5121
Fax: 518-877-5121
Email: mleone@center.colgate.edu

Summer Contact Information
Colgate University
Dana Arts Center, Hamilton NY 13346-139
Tel: 315-824-7041
Fax: 315-824-7975
Email: mleone@center.colgate.edu

General
Total enrollment: 180. *Minimum age or age range:* 10 to 19. *Level of program:* intermediate, advanced.

High school credit available? yes. *College credit available?* no.

Services
Housing options: on-campus dorms.

Application Information
Program dates: 6/29-7/27 (2-4 week sessions). *Application fee:* $275. *Enrollment full by:* 6/15.

Audition Information
Audition not required.

Costs & Financial Aid
Financial aid available? partial scholarship.

Curriculum, Students, and Faculty
Offered courses: audition preparation, band, brass ensemble, chamber ensemble, choir, chorus, composition studies program, concerto, conducting, guitar, jazz ensemble, master classes, music history, music theory, orchestra, percussion, piano, private lessons, repertory, saxophone, string, vocal jazz, woodwind. Curriculum fixed.

Selectivity for males: most admitted, but not all. *Selectivity for females:* most admitted, but not all.

Full-time faculty: 40. *Guest faculty*: 10.

Performance Information
Performance opportunities and frequency: weekly. *Specific performance opportunities:* weekly recitals, weekly concerts. *Orchestra seating:* by audition. *Seat rotation:* rotated once per week. *Performance casting:* auditioned. *Performances by visiting artists?* yes. *Recent guests:* John Oberbrunner, David T. Brown.

Rehearsal facilities: air conditioned private practice rooms at modern arts center on Colgate University campus. *Performance facilities:* modern air-conditioned theater in arts center on Colgate University campus.

FRENCH WOODS FESTIVAL OF THE PERFORMING ARTS

Winter Contact Information
P.O. Box 770086, Coral Springs FL 33077
Tel: 800-634-1703
Fax: 954-346-7564
Email: frenchwood@aol.com
Contact: Ronald Schaefer

Summer Contact Information
RR 1 Box 228
Hancock, NY 13783
Tel: 914-887-5600
Fax: 914-887-5075
Email: frenchwood@aol.com
Contact: Ronald Schaefer

General
Total enrollment: 400. *Minimum age or age range:* 7 to 17. *Level of program:* beginning, intermediate, advanced.

High school credit available? no. *College credit available?* no.

Services
Housing options: on-campus cabins.

Application Information
Program dates: 6/25-8/24. *Application deadline:* none. *Application fee:* $30. *Enrollment full by:* March.

Audition Information
Audition not required.

Audition evaluation criteria: ability to play standard chamber music repertoire.

Costs & Financial Aid
Financial aid available? partial scholarship. *Scholarship notification:* after applying. *Students*

receiving financial aid: 15%. *Procedure for applying for financial aid:* submit scholarship form.

Curriculum, Students, and Faculty

Offered courses: audition preparation, master classes, movement, musical theater. Curriculum fixed. *Program concentration:* instrumental (band, orchestra, jazz) vocal (musical theatre).

Selectivity for males: approximately 60% admitted. *Selectivity for females:* approximately 60% admitted.

Full-time faculty: 8. *List of some faculty and their affiliations:* Darrell Rosenbluth, Min Young Song, Florence Altenburger, London Symphony, David Wallace, NY Philharmonic.

Performance Information

Performance opportunities and frequency: each week. *Specific performance opportunities:* many chamber performances, some solo performances.

Rehearsal facilities and hours: cabins, outdoors. *Performance facilities:* on campus and in surrounding community concert halls.

HARTWICK COLLEGE SUMMER MUSIC FESTIVAL & INSTITUTE

Winter Contact Information

Hartwick College Summer Music Festival and Institute
Oneonta NY 13820
Tel: 800-388-0337
Fax: 607-431-4813
Email: wingr@hartwick.edu
Contact: Rhonda E. Wing

Summer Contact Information

Hartwick College Summer Music Festival and Institute
Oneonta NY 13820
Tel: 800-388-0337
Fax: 607-431-4813
Email: wingr@hartwick.edu
Contact: Rhonda E. Wing

General

Total enrollment: 400. *Minimum age or age range:* 9 to 22. *Level of program:* beginning, intermediate, advanced.

High school credit available? yes. *College credit available?* yes.

Services

Housing options: on-campus dorms.

Application Information

Requirements: recommendation. *Program dates:* 6/27-8/9. *Application deadline:* rolling. *Application fee:* $300. *Enrollment full by:* 6/15.

Audition Information

Audition required. No audition fee. Audition includes: cassette tape audition.

Costs & Financial Aid

Lessons: $44 per hour.

Financial aid available? partial scholarship.

Curriculum, Students, and Faculty

Offered courses: acting for singers, audition preparation, band, chamber ensemble, chorus, coaching, conducting, diction, master classes, movement, music history, music theory, musical theater, orchestra, private lessons, repertory, seminar on the business of music. Curricula choices. *Program concentration:* choral, band, orchestra, jazz, music theatre.

Selectivity for males: most admitted, but not all. *Selectivity for females:* most admitted, but not all.

Renowned alumni: Fred Mills.

List of some faculty and their affiliations: Robert Cafaro, The Philadephia Orchestra; Jungeun Kim, The Philadelphia Orchestra; Fred Mills, University of Georgia, Canadian Brass, Erez Ofer, The Philadelphia Orchestra.

Performance Information

Performance opportunities and frequency: varies. *Orchestra seating:* by audition. *Seat rotation:* rotated weekly. *Performance casting:* auditioned. *Performances by visiting artists?* yes. *Recent guests:* Howard Aibel, Jeffrey Kahner, Philip Smith, Philip Meyers, Joseph Alessi, Don Harry.

Rehearsal facilities: Anderson Center for the Arts. *Performance facilities:* Anderson Center for the Arts Theater and Slade Theater.

Affiliations

Summer program is affiliated with other program(s): future students recruited from the program.

JAZZ WORKSHOP

Winter Contact Information
Summer Jazz Workshop, Manhattan School of Music, 120 Claremont Avenue, New York NY 10027-4698
Tel: 212-749-2802, 525
Fax: 212-749-5471
Email: admission@msmnyc.edu
Contact: Yuzuru Sadashige

Summer Contact Information
Summer Jazz Workshop, Manhattan School of Music, 120 Claremont Avenue, New York NY 10027-4698
Tel: 212-749-2802, 525
Fax: 212-749-5471
Email: admission@msmnyc.edu
Contact: Yuzuru Sadashige

General

Minimum age or age range: all ages. *Level of program:* beginning, intermediate, advanced.

High school credit available? no. *College credit available?* no.

Services

Housing options: on-campus dorms.

Application Information

Program dates: last week of June, last 2 weeks of July (3 weeks). *Application deadline:* 1 week prior workshop. *Enrollment full by:* unlimited.

Audition Information

Audition not required.

Costs & Financial Aid

Financial aid available? no.

Curriculum, Students, and Faculty

Offered courses: chamber ensemble, coaching, jazz music theory, master classes. Curriculum fixed. *Program concentration:* jazz performance (ensembles, master classes, elective classes).

Selectivity for males: admit all who apply. *Selectivity for females:* admit all who apply.

Full-time faculty: 10. *Guest faculty:* 2. *List of some faculty and their affiliations:* Hal Lieberman, Steve Slagle, Barry Harris, Harvie Swarts, Dave Lalama.

Performance Information

Performance opportunities and frequency: 1 per week.

Rehearsal facilities and hours: open practice rooms with pianos, 8:00 am-10:30 pm. *Performance facilities:* Hubbard Recital Hall at Manhattan School of Music.

MUSIC HORIZONS, JAZZ STUDIES, SUMMER WIND ENSEMBLE, PIANO WORKSHOP/ COMPETITION

Winter Contact Information
Eastman School of Music, 26 Gibbs Street, Rochester NY 14604
Tel: 716-274-1400
Fax: 716-274-1088
Email: cplr@uhura.cc.rochester.edu
Contact: Celia Palmer

Summer Contact Information
Eastman School of Music, 26 Gibbs Street, Rochester NY 14604
Tel: 716-274-1400
Fax: 716-274-1088
Email: cplr@uhura.cc.rochester.edu
Contact: Celia Palmer

General

Total enrollment: 118. *Minimum age or age range:* 14 to 18. *Level of program:* intermediate, advanced.

High school credit available? no. *College credit available?* no.

Services

Housing options: on-campus dorms, commuting is possible.

Application Information

Requirements: recommendation. *Program dates:* 7/14-8/8, 7/14-8/8, 7/21-7/27, 7/28-8/8. *Application deadline:* 4/1, 4/1, 5/1, 5/20. *Acceptance notification:* May.

Audition Information

Audition required; video. *Audition fee:* $25. *Audition includes:* any 3 selections for Muic Horizons, Summer Wind Ensemble, and Piano Workshop; specific items to illustrate range, technique, jazz conception and improvisation for Jazz Studies. *Accompanist provided?* no.

Costs & Financial Aid

Tuition (full): $325-$750. *Room:* $250. *Board:* $975.

Financial aid available? partial scholarship. *Scholarship notification:* May and June. *Students receiving financial aid:* 30%. *Procedure for applying for financial aid:* check the line requesting consideration.

Curriculum, Students, and Faculty

Offered courses: band, career counseling, chamber ensemble, chorus, coaching, improvisation, jazz combo, master classes, music history, music theory, piano seminar, private lessons, repertory, voice. *Specific curriculum information:* curriculum is fixed for Summer Wind Ensemble and Jazz Studies, choices are available in Music Horizons *Program concentration:* Individual solo performance and skills, jazz performance and individual skills, group performance, solo piano performance.

Selectivity for males: approximately 60% admitted. *Selectivity for females:* approximately 60% admitted.

Full-time faculty: 4. *Guest faculty:* 70.

Performance Information

Performance opportunities and frequency: 5 Music Horizons performances, 3 Jazz Studies performances, 2 Summer Wind Ensemble performances, 1-10 Piano Workshop performances. *Specific performance opportunities:* weekly repertory class and festival day for Music Horizons, 3 performances for Jazz Studies, 2 concerts for Summer Wind Ensemble, competition and 2 final concerts for Piano Workshop. *Orchestra seating:* By audition tape. *Performances by visiting artists?* yes. *Recent guests:* Gene Bertoncini, John Arrucci, Mitzie Collins.

Rehearsal facilities and hours: more than 50 rooms, most with pianos, available 8:00 am-10:00 pm. *Performance facilities:* Eastman Theater, Kilbourn Hall, Ciminelli Lounge.

Affiliations

Summer program is affiliated with other program(s): future students recruited from the program.

PROFESSIONAL MUSICAL THEATER WORKSHOP

Winter Contact Information

Manhattan School of Music, New York NY 10027-4698
Tel: 212-749-2802, ext. 525
Fax: 212-749-5471
Email: admission@msmnyc.edu
Contact: Yuzuru Sadoshige

Summer Contact Information

Manhattan School of Music, New York NY 10027-4698
Tel: 212-749-2802, 525
Fax: 212-749-5471
Email: admission@msmnyc.edu
Contact: Yuzuru Sadoshige

General

Total enrollment: 16. *Minimum age or age range:* all ages. *Level of program:* advanced.

High school credit available? no. *College credit available?* no.

Application Information

Program dates: 3 weeks in June. *Application deadline:* 1 month prior to workshop. *Application fee:* $20. *Acceptance notification:* within 1-2 days after audition.

Audition Information

Audition required: live, video, on-site. *Audition fee:* $30. *Audition includes:* 1 up-tempo song, 1 ballad song, 2-minute monologue from play or musical. *Accompanist provided?* no.

Costs & Financial Aid

Tuition (full): $145.

Curriculum, Students, and Faculty

Offered courses: audition preparation, master classes, movement, musical theater. Curriculum fixed. *Program concentration:* musical theatre performance.

Selectivity for males: most admitted, but not all. *Selectivity for females:* most admitted, but not all.

Full-time faculty: 4.

Performance Information

Performance opportunities and frequency: 1 per session. *Specific performance opportunities:* each camp session culminates in a group recital that presents camp activities and compositions.

Affiliations

Summer program is affiliated with a conservatory: future students are recruited from the program.

SKIDMORE JAZZ INSTITUTE

Winter Contact Information

Office of the Dean of Special Programs, Skidmore College, Saratoga Springs NY 12866
Tel: 518-580-5590
Fax: 518-584-7963
Email: mmccoll@skidmore.edu
Contact: Maria McColl

Summer Contact Information

Office of the Dean of Special Programs, Skidmore College, Saratoga Springs NY 12866
Tel: 518-580-5591
Fax: 518-584-7964
Email: mmccoll@skidmore.edu
Contact: Maria McColl

General

Minimum age or age range: 14 and up. *Level of program:* intermediate, advanced.

High school credit available? no. *College credit available?* yes.

Services

Housing options: on-campus dorms.

Application Information

Requirements: essay, recommendation. *Program dates:* 2 weeks in June, July. *Application deadline:* 5/1. *Application fee:* $30. *Enrollment full by:* 5/6. *Acceptance notification:* 1st week of May.

Audition Information

Audition required. No audition fee. Audition includes: application, audiotape with specific musical selections, application fee. *Accompanist provided?* no.

Audition evaluation criteria: intermediate/advanced musical proficiency.

Costs & Financial Aid

Tuition (full): $850. *Lessons:* $250. *Room:* $230.

Financial aid available? full scholarship, partial scholarship. *Scholarship notification:* acceptance date. *Students receiving financial aid:* 30%. *Procedure for applying for financial aid:* written application.

Curriculum, Students, and Faculty

Offered courses: master classes. Curriculum fixed. *Program concentration:* jazz.

Selectivity for males: approximately 33% admitted. *Selectivity for females:* approximately 33% admitted.

Full-time faculty: 7. *Guest faculty:* 6. *List of some faculty and their affiliations:* Milt Hinton, Ed Shangh Nessy, Jackie McLean, Ray Brown.

Performance Information

Performance opportunities and frequency: 1 per week. *Specific performance opportunities:* 2 student performances. *Performances by visiting artists?* yes. *Recent guests:* Jackie McLean, Ray Brown, Benny Green.

Rehearsal facilities and hours: state-of-the-art facilities within small liberal arts college, 8:00 am-11:00 pm daily. *Performance facilities:* campus recital hall or theater.

Affiliations

Summer program is affiliated: future students are recruited from the program.

USDAN CENTER FOR THE CREATIVE AND PERFORMING ARTS

Winter Contact Information

420 East 79th St., New York, NY 10021
Tel: 212-772-6060
Fax: 212-772-6079
Contact: Dale Lewis

Summer Contact Information

185 Colonial Springs Rd., Wheatley Heights, NY 11798
Tel: 516-643-7900
Fax: 516-643-7929

General

Total enrollment: 1500. *Minimum age or age range:* 8 to 18. *Level of program:* beginning, intermediate, advanced.

High school credit available? no. *College credit available?* yes.

Application Information

Program dates: 7 weeks in July, August. *Application deadline:* rolling, from late December. *Application fee:* $75. *Acceptance notification:* within 10 days of audition.

Audition Information

Audition required; live, on-site. *No audition fee. Audition includes:* student should call for specifics. *Accompanist provided?* yes.

Costs & Financial Aid

Tuition (full): $1,550.

Financial aid available? full scholarship, partial scholarship. *Scholarship notification:* rolling. *Students receiving financial aid:* 20%. *Procedure for applying for financial aid:* call for application.

Curriculum, Students, and Faculty

Offered courses: acting for singers, band, chamber ensemble, chorus, coaching, master classes, movement, musical theater, orchestra, Curricula choices. *Program concentration:* band, orchestra, choral, jazz studies, piano, dance, theater, visual art, creative writing, chess.

Selectivity for males: most admitted, but not all. *Selectivity for females:* most admitted, but not all.

Renowned alumni: Lawrence Yarman, Joanne Borts, Gordon Leeds, Miriam Mahdaviani, Mariah Carey.

Full-time faculty: 150. *Guest faculty:* 10. *List of some faculty and their affiliations:* Dale Lewis, Elliot J. Bean, Long Island Chorale; A. Bradford DeMilo, Nassau Symphony; Elaine L. Gates, Gary Hodges, Margaretha Maimone, Delta Ensemble;

Amelia Roosevelt, Steven Schopp, Susan Shaw, Queens Symphony, Lake George Opera, NY Gilbert and Sullivan Players; Richard Titone, Mostly Mozart Festival, Bach Ensemble.

Performance Information

Performance opportunities and frequency: daily concerts. *Orchestra seating:* by audition in class. *Performance casting:* in class. *Performances by visiting artists?* yes. *Recent guests:* The Canadian Brass, Tokyo String Quartet, Elliot Fisk, Emanuel Ax, Yo-Yo Ma, Jimmy Heath, Bill Taylor, Ruggiero Ricci.

Rehearsal facilities and hours: classes, 10:00 am-3:00 pm. *Performance facilities:* assembly amphitheater, studios.

WESTERN WIND WORKSHOP IN ENSEMBLE SINGING

Winter Contact Information

The Western Wind Vocal Ensemble, Inc., 263 West 86th Street, New York NY 10024
Tel: 212-873-2848
Fax: 212-873-2849
Email: workshops@westernwind.org
Contact: Zach Nelson

Summer Contact Information

The Western Wind Vocal Ensemble, Inc., 263 West 86th Street, New York NY 10024
Tel: 212-873-2849
Fax: 212-873-2850
Email: workshops@westernwind.org
Contact: Zach Nelson

General

Minimum age or age range: all ages. *Level of program:* beginning, intermediate, advanced.

High school credit available? no. *College credit available?* no.

Services

Housing options: on-campus Victorian dorm, off-campus housing-local hotels and motels.

Application Information

Program dates: late-June, early-August. *Application deadline:* 5/15, 6/15. *Enrollment full by:* 6/1, 6/15.

Audition Information

Audition required. No audition fee. Audition evaluation criteria: self-survey, read through with faculty (not criteria for acceptance).

Costs & Financial Aid

Financial aid available? partial scholarship. *Scholarship notification:* 6/1. *Students receiving financial aid:* 5%. *Procedure for applying for financial aid:* send letter, deadline 4/15.

Curriculum, Students, and Faculty

Offered courses: chorus, master classes, repertory. Curricula choices. *Program concentration:* Renaissance, early American, classical, romantic, modern, jazz, pop.

Selectivity for males: most admitted, but not all. *Selectivity for females:* most admitted, but not all.

List of some faculty: Phyllis Clark, Kathy Theil, William Zukof, Michael Steinberger, Tim Evens, Elliot Levine, Bob Einstein, Grant Herreid.

Performance Information

Performance opportunities and frequency: 1 master class performance per day. *Specific performance opportunities:* daily seminar, master classes. *Performances by visiting artists?* yes.

Rehearsal facilities and hours: Smith College Music Department practice room with piano, available continuously. *Performance facilities:* Smith College Music Department concert hall.

Additional Comments

Although the focus of this workshop is more general, talented high school and college students can apply for scholarships.

NORTH CAROLINA

BREVARD MUSIC CENTER

Winter Contact Information

P.O. Box 312, Brevard NC 28712-0312
Tel: 704-884-2011
Fax: 704-884-2036
Email: dnickson@brevardmusic.org
Contact: Don Nickson

Summer Contact Information

P.O. Box 312, Brevard NC 28712-0312
Tel: 704-884-2011
Fax: 704-884-2036
Email: dnickson@brevardmusic.org
Contact: Don Nickson

General

Total enrollment: 375.

Services

Housing options: On-campus cabins; housing with families is for faculty only.

Audition Information

Audition required; off-site. *Accompanist provided?* no.

Curriculum, Students, and Faculty

Offered courses: master classes, movement (5 classes per week), musical theater. *Program concentration:* musical performance and repertoire, individual and ensemble instruction.

Performance Information

Performance opportunities and frequency: 2 orchestra performances weekly, 1 chorus performance. *Specific performance opportunities:* 4 orchestra concerts, 2 chorus concerts, daily chamber and solo concerts at lunch. *Orchestra seating:* initially by audition, subsequently decided by orchestra faculty. *Seat rotation:* rotated for each concert. *Performances by visiting artists?* yes. *Recent guests:* Kathryn Sleeper, Willie Hill, George Shaw.

Rehearsal facilities and hours: practice and/or private lessons, 1:00 pm-3:00pm and whatever time students can carve out from group and/sectional rehearsals.

CANNON MUSIC CAMP

Winter Contact Information

Appalachian State University, Boone NC 28608
Tel: 704-262-4091
Fax: 704-262-6446
Email: jacksnjc@appstate.edu
Contact: Jay C. Jackson

Summer Contact Information

Appalachian State University, Boone NC 28608
Tel: 704-262-4091
Fax: 704- 262-6446
Email: jacksnjc@appstate.edu
Contact: Jay C. Jackson

Services

Housing options: On-site housing.

Audition Information

Audition not required.

Curriculum, Students, and Faculty

Offered courses: Alexander technique, master classes.

EASTERN MUSIC FESTIVAL

Winter Contact Information

P.O. Box 22026, Greensboro NC 27420
Tel: 910-333-7450
Fax: 910-333-7454
Email: emf@nr.infi.net
Contact: Kathleen Tesar

Summer Contact Information

P.O. Box 22026, Greensboro NC 27420
Tel: 910-333-7451
Fax: 910-333-7455
Email: emf@nr.infi.net
Contact: Kathleen Tesar

General

Total enrollment: 205.

Services

Housing options: On-campus air-conditioned dorms.

Audition Information

Audition required; live, on-site. *Audition includes:* 1 lyrical piece and 1 technical piece by different composers, sight-reading. *Accompanist provided?* no.

Curriculum, Students, and Faculty

Offered courses: Alexander technique, audition preparation, master classes. *Program concentration:* Symphony orchestra, piano, chamber music, master classes, private lessons.

Performance Information

Performance opportunities and frequency: 5 weekends. *Specific performance opportunities:* artists attend only to rehearse and are not assured of performing. *Performances by visiting artists?* no. *Recent guests:* Rudolf Serkin, Adolf Busch, Herman Busch, Pablo Casals, Mieczyslaw Horszowski, Alexander Schneider, Pina Carmirelli, Sandor Vegh.

GLICKMAN-POPKIN BASSOON CAMP/ MARK POPKIN'S BASSOON CAMP BY-THE-SEA

Winter Contact Information

740 Arbor Road, Winston-Salem NC 27104-2210
Tel: 910-725-5681
Fax: 910-777-8254
Email: elsiepop@aol.com
Contact: Mark A. Popkin

Summer Contact Information
740 Arbor Road, Winston-Salem NC 27104-2210
Tel: 910-725-5681
Fax: 910-777-8254
Email: elsiepop@aol.com
Contact: Mark A. Popkin

General

Minimum age or age range: all ages. *Level of program:* beginning, intermediate, advanced.

High school credit available? no. *College credit available?* no.

Services

Housing options: semi-private room with private bath or semi-private with shared bath.

Application Information

Program dates: second, third weeks of June. *Application deadline:* none. *Application fee:* $25. *Enrollment full by:* 6/1.

Audition Information

Audition not required.

Costs & Financial Aid

Tuition (full): $280.

Curriculum, Students, and Faculty

Offered courses: audition preparation, master classes. Curriculum fixed. *Program concentration:* bassoon performance practices, reed making, maintenance.

Selectivity for males: admit all who apply. *Selectivity for females:* admit all who apply.

Full-time faculty: 2. *List of some faculty and their affiliations:* Ashley Heinzen, Ann Adams.

Performance Information

Specific performance opportunities: faculty performance, student performance at the end of the week.

Affiliations

Summer program is affiliated with a conservatory: future students are recruited from the program.

NORTH CAROLINA SCHOOL OF THE ARTS SUMMER SESSION (NCSA)

Winter Contact Information
200 Waughtown Street, Winston-Salem NC 27117-2189
Tel: 910-770-3204
Fax: 910-770-3375
Email: raineyb@ncsavx.ncarts.edu
Contact: Bill Rainey

Summer Contact Information
200 Waughtown Street, Winston-Salem NC 27117-2189
Tel: 910-770-3204
Fax: 910-770-3375
Email: raineyb@ncsavx.ncarts.edu
Contact: Bill Rainey

General

Total enrollment: 70. *Minimum age or age range:* 15 to 18. *Level of program:* intermediate, advanced.

High school credit available? yes. *College credit available?* yes.

Services

Housing options: on-campus dorms.

Application Information

Requirements: recommendation. *Program dates:* 6/22-7/25. *Application deadline:* 5/1. *Application fee:* $35. *Enrollment full by:* 6/1.

Audition Information

Audition required: *No audition fee. Audition includes:* 2 excerpts of current technical level. *Accompanist provided?* no.

Costs & Financial Aid

Room: $660.

Financial aid available? partial scholarship. *Scholarship notification:* ASAP. *Students receiving financial aid:* 10%. *Procedure for applying for financial aid:* letter.

Curriculum, Students, and Faculty

Offered courses: band, chamber ensemble, chorus, coaching, master classes, movement, music history, music theory, opera workshop, orchestra, private lessons. Curriculum fixed.

Selectivity for males: approximately 60% admitted. *Selectivity for females:* approximately 60% admitted.

Renowned alumni: Ransom Wilson, Sharon Robinson.

Full-time faculty: 10. *List of some faculty:* Philip Dunigan, Robert Ustokin, James Kalyn, David Winkleman, Lawrence Dillon, James Allbritton, Michael Rothkopf.

Performance Information

Performance opportunities and frequency: 10 student concerts and recitals. *Specific performance opportunities:* each student performs in an ensemble and/or recital. *Orchestra seating:* by conductor.

Rehearsal facilities: NCSA, 2 concerts halls, practice rooms, and classrooms. *Performance facilities:* Crawford and recital halls on the NCSA campus.

Affiliations

Summer program is affiliated with other program(s): future students recruited from the program.

WILDACRES FLUTE RETREAT

Winter Contact Information

3530 Bear Creek Road, Tallahassee FL 32308
Tel: 904-942-6520
Fax: 904-942-6520
Email: kbarton@freenet.tlh.fl.us
Contact: Karl Barton

Summer Contact Information

Tel: 704-756-4573
Fax: 704-756-4586
Email: kbarton@freenet.tlh.fl.us
Contact: Karl Barton

General

Total enrollment: 90. *Minimum age or age range:* 14 to 65. *Level of program:* advanced.

High school credit available? no. *College credit available?* no.

Services

Housing options: lodges, local motels, chalets.

Application Information

Program dates: 6/20-6/26. *Application deadline:* performers 4/1, general program 6/1. *Application fee:* $50. *Enrollment full by:* 4/1. *Acceptance notification:* 5/1.

Audition Information

Audition required. *No audition fee. Audition includes:* prepared study, standard repertoire. *Accompanist provided?* no.

Audition evaluation criteria: committee review of taped audition.

Costs & Financial Aid

Tuition (full): $500. *Lessons:* $75.

Financial aid available? partial scholarship. *Scholarship notification:* 5/1. *Students receiving financial aid:* 10%. *Procedure for applying for financial aid:* preliminary written request, scholarship application requires personal essay, need-based scholarship.

Curriculum, Students, and Faculty

Offered courses: Alexander technique, flute repair, master classes, multicultural flutes, pedagogy, private lessons. Curriculum fixed. *Program concentration:* flute performance.

Selectivity for males: approximately 60% admitted. *Selectivity for females:* approximately 60% admitted.

Full-time faculty: 10. *List of some faculty and their affiliations:* William Bennett, English Chamber Orchestra, Royal Academy of Music; Stephen Preston, Academy of Ancient Music, Royal College of Music.

Performance Information

Specific performance opportunities: in master classes, afternoon recitals.

Rehearsal facilities and hours: practicing allowed in rooms, 8:00 am-11:00 pm. *Performance facilities:* Wildcrest Retreat Main Auditorium.

OHIO

BALDWIN-WALLACE COLLEGE CONSERVATORY OF MUSIC, SUMMER MUSIC CLINIC

Winter Contact Information

275 Eastland Road, Berea OH 44017
Tel: 216-826-2367
Fax: 216-826-3239
Email: thecon@bw.edu
Contact: Anita S. Evans

Summer Contact Information

275 Eastland Road, Berea OH 44017
Tel: 216-826-2368
Email: thecon@bw.edu
Contact: Anita S. Evans

General

Total enrollment: 200. *Minimum age or age range:* 14 to 18. *Level of program:* intermediate, advanced.

Services

Housing options: on-campus supervised single sex residence halls.

Application Information

Program dates: 6/21-7/5. *Application deadline:* 5/10.

Audition Information

Audition not required.

Costs & Financial Aid

Tuition (full): $375. *Lessons:* included in the tuition. *Room:* $310.

Financial aid available? full scholarship, partial scholarship. *Students receiving financial aid:* 10%. *Procedure for applying for financial aid:* Application, audition videotape, music teacher evaluation.

Curriculum, Students, and Faculty

Offered courses: band, beginner guitar, beginner piano, chamber ensemble, chorus, music theory, orchestra, piano seminar, private lessons. Curricula choices. *Program concentration:* 2 weeks of intensive music study centering around major ensemble and private lesson instruction.

Full-time faculty: 20. *Guest faculty:* 3. *List of some faculty and their affiliations:* James Darling, Cleveland Orchestra; Elizabeth Camus, Cleveland Orchestra; Robert Mayerovitch, Elysian Trio; Julian Ross, Elysian Trio; Dwight Oltman, Beach Festival, Cleveland Ballet Conductor.

Performance Information

Performance opportunities and frequency: 1 recital, 1 concert. *Specific performance opportunities:* each week culminates in a mass concert for all major ensembles, solo night, piano seminar recital, chamber music recitals. *Orchestra seating:* All major ensembles are auditioned on the first day of clinic.

Rehearsal facilities and hours: 50 unassigned rooms, grand piano available for piano students. *Performance facilities:* Fanny Nast Gamble Auditorium, 600 seats, largest performing venue on campus, Fynette H. Kulas Chamber Hall, 100-seat, intimate performing hall for small chamber groups.

Affiliations

Summer program is affiliated with other program(s): future students recruited from the program.

BOWLING GREEN STATE UNIVERSITY SUMMER MUSIC INSTITUTE

Winter Contact Information

College of Musical Arts, Bowling Green, OH 43403
Tel: 419-372-2182
Fax: 419-372-2938
Deborah L. Meth

Summer Contact Information

College of Musical Arts, Bowling Green OH 43403
Tel: 419-372-2182
Fax: 419-372-2938
Contact: Deborah L. Meth

General

Total enrollment: 175. *Level of program:* intermediate, advanced.

Services

Housing options: on-campus dorms.

Application Information

Requirements: recommendation. *Program dates:* mid-June to mid-July. *Application deadline:* 5/1.

Audition Information

Audition not required.

Costs & Financial Aid

Financial aid available? Yes; partial scholarship.

Curriculum, Students, and Faculty

Offered courses: audition preparation, band, chamber ensemble, chorus, coaching, master classes, music theory, orchestra, private lessons, repertory. Curriculum fixed. *Program concentration:* piano, saxophone, flute, strings, jazz, choir, band, recording technology.

Selectivity for males: most admitted, but not all. *Selectivity for females:* most admitted, but not all.

Performance Information

Performance opportunities and frequency: 2 public performances per camp week. *Specific performance opportunities:* recitals, chamber music, orchestra. *Orchestra seating:* by conductor.

Rehearsal facilities and hours: College of Musical Arts daily practice scheduled. *Performance facilities:* all performances in Bryan Recital Hall.

ENCORE SCHOOL FOR STRINGS

Winter Contact Information

The Cleveland Institute of Music, 11021 East Boulevard, Cleveland OH 44106-1776
Tel: 216-791-5000
Fax: 216-791-1530
Contact: Sandie Poole-Fabian

Summer Contact Information

Western Reserve Academy, 110 College Street, Hudson OH 44236
Tel: 216-650-9744
Fax: 216-650-9754
Contact: Sandie Poole-Fabian

General

Total enrollment: 160. *Minimum age or age range:* 10 to 25. *Level of program:* advanced.

High school credit available? no. *College credit available?* no.

Services

Housing options: on-campus dorms, limited off-campus independent housing.

Application Information

Program dates: 6/28-8/8. *Application deadline:* 3/1. *Application fee:* $25. *Enrollment full by:* 3/7. *Acceptance notification:* 4/1.

Audition Information

Audition required. No audition fee. Audition includes: 1 movement of standard concerto, 1 movement of a solo Bach Sonata, Partita, or Suite. *Accompanist provided?* no.

Costs & Financial Aid

Tuition (full): $3,250.

Financial aid available? Yes; partial scholarship. *Scholarship notification:* end of April. *Students receiving financial aid:* 15%. *Procedure for applying for financial aid:* send written request with application.

Curriculum, Students, and Faculty

Offered courses: chamber ensemble, coaching, *Program concentration:* violin, viola, cello-solo and chamber music.

Selectivity for males: approximately 33% admitted. *Selectivity for females:* approximately 33% admitted.

Renowned alumni: Ivan Chan, Leila Josefowicz, Lara St. John, Scott St. John, Hilary Hahn, Juliette Kang, Soovin Kim, Jasper Wood, Robert Chen, Martin Beaver, Sherye Staples.

Full-time faculty: 25.

Performance Information

Specific performance opportunities: bi-weekly concerts open to the public, luncheon chamber concerts, community outreach concerts. *Performances by visiting artists?* yes. *Recent guests:* Miami Quartet, Lara St. John, Soovin Kim, Henry Roth.

Rehearsal facilities and hours: dorm rooms, studios. *Performance facilities:* chapel.

FRIENDS MUSIC CAMP

Winter Contact Information

P.O. Box 427, Yellow Springs OH 45387
Tel: 937-767-1311
Contact: Peg Champney

Summer Contact Information

Olney Friends School, Barnesville OH 43713
Tel: 614-425-3655
Fax: 614-425-3202
Contact: Peg Champney

General

Total enrollment: 75. *Minimum age or age range:* 10 to 18. *Level of program:* beginning, intermediate, advanced.

High school credit available? no. *College credit available?* no.

Services

Housing options: on-campus dorms.

Application Information

Program dates: 7/6-8/3. *Application deadline:* rolling. *Application fee:* $50. *Enrollment full by:* 3/31. *Acceptance notification:* 1 week after application received.

Audition Information

Audition not required.

Costs & Financial Aid

Tuition (full): $1,160.

Financial aid available? Yes; partial scholarship. *Scholarship notification:* usually within 2 weeks of receiving application. *Students receiving financial aid:* 30%. *Procedure for applying for financial aid:* apply early with definite request.

Curriculum, Students, and Faculty

Offered courses: band, chamber ensemble, chorus, music history, music theory, musical theater, orchestra, private lessons. Curricula choices. *Program concentration:* instrumental music and voice.

Selectivity for males: most admitted, but not all. *Selectivity for females:* most admitted, but not all.

Full-time faculty: 19. *List of some faculty and their affiliations:* Wendy Champhey, Carmina Quartet, Luba Fedorov.

Performance Information

Performance opportunities and frequency: 1-4 individual performances during session. *Specific performance opportunities:* 1 student recital each week, 4 large group concerts during camp, 1 musical theater production. *Orchestra seating:* According to the conductor. *Seat rotation:* some rotating by skill level.

Rehearsal facilities and hours: individual rooms, daily one hour practice. *Performance facilities:* auditorium of main building on campus.

OKLAHOMA

OKLAHOMA SUMMER ARTS INSTITUTE

Winter Contact Information
P.O. Box 18154, Oklahoma City OK 73154
Tel: 405-842-0890
Fax: 405-848-4538
Email: okarts@telepath.com
Contact: Mary Gordon Taft

Summer Contact Information
P.O. Box 18154, Oklahoma City OK 73154
Tel: 405-842-0890
Fax: 405-848-4538
Email: okarts@telepath.com
Contact: Mary Gordon Taft

General

Total enrollment: 126. *Minimum age or age range:* 14 to 18. *Level of program:* advanced

High school credit available? no. *College credit available?* yes.

Services

Housing options: on-campus dorms and cabins—students are housed with counselors.

Application Information

Requirements: essay, recommendation. *Program dates:* 6/13-6/28 (2 weeks). *Application deadline:* at time of audition. *Application fee:* $5. *Enrollment full by:* 3/1. *Acceptance notification:* early April.

Audition Information

Audition required; live, video, off-site. *Audition fee:* $5. *Audition includes:* 2 octave scales of student's choice, sight-reading and brief solo for orchestra; solo, sight-reading, range testing, and tonal memory exercise for chorus; all auditions are video-taped. *Accompanist provided?* no.

Audition evaluation criteria: vocal quality, sight-reading, musicality, tonal retention, technique.

Costs & Financial Aid

Tuition (full): $75. *Lessons:* included in the tuition.

Financial aid available? Yes; partial scholarship. *Procedure for applying for financial aid:* All students receive a $750 scholarship from the state department of education upon acceptance.

Curriculum, Students, and Faculty

Offered courses: chamber ensemble, chorus, coaching, conducting, master classes, movement, orchestra, private lessons. Curriculum fixed. *Program concentration:* orchestral music and chorus.

Selectivity for males: approximately 10% admitted. *Selectivity for females:* approximately 10% admitted.

Renowned alumni: Yolanda Kandonassis.

Guest faculty: 25. *List of some faculty and their affiliations:* Kate Tamarkin, East Texas Symphony, Vermont Symphony; Thomas Sleeper, University of Miami Symphony; Patrick Gardener, Rutgers University; Jo Michael Scheibe, University of Miami.

Performance Information

Performance opportunities and frequency: 2 orchestra performances each week, 1 chorus performance each week. *Specific performance opportunities:* 4 orchestra concerts, 2 chorus concerts, daily chamber and solo concerts at lunch. *Orchestra seating:* Initially by audition scores, subsequently decided by orchestra faculty. *Seat rotation:* rotated for each concert. *Performances by visiting artists?* yes. *Recent guests:* Katheyn Sleeper, Willie Hill, George Shaw.

Rehearsal facilities and hours: practice and/or private lessons, 1:00 pm-3:00 pm and whatever time students can carve out from group and sectional rehearsals. *Performance facilities:* in process of building 750-seat which will include a small recital hall and practice spaces.

OREGON

OREGON BACH FESTIVAL

Winter Contact Information
1257 University of Oregon, Eugene OR 97403
Email: mlowen@oregon.uoregon.edu
Contact: Marla Lowen

Summer Contact Information
1257 University of Oregon, Eugene OR 97403
Email: mlowen@oregon.uoregon.edu
Contact: Marla Lowen

General

Minimum age or age range: 21 and up. *Level of program:* advanced.

High school credit available? no. *College credit available?* no.

Services

Housing options: on-campus dorms.

Application Information

Program dates: last week of June-first week of July. *Application deadline:* 3/1. *Enrollment full by:* 6/1. *Acceptance notification:* 4/1.

Audition Information

Audition required; video. *No audition fee. Accompanist provided?* no.

Costs & Financial Aid

Financial aid available? no.

Curriculum, Students, and Faculty

Offered courses: master classes. Curriculum fixed. *Program concentration:* master class in choral/orchestral conducting/classical.

TWENTIETH ANNUAL SUMMER MUSIC DAY CAMPS SPONSORED BY THE CHAMBER MUSIC SOCIETY OF OREGON AT PORTLAND STATE UNIVERSITY

Winter Contact Information

1935 Northeast 59th Avenue, Portland OR 97213-4117
Tel: 503-287-2175
Contact: Hazel M. Delorenzo

Summer Contact Information

1935 Northeast 59th Avenue, Portland OR 97213-4117
Tel: 503-287-2176
Fax: 503-287-2176
Contact: Hazel M. Delorenzo

Services

Housing options: on-campus dorms.

Audition Information

Audition not required.

Curriculum, Students, and Faculty

Program concentration: piano, strings, woodwinds, brass.

Performance Information

Specific performance opportunities: 8 concerts in 8 weeks. *Performances by visiting artists?* yes. *Recent guests:* Michael Tree, Guarneri Quartet; Stephen Geber, Cleveland Symphony.

Rehearsal facilities: dorm rooms and private rooms, some with piano.

PENNSYLVANIA

LEBANON VALLEY COLLEGE

Winter Contact Information

Summer Music Camp, 101 N. College Avenue, Annville PA 17003
Tel: 717-867-6289
Fax: 717-867-6124
Email: hearson@luc.edu
Contact: Dr. Robert H. Hearson

Summer Contact Information

Summer Music Camp, 101 N. College Avenue, Annville PA 17003
Tel: 717-867-6289
Fax: 717-867-6124
Email: hearson@luc.edu
Contact: Dr. Robert H. Hearson

General

Total enrollment: 130. *Level of program:* intermediate, advanced.

High school credit available? no. *College credit available?* no.

Services

Housing options: on-campus dorms.

Application Information

Requirements: recommendation. *Program dates:* 7/12-7/17. *Application deadline:* 6/30. *Enrollment full by:* 5/30. *Acceptance notification:* upon receipt of application.

Audition Information

Audition required. No audition fee. Accompanist provided? no.

Audition evaluation criteria: level of performance.

Costs & Financial Aid

Tuition (full): $375. *Lessons:* $15 per half hour.

Curriculum, Students, and Faculty

Offered courses: audition preparation, band, chamber ensemble, master classes, music theory, orchestra, private lessons, repertory, seminar on the business of music. Curricula choices. *Program concentration:* concert band, strings, piano, guitar, jazz band, percussion ensemble, chamber ensembles.

Selectivity for males: most admitted, but not all. *Selectivity for females:* most admitted, but not all.

Full-time faculty: 11. *Guest faculty:* 3. *List of some faculty and their affiliations:* Robert Hearson, James Erdman, The President's Own U.S. Marine Band; Erwin Chandler, Jill Klinger, Joseph Mixon, Robert Nowak.

Performance Information

Performance opportunities and frequency: 1 recital, 1 concert. *Specific performance opportunities:* band, orchestra, jazz band, percussion ensemble, brass choir, chamber ensembles. *Orchestra seating:* first day auditions.

Rehearsal facilities and hours: modern, air-conditioned, 7:30 am-10:30 pm. *Performance facilities:* 600-seat auditorium.

Affiliations

Summer program is affiliated with a university: future students are recruited from the program.

PRECOLLEGE—SCHOOL OF MUSIC, CARNEGIE MELLON UNIVERSITY

Winter Contact Information

Pittsburgh PA 15213-3890
Tel: 412-268-2382
Fax: 412-268-1431
Email: precollege@andrew.cmu.edu
Contact: Natalie L. Ozeas

Summer Contact Information

Pittsburgh PA 15213-3890
Tel: 412-268-2382
Fax: 412-268-1431
Email: precollege@andrew.cmu.edu
Contact: Natalie L. Ozeas

General

Total enrollment: 100. *Minimum age or age range:* 16 to 17. *Level of program:* intermediate, advanced.

High school credit available? no. *College credit available?* no.

Services

Housing options: On-site housing.

Application Information

Application deadline: 5/1. *Application fee:* $25. *Acceptance notification:* rolling.

Audition Information

Audition required. No audition fee. Audition includes: taped performance representative of level of performance, or scores of original compositions. *Accompanist provided?* no.

Costs & Financial Aid

Tuition (full): $3,250.

Financial aid available? Yes; partial scholarship. *Scholarship notification:* end of April. *Students receiving financial aid:* 15%. *Procedure for applying for financial aid:* send written request with application.

Curriculum, Students, and Faculty

Offered courses: audition preparation, master classes, movement, musical theater. Curriculum fixed. *Program concentration:* performance, composition, technology, voice, piano.

Selectivity for males: approximately 33% admitted. *Selectivity for females:* approximately 33% admitted.

Renowned alumni: Sheryl Staples, Ivan Chan, Leila Josefowicz, Lara St. John, John St. John, Hilary Hahn, Juliette Kang, Soovin Kim, Jasper Wood, Robert Chen, Martin Beaver.

Full-time faculty: 25.

Performance Information

Performance opportunities and frequency: biweekly. *Specific performance opportunities:* concerts open to public, luncheon chamber music concerts, community outreach concerts. *Performances by visiting artists?* yes. *Recent guests:* Miami Quartet, Lara St. John, Soovin Kim, Henry Roth.

Rehearsal facilities and hours: dorm rooms, studios. *Performance facilities:* The Chapel.

QUARTET PROGRAM

Winter Contact Information

1163 East Avenue, Rochester NY 14607
Tel: 716-274-1592
Fax: 716-442-4282
Email: ccastleman@aol.com
Contact: Charles Castleman

Summer Contact Information

Bucknell University, P.O. Box C-4000, Lewisburg PA 17837
Tel: 717-523-4911
Fax: 717-523-4910
Email: ccastleman@aol.com
Contact: Charles Castleman

General

Total enrollment: 36. *Minimum age or age range:* 14 to 35. *Level of program:* advanced.

High school credit available? no. *College credit available?* no.

Services

Housing options: on-campus dorms—students have their own rooms.

Application Information

Program dates: late June-early August (7 weeks). *Application deadline:* 3/15. *Acceptance notification:* 4/10.

Audition Information

Audition required; live, video, off-site. *No audition fee. Audition includes:* 2 contrasting works, 15 minutes long. *Accompanist provided?* no.

Audition evaluation criteria: auditions for campers are for placement only.

Costs & Financial Aid

Tuition (full): $375.

Financial aid available? yes.

Curriculum, Students, and Faculty

Offered courses: master classes. Curriculum fixed. *Program concentration:* violin, viola, cello-solo and chamber music.

Selectivity for males: admit all who apply. *Selectivity for females:* admit all who apply.

Affiliations

Summer program is affiliated with a conservatory: future students are recruited from the program.

TENNESSEE

SEWANEE SUMMER MUSIC CENTER

Winter Contact Information
735 University Avenue, Sewanee TN 37383-1000
Tel: 615-598-1225
Fax: 615-598-1706
Contact: Martha McCrory

Summer Contact Information
735 University Avenue, Sewanee TN 37383-1000
Tel: 615-598-1225
Fax: 615-598-1706
Contact: Martha McCrory

General

Total enrollment: 220. *Minimum age or age range:* 12 and up. *Level of program:* intermediate.

High school credit available? no. *College credit available?* no.

Services

Housing options: on-campus dorms.

Application Information

Program dates: 6/27-8/2.

Audition Information

Audition required. No audition fee. Accompanist provided? yes.

Audition evaluation criteria: self-survey, read through with faculty (not a criteria for acceptance).

Costs & Financial Aid

Tuition (full): $2,000. *Lessons:* $80 per half hour.

Financial aid available? Yes; partial scholarship. *Students receiving financial aid:* 20%.

Curriculum, Students, and Faculty

Offered courses: chamber ensemble, conducting, master classes, music theory, orchestra, private lessons, repertory. Curriculum fixed.

Selectivity for males: approximately 33% admitted. *Selectivity for females:* approximately 33% admitted.

Full-time faculty: 30. *Guest faculty:* 7. *List of some faculty:* Martha McCrory, Leonid Kerbel, Norman Paulu, Grace Mihi Bahng, Marian Shaffer, Michael Gurt, Eldred Spell, Bruce Dinkins, James Lotz, Lynn Mostoller, Laura Rickets Hoffman, Cyrus Ginwala.

Performance Information

Performance opportunities and frequency: weekly orchestra, chamber performance. *Specific performance opportunities:* an average of 20 conerts per season. *Orchestra seating:* By audition. *Performances by visiting artists?* yes. *Recent guests:* Alan Balter, Peter Vronsky, Donald Johanas, Menahem Nebenhaus, Tokyo String Quartet, The Ying Quartet, Dale Clevenger.

Rehearsal facilities and hours: Guerry Hall and the outdoor splendor of the campus, 7:00 am-10:00 pm. *Performance facilities:* 1000-seat Guerry Auditorium, Guerry Garth outdoor stage set among the University of the South's gothic structure.

TEXAS

FESTIVAL-INSTITUTE AT ROUND TOP

Winter Contact Information
P.O. Drawer 89, Round Top TX 78954-0089
Tel: 409-249-3129
Fax: 409-249-5078
Email: festinst@fais.net
Contact: James Dick

Summer Contact Information
P.O. Drawer 89, Round Top TX 78954-0089
Tel: 409-249-3129Fax: 409-249-5078
Email: festinst@fais.net
Contact: Alain Declert or James Dick

General
Total enrollment: 100. *Minimum age or age range:* 18 to 28. *Level of program:* advanced.

High school credit available? yes. *College credit available?* no.

Services
Housing options: 3-4 people per rooms with air-conditioning and bath.

Application Information
Requirements: recommendation. *Program dates:* 6/1-7/12. *Application deadline:* 3/1. *Enrollment full by:* April. *Acceptance notification:* 4/1.

Audition Information
Audition required; live, off-site. *No audition fee. Audition includes:* solo piece, orchestral excerpts. *Accompanist provided?* no.

Audition evaluation criteria: rhythm, articulation, projection.

Costs & Financial Aid
Financial aid available? full scholarship, partial scholarship. *Students receiving financial aid:* 99%.

Curriculum, Students, and Faculty
Offered courses: audition preparation, chamber ensemble, coaching, conducting, master classes, music history, orchestra, private lessons, repertory, seminar on the business of music. Curriculum fixed. *Program concentration:* orchestral, chamber and string quartets.

Selectivity for males: approximately 33% admitted. *Selectivity for females:* approximately 33% admitted.

Renowned alumni: Peter Rejto, Sheryl Staples.

Full-time faculty: 12. *Guest faculty:* 2. *List of some faculty and their affiliations:* James Dick, Thomas Booth, Dallas Symphony; Karl Kraber, The Chamber Soloists of Austin, Jorja Fleezanis, Minnesota Orchestra.

Performance Information
Performance opportunities and frequency: every week. *Specific performance opportunities:* orchestral and chamber. *Orchestra seating:* by faculty.

Rehearsal facilities and hours: 35 individual studios, 6 ensemble studios, one concert hall, 8:00 am-12:00 am. *Performance facilities:* Festival Concert Hall, 1,200 seats, Edythe Bates Old Chapel, 170 seats.

SUMMER MUSIC PROGRAMS

Winter Contact Information
School of Music, Baylor University, Waco TX 76798
Tel: 254-755-1122
Fax: 254-755-3574
Contact: Barry Hopper

Summer Contact Information
School of Music, Baylor University, Waco TX 76798
Tel: 254-755-1122
Fax: 254-755-3574
Contact: Barry Hopper

General
Level of program: intermediate, advanced.

High school credit available? no. *College credit available?* no.

Services
Housing options: on-campus dorms.

Audition Information
Audition not required.

Costs & Financial Aid
Tuition (full): $300.

Financial aid available? full scholarship, partial scholarship. *Students receiving financial aid:* 20%.

Curriculum, Students, and Faculty
Offered courses: band, chamber ensemble, chorus, orchestra. Curriculum fixed.

Selectivity for males: approximately 60% admitted. *Selectivity for females:* approximately 60% admitted.

Performance Information
Performance opportunities and frequency: 2 performances. *Specific performance opportunities:* 1 chamber concert, 1 formal orchestra for wind ensemble. *Orchestra seating:* By audition.

Rehearsal facilities: 60 university practice rooms. *Performance facilities:* Jones Concert Hall.

Affiliations
Summer program is affiliated with a university: future students are recruited from the program.

VERMONT

ADAMANT MUSIC SCHOOL

Winter Contact Information
130 West 67th Street Apartment 25-F, New York NY 10023-5914
Tel: 212-496-2069
Fax: 212-496-2069
Email: MLFADAMANT@MSN.com
Contact: Mary Lou Francis

Summer Contact Information
On Adamant Green, Adamant VT 05640
Tel: 802-229-9297
Fax: 802-223-0915
Email: MLFADAMANT@MSN.com
Contact: Mary Lou Francis

General

Total enrollment: 32. *Minimum age or age range:* 14 and up. *Level of program:* advanced.

High school credit available? yes. *College credit available?* yes.

Services

Housing options: 5 resident houses with 39 bedrooms.

Application Information

Requirements: recommendation. *Program dates:* last 2 weeks of July-mid August. *Application deadline:* 4/1. *Enrollment full by:* 4/1. *Acceptance notification:* 4/15-4/30.

Audition Information

Audition required. No audition fee. Audition includes: 3 pieces of contrasting styles, 1 piece must be a sonata by Haydn, Beethoven or Mozart.

Costs & Financial Aid

Tuition (full): $1,400.

Financial aid available? full scholarship, partial scholarship. *Scholarship notification:* 4/30. *Students receiving financial aid:* 50%. *Procedure for applying for financial aid:* submit family income disclosure form.

Curriculum, Students, and Faculty

Offered courses: coaching, master classes, repertoire, solo repertoire. *Program concentration:* The program is for piano students only.

Selectivity for males: approximately 60% admitted.

List of some faculty: Mary Lou Francis, Lynn Rice-See, George Burde.

Performance Information

Performance opportunities and frequency: 2-3 per week. *Specific performance opportunities:* as many as the student wishes or requires. *Performances by visiting artists?* yes. *Recent guests:* Peter Orth, Nicolai Lomou.

Rehearsal facilities: 29 practice studios, 32 grand pianos. *Performance facilities:* 2 performance halls in Adamant.

BENNINGTON COLLEGE JULY PROGRAM

Winter Contact Information
Bennington VT 05201
Tel: 802-442-5401, ext. 367
Fax: 802-442-6164
Email: july_program@bennington.edu
Contact: Vallerie Malkin

Summer Contact Information
Bennington College, Bennington VT 05201
Tel: 802-442-5402, ext. 367
Fax: 802-442-6165
Email: july_program@bennington.edu
Contact: Vallerie Malkin

General

Total enrollment: 250. *Minimum age or age range:* 15 to 18. *Level of program:* beginning, intermediate, advanced.

High school credit available? yes. *College credit available?* yes.

Services

Housing options: on-site housing.

Application Information

Requirements: essay, recommendation. *Application deadline:* rolling. *Application fee:* $30. *Enrollment full by:* late June. *Acceptance notification:* July.

Audition Information

Audition not required. Accompanist provided? yes.

Costs & Financial Aid

Tuition (full): $2,875. *Lessons:* $37.50.

Financial aid available? full scholarship, partial scholarship. *Students receiving financial aid:* 33%. *Procedure for applying for financial aid:* fill out application, deadline 5/15.

Curriculum, Students, and Faculty

Offered courses: acting, dance, music, performance on stage, rhythm movement, voice. Curriculum fixed. *Program concentration:* all instruments: classical and jazz, voice, percussion.

Selectivity for males: most admitted, but not all.

Renowned alumni: Carol Channing, Tim Duley.

Full-time faculty: 60. *Guest faculty:* 25. *List of some faculty and their affiliations:* Jonathan Golore, New Jazz Orchestra of Buffalo; Amy Williams.

Affiliations

Summer program is affiliated with other program(s): future students recruited from the program.

CHAMBER MUSIC CONFERENCE AND COMPOSERS' FORUM OF THE EAST

Winter Contact Information

P.O. Box 1346, Melville NY 11747-0422
Tel: 617-625-9557
Contact: Dorothy Kalson, Beth Anderson

Summer Contact Information

Bennington College, Bennington VT 05201
Tel: 802-442-5401
Contact: Dorothy Kalson, Beth Anderson

General

Total enrollment: 300. *Level of program:* intermediate, advanced.

High school credit available? no. *College credit available?* no.

Services

Housing options: on-campus dorms.

Application Information

Requirements: recommendation. *Program dates:* 7/21-8/24. *Application deadline:* 4/1. *Application fee:* $150. *Enrollment full by:* 5/15. *Acceptance notification:* as soon as possible.

Audition Information

Audition required; live, video. *No audition fee. Audition includes:* prepared selections of chamber and/or solo repertoire, sight-reading. *Accompanist provided?* no.

Audition evaluation criteria: compare musician's playing to other conference participants.

Costs & Financial Aid

Tuition (full): $740.

Financial aid available? partial scholarship. *Scholarship notification:* 6/10. *Students receiving financial aid:* 5%. *Procedure for applying for financial aid:* complete financial aid forms.

Curriculum, Students, and Faculty

Offered courses: chamber ensemble. Curricula choices. *Program concentration:* chamber music.

Selectivity for males: approximately 10% admitted. *Selectivity for females:* approximately 10% admitted.

Full-time faculty: 50. *Guest faculty:* 10. *List of some faculty:* Joel Berman, Cynthia Adler, Martin Bresnick, Eriko Sato, Eugene Becker, Michael Finckel, Jo-Ann Sternberg, Joanna Jenner.

Performance Information

Performance opportunities and frequency: 2 performances. *Specific performance opportunities:* 2 participant recitals weekly. *Performances by visiting artists?* yes.

Rehearsal facilities and hours: Bennington College music building, Jennings Hall, 24 hours. *Performance facilities:* Carriage Barn faculty concerts, Greenwall Auditorium, Visual Arts/Performing Arts (VAPA) Building.

Additional Comments

We are a chamber music organization for adult amateurs. Each year we have about 5 college-age students as part of our total participant population. The age is primarily late 20s to late 60s.

KILLOOLEET CAMP

Winter Contact Information

70 Trull Street, Somerville MA 02145
Tel: 617-666-1484
Fax: 617-666-0378
Email: killooleet.com
Contact: Kate Seeger

Summer Contact Information

P.O. Box 70, Hancock VT 05748
Tel: 802-767-3152
Email: killooleet.com
Contact: Kate Seeger

General

Total enrollment: 100. *Minimum age or age range:* 9-14. *Level of program:* beginning, intermediate, advanced.

High school credit available? no. *College credit available?* no.

Services

Housing options: on-site housing.

Application Information

Requirements: interview. *Program dates:* 6/29-8/23. *Application deadline:* fall, winter. *Enrollment full by:* February.

Audition Information

Audition not required.

Audition evaluation criteria: guest artists evaluate students.

Costs & Financial Aid

Financial aid available? partial scholarship. *Scholarship notification:* most available in early fall. *Students receiving financial aid:* 8%. *Procedure for applying for financial aid:* call for information.

Curriculum, Students, and Faculty

Offered courses: band, musical theater, performance arts. Curricula choices. *Program concentration:* We concentrate in many areas and encourage specialization music (performing and singing alone in groups), bring instruments (several rhythm and blues bands), small groups, dramatics and dance (small creative production, musical of summer).

Selectivity for males: admit all who apply. *Selectivity for females:* admit all who apply.

Renowned alumni: Andy Stein, Rory Block.

Full-time faculty: 30.

Performance Information

Specific performance opportunities: constant informal performances.

Rehearsal facilities and hours: rest hour, morning periods for band, 4 periods a day, 1/2 hour each.

KINHAVEN MUSIC SCHOOL

Winter Contact Information

1704 Sycamore Street, Bethlehem PA 18017
Tel: 610-868-9200
Fax: 610-868-9200
Contact: Nancy Bidlack

Summer Contact Information

P.O. Box 68
Weston VT 05161
Tel: 802-824-4332
Fax: 802-824-4332
Contact: Nancy Bidlack

General

Total enrollment: 90. *Minimum age or age range:* 13 to summer after high school graduation. *Level of program:* intermediate, advanced.

High school credit available? no. *College credit available?* no.

Services

Housing options: on-campus cabins.

Application Information

Program dates: 6/26-8/9. *Application fee:* $100. *Enrollment full by:* March-April. *Acceptance notification:* March-April.

Audition Information

Audition required; live, video. *No audition fee. Audition includes:* 2 contrasting selections, 5-10 minutes long. *Accompanist provided?* no.

Costs & Financial Aid

Tuition (full): $3,700.

Financial aid available? Yes; partial scholarship. *Scholarship notification:* March-April. *Students receiving financial aid:* 30%. *Procedure for applying for financial aid:* request information from office.

Curriculum, Students, and Faculty

Offered courses: chamber ensemble, chorus, coaching, orchestra, private lessons. Curriculum fixed. *Program concentration:* chamber music, orchestra.

Selectivity for males: approximately 60% admitted. *Selectivity for females:* approximately 60% admitted.

Renowned alumni: Steven Kates, Elliot Fisk, Fenwick Smith, Ashley Richardson, Yari Bond, Richard Brice, Basi Vendr Mischa Amory, Peggy Pearson.

Full-time faculty: 20. *List of some faculty and their affiliations:* Jerry T. Bidlack, Young Peoples' Philharmonic of the Lehigh Valley; Marita Abner, Kansas City Chamber Orchestra; Kate Boyd, Dominick Fiore, Lloyd Goldstein, Florida Orchestra; Sarah Hewitt, Brooklyn Philharmonic.

Performance Information

Specific performance opportunities: orchestra and every chamber group perfoms weekly. *Seat rotation:* rotated for each piece.

Rehearsal facilities and hours: every student is assigned to a practice room. *Performance facilities:* concert hall on the grounds.

MANCHESTER MUSIC FESTIVAL

Winter Contact Information
P.O. Box 1165, Manchester Center VT 05255
Tel: 802-362-1956
Fax: 802-362-0711
Email: mms@vermontel.com
Contact: Michele Sargent

Summer Contact Information
P.O. Box 1165, Manchester Center VT 05255
Tel: 802-362-1957
Fax: 802-362-0712
Email: mms@vermontel.com
Contact: Michele Sargent

General

Total enrollment: 25. *Minimum age or age range:* 18 to 35. *Level of program:* advanced.

High school credit available? no. *College credit available?* no.

Services

Housing options: off-campus housing.

Application Information

Requirements: recommendation. *Program dates:* 7/5-8/16. *Application deadline:* May. *Application fee:* $50. *Enrollment full by:* April. *Acceptance notification:* within one week after tape or live audition.

Audition Information

Audition required; live. *No audition fee. Audition includes:* 20 minutes of contrasting musical styles. *Accompanist provided?* no.

Costs & Financial Aid

Tuition (full): $1,200. *Room:* $400.

Financial aid available? full scholarship, partial scholarship. *Students receiving financial aid:* 99%. *Procedure for applying for financial aid:* send letter stating need.

Curriculum, Students, and Faculty

Offered courses: chamber ensemble, coaching, master classes, orchestra, private lessons. Curriculum fixed.

Full-time faculty: 8. *Guest faculty:* 3.

Performance Information

Performance opportunities and frequency: 5 student concerts per week. *Rehearsal facilities and hours:* First Congregational Church in Manchester and diverse locations, 8:00 am-10:00 pm. *Performance facilities:* Arkell Pavillion of the Southern Vermont Art Center, Smith Center for the Arts.

MARLBORO MUSIC SCHOOL AND FESTIVAL

Winter Contact Information
135 South 18th Street, Philadelphia PA 19103
Tel: 215-569-4690
Fax: 215-569-9497
Contact: Carol Fais

Summer Contact Information
Marlboro VT 05344
Tel: 802-254-2394
Fax: 802-254-4307
Contact: Carol Fais

General

Level of program: advanced.

High school credit available? no. *College credit available?* no.

Services

Housing options: on-campus dorms.

Application Information

Requirements: recommendation. *Program dates:* late June to mid August. *Application deadline:* 12/5.

Audition Information

Audition required; live, off-site. *No audition fee. Audition includes:* chamber music excerpts, solo works. *Accompanist provided?* yes.

Costs & Financial Aid

Financial aid available? full scholarship, partial scholarship. *Students receiving financial aid:* 99%.

Curriculum, Students, and Faculty

Curriculum fixed. *Program concentration:* advanced study center for exceptionally gifted young professionals.

Selectivity for males: approximately 10% admitted.

Full-time faculty: 2.

Performance Information

Performance opportunities and frequency: 5 weekends. *Specific performance opportunities:* artists attend only to rehearse and are not assured of performing.

Rehearsal facilities and hours: campus of Marlboro College. *Performance facilities:* 680-seat audititorium.

POINT COUNTER POINT CHAMBER MUSIC CAMP

Winter Contact Information
P.O. Box 3181, Terre Haute IN 47803
Tel: 812-877-3745
Fax: 812-877-2174
Email: pointcp@aol.com
Contact: Dr. Paul Roby

Summer Contact Information
RD2 Box 2322, Brandon VT 05733
Tel: 802-247-8467
Fax: 812-877-2174
Email: pointcp@aol.com
Contact: Dr. Paul Roby

General
Total enrollment: 100. *Minimum age or age range:* 11 to 17. *Level of program*: intermediate, advanced.

High school credit available? no. *College credit available?* no.

Services
Housing options: on-campus cabins.

Application Information
Requirements: recommendation. *Program dates:* 6/29-7/19, 7/20-8/16, 6/29-8/16. *Application fee:* $30. *Enrollment full by:* 6/1. *Acceptance notification:* upon receipt of completed application.

Audition Information
Audition required: video. *Audition fee*: $30. *Audition includes:* 10 minutes of applicant's best playing. *Accompanist provided?* no.

Audition evaluation criteria: ability to play standard chamber music repertoire.

Costs & Financial Aid
Tuition (full): $2,250.

Financial aid available? partial scholarship. *Scholarship notification:* after applying. *Students receiving financial aid:* 15%. *Procedure for applying for financial aid*: submit scholarship form.

Curriculum, Students, and Faculty
Offered courses: chamber ensemble, coaching (6 classes per week, master classes, music history, music theory, private lessons (2 classes per week). Curriculum fixed. *Program concentration:* chamber music.

Selectivity for males: approximately 60% admitted. *Selectivity for females:* approximately 60% admitted.

Full-time faculty: 8. *Guest faculty:* 8. *List of some faculty and their affiliations:* Darrell Rosenbluth, Ming Young Song, Florence Altenburger, London Symphony; David Wallace, NY Philharmonic.

Performance Information
Performance opportunities and frequency: each week. *Specific performance opportunities:* many chamber performances, some solo performances. *Performances by visiting artists?* no.

Rehearsal facilities and hours: cabins, outdoors. *Performance facilities:* on campus and in surrounding community concert halls.

WASHINGTON

CHAMBER MUSIC INSTITUTE

Winter Contact Information
P.O. Box 45776, Seattle WA 98145
Tel: 206-527-8839
Fax: 206-526-8621
Email: olymusic@brigadoon.com
Contact: Alan Iglitzin

Summer Contact Information
P.O. Box 45776, Seattle WA 98145
Tel: 206-527-8840
Email: olymusic@brigadoon.com
Contact: Alan Iglitzin

General
Total enrollment: 20. *Minimum age or age range:* 14 to 18. *Level of program:* advanced.

High school credit available? no. *College credit available?* no.

Services
Housing options: on-campus cabins.

Application Information
Requirements: essay, recommendation. *Program dates:* 7/5-7/26. *Application deadline:* rolling. *Application fee:* $40. *Enrollment full by:* 5/1.

Audition Information
Audition required; live, video, on-site, off-site. *No audition fee. Audition includes:* 2 solo works in contrasting styles, an etude, and materials sent upon receipt of application. *Accompanist provided?* no.

Costs & Financial Aid
Tuition (full): $1,500. *Room:* $1,200.

Financial aid available? Yes; partial scholarship. *Scholarship notification:* 4/15. *Students receiving financial aid:* 50%. *Procedure for applying for financial aid:* separate application form, including essay explaining need.

Curriculum, Students, and Faculty

Offered courses: chamber ensemble, coaching, master classes, movement. Curriculum fixed. *Program concentration:* string quartets.

Selectivity for males: approximately 33% admitted. *Selectivity for females:* approximately 33% admitted.

Full-time faculty: 4. *Guest faculty:* 2. *List of some faculty and their affiliations:* Alan Iglitzin, Olympic Musical Festival, Philadelphia String Quartet; Irwin Elsenberg, Chamber Music Institute, Philadelphia String Quartet; Carter Enyeart, Eastman School of Music, Robin Sharp, San Francisco Conservatory.

Performance Information

Performance opportunities and frequency: 1 performance per week. *Specific performance opportunities:* 3 performances.

Rehearsal facilities and hours: cabins located throughout the festival grounds, 9:30 am-12:00 pm, 1:00 pm-3:00 pm daily. *Performance facilities:* most concerts take place in renovated turn of the century dairy barn, seats 425, other performances in area churches and halls.

SUMMER MUSIC FESTIVAL MAX ARONOFF VIOLA INSTITUTE

Winter Contact Information

6302 54th Avenue Court West, Tacoma WA 98467
Tel: 253-474-6922
Fax: 253-756-3500
Contact: Joyce A. Ramee

Summer Contact Information

6302 54th Avenue Court West, Tacoma WA 98467
Tel: 253-474-6923
Fax: 253-756-3501
Contact: Joyce A. Ramee

General

Total enrollment: 50. *Minimum age or age range:* 14 and up. *Level of program:* beginning, intermediate, advanced.

High school credit available? no. *College credit available?* no.

Services

Housing options: on-campus dorms, option for local residents to commute.

Application Information

Program dates: 6/28-7/3. *Application deadline:* 5/15. *Application fee:* $32. *Enrollment full by:* 5/15.

Audition Information

Audition required. No audition fee. Accompanist provided? no.

Audition evaluation criteria: intonation, rhythm, note accuracy, style, level of repertoire, years of study, age of student.

Costs & Financial Aid

Tuition (full): $245. *Room:* $250.

Financial aid available? full scholarship, partial scholarship. *Scholarship notification:* 5/20. *Students receiving financial aid:* 40%. *Procedure for applying for financial aid:* submit tax return.

Curriculum, Students, and Faculty

Offered courses: audition preparation, master classes, movement. Curriculum fixed. *Program concentration:* audition preparation, chamber music, technical workshops, improving individual musical skills at any level, private lessons, master classes.

Selectivity for males: approximately 33% admitted. *Selectivity for females:* approximately 33% admitted.

Renowned alumni: Karen Bentley, David Filner, James Freeman.

Full-time faculty: 13. *List of some faculty:* Deborah Clasquin, Carol Jacobson, Terrie Baune, John Brecher,David Filner, Nicolas Marlowe, Cindy Moyer, Laurette Goldberg, Lisa Byrnes, Armand Ambrosini, Tom Nugent, Jerri Taylor, William Harrington.

Performance Information

Performance opportunities and frequency: 5 concerts in 6 days. *Specific performance opportunities:* daily evening concerts. *Seat rotation:* chamber assignment changes daily.

WISCONSIN

AMERICAN SUZUKI INSTITUTE

Winter Contact Information
University of WI- Stevens Point, Stevens Point WI 54481-3897
Tel: 715-346-3033
Fax: 715-346-3858
Email: dmartz@uwsp.edu
Contact: Dee Martz

Summer Contact Information
University of WI- Stevens Point, Stevens Point WI 54481-3897
Tel: 715-346-3033
Fax: 715-346-3858
Email: dmartz@uwsp.edu
Contact: Dee Martz

General

Total enrollment: 1,400. *Minimum age or age range:* 3 and up. *Level of program:* beginning, intermediate, advanced.

High school credit available? no. *College credit available?* yes.

Services

Housing options: dorms.

Application Information

Program dates: first 2 weeks of August. *Application deadline:* first week of June. *Application fee:* $90. *Enrollment full by:* second-third week of June. *Acceptance notification:* as soon as possible.

Audition Information

Audition required. *No audition fee. Audition includes:* two pieces from Suzuki volumes. *Accompanist provided?* no.

Costs & Financial Aid

Financial aid available? Yes; partial scholarship. *Scholarship notification:* ASAP. *Students receiving financial aid:* 1%. *Procedure for applying for financial aid:* request information.

Curriculum, Students, and Faculty

Offered courses: chamber ensemble, master classes, music history, music theory, orchestra, private lessons, repertory. Curriculum fixed. *Program concentration:* Suzuki talent education method for bass, cello, flute, harp, piano, viola, violin; for students and teacher trainees.

Selectivity for males: admit all who apply. *Selectivity for females:* admit all who apply.

Full-time faculty: 100.

Performance Information

Performance opportunities and frequency: 1 performance. *Specific performance opportunities:* solo recitals. *Orchestra seating:* Conductor's choice. *Performance facilities:* large gymnasium, concert hall.

INTERNATIONAL WORKSHOPS, SUMMER MUSIC WORKSHOP

Winter Contact Information
187 Aqua View Drive, Cedarburg WI 53012
Tel: 414-377-7062
Fax: 414-377-7096
Email: thintz@execpc.com
Contact: Tori Hintz

Summer Contact Information
187 Aqua View Drive, Cedarburg WI 53012
Tel: 414-377-7062
Fax: 414-377-7096
Email: thintz@execpc.com
Contact: Tori Hintz

General

Total enrollment: 400. *Level of program:* beginning, intermediate, advanced.

High school credit available? no. *College credit available?* yes.

Services

Housing options: on-campus hotels.

Application Information

Program dates: 7/18-7/31, 7/2-7/15. *Application deadline:* 6/15.

Audition Information

Audition not required.

Costs & Financial Aid

Tuition (full): $1,450. *Room:* $150.

Financial aid available? Yes; partial scholarship. *Scholarship notification:* 6/15. *Students receiving financial aid:* 5%. *Procedure for applying for financial aid:* application letter.

Curriculum, Students, and Faculty

Offered courses: chamber ensemble, chorus, conducting, master classes, movement, orchestra, private lessons, repertory. Curricula choices. *Program concentration:* strings, piano, orchestral conducting, choral conducting, general music.

Selectivity for males: admit all who apply. *Selectivity for females:* admit all who apply.

Full-time faculty: 30. *Guest faculty:* 10. *List of some faculty:* Gerald Fischbach, Don McInnes, Phyllis Young, Francois Rabbath, Nelita True, Rodney Eichenberger, Sandra Stauffer.

Performance Information

Performance opportunities and frequency: varies during two weeks. *Specific performance opportunities:* master classes, soloist recitals, chamber music recitals. *Orchestra seating:* by questionnaire and pervious playing. *Performances by visiting artists?* yes. *Recent guests:* Eduard Melkus, Don McInnes, Nelita True, Igor Ozim.

Rehearsal facilities and hours: many practice rooms, with and without piano, open all day. *Performance facilities:* depends on venue, differs each summer, concert hall, university auditorium or cathedral.

MADELINE ISLAND MUSIC CAMP

Winter Contact Information
118 East 26th Street, Minneapolis MN 55404
Tel: 612-871-7781
Fax: 612-871-3356
Contact: Thomas M. George

Summer Contact Information
P.O. Box 254
LaPointe WI 54850
Contact: Thomas M. George

Services

Housing options: on-campus cabin and condos.

Application Information

Application fee: $20.

Audition Information

Audition required; live, video, on-site, off-site. *Audition includes:* call for details.

Costs & Financial Aid

Financial aid available? full scholarship, partial scholarship. *Scholarship notification:* April. *Students receiving financial aid:* 50%. *Procedure for applying for financial aid:* Submit parent's 1040 form.

Curriculum, Students, and Faculty

Offered courses: chamber ensemble, coaching, master classes, private lessons. Curriculum fixed. *Program concentration:* chamber music.

Selectivity for males: approximately 60% admitted.

Renowned alumni: Kirsten Docter, Cavanmi String Quartet.

Full-time faculty: 7. *Guest faculty:* 1. *List of some faculty and their affiliations:* Mary Lou Francis, Lynn Rice-See, George Burde, Eugene Barban, Gwen Beamish, Elaine Greenfield, Daniel Paul Horn, Freda Rosenblatt, Golda Wainberg-Tatz.

Performance Information

Performance opportunities and frequency: weekly. *Specific performance opportunities:* weekly performances, touring. *Orchestra seating:* By program coordinator. *Performances by visiting artists?* yes. *Recent guests:* Peter Orth, Nicolai Lomov.

Rehearsal facilities and hours: new ensemble room, solo practice rooms. *Performance facilities:* Island Restaurant.

RESIDENTIAL VOCAL PERFORMANCE WORKSHOP: THE COMPLETE SINGER

Winter Contact Information
University of Wisconsin, Division of Continuing Education, 800 Algoma Boulevard, Oshkosh WI 54901-8623
Tel: 920-424-4224
Fax: 920-424-1266
Email: jandrews@uwosh.edu
Contact: Joyce Andreus

Summer Contact Information
University of Wisconsin, Division of Continuing Education, 800 Algoma Boulevard, Oshkosh WI 54901-8623
Tel: 920-424-4224
Fax: 920-424-1266
Email: jandrews@uwosh.edu
Contact: Joyce Andreus

General

Total enrollment: 18. *Minimum age or age range:* 14 to 18. *Level of program:* beginning, intermediate, advanced.

High school credit available? no. *College credit available?* no.

Services

Housing options: on-campus dorms.

Application Information

Program dates: second week of June (1week). *Application deadline:* late May. *Enrollment full by:* early May.

Audition Information

Audition not required.

Costs & Financial Aid

Tuition (full): $299.

Financial aid available? no.

Curriculum, Students, and Faculty

Offered courses: acting for singers, audition preparation, chamber ensemble, coaching, master classes, movement, musical theater, private lessons, repertory. *Specific curriculum information*: program usually also offers classes in costuming/make up for musical theater or recording studio techniques. Curriculum fixed. *Program concentration:* daily classes for singers in voice technique and repertoire, dance and movement, and theater/acting classes.

Selectivity for males: most admitted, but not all. *Selectivity for females:* most admitted, but not all.

Full-time faculty: 4. *Guest faculty:* 1. *List of some faculty and their affiliations:* Frank Hoffmeister, Tom Manning, Missy Allen.

Performance Information

Specific performance opportunities: 1 program of classical art song and 1 program of musical theater and acting scenes performed for friends and family of participants. *Performance facilities:* all classes and performances are held in the music department and theater department stages and rehearsal rooms of the University of Wisconsin-Oshkosh.

UNIVERSITY OF WISCONSIN—GREEN BAY SUMMER MUSIC CAMP

Winter Contact Information

Office of Outreach and Extension
University of Wisconsin-Gr, 2420 Nicolet Drive,
Green Bay WI 54311-7001
Tel: 920-465-2267
Fax: 920-465-2552
Email: searl@uwgb.edu
Contact: Laura Aaron Sear

Summer Contact Information

Office of Outreach and Extension, 2420 Nicolet Drive,
Green Bay WI 54311-7001
Tel: 920-465-2267
Fax: 920-465-2552
Email: searl@uwgb.edu
Contact: Laura Aaron Sear

General

Total enrollment: 1,550. *Minimum age or age range:* 9 to 18. *Level of program:* beginning, intermediate, advanced.

High school credit available? no. *College credit available?* no.

Services

Housing options: on-campus residence halls.

Application Information

Requirements: recommendation. *Program dates:* mid June-mid August. *Application deadline:* 2 weeks prior to start of individual camp.

Audition Information

Audition required. No audition fee. Audition includes: sight-reading, scales, and often a prepared piece. *Accompanist provided?* no.

Audition evaluation criteria: range and sight-reading ability, for placement only.

Costs & Financial Aid

Financial aid available? Students receiving financial aid: 2%.

Curriculum, Students, and Faculty

Offered courses: acting for singers, band, chamber ensemble, chorus, conducting, master classes, music theory, orchestra. *Specific curriculum information*: curriculum is fixed for students in grades 4-8, choices are available for students in grades 9-12. *Program concentration:* keyboard (piano, pipe organ, digital keyboard), jazz, vocal jazz and show cjoir, guitar, middle school band, orchestra, choir, senior high band, orchestra.

Selectivity for males: most admitted, but not all. *Selectivity for females:* most admitted, but not all.

Renowned alumni: Lyle Ma Dave Charles, Henry Greve, Carl Allen.

Full-time faculty: 90. *List of some faculty:* Kevin Collins, Cheryl Grosso, John Salerno, Chris Salerno, Lovell Ives, Thomas PF Otenhouer, Arthur Cohrs.

Performance Information

Specific performance opportunities: all programs have a final public concert, many of which take place at the Weidner Center for the Performing Arts. Some programs also include less formal (non-public) talent shows during the week. *Orchestra seating:* Final assignments based upon class performance. *Seat rotation:* rotated throughout week. *Performances by visiting artists?* yes. *Recent guests:* Therese Gigot, Kathy DeJardin, Cheryl Grosso, Janet Planet, Chris Salerno.

Rehearsal facilities and hours: 25 practice rooms, 4 rehearsal halls, 20 classrooms used on a daily basis. *Performance facilities:* Weidner Center for the Performing Arts, seats 2000, University Theater, seats 400.

Affiliations

Summer program is affiliated with a university: future students are recruited from the program.

UNIVERSITY OF WISCONSIN, MADISON SUMMER MUSIC CLINIC

Winter Contact Information
455 North Park Street, Madison WI 53706
Tel: 608-263-2242
Fax: 608-262-8876
Email: maaley@facstaff.wisc.edu
Contact: Anne Aley

Summer Contact Information
455 North Park Street, Madison WI 53706
Tel: 608-263-2242
Fax: 608-262-8876
Email: maaley@facstaff.wisc.edu
Contact: Anne Aley

General

Total enrollment: 1,150. *Minimum age or age range:* 12 to 18. *Level of program:* beginning, intermediate, advanced.

High school credit available? no. *College credit available?* no.

Services

Housing options: on-campus dorms.

Application Information

Requirements: recommendation. *Program dates:* junior high school: 6/21-6/27, senior high school: 6/28-7/3. *Application deadline:* 5/15.

Audition Information

Audition required; live, on-site. *Accompanist provided?* no.

Costs & Financial Aid

Room & board: $150.

Financial aid available? no.

Curriculum, Students, and Faculty

Offered courses: acting for singers, band, chamber ensemble, chorus, conducting, master classes, movement, music history, music theory, musical theater, opera workshop, orchestra, relaxation technique, repertory, seminar on the business of music. Curricula choices. *Program concentration:* Performance, theory, band, orchestra, choir, jazz ensmble, musical theater.

Selectivity for males: admit all who apply. *Selectivity for females:* admit all who apply.

Renowned alumni: John Zirbel, Montreal Symphony.

Performance Information

Specific performance opportunities: final concerts for ensembles at conclusion of each camp, chamber music and recitals ongoing throughout camp. *Orchestra seating:* by audition. *Performances by visiting artists?* yes.

Rehearsal facilities and hours: practice rooms available through School of Music. *Performance facilities:* Mills Auditorium, UW Madison campus, Music Hall, Morphy Recital Hall.

AUSTRIA

AIMS SUMMER VOCAL INSTITUTE IN GRAZ, AUSTRIA

Winter Contact Information
6621 Snider Plaza, Dallas TX 75205-1351
Tel: 214-363-2683
Fax: 214-363-6474
Email: aims@cyberramp.net
Contact: Nora Sands

Summer Contact Information
Elisabethstrasse 93, A-8010, Graz Austria
Tel: 011-43-316-32-70-66
Fax: 011-43-316-32-55-74
Email: aims@sime.com
Contact: Nora Sands

General

Total enrollment: 90. *Minimum age or age range:* 18 to 40. *Level of program:* intermediate, advanced.

High school credit available? no. *College credit available?* yes.

Services

Housing options: on-campus dorms.

Application Information

Requirements: interview. *Program dates:* early July to mid-August. *Application deadline:* flexible. *Enrollment full by:* 5/31. *Acceptance notification:* 2 weeks after audition.

Audition Information

Audition required. *Audition fee:* $30. *Audition includes:* 2 selections from students's list for singers; solo work, accompanying, and sight reading for pianists. *Accompanist provided? yes.*

Costs & Financial Aid

Financial aid available? partial scholarship. *Scholarship notification:* Beginning 3/15. *Students receiving financial aid:* 40%. *Procedure for applying for financial aid:* make note on audition interview questionnaire.

Curriculum, Students, and Faculty

Offered courses: acting for singers, audition preparation, coaching (2 classes per week), diction, foreign language study, master classes, movement, orchestra, private lessons, repertory, seminar on the business of music. Curricula choices. *Program concentration:* Opera and lieder.

Selectivity for males: most admitted, but not all.

Renowned alumni: Barbara Daniels, Chris Merritt, Andrew Litton, Mary Mills, Constance Haumann, Helen Bickers, Deborah Polaski.

Full-time faculty: 60. *Guest faculty:* 2.

Performance Information

Specific performance opportunities: 5 with orchestra, 25 small groups (arias, duets, etc.). *Seat rotation:* rotated for every concert. *Performance casting:* after hearings in Graz. *Performances by visiting artists?* no.

Rehearsal facilities and hours: 10 rooms in dorm, 8:00 am-9:00 pm, 15 rooms in teaching facility, 9:00 am-6:00 pm. *Performance facilities:* major concert hall, small recital halls, churches, hotels, open air courtyards.

FOGOTISSIMO (SINCE 1972)

Winter Contact Information

Eichendorff's Ruh, A-2564 Furth, Vienna Austria
Fax: 011-0043-1-7141710
Contact: Walter Hermann Sallagar

Summer Contact Information

Eichendorff's Ruh, A-2564 Furth, Vienna Austria
Tel: 011-0043-2674-88265
Contact: Walter Hermann Sallagar

General

Total enrollment: 4. *Level of program:* beginning, intermediate, advanced.

High school credit available? no. *College credit available?* no.

Services

Housing options: on-campus hunter's lodge.

Application Information

Program dates: 7/12-7/19. *Application deadline:* one month prior to workshop.

Audition Information

Audition not required.

Costs & Financial Aid

Financial aid available? no.

Curriculum, Students, and Faculty

Offered courses: coaching, ensemble, private lessons. *Specific curriculum information*: individual training in repair. *Program concentration:* bassoon professional repair mixed with ensemble playing.

Selectivity for males: approximately 33% admitted. *Selectivity for females:* approximately 33% admitted.

Renowned alumni: Chris Weait, Stefan Weidenaver, Chip Owen, Fox Factory, Alan Smith, Peter Di Wit.

Performance Information

Specific performance opportunities: sometimes play with the church ensemble for fun. *Rehearsal facilities and hours:* 9:00 am-12:00 pm, 2:00 pm-5:00 pm, evenings with playing. *Performance facilities:* concert hall, chapel.

INTERNATIONAL SUMMER ACADEMY OF THE MOZARTEUM

Winter Contact Information

Mirabell Platz 1, Salzburg A-5020 Austria
Tel: 011-443-662-88908400
Fax: 011-443-662-872659
Email: micaela.bartsch@moz.ac.at
Contact: Michaela Bartsch

Summer Contact Information

Mirabell Platz 1, Salzburg A-5020 Austria
Tel: 011-443-662-88908400
Fax: 011-443-662-872659
Email: micaela.bartsch@moz.ac.at
Contact: Michaela Bartsch

General

Total enrollment: 1,000. *Minimum age or age range:* 20 to 30. *Level of program:* advanced.

High school credit available? no. *College credit available?* no.

Services

Housing options: off-campus housing

Application Information

Program dates: 7/13-8/22. *Application deadline:* 6/1. *Application fee:* $1,500. *Enrollment full by:* 6/1.

Audition Information

Audition required; live, on-site. *Audition includes:* 1-2 pieces. *Accompanist provided?* yes.

Costs & Financial Aid

Financial aid available? Yes; partial scholarship. *Scholarship notification:* 6/30. *Students receiving financial aid:* 10%. *Procedure for applying for financial aid:* send scholarship request with letter of recommendation from teacher.

Curriculum, Students, and Faculty

Offered courses: master classes. Curricula choices. *Program concentration:* voice and instrumental master classes.

Selectivity for males: approximately 60% admitted. *Selectivity for females:* approximately 60% admitted.

Performance Information

Performance opportunities and frequency: daily. *Specific performance opportunities:* daily student concerts. *Orchestra seating:* by teacher. *Performance casting:* assigned by teacher. *Performances by visiting artists?* yes.

Rehearsal facilities and hours: 8:00 am-8:00 pm. *Performance facilities:* 900-seat concert hall, 200-seat recital hall.

CANADA

COURTENAY YOUTH MUSIC CENTRE SUMMER

Winter Contact Information

Music School and Festival, P.O. Box 3056, Courtney BC V9N5N3
Canada
Tel: 250-338-7463
Fax: 250-334-2934
Email: cymcreg@island.net
Contact: Stacey Wright

Summer Contact Information

Music School and Festival, P.O. Box 3056, Courtney BC V9N5N3
Canada
Tel: 250-334-5749
Fax: 250-334-5719
Email: cymcreg@island.net
Contact: Stacey Wright

General

Minimum age or age range: 12 and up. *Level of program:* beginning, intermediate, advanced.

High school credit available? no. *College credit available?* no.

Services

Housing options: on-campus housing, privately owned ski chalets.

Application Information

Requirements: recommendation. *Program dates:* 6/28-8/3. *Application deadline:* 4/15, 5/31. *Application fee:* $40.

Audition Information

Audition required. *No audition fee. Audition includes:* sample of ability. *Accompanist provided?* no.

Audition evaluation criteria: tape sent to faculty.

Costs & Financial Aid

Tuition (full): $500.

Financial aid available? full scholarship, partial scholarship. *Scholarship notification:* 2 months prior to camp. *Students receiving financial aid:* 50%. *Procedure for applying for financial aid:* application form, audio tape, letter of reference.

Curriculum, Students, and Faculty

Offered courses: audition preparation, band, chamber ensemble, chorus, coaching, master classes, music history, music theory, musical theater, orchestra, private lessons. Curriculum fixed. *Program concentration:* jazz workshop, musical theatre program, festival program, chamber music programs, baroque, percussion, voice, classical guitar, harp and band program.

Selectivity for males: most admitted, but not all. *Selectivity for females:* most admitted, but not all.

Full-time faculty: 48. *Guest faculty:* 4.

Performance Information

Orchestra seating: By placement audition. *Performance casting:* auditioned. *Performances by visiting artists?* yes. *Recent guests:* Martin Beaver, Eiji Hashimoto, Douglas McNabrey.

Rehearsal facilities and hours: instruction 8:30 am-5:30 pm daily, rehearsals held on campus in band facility. *Performance facilities:* concerts held on campus in Memorial Union, recitals held in band rehearsal hall.

DOMAINE FORGET MUSIC AND DANCE ACADEMY

Winter Contact Information
398 Chemin les Bains, ST-Irenee QC G0T1V0 Canada
Tel: 418-452-8111
Fax: 418-452-3503
Email: dforget@cite.net
Contact: Ginette Gauthier, Edith Allaire

Summer Contact Information
398 Chemin les Bains, ST-Irenee QC G0T1V0 Canada
Tel: 418-452-8112
Fax: 418-452-3504
Email: dforget@cite.net
Contact: Ginette Gauthier, Edith Allaire

General

Minimum age or age range: 12 to 60. *Level of program:* intermediate, advanced.

High school credit available? no. *College credit available?* no.

Services

Housing options: On-campus studios and dorms for younger students.

Application Information

Requirements: recommendation. *Program dates:* first weekend of June to last Sunday of August. *Application deadline:* 5% discount before May 1st. *Application fee:* $40. *Enrollment full by:* depends on the session and instrument. *Acceptance notification:* as soon as possible.

Audition Information

Audition required; live, on-site. *No audition fee. Audition includes:* 2 solo pieces of contrasting styles. *Accompanist provided?* no.

Costs & Financial Aid

Lessons: $50.

Financial aid available? partial scholarship. *Procedure for applying for financial aid:* Free tuition depending on previous year's results.

Curriculum, Students, and Faculty

Offered courses: audition preparation, band, chamber ensemble, chorus, coaching, conducting, master classes, movement, music theory, orchestra, private lessons, repertory. Curricula choices. *Program concentration:* brass, woodwinds, dance guitar, jazz, strings, choral singing, new music, chamber music, band conducting.

Selectivity for males: most admitted, but not all. *Selectivity for females:* most admitted, but not all.

Full-time faculty: 80. *Guest faculty:* 20.

Performance Information

Specific performance opportunities: 1 student concert at the end of each session. *Orchestra seating:* by audition. *Seat rotation:* rotated rarely. *Performances by visiting artists?* yes. *Recent guests:* Ik-Hwan Bae, Ian Swensen, Paul Katz, Ken Slowick, Trio Gagne-Richards, Ellis Marsalis, Capriccio Stravagante, Guillemette Lauren, Jay Bernfeld, Skip Sempe.

Rehearsal facilities and hours: studios, practice huts, during free time before 11:00 pm. *Performance facilities:* Francoys-Bernier Concert Hall.

GAELIC COLLEGE OF CELTIC ARTS AND CRAFTS

Winter Contact Information
P.O. Box 9, Baddeck NS B0E 1B0 Canada
Tel: 902-295-3411
Fax: 902-295-2912
Email: gaelcoll@atcon.com
Contact: Sam MacPhee

Summer Contact Information
P.O. Box 9, Baddeck NS B0E 1B0 Canada
Tel: 902-295-3411
Fax: 902-295-2912
Email: gaelcoll@atcon.com
Contact: Sam MacPhee

General

Total enrollment: 525. *Minimum age or age range:* 5 and up. *Level of program:* beginning, intermediate, advanced.

College credit available? no.

Services

Housing options: on-campus dorms, off-campus bed and breakfast, motels, campgrounds nearby.

Application Information

Application deadline: registration date. *Application fee:* $30. *Enrollment full by:* 5/30. *Acceptance notification:* within 30 days after application is received.

Audition Information

Audition not required.

Costs & Financial Aid

Financial aid available? full scholarship, partial scholarship. *Scholarship notification:* 6/5. *Students receiving financial aid:* 10%. *Procedure for applying for financial aid:* application.

Curriculum, Students, and Faculty

Offered courses: band, Gaelic language study. Curricula choices. *Program concentration:* piping, dance, Cape Breton fiddle, Scottish small pipes, piano, harp, and Gaelic language and song.

Selectivity for males: most admitted, but not all. *Selectivity for females:* most admitted, but not all.

Full-time faculty: 30.

Performance Information

Performance opportunities and frequency: daily. *Specific performance opportunities:* daytime, daily student recitals. *Performance facilities:* outside performance center and in hall.

INTERPROVINCIAL MUSIC CAMP

Winter Contact Information

77 Ingram Drive, Toronto ON M6M 2L7 Canada
Tel: 416-488-3316
Email: mgm@imconline.org
Contact: Anne Fleming-Read

Summer Contact Information

McKellar ON M6M 2L7 Canada
Tel: 705-389-2410
Fax: 705-389-3079
Email: mgm@imconline.org
Contact: Anne Fleming-Read

General

Minimum age or age range: 10 to 19. *Level of program:* beginning, intermediate, advanced.

High school credit available? no. *College credit available?* no.

Services

Housing options: on-campus cabins—8 campers and 1 counselor.

Application Information

Program dates: last 2 weeks of August. *Enrollment full by:* 8/1.

Audition Information

Audition required; live, on-site. *No audition fee. Accompanist provided?* no.

Costs & Financial Aid

Financial aid available? full scholarship, partial scholarship. *Scholarship notification:* 5/30. *Students receiving financial aid:* 10%. *Procedure for applying for financial aid:* request scholarship application.

Curriculum, Students, and Faculty

Offered courses: band, chamber ensemble, coaching, master classes, musical theater, orchestra, private lessons, seminar on the business of music. Curriculum fixed. *Program concentration:* classical band/orchestra/chamber music, jazz camp: bigband/combo/swing, camprock: rock & roll.

Selectivity for males: most admitted, but not all. *Selectivity for females:* most admitted, but not all.

Performance Information

Specific performance opportunities: large performance at end of session, chamber music throughout program. *Orchestra seating:* by audition. *Performance casting:* auditioned. *Performances by visiting artists?* yes. *Recent guests:* Cho Liang-Lin, Quartetto Gelato.

Rehearsal facilities and hours: small practice cabin, available any time not in classes until 10:00 pm. *Performance facilities:* barn that has been converted into a theater with complete lighting and sound system, used for concerts/rehearsals/musical theater.

MANITOU

Winter Contact Information

77 Ingram Drive, Suite 200,
Toronto ON M0M2L7 Canada
Tel: 416-245-0605
Fax: 416-245-6844
Email: camp@manitou-online.com
Contact; Jordanna Lipson

Summer Contact Information

POG1CO, McKeller ON Canada
Tel: 705-389-2410
Fax: 705-389-3079
Email: camp@manitou-online.com
Contact: Jordanna Lipson

General

Minimum age or age range: 8 to 17. *Level of program:* beginning, intermediate, advanced

High school credit available? no. *College credit available?* no.

Services

Housing options: on-campus cabin.

Application Information

Program dates: musical theater: July-Aug, Interprovincial Music Camp: late August, Camp Rock: June- Aug, "Jazz" camp: Aug.

Audition Information
Audition not required.

Costs & Financial Aid
Financial aid available? no.

Curriculum, Students, and Faculty
Curriculum fixed.

Selectivity for males: admit all who apply. *Selectivity for females:* admit all who apply.

Guest faculty: 20.

Performance Information
Specific performance opportunities: final concert at end of week. *Performances by visiting artists?* yes. *Recent guests:* Dr. Marc Dickman, Mr Robert W. Smith. *Performance facilities:* Smith Hall Auditorium.

Affiliations
Summer program is affiliated with a conservatory: future students are recruited from the program.

VANCOUVER EARLY MUSIC PROGRAMME AND FESTIVAL

Winter Contact Information
1254 West 7th Avenue, Vancouver BC V6H 1B6 Canada
Tel: 604-732-1610
Fax: 604-732-1602
Email: earlymus@istar.ea
contact: Jose Verstappen

Summer Contact Information
1254 West 7th Avenue, Vancouver BC V6H1B6 Canada
Tel: 604-732-1610
Fax: 604-732-1602
Email: earlymus@istar.ea
Contact: Jose Verstappen

General
Minimum age or age range: adults. *Level of program:* beginning, intermediate, advanced.

High school credit available? no. *College credit available?* no.

Services
Housing options: on-campus dorms.

Application Information
Requirements: recommendation. *Program dates:* mid July-mid August. *Application deadline:* varies. *Application fee:* $75.

Audition Information
Audition required. *No audition fee.*

Costs & Financial Aid
Tuition (full): $715.

Financial aid available? Yes; partial scholarship. *Scholarship notification:* early May. *Students receiving financial aid:* 10%. *Procedure for applying for financial aid:* send letter stating need and level.

Curriculum, Students, and Faculty
Offered courses: acting for singers, aspects of performance practice, chamber ensemble, chorus, master classes, orchestra, repertory. Curricula choices. *Program concentration:* medieval, renaissance, baroque, early classical.

Selectivity for males: approximately 60% admitted. *Selectivity for females:* approximately 60% admitted.

Renowned alumni: Derek Lee Ragire, Suzee Leblanc, John Fleagle, Ronn McFarlance, Baltimore Consort.

Performance Information
Specific performance opportunities: student recitals at end of each workshop. *Performances by visiting artists?* yes. *Recent guests:* Pacific Baroque Orchestra, Sequentia, Peter Hannan, Alison Melvill, Nan Mackie, Benjamin Bagby, Sanford Sylvan, David Douglas.

Rehearsal facilities and hours: all workshops at University of British Columbia Music School, building open 7:00 am-11:00 pm. *Performance facilities:* recital hall at university.

CZECH REPUBLIC

SUMMER CAMP FOR STRINGS

Winter Contact Information
HUDEBNI MLA'DEZ (Jeunesses musicales)
RYCHNOV N KN Music, 8-KRIZIKOVA 64, Prague 18000
Czech Republic
Tel: 011-02-232-2470
Fax: 011-02-232-2470
Contact: Jana Klimtova

Summer Contact Information
Rychnov NKN Music School,
Tel: 011-0445-22882
Contact: Jana Klimtova

General

Minimum age or age range: 16 to 23. *Level of program:* intermediate.

High school credit available? no. *College credit available?* no.

Services

Housing options: on-campus, 2 bedroom home.

Application Information

Program dates: 8/18-8/28. *Application deadline:* 6/1. *Enrollment full by:* 4/1.

Audition Information

Audition required, on-site. *No audition fee. Audition includes:* etude and solo piece, 2-3 minutes long. *Accompanist provided?* no.

Costs & Financial Aid

Financial aid available? no.

Curriculum, Students, and Faculty

Offered courses: string orchestra. *Program concentration:* Handel, Concerti Grossi, Grieg, Holdberg.

Selectivity for males: most admitted, but not all. *Selectivity for females:* most admitted, but not all.

Performance Information

Performances by visiting artists? yes. *Recent guests:* Wilham Quartet, Stamic Quartet, Daniel Veis. *Performance facilities:* hall of the music school, churches for orchestra concerts.

ENGLAND

BRITTEN-PEARS SCHOOL FOR ADVANCED MUSICAL STUDIES

Winter Contact Information

High Street, Aldeburgh, Suffolk, IP155AX England
Tel: 0172-845-2935
Fax: 0172-845-2715
Contact: Elizabeth Webb

Summer Contact Information

High Street, Aldeburgh, Suffolk 1P155AX England
Tel: 0172-845-2935
Fax: 0172-845-2715
Contact: Elizabeth Webb

General

Total enrollment: 300. *Minimum age or age range:* 18 to 35. *Level of program:* advanced.

High school credit available? no. *College credit available?* no.

Services

Housing options: off-campus housing.

Application Information

Requirements: interview, essay, recommendation. *Program dates:* varies. *Application deadline:* mid December. *Enrollment full by:* deadline. *Acceptance notification:* late March.

Audition Information

Audition required; live, off-site. *Audition fee:* $40. *Audition includes:* material suitable for course to which student applied, no sight reading or set pieces except for orchestra. *Accompanist provided?* yes.

Audition evaluation criteria: depends on courses, high technical level (post graduate / young professional).

Costs & Financial Aid

Financial aid available? Yes; partial scholarship. *Scholarship notification:* end of March. *Students receiving financial aid:* 99%. *Procedure for applying for financial aid:* bursary form available at audition.

Curriculum, Students, and Faculty

Offered courses: chamber ensemble, master classes, opera workshop, orchestra. Curriculum fixed. *Program concentration:* voice, chamber, orchestra.

Selectivity for males: approximately 33% admitted. *Selectivity for females:* approximately 33% admitted.

Renowned alumni: Anthony Rolfe Johnson, Ian Bostridge, Robert Cohen, Nicholas Daniel, Katarina Karneys.

Performance Information

Specific performance opportunities: end of course public recital, public performances for opera courses. *Orchestra seating:* based on standard of playing. *Seat rotation:* rotation differs for each course but is fixed within each course. *Performance casting:* auditioned. *Performances by visiting artists?* yes. *Recent guests:* as part of Aldeburgh Festival.

Rehearsal facilities and hours: 1 recital room, 1 large room, 4 practice room for chamber music, 6 practice rooms for individuals, all with piano. *Performance facilities:* recital room adjoining.

FINLAND

LIEKSA BRASS WEEK

Winter Contact Information
Koski-Jaakonkatu 4, Lieksa 81700 Finland
Tel: 358-13-523-134
Fax: 358-13-523-133
Email: brass.week@lieksa.inet.fi
Contact: Mr. Jouni Kuramo

Summer Contact Information
Koski-Jaakonkatu 4, Lieksa 81700 Finland
Tel: 358-13-523-134
Fax: 358-13-523-133
Email: brass.week@lieksa.inet.fi
Contact: Mr. Jouni Kuramo

General

Minimum age or age range: 17 to 50. *Level of program:* beginning, intermediate, advanced.

High school credit available? no. *College credit available?* no.

Services

Housing options: on-campus dorms, class accommodations.

Application Information

Requirements: essay. *Program dates:* 7/25-8/8. *Application deadline:* 4/30.

Audition Information

Audition required; live. *No audition fee. Accompanist provided? yes.*

Costs & Financial Aid

Financial aid available? no.

Curriculum, Students, and Faculty

Offered courses: band, master classes, private lessons. *Program concentration:* Brass, big band and septet music.

Performance Information

Performance opportunities and frequency: 1-3 performances. *Specific performance opportunities:* mid-day music.

Rehearsal facilities and hours: school rooms. *Performance facilities:* concert hall of Lieksa.

HONG KONG

HONG KONG YOUTH MUSIC CAMP

Winter Contact Information
Professional Urban Council and Professional Regional Council, 25/F. Wanchai Tower, 12 Harbor Road, Wanchai, Hong Kong
Tel: 852-2582-5328
Fax: 852-2802-8440
Contact: Ms. Winnie Lin

Summer Contact Information
Professional Urban Council and Professional Regional Council, 25/F. Wanchai Tower, 12 Harbor Road, Wanchai, Hong Kong
Tel: 852-2582-5328
Fax: 852-2802-8440
Contact: Ms. Winnie Lin

General

Total enrollment: 450. *Minimum age or age range:* 10 to 23. *Level of program:* intermediate, advanced.

High school credit available? no. *College credit available?* no.

Services

Housing options: on-campus dorms.

Application Information

Requirements: interview. *Program dates:* mid July to early August (two 7-8 day sessions). *Application deadline:* late April. *Enrollment full by:* early June. *Acceptance notification:* early June.

Audition Information

Audition required; live. *No audition fee. Audition includes:* scales, arpeggios, work of student's choice, sight-reading. *Accompanist provided?* no.

Audition evaluation criteria: proficiency on instrument, orchestral experience.

Costs & Financial Aid

Tuition (full): $100.

Financial aid available? Yes; partial scholarship. *Students receiving financial aid:* 1%. *Procedure for applying for financial aid:* financial aid available for local applicants only.

Curriculum, Students, and Faculty

Offered courses: band, chorus, orchestra. Curriculum fixed. *Program concentration:* string orchestra, symphony, band, Chinese orchestra, choir.

Selectivity for males: approximately 60% admitted. *Selectivity for females:* approximately 60% admitted.

Full-time faculty: 25. *Guest faculty:* 4.

Performance Information

Performance opportunities and frequency: 1 solo and 1 chamber in-camp concert, 1 finale orchestral concert. *Specific performance opportunities:* concerts. *Orchestra seating:* based on audition results.

Rehearsal facilities and hours: daily rehearsal, 9:00 am-12:00 pm, daily recreation hours, 3:30 pm-6:00 pm, daily evening programs, 7:00 pm-9:00 pm. *Performance facilities:* in-camp concerts in assembly hall at campsite, finale concerts in concert halls managed by the Professional Urban and Regional Councils.

ISRAEL

THE JERUSALEM RUBIN ACADEMY SUMMER SESSION

Winter Contact Information

Academy Secretariat, GivatRam Campus 91904, Jerusalem Israel
Tel: 02-6759911
Fax: 02-6527713
Contact: Rina Gordon

Summer Contact Information

Academy Secretariat, GivatRam Campus 91904, Jerusalem Israel
Tel: 02-6759912
Fax: 02-6527714
Contact: Rina Gordon

General

Minimum age or age range: 16 to 25. *Level of program:* advanced.

High school credit available? no. *College credit available?* no.

Services

Housing options: on-campus dorms.

Application Information

Program dates: July, August. *Application deadline:* 6/30. *Application fee:* $25. *Enrollment full by:* 6/30. *Acceptance notification:* 1 month after application is received.

Audition Information

Audition required; video, off-site. *Audition fee:* $50. *Audition includes:* 10 minutes of repertoire including at least 2 genres. *Accompanist provided?* no.

Costs & Financial Aid

Room: $545.

Financial aid available? full scholarship, partial scholarship. *Scholarship notification:* 3/15. *Students receiving financial aid:* 75%. *Procedure for applying for financial aid:* application and audition.

Curriculum, Students, and Faculty

Offered courses: master classes, movement. Curriculum fixed. *Program concentration:* individual lessons in different instruments according to requests, chamber music groups, conducting, composition.

ITALY

BERKLEE IN UMBRIA

Winter Contact Information

Umbria Jazz Clinics, Sede Amministrativa, Viat. Albinoni 30-06132 S. Sisto Perugia, Italy
Tel: 39-75-573-24325
Fax: 39-75-572-2656
Contact: Cristina Ventura

Summer Contact Information

Umbria Jazz Clinics, Sede Amministrativa, Viat. Albinioni 30-06132 S. Sisto Perugia, Italy
Tel: 39-75-573-24325
Fax: 39-75-572-2656
Contact: Cristina Ventura

General

Total enrollment: 225.

High school credit available? no. *College credit available?* no.

Services

Housing options: on-site housing.

Application Information

Program dates: mid July. *Application deadline:* late June. *Enrollment full by:* July.

Audition Information

Audition required; live, on-site. *No audition fee. Accompanist provided?* no.

Curriculum, Students, and Faculty

Offered courses: blues history, ensemble, music theory. Curriculum fixed. *Program concentration:* jazz, improvisation, blues, theory.

Full-time faculty: 10.

Performance Information

Specific performance opportunities: during ensemble classes, student concert at the end of the program. *Performances by visiting artists?* yes. *Recent guests:* Gary Burton, John Scofield, Bill Pierce.

Rehearsal facilities and hours: practice rooms based on availability during program. *Performance facilities:* outdoors, Morlucchi Theatre in Perugia.

ROME FESTIVAL SUMMER INSTITUTE

Winter Contact Information
Empire State Building, Suite 3304, New York NY 10118
Tel: 908-233-7214
Fax: 908-233-2979
Email: mbarber151@aol.com
Contact: Molly Barber

Summer Contact Information
Via F. Duodo 47, Rome Italy
Tel: 011-39-6-39-74-98-68
Fax: 908-233-2979
Email: mbarber151@aol.com
Contact: Molly Barber

General

Total enrollment: 90. *Minimum age or age range:* 20 to 55 (summer institute), 15 to 19 (young artists). *Level of program:* advanced.

High school credit available? no. *College credit available?* yes.

Services

Housing options: Hotels in historic center of Rome.

Application Information

Requirements: interview (reommendation). *Program dates:* mid June to late July. *Application deadline:* rolling. *Application fee:* $33. *Acceptance notification:* 10 days after audition.

Audition Information

Audition required; live, video. *Audition fee:* $33. *Accompanist provided?* no.

Costs & Financial Aid

Tuition (full): $2,494.

Financial aid available? full scholarship, partial scholarship. *Scholarship notification:* when admitted. *Students receiving financial aid:* 99%. *Procedure for applying for financial aid:* complete application.

Curriculum, Students, and Faculty

Offered courses: acting for singers, ballet, chamber ensemble, chorus, coaching (2 classes per week, years to complete), conducting, cultural visits, diction, Italian language study, master classes, movement, opera, orchestra, repertory. Curricula choices. *Program concentration:* opera, symphonic, chamber music, ballet, choral, classical guitar, pianoforte, conducting.

Full-time faculty: 15. *Guest faculty:* 5.

Performance Information

Orchestra seating: by musical director. *Seat rotation:* some rotation by concert or opera. *Performance casting:* audition prior to arrival *Performances by visiting artists?* yes.

Rehearsal facilities and hours: at concert site and several nearby church schools, 8:00 am-1:00 pm and 4:30 pm-8:00 pm (Mon- Fri). *Performance facilities:* Giardino Auditorium, P2 San Salvatore inlauro, 15 Roma, in historic center between Piazzo Navona and Castel San Angelo.

Additional Comments

Rome Festival Summer Institute is only for performers, must be able to sing opera in 10 days of rehearsals or perform standard orchestral repertoire in 3 rehearsals.

SPOLETO ARTS SYMPOSIA

Winter Contact Information
760 West End Avenue, Suite 3A, New York NY 10025
Tel: 212-663-4440
Fax: 212-663-4440
Email: clintoneve@aol.com
Contact: C.J. Everett

Summer Contact Information
c/o Azienda di Turismo, Piazza della Liberta, Spoleto 06049 Italy
Fax: 011-39-0743-46-241
Email: clintoneve@aol.com
Contact: C.J. Everett

General

Total enrollment: 100. *Level of program:* beginning, intermediate, advanced.

High school credit available? no. *College credit available?* no.

Services

Housing options: double rooms in a 15th century convent; arrangements can be made for living with families or in apartments.

Application Information

Program dates: mid-July to mid-August. *Application deadline:* rolling. *Application fee:* $50. *Enrollment full by:* May. *Acceptance notification:* 2 weeks after audition.

Audition Information

Audition required. live, audio, video. *Audition includes:* 2 musical selections. *Accompanist provided?* yes.

Costs & Financial Aid

Tuition (full): $2,200.

Financial aid available? partial scholarship. *Scholarship notification:* late May. *Students receiving financial aid:* 5%. *Procedure for applying for financial aid:* Send copy of IRS tax form.

Curriculum, Students, and Faculty

Offered courses: acting for singers, audition preparation, coaching, diction, Italian language study, master classes, opera workshop, private lessons, repertory, seminar on the business of music, Curricula choices. *Program concentration:* voice, opera, flute, cooking.

Selectivity for males: approximately 60% admitted. *Selectivity for females:* approximately 60% admitted.

Renowned alumni: Judd Ernster, Kirstin Dickerson, Teresa Santiago.

List of some faculty and their affiliations: Judith Coen, Metropolitan Opera; Roberts Wesleyan College; Enza Ferrari, teacher of Maria Callas.

Performance Information

Specific performance opportunities: singers usually perform in 4-5 public concerts, daily master classes, flutists have outdoor concerts. *Performances by visiting artists?* yes.

Rehearsal facilities and hours: in a music school, 9:00 am-9:00 pm. *Performance facilities:* 12th century church, 18th century opera house.

Additional Comments

There are concurrent programs for writers and also a cooking school.

NETHERLANDS

HOLLAND MUSIC SESSIONS

Winter Contact Information

P.O. Box 250, 1860 AG Bergen, The Netherlands
Tel: 0031-72-582-1300
Fax: 0031-72-582-1299
Contact: Frans Wolfkamp

Summer Contact Information

P.O. Box 250, 1860 AG Bergen, The Netherlands
Tel: 0031-72-582-1300
Fax: 003-72-582-1299
Contact: Frans Wolfkamp

General

Total enrollment: 300. *Level of program:* advanced.

High school credit available? yes. *College credit available?* yes.

Services

Housing options: hotel, guest-families.

Application Information

Requirements: interview, essay, recommendation. *Program dates:* 6/26-8/10. *Application deadline:* 4/1. *Application fee:* $100. *Acceptance notification:* 4/1.

Audition Information

Audition required. *Audition fee:* $100. *Audition includes:* performance. *Accompanist provided?* yes.

Costs & Financial Aid

Tuition (full): $975.

Financial aid available? full scholarship, partial scholarship. *Scholarship notification:* 4/1. *Students receiving financial aid:* 20%. *Procedure for applying for financial aid:* letter.

Curriculum, Students, and Faculty

Offered courses: chamber ensemble, master classes, orchestra, repertory, Curricula choices. *Program concentration:* solo and chamber music.

Selectivity for males: approximately 10% admitted. *Selectivity for females:* approximately 10% admitted.

Renowned alumni: Philippe Giusiano, Niemolas Angelica.

Full-time faculty: 38. *Guest faculty:* 2. *List of some faculty:* Lazar Berman, John O'Connor, John Perry, Erick Friedman, Viktor Liberman, Anner

Bijlsma, Iwan Monighetti, Annele Nicolet, Elly Ameling, Thom Bollen.

Performance Information

Performance opportunities and frequency: 1-2 performances. *Specific performance opportunities:* 4 levels. *Performance casting: Performances by visiting artists?* no.

Rehearsal facilities and hours: conservatories, piano studios. *Performance facilities:* concert halls.

PUERTO RICO

FESTIVAL OF THE SYMPHONIE YOUTH ORCHESTRA OF THE AMERICAS

Winter Contact Information

P.O. Box 41227, San Juan PR 00940-1227
Tel: 787-721-7727, 7144
Fax: 787-723-5843
Contact: Maria E. Fernandez-Net, Annabel Delgado

Summer Contact Information

P.O. Box 41227, San Juan PR 00940-1227
Tel: 787-721-7728, 7144
Fax: 787-723-5844
Contact: Maria E. Fernandez-Net, Annabel Delgado

General

Level of program: intermediate, advanced.

High school credit available? no. *College credit available?* no.

Services

Housing options: hotel paid by festival.

Application Information

Program dates: 6/7-6/21. *Application deadline:* 3/31. *Application fee:* $125. *Acceptance notification:* May.

Audition Information

Audition not required. Audition includes: pieces selected by music director. *Accompanist provided?* no.

Costs & Financial Aid

Tuition (full): $250. *Lessons:* optional. *Room:* $250.

Financial aid available? no.

RUSSIA

MOSCOW CONSERVATORY INTERNATIONAL SUMMER SCHOOL

Winter Contact Information

111 Munn Lane, Cherry Hill NJ 08034
Tel: 609-795-1830
Fax: 609-427-6733

Summer Contact Information

B. Nikotskega 13, Moscow Russia
Tel: 011-7-095-229-6833
Fax: 011-7-095-229- 6833

General

Level of program: advanced.

High school credit available? no. *College credit available?* yes.

Services

Housing options: on-campus dorms.

Application Information

Requirements: recommendation. *Program dates:* first 3 weeks of August. *Application deadline:* 5/1. *Application fee:* $250. *Enrollment full by:* unlimited. *Acceptance notification:* 6/1.

Audition Information

Audition required. No audition fee. Audition includes: several works of contrasting styles. *Accompanist provided?* yes.

Costs & Financial Aid

Tuition (full): $2,580. *Lessons:* 3 lessons per week included in tuition.

Curriculum, Students, and Faculty

Offered courses: chamber ensemble, competition preparation, conducting, foreign language study, master classes, music history, private lessons, repertory. Curricula choices. *Program concentration:* solo performance, pedagogy, chamber music.

Selectivity for males: approximately 60% admitted. *Selectivity for females:* approximately 60% admitted.

Renowned alumni: Edith Chen.

Full-time faculty: 30. *List of some faculty and their affiliations:* Lev Naumov, Moscow Conservatory; S. Dovensky, Moscow Conservatory; M. Lashvili, Moscow Conservatory.

Performance Information

Specific performance opportunities: bi-weekly public performances in Rachmoninoff Hall, Moscow. *Performances by visiting artists?* yes. *Recent guests:* Irina Plafnikova, Alexei Nasedkin, Sergei Kavikenko, Marina Iashvili.

Rehearsal facilities and hours: Moscow Conservatory, 3 hours practice guaranteed, upright piano in each dorm room. *Performance facilities:* Rachmoninoff Hall, Moscow.

Affiliations

Summer program is affiliated with other program(s): future students recruited from the program.

SWITZERLAND

ATELIER DU JAZZ ET ART

Winter Contact Information
55 Bethune St., Suite B645, New York NY 10014
Tel: 212-727-1756
Fax: 212-691-0631
Email: st172@columbia.edu

Summer Contact Information
Conservatoire du Musique
La Chaux-de-Fonds, Switzerland

General

Housing options: with families.

Appllication Information

Program Dates: 3 weeks in July-August.

Audition Information

Audition required: tape.

INDEX

HIGH SCHOOL PROGRAMS

DANCE

DRAMA

MUSIC

COLLEGE PROGRAMS

DANCE

DRAMA

MUSIC

SUMMER DANCE PROGRAMS

SUMMER DRAMA PROGRAMS

SUMMER MUSIC PROGRAMS

APPENDIXES

HELPFUL BOOKS

DANCE

Anderson, Jack. *Ballet and Modern Dance: A Concise History*, 2nd edition, Princeton Book Company, Pennington, NJ, 1991.

Arnheim, Daniel, D. *Dance Injuries: Their Prevention and Care*, 3rd edition, Princeton Book Company, Pennington, NJ, 1991.

Balanchine, George and Mason, Francis. *101 Stories of Great Ballets*, Anchor Books/ Doubleday, New York, NY, 1975.

Barringer, Janice and Schlesinger, Sarah. *The Pointe Book: Shoes, Training and Technique*, Princeton Book Company, Pennington, NJ, 1997.

Bentley, Toni. *Winter Season*, Vintage Books/Random House, New York, NY, 1982.

Bruneau, Daniel. *L'Enseignement de la Musique et la Danse*, Paris, France, 1991.

College Music Society. *Directory of Dance Faculties in Colleges and Universities: U.S. and Canada*, CMS Publications, Missoula, MT, 1997.

Dance Fair NRW (Tanzmesse NRW) *Gesellschaft Fur Zeitgenossischen Tanz* (NRW) Landesburo Tanz; Koln, Germany.

De Mille, Agnes. *Dance to the Piper*, Da Capo Press, New York, NY, 1982.

Denby, Edwin. *Dancers, Buildings and People in the Streets*, Popular Library, Fawcett, New York, NY, 1965.

Grant, Gail. *Technical Manual and Dictionary of Classical Ballet*, Dover Books, New York, NY, 1982.

Hamilton, Linda H. *Advice for Dancers, Emotional Council and Practical Strategies*, Jossey-Bass, San Francisco, CA, 1998.

Humphrey, Doris. *The Art of Making Dances*, Princeton Book Company, Pennington, NJ, 1987.

Karsavina, Tamara. *Theatre Street*, Dance Books Ltd., London, England, 1981.

Koegler, Horst. *The Concise Oxford Dictionary of Ballet*, Oxford University Press, London, England, 1977.

McCormack, Allen E., ed. *Stern's Performing Arts Directory*, Dance Magazine, New York, NY, published annually.

Noverre, Jean Georges. *Letters on Dancing and Ballets*, Dance Horizons, New York, NY, 1975.

Sidimus, Joysanne. *Exchanges: Life After Dance*, Press of Terpsichore, Toronto, Canada, 1987.

Siegel, Marcia. *The Shapes of Change*, Avon Books, New York, NY, 1981.

Tracy, Robert. *Goddess*, Limelight Editions, New York, NY, 1997.

Vincent, Richard. *The Dancer's Book of Health*, Princeton Book Company, Pennington, NJ, 1988.

Whitehill, Angela and Noble, William. *The Young Professional's Book of Ballet*, Princeton Books, Pennington, NJ, 1990.

Whitehill, Angela and Noble, William. *The Parent's Book of Ballet*, Meriwether Publishing Ltd., Colorado Springs, CO, 1988.

DRAMA

Caine, Michael. *Acting in Film*, Applause Books, New York, NY, 1990.

Charles, Jill, ed. *Directory of Theatre Training Programs, II*, 2nd edition, Theatre Directories, Dorset, VT, 1989.

Cohen, Robert. *Acting Professionally: Raw Facts About Careers in Acting*, Mayfield Publications, Mountain View, CA, 1990.

College Music Society. *Directory of Theatre Faculties in Colleges and Universities, U.S. and Canada*, CMS Publications, Missoula, MT, 1997.

Donnelly, Kyle, ed. *Classical Monologues for Men and Women*, Heinemann, Portsmouth, NH, 1992.

Eaker, Sherry, ed. *The Back Stage Handbook for Performing Artists*, Watson-Guptill Publications/BPI Communications, Inc., 1996.

Musical America, Musical America Publications, New York, NY, published annually.

O'Neill, Brian. *Acting as a Business: Strategies for Success*, Heinemann, Inc., Portsmouth, NH, 1993.

Hagan, Uta. *A Challenge for the Actor*, Charles Scribner and Sons, New York, NY, 1991.

Hunt, Gordon. *How to Audition: A Casting Director's Guide for Actors*, Dramatic Publishing Company, New York, NY, 1977.

Laurie, Rona. *Auditioning: A Practical Guide for the Would-Be Actor and Drama Student*, J. Garnet Miller, Ltd., Worcestershire, England, 1985.

MUSIC

College Music Society, *Directory of Music Faculties in Colleges and Universities, U.S. and Canada*, CMS Publications, Missoula, MT, 1996.

Directory of Canadian Orchestras and Youth Orchestras, Association of Canadian Orchestras, Toronto, Canada, 1997.

Highstein, Ellen. *Making Music in Looking Glass Land: A Guide to Survival and Business Skills for the Classical Musician*, 2nd edition, Writer's Digest Books, Cincinnati, OH, 1984.

Reid, Wendy and Wealt, Christopher. *Auditions are Just the Beginning: A Career Guide to Orchestras*, Association of Canadian Orchestras, Toronto, Canada, 1991.

Uscher, Nancy. *Your Own Way in Music: A Career and Resource Guide*, St. Martin's Press, New York, NY, 1990.

GENERAL

Custard, Edward. *The Princeton Review Guide to the Best 311 Colleges*, Random House, NY, 1998.

Custard, Edward; ed. *The Complete Book of Colleges*, Random House, NY, 1998.

Vuturo, Chris. *The Scholarship Advisor*, Random House, NY 1998.

PERIODICALS OF INTEREST

DANCE

Ballet Review
46 Morton Street
New York, NY 10014

Choreography and Dance
Harwood Academic Publishers
P.O. Box 90
Reading
Berkshire RG1 8JL, England

Dance and the Arts
Dance Pages
P.O. Box 916
Ansonia Station
New York, NY 10023

Dance Chronicle
Marcel Dekker
P.O. Box 5005
Monticello, NY 12701-5185

Dance Magazine
31 West 60th Street
New York, NY 10023

Dance Now
Dance Books Ltd.
15 Cecil Court
London, WC2N 4EZ, England

Dance Research
Oxford Journals
Oxford University Press
Oxford OX2 6DP, England

Dance Research Journal
CORD
SUNY Brockport
Department of Dance
350 New Campus Drive
Brockport, NY 14420-2939

Dance Teacher Now
P.O. Box 41204
Raleigh, NC 27629

Dance Theatre Journal
Laban Center
Laurie Grove
New Cross
London, SE14 6NH, England

Dance View
P.O. Box 34435
Martin Luther King Station
Washington, DC 20043

DRAMA

American Theatre
355 Lexington Ave.
New York, NY 10017

Asian Theatre Journal
Univ. of Hawaii Press
Journals Department
2840 Kolwalu Street
Honolulu, HI 96822

Backstage Publications, Inc.
Watson-Guptill Publications
1515 Broadway
New York, NY 10036-8986

New Theatre Quarterly
Journals Department
40 West 20th Street
New York, NY 10011-4211

Plays and Players
Subscriptions
Media House
55 Lower Addiscombe Road
Croydon
Surrey, CRO 6PQ, England

Theatre
222 York Street
New Haven, CT 06520

Variety
154 West 46th Street
New York, NY 10036

MUSIC

Chamber Music Magazine
Chamber Music America
545 8th Avenue
9th Floor
New York, NY 10018

Das Orchester
Postfach 3540
Weihergarten 1-11
D-6500 Mainz, Germany

The Instrumentalist
200 Northfield Road
Northfield, IL 60093

Orchestra/Orchestres Canada
Association of Canadian Orchestras
56 The Esplanade
Suite 311
Toronto, Ontario
M5E 1A7, Canada

Symphony Magazine
American Symphony Orchestra League
777 14th Street NW
Washington, DC 20005

Flute Talk
Instrumental Publishing Company
200 Northfield Road
Northfield, IL 60093

Flutists Quarterly
National Flute Association, Inc.
Phyllis Pemberton
P.O. Box 800598
Santa Clara, CA 91380-0597

Horn Call
International Horn Society
c/o Dept. of Music
Southeastern Oklahoma State University
Durant, OK 74701

Double Reed
International Double Reed Society
c/o Lowry Riggins, Executive Secretary-Treasurer
626 Lakeshore Drive
Munroe, LA 71203-4032

The Brass Player
N.Y. Brass Conference for Scholarships
315 W. 53rd Street
New York, NY 10019

Brass Bulletin
P.O. 10-12478-1
Zurich, Switzerland

International Trumpet Guild Journal
Box 50183
Columbia, SC 29250

International Trombone Association Journal
Box 5336
Denton, TX 76203

Clavier
200 Northfield Road
Northfield, IL 60093

Piano Today
352 Evelyn Street
Paramus, NJ 07652

Keyboard Magazine
GPI Publications
20085 Stevens Creek
Cupertino, CA 95014

Piano Guild Notes
National Guild of Piano Teachers
Box 1807
Austin, TX 78767

Piano Journal
28 Emperor's Gate
London SW7 4HS, England

Piano and Keyboard
String Letter Press
P.O. Box 767
San Anselmo, CA 94979-0767

The American Organist
475 Riverside Drive
Suite 1260
New York, NY 10025

Diapason
Scranton Gillette Communications, Inc.
380 East Northwest Highway
Des Plaines, IL 60016-2282

Organ Yearbook
c/o Vitgerverij Frits
Knuf, B.V.
Box 720
4116, ZJ
Buren, The Netherlands

Tracker
The Organ Historical Society, Inc.
P.O. Box 26811
Richmond, VA 23261

American Harp Journal
American Harp Society
P.O. Box 38334
Los Angeles, CA 90038

Modern Drummer
P.O. Box 480
Mt. Morris, IL 61054-0480

Percussive Notes Magazine
Percussive Arts Society
214 West Main Street
Box 697
Urbana, IL 61801-0697

IDRS
4663 Glenway Avenue
Cincinnati, OH 95238

American String Teacher
American String Teacher Association
4020 McEwen
Suite 10E
Dallas, TX 75244

The Strad
Hainault Road
Little Heath
Rumford
Essex, RM6 5NP, England

Strings
P.O. Box 767
San Anselmo, CA 94960

Violin Society of America Journal
c/o Edward C. Campbell
Chimneys Violin Shop
614 Lerew Road
Boiling Springs, PA 17007

Journal of the American Viola Society
c/o BYU music
Harris Fine Arts Center
Provo, UT 84602

Vioexchange
P.O. Box 6046
Ann Arbor, MI 48106

Bass World
c/o School of Music
Northwestern University
Evanston, IL 60208

Double Bassist
P. O. Box 648
Harrow
Middlesex, HA1 2NW, England

Acoustic Guitar
P.O. Box 767
San Anselmo, CA 94979-0767

Guitar Review
Albert Augustine, Ltd.
40 West 25th Street
New York, NY 10010

The NATS Journal
National Association of
Teachers of Singing
250 West 57th Street
Suite 2129
New York, NY 10107

Classical Singer Newsletter
153 Maplewood Drive
Maplewood, NJ 07040

Opera
c/o Opera, D5B
2a Sopwith Crescent
Hurrican Way
Shotgate, Wickford
Essex, SS11 8YU England

Opera Canada
Foundation for Coast to Coast
Opera Publication
366 Adelaide Street East #433
Toronto, Ontario
M5A 3X9 Canada

Opera Journal
National Opera Association
c/o Marajean Marvin, Executive Secretary
School of Music
Ohio State University
Columbus, OH 43210

Opera News
Metropolitan Opera Guild
70 Lincoln Center Plaza
New York, NY 10023

Vocals
142 N. Milpitas Blvd.
Suite 280
Milpitas, CA 95035-4400

American Symphony Orchestra League Bulletin
American Symphony Orchestra League
777 14th Street NW
Washington, DC 20005

Journal of the Conductors Guild
P.O. Box 3361
West Chester, PA 19381

American Choral Review
American Choral Foundation
2111 Sansom Street
Philadelphia, PA 19103

Computer Music Journal
Journals Department
MIT Press
28 Carleton Street
Cambridge, MA 02142

Coda
Journal of Jazz and Improvised Music
33 Winton Lodge
Imperial Avenue
Westcliff-on-Sea
Essex, England

Down Beat
180 West Park Avenue
Elmhurst, IL 60126

Jazz Journal International
113-117 Farringdon Road
London, EC1R 3BT, England

Billboard
P.O. Box 2071
Mahopec, NY 10541-2071

Rolling Stone
625 Third Street
San Francisco, CA 94107

USEFUL ADDRESSES FOR PERFORMING ARTS ORGANIZATIONS

American Symphony Orchestra League (ASOL)
777 14th Street, NW
Washington DC, 20005

Association for Theatre in Higher Education (ATHE)
P.O. Box 15282
Evansville, IN 47716

Dance Notation Bureau
31 West 21st Street
New York, NY 10010

Dance Professionals Association
440 East 81st Street
Suite 6G
New York, NY 10028

Dancesource
P.O. Box 15038
Dallas, TX 75201

Dance/USA
1156 15th Street
Washington, DC 20005-1704

Educational Theatre Association
3368 Central Parkway
Cincinnati, OH 45225

Independent Educational Consultants Association (IECA)
Cove Road P.O. Box 125
Forestdale, MA 02644

Miller Institute for the Performing Artist
St. Luke's/Roosevelt Hospital
10th Avenue and West 59th Street
New York, NY 10019

Music Educators National Conference (MENC)
1902 Association Drive
Reston, VA 22091

National Arts Medicine Center
National Rehabilitation Hospital
Bethesda, MD 20813

National Association of College Admissions Counselors
1800 Diagonal Road
Suite 430
Alexandria, VA 22314

National Association of Schools of Music (NASM)
11250 Roger Bacon Drive
Suite 21
Reston, VA 22090

National Association of Schools of Theatre (NAST)
11250 Roger Bacon Drive
Suite 21
Reston, VA 22090

National Association of Schools of Dance (NASD)
11250 Roger Bacon Drive
Suite 21
Reston, VA 22090

National Dance Association
1900 Association Drive
Reston, VA 22091

National Foundation for Advancement in the Arts (NFAA) (ARTS)
800 Brickell Avenue
Miami, FL 33137

Network of Visual and Performing Arts Schools
5505 Connecticut Avenue, NW
#280
Washington, DC 20015

Regional Dance America
1570 Dairy Ashford
Houston, TX 77077

University/Resident Theatre Association (U/RTA)
1560 Broadway
Suite 903
New York, NY 10036

SAMPLE RÉSUMÉS

Sample Dance Résumé

Suzy Jones

19 Backwater Street
Boston, MA 00000
617-444-4444
Fax: 617-444-4443

Training:

The Dolly Dinkle School
5 years, once weekly Ballet, Toe, Tap, Jazz
Massachusetts School of Dance
3 years, 3 times weekly Ballet, Pointe, Variations
School of United States Labanotation
2 Summer Intensives Ballet, Modern Dance, Nutrition

Non-Dance Qualifications:

2 Years flute lessons
Honors student
Advanced Placement French, American Literature

Performance Experience:

Finian's Rainbow–Jeanie McClaren–High School Production, 1995
Nutcracker–Mouse–Mass. Regional Ballet, 1994–96
The Stranger–Ensemble–Regional Dance America Northeast Festival, 1996

Choreography:

I Grow Up–Solo–School Show, 1997

Vital Statistics:

Height: 5'4"
Weight: 110 pounds

Sample Drama Résumé—Applying to ARTS High School

Comment: Although this would seem quite complete and age appropriate, other categories you might mention include: technical theater work, any awards received, or any competitions for which you received recognition. In applying to high schools, you do not need to provide your entire life story, but your junior high or middle school years should certainly be highlighted.

Mary Smith

14 Maiden Lane
Candyland, MS 12345
565-666-9908
e-mail address: msmith@net.com

Education

Martha Washington Junior High School, Chocolate, MS, Grades 5–8

Performance Experience

- **Sound of Music** *Liesl* Martha Washington School, 1997
- **Cinderella** *Stepsister* Candyland Community Theatre, 1996
- **Alice in Wonderland** *Alice* Tonowanda Summer Camp, 1995

Training and Extra Activities

- **Two years of drama/acting class** Martha Washington School
- **Five years of ballet** Miss Suzy's Dance Class
- **Two years of tap** Shuffles Tap Classes
- **Drama Club** Martha Washington School

Other Interests and Hobbies

- Stamp collecting
- Babysitting
- Dog walking
- Juggling

Sample Drama Résumé—Applying to Conservatory

Gaylord Hitchcock

125 Westerly Blvd, Overlook, NE 46809 345-678-9123
e-mail address: ghitch@aol.net

Height: 6'1"
Weight: 180 pounds
Hair: Brown
Eyes: Blue

Education

Fleetwater Valley High School, Fleetwater, MD. Diploma anticipated, 1998
3.8 grade point average
Honors courses
Member of National Honor Society

Theater Experience

Picnic	Hal	Theater in the Round, Westerly, RI
Cat on a Hot Tin Roof	Brick	Williamsville Theater, Bend, OR

Television and Film

The Moving Galaxy	Guy	WEX-TV (Four segments)
Ice Freezes	Walk-on	John Fox, producer and director

Commercials

Ice Cream Man		Good Humor ad, 1996

Summers

Apprentice, Williamstown Theatre Festival, 1997
Interlochen Arts Academy, 1994–96

Training

Commercials:	Classes at Sell-On Technique
Acting Classes:	Fleetwater High School
	Interlochen Arts Camp
	Circle Theater Acting Workshop
Dance:	Fleetwater Ballet, Tap, and Jazz Studio
Voice:	Lessons with Margaret Warbler for four years

Special Skills

Excellent whistler. Certified scuba diver. Rollerblader. Weight lifter.

Sample Résumé for an Instrumentalist

Peter Schaeffer, *Clarinet*

22 Beekman Lane • Edgewater, NJ 06034 • (201)-876-5

orchestral experience~

All-State Orchestra, principal clarinet, 1998
New Jersey Youth Symphony, 1997–98
Edgewater Symphony, 1995–98

band experience~

Marching Midgets, Marshfield, PA, 1994–97

competitions~

Winner, Swiners Club Competition, 1998

education~

Edgewater High School, New Jersey
High School Diploma, 1998

Clarinet teachers: Harvey Nuttle, Douglas Kramer
Piano teacher: Mary Goldfinger

summer program~

Idyllwild Summer Music Program, California, Summer, 1996

references: available upon request

Sample Résumé for a Singer

Edith Warbler

1996 Cabrini Boulevard, Apt. 14G New York, NY 10045
212.232.4456

Singing Experience:

• Soprano section leader	New Dutchland Singers, NYC	1997–present
• Soprano soloist	Ukranian Choir, NYC	1995–97
• Soprano soloist	Church of the Holy Savior, NYC	1991–94

Roles:

• Nursing Sister	*Suor Angelica*, Kentucky Valley Opera	1996
• Monica	*The Medium*, Hudson River Opera	1995

Oratorio:

• Soprano soloist	Bach, *Magnificat*, Westchester Philharmonia	1998
• Soprano soloist	Hadyn, *Creation*, Loyola Handel and Hadyn	1997

Education:

- Woeffle School of Singing, New York, NY, Master of Music — 1997
- Snow Shoe University, Booser, Montana
  Bachelor of Arts, French major — 1996

Voice Teachers: Dorothea Laringetti, Luciano Piano, Alan Fall

Coaches: Frank Huffer, Brendon Ferris

Diction: Nicholas Castle

Languages: Fluent in French, Conversational German

Other musical studies: Ten years of piano, five years of violin

Dance: Six years of ballet

References: Available upon request

ABOUT THE AUTHORS

Carole Everett is an educator and renowned mezzo-soprano who has performed with opera companies and orchestras and on recital tours around the world. She is an honors graduate of Barnard College of Columbia University and holds advanced degrees from the Universitá di Siena, Italy. For seven years, 1986–1993, she served as the director of admissions at The Juilliard School in New York City, overseeing admissions for dance, drama, and music at the undergraduate and graduate levels. She has been an adjudicator of the Metropolitan Opera Regional Council Auditions for Young Artists and also for the New York Youth Symphony Concerto Competition.

Ms. Everett is the co-founder and co-director of the Spoleto Arts Symposia, a series of summer programs in Italy for singers, flutists, writers, and cooks. She speaks and consults frequently on college and graduate school admissions and has taught voice, public speaking, and Latin at junior high through post-secondary levels. She is the author of *The Performing Art Major's College Guide: Dance, Drama, Music* (Simon and Schuster / Arco), now in its third edition, which includes opinions about various programs. Ms. Everett is a native of Wellesley, Massachusetts, and lives in New York City and Spoleto, Italy, with her husband, son, and golden retriever.

Muriel Topaz is currently writer and senior editor for *Dance Magazine*, and for Gordon and Breach publisher's scholarly journal *Choreography and Dance* and book series *Choreography and Dance Studies*. She has been active as a reconstructor, having recently staged *Jardin Aux Lilas* (Tudor) for the Milwaukee Ballet, and *Continuo* (Tudor) for the Paris Conservatory. A world authority on Labanotation, Topaz was organizer and co-chair of two International Congresses on Movement Notation, the first interchanges among the various notation systems currently in use. She has written dance scores for some of the most notable choreographers of our time, including Humphrey, Jooss, Robbins, Sokolow, Taylor, and Tudor, and, most recently, Limón's *Moor's Pavane*. She has taught Labanotation throughout the United States and in Argentina, Mexico, France, and England. She is currently the chair of the International Council of Kinetography Laban.

From 1985 until 1993, Ms. Topaz was director of the Dance Division of the Juilliard School, and from 1977 to 1985, executive director of the Dance Notation Bureau. Ms. Topaz has served on the advisory board of Regional Dance America, chaired the dance panel of the New York State Council on the Arts, and evaluated dance companies for the Canada Council, the National Endowment for the Arts, Ballet Builders, the New Jersey State Council on the Arts, and the Massachusetts Cultural Council. Her distinguished career has included work as dancer, teacher, choreographer, reconstructor, author, Labanotator, dance panelist, administrator, adjudicator, editor, and board member. In 1997 she was awarded a John Simon Guggenheim Foundation Fellowship to pursue research for a biography of Antony Tudor.

Ms. Topaz was married to the distinguished American composer, Jacob Druckman, until his untimely death in 1996. She has two children; Karen Jeanneret, an attorney who resides in Switzerland, and Daniel Druckman, percussionist with the New York Philharmonic Orchestra, and three grandchildren. She resides in Connecticut and the Florida Keys.